Where participation leads to action!

Welcome to MyPoliSciLab, where participation leads to action!

MyPoliSciLab is a state-of-the-art, interactive, and instructive online solution for introducing students to American Government. Designed to amplify and supplement a traditional lecture course or completely administer an online course, MyPoliSciLab combines multimedia – simulations, videos, news feeds and archives, quizzes and tests – to make teaching and learning more effective and fun!

WHAT STUDENTS ARE SAYING ABOUT ONLINE EXAMS AND QUIZZES

"I love it. I keep trying until I get a perfect grade and after a couple times you know the content like the back of your hand!"

"I liked being able to view the results of the quizzes immediately instead of having to wait for them to be graded by the instructor."

WHAT STUDENTS ARE SAYING ABOUT ONLINE ACTIVITIES

"The activities were my favorite part of the course. They took a different approach to an interesting subject, and made it more applicable to real-life situations. This made the subject seem even more real than before."

ONE PLACE.
Everything your students need to succeed.

MyPoliSciLab is a state-of-the-art, interactive, and instructive online solution for your American Government course.

Pre-Test, Post Test, and Chapter Exam
For each chapter of the printed textbook, students will navigate through a pre-test, post-test, and a full-chapter exam — all fully integrated with the online E-book so students can assess, review, and improve their understanding of the material in each chapter.

Chapter Review
For each chapter, students will find additional resources such as a complete study guide, learning objectives, and a summary.

E-book.
Matching the exact layout of the printed textbook, the E-book contains multimedia icons in the margins that launch a wealth of exciting resources.

The *New York Times* Online Feed & the *New York Times* Search by Subject™ Archive
Both provide free access to the full text of the *New York Times* and articles from the world's leading journalists of the *Times*. The online feed provides students with updated headlines and political news on an **hourly** basis.

Online Administration
Instructors can easily track students' work on the site and monitor their progress on each activity. The *Instructor Gradebook,* which now includes upgraded functionality, provides maximum flexibility for allowing instructors to sort by student, activity, or to view the entire class in spreadsheet view.

Research Navigator™
This database provides thousands of articles from journals as well as popular periodicals, such as *Newsweek* and *USA Today,* that give students and professors access to scholarly and topical content from a variety of sources.

Interactive Activities
Students will find over 100 simulations, interactive timelines, videos, comparative exercises, and more — all integrated with the online E-book through icons that appear in the margins. Now fully updated with brand-new activities!

SIMULATION. Students are given a role to play — such as congress member, lobbyist, or police officer — so they can experience the challenges and excitement of politics firsthand.

TIMELINE. With an abundance of media and graphics, students can step through the evolution of an aspect of our political system.

VISUAL LITERACY. Students interpret and apply data about intriguing political topics. Each activity begins with an interactive primer on reading graphs and charts.

PARTICIPATION. Bringing the importance of politics home, these activities appear as three types: 1) Debates, 2) Surveys, and 3) "Get Involved" activities.

COMPARATIVE. Students compare the U.S. political system to those of other countries.

CONTINUOUSLY UPDATED MULTIMEDIA MAPPED TO CHAPTER CONTENT

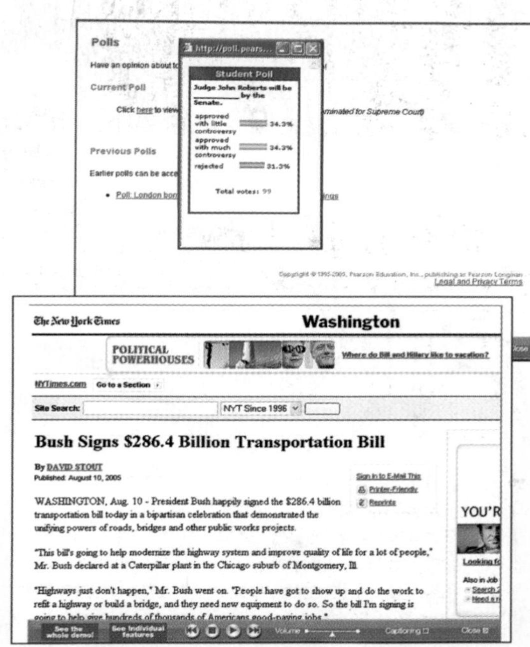

NEW FEATURES

Student Polling

Updated weekly with timely, provocative questions, this new feature allows students to participate in nationwide polls on hot topics. Students are asked to vote on questions such as "Should flag burning be permitted?" Results of student responses around the country are immediately displayed.

PoliSci News

PoliSci News contains 1) an online feed from the *New York Times* that is updated hourly, 2) an exclusive *New York Times* database that allows students to browse by subject area or search for a specific topic, and 3) PoliSci News Review — a series of articles selected by a political science professor that recaps the previous week's most important political events and are followed by quizzes.

Roundtable Discussion Video Clips

Video clips consist of three professors discussing important concepts covered in the text. Key concepts such as campaign finance reform and critical questions such as "Is Federalism Dead?" are discussed from a wide range of perspectives and viewpoints — providing students with a balanced review of key course material. Each discussion is accompanied by critical thinking prompts, multiple choice questions, and a transcript for reference.

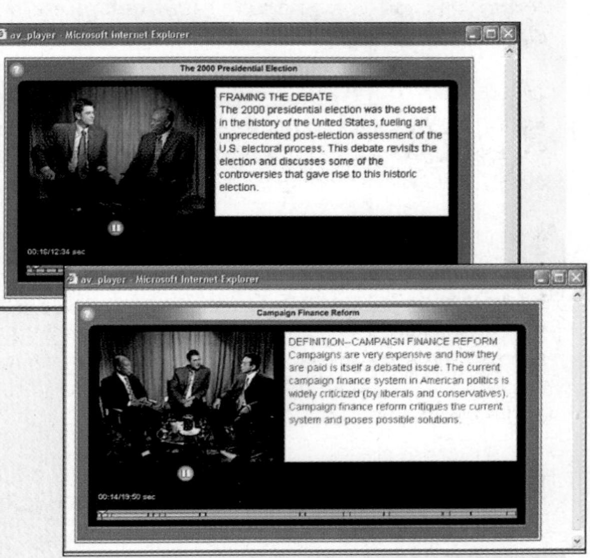

Debate Video Clips

Offering lively, challenging debates from two sides of an issue, these clips feature two professors discussing hot-button issues and answering pressing questions such as "Does the Patriot Act violate American civil liberties?" Each debate is accompanied by critical thinking prompts, multiple choice questions, and a transcript for reference.

INSTRUCTOR: WE CAN HELP YOU EASILY INTEGRATE THESE AMAZING ASSETS INTO YOUR COURSE...HOW?

Author's Choice

With so many incredible activities to assign, we have asked our authors to hand select one or two activities that best complement or amplify each chapter. You have the work done for you in easy-to-use, pre-packaged MyPoliSciLab assignments. If you only have time to assign and complete one activity for the chapter, the Author's Choice designation makes it easy!

Go to mypoliscilab.com to see a sample chapter!

Student Survey Results

Recently, Longman Publishers conducted a nationwide survey of students to determine just how useful they find MyPoliSciLab and its individual features. The sample included hundreds of students from both 2-year and 4-year schools.

The results are impressive. Not only do they show that students find MyPoliSciLab to be an effective supplement, but they show how each specific feature of MyPoliSciLab enhances students' learning experience and engages them with the course material. See for yourself!

Very low learning value → 1 ... 5 ← Very high learning value

	1	2	3	4	5	4s & 5s
Online Quizzes	1.3%	1.3%	8.8%	26.8%	61.9%	88.7%
Chapter Exams	0.8%	5.0%	8.4%	18.4%	67.4%	85.8%
Debate Videos	2.2%	3.5%	15.8%	27.6%	50.9%	78.5%
Roundtable Videos	3.0%	3.0%	16.5%	32.0%	45.5%	77.5%
Chapter Activities	0.9%	5.2%	16.5%	23.9%	53.5%	77.4%
Online E-Book	5.4%	8.3%	15.1%	17.6%	53.7%	71.2%
PS News Review	5.0%	4.5%	23.2%	23.2%	44.1%	67.3%
Homepage Updates	8.0%	11.7%	16.9%	23.9%	39.4%	63.4%
Polling Questions	7.6%	9.0%	27.0%	20.9%	35.5%	56.4%

WHAT STUDENTS ARE SAYING ABOUT ONLINE E-BOOK

"It helped a lot, especially since you could magnify the words. Also, it was great to be able to type in a key word and see exactly where it appears in the text."

WHAT STUDENTS ARE SAYING ABOUT ROUNDTABLE VIDEOS

"All videos were fantastic and allowed each topic to be discussed from each viewpoint but was kept objective by the moderator."

WHAT STUDENTS ARE SAYING ABOUT POLISCI NEWS

"I really liked this feature. I don't get a chance to catch up on political news very often, so this was very helpful."

WHAT STUDENTS ARE SAYING ABOUT POLLING QUESTIONS

"The polling questions are fun. Sometimes I was very surprised at other students' responses."

GOVERNMENT IN AMERICA

PEOPLE, POLITICS, AND POLICY

Brief Ninth Edition

GEORGE C. EDWARDS III
Texas A & M University

MARTIN P. WATTENBERG
University of California, Irvine

ROBERT L. LINEBERRY
University of Houston

New York San Francisco Boston
London Toronto Sydney Tokyo Singapore Madrid
Mexico City Munich Paris Cape Town Hong Kong Montreal

Editor-in-Chief: Eric Stano
Assistant Development Manager: David B. Kear
Senior Marketing Manager: Elizabeth Fogarty
Supplements Editor: Brian Belardi
Media Supplements Editor: Beth Crippen Strauss
Production Manager: Denise Phillip
Project Coordination, Text Design, and Electronic Page Makeup: GGS Book Services
Cover Design Manager: John Callahan
Cover Designer: Maria Ilardi
Cover Photos: Eagle courtesy Minden Pictures; George W. Bush courtesy Aurora Photos; the Constitution courtesy PhotoEdit; Immigration rally (people with flags) courtesy AP Images.
Photo Researcher: Photosearch, Inc.
Senior Manufacturing Buyer: Dennis J. Para
Printer and Binder: Quebecor World
Cover Printer: Phoenix Color Corporation

For permission to use copyrighted material, grateful acknowledgment is made to the copyright holders on pp. 686–687, which are hereby made part of this copyright page.

Library of Congress Cataloging-in-Publication Data

Edwards, George C.
Government in America: people, politics, and policy / George C. Edwards III, Martin P. Wattenberg, Robert L. Lineberry.—Brief 9th ed.
p. cm.
Includes bibliographical references and index.
ISBN 0-321-44278-4
1. United States—Politics and government—Textbooks. I. Wattenberg, Martin P. II. Lineberry, Robert L. III. Title.

JK276.E39 2008
320.473—dc22

2006029133

Please visit us at www.ablongman.com

ISBN-13: 978-0-321-44278-9
ISBN-10: 0-321-44278-4

1 2 3 4 5 6 7 8 9 10—QWT—10 09 08 07

Contents

17 National Security Policymaking 546

Preface

Politics matters. That is the core message of this book. The national government provides important services, ranging from retirement security and health care to recreation facilities and weather forecasts. The national government may also send us to war or negotiate peace with our adversaries, expand or restrict our freedom, raise or lower our taxes, and increase or decrease aid to education. In the twenty-first century, decision makers of both political parties are facing difficult questions regarding American democracy and the scope of our government. Students need a framework for understanding these questions.

Focus

We write *Government in America, Brief Edition,* to provide our readers with a better understanding of our fascinating political system. This ninth edition continues to frame its content with a public policy approach to government in the United States. We continually ask—and answer—the question, "What difference does politics make to the policies governments produce?" It is one thing to describe the Madisonian system of checks and balances and separation of powers or the elaborate and unusual federal system of government in the United States; it is something else to ask how these features of our constitutional structure affect the policies governments generate.

We find that this focus engages students' interest. Students, like their instructors, quickly recognize that the principal reason for studying politics is to understand why government produces the policies it does. What many see as "dry" subjects become interesting when they are tied to outcomes that directly affect each of us. Even introductory students feel comfortable asking, "So what?" To reinforce this interest, we have a feature in the margins titled **Why It Matters** in which we ask students to think critically about some aspect of our system and how things might be if it worked differently.

We do not discuss policy at the expense of politics, however. We provide extensive coverage of four core subject areas: constitutional foundations, patterns of political behavior, political institutions, and public policy outputs, but we try to do so in a more analytically significant—and interesting—manner. We take special pride in introducing students to relevant work from current political scientists, such as the role of political action committees (PACs) or the impact of divided government—something we have found instructors appreciate.

It is not enough to arouse students' interest, however. To be a useful teaching tool, a text must be accessible to students and enjoyable to read. We believe a principal reason for the success of *Government in America, Brief Edition,* is its high level of readability. To ensure that the material is not only clearly presented but also meaningful, we make special efforts to illustrate points with interesting examples to which students can relate. The ability of Congress to indirectly regulate behavior in the states becomes more meaningful when the power is illustrated with a discussion of raising the drinking age. In addition, this is neither a conservative nor a liberal book. Instead, we make every effort to present material in an evenhanded manner. As a result, over the years we have received many letters in which students have told us how much they enjoyed reading the book. Needless to say, we find this response very gratifying.

Two Themes

To render the policy focus in concrete terms, two important themes appear throughout the book: the nature of democracy and the scope of government. Each chapter begins with a preview of the relevancy of these themes to the chapter's subject, refers to the themes at points within the chapter, and ends with specific sections on the two themes under the heading "Understanding . . . " that show how the themes illuminate the chapter's subject matter.

The first great question central to governing, a question every nation must answer, is *How should we govern?* In the United States, our answer is "democracy." Yet democracy is an evolving and somewhat ambiguous concept. In Chapter 1, we define democracy as a means of selecting policymakers and of organizing government so that policy represents and responds to citizens' preferences. As with previous editions, we continue to incorporate theoretical issues in our discussions of different models of American democracy. We try to encourage students to think analytically about the theories and to develop independent assessments of how well the American system lives up to citizens' expectations of democratic government. To help them do this, in every chapter we raise questions about democracy. For example, does Congress give the American people the policies they want? Is a strong presidency good for democracy? Does our mass media make us more democratic? Are powerful courts that make policy decisions compatible with democracy?

A common complaint about the national government is that it cannot respond to the needs of its citizens, that it suffers from *gridlock.* A subtheme to our discussion of democracy is whether America's diversity and the openness of our political system have the drawback of incapacitating government. The diversity of the American people is reflected in the variety of political interests represented in the political system. This system is so open that many different interests find access to policymakers. In our system of checks and balances, opposition by one set of policymakers can sometimes frustrate the will of the majority. We leave it to the reader to determine whether the difficulty of achieving policy change, be it the Bill Clinton health care reform plan or the George W. Bush tax cut, is a positive feature of our system. Our goal is to promote understanding of the consequences of the American democratic system and to provoke discussion about these consequences. We find that students are especially interested in why government does not "do something."

The second theme, the scope of government, focuses on another great question of governing: *What should government do?* Here we discuss alternative views concerning the proper role and size for American government and how this scope is influenced by the workings of institutions and politics. The government's scope is the core question around which politics revolves in contemporary America, pervading many crucial issues: To what degree should Washington impose national standards such as speed limits on state policies? How high should taxes be? Do elections encourage politicians to promise more governmental services? Questions about the scope of government are policy questions and thus obviously directly related to our policy approach. Since the scope of government is *the* pervasive question in American politics today, students will have little problem finding it relevant to their lives and interests.

A subtheme of the scope of government is the role of *individualism* in American political life. The people who immigrated to America may have been diverse, but many adopted a common dream of America as a place where people could make it on their own without interference from government. Today, individualism remains a powerful influence in the United States. Americans' strong preference for free markets and limited government has important consequences for public policy. For example, it substantially constrains efforts to intervene in the economy, efforts that have long been the norm in other developed democracies.

At the same time, a central contest in American politics has been between two kinds of individualism. Economic individualism embraces the doctrines of capitalism. The purpose of government is to protect the creativity of entrepreneurs and markets, which leads to well-being. Democratic individualism appeals to government to redress the social inequalities that result from economic individualism. Puritans, abolitionists, agrarian populists, prohibitionists, civil rights crusaders, feminists, and the contemporary religious right have preached collective purpose against individualism. Thus, we often employ the concept of individualism in our analysis of the scope of government.

We hope that students—long after reading *Government in America, Brief Edition*—will employ these perennial questions about the nature of our democracy and the scope of our government when they examine political events. The specifics of policy issues will change, but questions about whether the government is responsive to the people or whether it should expand or contract its scope will always be with us.

Features

Eight features appear throughout *Government in America, Brief Edition*: (1) **Issues of the Times**, (2) **You Are the Policymaker/Judge**, (3) **Young People and Politics**, (4) **A Generation of Change**, (5) **How You Can Make a Difference**, (6) **Why It Matters**, and (7) **Get Connected**. Each of the features plays a particular role in the text to support our approach to American government.

We believe students should stay on top of current and enduring issues in American politics and government by reading a newspaper every day. To that end, we include a feature called **Issues of the Times**. This feature presents thought-provoking articles directly from the *New York Times* on important issues in the news along with useful pedagogy that helps students understand and think critically about the issue presented and become comfortable reading politically-oriented newspaper articles. We refer to the feature within each chapter but have placed the actual articles from all the chapters together near the end of the book so instructors can use them flexibly as a built-in reader.

You Are the Policymaker

You Are the Judge

We also believe it is important that students recognize and think critically about difficult policy choices they must face as citizens. **You Are the Policymaker** asks students to read arguments on both sides of a specific current issue, such as whether we should prohibit PACs, and then to make a policy decision. In Chapters 4 and 5 (Civil Liberties and Civil Rights), this feature is titled **You Are the Judge** and presents the student with an actual court case. This feature directly supports our policy approach.

Young People and Politics

One of the greatest challenges to teaching is overcoming student apathy, even in the face of the September 11 attacks and the Iraq War. Students quite naturally want to know how politics impacts them and how their generation is different. As an extension of our central focus on *politics matters*, our popular **Young People and Politics** feature illustrates how policies specifically impact young adults, how their political behavior patterns are unique and important, and how their particular policy desires are being met or largely ignored by public officials. These features are also especially useful for instructors since there is relatively little written on the topic.

A Generation of Change

Students, particularly students between the ages of 18 and 22, also need historical perspective on contemporary issues. In our new **A Generation of Change** feature, we provide students insight into how various aspects of American politics have changed dramatically over just the course of their lifetime. Some examples of A Generation of Change include the change in network news broadcasts, partisan realignment in the South, and the increase in polarization of Democratic and Republican voters.

How You Can Make a Difference

How You Can Make a Difference provides students with information on how they can get involved with issues in order to influence how government works or what policies are established. This feature is a natural extension of our core message that politics matters.

Why It Matters

We mentioned earlier our feature that appears several times in each chapter's margins titled **Why It Matters**. Here we encourage students to think critically about an aspect of government, politics, or policy and ask them to consider the impact—usually on themselves—if things worked differently.

Get Connected

Our **Get Connected** feature gets students involved in the study of politics and government via the Internet. These user-friendly exercises appear at the end of every chapter and have students research a particular topic covered in the chapter by visiting one or more related Web sites and points out the relevancy of the material presented to their own lives.

To bring some of our new and existing features together and prepare students for making the most of them, we have included a section at the beginning of the book called "Tools for Understanding *Government in America*." This "primer" provides helpful guidance on how to read newspapers, study charts and graphs, and understand the Internet.

Each chapter concludes with a contemporary bibliography, a listing of key terms, and Internet resources relevant to the chapter. (The URLs included at the end of each chapter were current when the book went to press. However, changes or updates may have been made to the site at the discretion of the individual site owner or webmaster.)

Finally, as an additional study aid, we also define key terms in the margins of the text when they are first introduced.

Currency

This ninth edition of *Government in America, Brief Edition*, is completely up to date and incorporates the best recent scholarship on U.S. government. Our emphasis in each chapter on the scope of government is also very timely, as it remains at the core of debates about taxation, regulating the environment, campaign finance, and access to health care. We provide comprehensive coverage of the 2006 midterm elections—both the campaigns and the results—in Chapters 8 to 9 and 11 to 12. We also include the latest Supreme Court decisions from 2006 on federalism, civil liberties, civil rights, and other relevant topics. From the numbers for the 2007 budget to the backgrounds of members of Congress, the text, tables, and figures reflect the most recent available data. Naturally, we devote considerable attention to the Bush administration in Chapter 12 and to the efforts of both the president and Congress to deal with the budget (Chapter 15), which has become central to American politics and policy. Finally, we cover the war on terrorism and the war with Iraq, especially in Chapter 17.

Graphics play an important role in textbooks, and we continue to upgrade our figures, graphs, tables, and charts. We employ vibrant colors and worked hard to make all our graphics easier and more interesting to read. We also provide a brief guide to using graphics following this preface.

New to This Edition

We have mentioned our new feature called **A Generation of Change**, which compares various current aspects of politics, government, and public policy to those of a generation ago. An 18-year-old student in 2007 was born in 1989, when President Reagan was finishing up his term and the first President Bush took office. Because students often have little idea of just how much things have changed in their lifetime (indeed, we often find ourselves surprised!), the **A Generation of Change** feature provides students some historical perspective.

The **Issues of the Times Reader**, included at the back of the book, presents thought-provoking articles directly from the *New York Times* on important issues in the news along with useful pedagogy that helps students understand and think critically about the issues. There is a separate article for each chapter.

Chapter 1 now includes a section on American Political Culture and Democracy, which looks at the overall set of values widely shared within American society. This section discusses five aspects of this culture, including liberty, egalitarianism, individualism, laissez-faire, and populism. Following this section is a new section, A Culture War?, which asks whether America is now polarized into widely separated camps.

In response to feedback from those using this book, we have split the old Chapter 4 on Civil Liberties and Civil Rights into two chapters. Chapter 4 covers Civil Liberties and Chapter 5 focuses on Civil Rights.

In Chapter 7, we have revised the section on Narrowcasting: Cable TV and the Internet by separating these two topics and expanding on them and their impact on politics and the mass media. The new section From Broadcasting to Narrowcasting: The Rise of the Cable News Channels focuses on the rise of cable news channels and explores the proliferation of channels appealing to a specialized audience and their impact on the overall quality of political journalism. The new section The Impact of the Internet looks at the expanding role of the Internet in the political process and asks whether the educational potential of the Internet has been realized or whether it simply reinforces predispositions. The section also explores how the Internet facilitates communication, brings activists together through Web sites and blogs, and provides information and news as an alternative to other media.

In Chapter 8, we have expanded the discussion of 1968–Present in the section on Party Eras in American History to include an analysis of the Southern Realignment.

In Chapter 17, we elevated and expanded the section on The War on Terrorism and included a new component on Afghanistan and Iraq. In addition, our new section on The Changing Role of Military Power includes a new subsection on Humanitarian Interventions.

As we mentioned previously, we have updated the entire text to reflect recent changes in politics, policy, and participation, including examples that support the discussion. We have also updated *all* the figures and tables to include the most recent data available. We have updated or replaced approximately 25 to 30 percent of the photos and their captions, which we use to support, expand, and illustrate the discussion.

Appendix

The Appendix continues to include the Constitution and the Declaration of Independence, *Federalist Papers #10* and *#51*, a table on presidents and presidential elections, and a glossary of key terms. We continue to provide a list of key terms in Spanish.

Briefing a Text

Creating a brief version of a larger text is not—and *should not* be—an easy task. Unlike many authors, we do not hire others to cut our full-length versions. We believe students deserve the work of those closest to the text—the original authors. Moreover, we have chosen to rewrite material for the brief version rather than simply delete chapters, features, and tables from the longer text. It is more time consuming, of course, but it is the only way to ensure the highest-quality work. That, as always, is our ultimate goal.

Supplements

Instructor Supplements for Qualified College Adopters

Instructor's Manual (ISBN: 0-321-371641-1) Written by R. Mark Tiller of Houston Community College, Westgate, this comprehensive manual includes a list of pedagogical features, learning objectives, chapter outlines, narrative chapter overviews, key terms and definitions, suggestions for further study, media suggestions, and ideas for class discussion.

Test Bank (ISBN: 0-321-371641-2) This test bank, prepared by Dennis Plane of Juniata College, has been completely revised and contains thousands of challenging multiplechoice, true-false, short answer, and essay questions along with a page-referenced answer key.

TestGen-EQ Computerized Testing System (ISBN: 0-321-371641-3) This flexible, easy-to-use computer test bank includes all the test items in the printed test bank. The software allows professors to edit existing questions and to add their own items. Tests can be printed in several different formats and can include features such as graphs and tables.

PowerPoint® Presentations PowerPoint® presentations that include a lecture outline of the new edition, along with graphics from the book, are available on the Instructor Resource Center at *www.ablongman.com/irc*. Contact your local Longman representative for access to this site.

Transparencies (ISBN: 0-321-371641-6) A set of four-color acetate transparencies includes figures, graphs, and tables from the text.

Digital Media Archive Presentation CD-ROM (ISBN: 0-321-27068-1) This complete multimedia presentation tool provides instructors with the following: a built-in presentation maker; approximately 100 photos and 150 figures, graphs; and tables from Longman American government textbooks; 40 video clips; and more. All items can be imported into an instructor's existing presentation program, such as PowerPoint®.

Longman Political Science Video Program Qualified adopters can peruse our list of videos for the American government classroom. Contact your local Longman representative for more information.

Study Site for American Government (*www.longmanamericangovernment.com*) This online course companion provides a wealth of resources for students and instructors using Longman American government texts. Containing practice tests, flashcards, and Web explorations, the Study Site for American government helps students quickly master the fundamentals, review a subject for understanding, or prepare for an exam.

Student Supplements for Qualified College Adopters

Longman's MyPoliSciLab This state-of-the-art, interactive, online solution for the American government course, fully integrated in the course management system of your choice—Course Compass®, WebCT, or Backboard—or as an independent website, free of a course management system altogether, is available at no additional charge when bundled with a copy of *Government in America* and contains the following features:

- **Assessment.** For each chapter of the text, students will navigate through a comprehensive pre-test, post-test, and a full chapter exam, all fully integrated with an online e-book version of this text so students can assess, review, and improve their understanding of the text chapters.
- **Interactive Activities.** Developed and revised by a team of more than 15 political science faculty, *MyPoliSciLab* features more than 100 highly interactive activities, all updated and revised—including comparative activities, visual literacy exercises, interactive timelines, participation exercises, and **more than 30 simulations**—for all the major topics in the course.

- **Roundtable Discussion Videos.** Added and updated throughout the semester, these 10–12 minute video clips consist of three professors discussing important concepts covered in the text. Dozens of key concepts (such as campaign finance reform) and critical questions (such as, "Is Federalism Dead?") are discussed from a wide range of perspectives and viewpoints, providing students with a balanced review of key course material. Each discussion is accompanied by critical thinking prompts, multiple-choice questions, and transcripts for reference.

- **Debate Videos.** Updated throughtout the semester and offering lively, challenging debates from two sides of an issue, these 10–12 minute clips feature two professors discussing hot-button issues and answering pressing questions such as, "Does the Patriot Act violate American civil liberties?" Each discussion is accompanied by critical thinking prompts, multiple-choice questions, and transcripts for reference.

- **Student Polling.** Updated weekly with timely, provocative questions, this new feature allows students to participate in nationwide polls on hot topics. Students are asked to vote on questions such as, "Should flag burning be permitted?" Results of the thousands of student responses around the country are immediately displayed.

- **PoliSci News.** PoliSci News contains an online feed from the *New York Times* that is updated hourly; an exclusive *New York Times* database that allows students to browse by subject area or search for a specific topic; and PoliSci News Review, a series of articles selected by a political science professor that recaps the previous week's most important political events and are followed by quizzes and critical thinking questions.

- **Author's Choice.** With so many incredible activities to assign, the authors of this book have hand selected one or two activities that best complement or amplify each chapter. You have the work done for you in easy-to-use, prepackaged *MyPoliSciLab* assignments. If you only have time to assign and complete one activity for the chapter, the Author's Choice designation makes it easy!
- **Research Navigator**™. The EBSCO ContentSelect Academic Journal Database content is collected from thousands of articles organized by discipline and fully searchable. Articles in popular periodicals, such as *Newsweek* and *USA Today*, are included, giving students and professors access to topical content from a variety of sources.
- **Link Library.** Offers editorially selected "Best of the Web" sites. Libraries are continually scanned and kept up-to-date, providing the most relevant and accurate links for research assignments.
- **Writing Resources.** Topics include Avoiding Plagiarism, Finding Sources, Using your Library, Start Writing, Internet Research, and Citing Sources.
- **Online E-book.** Matching the exact layout of the printed textbook, the online E-book contains multimedia icons in the margins that launch to exciting resources (e.g., simulations or videos), which expand on key topics students encounter as they read through the text.
- **Online Administration.** Instructors can easily track student work on the site and monitor students' progress on each activity. The *Instructor Gradebook*, which includes upgraded functionality to ensure a truly seamless experience for users, provides maximum flexibility allowing instructors to sort by student, activity, or to view the entire class in spreadsheet view.

See the advertisement at the front of this text for more information.

Study Site for American Government (*www.longmanamericangovernment.com*) This online course companion provides a wealth of resources for students and instructors using Longman American government texts. Containing practice tests, flashcards, and Web explorations, the Study Site for American government helps students quickly master the fundamentals, review a subject for understanding, or prepare for an exam.

Study Guide (ISBN: 0-321-48299-9) Written by Charles Matzke of Michigan State University, the Study Guide helps students reinforce themes and concepts they encounter in the text. It includes chapter outlines, key terms, multiple choice, fill-in-the-blank, essay questions, and exercises that help students test their understanding of the material with real-world applications.

Great Questions in Politics

Written by some of the most influential scholars and thinkers in political science, each book in this series examines a major question in American politics, offers a new perspective on our political system, and challenges conventional wisdom and prevailing attitudes.

Package any of the Great Questions in Politics books with *Government in America* and receive a 10 percent discount.

Culture War? The Myth of a Polarized America By Morris P. Fiorina, Stanford University; Samuel J. Abrams, Harvard University; and Jeremy C. Pope, Stanford University (ISBN: 0-321-36606-9). *Culture War? The Myth of a Polarized America* combines polling data with a compelling narrative to debunk commonly believed myths about American politics—particularly the claim that Americans are deeply divided in their fundamental political views.

Governing by Campaigning: The Politics of the Bush Presidency, 2007 Edition By George C. Edwards III, Texas A&M University (ISBN: 0-205-52962-3). This brief volume, by one of the foremost experts on the presidency, explores how the Bush administration has attempted sweeping changes in public policy—without broad support for doing so—by taking its case to the American public more than any other president in history.

A Divider, Not a Uniter: George W. Bush and the American People: The 2006 Election and Beyond By Gary C. Jacobson, University of California, San Diego (ISBN: 0-205-52974-7). This brief, engaging book is rich in data and analyzes the reasons why the public is so divided along party lines about George W. Bush.

Is Voting for Young People? With Postscript on New Forms of Citizen Engagement By Martin P. Wattenberg, University of California, Irvine (ISBN: 0-205-51867-9). This accessible, provocative, and brief book explores the reasons why the young are less and less likely to follow politics and vote in the United States, as well as many other established democracies, and suggests ways of changing that.

Seven Sins of American Foreign Policy By Loch K. Johnson, University of Georgia (ISBN: 0-321-41585-X). This brief, accessible book by renowned intelligence and foreign policy expert, Loch Johnson, examines seven major shortcomings— "sins"—in American foreign policy over several administrations that have generated pervasive negative attitudes toward the United States, cost us friendship and support, and impaired our ability to advance our international interests.

Congressional Travels: Places, Connections and Authenticity By Richard F. Fenno Jr., University of Rochester (ISBN: 0-321-47071-0). This book argues that authenticity—knowing what a representative is like in his or her district and looking beyond mere roll-call voting—contributes significantly to understanding the full body of work done by our members of Congress. It further posits, by recounting Fenno's life's work, that the best way to gain a sense of authenticity is to do what Fenno is most famous for—making multiple trips and spending a great deal of time observing representatives at home, with their constituents, in their districts.

Additional Supplemental Student Reading

Discount Subscription to the *New York Times* A 10-week subscription for only $20. Contact your local Longman representative for more information.

Discount Subscription to *Newsweek* Magazine Students receive 12 issues of *Newsweek* at more than 80 percent off the regular price. An excellent way for students to keep up with current events.

***You Decide! Current Debates in American Politics,* 2007 Edition (ISBN: 0-321-43016-6)** Edited by John T. Rourke, University of Connecticut, this exciting debate-style reader examines provocative issues in American politics today. The topics have been selected for their currency, importance, and student interest, and the pieces that argue various sides of a given issue come from recent journals, congressional hearings, think tanks, and periodicals. Available at no additional charge when packaged with this text.

***Voices of Dissent: Critical Readings in American Politics,* Seventh Edition (ISBN: 0-205-56001-6)** Edited by William F. Grover, St. Michael's College, and Joseph G. Peschek, Hamline University, this collection of critical essays goes beyond the debate between mainstream liberalism and conservatism to fundamentally challenge the status quo. Available at a discount when ordered packaged with the text.

***American Government: Readings and Cases,* Seventeenth Edition (ISBN: 0-321-47314-0)** Edited by Peter Woll, Brandeis University, this longtime best-selling reader provides a strong, balanced blend of classic readings and cases that illustrate and amplify important concepts in American government, alongside extremely current selections drawn from today's issues and literature. Available at a discount when ordered packaged with this text.

***Ten Things That Every American Government Student Should Read* (ISBN: 0-205-28969-X)** Edited by Karen O'Connor of American University. We asked American government instructors across the country to vote for the 10 things beyond the text that they believe every student should read and put them in this brief and useful reader. Available at no additional charge when ordered packaged with the text.

Choices: An American Government Database Reader This customizable reader allows instructors to choose from a database of over 300 readings to create a reader that exactly matches their course needs. Go to *www.pearsoncustom.com/database/choices.html* for more information.

Penguin-Longman Value Bundles Longman offers 25 Penguin Putnam titles at more than a 60 percent discount when packaged with any Longman text. A totally unique offer and a wonderful way to enhance students' understanding of concepts in American government. Go to *www.ablongman.com/penguin* for more information.

***Writing in Political Science,* Third Edition (ISBN: 0-321-21735-7)** Written by Diane Schmidt, California State University–Chico, this guide takes students step-by-step through all aspects of writing in political science. Available at a discount when ordered packaged with any Longman textbook.

Longman State Politics Series

***Texas,* Fourth Edition (ISBN: 0-321-38459-8)** By Debra St. John, Collin County Community College. A ninety-page primer on state and local government and political issues in Texas. Available at no extra cost when shrink-wrapped with the text.

***California,* Fifth Edition (ISBN: 0-321-42764-5)** By Pamela Fiber, California State University–Long Beach. A seventy-page primer on state and local government and political issues in California. Available at no extra cost when shrink-wrapped with the text.

***Florida* (ISBN: 0-321-42763-7)** By George A. Gonzales, University of Miami. A fifty-page primer on state and local government and political issues in Florida. Available at no extra cost when shrink-wrapped with the text.

***Georgia* (ISBN: 0-321-42765-3)** By Said L. Sewell, University of West Georgia, and F. Carl Walton, Lincoln University. A seventy-page primer on state and local government and political issues in Georgia. Available at no extra cost when shrink-wrapped with the text.

***Annotated 1876 Texas Constitution* (ISBN: 0-321-35533-4)** Annotated by Stefan D. Haag, Austin Community College. This supplement offers the full 1876 Texas Constitution integrated with a detailed primer examining the meaning and context of the Constitution's most significant language. This ancillary helps give students a deep understanding of what the 1876 Texas Constitution says, why it included the language it did, and what role this seminal document plays in the lives of Texans today.

Acknowledgments

Many colleagues have kindly given us comments on the drafts of the ninth edition of *Government in America, Brief Edition.* They are Sean K. Anderson, Idaho State University; Stephen Bennett, University of Southern Indiana; D'Linell Finley, Auburn University, Montgomery; C. Todd Kent, Texas A&M University; Jeffrey Peake, Bowling Green State University; Sherri L. Wallace, University of Louisville; and Reed L. Welch, West Texas A&M University.

There are also many reviewers of previous editions to whom we owe our continued gratitude: Donald Aiesi, Furman University; Audrey Ambsino, Middlesex Community College; Jeffrey C. Berry, South Texas Community College; Allison Calhoun-Brown, Georgia State University; Montgomery Buell, Walla Walla

College; Don Cothran, Northern Arizona State University; Jim Cox, Georgia Perimeter College; Rebecca E. Deen, University of Texas at Arlington; Donald Kent Douglas, Long Beach City College; Paul R. Fessler, Culver–Stockton College; Christopher P. Gilbert, Gustavus Adolphus College; Forest Grieves, University of Montana; Martin Gruberg, University of Wisconsin; Stefan Haag, Austin Community College; Dick Hernandez, Orange Coast College; Elizabeth Hodges, Lenoir Community College; William Kelly, Auburn University; Haroon A. Khan, Henderson State University; Fred A. Kramer, University of Massachusetts; Ashlyn Kuersten, Western Michigan University; James J. Lopach, University of Montana; John Messmer, St. Louis Community College; Michael K. Moore, University of Texas at Arlington; Richard Pious, Barnard College; William R. Thomas, Georgia State University; Shad Shatterth Waite, University of Oklahoma; Reed Welch, West Texas A & M University.

A number of editors have provided valuable assistance in the production of this ninth edition of *Government in America, Brief Edition.* Editor-in-Chief Eric Stano provided valuable guidance. David Kear was a superb Developmental Editor, coordinating every aspect of the book. We are grateful to both of them.

George C. Edwards III
Martin P. Wattenberg
Robert L. Lineberry

Tools for Understanding *Government in America*

A Student Guide to Reading Charts and Graphs

Information such as voting turnout in the last election, the president's job approval rating, or expenditures on national defense is often presented in quantitative form—that is, through the use of numbers. To help you understand this information, we employ charts and graphs. These figures provide a straightforward, visual representation of quantitative information. Yet charts and graphs can be confusing if you do not understand how to read them.

When you come across one of the charts and graphs in this book, you should ask three questions: First, *what is being measured?* This could be money, public opinion, seats in Congress, or a wide range of other subjects. Second, *what is the unit of measurement?* Is it 50 Americans or 50 percent of Americans? Obviously, it makes a difference. Finally, *what is the purpose of the figure?* Does it show changes over time? Does it compare two or more groups of people or countries? In most instances, captions are provided to explain the purpose of a figure.

The Federal Government Dollar (Fiscal Year 2007 Estimate)

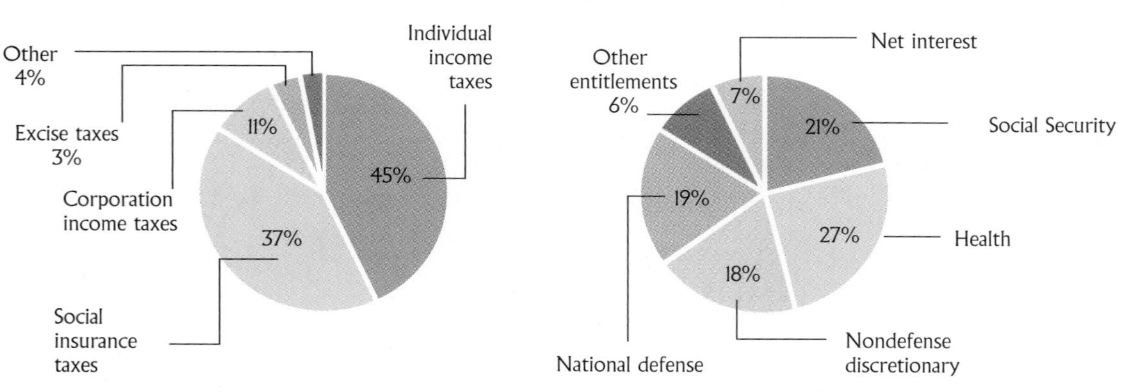

Source: Budget of the United States, Fiscal Year 2007, Historical Tables (Washington, D.C.: U.S. Government Printing Office, 2006), Tables 2.2, 8.3, 16.1.

After answering these general questions, examine the specific type of figure. This text relies on three main types of figures: pie charts, bar graphs, and line graphs. A *pie chart* is a circle divided into wedge-shaped "slices," or segments. Pie charts show the relative sizes of the segments to one another and to the whole. For example, by glancing at the following chart, you can quickly see that the federal government spends more of its funds on Social Security (21 percent) than on national defense (19 percent). The area of each segment is the same percent of the total circle as the number it represents is of the sum of all the numbers in the chart. Since Social Security accounts for 21 percent of federal expenditures, its corresponding segment covers 21 percent of the area of the pie chart.

The second kind of figure, a *bar graph*, displays quantitative information by using rectangles (bars) set within two perpendicular lines, a vertical axis and a horizontal axis. Bar graphs are most frequently used to show and compare the values of multiple entities at a given point in time. Categories (such as groups of people or countries) are set along one axis and a scale (time or numbers, for example) is on the other axis. The length of each bar corresponds to its value on the scale. This makes it easy to visually contrast the values for multiple entities. For example, in the bar graph shown here, which uses a scale measuring poverty rates, you can see that the bars representing persons of African American origin, young people, and unmarried females are the longest, indicating that they are the most likely to be living in poverty. The characteristics of people are on the vertical axis and on the bars themselves, and the scale representing the percentage of people in poverty is on the horizontal axis.

The third type of figure, a *line graph*, illustrates quantitative information by means of lines. Typically, the vertical axis of a line graph represents a quantitative scale (such as percentages) and the horizontal axis represents a category (such as presidents or a sequence of dates). Specific numbers are represented as points on the graph between

Poverty Rates for Persons With Selected Characteristics

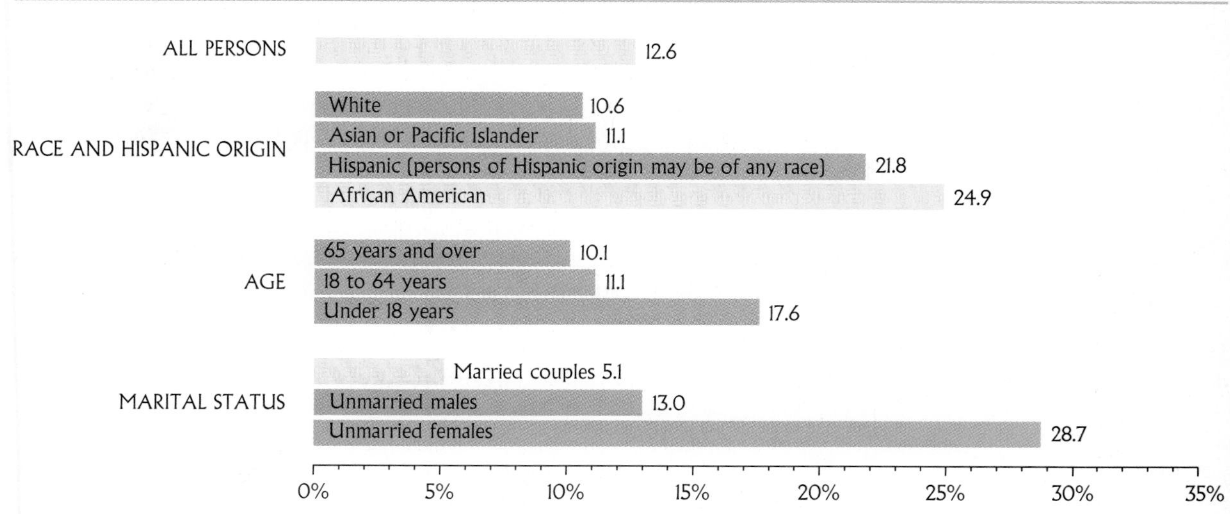

Source: U.S. Census Bureau, 2006.

The Decline of Turnout in Presidential Elections, 1892–2004

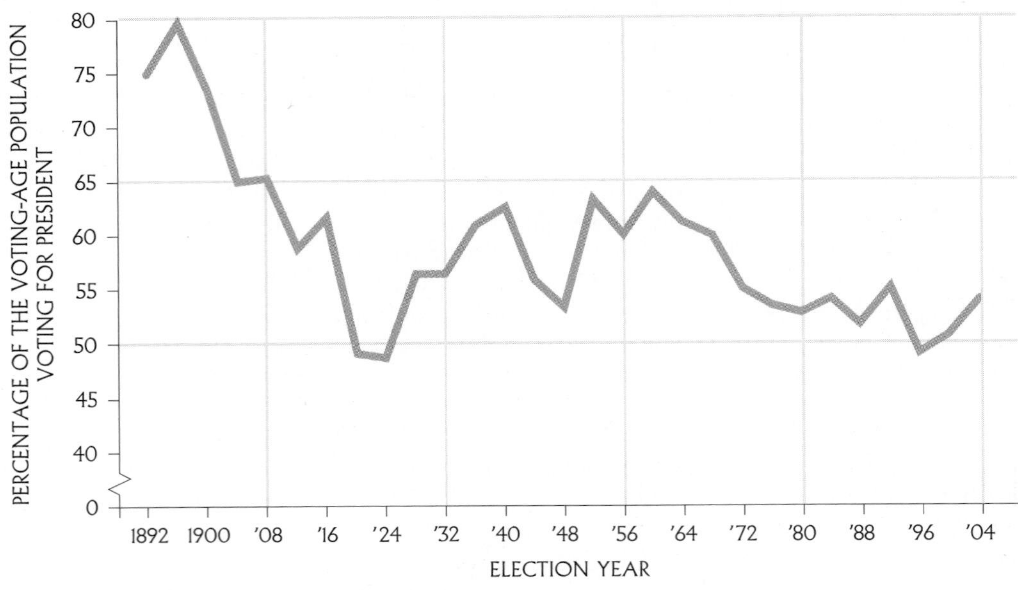

Source: For data up to 1968, *Historical Statistics of the United States* (Washington, D.C.: Government Printing Office, 1975), part 2, 1,071. For 1972–1988. *Statistical Abstract of the United States,* 1990 (Washington, D.C.:Government Printing Office, 1990), 264, Subsequent years from census reports and authors' calculations.

the two axes and are connected with a line. Sometimes there is more than one line on a graph, as when numbers are shown for two different sets of information—for example, elections for both the House and the Senate, state and federal expenditures, or exports and imports. The two lines can be compared to each other, or, in some cases, the distance between the two lines can be analyzed. In the following line graph, which charts a single set of quantitative information, the percentage of the voting-age population that actually voted is shown on the vertical axis, and the horizontal axis represents years of presidential elections. The falling line indicates that turnout has declined since 1892.

By remembering these key features of charts and graphs, you can more accurately assess the information presented in *Government in America* as well as interpret such figures wherever you encounter them—in other textbooks, in newspapers and magazines, or on the Web.

A Student Guide to Reading Newspapers

Although there are a number of good ways to stay on top of what is happening in American government and politics—for example, television and radio news broadcasts—one of the best ways to stay informed is to read a newspaper every day.

Newspapers offer more in-depth information on a particular issue than you might get in a 30-second or one-minute broadcast news story. Here are some guidelines to help you become a better-informed newspaper reader.

Choose Your Newspaper Wisely Not all newspapers are the same; they vary greatly in the type and amount of coverage devoted to specific issues. Most newspapers will cover the big stories of the day—terrorist threats, a devastating hurricane, or the presidential campaign. However, they differ when it comes to how much emphasis they give to various stories. For example, a newspaper with a more sensationalistic approach may give front-page coverage to a scandal involving a well-known celebrity and relegate a major story of national interest to page 2 or 3 or even later. A less sensationalistic newspaper would be more likely to feature a national or international news event on the front page and cover the celebrity scandal much further into the newspaper or not at all. Be aware of how your newspaper covers the important stories of the day.

You should also be aware of which newspapers have a more national focus and which are more locally oriented. Many local papers have good national and international coverage. However, there are a few papers that are considered national in scope and that have excellent coverage of national and international affairs. The *New York Times*, the *Washington Post*, the *Wall Street Journal*, the *Christian Science Monitor*, and *USA Today* all fall in this category.

Develop a Reading Strategy Some people prefer to go right to the sports section and work their way back to the national and international news of the day. Others scan the headlines first and then decide which articles they will read. Only you can determine what works best for you. Remember, however, that reading just the gossip and horoscope sections of a newspaper will not do much to promote your understanding of politics and government. This is not to say that you should not read those sections of the paper that most interest you. However, you may want to *first* spend some time reading the national and international news of the day before moving onto other sections of the newspaper.

Most newspapers contain a section called the "op-ed" page (which is short for opinion-editorial). It is also known simply as the editorial page. This section typically contains opinion pieces about current events and issues written by newspaper staff, regular columnists, or other commentators. These pieces can help give you a broad range of opinion and show you the arguments, pro and con, people are making regarding issues in the news. The letters to the editor, which are also usually in the op-ed section, will give the point of view of newspaper readers like yourself. Newspaper editors try to select a range of letters that express a variety of opinions.

Newspapers have a lot of coverage, and few people read them cover to cover each day. Develop your own strategy for reading a newspaper regularly and in the time you have available. You can scan the headlines or look at the index or contents page if the news paper has one in order to see which articles are of interest to you. (The index or contents page often has a brief summary of articles, which can give you a good overview.) If you don't have time to read entire articles, try reading the first four or five paragraphs of those that interest you; that should give you a pretty good grasp of the issue being covered.

Once you have scanned the major stories and read those of interest, try reading or scanning the op-ed page to see what people are saying about those stories. Between reading the key stories and the op-ed pieces about them, you will hone your own critical thinking skills and you can do a better job of forming and supporting your own opinions about the issues of the day.

Be a Critical Consumer of What You Read Do not take what you read at face value. Be sure to read between the lines by questioning the sources and data provided in the article. For example, an article on gun control would more than likely include several quotes and data from members of the National Rifle Association along with quotes and data from opposing groups. Neither of these groups are neutral about this issue; they both have a particular agenda to promote. You will need to carefully weigh both sides of the argument before coming to your own conclusions about the issue.

Also, question material that comes from anonymous sources. Ask yourself why a particular person does not want his or her identity noted in the article. Is this a government official attempting to promote a particular agenda? An official who wants to test out public opinion on a particular program? Keep in mind there is always a reason why sources go unidentified.

When you read a column or editorial on the op-ed page, the writer's perspective is usually evident because the writer often states his or her opinion at the outset. Editorials by a newspaper's staff are usually anonymous, and these pieces often reflect the general opinion of the newspaper's management and staff. Thus, as you become familiar with a newspaper's editorials, you will gain a sense of the newspaper's perspective. Editorial pieces by people other than newspaper staff are usually identified, along with the writer's affiliation. You should be aware of the writer's affiliation because it will often give you clues about the writer's opinion and perspective.

Develop Your Own Opinions Reading a newspaper every day should not only inform you of what is going on in the world around you but also help you to develop and expand your own opinions on national and world events based on the material you've read. Do not be a neutral reader; that is, do not just read an article or an editorial and move on to the next one. Take a few minutes to think about the implications of the material you read. For example, you may read an article that challenges your beliefs about a particular group or way of life. Use the material you gleaned from the article to develop and perhaps expand your opinions. Even editorials or columns you do not agree with will help you think about the opinions you hold.

Issues of the Times

To give you experience in critically reading and analyzing a newspaper article, every chapter of *Government in America* includes a reference to the feature Issues of the Times, which is included at the back of the book. This feature focuses on articles from the *New York Times* on current and enduring issues in American government and politics. Before you begin each article, pay special attention to The Issue section that precedes it, which will give you valuable background material on the article you are about to read.

The Issue: Affirmative Action

Nearly everyone in America supports equal opportunity for employment, promotion, or admission to universities. Few people believe any group should be at a disadvantage. However, consensus breaks down when the focus turns to equal results in obtaining these jobs or university slots. There is little support for giving some people a special advantage, even if it is to overcome past discrimination.

How do we reconcile these views with the following facts: (1) not everyone has the same chance to take advantage of a theoretical opportunity, (2) discrimination still occurs in some quarters of society, and (3) the nation is becoming more diverse and the legitimacy of institutions requires that they be broadly representative of American society?

As you read the article, pay attention to call-outs within the article that point out different aspects for you to think about.

This decision was affirmative action in its purest, most elemental form. But 25 years of distortion and political warfare over this issue have made it difficult for most people to speak clearly on the subject or even to recognize affirmative action when they see it. Loaded terms such as "quotas" and "reverse discrimination" have made it all but impossible to see affirmative action as a constructive and vitally important policy for the United States.

Loaded terms such as "quotas" and "reverse discrimination" have made it all but impossible to see affirmative action as a constructive and vitally important policy for the United States.

When you finish reading the article, go through each of the Think About It questions and come to your own opinion about the material presented.

Think About It

- Do you support the army's approach to affirmative action?
- Does the army's approach to promotion help get minorities into the army in the first place?
- Can the army's approach to affirmative action be used to rectify the imbalance of minorities in the nation's leading universities or in the most prestigious and lucrative positions in business?
- Do most organizations have a similar hierarchy to that in the army?

A Student Guide to Using the Internet

There are a number of ways the Internet can help you understand government in America. You may, for example, go to the Internet to follow up on a specific issue or agency you learned about in class. Or your instructor may ask you to write a paper on a topic based on material gathered from the Internet and library. In either case, you can find a wealth of information on the Internet. Whether you know just a little about the Internet or you are a sophisticated user, this guide will help you make the most of this electronic research tool.

Finding Information on the Internet

The Internet has changed the way college students work. In addition to using the library, students can now find a wealth of information with just a few keystrokes on a computer keyboard. When looking for information on the Internet, first start with a good search engine. Search engines catalog Web sites in a series of directories and allow you to do searches by typing in a few key words. There are several good search engines to choose from, for example, Yahoo! (*www.yahoo.com*), AltaVista (*www.altavista.com*), and Lycos (*www.lycos.com*). Many political scientists use the Google search engine (www.google.com) because it is fast and helpful in doing research. Use a search engine to research topics when you don't have the name of a particular Web site. You just type in the particular topic you want to learn about into the search screen. Try to be as precise as possible when performing the search, or else you can quickly get information overload. For example, typing in a word like "voting" into the Google search engine will yield over 5 million references to voting. A way to avoid this information overload is to put in a more exact phrase, such as "voting trends in the 2006 midterm elections."

Helpful Web Sites for Studying Government in America

Each chapter of *Government in America* concludes with a list of informative Web sites focusing on material covered in that chapter. Here is a list of Web sites that are especially useful in keeping up with government and politics in general.

You can follow politics, government, and policy issues daily through online editions of newspapers (you may want to make one of these online publications your home page):

New York Times
www.newyorktimes.com

Washington Post
www.washingtonpost.com

Chicago Tribune
www.chicagotribune.com

USA Today
www.usatoday.com

The cable news networks also maintain great Web sites for keeping you up to date about politics and government:

www.cnn.com
www.msnbc.com

You can locate information on virtually every part of the U.S. government by visiting its official Web portal at *www.firstgov.gov*. This site also provides information on state, local, and tribal governments in the United States. Nine times out of 10, you can find a government agency's Web site by simply entering the name of the agency into a search engine. Or you can use agency initials followed by ".gov." For example, "FBI.gov" will take you to the Federal Bureau of Investigation. "INS.gov" will yield the Immigration and Naturalization Service.

Evaluating Information from the Internet

It is important to carefully evaluate material you get from the Internet. Just because something is printed on a Web site doesn't mean it is reliable. *Anyone* can publish material on the Internet—your searches can bring up materials published by reliable governmental sources; however, you will also find material published by people who have a particular ax to grind but have no substance or data to back up their claims. Follow these guidelines when evaluating sources:

- *Check the abbreviation that follows the electronic address.* For example, Web site addresses that end with abbreviations like *.gov* (government body), *.org* (nonprofit organization), and *.edu* (educational institution) are usually reliable places to start your search.
- *Find out who is responsible for the site.* Many Web sites you'll visit clearly identify who is responsible for maintaining the site. Once you determine who is responsible for the site, you may want to do some further research on the person or group responsible (if it is not a well-known source). If you cannot easily find who is responsible for the material on the site or any kind of mission statement for the group or if what you find doesn't seem credible, be wary of the material posted.
- *Determine the purpose of the site.* Determining the purpose of the sites you visit will help you make better choices about the material presented at the site. Ask

yourself the following questions: Does the site communicate information about government and politics from a reliable source? (As noted, check to see who is responsible for the site.) Does the site promote the ideals of a particular interest group? (If so, you should recognize that the material you find usually presents just one side of an issue.) Is the language and material on the site unusually harsh and abrasive? (In this case, you have probably found the site of a political crackpot. Beware of these kinds of sites.)

Get Connected to Government in America

At the end of each chapter in *Government in America,* we introduce an Internet exercise—Get Connected—to help you understand government, politics, and policy. These exercises offer interesting and fun ways to learn about government and politics and will also allow you to practice using some of the guidelines presented in this section.

About the Authors

George C. Edwards III is Distinguished Professor of political science at Texas A&M University. He also holds the Jordan Chair in Presidential Studies in the Bush School and has served as the Olin Professor of American Government at Oxford and the John Adams Fellow at the University of London and held senior visiting appointments at Peking University, Hebrew University in Jerusalem, and the U.S. Military Academy at West Point. He was the founder and from 1991 to 2001 the director of The Center for Presidential Studies.

When he determined that he was unlikely to become shortstop for the New York Yankees, he turned to political science. Today, he is one of the country's leading scholars of the presidency. He has authored dozens of articles and written or edited 21 books on American politics and public policymaking, including *At the Margins: Presidential Leadership of Congress, Presidential Approval, Presidential Leadership, National Security and the U.S. Constitution, Implementing Public Policy*, and *Researching the Presidency*. He is also editor of *Presidential Studies Quarterly* and consulting editor of the *Oxford Handbook of American Politics* series. Among his latest books, *On Deaf Ears: The Limits of the Bully Pulpit* is a study of the effectiveness of presidential leadership of public opinion, *Why the Electoral College Is Bad for America* advocates direct election of the president, and *Governing by Campaigning* focuses on the politics of the Bush presidency.

Professor Edwards has served as president of the Presidency Research Section of the American Political Science Association and on many editorial boards. He has received the Decoration for Distinguished Civilian Service from the U.S. Army and the Pi Sigma Alpha Prize from the Southern Political Science Association and is a member of the Council on Foreign Relations. He has spoken to more than 200 universities and other groups in the United States and abroad, keynoted numerous national and international conferences, given hundreds of interviews with the national and international press, and can often be heard on National Public Radio. His work has been funded by grants from the National Science Foundation, the Smith-Richardson Foundation, and the Ford Foundation. He serves on the Board of Directors of the Roper Center and the Board of Trustees of the Center for the Study of the Presidency.

Dr. Edwards also applies his scholarship to practical issues of governing, including advising Brazil on its constitution and the operation of its presidency, Russia on building a democratic national party system, Mexico on elections, and Chinese scholars on democracy, and authoring studies for the 1988 and 2000 U.S. presidential transitions.

When not writing, speaking, or advising, he prefers to spend his time with his wife Carmella, sailing, skiing, scuba diving, traveling, or attending art auctions.

Martin P. Wattenberg is Professor of political science at the University of California, Irvine. His first regular paying job was with the Washington Redskins, from which he moved on to receive a Ph.D. at the University of Michigan. He is the author of *Is Voting for Young People?*, part of Longman's Great Questions in Politics series. In addition, he is the author of several books published by Harvard University Press: *Where Have All the Voters Gone?* (2002), *The Decline of American Political Parties* (1998), and *The Rise of Candidate-Centered Politics* (1991).

Professor Wattenberg has lectured about American politics on all of the inhabited continents. His travels have led him to become interested in electoral politics around the world. He has coedited two books published by Oxford University Press—one on party systems in the advanced industrialized world and the other on the recent trend toward mixed-member electoral systems.

Robert L. Lineberry is Professor of political science at the University of Houston and has been its senior vice president. He served from 1981 to 1988 as dean of the College of Liberal Arts and Sciences at the University of Kansas in Lawrence.

A native of Oklahoma City, he received a B.A. degree from the University of Oklahoma in 1964 and a Ph.D. in political science from the University of North Carolina in 1968. He taught for seven years at Northwestern University.

Dr. Lineberry has been president of the Policy Studies Section of the American Political Science Association and is currently the editor of *Social Science Quarterly*. He is the author or coauthor of numerous books and articles in political science. In addition, for the past 35 years he has taught regularly the introductory course in American government.

He has been married to Nita Lineberry for 43 years. They have two children, Nikki, who works in Denver, and Keith, who works in Houston. They have six grandchildren—Lee, Hunter, Callie, Arwen, Elijah, and Eleanor.

CHAPTER 1

Introducing Government in America

Chapter Outline

Government

Politics

The Policymaking System

Democracy

The Scope of Government in America

Summary

POLITICS AND GOVERNMENT MATTER—that is the single most important message of this book. Consider, for example, the following list of ways that government and politics may have already impacted your life:

- Any public schools you attended were prohibited by the federal government from discriminating against females and minorities and from holding prayer sessions led by school officials. Municipal school boards regulated your education, and the state certified and paid your teachers.
- The ages at which you could get your driver's license, drink alcohol, and vote were all determined by state and federal governments.

College students, like all Americans, are impacted by governmental policies. Yet many young people today do not seem to think politics matters. The political apathy of today's youth can be seen in low levels of voter turnout, interest in politics, and knowledge of political affairs. This lack of political interest does not mean that this is a generation of couch potatoes, however. In fact, their level of volunteerism in community affairs is very high.

- Before you could get a job, the federal government had to issue you a Social Security number, and you have been paying Social Security taxes every month that you have been employed. If you worked at a relatively low-paying job, your starting wages were determined by state and federal minimum-wage laws.
- As a college student, you may be drawing student loans financed by the government. The government even dictates certain school holidays.
- Even though gasoline prices have recently risen quite a lot, federal policy continues to make it possible for you to drive long distances relatively cheaply compared to citizens in most other countries. In many other advanced industrialized nations, such as England and Japan, gasoline is twice as expensive as in the United States because of high taxes their governments impose on fuel.
- If you have ever rented an apartment, federal law prohibits landlords from discriminating against you because of your race or religion.

Yet, many Americans—especially young people—are apathetic about politics and government. For example, before his historic return to space, former U.S. Senator John Glenn remarked that he worried "about the future when we have so many young people who feel apathetic and critical and cynical about anything having to do with politics. They don't want to touch it. And yet politics is literally the personnel system for democracy."[1]

Stereotypes can be mistaken; unfortunately this is one case where widely held impressions are overwhelmingly supported by solid evidence, which will be reviewed briefly here. This is not to say that young people are inactive in American society. As Harvard students Ganesh Sitaraman and Previn Warren write in *Invisible Citizens: Youth Politics After September 11*: "Young people are some of the most active members of their communities and are devoting increasing amounts of their

Figure 1.1 The Political Disengagement of College Students Today

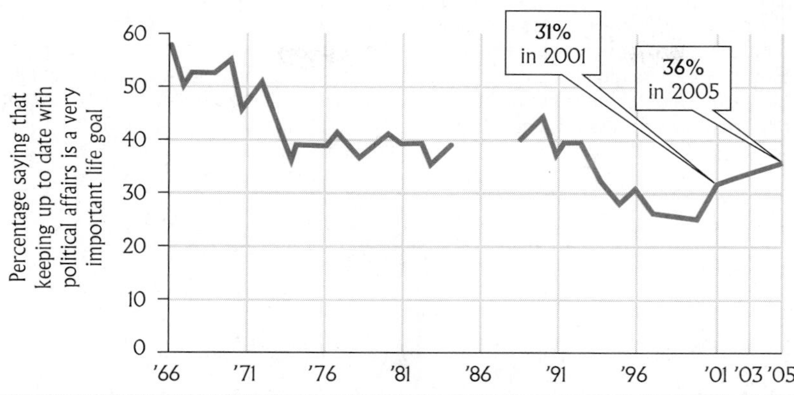

Source: UCLA Higher Education Research Institute.

time to direct service work and volunteerism."[2] It is only when it comes to politics that young people seem to express indifference about getting involved. Whether because they think they can't make a difference, the political system is corrupt, or they just don't care, young Americans are clearly apathetic about public affairs. And while political apathy isn't restricted to young people, a tremendous gap has opened up between the young (defined as under age 25) and the elderly (defined as over age 65) on measures of political interest, knowledge, and participation.

Political Participation and the Young

An annual nationwide study of college freshmen found in 2005 that only 36 percent said that "keeping up with politics" was an important priority for them. As shown in Figure 1.1, since the terrorist attacks of September 11, there has been some resurgence of political interest among college students, but nevertheless it remains far below what researchers found in the 1960s. Furthermore, political interest among young people as a whole is quite low. In 2004, the National Election Study asked a nationwide sample about their general level of interest in politics. Only 52 percent of young people interviewed said they followed politics most or some of the time compared to 86 percent of senior citizens. Yet there was no generation gap in terms of political interest when 18- to 20-year-olds first became eligible to vote in the early 1970s. Back then, 69 percent of young people expressed at least some interest in politics compared to 65 percent of the elderly.

Because they pay so little attention to public affairs, American youth are less likely to be well informed about politics and government compared to senior citizens. The current pattern of political knowledge increasing with age has become well known in recent years. But it was not always that way. The 1964 and 2004 National Election Studies each contain a substantial battery of political knowledge questions that enable this point to be clearly demonstrated. Figure 1.2 shows the percentage of correct answers to eight questions in 1964 and six questions in 2004 by age category.[3] In 1964, there was virtually no pattern by age, with those under 30 actually scoring 5 percent higher on this test than senior citizens. By contrast, in

Figure 1.2 Age and Political Knowledge: 1964 and 2004 Compared

Note: Entries are based on the percentage of accurate responses to a series of eight questions in 1964 and six questions in 2004. In 1964, respondents were given credit for knowing that Goldwater was from Arizona, Johnson was from Texas, Goldwater and Johnson were Protestants, Democrats had the majority in Congress both before and after the election, Johnson had supported civil rights legislation, and Goldwater had opposed it. In 2004, respondents were given credit for knowing that the Republicans had the majority in the House and Senate before the election and for correctly identifying Dennis Hastert (Speaker of the House), Dick Cheney (vice president), Tony Blair (prime minister of Great Britain), and William Rehnquist (chief justice of the Supreme Court).

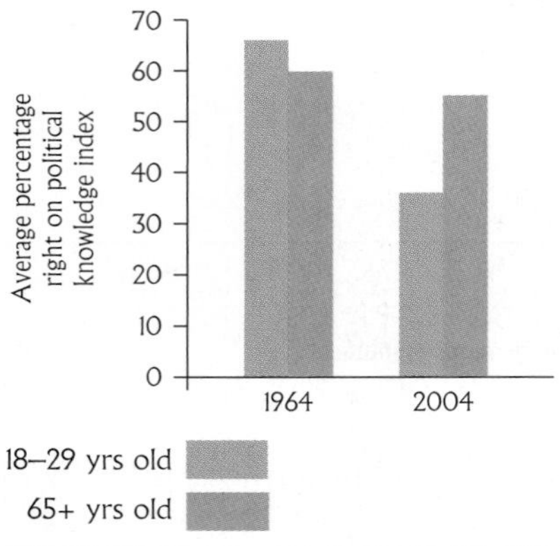

Source: Authors' analysis of 1964 and 2004 National Election Studies.

2004 young people provided the correct answer to only one out of every three questions, whereas people over 65 were correct more than half the time. Regardless of whether the question concerned identifying current U.S. or foreign political leaders or partisan control of the Congress, the result was the same: Young people were clearly less knowledgeable than the elderly.

Thomas Jefferson once said that there has never been, nor ever will be, a people who are politically ignorant and free. If this is indeed the case, write Stephen Bennett and Eric Rademacher, then "we can legitimately wonder what the future holds if Xers remain as uninformed as they are about government and public affairs."[4] While this may well be an overreaction, there definitely are important consequences when citizens lack political information. In *What Americans Know About Politics and Why It Matters*, Michael Delli Carpini and Scott Keeter make a strong case for the importance of staying informed about public affairs. Political knowledge, they argue: (1) fosters civic virtues, such as political tolerance; (2) helps citizens to identify what policies would truly benefit them and then incorporate this information in their voting behavior; and (3) promotes active participation in politics.[5] If you've been reading about the debate on health care reform, for example, you'll be able to understand proposed legislation on managed care and patient's rights. This knowledge will then help you identify and vote for candidates whose views agree with yours.

Lacking such information about political issues, however, fewer young Americans are heading to the polls compared to previous generations. This development has pulled the nationwide voter turnout rate down substantially in recent years. In 1996,

Figure 1.3 Presidential Election Turnout Rates by Age, 1972–2004

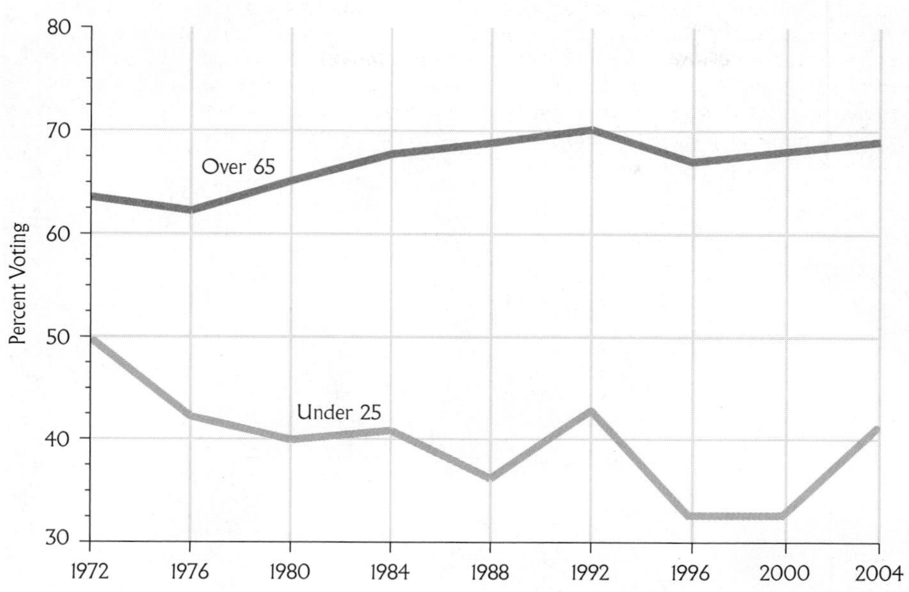

Source: U.S. Census Bureau Current Population Surveys. Data can be found at *www.census.gov/population/www/socdemo/voting.html.*

presidential election turnout fell below the 50 percent mark for the first time since the early 1920s—when women had just received suffrage and not yet begun to use it as frequently as men. Young people have always had the lowest turnout rates, perhaps the reason why there was relatively little opposition in 1971 to lowering the voting age to 18. But even the most pessimistic analysts could not have foreseen the record-low participation rates of young people in recent years.

Why does voter turnout matter? As you will see throughout this book, those who participate in the political process are more likely to benefit from government programs and policies. Young people often complain that the elderly have far more political clout than they do—turnout statistics make it clear why this is the case. As shown in Figure 1.3, the voter turnout rate for people under 25 has consistently been much lower in recent years compared to senior citizens. Whereas turnout rates for the young have generally been going down, turnout among people over 65 years of age has actually gone up slightly over the same period. Political scientists used to write that the frailties of old age led to a decline in turnout after age 60; now such a decline occurs only after 80 years of age. Greater access to medical care provided to today's elderly population because of the passage of Medicare in 1965 must surely be given some of the credit for this change. Who says politics doesn't make a difference?

Of course, today's youth have not had any policy impact them the way that Medicare has benefited their grandparents or that the draft and the Vietnam War affected their parents. However, the cause of young people's political apathy probably

The narrow 537-vote margin by which George W. Bush carried the state of Florida in 2000 proved the old adage that every vote counts. Here, an election official strains to figure out how to interpret a voter's punch in the tedious process of recounting ballots by hand.

runs deeper. A broader reason is that today's youth have grown up in an environment in which public affairs news has not been as readily visible as it has been in the past. It has become particularly difficult to convince a generation that has channel surfed all their lives that politics really does matter.

Major political events were once shared national experiences. Consider how nearly everyone in America was glued to their television to follow the events of September 11, 2001. For many young people, this was the first time in their lives that they closely followed a major national event along with everyone else. With this lone exception, the current generation of young people has been the first to grow up in a media environment in which there are few such shared experiences. Growing up in a fragmented media environment with dozens of TV channels and thousands of Internet sites has offered today's youth a rich and varied socialization experience but also one that has enabled them to easily avoid political events.

Technological Innovations That Have Changed the Political Landscape

In contrast, when CBS, NBC, and ABC dominated the airwaves, their blanket coverage of presidential speeches, political conventions, and presidential debates sometimes left little else to watch on TV. As channels have proliferated over the past two decades, though, it has become much easier to avoid exposure to politics altogether by simply grabbing the remote control. Whereas President Nixon got an average rating of 50 for his televised addresses to the nation (meaning that half the population was watching), President Clinton averaged only about 30 in his first term.[6] Political conventions, which once received more TV coverage than the Summer Olympics, have been relegated to an hour per night and draw abysmal ratings. The 2004 presidential debates drew a respectable average rating of 33, but this was only about three-fifths of the size of the typical debate audience during the 1960–1980 period. In sum, young people have never known a time when most citizens paid attention to major political events. As a result, most of them have yet to get into the habit of following and participating in politics. Initially, there was some hope that September 11 might get more young people to follow national affairs. But to date there has been little evidence of this taking place. For example, a May 2004 Pew Research Center survey revealed that 36 percent of young adults said they enjoyed keeping up with the news compared to 65 percent of senior citizens.

Democracy and the Internet

The revolutionary expansion of channels and Web sites presents both opportunities and challenges for political involvement in the future, especially for today's youth. Some optimistic observers see these developments as offering "the prospect of a revitalized democracy characterized by a more active and informed citizenry."[7] Political junkies will certainly find more political information available than ever before, and electronic communications will make it easier for people to express their political views in various forums and directly to public officials. However, with so many Web sites for so many specific interests, it will also be extraordinarily easy to avoid the subject of public affairs. Thus, groups that are concerned about low youth turnout are focusing on innovative ways of reaching out to young people to make them more aware of politics. You can read about various efforts that were made to get young people interested in the 2004 presidential campaign in "Issues of the Times: How Can Young People's Interest in Politics Be Increased?" which is printed in the *Times Reader* at the back of this book.

It is our hope that after reading this book, you will be persuaded that paying attention to politics and government is important. As noted at the beginning of this chapter, government has a substantial impact on all our lives. But it is also true that we have the opportunity to have a substantial impact on government. Involvement in public affairs can take many forms, ranging from simply becoming better informed by browsing through political Web sites to running for elected office. In between are countless opportunities for everyone to make a difference.

Government

The institutions that make authoritative decisions for any given society are collectively known as **government**. In our own national government, these institutions are Congress, the president, the courts, and federal administrative agencies ("the bureaucracy"). Thousands of state and local governments also make policies that influence our lives. There are roughly 500,000 elected officials in the United States, which means that policies that affect you are being made almost constantly.

government
The institutions and processes through which **public policies** are made for a society.

Because government shapes how we live it is important to understand the process by which decisions are made as well as what is actually decided. Two fundamental questions about governing will serve as themes throughout this book:

How should we govern? Americans take great pride in calling their government democratic. This chapter examines the workings of democratic government; the chapters that follow will evaluate the way American government actually works compared to the standards of an "ideal" democracy. We will continually ask, "Who holds power and who influences the policies adopted by government?"

What should government do? This text explores the relationship between *how* American government works and *what* it does. In other words, "Does our government do what we want it to do?" Debates over this question concerning the scope of government are among the most important in American political life today. Some people would like to see the government take on more responsibilities; others believe it already takes on too much and that America needs to promote individual responsibility instead.

While citizens often disagree about what their government should do for them, all governments have certain functions in common. National governments throughout the world perform the following functions:

Maintain a national defense. A government protects its national sovereignty, usually by maintaining armed forces. In the nuclear age, some governments possess awesome power to make war through highly sophisticated weapons. The United States currently spends over $400 billion a year on national defense. Since September 11, the defense budget has increased substantially, in part to cope with the threat of terrorism on U.S. soil.

Provide public services. Governments in this country spend billions of dollars on schools, libraries, weather forecasting, halfway houses, and dozens of other public policies. Some of these services, like highways and public parks, can be shared by everyone and cannot be denied to anyone. These kinds of services are called **public goods**. Other services, such as a college education or medical care, can be restricted to individuals who meet certain criteria but may be provided by the private sector as well. Governments typically provide these services to make them accessible to people who may not be able to afford privately available services.

public goods

Goods such as clean air and clean water that everyone must share.

Preserve order. Every government has some means of maintaining order. When people protest in large numbers, governments may resort to extreme measures to restore order. For example, the National Guard was called in to stop the looting and arson after rioting broke out in Los Angeles after the 1992 Rodney King verdict.

Socialize the young. Most modern governments pay for education and use it to instill national values among the young. School curricula typically offer a course on the theory and practice of the country's government. Rituals like the daily Pledge of Allegiance seek to foster patriotism and love of country.

Collect taxes. Approximately one out of every three dollars earned by an American citizen is used to pay national, state, and local taxes—money that pays for the public goods and services provided by the government.

All these governmental tasks add up to weighty decisions that must be made by our political leaders. For example, how much should we spend on national defense as opposed to education? How high should taxes for Medicare and Social Security be? The way we answer such questions is through politics.

Politics

Politics determines whom we select as our governmental leaders and what policies these leaders pursue. Political scientists often cite Harold D. Lasswell's famous definition of politics: "Who gets what, when, and how."[8] It is one of the briefest and most useful definitions of politics ever penned. Admittedly, this broad definition covers a lot of ground (office politics, sorority politics, and so on) in which political scientists are not interested. They are interested primarily in politics related to governmental decision making.

politics
The process that determines who we select as our governmental leaders and what policies these leaders pursue. Politics produces authoritative decisions about public issues.

The media usually focus on the *who* of politics. At a minimum, this includes voters, candidates, groups, and parties. *What* refers to the substance of politics and government—benefits, such as medical care for the elderly, and burdens, such as new taxes. In this sense, government and politics involve winners and losers. *How* people participate in politics is important, too. They get what they want through voting, supporting, compromising, lobbying, and so forth.

The Policymaking System

Americans frequently expect government to do something about their problems. For example, the president and members of Congress are expected to keep the economy humming along; voters will penalize them at the polls if they do not. The **policymaking system** reveals the way our government responds to the priorities of its people. Figure 1.4 shows a skeletal model of this system. The rest of this book will flesh out this model, but for now it will help you understand how government policy comes into being and evolves over time.

policymaking system
The process by which policy comes into being and evolves over time. People's interests, problems, and concerns create political issues for government policymakers. These issues shape policy, which in turn impacts people, generating more interests, problems, and concerns.

People Shape Policy

The policymaking system begins with people. All Americans have interests, problems, and concerns that are touched on by public policy. Some people may think the government should help train people for jobs in today's new technological environment; others may think that their taxes are too high and that the country would be best served by a large tax cut. Some people may expect government to do something to curb domestic violence; others may be concerned about prospects that the government may make it much harder to buy a handgun.

What do people do to express their opinions in a democracy? There are numerous avenues for action, such as voting for candidates who represent their opinions, joining political parties, posting messages to Internet chat groups, and forming interest groups. In this way, people's concerns enter the **linkage institutions** of the policymaking system. Linkage institutions transmit the preferences of Americans to the policymakers in government. Parties and interest groups strive to ensure that

linkage institutions
The political channels through which people's concerns become political issues on the policy agenda. In the United States, linkage institutions include elections, political parties, interest groups, and the media.

Figure 1.4 The Policymaking System

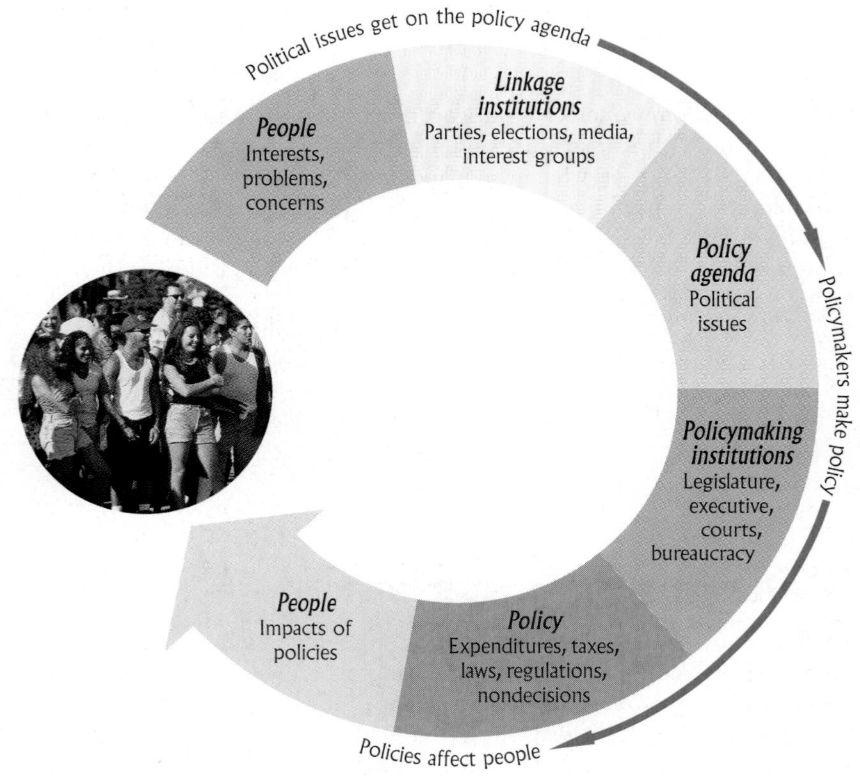

policy agenda
The issues that attract the serious attention of public officials and other people actually involved in politics at any given point in time.

You Are the Director of Economic Development for the City of Los Angeles, California

their members' concerns receive appropriate political attention. The media investigate social problems and inform people about them. Elections allow citizens the chance to make their opinions heard by choosing their public officials.

All these institutions help to shape the government's **policy agenda**, which consists of the issues that attract the serious attention of public officials and other people actively involved in politics at any given time. Some issues will be considered, and others will not. If politicians want to get elected, they must pay attention to the problems that concern the voters. When you vote, you are partly looking at whether a candidate shares your agenda. If you are worried about rising health care costs and unemployment, and a certain candidate talks only about America's moral decay and ending legalized abortions, you will probably support another candidate.

A government's policy agenda changes regularly. When jobs are scarce and business productivity is falling, economic problems occupy a high position on the government's agenda. If the economy is doing well and trouble spots around the world occupy the headlines, foreign policy questions are bound to dominate the agenda. In general, bad news—particularly about a crisis situation—is more likely than good news to draw sufficient media attention to put a subject on the policy agenda. As they say in journalism schools, "Good news is no news." When unemployment rises sharply it leads the news; when jobs are plentiful, the latest unemployment report is much less of a news story. Thus, the policy agenda responds more to societal failures than successes. The question politicians constantly ask is, "How can we as a people do better?"

People, of course, do not always agree on what government should do. Indeed, one group's concerns and interests are often at odds with those of another group. A **political issue** is the result of people disagreeing about a problem or about the public policy needed to fix it. There is never a shortage of political issues; government, however, will not act on any issue until it is high on the policy agenda.

political issue
An issue that arises when people disagree about a problem and how to fix it.

Policymakers stand at the core of the political system, working within the three **policymaking institutions** established by the U.S. Constitution: the Congress, the presidency, and the courts. Policymakers scan the issues on the policy agenda, select those that they consider important, and make policies to address them. Today, the power of the bureaucracy is so great that most political scientists consider it a fourth policymaking institution.

policymaking institutions
The branches of government charged with taking action on political issues. The U.S. Constitution established three policymaking institutions—the Congress, the presidency, and the courts. Today, the power of the bureaucracy is so great that most political scientists consider it a fourth policymaking institution.

Very few policies are made by a single policymaking institution. Environmental policy is a good example. Some presidents have used their influence with Congress to urge clean-air and clean-water policies. When Congress responds by passing legislation to clean up the environment, bureaucracies have to implement the new policies. The bureaucracies, in turn, create extensive volumes of rules and regulations that define how policies are to be implemented. In addition, every law passed and every rule made can be challenged in the courts. Courts make decisions about what the policies mean and whether they conflict with the Constitution.

Policies Impact People

Every decision that government makes—every law it passes, budget it establishes, and ruling it hands down—is **public policy.** There are many types of public policies. Table 1.1 lists some of the most important types.

public policy
A choice that **government** makes in response to a political issue. A policy is a course of action taken with regard to some problem.

Policies can also be established through inaction as well as action. Doing nothing—or nothing different—can prove to be a very consequential governmental decision. Reporter Randy Shilts's book traces the staggering growth in the number of

Table 1.1 Types of Public Policies

TYPE	DEFINITION	EXAMPLE
Congressional statute	Law passed by Congress	Social Security Act
Presidential action	Decision by president	American troops invade Iraq
Court decision	Opinion by Supreme Court or other court	Supreme Court ruling that school segregation is unconstitutional
Budgetary choices	Legislative enactment of taxes and expenditures	The federal budget
Regulation	Agency adoption of regulation	Food and Drug Administration's approval of a new drug

people with AIDS and reveals how governments in Washington and elsewhere did little or debated quietly about what to do.[9] Shilts claims that because politicians viewed AIDS as a gay person's disease, they were reluctant to support measures to deal with it, fearful of losing the votes of antigay constituents. The issue thus remained a low priority on the government's policy agenda until infections started to spread to the general population, including celebrities like basketball star Magic Johnson.

How to Satisfy Aunt Martha

Once policies are made and implemented, they affect people. Policy impacts are the effects that a policy has on people and on society's problems. People want policy that addresses their interests, problems, and concerns. A new law, executive order, bureaucratic regulation, or court judgment doesn't mean much if it doesn't work. Environmentalists want an industrial emissions policy that not only claims to prevent air pollution but also does so. Minority groups want a civil rights policy that not only promises them equal treatment but also ensures it.

Having a policy implies a goal. Whether we want to reduce poverty, cut crime, clean the water, or hold down inflation, we have a goal in mind. Policy impact analysts ask how well a policy achieves its goal—and at what cost. The analysis of policy impacts carries the political system back to its point of origin: the concerns of the people. Translating people's desires into effective public policy is crucial to the workings of democracy.

Democracy

In 1848, Karl Marx and Friedrich Engels published *The Communist Manifesto*, one of the most famous political documents ever written. It began with these words: "A specter is haunting Europe. It is the specter of communism." Today one could write, "A specter is haunting the world. It is the specter of democracy." In recent years, democratic forms of governments have emerged in Eastern European countries that were formerly communist, in Latin American countries that were controlled by military dictatorships, and in South Africa, where apartheid denied basic rights to the Black majority. Yet despite this global move toward democracy, not everyone defines democracy the way Americans do—or think they do.

Defining Democracy

democracy
A system of selecting policymakers and of organizing government so that policy represents and responds to the public's preferences.

Democracy is a means of selecting policymakers and of organizing government so that policy reflects citizens' preferences. Today, the term *democracy* takes its place among terms like *freedom*, *justice*, and *peace* as a word that seemingly has only positive connotations. Yet the writers of the U.S. Constitution had no fondness for democracy, as many of them doubted the ability of ordinary Americans to make informed judgments about what government should do. Roger Sherman, a delegate to the Constitutional Convention, said the people "should have as little to do as may be with the government." Only much later did Americans come to cherish democracy and believe that all citizens should actively participate in choosing their leaders.

Most Americans would probably say that democracy is "government by the people." This phrase, of course, is part of Abraham Lincoln's famous definition of

Just as a multitude of statues of Lenin were pulled down as communism fell in eastern Europe in 1989, so the statues of Saddam Hussein were pulled down in Iraq in 2003. The formerly communist eastern European countries are now democracies, and one goal of the U.S. government for the rebuilding of Iraq is to ensure that it too becomes a democracy.

democracy from his Gettysburg Address: "Government of the people, by the people, and for the people." How well each of these aspects of democracy is being met is a matter crucial to evaluating how well our government is working. Certainly, government has always been "of the people" in the United States, for the Constitution forbids granting titles of nobility. On the other hand, it is a physical impossibility for government to be "by the people" in a society of 300 million people. Therefore, our democracy involves choosing people from among our midst to govern. Where the serious debate begins is whether political leaders govern "for the people," as there always are significant biases in how the system works. Democratic theorists have elaborated a set of more specific goals for evaluating this crucial question.

American Democracy and Human Rights

Traditional Democratic Theory

Traditional democratic theory rests on a number of key principles that specify how governmental decisions are arrived at in a democracy. Robert Dahl, one of America's leading theorists, suggests that an ideal democratic process should satisfy the following five criteria:

Equality in voting. The principle of "one person, one vote" is basic to democracy. Voting need not be universal, but it must be representative.

Effective participation. Citizens must have adequate and equal opportunities to express their preferences throughout the decision-making process.

Self Government

Enlightened understanding. A democratic society must be a marketplace of ideas. A free press and free speech are essential to civic understanding. If one group monopolizes and distorts information, citizens cannot truly understand issues.

Citizen control of the agenda. Citizens should have the collective right to control the government's policy agenda. If wealthy individuals or groups distort the agenda, the people cannot make government address the issues they feel are most important.

Inclusion. The government must include, and extend rights to, all those subject to its laws. Citizenship must be open to all within a nation if the nation is to call itself democratic.[10]

majority rule
A fundamental principle of **traditional democratic theory**. In a democracy, choosing among alternatives requires that the majority's desire be respected.

minority rights
A principle of **traditional democratic theory** that guarantees rights to those who do not belong to majorities and allows that they might join majorities through persuasion and reasoned argument.

representation
A basic principle of **traditional democratic theory** that describes the relationship between the few leaders and the many followers.

Only by following these principles can a political system be called "democratic." Furthermore, democracies must practice **majority rule**, meaning that in choosing among alternatives, the will of more than half the voters should be followed. At the same time, most Americans would not want to give the majority free rein to do anything they can agree on. Restraints on the majority are built into the American system of government in order to protect the minority. Basic principles such as freedom of speech and assembly are inviolable **minority rights** that the majority cannot infringe on.

In a society too large to make its decisions in open meetings, a few will have to look after the concerns of many. The relationship between the few leaders and the many followers is one of **representation**. The literal meaning of representation is to make present once again. In politics, this means that the desires of the people should be replicated in government through the choices of elected officials. The closer the correspondence between representatives and their constituents, the closer the approximation to an ideal democracy. As might be expected for such a crucial question, theorists disagree widely about the extent to which this actually occurs in America.

Three Contemporary Theories of American Democracy

Theories of American democracy are essentially theories about who has power and influence. All, in one way or another, ask the question "Who really governs our nation?" Each focuses on a key aspect of politics and government, and each reaches a somewhat different conclusion.

pluralist theory
A theory of government and politics emphasizing that politics is mainly a competition among groups, each one pressing for its own preferred policies.

Pluralist Theory. One important theory of American democracy, **pluralist theory**, states that groups with shared interests influence public policy by pressing their concerns through organized efforts. Pluralists are generally optimistic that the public interest will eventually prevail in creating public policy through a complex process of bargaining and compromise. They believe that rather than speaking of majority rule we should speak of groups of minorities working together. Robert Dahl expresses this view well when he writes that in America "all active and legitimate groups in the population can make themselves heard at some crucial stage in the process."[11]

Elite and Class Theory. Critics of pluralism believe that it paints too rosy a picture of American political life. By arguing that almost every group can get a piece of the pie, they say that pluralists miss the larger question of how the pie is distributed. **Elite and class theory** contends that our society, like all societies, is divided along class lines and that an upper-class elite pulls the strings of government. Wealth—the holding of assets such as property, stocks, and bonds—is the basis of this power. Over a third of the nation's wealth is currently held by just 1 percent of the population. Elite and class theorists believe that this 1 percent of Americans controls most policy decisions because they can afford to finance election campaigns and control key institutions such as large corporations. According to elite and class theory, a few powerful Americans do not merely influence policymakers—they *are* the policymakers.

elite and class theory
A theory of government and politics contending that societies are divided along class lines and that an upper-class elite will rule, regardless of the formal niceties of governmental organization.

Since George W. Bush assumed the presidency, many scholars have argued that the political deck has become increasingly stacked in favor of the superrich. For example, political scientists Jacob Hacker and Paul Pierson wrote in 2005 that "America's political market no longer looks like the effectively functioning markets that economics textbooks laud. Rather, it increasingly resembles the sort of market that gave us the Enron scandal, in which corporate bigwigs with privileged information got rich at the expense of ordinary shareholders, workers, and consumers."[12] A report on rising inequality issued by the American Political Science Association in 2004 concluded, "Citizens with lower or moderate incomes speak with a whisper that is lost on the ears of inattentive government officials, while the advantaged roar with a clarity and consistency that policymakers readily hear and routinely follow."[13]

Hyperpluralism. A third theory, **hyperpluralism**, offers a different critique of pluralism. Hyperpluralism is pluralism gone sour. In this view, groups are so strong that government is weakened, as the influence of many groups cripples government's ability to make policy. Hyperpluralism states many groups—not just the elite ones—are so strong that government is unable to act. These powerful groups divide the government and its authority. Hyperpluralist theory holds that government gives in to every conceivable interest and single-issue group. When politicians try to placate every group, the result is confusing, contradictory, and muddled policy—if politicians manage to make policy at all. Like elite and class theorists, hyperpluralist theorists suggest that the public interest is rarely translated into public policy.

hyperpluralism
A theory of government and politics contending that groups are so strong that government is weakened. Hyperpluralism is an extreme, exaggerated, or perverted form of **pluralism**.

Challenges to Democracy

Regardless of which theory is most convincing, there are a number of continuing challenges to democracy. Many of these challenges apply to American democracy as well as to the fledgling democracies around the world.

Increased Technical Expertise. Traditional democratic theory holds that ordinary citizens have the good sense to reach political judgments and that government has the capacity to act on those judgments. Today, however, we live in a society of experts whose technical knowledge overshadows the knowledge of the general population. What, after all, does the average citizen—however conscientious—know about eligibility criteria for welfare, agricultural price supports, foreign competition, and the hundreds of other issues that confront government each year? Years ago, the power of the few—the elite—might have been based on property holdings. Today, the elite are likely to be those who command knowledge, the experts. Even the most rigorous democratic theory does not demand that citizens be experts on everything; but as human knowledge has expanded, it has become increasingly difficult for individual citizens to make well-informed decisions.

Limited Participation in Government. When citizens do not seem to take their citizenship seriously, democracy's defenders worry. There is plenty of evidence that Americans know little about who their leaders are, much less about their policy decisions, as we will discuss at length in Chapter 6. Furthermore, Americans do not take full advantage of their opportunities to shape government or select its leaders. Limited participation in government challenges the foundation of democracy. In particular, because young people represent the country's future, their abysmal voting turnout rates point to an even more serious challenge to democracy on the horizon.

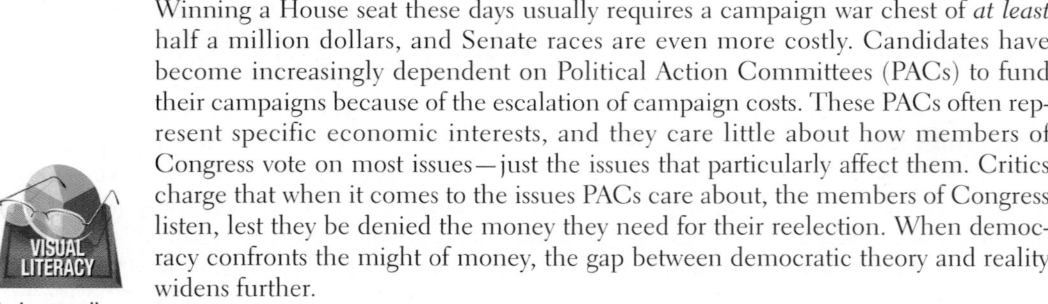

Escalating Campaign Costs. Many political observers worry about the close connection between money and politics, especially in congressional elections. Winning a House seat these days usually requires a campaign war chest of *at least* half a million dollars, and Senate races are even more costly. Candidates have become increasingly dependent on Political Action Committees (PACs) to fund their campaigns because of the escalation of campaign costs. These PACs often represent specific economic interests, and they care little about how members of Congress vote on most issues—just the issues that particularly affect them. Critics charge that when it comes to the issues PACs care about, the members of Congress listen, lest they be denied the money they need for their reelection. When democracy confronts the might of money, the gap between democratic theory and reality widens further.

Understanding Who We Are

Diverse Political Interests. The diversity of the American people is reflected in the diversity of interests represented in the political system. As will be shown in this book, this system is so open that interests find it easy to gain access to policymakers. Moreover, the distribution of power within the government is so decentralized that access to a few policymakers may be enough to determine the outcome of public policy battles.

When interests conflict, which they often do, no coalition may be strong enough to form a majority and establish policy. But each interest may use its influence to thwart those whose policy proposals they oppose. In effect, they have a veto over policy, creating what is often referred to as **policy gridlock**. In a big city,

policy gridlock
A condition that occurs when no coalition is strong enough to form a majority and establish policy. The result is that nothing may get done.

gridlock occurs when there are so many cars on the road that no one can move. In politics, it occurs when each policy coalition finds its way blocked by others. This political problem is magnified when voters choose a president of one party and congressional majorities of the other party, as was often the case in the 1980s and 1990s. Thus, a major challenge to democracy in America is to overcome the diversity of interests and fragmentation of power in order to deliver policies that are responsive to citizens' needs.

American Political Culture and Democracy

The key factor that holds American democracy together in the view of many scholars is its **political culture**—the overall set of values widely shared within American society. As Ronald Inglehart and Christian Welzel argue in their recent book on cultural change and democracy, "Democracy is not simply the result of clever elite bargaining and constitutional engineering. It depends on deep-rooted orientations among the people themselves. These orientations motivate them to demand freedom and responsive government. . . . Genuine democracy is not simply a machine that, once set up, functions by itself. It depends on the people."[14]

political culture
An overall set of values widely shared within a society.

Far more than most countries, the political culture of the United States is crucial to understanding its government, as Americans are so diverse in terms of ancestries, religions, and heritages. What unites Americans more than anything else is a set of shared beliefs and values. As G. K. Chesterton, the noted British observer of American politics, wrote in 1922, "America is the only nation in the world that is founded on a creed. That creed is set forth with dogmatic and even theological lucidity in the Declaration of Independence."[15] Arguing along the same lines, Seymour Martin Lipset writes that "the United States is a country organized around an ideology which includes a set of dogmas about the nature of good society."[16] Lipset argues that the American creed can be summarized by five elements: liberty, egalitarianism, individualism, laissez-faire, and populism.[17] We will review each of these aspects of American political culture briefly below.

What Are American Civic Values?

Liberty. One of the most famous statements of the American Revolution was Patrick Henry's "Give me liberty or give me death." During the Cold War, a common bumper sticker was "Better Dead Than Red," reflecting many Americans' view that they would prefer to fight to the bitter end than submit to the oppression of communist rule. To this day, New Hampshire's official state motto is "Live Free or Die." When immigrants are asked why they came to America, by far the most common response is to live in freedom.

Freedom of speech and religion are fundamental to the American way of life. In the Declaration of Independence, Thomas Jefferson placed liberty right along with life and the pursuit of happiness as an "unalienable right" (that is, a right not awarded by human power, not transferable to another power, and incapable of repudiation).

Egalitarianism. The most famous phrase in the history of democracy is the Declaration of Independence's statement "We hold these truths to be self-evident that all men are created equal." As the French observer Alexis de Tocqueville noted long ago, egalitarianism in the United States involves equality of opportunity and respect in the absence of a monarchy and aristocracy. Americans have never been equal in terms of condition. What is most critical to this part of the American creed is that everyone has a chance to be rich—not that everyone will be rich.

Tocqueville accurately saw into the American future that the social equality he observed in American life in the 1830s would eventually lead to political equality. Although relatively few Americans then had the right to vote, he predicted that all Americans would be given these rights because, in order to guarantee equality of opportunity, everyone must have an equal opportunity to participate in democratic governance. Thus, another key aspect of egalitarianism is political equality, which involves equal voting rights for all American citizens.

Individualism. One of the aspects of American political culture that has shaped the development of American democracy has been individualism—the belief that people can and should get ahead on their own. The immigrants who founded American society may have been diverse, but many shared a common dream of America as a place where one could make it on one's own without interference from government. Louis Hartz's *The Liberal Tradition in America* is a classic analysis of the dominant political beliefs during America's formative years. Hartz argues that the major force behind limited government in America is that it was settled by people who fled from the feudal and clerical oppressions of the Old World. Once in the New World, they wanted little from government other than for it to leave them alone.[18]

Another explanation for American individualism is the existence of a bountiful frontier—at least up until the start of the twentieth century. Not only did many people come to America to escape from governmental interference, but the frontier allowed them to get away from government almost entirely once they arrived. Frederick Jackson Turner's famous work on the significance of the frontier in American history argues that "the frontier is productive of individualism."[19] According to Turner, being in the wilderness and having to survive on one's own left settlers with an aversion to any control from the outside world—particularly from the government.

Laissez-faire. An important result of American individualism has been a clear tendency to prefer laissez-faire economic policies, which promote free markets and limited government. As John Kingdon writes in his book *America the Unusual*, "Government in the United States is much more limited and much smaller than government in virtually every other advanced industrialized country on earth."[20] Compared to most other economically developed nations, the United States devotes a smaller percentage of its resources to government. As we will see in Chapter 15, the tax burden on Americans is small compared to other democratic nations.

Further, most advanced industrial democracies have a system of national insurance that provides most health care; the United States does not, though Bill Clinton unsuccessfully tried to establish such a system. In other countries, national governments have taken it on themselves to start up airline, telephone, and communications companies. Governments have built much of the housing in most Western nations, compared to only a small fraction of the housing in America. Thus, in terms of its impact on citizens' everyday lives, government in the United States actually does less than the governments of similar countries.

Populism. Abraham Lincoln summarized American democracy as a "government of the people, for the people, and by the people." Such an emphasis on *the people* is at the heart of populism, which can best be defined as a political philosophy supporting the rights of average citizens in their struggle against privileged elites. As Lipset writes, American populist thought holds that the people at large "are possessed of some kind of sacred mystique, and proximity to them endows the politician with esteem—and with legitimacy."[21]

In America, being on the side of the ordinary people against big interests is so valued that liberal and conservative politicians alike frequently claim this mantle. Liberals are inclined to argue that they will stand up to big multinational corporations and protect the interests of ordinary Americans. Conservatives, on the other hand, are likely to repeat Ronald Reagan's famous promise to get big government off the backs of the American people. A populist pledge to "put the people first" is always a safe strategy in the American political culture.

A Culture War?

Although Americans are widely supportive of cultural values like liberty and egalitarianism, some scholars are concerned that a sharp polarization into rival political camps with different political cultures has taken place in recent years. James Q. Wilson defines such a polarization as "an intense commitment to a candidate, a culture, or an ideology that sets people in one group definitively apart from people in another, rival group."[22] Wilson believes that America is a more polarized nation today than in any time in living memory. He argues that the intensity of political divisions in twenty-first-century America is a major problem, writing that "a divided America encourages our enemies, disheartens our allies, and saps our resolve— potentially to fatal effect."[23]

Other scholars, however, believe that there is relatively little evidence of a so-called culture war going on among ordinary American citizens. Morris Fiorina concludes, "There is little indication that voters are polarized now or that they are becoming more polarized—even when we look specifically at issues such as abortion that supposedly are touchstone issues in the culture war. If anything, public opinion has grown more centrist on such issues and more tolerant of the divergent views, values, and behavior of other Americans."[24] Wayne Baker outlines three ways in which America might be experiencing a crisis of cultural values: 1) a loss over time of traditional values, such as the importance of religion and family life; 2) an unfavorable comparison with the citizens of other countries in terms of values such as patriotism or support for moral principles; and 3) the division of society into opposed groups with irreconcilable moral differences. Baker tests each of these three possibilities thoroughly with recent survey data from the United States and other countries and finds little evidence of an ongoing crisis of values in America.[25]

Preview Questions About Democracy

Throughout *Government in America* you will be asked to evaluate American democracy. The chapters that follow will acquaint you with the development of democracy in the United States. For example, the next chapter will show that the U.S. Constitution was not originally designed to promote democracy but has slowly evolved to its current form. Much of America's move toward greater democracy has centered on the extension of civil liberties and civil rights we review in Chapters 4 and 5. Probably the most important civil right is the right to vote. Upcoming chapters will examine voting behavior and elections and ask the following questions about how people form their opinions and to what extent they express these opinions via elections:

- Are people knowledgeable about matters of public policy?
- Do they apply what knowledge they have to their voting choices?
- Are American elections designed to facilitate public participation?

Linkage institutions, such as interest groups, political parties, and the media, help translate input from the public into output from the policymakers. When you explore these institutions, consider the extent to which they either help or hinder democracy.

- Does the interest group system allow for all points of view to be heard, or do significant biases give advantages to particular groups?
- Do political parties provide voters with clear choices, or do they intentionally obscure their stands on issues in order to get as many votes as possible?
- If there are choices, do the media help citizens understand them?

The Initiative and Referendum

It is up to public officials actually to make the policy choices because American government is a representative democracy. For democracy to work well, elected officials must be responsive to public opinion.

- Is the Congress representative of American society, and is it capable of reacting to changing times?
- Does the president look after the general welfare of the public, or has the office become too focused on the interests of the elite?

These are some of the crucial questions you will address in discussing the executive and legislative branches of government. In addition, the way our non-elected institutions—the bureaucracy and the courts—function is crucial to evaluating how well American democracy works. These institutions are designed to implement and interpret the law, but bureaucrats and judges often cannot avoid making public policy as well. When they do so, are they violating democratic principles for policy decisions, given that neither institution can be held accountable at the ballot box?

All these questions concerning democracy in America have more than one answer. A goal of *Government in America* is to offer different ways to evaluate and answer these questions. One way to approach the preceding questions is to address one of the most important questions facing modern American democracy: Is the scope of government responsibilities too vast, just about right, or not comprehensive enough?

The Scope of Government in America

Comparing Political Landscapes

In his first presidential address to Congress in 1993, Bill Clinton stated, "I want to talk to you about what government can do because I believe government must do more." Toward this end, President Clinton later proposed a comprehensive government program to require businesses to provide a basic level of health insurance for their employees. Congressional Republicans lined up solidly against Clinton's plan for national health insurance, arguing that government intervention in the affairs of individual citizens and businesses does more harm than good.

Those who are inclined to support government involvement in matters such as health care argue that intervention is the only means of achieving important goals in American society. How else, they ask, can we ensure that everyone has enough to eat, clean air and water, and affordable housing? How else can we ensure that the disadvantaged are given opportunities for education and jobs and are not discriminated against? Opponents of widening the scope of government agree that these are worthwhile goals but challenge whether involving the federal government is an effective way to pursue them. Dick Armey, who served as the Republicans' majority leader in the House from 1995 to 2002, expressed this view well when he wrote, "There is more wisdom in millions of individuals making decisions in their own self-interest than there is in even the most enlightened bureaucrat (or congressman) making decisions on their behalf."[26] Or, as President George W. Bush regularly told supporters during the 2000 presidential campaign, "Our opponents trust the government; we trust the people."

To understand the dimensions of this debate, it is important first to get some sense of the current scope of the federal government's activities.

How Active Is American Government?

In terms of dollars spent, government in America is vast. Altogether, our governments—national, state, and local—spend about 29 percent of our **gross domestic product**, the total value of all goods and services produced annually by the United States. Government not only spends large sums of money but also employs large numbers of people. About 18 million Americans work for our government, mostly at the state and local level as teachers, police officers, university professors, and so on. Consider some facts about the size of our national government:

gross domestic product
The sum total of the value of all the goods and services produced in a nation.

- It spends about $2.8 trillion annually (printed as a number, that's $2,800,000,000,000 a year).
- It employs nearly 2 million people.
- It owns one-third of the land in the United States.
- It occupies 2.6 billion square feet of office space, more than four times the office space located in the nation's 10 largest cities.
- It owns and operates more than 400,000 nonmilitary vehicles.

How does the American national government spend $2.8 trillion a year? National defense takes about one-sixth of the federal budget, a much smaller percentage than it did three decades ago. Social Security consumes more than one-fifth of the budget. Medicare is another big-ticket item, requiring a little over one-tenth of the budget. State and local governments also get important parts of the federal government's budget. The federal government helps fund highway and airport construction, police departments, school districts, and other state and local functions.

When expenditures grow, tax revenues must grow to pay the additional costs. When taxes do not grow as fast as spending, a budget deficit results. The federal government ran a budget deficit every year from 1969 through 1997. The last few Clinton budgets showed surpluses, but soon after George W. Bush took over the government was running a deficit once again. In fiscal year 2006, the deficit for the year was over $300 billion. No doubt the events of September 11 contributed to the reappearance of deficit spending due to the negative impact they had on the U.S. economy as well as the added security expenses the government suddenly encountered. But opponents of President Bush have put much of the blame on the large tax cut the president proposed in the 2000 campaign and then delivered early in his presidency. In any event, years of deficits have left the country with a national debt of over $8 trillion, which will continue to pose a problem for policymakers for decades to come.

Whatever the national problem—pollution, AIDS, hurricane relief, homelessness, hunger, sexism—many people expect Congress to solve it with legislation. Thus, American government certainly matters tremendously in terms of dollars spent, persons employed, and laws passed. Our concern, however, is less about the absolute size of government and more about whether government activity is what we want it to be.

Preview Questions About the Scope of Government

Debate over the scope of government is central to contemporary American politics, and it is a theme this text will examine in each chapter. Our goal is not to determine for you the proper role of the national government. Instead, you will explore the implications of the way politics, institutions, and policy in America affect the scope of government. By raising questions such as those listed in the next few paragraphs, you may draw your own conclusions about the appropriate role of government in America. Part One of *Government in America* examines the constitutional foundations of American government. A concern with the proper scope of government leads to a series of questions regarding the constitutional structure of American politics, including the following:

- What role did the Constitution's authors foresee for the federal government?
- Does the Constitution favor a government with a broad scope, or is it neutral on this issue?

- Why did the functions of government increase, and why did they increase most at the national rather than the state level?
- Has bigger, more active government constrained freedom, or does the increased scope of government serve to protect civil liberties and civil rights?

Part Two focuses on those who make demands on government, including the public, political parties, interest groups, and the media. Here you will seek answers to questions such as the following:

- Does the public favor a large, active government?
- Do competing political parties predispose the government to provide more public services?
- Do elections help control the scope of government, or do they legitimize an increasing role for the public sector?
- Are pressures from interest groups necessarily translated into more governmental regulations, bigger budgets, and the like?
- Has media coverage of government enhanced government's status and growth, or have the media been an instrument for controlling government?

One of the most debated issues in recent years has been gun control. Critics of gun control argue that it involves an expansion of the size of government, which infringes on freedom, whereas proponents maintain it is well within the scope of reasonable governmental activities. Here, advocates of restrictions on gun sales express their point of view.

Governmental institutions themselves obviously deserve close examination. Part Three discusses these institutions and asks the following:

- Has the presidency been a driving force behind increasing the scope and power of government (and thus of the president)?
- Can the president control a government with so many programs and responsibilities?
- Is Congress, because it is subject to constant elections, predisposed toward big government?
- Is Congress too responsive to the demands of the public and organized interests?

The nonelected branches of government, which are also discussed in these chapters, are especially interesting when we consider the issue of the scope of government. For instance:

- Are the federal courts too active in policymaking, intruding on the authority and responsibility of other branches and levels of government?
- Is the bureaucracy too acquisitive, constantly seeking to expand its budgets and authority, or is it simply a reflection of the desires of elected officials?
- Is the bureaucracy too large and thus a wasteful menace to efficient and fair implementation of public policies?

The next 17 chapters will search for answers to these and many other questions regarding the scope of government and why it matters. You will undoubtedly add a few questions of your own as you seek to resolve the issue of the proper scope of government involvement.

Summary

Evidence abounds that young people today are politically apathetic. They shouldn't be. Politics and government matter a great deal to everyone and affect many aspects of life. If nothing else, we hope this text will convince you of this.

Government consists of those institutions that make authoritative public policies for society as a whole. In the United States, four key institutions make policy at the national level: Congress, the presidency, the courts, and the bureaucracy. Politics is, very simply, who gets what, when, and how. The result of government and politics is public policy.

The first question central to governing is, "How should we govern?" Americans are fond of calling their government democratic. Democratic government includes, above all else, a commitment to majority rule and minority rights. American political culture can be characterized by five key concepts: liberty, egalitarianism, individualism, laissez-faire, and populism. This text will help you compare the way American government works with the standards of democracy and will continually address questions about who holds power and who influences the policies adopted by government.

The second fundamental question regarding governing is, "What should government do?" One of the most important issues about government in America has to do with its scope. Conservatives often talk about the evils of intrusive government; liberals see the national government as rather modest in comparison both to what it could do and to the functions governments perform in other democratic nations.

Internet Resources

www.policyalmanac.org
Contains a discussion of major policy issues of the day and links to resources about them.

http://thomas.loc.gov/home/histdox/fedpapers.html
The complete collection of the *Federalist Papers.*

www.tocqueville.org
Information and discussion about Tocqueville's classic work *Democracy in America.*

www.bowlingalone.com
A site designed to accompany Robert Putnam's work, which contains information concerning the data he used and projects he is working on to reinvigorate American communities.

www.yahoo.com/Government
A good place to go to search for information about government and politics.

Get Connected

The Policymaking System

Americans frequently want government to enact specific policies in order to address various problems. However, not all problems are the same. In addition, not all Americans agree on which problems government should solve or on how government should solve them. As Figure 1.4 illustrates, the policymaking system in the United States is complex with many actors and institutions involved. Political parties—one of the many linkage institutions within the policymaking system—play a key role because they bring the people's concerns to the policy agenda. In order to examine this part of the policymaking system up close, let us take a look at a concern shared by many Americans—Social Security insurance and its continued availability—and the proposed policies of key political parties to address this concern.

Search the Web

Go to the Web sites for the platforms of the Green Party, *www.gp.org/platform/2004/socjustice.html#1000939*; the Republican Party, *www.gop.com/Issues/SocialSecurity/*; the Democratic Party, *www.democrats.org/a/national/secure_retirement/*; and the Libertarian Party, *www.lp.org/issues/social-security.shtml*. Review the portion of each platform that relates to Social Security. Get a sense of each party's position on Social Security reform. Write down the key terms and phrases each platform uses.

Questions to Ask

- Based on what you have read, do you think the different political parties have different views on Social Security insurance?
- Which party appears to propose the least significant changes in the Social Security program?
- Which party appears to propose the most significant changes in the Social Security program?
- After reading each party's position, which do you most agree with?

Why It Matters

We all pay Social Security, and it is hoped that we will all have a chance to collect it when the time comes. However, there are many proposals to change the Social Security system. Some of the proposals might make it more difficult to collect. Others might make it more costly. Still others might make it possible for citizens to invest part of their Social Security in the stock market. It is important to understand these proposals and to support the party that best reflects your view on what should happen to Social Security insurance.

Get Involved

Go to the Web and try to find your major state political party Web sites. See how each of the parties proposes solving the problems you think are most pressing in your state. For instance, how do the parties propose paying for education or roads? Or, what are their positions on the environment and declining population in rural areas? If you find that you agree with one of them, you might want to consider sending an e-mail asking about how you can become involved with that party.

For more excercises, go to www.longmanamericangovernment.com.

For Further Reading

Bok, Derek. *The State of the Nation: Government and the Quest for a Better Society*. Cambridge, MA: Harvard University Press, 1996. An excellent analysis of how America is doing, compared to other major democracies, on a wide variety of policy aspects.

de Tocqueville, Alexis. *Democracy in America*. New York: Mentor Books, 1956. This classic by a nineteenth-century French aristocrat remains one of the most insightful works on the nature of American society and government.

Hartz, Louis. *The Liberal Tradition in America*. New York: Harcourt, Brace, 1955. A classic analysis of why the scope of American government has been more limited than in other democracies.

Kingdon, John W. *Agendas, Alternatives, and Public Policies*. 2nd ed. New York: HarperCollins, 1995. One of the first efforts by a political scientist to examine the political agenda.

Macedo, Stephen, et al. *Democracy at Risk: How Political Choices Undermine Citizen Participation, and What We Can Do About It*. Washington, DC: Brookings, 2005. An insightful review of many aspects of political participation in America.

Putnam, Robert. *Bowling Alone: The Collapse and Revival of American Community*. New York: Simon & Schuster, 2000. Putnam's highly influential work shows how Americans have become increasingly disconnected from one another since the early 1960s.

Sitaraman, Ganesh, and Previn Warren. *Invisible Citizens: Youth Politics After September 11*. New York: iUniverse, Inc., 2003. Two Harvard students examine why it is that today's youth demonstrate a commitment to community service while at the same largely neglect involvement in politics.

Stanley, Harold W., and Richard G. Niemi. *Vital Statistics on American Politics, 2005–2006*. Washington, DC: Congressional Quarterly Press, 2006. Useful data on government, politics, and policy in the United States.

CHAPTER 2

The Constitution

Chapter Outline

POLITICS IN ACTION: AMENDING THE CONSTITUTION Gregory Lee Johnson knew little about the Constitution, but he knew he was upset. He felt that the buildup of nuclear weapons in the world threatened the planet's survival, and he wanted to protest presidential and corporate policies concerning nuclear weapons. Yet he had no money to hire a lobbyist or to purchase an ad in a newspaper. So he, along with some other demonstrators, marched through the streets of Dallas, chanting political slogans and stopping at several corporate locations to stage "die-ins" intended to dramatize the consequences of nuclear war. The demonstration ended in front of Dallas City Hall, where Gregory doused an American flag with kerosene and set it on fire.

Burning the flag violated the law, and Gregory was convicted of "desecration of a venerated object," sentenced to one year in prison, and fined $2,000. He appealed his conviction, claiming the law that prohibited burning the flag violated his freedom of speech. The U.S. Supreme Court agreed in the case of *Texas v. Gregory Lee Johnson.*

Gregory was pleased with the Court's decision, but he was nearly alone. The public howled its opposition to the decision, and President George H. W. Bush called for a constitutional amendment authorizing punishment of flag desecraters. Many public officials vowed to support the amendment, and organized opposition to the amendment was scarce. However, an amendment to prohibit burning the American flag did not obtain the two-thirds vote in each house of Congress necessary to send a constitutional amendment to the states for ratification.

Instead, Congress passed a law—the Flag Protection Act—that outlawed the desecration of the American flag. The next year, however, in *United States v. Eichman,* the Supreme Court found the act an impermissible infringement on free speech.

After years of political posturing, legislation, and litigation, little has changed. Burning the flag remains a legally protected form of political expression despite the objections of the overwhelming majority of the American public. Gregory Johnson did not prevail because he was especially articulate, nor did he win because he had access to political resources such as money or powerful supporters. He won because of the nature of the Constitution.

Understanding how an unpopular protestor like Gregory Lee Johnson could prevail against the combined forces of the public and its elected officials is central to understanding the American system of government. The Constitution supersedes ordinary law, even when the law represents the wishes of a majority of citizens. The Constitution not only guarantees individual rights but also decentralizes power. Even the president, "the leader of the free world," cannot force Congress to act, as George Bush could not force Congress to start the process of amending the Constitution. Power is not concentrated efficiently in one person's hands, such as the president's. Instead, there are numerous checks on the exercise of power and many obstacles to change. Some complain that this system produces stalemate, while others praise the way it protects minority views. Both positions are correct.

Gregory Johnson's case raises some important questions about government in America. What does democracy mean if the majority does not get its way? Is this how we should be governed? And is it appropriate that the many limits on the scope of government action, both direct and indirect, prevent action desired by most people?

---

constitution

A nation's basic law. It creates political institutions, assigns or divides powers in government, and often provides certain guarantees to citizens. Constitutions can be either written or unwritten. See also **U.S. Constitution.**

A **constitution** is a nation's basic law. It creates political institutions, allocates power within government, and often provides guarantees to citizens. A constitution is also an unwritten accumulation of traditions and precedents that have established acceptable styles of behavior and policy outcomes.

A constitution sets the broad rules of the game of politics, allowing certain types of competition among certain players. *These rules are never neutral,* however. Instead, they give some participants and some policy options advantages over others in the policymaking process. To understand government and to answer questions about how we are governed and what government does, we must first understand the Constitution.

The Origins of the Constitution

In the summer of 1776, a small group of men met in Philadelphia and passed a resolution that began an armed rebellion against the government of the most powerful nation on Earth. The resolution was, of course, the Declaration of Independence; the armed rebellion was the American Revolution.

The Road to Revolution

By eighteenth-century standards, life was not bad for most people in America at the time of the Revolution (slaves and indentured servants being major exceptions). In fact, White colonists "were freer, more equal, more prosperous, and less burdened with cumbersome feudal and monarchical restraints than any other part of mankind."[1] Although the colonies were part of the British Empire, the king and Parliament generally confined themselves to governing America's foreign policy and trade. Almost everything else was left to the discretion of individual colonial governments. Although commercial regulations irritated colonial shippers, planters, land speculators, and merchants, these rules had little influence on the vast bulk of the population, who were self-employed farmers or artisans.

As you can see in Figure 2.1, Britain obtained an enormous new territory in North America after the French and Indian War (also known as the Seven Years'

Figure 2.1 European Claims in North America

Following its victory in the French and Indian War in 1763, Britain obtained an enormous new territory to govern. To raise revenues to defend and administer the territory, it raised taxes on the colonists and tightened enforcement of trade regulations.

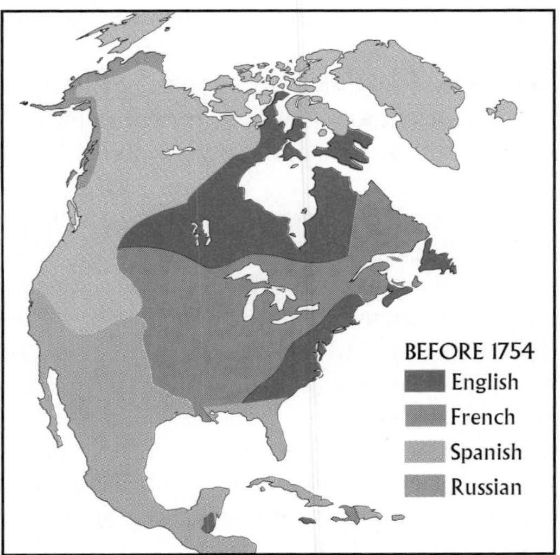

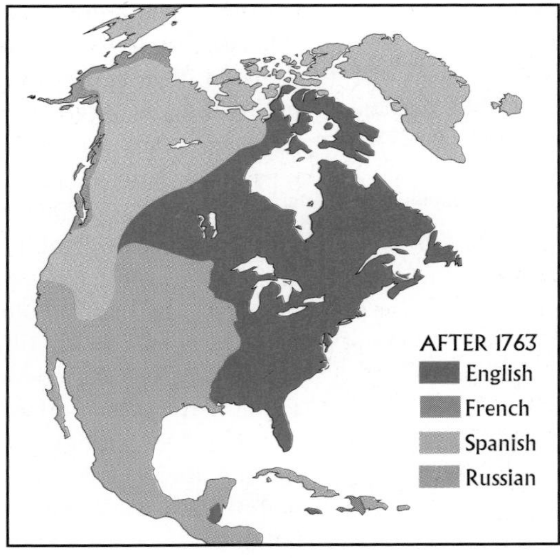

War) ended in 1763. The cost of defending this territory against foreign adversaries was large, and Parliament reasoned that it was only fair that those who were the primary beneficiaries—the colonists—should contribute to their own defense. Thus, in order to raise revenue for colonial administration and defense, the British Parliament passed a series of taxes on official documents, newspapers, paper, glass, paint, and tea. Britain also began tightening enforcement of its trade regulations, which were designed to benefit the mother country, not the colonists.

The colonists lacked direct representation in Parliament and resented the legislature imposing taxes without their consent. They protested, boycotted the taxed goods, and as a symbolic act of disobedience even threw 342 chests of tea into Boston Harbor. Britain reacted by applying economic pressure through a naval blockade of the harbor, further fueling the colonists' anger. The colonists responded by forming the First Continental Congress in September 1774, sending delegates from each colony to Philadelphia to discuss the future of relations with Britain.

Declaring Independence

As colonial discontent with the English festered, the Continental Congress was in almost continuous session during 1775 and 1776. In May and June of 1776, the Continental Congress began debating resolutions about independence. On June 7, Richard Henry Lee of Virginia moved "that these United States are and of rights ought to be free and independent states." A committee composed of Thomas Jefferson of Virginia, John Adams of Massachusetts, Benjamin Franklin of Pennsylvania, Roger Sherman of Connecticut, and Robert Livingston of New York was formed to draft a document to justify the inevitable declaration. On July 2, Lee's motion to declare independence from England was formally approved. The Congress adopted the famous **Declaration of Independence,** written primarily by Jefferson, two days later, on July 4.

Declaration of Independence
The document approved by representatives of the American colonies in 1776 that stated their grievances against the British monarch and declared their independence.

The Declaration of Independence quickly became one of the most widely quoted and revered documents in America. Filled with fine principles and bold language, it can be read as both a political tract and a philosophical treatise. (It is reprinted in the Appendix of this book.)

Politically, the Declaration was a polemic, announcing and justifying a revolution. Most of the document—27 of its 32 paragraphs—lists the ways the king had abused the colonies. George III was accused of all sorts of evil deeds, even though he personally had little to do with Parliament's colonial policies. King George was even blamed for inciting the "merciless Indian savages" to make war on the colonists. The king received the blame because the Convention delegates held that Parliament lacked authority over the colonies.

The Declaration's polemical aspects were important because the colonists needed foreign assistance to take on the British. France, which was engaged in a war with Britain, was a prime target for the delegates' diplomacy and eventually provided aid that was critical to the success of the Revolution.

Today, the Declaration of Independence is studied more as a statement of philosophy than as a political call to arms. In just a few sentences, Jefferson set forth the American democratic creed, the most important and succinct statement of the philosophy underlying American government—as applicable today as it was in 1776.

The English Heritage: The Power of Ideas

Philosophically, the Jeffersonian pen put on paper ideas that were by then common knowledge on both sides of the Atlantic, especially among those people who wished to challenge the power of kings. Franklin, Jefferson, James Madison of Virginia, Robert Morris of Pennsylvania, Alexander Hamilton of New York, and other intellectual leaders in the colonies were learned and widely read men, familiar with the works of English, French, and Scottish political philosophers. These leaders corresponded about the ideas they were reading, quoted philosophers in their debates over the Revolution, and applied those ideas to the new government they formed through the framework of the Constitution.

John Locke was one of the most influential philosophers read by the colonists. His writings, especially *The Second Treatise of Civil Government* (1689), profoundly influenced American political leaders.[2]

The foundation on which Locke built his powerful philosophy was a belief in **natural rights**—rights inherent in human beings, not dependent on governments. Before governments arise, Locke held, people exist in a state of nature in which there are no formal laws or governments. Instead, the laws of nature govern people, laws determined by people's innate moral sense. This natural law brings natural rights, including life, liberty, and property. Natural law can even justify a challenge to the rule of a tyrannical king because it is superior to human law. Government, Locke argued, must be built on the **consent of the governed;** in other words, the people must agree on who their rulers will be. It should also be a **limited government;** that is, there must be clear restrictions on what rulers can do. Indeed, the sole purpose of government, according to Locke, was to protect natural rights. The idea that certain things were beyond the realm of government contrasted sharply with the traditional notion that kings had been divinely granted absolute rights over subjects.

Two limits on government were particularly important to Locke. First, governments must provide standing laws so that people know in advance whether their acts will be acceptable. Second, and Locke was very forceful on this point, "the supreme power cannot take from any man any part of his property without his consent." To Locke, "the preservation of property was the end of government." The sanctity of property was one of the few ideas absent in Jefferson's draft of the Declaration of Independence. Even though Jefferson borrowed from and even paraphrased Lockean ideas, he altered Locke's phrase "life, liberty, and property" to "life, liberty, and the pursuit of happiness." We shall soon see, though, how the Lockean idea of the sanctity of property figured prominently at the Constitutional Convention. James Madison, the most influential member of that

natural rights
Rights inherent in human beings, not dependent on governments, which include life, liberty, and property. The concept of natural rights was central to English philosopher John Locke's theories about government and was widely accepted among America's Founders.

consent of the governed
The idea that government derives its authority by sanction of the people.

limited government
The idea that certain restrictions should be placed on government to protect the **natural rights** of citizens.

body, directly echoed Locke's view that the preservation of property is the purpose of government.

Locke argued that in an extreme case people have a right to revolt against a government that no longer has their consent, but he also emphasized that people should not revolt until injustices become deeply felt. The Declaration of Independence accented the same point, declaring that "governments long established should not be changed for light and transient causes." But when matters went beyond "patient sufferance," severing these ties was not only inevitable but also necessary.

Jefferson's Handiwork: The American Creed

There are some remarkable parallels between Locke's thought and Jefferson's language in the Declaration of Independence (see Table 2.1). Jefferson, like Locke, finessed his way past the issue of how the rebels knew men had rights. Jefferson simply declared that it was "self-evident" that men were equally "endowed by their Creator with certain unalienable rights," including "life, liberty, and the pursuit of happiness." Because it was the purpose of government to "secure" these rights, if it failed to do so, the people could form a new government.[3]

Locke represented only one element of revolutionary thought from which Jefferson borrowed. In the English countryside, there was also a well-established tradition of opposition to the executive power of the Crown and support for recovering the rights of the people. An indigenous American republicanism—stressing moral virtue, patriotism, relations based on natural merit, and the equality of independent citizens—intensified the radicalism of this "country" ideology and linked it with older currents of European thought stretching back to antiquity.

It was in the American colonies that the powerful ideas of European political thinkers took root and grew into what Seymour Martin Lipset has termed the "first new nation."[4] With these revolutionary ideas in mind, Jefferson claimed in the Declaration of Independence that people should have primacy over governments, that they should rule instead of be ruled. Moreover, each person was important as an individual, "created equal" and endowed with "unalienable rights." Consent of the governed, not divine rights or tradition, made the exercise of political power legitimate.

No government had ever been based on these principles. Ever since 1776, Americans have been concerned about fulfilling the high aspirations of the Declaration of Independence.

Winning Independence

The pen may be mightier than the sword, but declaring independence did not win the Revolution—it merely announced its beginning. John Adams wrote to his wife Abigail, "You will think me transported with enthusiasm, but I am not. I am well

Table 2.1 Locke and the Declaration of Independence: Some Parallels

LOCKE	DECLARATION OF INDEPENDENCE
Natural Rights	
"The state of nature has a law to govern it"	"Laws of Nature and Nature's God"
"life, liberty, and property"	"life, liberty, and the pursuit of happiness"
Purpose of Government	
"to preserve himself, his liberty, and property"	"to secure these rights"
Equality	
"men being by nature all free, equal and independent"	"all men are created equal"
Consent of the Governed	
"for when any number of men have, by the consent of every individual, made a community, with a power to act as one body, which is only by the will and determination of the majority"	"Governments are instituted among men, deriving their just powers from the consent of the governed."
Limited Government	
"Absolute arbitrary power, or governing without settled laws, can neither of them consist with the ends of society and government." "As usurpation is the exercise of power which another has a right to, so tyranny is the exercise of power beyond right, which nobody can have a right to."	"The history of the present King of Great Britain is a history of repeated injuries and usurpations."
Right to Revolt	
"The people shall be the judge. . . . Oppression raises ferments and makes men struggle to cast off an uneasy and tyrannical yoke."	"Prudence, indeed, will dictate that Governments long established should not be changed for light and transient causes. . . . But when a long train of abuses and usurpations, pursuing invariably the same Object evinces a design to reduce them under absolute Despotism, it is their right, it is their duty, to throw off such Government."

IN CONGRESS. JULY 4, 1776.

The unanimous Declaration of the thirteen united States of America.

aware of the toil, blood, and treasure that it will cost us to maintain this Declaration, and support and defend these states." Adams was right. The colonists seemed little match for the finest army in the world, whose size was nearly quadrupled by hired guns from the German state of Hesse and elsewhere. In 1775, the British had 8,500 men stationed in the colonies and had hired nearly 30,000 mercenaries. Initially, the colonists had only 5,000 men in uniform, and their number waxed and waned as the war progressed. Nevertheless, in 1783, the American colonies won their war of independence. How they eventually won is a story best left to history books. However, we will explore how they formed a new government in the following sections.

The "Conservative" Revolution

Revolutions such as the 1789 French Revolution, the 1917 Russian Revolution, and the 1978–1979 Iranian Revolution produced great societal change—as well as plenty of bloodshed. The American Revolution was different. Although many people lost their lives during the Revolutionary War, the Revolution itself was essentially a conservative movement that did not drastically alter the colonists' way of life. Its primary goal was to restore rights the colonists felt were already theirs as British subjects.

American colonists did not feel the need for great social, economic, or political upheavals. They "were not oppressed people; they had no crushing imperial shackles to throw off."[5] As a result, the Revolution did not create class conflicts that would split society for generations to come. The colonial leaders' belief that they needed the consent of the governed blessed the new nation with a crucial element of stability—a stability the nation would need.

The Government That Failed: 1776–1787

The Continental Congress that adopted the Declaration of Independence was only a voluntary association of the states. In 1776, the Congress appointed a committee to draw up a plan for a permanent union of the states. That plan, our first constitution, was the **Articles of Confederation.**[6]

The Articles of Confederation

Articles of Confederation The first constitution of the United States, adopted by Congress in 1777 and enacted in 1781. The Articles established a national legislature, the Continental Congress, but most authority rested with the state legislatures.

The Articles established a government dominated by the states. The United States, according to the Articles, was a confederation, a "league of friendship and perpetual union" among 13 states. The Articles established a national legislature with one house; states could send as many as seven delegates or as few as two, but each state had only one vote. There was no president and no national court, and the powers of the national legislature—the Congress—were strictly limited. Most authority rested with the state legislatures because the new nation's leaders feared that a strong central government would become as tyrannical as British rule.

Because unanimous consent of the states was needed to put the Articles into operation, the Articles adopted by Congress in 1777 did not go into effect until

1781, when laggard Maryland finally ratified them. In the meantime, the Continental Congress barely survived, lurching from crisis to crisis. At one point during the war, some of Washington's troops threatened to create a monarchy with him as king unless Congress paid their overdue wages.

The Congress had few powers outside maintaining an army and navy—and little money to do even that. It had to request money from the states because it had no power to tax. If states refused to send money (which they often did), Congress did without. In desperation, Congress sold off western lands (land east of the Mississippi and west of the states) to speculators, issued securities that sold for less than their face value, or used its own presses to print money that was virtually worthless. Congress also voted to disband the army despite continued threats from Britain and Spain.

Articles of Confederation

Congress lacked the power to regulate commerce, which inhibited foreign trade and the development of a strong national economy. It did, however, manage to develop sound policies for the management of the western frontiers, passing the Northwest Ordinance of 1787 that encouraged the development of the Great Lakes region.

In general, the weak and ineffective national government could take little independent action. All government power rested in the states. The national government could not compel the states to do anything, and it had no power to deal directly with individual citizens. The weakness of the national government prevented it from dealing with the hard times that faced the new nation. There was one benefit of the Articles, however: When the nation's leaders began to write a new Constitution, they could look at the provisions of the Articles of Confederation and know some of the things they should avoid.

Why It Matters

A Strong National Government

One of the most important features of the Constitution is the creation of a strong national government. If the framers had retained a weak national government, as under the Articles of Confederation, Congress could not create a great national economic market through regulating interstate commerce, the president could not conduct a vigorous foreign policy, federal courts could not issue orders to protect civil rights, and the federal government could not raise the funds to pay for Social Security benefits.

Changes in the States

What was happening in the states was more important than what was happening in the Congress. The most important change was a dramatic increase in democracy and liberty, at least for White males. Many states adopted bills of rights to protect freedoms, abolished religious qualifications for holding office, and liberalized requirements for voting. Expanded political participation brought a new middle class to power.

The structure of government in the states also became more responsive to the people. State constitutions concentrated power in the legislatures because most people considered legislators to be closer to the voters than governors or judges. Legislatures often selected the governors and kept them on a short leash, with brief tenures and limited veto and appointment powers. Legislatures also overruled court decisions and criticized judges for unpopular decisions.

The idea of equality was driving change throughout the nation. Although the Revolutionary War itself did not transform American society, it unleashed the republican tendencies in American life. Americans were in the process of becoming "the most liberal, the most democratic, the most commercially minded, and the most modern people in the world."[7] Members of the old colonial elite found this turn of affairs quite troublesome because it challenged their hold on power.

Economic Turmoil

After the Revolution, James Madison observed that "the most common and durable source of factions [special interests] has been the various and unequal division of property."[8] The post-Revolutionary legislatures epitomized Madison's argument that economic inequality played an important role in shaping public policy. Economic issues were at the top of the political agenda. A postwar depression had left many small farmers unable to pay their debts and threatened them with mortgage foreclosures. Now under control of people more sympathetic to debtors, the state legislatures listened to the demands of small farmers. A few states, notably Rhode Island, demonstrated their support of debtors, passing policies favoring them over creditors. Some printed tons of paper money and passed "force acts" requiring reluctant creditors to accept the almost worthless money. Debtors could thus pay big debts with cheap currency.

Shays' Rebellion
A series of attacks on courthouses by a small band of farmers led by Revolutionary War Captain Daniel Shays to block foreclosure proceedings.

Shays' Rebellion

Policies favoring debtors over creditors did not please the economic elite who had once controlled nearly all the state legislatures. They were further shaken when, in 1786, a small band of farmers in western Massachusetts rebelled at losing their land to creditors. Led by Revolutionary War Captain Daniel Shays, this rebellion, called **Shays' Rebellion,** was a series of armed attacks on courthouses to prevent judges from foreclosing on farms. Farmers in other states—though never in large numbers—were also unruly. Jefferson was not distressed at this behavior, calling the attack a "little rebellion," but it remained on the minds of the economic elite. They were scared at the thought that people had taken the law into their own hands and violated the property rights of others. Neither Congress nor the state was able to raise a militia to stop Shays and his followers, and elites assembled a privately paid force to do the job, which further fueled dissatisfaction with the weakness of the Articles of Confederation system.

Shays' Rebellion, in which farmers physically prevented judges from foreclosing on farms, helped spur the birth of the Constitution. News of the small rebellion spread quickly around the country, and some of the Philadelphia delegates thought a full-fledged revolution would result. The event reaffirmed the framers' belief that the new federal government needed to be a strong one.

The Aborted Annapolis Meeting

In September 1786, a handful of leaders assembled at Annapolis, Maryland, to discuss problems with the Articles of Confederation and suggest solutions. The assembly was an abortive attempt at reform. Only five states—New York, New Jersey, Delaware, Pennsylvania, and Virginia—were represented at the meeting; the 12 delegates were few enough in number to meet around a dinner table. Called to consider commercial conflicts that had arisen among the states under the Articles of Confederation, the Annapolis delegates decided that a larger meeting and a broader proposal were needed to organize the states. Holding most of their meetings at a local tavern, this small and unofficial band of reformers issued a call for a full-scale meeting of the states in Philadelphia the following May—in retrospect, a rather bold move by so small a group. The Continental Congress granted their request, however, and called for a meeting of all the states. In May 1787, what we now call the Constitutional Convention got down to business in Philadelphia.

Making a Constitution: The Philadelphia Convention

Representatives from 12 states came to Philadelphia to heed the Continental Congress's call to "take into consideration the situation in the United States." Only Rhode Island, a stronghold of paper-money interests, refused to send delegates.

The delegates were ordered to meet "for the sole and express purpose of revising the Articles of Confederation." The Philadelphia delegates did not pay much attention to this order, however, because amending the Articles required the unanimous consent of the states, which they knew would be impossible. Thus the 55 delegates ignored their instructions and began writing what was to become the **U.S. Constitution.**

U.S. Constitution
The document written in 1787 and ratified in 1788 that sets forth the institutional structure of U.S. government and the tasks these institutions perform. It replaced the Articles of Confederation.

Gentlemen in Philadelphia

Who were these 55 men? This select group of economic and political notables included mostly wealthy planters, successful (or once successful) lawyers and merchants, and men of independent wealth. Many were college graduates, and most had practical political experience. Most were coastal residents rather than residents of the expanding western frontiers, and a significant number were urbanites rather than part of the primarily rural American population.

Intent of the Framers

Philosophy into Action

The delegates in Philadelphia were an uncommon combination of philosophers and shrewd political architects. The debates moved from high principles on the big issues to self-interest on the small ones.[9] The first two weeks were devoted mainly to general debates about the nature of republican government (government in which ultimate power rests with the voters). After that, practical and divisive issues sometimes threatened to dissolve the meeting.

Obviously, these 55 men did not share the same political philosophy. Democratic Benjamin Franklin held very different views from a number of delegates who were wary of democracy. Yet at the core of their ideas existed a common center. The group agreed on questions of (1) human nature, (2) the causes of political conflict, (3) the objects of government, and (4) the nature of a republican government.

Human Nature. In his famous work titled *Leviathan* written in 1651, Thomas Hobbes argued that man's natural state was war and that a strong absolute ruler was necessary to restrain man's bestial tendencies. Without a strong government, Hobbes wrote, life would be "solitary, poor, nasty, brutish, and short." The delegates were not convinced of the need for a monarch, but they did hold a cynical view of human nature.

People, they thought, were self-interested. Franklin and Hamilton, poles apart philosophically, both voiced this sentiment. Said Franklin, "There are two passions which have a powerful influence on the affairs of men: the love of power and the love of money." Hamilton agreed in his characteristically straightforward manner: "Men love power." The men at Philadelphia believed that government should play a key role in containing the natural self-interest of people.[10]

Political Conflict. Of all the words written by and about the delegates, none have been more widely quoted than these by James Madison: "The most common and durable source of factions has been the various and unequal distribution of property." In other words, *the distribution of wealth* (land was the main form of wealth in those days) *is the source of political conflict.* "Those who hold and those who are without property," Madison went on, "have ever formed distinct interests in society." Other sources of conflict included religion, views of governing, and attachment to various leaders.[11]

factions
Interest groups arising from the unequal distribution of property or wealth that James Madison attacked in ***Federalist Paper*** *#10*. Today's parties or interest groups are what Madison had in mind when he warned of the instability in government caused by factions.

Arising from these sources of conflict are **factions,** which we might call parties or interest groups. A majority faction might well be composed of the many who have little or no property; the minority faction, of those with property. If unchecked, the delegates thought, one of these factions would eventually tyrannize the other. The majority would try to seize the government to reduce the wealth of the minority; the minority would try to seize the government to secure its own gains. Governments that are run by factions, the Founders believed, are prone to instability, tyranny, and even violence. The Founders intended to check the effects of factions.

Objects of Government. To Gouverneur Morris of Pennsylvania, the preservation of property was the "principal object of government." Morris's remark typifies the philosophy of many of the delegates. As property holders themselves, these delegates could not imagine a government that did not make its principal objective an economic one: the preservation of individual rights to acquire and hold wealth. A few (like Morris) were intent on shutting out the propertyless altogether.

Nature of Government. Given their beliefs about human nature, the causes of political conflict, the need to protect property, and the threat of tyranny by a faction, what sort of government did the delegates believe would work? They answered in different ways, but the message was always the same. Power should be set against power so that no one faction would overwhelm the others. The secret of good government is "balanced" government. They were influenced in their thinking by writings of a French aristocrat, Baron Montesquieu, who advocated separate branches of government with distinct powers and the ability to check the other branches. The Founders agreed, concluding that a limited government would have to contain checks on its own power. So long as no faction could seize the whole of government at once, tyranny could be avoided. A balanced government required a complex network of checks, balances, and separation of powers.

The Agenda in Philadelphia

The delegates in Philadelphia could not merely construct a government from ideas. They wanted to design a government that was consistent with their political philosophy, but they also had to confront some of the thorniest issues confronting the fledgling nation at the time—issues of equality, the economy, and individual rights.

The Equality Issues

The Declaration of Independence states that all men are created equal; the Constitution, however, is silent on equality. Nevertheless, some of the most important issues on the policy agenda in Philadelphia concerned equality. Three issues occupied more attention than almost any others: whether the states were to be equally represented, what to do about slavery, and whether to ensure political equality.

Equality and Representation of the States. One crucial policy issue was how to constitute the new Congress. The **New Jersey Plan,** proposed by William Paterson of New Jersey, called for each state to be equally represented in the new Congress. The opposing strategy, suggested by Edmund Randolph of Virginia, is usually called the **Virginia Plan.** It called for giving each state representation in Congress based on the state's share of the American population.

The delegates resolved this conflict with a compromise devised by Roger Sherman and William Johnson of Connecticut. The solution proposed by this **Connecticut Compromise** was to create two houses in Congress. One body, the Senate, would have two members from each state (the New Jersey Plan), and the second body, the House of Representatives, would have representation based on population (the Virginia Plan). The U.S. Congress is still organized in exactly the same way. Each state has two senators, and the state's population determines its representation in the House.

Although the Connecticut Compromise was intended to maximize equality among the states, it actually gives more power to people who live in states with small populations than to those who live in more heavily populated states. Every state has two senators and at least one member of the House, no matter how small its population. To take the most extreme case, Wyoming and California have the same number of votes in the Senate (two), although Wyoming has less than 2 percent of California's population. Thus a citizen of Wyoming has more than 50 *times* the representation in the Senate as does a citizen of California.[12]

Because it is the Senate, not the House, that ratifies treaties, confirms presidential nominations, and hears trials of impeachment, citizens in less populated states

New Jersey Plan
The proposal at the Constitutional Convention that called for equal **representation** of each state in Congress regardless of the state's population.

Virginia Plan
The proposal at the Constitutional Convention that called for **representation** of each state in Congress in proportion to that state's share of the U.S. population.

Connecticut Compromise
The compromise reached at the Constitutional Convention that established two houses of Congress: the House of Representatives, in which **representation** is based on a state's share of the U.S. population, and the Senate, in which each state has two representatives.

Why It Matters

Representation in the Senate

The Senate both creates a check on the House and overrepresents states with small populations. If there were only one house of Congress, governance would be more efficient. If representation were based on population, interests centered in states with small populations would lose an advantage. At the same time, there would be one less important check on government action and perhaps a closer correspondence between public opinion and public policy. Which do you prefer?

have a greater say in these key tasks. In addition, the electoral college (which is the body that actually elects the president and is discussed in Chapter 9) gives small states greater weight. If no presidential candidate receives a majority in the electoral college, the House of Representatives makes the final decision—with each state having one vote. In such a case (which has not occurred since 1824), the votes of citizens of Wyoming would again carry more than 50 times as much weight as those of Californians.

Whether representation in the Senate is "fair" is a matter of debate. What is not open to question is that the delegates to the 1787 convention had to accommodate various interests and viewpoints in order to convince all the states to join an untested union.

Slavery. The second equality issue was slavery. The contradictions between slavery and the sentiments of the Declaration of Independence are obvious, but slavery was legal in every state except Massachusetts. It was concentrated in the South, however, where slave labor was commonplace in agriculture. The delegates did agree that Congress could limit future *importing* of slaves (they allowed it to be outlawed after 1808), but they did not forbid slavery itself. The Constitution, in fact, inclined toward recognizing slavery; it stated that persons legally "held to service or labour" (referring to slaves) who escaped to free states had to be returned to their owners.

Another difficult question about slavery arose at the Convention. How should slaves be counted in determining representation in Congress? Southerners were happy to see slaves counted toward determining their representation in the House of Representatives (though reluctant to count them for apportionment of taxation). Here the result was the famous *three-fifths compromise.* Representation and taxation were to be based on the "number of free persons," plus three-fifths of the number of "all other persons." Everyone, of course, knew who those other persons were.

When the Constitution was written, many northern and southern delegates assumed that slavery, being relatively unprofitable, would soon die out. A single invention—Eli Whitney's cotton gin—made it profitable again. Although Congress did act to control the growth of slavery, the slave economy became entrenched in the South.

Political Equality. The delegates dodged one other issue on equality. A handful of delegates, led by Franklin, suggested that national elections should require universal manhood suffrage (that is, a vote for all free adult males). This still would have left a majority of the population disenfranchised, but for those still smarting from Shays' Rebellion and the fear of mob rule, the suggestion was too democratic. Many delegates wanted to put property qualifications on the right to vote. Ultimately, as the debate wound down, they decided to leave the issue to the states. People qualified to vote in state elections could also vote in national elections (see Table 2.2).

The Economic Issues

The Philadelphia delegates were deeply concerned about the state of the American economy. Economic issues were high on the Constitution writers' policy agenda. People disagreed (in fact, historians still disagree) as to whether the postcolonial economy was in a shambles. Advocates of the Constitution, called Federalists, emphasized the economy's "weaknesses, especially in the commercial sector, and Anti-Federalists (those opposed to a strong national government, and thus opposed to a new constitution) countered with charges of exaggeration."[13] The writers of the Constitution, already committed to a strong national government, charged that the economy was indeed in disarray and that they needed to address the following problems:

- The states had erected tariffs against products from other states.
- Paper money was virtually worthless in some states, but many state governments, which were controlled by debtor classes, forced it on creditors anyway.
- The Congress was having trouble raising money because the economy was in a recession.

Table 2.2 How Three Issues of Equality Were Resolved: A Summary

PROBLEM	SOLUTION
Equality of the States	
Should states be represented equally (the New Jersey Plan) or in proportion to their population (the Virginia Plan)?	Both, according to the Connecticut Compromise. States have equal representation in the Senate, but representation in the House is proportionate to population.
Slavery	
What should be done about slavery?	Although Congress was permitted to stop the importing of slaves after 1808, the Constitution is mostly silent on the issue of slavery.
How should slaves be counted for representation in the House of Representatives?	Count each slave as three-fifths of a person.
Political Equality	
Should the right to vote be based on universal manhood suffrage, or should it be very restricted?	Finesse the issue. Let the states decide qualifications for voting.

Understanding something about the delegates and their economic interests gives us insight into their views on political economy. They were, by all accounts, the nation's postcolonial economic elite. Some were budding capitalists. Others were creditors whose loans were being wiped out by cheap paper money. Many were merchants who could not even carry on trade with a neighboring state. Virtually all of them thought a strong national government was needed to bring economic stability to the chaotic union of states that existed under the Articles of Confederation.[14]

It is not surprising, then, that the framers of the Constitution would seek to strengthen the economic powers (and thus the scope) of the new national government. One famous historian, Charles A. Beard, claimed that their principal motivation for doing so was to increase their personal wealth. The framers, he said, not only were propertied, upper-class men protecting their interests but also held bonds and investments whose value would increase if the Constitution were adopted. The best evidence, however, indicates that although they were concerned about protecting property rights, the Founders' motivations were in the broad sense of building a strong economy rather than in the narrow sense of increasing their personal wealth.[15]

The delegates made sure that the Constitution clearly spelled out the economic powers of Congress (see Table 2.3). Consistent with the general allocation of power in the Constitution, Congress was to be the chief economic policymaker. It could obtain revenues through taxing and borrowing. These tools, along with the power to appropriate funds, became crucial instruments for influencing the economy. By maintaining sound money and guaranteeing payment for the national debt, Congress was to encourage economic enterprise and investment in the United States. The Constitution also allocates to Congress power to build the nation's infrastructure by constructing post offices and roads and to establish standard weights and measures. To protect property rights, Congress was charged with punishing counterfeiters and pirates, ensuring patents and copyrights, and legislating rules for bankruptcy. Equally important (and now a key congressional power, with a wide range of implications for the economy) was Congress's new ability to regulate interstate and foreign commerce. In sum, the Constitution granted Congress the power to create the conditions within which markets could flourish.

In addition, the framers prohibited practices in the states that they viewed as inhibiting economic development, such as maintaining individual state monetary systems, placing duties on imports from other states, and interfering with lawfully contracted debts. Moreover, the states were to respect civil judgments and contracts made in other states, and they were to return runaway slaves to their owners. (This last protection of "property" rights is now, of course, defunct as a result of the Thirteenth Amendment, which outlawed slavery.) To help the states, the national government guaranteed them "a republican form of government" to prevent a recurrence of Shays' Rebellion, in which some people used violence, instead of legislation and the courts, to resolve commercial disputes.

The Constitution also obligated the new government to repay all the public debts incurred under the Continental Congress and the Articles of Confederation—debts that totaled $54 million. Although this requirement may seem odd, there was sound economic reason for it. Paying off the debts would

Table 2.3 Economics in the Constitution

Powers of Congress

1. Levy taxes.
2. Pay debts.
3. Borrow money.
4. Coin money and regulate its value.
5. Regulate interstate and foreign commerce.
6. Establish uniform laws of bankruptcy.
7. Punish piracy.
8. Punish counterfeiting.
9. Create standard weights and measures.
10. Establish post offices and post roads.
11. Protect copyrights and patents.

Prohibitions on the States

1. States cannot pass laws impairing the obligations of contract.
2. States cannot coin money or issue paper money.
3. States cannot require payment of debts in paper money.
4. States cannot tax imports or exports from abroad or from other states.
5. States cannot free runaway slaves from other states (now defunct).

Other Key Provisions

1. The new government assumes the national debt contracted under the Articles of Confederation.
2. The Constitution guarantees a republican form of government.
3. The states must respect civil court judgments and contracts made in other states.

ensure from the outset that money would flow into the American economy and would also restore the confidence of investors in the young nation. Even today, people trade in government debt (in the form of bonds) just as they do in the stocks of corporations. Thus, the Constitution helped to spur a capitalist economy.

The Individual Rights Issues

Another major item on the Constitutional Convention agenda for the delegates was designing a system that would preserve individual rights. There was no dispute about the importance of safeguarding individualism, and the Founders believed that this would be relatively easy. After all, they were constructing a limited government that, by design, could not threaten personal freedoms. In addition, they dispersed power among the branches of the national government and between the national and state governments so each branch or level could restrain the other. Also, most of the delegates believed that the various states were already doing a sufficient job of protecting individual rights.

As a result, the Constitution says little about personal freedoms. The protections it does offer are the following:

- It prohibits suspension of the **writ of habeas corpus** (except during invasion or rebellion). Such a court order enables persons detained by authorities to secure an immediate inquiry into the causes of their detention. If no proper explanation is offered, a judge may order their release. (Article I, Section 9)

writ of habeas corpus
A court order requiring jailers to explain to a judge why they are holding a prisoner in custody.

- It prohibits Congress or the states from passing bills of attainder (which punish people without a judicial trial). (Article I, Section 9)
- It prohibits Congress or the states from passing *ex post facto* laws (which punish people or increase the penalties for acts that were not illegal or not as punishable when the act was committed). (Article I, Section 9)
- It prohibits the imposition of religious qualifications for holding office in the national government. (Article VI)
- It narrowly defines and outlines strict rules of evidence for conviction of treason. To be convicted, a person must levy war against the United States or adhere to and aid its enemies during war. Conviction requires confession in open court or the testimony of *two* witnesses to the *same* overt act. The framers of the Constitution would have been executed as traitors if the Revolution had failed, and they were therefore sensitive to treason laws. (Article III, Section 3)
- It upholds the right to trial by jury in criminal cases. (Article III, Section 2)

The delegates were content with their document. When it came time to ratify the Constitution, however, there was widespread criticism of the absence of specific protections of individual rights, such as free expression and the rights of the accused.

The Madisonian Model

The framers believed that human nature was self-interested and that inequalities of wealth were the principal source of political conflict. Regardless, they had no desire to remove the divisions in society by converting private property to common ownership; they also believed that protecting private property was a key purpose of government. Their experience with state governments under the Articles of Confederation reinforced their view that democracy was a threat to property. Many of them felt that the nonwealthy majority—an unruly mob—would tyrannize the wealthy minority if given political power. Thus the delegates to the Constitutional Convention faced the challenge of reconciling economic inequality with political freedom.

Thwarting Tyranny of the Majority

James Madison was neither wealthy nor a great orator. He was, however, a careful student of politics and government and became the principal architect of the government's final structure.[16] He and his colleagues feared both majority and minority factions. Either could take control of the government and use it to their own advantage. Factions of the minority, however, were easy to handle; the majority could simply outvote them. Factions of the majority were harder to handle. If the majority united around some policy issue, such as the redistribution of wealth, they could oppress the minority, violating the latter's basic rights.[17]

As Madison would later explain in the *Federalist Papers*,

> *Ambition must be made to counteract ambition. . . . If men were angels, no government would be necessary. If angels were to govern men, neither external nor internal controls would be necessary. In framing a government which is to be administered by men over men, the great difficulty lies in this: you must first enable the government to control the governed; and then in the next place oblige it to control itself.*[18]

To prevent the possibility of a tyranny of the majority, Madison proposed the following:

1. Place as much of the government as possible beyond the direct control of the majority.
2. Separate the powers of different institutions.
3. Construct a system of checks and balances.

Limiting Majority Control. Madison believed that to thwart tyranny by the majority, it was essential to keep most of the government beyond their power. His plan placed only one element of government, the House of Representatives, within direct control of the votes of the majority. In contrast, state legislatures were to elect senators, and special electors were to select the president; in other words, government officials would be elected by a small minority, not by the people themselves. The president was to nominate judges (see Figure 2.2). Even if the majority seized control of the House of Representatives, they still could not enact policies without the agreement of the Senate and the president. To further insulate governmental officials from public opinion, the Constitution gave judges lifetime tenure

The American System of Checks and Balances

Figure 2.2 The Constitution and the Electoral Process: The Original Plan

Under Madison's plan, which was incorporated in the Constitution, voters' electoral influence was limited. Only the House of Representatives was directly elected. Senators and presidents were indirectly elected, and judges were nominated by the president. Over the years, Madison's original model has been substantially democratized. The Seventeenth Amendment (1913) established direct election of senators by popular majorities. Today, the electoral college has become largely a rubber stamp, voting the way the popular majority in each state votes.

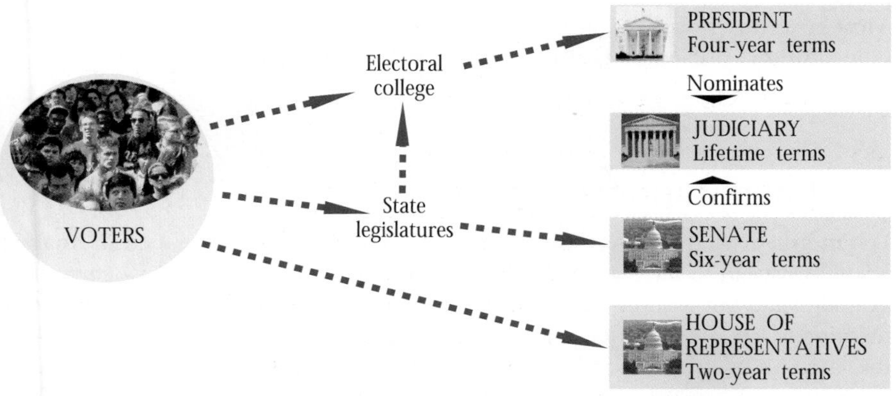

separation of powers
A feature of the Constitution that requires each of the three branches of government—executive, legislative, and judicial—to be relatively independent of the others so that one cannot control the others. Power is shared among these three institutions.

checks and balances
Features of the Constitution that limit government's power by requiring that power be balanced among the different governmental institutions. These institutions continually constrain one another's activities. This system reflects Madison's goal of setting power against power.

Why It Matters

Checks and Balances
The checks and balances in the Constitution favor the status quo. They force contending sides to compromise if legislation is going to pass. They also create the potential for gridlock in which no change occurs.

and senators terms of six years, with only one-third elected every two years, compared with the two-year election intervals of all members of the House of Representatives.

Separating Powers. The Madisonian scheme also provided for a **separation of powers.** Each of the three branches of government—executive (the president), legislative (Congress), and judicial (the courts)—would be relatively independent of one another so that no single branch could control the others. The Founders gave the president, Congress, and the courts independent elements of power. The Constitution does not divide power absolutely, however; rather, it *shares* it among the three institutions.

Creating Checks and Balances. Because powers were not completely separate, each branch required the consent of the others for many of its actions. This created a system of **checks and balances** that reflected Madison's goal of setting power against power to constrain government actions. He reasoned that if a faction seized one institution, it still could not damage the whole system. The system of checks and balances was an elaborate and delicate creation. The president checks Congress by holding veto power; Congress holds the purse strings of government and must approve presidential appointments.

The courts also figured into the system of checks and balances. Presidents could nominate judges, but their confirmation by the Senate was required. The Supreme Court itself, in *Marbury v. Madison* (1803), asserted its power to check the other branches through judicial review: the right to hold actions of the other two branches unconstitutional. This right, which is not specifically outlined in the Constitution, considerably strengthened the Court's ability to restrain the other branches of government. For a summary of separation of powers and the checks and balances system, see Figure 2.3.

Establishing a Federal System. As we will discuss in detail in Chapter 3, the Founders also established a federal system of government that divided the power of government between a national government and the individual states. Most government activity at the time occurred in the states. The framers of the Constitution anticipated that this would be an additional check on the national government.

The Constitutional Republic

republic
A form of government in which the people select representatives to govern them and make laws.

When asked what kind of government the delegates had produced, Benjamin Franklin is said to have replied, "A republic . . . if you can keep it." Because the Founders did not wish to have the people directly make all decisions (as in a town meeting where everyone has one vote), and because even then the country was far too large for such a proposal to be feasible, they did not choose to create a direct democracy. Their solution was to establish a **republic:** a system based on the

Figure 2.3 Separation of Powers and Checks and Balances in the Constitution

The doctrine of separation of powers allows the three institutions of government to check and balance one another. Judicial review—the power of courts to hold executive and congressional policies unconstitutional—was not explicit in the Constitution but was asserted by the Supreme Court in *Marbury v. Madison.*

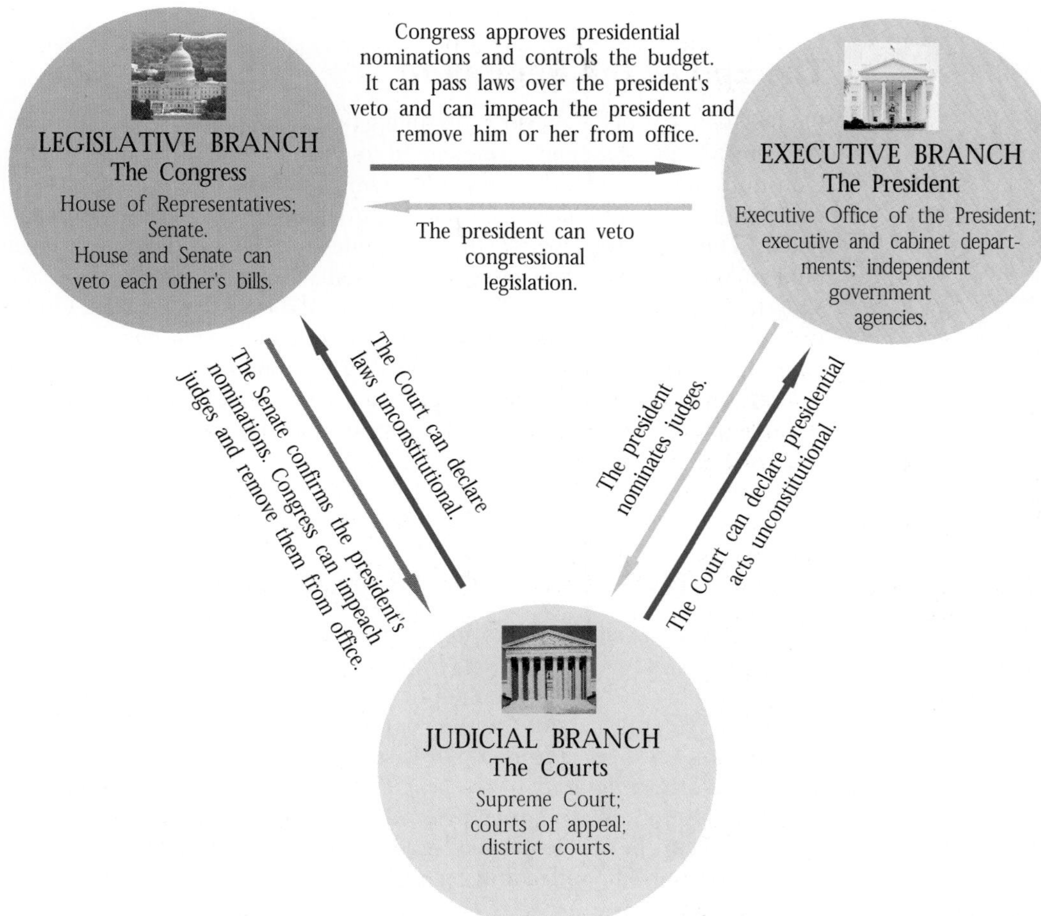

consent of the governed in which representatives of the public exercise power. This deliberative democracy required and encouraged reflection and refinement of the public's views through an elaborate decision-making process.

The system of checks and balances and separation of powers favors the status quo. People who desire change must usually have a sizable majority, not just a simple majority of 51 percent. Those opposed to change need only win at one point in the policymaking process—say in obtaining a presidential veto—whereas those who favor change must win *every* battle along the way. Change usually comes slowly, if at all. As a result, the Madisonian system encourages moderation and compromise and slows change. It is difficult for either a minority or a majority to tyrannize, and both property rights and personal freedoms (with only occasional lapses) have survived.

The End of the Beginning

On the 109th day of the meetings, in stifling heat made worse because the windows of the Pennsylvania statehouse were closed to ensure secrecy, the final version of the Constitution was read aloud. Then Benjamin Franklin rose with a speech he had written but was so enfeebled that he had to ask James Wilson to deliver it. In it, Franklin noted, "There are several parts of this Constitution of which I do not at present approve, but I am not sure that I shall never approve them." Nonetheless, Edmund Randolph of Virginia rose to announce apologetically that he did not intend to sign. On Franklin's motion, a vote was taken. Ten states voted yes, and none voted no, but South Carolina's delegates were divided. After the document was signed, the members adjourned to a tavern. The experience of the last few hours, when conflict intermingled with consensus, reminded them that implementing this new document would be no small feat.

Ratifying the Constitution

The Constitution did not go into effect once the Constitutional Convention in Philadelphia was over. It had to be ratified by the states. Our awe of the Founders sometimes blinds us to the bitter politics of the day. There is no way of determining the public's feelings about the new document, but as John Marshall (who later became chief justice) suggested, "It is scarcely to be doubted that *in some of the adopting states, a majority of the people were in opposition*" (emphasis added).[19] The Constitution itself required that only 9 of the 13 states approve the document before it could be implemented, ignoring the requirement that the Articles of Confederation be amended only by unanimous consent.

Federalists
Supporters of the **U.S. Constitution** at the time the states were contemplating its adoption.

Anti-Federalists
Opponents of the **U.S. Constitution** at the time when the states were contemplating its adoption.

Federalist Papers
A collection of 85 articles written by Alexander Hamilton, John Jay, and James Madison under the name "Publius" to defend the **Constitution** in detail.

Federalists and Anti-Federalists

Throughout the states, a fierce battle erupted between the **Federalists,** who supported the Constitution, and the **Anti-Federalists,** who opposed it. Newspapers were filled with letters and articles, many written under pseudonyms, praising or condemning the document. In praise of the Constitution, three men—James Madison, Alexander Hamilton, and John Jay—wrote a series of articles under the name Publius. These articles, known as the ***Federalist Papers,*** are second only to the Constitution itself in reflecting the thinking of the framers.

George Washington presides over the signing of the Constitution. "The business being closed," he wrote, "the members adjourned to the City Tavern, dined together and took cordial leave of each other."

Beginning on October 27, 1787, barely a month after the Convention ended, the *Federalist Papers* began to appear in New York newspapers as part of the ratification debate in New York. Eighty-five were eventually published. They not only defended the Constitution detail by detail but also represented an important statement of political philosophy. (The essays influenced few of the New York delegates, however, who voted to ratify the Constitution only after New York City threatened to secede from the state if they did not.)

Far from being unpatriotic or un-American, the Anti-Federalists sincerely believed that the new government was an enemy of freedom, the very freedom they had just fought a war to ensure. Adopting names like Aggrippa, Cornelius, and Monteczuma, the Anti-Federalists launched bitter, biting, even brilliant attacks on the Philadelphia document. They frankly questioned the motives of the Constitution writers.

One objection was central to the Anti-Federalists' attacks: The new Constitution was a class-based document, intended to ensure that a particular economic elite controlled the public policies of the national government. According to one Anti-Federalist,

> *These lawyers, men of learning, and moneyed men . . . expect to get into Congress themselves . . . so they can get all the power and all the money into their own hands.*[20]

Remember that these charges of conspiracy and elitism were being hurled at the likes of Washington, Madison, Franklin, and Hamilton.

The Anti-Federalists had other fears. Not only would the new government be run by a few, but it would also erode fundamental liberties. In the South Carolina ratifying convention, James Lincoln declared that he "would be glad to know why, in this Constitution, there is a total silence with regard to the liberty of the press. Was it forgotten? Impossible! Then it must have been purposely omitted; and with what design, good or bad, I leave the world to judge." You can compare the views of the Federalists and Anti-Federalists in Table 2.4.

You Are James Madison

These arguments about the lack of protections of individual rights were persuasive. To allay fears that the Constitution would restrict personal freedoms, the Federalists promised to add amendments to the document specifically protecting individual liberties. They kept their word; James Madison introduced 12 constitutional amendments during the First Congress in 1789. Ten were ratified by the states and took effect in 1791. These first 10 amendments to the Constitution, which restrain the national government from limiting personal freedoms, have come to be known as the **Bill of Rights** (see Table 2.5). Another of Madison's original 12 amendments, one dealing with congressional salaries, was ratified 201 years later as the Twenty-seventh Amendment (see the Appendix in this book).

Bill of Rights
The first 10 amendments to the **U.S. Constitution,** drafted in response to some of the **Anti-Federalist** concerns. These amendments define such basic liberties as freedom of religion, speech, and press and guarantee defendants' rights.

Opponents also feared that the Constitution would weaken the power of the states (which it did). Many state political leaders feared that their own power would be diminished as well.

Finally, not everyone wanted the economy placed on a more sound foundation. Creditors opposed the issuance of paper money because it would produce inflation and make the money they received as payment on their loans decline in value. Debtors favored paper money, however. Their debts (such as the mortgages on their farms) would remain constant, but if money became more plentiful, it would be easier for them to pay off their debts.

Table 2.4 Federalists and Anti-Federalists Compared

	ANTI-FEDERALISTS	FEDERALISTS
Backgrounds	Small farmers, shopkeepers, laborers	Large landowners, wealthy merchants, professionals
Government Preferred	Strong state government Weak national government Direct election of officials Shorter terms Rule by the common man Strengthened protections for individual liberties	Weaker state government Strong national government Indirect election of officials Longer terms Government by the elite Expected few violations of individual liberties

Table 2.5 The Bill of Rights (Arranged by Function)

Protection of Free Expression	
Amendment 1:	Freedom of speech, press, and assembly Freedom to petition government
Protection of Personal Beliefs	
Amendment 1:	No government establishment of religion Freedom to exercise religion
Protection of Privacy	
Amendment 3:	No forced quartering of troops in homes during peacetime
Amendment 4:	No unreasonable searches and seizures
Protection of Defendants' Rights	
Amendment 5:	Grand jury indictment required for prosecution of serious crime No second prosecution for the same offense No compulsion to testify against oneself No loss of life, liberty, or property without due process of law
Amendment 6:	Right to a speedy and public trial by a local, impartial jury Right to be informed of charges against oneself Right to legal counsel Right to compel the attendance of favorable witnesses Right to cross-examine witnesses
Amendment 7:	Right to jury trial in civil suit where the value of controversy exceeds $20
Amendment 8:	No excessive bail or fines No cruel and unusual punishments
Protection of Other Rights	
Amendment 2:	Right to bear arms
Amendment 5:	No taking of private property for public use without just compensation
Amendment 9:	Unlisted rights are not necessarily denied
Amendment 10:	Powers not delegated to the national government or denied to the states are reserved for the states or the people

Ratification

Federalists may not have had the support of the majority, but they made up for it in shrewd politicking. They knew that many members of the legislatures of some states were skeptical of the Constitution and that state legislatures were populated with political leaders who would lose power under the Constitution. Thus, the Federalists specified that the Constitution be ratified by special conventions in each of the states—not by state legislatures.

Delaware was the first to approve, on December 7, 1787. Only six months passed before New Hampshire's approval (the ninth) made the Constitution official. Virginia and New York then voted to join the new union. Two states were holdouts: North Carolina and Rhode Island made the promise of the Bill of Rights their price for joining the other states.

With the Constitution ratified, it was time to select officeholders. The framers of the Constitution assumed that George Washington would be elected the first president of the new government—even giving him the Convention's papers for safekeeping—and they were right. The general was the unanimous choice of the electoral college for president. He took office on April 30, 1789, in New York City, the first national capital. New Englander John Adams became "His Superfluous Excellence," as Franklin called the vice president.

Constitutional Change

You Are Attempting to Revise the California State Constitution

"The Constitution," said Jefferson, "belongs to the living and not to the dead." The U.S. Constitution is frequently—and rightly—referred to as a living document. It is constantly being tested and altered.

Generally, constitutional changes are made either by formal amendments or by a number of informal processes. Formal amendments change the letter of the Constitution. There is also an unwritten body of tradition, practice, and procedure that, when altered, may change the spirit of the Constitution. In fact, not all nations, even those such as Britain that we call democratic, have written constitutions.

The Formal Amending Process

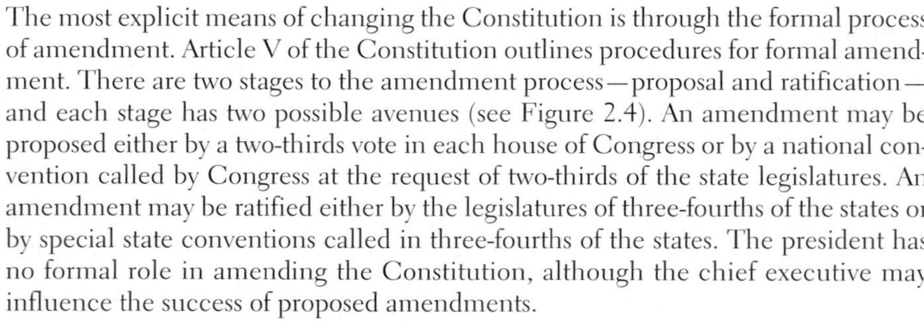

The most explicit means of changing the Constitution is through the formal process of amendment. Article V of the Constitution outlines procedures for formal amendment. There are two stages to the amendment process—proposal and ratification—and each stage has two possible avenues (see Figure 2.4). An amendment may be proposed either by a two-thirds vote in each house of Congress or by a national convention called by Congress at the request of two-thirds of the state legislatures. An amendment may be ratified either by the legislatures of three-fourths of the states or by special state conventions called in three-fourths of the states. The president has no formal role in amending the Constitution, although the chief executive may influence the success of proposed amendments.

Why It Matters

Amending the Constitution Amending the Constitution is difficult. The challenge of passing an amendment can constrain liberal interests as in the case of the ERA or more conservative interests as in the case of the proposed ban on burning the American flag. In these and other instances, the rules for amending the Constitution also function against writing short-term political impulses into the fundamental law of the land.

All but one of the successful amendments to the Constitution have been proposed by Congress and ratified by the state legislatures. The exception was the Twenty-first Amendment, which repealed the short-lived Eighteenth Amendment—the prohibition amendment that outlawed the sale and consumption of alcohol. The amendment was ratified by special state conventions rather than by state legislatures. Because proponents of repeal doubted that they could win in conservative legislatures, they persuaded Congress to require that state conventions be called.

Unquestionably, formal amendments have made the Constitution more egalitarian and democratic. Amendments that emphasize equality and increase the ability of a popular majority to affect government now provide a balance to the emphasis on economic issues in the original document. The Bill of Rights, which Chapter 4 will discuss in detail, head the amendments (see Table 2.5). Later amendments, including the Thirteenth Amendment abolishing slavery, forbid various political and social inequalities based on race, gender, and age (Chapter 5 discusses these amendments). Other amendments, discussed later in this chapter, have

Figure 2.4 How the Constitution Can Be Amended

The Constitution sets up two alternative routes for proposing amendments and two for ratifying them. One of the four combinations has been used in every case but one.

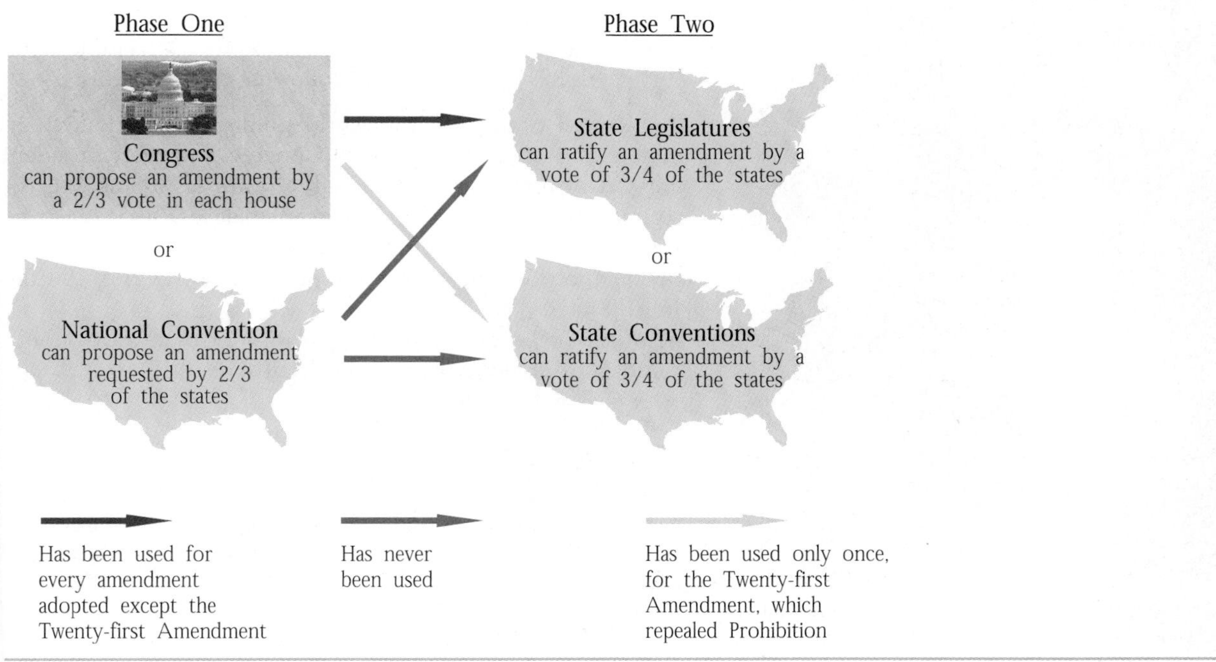

Has been used for every amendment adopted except the Twenty-first Amendment

Has never been used

Has been used only once, for the Twenty-first Amendment, which repealed Prohibition

democratized the political system, making it easier for voters to influence the government. Only one existing amendment specifically addresses the economy—the Sixteenth, or "income tax," Amendment. Overall, it is clear that the most important effect of these constitutional amendments has been to expand liberty and equality in the United States.

Some amendments have been proposed but not ratified. The best known of these in recent years is the **Equal Rights Amendment,** or **ERA.** First introduced in Congress in 1923 by the nephew of suffragist Susan B. Anthony, the ERA had to wait 49 years—until 1972—before Congress passed it and sent it to the states for ratification. The ERA stated simply, "Equality of rights under the law shall not be denied or abridged by the United States or by any State on account of sex."

Equal Rights Amendment

A constitutional amendment passed by Congress in 1972 and sent to the state legislatures for ratification, stating that "equality of rights under the law shall not be denied or abridged by the United States or by any state on account of sex." The amendment failed to acquire the necessary support from three-fourths of the state legislatures.

This seemingly benign amendment sailed through Congress and the first few state legislatures. Public opinion polls showed substantial support for the ERA, even among people who held traditional views of women's roles.[21]

Nevertheless, the ERA was not ratified. It failed, in part, because of the system of checks and balances. The ERA had to be approved not by a national majority but by three-fourths of the states. Many conservative Southern states opposed it, thus exercising their veto power despite approval by a majority of Americans.

Amending the constitution to give women the right to vote was an important step in the women's rights movement.

Marbury v. Madison

The 1803 case in which Chief Justice John Marshall and his associates first asserted the right of the **Supreme Court** to determine the meaning of the **U.S. Constitution.** The decision established the Court's power of **judicial review** over acts of Congress, in this case the Judiciary Act of 1789.

judicial review

The power of the courts to determine whether acts of Congress and, by implication, the executive are in accord with the **U.S. Constitution.** Judicial review was established by John Marshall and his associates in ***Marbury v. Madison.***

The Informal Process of Constitutional Change

Think for a moment of all the changes in American government that have taken place without altering a word or a letter of the written document. In fact, there is not a word in the Constitution that would lead us to suspect any of the following developments:

- The United States has the world's oldest two-party system, wherein almost every member of Congress and every president since Washington has declared, "I am a Democrat (or Republican, or Federalist, or Whig, or whatever)."
- Abortions through the second trimester of pregnancy (when the fetus cannot live outside the mother's womb) are legal in the United States.
- Members of the electoral college consider themselves honor bound (and in some places even legally bound) to follow the preference of their state's electorate.
- Proceedings of both the Senate and the House are on television, and television influences our political agenda and guides our assessments of candidates and issues.
- Government now taxes and spends about one-third of our gross domestic product, an amount the Convention delegates might have found gargantuan.

None of these things is "unconstitutional." The parties emerged, first technology and then the law permitted abortions, television came to prominence in American life—all without having to tinker with the Founders' handiwork. These developments could occur because the Constitution changes *informally* as well as formally. There are several ways in which the Constitution changes informally: through judicial interpretation, through political practice, and as a result of changes in technology and changes in the demands on policymakers.

Judicial Interpretation. Disputes often arise about the meaning of the Constitution. If it is the "supreme law of the land," then someone has to decide how to interpret the Constitution when disputes arise. In 1803, in the famous case of ***Marbury v. Madison,*** the Supreme Court decided it would be the one to resolve differences of opinion. It claimed for itself the power of **judicial review.** Implied but never explicitly stated in the Constitution,[22] this power gives courts the right to decide whether the actions of the legislative and executive branches of state and national governments are in accord with the Constitution (see "In Focus: John Marshall and the Growth of Judicial Review").

Judicial interpretation can profoundly affect how the Constitution is understood because the Constitution usually means what the Supreme Court says it means. For example, in 1896 the Supreme Court decided that the Constitution allowed racial discrimination despite the presence of the Fourteenth Amendment. Fifty-eight years

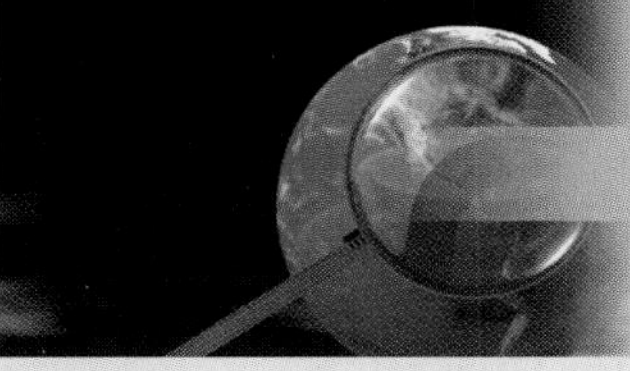

IN FOCUS

John Marshall and the Growth of Judicial Review

Scarcely was the government housed in its new capital when Federalists and Democrats clashed over the courts. In the election of 1800, Democrat Thomas Jefferson beat Federalist John Adams. Determined to leave at least the judiciary in trusted hands, Adams tried to fill it with Federalists. He allegedly stayed at his desk until 9:00 p.m. signing commissions on his last night in the White House (March 3, 1801).

In the midst of this flurry, Adams appointed William Marbury to the minor post of justice of the peace in the District of Columbia. In the rush of last-minute business, however, Secretary of State John Marshall failed to deliver commissions to Marbury and 16 others. He left the commissions to be delivered by incoming Secretary of State James Madison.

Madison and Jefferson were furious at Adams's actions and refused to deliver the commissions. Marbury and three others in the same situation sued Madison, asking the Supreme Court to order him to give them their commissions. They took their case directly to the Supreme Court under the Judiciary Act of 1789, which gave the Court original jurisdiction in such matters.

The new chief justice was none other than Adams's secretary of state and arch-Federalist John Marshall, himself one of Adams's "midnight appointments." Marshall and his Federalist colleagues were in a tough spot. Threats of impeachment came from Jeffersonians, who were fearful that the Court would vote for Marbury. Moreover, if the Court ordered Madison to deliver the commissions, he was likely to ignore it, thereby risking ridicule for the nation's highest court over a minor issue. Marshall had no means of compelling Madison to act.

The Court could also deny Marbury's claim. Taking that option, however, would concede the issue to the Jeffersonians and give the appearance of retreat in the face of opposition, thereby reducing the power of the Court.

Marshall devised a shrewd solution to the case *Marbury v. Madison*. In February 1803, he delivered the unanimous opinion of the Court. First, Marshall and his colleagues argued that Madison was wrong to withhold Marbury's commission. The Court also found, however, that the Judiciary Act of 1789 contradicted the plain words of the Constitution about the Court's original jurisdiction. Thus, Marshall dismissed Marbury's claim, saying that the Court, according to the Constitution, had no power to require that the commission be delivered.

Conceding a small battle over Marbury's commission (he did not get it), Marshall won a much larger war, asserting for the courts the power to determine what is and is not constitutional. As Marshall wrote, "An act of the legislature repugnant to the Constitution is void," and "it is emphatically the province and duty of the judicial department to say what the law is." Thus, the chief justice established the power of judicial review, the power of the courts to hold acts of Congress and, by implication, the executive, in violation of the Constitution.

After *Marbury*, angry members of Congress, together with other Jeffersonians, claimed that Marshall was a "usurper of power," setting himself above Congress and the president.

This view, however, was unfair. State courts, before and after the Constitution, had declared acts of their legislatures unconstitutional. In *Federalist Paper* #78, Alexander Hamilton had declared the courts had a "duty . . . to declare all acts contrary to the manifest tenor of the Constitution void," and the federal courts had actually done so. *Marbury* was not even the first case of striking down an act of Congress; a lower federal court had done so in 1792, and the Supreme Court itself had approved a law after a constitutional review in 1796. Marshall was neither inventing nor imagining his right to review laws for their constitutionality.

The case also illustrates that the courts must be politically astute in exercising their power over the other branches. By in effect reducing its own power—the authority to hear cases such as Marbury's under its original jurisdiction—the Court was able to assert the right of judicial review in a fashion that the other branches could not easily rebuke.

later, it overruled itself and concluded that segregation by law violated the Constitution. In 1973, the Supreme Court decided that the Constitution protected a woman's right to an abortion during the first two trimesters of pregnancy when the fetus is not viable outside the womb—an issue the Founders never imagined. (We discuss these cases in Chapters 4 and 5.)

Changing Political Practice. Current political practices also change the Constitution—stretching it, shaping it, and giving it new meaning. Probably no changes are more important than those related to parties and presidential elections.

Political parties as we know them did not exist when the Constitution was written. In fact, its authors would have disliked the idea of parties, which encourage factions. Regardless, by 1800 a party system had developed, and it plays a key role in making policy today. American government would be radically different if there were no political parties, even though the Constitution is silent about them.

Changing political practice has also altered the role of the electoral college, which has now been reduced to a clerical one in selecting the president. The writers of the Constitution, eager to avoid giving too much power to the uneducated

HOW YOU CAN MAKE A DIFFERENCE

Birthright Citizenship

In late 2005, Representative Nathan Deal (R-Ga) and over 70 cosponsors offered an amendment to the Border Protection, Antiterrorism and Illegal Immigration Act that would have automatically restricted citizenship at birth to children of U.S. citizens and residents. Currently, anyone born in the United States, regardless of the immigration status of their parents, is automatically granted citizenship under the 14th Amendment of the U.S. Constitution. This new proposal would have changed that practice. Deal argued that many illegal immigrants use the birthright citizenship of their American-born children to establish a foothold for themselves, since the children are eligible for government services, and can later petition for their parents' residency.

Making a Difference

The League of United Latin American Citizens (www.lulac.org) and the "Keep Our Families Together" Campaign of the National Alliance of Latin American and Caribbean Communities (NALACC) (www.nalacc.org) were two of the groups that opposed this amendment. By reaching out to their members, and through e-mail and press campaigns, these groups lead the fight to reject this amendment. Republican House leaders did not let the amendment come to a vote. However, the issue of birthright citizenship remains one part of the larger, ongoing debates about immigration reform.

What you can do:

- Download and distribute campaign materials either in support of groups like NALACC (http://www.nalacc.org/materiales.html) and LULAC, or to support changing birthright citizenship, from the Federation for American Immigration Reform (www.fairus.org.)
- Become members of these advocacy groups. If you are not the type to join advocacy groups, you can always contact your members of Congress with proposed amendments of your own.
- To add weight to your proposal, you can also do research online or in a library to see if there are others who share your concern, and you can then contact these like-minded citizens to have them request *their* congressional members to introduce similar amendments.

majority, intended that there be no popular vote for the president; instead, state legislatures or the voters (depending on the state) would select wise electors who would then choose a "distinguished character of continental reputation" (as the *Federalist Papers* put it) to be president. These electors formed the electoral college. Each state would have the same number of electors to vote for the president as it had senators and representatives in Congress.

In 1796, the first election in which George Washington was not a candidate, electors scattered their votes among 13 candidates. By the election of 1800, domestic and foreign policy issues had divided the country into two political parties. To avoid dissipating their support, the parties required electors to pledge in advance to vote for the candidate who won their state's popular vote, leaving electors with a largely clerical function.

Although electors are now rubber stamps for the popular vote, nothing in the Constitution prohibits an elector from voting for any candidate. Every so often, electors have decided to cast votes for their own favorites; some state laws require electors to vote for the candidate chosen by a plurality of their state's citizens, but such laws have never been enforced. The idea that the electoral college would exercise wisdom independent of the majority of people is now a constitutional anachronism, changed not by formal amendment but by political practice.

Technology. The Constitution has also been changed greatly by technology. The media have always played an important role in politics—questioning governmental policies, supporting candidates, and helping shape citizens' opinions. Modern technology, however, has spurred the development of a *mass* media that can rapidly reach huge audiences, something unimaginable in the eighteenth century. The bureaucracy has grown in importance with the development of computers, which create new potential for bureaucrats to serve the public (such as writing more than 40 million Social Security checks each month)—and, at times, create mischief. Electronic communications and the development of atomic weapons have given the president's role as commander in chief added significance, increasing the power of the president in the constitutional system. More recently, the Internet has fundamentally changed the way we select elected officials (see "Issues of the Times: How Is the Internet Changing Politics?").

Increasing Demands on Policymakers. The significance of the presidency has also grown as a result of increased demands for new policies. The evolution of the United States in the realm of international affairs—from an insignificant country that kept to itself to a superpower with an extraordinary range of international obligations—has concentrated additional power in the hands of the chief executive, who is designated to take the lead in foreign affairs. Similarly, the increased demands of domestic policy have positioned the president in a more prominent role in preparing the federal budget and a legislative program. (You can see the impact of the 9/11 terrorists' attacks on presidential power in "A Generation of Change: The War on Terrorism.")

The Importance of Flexibility

The Constitution, even with all 27 amendments, is a short document containing fewer than 8,000 words. It does not prescribe in detail the structure and functioning of the national government. Regarding the judiciary, the Constitution simply tells

A GENERATION OF CHANGE

The War on Terrorism

All wars increase presidential power because they place additional demands on the commander in chief. Congress of necessity delegates to the president the authority to prosecute a war, which involves a multitude of decisions, ranging from military strategy to logistics. The war on terrorism has taken delegation of authority one step further, however.

Because the enemy may not be a country but rather an amorphous group of people who employ the weapons of terrorism as political instruments, it is more difficult for Congress to specify the president's authority. Thus, a few days following the terrorist attacks of September 11, 2001, Congress passed a broad resolution authorizing him to use force against those nations, organizations, or persons that he alone determined were involved in the attacks. Thus, Congress asked the president to determine the identity of the enemy. This resolution served as the legal basis for the war in Afghanistan in 2002.

In October 2002, Congress passed another resolution authorizing the president to use "all means necessary and appropriate," which included the use of military force, to defend the United States against Iraq and enforce UN resolutions regarding Iraq. Congress delegated to the president the right to determine if and when the United States would go to war. This broad grant of power provided the authority to invade Iraq in March 2003. The president also interpreted this resolution as authorizing him to order the National Security Agency to monitor secretly the international telephone calls and e-mail messages of people inside the United States who might be communicating with terrorists abroad.

In addition to fighting terrorists abroad, securing the homeland also became a highly salient issue. Only six weeks after the terrorist attacks, Congress passed the USA Patriot Act. This law gave the executive branch broad new powers for the wiretapping, surveillance, and investigation of terrorism suspects. The act gave the federal government the power to examine a suspect's records held by third parties such as doctors, libraries, bookstores, universities, and Internet service providers. It also allowed searches of private property without probable cause and without prior notice to the owner, limiting a person's opportunities to challenge a search.

Thus, the war on terrorism has resulted in substantially increased demands on the president and a notable increase in authority to meet those demands. Whether Congress or the courts will reassert their own authority is an open question. In the meantime, the war on terrorism has altered the balance of power in our constitutional system.

Congress to create a court system as it sees fit. The Supreme Court is the only court required by the Constitution, and even here the Constitution leaves the number of justices and their qualifications up to Congress. Similarly, many of the governing units we have today—such as the executive departments, the various offices in the White House, the independent regulatory commissions, and the committees of Congress, to name only a few examples—are not mentioned at all in the Constitution.

Explore Your State Constitution

It is easy to see that the document the framers produced over 200 years ago was not meant to be static, written in stone. Instead, the Constitution's authors created a flexible system of government, one that could adapt to the needs of the times without sacrificing personal freedom. The framers allowed future generations to determine their own needs. As muscle grows on the constitutional skeleton, it inevitably gives new shape and purpose to the government. This flexibility has helped ensure the Constitution's—and the nation's—survival. Although the United States is young compared to other Western nations, it has the oldest functioning Constitution. France, which experienced a revolution in 1789, the same year the Constitution took effect, has had 12 constitutions over the past two centuries. Despite the great diversity of the American population, the enormous size of the country, and the extraordinary changes that have taken place over the nation's history, the U.S. Constitution is still going strong.

Understanding the Constitution

As the body of rules that govern our nation, the Constitution has an impact on our everyday lives. Our theme of the scope of government runs throughout this chapter, which focuses on what the national government can and cannot do. A nation that prides itself on being "democratic" must evaluate the Constitution according to democratic standards, the core of our other theme.

The Constitution and Democracy

Although the United States is often said to be one of the most democratic societies in the world, few describe the Constitution as democratic. This paradox is hardly surprising, considering the political philosophies of the men who wrote it. Among eighteenth-century upper-class society, democratic government was generally despised. If democracy was a way of permitting the majority's preference to become policy, the Constitution's authors wanted no part of it. The American government was to be a government of the "rich, well-born, and able," as Hamilton said, a government where John Jay's wish that "the people who own the country ought to govern it" would be a reality. Few people today would consider these thoughts democratic.

The Constitution did not, however, create a monarchy or a feudal aristocracy. It created a republic, a representative form of democracy modeled after the Lockean tradition of limited government. Thus, the undemocratic—even antidemocratic—Constitution established a government that permitted substantial movement toward democracy.

One of the central themes of American history is the gradual democratization of the Constitution. What began as a document characterized by numerous restrictions on direct voter participation has slowly become much more democratic. Today, few people share the Founders' fear of democracy. The expansion of voting rights has moved the American political system away from the elitist model of democracy and toward the pluralist model.

The History of Constitutional Amendments

The Constitution itself offered no guidelines on voter eligibility, leaving it to each state to decide. As a result, only a small percentage of adults could vote; women and slaves were excluded entirely. Of the 17 constitutional amendments passed since the Bill of Rights, five have focused on the expansion of the electorate. The Fifteenth Amendment (1870) prohibited discrimination on the basis of race in determining voter eligibility (although it took the Voting Rights Act of 1965, discussed in Chapter 4, to make the amendment effective). The Nineteenth

YOUNG PEOPLE AND POLITICS

Lowering the Voting Age

The 1960s was a tumultuous era, and massive Vietnam War protests organized by students and other young people were common in the last half of the decade. Many young people felt that protesting was the best they could do because the voting age was 21 in most states—even though 18-year-olds were old enough to marry, work, and pay taxes as others adults did. In the Vietnam War, the average age of U.S. soldiers was 19, and young citizens often asserted, "If we're old enough to fight, we're old enough to vote."

Majorities in both houses of Congress agreed that the voting age was unfair and passed the Voting Rights Act of 1970, lowering the voting age to 18 in both federal and state elections. The Supreme Court, however, held that Congress had exceeded its authority and only could set voting ages in national elections.

In 1971, Senator Jennings Randolph, a Democrat of West Virginia, proposed a constitutional amendment to lower the voting age to 18 years: "The right of citizens of the United States, who are eighteen years of age or older, to vote shall not be denied or abridged by the United States or by any State on account of age." Randolph was a warrior for peace and had great faith in young people, arguing, "They possess a great social conscience, are perplexed by the injustices in the world, and are anxious to rectify those ills."

Randolph had introduced legislation lowering the voting age 11 times, beginning in 1942. This time, aided by appreciation of the sacrifices of young soldiers in Vietnam, he was successful. The amendment passed the Senate unanimously, and it passed the House of Representatives by a vote of 400 to 19. It was then sent to the states to be ratified. No state wanted to maintain two sets of voter registration books and go to the expense of running separate election systems for federal elections and for all other elections. Thus, the states were receptive to the proposed amendment, and in just 100 days three-fourths of the states ratified it.

On July 5, the Twenty-sixth Amendment was formally adopted into the Constitution, adding 11 million potential voters to the electorate. Half of these young voters cast their ballots in the 1972 presidential election.

Questions for Discussion

- There are proposals in some states to lower the voting age below 18. What is the appropriate age for voting?
- Would it be appropriate for different states to have diferent ages for voting?

You Are Proposing a Constitutional Amendment

Amendment (1920) gave women the right to vote (although some states had already done so). The Twenty-third Amendment (1961) accorded the residents of Washington, D.C., the right to vote in presidential elections. Three years later, the Twenty-fourth Amendment prohibited poll taxes (which discriminated against the poor). Finally, the Twenty-sixth Amendment (1971) lowered the voter eligibility age to 18 (see "Young People and Politics: Lowering the Voting Age").

Not only are more people eligible to vote, but voters now have more officials to elect. The Seventeenth Amendment (1913) provided for direct election of senators. Presidential elections have been fundamentally altered by the development of political parties. By placing the same candidate on the ballot in all the states and requiring members of the electoral college to support the candidate who receives the most votes, parties have increased the probability that the candidate for whom most Americans vote will also receive a majority of the electoral college vote. (For more on the electoral college, see Chapter 9.) Nevertheless, it is possible for the candidate who receives the most popular votes to lose the election, as occurred in 1824, 1876, 1888, and 2000.

Technology has also diminished the separation of the people from those who exercise power. Officeholders communicate directly with the public through television, radio, and targeted mailings. Air travel makes it easy for members of Congress to commute regularly between Washington and their districts. Similarly, public opinion polls, the telephone, and e-mail enable officials to stay apprised of citizens' opinions on important issues. Even though the American population has grown from fewer than 4 million to 300 million people since the first census was taken in 1790, the national government has never been closer to those it serves.

The Constitution and the Scope of Government

Comparing Constitutions

The Constitution created political institutions and the rules for politics and policymaking. Many of these rules limit government action. This limiting function is what the Bill of Rights and related provisions in the Constitution are all about. No matter how large the majority, for example, it is unconstitutional to establish a state-supported church.

The goal of most of these limitations is primarily to protect liberty and to open the system to a broad range of participants. The potential range of action for the government is actually quite wide. Thus, it is constitutionally permissible, although highly unlikely, for the United States either to abolish Social Security payments to the elderly or to take over ownership of the oil industry or the nation's airlines.

Yet the system of government created by the Constitution has profound implications for what the government does. On one hand, the system reinforces individualism at every turn. The separation of powers and the checks and balances established by the Constitution allow almost all groups some place in the political system where their demands for public policy can be heard. Because many institutions share power, groups can usually find at least one sympathetic ear in government. Even if the president opposes the policies a particular group favors, Congress, the courts, or some other institution can help the group achieve its policy goals. In the early days of the civil rights movement, for example, African Americans found Congress and the president unsympathetic, so they turned to the Supreme Court. Getting their interests on the political agenda would have been much more difficult if the Court had not had important constitutional power.

On the other hand, the Constitution encourages stalemate. By providing effective access for so many interests, the Founders created a system of policymaking in which it is difficult for the government to act. The separation of powers and the system of checks and balances promote the politics of bargaining, compromise, and playing one institution against another. The system of checks and balances implies that one institution is checking another. *Thwarting*, *blocking*, and *impeding* are synonyms for checking. But if I block you, and you block someone else, and that person blocks me, none of us is going to accomplish anything, and we have gridlock.

If the president, Congress, and the courts all pull in different directions on policy, the result may be either no policy at all (gridlock) or an inadequate, makeshift policy. The outcome may be nondecisions when the country requires that difficult decisions be made. If government cannot respond effectively because its policymaking processes are too fragmented, then its performance will be inadequate. Perhaps the Madisonian model has reduced the ability of government to reach effective policy decisions. Certainly, radical departures from the status quo are atypical in American politics.

Summary

The year 1787 was crucial in building the American system of government. The 55 men who met in Philadelphia created a policymaking system that responded to a complex policy agenda. Critical conflicts over equality led to key compromises in the New Jersey and Virginia Plans, the three-fifths compromise on slavery, and the decision to leave the issue of voting rights to the states. There was more consensus, however, about the economy. These merchants, lawyers, and large landowners believed that the American economy was in a shambles, and they intended to make the national government an economic stabilizer. The specificity of the powers assigned to Congress left no doubt that Congress was to forge national economic policy. The delegates knew, too, that the global posture of the fledgling nation was pitifully weak. A strong national government would be better able to ensure its own security and that of the nation.

Madison and his colleagues were less clear about the protection of individual rights. Because they believed that the limited government they had constructed would protect freedom, they said little about individual rights in the Constitution. However, the ratification struggle revealed that protection of personal freedoms was much on the public's mind. As a result, the Bill of Rights was proposed. These first 10 amendments to the Constitution, along with the Thirteenth and Fourteenth Amendments, provide Americans with protection from governmental restraints on individual freedoms.

It is important to remember that 1787 was not the only year of nation building. The nation's colonial and revolutionary heritage shaped the meetings in Philadelphia. Budding industrialism in a basically agrarian nation put economic issues on the Philadelphia agenda. What Madison was to call an "unequal division of property" made equality an issue, particularly after Shays' Rebellion. The greatest inequality of all, that between slavery and freedom, was so contentious an issue that the Founders simply avoided addressing it in the Constitution.

Nor did ratification of the Constitution end the nation-building process. Constitutional change—both formal and informal—continues to shape and alter the letter and the spirit of the Madisonian system.

Because that system includes separate institutions sharing power, it results in many checks and balances. Today, some Americans complain that this system has created a government too responsive to too many interests and too fragmented to act. Others praise the way it protects minority views. In Chapter 3, we will look at yet another way in which the Constitution divides governmental power: between the national and the state governments.

Internet Resources

www.law.emory.edu/FEDERAL/federalist/
The *Federalist Papers*. Allows you to search the essays using key words.

www.law.emory.edu/erd/docs/usconst.html
The Constitution. Allows you to search the document using key words.

www.archives.gov/national-archives-experience/charters/constitution_founding_fathers.html
Biographies of the Founders.

www.earlyamerica.com/earlyamerica/milestones/articles/text.html
The Articles of Confederation. Also provides access to a wide range of documents from the founding period.

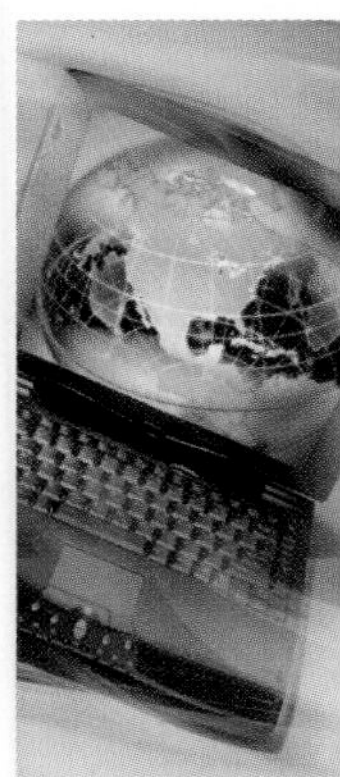

Get Connected

Constitutional Change

The Founders did not intend for the Constitution, the rules of our political system, to be static. Instead, they designed the Constitution specifically so that it could be changed—added to or subtracted from—as needed. Figure 2.4 illustrates the ways the Constitution can be changed. Although proposed constitutional changes can originate from national and state conventions, all constitutional changes to date have originated in Congress. So far there have been 27 amendments, but there have been many more proposed changes. Even now, there are several proposed changes to the Constitution being debated in the chambers of Congress and in the media. One of the most controversial is an amendment defining marriage and reads,

> *Marriage in the United States shall consist only of the union of a man and a woman. Neither this Constitution nor the constitution of any State, nor state or federal law, shall be construed to require that marital status or the legal incidents thereof be conferred upon unmarried couples or groups.*

Search the Web

Go to the Web sites of a number of groups and people who are on opposite sides of the marriage constitutional amendment debate, including the Alliance for Marriage, *www.allianceformarriage.org/site/PageServer*; the American Civil Liberties Union, *www.aclu.org/marriageamendment*; Focus on the Family, *www.family.org/cforum/fosi/marriage/ssuap*; the Human Rights Campaign, *www.hrc.org/marriage*; and the Log Cabin Republicans, *www.logcabin.org/logcabin/defendconstitution.html*, and review their positions on the proposed constitutional amendment defining marriage. For additional information, review the Guidelines for Constitutional Amendments developed by Citizens for the Constitution, *www.constitutionproject.org/pdf/guidelines.pdf* (the guidelines are listed on page 7 of the publication, which requires a PDF reader to view).

Questions to Ask

- Why is the idea of amending a definition of marriage into the U.S. Constitution controversial?
- Which of these groups favor the proposed amendment, and what are their reasons?
- Which of these groups oppose the amendment and why?
- What is your position on the proposed amendment, and why did you reach that conclusion?
- Does the proposed marriage amendment violate the spirit of the separation of church and state found in the First Amendment?

Why It Matters

Some say the process of amending the Constitution is too difficult and prevents necessary constitutional change. Other observers argue that the obstacles to amending the Constitution are good because they keep proposals like the gay marriage amendment, on which opinion may change in the next decade, from becoming part of the document. Would our nation be improved if the Constitution were more easily amended? Should constitutional amendments only change governmental structures, or should they deal with social issues such as marriage?

Get Involved

The definition of marriage amendment is just one of the many proposals introduced in Congress to amend the Constitution. Can you think of amendments you would like to see added to the Constitution? Make a list of your proposed amendments and compare your list with those of other students in class.

For more exercises, go to www.longmanamericangovernment.com.

For Further Reading

Bailyn, Bernard. *The Ideological Origins of the American Revolution.* Cambridge, MA: Harvard University Press, 1967. A leading work on the ideas that spawned the American Revolution.

Becker, Carl L. *The Declaration of Independence: A Study in the History of Political Ideas.* New York: Random House, 1942. Classic work on the meaning of the Declaration.

Dahl, Robert A. *How Democratic Is the American Constitution?* 2nd ed. New Haven, CT: Yale University Press, 2003. Questions the extent to which the Consitution furthers democratic goals.

Hamilton, Alexander, James Madison, and John Jay. *The Federalist Papers.* 2nd ed. Edited by Roy P. Fairfield. Baltimore: Johns Hopkins University Press, 1981. Key tracts in the campaign for the Constitution and cornerstones of American political thought.

Higginbotham, A. Leon, Jr. *In the Matter of Color: Race and the American Legal Process, the Colonial Period.* New York: Oxford University Press, 1978. Chronicles how colonial governments established the legal foundations for the enslavement of African Americans.

Jensen, Merrill. *The Articles of Confederation.* Madison: University of Wisconsin Press, 1940. Definitive and balanced treatment of the Articles.

Jillson, Calvin C. *Constitution Making: Conflict and Consensus in the Federal Convention of 1787.* New York: Agathon, 1988. Sophisticated analysis of the drafting of the Constitution.

Lipset, Seymour Martin. *The First New Nation.* New York: Basic Books, 1963. Political sociologist Lipset sees the early American experience as one of nation building.

Maier, Pauline. *American Scripture.* New York: Knopf, 1997. Argues that the Declaration was the embodiment of the American mind and historical experience.

McDonald, Forrest B. *Novus Ordo Seclorum: The Intellectual Origins of the Constitution.* Lawrence: University Press of Kansas, 1986. Discusses the ideas behind the Constitution.

Morris, Richard B. *The Forging of the Union, 1781–1789.* New York: Harper & Row, 1987. Written to coincide with the bicentennial of the Constitution, this is an excellent history of the document's making.

Norton, Mary Beth. *Liberty's Daughters.* Boston: Little, Brown, 1980. Examines the role of women during the era of the Revolution and concludes that the Revolution transformed gender roles, setting women on the course of equality.

Rossiter, Clinton. *1787: The Grand Convention.* New York: Macmillan, 1966. A well-written study of the making of the Constitution.

Storing, Herbert J. *What the Anti-Federalists Were For.* Chicago: University of Chicago Press, 1981. Analysis of the political views of those opposed to ratification of the Constitution.

Wood, Gordon S. *The Creation of the American Republic.* Chapel Hill: University of North Carolina Press, 1969. In-depth study of American political thought prior to the Constitutional Convention.

Wood, Gordon S. *The Radicalism of the American Revolution.* New York: Vintage, 1993. Shows how American society and politics were thoroughly transformed in the decades following the Revolution.

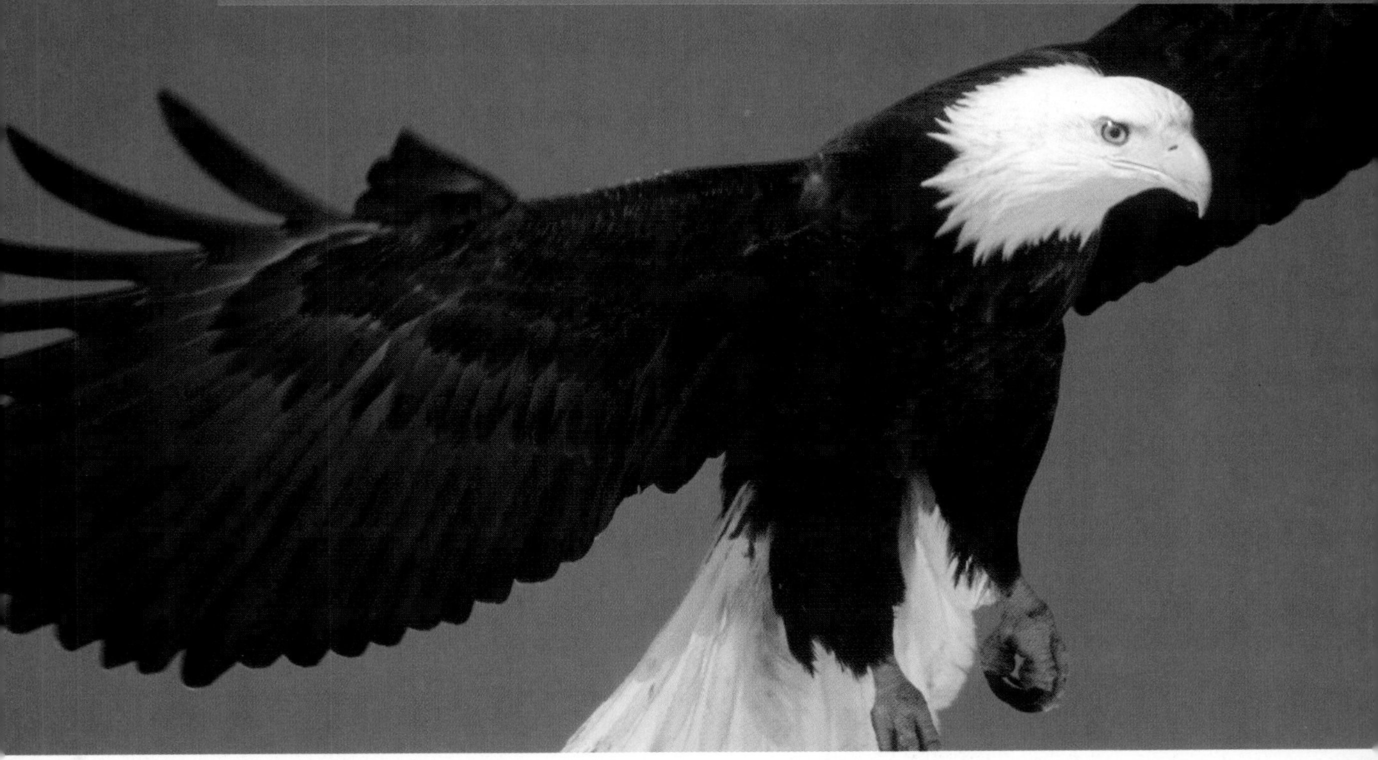

Federalism

Chapter Outline

POLITICS IN ACTION: AIDING DISASTER VICTIMS On August 29, 2005, Hurricane Katrina, a category 5 storm, swept across the Mississippi Gulf Coast, devastating New Orleans and parts of Mississippi and Alabama. Levees that had protected New Orleans for generations gave way to the force of the storm, stranding thousands of citizens without electricity, food, water, health care, communications, or police protection.

State and local governments are the first responders to natural disasters, but the breadth of the disaster quickly overwhelmed most of the local infrastructure. The national government is supposed to supplement state and local efforts; instead, a virtual standoff between hesitant federal officials and besieged authorities in Louisiana deepened the crisis in New Orleans.

Chaos reigned as the fractured division of responsibility meant no one person or agency was in charge. Federal and state officials clashed over the issue of "federalizing" the Louisiana National Guard, which the governor was reluctant to do because she feared losing authority over it and lacked confidence in the national government.

State and local officials assumed that Washington would provide rapid and substantial aid, but leaders in Louisiana and New Orleans were not always sure what they needed. Thus, desperate state and local officials made open-ended pleas for help, which federal officials found difficult to interpret. Rather than initiate relief efforts—such as providing buses, food and water, troops, diesel fuel, and rescue boats—federal officials waited for specific requests and, weighing legalities and logistics, proceeded at a deliberate pace.

As a result, Americans watched in horror as their favorite news anchors reported from New Orleans standing beside suffering victims while federal officials were still unable to move the necessary personnel (including members of the world's mightiest military force) and supplies to aid those stricken by the storm.

Aid did arrive eventually, but it was followed very closely by a public relations battle to assign blame for what everyone agreed was a wholly inadequate response at all levels. The issue was not the goal of aiding disaster victims. Everyone agreed with that. Instead, the issue was the appropriate federal and state powers and responsibilities—an issue over which America has fought a civil war.

Contemporary Federalism

The issue of federalism and the delegation of responsibility to different levels of government is a crucial political battleground—policymakers' answers to the questions of how we should be governed (in this case, by the states or by the federal government) and what should be the scope of the national government in shaping public policies.

It is important to understand American federalism, the complex relationships between different levels of government in the United States. We will be especially attentive to our themes of democracy and the scope of government. Does federalism, the vertical division of power, enhance democracy in the United States? Does the additional layer of policymakers make government more responsive to public opinion or merely more complicated? Does it enhance the prospects that a national majority of Americans have their way in public policy? And what are the implications of federalism for the scope of the national government's activities? Why has the national government grown so much in relation to state governments, and has this growth been at the expense of the states?

The relationships between governments at the local, state, and national levels often confuse Americans. Neighborhood schools are run by locally elected school boards but also receive state and national funds, and with those funds come state and national rules and regulations. Local airports, sewage systems, pollution control systems, and police departments also receive a mix of local, state, and national funds, so they operate under a complex web of rules and regulations imposed by each level of government.

Sometimes this complex system is almost impossible to understand, especially given the size of the country and the large number of governmental units within it. Even the national government has difficulty keeping track of about $450 billion in federal aid distributed each year to states and cities. In 1972, when the U.S. Treasury Department first sent revenue-sharing checks to 50 states and 38,000 local governments, some 5,000 checks were returned, marked "addressee unknown," by the Postal Service.[1] If the Postal Service has trouble keeping up with all the governments in America, it's no wonder citizens do, too.

Defining Federalism

Federalism is a rather unusual system for governing, with particular consequences for those who live within it. This section explains the federal system and how it affects Americans living in such a system.

What Is Federalism?

Federalism is a way of organizing a nation so that two or more levels of government have formal authority over the same area and people. It is a system of shared power between units of government. For example, the state of California has formal authority over its inhabitants, but the national government can also pass laws and establish policies that affect Californians. We are subject to the formal authority of both the state and the national governments.

federalism
A way of organizing a nation so that two or more levels of government have formal authority over the same land and people. It is a system of shared power between units of government.

Although federalism is not unique to the United States, it is not a common method of governing. Only 11 of the 190 or so nations of the world have federal systems, and these countries, which include Germany, Mexico, Argentina, Canada, Australia, India, and the United States, share little else.

Most governments in the world today are not federal but **unitary governments**, in which all power resides in the central government. If the French Assembly, for instance, wants to redraw the boundaries of local governments or change their forms of government, it can (and has). However, if the U.S. Congress wants to abolish Alabama or Oregon, it cannot.

unitary governments
A way of organizing a nation so that all power resides in the central government. Most national governments today are unitary governments.

American states are unitary governments with respect to their local governments. Local governments get their authority from the states; they can be created or abolished by the states. States also have the power to make rules for their own local governments. They can tell them what their speed limits will be, the way in which they should be organized, how they can tax people, on what they can spend money, and so forth. States, however, receive their authority not from the national government but *directly* from the Constitution.

Comparing Federal and Unitary Systems

There is a third form of governmental structure, a *confederation*. The United States began as such under the Articles of Confederation. In a confederation, the national government is weak, and most or all the power is in the hands of its components—for example, the individual states. Today, confederations are rare except in international organizations such as the United Nations (see Chapter 17). Table 3.1 provides a summary of the authority relations in the three systems of government.

The workings of the federal system are sometimes called **intergovernmental relations.** This term refers to the entire set of interactions among national, state, and local governments.[2]

intergovernmental relations
The workings of the federal system—the entire set of interactions among national, state, and local governments.

In the U.S. federal system, two governments may have authority in the same policy area. For example, the interstate highway system was constructed with a combination of national and state dollars.

Table 3.1 Authority Relations in Three Systems of Government

	UNITARY	FEDERAL	CONFEDERATE
Central government	Holds primary authority Regulates activities of states	Shares power with states	Limited powers to coordinate state activities
State government	Few or no powers Duties regulated by central government	Shares power with central government	Sovereign Allocate some duties to central government
Citizens	Vote for central government officials	Vote for both state and central government officials	Vote for state government officials

Why It Matters

The Bill of Rights

State constitutions guarantee many basic rights. However, few Americans would feel comfortable with only state protections for their liberties. The Bill of Rights in the U.S. Constitution is the ultimate legal defense of freedom.

Why Is Federalism So Important?

The federal system in America *decentralizes our politics*. Senators are elected as representatives of individual states, not of the entire nation. On Election Day in November, there are actually 51 presidential elections, one in each state and one in Washington, D.C. (see Chapter 9). It is even possible—as happened in 2000—for a candidate who receives the most popular votes in the country to lose the election because of the way the electoral votes are distributed by state.

The federal system decentralizes our politics in more fundamental ways than our electoral system. With more layers of government, more opportunities exist for political participation. With more people wielding power, there are more points of access in government and more opportunities for interests to have their demands for public policies satisfied. With more decisions made in the states, there are fewer sources of conflict at the national level.

As we will see, federalism also enhances judicial power. Dividing government power and responsibilities necessitates umpires to resolve disputes between the two levels of government. In the American system, judges serve as the umpires. Thus when the national government places prohibitions or requirements on the states, inevitably issues arise for the courts to decide.

The federal system not only decentralizes our politics but also *decentralizes our policies*. The history of the federal system demonstrates the tension between the states and the national government about policy: who controls it and what it should be. In the past, people debated whether the states or the national government should regulate the railroads, pass child labor laws, or adopt minimum-wage legislation. Today, people debate whether the states or the national government should regulate abortions, set standards for public schools, determine speed limits on highways, or tell 18-year-olds they cannot drink alcohol.[3]

Policies about equality, the economy, the environment, and other matters are subject to both the centralizing force of the national government and the dispersing force of the states. The overlapping powers of the two levels of government mean that most of our public policy debates are also debates about federalism.

States are responsible for most public policies dealing with social, family, and moral issues. The Constitution does not give the national government the power to pass laws that *directly* regulate drinking ages, marriage and divorce, or speed limits. These policy prerogatives belong to the states. They become national issues, however, when aggrieved or angry groups take their cases to Congress or the federal courts in an attempt to use the power of the national government to *influence* states or to get federal courts to find a state's policy unconstitutional.

A good example of this process is the federal requirement that states raise their drinking age to 21 in order to receive highway funds. Candy Lightner, a California real estate broker suffering from the death of her 13-year-old daughter at the hands of a drunk driver, formed Mothers Against Drunk Driving (MADD). MADD lobbied Congress to pass a law withholding federal highway funds from any state that did not raise its drinking age. Today, every state has a legal drinking age of 21.

You Are a Restaurant Owner

The American states have always been policy innovators.[4] The states overflow with reforms, new ideas, and new policies. From clean-air legislation to welfare reform, the states constitute a national laboratory to develop and test public policies and share the results with other states and the national government. Almost every policy the national government has adopted had its beginnings in the states. One or more states pioneered child labor laws, minimum-wage legislation, unemployment compensation, antipollution legislation, civil rights protections, and the income tax. More recently, states have been active in reforming health care, education, and welfare—and the national government is paying close attention to their efforts.

Federalism is an important key to unlocking the secrets of the American political system. Which president is elected, which policy innovations are developed, at what age young men and women can legally drink, and many other issues are profoundly affected by the workings of the federal system.

The Constitutional Basis of Federalism

The word *federalism* is absent from the Constitution, and not much was said about it at the Constitutional Convention. Eighteenth-century Americans had little experience in thinking of themselves as Americans first and state citizens second. In fact, loyalty to state governments was so strong that the Constitution would have been resoundingly defeated had it tried to abolish them. In addition, a central

HOW YOU CAN MAKE A DIFFERENCE

Federalism

Because governmental authority in the United States is divided into local, state, and national levels, the American constitutional system offers numerous political offices and positions. The sheer number of offices gives Americans ample opportunity to actively participate in the political process. By running as a candidate, the federal principle allows concerned citizens to directly influence the politics and policy they deem important. And you need not win an election to have an effect on local policy, as simply running for office can bring issues into the public consciousness.

Making a Difference

Take, for instance, the example of Leigh Ann Ellis, who was a PTA mother concerned with local school district corruption. Leigh Ann ran for a place on the board of the Dallas Independent School District and ended up ousting the possibly incompetent local school board representative. Due to her alarm over the quality of her child's education, she took advantage of American federalism to stand for election and make a difference in her community.

What you can do:

- You, too, have the opportunity to run for local office and help change the policies that directly affect your daily life. You can run for student government, your state's legislature (18-year-old Derrick Seaver won a seat in the Ohio State Legislature in 2000) or for most local offices of your own choosing.
- You can attend school board and city council meetings or engage in local activism by organizing petition drives or letter-writing campaigns. State and local officials tend to be very much in tune with the activities of their constituents, since it takes fewer resources for citizens to remove these officials from office or to generate publicity for local problems.
- Identify three local offices in which you are eligible to run for election. What are the age and residency requirements to run for your state's legislature and local offices?

government, working alone, would have had difficulty trying to govern eighteenth-century Americans. The people were too widely dispersed and the country's transportation and communication systems too primitive to allow governing from a central location. There was no other practical choice in 1787 but to create a federal system of government.

The Division of Power

Governors

The Constitution's writers carefully defined the powers of state and national governments (see Table 3.2). Although they favored a stronger national government, the framers still made states vital cogs in the machinery of government. The Constitution guaranteed states equal representation in the Senate (and even made this provision unamendable in Article V). It also made states responsible for both state and national elections—an important power. Further, the Constitution virtually guaranteed the continuation of each state; Congress is forbidden to create new states by chopping up old ones, unless a state's legislature approves (an unlikely event).

Table 3.2 The Constitution's Distribution of Powers

TO THE NATIONAL GOVERNMENT	TO BOTH THE NATIONAL AND STATE GOVERNMENTS	TO THE STATE GOVERNMENTS
SOME POWERS GRANTED BY THE CONSTITUTION		
Coin money Conduct foreign relations Regulate commerce with foreign nations and among states Provide an army and a navy Declare war Establish courts inferior to the Supreme Court Establish post offices Make laws necessary and proper to carry out the foregoing powers	Tax Borrow money Establish courts Make and enforce laws Charter banks and corporations Spend money for the general welfare Take private property for public purposes, with just compensation	Establish local government Regulate commerce within a state Conduct elections Ratify amendments to the federal Constitution Take measures for public health, safety, and morals Exert powers the Constitution does not delegate to the national government or prohibit the states from using
SOME POWERS DENIED BY THE CONSTITUTION		
Tax articles exported from one state to another Violate the Bill of Rights Change state boundaries	Grant titles of nobility Permit slavery (Thirteenth Amendment) Deny citizens the right to vote because of race, color, or previous servitude (Fifteenth Amendment) Deny citizens the right to vote because of gender (Nineteenth Amendment)	Tax imports or exports Coin money Enter into treaties Impair obligations of contracts Abridge the privileges or immunities of citizens or deny due process and equal protection of the law (Fourteenth Amendment)

The Constitution also created obligations of the national government toward the states; it is to protect states against violence and invasion, for example. At times, though, the states find the national government deficient in meeting its obligations, as we will discuss later in this chapter.

In Article VI of the Constitution, the framers dealt with what remains a touchy question: In a dispute between the states and the national government, which prevails? The answer that the delegates provided, often referred to as the **supremacy clause**, seems clear enough. They stated that the following three items were the supreme law of the land:

supremacy clause
Article VI of the Constitution, which makes the Constitution, national laws, and treaties supreme over state laws when the national government is acting within its constitutional limits.

1. The Constitution
2. Laws of the national government (when consistent with the Constitution)
3. Treaties (which can be made only by the national government)

Judges in every state were specifically directed to obey the Constitution, even if their state constitutions or state laws directly contradicted it. Today, all state executives, legislators, and judges are bound by oath to support the Constitution.

Tenth Amendment
The constitutional amendment stating, "The powers not delegated to the United States by the Constitution, nor prohibited by it to the states, are reserved to the states respectively, or to the people."

The national government, however, can operate only within its appropriate sphere. It cannot usurp the states' powers. But what are the boundaries of the national government's powers? According to some commentators, the **Tenth Amendment** provides part of the answer. It states that the "powers not delegated to the United States by the Constitution, nor prohibited by it to the states, are reserved to the states respectively, or to the people." To those advocating states' rights, the amendment clearly means that the national government has only those powers specifically assigned to it by the Constitution. The states or people have supreme power over any activity not mentioned there. Despite this interpretation, in 1941 the Supreme Court (in *United States v. Darby*) called the Tenth Amendment a constitutional truism, a mere assertion that the states have independent powers of their own—not a declaration that state powers are superior to those of the national government.

The Court seemed to backtrack on this ruling in favor of national government supremacy in a 1976 case, *National League of Cities v. Usery*, in which it held that extending national minimum-wage and maximum-hours standards to employees of state and local governments was an unconstitutional intrusion of the national government into the domain of the states. In 1985, however (in *Garcia v. San Antonio Metro*), the Court overturned the *National League of Cities* decision. The Court held, in essence, that it was up to Congress, not the courts, to decide which actions of the states should be regulated by the national government. Once again, the Court ruled that the Tenth Amendment did not give states power superior to that of the national government for activities not mentioned in the Constitution.

Occasionally, issues arise in which states challenge the authority of the national government. In the late 1980s, the governors of several states refused to allow their state National Guards to engage in training exercises in Central America. National Guards are state militias, but the Constitution provides that the president can nationalize them. In 1990, the Supreme Court reiterated the power of the national government by siding with the president. Similarly, South Dakota sued the federal government over its efforts to raise states' drinking-age laws and over its efforts to mandate a 55-mile-per-hour speed limit on highways. The state lost both cases. (In 1995, however, Congress changed the law on speed limits, deciding to leave it up to the states.) Several states are in the process of challenging federal education regulations resulting from the No Child Left Behind Act.

You Are a Federal Judge

Federal courts can order states to obey the Constitution or federal laws and treaties. However, in deference to the states, the *Eleventh Amendment* prohibits individual damage suits against state officials (such as a suit against a police officer for violating one's rights) and protects state governments from being sued against their consent by private parties in federal courts or in state courts,[5] or before federal administrative agencies.[6] In 2001, the court voided the application of the Americans with Disabilities Act to the states, finding it a violation of the Eleventh Amendment (*Board of Trustees of University of Alabama, et al. v. Garrett, et al.*). Cases arising under the Fourteenth Amendment (usually cases regarding racial discrimination) are an exception.[7] Suits may also be brought by the federal government against states in federal courts and by individuals against state officials seeking to prohibit future illegal actions.

Recently the Supreme Court has made it easier for citizens to control the behavior of local officials. The Court ruled that a federal law passed in 1871 to protect newly freed slaves permits individuals to sue local governments for damages or to seek injunctions against any local official acting in an official capacity who they believe has deprived them of any right secured by the Constitution or by federal law.[8] Such suits are now common in the federal courts.

Establishing National Supremacy

Why is it that the federal government has gained power relative to the states? Four key events have largely settled the issue of how national and state powers are related: (1) the elaboration of the doctrine of implied powers, (2) the definition of the commerce clause, (3) the Civil War, and (4) the long struggle for racial equality.

Implied Powers. As early as 1819, the issue of state versus national power came before the Supreme Court in the case of ***McCulloch v. Maryland***. The new American government had moved quickly on many economic policies. In 1791, it created a national bank, a government agency empowered to print money, make loans, and engage in many other banking tasks. A darling of Alexander Hamilton and his allies, the bank was hated by those opposed to strengthening the national government's control of the economy. Those opposed—including Thomas Jefferson, farmers, and state legislatures—saw the bank as an instrument of the elite. The First Bank of the United States was allowed to expire, but then the Second Bank was created during James Madison's presidency, fueling a great national debate.

McCulloch v. Maryland
An 1819 Supreme Court decision that established the supremacy of the national government over state governments. In deciding this case, Chief Justice John Marshall and his colleagues held that Congress had certain **implied powers** in addition to the **enumerated powers** found in the Constitution.

Railing against the "Monster Bank," the state of Maryland passed a law in 1818 taxing the national bank's Baltimore branch $15,000 a year. The Baltimore branch refused to pay, whereupon the state of Maryland sued the cashier, James McCulloch, for payment. When the state courts upheld Maryland's law and its tax, the bank appealed to the U.S. Supreme Court. John Marshall was chief justice when two of the country's most capable lawyers argued the case before the Court.

Daniel Webster, widely regarded as one of the greatest senators in U.S. history, argued for the national bank, and Luther Martin, a delegate to the Constitutional Convention, argued for Maryland. Martin maintained that the Constitution was very clear about the powers of Congress (as outlined in Article I). The power to create a national bank was not among them. Thus, Martin concluded, Congress had exceeded its powers, and Maryland had a right to tax the bank. On behalf of the bank, Webster argued for a broader interpretation of the powers of the national government. The Constitution was not meant to stifle congressional powers, he said, but rather to permit Congress to use all means "necessary and proper" to fulfill its responsibilities.

Marshall, never one to sidestep a big decision, wrote his ruling in favor of the bank before the arguments ended—some said before they even began. He and his colleagues set forth two great constitutional principles in their decision. The first was the *supremacy of the national government over the states*. Marshall wrote, "If any one proposition could command the universal assent of mankind, we might expect it to be this—that the government of the United States, though limited in its power, is supreme within its sphere of action." As long as the national government behaved in accordance with the Constitution, said the Court, its policies took precedence over state policies. Accordingly, federal laws or regulations, such as many civil rights acts and rules regulating hazardous substances, water quality, and clean-air standards, *preempt* state or local laws or regulations and thus preclude their enforcement.

The other key principle of *McCulloch* was that *the national government has certain implied powers that go beyond its enumerated powers*. The Court held that Congress was behaving consistently with the Constitution when it created the national bank. It was true, Marshall admitted, that Congress had certain **enumerated powers**, powers *specifically* listed in Article I, Section 8, of the Constitution. Congress could coin money, regulate its value, impose taxes, and so forth. Creating a bank was not enumerated. But the Constitution added that Congress has the power to "make all laws necessary and proper for carrying into execution the foregoing powers." That, said Marshall, gave Congress certain **implied powers.** It could make economic policy consistent with the Constitution in a number of ways.

enumerated powers
Powers of the federal government that are specifically addressed in the Constitution; for Congress, these powers are listed in Article I, Section 8, and include the power to coin money, regulate its value, and impose taxes.

implied powers
Powers of the federal government that go beyond those enumerated in the Constitution. The Constitution states that Congress has the power to "make all laws necessary and proper for carrying into execution" the powers enumerated in Article I.

Today, the notion of implied powers has become like a rubber band that can be stretched without breaking; the "necessary and proper" clause of the Constitution is often referred to as the **elastic clause.** Hundreds of congressional policies involve powers not specifically mentioned in the Constitution, especially in the domain of economic policy. Federal policies to regulate food and drugs, build interstate highways, protect consumers, clean up dirty air and water, and do many other things are all justified as implied powers of Congress.

elastic clause
The final paragraph of Article I, Section 8, of the Constitution, which authorizes Congress to pass all laws "necessary and proper" to carry out the enumerated powers.

Commerce Power. The Constitution gives Congress the power to regulate interstate and international commerce. American courts have spent many years trying to define commerce. In 1824, the Supreme Court, in deciding the case of **Gibbons v. Ogden**, defined commerce very broadly to encompass virtually every form of commercial activity. Today, commerce covers not only the movement of goods, but also radio signals, electricity, telephone messages, the Internet, insurance transactions, and much more.

Gibbons v. Ogden
A landmark case decided in 1824 in which the Supreme Court interpreted very broadly the clause in Article I, Section 8, of the Constitution giving Congress the power to regulate interstate commerce, encompassing virtually every form of commercial activity.

The Supreme Court's decisions establishing the national government's implied powers (*McCulloch v. Maryland*) and a broad definition of interstate commerce (*Gibbons v. Ogden*) created a source of national power as long as Congress employed its power for economic development through subsidies and services for business interests. In the latter part of the nineteenth century, however, Congress sought to use these same powers to regulate the economy rather than to promote it. The Court then interpreted the interstate commerce power as giving Congress no constitutional right to regulate local commercial activities such as establishing safe working conditions for laborers or protecting children from working long hours.

When the Great Depression hit, new demands were placed on the national government. Beginning in 1933, the New Deal of President Franklin D. Roosevelt produced an avalanche of regulatory and social welfare legislation, much of which was voided by the Supreme Court (see Chapter 14). But in 1937 the Court reversed itself and ceased trying to restrict the efforts of the national government to regulate commerce at any level. In 1964, Congress prohibited racial discrimination in places of public accommodation such as restaurants, hotels, and movie theaters on the basis of its power to regulate interstate commerce. Thus regulating commerce is one of the national government's most important sources of power.

In recent years the Supreme Court has scrutinized the use of commerce power with a skeptical eye, however. In 1995 the Court held in *United States v. Lopez* that the federal Gun-Free School Zones Act of 1990, which forbade the possession of firearms in public schools, exceeded Congress's constitutional authority to regulate commerce. Guns in a school zone, the majority said, have nothing to do with commerce. Similarly, in 2000 the Court ruled in *United States v. Morrison* that the power to regulate interstate commerce did not provide Congress with authority to enact the 1994 Violence Against Women Act, which provided a federal civil remedy for the victims of gender-motivated violence. Gender-motivated crimes of violence are not, the Court said, in any sense economic activity.

Federalism and the Supreme Court

The Supreme Court announced another limitation on commerce power in 1996. In *Seminole Tribe of Florida v. Florida*, the Court dealt with the case of a right Congress had given Indian tribes to sue state officials to force good-faith negotiations (in this case over a license to run a casino). Contrary to previous decisions, the Court declared that the Eleventh Amendment prohibits Congress from using the interstate commerce power to revoke states' immunity from such lawsuits by private parties. The principal effect of the decision is to limit suits seeking to enforce rights granted by Congress within its authority under the Commerce Clause (which encompasses much of modern federal regulation).

Several other recent cases have had important implications for federalism. In *Printz v. United States* and *Mack v. United States* (1997), the Supreme Court voided the congressional mandate in the Brady Handgun Violence Prevention Act that the chief law enforcement officer in each local community conduct background checks on prospective gun purchasers. According to the Court, "The federal government may neither issue directives requiring the states to address particular problems, nor command the states' officers, or those of their political subdivision, to administer or enforce a federal regulatory program."

The Civil War. What *McCulloch* pronounced constitutionally the Civil War (1861–1865) settled militarily. The Civil War is often thought of mainly as a struggle over slavery; but it was also, and perhaps more importantly, a struggle between states and the national government. In fact, Abraham Lincoln announced in his 1861 inaugural address that he would willingly support a constitutional amendment guaranteeing slavery if it would save the Union. Instead, it took a bloody civil war for the national government to assert its power over the Southern states' claim of sovereignty.

The Struggle for Racial Equality. A century later, conflict between the states and the national government again erupted over states' rights and national power. In 1954, in *Brown v. Board of Education*, the Supreme Court held that school segregation was unconstitutional. Southern politicians responded with what they called "massive resistance" to the decision. When a federal judge ordered the admission of two African American students to the University of Alabama in 1963,

Governor George Wallace literally blocked the school entrance to prevent federal marshals and the students from entering the admissions office. Despite Wallace's efforts, the students were admitted and throughout the 1960s the federal government enacted laws and policies to end segregation in schools, housing, public accommodations, voting, and jobs. In 1979 (after African Americans began voting in large numbers in Alabama), George Wallace himself said of his stand in the schoolhouse door: "I was wrong. Those days are over and they ought to be over." The conflict between states and the national government over equality issues was decided in favor of the national government. National standards of racial equality prevailed.

The national government is supreme within its sphere, but the sphere for the states remains a large and important one.

States' Obligations to Each Other

Federalism involves more than relationships between the national government and state and local governments. The states must deal with each other as well, and the Constitution outlines certain obligations that each state has to every other state.

Full Faith and Credit. Suppose that, like millions of other Americans, a person divorces and then remarries. For each marriage this person purchases a marriage license, which registers the marriage with a state. On the honeymoon for the second marriage, the person travels across the country. Is this person married in

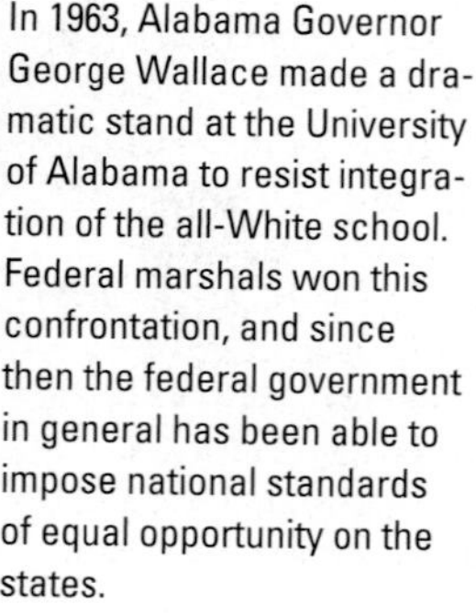
In 1963, Alabama Governor George Wallace made a dramatic stand at the University of Alabama to resist integration of the all-White school. Federal marshals won this confrontation, and since then the federal government in general has been able to impose national standards of equal opportunity on the states.

each state passed through, even though the marriage license is registered with only one state? Can the person be arrested for bigamy because the divorce occurred in only one state?

The answer, of course, is that a marriage license and a divorce, like a driver's license and a birth certificate, are valid in all states. Article IV of the Constitution requires that states give **full faith and credit** to the public acts, records, and civil judicial proceedings of every other state. This reciprocity is essential to the functioning of society and the economy. Without the full faith and credit clause, people could avoid their obligations, say, to make payments on automobile loans simply by crossing a state boundary. In addition, because contracts between business firms can be enforced across state boundaries, firms incorporated in one state can do business in another.

full faith and credit
A clause in Article IV, Section 1, of the Constitution requiring each state to recognize the official documents and civil judgments rendered by the courts of other states.

Usually, the full faith and credit provision in the Constitution poses little controversy. An exception occurred in 1996 when courts in Hawaii recognized same-gender marriages. What would happen in other states that did not recognize Hawaiian marriages between same-gender partners? Congress answered with the Defense of Marriage Act, which permits states to disregard gay marriages, even if they are legal elsewhere in the United States. Hawaii has since overturned recognition of gay marriages, but in 2000 Vermont accorded legal status to gay civil unions. In 2003 the Massachusetts supreme court held that the state constitution guaranteed full marriage rights for gay couples. It remains to be seen whether courts will uphold Congress's power to make exceptions to the full faith and credit clause.

Because of the full faith and credit clause of the Constitution, marriage certificates issued by one state are valid in every state. People are also entitled to most of the benefits—and subject to most of the obligations—of citizenship in any state they visit, thanks to the privileges and immunities clause. Gay marriage is straining these principles, however, as most states refuse to recognize marriages between same-gender partners.

Extradition. What about criminal penalties? Almost all criminal law is state law. If someone robs a store, steals a car, or commits a murder, chances are that this person is breaking a state, not a federal, law. The Constitution says that states are required to return a person charged with a crime in another state to that state for trial or imprisonment, a practice called **extradition.** Although there is no way to force states to comply, they usually are happy to do so, not wishing to harbor criminals and hoping that other states will reciprocate. Thus a lawbreaker cannot avoid punishment by simply escaping to another state.

extradition

A legal process whereby an alleged criminal offender is surrendered by the officials of one state to officials of the state in which the crime is alleged to have been committed.

Privileges and Immunities. The most complicated obligation among the states is the requirement that citizens of each state receive all the **privileges and immunities** of any other state in which they happen to be. The goal of this constitutional provision is to prohibit states from discriminating against citizens of other states. If, for example, a Texan visits California, the Texan will pay the same sales tax and receive the same police protection as residents of California.

privileges and immunities

A clause in Article IV, Section 2, of the Constitution according citizens of each state most of the privileges of citizens of other states.

There are many exceptions to the privileges and immunities clause, however. Many of you attend public universities. If you reside in the same state as your university, you generally pay a tuition substantially lower than that paid by your fellow students from out of state. Similarly, only residents of a state can vote in state elections. States often attempt to pass the burdens of financing the state government to those outside the state, such as through taxes on minerals mined in the state but consumed elsewhere or special taxes on hotel rooms rented by tourists.

The Supreme Court has never clarified just which privileges a state must make available to all Americans and which privileges can be limited to its own citizens. In general, the more fundamental the rights—such as owning property or receiving police protection—the less likely it is that a state can discriminate against citizens of another state. In 1999, the Supreme Court held in *Saenz v. Roe* that California could not require a new resident to wait a year before becoming eligible for welfare benefits that exceeded those available in the state from which the new resident came.

Explaining Differences in State Laws

Intergovernmental Relations Today

The past two centuries have seen dramatic changes in American federalism. These changes are apparent in two main areas. First, there has been a gradual shift from a dual federalism to a cooperative federalism, which emphasizes sharing power between two levels of government.[9] The second major change has been the rise of fiscal federalism, the elaborate assortment of federal grants-in-aid to the states and localities.

From Dual to Cooperative Federalism

One way to understand the changes in American federalism over the past 200 years is to contrast two types of federalism. The first type is called **dual federalism**, in which both the national government and the states remain supreme within their

dual federalism

A system of government in which both the states and the national government remain supreme within their own spheres, each responsible for some policies.

own spheres. The states are responsible for some policies, the national government for others. For example, the national government has exclusive control over foreign and military policy, the postal system, and monetary policy. States are exclusively responsible for schools, law enforcement, and road building. In dual federalism, the powers and policy assignments of the layers of government are distinct, as in a layer cake, and proponents of dual federalism believe that the powers of the national government should be interpreted narrowly.

Most politicians and political scientists today argue that dual federalism is outdated. They are more likely to describe the current American federal system as one of **cooperative federalism**, where powers and policy assignments are shared between states and the national government.[10] Instead of a layer cake, they see American federalism as more like a marble cake, with mingled responsibilities and blurred distinctions between the levels of government. After the terrorist attacks on September 11, 2001, the national government asked state and local governments to investigate suspected terrorists, and both national and state public health officials dealt with the threat caused by anthrax in the mail in Florida, New York, and Washington, D.C.

cooperative federalism
A system of government in which powers and policy assignments are shared between states and the national government. They may also share costs, administration, and even blame for programs that work poorly.

Before the national government began to assert its dominance over state governments, the American federal system leaned toward dual federalism. The American system, however, was never neatly separated into purely state and purely national responsibilities. For example, education was usually thought of as being mainly a state and local responsibility, yet even under the Articles of Confederation, Congress set aside land in the Northwest Territory to be used for schools. During the Civil War, the national government adopted a policy to create land grant colleges. Important American universities such as Wisconsin, Texas A & M, Illinois, Ohio State, North Carolina State, and Iowa State owe their origins to this national policy. (To learn more about how federalism affects college education, see "Young People and Politics: Federal Support for Colleges and Universities.")

In the 1950s and 1960s, the national government began supporting public elementary and secondary education. In 1958 Congress passed the National Defense Education Act, largely in response to Soviet success in the space race. The act provided federal grants and loans for college students and financial support for elementary and secondary education in science and foreign languages. In 1965, Congress passed the Elementary and Secondary Education Act, which provided federal aid to numerous schools. Although these policies expanded the national government's role in education, they were not a sharp break with the past.

Federalism and Regulations

Today, the federal government's presence is felt in every schoolhouse. Almost all school districts receive some federal assistance. To do so, they must comply with federal rules and regulations. They must, for example, maintain desegregated and nondiscriminatory programs. In addition, as we will see in Chapters 4 and 5, federal courts have ordered local schools to implement elaborate desegregation plans and have placed constraints on school prayers.

Highways are another example of the movement toward cooperative federalism. In an earlier era, states and cities were largely responsible for building roads, although the Constitution does authorize Congress to construct "post roads." In 1956, Congress passed an act creating an interstate highway system. Hundreds of red, white, and blue signs were planted at the beginnings of interstate construction projects. The signs announced that the interstate highway program was a joint

YOUNG PEOPLE AND POLITICS

Federal Support for Colleges and Universities

Because most colleges and universities are public institutions created by state and local governments, federalism has direct consequences for students. State and local governments provide most of the funding for public colleges and universities, but almost everyone agrees that this funding is inadequate. In response to this problem, the national government has stepped in to support postsecondary education programs.

One could argue that as the primary source of financial aid, the federal government makes it possible for many students to attend college at all. The federal government provides more than $17 billion in financial assistance (including grants, loans, and work-study assistance) to more than 8 million postsecondary students each year. Nearly 60 percent of all full-time undergraduates receive some form of financial aid from the federal government, compared to about 52 percent who receive aid from all other sources.

The federal government also provides several billion dollars of direct grants to colleges and universities across the nation. Billions more in federal funds support research and training in certain areas, especially science and engineering—which receive about $20 billion a year. The chances are that the library, laboratories, and the buildings in most colleges and universities have been assisted by funds from the federal government.

Each year the federal government provides about 11 percent of the revenue for public colleges and universities (10 percent for private schools). Few colleges and universities could withstand an 11 percent budget cut and the loss of most of the financial assistance for its students. Federalism, then, matters quite a lot to college students.

Questions for Discussion

- Why do state institutions of higher education require aid from the federal government? Why don't the states provide adequate funds to run their own colleges and universities?
- Federal aid comes with strings attached. Would it be better to rely completely on state support?

federal–state project and specified the cost and sharing of funds. In this and many other areas, the federal system has promoted a partnership between the national and state governments.

Cooperative federalism today rests on several standard operating procedures. For hundreds of programs, cooperative federalism involves the following:

- *Shared costs*. Washington foots part of the bill, but states or cities that want to get their share must pay part of a program's costs. Cities and states can get federal money for airport construction, sewage treatment plants, youth programs, and many other programs, but only if they pay some of the costs.
- *Federal guidelines*. Most federal grants to states and cities come with strings attached. Congress spends billions of dollars to support state highway construction, for example, but to get their share, states must adopt and enforce limits on the legal drinking age.
- *Shared administration*. State and local officials implement federal policies, but they have administrative powers of their own. The U.S. Department of Labor,

Cooperative federalism began during the Great Depression of the 1930s. In this photo, Works Progress Administration workers, paid by the federal government, build a local road in New York. In subsequent decades, the entire interstate highway system was constructed with a combination of national and state dollars.

for example, gives billions of dollars to states for job retraining, but states have considerable latitude in spending the money.

The cooperation between the national government and state governments is such an established feature of American federalism that it persists even when the two levels of government are in conflict on certain matters. For example, in the 1950s and 1960s, Southern states cooperated well with Washington in building the interstate highway system while they clashed with the national government over racial integration.

In his first inaugural address, Ronald Reagan articulated a traditional conservative view when he argued that the states had primary responsibility for governing in most policy areas, and he promised to "restore the balance between levels of government." Few officials at either the state or the national level agreed with Reagan about ending the national government's role in domestic programs. Nevertheless, Reagan's opposition to the national government's spending on domestic policies and the huge federal deficits of the 1980s forced a reduction in federal funds for state and local governments and shifted some responsibility for policy back to the states.

Despite Reagan's move toward a more dual federalism, most Americans embrace a pragmatic view of governmental responsibilities, seeing the national government as more capable of—and thus responsible for—handling some issues (such as managing the economy, ensuring access to health care and that food and medicines are safe, preserving the environment, and providing income security for the elderly), while they view state and local governments as better at managing others (such as crime, welfare, and education).[11] Politicians are also pragmatic in their embrace of federal principles, as you can see in "A Generation of Change: Principles versus Pragmatism."

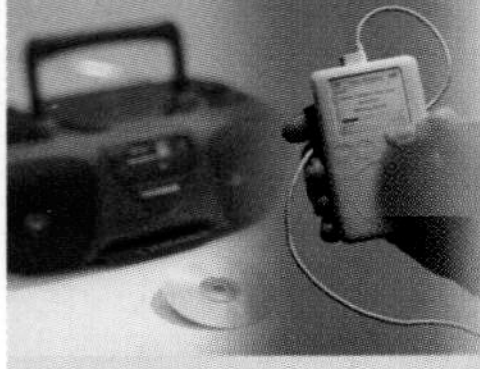

A GENERATION OF CHANGE

Principles versus Pragmatism

For most of the Twentieth Century, Democrats increased the power of the federal government in order to advance policies ranging from child labor laws and education to Social Security and health care. Republicans, as epitomized by Ronald Reagan, generally opposed these policies and favored states taking responsibility for these issues. They often articulated their opposition to increased federal power in terms of a defense of state authority in a federal system.

However, when the Republicans captured Congress in the 1994 elections, the first time they had majorities in both houses in 40 years, they were less concerned with abstract principles and more with adopting a pragmatic approach to federalism to accomplish their goals. On the one hand, they often referred to a "revolution" in public policy, one aimed primarily at restricting the scope of the national government. At the same time, Republicans found turning to the federal government the most effective way to achieve many of their policy objectives.

Restricting the Scope of Federal Government	Expanding the Scope of Federal Government
THE REPUBLICAN CONGRESS . . .	THE REPUBLICAN CONGRESS . . .
overhauled welfare policy to allow states to devise innovative ways to lift people out of poverty while reducing federal spending and cutting some benefits for the poor	designated the federal government the sole regulator of products as diverse as mutual funds and agricultural chemicals to reduce government interference in the marketplace
made it more difficult for the federal government to impose requirements on states without providing money to pay for them, making it more difficult to enact new environmental protection legislation	nullified state laws that restricted telecommunications competition
repealed national speed limits	set national standards requiring insurers to cover at least 48 hours of hospitalization for mothers and newborns
made it more difficult for prisoners to challenge the constitutionality of their sentences in federal court or to appeal to federal officials for relief from poor prison conditions	required state and local officials to meet new federal antifraud specifications for birth certificates and driver's licenses to control immigration
	extended federal criminal penalties to cover crimes such as stalking, domestic terrorist activities, and rape during carjacking
	threatened to cut off federal grants to states that failed to keep criminals behind bars for about 85 percent of their sentences or to increase arrests of violent criminals
	imposed penalties on states that fail to meet new federal targets for placing welfare recipients in jobs
	required states to create registries to track child-support orders, or face a considerable loss of federal funds
	required states to study local drinking water sources, map certain watersheds, and publish annual reports on drinking water violations
	placed significant new requirements on state and local school authorities when it passed the No Child Left Behind Act in 2001
	removed most class-action lawsuits from state courts in 2005

Thus, politicians often employ the rhetoric of principled federalism to make political points, but the reality of governing just as often has turned these officials in a pragmatic direction to accomplish their goals.

Fiscal Federalism

The cornerstone of the national government's relations with state and local governments is **fiscal federalism:** the pattern of spending, taxing, and providing grants in the federal system. Subnational governments can influence the national government through local elections for national officials, but the national government has a powerful source of influence over the states—money. Grants-in-aid, federal funds appropriated by Congress for distribution to state and local governments, are the main instrument the national government uses for both aiding and influencing states and localities.

fiscal federalism
The pattern of spending, taxing, and providing grants in the federal system; it is the cornerstone of the national government's relations with state and local governments.

Despite the Reagan administration's policy to reduce aid to states and cities, federal aid (including loan subsidies) amounted to about $460 billion in 2007. Figure 3.1 illustrates the growth in the amount of money spent on federal grants. Federal aid, covering a wide range of policy areas (see Figure 3.2), accounts for about one-fourth of all the funds spent by state and local governments and for about 17 percent of all federal government expenditures in 2007.[12]

Why It Matters

Grants-in-Aid
The federal system of grants-in-aid sends revenues from federal taxes to state and local governments. This transfers the burden of paying for services from those who pay state and local taxes, such as taxes on sales and property, to those who pay national taxes, especially the federal income tax.

The Grant System: Distributing the Federal Pie. The national government regularly publishes the *Catalogue of Federal Domestic Assistance*, a massive volume listing the federal aid programs available to states, cities, and other local governments. The book lists federal programs that support energy assistance for the elderly poor, housing allowances for the poor, drug abuse services, urban rat control efforts, community arts programs, state disaster preparedness programs, and many more.

There are two major types of federal aid for states and localities: categorical grants and block grants. **Categorical grants** are the main source of federal aid to state and local governments. These grants can be used only for one of several hundred specific purposes, or categories, of state and local spending.

Because direct orders from the federal government to the states are rare (an exception is the Equal Opportunity Act of 1982, barring job discrimination by state and local governments), most federal regulation is accomplished in a more indirect manner. Instead of issuing edicts that tell citizens or states what they can and cannot do, Congress attaches conditions to the grants that states receive. The federal government has been especially active in appending restrictions to grants since the 1970s.

categorical grants
Federal grants that can be used only for specific purposes, or "categories," of state and local spending. They come with strings attached, such as nondiscrimination provisions. Compare **block grants.**

One string commonly attached to categorical and other federal grants is a nondiscrimination provision, stating that aid may not be used for purposes that discriminate against minorities, women, or other groups. Another string, a favorite of labor unions, is that federal funds may not support construction projects that pay below the local union wage. Other restrictions may require an environmental impact statement for a federally supported construction project or provisions for community involvement in the planning of the project.

The federal government may also employ *crossover sanctions*—using federal dollars in one program to influence state and local policy in another, such as when funds are withheld for highway construction unless states raise the drinking age to 21 or establish highway beautification programs.

Figure 3.1 Fiscal Federalism: Federal Grants to State and Local Governments

Federal grants to state and local governments have grown rapidly in recent decades and now amount to about $460 billion per year.

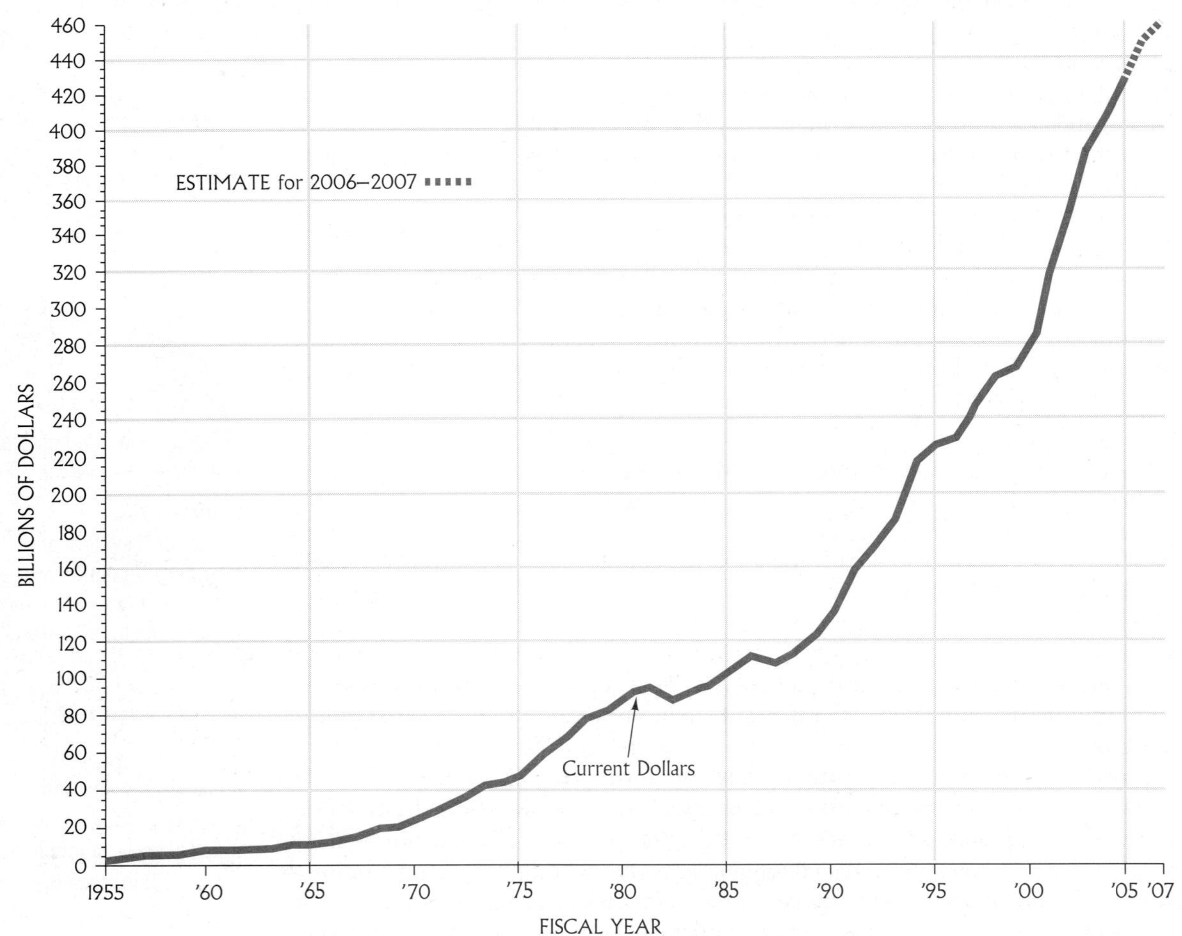

Source: Office of Management and Budget, *Budget of the United States Government, Fiscal Year 2007: Historical Tables* (Washington, DC: U.S. Government Printing Office, 2006), table 12.1.

Crosscutting requirements occur when a condition on one federal grant is extended to all activities supported by federal funds, regardless of their source. The grandfather of these requirements is Title VI of the 1964 Civil Rights Act (see Chapter 5), which bars discrimination in the use of federal funds because of race, color, national origin, gender, or physical disability. For example, if a university discriminates illegally in one program—such as athletics—it may lose the federal aid it receives for all its programs. There are also crosscutting requirements dealing with environmental protection, historic preservation, contract wage rates, access to government information, the care of experimental animals, the treatment of human subjects in research projects, and a host of other policies.

Figure 3.2 Functions of Federal Grants

Health care receives the largest percentage of federal grants, followed by income security, education and training, and transportation.

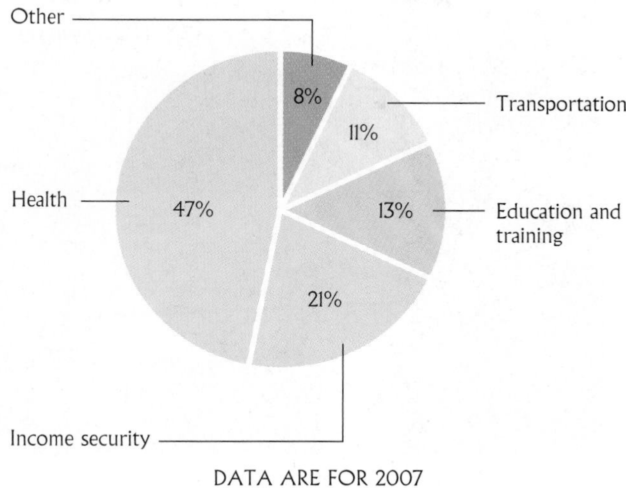

Source: Office of Management and Budget, *Budget of the United States Government, Fiscal Year 2007: Historical Tables* (Washington, DC: U.S. Government Printing Office, 2006), table 12.2.

There are two types of categorical grants. The most common type is a project grant. A **project grant** is awarded on the basis of competitive applications. National Science Foundation grants obtained by university professors are examples of project grants.

project grants
Federal **categorical grants** given for specific purposes and awarded on the basis of the merits of applications.

As their name implies, **formula grants** are distributed according to a formula. These formulas vary from grant to grant and may be computed on the basis of population, per capita income, percentage of rural population, or some other factor. A state or local government does not apply for a formula grant; a grant's formula determines how much money the particular government will receive. As a result, Congress is the site of vigorous political battles over the formulas themselves. The most common formula grants are those for Medicaid, child nutrition programs, sewage treatment plant construction, public housing, community development programs, and training and employment programs.

formula grants
Federal categorical grants distributed according to a formula specified in legislation or in administrative regulations.

Applications for categorical grants typically arrive in Washington in boxes, not envelopes. Complaints about the cumbersome paperwork and the many strings attached to categorical grants led to the adoption of the other major type of federal aid, **block grants**. These grants are given more or less automatically to states or communities, which then have discretion within broad areas in deciding how to spend the money. First adopted in 1966, block grants are used to support programs in areas like community development and social services. The percentage of federal aid to state and local governments in the form of block grants began increasing in 1995 as the new Republican majority in Congress passed more federal aid in the form of block grants, including grants for welfare programs.

block grants
Federal grants given more or less automatically to states or communities to support broad programs in areas such as community development and social services.

The federal government often uses grants-in-aid as an incentive for the states. For example, aid has been withheld from some cities until police departments have been racially and sexually integrated.

The Scramble for Federal Dollars. With more than $460 billion in federal grants at stake, most states and many cities have established full-time staffs in Washington.[13] Their task is to keep track of what money is available and to help their state or city get some of it. There are many Washington organizations of governments—the U.S. Conference of Mayors and the National League of Cities, for example—that act like other interest groups by lobbying Congress. Senators and representatives regularly go to the voters with stories of their influence in securing federal funds for their constituencies. They need continued support at the polls, they say, so they will rise in seniority and get key posts to help "bring home the bacon."

A general rule of federalism is that the more money there is at stake, the more fervently people will argue about its distribution. There are some variations in the amount of money states give to, and get back from, the national government. On the whole, however, federal grant distribution follows the principle of *universalism:* something for everybody. The vigilance of senators and representatives keeps federal aid reasonably well spread among the states. Indeed, federal aid to states and cities is more equitably distributed than most other things in America, including income, access to education, and taxes.

This equality makes good politics, but it also may undermine public policy. Chapter I of the 1965 Elementary and Secondary Education Act is the federal government's principal endeavor to assist public schools. The primary intent of Chapter I was to give extra help to poor children. Yet the funds are allocated to 95 percent of all the school districts in the country. President Clinton's proposal to concentrate Chapter I funds on the poorest students failed when it ran into predictable opposition in Congress.

The Mandate Blues. States and localities are usually pleased to receive aid from the national government, but there are times when they would just as soon not have it. For example, say Congress decides to extend a program administered by the states and funded, in part, by the national government. It passes a law requiring the states to extend the program if they want to keep receiving aid, which most states do. Requirements that direct states or local governments to comply with federal rules under threat of penalties or as a condition of receipt of a federal grant are called *mandates*. Congress usually (though not always) appropriates some funds to help pay for the new policy, but either way, the states suddenly have to budget more funds for the project just to receive federal grant money.

Medicaid, which provides health care for poor people, is a prime example of a federal grant program that puts states in a difficult situation. Administered by the states, Medicaid receives wide support from both political parties. The national government pays the majority of the bill, and the states pick up the rest. In the past two decades, Congress has moved aggressively to expand Medicaid to specific populations, requiring the states to extend coverage to certain children, pregnant women, and elderly poor. Congress has also increased its funding for the program, but new requirements have meant huge new demands on state budgets as well. In effect, Congress has set priorities for the states.

A related problem arises when Congress passes a law creating financial obligations for the states but provides no funds to meet these obligations. For example, in 1990 Congress passed the Americans with Disabilities Act, requiring states to make facilities, such as state colleges and universities, accessible to individuals with disabilities. Congress allocated no funds to implement this policy, however. Similarly, the Clean Air Act of 1970 established national air quality standards but requires states to administer them and to appropriate funds for their implementation.

In 1995, the newly elected Republican majorities in Congress made limiting unfunded and underfunded mandates on state and local governments a high priority. Congress passed, and President Clinton signed, a law that requires both chambers to take a separate, majority vote in order to pass any bill that would impose unfunded mandates of more than $50 million on state and local governments. The law also requires the Congressional Budget Office to estimate the costs of all bills that impose such mandates. All antidiscrimination legislation and most legislation requiring state and local governments to take various actions in exchange for continued federal funding (such as grants for transportation) are exempt from this procedure.

State and local governments are the first responders in most emergencies, as we have seen in the case with Hurricane Katrina. Their police forces provide most of the nation's internal security, they maintain most of the country's transportation infrastructure (such as highways, mass transit, port facilities, and airports), and they are responsible for protecting the public's health and providing emergency health care. The heightened concern for homeland security since September 11, 2001, has led Congress to impose sizable new mandates on the states to increase their ability to deal with acts of terrorism, but it has not provided all the resources necessary to increase state and local capabilities. Similarly, the No Child Left Behind Act, passed in 2002, threatens school systems with the loss of federal funds if their schools do not improve student performance. Such improvements cost money, however, and the federal government has provided only a modest increase in funding.

Federal courts also create unfunded mandates for the states. In recent years, federal judges have issued states orders in areas such as prison construction and management, school desegregation, and facilities in mental health hospitals, sometimes even temporarily taking them over. These court orders often require states to spend funds to meet standards imposed by the judge.

A combination of federal regulations and inadequate resources may also put the states in a bind. The national government requires that a local housing authority build or acquire a new apartment for each one it demolishes. But for years Congress has provided little money for the construction of public housing. As a result, a provision intended to help the poor by ensuring a stable supply of housing actually hurts them because it discourages local governments from demolishing unsafe and inadequate housing.

The federal government may also unintentionally create financial obligations for the states. In 1994, California, New York, Texas, Florida, and other states sued the federal government for reimbursement for the cost of health care, education, prisons, and other public services that the states provide to illegal residents. The states charged that the federal government's failure to control its borders was the source of huge new demands on their treasuries and that Washington, not the states, should pay for the problem. Although the states did not win their cases, their point is a valid one.

Understanding Federalism

The federal system is central to politics, government, and policy in America. The division of powers and responsibilities among different levels of government has implications for both the themes of democracy and the scope of government.

Federalism and Democracy

One of the reasons the Founders established a federal system was to allay the fears of those who believed that a powerful and distant central government would tyrannize the states and limit their voice in government. By decentralizing the political system, federalism was designed to contribute to democracy—or at least to the limited form of democracy supported by the Founders. Has it done so?

Advantages for Democracy. The more levels of government, the more opportunities there are for participation in politics. State governments provide thousands of elected offices for which citizens may vote and/or run.

Additional levels of government also contribute to democracy by increasing access to government. Because different citizens and interest groups will have better access to either state-level governments or the national government, the two levels increase the opportunities for government to be responsive to demands for policies. For example, in the 1950s and 1960s when advocates of civil rights found themselves stymied in Southern states, they turned to the national level for help in achieving racial equality. Business interests, on the other hand, have traditionally found state governments to be more responsive to their demands. Organized labor is not well established in some states, but it can usually depend on some sympathetic officials at the national level who will champion its proposals.

Different economic interests are concentrated in different states: energy in Texas, tobacco farming in Virginia, and copper mining in Montana, for example. The federal system allows an interest concentrated in a state to exercise substantial influence in the election of that state's officials, both local and national. In turn, these officials promote policies advantageous to the interest in both Washington and the state capital. This is a pluralism of interests that James Madison, among others, valued within a large republic.

State and local bases have another advantage. Even if a party loses at the national level, it can rebuild in its areas of strength and develop leaders under its banner at the state and local levels. As a result, losing an election becomes more acceptable, and the peaceful transfer of power is more probable. This was especially important in the early years of the nation before our political norms had become firmly established.

Because the federal system assigns states important responsibilities for public policies, it is possible for the diversity of opinion within the country to be reflected in different public policies among the states. If the citizens of Texas wish to have a death penalty, for example, they can vote for politicians who support it, whereas those in Wisconsin can vote to abolish the death penalty altogether (see "You Are the Policymaker: Should *Whether* You Live Depend on *Where* You Live?"). Similarly, there are large differences in the amounts that states provide for the poor, ranging from $631 per month for a family of three in Alaska to $161 per month in Arkansas.[14]

States may also take initiatives on what most people view as national policies when the federal government acts contrary to the views of people within those states. Congress has not raised the minimum wage since 1997, but more than a dozen states have raised it for those who work in them. In another example, California's voters passed an initiative pouring $3 billion into laboratories devoted to researching stem cells after George W. Bush severely restricted federal stem cell research. There are important limitations on such actions, however, as you can read about in "Issues of the Times: Can States Compensate for Federal Inaction?"

By handling most disputes over policy at the state and local levels, federalism also reduces decision making and conflict at the national level. If every issue had to be resolved in Washington, the national government would be overwhelmed.

Disadvantages for Democracy. Despite its advantages for democracy, relying on states to supply public services has some drawbacks. States differ in the resources they can devote to services like public education. Thus the quality of education a child receives is heavily dependent on the state in which the child's parents happen to reside. In 2004, New York state and local governments spent an average of $12,408 for each child in the public schools; in Utah the figure was only $5,556.[15]

Is Federalism Dead and Should It Be?

Diversity in policy can also discourage states from providing services that would otherwise be available. Political scientists have found that generous welfare benefits can strain a state's treasury by attracting poor people from states with

YOU ARE THE POLICYMAKER

Should *Whether* You Live Depend on *Where* You Live?

Because the federal system allocates major responsibilities for public policy to the states, policies often vary with the different views of the population in different locations. The differences among public policies are especially dramatic in the criminal justice system.

A conviction for first-degree murder in 38 states may well mean the death penalty for the convicted murderer. In 12 other states and the District of Columbia, first-degree murderers are subject only to a maximum penalty of life behind bars.

Some people see diversity in public policy as one of the advantages of federalism. Others may argue that citizens of the same country ought to be subject to uniform penalties. What do *you* think? Should *whether* you live depend on *where* you live?

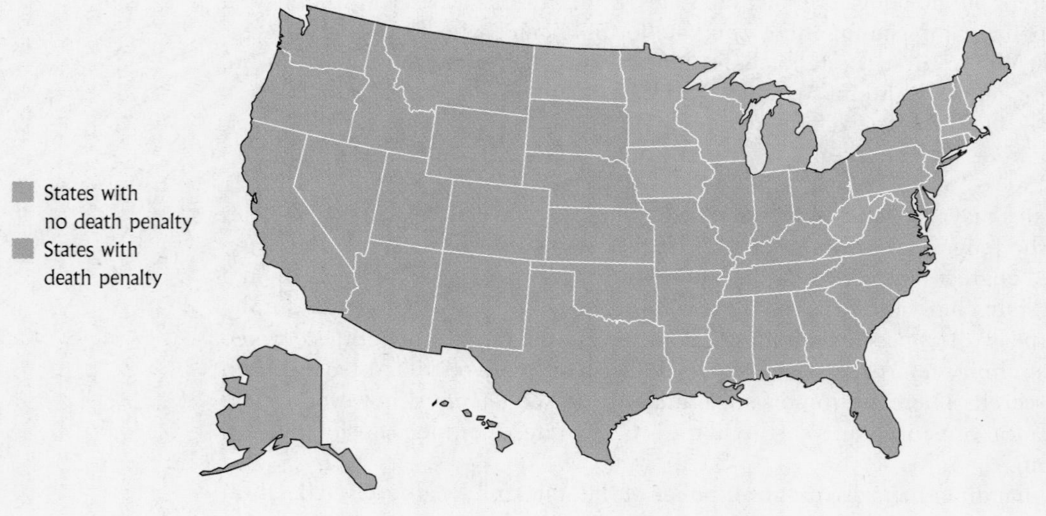

lower benefits. As a result, states are deterred from providing generous benefits to those in need. A national program with uniform welfare benefits would provide no incentive for welfare recipients to move to another state in search of higher benefits.[16]

Federalism may also have a negative effect on democracy insofar as local interests are able to thwart national majority support of certain policies. As discussed earlier in this chapter, in the 1960s the states—especially those in the South—became battlegrounds when the national government tried to enforce national civil rights laws and court decisions. Federalism complicated and delayed efforts to end racial discrimination because state and local governments were responsible for public

Table 3.3 The Number of Governments in America

GOVERNMENT LEVEL	NUMBER OF GOVERNMENTS
U.S. government	1
States	50
Counties	3,034
Municipalities	19,429
Townships or towns	16,504
School districts	13,506
Special districts	35,052
Total	**87,576**

Source: U.S. Department of Commerce, *Statistical Abstract of the United States, 2005–2006* (Washington, D.C.: US Government Printing Office, 2006), 272.

education and voting eligibility, for example, and because they had passed most of the laws supporting racial segregation.

Finally, the sheer number of governments in the United States is, at times, as much a burden as a boon to democracy. Program vendors at baseball games say, "You can't tell the players without a scorecard"; unfortunately, scorecards are not available for local governments where the players are numerous and sometimes seem to be involved in different games. The U.S. Bureau of the Census counts not only people but also governments. Its latest count revealed an astonishing 87,576 American governments (see Table 3.3).

Comparing State and Local Governments

Certainly, 87,000 governments ought to be enough for any country. Are there too many? Americans speak eloquently about their state and local governments as grassroots governments, close to the people. Yet having so many governments makes it difficult to know which governments are doing what. Exercising democratic control over them is even more difficult; voter turnout in local elections is often less than 20 percent.

Federalism and the Scope of the National Government

One of the most persistent questions in American politics has been the scope of the national government relative to that of the states. To understand the relative roles of the two levels of government, we must first understand why the national government grew and then ask whether this growth was at the expense of the states or whether it occurred because of the unique capabilities and responsibilities of the national government.

President Ronald Reagan negotiated quotas on imports of Japanese cars in order to give advantages to the American auto industry, raising the price of all automobiles in the process. At the behest of steel companies, President George Bush exercised his authority to continue Reagan's quotas on the amount of steel that could be imported (thereby making steel products more expensive). The first major piece of legislation his administration sent to Congress in 1989 was a bailout plan for the savings and loan industry, which had gotten into financial trouble through a combination of imprudent loans, declining property values, deregulation of banking, incompetence, and corruption. In 2002, President George W. Bush raised tariffs on imported steel—contrary to his position in favor of the open marketplace. He also signed bills providing tax breaks and loan guarantees to oil and pipeline companies.

In each of these cases and dozens of others, the national government has involved itself (some might say interfered) in the economic marketplace with quotas and subsidies intended to help American businesses. As Chapter 2 explained, the national government took a direct interest in economic affairs from the very founding of the republic. As the United States changed from an agricultural to an industrial nation, new problems arose and with them new demands for governmental action. The national government responded with a national banking system, subsidies for railroads and airlines, and a host of other policies that dramatically increased its role in the economy.

The industrialization of the country raised other issues as well. With the formation of large corporations in the late nineteenth century—Cornelius Vanderbilt's New York Central Railroad and John D. Rockefeller's Standard Oil Company, for example—came the potential for such abuses as monopoly pricing. If there is only one railroad in town, it can charge farmers inflated prices to ship their grain to market. If a single company distributes most of the gasoline in the country, it can set the price at which gasoline sells. Thus many interests asked the national government to restrain monopolies and to encourage open competition.

There were additional demands on the national government for new public policies. Farmers sought services such as agricultural research, rural electrification, and price supports. Unions wanted the national government to protect their rights to organize and bargain collectively and to help provide safer working conditions, a minimum wage, and pension protection. Along with other groups, labor unions supported a wide range of social welfare policies, from education to health care, that would benefit the average worker. As the country became more urbanized, new problems arose in the areas of housing, welfare, the environment, and transportation. In each case, the relevant interest turned to the national government for help.

Why not turn to the state governments instead? In most cases, the answer is simple: A problem or policy requires the authority and resources of the national government. The Constitution forbids states from having independent defense policies. And even if it did not, how many states would want to take on a responsibility that represents more than half the federal workforce and about one-fifth of federal expenditures?

It is constitutionally permissible but not sensible for the states to handle a wide range of other issues. It makes little sense for Louisiana to pass strict controls on polluting the Mississippi River if most of the river's pollution occurs upstream, where Louisiana has no jurisdiction. Rhode Island has no incentive to create an energy policy because no natural energy reserves are located in the state. Similarly, how effectively can a state regulate an international conglomerate such as General Motors? How can each state, acting individually, manage the nation's money supply?

Each state could have its own space program, but it is much more efficient if the states combine their efforts in one national program. The largest category of federal expenditures is that for economic security, including the Social Security program. Although each state could have its own retirement program, how could state governments determine which state should pay for retirees who move to Florida or Arizona? A national program is the only feasible method of ensuring the incomes of the mobile elderly of today's society.

Figure 3.3 shows that the national government's share of American governmental expenditures has grown rapidly since 1929; most of this growth occurred during the Great Depression. Then, the national government spent an amount equal to only 2.5 percent of the size of our economy, our gross domestic product (GDP); today, it spends about 20 percent of our GDP (this includes grants to states and localities). The proportion of our GDP spent by state and local governments has grown less rapidly than the national government's share. States and localities spent 7.4 percent of our GDP in 1929; they spend about 11 percent today (not including federal grants).[17]

Figure 3.3 Fiscal Federalism: The Public Sector and the Federal System

The federal government's spending increased rapidly during the Great Depression and World War II. In recent years, the role of both federal and state governments has declined slightly.

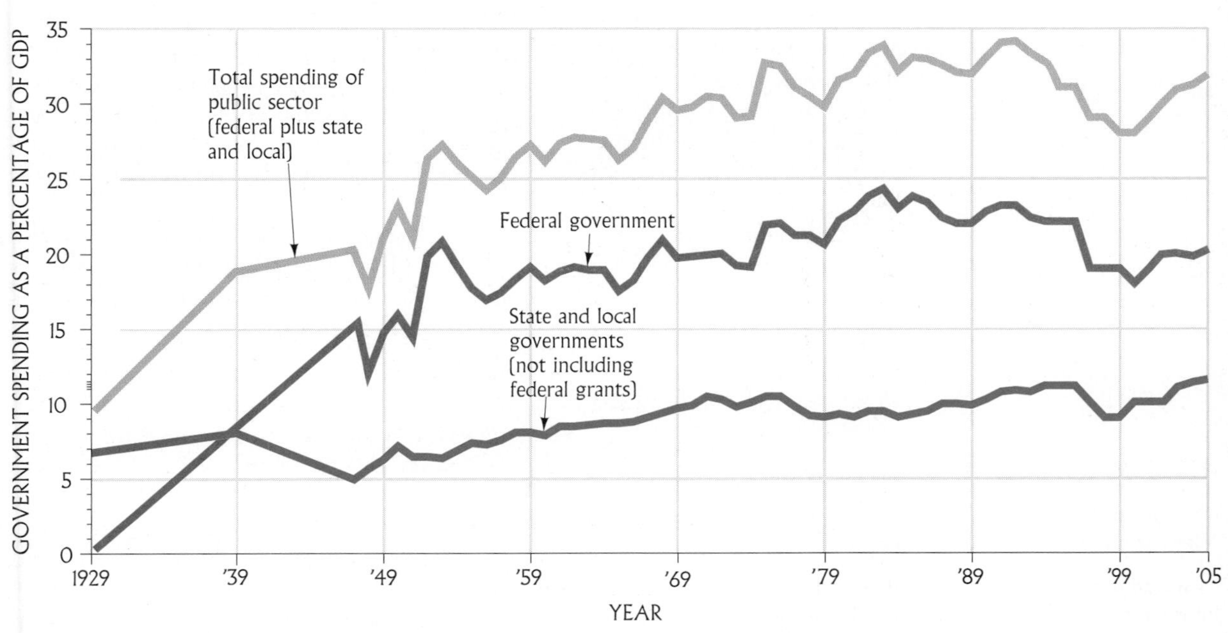

Source: Office of Management and Budget, *Budget of the United States Government, Fiscal Year 2007: Historical Tables* (Washington, DC: U.S. Government Printing Office, 2006), table 15.3.

Figure 3.3 demonstrates that the states have not been supplanted by the national government; indeed, they carry out virtually all the functions they always have. Instead, with the support of the American people, the national government has taken on new responsibilities. In addition, the national government has added programs to help the states meet their own responsibilities.

Summary

Federalism is a governmental system in which power is shared between a central government and other governments. Federalism is much less common than are the unitary governments typical of most parliamentary democracies. American federalism consists of 50 state governments joined in an "indestructible union" (as the Supreme Court once called it) under one national government. Today, federal power over the states is indisputable; the Supreme Court cases *McCulloch v. Maryland* and *Gibbons v. Ogden*, the Civil War, and the struggle for racial equality all helped to determine national supremacy. The federal government often uses its fiscal leverage to influence state and local policies.

The United States has moved from a system of dual federalism to one of cooperative federalism, in which the national and state governments share responsibility for public policies. Fiscal federalism is of great help to states. Even after the Reagan administration reductions, the federal government distributes about $460 billion in federal funds to states and cities each year.

The Founders instituted federalism largely to enhance democracy in America, and it strengthens democratic government in many ways. At the same time, diverse state policies and the sheer number of local governments cause problems as well. Demands for new policies and the necessity for national policy on certain issues have contributed to the growth of national government relative to state governments. Yet the state governments continue to play a central role in governing the lives of Americans.

Although American federalism concerns state power and national power, it is not a concept removed from most Americans' lives. Federalism affects a vast range of social and economic policies. Slavery, school desegregation, abortion, and teenage drinking have all been debated in terms of federalism.

Internet Resources

www.cfda.gov
Allows you to search through hundreds of federal grants.

www.ncsl.org/statefed/statefed.htm
Information and discussion of issues on federal–state relations.

www.census.gov/compendia/statab
The *Statistical Abstract of the United States*, containing a wealth of data on state public policies.

www.csg.org/CSG/default.htm
Council of State Governments Web site with information on states and state public policies.

www.thirteen.org/federalist
Discussions of the *Federalist Papers* and short articles and debates on issues regarding federalism.

Get Connected

Intergovernmental Relations

Even though education, like public safety and public health, is the responsibility of the states, the national government still finds ways to shape education policy. In January 2002, President George W. Bush signed the No Child Left Behind Act into law. This act sets federal standards for education and then makes federal grants available to states that agree to achieve these new national standards. Let us take a closer look at this federal law to determine its impact on federalism.

Search the Web

Reviewing a federal law can be challenging. This review will not be that difficult, however. First, review the Statement of Purposes (just review sec. 1001) of the No Child Left Behind Act, *www.ed.gov/policy/elsec/leg/esea02/pg1.html#sec1001*, so you can gain a basic understanding of the intent of the legislation. Now review the part of the bill that says what the federal government will do for the states (just review secs. 6111 and 6112), *www.ed.gov/policy/elsec/leg/esea02/pg87.html#sec6111*. Finally, read what the states must do in order to receive federal money (review sec. 1111), *www.ed.gov/policy/elsec/leg/esea02/pg2.html#sec1111*. The National Education Association, *www.nea.org/esea/memberspeakout1.html*, is a critic of No Child Left Behind. The C-SPAN Web site, *www.c-span.org/guide/congress/glossary/ unfunded.htm*, has a definition of "unfunded mandate."

Questions to Ask

- What do states get from the federal government under this act?
- What are some of the things states have to do in order to get the federal money?
- On what does the National Education Association base its criticism of the No Child Left Behind Act?
- Is the No Child Left Behind Act an unfunded mandate?

Why It Matters

Even though the United States is a federal system of governance, increasingly the national government establishes national standards and then encourages states to comply with those standards through a system of spending, taxing, and providing grants—all of which can have a direct effect on you.

Get Involved

Talk to an elementary or high school teacher or a school board member in your community about the No Child Left Behind Act. How does it affect them? How do they think this Act will affect the quality of education in the community?

For more exercises, go to www.longmanamericangovernment.com.

For Further Reading

Anton, Thomas. *American Federalism and Public Policy*. Philadelphia: Temple University Press, 1989. An overview of how the national, state, and local governments share responsibility for policies.

Beer, Samuel H. *To Make a Nation: The Rediscovery of American Federalism*. Cambridge, MA: Harvard University Press, 1993. An excellent study of the philosophical bases of American federalism.

Conlan, Timothy J. *From New Federalism to Devolution: Twenty-Five Years of Intergovernmental Reform*. Washington, DC: Brookings Institution, 1998. An analysis of the efforts to restructure intergovernmental relations since the late 1960s.

Dye, Thomas R. *American Federalism: Competition Among Governments*. Lexington, MA: Lexington Books, 1990. Analyzes competitive federalism, in which states and local governments compete to offer public services at low costs.

Elazar, Daniel J. *American Federalism: A View from the States*. 3rd ed. New York: Harper & Row, 1984. A well-known work surveying federalism from the standpoint of state governments.

Kettl, Donald F. *The Regulation of American Federalism*. Baltimore: Johns Hopkins University Press, 1987. Examines the regulations that the national government imposes on state and local governments.

Peterson, Paul E. *The Price of Federalism*. Washington, DC: Brookings Institution, 1995. A good assessment of the costs and benefits of federalism.

Peterson, Paul, Barry G. Rabe, and Kenneth K. Wong. *When Federalism Works*. Washington, DC: Brookings Institution, 1986. Examines federal grants-in-aid programs and explains why they are implemented better in some areas than in others.

Walker, David B. *The Rebirth of Federalism*. 2nd ed. Chatham, NJ: Chatham House, 2001. A history of American federalism and an analysis of its current condition.

Wright, Deil S. *Understanding Intergovernmental Relations*. 4th ed. Belmont, CA: Wadsworth, 2003. A review of the relations among the local, state, and national levels of government.

Civil Liberties

Chapter Outline

POLITICS IN ACTION: FREE SPEECH ON CAMPUS The Board of Regents of the University of Wisconsin System requires students at the university's Madison campus to pay a segregated activity fee. The fee supports various campus services and extracurricular student activities. In the university's view, such fees enhance students' educational experiences by promoting extracurricular activities, stimulating advocacy and debate on diverse points of view, enabling participation in campus administrative activity, and providing opportunities to develop social skills, all consistent with the university's broad educational mission. Registered student organizations (RSOs) engaging in a number of diverse expressive activities are eligible to receive a portion of the fees, which are administered by the student government subject to the university's approval.

There has been broad agreement that the process for reviewing and approving RSO applications for funding is administered in a viewpoint-neutral fashion. RSOs may also obtain funding through a student referendum. Some students, however, sued the university, alleging that the activity fee violated their First Amendment rights and that the university must grant them the choice not to fund RSOs that engage in political and ideological expression offensive to their personal beliefs.

In 2000, the Supreme Court held in a unanimous decision in *Board of Regents of University of Wisconsin System v. Southworth* that if a university determines that its mission is well served if students have the means to engage in dynamic discussion on a broad range of issues, it may impose a mandatory fee to sustain such dialogue. The Court recognized that it was all but inevitable that the fees will subsidize speech that some students find objectionable or offensive. Thus, the Court required that a university provide some protection to its students' First Amendment interests by requiring viewpoint neutrality in the allocation of funding support.

The University of Wisconsin case is the sort of complex controversy that shapes American civil liberties. Debates about the right to abortion, the right to bear arms, the separation of church and state, and similar issues are constantly in the news. Some of these issues arise from conflicting interests. The need to protect society against crime often conflicts with society's need to protect the rights of people accused of crime. Other conflicts derive from strong differences of opinion about what is ethical, moral, or right. To some Americans, abortion is murder, the taking of a human life. To others, a woman's choice whether to bear a child, free of governmental intrusion, is a fundamental right. Everyone, however, is affected by the extent of our civil liberties.

Deciding complex questions about civil liberties requires balancing competing values, such as maintaining an open system of expression while protecting individuals from the excesses such a system may produce. As we learned in Chapter 1, civil liberties are essential to democracy. How could we have free elections without free speech, for example? But does it follow that critics of officials should be able to say whatever they want, no matter how untrue? And who should decide the extent of our liberty? Should it be a representative institution such as Congress or a judicial elite such as the Supreme Court?

The role of the government in resolving civil liberties controversies is also the subject of much debate. Conservatives usually advocate narrowing the scope of government, yet many strongly support government-imposed limits on abortion and government-sanctioned prayers in public schools. They also want government to be less hindered by concern for defendants' rights. Liberals, who typically support a broader scope of government, usually want to limit government's role in prohibiting abortion and encouraging religious activities and to place greater constraints on government's freedom of action in the criminal justice system.

---

civil liberties

The legal constitutional protections against government. Although our civil liberties are formally set down in the **Bill of Rights,** the courts, police, and legislatures define their meaning.

Bill of Rights

The first ten amendments to the **U.S. Constitution,** which define such basic liberties as freedom of religion, speech, and press and guarantee defendants' rights.

Civil liberties are individual legal and constitutional protections against the government. Americans' civil liberties are set down in the **Bill of Rights**, the first 10 amendments to the Constitution. At first glance, many questions about civil liberties look easy. The Bill of Rights' guarantee of a free press seems straightforward; either Americans can write what they choose, or they cannot. In the real world of American law, however, these issues are subtle and complex.

Issues of civil liberties present many vexing problems for the courts to resolve. For example, is burning the American flag desecration of a sacred patriotic symbol, or is it an expression of opposition to government policy protected by the Constitution?

Throughout this chapter you will find special features titled "You Are the Judge." Each feature describes an actual case brought before the courts and asks you to apply your sense of fairness and your standards to arrive at a judgment.

To understand the specifics of American civil liberties, we must first understand the Bill of Rights.

The Bill of Rights—Then and Now

By 1787, all state constitutions had bills of rights, some of which survive, intact, to this day. Although the new U.S. Constitution had no bill of rights, the state ratifying conventions made its inclusion a condition of ratification.

The Bill of Rights, formally added to the Constitution in 1791, ensures Americans' basic liberties such as freedom of speech and religion, and protection against arbitrary searches and being held for long periods without trial (you can review these amendments in the Appendix).

Political scientists have discovered that people are devotees of rights in theory but that their support wavers when it comes time to put those rights into practice.[1] For example, Americans in general believe in freedom of speech, but many citizens would not let the Ku Klux Klan speak in their neighborhood or allow their public schools to teach about atheism or homosexuality. In addition, Americans seem willing to trade off civil liberties for security when they feel that the nation is threatened, as in the case of terrorism.[2] Few rights are absolute; we cannot avoid the difficult questions of balancing civil liberties and other individual and societal values.

First Amendment
The constitutional amendment that establishes the four great liberties: freedom of the press, of speech, of religion, and of assembly.

The Bill of Rights and the States

Take another look at the **First Amendment**. Note the first words: "Congress shall make no law . . ." The Founders wrote the Bill of Rights to restrict the powers of the new national government. In 1791, Americans were comfortable with their state governments; after all, every state constitution had its own bill of rights. Thus, a literal reading of the First Amendment suggests that it does not prohibit a state government from passing a law prohibiting the free exercise of religion, free speech, or freedom of the press.

What happens, however, if a state passes a law violating one of the rights protected by the federal Bill of Rights and the state's constitution does not prohibit this abridgment of freedom? In 1833, the answer to that question was "nothing." The Bill of Rights, said the Court in ***Barron v. Baltimore***, restrained only the national government, not states and cities.

Almost a century later, however, the Court ruled that a state government must respect some First Amendment rights. The 1925 ruling in ***Gitlow v. New York*** relied not on the First Amendment but on the Fourteenth—the second of three "Civil War Amendments" that ended slavery, gave former slaves legal protection, and ensured their voting rights. Ratified in 1868, the **Fourteenth Amendment** declared,

> *No state shall make or enforce any law which shall abridge the privileges or immunities of citizens of the United States nor shall any state deprive any person of life, liberty, or property, without due process of law; nor deny to any person within its jurisdiction the equal protection of the laws.*

In *Gitlow*, the Court announced that freedoms of speech and press "were fundamental personal rights and liberties protected by the **due process clause** of the Fourteenth Amendment from impairment by the states." In effect, the Court interpreted the Fourteenth Amendment to say that states could not abridge the freedoms of expression protected by the First Amendment. This decision began the development of the **incorporation doctrine**, the legal concept under which the Supreme Court has nationalized the Bill of Rights by making most of its provisions applicable to the states through the Fourteenth Amendment. However, not everyone agreed that the Fourteenth Amendment incorporated parts of the Bill of Rights into state laws. For example, Edwin Meese, who served as attorney general under Ronald Reagan, strongly criticized *Gitlow* and called for "disincorporation" of the Bill of Rights.

Initially, only parts of the First Amendment were held binding on the states as a result of *Gitlow*. Gradually, especially during the 1960s when Earl Warren was chief justice, the Supreme Court applied most of the Bill of Rights to the states (see Table 4.1). Many of the court decisions that empowered the Bill of Rights were controversial, but today the Bill of Rights guarantees individual freedoms against infringement by state and local governments as well as by the national government. Only the Second, Third, and Seventh Amendments, the grand jury requirement of the Fifth Amendment, and the prohibition against excessive fines and bail in the Eighth Amendment have not been applied specifically to the states.

Barron v. Baltimore
The 1833 Supreme Court decision holding that the Bill of Rights restrained only the national government, not the states and cities.

Gitlow v. New York
The 1925 Supreme Court decision holding that freedoms of press and speech are "fundamental personal rights and liberties protected by the **due process clause** of the **Fourteenth Amendment** from impairment by the states" as well as by the federal government.

Fourteenth Amendment
The constitutional amendment adopted after the Civil War that states, "No State shall make or enforce any law which shall abridge the privileges or immunities of citizens of the United States; nor shall any state deprive any person of life, liberty, or property, without due process of law; nor deny to any person within its jurisdiction the **equal protection of the laws**." See also **due process clause**.

due process clause
Part of the **Fourteenth Amendment** guaranteeing that persons cannot be deprived of life, liberty, or property by the United States or state governments without due process of law. See also ***Gitlow v. New York***.

incorporation doctrine
The legal concept under which the **Supreme Court** has nationalized the **Bill of Rights** by making most of its provisions applicable to the states through the **Fourteenth Amendment**.

Table 4.1 The Nationalization of the Bill of Rights

DATE	AMENDMENT	RIGHT	CASE
1925	First	Freedom of speech	*Gitlow v. New York*
1931	First	Freedom of the press	*Near v. Minnesota*
1937	First	Freedom of assembly	*De Jonge v. Oregon*
1940	First	Free exercise of religion	*Cantwell v. Connecticut*
1947	First	Establishment of religion	*Everson v. Board of Education*
1958	First	Freedom of association	*NAACP v. Alabama*
1963	First	Right to petition government	*NAACP v. Button*
	Second	Right to bear arms	Not incorporated[a]
	Third	No quartering of soldiers	Not incorporated[b]
1949	Fourth	No unreasonable searches and seizures	*Wolf v. Colorado*
1961	Fourth	Exclusionary rule	*Mapp v. Ohio*
1897	Fifth	Guarantee of just compensation	*Chicago, Burlington, and Quincy RR v. Chicago*
1964	Fifth	Immunity from self-incrimination	*Mallory v. Hogan*
1969	Fifth	Immunity from double jeopardy	*Benton v. Maryland*
	Fifth	Right to grand jury indictment	Not incorporated
1932	Sixth	Right to counsel in capital cases	*Powell v. Alabama*
1948	Sixth	Right to public trial	*In re Oliver*
1963	Sixth	Right to counsel in felony cases	*Gideon v. Wainwright*
1965	Sixth	Right to confrontation of witnesses	*Pointer v. Texas*
1966	Sixth	Right to impartial jury	*Parker v. Gladden*
1967	Sixth	Right to speedy trial	*Klopfer v. North Carolina*
1967	Sixth	Right to compulsory process for obtaining witnesses	*Washington v. Texas*
1968	Sixth	Right to jury trial for serious crimes	*Duncan v. Louisiana*
1972	Sixth	Right to counsel for all crimes involving jail terms	*Argersinger v. Hamlin*
	Seventh	Right to jury trial in civil cases	Not incorporated
1962	Eighth	Freedom from cruel and unusual punishment	*Robinson v. California*
	Eighth	Freedom from excessive fines or bail	Not incorporated
1965	Ninth	Right of privacy	*Griswold v. Connecticut*

[a] The Supreme Court has upheld limits on the rights of private citizens to bear arms.
[b] The quartering of soldiers has not occurred under the Constitution.

Freedom of Religion

The First Amendment contains two elements regarding religion and government. These elements are commonly referred to as the **establishment clause** and the **free exercise clause**. The establishment clause states that "Congress shall make no law respecting an establishment of religion." The free exercise clause prohibits the abridgment of citizens' freedom to worship or not to worship as they please. Sometimes these freedoms conflict. The government's practice of providing chaplains on military bases is one example of this conflict; some accuse the government of establishing religion in order to ensure that members of the armed forces can freely practice their religion. Usually, however, establishment clause and free exercise clause cases raise different kinds of conflicts.

establishment clause
Part of the **First Amendment** stating that "Congress shall make no law respecting an establishment of religion."

free exercise clause
A **First Amendment** provision that prohibits government from interfering with the practice of religion.

Lemon v. Kurtzman
The 1971 Supreme Court decision that established that aid to church-related schools must (1) have a secular legislative purpose, (2) have a primary effect that neither advances nor inhibits religion, and (3) not foster excessive government entanglement with religion.

Why It Matters

The Establishment Clause
What if the Constitution did not prohibit the establishment of religion? If a dominant religion received public funds and was in a position to control health care, public education, and other important aspects of public policy, these policies might be quite different from what they are today. In addition, the potential for conflict between followers of the established religion and adherents to other religions would be substantial.

The Establishment Clause

Some nations, such as Great Britain, have an established church that is officially supported by the government and recognized as a national institution. A few American colonies had official churches, but the religious persecutions that incited many colonists to move to America discouraged any desire for the First Congress to establish a national church in the United States. Thus an established national religion is prohibited by the First Amendment.

It is much less clear, however, what else the first Congress intended to be included in the establishment clause. Some people argued that it meant only that the government could not favor one religion over another. In contrast, Thomas Jefferson argued that the First Amendment created a "wall of separation" between church and state, forbidding not just favoritism but also any support for religion at all. These interpretations continue to provoke argument, especially when religion is mixed with education.

Debate is especially intense over aid to church-related schools and prayers in the public schools. In ***Lemon v. Kurtzman*** (1971), the Supreme Court declared that aid to church-related schools must do the following:

1. Have a secular legislative purpose
2. Have a primary effect that neither advances nor inhibits religion
3. Not foster an excessive government "entanglement" with religion

There is a fine line between aid that is permissible and aid that is not. For instance, the Court has allowed religiously affiliated colleges and universities to use public funds to build buildings. Tax funds may also be used to provide students in parochial schools with textbooks, computers and other instructional equipment, lunches, and transportation to and from school and to administer standardized testing services. Public funds cannot, however, be used to pay teacher salaries or provide transportation for students on field trips. The theory underlying these decisions is that it is possible to determine that buildings, textbooks, lunches, school buses, and national tests are not used to support sectarian education. However, determining how teachers handle a subject in class or focus a field trip may require complex and constitutionally impermissible regulation of religion.

In an important loosening of its constraints on aid to parochial schools, however, the Supreme Court decided in 1997 in *Agostini v. Felton* that public school systems could send teachers into parochial schools to teach remedial and supplemental classes to needy children. In a landmark decision in 2002, the Court in ***Zelman v. Simmons-Harris*** upheld a program that provided some families in Cleveland, Ohio, vouchers that could be used to pay tuition at religious schools.

Zelman v. Simmons-Harris
The 2002 Supreme Court decision that upheld a state providing families with vouchers that could be used to pay for tuition at religious schools.

Controversy over aid to schools is not limited to Roman Catholic schools or any other single religion. In 1994, the Supreme Court ruled in *Kiryas Joel v. Grumet* that New York state had gone too far in favoring religion when it created a public school district for the benefit of a village of Hasidic Jews.

At the same time, the Supreme Court has been opening public schools to religious activities. The Court decided that public universities that permit student groups to use their facilities must allow student religious groups on campus to use the facilities for religious worship.[3] In the 1984 Equal Access Act, Congress made it unlawful for any public high school receiving federal funds (almost all of them do) to keep student groups from using school facilities for religious worship if the school opens its facilities for other student meetings.[4] Similarly, in 1993 the Court required public schools that rent facilities to organizations to do the same for religious groups.[5] In 2001, the Supreme Court extended this principle to public elementary schools.[6]

In 1995, the Court held that the University of Virginia was constitutionally required to subsidize a student religious magazine on the same basis as other student publications.[7] However, in 2004 the Court held that the state of Washington was within its rights when it excluded students pursuing a devotional theology degree from its general scholarship program.[8]

Church and State

The threshold of constitutional acceptability becomes higher when public funds are used in a more direct way to support education. Thus school authorities may not permit religious instructors to come into public school buildings during the school day to provide religious education,[9] but they may release students from part of the compulsory school day to receive religious instruction elsewhere.[10] In 1980, the Court also prohibited posting the Ten Commandments on the walls of public classrooms.[11]

School prayer is perhaps the most controversial religious issue. In 1962 and 1963, the Court aroused the wrath of many Americans by ruling that voluntary recitations of prayers or Bible passages, when done as part of classroom exercises in public schools, violated the establishment clause. In ***Engel v. Vitale*** and ***School District of Abington Township, Pennsylvania v. Schempp*** the justices observed that "the place of religion in our society is an exalted one . . . [but] in the relationship between man and religion, the State is firmly committed to a position of neutrality."

Engel v. Vitale
The 1962 Supreme Court decision holding that state officials violated the **First Amendment** when they wrote a prayer to be recited by New York's schoolchildren.

School District of Abington Township, Pennsylvania v. Schempp
A 1963 Supreme Court decision holding that a Pennsylvania law requiring Bible reading in schools violated the **establishment clause** of the **First Amendment.**

It is *not* unconstitutional, of course, to pray in public schools. Students may pray silently as much as they wish. What the Constitution forbids is the sponsorship or encouragement of prayer, directly or indirectly, by public school authorities. Thus in 1992, the Court ruled that a school-sponsored prayer at a public-school graduation violated the constitutional separation of church and state.[12] In 2000, the Court held that student-led prayer at football games was also unconstitutional.[13] Three Alabama laws authorized schools to hold one-minute periods of silence for "meditation or voluntary prayer," but the Court rejected this approach because the state made it clear that the purpose of the statute was to return prayer to the schools. The Court did indicate, however, that a less clumsy approach would pass its scrutiny.[14]

Political scientist Kenneth D. Wald observes that a great ferment in the relationship between religion and American political life has marked recent years. Religious issues and controversies have assumed much greater importance in political debate than they commanded before.[15] Much of this new importance is due to fundamentalist religious groups that have spurred their members to political action. Many school districts have simply ignored the Supreme Court's ban on school prayer and continue to allow prayers in their classrooms. Some religious groups and many members of Congress, especially conservative Republicans, have pushed for a constitutional amendment permitting prayer in school.

Fundamentalist Christian groups have pressed some state legislatures to mandate the teaching of "creation science"—their alternative to Darwinian theories of evolution—in public schools. Louisiana, for example, passed an act requiring schools that taught Darwinian theory to teach creation science, too. Regardless, the Supreme Court ruled in 1987 that this law violated the establishment clause.[16] The Court had already held in a 1968 case that states cannot prohibit Darwin's theory of evolution from being taught in public schools.[17] More recently, some groups have advocated "intelligent design" as an alternative to evolution. Although they claim that their belief has no religious implications, lower courts have begun to rule that requiring teachers to present intelligent design as an alternative to evolution is a constitutionally unacceptable promotion of religion in the classroom.

Political Correctness

The Supreme Court's struggle to interpret the establishment clause is also evident in areas other than education. In 2005, the Supreme Court found that two Kentucky counties violated the establishment clause value of official religious neutrality when they posted large, readily visible copies of the Ten Commandments in their courthouses. The Court concluded that the counties' ostensible and predominant purpose was to advance religion.[18] However, the Court did not hold that a governmental body can never integrate a sacred text constitutionally into a governmental display on law or history. Thus, in 2005 the Court also upheld the inclusion of a monolith inscribed with the Ten Commandments among the 21 historical markers and 17 monuments surrounding the Texas State Capitol. The Court argued that simply having religious content or promoting a message consistent with a religious doctrine does not run afoul of the establishment clause. Texas's placement of the Commandments monument on its capitol grounds was a far more passive use of those texts than where they confront elementary school students every day and also served a legitimate historical purpose.[19]

Displays of religious symbols during the holidays have prompted considerable controversy. In 1984, the Court found that Pawtucket, Rhode Island, could set up a Christmas nativity scene on public property—along with Santa's house and sleigh, Christmas trees, and other symbols of the Christmas season.[20] Five years later, the Court extended the principle to a Hanukkah menorah placed next to a Christmas tree. The Court concluded that these displays had a secular purpose and provided little or no benefit to religion. At the same time, the Court invalidated a display of the nativity scene without secular symbols in a courthouse because, in this context, the county gave the impression of endorsing the display's religious message.[21]

In this case, the Court said the Constitution does not require complete separation of church and state; it mandates accommodation of all religions and forbids hostility toward any. At the same time, the Constitution forbids government endorsement of religious beliefs. Drawing the line between neutrality toward religion and promotion of it is not easy; this dilemma ensures that cases involving the establishment of religion will continue to come before the Court.

The Free Exercise Clause

The First Amendment also guarantees the free exercise of religion. This guarantee seems simple enough. Whether people hold no religious beliefs, practice voodoo, or go to church, temple, or mosque, they should have the right to practice religion as they choose. The matter is more complicated, of course. Religions sometimes

Cassius Clay was the world heavyweight boxing champion before he converted to Islam, changed his name to Muhammad Ali, and was drafted during the war in Vietnam. Arguing that he opposed war on religious grounds, he refused to join the army. The federal government prosecuted him for draft dodging, and the boxing commission stripped him of his title. In 1971, the Supreme Court overturned his conviction for draft evasion. He is pictured here at the Houston induction center in 1967.

forbid actions that society thinks are necessary; or, conversely, religions may require actions that society finds unacceptable. For example, what if a religion justifies multiple marriages or the use of illegal drugs? Muhammad Ali, the boxing champion, refused induction into the armed services during the Vietnam War because, he said, military service would violate his Muslim faith. Amish parents often refuse to send their children to public schools. Because of their beliefs, Jehovah's Witnesses and Christian Scientists may refuse to accept blood transfusions and certain other kinds of medical treatment for themselves or their children.

Consistently maintaining that people have an inviolable right to *believe* what they want, the courts have been more cautious about the right to *practice* a belief. What if, the Supreme Court once asked, a person "believed that human sacrifices were a necessary part of religious worship?" In *Employment Division v. Smith* (1988), the Court discarded its previous requirement for a *compelling interest* before a government could even indirectly limit or prohibit religious practices. In *Smith*, the Court decided that state laws interfering with religious practices but not specifically aimed at religion are constitutional. As long as a law does not single out and ban religious practices because they are engaged in for religious reasons, or only because of the religious belief they display, a general law may be applied to conduct even if the conduct is religiously inspired (denying people unemployment compensation is an exception). In *Smith*, the state of Oregon was allowed to prosecute persons who used the drug peyote as part of their religious rituals.

Even before this decision, the Supreme Court had never permitted religious freedom to be an excuse for any and all behaviors. The Court had upheld laws and regulations forbidding polygamy, outlawing business activities on Sunday as applied to Orthodox Jews, denying tax exemptions to religious schools that discriminate on the basis of race,[22] approving building a road through ground sacred to some Native

Americans, and even prohibiting a Jewish air force captain from wearing his yarmulke (Congress later intervened to permit military personnel to wear yarmulkes).

Congress and the Supreme Court have granted protection to other religiously motivated practices under the free exercise clause. The Court allowed Amish parents to take their children out of school after the eighth grade. Reasoning that the Amish community was well established and that its children would not burden the state, the Court held that religious freedom took precedence over compulsory education laws.[23] More broadly, although a state can compel parents to send their children to an accredited school, parents have a right to choose religious schools rather than public schools for their children's education. A state may not require Jehovah's Witnesses or members of other religions to participate in public school flag-saluting ceremonies. Congress has also ruled—and the courts have upheld—that people can become conscientious objectors to war on religious grounds. You can examine another free exercise case in "You Are the Judge: The Case of Animal Sacrifices."

In the Religious Freedom Restoration Act of 1993, Congress attempted to overturn the principle the Court articulated in *Smith*. This act conferred on all persons the right to perform their religious rituals unless the government can show that the law or regulation in question is narrowly tailored and in pursuit of a "compelling interest." In 1997, however, the Supreme Court declared this act an unconstitutional

YOU ARE THE JUDGE

The Case of Animal Sacrifices

The church of Lukumi Babalu Aye, in Hialeah, Florida, practiced Santeria, a Caribbean-based mix of African ritual, voodoo, and Catholicism. Central to Santeria is the ritual sacrifice of animals—at birth, marriage, and death rites as well as at ceremonies to cure the sick and initiate new members.

Offended by these rituals, the city of Hialeah passed ordinances prohibiting animal sacrifices in religious ceremonies. The church challenged the constitutionality of these laws, claiming they violated the free exercise clause of the First Amendment because the ordinances essentially barred the practice of Santeria. The city, the Santerians claimed, was discriminating against a religious minority. Besides, many other forms of killing animals were legal, including fishing, using animals in medical research, selling lobsters to be boiled alive, and feeding live rats to snakes.

You Be the Judge: Do the Santerians have a constitutional right to sacrifice animals in their religious rituals? Does the city's interest in protecting animals outweigh the Santerians' requirement for animal sacrifice?

Answer: In 1993, the Court overturned the Hialeah ordinances that prohibited the use of animal sacrifice in religious ritual. In *Church of the Lukumi Babalu Aye, Inc. v. City of Hialeah,* the justices concluded that governments that permit other forms of killing of animals may not then ban sacrifices or ritual killings. In this instance, the Court found no compelling state interest that justified the abridgement of the freedom of religion.

The free exercise of religious beliefs sometimes clashes with society's other values or laws, as when the Amish—who prefer to lead simple, traditional lives—refused to send their children to public schools. The Supreme Court eventually held in favor of the Amish, arguing that Amish children, living in such a close-knit community, were unlikely to become dependent on the state.

intrusion by Congress into the states' prerogatives for regulating the health and welfare of citizens.[24] The law still applies to the federal government, however, and in 2006 the Court allowed a small religious sect to use an hallucinogenic tea in its rituals.[25]

Freedom of Expression

Comparing Civil Liberties

A democracy depends on the free expression of ideas. Thoughts that are muffled, speech that is forbidden, and meetings that cannot be held are enemies of the democratic process. Totalitarian governments know this, which is why they go to enormous trouble to limit expression.

Americans pride themselves on their free and open society. Freedom of conscience is absolute; Americans can *believe* whatever they want. The First Amendment plainly forbids the national government from limiting freedom of *expression*—that is, the right to say or publish what one believes. Is freedom of expression, then, like freedom of conscience, also *absolute*? Supreme Court Justice Hugo Black thought so; he was fond of pointing out that the First Amendment said Congress shall make *no* law. "I read no law abridging to mean no law abridging." In contrast, Justice Oliver Wendell Holmes offered a classic example of impermissible speech in 1919: "The most stringent protection of free speech would not protect a man in falsely shouting 'fire' in a theater and causing a panic."

The courts have been called on to decide where to draw the line separating permissible from impermissible speech. In doing so, judges have had to balance freedom of expression against competing values like public order, national security, and the right to a fair trial. One controversial freedom of expression issue involves so-called hate speech. In 1992, the Supreme Court ruled that legislatures and universities may not single out racial, religious, or sexual insults or threats for prosecution as "hate speech" or "bias crimes."[26] (See "Issues of the Times: Should Universities Regulate Hate Speech?")

The courts have also had to decide what kinds of activities do and do not constitute *speech* (or press) within the meaning of the First Amendment. Holding a political rally to attack an opposing candidate's stand on important issues gets First Amendment protection. Obscenity and libel, which are also expressions, do not. To make things more complicated, certain forms of nonverbal speech, such as picketing, are considered symbolic speech and receive First Amendment protection. The courts consider other forms of expression, such as fraud and incitement to violence, to be action rather than speech. Government can limit action more easily than it can limit expression.

The one thing all freedom-of-expression cases have in common is the question of whether a certain expression receives the protection of the Constitution.

Prior Restraint

prior restraint
A government preventing material from being published. This is a common method of limiting the press in some nations, but it is usually unconstitutional in the United States, according to the **First Amendment** and as confirmed in the 1931 Supreme Court case of ***Near v. Minnesota***.

Near v. Minnesota
The 1931 Supreme Court decision holding that the **First Amendment** protects newspapers from **prior restraint**.

One principle stands out clearly in the complicated history of freedom of expression laws: Time and time again, the Supreme Court has struck down prior restraint on speech and the press. **Prior restraint** refers to a government's actions that prevent material from being published; in a word, prior restraint is censorship. In the United States, the First Amendment ensures that even if the government frowns on certain material, a person's right to publish it is all but inviolable. A landmark case involving prior restraint is ***Near v. Minnesota*** (1931). A blunt newspaper editor called local officials a string of names including "grafters" and "Jewish gangsters." The state closed down his business, but the Supreme Court ordered the paper reopened.[27] Of course, the newspaper editor—or anyone else—could later be punished for violating a law or someone's rights *after* publication.

The extent of an individual's or group's freedom from prior restraint does depend in part, however, on who that individual or group is. In 1988, the Supreme Court ruled that a high school newspaper was not a public forum and could be regulated in "any reasonable manner" by school officials.[28]

The Supreme Court has also upheld restrictions on the right to publish in the name of national security. Wartime often brings censorship to protect classified information. Critics of the press during the Persian Gulf War complained that press reporting might have helped to pinpoint locations of SCUD missile attacks, knowledge of which could be used to aim future missiles more precisely. Defenders of the freedom of the press complained that never before had the press been as "managed" as in that conflict: Reporters could get to the field only in the company of official Pentagon press representatives—and some who tried other ways of getting in the field were captured by the Iraqis.

Nevertheless, the courts are reluctant to issue injunctions prohibiting the publication of material even in the area of national security. The most famous case regarding prior restraint and national security involved the publication of stolen Pentagon papers. You can examine this case in "You Are the Judge: The Case of the Purloined Pentagon Papers."

YOU ARE THE JUDGE

The Case of the Purloined Pentagon Papers

During the Johnson administration, the Department of Defense had amassed an elaborate secret history of American involvement in the Vietnam War. Hundreds of documents, many of them secret cables, memos, and war plans, were included. Many documented American ineptitude and South Vietnamese duplicity. One former Pentagon official, Daniel Ellsberg, who had become disillusioned with the Vietnam War, managed to retain access to a copy of these Pentagon papers. Hoping that revelations of the Vietnam quagmire would help end American involvement, he decided to leak the Pentagon papers to the *New York Times*.

The Nixon administration pulled out all the stops in its effort to embarrass Ellsberg and prevent publication of the Pentagon papers. Nixon's chief domestic affairs adviser, John Ehrlichman, approved a burglary of Ellsberg's psychiatrist's office, hoping to find damaging information on Ellsberg. (The burglary was bungled, and it eventually led to Ehrlichman's conviction and imprisonment.) In the courts, Nixon administration lawyers sought an injunction against the *Times* that would have ordered it to cease publication of the secret documents. Government lawyers argued that national security was being breached and that Ellsberg had stolen the documents from the government. The *Times* argued that its freedom to publish would be violated if an injunction were granted. In 1971 the case of *New York Times v. United States* was decided by the Supreme Court.

You Be the Judge: Did the *Times* have a right to publish secret, stolen Department of Defense documents?

Answer: In a 6-to-3 decision, a majority of the justices agreed that the "no prior restraint" rule prohibited prosecution before the papers were published. The justices also made it clear that if the government brought prosecution for theft, the Court might be sympathetic. No such charges were filed.

Free Speech and Public Order

Not surprisingly, government has sometimes been a zealous opponent of speech that opposes government policies. In wartime and peacetime, the biggest conflict between press and government has been about the connection between a free press and the need for public order. During World War I, Charles T. Schenck, the secretary of the American Socialist Party, distributed thousands of leaflets urging young men to resist the draft. Schenck was charged with impeding the war effort. The Supreme Court upheld his conviction in 1919 (*Schenck v. United States*). Justice Holmes declared that government could limit speech if it provokes a clear and present danger of substantive evils. Only when such danger exists can government restrain speech. It is difficult to say, of course, when speech becomes dangerous rather than simply inconvenient for the government.

Civil Liberties and National Security

The courts confronted the issue of free speech and public order during the 1950s. In the late 1940s and early 1950s there was widespread fear that Communists had infiltrated the government. Senator Joseph McCarthy and others in Congress were persecuting people they thought subversive, based on the Smith Act of 1940, which forbade advocating the violent overthrow of the American government. In *Dennis v. United States* (1951), the Supreme Court upheld prison sentences for several Communist Party leaders for conspiring to advocate the violent overthrow of the government—even in the absence of evidence that they actually urged people to commit specific acts of violence. The Court ruled that a Communist takeover was so grave a danger that government should squelch their threat.

Soon the political climate changed, however, and the Court narrowed the interpretation of the Smith Act, making it more difficult to prosecute dissenters. In later years, the Court has found that it is permissible to advocate the violent overthrow of the government in the abstract but not actually to incite anyone to imminent lawless action (*Yates v. United States* [1957]; *Brandenburg v. Ohio* [1969]). Courts have been quite supportive of the right to protest, pass out leaflets, or gather signatures on petitions—as long as it is done in public places. Campaign literature may even be distributed anonymously.[29]

HOW YOU CAN MAKE A DIFFERENCE

Free Speech on Campus

In order to have a healthy, dynamic and vibrant republic, free-speech rights must receive constitutional security. With an increasingly politically polarized electorate, and with the increasing intensity of hot-button issues such as the War on Terror, illegal immigration, and energy consumption, it is crucial that open and honest debate by those on all sides of a question be protected. This is equally true in the universities, since it is a mission of academia to foster new ideas and policies in the hope of improving the national community and the human condition. Nevertheless, there has been a trend on campuses across the country to silence speech that professors and universities deem offensive, with the resulting effect of squashing student's First Amendment protected speech. As a student, you are in a unique position to make a difference regarding this issue.

Making a Difference

When New York University recently prohibited the student group the Objectivist Club from displaying censored cartoons in the club's "Free Speech and the Danish Cartoons" forum, the NYU students fought back. The forum had planned to discuss the suppression in Europe of religious cartoons portraying the Prophet Mohammad. The NYU students went public by contacting the Foundation for Individual Rights in Education (otherwise known as FIRE, *http://www.thefire.org/*), and their story was published in *USA Today*.

What you can do:

- You can be a "watchdog" to ensure that full and open debate is allowed to flourish in both the classroom and on campus and you can engage in student activism.
- You can also help monitor the current controversy regarding the Academic Bill of Rights movement (*http://www.studentsforacademicfreedom.org/*). This movement is an attempt to place into law policies guaranteeing students and professors the ability to express their First Amendment speech freedoms. You can contact your local state representative or university legal affairs officer to air your views on the potential effectiveness or harmfulness of this movement.
- Identify organizations dedicated to helping students obtain an atmosphere of free inquiry on university campuses, and join those organizations.

Free speech sometimes conflicts with public order. The Constitution protects the rights of protestors, such as those pictured here opposing the war with Iraq, to have their say.

Constitutional protections diminish once a person steps on private property, such as most shopping centers. The Supreme Court has held that federal free-speech guarantees did not apply when a person was on private property.[30] However, it upheld a state's power to include politicking in shopping centers within its own free-speech guarantee,[31] and in 1994, the Supreme Court ruled that cities cannot bar residents from posting signs on their own property.[32]

Free Press and Fair Trials

The Bill of Rights is an inexhaustible source of potential conflicts among different types of freedoms. One is the conflict between the right of the press to print what it wants and the right to a fair trial. The quantity of press coverage given the trial (and pretrial hearings) of football star O. J. Simpson, accused of murdering his wife and her friend, surpassed that given the Super Bowl, and little of it was sympathetic to Simpson. Does such extensive media coverage compromise the fairness of the trial? Defense attorneys argue that such publicity can inflame the community—and potential jurors—against defendants. It may very well. The trouble is that the Constitution's guarantee of freedom of the press entitles journalists to cover every trial.

In addition to arguing that the public has a right to know, some journalists hope to capitalize on their coverage of lurid crime stories to sell newspapers, gain ratings, or attract advertisers. Those motivations have prompted newspapers to challenge courts' restrictions on media coverage of trials. When a Nebraska judge issued a gag order forbidding the press to report any details of a particularly gory murder (or even to report the gag order itself), the outraged Nebraska Press Association took the case to the Supreme Court. The Court sided with the editors and revoked the gag order.[33] In 1980, the Court reversed a Virginia judge's order to close a murder trial to the public and the press.[34] A pretrial hearing, though, is a different matter. A 1979 case permitted a closed hearing on the grounds that pretrial publicity might compromise the defendant's right to fairness.

Although reporters always want access to trials, they do not always want the courts to have access to their files. Occasionally a reporter withholds some critical evidence that either the prosecution or the defense wants in a criminal case. Reporters argue that protecting their sources should exempt them from revealing notes from confidential informants. More than one reporter has gone to jail for this principle, arguing that they had no obligation to produce evidence that might bear on the guilt or innocence of a defendant. *New York Times* reporter Judith Miller spent several months in jail in 2005 for refusing to turn over her notes relevant to the investigation of a leak that revealed the identity of CIA operative Valerie Plame.

Some states have passed *shield laws* to protect reporters in these situations. In most states, though, reporters have no more rights than other citizens once a case has come to trial. The Supreme Court ruled in *Branzburg v. Hayes* (1972) that in the absence of shield laws, the right of a fair trial preempts the reporter's right to protect sources. This issue came to a head in one celebrated case involving the student newspaper at Stanford University. After a violent confrontation with student protestors, the police got a search warrant and marched off to the *Stanford Daily*, which they believed to have pictures of the scene—from which they could make arrests. The paper argued that its files were protected by the First Amendment, but the decision in *Zurcher v. Stanford Daily* (1978) sided with the police, not the paper.

It is one thing to attempt to obtain the press's cooperation in trials and quite another to limit the press's coverage of judicial proceedings. The balance between a free press and a fair trial is not an even one. The Court has *never* upheld a restriction on the press in the interest of a fair trial. Ultimately, the only feasible measure the judicial system can take against the influence of publicity in high profile cases is to sequester the jury, thereby isolating it from the media and public opinion.

Obscenity

VISUAL LITERACY

What Speech Is Protected by the Constitution?

In *The Brethren*, a gossipy portrayal of the Supreme Court, Bob Woodward and Scott Armstrong recount the tale of Justice Thurgood Marshall's lunch with some law clerks. Glancing at his watch at about 1:50 P.M., the story goes, Marshall exclaimed, "My God, I almost forgot. It's movie day, we've got to get back."[35] Movie day at the Court was an annual event when movies brought before the Court on obscenity charges were shown in a basement storeroom.

Several justices boycotted these showings, arguing that obscenity should never be banned and so how "dirty" a movie is has no relevance. In 1957, however, the majority held that "obscenity is not within the area of constitutionally protected speech or press" (***Roth v. United States***). The doctrine set forth in this case still prevails. Deciding what is obscene, though, has never been an easy matter. In a line that would haunt him for the rest of his life, Justice Potter Stewart once remarked that although he could not define obscenity, "I know it when I see it."

Roth v. United States

A 1957 Supreme Court decision ruling that "obscenity is not within the area of constitutionally protected speech or press."

Although the Supreme Court ruled in *Roth v. United States* that obscenity is not protected by the First Amendment, determining just what is obscene has proven difficult. Popular radio personality Howard Stern pressed the limits of obscenity rules when he worked for radio stations using the public airwaves. Ultimately, he moved to satellite radio, where the rules are much less restrictive.

Efforts to define obscenity have perplexed the courts for years. Obviously, public standards vary from time to time, place to place, and person to person. Much of today's MTV would have been banned a decade or two ago. At one time or another, the works of Aristophanes, those of Mark Twain, and even the "Tarzan" stories by Edgar Rice Burroughs were banned. The state of Georgia banned the acclaimed film *Carnal Knowledge*—a ban the Supreme Court struck down in 1974.[36]

The Court tried to clarify its doctrine by spelling out what could be classified as obscene and thus outside First Amendment protection in the 1973 case of ***Miller v. California***. Then Chief Justice Warren Burger wrote that materials were obscene under the following circumstances:

Miller v. California
A 1973 Supreme Court decision that avoided defining obscenity by holding that community standards be used to determine whether material is obscene in terms of appealing to a "prurient interest" and being "patently offensive" and "lacking in value."

1. The work, taken as a whole, appealed "to a prurient interest in sex."
2. The work showed "patently offensive" sexual conduct that was specifically defined by an obscenity law.
3. The work, taken as a whole, lacked "serious literary, artistic, political, or scientific value."

Decisions regarding whether material was obscene, said the Court, should be based on average people (in other words, juries) applying the contemporary standards of local—not national—communities.

The Court did provide "a few plain examples" of what sort of material might fall within this definition of obscenity. Among these examples were "patently offensive representations of ultimate sexual acts, . . . actual or simulated," "patently offensive representations of masturbation or excretory functions," or "lewd exhibition of the genitals." Cities throughout the country duplicated the language of *Miller* in their obscenity ordinances. The difficulty remains in determining what is *lewd* or *offensive*. Laws must satisfy these qualifying adjectives to prevent communities from banning anatomy texts, for example, as obscene.

Another reason why obscenity convictions can be difficult to obtain is that no nationwide consensus exists that offensive material should be banned—at least not when it is restricted to adults. In many communities the laws are lenient regarding pornography, and prosecutors know that they may not get a jury to convict, even when the disputed material is obscene as defined by *Miller*. Thus obscene material is widely available in adult bookstores, video stores, and movie theaters.

Courts have consistently ruled that states may protect children from obscenity, since they are considered more vulnerable to its harmful influences. The rating scheme of the Motion Picture Association of America is one example, as is the more recent TV ratings system. Equally popular are laws designed to protect the young against pornographic exploitation. It is a violation of federal law to receive sexually explicit photographs of children through the mail or over the Internet, and in 1990 the Supreme Court upheld Ohio's law forbidding the possession of child pornography.[37]

Advances in technology have created a new wrinkle in the obscenity issue. The Internet and the World Wide Web make it easier to distribute obscene material rapidly, and a number of online information services have taken advantage of this opportunity. Congress, especially concerned with protecting minors from exposure to pornography, has recently decided that the Internet is not the electronic equivalent of the printing press and thus does not deserve the free-speech protection of the First Amendment. Instead, it regards the Internet as a broadcast medium, subject to government regulation (discussed later in this chapter).

In 1996, Congress passed the Communications Decency Act, banning obscene material and criminalizing the transmission of indecent speech or images to anyone under 18 years of age. The new law made no exception for material that has serious literary, artistic, political, or scientific merit as outlined in *Miller v. California*. In 1997, the Supreme Court overturned this law as being overly broad and vague and a violation of free speech.[38] In 2002, the Court overturned a law banning virtual child pornography on similar grounds.[39] Apparently the Supreme Court views the Internet similarly to print media, with similar protections against government regulation. In 1999, however, the Court upheld prohibitions on obscene e-mail and faxes.

Despite the Court's best efforts to define obscenity and determine when it can be banned, state and local governments continue to struggle with the application of these rulings. In one famous case, a small New Jersey town tried to get rid of a nude dancing parlor by using its zoning power to ban all live entertainment. The Court held that the measure was too broad and thus unlawful.[40] But the Court upheld laws banning nude dancing when their effect on overall expression was minimal.[41] Jacksonville, Florida, tried to ban drive-in movies containing nudity. We can examine the Court's reaction in "You Are the Judge: The Case of the Drive-in Theater."

Hate Speech

Other attempts to restrict obscenity have been proposed by some women's groups, which claim that pornography degrades and dehumanizes women. Legal scholar Catherine MacKinnon claims that "pornography is an . . . industry of rape and battery and sexual harassment."[42] Some cities, at the urging of an unusual alliance of conservative Christians and feminists, have passed antipornography ordinances on the grounds that pornography harms women. So far, however, courts

YOU ARE THE JUDGE

The Case of the Drive-in Theater

Almost everyone concedes that *sometimes* obscenity should be banned by public authorities. One instance might be when a person's right to show pornographic movies clashes with another's right to privacy. Presumably, no one wants hard-core pornography shown in public places where schoolchildren might see it. Showing dirty movies in an enclosed theater or in the privacy of your own living room is one thing. Showing them in public is something else. Or is it?

The city of Jacksonville, Florida, wanted to limit the showing of certain kinds of movies at drive-in theaters. Its city council reasoned that drive-ins were public places and that drivers passing by would be involuntarily exposed to movies they might prefer not to see. Some members of the council argued that drivers distracted by steamy scenes might even cause accidents. So the council passed a local ordinance forbidding movies showing nudity (defined in the ordinance as "bare buttocks . . . female bare breasts, or human bare pubic areas") at drive-in theaters.

Arrested for violating the ordinance, a Mr. Erznoznik challenged the constitutionality of the ordinance. He claimed the law was overly broad and banned nudity, not obscenity. The lawyers for the city insisted that the law could be squared with the First Amendment. The government, they claimed, had a responsibility to forbid a "public nuisance," especially one that might cause a traffic hazard.

You Be the Judge: Did Jacksonville's ban on nudity in movies at drive-ins go too far, or was it a constitutional limit on free speech?

Answer: In *Erznoznik v. Jacksonville* (1975), the Supreme Court held that Jacksonville's ordinance was unconstitutionally broad. The city council had gone too far; it could end up banning movies that might not be obscene. The ordinance would, said the Court, ban a film "containing a picture of a baby's buttocks, the nude body of a war victim or scenes from a culture where nudity is indigenous." Said Justice Powell for the Court, "Clearly, all nudity cannot be deemed obscene."

have struck these ordinances down on First Amendment grounds. No such case has reached the Supreme Court—yet.

Libel and Slander

Another type of expression not protected by the First Amendment is **libel**: the publication of false statements that are malicious and damage a person's reputation. *Slander* refers to spoken defamation, whereas libel refers to written defamation. Of course, if politicians could collect damages for every untrue thing said about them, the right to criticize the government—which the Supreme Court termed "the central meaning of the First Amendment"—would be stifled. No one would dare be critical for fear of making a factual error.

To encourage public debate, the Supreme Court has held in cases such as ***New York Times v. Sullivan*** (1964) that statements about public figures are libelous only if made with malice and reckless disregard for the truth. Public figures have to prove to a jury, in effect, that whoever wrote or said untrue statements about them knew that the statements were untrue and intended harm. This standard makes libel

libel
The publication of false or malicious statements that damage someone's reputation.

New York Times v. Sullivan
Decided in 1964, this case established the guidelines for determining whether public officials and public figures could win damage suits for libel. To do so, such individuals must prove that the defamatory statements were made with "actual malice" and reckless disregard for the truth.

Why It Matters

Libel Law
It is difficult for public figures to win libel cases. Public figures will likely lose even if they can show that the defendant made defamatory falsehoods about them. This may not be fair, but it is essential for people to feel free to criticize public officials. Fear of losing a lawsuit would have chilling effect on democratic dialogue.

cases difficult for public figures to win because it is difficult to prove that a publication was intentionally malicious.[43]

Private individuals have a lower standard to meet for winning libel lawsuits. They need show only that statements made about them were defamatory falsehoods and that the author was negligent. Nevertheless, it is unusual for someone to win a libel case; most people do not wish to draw attention to critical statements about themselves.

Libel cases must balance freedom of expression with respect for individual reputations. If public debate is not free, there can be no democracy. On the other hand, some reputations will be damaged (or at least bruised) in the process. In one widely publicized case, General William Westmoreland, once the commander of American troops in South Vietnam, sued CBS for the 1982 broadcast of a documentary called "The Uncounted Enemy." It claimed that American military leaders in Vietnam, including Westmoreland, systematically lied to Washington about their success there to make it appear that the United States was winning the war. All the evidence, including CBS's own internal memoranda, showed that the documentary made errors of fact. Westmoreland sued CBS for libel. Ultimately, the power of the press—in this case, a sloppy, arrogant press—prevailed. Fearing defeat at the trial, Westmoreland settled for a mild apology.[44]

Symbolic Speech

Freedom of speech, more broadly interpreted, is a guarantee of freedom of expression. In 1965, when two Iowa high school students were suspended from school for wearing black armbands to protest the Vietnam War, the Supreme Court held that the suspension violated the students' First Amendment rights. The right to freedom of speech, said the Court, went beyond the spoken word.[45]

Texas v. Johnson
A 1989 case in which the Supreme Court struck down a law banning the burning of the American flag on the grounds that such action was **symbolic speech** protected by the **First Amendment.**

symbolic speech
Nonverbal communication, such as burning a flag or wearing an armband. The Supreme Court has accorded some symbolic speech protection under the **First Amendment.**

When Gregory Johnson set a flag on fire at the 1984 Republican National Convention in Dallas to protest nuclear arms buildup, the Supreme Court decided that the state law prohibiting flag desecration violated the First Amendment (***Texas v. Johnson*** [1989]). Burning the flag, the Court said, constituted speech and not just dramatic action.[46] When Massachusetts courts ordered the organizers of the annual St. Patrick's Day parade to include the Irish-American Gay, Lesbian, and Bisexual Group of Boston, the Supreme Court declared that a parade is a form of protected speech and thus that the organizers are free to include or exclude whomever they want.

Wearing an armband, burning a flag, and marching in a parade are examples of **symbolic speech:** actions that do not consist of speaking or writing but that express an opinion. Court decisions have classified these activities somewhere between pure speech and pure action. The doctrine of symbolic speech is not precise; for example, although burning a flag is protected speech, burning a draft card is not.[47] In 2003, the Court held that states may make it a crime to burn a cross with a purpose to intimidate, as long as the law clearly gives prosecutors the burden of proving that the act was intended as a threat and not as a form of symbolic expression.[48] The relevant cases make it clear, however, that First Amendment rights are not limited by a rigid definition of what constitutes speech.

Commercial Speech

Not all forms of communication receive the full protection of the First Amendment. **Commercial speech,** such as advertising, is restricted far more extensively than expressions of opinion on religious, political, or other matters. The Federal Trade Commission (FTC) decides what kinds of goods may be advertised on radio and television and regulates the content of such advertising. These regulations have responded to changes in social mores and priorities. Thirty years ago, for example, tampons could not be advertised on TV, whereas cigarette commercials were everywhere. Today the situation is reversed.

commercial speech
Communication in the form of advertising. It can be restricted more than many other types of speech but has been receiving increased protection from the Supreme Court.

The FTC attempts to ensure that advertisers do not make false claims for their products, but "truth" in advertising does not prevent misleading promises. For example, when ads imply that the right mouthwash or deodorant will improve one's love life, that dubious message is perfectly legal.

Nevertheless, commercial speech on the airwaves is regulated in ways that would clearly be impossible in the political or religious realm—even to the point of forcing a manufacturer to say certain words. For example, the makers of Excedrin pain reliever were forced to add the words "on pain other than headache" in their commercials describing tests that supposedly supported the product's claims of superior effectiveness. (The test results were based on the pain experienced after giving birth.)

Although commercial speech is regulated more rigidly than other types of speech, the courts have been broadening its protection under the Constitution. For years, many states had laws that prohibited advertising for professional services—such as legal and engineering services—and for certain products ranging from eyeglasses and prescription drugs to condoms and abortions. Advocates of these laws claimed that they were designed to protect consumers against misleading claims, while critics charged that the laws prevented price competition. In recent years, the courts have struck down many such restrictions as violations of freedom of speech. In 1999, the Court overturned restrictions on advertising casino gambling in states where such gambling is legal.[49] In general, regulation of commercial speech is allowed when the speech concerns unlawful activity or is misleading but otherwise must advance a substantial government interest and be no more extensive than necessary to serve that interest.[50]

Regulation of the Public Airwaves

The Federal Communications Commission (FCC) regulates the content, nature, and very existence of radio and television broadcasting. Although newspapers do not need licenses, radio and television stations do. A licensed station must comply with regulations, including the requirement that they devote a certain percentage of broadcast time to public service, news, children's programming, political candidates, or views other than those its owners support. The rules are more relaxed for cable channels, which can specialize in a particular type of broadcasting because consumers pay for, and thus have more choice about, the service.

This sort of governmental interference would clearly violate the First Amendment if it were imposed on the print media. For example, the state of Florida passed a law requiring newspapers in the state to provide space for political candidates to reply to

Miami Herald Publishing Company v. Tornillo
A 1974 case in which the Supreme Court held that a state could not force a newspaper to print replies from candidates it had criticized, illustrating the limited power of government to restrict the **print media.**

Red Lion Broadcasting Company v. Federal Communications Commission
A 1969 case in which the Supreme Court upheld restrictions on radio and television broadcasting. These restrictions on the **broadcast media** are much tighter than those on the **print media** because there are only a limited number of broadcasting frequencies available.

newspaper criticisms. The Supreme Court, without hesitation, voided this law (***Miami Herald Publishing Company v. Tornillo*** [1974]). Earlier, in ***Red Lion Broadcasting Company v. Federal Communications Commission*** (1969), the Court upheld similar restrictions on radio and television stations, reasoning that such laws were justified because only a limited number of broadcast frequencies were available.

One FCC rule regulating the content of programs restricts the use of obscene words. Comedian George Carlin has a famous routine called "Filthy Words" that could never be said over the airwaves. A New York City radio station tested Carlin's assertion by airing his routine. The ensuing events proved Carlin right. In 1978, the Supreme Court upheld the commission's policy of barring these words from radio or television when children might hear them.[51]

Similarly, the FCC has twice fined New York disc jockey Howard Stern $600,000 for indecency. It is especially interesting that if cable or satellite, instead of the airwaves, had carried Stern's commentaries, he could have expressed himself with impunity. Technological change has blurred the line between broadcasting and private communications between individuals. With cable television now in most American homes, the Supreme Court is faced with ruling on the application of free-speech guidelines to cable broadcasting.

Freedom of Assembly

The last of the great rights guaranteed by the First Amendment is the freedom to "peaceably assemble." This freedom is often neglected alongside the more trumpeted freedoms of speech, press, and religion, yet it is the basis for forming interest groups, political parties, and professional associations, as well as for picketing and protesting.

Right to Assemble

There are two facets of the freedom of assembly. First is the literal right to assemble—that is, to gather together in order to make a statement. This freedom can conflict with other societal values when it disrupts public order, traffic flow, peace and quiet, or bystanders' freedom to go about their business without interference. Within reasonable limits, called *time, place,* and *manner restrictions,* freedom of assembly includes the rights to parade, picket, and protest. Whatever a group's cause, it has the right to demonstrate, but no group can simply hold a spontaneous demonstration any time, anywhere, and any way it chooses. Usually, a group must apply to the local city government for a permit and post a bond of a few hundred dollars—a little like making a security deposit on an apartment. The governing body must grant a permit as long as the group pledges to hold its demonstration at a time and place that allows the police to prevent major disruptions. There are virtually no limitations on the content of a group's message. In one important case, the American Nazi Party applied to the local government to march in the streets of Skokie, Illinois, a Chicago suburb with a sizable Jewish population, including many survivors of Hitler's death camps. You can examine the Court's response in "You Are the Judge: The Case of the Nazis' March in Skokie."

The balance between freedom and order is tested when protest verges on harassment. Protestors lined up outside abortion clinics have been a common sight.

Members of groups such as "Operation Rescue" try to shame clients into staying away and may harass them if they do visit a clinic. Rights are in conflict in such cases: A woman seeking to terminate her pregnancy has the right to obtain an abortion; the demonstrators have the right to protest the very existence of the clinic. The courts have acted to restrain these protestors, setting limits on how close they may come to the clinics and upholding damage claims of clients against the protestors. In one case, pro-life demonstrators in a Milwaukee, Wisconsin, suburb paraded outside the home of a physician who was reported to perform abortions. The town board forbade future picketing in residential neighborhoods. In 1988, the Supreme Court agreed that the right of residential privacy was a legitimate local concern and upheld the ordinance.[52] In 1994, Congress passed a law enacting broad new penalties against abortion protesters.

Right to Associate

The second facet of freedom of assembly is the right to associate with people who share a common interest, including an interest in political change. In a famous case at the height of the civil rights movement, Alabama tried to harass the state chapter of the National Association for the Advancement of Colored People (NAACP) by

YOU ARE THE JUDGE

The Case of the Nazis' March in Skokie

Hitler's Nazis slaughtered 6 million Jews in death camps like Bergen-Belsen, Auschwitz, and Dachau. Many of the survivors migrated to the United States, and many settled in Skokie, Illinois. Skokie, with 80,000 people, is a suburb just north of Chicago. In its heavily Jewish population are thousands of survivors of German concentration camps.

The American Nazi Party was a ragtag group of perhaps 25 to 30 members. Their headquarters was a storefront building on the West Side of Chicago, near an area of an expanding African American population. After being denied a permit to march in an African American neighborhood of Chicago, the American Nazis announced their intention to march in Skokie. Skokie's city government required that they post a $300,000 bond to get a parade permit. The Nazis claimed that the high bond was set in order to prevent their march and that it infringed on their freedoms of speech and assembly. The American Civil Liberties Union (ACLU), despite its loathing of the Nazis, defended the Nazis' claim and their right to march. The ACLU lost half its Illinois membership because it took this position.

You Be the Judge: Do Nazis have the right to parade, preach anti-Jewish propaganda, and perhaps provoke violence in a community peopled with survivors of the Holocaust? What rights or obligations does a community have to maintain order?

Answer: A federal district court ruled that Skokie's ordinance did restrict freedom of assembly and association. No community could use its power to grant parade permits to stifle free expression. In *Collins v. Smith* (Collins was the Nazi leader, and Smith was the mayor of Skokie), the Supreme Court let this lower-court decision stand. In fact, the Nazis did not march in Skokie, settling instead for some poorly attended demonstrations in Chicago.

White supremacists and anti–White supremacists square off. The Supreme Court has generally upheld the right of any group, no matter how controversial or offensive, to peaceably assemble, as long as the group's demonstrations remain on public property.

NAACP v. Alabama

The Supreme Court protected the right to assemble peaceably in this 1958 case when it decided the NAACP did not have to reveal its membership list and thus subject its members to harassment.

requiring it to turn over its membership list. The Court found this demand an unconstitutional restriction on freedom of association (***NAACP v. Alabama*** [1958]).

In 2006, some law schools argued that Congress's insistence that law schools grant military recruiters access to their students violated the schools' freedom of speech and association. The Supreme Court concluded that the law regulated conduct, not speech. In addition, nothing about recruiting suggests that law schools agree with any speech by recruiters, and nothing in the law restricts what they may say about the military's policies. Nor does the law force a law school to accept members it does not desire, and students and faculty are free to associate to voice their disapproval of the military's message.[53]

The four freedoms guaranteed by the First Amendment—religion, speech, press, and assembly—are one key part of Americans' civil liberties. When people confront the American legal system as suspected or convicted criminals, they also have certain rights under the Constitution. These rights regulate how the government can investigate, interrogate, try, and punish them.

Rights of the Accused

Defendants' Rights

The Bill of Rights contains only 45 words that guarantee the freedoms of religion, speech, press, and assembly. Most of the remaining words concern the rights of people accused of crimes. These rights were originally intended to protect the accused in *political* arrests and trials; British abuse of colonial political leaders was still fresh in the memory of American citizens. Today the courts apply the protections in the Fourth, Fifth, Sixth, Seventh, and Eighth Amendments mostly in criminal justice cases.

It is useful to think of the stages of the criminal justice system as a series of funnels decreasing in size. Generally speaking, a *crime* is (sometimes) followed by an *arrest*, which is (sometimes) followed by a *prosecution*, which is (sometimes) followed by a *trial*, which (usually) results in a *verdict* of innocence or guilt. The funnels get smaller and smaller, each dripping into the next. Many more crimes occur than are reported, many more crimes are reported than arrests are made (the ratio is about five to one), many more arrests are made than prosecutors prosecute, and many more prosecutions occur than jury trials. At each stage of the criminal justice system, the Constitution protects the rights of the accused (see Table 4.2).

Interpreting Defendants' Rights

Civil Liberties in Today's World: Privacy and the Rights of the Accused

The Bill of Rights sets out civil liberties that American citizens have if they are arrested or brought to court. At every stage of the criminal justice system, police, prosecutors, and judges must behave in accordance with the Bill of Rights. Any misstep may invalidate a conviction.

The language of the Bill of Rights comes from the late 1700s and is often vague. For example, just how speedy is a "speedy trial"? How "cruel and unusual" does a punishment have to be in order to violate the Eighth Amendment? The courts continually must rule on the constitutionality of actions by police, prosecutors, judges, and legislatures—actions that a citizen or group could claim violate certain rights. Defendants' rights, just like those rights protected by the First Amendment, are not clearly defined in the Bill of Rights.

One thing is clear, however. The Supreme Court's decisions have extended specific provisions of the Bill of Rights—one by one—to the states as part of the general process of incorporation we discussed earlier. Virtually all the rights we discuss in the following sections affect the actions of both the national and state authorities.

Table 4.2 The Constitution and the Stages of the Criminal Justice System

Although our criminal justice system is complex, it can be broken down into stages. The Constitution protects the rights of the accused at every stage.

STAGE	PROTECTIONS
1. Evidence gathered	"Unreasonable search and seizure" forbidden (Fourth Amendment)
2. Suspicion cast	Guarantee that "writ of habeas corpus" will not be suspended, forbidding imprisonment without evidence (Article I, Section 9)
3. Arrest made	Right to have the "assistance of counsel" (Sixth Amendment)
4. Interrogation held	Forced self-incrimination forbidden (Fifth Amendment) "Excessive bail" forbidden (Eighth Amendment)
5. Trial held	"Speedy and public trial" by an impartial jury required (Sixth Amendment) "Double jeopardy" (being tried twice for the same crime) forbidden (Fifth Amendment) Trial by jury required (Article III, Section 2) Right to confront witnesses (Sixth Amendment)
6. Punishment imposed	"Cruel and unusual punishment" forbidden (Eighth Amendment)

Searches and Seizures

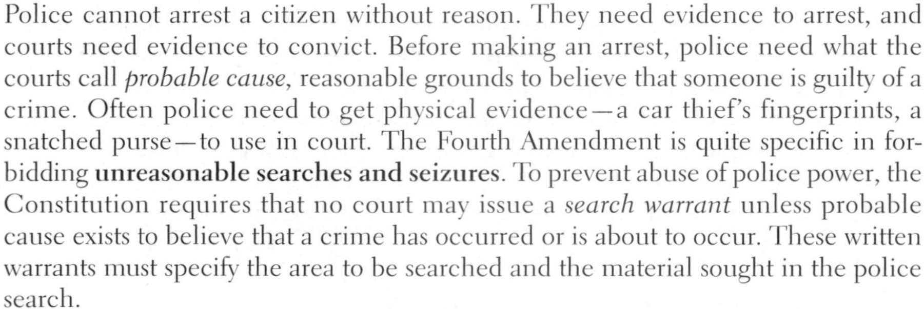

Police cannot arrest a citizen without reason. They need evidence to arrest, and courts need evidence to convict. Before making an arrest, police need what the courts call *probable cause*, reasonable grounds to believe that someone is guilty of a crime. Often police need to get physical evidence—a car thief's fingerprints, a snatched purse—to use in court. The Fourth Amendment is quite specific in forbidding **unreasonable searches and seizures**. To prevent abuse of police power, the Constitution requires that no court may issue a *search warrant* unless probable cause exists to believe that a crime has occurred or is about to occur. These written warrants must specify the area to be searched and the material sought in the police search.

You Are a Police Officer

A warrant is not a constitutional requirement for a reasonable police search, however. Most searches in this country take place without warrants. Such searches are valid if probable cause of a crime exists, if the search is necessary to protect an officer's safety, or if the search is limited to material relevant to the suspected crime or within the suspect's immediate control. The Supreme Court has also held that police may enter a home without a warrant when they have an objective reasonable basis for believing that an occupant is seriously injured or imminently threatened with such injury.[54]

unreasonable searches and seizures
Obtaining evidence in a haphazard or random manner, a practice prohibited by the Fourth Amendment. Probable cause and/or a **search warrant** are required for a legal and proper search for and seizure of incriminating evidence.

Normally, if police find anything in a search, they find what they have probable cause to believe is there. In two cases involving Fourth Amendment issues, authorities used aerial searches to secure the evidence they needed. The first case involved a marijuana grower named Ciraolo. When police, responding to a tip, went to look at his place, they found it surrounded by 10-foot fences. The police then rented a private plane, took pictures of the crop, and secured a conviction. Environmental

One of the most important principles of constitutional law is that defendants in criminal cases have rights. Probable cause and/or a search warrant are required for a legal search for and seizure of incriminating evidence. Here police officers read the suspect his rights based on the Supreme Court's decision in *Miranda v. Arizona.*

Protection Agency officials took a similar aerial photo of Dow Chemical's Midland, Michigan, plant and located environmental violations. Both Ciraolo and Dow sued, claiming they were the victims of unconstitutional search and seizure. Both lost, however, when their cases came before the Supreme Court. Since then, the Court has also upheld roadside checkpoints in which police randomly examine drivers for signs of intoxication[55] and the use of narcotics-detecting dogs at a routine stop for speeding. [56] The Court has, however, voided more general vehicle checkpoints.[57]

exclusionary rule
The rule that evidence, no matter how incriminating, cannot be introduced into a trial if it was not constitutionally obtained. The rule prohibits use of evidence obtained through **unreasonable search and seizure.**

Ever since 1914, the Supreme Court has used an **exclusionary rule** to weigh evidence in criminal cases. This rule prevents illegally seized evidence from being introduced in court, but until 1961 the rule applied only to the federal government. The Supreme Court broadened the application in the case of a Cleveland woman named Dollree Mapp, who was under suspicion for illegal gambling activities. The police broke into her home looking for a fugitive, and while there, they searched the house and found a cache of obscene materials. Mapp was convicted of possessing them. She appealed her case to the federal courts, claiming that the exclusionary rule should be made a part of the Fourth Amendment. Since the local police had no probable cause to search for obscene materials—only for materials related to gambling—she argued, the evidence should not be used against her. In an important decision (***Mapp v. Ohio*** [1961]), the Supreme Court ruled that the evidence had been seized illegally and the Court reversed Mapp's conviction. Since then, the exclusionary rule has been part of the Fourth Amendment and has been incorporated within the rights that restrict the states, as well as the federal government.

Mapp v. Ohio
The 1961 Supreme Court decision ruling that the Fourth Amendment's protection against **unreasonable searches and seizures** must be extended to the states as well as the federal government.

Critics of the exclusionary rule, including some Supreme Court justices, argue that its strict application may permit guilty persons to go free because of police carelessness or innocent errors. The guilty, they say, should not go free because of a "technicality." Supporters of the exclusionary rule respond that the Constitution is not a technicality and that defendants' rights protect the *accused* —because everyone is presumed innocent until proven otherwise. You can examine one contemporary search-and-seizure case in "You Are the Judge: The Case of Ms. Montoya."

Why It Matters

The Exclusionary Rule
One of the most controversial aspects of the courts' efforts to uphold defendants' rights has been their use of the exclusionary rule in which they disregard evidence obtained illegally. Although some may view the exclusionary rule as a technicality that helps criminals to avoid justice, this rule protects defendants (who have *not* been proven guilty) from abuses of police power.

An increasingly conservative Court made some exceptions to the exclusionary rule beginning in the 1980s. The Court allowed the use of illegally obtained evidence when this evidence led police to a discovery that they eventually would have made without it.[58] The justices also decided to establish the good-faith exception to the rule; evidence could be used if the police who seized it mistakenly thought they were operating under a constitutionally valid warrant.[59] In 1995, the Court held that the exclusionary rule does not bar evidence obtained illegally as the result of clerical errors.[60] In 2006, it held that a police violation of the knock-and-announce rule was not a justification for suppressing the evidence they found upon entry with a warrant.[61]

However, some decisions offer more protection against searches. An Iowa police officer stopped Patrick Knowles for speeding and issued him a citation. The officer then conducted a full search of the car without either Knowles's consent or probable cause, found marijuana and a "pot pipe," and arrested Knowles. The Supreme Court held that the search of Knowles's car violated the Fourth Amendment. The Court said that although officers may order a driver and passengers out of a car while issuing a traffic citation and may search for weapons to

YOU ARE THE JUDGE

The Case of Ms. Montoya

Rose Elviro Montoya de Hernandez arrived at the Los Angeles International Airport on Avianca Flight 080 from Bogotá, Colombia. Her first official encounter was with U.S. Customs inspector Talamantes, who noticed that she spoke no English. Interestingly, Montoya's passport indicated eight recent quick trips from Bogotá to Los Angeles. She had $5,000 in cash but no pocketbook or credit cards.

Talamantes and the other customs officers were suspicious. Stationed in Los Angeles, they were hardly unaware of the fact that Colombia was a major drug supplier. They questioned Montoya, who explained that her husband had a store in Bogotá and that she planned to spend the $5,000 at Kmart and JC Penney, stocking up on items for the store.

The inspector, somewhat wary, handed Montoya over to female customs inspectors for a search. These agents noticed what the Supreme Court later referred to delicately as a "firm fullness" in Montoya's abdomen. Suspicions, already high, increased. The agents applied for a court order to conduct pregnancy tests, X-rays, and other examinations, and eventually they found 88 balloons containing 80 percent pure cocaine in Montoya's alimentary canal.

Montoya's lawyer argued that this constituted unreasonable search and seizure and that her arrest and conviction should be set aside. There was, he said, no direct evidence that would have led the officials to suspect cocaine smuggling. The government argued that the arrest had followed from a set of odd facts leading to reasonable suspicion that something was amiss.

You Be the Judge: Was Montoya's arrest based on a search-and-seizure incident that violated the Fourth Amendment?

Answer: Justice Rehnquist wrote the majority opinion, holding that U.S. Customs agents were well within their constitutional authority to search Montoya. Even though collection of evidence took the better part of two days, Justice Rehnquist remarked wryly that "the rudimentary knowledge of the human body which judges possess in common with the rest of mankind tells us that alimentary canal smuggling cannot be detected in the amount of time in which other illegal activities may be investigated through brief . . . stops."

protect themselves from danger, Knowles presented no threat to the officer's safety and thus provided no justification for the intrusion of a search of his car.[62] Similarly, the Supreme Court prohibited highway checkpoints designed to detect ordinary criminal wrongdoing, such as possessing illegal drugs,[63] and it ruled that an anonymous tip that a person is carrying a gun is not sufficient justification for a police officer to stop and frisk that person.[64] In addition, the Court found that police use of a thermal imaging device to detect abnormal heat (needed for growing marijuana) in a home violated the Fourth Amendment.[65]

The *USA Patriot Act*, passed just six weeks after the September 11, 2001, terrorist attacks, gave the government broad new powers for the wiretapping, surveillance, and investigation of terrorism suspects. Attorney General John Ashcroft also eased restrictions on domestic spying in counterterrorism operations, allowing agents to monitor political or religious groups without any connection to a criminal investigation. The Patriot Act gave the federal government the power to examine a terrorist suspect's records held by a third parties such as doctors, libraries, bookstores, universities, and Internet service providers. It also allowed searches of private property without probable cause and without notice to the owner until after the search had been executed, limiting a person's opportunities to challenge a search. In December 2005, reports revealed that the president had ordered the National Security Agency, without the court-approved warrants ordinarily required for domestic spying, to monitor the international telephone calls and e-mail messages of people inside the United States. Such broad powers have concerned those at both ends of the political spectrum and are sure to invite Supreme Court decisions.

The Patriot Act

Self-Incrimination

In the American system, the burden of proof rests on the police and the prosecutors. Suspects cannot be forced to help with their own conviction by, say, blurting out a confession in the stationhouse. The ***Fifth Amendment*** forbids forced **self-incrimination**, stating that no person "shall be compelled to be a witness against himself." Whether in a congressional hearing, a courtroom, or a police station, suspects need not provide evidence that can later be used against them. Under law, though, the government may guarantee suspects *immunity*—exemption from prosecution in exchange for suspects' testimony regarding their own and others' misdeeds.

Fifth Amendment
The constitutional amendment designed to protect the rights of persons accused of crimes, including protection against double jeopardy, **self-incrimination,** and punishment without due process of law.

self-incrimination
The situation occurring when an individual accused of a crime is compelled to be a witness against himself or herself in court. The **Fifth Amendment** forbids self-incrimination.

Miranda v. Arizona
The 1966 Supreme Court decision that sets guidelines for police questioning of accused persons to protect them against **self-incrimination** and to protect their right to counsel.

You have probably seen television shows in which an arrest is made and the arresting officers recite, often from memory, a set of rights to the arrestee. These rights are authentic and originate from a famous court decision—perhaps the most important modern decision in criminal law.[66]

Ernesto Miranda was picked up as a prime suspect in the rape and kidnapping of an 18-year-old girl. Identified by the girl from a police lineup, Miranda was questioned for two hours. During this time, he was told of neither his constitutional right against self-incrimination nor his right to counsel. He said enough to lead eventually to a conviction. The Supreme Court reversed his conviction on appeal, however. In ***Miranda v. Arizona*** (1966), the Court established guidelines for police questioning. Suspects must be told the following:

- That they have a constitutional right to remain silent and may stop answering questions at any time
- That what they say can be used against them in a court of law
- That they have a right to have a lawyer present during questioning and that the court will provide an attorney if they cannot afford their own lawyer

In the decades since the *Miranda* decision, the Supreme Court has made a number of exceptions to its requirements. In 1991, for example, the Court held that a coerced confession introduced in a trial does not automatically taint a conviction. If other evidence is enough for a conviction, then the coerced confession is a "harmless error" that does not necessitate a new trial.[67] Nevertheless, in 2000 in *Dickerson v. United States,* the Court made it clear that it supported *Miranda* and that Congress was not empowered to change it.

YOU ARE THE JUDGE

The Case of the Dirty Old Man

In 1984, Keith Jacobson, a 56-year-old farmer who supported his elderly father in Nebraska, ordered two magazines and a brochure from a California adult bookstore. He expected nude photographs of adult males but instead found photographs of nude boys. He ordered no other magazines.

Three months later the current federal law was changed to make the receipt of such materials illegal. Finding his name on the mailing list of the California bookstore, two government agencies repeatedly enticed Jacobson through five fictitious organizations and a bogus pen pal with solicitations for sexually explicit photographs of children. After 26 months of enticement, Jacobson finally ordered a magazine and was arrested for violating the Child Protection Act.

He was convicted of receiving child pornography through the mail, which he undoubtedly did. Jacobson claimed, however, that he had been entrapped into committing the crime.

You Be the Judge: Was Jacobson an innocent victim of police entrapment, or was he a dirty old man seeking child pornography?

Answer: The Court agreed with Jacobson. In *Jacobson v. United States* (1992), it ruled that the government had overstepped the line between setting a trap for the "unwary innocent" and the "unwary criminal" and failed to establish that Jacobson was independently predisposed to commit the crime for which he was arrested. Jacobson's conviction was overturned.

The Fifth Amendment prohibits not only coerced confessions but also coerced crimes. The courts have overturned convictions based on *entrapment*—when law enforcement officials encourage persons to commit crimes (such as accepting bribes or purchasing illicit drugs) that they otherwise would not commit. "You Are the Judge: The Case of the Dirty Old Man" addresses this issue.

Sixth Amendment
The constitutional amendment designed to protect individuals accused of crimes. It includes the right to counsel, the right to confront witnesses, and the right to a speedy and public trial.

Gideon v. Wainwright
The 1963 Supreme Court decision holding that anyone accused of a felony where imprisonment may be imposed, however poor he or she might be, has a right to a lawyer.

The Right to Counsel

One of the most important of the *Miranda* rights is the right to secure counsel. Although the ***Sixth Amendment*** has always ensured the right to be represented by an attorney in federal courts, this right was not extended to people tried in state courts until the 1960s. Until the 1930s, individuals were tried and sometimes convicted for capital offenses (those in which the death penalty could be imposed) without a lawyer. In 1932, the Supreme Court ordered the states to provide an attorney for indigent (poor) defendants accused of a capital crime (*Powell v. Alabama*).

Most crimes are not capital crimes, however, and most crimes are tried in state courts. It was not until 1963, in ***Gideon v. Wainwright***,[68] that the Supreme Court extended the right to an attorney for everyone accused of a felony in a state court. Subsequently, the Court went a step further than *Gideon* and held that whenever imprisonment could be imposed, a lawyer must be provided for the accused (*Argersinger v. Hamlin* [1972]). In addition, the Supreme Court found that a trial court's erroneous deprivation of a criminal defendant's *choice* of counsel entitles him to reversal of his conviction.[69]

Trials

Television's portrayal of courts and trials is almost as dramatic as its portrayal of detectives and police officers—both often vary from reality. If you visit a typical American criminal courtroom, you will rarely see a trial complete with judge and jury. In American courts, 90 percent of all cases begin and end with a guilty plea. Most cases are settled through a process called **plea bargaining**. A plea bargain results from a bargain struck between a defendant's lawyer and a prosecutor to the effect that a defendant will plead guilty to a lesser crime (or fewer crimes) in exchange for a state's not prosecuting that defendant for a more serious (or additional) crime.

plea bargaining
A bargain struck between the defendant's lawyer and the prosecutor to the effect that the defendant will plead guilty to a lesser crime or fewer crimes in exchange for the state's promise not to prosecute the defendant for a more serious crime or additional crimes.

Critics of the plea-bargaining system believe it permits many criminals to avoid the full punishment they deserve. However, the process works to the advantage of both sides; it saves the state the time and money that would otherwise be spent on a trial, and it permits defendants who think they might be convicted of a serious charge to plead guilty to a lesser one.

Whether plea bargaining serves the ends of justice is much debated. To its critics, plea bargaining benefits defendants. A study of sentencing patterns in three California counties discovered that a larger proportion of defendants who went to trial (rather than plea bargained) ended up going to prison compared with those who pleaded guilty and had no trial. In answer to their question "Does it pay to plead guilty?" the researchers gave a qualified yes.[70] Good or bad, plea bargaining is a practical necessity. Only by a vast increase in resources could the court system cope with a trial for every defendant.

The defendants in the 300,000 cases per year that actually go to trial are entitled to many rights, including the Sixth Amendment's provision for a speedy trial by an impartial jury. An impartial jury includes one that is not racially biased.[71] The Constitution does not specify the size of a jury; in principle, it could be anywhere from 1 to 100 people. Tradition in England and America has set jury size at 12, although in petty cases six jurors are sometimes used. Whereas traditionally a jury had to be unanimous in order to convict, the Supreme Court eroded those traditions, permitting states to use fewer than 12 jurors and to convict with a less-than-unanimous vote. Federal courts still employ juries of 12 persons and require unanimous votes for a criminal conviction.

In recent years the Supreme Court has aggressively defended the jury's role in the criminal justice process—and limited the discretion of judges in sentencing. In several cases the Court has held that other than a previous conviction, any fact that increases the penalty for a crime beyond the prescribed statutory maximum or even the ordinary range must be submitted to a jury and proved beyond a reasonable doubt.[72] These decisions ensure that the judge's authority to sentence derives wholly from the jury's verdict.

The Sixth Amendment (and the protection against the suspension of the writ of *habeas corpus*) also guarantees that persons who are arrested have a right to be brought before a judge. This occurs at two stages of the judicial process. First, those detained have a right to be informed of the accusations against them. Second, they have a right to a *speedy and public trial.* Normally, these guarantees present few issues. However, in the aftermath of the September 11, 2001, terrorist attacks, the FBI detained more than 1,200 persons as possible dangers to national security. Of these persons, 762 were illegal aliens (mostly Arabs and Muslims), and many of them languished in jail for months until cleared by the FBI.

For the first time in U.S. history, the federal government withheld the names of detainees, reducing their opportunities to exercise their rights to access to the courts and to counsel. The government argued that releasing the names and details of those arrested would give terrorists a window on the terror investigation. In 2004, the Supreme Court refused to consider whether the government properly withheld names and other details about these prisoners. However, in other cases the Court found that detainees held both in the United States and at the naval base at Guantánamo Bay, Cuba, had the right to challenge their detention before a judge or other neutral decision maker (*Hamdi v. Rumsfeld* and *Rasul v. Bush* [2004]).

Balancing Liberty and Security in a Time of War

In addition, defendants have the right to confront the witnesses against them. The Supreme Court has held that testimony cannot be introduced into a trial unless the witness can be cross-examined by the accused (*Crawford v. Washington* [2004]).

In an historic decision in 2006 (*Hamdan V. Rumsfeld*), the Supreme Court held that the procedures President Bush had approval for trying prisoners at Guantánamo Bay lacked congressional authorization and violated both the Uniform code of Military Justice and the Geneva Conventions. The flaws the Court cited were the failure to guarantee defendants the right to attend their trial and the prosecution's ablity under the rules to introduce hearsay evidence, unsworn testimony, and evidence obtained through coercion. Equally important, the Constitution did not empower the president to establish judical procedures on his own.

Eighth Amendment
The constitutional amendment that forbids **cruel and unusual punishment,** although it does not define this phrase. Through the **Fourteenth Amendment,** this **Bill of Rights** provision applies to the states.

cruel and unusual punishment
Court sentences prohibited by the **Eighth Amendment**. Although the Supreme Court has ruled that mandatory death sentences for certain offenses are unconstitutional, it has not held that the death penalty itself constitutes cruel and unusual punishment.

Cruel and Unusual Punishment

Citizens convicted of a crime can expect some punishment ranging from mild to severe, the mildest being some form of probation and the most severe, of course, being the death penalty. The ***Eighth Amendment*** forbids **cruel and unusual punishment**, although it does not define the phrase. Through the Fourteenth Amendment, this provision of the Bill of Rights applies to the states.

Almost the entire constitutional debate over cruel and unusual punishment has centered on the death penalty (an exception can be found in "You Are the Judge: The Case of the First Offender"). About 3,600 people are currently on death row, about a quarter of them in Florida and Texas. In 1968, the Court overturned a death sentence because opponents of the death penalty had been excluded from the jury at sentencing (*Witherspoon v. Illinois*), a factor that stacked the cards, said the Court, in favor of the extreme penalty.

The Court first confronted the question of whether the death penalty is inherently cruel and unusual punishment in *Furman v. Georgia* (1972). Although

YOU ARE THE JUDGE

The Case of the First Offender

Ronald Harmelin of Detroit was convicted of possessing 672 grams of cocaine (a gram is about one-thirtieth of an ounce). Michigan's mandatory sentencing law required the trial judge to sentence Harmelin, a first-time offender, to life imprisonment without possibility of parole. Harmelin argued that this was cruel and unusual punishment because it was "significantly disproportionate," meaning that, as we might say, the punishment did not fit the crime. Harmelin's lawyers argued that many other crimes more serious than cocaine possession would net similar sentences.

You Be the Judge: Was Harmelin's sentence cruel and unusual punishment?

Answer: The Court upheld Harmelin's conviction in *Harmelin v. Michigan* (1991), spending many pages to explain that severe punishments were quite commonplace, especially when the Bill of Rights was written. Severity alone does not qualify a punishment as "cruel and unusual." The severity of punishment was up to the legislature of Michigan, which, the justices observed, knew better than they the conditions on the streets of Detroit.

Furman sent a message, it was a confusing one. Four justices said that the death penalty was not cruel and unusual punishment, yet the Court overturned Georgia's death penalty law because its imposition was "freakish" and "random." Warned by *Furman*, 35 states passed new laws permitting the death penalty. Some states, to prevent arbitrariness in punishment, went to the other extreme, mandating death penalties for some crimes. In *Woodson v. North Carolina* (1976), the Supreme Court ruled against mandatory death penalties.

Since then the Court has come down more clearly on the side of the death penalty. Troy Gregg had murdered two hitchhikers and was awaiting execution in Georgia's state prison. Gregg's attorney argued that the death penalty was cruel and unusual punishment. In ***Gregg v. Georgia*** (1976), the Court disagreed. "Capital punishment," it said, "is an expression of society's outrage at particularly offensive conduct. . . . It is an extreme sanction, suitable to the most extreme of crimes." Even though not everyone committing the same crime is equally likely to receive the death penalty, the Supreme Court held in ***McCleskey v. Kemp*** (1987) that the death penalty did not violate the equal protection of the law guaranteed by the Fourteenth Amendment.

Today, the death penalty is a part of the American criminal justice system, and more than 1,000 persons have been executed since the Court's decision in *Gregg*. The Court has also made it more difficult for death row prisoners to file petitions that would force legal delays and appeals to stave off their appointed executions, and it has allowed "victim impact" statements detailing the character of murder victims and their families' suffering to be used against a defendant.

Not everyone is convinced about the fairness of the death penalty, however.[73] You can read about litigation over the past generation in "A Generation of Change:

Gregg v. Georgia

The 1976 Supreme Court decision that upheld the constitutionality of the death penalty, stating, "It is an extreme sanction, suitable to the most extreme of crimes." The court did not, therefore, conclude that the death sentence constitutes **cruel and unusual punishment.**

McCleskey v. Kemp

The 1987 Supreme Court decision that upheld the constitutionality of the death penalty against charges that it violated the **Fourteenth Amendment** because minority defendants were more likely to receive the death penalty than were White defendants.

YOUNG PEOPLE AND POLITICS

College Students Help Prevent Wrongful Deaths

The Center on Wrongful Convictions at Northwestern University investigates possible wrongful convictions and represents imprisoned clients with claims of actual innocence. The young staff, including faculty, cooperating outside attorneys, and Northwestern University law students, pioneered the investigation and litigation of wrongful convictions—including the cases of nine innocent men sentenced to death in Illinois.

Undergraduates as well as law students have been involved in establishing the innocence of men who had been condemned to die. One instance involved the case of a man with an IQ of 51. The Illinois Supreme Court stayed his execution, just 48 hours before it was due to be carried out, because of questions about his mental fitness. This stay provided a professor and students from a Northwestern University investigative journalism class an opportunity to investigate the man's guilt.

They tracked down and reinterviewed witnesses. One eyewitness recanted his testimony, saying that investigators had pressured him into implicating the man. The students found a woman who pointed to her ex-husband as the killer. Then a private investigator interviewed the ex-husband, who made a videotaped statement claiming he killed in self-defense. The students literally helped to save the life of an innocent man.

On January 11, 2003, Governor George H. Ryan of Illinois chose Lincoln Hall at Northwestern University's School of Law to make an historic announcement. He commuted the death sentences of all 167 death row prisoners in Illinois (he also pardoned four others based on innocence the previous day). The governor felt it was fitting to make the announcement there before "the students, teachers, lawyers, and investigators who first shed light on the sorrowful conditions of Illinois' death penalty system."

In addition to saving the lives of wrongfully convicted individuals in Illinois, the Northwestern investigations have also helped trigger a nationwide reexamination of the capital punishment system. To learn more about the Center on Wrongful Convictions, visit its Web site at *www.law.northwestern.edu/wrongfulconvictions/*.

Questions for Discussion

- Why do you think college students and others were able to determine the truth about the innocence of condemned men better than the police and prosecuters at the original trials?
- Are there other areas of public life in which students can make important contributions through their investigations?

Contesting the Death Penalty," and you can see what some students are doing about what they see as the injustices in the death penalty system in "Young People and Politics: College Students Help Prevent Wrongful Deaths."

The Right to Privacy

The members of the First Congress who drafted the Bill of Rights and enshrined American civil liberties would never have imagined that Americans would go to court to argue about wiretapping, surrogate motherhood, abortion, or pornography. New technologies have raised ethical issues unimaginable in the eighteenth century. Today, one of the greatest debates concerning Americans' civil liberties lies in the emerging area of privacy rights.

A GENERATION OF CHANGE

Contesting the Death Penalty

The death penalty has been a long-running concern of those interested in criminal justice. Most Americans support it. On the other hand, the European Union prohibits it in member countries. We saw in Chapter 3 that 12 states and the District of Columbia have eliminated it altogether, and the courts in many other states rarely sentence a defendant to death.

Shortly before retiring from the bench in 1994, Supreme Court Justice Harry Blackmun declared that the administration of the death penalty "fails to deliver the fair, consistent and reliable sentences of death required by the Constitution" (*Callins v. Callins* [1994]).[79] Social scientists have shown that minority defendants and murderers whose victims were White are more likely to receive death sentences than are White murderers or those whose victims were not White. For example, about 80% of the murder victims in cases resulting in an execution were White, even though only 50% of murder victims generally are White.

Nevertheless, in *McCleskey v. Kemp* (1987), the Supreme Court concluded that the death penalty did not violate the equal protection of the law guaranteed by the Fourteenth Amendment. The Court insisted that the unequal distribution of death penalty sentences was constitutionally acceptable because there was no evidence that juries intended to discriminate on the basis of race. The Court, it seemed, had made a final determination about the constitutional validity of the death penalty.

In recent years, however, evidence that courts have sentenced innocent people to be executed has reinvigorated the debate over the death penalty. Attorneys have employed the new technology of DNA evidence in a number of states to obtain the release of dozens of death row prisoners. Governor George Ryan of Illinois declared a moratorium on executions in his state after researchers proved that 13 people on death row were innocent. Later, he commuted the death sentences of all prisoners in the state.

In addition, in 2002 the Supreme Court took another look at the application of the death penalty. In *Atkins v. Virginia*, the Court prohibited the execution of mentally retarded persons. In 2005, the Court limited the application of the death penalty further when it overturned a 1989 decision and held in *Roper v. Simmons* that the Eighth and Fourteenth Amendments forbid the death penalty for offenders who were under the age of 18 when their crimes were committed. In addition, the Court has required that a jury, not just a judge, find an aggravating circumstance necessary for imposition of the death penalty (*Ring v. Arizona*). The Court also required lawyers for defendants in death penalty cases to make reasonable efforts to fight for their clients at a trial's sentencing phase (*Rompilla v. Beard* [2005]).

These decisions mark important changes over the past generation, although they did not focus on the fundamental principle of the constitutionality of the death penalty. Nevertheless, Supreme Court decisions, new DNA technology, and perhaps a growing public concern about the fairness of the death penalty have resulted in the number of death sentences dropping dramatically—from 300 in 1998 to 96 in 2005.

YEAR	DEATH SENTENCES	EXECUTIONS
1998	300	68
1999	276	98
2000	232	85
2001	163	66
2002	168	71
2003	152	65
2004	124	59
2005	96	60

Source: Death Penalty Information Center.

Is There a Right to Privacy?

Nowhere does the Bill of Rights say that Americans have a **right to privacy**. Clearly, however, the First Congress had the concept of privacy in mind when it crafted the first 10 amendments. Freedom of religion implies the right to exercise private

right to privacy
The right to a private personal life free from the intrusion of government.

beliefs, protections against "unreasonable searches and seizures" make persons secure in their homes, and private property cannot be seized without "due process of law." In 1928, Justice Brandeis hailed privacy as "the right to be left alone—the most comprehensive of the rights and the most valued by civilized men."

The idea that the Constitution guarantees a right to privacy was first enunciated in a 1965 case involving the conviction of a doctor and a family planning specialist for disseminating birth control devices in violation of a little-used Connecticut law. The state reluctantly brought them to court, and they were convicted. After wrestling with the privacy issue in *Griswold v. Connecticut*, seven Supreme Court justices finally decided that various portions of the Bill of Rights cast "penumbras" (or shadows)—unstated liberties implied by the explicitly stated rights—protecting a right to privacy, including a right to family planning between husband and wife. Supporters of privacy rights argued that this ruling was a reasonable interpretation of the Fourth Amendment. Critics of the ruling—and there were many of them—claimed that the Supreme Court was inventing protections not specified by the Constitution.

The most important application of privacy rights, however, came not in the area of birth control but in the area of abortion. The Supreme Court unleashed a constitutional firestorm in 1973 that has not yet abated.

Controversy over Abortion

In the summer of 1972, Supreme Court Justice Harry Blackmun returned to Minnesota's famous Mayo Clinic, where he had once served as general counsel. The clinic lent him a tiny desk in the corner of a librarian's office, where he worked quietly for two weeks. His research during this short summer vacation focused on the medical aspects of abortion. The Court had assigned Blackmun the task of writing the majority opinion in one of the most controversial cases ever to come before the Court. Under the pseudonym of "Jane Roe," a Texas woman named Norma McCorvey sought an abortion. She argued that the state law allowing the procedure only to save the life of a mother was unconstitutional. Texas argued that states had the power to regulate moral behavior, including abortions.

Roe v. Wade
The 1973 Supreme Court decision holding that a state ban on all abortions was unconstitutional. The decision forbade state control over abortions during the first trimester of pregnancy, permitted states to limit abortions to protect the mother's health in the second trimester, and permitted states to protect the fetus during the third trimester.

The opinion in ***Roe v. Wade*** (1973) followed medical authorities in dividing pregnancy into three equal trimesters. *Roe* forbade any state control of abortions during the first trimester; it permitted states to regulate abortion procedures, but only in a way that protected the mother's health, in the second trimester; and it allowed the states to ban abortion during the third trimester, except when the mother's life or health was in danger. This decision unleashed a storm of protest. The Court's staff needed extra mailboxes to handle the correspondence, some of which contained death threats.[74] Eventually, states adjusted to the new decision, doctors and hospitals cooperated, and, however awkward the reasoning or controversial the result, the decision governed public policy. Since *Roe v. Wade*, about 1.5 million legal abortions have been performed annually.

Yet the furor has never subsided. Congress has passed numerous statutes forbidding the use of federal funds for abortions. Many states have passed similar restrictions. Missouri went as far as any other state, forbidding the use of state funds or state employees to perform abortions. A clinic in St. Louis challenged the law as unconstitutional, but in *Webster v. Reproductive Health Services* (1989), the Court upheld the law. It has also upheld laws requiring minors to notify one or both parents or a judge before obtaining an abortion.

In 1991, the conservative Court went even further in upholding restrictions on abortions. In *Rust v. Sullivan,* the Court found that a Department of Health and Human Services ruling—specifying that family planning services receiving federal funds could not provide women any counseling regarding abortion—was constitutional. This decision was greeted by a public outcry that the rule would deny many poor women abortion counseling and limit the First Amendment right of a medical practitioner to counsel a client. On his third day in office, President Clinton lifted the ban on abortion counseling.

In 1992, in ***Planned Parenthood v. Casey,*** the Court changed its standard for evaluating restrictions on abortion from one of "strict scrutiny" of any restraints on a "fundamental right" to one of "undue burden" that permits considerably more regulation. The Court upheld a 24-hour waiting period, a parental or judicial consent requirement for minors, and a requirement that doctors present women with information on the risks of the operation. The Court struck down a provision requiring a married woman to tell her husband of her intent to have an abortion. At the same time, the majority also affirmed their commitment to the basic right of a woman to obtain an abortion. In 2000, the Court held in *Sternberg v. Carhart* that Nebraska's prohibition of "partial birth" abortions was unconstitutional because it placed an undue burden on women seeking an abortion by limiting their options to less safe procedures and because the law provided no exception for cases where the health of the mother was at risk. In 2003, Congress passed a law banning partial birth abortions. It remains to be seen whether the Court will uphold it.

Planned Parenthood v. Casey

A 1992 case in which the Supreme Court loosened its standard for evaluating restrictions on abortion from one of "strict scrutiny" of any restraints on a "fundamental right" to one of "undue burden" that permits considerably more regulation.

Americans are deeply divided on the issue of abortion. Proponents of choice believe that access to abortion is essential if women are to be fully autonomous human beings. Opponents call themselves pro-life because they believe that the fetus is fully human; therefore, an abortion deprives a fetus of the right to life. These positions are irreconcilable, making abortion a politician's nightmare. Wherever a politician stands on this divisive issue, a large number of voters will be enraged.

Abortion

Because passions run so strongly on the issue, advocates may take extreme action. In the last two decades abortion opponents have bombed a number of abortion clinics, and they murdered two physicians who performed abortions in Pensacola, Florida.

Efforts to protect women's access to clinics sometimes clash with protesters' rights to free speech and assembly. In 1994, the Court consolidated the right to abortion established in *Roe* with the protection of a woman's right to enter an abortion clinic to exercise that right. Citing the government's interest in preserving order and maintaining women's access to pregnancy services, the Court upheld a state court's order of a 36-foot buffer zone around a clinic in Melbourne, Florida.[75] That same year Congress passed the Freedom of Access to Clinic Entrances Act, which makes it a federal crime to intimidate abortion providers or women seeking abortions. In 2000, it upheld a 100-foot restriction on approaching someone at a health care facility to discourage abortions.[76] In another case, the Court decided that abortion clinics could invoke the federal racketeering law to sue violent antiabortion protest groups for damages.[77]

Passions sometimes rule in the debate over abortion. Paul Hill went so far as to murder a physician who performed abortions, arguing that he had a right to do so to save the lives of the unborn. The jury did not agree, and Hill was sentenced to death.

Understanding Civil Liberties

American government is both democratic and constitutional. America is democratic because it is governed by officials who are elected by the people and, as such, are accountable for their actions. The American government is constitutional because it has a fundamental organic law, the Constitution, that limits the things government may do. By restricting the government, the Constitution limits what the people can empower the government to do. The democratic and constitutional components of government can produce conflicts, but they also reinforce one another.

Civil Liberties and Democracy

The rights ensured by the First Amendment—the freedoms of speech, press, and assembly—are essential to a democracy. If people are to govern themselves, they need access to all available information and opinions in order to make intelligent, responsible, and accountable decisions. If the right to participate in public life is to be open to all, then Americans—in all their diversity—must have the right to express their opinions.

Individual participation and the expression of ideas are crucial components of democracy, but so is majority rule, which can conflict with individual rights. The majority does not have the freedom to decide that there are some ideas it would rather not hear, although at times the majority tries to enforce its will on the minority. The conflict is even sharper in relation to the rights guaranteed by the Fourth,

Fifth, Sixth, Seventh, and Eighth Amendments. These rights protect all Americans, but they also make it more difficult to punish criminals. It is easy—though misleading—for the majority to view these guarantees as benefits for criminals at the expense of society.

With some notable exceptions, the United States has done a good job in protecting the rights of diverse interests to express themselves. There is little danger that a political or economic elite will muffle dissent. Similarly, the history of the past five decades is one of increased protections for defendants' rights, and defendants are typically not among the elite. Ultimately, the courts have decided what constitutional guarantees mean in practice. Although federal judges, appointed for life, are not directly accountable to popular will,[78] "elitist" courts have often protected civil liberties from the excesses of majority rule.

Civil Liberties and the Scope of Government

Civil liberties in America are both the foundation for and a reflection of our emphasis on individualism. When there is a conflict between an individual or a group attempting to express themselves or worship as they please and an effort by a government to constrain them in some fashion, the individual or group usually wins. If protecting the freedom of an individual or group to express themselves results in inconvenience or even injustice for the public officials they criticize or the populace they wish to reach, so be it. Every nation must choose where to draw the line between freedom and order. In the United States, we generally choose liberty.

Today's government is huge and commands vast, powerful technologies. Americans' Social Security numbers, credit cards, driver's licenses, and school records are all on giant computers to which the government has immediate access. It is virtually impossible to hide from the police, the FBI, the Internal Revenue Service, or any governmental agency. Because Americans can no longer avoid the attention of government, strict limitations on governmental power are essential. The Bill of Rights provides these vital limitations.

Thus, in general, civil liberties limit the scope of government. Yet substantial government efforts are often required to protect the expansion of rights that we have witnessed thus far. Those seeking abortions may need help reaching a clinic, defendants may demand that lawyers be provided them at public expense, advocates of unpopular causes may require police protection, and litigants in complex lawsuits over matters of birth or death may rely on judges to resolve their conflicts. It is ironic—but true—that an expansion of freedom may require a simultaneous expansion of government.

Summary

Civil liberties are an individual's protection against the government. The Bill of Rights makes it clear that American government is a constitutional democracy in which individual rights limit government. Disputes about civil liberties are frequent because the issues involved are complex and divisive. Legislatures and courts are constantly defining in practice what the Bill of Rights guarantees in theory.

In a way, the notion that government can protect people from government is contradictory. Thomas Jefferson wrote in the Declaration of Independence that all people "are endowed by their creator with certain unalienable rights." Jefferson's next "self-evident truth" was that "to secure these rights, governments are instituted." People, said Jefferson, do not get their rights from government. Instead, rights precede government, which then gets its power to rule from the people. The Bill of Rights does not give Americans freedom of religion or the right to a fair trial; these amendments merely recognize that these rights exist. People often speak, however, as though rights are things that government gives them.

The First Amendment guarantees freedoms of religion, expression, and assembly. The Bill of Rights also contains protections that are especially important to those accused or convicted of crimes. Together, these rights provide Americans with more liberty than that enjoyed by most other people on Earth.

One task that government must perform is to resolve conflicts between rights. Often, First Amendment rights and rights at the bar of justice exist in uneasy tension; a newspaper's right to inform its readers may conflict with a person's right to a fair trial. Today, the Supreme Court has extended to the states most of the rights enjoyed under the U.S. Constitution.

Today's technologies raise key questions about ethics and the Constitution. Although the Constitution does not specifically mention a right to privacy, the Supreme Court found this right implied by several guarantees in the Bill of Rights. The most controversial application of privacy rights has been in abortion cases.

Internet Resources

www.freedomforum.org
Background information and recent news on First Amendment issues.

www.eff.org
Web site concerned with protecting online civil liberties.

www.aclu.org
Home page of the American Civil Liberties Union offering links to many other sites concerned with civil liberties.

www.firstamendmentcenter.org/rel_liberty/overview.aspx
Overview of freedom of religion in the United States.

www.law.cornell.edu/wex/index.php/Criminal_law
The text of the landmark cases on criminal justice and background material.

www.law.cornell.edu/wex/index.php/First_amendment
The text of the landmark cases on freedom of religion, speech, press, and assembly and background material.

www.cc.org/
Christian Coalition home page containing background information and discussion of current events.

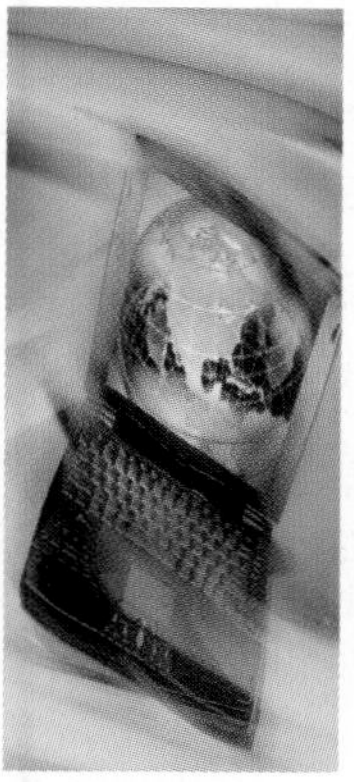

Get Connected

The Bill of Rights and the Pledge of Allegiance

The U.S. Constitution did not originally include basic civil liberties such as those found in the Bill of Rights. In fact, as the text notes, the states made inclusion of the Bill of Rights a condition for ratification of the Constitution. The United States was the first nation to guarantee these basic rights to its citizens. The First Amendment provides that "Congress shall make no law respecting an establishment of religion, or prohibiting the free exercise thereof. . ." In its 2003–2004 term, the U.S. Supreme Court was asked to decide a case, *Elk Grove v. Newdow,* in which a man challenged the inclusion of the words "under God" in the Pledge of Allegiance. The Court ultimately held that the man bringing the case, Dr. Newdow, did not have legal standing to sue, but a similar case is likely in the near future.

Search the Web

After reviewing the U.S. Bill of Rights in the Appendix, visit the Pledge of Allegiance Resource page at the Pew Forum on Religion and Public Life, *http://pewforum.org/religion-schools/pledge/*. Read the summary of the case's progress through the federal judicial system, then scroll down to the list of *amicus* briefs. Click on several of the *amicus* briefs in support of the petitioner and several in support of the respondent. The briefs' arguments usually are summarized in the "Interest of Amicus" section near the beginning of each document.

Questions to Ask

- In your opinion, should people, especially children, be forced to repeat a pledge that violates their beliefs? What if the pledge violates their parents' beliefs—or one of their parent's beliefs?
- After reading several of the *amicus* briefs, why did some of the people and groups think "under God" should be removed from the Pledge?
- Why did other groups think "under God" should stay in the Pledge of Allegiance?
- Do the words "under God" in the Pledge of Allegiance violate the First Amendment? Why or why not?

Why It Matters

Any survey of the world shows that religion is a source of intense conflict, often within a single nation. The Bill of Rights guarantees American citizens certain protections from government, including against the establishment of religion. The question is how to prevent the establishment of religion without restricting the free exercise of religion. It is important—but often difficult—to draw the line properly between government neutrality toward religion on the one hand and government support of it on the other.

Get Involved

Examine some of the other religious liberty cases identified on the Pew Forum's Religion and Public Schools Issues page to compare the Pledge case with previous cases.

For more exercises, go to www.longmanamericangovernment.com.

For Further Reading

Adler, Renata. *Reckless Disregard.* New York: Knopf, 1986. The story of two monumental conflicts between free press and individual reputations.

Baker, Liva. *Miranda: The Crime, the Law, the Politics.* New York: Atheneum, 1983. An excellent book-length treatment of one of the major criminal cases of our time.

Craig, Barbara Hickson, and David M. O'Brien. *Abortion and American Politics.* Chatham, NJ: Chatham House, 1993. Provides a history of the abortion issue since 1973.

Garrow, David J. *Liberty and Sexuality.* New York: Macmillan, 1994. The most thorough treatment of the development of the law on the right to privacy and abortion.

Heymann, Philip B. *Terrorism, Freedom, and Security.* Cambridge, MA: MIT Press, 2004. Thoughtfully balances concerns for freedom with those of safety from terrorism.

Irons, Peter. *The Courage of Their Convictions: Sixteen Americans Who Fought Their Way to the Supreme Court.* New York: Penguin Books, 1990. Accounts of 16 Americans over a period of 50 years who took their cases to the Supreme Court in defense of civil liberties.

Levy, Leonard W. *The Emergence of a Free Press.* New York: Oxford University Press, 1985. A major work on the framers' intentions regarding freedom of expression.

Levy, Leonard W. *The Establishment Clause: Religion and the First Amendment.* New York: Macmillan, 1986. The author argues that it is unconstitutional for government to provide aid to any religion.

Lewis, Anthony. *Make No Law: The Sullivan Case and the First Amendment.* New York: Random House, 1991. A well-written story of the key case regarding American libel law and an excellent case study of a Supreme Court case.

Rosenblatt, Roger. *Life Itself: Abortion in the American Mind.* New York: Random House, 1992. The author seeks to reconcile the clash of absolutes in the abortion controversy with scholarly analysis and interview data.

Civil Rights

Chapter Outline

POLITICS IN ACTION: LAUNCHING THE CIVIL RIGHTS MOVEMENT A 42-year-old seamstress named Rosa Parks was riding in the "colored" section of a Montgomery, Alabama, city bus on December 1, 1955. A White man got on the bus and found that all the seats in the front, which were reserved for Whites, were taken. He moved on to the equally crowded colored section. J. F. Blake, the bus driver, then ordered all four passengers in the first row of the colored section to surrender their seats because the law prohibited Whites and African Americans from sitting next to or even across from one another.

Three of the African Americans hesitated and then complied with the driver's order. But Rosa Parks, a politically active member of the National Association for the Advancement of Colored People, said no. The driver threatened to have her arrested, but she refused to move. He then called the police, and a few minutes later two officers boarded the bus and arrested her.

At this moment the civil rights movement was born. There had been substantial efforts—and some important successes—to use the courts to end racial segregation, but Rosa Parks's refusal to give up her seat led to extensive mobilization of African Americans. Protestors employed a wide range of methods to end segregation, including nonviolent resistance. A new preacher in town, Martin Luther King Jr. of Atlanta, organized a boycott of the city buses. He was jailed, his house was bombed, and his wife and infant daughter were almost killed, but neither he nor the African American community wavered. Although they were harassed by the police and went without motor transportation by walking or even riding mules, they persisted in boycotting the buses.

It eventually took the U.S. Supreme Court to end the boycott. On November 13, 1956, the Court declared that Alabama's state and local laws requiring segregation on buses were illegal. On December 20, federal injunctions were served on the city and bus company officials, forcing them to follow the Supreme Court's ruling.

On December 21, 1956, Rosa Parks boarded a Montgomery city bus for the first time in over a year. She could sit wherever she liked and chose a seat near the front.

Americans have never fully come to terms with equality. Most Americans favor equality in the abstract—a politician who advocated inequality would not attract many votes—yet the concrete struggle for equal rights under the Constitution has been our nation's most bitter battle. It pits person against person, as in the case of Rosa Parks and the nameless White passenger, and group against group. Those people who enjoy privileged positions in American society have been reluctant to give them up.

Individual liberty is central to democracy. So is a broad notion of equality, such as that implied by the concept of "one person, one vote." Sometimes these values conflict, as when individuals or a majority of the people want to act in a discriminatory fashion. How should we resolve such conflicts between liberty and equality? Can we have a democracy if some citizens do not enjoy basic rights to political participation or suffer discrimination in employment? Can we or should we try to remedy past discrimination against minorities and women?

In addition, many people have called on government to protect the rights of minorities and women, increasing the scope and power of government in the process. Ironically, this increase in government power is often used to *check* government, as when the federal courts restrict the actions of state legislatures. It is equally ironic that society's collective efforts to use government to protect civil rights are designed not to limit individualism but to enhance it, freeing people from suffering and from prejudice. But how far should government go in these efforts? Is an increase in the scope of government to protect some people's rights an unacceptable threat to the rights of yet other citizens?

---

civil rights
Policies designed to protect people against arbitrary or discriminatory treatment by government officials or individuals.

The phrase "all men are created equal" is at the heart of American political culture, yet implementing this principle has proved to be one of our nation's most enduring struggles. Throughout our history, issues involving African Americans, women, and other minorities have raised constitutional questions about slavery, segregation, equal pay, and a host of other issues. Their rallying cry has been **civil rights**, which are policies designed to protect people against arbitrary or discriminatory treatment by government officials or individuals.

The resulting controversies have been fought in the courts, Congress, and the bureaucracy, but the meaning of *equality* remains as elusive as it is divisive. Today's equality debates center on these key types of inequality in America:

- *Racial discrimination*. Two centuries of discrimination against racial minorities have produced historic Supreme Court and congressional policies that seek to eliminate racial discrimination from the constitutional fabric. Americans have yet to resolve issues such as the appropriate role of affirmative action programs, however.
- *Gender discrimination*. The role of women in American society has changed substantially since the 1700s. However, equal rights for women have yet to be constitutionally guaranteed. The Equal Rights Amendment was not ratified, and women continue to press for equality and to seek protection from sexual harassment.
- *Discrimination based on age, disability, sexual orientation, and other factors*. As America is "graying," older Americans are demanding a place under the civil rights umbrella. People with disabilities are among the newest claimants for civil rights. Also seeking constitutional protections against discrimination are groups such as gays and lesbians, people with acquired immunodeficiency syndrome (AIDS), and the homeless.

Racial Equality: Two Centuries of Struggle

The struggle for equality has been a persistent theme in our nation's history. Slaves sought freedom, free African Americans fought for the right to vote and to be treated as equals, women pursued equal participation in society, and the economically disadvantaged called for better treatment and economic opportunities. This fight for equality affects all Americans. Philosophically, the struggle involves defining the term *equality*. Constitutionally, it involves interpreting laws. Politically, it often involves power.

Conceptions of Equality

What does *equality* mean? Jefferson's statement in the Declaration of Independence that "all men are created equal" did not mean that he believed everybody was exactly alike or that there were no differences among human beings. Jefferson insisted throughout his long life that African Americans were genetically inferior to Whites. The Declaration went on to speak, however, of "inalienable rights" to which all were equally entitled. A belief in *equal rights* has often led to a belief in *equality of opportunity*; in other words, everyone should have the same chance. What individuals make of that equal chance depends on their abilities and efforts.

American society does not emphasize *equal results* or *equal rewards*; few Americans argue that everyone should earn the same salary or have the same amount of property. In some other countries, such as the Scandinavian nations, the government uses its taxing power to distribute resources much more equally than in the United States. These countries thus have much less poverty. On the other hand, critics of these more egalitarian countries often complain that emphasis on the equal distribution of resources stifles initiative and limits opportunity.

Early American Views of Equality

More than 200 years ago, Virginia lawyer Richard Bland proclaimed, "I am speaking of the rights of a people, rights imply equality." Bland's interpretation of the meaning of the American Revolution was not widely shared. Few colonists were eager to defend slavery, and the delegates to the Constitutional Convention did their best to avoid facing the tension between slavery and the principles of the Declaration of Independence. Women's rights got even less attention than slavery at the Convention. John Adams, for instance, was uncharacteristically hostile to his wife Abigail's feminist opinions. Abigail's claim that "if particular care and attention is not paid to the ladies, we are determined to foment a rebellion" prompted her husband to reply, "I cannot but laugh."[1]

Equality

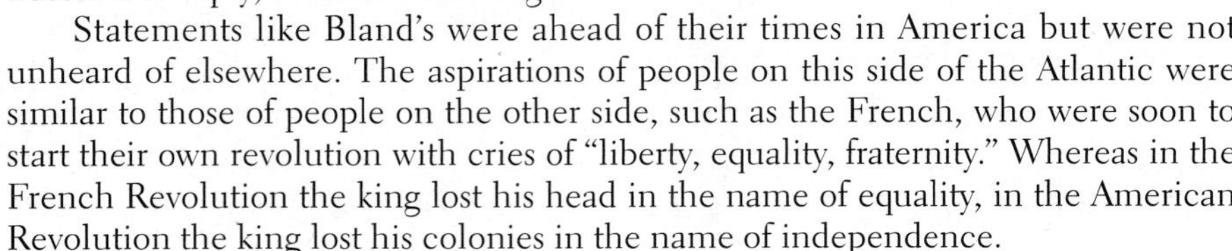

Statements like Bland's were ahead of their times in America but were not unheard of elsewhere. The aspirations of people on this side of the Atlantic were similar to those of people on the other side, such as the French, who were soon to start their own revolution with cries of "liberty, equality, fraternity." Whereas in the French Revolution the king lost his head in the name of equality, in the American Revolution the king lost his colonies in the name of independence.

The Constitution and Inequality

Perhaps the presence of conflicting views of equality in eighteenth-century America explains why the word *equality* does not appear in the original Constitution. In addition, America in 1787 was a place far different from contemporary America, with far different values. The privileged delegates to the Constitutional Convention would have been baffled, if not appalled, at discussions of equal rights for 12-year-old children, deaf students, gay soldiers, or female road dispatchers. The delegates created a plan for government, not guarantees of individual rights.

Not even the Bill of Rights mentions equality. It does, however, have implications for equality in that it does not limit the scope of its guarantees to specified groups within society. It does not say, for example, that only Whites have freedom from compulsory self-incrimination or that only men are entitled to freedom of speech. The First Amendment guarantees of freedom of expression, in particular, are important because they allow those who are discriminated against to work toward achieving equality. This kind of political activism, for instance, led to the constitutional amendment that enacted a guarantee of equality, the Fourteenth Amendment.

The first and only place in which the idea of equality appears in the Constitution is in the **Fourteenth Amendment**, one of the three amendments passed after the Civil War. (The Thirteenth abolishes slavery, and the Fifteenth extends the right to vote to African Americans.) The Fourteenth Amendment forbids

Fourteenth Amendment
The constitutional amendment adopted after the Civil War that states, "No State shall make or enforce any law which shall abridge the privileges or immunities of citizens of the United States; nor shall any state deprive any person of life, liberty, or property, without due process of law; nor deny to any person within its jurisdiction the **equal protection of the laws**." See also **due process clause**.

the states from denying to anyone "equal protection of the laws." Those five words represent the only reference to the idea of equality in the entire Constitution, yet within them was enough force to begin ensuring equal rights for all Americans. The full force of the amendment was not felt for nearly 100 years, for it was not until the mid-twentieth century that the Fourteenth Amendment was used as an instrument for unshackling disadvantaged groups. Once dismissed as "the traditional last resort of constitutional arguments," the equal protection clause now has few rivals in generating legal business for the Supreme Court.

But what does **equal protection of the laws** mean? The Fourteenth Amendment does not say that "the states must treat everybody exactly alike" or that "every state must promote equality among all its people." Presumably, it means, as one member of Congress said during the debate on the amendment, "equal protection of life, liberty, and property" for all. Thus, a state cannot confiscate an African American's property under the law while letting Whites keep theirs or otherwise give Whites privileges denied to African Americans. Some members of Congress interpreted the clause to be a much more lavish protection of rights than this interpretation. But shortly after the amendment was ratified in 1868, the narrow interpretation won out in the courts. In *Strauder v. West Virginia* (1880), the Supreme Court invalidated a law barring African Americans from jury service, but the Court refused to extend the amendment to remedy more subtle kinds of discrimination.

equal protection of the laws
Part of the **Fourteenth Amendment** emphasizing that the laws must provide equivalent "protection" to all people.

Over the past 100 years, however, the equal protection clause has become the vehicle for more expansive constitutional interpretations. In order to determine whether a particular form of discrimination is permissible, the Supreme Court developed three levels of scrutiny, or analysis, called standards of review (see Table 5.1). The Court has ruled that most classifications that are *reasonable*—that bear a rational relationship to some legitimate governmental purpose—are constitutional.

The African American struggle for equality paved the way for civil rights movements by women and other minorities. Here, civil rights leaders Roy Wilkins, James Farmer, Martin Luther King Jr., and Whitney Young meet with President Lyndon B. Johnson.

Table 5.1 Supreme Court's Standards for Classifications Under the Equal Protection Clause of the Fourteenth Amendment

BASIS OF CLASSIFICATION	STANDARD OF REVIEW	APPLYING THE TEST
Race	Inherently suspect (difficult to meet)	Is the classification necessary to accomplish a compelling governmental purpose and the least restrictive way to reach the goal?
Gender	Intermediate standard (moderately difficult to meet)	Does the classification bear a substantial relationship to an important governmental goal?
Other (age, wealth, etc.)	Reasonableness (easy to meet)	Does the classification have a rational relationship to a legitimate governmental goal?

The person who challenges these classifications has the burden of proving that they are arbitrary. Thus, for example, the states can restrict the right to vote to people over the age of 18; age is a reasonable classification and hence a permissible basis for determining who may vote. A classification that is arbitrary—a law singling out, say, people with red hair or blue eyes for inferior treatment—is invalid.

The Court has also ruled that racial and ethnic classifications are *inherently suspect*. Courts presume these classifications to be invalid and uphold them only if they serve a "compelling public interest" and there is no other way to accomplish the purpose of the law. In this case, the burden of proof is on the state. Classifications by race and ethnicity, such as for college admissions, may be acceptable if they are made in laws seeking to remedy previous discrimination. However, as we will see in our discussion of affirmative action, the future of such laws is in doubt.

Classifications based on gender fit *somewhere between* these two extremes; the courts presume them to be neither constitutional nor unconstitutional. A law that discriminates on the basis of gender must bear a substantial relationship to an important legislative purpose. If these three levels of judicial scrutiny (reasonable, inherently suspect, and somewhere in between) appear confusing, indeed they are—even judges and legal scholars struggle to interpret these standards.

Today courts interpret the equal protection clause broadly enough to forbid racial segregation in public schools, prohibit job discrimination, reapportion state legislatures, and permit court-ordered busing and affirmative action. Conditions for women and minorities would be radically different if it were not for the "equal protection" clause.[2] The next three sections show how equal protection litigation has worked to the advantage of minorities, women, and other groups seeking protection under the civil rights umbrella.

Race, the Constitution, and Public Policy

Throughout American history, African Americans have been the most visible minority group in the United States. These individuals have blazed the constitutional trail for securing equal rights for all Americans. Three eras delineate African

Americans' struggle for equality in America: (1) the era of slavery, from the beginnings of colonization until the end of the Civil War in 1865; (2) the era of reconstruction and resegregation, from roughly the end of the Civil War until 1953; and (3) the era of civil rights, roughly from 1954 to the present.

The Era of Slavery

The first African immigrants to America were kidnapped from their home countries. Most African Americans lived in slavery for the first 250 years of American settlement. Slaves were the property of their masters. They could be bought and sold, and they could neither vote nor own property. The Southern states, whose plantations required large numbers of unpaid workers, were the primary market for slave labor.

The Struggle for Equal Protection

During the slavery era, any public policy of the slave states or the federal government had to accommodate the property interests of slave owners, who were often wealthy and enjoyed substantial political influence. The Supreme Court got into the act, too, along with the legislative and executive branches (see Table 5.2). The boldest decision supporting slavery was ***Scott v. Sandford*** (1857), wherein Chief Justice Taney bluntly announced that a Black man, slave or free, was "chattel" and had no rights under a White man's government and that Congress had no power to ban slavery in the Western territories. This decision invalidated the hard-won Missouri Compromise, which allowed Missouri to become a slave state on the condition that Northern territories would remain free of slavery. As a result, the *Scott* decision was an important milestone on the road to the Civil War.

Scott v. Sandford
The 1857 Supreme Court decision ruling that a slave who had escaped to a free state enjoyed no rights as a citizen and that Congress had no authority to ban slavery in the territories.

The Union victory in the Civil War and the ratification of the **Thirteenth Amendment** ended slavery. The promises implicit in this amendment and the other two Civil War amendments introduced the era of reconstruction and resegregation in which these promises were first honored and then broken.

Thirteenth Amendment
The constitutional amendment ratified after the Civil War that forbade slavery and involuntary servitude.

Table 5.2 Toward Racial Equality: Milestones in the Era of Slavery

1600–1865
Slavery takes hold in the South, comes to characterize almost all relations between African Americans and Whites, is constitutionally justified, and is finally abolished.

1619	Slaves from Africa are brought to Jamestown and sold to planters.
1776	The Continental army enlists African Americans to fight the British after the British offer freedom to slaves who would fight on their side.
1787	The Constitution provides for a slave to be counted as three-fifths of a person in representation and taxation and permits Congress to forbid the importation of new slaves after 1808.
1808	Congress prohibits importation of slaves.
1857	The *Scott v. Sandford* decision holds that slaves may not gain freedom by escaping to a free state or territory; it upholds the constitutionality of the slave system.
1862	President Lincoln issues the Emancipation Proclamation.
1865	The Thirteenth Amendment abolishes slavery and involuntary servitude.

The Era of Reconstruction and Resegregation

After the Civil War ended, Congress imposed strict conditions on the former confederate states before it would seat their representatives and senators. No one who had served in secessionist state governments or in the Confederate Army could hold state office, the legislatures had to ratify the new amendments, and the military would govern the states like "conquered provinces" until they complied with the tough federal plans for reconstruction. Many African American men held state and federal offices during the 10 years following the war. Some government agencies, such as the Freedmen's Bureau, provided assistance to former slaves who were making the difficult transition to independence.

To ensure his election in 1876, Rutherford Hayes promised to pull the troops out of the South and let the old slave states resume business as usual. This done, Southerners lost little time reclaiming power and imposing a code of *Jim Crow laws*, or segregational laws, on African Americans. ("Jim Crow" was the name of a stereotypical African American in a nineteenth-century minstrel song.) These laws relegated African Americans to separate public facilities, separate school systems, and even separate restrooms. Most Whites lost interest in helping former slaves. And what the Jim Crow laws mandated in the South was also common practice in the North. Indeed, the national government practiced segregation in the armed forces, employment, housing programs, and prisons.[3] In this era, racial segregation affected every part of life, from the cradle to the grave. African Americans were delivered by African American physicians or midwives and buried in African American cemeteries. Groups such as the Ku Klux Klan terrorized African Americans who violated the norms of segregation, lynching hundreds of them during this era.

Plessy v. Ferguson
An 1896 Supreme Court decision that provided a constitutional justification for segregation by ruling that a Louisiana law requiring "equal but separate accommodations for the White and colored races" was constitutional.

The Supreme Court provided a constitutional justification for segregation in the 1896 case of ***Plessy v. Ferguson***. The Louisiana legislature required "equal but separate accommodations for the White and colored races" in railroad transportation. Although Homer Plessy was seven-eighths White, he had been arrested for refusing to leave a railway car reserved for Whites. The Court upheld the law, saying that segregation in public facilities was not unconstitutional as long as the separate facilities were substantially equal. In subsequent decisions, the Court paid more attention to the "separate" than to the "equal" part of this principle. For example, Southern states were allowed to maintain high schools and professional schools for Whites even when there were no such schools for African Americans. A measure of segregation in both the South and the North existed as late as the 1960s; nearly all the African American physicians in the United States were graduates of two medical schools, Howard University in Washington, D.C., and Meharry Medical College in Tennessee.

Nevertheless, some progress on the long road to racial equality was made in the first half of the twentieth century. The Supreme Court and the president began to prohibit a few of the most egregious practices of segregation (see Table 5.3), paving the way for a new era of civil rights.

The Era of Civil Rights

After searching carefully for the perfect case to challenge legal school segregation, the Legal Defense Fund of the National Association for the Advancement of Colored People (NAACP) selected the case of Linda Brown. Brown was an African

Table 5.3 Toward Racial Equality: Milestones in the Era of Reconstruction and Resegregation

1866–1953

Segregation is legally required in the South and sanctioned in the North, lynchings of African Americans occur in the South, and civil rights policy begins to appear.

1868	The Fourteenth Amendment makes African Americans U.S. citizens and guarantees "equal protection of the law." This guarantee is widely ignored for nearly a century.
1870	The Fifteenth Amendment forbids racial discrimination in voting, although many states find ways to prevent or discourage African Americans from voting.
1877	End of Reconstruction. African American gains made in the South (such as antidiscrimination laws) are reversed as former Confederates return to power. Jim Crow laws flourish, making segregation legal.
1883	In the *Civil Rights Cases* the Supreme Court rules that the Fourteenth Amendment does not prohibit discrimination by private businesses and individuals.
1896	The *Plessy v. Ferguson* decision permits "separate but equal" public facilities, providing a constitutional justification for segregation.
1909	The National Association for the Advancement of Colored People (NAACP) is founded by African Americans and Whites.
1915	*Guinn v. United States* bans the grandfather clause that had been used to prevent African Americans from voting.
1941	Executive order forbids racial discrimination in defense industries.
1944	The *Smith v. Allwright* decision bans all-White primaries.
1948	President Truman orders the armed forces desegregated.
1950	*Sweatt v. Painter* finds the "separate but equal" formula generally unacceptable in professional schools.

American student in Topeka, Kansas, required by Kansas law to attend a segregated school. In Topeka, the visible signs of education—teacher quality, facilities, and so on—were equal between African American and White schools. Thus, the NAACP chose the case in order to test the *Plessy v. Ferguson* doctrine of "separate but equal." It wanted to force the Court to rule directly on whether school segregation was inherently unequal and thereby violated the Fourteenth Amendment's requirement that states guarantee "equal protection of the laws."

President Eisenhower had just appointed Chief Justice Earl Warren. So important was the case that the Court had already heard one round of arguments before Warren joined the Court. The justices, after hearing the oral arguments, met in the Supreme Court's conference room. Believing that a unanimous decision would have the most impact, the justices negotiated a broad agreement and then determined that Warren himself should write the opinion.

In ***Brown v. Board of Education*** (1954), the Supreme Court set aside its precedent in *Plessy* and held that school segregation was inherently unconstitutional because it violated the Fourteenth Amendment's guarantee of equal protection. Legal segregation had come to an end.

A year after its decision in *Brown*, the Court ordered lower courts to proceed with "all deliberate speed" to desegregate public schools. Desegregation proceeded slowly in the South, however. A few counties threatened to close their public

Brown v. Board of Education
The 1954 Supreme Court decision holding that school segregation in Topeka, Kansas, was inherently unconstitutional because it violated the **Fourteenth Amendment's** guarantee of **equal protection.** This case marked the end of legal segregation in the United States.

Why It Matters

Brown v. Board of Education

In *Brown v. Board of Education*, the Supreme Court overturned its decision in *Plessy v. Ferguson*. This decision was a major step in changing the face of America. Just imagine what the United States would be like today if we still had segregated public facilities and services like universities and restaurants.

schools; enrollment in private schools by Whites soared. In 1957, President Eisenhower had to send troops to desegregate Central High School in Little Rock, Arkansas. In 1969, 15 years after its first ruling that school segregation was unconstitutional and in the face of continued massive resistance, the Supreme Court withdrew its earlier grant of time to school authorities and declared, "Delays in desegregating school systems are no longer tolerable" (*Alexander v. Holmes County Board of Education*). In 1964, under the Civil Rights Act, Congress prohibited federal aid to schools that remained segregated. Thus, after nearly a generation of modest progress, Southern schools were suddenly integrated.

The Court found that if schools were legally segregated before, authorities had an obligation to overcome past discrimination. This could include the distribution of students and pupils on a racial basis. Some federal judges ordered the busing of students to achieve racially balanced schools, a practice upheld (but not required) by the Supreme Court in *Swann v. Charlotte-Mecklenberg County Schools* (1971).

Not all racial segregation is what is called *de jure* ("by law") segregation. *De facto* ("in reality") segregation results, for example, when children are assigned to schools near their homes and those homes are in neighborhoods that are racially segregated for social and economic reasons. Sometimes the distinction between *de jure* and *de facto* segregation has been blurred by past official practices. Because minority groups and federal lawyers demonstrated that Northern schools, too, had purposely drawn district lines to promote segregation, school busing came to the North as well. Denver, Boston, and other cities instituted busing for racial balance, just as Southern cities did.

Majorities of both Whites and African Americans have opposed busing, which is one of the least popular remedies for discrimination. In recent years, it has

On September 25, 1957, troops of the 101st Airborne Division escorted nine African American students to Central High School in Little Rock, Arkansas. A court had ordered the school's desegregation in response to *Brown v. Board of Education*, but Arkansas Governor Orval Faubus fought the ruling. President Eisenhower used the National Guard to provide continuing protection for the students.

become less prominent as a judicial instrument. In addition, courts do not have the power to order busing between school districts; thus, school districts that are composed largely of minorities must rely on other means to integrate.

The civil rights movement organized both African Americans and Whites to end the policies and practices of segregation. Sit-ins, marches, and civil disobedience were key strategies of the civil rights movement, which sought to establish equal opportunities in the political and economic sectors and to end policies that put up barriers between people because of race (see "Young People and Politics: Freedom Riders"). The movement's trail was long and sometimes bloody. Police turned their dogs on nonviolent marchers in Birmingham, Alabama. Racists murdered other activists in Meridian, Missississippi, and Selma, Alabama. Fortunately, the goals of the civil rights movement appealed to the national conscience. By the 1970s, overwhelming majorities of White Americans supported racial integration.[4] Today, the principles established in *Brown* have near-universal support.

Civil Rights Movement

It was the courts as much as the national conscience that put civil rights goals on the nation's policy agenda. *Brown v. Board of Education* was only the beginning of a string of Supreme Court decisions holding various forms of discrimination unconstitutional. *Brown* and these other cases gave the civil rights movement momentum that would grow in the years that followed (see Table 5.4).

As a result of national conscience, the courts, the civil rights movement, and the increased importance of African American voters, the 1950s and 1960s saw a marked increase in public policies seeking to foster racial equality. These innovations included policies to promote voting rights, access to public accommodations, open housing, and nondiscrimination in many other areas of social and economic life. The **Civil Rights Act of 1964** did the following:

Civil Rights Act of 1964
The law that made racial discrimination against any group in hotels, motels, and restaurants illegal and forbade many forms of job discrimination.

- Made racial discrimination illegal in hotels, motels, restaurants, and other places of public accommodation
- Forbade discrimination in employment on the basis of race, color, national origin, religion, or gender[5]
- Created the Equal Employment Opportunity Commission (EEOC) to monitor and enforce protections against job discrimination
- Provided for withholding federal grants from state and local governments and other institutions that practiced racial discrimination
- Strengthened voting rights legislation
- Authorized the U.S. Justice Department to initiate lawsuits to desegregate public schools and facilities

The Voting Rights Act of 1965 (discussed next) was the most extensive federal effort to crack century-old barriers to African American voting in the South. The *Open Housing Act of 1968* took steps to forbid discrimination in the sale or rental of housing.

Congressional and judicial policies attacked virtually every type of segregation after 1954. By the 1980s, there were few, if any, forms of racial discrimination left to legislate against. Efforts for legislation were successful, in part, because by the mid-1960s federal laws effectively protected the right to vote, in fact as well as on paper. Members of minority groups thus had some power to hold their legislators accountable.

YOUNG PEOPLE AND POLITICS

Freedom Riders

Most political activity is quite safe. There have been occasions, however, when young adults have risked bodily harm and even death to fight for their beliefs. Years after *Brown v. Board of Education* (1954), segregated transportation continued in some parts of the Deep South. To change this system, the Congress of Racial Equality (CORE) organized freedom rides in 1961. Young Black and White volunteers in their teens and early twenties traveled on buses through the Deep South. In Anniston, Alabama, one bus was destroyed, and riders on another were attacked by men armed with clubs, bricks, iron pipes, and knives. In Birmingham, the passengers were greeted by members of the Ku Klux Klan with further acts of violence. At Montgomery, the state capital, a White mob beat the riders with chains and ax handles.

The Ku Klux Klan hoped that this violent treatment would stop other young people from taking part in freedom rides. It did not. Over the next six months, more than a thousand people took part in freedom rides. A young White man from Madison, Wisconsin, James Zwerg, was badly injured by a mob and left in the road for over an hour. White-run ambulances refused to take him to the hospital. In an interview afterward, he reflected the grim determination of the freedom riders: "Segregation must be stopped. It must be broken down. Those of us on the Freedom Ride will continue. No matter what happens we are dedicated to this. We will take the beatings. We are willing to accept death."

As with the Montgomery bus boycott and the conflict at Little Rock, the freedom riders gave worldwide publicity to the racial discrimination suffered by African Americans, and in doing so they helped to bring about change. Attorney General Robert Kennedy petitioned the Interstate Commerce Commission (ICC) to draft regulations to end racial segregation in bus terminals. The ICC was reluctant, but in September 1961 it issued the necessary orders.

The freedom riders did not limit themselves to desegregating buses. During the summer of 1961, they also sat together in segregated restaurants, lunch counters, and hotels. Typically they were refused service, and they were often threatened and sometimes attacked. The sit-in tactic was especially effective when it focused on large companies that feared boycotts in the North and that began to desegregate their businesses.

In the end, the courage of young people committed to racial equality prevailed. They helped to change the face of America.

Questions for Discussion

- What are young adults doing to fight racism today?
- Does civil disobedience have a role in contemporary America?

suffrage
The legal right to vote, extended to African Americans by the **Fifteenth Amendment**, to women by the **Nineteenth Amendment**, and to people over the age of 18 by the **Twenty-sixth Amendment**.

Fifteenth Amendment
The constitutional amendment adopted in 1870 to extend **suffrage** to African Americans.

Getting and Using the Right to Vote

When the Constitution was written, no one thought about extending the right to vote to African Americans (most of whom were slaves) or to women. The early Republic limited **suffrage**, the legal right to vote, to a handful of the population—mostly property-holding White males. Only after the Civil War was the right to vote extended, slowly and painfully, to African American males and then to other minority groups.

The **Fifteenth Amendment**, adopted in 1870, guaranteed African Americans the right to vote—at least in principle. It said, "The right of citizens to vote shall not be abridged by the United States or by any state on account of race, color, or previous condition of servitude." The gap between these words and their implementation,

Table 5.4 Toward Racial Equality: Milestones in the Era of Civil Rights

1954–2007

Integration becomes a widely accepted goal; the civil rights movement grows, followed by urban racial disorders in the 1960s; African American voting increases; and attention shifts to equal results and affirmative action.

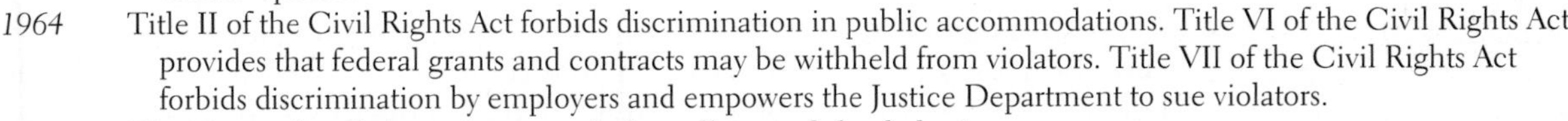

1954	*Brown v. Board of Education* holds that segregated schools are inherently unequal and violate the Fourteenth Amendment's equal protection clause.
1955	Martin Luther King Jr. leads a bus boycott in Montgomery, Alabama.
1957	Federal troops enforce desegregation of a Little Rock, Arkansas, high school.
1963	Civil rights demonstrators numbering 250,000 march on Washington, D.C. Martin Luther King Jr. delivers "I have a dream" speech.
1964	Title II of the Civil Rights Act forbids discrimination in public accommodations. Title VI of the Civil Rights Act provides that federal grants and contracts may be withheld from violators. Title VII of the Civil Rights Act forbids discrimination by employers and empowers the Justice Department to sue violators.
	The Twenty-fourth Amendment ends the poll tax in federal elections.
1965	The Voting Rights Act sends federal registrars to Southern states and counties to protect African Americans' right to vote and gives registrars the power to impound ballots in order to enforce the act.
	Executive order requires companies with federal contracts to take affirmative action to ensure equal opportunity.
	Riots occur in Watts, California, and other cities and reappear every summer in various cities for the next five years.
1966	*Harper v. Virginia* holds that the Fourteenth Amendment forbids making payment of a tax a condition of voting in any election.
1967	Cleveland becomes the first major city to elect an African American mayor (Carl Stokes).
1968	The *Jones v. Mayer* decision and the Civil Rights Act of 1968 make all racial discrimination in the sale or rental of housing illegal.
	Martin Luther King Jr. assassinated.
1971	The *Swann v. Charlotte-Mecklenberg County Schools* decision approves busing as a means of combating state-enforced segregation.
1978	*California Board of Regents v. Bakke* forbids rigid racial quotas for medical school admissions but does not forbid considering race as a factor when deciding admissions.
1979	*United Steelworkers of America v. Weber* permits an affirmative action program to favor African Americans if the program is designed to remedy past discrimination.
	Dayton Board of Education v. Brinkman upholds school busing to remedy Northern school segregation.
1984	Jesse Jackson becomes the first African American candidate for president to receive substantial support in the primaries.
	Grove City College v. Bell forbids the federal government from withholding all federal funds from a college that refuses to file forms saying that it does not discriminate. (Only a specific program risked its federal funds.)
1988	Congress rewrites the Civil Rights Act to "overturn" the implications of *Grove City College*.
1991	After three years of conflict, Congress enacts the Civil Rights and Women's Equity in Employment Act, which counters the effects of several Supreme Court decisions making it more difficult for workers to bring and win job discrimination suits.
1995	*Adarand Constructors v. Pena* holds that affirmative action programs must undergo strict scrutiny to determine that they are narrowly tailored to serve a compelling governmental interest.
2003	*Grutter v. Bollinger* approves use of race as one factor in college admissions.

however, remained wide for a full century. States seemed to outdo one another in developing ingenious methods of circumventing the Fifteenth Amendment.

Many states required potential voters to complete literacy tests before registering to vote. These tests typically required prospective voters to read, write, and understand their state constitution or the U.S. Constitution. In practice, however, registrars rarely administered the literacy tests to Whites, while the standard of literacy they required of Blacks was so high that few were ever able to pass the test. In addition, Oklahoma and other Southern states used a *grandfather clause* that exempted persons whose grandfathers were eligible to vote in 1860 from taking these tests. This exemption did not apply, of course, to the grandchildren of slaves but did allow illiterate Whites to vote. The law was blatantly unfair; it was also unconstitutional, said the Supreme Court in the 1915 decision *Guinn v. United States*.

poll taxes

Small taxes levied on the right to vote that often fell due at a time of year when poor African American sharecroppers had the least cash on hand. This method was used by most Southern states to exclude African Americans from voting. Poll taxes were declared void by the **Twenty-fourth Amendment** in 1964.

White primary

One of the means used to discourage African American voting that permitted political parties in the heavily Democratic South to exclude African Americans from primary elections, thus depriving them of a voice in the real contests. The Supreme Court declared White primaries unconstitutional in 1944.

Twenty-fourth Amendment

The constitutional amendment passed in 1964 that declared **poll taxes** void in federal elections.

Voting Rights Act of 1965

A law designed to help end formal and informal barriers to African American **suffrage**. Under the law, hundreds of thousands of African Americans were registered to vote, and the number of African American elected officials increased dramatically.

To exclude African Americans from registering to vote, most Southern states also relied on **poll taxes**, which were small taxes levied on the right to vote that often fell due at a time of year when poor sharecroppers had the least cash on hand. To render African American votes ineffective, most Southern states also used the **White primary**, a device that permitted political parties in the heavily Democratic South to exclude African Americans from voting in primary elections, thus depriving them of a voice in the most important contests and letting them vote only when it mattered least. The Supreme Court declared White primaries unconstitutional in 1944 in *Smith v. Allwright*.

The civil rights movement put suffrage high on its political agenda; one by one, the barriers to African American voting fell during the 1960s. The **Twenty-fourth Amendment**, which was ratified in 1964, prohibited poll taxes in federal elections. Two years later, the Supreme Court voided poll taxes in state elections in *Harper v. Virginia State Board of Elections*.

To combat the use of discriminatory voter registration tests—requiring literacy or an understanding of the Constitution, for example—the **Voting Rights Act of 1965** prohibited any government from using voting procedures that denied a person the vote on the basis of race or color and abolished the use of literacy requirements for anyone who had completed the sixth grade. The federal government sent election registrars to areas with long histories of discrimination, and these same areas had to submit all proposed changes in their voting laws or practices to a federal official for approval. As a result of these provisions, hundreds of thousands of African Americans registered to vote in Southern states.

The effects of these efforts were swift and certain, as the civil rights movement turned from protest to politics.[6] When the Voting Rights Act passed in 1965, only 70 African Americans held public office in the 11 Southern states. By the early 1980s, more than 2,500 African Americans held elected offices in those states, and the number has continued to grow. There are currently more than 9,000 African American elected officials in the United States.[7]

The Voting Rights Act of 1965 not only secured the right to vote for African Americans but also attempted to ensure that their votes would not be diluted through racial gerrymandering (drawing district boundaries to advantage a specific group). For example, White-majority districts frequently elected members of a city council in at-large seats (in which council members were elected from the entire city) and prevented a geographically concentrated minority from electing a minority council member. When Congress amended the Voting Rights Act in 1982, it further insisted that minorities be able to "elect representatives of their choice" when their numbers and configuration permitted. Thus, redrawing district boundaries was to avoid discriminatory *results* and not just discriminatory *intent*. In 1986, the Supreme Court upheld this principle in *Thornburg v. Gingles*.

Officials in the Justice Department, which was responsible for enforcing the Voting Rights Act, and state legislatures that drew new district lines interpreted these actions as a mandate to create minority-majority districts. Consequently, when congressional district boundaries were redrawn following the 1990 census, several states, including Florida, North Carolina, Texas, Illinois, New York, and Louisiana, created odd-shaped districts that were designed to give minority-group voters a numerical majority. Fourteen new U.S. House districts were drawn specifically to help elect African Americans to Congress, and six districts were drawn to elect new Hispanic members (these efforts worked, as we will see in Chapter 11).

However, in 1993, the Supreme Court heard a challenge to a North Carolina congressional district that in some places was cut no wider than a superhighway to create an African American majority winding snakelike for 160 miles. In its decision in *Shaw v. Reno*, the Court decried the creation of districts based solely on racial composition, as well as the district drawers' abandonment of traditional redistricting standards such as compactness and contiguity. Thus, the Court gave legal standing to challenges to any congressional map with an oddly shaped minority-majority district that may not be defensible on grounds other than race (such as shared community interest or geographical compactness). The next year, in *Johnson v. DeGrandy*, the Court ruled that a state legislative redistricting plan does not violate the Voting Rights Act if it does not create the greatest possible number of districts in which minority-group votes would make up a majority.

In 1995, in *Miller v. Johnson*, the Court rejected the efforts of the Justice Department to achieve the maximum possible number of minority districts. It held that the use of race as a "predominant factor" in drawing district lines should be presumed to be unconstitutional. The next year, in *Bush v. Vera* and *Shaw v. Hunt*, the Supreme Court voided three convoluted districts in Texas and one in North Carolina on the grounds that race had been the primary reason for abandoning compact district lines and that the state legislatures had crossed the line into unconstitutional racial gerrymandering.

In yet another turn, in 1999 the Court declared in *Hunt v. Cromartie* that conscious consideration of race is not automatically unconstitutional if the state's primary motivation was potentially political rather than racial. We can expect continued litigation concerning this question, especially since the Court has decided that state legislatures may redraw district boundaries at any time and not only after a census.[8]

Why It Matters

The Voting Rights Act
In passing the Voting Rights Act of 1965, Congress enacted an extraordinarily strong law to protect the rights of minorities to vote. There is little question that officials pay more attention to minorities when they can vote. And many more members of minority groups are elected to high public office.

Other Minority Groups

As we discuss in Chapter 6, America is heading toward a *minority majority*: a situation in which minority groups will outnumber Caucasians of European descent. African Americans are not the only racial group that has suffered legally imposed discrimination, and as of 2001, African Americans are no longer the largest minority group in the United States. Even before the civil rights struggle, Native Americans, Hispanics, and Asians learned how powerless they could become in a society dominated by Whites. The civil rights laws for which African Americans fought have benefited members of these groups as well. In addition, social movements tend to beget new social movements; thus, the African American civil rights movement of the 1960s spurred other minorities to mobilize to protect their rights.

Native Americans. The earliest inhabitants of the continent, the American Indians, are, of course, the oldest minority group. Nearly 2 million people identify themselves as Native Americans. The history of poverty, discrimination, and exploitation experienced by American Indians is a long one. For generations, U.S. policy promoted westward expansion at the expense of Native Americans' lands. The government first isolated Native Americans on reservations, where they lost their lands and their rights in the process. After the Dawes Act of 1887, the federal government switched strategies and focused on assimilating Native Americans into mainstream American life. The government sent children to boarding schools off the reservations and banned tribal rituals and languages.

Finally, in 1924 Congress made American Indians citizens of the United States and gave them the right to vote, a status that African Americans had achieved a half century before. Not until 1946 did Congress establish the Indian Claims Act to settle financial disputes arising from lands taken from the American Indians.[9] Today, most Native Americans still live in poverty and ill health, almost half on or near a reservation. American Indians know, perhaps better than any other group, the significance of the gap between public policy and private realization regarding discrimination.

But progress is being made. The civil rights movement of the 1960s created a more favorable climate for Native Americans to secure guaranteed access to the polls, to housing, and to jobs and to reassert their treaty rights. The Indian Bill of Rights was adopted as Title II of the Civil Rights Act of 1968, applying most of the provisions of the Constitution's Bill of Rights to tribal governments. In *Santa Clara Pueblo v. Martinez* (1978), the Supreme Court strengthened the tribal power of individual tribe members and furthered self-government by Indian tribes.

American Indian activists such as Dennis Means of the American Indian Movement (AIM), Vine Deloria, and Dee Brown drew attention to the plight of American Indian tribes. Several Native Americans seized Alcatraz Island in San Francisco Bay in 1969 to protest the loss of Indian lands. In 1973, armed members of AIM seized 11 hostages at Wounded Knee, South Dakota—the site of an 1890 massacre of 200 Sioux (Lakota) by U.S. cavalry—and remained there for 71 days until the federal government agreed to examine Indian treaty rights. Ben Nighthorse Campbell won election as a U.S. senator from Colorado in 1992, the first Native American elected to Congress in more than 20 years.

Equally important, Indians began to use the courts to protect their rights. The Native American Rights Fund (NARF), founded in 1970, has won important victories concerning hunting, fishing, and land rights. Native Americans are also retaining access to their sacred places and have had some success in stopping the building of roads and buildings on ancient burial grounds or other sacred spots. Several tribes have won court cases protecting them from taxation of tribal profits.

As in other areas of civil rights, the preservation of Native American culture and the exercise of Native American rights sometimes conflict with the interests of the majority. For example, there is conflict over special rights that some tribes have to fish and even hunt whales. Anglers concerned with the depletion of fishing stock and environmentalists worried about loss of the whale population have voiced protests. Similarly, Native American rights to run businesses denied to others by state law and to avoid taxation on tribal lands have made running gambling casinos a lucrative option for Indians. This has irritated both those who oppose gambling and those who are offended by the tax-free competition.

Hispanic Americans. Hispanic Americans (or Latinos, as some prefer to be called)—chiefly from Mexico, Puerto Rico, and Cuba but also from El Salvador, Honduras, and other countries in Central America—have displaced African Americans as the largest minority group. Today they compose about 14 percent of the U.S. population.

The first major efforts on behalf of civil rights for Hispanics date only from the mid-1960s. Hispanic leaders drew from the tactics of the African American civil rights movement and used sit-ins, boycotts, marches, and related activities to draw attention to their cause. Inspired by the NAACP's Legal Defense Fund, they also created the Mexican American Legal Defense and Education Fund (MALDEF) in 1968 to help argue their cause in court. In addition, Hispanic groups began mobilizing in other ways to protect their interests. An early prominent example was the United Farm Workers, led by Cesar Chavez, who publicized the plight of migrant workers, a large proportion of whom are Hispanic.

The growing numbers of Hispanic Americans will soon make them the largest minority group in the United States. Their political power is reflected in Alberto Gonzales's selection for President George W. Bush's cabinet and in the two dozen members of the U.S. House of Representatives, such as Loretta and Linda Sanchez of California.

Like Native Americans, Hispanic Americans benefit from the nondiscrimination policies originally passed to protect African Americans. Provisions of the Voting Rights Act of 1965 covered San Antonio, Texas, and thereby permitted Hispanic voters to lend weight to the election of Mayor Henry Cisneros. There are now more than 4,400 elected Hispanic officials in the United States,[10] and Hispanic Americans play a prominent role in the politics of such major cities as Houston, Miami, Los Angeles, and San Diego. In 1973, Hispanics won a victory when the Supreme Court found that multimember electoral districts (in which more than one person represents a single district) in Texas discriminated against minority groups because they decreased the probability of a minority being elected.[11] Nevertheless, poverty, discrimination, and language barriers continue to depress Hispanic voter registration and turnout.

Asian Americans. Asian Americans are the fastest-growing minority group; their representation in the American population rose from 0.5 percent to 4 percent from 1960 to 2000. Asian Americans suffered discrimination in education, jobs, and housing as well as restrictions on immigration and naturalization for more than a hundred years prior to the civil rights acts of the 1960s. Discrimination was especially egregious during World War II when the U.S. government, beset by fears of a Japanese invasion of the Pacific Coast, rounded up more than 100,000 Americans of Japanese descent and herded them into encampments. These internment camps were, critics claimed, America's concentration camps. The Supreme Court, however, in ***Korematsu v. United States*** (1944), upheld the internment as constitutional. Congress has since authorized benefits to the former internees. Today, Americans of Chinese, Japanese, Korean, Vietnamese, and other Asian cultures have assumed prominent positions in U.S. society.

Korematsu v. United States
A 1944 Supreme Court decision that upheld as constitutional the internment of more than 100,000 Americans of Japanese descent in encampments during World War II.

Other Groups. There are more than 1.2 million persons of Arab ancestry in the United States. Since the terrorist attacks of September 11, 2001, Arab, Muslim, Sikh, and South Asian Americans and those perceived to be members of these groups have been the victims of increased numbers of bias-related assaults, threats, vandalism, and arson. The incidents have consisted of telephone, Internet, mail, and face-to-face threats; minor assaults as well as assaults with dangerous weapons and assaults resulting in serious injury and death; and vandalism, shootings, arson, and bombings directed at homes, businesses, and places of worship. Members of these groups have also experienced discrimination in employment, housing, education, and access to public accommodations and facilities.

Comparing Civil Rights

As we saw in Chapter 4, in the wake of the September 11, 2001, terrorist attacks, the FBI detained more than 1,200 persons as possible threats to national security. About two-thirds of these persons were illegal aliens—mostly Arabs and Muslims—and many of them languished in jail for months until cleared by the FBI. This process seemed to violate the right of detainees to be informed of accusations against them found in the Sixth Amendment and the protection against the suspension of the writ of habeas corpus. As we have seen, in 2004 the Supreme Court declared that detainees had the right to challenge their detention before a judge or other neutral decision maker.

One of the low points in the protection of civil rights in the United States occurred during World War II when more than 100,000 Americans of Japanese descent were moved to internment camps.

The struggle for equal rights has not been limited to racial minorities, however. Political activity on behalf of women has been so energetic and so far-reaching that a separate section is needed to examine this struggle for equality.

Women, the Constitution, and Public Policy

Abigail Adams may have been practically alone in her feminist views in the 1770s, but the next century brought significant feminist activity. The first women's rights activists were products of the abolitionist movement, where they often encountered sexist opposition. Noting that the status of women shared much in common with that of slaves, some leaders resolved to fight for women's rights.

Two of these women, Lucretia Mott and Elizabeth Cady Stanton, organized a meeting at Seneca Falls in upstate New York. They had much to discuss. Not only were women denied the vote, but they were also subjected to patriarchal (male-dominated) family law and denied educational and career opportunities. The legal doctrine known as *coverture* deprived married women of any identity separate from that of their husbands; wives could not sign contracts or dispose of property. Divorce law was heavily biased in favor of husbands. Even abused women found it almost impossible to end their marriages, and men had the legal advantage in securing custody of the children.

The Battle for the Vote

On July 19, 1848, 100 men and women signed the Seneca Falls Declaration of Sentiments and Resolutions. Patterned after the Declaration of Independence, it proclaimed, "The history of mankind is a history of repeated injuries and usurpations on the part of man toward woman, having in direct object the establishment of an absolute tyranny over her." Thus began the movement that would culminate in the ratification of the **Nineteenth Amendment** 72 years later, giving women the vote. Charlotte Woodward, 19 years old in 1848, was the only signer of the Seneca Falls Declaration who lived to vote for the president in 1920.

Nineteenth Amendment
The constitutional amendment adopted in 1920 that guarantees women the right to vote. See also **suffrage**.

Advocates of women's suffrage hoped that women would be included in the Fifteenth Amendment but were disappointed when they were excluded from protections accorded to newly freed slaves. Thus, the battle for women's suffrage was fought mostly in the late nineteenth and early twentieth centuries. Leaders like Stanton and Susan B. Anthony were prominent in the cause, which emphasized the vote but also addressed women's other grievances. The suffragists had considerable success in the states, especially in the West. Several states allowed women to vote before the constitutional amendment passed. The feminists lobbied, marched, protested, and even engaged in civil disobedience.[12]

The "Doldrums": 1920–1960

Winning the right to vote did not automatically win equal status for women. In fact, the feminist movement seemed to lose rather than gain momentum after winning the vote, perhaps because the vote was about the only goal on which all feminists agreed. There was considerable division within the movement on other priorities.

Many suffragists accepted the traditional model of the family. Fathers were breadwinners, mothers bread bakers. Although most suffragists thought that women should have the opportunity to pursue any occupation they chose, many also believed that women's primary obligations revolved around the roles of wife and mother. Many suffragists had defended the vote as basically an extension of the maternal role into public life, arguing that a new era of public morality would emerge when women could vote. These *social feminists* were in tune with prevailing attitudes.

Public policy toward women continued to be dominated by protectionism rather than by the principle of equality. Laws protected working women from the burdens of overtime work, long hours on the job, and heavy lifting. The fact that these laws also protected male workers from female competition received little attention. State laws tended to reflect—and reinforce—traditional family roles. These laws concentrated on limiting women's work opportunities outside the home so they could concentrate on their duties within it. The laws in most states required husbands to support their families (even after a divorce) and to pay child support, though divorced fathers did not always pay. When a marriage ended, mothers almost always got custody of the children, although husbands had the legal advantage in custody battles. Public policy was designed to preserve traditional motherhood and hence, supporters claimed, to protect the family and the country's moral fabric.[13]

Only a minority of feminists challenged these assumptions. Alice Paul, the author of the original **Equal Rights Amendment (ERA)**, was one activist who claimed that the real result of protectionist law was to perpetuate gender inequality. Simply worded, the ERA reads, "Equality of rights under the law shall not be denied or abridged by the United States or by any state on account of sex." Most people saw the ERA as a threat to the family when it was introduced in Congress in 1923. It gained little support. In fact, women were less likely to support the amendment than men were.

Equal Rights Amendment

A constitutional amendment originally introduced in Congress in 1923 and passed by Congress in 1972, stating that "equality of rights under the law shall not be denied or abridged by the United States or by any state on account of sex." Despite public support, the amendment failed to acquire the necessary support from three-fourths of the state legislatures.

The Second Feminist Wave

The civil rights movement of the 1950s and 1960s attracted many female activists, some of whom also joined student and antiwar movements. These women often met with the same prejudices as had women abolitionists. Betty Friedan's book *The Feminine Mystique*, published in 1963, encouraged women to question traditional assumptions and to assert their own rights. Groups such as the National Organization for Women (NOW) and the National Women's Political Caucus were organized in the 1960s and 1970s.

Before the advent of the contemporary feminist movement, the Supreme Court upheld virtually any instance of gender-based discrimination. The state and federal governments could discriminate against women—and, indeed, men—as they chose. In the 1970s, the Court began to take a closer look at gender discrimination. In ***Reed v. Reed*** (1971), the Court ruled that any "arbitrary" gender-based classification violated the equal protection clause of the Fourteenth Amendment. This was the first time the Court declared any law unconstitutional on the basis of gender discrimination. Five years later, ***Craig v. Boren*** established a "medium scrutiny" standard: Gender discrimination would be presumed to be neither valid nor invalid. The courts were to show less deference to gender classifications than to more routine classifications but more deference than to racial classifications. Nevertheless, the Court has repeatedly said that there must be an "exceedingly persuasive justification" for any government to classify people by gender. Table 5.5 lists important policy milestones on gender equality.

Reed v. Reed

The landmark case in 1971 in which the Supreme Court for the first time upheld a claim of gender discrimination.

Craig v. Boren

In this 1976 ruling, the Supreme Court established a "medium scrutiny" standard for determining gender discrimination.

The Supreme Court has struck down many laws and rules for discriminating on the basis of gender. For example, the Court voided laws giving husbands exclusive control over family property.[14] The Court also voided employers' rules that denied women equal monthly retirement benefits because they live longer than men.[15]

In fact, many of the litigants in cases raising constitutional questions about gender discrimination have been men seeking equality with women in their treatment under the law. For example, the Court has voided laws that allowed the following:

- Provided for alimony payments to women only (*Orr v. Orr* [1979])
- Closed a state's nursing school to men (*Mississippi v. Hogan* [1982])
- Set a higher age for drinking for men than for women (*Craig v. Boren* [1976])
- Set a higher age for reaching legal adult status for men than for women (*Stanton v. Stanton* [1975])

Men have not always prevailed in their efforts for equal treatment, however. The Court upheld a statutory rape law applying only to men[16] and the male-only

Table 5.5 Toward Gender Equality: Public Policy Milestones

1969–2007	
1969	Executive order declares that offering equal opportunities for women at every level of federal service is to be national policy and establishes a program for implementing the policy.
1971	In *Reed v. Reed*, the Supreme Court invalidates a state law preferring men to women in court selection of an estate's administrator.
1972	Provisions of Title VII of the Civil Rights Act of 1964 are extended to cover the faculty and professional staffs of colleges and universities.
	The Education Act forbids gender discrimination in public schools (with some exceptions for historically single-gender schools).
	The ERA is proposed by Congress and sent to the states for ratification.
1974	A woman—Ella Grasso of Connecticut—is elected governor for the first time without succeeding her husband to the office.
1975	Congress opens armed services academies to women.
1976	Courts strike down an Oklahoma law setting different legal drinking ages for men and women.
1977	Supreme Court voids arbitrary height and weight requirements for employees in *Dothard v. Rawlinson*.
1978	The deadline for ratification of the ERA is extended.
	Congress passes the Pregnancy Discrimination Act.
1981	The Supreme Court rules that male-only military draft registration is constitutional.
	Sandra Day O'Connor becomes the first woman Supreme Court justice.
1982	The ERA ratification deadline passes without ratification of the amendment.
1984	Geraldine Ferraro is nominated as the first woman vice-presidential candidate of a major party.
1988	The Supreme Court unanimously upholds a 1984 New York City law aimed primarily at requiring the admission of women to large, private clubs that play an important role in professional life.
1991	After three years of conflict, Congress enacts the Civil Rights and Women's Equity in Employment Act, which counters the effects of several Supreme Court decisions, making it more difficult for workers to bring and win job discrimination suits.
1992	California becomes the first state to be represented by two female U.S. senators.
1993	Supreme Court in *Harris v. Forklift Systems* lowers the threshold for proving sexual harassment in the workplace.
1994	Forty-eight women elected to U.S. House and eight to the Senate, the most in history.
1996	In *United States v. Virginia et al.*, the Supreme Court declares categorical exclusion of women from state-funded colleges unconstitutional.
1997	Madeline Albright appointed secretary of state, the first woman to serve in that role.
2001	Condoleezza Rice appointed national security adviser, the first woman to hold that post.
2002	Representative Nancy Pelosi is elected by her colleagues as House Democratic Leader, becoming the first woman to head her party in Congress.
2007	Nancy Pelosi elected as Speaker of the House of Representatives, the first woman to hold that position.

draft, which we will discuss shortly. The Court also allowed a Florida law giving property tax exemptions only to widows, not to widowers.[17]

Contemporary feminists have suffered defeats as well as victories. The ERA was revived when Congress passed it in 1972 and extended the deadline for ratification until 1982. Nevertheless, the ERA was three states short of ratification when time ran out. Paradoxically, the defeat of the ERA had just the opposite effect of

HOW YOU CAN MAKE A DIFFERENCE

Gender Discrimination

In the decades since the civil rights moment and the federal intervention in the 1960s and 1970s, the drive for gender and racial equality has made big strides. Legal forms of discrimination have all but disappeared as a result of increased government oversight and heightened public awareness. However, gender discrimination still persists in subtler ways, and a number of individuals and organizations remain focused on assuring and expanding women's rights.

Making a Difference

An Idaho law enacted in 1864 held that males must be preferred to females in cases where parents otherwise had equal claims (and equal qualifications) to serve as administrator of their child's estate. Sally Reed challenged this law after her 16-year-old son died without a will in 1967. Sally Reed and her estranged husband, Cecil Reed, each filed petitions to be appointed as the administrator of their son's estate. The probate court chose Cecil, and Sally contested the appointment. In 1971, the Supreme Court held in *Reed v. Reed* that the arbitrary preference established in favor of males in the Idaho law violated the Equal Protection Clause of the Fourteenth Amendment—the first time that any law had been voided on the basis of gender discrimination.

What you can do:

- Celebrate Women's Equality Day (August 26th) in your school or workplace.
- Sign the National Organization for Women's (NOW) petition to Prospective 2008 Candidates for President, urging them to end discrimination against women and restore women's rights (www.now.org).
- Write your legislators to support legislation to end sex tourism and trafficking. Visit Equality Now (www.equalitynow.org) for more information.

that which the 1920 suffrage victory had on feminism. Far from weakening the movement, losing the ERA battle stimulated vigorous feminist activity. Proponents have vowed to keep reintroducing the amendment in Congress and continue to press hard for state and federal action on women's rights.

Women in the Workplace

One reason why feminist activism persists has nothing to do with ideology or other social movements. The family pattern that traditionalists sought to preserve—father at work, mother at home—is becoming a thing of the past. The female civilian labor force amounts to 68 million (as compared to 79 million males), representing 59 percent of adult women. Fifty-two percent of these women are married. There are also 33 million female-headed households (8 million of which include children), and about two-thirds of American mothers who have children below school age are in the labor force.[18] As conditions have changed, public opinion and public policy demands have changed, too. Protectionism is not dead. Women still assume more duties inside the home than men do, and debates over policies like the "mommy track" (reduced work responsibilities for women workers with children) parental leaves to women reflect this social phenomenon. Demands for equality, however, keep nudging protectionism into the background.

Congress has made some important progress, especially in the area of employment. The Civil Rights Act of 1964 banned gender discrimination in employment. The protection of this law has been expanded several times. For example, in 1972, Congress gave the EEOC the power to sue employers suspected of illegal discrimination. Title IX of the Education Act of 1972 forbade gender discrimination in federally subsidized education programs, including athletics. The Pregnancy Discrimination Act of 1978 made it illegal for employers to exclude pregnancy and childbirth from their sick leave and health benefits plans. The Civil Rights and Women's Equity in Employment Act of 1991 shifted the burden of proof in justifying hiring and promotion practices to employers, who must show that employment practices are related to job performance and that they are consistent with "business necessity" (an ambiguous term, however).

The Supreme Court also weighed in against gender discrimination in employment and business activity. In 1977, it voided laws and rules barring women from jobs through arbitrary height and weight requirements (*Dothard v. Rawlinson*). Any such prerequisites must be directly related to the duties required in a particular position. Women have also been protected from being required to take mandatory pregnancy leaves from their jobs[19] and from being denied a job because of an employer's concern for harming a developing fetus.[20] Many commercial contacts are made in private business and service clubs, which often have excluded women from membership. The Court has upheld state and city laws that prohibit such discrimination.[21]

Why It Matters

Changes in the Workplace

Laws and Supreme Court decisions striking down barriers to employment for women are not just ornaments. Instead, they have important consequences for employment opportunities for millions of women and have helped them make substantial gains in entering careers formerly occupied almost entirely by men.

Education is closely related to employment. Title IX of the Education Act of 1972 forbids gender discrimination in federally subsidized education programs (which include almost all colleges and universities). But what about single-gender schooling? In 1996, the Supreme Court declared that Virginia's categorical exclusion of women from education opportunities at the state-funded Virginia Military Institute (VMI) violated women's rights to equal protection of the law.[22] A few days later, The Citadel, the nation's only other state-supported all-male college, announced that it would also admit women.

Women have made substantial progress in their quest for equality, but debate continues as Congress considers new laws. Three of the most controversial issues that legislators will continue to face are wage discrimination, the role of women in the military, and sexual harassment.

Wage Discrimination and Comparable Worth

Traditional women's jobs often pay much less than men's jobs that demand comparable skill; a female secretary often earns far less than a male accounts clerk with the same qualifications. Median annual earnings for full-time women workers are only 80 percent as much as the wages of men.[23] In other words, women earn $0.80 for every $1.00 men make.

comparable worth
The issue raised when women who hold traditionally female jobs are paid less than men for working at jobs requiring comparable skill.

In 1983, the Washington State Supreme Court ruled that its state government had discriminated against women for years by denying them equal pay for jobs of **comparable worth**. The U.S. Supreme Court has remained silent so far on the merits of this issue. The executive branch under Ronald Reagan consistently

As women have become more active in politics, they have begun to assume more leadership roles. Here, Dianne Feinstein and Barbara Boxer of California hold a joint press conference. Their 1992 victories marked the first time a state had been represented in the Senate by two female senators.

opposed the idea of comparable worth. The late Clarence Pendleton, Ronald Reagan's appointee as head of the U.S. Civil Rights Commission, argued that lawsuits based on comparable worth would interfere with the free market for wages by reducing incentives for women to seek higher-paying, traditionally male jobs. Pendleton called comparable worth "the craziest idea since Looney Tunes." Ridicule has not made this serious dispute go away, however.

Women in the Military

Military service is another controversial aspect of gender equality. Women have served in every branch of the armed services since World War II. Originally, they served in separate units such as the WACS (Women's Army Corps), the WAVES (Women Accepted for Volunteer Emergency Service in the navy), and the Nurse Corps. The military had a 2 percent quota for women (which was never filled) until the 1970s. Now women are part of the regular service. They make up 15 percent of the armed forces (19 percent of the air force), and compete directly with men for promotions. Congress opened all the service academies to women in 1975. Women have done well, including graduating first at the U.S. Naval Academy in Annapolis and serving as first captain of the Corps of Cadets at West Point.

Two important differences between the treatment of men and that of women persist in military service. First, only men must register for the draft when they turn 18 (see "You Are the Judge: Is Male-Only Draft Registration Gender Discrimination?"). Second, statutes and regulations also prohibit women from serving in combat.

In the past few years, women have overcome many obstacles to serving in the military, performing well in a variety of nontraditional roles, such as piloting helicopters and patrolling in combat vehicles.

A breach exists between policy and practice, however, as the Persian Gulf War and the war in Iraq showed. Women piloted helicopters at the front and helped to operate antimissile systems; some were taken as prisoners of war. Women are now permitted to serve as combat pilots in the navy and air force and to serve on navy warships. However, they are still not permitted to serve in ground combat units in the army or marines.

These actions have reopened the debate over whether women should serve in combat. Some experts insist that because women, on average, have less upper-body strength than men, they are less suited for combat. Others argue that men will not be able to fight effectively beside wounded or dying women. Critics of these views point out that some women surpass some men in upper-body strength and that we do not know how well men and women will fight together. This debate is not only a controversy about ability; it also touches on the question of whether engaging in combat is a burden or a privilege. Clearly some women—and some who would deny them combat duty—take the latter view.

Sexual Harassment

Whether in the military, on the assembly line, or in the office, women for years have voiced concern about sexual harassment, which, of course, does not affect only women. In 1986, the Supreme Court articulated this broad principle: Sexual harassment that is so pervasive as to create a hostile or abusive work environment is a form of gender discrimination, which is forbidden by the 1964 Civil Rights Act.[24] In 1993, in *Harris v. Forklift Systems*, the Court reinforced its decision. No single factor, the Court said, is required to win a sexual harassment case under Title VII of the 1964 Civil Rights Act. The law is violated when the workplace environment

YOU ARE THE JUDGE

Is Male-Only Draft Registration Gender Discrimination?

There is no military conscription at present (the United States has had a volunteer force since 1973), but President Jimmy Carter asked Congress to require both men and women to register for the draft after the Soviet Union invaded Afghanistan in 1979. Registration was designed to facilitate any eventual conscription. In 1980, Congress reinstated registration for men only, a policy that was not universally popular. Federal courts ordered registration suspended while several young men filed a suit. These men argued that the registration requirement was gender-based discrimination that violated the due process clause of the Fifth Amendment.

You Be the Judge: Does requiring only males to register for the draft unconstitutionally discriminate against them?

Answer: The Supreme Court displayed its typical deference to the elected branches in the area of national security when it ruled in 1981 in *Rostker v. Goldberg* that male-only registration did not violate the Fifth Amendment. The Court found that male-only registration bore a substantial relationship to Congress's goal of ensuring combat readiness and that Congress acted well within its constitutional authority to raise and regulate armies and navies when it authorized the registration of men and not women. Congress, the Court said, was allowed to focus on the question of military need rather than "equity."

"would reasonably be perceived, and is perceived, as hostile or abusive." Thus, workers are not required to prove that the workplace environment is so hostile as to cause them "severe psychological injury" or that they are unable to perform their jobs. The protection of federal law comes into play before the harassing conduct leads to psychological difficulty.

In 1998 the Supreme Court again spoke expansively about sexual harassment in the workplace. In *Faragher v. City of Boca Raton*, the Court made it clear that employers are responsible for preventing and eliminating harassment at work. They can be held liable for even those harassing acts of supervisory employees that violate clear policies and of which top management has no knowledge. In 2004 in *Pennsylvania State Police v. Suders*, the Court held that if harassment culminates in a tangible action such as a discharge or demotion, an employer is strictly liable if there is no legal defense such as one showing that the employer had set up a system for reporting and correcting sexual harassment but that the employee had unreasonably failed to use that system.

In *Burlington Industries, Inc. v. Ellerth*, the Court found that an employee could sue for sexual harassment even without being able to show job-related harm. Victims must have availed themselves of effective complaint policies and other protection offered by the company first, however. The Court has also held that the 1964 Civil Rights Act's prohibition against employer retaliation against someone filing a complaint about sexual harassment extends beyond being fired or demoted to include a change in work assignments.[25] The Court also made it clear that the law also prevents sexual harassment by people of the same gender (*Oncale v. Sundower Offshore Services*).

In 1999, the Court turned its attention to sexual harassment in public schools. It held that school districts can be held liable for sexual harassment in cases of student-on-student harassment where the school district has knowledge of the harassment or is deliberately indifferent to it. The harassment must be so severe, pervasive, and objectively offensive that it can be said to deprive the victims of access to the educational opportunities or benefits provided by the school (*Davis v. Monroe County Board of Education*).

Sexual harassment can occur anywhere but may be especially prevalent in male-dominated occupations such as the military. A 1991 convention of the Tailhook Association, an organization of naval aviators, made the news after reports surfaced of drunken sailors jamming a hotel hallway and sexually assaulting female guests, including naval officers, as they stepped off the elevator. After the much-criticized initial failure of the navy to identify the officers responsible for the assault, heads rolled, including those of several admirals and the secretary of the navy. In 1996 and 1997, a number of army officers and noncommissioned officers had their careers ended—and some went to prison—for sexual harassment of female soldiers in training situations. Behavior that was once viewed as simply male high jinks is now recognized as intolerable. The Pentagon removed top officials at the Air Force Academy in 2003 following charges that female cadets were frequently raped by male cadets.

Newly Active Groups Under the Civil Rights Umbrella

Racial and ethnic minorities and women are not the only Americans who can claim civil rights; policies enacted to protect one or two groups can be applied to others. Three recent entrants into the civil rights arena are aging Americans, people with disabilities, and homosexuals. All these groups claim equal rights, as racial minorities and women do, but represent different challenges to mainstream America.

Civil Rights and the Graying of America

America is aging rapidly. People in their 80s make up the fastest-growing age-group in this country. John Glenn, a 77-year-old senator from Ohio, made history in October 1998 as the oldest person in space when he accompanied a crew of six other astronauts aboard the space shuttle *Discovery*.

When the Social Security program began in the 1930s, 65 was the retirement age. Although this age was apparently chosen arbitrarily, it soon became the mandatory retirement age for many workers. Although many workers might prefer to retire while they are still healthy and active enough to enjoy leisure, not everyone wants or can afford to do so. Social Security is not—and was never meant to be—an adequate income, and not all workers have good pension plans or retirement savings plans.

Although many elderly people wished to work, employers routinely refused to hire people over a certain age. Graduate and professional schools often rejected applicants in their 30s on the grounds that their professions would get fewer years—and thus less return—out of them. This policy had a severe impact on housewives and veterans who wanted to return to school.

As early as 1967, Congress banned some kinds of age discrimination. In 1975, civil rights law denied federal funds to any institution discriminating against people over the age of 40 because of their age. Congress amended the Age Discrimination in Employment Act in 1978 to raise the general compulsory retirement age to 70. Now compulsory retirement has been phased out altogether. No one knows what other directions the *gray liberation movement* may take as its members approach the status of a minority majority. In 1976 the Supreme Court, however, declared that it would not place age in the suspect classification category when it upheld a state law requiring police officers to retire at the age of 50. Age classifications would fall under the rational basis test.[26]

Job bias is often hidden, and proving it depends on inference and circumstantial evidence. The Supreme Court made it easier to win cases of job bias in 2000 when it held in *Reeves v. Sanderson* that a plaintiff's evidence of an employer's bias, combined with sufficient evidence to find that the employer's asserted justification is false, may permit juries and judges to conclude that an employer unlawfully discriminated. Five years later the Court found that employers can be held liable for discrimination even if they never intended any harm. Older employees need only show an employer's policies disproportionately harmed them—and that there was no reasonable basis for the employer's policy.[27] Thus, employees can win lawsuits without direct evidence of an employer's illegal intent. The impact of these decisions is likely to extend beyond questions of age discrimination to the litigation of race and gender discrimination cases brought under Title VII of the Civil Rights Act of 1964 as well as cases brought under the Americans with Disabilities Act.

Civil Rights and People with Disabilities

Americans with disabilities have suffered from both direct and indirect discrimination. Governments and employers have often denied them rehabilitation services (a kind of affirmative action), education, and jobs. Many people with disabilities have been excluded from the workforce and isolated without overt discrimination. Throughout most of American history, public and private buildings have been hostile to the blind, deaf, and mobility impaired. Stairs, buses, telephones, and other necessities of modern life have been designed in ways that keep these individuals out of offices, stores, and restaurants. As one slogan said, "Once, blacks had to ride at the back of the bus. We can't even get on the bus."

The first rehabilitation laws were passed in the late 1920s, mostly to help veterans of World War I. Accessibility laws had to wait another 50 years. The Rehabilitation Act of 1973 (twice vetoed by Richard Nixon as "too costly") added people with disabilities to the list of Americans protected from discrimination. Because the law defines an inaccessible environment as a form of discrimination, wheelchair ramps, grab bars on toilets, and Braille signs have become common features of American life. The Education of All Handicapped Children Act of 1975 entitled all children to a free public education appropriate to their needs. The **Americans with Disabilities Act of 1990 (ADA)** strengthened these protections, requiring employers and administrators of public facilities to make "reasonable accommodations" and prohibiting employment discrimination against people with disabilities.

Americans with Disabilities Act of 1990
A law passed in 1990 that requires employers and public facilities to make "reasonable accommodations" for people with disabilities and prohibits discrimination against these individuals in employment.

Determining who is "disabled" has generated controversy. Are people with AIDS entitled to protections? In 1998 the Supreme Court answered yes. It ruled that the ADA offered protection against discrimination to people with AIDS.[28] What about people with bad eyesight or high blood pressure? In 1999 the Supreme Court ruled that people with physical impairments who can function normally when they wear glasses or take their medicine cannot be considered disabled and thus do not fall under the ADA's protection against employment discrimination.[29]

Nobody wants to oppose policies beneficial to people with disabilities. After all, people like Helen Keller and Franklin Roosevelt are popular American heroes. Nevertheless, civil rights laws designed to protect the rights of these individuals have met with vehement opposition and, once passed, with sluggish enforcement. The source of this resistance is the same concern that troubled Nixon: cost. Budgeting for such programs is often shortsighted, however. People often forget that changes allowing people with disabilities to become wage earners, spenders, and taxpayers are a gain rather than drain on the economy.

You Are the Mayor

Americans with disabilities are among the successors to the 1960s civil rights activists. Recently, they have been active in demanding government benefits.

Gay and Lesbian Rights

Gay and lesbian activists may face the toughest battle for equality. *Homophobia*—fear and hatred of homosexuals—has many causes; some are very powerful. Some religious groups, for instance, condemn homosexuality. Such attitudes continue to characterize a large segment of the American public despite some changes over the past few years (see "A Generation of Change: Discrimination against Homosexuals"). Homophobia appeared to be the motive for the brutal 1998 killing of Matthew Shepard, a 21-year-old political science freshman at the University of Wyoming. Students attacked Shepard after he attended a meeting for Gay Awareness Week events on campus. He was found tied to a fence, where his assailants had hit him in the head with a pistol 18 times and repeatedly kicked him in the groin.

Even by conservative estimates, several million Americans are homosexual, representing every social stratum and ethnic group. Gays and lesbians often face

A GENERATION OF CHANGE

Discrimination Against Homosexuals

A substantial percentage of the American public has opposed allowing homosexuals to enter many common occupations. However, attitudes toward job discrimination grew substantially more liberal from 1992 through 2003. It appeared that the long-term trend would eventually provide the basis for largely eliminating discrimination. Yet the latest public opinion data tell a different story. In 2005, acceptance to hiring homosexuals decreased for every occupation in the table, especially for school teachers and the clergy. This trend could be the result of heightened sensitivity about homosexuality in response to the issue of gay marriage and the fact that some conservative groups supporting George W. Bush emphasized it in the 2004 presidential election.

Do you think homosexuals should or should not be hired for each of the following occupations?

	% Saying "Yes, should be hired"					
	1992	1996	1999	2001	2003	2005
Salesperson	82%	90%	90%	91%	92%	90%
Armed forces	57	65	70	72	80	76
Doctors	53	69	75	78	82	78
High school teachers	47	60	61	63	67	62
Clergy	43	53	54	54	56	49
Elementary school teachers	41	55	54	56	61	54

Source: Gallup Poll, April 1999, May 2001, May 2003, May 2005.

Suspect Classfications and Gay Marriage

discrimination in hiring, education, access to public accommodations, and housing. Of particular concern to the gay community is the AIDS virus, which had an especially devastating effect on male homosexuals when the epidemic struck in the early 1980s.

A notorious incident in a New York City bar in 1969 stimulated the growth of the gay rights movement. Police raided the Stonewall bar, frequented by gay men. Unwarranted violence, arrests, and injury to persons and property resulted. Both gay men and lesbians organized throughout the 1970s and 1980s in an effort to protect their civil rights. During this time, they developed political skills and formed significant interest groups.

The record of gay rights is mixed. In 1986 the Supreme Court, in *Bowers v. Hardwick*, allowed states to ban homosexual relations. In 2000 the Supreme Court held that the Boy Scouts could exclude a gay man from being an adult member because homosexuality violates the organization's principles.[30]

In the summer of 1993, after months of negotiation with the Pentagon and an avalanche of criticism, President Clinton announced a new policy that barred the Pentagon from asking military recruits or service personnel to disclose their sexual orientation. Popularly known as the "don't ask, don't tell" policy, it also reaffirmed the Defense Department's strict prohibition against homosexual conduct. Service members who declare their homosexuality face discharge unless they can prove they will remain celibate, and they are barred from even disclosing to a friend in private conversation that they are gay or bisexual. The policy also requires commanders to have "credible information" that the policy is being violated before launching an investigation.

Gay activists have also won important victories. Seven states, including California, and more than 100 communities have passed laws protecting homosexuals against some forms of discrimination.[31] Most colleges and universities now have gay rights organizations on campus. In 1996, in *Romer v. Evans*, the Supreme Court voided a state constitutional amendment approved by the voters of Colorado that denied homosexuals protection against discrimination. The Court found that the Colorado amendment violated the U.S. Constitution's guarantee of equal protection of the law. In 2003, in *Lawrence v. Texas*, the Supreme Court overturned *Bowers v. Hardwick* when it voided a Texas anti-sodomy law on the grounds that such laws were unconstitutional intrusions of the right to privacy.

Civil Rights and Gay Adoption

The newest issue concerning gay rights is gay marriage. Most states have laws banning same-sex marriage and the recognition of such marriages that occur in other states. In 1996, Congress passed the Defense of Marriage Act, which permits states to disregard gay marriages, even if they are legal elsewhere in the United States. However, the states of Vermont and Connecticut recognize gay "civil unions," and several states, including California, Hawaii, Maine, and New Jersey, provide domestic partnership benefits to same-sex couples. In November 2003, the Massachusetts Supreme Court declared that the state's constitution guaranteed same-sex couples the right to marry. From San Francisco to Boston, gays rushed to the altar, provoking a strong backlash from social conservatives. President Bush called for a constitutional amendment to ban gay marriage.

When the Massachusetts Supreme Court held that the state's constitution required recognition of gay marriage, the issue became a factor in the 2004 presidential election. Here supporters and opponents of gay marriage protest outside the Massachusetts State House as the legislators considered amending the Massachusetts constitution to overturn the court's decision.

Amending the Constitution is difficult, and both the public and elected officials are divided on the wisdom of doing so. In the meantime, gays push for benefits associated with marriage, including health insurance, taxes, Social Security payments, hospital visitation rights, and many other aspects of life that most people take for granted.

Affirmative Action

The public policy paths for women and minorities have not been identical. However, they have converged in the debate about affirmative action to overcome the effects of past discrimination. Some people argue that groups that have suffered invidious discrimination require special efforts to provide them access to education and jobs. **Affirmative action** involves efforts to bring about increased employment, promotion, or admission for members of such groups. The goal is to move beyond *equal opportunity* (in which everyone has the same chance of obtaining good jobs, for example) toward *equal results* (in which different groups have the same percentage of success in obtaining those jobs). This goal might be accomplished through special rules in the public and private sectors that recruit or otherwise give preferential treatment to previously disadvantaged groups. Numerical quotas that ensure that a portion of government contracts, law school admissions, or police department promotions go to minorities and women are the strongest and most controversial form of affirmative action.

affirmative action
A policy designed to give special attention to or compensatory treatment of members of some previously disadvantaged group.

The constitutional status of affirmative action is not clear. New state and federal laws have discriminated *in favor of* these previously disadvantaged groups. Some state governments adopted affirmative action programs to increase minority enrollment, job holding, or promotion. Eventually, the federal government mandated that all state and local governments, as well as each institution receiving aid from or contracting with the federal government, adopt an affirmative action program. (See "Issues of the Times: Affirmative Action.")

The University of California at Davis (UC–Davis) introduced one such program. Eager to produce more minority physicians in California, the medical school set aside 16 of 100 places in the entering class for "disadvantaged groups." One White applicant who did not make the freshman class was Allan Bakke. After receiving his rejection letter from Davis for two straight years, Bakke learned that the mean scores on the Medical College Admissions Test of students admitted under the university's program were the 46th percentile on verbal tests and the 35th on science tests. Bakke's scores on the same tests were at the 96th and 97th percentiles, respectively. He sued UC–Davis, claiming that it had denied him equal protection of the laws by discriminating against him because of his race.

Regents of the University of California v. Bakke
A 1978 Supreme Court decision holding that a state university could not admit less qualified individuals solely because of their race.

The result was an important Supreme Court decision in Bakke's favor, ***Regents of the University of California v. Bakke*** (1978).[32] The Court ordered Bakke admitted, holding that the UC–Davis Special Admissions Program did discriminate against him because of his race. Yet the Court refused to order UC–Davis never to use race as a criterion for admission. A university could, said the Court, adopt an "admissions program where race or ethnic background is simply one element—to be weighed fairly against other elements—in the selection process." It could *not*, as the UC–Davis Special Admissions Program did, set aside a quota of spots for particular groups.

Although Bakke ended up in medical school, Brian Weber did not get into an apprenticeship program he wanted to enter in Louisiana. In *United Steelworkers of America, AFL-CIO v. Weber* (1979), the Court found that the Kaiser Aluminum Company intended its special training program, which employed a quota for minorities, to rectify years of past employment discrimination at Kaiser. Thus, said the Court, a voluntary union- and management-sponsored program to take more African Americans than Whites did *not* discriminate against Weber.

Until 1995, the Court was more deferential to Congress than to local government in upholding affirmative action programs. In 1989, the Court found a Richmond, Virginia, plan that reserved 30 percent of city subcontracts for minority firms to be unconstitutional.[33] In 1980, on the other hand, the Court upheld a federal rule setting aside 10 percent of all federal construction contracts for minority-owned firms.[34] In 1990, the Court agreed that Congress may require preferential treatment for minorities to increase their ownership of broadcast licenses.[35] This event marked the first time the Supreme Court upheld a specific affirmative action program that was not devised to remedy past discrimination.

Adarand Constructors v. Pena
A 1995 Supreme Court decision holding that federal programs that classify people by race, even for an ostensibly benign purpose such as expanding opportunities for minorities, should be presumed to be unconstitutional.

Things changed in 1995, however. In ***Adarand Constructors v. Pena***, the Court overturned the decision regarding broadcast licenses and cast grave doubt on its holding regarding contracts set aside for minority-owned firms. It held that federal programs that classify people by race, even for an ostensibly benign purpose such as expanding opportunities for members of minorities, should be presumed to be unconstitutional. Such programs must be subject to the most searching judicial inquiry and can survive only if they are "narrowly tailored" to accomplish a "compelling governmental interest." In other words, the Court applied criteria for evaluating affirmative action programs similar to those it applies to other racial classifications, the less benign suspect classifications we discussed earlier in the chapter. These are also the same criteria the Court has applied to state affirmative action programs since 1989. Although *Adarand Constructors v. Pena* did not void federal affirmative action programs in general, it certainly limits their potential impact.

On other matters, the Court has approved preferential treatment of minorities in promotions,[36] and it has also ordered quotas for minority union memberships.[37] We examine a case of a public employer using affirmative action promotions to counter underrepresentation of women and minorities in the workplace in "You Are the Judge: The Case of the Santa Clara Dispatcher."

Affirmative Action

On the other hand, the Court has ruled that affirmative action does not exempt recently hired minorities from traditional work rules specifying the "last hired, first fired" order of layoffs.[38] In 1986, the Court found unconstitutional an effort to give preference to African American teachers in layoffs because this policy punished innocent White teachers and the African American teachers had not been the actual victims of past discrimination.[39]

Not everyone agrees that affirmative action is a wise or fair policy. There is little support from the general public for programs such as those that set aside jobs or

YOU ARE THE JUDGE

The Case of the Santa Clara Dispatcher

For four years, Diane Joyce patched asphalt with a Santa Clara county road crew around San Jose, California, and its suburbs. She applied for a promotion, hoping to work in the less strenuous and better-paid position of dispatcher. Another applicant for the job was Paul Johnson, a White male who had worked for the agency for 13 years.

Like Diane, Paul did well on the exam given to all applicants; in fact, the two scored among the top six applicants, Diane with a score of 73 and Paul with 75. Knowing that Paul's score was a shade better and his work experience longer, the supervisor decided to hire him. The county's affirmative action officers overruled the supervisor, however, and Diane got the job. Paul decided to get a lawyer.

Paul's lawyer argued that Diane's promotion violated Title VII of the Civil Rights Act of 1964. This law, originally passed to guarantee minority access to jobs and promotions, makes it unlawful for an employer to deprive any individual of employment opportunities because of their race, color, religion, gender, or national origin.

You Be the Judge: Should Diane Joyce have been promoted?

Answer: In *Johnson v. Transportation Agency, Santa Clara County* (1987), the Supreme Court held that public employers may use carefully constructed affirmative action promotion plans, designed to remedy specific past discriminations, to counter women's and minorities' underrepresentation in the workplace. Thus, Diane Joyce kept her job. In a stinging dissent, Justice Scalia complained that the Court was "converting [the law] from a guarantee that race or sex will not be a basis for employment determinations, to a guarantee that it often will."

employ quotas for members of minority groups. Opposition is especially strong when people view affirmative action as *reverse discrimination*—as in the case of individuals like Allan Bakke who are themselves blameless—and less qualified individuals are hired or admitted to educational or training programs because of their minority status.

Critics of reverse discrimination argue that any race or gender discrimination is wrong, even when its purpose is to rectify past injustices rather than to reinforce them. After all, Bakke and Johnson could no more help being White and male than Diane Joyce could help being a woman. Opponents of affirmative action believe that merit is the only fair basis for distributing benefits. Bakke and Johnson found that the rules by which institutions operated had suddenly changed—and they suffered as a result. It is easy to sympathize with them.

In 1996, California voters passed Proposition 209, which banned state affirmative action programs based on race, ethnicity, or gender in public hiring, contracting, and educational admissions (Washington State passed a similar ban in 1998). Opponents immediately filed a lawsuit in federal court to block enforcement of the law, claiming that it violated the Fourteenth Amendment, but courts upheld the law. There is little question that support for Proposition 209 represents a widespread skepticism about affirmative action programs.

In 2003, the Supreme Court made two important decisions on affirmative action in college admissions. First, the Court agreed that there was a compelling interest in promoting racial diversity on campus. The Court upheld the University of Michigan law school's use of race as one of many factors in admission in *Grutter v. Bollinger* (2003). The Court found that the law school's use of race as a plus in the admissions process was narrowly tailored and that it made individualistic, holistic reviews of applicants in a nonmechanical fashion. In 2006, Michigan voters passed a ballot initiative banning affirmative action in college admissions and government hiring.

In *Gratz v. Bollinger* (2003), however, the Court struck down the University of Michigan's system of undergraduate admissions in which every applicant from an underrepresented racial or ethnic minority group was automatically awarded 20 points of the 100 needed to guarantee admission. The Court said that the system was tantamount to using a quota, which it outlawed in *Bakke*, because it made the factor of race decisive for virtually every minimally qualified underrepresented minority applicant. The 20 points awarded to minorities were more than the school awarded for some measures of academic excellence, writing ability, or leadership skills.

On the other hand, the case for affirmative action is also persuasive. Proponents of these policies argue that what constitutes merit is highly subjective and can embody prejudices of which the decision maker may be quite unaware. Experts suggest that a man can "look more like" a road dispatcher and thus get a higher rating from interviewers than a woman might. Affirmative action supporters believe that increasing the number of women and minorities in desirable jobs is such an important social goal that it should be considered when determining an individual's qualifications. They claim that what White males lose from affirmative action programs are privileges to which they were never entitled in the first place; after all, nobody has the right to be a doctor or a road dispatcher. Research has found that affirmative action offers significant benefits for women and minorities with relatively small costs for White males.[40]

Understanding Civil Rights and Public Policy

The original Constitution is silent on the issue of equality. The only direct reference is in the Fourteenth Amendment, which forbids the states to deny "equal protection of the laws." Those five words have been the basis for major civil rights statutes and scores of judicial rulings protecting the rights of minorities and women. These laws and decisions, granting people new rights, have empowered groups to seek and gain still more victories. The implications of their success for democracy and the scope of government are substantial.

Race and the Death Penalty

Civil Rights and Democracy

Equality is a basic principle of democracy. Every citizen has one vote because democratic government presumes that each person's needs, interests, and preferences are neither any more nor any less important than the needs, interests, and preferences of every other person. Individual liberty is an equally important democratic principle, one that can conflict with equality.

Equality tends to favor majority rule. Because under simple majority rule everyone's wishes rank equally, the policy outcome that most people prefer seems to be the fairest choice in cases of conflict. What happens, however, if the majority wants to deprive the minority of certain rights? In situations like these, equality threatens individual liberty. Thus, the principle of equality can invite the denial of minority rights, whereas the principle of liberty condemns such action.[41]

Majority rule is not the only threat to liberty. Politically and socially powerful minorities have suppressed majorities as well as other minorities. Women have long outnumbered men in America, about 53 percent to 47 percent. In the era of segregation, African Americans outnumbered Whites in many Southern states. Inequality persisted, however, because customs that reinforced it were entrenched within the society and because inequality often served the interests of the dominant groups. When slavery and segregation existed in an agrarian economy, Whites could get cheap agricultural labor. When men were breadwinners and women were homemakers, married men had a source of cheap domestic labor.

Both African Americans and women made many gains even when they lacked one essential component of democratic power: the vote. They used other rights—such as their First Amendment freedoms—to fight for equality. When Congress protected the right of African Americans to vote in the 1960s, the nature of Southern politics changed dramatically. The democratic process is a powerful vehicle for disadvantaged groups to press their claims.

Civil Rights and the Scope of Government

Civil rights laws increase the scope and power of government. These laws regulate the behavior of individuals and institutions. Restaurant owners must serve all patrons regardless of race. Professional schools must admit women. Employers must accommodate people with disabilities and make an effort to find minority workers, whether they want to or not. Those who want to reduce the scope of government are uneasy with these laws, if not downright hostile to them.

The Founders might be greatly perturbed if they knew about all the civil rights laws the government has enacted; these policies do not conform to the eighteenth-century idea of limited government. But the Founders would expect the national government to do whatever is necessary to hold the nation together. The Civil War showed that the original Constitution did not adequately deal with issues like slavery that could destroy the society the Constitution's writers had struggled to secure.

However, civil rights, like civil liberties, is an area in which increased government activity in protecting basic rights can lead to greater checks on government by those who benefit from such protections. Remember that much of segregation was *de jure*, established by governments. Moreover, we can view government action in the area of civil rights as the protection of individualism. Basic to the notion of civil rights is that individuals are not to be judged according to characteristics they share with a group. Thus, civil rights protect the individual against collective discrimination.

The question of where to draw the line in the government's efforts to protect civil rights has received different answers at different points in American history, but few Americans want to turn back the clock to the days of *Plessy v. Ferguson* and Jim Crow laws or to the exclusion of women from the workplace.

Summary

Racial minorities have struggled for equality since the very beginning of the Republic. In the era of slavery, the Supreme Court upheld the practice and denied slaves any rights. After the Civil War and Reconstruction ended, governments at all levels established legal segregation. For a time, the Supreme Court sanctioned Jim Crow laws, but in 1954, the *Brown v. Board of Education* case held that *de jure* racial segregation violated equal protection of the laws, which was guaranteed by the Fourteenth Amendment. This event marked the beginning of the era of civil rights. *Brown* inaugurated a movement that succeeded in ending virtually every form of legal discrimination against minorities.

Although feminists have not ignored the courts, the struggle for women's equality has emphasized legislation over litigation. Women won the right to vote in 1920, but the states failed to ratify the Equal Rights Amendment. This defeat did not kill the feminist movement, however. Comparable worth, women's role in the military, sexual harassment, and the balance between work and family are among the many controversial women's issues society is still debating.

The interests of women and minorities have converged on the issue of affirmative action—that is, policies requiring special efforts on behalf of disadvantaged groups. In the *Bakke* case and in decisions like *Johnson v. Santa Clara*, the Court ruled that affirmative action plans were both legal and constitutional. However, there is substantial opposition to what many see as reverse discrimination.

The civil rights umbrella is a large one. Increasing numbers of groups seek protection for their rights. Older Americans, people with disabilities, and homosexuals have used the laws to ensure their equality. People with AIDS and other chronically ill people may yet mount battles in the political arena. It is difficult to predict what controversies the twenty-first century will bring, when minority groups will outnumber the current majority.

Internet Resources

www.law.cornell.edu/wex/index.php/Equal_protection
The background material and text of the landmark cases on equal protection.

www.usdoj.gov/crt/
Home page of the Civil Rights Division of the U.S. Department of Justice containing background information and discussion of current events.

www.usdoj.gov/crt/ada/adahom1.htm
Home page of the Americans with Disabilities Act of the U.S. Department of Justice containing background information and discussion of current events.

www.naacp.org
Home page of the NAACP containing background information and discussion of current events.

www.civilrightsproject.harvard.edu/
Home page of the Civil Rights Project at Harvard University, with background information and other resources on civil rights.

www.usccr.gov/
U.S. Commission on Civil Rights home page, with news of civil rights issues around the country.

www.hrc.org/
Human Rights Campaign home page, with information on lesbian, gay, bisexual, and transgender rights.

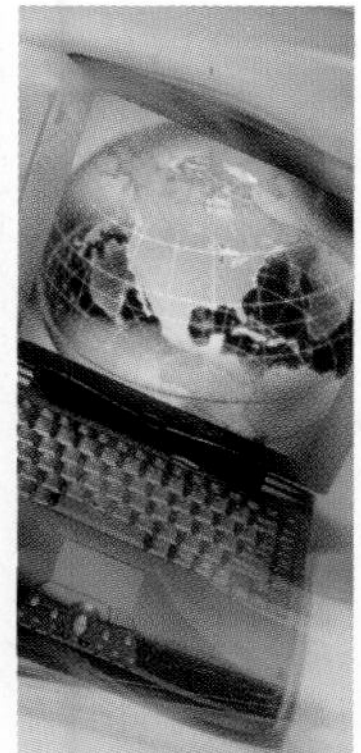

Get Connected

Race, Affirmative Action, and Equal Opportunity

Race is an enduring issue in American politics. Historically, the debate has focused on relations between Blacks and Whites, but demographic trends and immigration are changing the debate. The Hispanic population in the United States is growing, adding to the complexity of race relations. Decision makers have been asked to develop ways to provide for equal opportunities for all races without creating a system of race-based quotas. Let us compare several strategies for implementing affirmative action and/or equal opportunity.

Search the Web

Go the Civil Rights.org Web page on affirmative action, *www.civilrights.org/issues/affirmative/*. You may want to read the information on affirmative action in university admissions decisions more closely. Also visit the Center for Equal Opportunity's Web site, *www.ceousa.org/*. You will find some information on affirmative action in university admissions as well.

Questions to Ask

- What is affirmative action? Do the two groups define affirmative action differently?
- What evidence does Civil Rights.org use to defend affirmative action? What evidence does the Center for Equal Opportunity use to oppose affirmative action?
- What do the two groups think should be done to increase access to higher education for all people regardless of race?

Why It Matters

Equality is central to our political culture. One of the most difficult tasks of policymakers is bridging the gap between equality of opportunity and equality of results. It is critical that they integrate all citizens fully into American life, but they must do so in a manner that most citizens perceive to be fair to those who have not suffered from past discrimination.

Get Involved

Look at the other students in the class. How many are of a race different than yours? How many are of the opposite gender? Ask several of those students about racial preferences in college admissions decisions. Are the other students' views about racial preferences different from your own?

For more exercises, go to www.longmanamericangovernment.com.

For Further Reading

Arsenault, Raymond. *Freedom Riders: 1961 and the Struggle for Racial Justice*. New York: Oxford University Press, 2006. The story of the freedom riders' efforts to desegregate the South.

Baer, Judith A. *Women in the Law: The Struggle Toward Equality from the New Deal to the Present*. 3rd rev. ed. New York: Holmes and Meier, 2003. An excellent analysis of women's changing legal status.

Berger, Raoul. *Government by Judiciary: The Transformation of the Fourteenth Amendment*. Cambridge, MA: Harvard University Press, 1977. Berger is not one who favors use of the Fourteenth Amendment to expand equality.

Bergman, Barbara R. *In Defense of Affirmative Action*. New York: Basic Books, 1996. An argument on behalf of affirmative action policies.

Berry, Mary F. *Why ERA Failed*. Bloomington: Indiana University Press, 1986. An excellent account of public policies affecting women, with particular attention to the demise of the Equal Rights Amendment.

Bowen, William G., and Derek Bok. *The Shape of the River: The Long-Term Consequences of Considering Race in College and University Admissions*. Princeton, NJ: Princeton University Press, 1998. Former presidents of Harvard and Princeton discuss affirmative action in higher education.

García, John A. *Latino Politics in America: Community, Culture, and Interests*. Lanham, MD: Rowman & Littlefield, 2003. An insightful view of Latino politics.

Greenberg, Jack. *Crusader in the Courts*. New York: Basic Books, 1994. The story of litigation in the civil rights era as told by one of the chief participants.

Kluger, Richard. *Simple Justice*. New York: Knopf, 1976. The story of the *Brown* case.

Mansbridge, Jane. *Why We Lost the ERA*. Chicago: University of Chicago Press, 1986. The politics of women's rights.

McClain, Paula D., and Joseph Stewart. *"Can't We All Get Along?"* 4th ed. Boulder, CO: Westview, 2005. Racial and ethnic minorities in American politics.

McGlen, Nancy, and Karen O'Connor. *Women's Rights: The Struggle for Equality in the Nineteenth and Twentieth Centuries*. New York: Praeger, 1983. A good account of the struggle for equal rights for women.

Nakanishi, Don T., and James S. Lai, eds. *Asian American Politics: Law, Participation, and Policy*. Lanham, MD: Rowman & Littlefield, 2003. Essays focusing on Asian American politics.

Urofsky, Melvin I. *A Conflict of Rights: The Supreme Court and Affirmative Action*. New York: Scribner's, 1991. A case study of the issues, people, and events surrounding the case of *Joyce v. Johnson*.

Wilkins, David E. *American Indian Politics and the American Political System*. Rev. ed. Lanham, MD: Rowman & Littlefield, 2003. Excellent treatment of Native American issues and politics.

Woodward, C. Vann. *The Strange Career of Jim Crow*. 2nd ed. New York: Oxford University Press, 1966. Examines the evolution of Jim Crow laws in the South.

Public Opinion and Political Action

Politics in Action: A Rare Moment of Consensus in Public Opinion American public opinion about the events of September 11, 2001, and the subsequent war in Afghanistan reflected a unanimity that is rarely seen. Normally, analysts find a great diversity of views among the American public, and public opinion surveys usually reveal many conflicting attitudes that frequently reflect ambivalence. But such was not the case in this instance. Hundreds of millions of Americans responded with remarkably near-unanimous opinions. Most everyone agreed that the attacks were an act of war that demanded an immediate response by force. Partisan differences, racial differences, and regional differences mattered little in understanding attitudes about the events of September 11 and the war against terrorism.

Chapter Outline

A CNN/*USA Today* poll conducted on September 11, 2001, found that 86 percent felt the attacks that day had been an act of war. A *Washington Post*/ABC poll conducted on September 13 found 93 percent favored military action when asked, "If the United States can identify the groups or nations responsible for the attacks, would you support or oppose taking military action against them?" The same poll found that 85 percent favored striking at Afghanistan if Osama Bin Laden was found to be culpable and Afghanistan refused to turn him over. Support for military action dropped a bit when people were asked if it meant innocent civilians might be hurt or killed and a bit more when posed with the scenario of a long war with large numbers of U.S. troops killed or injured. But 69 percent of the population nevertheless supported the use of force even under the conditions of Afghan civilian casualties and high military costs to the United States.

War, Peace, and Public Opinion

Not only did the vast majority of the American public immediately give their support for military action, but they continued to support such action once hostilities commenced in Afghanistan. At *www.pollingreport.com*, we found reports of 18 different public opinion polls that asked people whether they approved or disapproved of U.S. military action being taken in response to the terrorist attacks. The level of support was consistently high, ranging from 86 to 92 percent. Such support levels exceeded public support levels for the Persian Gulf War in 1991, which is typically thought of as an overwhelmingly supported military operation.

The case of September 11 is clearly an exception to the rule regarding public opinion. Usually, public opinion polls are taken to find out the level of disagreement in the country and what sorts of people favor which actions. As will be seen in this chapter, the degree of unanimity apparent in public opinion immediately after the terrorist attacks is most unusual.

Politicians and columnists commonly intone the words "the American people" and then claim their view as that of the citizenry. Yet it would be hard to find a statement about the American people—who they are and what they believe—that is either 100 percent right or 100 percent wrong. The American people are wondrously diverse. There are about 300 million Americans, forming a mosaic of racial, ethnic, and cultural groups. America was founded on the principle of tolerating diversity and individualism, and it remains one of the most diverse countries in the world today. Most Americans view this diversity as one of the most appealing aspects of their society.

public opinion
The distribution of the population's beliefs about politics and policy issues.

The study of American **public opinion** aims to understand the distribution of the population's belief about politics and policy issues. Because there are many groups with a great variety of opinions in the United States, this is an especially complex task. This is not to say that public opinion would be easy to study even if America were a more homogeneous society; as you will see, measuring public opinion involves painstaking interviewing procedures and careful wording of questions. Further complicating the task is the fact that people are often not well informed about the issues. The least informed are also the least likely to participate in the political process, a phenomenon that creates imbalances in who takes part in political action.

For American government to work efficiently and effectively, the diversity of the American public and its opinions must be faithfully channeled through the political process. This chapter reveals just how difficult this task is.

The American People

One way of looking at the American public is through **demography**—the science of human populations. The most valuable tool for understanding demographic changes in America is the **census**. The U.S. Constitution requires that the government conduct an "actual enumeration" of the population every 10 years. The first census was conducted in 1790.

demography
The science of population changes.

census
A valuable tool for understanding demographic changes. The Constitution requires that the government conduct an "actual enumeration" of the population every 10 years.

The Census Bureau tries to conduct the most accurate count of the population humanly feasible. It isn't an easy job, even with the allocation of billions of federal dollars to the task. After the 1990 census was completed, the Census Bureau estimated that 4.7 million people were not counted. Furthermore, they found that members of minority groups were disproportionately undercounted, as they were apparently more suspicious of government and thus less willing to cooperate with census workers. In order to correct for such an undercount in 2000, the Clinton administration approved a plan to scientifically estimate the characteristics of those people who failed to respond to the census forms and follow-up visits from Census workers and then to incorporate this information into the official count. Conservatives maintain that such a procedure would be subject to manipulation, less accurate than a traditional head count, and unconstitutional. In the 1999 case of *Department of Commerce v. U.S. House of Representatives,* the Supreme Court ruled that sampling could not be used to determine the number of congressional districts each state is entitled to. However, they left the door open for the use of sampling procedures to adjust the count for other purposes, such as allocation of federal grants to states. In the end, the Bush administration decided not to use this sampling option.

Changes in the U.S. population, as reflected in census figures, impact our culture and political system in numerous ways, which will be examined in the next few sections.

Responding to criticisms that many minority groups had been undercounted in the previous census, the Census Bureau launched special advertising campaigns to improve cooperation rates in these communities in 2000. Here you can see a poster in Detroit targeted at the large number of Iraqi immigrants in the city.

The Immigrant Society

The United States has always been a nation of immigrants. As John F. Kennedy said, America is "not merely a nation but a nation of nations."[1] All Americans except Native Americans either descended from immigrants or are immigrants themselves. Today, federal law allows up to 800,000 new immigrants to be legally admitted into the country every year. This is equivalent to adding a city with the population of Indianapolis every year. In recent years, the illegal immigrants have outnumbered legal immigrants.

There have been three great waves of immigration to the United States:

- Prior to the late nineteenth century, northwestern Europeans (English, Irish, Germans, and Scandinavians) constituted the first wave of immigration.

- During the late nineteenth and early twentieth centuries, southern and eastern Europeans (Italians, Jews, Poles, Russians, and others) made up the second wave. Most of these passed through Ellis Island in New York (now a popular museum) as their first stop in the new world.
- In recent decades, a third wave of immigrants has consisted of Hispanics (from Cuba, Central America, and Mexico) and Asians (from Vietnam, Korea, the Philippines, and elsewhere). The 1980s saw the second-largest number of immigrants of any decade in American history, and these groups are continuing to immigrate in large numbers.

Immigrants bring with them their aspirations as well as their own political beliefs. For example, Cubans in Miami, who nearly constitute a majority of the city's population, first came to America to escape Fidel Castro's Marxist regime and have brought their anticommunist sentiments with them. Similarly, the Vietnamese came to America after a communist takeover there. Cubans and Vietnamese are just two recent examples of the many types of immigrants who have come to America over the years to flee an oppressive government. Other examples from previous periods of heavy immigration include the Irish in the first wave and the Russians in the second. Throughout American history, such groups have fostered a great appreciation for individualism in American public policy by their wish to be free of governmental control.

The American Melting Pot

melting pot
The mixing of cultures, ideas, and peoples that has changed the American nation. The United States, with its history of immigration, has often been called a melting pot.

minority majority
The emergence of a non-Caucasian majority, as compared with a White, generally Anglo-Saxon majority. It is predicted that by about 2060, Hispanic Americans, African Americans, and Asian Americans together will outnumber White Americans.

With its long history of immigration, the United States has often been called a **melting pot**. This phrase refers to a mixture of cultures, ideas, and peoples. As the third wave of immigration continues, policymakers have begun to speak of a new **minority majority**, meaning that America will eventually cease to have a White, generally Anglo-Saxon majority. The 2000 census data found an all-time low in the percentage of non-Hispanic White Americans—just over 69 percent of the population. African Americans made up 12 percent of the population, Hispanics 13 percent, Asians 4 percent, and Native Americans slightly less than 1 percent. Between 1980 and 1990, minority populations grew at a much faster rate than the White population. As you can see in Figure 6.1, the Census Bureau estimates that by the middle of the twenty-first century, Whites will represent only 52 percent of the population.

Until recently, the largest minority group in the country has been the African American population. One in eight Americans is a descendant of these reluctant immigrants: Africans who were brought to America by force as slaves. As we saw in Chapter 5, a legacy of racism and discrimination has left a higher proportion of the African American population economically and politically disadvantaged than the White population. In 2004, the Census Bureau found that 25 percent of African Americans lived below the poverty line, compared to about 11 percent of Whites.

Despite this economic disadvantage, African Americans have recently been exercising a good deal of political power. The number of African American elected officials has increased by over 500 percent since 1970.[2] African Americans have been elected as mayors of many of the country's biggest cities, including Los Angeles,

Figure 6.1 The Coming Minority Majority

Based on the basis of current birthrates and immigration rates, the Census Bureau estimates that the demographics of the country should change as shown in the accompanying graph. Extend the lines a bit beyond the year 2050, and it is clear that minority groups will soon be in the majority nationwide. Of course, should rates of birth and immigration change, so will these estimates. But already there are 65 congressional districts with a minority majority, about 85 percent of which are represented in the House by an African American, a Hispanic, or an Asian American.

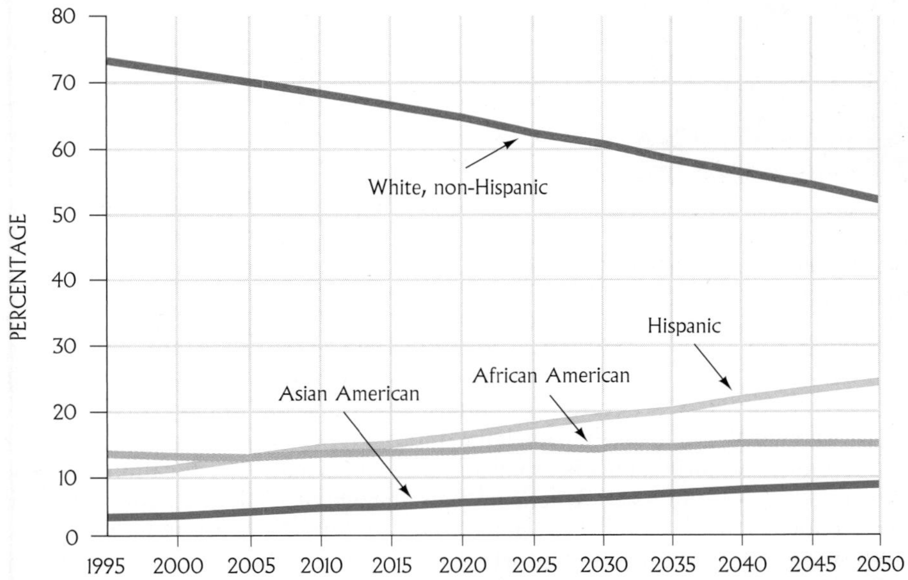

New York, and Chicago. In 2001, Colin Powell became the first African American secretary of state and Condoleezza Rice became the nation's first African American to serve as the president's national security advisor. (Rice later succeeded Powell as secretary of state.)

The familiar problems of African Americans sometimes obscure the problems of other minority groups, such as Hispanics (composed largely of Mexicans, Cubans, and Puerto Ricans). The 2000 census reported for the first time that the Hispanic population outnumbered the African American population. Like African Americans, Hispanics are concentrated in cities. Hispanics are rapidly gaining power in the Southwest, and cities such as San Antonio and Denver have elected mayors of Hispanic heritage. In recent years, the state legislatures of New Mexico, Texas, Arizona, Colorado, Florida, and California have each had at least 10 percent Hispanic representation.[3]

The Debate over Immigration

An issue of particular concern to the Hispanic community is what to do about the problem of illegal immigration. The Simpson-Mazzoli Act, named after its congressional sponsors, requires that employers document the citizenship of their employees. Whether people are born in Canton, Ohio, or Canton, China, they

Just north of San Diego, the problem of illegal immigration from Mexico has taken a dangerous turn. Seeking to make their way around a freeway checkpoint, immigrants sometimes attempt to cross the busy San Diego freeway. After a number of people were hit by cars, authorities posted signs like these to warn motorists to look out for people crossing the freeway.

must prove that they are either U.S. citizens or legal immigrants in order to work. Civil and criminal penalties can be assessed against employers who knowingly employ undocumented immigrants. However, it has proved difficult for authorities to establish that employers have knowingly accepted false Social Security cards and other forged identity documents. Hence, the Simpson-Mazzoli Act has proved to be inadequate in stopping illegal immigration from Mexico and other Latin American countries. One proposed solution that has been very controversial in recent years involves denying all benefits from government programs to people who cannot prove they are legal residents of the United States (see "You Are the Policymaker: Do We Need To Get Tougher With Illegal Immigrants?").

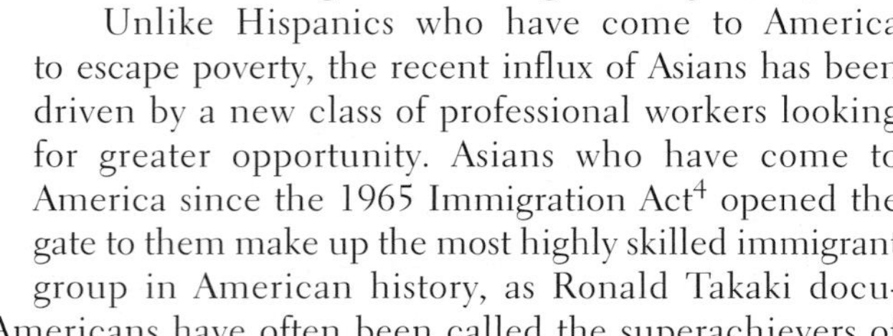

Unlike Hispanics who have come to America to escape poverty, the recent influx of Asians has been driven by a new class of professional workers looking for greater opportunity. Asians who have come to America since the 1965 Immigration Act[4] opened the gate to them make up the most highly skilled immigrant group in American history, as Ronald Takaki documents.[5] Indeed, Asian Americans have often been called the superachievers of the minority majority. This is especially true in the case of educational attainment—49 percent of Asian Americans over the age of 25 hold a college degree, almost twice the national average. As a result, their median family income has already surpassed that of non-Hispanic Whites. Although still a very small minority group, Asian Americans have had some notable political successes. In 1996, Gary Locke (a Chinese American) was elected governor of Washington, and in 2001 Norman Mineta (a Japanese American) was appointed secretary of transportation.

Illegal Immigration

The emergence of the minority majority is just one of several major demographic changes that have altered the face of American politics. In addition, the population has been moving and aging.

The Regional Shift

For most of American history, the most populous states have been concentrated in the states north of the Mason–Dixon Line and east of the Mississippi River. As you can see in Figure 6.2, though, over the past 60 years, much of America's population growth has been centered in the West and South. In particular, the populations of Florida, California, and Texas have grown rapidly as people moved to the Sun Belt. From 1990 to 2000, the rate of population growth was 24 percent in Florida, 14 percent in California, and 23 percent in Texas. In contrast, population growth in the Northeast was a scant 5 percent.

YOU ARE THE POLICYMAKER

Do We Need to Get Tougher With Illegal Immigrants?

Americans have traditionally welcomed immigrants with open arms. However, some immigrants have recently become less welcome: those who are in the country illegally. In states such as Texas and California, where many illegal immigrants from south of the border reside, there is concern that providing public services to these people is seriously draining state resources. This became the topic of heated debate when Californians voted on Proposition 187 in 1994. Labeled by its proponents as the "save our state initiative," this measure sought to cut illegal immigrants off from public services such as the right for their children to attend public schools and medical assistance for people with low incomes. According to its advocates, not only would Proposition 187 save the state treasury, it would also cut down on the number of illegal immigrants—many of whom, they argued, had come mostly to take advantage of the free goods offered in America.

Opponents replied that although illegal immigration is surely a problem, the idea of cutting off public services could easily do more harm than good. They pointed out the risks to public health of denying illegal immigrants basic health care such as immunizations that help control communicable diseases. And by throwing the children of illegal immigrants out of school, they argued that many would inevitably turn to crime with nothing to do all day. Besides, though they may be here illegally, these immigrants have to pay sales taxes on everything they buy and they pay rent—a portion of which indirectly goes to the state when their landlords pay their property taxes. Given that they contribute to the tax base that pays for public services, opponents of Proposition 187 argued that they should in all fairness be entitled to use them.

The proponents of Proposition 187 won at the ballot box. However, so far they have lost in their attempts to get the measure enforced. The courts have consistently ruled that the proposition violated the rights of illegal immigrants as well as national laws concerning eligibility for federally funded benefits. Overall, the proposition was held to be an unconstitutional state scheme to regulate immigration.

Because illegal immigrants continue to stream into the United States, the issue remains a hot one. In 2004, the Republican Party platform advocated "strong workplace enforcement with tough penalties against employees and employers who violate immigration laws." In contrast, the Democratic Party platform proposed that "Undocumented immigrants within our borders who clear a background check, work hard and pay taxes should have a path to earn full participation in America." The Republican platform called such a proposal "amnesty" and argued that this would "have the effect of encouraging illegal immigration and would give an unfair advantage to those who have broken our laws."

What do you think? Do you think a tough approach is the way to go, or do you favor incorporating illegal immigrants who prove themselves worthy into American society? What are the advantages and disadvantages of each approach?

Demographic changes are associated with political changes. States gain or lose congressional representation as their population changes, and thus power shifts as well. This **reapportionment** process occurs once a decade, after every census. After each census, the 435 seats in the House of Representatives are reallocated to the states on the basis of population changes. Thus, as California grew throughout the twentieth century, its representation in the House increased from just seven in 1900 to 53 as of the 2000 census. New York, on the other hand, has lost about one-third of its delegation over the past 50 years.

reapportionment
The process of reallocating seats in the House of Representatives every 10 years on the basis of the results of the census.

Figure 6.2 Shifting Population

These maps paint a population portrait of the United States over the past six decades. The states are drawn to scale on the basis of population. In 1940, the most populous states were concentrated east of the Mississippi River. New York, Pennsylvania, and Illinois stand out. By 2000 the national population picture—and the map—had changed considerably. Today the country's 300 million citizens are scattered more widely, and though large concentrations of population still dominate the East, there has been huge growth on the West Coast, in Texas, and in Florida.

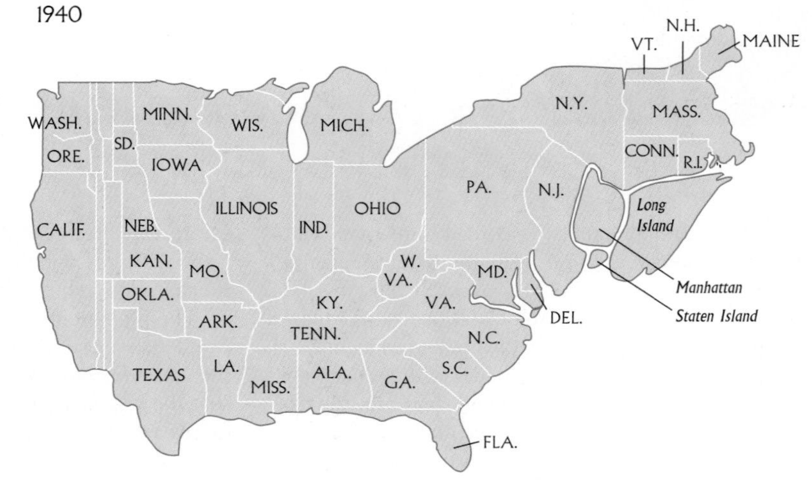

Source: The 1940 map was the work of the National Opinion Research Center, University of Denver, as printed in John Gunther's 1946 book *Inside U.S.A.*

The Graying of America

Florida, one of the three megastates, has grown in large part as a result of its attractiveness to senior citizens. Nationwide, the fastest-growing age-group in America is composed of citizens over 65. Not only are people living longer as a result of medical advances, but the birthrate has dropped substantially. About 60 percent of adult Americans living today grew up in families of four or more children. If the current "baby bust" continues, this figure will eventually be cut to 30 percent.[6]

Social Security is structured as a pay-as-you-go system. That means today's workers pay the benefits for today's retirees. In 1940, there were 42 workers per retiree; today there are 3. By 2040 there will be only 2, which will put tremendous pressure on the Social Security system. Begun under the New Deal, Social Security is exceeded only by national defense as America's most costly public policy. The current group of older Americans and those soon to follow can lay claim to trillions of dollars guaranteed by Social Security. People who have been promised benefits naturally expect to collect them, especially benefits for which they have made monthly contributions. Thus, both political parties have long treated Social Security benefits as sacrosanct. Whenever President Bush speaks on behalf of his proposal to allow younger workers to put part of their Social Security payroll taxes into personal retirement accounts, he carefully states his view that Social Security should remain unchanged for anyone born before 1950.

How Americans Learn About Politics: Political Socialization

As the most experienced segment of the population, the elderly have undergone the most **political socialization**. Political socialization is "the process through which an individual acquires his or her particular political orientations—his or her knowledge, feelings, and evaluations regarding his or her political world."[7] As people become more socialized with age, their political orientations grow firmer. It should not be surprising that governments aim their socialization efforts largely at the young, not the elderly.

political socialization
According to Richard Dawson, "the process through which an individual acquires his [or her] particular political orientations—his [or her] knowledge, feelings, and evaluations regarding his [or her] political world."

Only a small portion of Americans' political learning is formal. Civics or government classes in high school teach citizens some of the nuts and bolts of government—how many senators each state has, what presidents do, and so on. But such formal socialization is only the tip of the iceberg. Americans do most of their political learning without teachers or classes.

Informal learning is really much more important than formal, in-class learning about politics. Most informal socialization is almost accidental. Few parents sit down with their children and say, "Johnny, let us tell you why we're Republicans." Words like *pick up*, *absorb*, and *acquire* perhaps best describe the informal side of socialization.

Political Knowledge

Still, the family's role in socialization is central because of its monopoly on two crucial resources in the early years: time and emotional commitment. The powerful influence of the family is not easily undermined. Most students in an American

These children—the faces of the coming minority-majority population—suggest the unique problem of American political socialization: transforming people of diverse cultural backgrounds and beliefs into participating American citizens.

government class like to think of themselves as independent thinkers, especially when it comes to politics. Yet one can predict how the majority of young people will vote simply by knowing the political leanings of their parents.[8]

As children approach adult status, though, some degree of adolescent rebellion against parents and their beliefs often takes place. Witnessing the outpouring of youthful rebellion in the late 1960s and early 1970s, many people thought a generation gap was opening up. Radical youth supposedly condemned their backward-thinking parents. Although such a gap did exist in a few families, the overall evidence for it was slim. Eight years after Jennings and Niemi first interviewed a sample of high school seniors and their parents in the mid-1960s, they still found far more agreement than disagreement across the generational divide.[9] Recent research has demonstrated that one of the reasons for the long-lasting impact of parental influence on political attitudes is simply genetics, as shown by the data presented in Table 6.1.

The mass media are "the new parent" according to many observers. Average grade-school youngsters spend more time each week watching television than they spend at school. And television now displaces parents as the chief source of information as children get older.

Unfortunately, today's generation of young adults is significantly less likely to watch television news and read newspapers than their elders. One study attributed the relative lack of political knowledge of the youth of the 1990s to their media consumption or, more appropriately, to their lack of it.[10] In 1965, Gallup found virtually no difference between age categories in frequency of following politics through the media. In recent years, however, a considerable age gap has opened up, with older people paying the most attention to the news and young adults the least. Nielsen Media Research reported that the median age of viewers of the CBS, ABC, and NBC News from September 2003 through early February 2004 was almost exactly 60 years of age—18 years older than the audience for a typical prime-time program.[11] If you have ever turned on the TV news and wondered why so many of the commercials seem to be for various prescription drugs, now you know why.

Political learning does not, of course, end when one reaches 18 or even when one graduates from college. Politics is a lifelong activity. Because America is an aging society, it is important to consider the effects of growing older on political learning and behavior.

Aging increases political participation as well as strength of party attachment. Young adults (those 18 through 25) lack experience with politics. Because political behavior is to some degree learned behavior, there is some learning yet to do. Political participation rises steadily with age until the infirmities of old age make it harder to participate. Similarly, strength of party identification also increases as one grows older.

Table 6.1 The Role of Genetics in Transmitting Political Attitudes

In an article published in 2005, Alford, Funk, and Hibbing demonstrate the impact of genetics on political values by comparing identical and nonidentical twins. If the political similarity between parents and their offspring is completely due to environmental factors, then the correspondence between the beliefs of identical and nonidentical twins ought to be about equal because both types of twins share the same home environment. However, if genetics are an important factor, then identical twins should be found to agree with one another more often than nonidentical twins, as they share the same genes. In the world of genetics research, comparing different kinds of twins has become known as the "gold test," as it enables scholars to nicely control for environmental factors while varying genetic factors.

In the data that Alford, Funk, and Hibbing analyzed there was a Wilson-Patterson Attitude inventory. This involved presenting respondents with items like "the death penalty" and asking them whether they agreed or disagreed with this or were uncertain. In the following table, the correlations between twins are shown on a variety of items that relate to political issues. The higher the correlation, the more similarity there was in the attitudes of the twins. As you can see, in every case there was substantially more agreement among the identical twins—clearly demonstrating that genetics play an important role in shaping political attitudes.

	IDENTICAL TWINS	NONIDENTICAL TWINS
School prayer	.66	.46
The draft	.41	.21
Pacificism	.34	.15
Unions	.44	.26
Socialism	.43	.25
Foreign aid	.41	.23
Immigration	.45	.29
Women's liberation	.46	.30
The death penalty	.56	.40
Gay rights	.60	.46
Nuclear power	.42	.29
Abortion	.64	.52

Source: John R. Alford, Carolyn L. Funk, and John R. Hibbing, "Are Political Orientations Genetically Transmitted?," *American Political Science Review*, May 2005, 153–67.

Politics, like most other things, is thus a learned behavior. Americans learn to vote, to pick a political party, and to evaluate political events in the world around them. One of the products of all this learning is what is known as public opinion.

Measuring Public Opinion and Political Information

Before examining the role that public opinion plays in American politics, it is essential to learn about the science of public opinion measurement. How do we really know the approximate answers to questions such as what percentage of young people favor abortion rights, how many Hispanics supported George W. Bush's 2004 campaign, or what percentage of the public continues to believe that Iraq had weapons of mass destruction before the U.S. invasion? Polls provide these answers, but there is much skepticism about polls. Many people wonder how accurately polling can be done by interviewing only 1,000 or 1,500 people around the country. This section provides an explanation of how polling works; it is hoped that this will enable you to become a well-informed consumer of polls.

How Polls Are Conducted

Public opinion polling is a relatively new science. It was first developed by a young man named George Gallup, who initially did some polling for his mother-in-law, a long-shot candidate for secretary of state in Iowa in 1932. With the Democratic landslide of that year, she won a stunning victory, thereby further stimulating Gallup's interest in politics. The mighty oak of public opinion polling has grown from that little acorn. The firm Gallup founded spread throughout the democratic world, and in some languages *Gallup* is actually the word used for an opinion poll.[12]

sample
A relatively small proportion of people who are chosen in a survey so as to be representative of the whole.

It would be prohibitively expensive and time consuming to ask every citizen his or her opinion on a whole range of issues. Instead, polls rely on a **sample** of the population—a relatively small proportion of people who are chosen to represent the whole. Herbert Asher draws an analogy to a blood test to illustrate the principle of sampling.[13] Your doctor does not need to drain a gallon of blood from you to determine whether you have mononucleosis, AIDS, or any other disease. Rather, a small sample of blood will reveal its properties.

random sampling
The key technique employed by sophisticated survey researchers, which operates on the principle that everyone should have an equal probability of being selected for the sample.

In public opinion polling, a sample of about 1,000 to 1,500 people can accurately represent the "universe" of potential voters. The key to the accuracy of opinion polls is the technique of **random sampling**, which operates on the principle that everyone should have an equal probability of being selected as part of the sample. Your chance of being asked to be in the poll should therefore be as good as that of anyone else—rich or poor, African American or White, young or old, male or female. If the sample is randomly drawn, about 12 percent of those interviewed will be African American, slightly over 50 percent female, and so forth, matching the population as a whole.

sampling error
The level of confidence in the findings of a public opinion poll. The more people interviewed, the more confident one can be of the results.

Remember that the science of polling involves estimation; a sample can represent the population with only a certain degree of confidence. The level of confidence is known as the **sampling error**, which depends on the size of the sample. The more people interviewed in a poll, the more confident one can be of the results. A typical poll of about 1,500 to 2,000 respondents has a sampling error of ±3 percent. What this means is that 95 percent of the time the poll results are within 3 percent of what the entire population thinks. If 60 percent of the sample say they approve of the job the president is doing, one can be pretty certain that the true figure is between 57 and 63 percent.

You Are a Polling Consultant

In order to obtain results that will usually be within sampling error, researchers must follow proper sampling techniques. In perhaps the most infamous survey ever, a 1936 *Literary Digest* poll underestimated the vote for President Franklin Roosevelt by 19 percent, erroneously predicting a big victory for Republican Alf Landon. The well-established magazine suddenly became a laughingstock and soon went out of business. Although the number of responses the magazine obtained for its poll was a staggering 2,376,000, its polling methods were badly flawed. In trying to reach as many people as possible, the magazine drew names from the biggest lists they could find: telephone books and motor vehicle records. In the midst of the Great Depression, the people on these lists were above the average income level (only 40 percent of the public had telephones then; fewer still owned cars) and were more likely to vote Republican. The moral of the story is this: Accurate representation, not the number of responses, is the most important feature of a public opinion survey. Indeed, as polling techniques have advanced over the past 60 years, typical sample sizes have been getting smaller, not larger.

The newest computer and telephone technology has made surveying less expensive and more commonplace. In the early days of polling, pollsters needed a national network of interviewers armed with a clipboard of questions to traipse door-to-door in their localities. Now most polling is done on the telephone with samples selected through **random-digit dialing**. Calls are placed to phone numbers within randomly chosen exchanges (for example, 512-471-xxxx) around the country. In this manner, both listed and unlisted numbers are reached at a cost of about one-fifth that of person-to-person interviewing. There are a couple of disadvantages, however. Seven percent of the population does not have a phone, and people are somewhat less willing to participate over the telephone than in person—it is easier to hang up than to slam the door in someone's face. These are small trade-offs for political candidates running for minor offices, for whom telephone polls are the only affordable method of gauging public opinion. However, in this era of cell phones, many pollsters are starting to worry whether this methodology will continue to work much longer. Federal regulations bar pollsters from calling people on their cell phones without permission because the recipients of the calls are obliged to pay the cost. If many people give up their land lines and rely entirely on their cell phones, then telephone pollsters will not be able to reach them.

random-digit dialing
A technique used by pollsters to place telephone calls randomly to both listed and unlisted numbers when conducting a survey.

From its modest beginning with George Gallup's 1932 polls for his mother-in-law in Iowa, polling has become a big business. Public opinion polling is one of those American innovations, like soft drinks and fast-food restaurants, that has spread throughout the world. From Manhattan to Moscow, from Tulsa to Tokyo, people want to know what other people think.

The Role of Polls in American Democracy

Polls help political candidates detect public preferences. Supporters of polling insist that it is a tool for democracy. With it, they say, policymakers can keep in touch with changing opinions on the issues. No longer do politicians have to wait until the next election to see whether the public approves or disapproves of the government's course. If the poll results suddenly turn, then government officials can make corresponding midcourse corrections. It was George Gallup's fondest hope that polling could contribute to the democratic process by providing a way for public desires to be heard at times other than elections.

Critics of polling, by contrast, say it makes politicians more concerned with following than leading. Polls might have told the constitutional convention delegates that the Constitution was unpopular or might have told President Thomas Jefferson that people did not want the Louisiana Purchase. Certainly they would have told William Seward not to buy Alaska, a transaction known widely at the time as

Public opinion polls these days are done mostly over the telephone. Interviewers, most of whom are young people (and frequently college students), sit in front of computer terminals and read the questions that appear on the screen to randomly chosen individuals they have reached on the phone. They then enter the appropriate coded responses directly into the computer database. Such efficient procedures make it possible for analysts to get survey results very quickly.

"Seward's Folly." Polls may thus discourage bold leadership, like that of Winston Churchill, who once said,

> *Nothing is more dangerous than to live in the temperamental atmosphere of a Gallup poll, always taking one's pulse and taking one's temperature. . . . There is only one duty, only one safe course, and that is to try to be right and not to fear to do or say what you believe.*[14]

Recent research by Jacobs and Shapiro argues that the common perception of politicians like Bill Clinton pandering to the results of public opinion polls may be mistaken. Their examination of major policy debates in the 1990s finds that political leaders "track public opinion not to make policy but rather to determine how to craft their public presentations and win public support for the policies they and their supporters favor."[15] Staff members in both the White House and the Congress repeatedly remarked that their purpose in conducting polls was not to set policies but rather to find the key words and phrases with which to promote policies already in place. Thus, rather than using polls to identify centrist approaches that will have the broadest popular appeal, Jacobs and Shapiro argue that elites use them to formulate strategies that enable them to avoid compromising on what they want to do. You can read about one interesting case of how the Bush Administration did this in "Issues of the Times: Should Presidents Be Using Theories of Public Opinion to 'Sell' Their Policies?" printed in the *Times Reader* at the back of this book.

Polls can also weaken democracy by distorting the election process. They are often accused of creating a *bandwagon effect.* In particular, they play to the media's interest in who's ahead in the race. The issues of recent presidential campaigns have sometimes been drowned out by a steady flood of poll results.

exit poll

Public opinion surveys used by major media pollsters to predict electoral winners with speed and precision.

Probably the most widely criticized type of poll is the Election Day **exit poll**. For this type of poll, voting places are randomly selected around the country. Workers are then sent to these places and told to ask every tenth person how they voted. The results are accumulated toward the end of the day, enabling television networks to project the outcomes of all but very close races before the polls even close. In the presidential elections of 1980, 1984, 1988, and 1996, the networks declared a national winner while millions on the West coast still had hours to vote. Critics have charged that this practice discourages many people from voting and thereby affects the outcome of some state and local races. Although many voters in the Western states have been outraged by this practice, careful analysis of survey data shows that few voters have actually been influenced by exit poll results.[16]

In 2000, the exit polls received much of the blame for the media's inaccurate calls of the Florida result on election night. The fact that the Florida exit poll showed a small advantage for Gore contributed to their inaccurate projection of a Gore victory. Then, in 2004, the leaking of incomplete exit poll data via the Internet led to the dissemination of stories leading people to expect a Kerry victory as the votes were being counted. This time, however, the television networks were much more cautious in interpreting exit poll results, having learned their lesson from 2000 that a winner shouldn't be declared until a candidate clearly establishes an insurmountable margin of votes over the other.

Perhaps the most pervasive criticism of polling is that by altering the wording of a question, pollsters can usually get the results they want. Sometimes subtle changes in question wording can produce dramatic differences. For example, in August 2005 the percentage of the public who thought we should withdraw from Iraq was 15 points higher in the Harris poll than in the ABC/*Washington Post* poll. The Harris poll asked the following question: "Do you favor keeping a large number of U.S. troops in Iraq until there is a stable government there or bringing most of our troops home in the next year?" The ABC/*Washington Post* poll posed the question somewhat differently: "Do you think the United States should keep its military forces in Iraq until civil order is restored there, even if that means continued U.S. military casualties, or, do you think the United States should withdraw its military forces from Iraq in order to avoid further military casualties, even if it means civil order is not restored there?"[17] Apparently, the wording in the ABC/*Washington Post* poll made people more think more about the possible negative consequences of withdrawing from Iraq, which in turn made them less likely to favor this option. This example illustrates why it is crucial to carefully evaluate how questions are posed when reading public opinion data. Fortunately, as the Internet has progressed, most newspapers and polling organizations have come to routinely post their questionnaires online, thereby making it much easier than ever before for everyone to scrutinize their work.

Polling sounds scientific with its talk of random samples and sampling error; it is easy to take results for solid fact. But being an informed consumer of polls requires more than just a nuts-and-bolts knowledge of how they are conducted. You should think about whether the questions are fair and unbiased before making too much of the results. The good—or the harm—that polls do depends on how well the data are collected and how thoughtfully the data are interpreted.

What Polls Reveal About Americans' Political Information

Abraham Lincoln spoke stirringly of the inherent wisdom of the American people: "It is true that you may fool all of the people some of the time; and you can even fool some of the people all of the time; but you can't fool all of the people all the time." Obviously, Lincoln recognized the complexity of public opinion.

Thomas Jefferson and Alexander Hamilton had very different views about the wisdom of common people. Jefferson trusted people's good sense and believed that education would enable them to take the tasks of citizenship ever more seriously. Toward that end, he founded the University of Virginia. Hamilton held a contrasting view. His infamous words "Your people, sir, are a great beast" do not reflect confidence in people's capacity for self-government.

If there had been polling data in the early days of the American republic, Hamilton would probably have delighted in throwing some of the results in Jefferson's face. If public opinion analysts agree about anything, it is that the level of public knowledge about politics is dismally low. As discussed, this is particularly true for young people, but the overall levels of political knowledge are not particularly encouraging either. For example, in the 2004 National Annenberg Election Study conducted by the University of Pennsylvania, a national sample of Democrats were asked a set of questions about the Democratic contenders during the 10 days prior to the New Hampshire primary. The results were:

- 59 percent knew which candidate had been a general (Clark)
- 42 percent knew which candidate had been a decorated Vietnam veteran (Kerry)
- 33 percent knew which candidate would repeal all the Bush tax cuts (Dean)
- 25 percent knew which candidate had been a trial lawyer (Edwards)

If so many voters did not know these very basic facts about the candidates, then there is little doubt that most were also unaware of the detailed policy platforms they were running on.

No amount of Jeffersonian faith in the wisdom of the common people can erase the fact that Americans are not well informed about politics. Polls have regularly found that less than half the public can name their representative in the House, and much less say how he or she generally votes. Asking most people to explain their opinion on whether trade policy toward China should be liberalized, on the proposed "Star Wars" missile defense system, or whether the strategic oil reserve should be tapped when gasoline prices skyrocket often elicits blank looks. When trouble flares in a far-off country, polls regularly find that people have no idea where that place is.

As Lance Bennett points out, these findings provide "a source of almost bitter humor in light of what the polls tell us about public information on other subjects."[18] He notes that more people know their astrological sign (76 percent) than know the name of their representative in the House. Slogans from TV commercials are better recognized than famous political figures. When people were asked in 1989 which vegetable President George Bush did not like in the late 1980s, a poll found that 75 percent could identify it as broccoli, but relatively few people knew his stand on a tax cut for capital gains.

How can Americans, who live in the most information-rich society in the world, be so ill informed about politics? Some blame the schools. E. D. Hirsch Jr. criticizes schools for a failure to teach "cultural literacy."[19] People, he says, often lack the basic contextual knowledge—for example, where Afghanistan is, what the Vietnam War was about, and so forth—necessary to understand and use the information they receive from the news media or from listening to political candidates.

Why It Matters

Political Knowledge of the Electorate

The average American clearly has less political information than most analysts consider to be desirable. While this level of information is surely adequate to maintain our democracy, survey data plainly show that citizens with above-average levels of political knowledge are more likely to vote and to have stable and consistent opinions on policy issues. If political knowledge were to increase overall, it would in all likelihood be good for American democracy.

Indeed, it has been found that increased levels of education over the past four decades have scarcely raised public knowledge about politics.[20] Despite the apparent glut of information provided by the media, Americans do not remember much about what they are exposed to through the media. (Of course, there are many critics who say that the media fail to provide much meaningful information, a topic that will be discussed in Chapter 7.)

The "paradox of mass politics," says Russell Neuman, is that the American political system works as well as it does given the discomforting lack of public knowledge about politics.[21] Part of the reason for this phenomenon is that people may not know the ins and outs of policy questions or the actors on the political stage, but they know what basic values they want upheld. When people feel that government is not working according to the values they subscribe to, the sleeping giant of public opinion may be stirred to action. Examining these values is thus of great importance.

What Americans Value: Political Ideologies

A coherent set of values and beliefs about public policy is a **political ideology.** Liberal ideology, for example, supports a wide scope for the central government, often involving policies that aim to promote equality. Conservative ideology, in contrast, supports a less active scope of government that gives freer reign to the private sector. Table 6.2 attempts to summarize some of the key differences between liberals and conservatives.

political ideology
A coherent set of beliefs about politics, public policy, and public purpose. It helps give meaning to political events, personalities, and policies.

Who Are the Liberals and Conservatives?

Who Are Liberals and Conservatives

Overall, more Americans consistently choose the ideological label of conservative over liberal. The 2004 General Social Survey found that of those who labeled themselves, 38 percent were conservatives, another 38 percent were moderates, and just 24 percent were liberals. The predominance of conservative thinking in America is one of the most important reasons for the relatively restrained scope of government activities compared to most European nations.

Yet there are some groups that are more liberal than others and thus would generally like to see the government do more. Among people under age 30, there are just as many liberals as conservatives, as shown in "Young People and Politics: How Younger and Older Americans Compare on the Issues." The younger the individual, the less likely that person is to be a conservative. The fact that younger people are also less likely to vote means that conservatives are overrepresented at the polls.

In general, groups with political clout tend to be more conservative than groups whose members have often been shut out from the halls of political power. This is because excluded groups have often looked to the government to rectify the inequalities they have faced. For example, African Americans benefited from government activism in the form of the major civil rights bills of the 1960s to bring them into the mainstream of American life. Many African American leaders currently

Table 6.2 How To Tell a Liberal from a Conservative

Liberal and *conservative*—these labels are thrown around in American politics as though everyone knows what they mean. Here are some of the political beliefs likely to be preferred by liberals and conservatives. This table, to be sure, is oversimplified.

	Liberals	Conservatives
FOREIGN POLICY		
Military spending	Believe we should spend less	Believe we should maintain peace through strength
Use of force	Less willing to commit troops to action, such as in Iraq War	More likely to support military intervention around the world
SOCIAL POLICY		
Abortion	Support "freedom of choice"	Support "right to life"
Prayer in schools	Are opposed	Are supportive
Affirmative action	Favor	Oppose
ECONOMIC POLICY		
Scope of government	View government as a regulator in the public interest	Favor free-market solutions
Taxes	Want to tax the rich more	Want to keep taxes low
Spending	Want to spend more on the poor	Want to keep spending low
CRIME		
How to cut crime	Believe we should solve the problems that cause crime	Believe we should stop "coddling criminals"
Defendants' rights	Believe we should guard them carefully	Believe we should stop letting criminals hide behind laws

YOUNG PEOPLE AND POLITICS

How Younger and Older Americans Compare on the Issues

The following table compares the views of young adults and senior citizens on a variety of issues. Because younger citizens are much less likely to vote than older people, the differences between the two groups give us some indication of how public opinion is not accurately reflected at the polls. As you can see, younger people are substantially more likely to call themselves liberal than senior citizens. Befitting their liberalism, they are more supportive of government policies to reduce income differences. And their spending priorities are more on the liberal side as well: They are more in favor of spending on education and environmental protection and less inclined than seniors to spend more on defense. Younger voters are also more supportive of gay rights.

However, younger people are not always more likely to take the liberal side of an issue. Younger people are also more supportive of investing Social Security funds in the stock market and more in favor of school vouchers to help parents send their children to private school. Both of these reform proposals have been primarily championed by conservative politicians such as George W. Bush. The fact that young adults are the most likely to support them suggests that the nation's youth are most open to new ideas, be they liberal or conservative.

Questions for Discussion

- Only a few issues could be covered in this table because of space limitations. Are there other issues on which you think there are likely to be differences of opinion between young and old people?
- Do you think the differences shown in the table are important? If so, what difference might it make to the American political agenda if young people were to vote at the same rate as the elderly?

	18–29 YEARS OLD	65 AND OLDER
Very liberal	7	2
Liberal	25	14
Moderate	39	39
Conservative	24	38
Very conservative	5	7
Favor investing Social Security funds in the stock market	71	45
Oppose investing Social Security funds in the stock market	29	55
Favor school vouchers	44	30
Oppose school vouchers	56	70
Spending on education should be increased	81	53
Spending on education is about right	16	34
Spending on education should be reduced	3	13
Military spending should be increased	35	65
Military spending is about right	49	30
Military spending should be reduced	16	5
Favor gays in the military	64	53
Oppose gays in the military	36	47
Favor government policies to reduce income differences	61	42
Oppose government policies to reduce income differences	39	58
Spending to protect the environment should be increased	77	59
Spending to protect the environment is about right	18	28
Spending to protect the environment should be decreased	5	13

Source: 2000 National Annenberg Election Study.

place a high priority on retaining social welfare and affirmative action programs in order to assist their progress. It should come as little surprise then that African Americans are more liberal than the national average. Similarly, Hispanics also are less conservative than Whites, and if this pattern continues into the twenty-first century, the influx of many more Hispanics into the electorate will move the country in a slightly more liberal direction.

Are You a Liberal or a Conservative?

gender gap

A term that refers to the regular pattern by which women are more likely to support Democratic candidates. Women tend to be significantly less conservative than men and are more likely to support spending on social services and to oppose higher levels of military spending.

Women are not a minority group, making up about 54 percent of the population, but they have nevertheless been politically and economically disadvantaged. Compared to men, women are more likely to support spending on social services and to oppose the higher levels of military spending, which conservatives typically advocate. These issues concerning the priorities of government rather than the issue of abortion—on which men and women actually differ very little—lead women to be significantly less conservative than men. This ideological difference between men and women has led to the **gender gap**, which refers to the regular pattern by which women are more likely to support Democratic candidates. Bill Clinton carried the women's vote while Bob Dole was preferred among men in 1996, making Clinton the first president who can be said to be elected via the support of only one gender. In 2004, exit polls showed that women were about 7 percent more likely to support John Kerry than men.

The gender gap is a relatively new predictor of ideological positions, dating back only to 1980, when Ronald Reagan was first elected. A much more traditional source of division between liberals and conservatives has been financial status, or what is often known as social class. But in actuality, the relationship between family income and ideology is now relatively weak. As a result, social class has become much less predictive of political behavior than it used to be.[22]

The role of religion in influencing political ideology has also changed greatly in recent years. Catholics and Jews, as minority groups who struggled for equality, have long been more liberal than Protestants. Today, Jews remain by far the most liberal demographic group in the country.[23] However, the ideological gap between Catholics and Protestants is now smaller than the gender gap. Ideology is now determined more by religiosity—that is, the degree to which religion is important in one's life—than by religious denomination. What is known as the new Christian Right consists of Catholics and Protestants who consider themselves fundamentalists or "born again." The influx of new policy issues dealing with matters of morality and traditional family values has recently tied this aspect of religious beliefs to political ideology. Those who identify themselves as born-again Christians are currently the most conservative demographic group. On the other hand, people who say they have no religious affiliation (roughly one-tenth of the population) are more liberal than conservative.

Just as some people are very much guided by their religious beliefs whereas others are not, the same is true for political ideology. It would probably be a mistake to assume that when conservative candidates do better than they have in the past, this necessarily means people want more conservative policies, for not everyone thinks in ideological terms.

Do People Think in Ideological Terms?

The authors of the classic study *The American Voter* first examined how much people rely on ideology to guide their political thinking.[24] They divided the public into four groups, according to ideological sophistication. Their portrait of the American electorate was not flattering. Only 12 percent of the people showed evidence of thinking in ideological terms and thus were classified as *ideologues*. These people could connect their opinions and beliefs with broad policy positions taken by parties or candidates.

They might say, for example, that they liked the Democrats because they were more liberal or the Republicans because they favored a smaller government. Forty-two percent of Americans were classified as *group benefits* voters. These people thought of politics mainly in terms of the groups they liked or disliked; for example, "Republicans support small business owners like me" or "Democrats are the party of the working person." Twenty-four percent of the population were *nature of the times* voters. Their handle on politics was limited to whether the times seemed good or bad to them; they might vaguely link the party in power with the country's fortune or misfortune. Finally, 22 percent of the voters were devoid of any ideological or issue content in their political evaluations. They were called the *no issue content* group. Most of them simply voted routinely for a party or judged the candidates solely by their personalities. Overall, at least during the 1950s, Americans seemed to care little about the differences between liberal and conservative politics.

There has been much debate about whether this portrayal accurately characterizes the public today. Nie, Verba, and Petrocik took a look at the changing American voter from 1956 to 1972 and argued that voters were more sophisticated in the 1970s than in the 1950s.[25] Others, though, have concluded that people seemed more informed and ideological only because the wording of the questions had changed.[26] If the exact same methods are used to update the analysis of *The American Voter* through more recent elections, one finds some increase in the proportion of ideologues, but not much. The last time these methods were employed was in 1988, and then just 18 percent were classified as ideologues, as compared to 12 percent in 1956. Given that George Bush continually labeled his 1988 opponent Michael Dukakis as "that liberal Governor from the most liberal state in the country," it is striking how few people actually evaluated the parties and candidates in ideological terms.

These findings do not mean that the vast majority of the population does not have a political ideology. Rather, for most people the terms *liberal* and *conservative* are just not as important as they are for the political elite such as politicians, activists, journalists, and the like. Relatively few people have ideologies that organize their political beliefs as clearly as shown in Table 6.2. Thus, the authors of *The American Voter* concluded that to speak of election results as indicating a movement of the public either left (to more liberal policies) or right (to more conservative policies) is not justified because most voters do not think in such terms. Furthermore, those who do are actually the least likely to shift from one election to the next. The relatively small percentage of voters who made up their minds in the last couple days of the Bush–Gore campaign in 2000 were more concerned with integrity and competence than ideology.

Morris Fiorina makes a similar argument with regard to the question of whether America is in the midst of a political culture war. In the media these days, one frequently hears claims that Americans are deeply divided on fundamental political issues, making it seem like there are two different nations—the liberal blue states versus the conservative red states. After a thorough examination of public opinion data, Fiorina concludes that "the views of the American citizenry look moderate, centrist, nuanced, ambivalent—choose your term—rather than extreme, polarized, unconditional, dogmatic."[27] He argues that the small groups of liberal and conservative activists who act as if they are at war with one another have left most Americans in a position analogous to "unfortunate citizens of some third-world countries who try to stay out of the crossfire while Maoist guerrillas and right-wing death squads shoot at each other."[28]

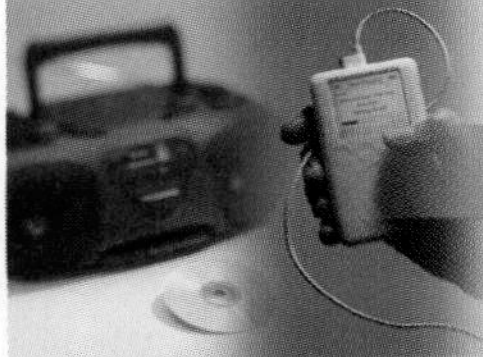

A GENERATION OF CHANGE

Attitudes Toward Gays and Lesbians by Political Ideology

It is often said that public opinion surveys are merely "snapshots in time." What this means is that public opinion can change from one time point to the next, as people's attitudes are subject to change. Furthermore, generational replacement can often produce substantial changes in pubic opinion over an extended period of time, as the attitudes of new entrants into the electorate are sometimes quite different from generations that are dying out. Such is the case with attitudes toward gays and lesbians over the past five presidential elections.

The American National Election Studies have regularly asked respondents to rate gays and lesbians on a "feeling thermometer" scale ranging from 0 to 100. They are told that 0 represents very cool feelings, whereas 100 represents very warm feelings, with 50 being the neutral point. The following graph displays the average ratings that liberals, moderates, and conservatives gave gays and lesbians from 1988 to 2004. It is interesting to note that as recently as 1988, all three ideological groups expressed more negative than positive feelings toward gays and lesbians, giving them an average rating well below 50 degrees. If reports of a culture war were correct, then we would have seen liberals become more positive toward homosexuals and conservatives turn even more negative. This has certainly not been the case. By 2004, the average rating given to gays and lesbians had risen by 21 points among liberals and 18 points among moderates and conservatives. Thus, societal attitudes have changed across the political spectrum. A key reason for this change is that young people have expressed more favorable ratings toward gays and lesbians within each ideological group. This is clearly a case of a generation of change being driven by a new generation of voters.

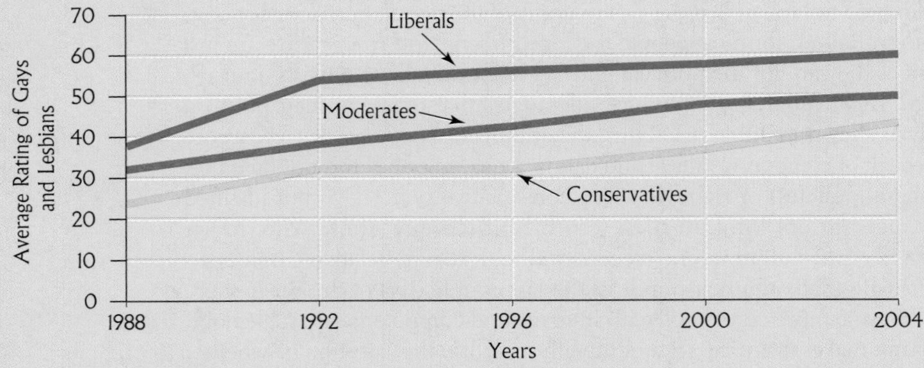

Source: Authors' analysis of American National Election Studies data.

One of the topics that many commentators believe have led to a political culture war is that of gay rights. However, as shown in "A Generation of Change: Attitudes Toward Gays and Lesbians by Political Ideology," the survey data over the past two decades show a growing acceptance of homosexuals among liberals, moderates, and conservatives alike. Rather than an ideological culture war, this example shows how all ideological groups have changed with the changing social mores of the times.

How Americans Participate in Politics

In politics, as in many other aspects of life, the squeaky wheel gets the grease. The way citizens "squeak" in politics is to participate. Americans have many avenues of political participation available to them:

- Mrs. Jones of Iowa City goes to a neighbor's living room to attend her local precinct's presidential caucus.
- Demonstrators against abortion protest at the Supreme Court on the anniversary of the *Roe v. Wade* decision.
- Parents in Alabama file a lawsuit to oppose textbooks that, in their opinion, promote "secular humanism."
- Mr. Smith, a Social Security recipient, writes to his senator to express his concern about a possible cut in his cost-of-living benefits.
- More than 120 million people vote in a presidential election.

All these activities are types of **political participation**, which encompasses the many activities in which citizens engage to influence the selection of political leaders or the policies they pursue.[29] Participation can be overt or subtle. The mass protests against communist rule throughout Eastern Europe in the fall of 1989 represented an avalanche of political participation, yet quietly writing a letter to your congressperson also represents political participation. Political participation can be violent or peaceful, organized or individual, casual or consuming.

political participation
All the activities used by citizens to influence the selection of political leaders or the policies they pursue. The most common, but not the only, means of political participation in a democracy is voting. Other means include **protest** and **civil disobedience.**

Generally, the United States has a culture that values political participation. Americans express very high levels of pride in their democracy: 79 percent say they are proud of how democracy works in the United States.[30] Nevertheless, just 55 percent of adult Americans voted in the presidential election of 2004, and only 40 percent turned out for the 2006 midterm elections. At the local level, the situation is even worse, with elections for city council and school board often drawing less than 10 percent of the eligible voters. (For more on voter turnout and why it is so low, see Chapter 9.)

Conventional Participation

Although the line is hard to draw, political scientists generally distinguish between two broad types of participation: conventional and unconventional. Conventional participation includes many widely accepted modes of influencing government—voting, trying to persuade others, ringing doorbells for a petition, running for office, and so on. In contrast, unconventional participation includes activities that are often dramatic, such as protesting, civil disobedience, and even violence.

Millions take part in political activities beyond simply voting. In two comprehensive studies of American political participation conducted by Sidney Verba and his colleagues, samples of Americans were asked in 1967 and 1987 about their role in various kinds of political activities, such as voting, working in campaigns, contacting government officials, signing petitions, working on local community issues, and participating in political protests.[31] Recently, Russell Dalton has extended the time series for some of these dimensions of political participation into the twenty-first century.[32] All told, voting is the only aspect of political participation that a majority of the population reported engaging in but also the only political activity for which there is evidence of a decline in participation in recent years. Substantial increases in participation have been found on the dimensions of giving money to candidates and contacting public officials, and small increases are evident for all the other activities. Thus, although the decline of voter turnout is a development Americans should rightly be concerned about (see Chapter 9), a broader look at political participation reveals some positive developments for participatory democracy.

Protest as Participation

protest
A form of **political participation** designed to achieve policy change through dramatic and unconventional tactics.

From the Boston Tea Party to burning draft cards to demonstrating against abortion, Americans have engaged in countless political protests. **Protest** is a form of political participation designed to achieve policy change through dramatic and unconventional tactics. The media's willingness to cover the unusual can make protest worthwhile, drawing attention to a point of view that many Americans might otherwise never encounter. For example, when an 89-year-old woman decided to try to walk across the country to draw attention to the need for campaign finance reform, she put this issue onto the front page of newspapers most everywhere she traveled. Using much more flamboyant means, the AIDS activist group appropriately called "ACT-UP" interrupts political gatherings to draw attention to the need for AIDS research. In fact, protests today are often orchestrated to provide television cameras with vivid images. Demonstration coordinators steer participants to prearranged staging areas and provide facilities for press coverage.

At the age of 89, Doris Haddock resolved to do something unusual that would draw people's attention to the issue of campaign finance reform: a cross-country walk from California to Washington, D.C. Moving at a pace of 10 miles per day, Granny D—the nickname Mrs. Haddock assumed for publicity purposes—made it all the way to Congress' front door. Along the way, she publicized her cause through numerous interviews and met with various politicians. The National Association of Secretaries of State issued a resolution commending her "for showing that one person can make a difference."

The right of political protest is constitutionally protected as an integral part of freedom of speech in the United States. Cindy Sheehan attracted national attention when she camped out in front of President Bush's Crawford ranch in the summer of 2005 to demonstrate against the U.S. military presence in Iraq.

Throughout American history, individuals and groups have sometimes used **civil disobedience** as a form of protest; that is, they have consciously broken a law they thought was unjust. In the 1840s, Henry David Thoreau refused to pay his taxes as a protest against the Mexican War and went to jail; he stayed only overnight because his friend Ralph Waldo Emerson paid the taxes. Influenced by India's Mahatma Gandhi, the Reverend Martin Luther King Jr. won a Nobel Peace Prize for his civil disobedience against segregationist laws in the 1950s and 1960s. His "Letter from a Birmingham Jail" is a classic defense of civil disobedience.[33]

civil disobedience
A form of **political participation** that reflects a conscious decision to break a law believed to be immoral and to suffer the consequences.

Sometimes political participation can be violent. The history of violence in American politics is a long one—not surprising, perhaps, for a nation born in rebellion. The turbulent 1960s included many outbreaks of violence. African American neighborhoods in American cities were torn by riots. College campuses were sometimes turned into battle zones as protestors against the Vietnam War fought police and National Guard units. At a number of campuses, demonstrations turned violent; students were killed at Kent State and Jackson State in 1970. Although supported by few people, violence has been a means of pressuring the government to change its policies throughout American history.

Class, Inequality, and Participation

The rates of political participation are unequal among Americans. Virtually every study of political participation has come to the conclusion that "citizens of higher social economic status participate more in politics. This generalization . . . holds true whether one uses level of education, income, or occupation as the measure of social status."[34]

HOW YOU CAN MAKE A DIFFERENCE

Political Participation

The one constant theme in democratic political theory is that mass public opinion has considerable influence over democratic governance. When public opinion is ignorant and motivated by feeling and passion and not by informed discussion, the quality of politics, lawmaking, and policy is significantly diminished. Partisans of both liberal and conservative views are often more likely to shout past each other, rather than engage in reasoned discourse. This is not helpful for debating the problems of the day, and it makes it difficult for real change to occur. Remember—the power to shape public opinion is held by every citizen and it should be used responsibly.

Making a Difference

Some residents of Hamtramck, Michigan, took issue with their City Council's approval of a noise ordinance that would allow the Muslim call to prayer to be broadcast on loud speakers from a local mosque in this increasingly diverse community. By organizing a petition drive, these residents forced the city to put the ordinance on hold, thus blocking its passage into law. The proponents of the petition drive claimed that their primary concern was the increased noise level and not the religious nature of the broadcasts. Though the ordinance was eventually passed, it was delayed for a significant amount of time by the actions and protests of these citizens.

What you can do:

- Educate yourself about American political institutions. By gaining an understanding of the origins, purposes, and functions of constitutional establishments, you can then bring informed judgment to political controversies.
- Get information about current events from both liberal- and conservative-leaning news sources and blogs. Keep an open mind and be willing to accept irrefutable facts and information that may be contrary to your own views.
- Make others aware of your opinions and beliefs. Write letters to newspaper editors or to local news producers, expressing your views on the issues.
- Create an Internet weblog where you air your opinions on the issues. Engage in thoughtful discourse with other bloggers who are writing about similar topics.

Figure 6.3 presents recent evidence on this score. Note that people with higher incomes are more likely not only to donate money to campaigns but also to participate in other ways that do not even require financial resources. Theorists who believe that America is ruled by a small, wealthy elite make much of this fact to support their view.

The scenes of despair among poor African Americans in New Orleans during the aftermath of Hurricane Katrina have refocused attention on racial inequalities in the United States. Some commentators have speculated that one of the reasons that the federal government was so slow in coming to the aid of African Americans in New Orleans is that they are less likely to vote. But in actuality, the difference in turnout rates between Whites and African Americans has been relatively small in Louisiana in recent years. In 2004, for example, 60 percent of Louisiana Whites over the age of 18 turned out to vote compared to 54 percent of African Americans in the state.[35] (Notably, in the area that encompasses the poverty-stricken lower Ninth Ward, the turnout rate of African Americans was exactly the same as it was statewide.)

One reason for this relatively small participation gap is that minorities have a group consciousness that gives them an extra incentive to vote. In fact, when African

Figure 6.3 Political Participation by Family Income

This graph shows, by their income status, the percentage of the adult population who said they participated in various forms of political activity.

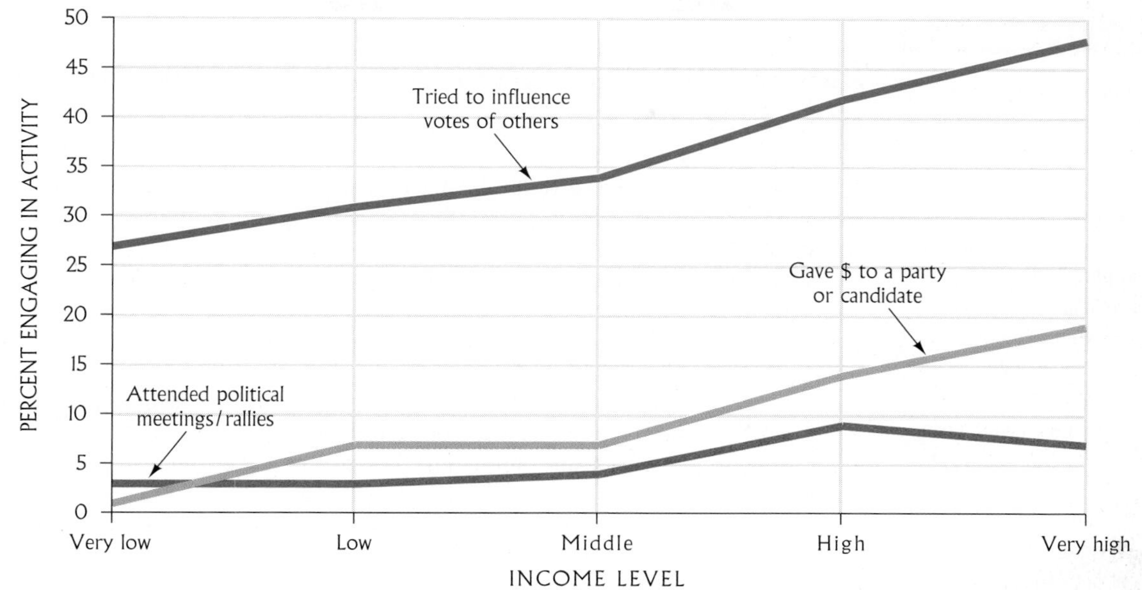

Source: 2000 National Election Study.

Americans and Whites of equal income and education are compared, the former actually participate more in politics.[36] In other words, a poor African American is more likely to participate than a poor White person. In general, lower rates of political participation among African-Americans are linked with lower socioeconomic status.

People who believe in the promise of democracy should definitely be concerned with the inequalities of political participation in America. Those who participate are easy to listen to; nonparticipants are easy to ignore. Just as the makers of denture cream do not worry too much about people with healthy teeth, many politicians don't concern themselves much with the views of groups with low participation rates, such as the young and people with low incomes. Who gets what in politics therefore depends in part on who participates.

Understanding Public Opinion and Political Action

Comparing Public Opinion

In many third world countries, there have been calls for more democracy in recent years. One often hears that citizens of developing nations want their political system to be like America's in the sense that ordinary people's opinions determine how the government is run. However, as this chapter has shown, there are many limits on the role public opinion plays in the American political system. The average person is not very well informed about political issues, including the crucial issue of the scope of government.

Why It Matters

Political Participation

Inequality in political participation is a problem in a representative democracy. Public policy debates and outcomes would probably be substantially different if people of all age-groups and income groups participated equally. If young adults participated more, politicians would be more inclined to work on ways by which the government could help young people get the training necessary to get good jobs. And if the poor participated at higher levels, government programs to alleviate poverty would likely be higher on the political agenda than it is today.

Public Attitudes Toward the Scope of Government

Central to the ideology of the Republican Party is the belief that the scope of American government has become too wide ranging. According to Ronald Reagan, probably the most admired Republican in recent history, government was not the solution to society's problems—it was the problem. He called for the government to "get off the backs of the American people."

Reagan's rhetoric about an overly intrusive government was reminiscent of the 1964 presidential campaign rhetoric of Barry Goldwater, who lost to Lyndon Johnson by a landslide. Indeed, Reagan first made his mark in politics by giving a televised speech on behalf of the embattled Goldwater campaign. Although the rhetoric was much the same when Ronald Reagan was first elected president in 1980, public opinion about the scope of government had changed dramatically. In 1964, only 30 percent of the population thought the government was getting too powerful; by 1980, this figure had risen to 50 percent.

For much of the population, however, questions about the scope of government have consistently elicited no opinion at all. Indeed, when this question was last asked in the 2000 National Election Study, 42 percent of those interviewed said they had not thought about the question (among those under 25 years of age, this figure was 60 percent). The question of government power is a complex one, but as *Government in America* will continue to emphasize, it is one of the key controversies in American politics today. Once again, it seems that the public is not nearly so concerned with political issues as would be ideal in a democratic society.

Nor does public opinion on different aspects of the same issue exhibit much consistency. Thus although more people today think the government is too big, a plurality has consistently called for more spending on such programs as education, health care, aid to cities, protecting the environment, and fighting crime. Many political scientists have looked at these contradictory findings and concluded that Americans are ideological conservatives but operational liberals—meaning that they oppose the idea of big government in principle but favor it in practice. The fact that public opinion is often contradictory in this respect sometimes leads to policy gridlock because it is hard for politicians to know which aspect of the public's attitudes to respond to.

Democracy, Public Opinion, and Political Action

Remember, though, that American democracy is representative rather than direct. As *The American Voter* stated many years ago, "The public's explicit task is to decide not what government shall do but rather who shall decide what government shall do."[37] When individuals under communist rule protested for democracy, what they wanted most was the right to have a say in choosing their leaders. Americans can—and often do—take for granted the opportunity to replace their leaders at the next election. Protest is thus directed at making the government listen to specific demands, not overthrowing it. In this sense, American citizens have become well socialized to democracy.

If the public's task in democracy is to choose who should lead, we must still ask whether it can choose wisely. If people know little about where candidates stand on issues, how can they make rational choices? Most choose performance criteria over policy criteria. As Morris Fiorina has written, citizens typically have one hard bit of data to go on: "They know what life has been like during the incumbent's administration. They need not know the precise economic or foreign policies of the incumbent administration in order to see or feel the results of those policies."[38] Thus, even if they are only voting according to the nature of the times, their voices are clearly being heard—holding public officials accountable for their actions.

Public Opinion and Leadership

Summary

American society is amazingly varied. The ethnic makeup of America is changing to a minority majority. Americans are moving toward warmer parts of the country and growing older as a society. All these changes have policy consequences. One way of understanding the American people is through demography—the science of population changes. Demography, it is often said, is destiny.

Another way to understand the American people is through examination of public opinion in the United States. What Americans believe—and what they believe they know—is public opinion, the distribution of people's beliefs about politics and policy issues. Polling is one important way of studying public opinion; polls give us a fairly accurate gauge of public opinion on issues, products, and personalities. On the positive side for democracy, polls help keep political leaders in touch with the feelings of their constituents. On the negative side, polls may lead politicians to "play to the crowds" instead of provide leadership.

Polls have revealed again and again that the average American has a low level of political knowledge. Far more Americans know their astrological sign than know the names of their representatives in Congress. Ideological thinking is not widespread in the American public, nor are people necessarily consistent in their attitudes. Often they are conservative in principle but liberal in practice; that is, they are against big government but favor more spending on a wide variety of programs.

Acting on one's opinions is political participation. Although Americans live in a participatory culture, their actual level of participation is less than spectacular. In this country, participation is a class-biased activity; certain groups participate more than others. Those who suffer the most inequality sometimes resort to protest as a form of participation. Perhaps the best indicator of how well socialized Americans are to democracy is that protest typically is aimed at getting the attention of the government, not overthrowing it.

Internet Resources

www.census.gov
The census is the best source of information on America's demography. Go to the list of topics to find out the range of materials that are available.

www.gallup.com
The Gallup poll regularly posts reports about their political surveys at this site.

www.census.gov/statab/www/
The *Statistical Abstract of the United States* contains a wealth of demographic and political information and is available in Adobe Acrobat format off the Internet.

www.demographics.com/publications/ad/index.htm
American Demographics magazine publishes many interesting stories that summarize how America's population is currently changing.

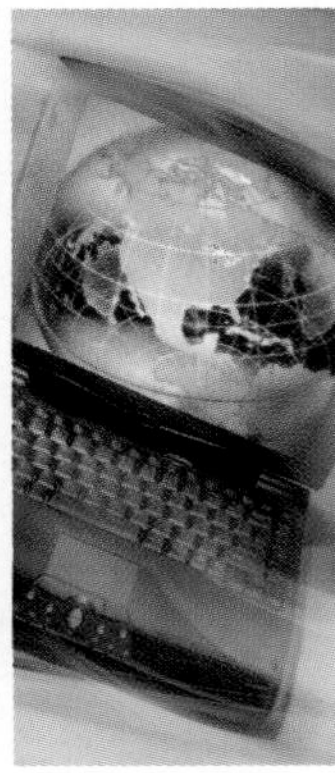

Get Connected

Public Opinion and SLOPs

Public opinion polls play an important role in American politics and government. Some observers even argue that policymakers keep an eye on polls when trying to develop policy, a practice that may be to the detriment of our system or government. There are polls that are conducted scientifically and provide useful information about what Americans are thinking. There are other polls called self-selected opinion polls, or SLOPs, that may provide biased or misleading information. You may have seen SLOPs on an interest group's Web site or even on the local news. How are scientific polls conducted, and how do the differ from SLOPs?

Search the Web

The Gallup Organization is one of the oldest public opinion polling firms in the country. Go to the "How Polls are Conducted" page at the Gallup Web site, *http://media.gallup.com/PDF/FAQ/HowArePolls.pdf*. Now review the National Council on Public Polls' "Statement About Internet Polls," *www.ncpp.org/internet.htm*. While the National Council on Public Polls' statement is about Internet polls, this type of public opinion poll could have the same shortcomings as the self-selected opinion poll you might see on television or find on an interest group's Web site.

Questions to Ask

- What are the important characteristics about Gallup's polling methods that allow people to have confidence in the findings revealed by the organization's polls?
- Why does the National Council on Public Polls think it is important to know if people were able to participate in the poll more than once?
- What are the shortcomings of any public opinion poll?

Why It Matters

The people are able to voice their opinions through public opinion polls, but polls may cause problems for our political system if they are not conducted correctly. It is important for the consumers of public opinion polls, including policymakers and voters, to have confidence in the information such polls present.

Get Involved

Find the results of an Internet poll at the CNN Web site, *www.cnn.com*; Fox News Channel's Web site, *www.foxnews.com*; or in your local media. Interest groups also run Internet polls. A list of interest groups and their Web addresses can be found at *www.csuchico.edu/~kcfount/index.html*. Evaluate the poll using the National Council on Public Polls' " Statement About Internet Polls." Contact the person or group that published the poll and ask them to answer the questions on the statement if the poll doesn't provide the answers directly. Consult this issue brief from the Pew Research Center for People and the Press, *http://people-press.org/commentary/display.php3?AnalysisID=20*, to offer suggestions on how to improve the poll.

For more exercises, go to www.longmanamericangovernment.com.

For Further Reading

Asher, Herbert. *Polling and the Public: What Every Citizen Should Know.* 6th ed. Washington, DC: Congressional Quarterly Press, 2004. A highly readable introduction to the perils and possibilities of polling and surveys.

Campbell, Andrea Louise. *How Policies Make Citizens: Senior Political Activism and the American Welfare State.* Princeton, NJ: Princeton University Press, 2003. Senior citizens have bucked the trend of declining political participation in recent years; Campbell explains why.

Campbell, Angus, et al. *The American Voter.* New York: Wiley, 1960. The classic study of the American voter, based on data from the 1950s.

Conway, M. Margaret. *Political Participation.* 3rd ed. Washington, DC: Congressional Quarterly Press, 2000. A good review of the literature on political participation.

Delli Carpini, Michael X., and Scott Keeter. *What Americans Know About Politics and Why It Matters.* New Haven, CT: Yale University Press, 1996. The best study of the state of political knowledge in the electorate.

DeSipio, Louis. *Counting on the Latino Vote.* Charlottesville: University Press of Virginia, 1996. An examination of the current state of Latino public opinion and how more Latinos could be politically mobilized in the future.

Fiorina, Morris P. *Culture War? The Myth of a Polarized America.* 2nd ed. New York: Longman, 2006. This book argues that the so-called culture war between the red and blue states is highly exaggerated, as most Americans possess relatively moderate and nuanced opinions on political issues.

Hetherington, Marc J. *Why Trust Matters.* Princeton, NJ: Princeton University Press, 2005. The author argues that the decline of trust in government in recent decades has weakened support for progressive policies to address problems of poverty and racial inequality.

Jacobs, Lawrence R., and Robert Y. Shapiro. *Politicians Don't Pander.* Chicago: University of Chicago Press, 2000. Contrary to popular notions that politicians hold their fingers to the wind and try to follow the polls, Jacobs and Shapiro argue that politicians use polls to figure out how to best persuade the public to support their preferred policies.

Nie, Norman H., Jane Junn, and Kenneth Stehlik-Barry. *Education and Democratic Citizenship in America.* Chicago: University of Chicago Press, 1996. An in-depth investigation of the role of education in fostering political tolerance and participation.

Tate, Katherine. *From Protest to Politics: The New Black Voters in American Elections,* enlarged edition. Cambridge, MA: Harvard University Press, 1998. An excellent examination of public opinion and participation in the African American community.

Verba, Sidney, and Norman H. Nie. *Participation in America.* New York: Harper & Row, 1972. A landmark study of American political participation.

Verba, Sidney, Kay Lehman Schlozman, and Henry E. Brady. *Voice and Equality: Civic Voluntarism in American Politics.* Cambridge, MA: Harvard University Press, 1995. A worthy update and extension to *Participation in America.*

Chapter Outline

The Mass Media and the Political Agenda

POLITICS IN ACTION: HOW TELEVISION HAS BROUGHT A SENSE OF IMMEDIACY TO GOVERNING In Washington's Smithsonian Museum, the television console used by President Lyndon Johnson in the mid-1960s can be seen on permanent display. Not wanting to miss anything on TV, Johnson asked for three screens to be installed in one console so he could monitor CBS, NBC, and ABC all at the same time. White House technicians rigged up a special remote control for the president, enabling him to switch the audio easily from one network to another. According to many observers, whenever he saw his picture appear, he immediately turned on the audio from that screen to hear what was being said about him.

As a piece of genuine Americana, LBJ's triple TV set symbolizes the tremendous importance television had assumed in U.S. politics by the mid-1960s. By bringing major events live into people's living rooms, television would sometimes set the stage for leaders to take quick action affecting the scope of government. The case of protests for minority voting rights in the South provides one such example. Lyndon Johnson was watching his triple-screen TV set when NBC interrupted its airing of "Judgment at Nuremberg" to show film that had just become available of civil rights demonstrators being brutally attacked by police in Selma, Alabama. Sensing the public outrage at this violence and injustice, Johnson soon proposed and pushed through the historic Voting Rights Act of 1965 (see Chapter 5).

Today, any time a president takes strong action on some important policy problem, television sets the stage by focusing attention on the issue and putting it high on the policy agenda. Recently, this process was clearly evident in the immediate aftermath of the catastrophic flooding of New Orleans caused by Hurricane Katrina. When TV reporters broadcast images of poor people stranded and desperately calling out for help, many Americans felt that the federal government should take quick action to deal with the situation. According to *Newsweek*, Dan Bartlett, counselor to the president, compiled a DVD of these reports to impress on President Bush the urgency of the problem. Soon after seeing these televised images, the president accelerated the military's response to the situation and started to develop a major reconstruction package of aid for the city.

The rise of television has had a profound impact on the two central questions we emphasize in this text—*How should we govern?* and *What should government do?* Television has brought an immediacy to how we govern, removing the filter of time from events. Whatever the problem or event, it is happening now—live on the TV screen. People thus have more reason than ever to expect immediate governmental responses. However, the Founding Fathers designed a very deliberative governing process in which problems would be considered by multiple centers of political power and acted on only after lengthy give-and-take. Given the difficulties of getting quick action through the American political system, it is no wonder the public has come to be generally more dissatisfied with our government in the television age.

The American political system has entered a new period of **high-tech politics**—a politics in which the behavior of citizens and policymakers, as well as the political agenda itself, is increasingly shaped by technology. The **mass media** are a key part of this technology. Television, radio, newspapers, magazines, the Internet, and other means of popular communication are called *mass media* because they reach and profoundly influence not only the elite but also the masses. This chapter examines media politics, focusing on the following:

- The rise of modern media in America's advanced technological society
- The making of the news and its presentation through the media
- The biases in the news
- The impact of the media on policymakers and the public

This chapter also reintroduces the concept of the policy agenda, in which the media play an important role.

high-tech politics
Politics in which the behavior of citizens and policymakers and the political agenda itself are increasingly shaped by technology.

mass media
Television, radio, newspapers, magazines, the Internet, and other means of popular communication.

The Mass Media Today

Whether promoting a candidate, drawing attention to a social issue, or generating a government program, effectively communicating a message is critical to political success. The key is gaining control over the political agenda, which involves getting one's priorities presented at the top of the daily news. Politicians have learned that one way to guide the media's focus successfully is to limit what they can report on to carefully scripted events. A **media event** is staged primarily for the purpose of being covered. If the media were not there, the event would probably not happen or would have little significance. For example, on the eve of the 2004 New Hampshire primary, John Kerry went door-to-door in a middle-class neighborhood with TV crews in tow. The few dozen people he met could scarcely have made a difference, but Kerry was not really there to win votes by personal contact. Rather, the point was to get television coverage of him reaching out to ordinary people. Getting the right image on TV news for just 30 seconds can easily have a greater payoff than a whole day's worth of handshaking. Whereas once a candidate's G.O.T.V. program stood for "Get Out the Vote," today it is more likely to mean "Get on TV."

media events

Events purposely staged for the media that nonetheless look spontaneous. In keeping with politics as theater, media events can be staged by individuals, groups, and government officials, especially presidents.

In addition, a large part of today's so-called 30-second presidency is the slickly produced TV commercial. Approximately 60 percent of presidential campaign spending is now devoted to TV ads. In recent presidential elections, about two-thirds of the prominently aired ads were negative commercials.[1] Many people are worried that the tirade of accusations, innuendoes, and countercharges in political advertising is poisoning the American political process and possibly even contributing to declining turnout.[2] Other democracies typically allocate their parties free air-time for longer ads that go into more depth than is possible with the American-style 30-second ad.

Image making does not stop with the campaign; it is also a critical element in day-to-day governing. Politicians' images in the press are seen as good indicators of their clout. Image is especially important for presidents, who in recent years have devoted much attention to maintaining a well-honed public image, as shown in the following internal White House memo written by President Nixon:

> *When I think of the millions of dollars that go into one lousy 30-second television spot advertising a deodorant, it seems to me unbelievable that we don't do a better job in seeing that presidential appearances always have the very best professional advice whenever they are to be covered on TV. . . . The President should never be without the very best professional advice for making a television appearance.*[3]

Few, if any, administrations devoted so much effort and energy to the president's media appearance as did Ronald Reagan's. It has often been said that Reagan played to the media as he had played to the cameras in Hollywood. According to journalist Mark Hertsgaard, news management in the Reagan White House operated on the following seven principles: (1) plan ahead, (2) stay on the offensive, (3) control the flow of information, (4) limit reporters' access to the president, (5) talk about the issues you want to talk about, (6) speak in one voice, and (7) repeat the same message many times.[4] To Ronald Reagan, the presidency was often a performance, and his aides helped to choreograph his public appearances. Like many recent presidents, Reagan realized that for a president to ignore the power of image and the media would be perilous. In today's high-tech age, presidents can hardly lead the country if they cannot communicate with it effectively. President Clinton once reflected on the unexpected dimensions of his job on *Larry King Live*: "The thing that has surprised me most is how difficult it is . . . to really keep communicating what you're about to the American people. That to me has been the most frustrating thing." According to Bob Woodward, Clinton confided to a friend that "I did not realize the importance of communications and the overriding importance of what is on the evening television news. If I am not on, or there with a message, someone else is, with their message."[5]

The Development of Media Politics

Three Hundred Years of American Mass Media

We clearly live in a mass media age, but it was not always this way. There was virtually no daily press when the First Amendment was written during Washington's presidency. The daily newspaper is largely a product of the mid-nineteenth century; radio and television have been around only since the first half of the twentieth century. As recently as the presidency of Herbert Hoover (1929–1933), reporters submitted their questions to the president in writing, and he responded in writing—if at all. As Hoover put it, "The President of the United States will not stand and be questioned like a chicken thief by men whose names he does not even know."[6]

Hoover's successor, Franklin D. Roosevelt (1933–1945), practically invented media politics. To Roosevelt, the media were a potential ally. Roosevelt promised reporters two **press conferences**—presidential meetings with reporters—a week, resulting in about 1,000 press conferences during his 12 years in the White House. FDR was also the first president to use radio, broadcasting a series of reassuring "fireside chats" to the Depression-ridden nation. Roosevelt's crafty use of radio helped him win four presidential elections. Theodore White tells the story of the time in 1944 when FDR found out that his opponent, Thomas E. Dewey, had purchased 15 minutes of airtime on NBC immediately following FDR's address. Roosevelt spoke for 14 minutes and then left 1 minute silent. Thinking that the network had experienced technical difficulties, many listeners changed their dials before Dewey came on the air.[7]

press conferences
Meetings of public officials with reporters.

Another of Roosevelt's talents was knowing how to feed the right story to the right reporter. He used presidential wrath to warn reporters off material he did not want covered, and he chastised news reports he deemed inaccurate. His wrath was rarely invoked, however, and the press revered him, never even reporting to the American public that the president was confined to a wheelchair. The idea that even a political leader's health status might be public business was alien to journalists in FDR's day.

This relatively cozy relationship between politicians and the press lasted through the early 1960s. ABC's Sam Donaldson said that when he first came to Washington in 1961, "many reporters saw themselves as an extension of the government, accepting, with very little skepticism, what government officials told them."[8] And coverage of a politician's personal life was generally off-limits. For example, as a young reporter R. W. Apple Jr. of the *New York Times* once observed a beautiful woman being escorted to President Kennedy's suite. Thinking he had a major

Franklin D. Roosevelt was the first president to use the media effectively. A favorite of reporters, FDR held more than 1,000 press conferences during more than 12 years in office. He was also the first president to use radio as a political tool, giving "fireside chats" to reassure the nation during the Great Depression.

scoop, he rushed to tell his editor. But he was quickly told, "Apple, you're supposed to report on political and diplomatic policies, not girlfriends. No story."[9]

The events of the Vietnam War and the Watergate scandal, though, soured the press on government. Today's newspeople work in an environment of cynicism. To them, politicians rarely tell the whole story; the press sees ferreting out the truth as their job. No one has demonstrated this attitude better in recent years than Sam Donaldson. In his book *Hold On, Mr. President!*, Donaldson wrote,

> *If you send me to cover a pie-baking contest on Mother's Day, I'm going to ask dear old Mom whether she used artificial sweetener in violation of the rules, and while she's at it, could I see the receipt for the apples to prove she didn't steal them. I maintain that if Mom has nothing to hide, no harm will have been done. But the questions should be asked.*[10]

When the Clinton–Lewinsky scandal broke, the entire press corps reacted in this fashion. So strong was the desire to find out what the president had to hide in his personal life that 75 percent of the questions asked during the daily White House press briefing concerned this scandal in the first week after the story broke.[11] The Middle East was in crisis, the United States was building up its forces against Iraq, and the president was preparing a State of the Union address. But on TV and radio talk shows programming could best be described as "All Monica, All the Time."

investigative journalism
The use of in-depth reporting to unearth scandals, scams, and schemes, at times putting reporters in adversarial relationships with political leaders.

Many political scientists are critical of **investigative journalism**—the use of detective-like reporting methods to unearth scandals—which often pits reporters against political leaders. There is evidence that TV's fondness for investigative journalism has contributed to greater public cynicism and negativity about politics.[12]

Most analysts would agree that the most important change in media coverage of politics in recent years has been the much greater scrutiny to which politicians are now subjected.

Scholars distinguish between two kinds of media: the **print media**, which include newspapers and magazines, and the **broadcast media**, which include radio, television, and the Internet. Each has reshaped political communication at different points in American history. It is difficult to assess the likely impact of the Internet at this point, but there is at least some reason to believe that political communication is being reshaped once again.

print media
Newspapers and magazines, as compared with **broadcast media**.

broadcast media
Television and radio, as compared with **print media**.

The Print Media

You Are the News Editor

The first American daily newspaper was printed in Philadelphia in 1783, but such papers did not proliferate until the technological advances of the mid-nineteenth century. The ratification of the First Amendment in 1791, guaranteeing freedom of speech, gave even the earliest American newspapers freedom to print whatever they saw fit. This has given the media a unique ability to display the government's dirty linen, a propensity that continues to distinguish the American press today.

Among the press there is a pecking order. Almost from the beginning, the *New York Times* was a cut above most newspapers in its influence and impact; it is the nation's "newspaper of record" and can be found online at *www.nytimes.com*. Its clearest rival in government circles is the *Washington Post* (*www.washingtonpost.com*), offering perhaps the best coverage inside Washington and a sprightlier alternative to the *Times*. Papers such as the *Chicago Tribune* (*www.chicagotribune.com*) and the *Los Angeles Times* (*www.latimes.com*), as well as those in Atlanta, Boston, and other big cities, are also major national institutions. For most newspapers in medium-sized and small towns, though, the main source of national and world news is the Associated Press wire service, whose stories are reprinted in small newspapers across the country. With 2,700 reporters, photographers, and editors scattered around every major location in the United States, the Associated Press has more news-gathering ability than any other news organization.

Ever since the rise of TV news, however, newspaper circulation rates have been declining. Whereas one newspaper was sold for every two adults in 1960, by 2004 only one paper was sold for every four adults. Most political scientists who have studied the role of media in politics believe this is an unfortunate trend, as studies invariably find that regular newspaper readers are better informed and more likely to vote.[13] This should hardly be surprising given the greater degree of information available in a newspaper compared to on TV. A major metropolitan newspaper averages roughly 100,000 words daily, whereas a typical broadcast of the nightly news on TV will amount to only about 3,600 words.[14] It remains to be seen whether the availability of most newspapers on the Web will lead more people to look at newspapers in the future, or rather will prove to be a desperate gasp for a fading business.

Magazines, the other component of the print media, are also struggling in the Internet age, especially when it comes to the few that are heavily concerned with political events. The so-called newsweeklies—mainly *Time*, *Newsweek*, and *U.S.*

News and World Report—rank well behind such popular favorites as *Reader's Digest*, *TV Guide*, and *National Geographic*. Although *Time*'s circulation is a bit better than that of the *National Enquirer*, *Playboy* and *People* edge out *Newsweek* in sales. Serious magazines of political news and opinion tend to be read by the educated elite; magazines such as the *New Republic*, *National Review*, and the *Atlantic Monthly* are outsold by American favorites such as *Hot Rod*, *Weightwatchers Magazine*, and *Organic Gardening*.

The Broadcast Media

Gradually, the broadcast media have displaced the print media as Americans' principal source of news and information. By the middle of the 1930s, radio ownership had become almost universal in America, and during World War II, radio went into the news business in earnest. The 1950s and early 1960s were the adolescent years for American television. During those years, the political career of Richard Nixon was made and unmade by television. In 1952, while running as Dwight Eisenhower's vice-presidential candidate, Nixon made a famous speech denying that he took gifts and payments under the table. He did admit accepting one gift—his dog, Checkers. Noting that his daughters loved the dog, Nixon said that regardless of his political future, they would keep it. His homey appeal brought a flood of sympathetic telegrams to the Republican National Committee, and party leaders had little choice but to leave him on the ticket.

In 1960, Nixon was again on television's center stage, this time in the first televised presidential debate against Senator John F. Kennedy. Nixon blamed his poor appearance in the first of the four debates for his narrow defeat in the election. Haggard from a week in the hospital and with his five-o'clock shadow and perspiration clearly visible, Nixon looked awful compared to the crisp, clean, attractive Kennedy. The poll results from this debate illustrate the visual power of television in American politics; people listening on the radio gave the edge to Nixon, but those who saw the debate on television thought Kennedy won. Russell Baker, who covered the event for the *New York Times*, writes in his memoirs that "television replaced newspapers as the most important communications medium in American politics" that very night.[15]

Just as radio had taken the nation to the war in Europe and the Pacific during the 1940s, television took the nation to the war in Vietnam during the 1960s. TV exposed governmental naïveté (some said it was outright lying) about the progress of the war. Napoleon once said that "four hostile newspapers are more to be feared than a thousand bayonets." Lyndon Johnson learned the hard way that three television networks could be even more consequential. Every night Americans watched the horrors of war in living color on television. President Johnson soon had two wars on his hands, one in faraway Vietnam and the other at home with antiwar protesters—both covered in detail by the media. In 1968, CBS anchor Walter Cronkite journeyed to Vietnam for a firsthand look at the state of the war. In an extraordinary TV special, Cronkite reported that the war was not being won, nor was it likely to be. Watching from the White House, Johnson sadly remarked that if he had lost Cronkite, he had lost the support of the American people.[16]

Television enables many more people to see candidates for elected office than would ever be possible in person. In fact, people have become so accustomed to seeing politicians' faces when they speak that giant TV screens are now often used to enable those attending political events to see the speakers' facial expressions.

The days of network anchors like Walter Cronkite being highly trusted and influential are clearly coming to an end, as cable news and the Internet have supplanted the nightly news shows. As *New York Times* media critic Frank Rich recently wrote, "The No. 1 cliché among media critics is that we're watching the 'last hurrah' of network news anchors as we have known them for nearly half a century."[17] You can see the evidence for this trend in "A Generation of Change: How Network News Broadcasts Are Going the Way of the Dinosaurs."

Government Regulation of the Broadcast Media

When broadcast media first appeared with the invention of radio, a number of problems that the government could help with (such as overlapping use of the same frequency) soon became apparent. In 1934, Congress created the Federal

A GENERATION OF CHANGE

How Network News Broadcasts Are Going the Way of the Dinosaurs

Over the past quarter century, the NBC, ABC, and CBS nightly news broadcasts have gone from being instrumental in setting the nation's agenda to the TV equivalent of dinosaurs on their last legs. By 1981, one could make a legitimate argument that network newscasts had played a significant role in the political downfall of Presidents Johnson, Nixon, and Carter because of the way they drew attention to these presidents' shortcomings. As Barbara Matusow wrote about the stars of the evening news in 1983, "They have taken their place beside presidents, congressmen, labor leaders, industrialists, and others who shape public policy and private attitudes."*

Between 1983 and 2004, Tom Brokaw, Peter Jennings, and Dan Rather anchored the nightly news at the NBC, ABC, and CBS, respectively. Throughout this period, these anchors saw their Nielsen ratings slip lower and lower, as you can see in the following graph. Usually, TV stars do not find that they have a job for very long once their shows start to sink in the Nielsen ratings. When Tom Brokaw was asked near the end of his career as anchor of the NBC Evening News what he perceived his mission to be, he simply responded "to survive." Because of the loyal viewership each of these three long-time anchors had built up, they were able to keep their news shows going. Whether their successors can do the same for another generation remains to be seen.

In its heyday, network TV news broadcasts put afternoon newspapers out of business. Too few people felt they needed an afternoon paper once one had the nightly news available every evening on television. Today, turning on the television to get the news at a set time early in the evening seems like a quaint remnant of the past in this era of 24-hour cable news channels and the Internet.

	COMBINED RATING OF ABC, NBC, & CBS NEWS
1981	37
1982	36
1983	35
1984	33
1985	33
1986	34
1987	31
1988	30
1989	29
1990	29
1991	28
1992	28
1993	28
1994	28
1995	26
1996	24
1997	23
1998	23
1999	22
2000	24
2001	23
2002	22
2003	21
2004	20

* Barbara Matusow, *The Evening Stars: The Making of the Network News Anchor* (Boston: Houghton Mifflin, 1983), 1.

Sources: 1981–1999: *Report on Television* (New York: Nielsen Media Research, 2000), 21; 2000–2004: *The State of the News Media, 2005*, *www.stateofthemedia.org/2005/index.asp* (accessed March 14, 2005).

Communications Commission (FCC) to regulate the use of airwaves. Today, the FCC regulates communications via radio, television, telephone, cable, and satellite. The FCC is an independent regulatory body, but in practice it is subject to many political pressures. Congress uses its control over the purse strings of the agency to influence the commission, and presidential appointments to it are naturally made with political considerations in mind.

The FCC has regulated the airwaves in three important ways. First, to prevent near monopolies of control over a broadcast market, it has instituted rules to limit the number of stations owned or controlled by one company. This once involved a variety of limitations but since 1996 has been simplified to state that no single owner can control more than 35 percent of the broadcast market. Second, the FCC conducts periodic examinations of the goals and performance of stations as part of its licensing authority. Congress long ago stipulated that in order to receive a broadcasting license, a station must serve the public interest. The FCC has on only rare occasions withdrawn licenses for failing to do so, such as when a Chicago station lost its license for neglecting informational programs and for presenting obscene movies. Third, the FCC has issued a number of fair treatment rules concerning access to the airwaves for political candidates and officeholders. The equal time rule stipulates that if a station sells advertising time to one candidate, it must be willing to sell equal time to other candidates for the same office. And the right-of-reply rule states if a person is attacked on a broadcast other than the news, then that person has a right to reply via the same station. For many years, the fairness doctrine was in place, which required broadcasters to give time to opposing views if they broadcast a program slanted to one side of a controversial issue. But with the development of so many TV channels via cable, this was seen as an unnecessary rule by the late 1980s, when it was abolished.

Censorship and the FCC

From Broadcasting to Narrowcasting: The Rise of Cable News Channels

The first major networks—ABC, NBC, and CBS—adopted the term "broadcasting" in the names of their companies because their signal was being sent out to a broad audience. As long as these networks dominated the industry, each would have to deal with general topics that the public as a whole was concerned with, such as politics and government. But with the development of cable TV, market segmentation has taken hold. Sports buffs can watch ESPN all day, music buffs can tune to MTV or VH1, history buffs can glue their dial to the History Channel, and so forth. If you are interested in politics, you can channel surf between C-SPAN, C-SPAN2, CNN, MSNBC, Fox News Channel, and others. Rather than appealing to a general audience, channels such as ESPN, MTV, and C-SPAN focus on a narrow particular interest. Hence, their mission can be termed **narrowcasting** rather than traditional "broadcasting." An analysis of media usage patterns by age shows that young adults are the least likely to be using newspapers and broadcast media, having grown up with the more recently established narrowcasting alternatives. (See "Young People and Politics: How the Under-30 Crowd Learns from Different Media Sources.")

narrowcasting
Media programming on cable TV or the Internet that is focused on one topic and aimed at a particular audience. Examples include MTV, ESPN, and C-SPAN.

With the growth of cable TV news channels, television has recently entered a new era of bringing the news to people—and to political leaders—as it happens.

YOUNG PEOPLE AND POLITICS

How the Under-30 Crowd Learns from Different Media Sources

In January 2004, the Pew Research Center asked a representative sample whether they regularly learned about the presidential campaign from a variety of media sources. This table shows the results, broken down by age. Notice that young people are substantially more likely to learn from the Internet and comedy TV shows. In contrast, older people are more likely to learn from the traditional sources of newspapers and network TV news (NBC, CBS, and ABC). Because so many young people are bypassing these sources, both are facing the likely prospect of declining audiences for some time to come.

Cable TV news—CNN, MSNBC, and the Fox News Channel—have seen their audiences expand in recent years, as Americans of all ages have come to rely on them fairly heavily. However, given how little time most people stay tuned to these channels, one has to be skeptical that people are getting much more than the basic headlines from these sources. In theory, the Internet offers all the details about public policy and government anyone could want. Whether very many of those who learn about politics via the Internet take advantage of the opportunities offered there remains to be seen. Comedy shows, on the other hand, offer very limited chances for learning about politics. Young people seem to enjoy them, though, and are at least having a good time learning from them.

Questions for Discussion

- How much do you think can really be learned about politics from the comedy shows that one out of five young people say they learn from?
- Why do you think young people are so much less likely to learn from the traditional major news sources—TV network news and newspapers?

% SAYING THEY REGULARLY LEARN SOMETHING ABOUT THE PRESIDENTIAL CAMPAIGN FROM:	AGE 18–29	AGE 30–49	AGE 50–64	AGE 65+
Cable news networks	37	37	43	37
Nightly network news	23	32	44	49
Daily newspaper	23	27	37	45
Comedy TV shows	21	6	5	2
Internet	20	16	11	3
Late-night TV talk shows like *Letterman* and *Leno*	13	7	7	9

Source: January 2004 survey by the Pew Research Center for the People and the Press, *http://peoplepress.org/reports/display.php3?ReportID=200.*

Michael Bohn writes that cable news has become a valuable source of breaking information in the White House Situation Room.[18] President George W. Bush and his aides regularly watched the cable news stations during the military campaign in Afghanistan; Osama Bin Laden's videotaped messages were regularly broadcast in part on them, enabling him to get his message out to a worldwide audience. A frequent response from U.S. officials to reporters' questions during the war against terrorism has been something along the lines of "I don't know any more than what you saw on CNN."

The future of political communication seems destined to bring more and more choices regarding what we can see about our government. About two-thirds of the American public currently subscribes to cable television, thereby giving them access to dozens of channels. Sometime in the not-too-distant future it is expected that most cable systems will offer 500 channels. As the number of channels proliferates, it is clear that political junkies will find more political information readily available than ever before.

Yet it is important to note that the potential of cable news is often not realized in practice. Although these channels have seemingly unlimited opportunities to cover political events and issues, their resources are far from up to the task. A recent content analysis of CNN, Fox News, and MSNBC programming confirms just how little substantive information is usually conveyed via cable news channels. Columbia University's Project for Excellence in Journalism analyzed 240 hours of cable news programming during 2003. Their report on this content analysis provides a telling indictment of the medium. Among their many findings were that 1) only 11 percent of the time was taken up with written and edited stories; 2) the role of the reporter was primarily to talk extemporaneously; 3) stories were repeated frequently, usually without any important new information; and 4) coverage of the news was spotty, ignoring many important topics. All in all, this comprehensive study paints a very unflattering portrait of what is shown on cable news networks, labeling much of it as simply "talk radio on television."[19]

Many scholars of the media feel that the transition from network news to cable news has reduced the overall quality of political journalism. As media critic Thomas Rosensteil writes, "Network journalism originally was designed not to make a profit but to create prestige. Cable is all about profit and keeping costs low. What is disappearing is an idealism about the potential of TV as a medium to better our politics and society."[20]

Why It Matters

The Increasing Speed of News Dissemination

When Samuel Morse sent the first telegraph message from the U.S. Capitol building, he tapped out a question, "What hath God wrought?" The answer back was, "What is the news from Washington?" Ever since then, the transmission of news via electronic means has become faster and faster. As a result, over time there has been less and less time for deliberative action to provide for the future, and the political agenda has come to focus more on the here and now.

The Impact of the Internet

Some scholars have expressed quite optimistic predictions that the development of the Internet will be a boon for American democracy. As any college student knows, the Internet is the ultimate research tool. Want to know something specific? The answer can usually be found by searching the Internet using a few key words. If you want to know how the presidential candidates stand on federal support for higher education, an Internet search should quickly reveal the answers. Or if you want to know how your two U.S. senators voted recently on Medicaid appropriations, the records of the Senate roll calls can be found on the Internet. In short, for anyone with basic computing skills, the ability to become well informed about political issues is now easier than ever before.

Yet simply because so much political information is at one's fingertips via the Internet doesn't necessarily mean that many people will take advantage of these unprecedented opportunities to become well informed. One of the things that makes the Internet different from TV is that it is purposive—that is, what people see is the product of their own intentional choices. Politics is only one of a myriad of subjects that one can find out about on the Internet. As we saw in the previous chapter on public opinion, most Americans' interest in politics is fairly limited. Most people with limited political interest will probably not be motivated to use the Internet to look up detailed information about politics very often. Indeed, the data on Lycos searches displayed in Table 7.1 indicate that even in the week before the

Table 7.1 The Top 25 Lycos Searches for the Week Before the 2004 Presidential Election

Every week the Lycos search engine lists the search terms that their users have most frequently sought information about on the Internet. Here you can find the top 25 searches for the week ending October 30, 2004 — the last full week before the 2004 presidential election. As you can see, only 2 of the top 25 search items reflected an interest in the election. More people were using the Internet to look up how to carve a pumpkin or to find out information about pop culture figures such as Britney Spears than they were to learn about the upcoming election.

The rankings reflect what Internet users are most interested in. Political scientists have long argued that politics are only a peripheral part of most people's lives, and these rankings clearly reflect that fact.

Soft News vs. Hard News

RANK	SEARCH TERM	RANK	SEARCH TERM
1.	Clay Aiken	14.	NFL
2.	Halloween Costumes	15.	Grand Theft Auto San Andreas
3.	Halloween	***16.***	***John Kerry***
4.	Pumpkin Carving	17.	NASCAR
5.	Paris Hilton	18.	Poker
6.	Britney Spears	19.	Dragonball
7.	Brooke Burke	20.	Usher
8.	Pam Anderson	21.	WWE
9.	Ashlee Simpson	22.	Lunar Eclipse
10.	Christmas	23.	Boston Red Sox
11.	KaZaA	***24.***	***George W. Bush***
12.	Baseball	25.	Lindsay Lohan
13.	Michelle Vieth		

Source: http://50.lycos.com/.

2004 presidential election, Americans were more likely to be looking for information on pop culture than politics.

The impact of the Internet on politics has thus far been more subtle than revolutionary. The major changes stem from the fact that the Internet facilitates more communication in every conceivable direction. Journalists, politicians, and interest group organizers can communicate more readily with the public at large, and ordinary citizens can now respond more easily and more frequently than ever before. Journalists who were once constrained by the amount of space in their newspaper or time on their TV show now have the ability to post additional information regarding their stories on the Internet. Perhaps more important, readers and viewers now have a way of challenging and supplementing media stories by posting their own material via blogs. For example, when Dan Rather and CBS News ran a story about documents that allegedly showed that George W. Bush had shirked his duties with the National Guard in the 1970s, a number of bloggers quickly raised questions concerning their authenticity. The bloggers were ultimately proven right, and CBS News apologized for running the story. You can read more about how the Internet is changing political reporting in "Issues of the Times: Can the Internet Provide the Means to Ensure Fairness in Political Reporting?" printed in the *Times Reader* at the back of this book.

HOW YOU CAN MAKE A DIFFERENCE

The Internet and the Media

Within the last five years, traditional print and broadcast media institutions have lost considerable standing with the American public. What is responsible for the traditional media's loss of power and influence? One of the major factors is the Internet. The nature of Internet news collection and dissemination is such that nearly anyone with Internet access and desire can be a part of this media revolution. People no longer have to wait for the evening news or the morning paper. Instead, they now have access to raw, unfiltered news data as it happens.

Making a Difference

One example of the immediacy of Internet news coverage is seen in the 2005 Hurricane Katrina coverage by NOLA.com, the online branch of the *New Orleans Times-Picayune*. For days the newspaper's coverage was carried exclusively on NOLA's blogs, as the paper had lost its presses and evacuated its building because of rising water levels. The site became an international focal point for information from local media, as well as a vital link for rescue operations and coordination. In the wake of these online-only efforts, the Pulitzer Committee for the first time opened all its categories to online entries.

What you can do:

- Use the technology available to you (cell phone cameras, text messages, e-mail, blogs, etc.) to keep others informed of the news and events that are important to you (as they happen).
- Create a political and news blog and join a group like Pajamas Media—an organization which solicits and dispenses real-time news and opinions from member bloggers and other interested persons as well.
- Check multiple Internet sources in order to ensure that the news you are receiving is as accurate as possible. Don't just believe the first Web site you visit!

Private Control of the Media

One of the main reasons America has such a rich diversity of media sources is that journalism has long been big business in the United States, with control of virtually all media outlets being in private hands. Only a relatively small number of TV stations are publicly owned in America, and these PBS stations play a minimal role in the news business, attracting low ratings. In contrast, in many other countries major TV networks are owned by the government. In Canada the most prominent stations are part of the state-run Canadian Broadcasting Company, and most anywhere in Europe the major networks are government owned. In these established democracies, government ownership is not supposed to inhibit journalists from criticizing the government because the journalists are assured autonomy. In underdeveloped countries like China, where democracy has yet to take root, it is a different story: Both television and newspapers are typically government enterprises and have to carefully avoid any criticism of their country's government. Private ownership of the media as well as the First Amendment right to free speech has long meant that American journalists have an unfettered capacity to criticize government leaders and policies.

Comparing News Media

Although the American media is free and independent when it comes to journalistic content, they are totally dependent on advertising revenues to keep their

Self-Censorship and the News

chains
Newspapers published by massive media conglomerates that account for much of the nation's daily circulation. Often these chains control **broadcast media** as well.

businesses going. Public ownership means that the media can serve the public interest without worrying about the size of their audience; private ownership means that getting the biggest audience is the primary—indeed, sometimes the only—objective. The major media in America are big business today and potentially the source of great profits. In recent years, the major television networks have been bought out by giant corporations. The Disney Corporation bought ABC, General Electric acquired NBC, Viacom (a conglomerate that owns many entertainment companies, including Blockbuster, Paramount Pictures, MTV, and Simon & Schuster) took over CBS, and CNN became part of Time Warner. Major metropolitan newspapers are owned mostly by **chains**, such as Gannett, Knight-Ridder, and Newhouse. Today's massive media conglomerates control newspapers with over 80 percent of the nation's daily circulation.[21] Thus, four of five Americans now read a newspaper owned not by a fearless local editor but by a corporation headquartered elsewhere. Often these chains control television and radio stations as well.

With corporate business managers increasingly calling the shots, American journalism has definitely been affected. For example, the major television networks once had bureaus all over the world and felt a responsibility to report on world affairs. Such foreign bureaus became an easy target for cost-cutting business executives, as they were expensive to operate and survey data showed that the public was not much interested in news from overseas. A study of network news broadcasts found that ABC, NBC, and CBS broadcast just 1,382 minutes of foreign news in 2000 compared to 4,032 minutes in 1989.[22] Consequently, by September 11, 2001, the American public was largely unfamiliar with overseas news, and the TV networks had to scramble to establish an ability to cover it. As we shall see in the following section, striving for profits greatly shapes how the news is reported in America.

Reporting the News

As journalism students will quickly tell you, news is what is timely and different. It is a man biting a dog, not a dog biting a man. An often-repeated speech on foreign policy or a well-worn statement on fighting drug abuse is less newsworthy than an odd episode. The public rarely hears about the routine ceremonies at state dinners, but when President Bush threw up all over the Japanese prime minister in 1992, the world's media jumped on the story. Similarly, when Howard Dean screamed to a crowd of supporters after the 2004 Iowa caucuses, the major networks and cable news channels played the clip over 600 times in the following four days, virtually obliterating any serious discussion of the issues. In its search for the unusual, the news media can give its audience a peculiar view of events and policymakers.

Millions of new and different events happen every day; journalists must decide which of them are newsworthy. A classic look into how the news is produced can be found in Edward J. Epstein's *News from Nowhere*,[23] which summarizes his observations from a year of observing NBC's news department from inside the organization. Epstein found that in their pursuit of high ratings, news shows are tailored to a fairly low level of audience sophistication. To a large extent, TV networks define news as what is entertaining to the average viewer. A dull and complicated story would have to be of enormous importance to get on the air; in contrast, relatively trivial stories can make the cut if they are interesting enough. Leonard Downie Jr. and Robert Kaiser argue that entertainment has increasingly pushed out information in the TV news business. In 2002, they wrote that the history of TV news can be summarized in a couple sentences:

> *As audiences declined, network executives decreed that news had to become more profitable. So news divisions sharply reduced their costs, and tried to raise the entertainment value of their broadcasts.*[24]

Regardless of the medium, it cannot be emphasized enough that news reporting is a business in America. Striving for the bottom line, profits, shapes how journalists define what is newsworthy, where they get their information, and how they present it. Because some types of news stories attract more viewers or readers than others, certain biases are inherent in what the American public sees and reads.

Finding the News

Americans' popular image of correspondents or reporters somehow uncovering the news is accurate in some cases, yet most news stories come from well-established sources. Major news organizations assign their best reporters to particular **beats**—specific locations from which news often emanates, such as Congress. For example, during the 1991 Persian Gulf War, more than 50 percent of the lead stories on TV newscasts came from the White House, Pentagon, and State Department beats.[25] Numerous studies of both the electronic and the print media show that journalists rely almost exclusively on such established sources to get their information.[26]

beats
Specific locations from which news frequently emanates, such as Congress or the White House. Most top reporters work a particular beat, thereby becoming specialists in what goes on at that location.

Those who make the news depend on the media to spread certain information and ideas to the general public. Sometimes they feed stories to reporters in the form of **trial balloons:** information leaked to see what the political reaction will be. For example, a few days prior to President Clinton's admission that he had an "inappropriate relationship" with Monica Lewinsky, top aides to the president leaked the story to Richard Berke of the *New York Times*. The timing of the leak was obvious; the story appeared just before Clinton had to decide how to testify before Kenneth Starr's grand jury. When the public reacted that it was about time he admitted this relationship, it was probably easier for him to do so—at least politically.

trial balloons
An intentional news leak for the purpose of assessing the political reaction.

Reporters and their official sources have a symbiotic relationship. News makers rely on journalists to get their message out at the same time that reporters rely on public officials to keep them in the know. When reporters feel that their access to information is being impeded, complaints of censorship become widespread. During the Gulf War, reporters' freedom of movement and observation was severely restricted. After the fighting was over, 15 influential news organizations sent a letter to the secretary of defense complaining that the rules for reporting the war were designed more to control the news than to facilitate it.[27] In response to complaints about the lack of access for reporters in the first Gulf War, the Pentagon embedded about 500 reporters with coalition fighting forces during the 2003 Iraq War, thus enabling them to report on combat activity as it happened. The public response to this new form of war reporting was largely positive.

During the 2003 Iraq War, a number of journalists were embedded with fighting units, meaning they traveled along with them day after day and literally became part of the unit. Being right in with the action enabled an immediacy of reporting that was never possible before. One much praised example of embedded reporting was that of NBC's David Bloom, who sent back stunningly clear pictures of what it was like to move through the desert with an infantry division. Sadly, Bloom was one of a number of journalists who died during the conflict with Iraq. He suffered a pulmonary embolism, a condition that may have been brought on by long hours confined to a very small space inside an armored tank.

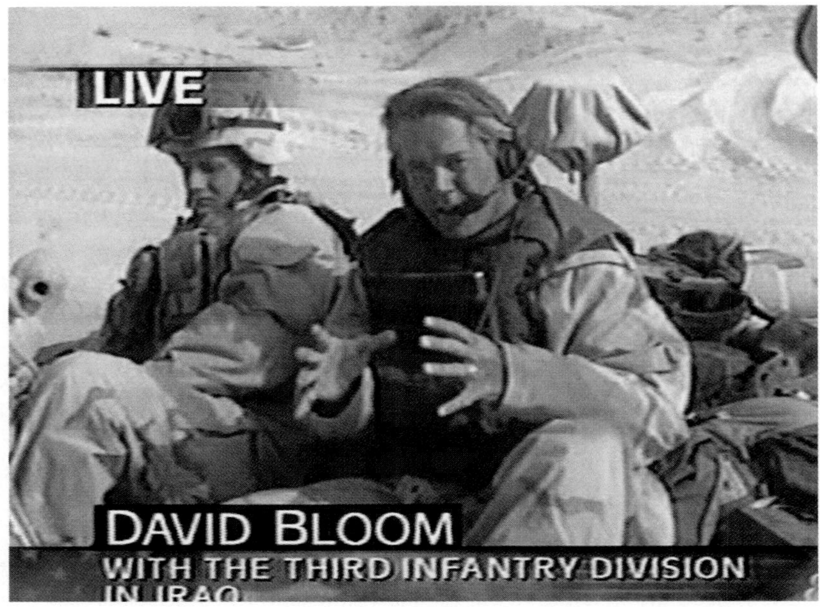

Presenting the News

Once the news has been "found," it has to be neatly compressed into a 30-second news segment or fit in among the advertisements in a newspaper. If you had to pick a single word to describe news coverage by the print and broadcast media, it would be *superficial*. "The name of the game," says former White House Press Secretary Jody Powell, "is skimming off the cream, seizing on the most interesting, controversial, and unusual aspects of an issue."[28] Editors do not want to bore or confuse their audience. TV news, in particular, is little more than a headline service. According to former CBS anchor Dan Rather, "You simply cannot be a well-informed citizen by just watching the news on television."[29]

Except for the little-watched but highly regarded *NewsHour* on PBS and ABC's late-night *Nightline*, analysis of news events rarely lasts more than a minute. Patterson's study of campaign coverage (see Chapter 9) found that only skimpy attention was given to the issues during a presidential campaign. Clearly, if coverage of political events during the height of an election campaign is thin, coverage of day-to-day policy questions is even thinner. Issues such as reforming the Medicare system, adjusting how the consumer price index is calculated, and deregulating the communications industry are highly complex and difficult to treat in a short news clip. A careful study of media coverage of President Clinton's comprehensive health care proposal found that the media focused much more on strategy and who was winning the political game than on the specific policy issues involved.[30]

Strangely enough, as technology has enabled the media to pass along information with greater speed, news coverage has become less thorough.[31] Modern high-tech communications equipment has helped reporters do their job faster but not necessarily better. Newspapers once routinely reprinted the entire text of important

Figure 7.1 The Incredible Shrinking Sound Bite

Following is the average length of time a presidential candidate was shown speaking uninterrupted on the evening network news from 1968 to 2004.

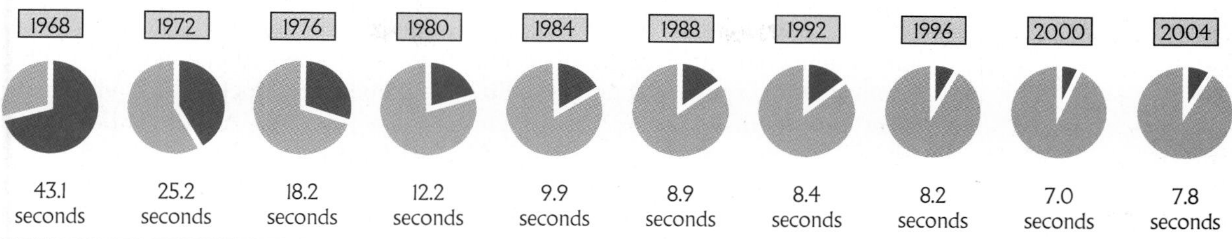

Source: Daniel Hallin, "Sound Bite News: Television Coverage of Elections," *Journal of Communications*, spring 1992; 1992–2004 data from studies by the Center for Media and Public Affairs.

political speeches; now the *New York Times* is virtually the only paper that does so—and even the *Times* has cut back sharply on this practice. In place of speeches, Americans now hear **sound bites** of 10 seconds or less on TV. As you can see in Figure 7.1, the average length of time that a presidential candidate has been given to talk uninterrupted on the TV news has declined precipitously from the late 1960s to the present day.

sound bites
Short video clips of approximately 10 seconds. Typically, they are all that is shown from a politician's speech on the nightly television news.

Even successful politicians sometimes feel frustrated by sound-bite journalism. A year after his election to the presidency, Jimmy Carter told a reporter that

> *it's a strange thing that you can go through your campaign for president, and you have a basic theme that you express in a 15- or 20-minute standard speech, . . . but the traveling press—sometimes exceeding 100 people—will never report that speech to the public. The peripheral aspects become the headlines, but the basic essence of what you stand for and what you hope to accomplish is never reported.*[32]

Rather than presenting their audience with the whole chicken, the media typically give just a McNugget. Why should politicians work to build a carefully crafted case for their point of view when a catchy line will do just as well? As former CBS anchor Walter Cronkite writes, "Naturally, nothing of any significance is going to be said in seven seconds, but this seems to work to the advantage of many politicians. They are not required to say anything of significance, and issues can be avoided rather than confronted."[33] Cronkite and others have proposed that in order to force candidates to go beyond sound bites they should be given blocks of free air time for a series of nights to discuss their opposing views (see "You Are the Policymaker: Should the Networks Have to Provide Free Air Time to Presidential Candidates?").

Over the past decade, politicians have found it increasingly difficult to get their message covered on the major networks, as ratings pressures have led to a decrease in political coverage, leaving the field to the much less watched channels like CNN and MSNBC. The three major networks *together* devoted an average of 12.6

YOU ARE THE POLICYMAKER

Should the Networks Have to Provide Free Air Time to Presidential Candidates?

In 1996, a group of prominent political and media figures proposed the idea of a series of free prime-time television appearances for presidential candidates to address the issues. The Coalition for Free Air Time called on the networks to turn over two to five minutes a night to the candidates in the month before the presidential election. Furthermore, the coalition suggested that these segments should be "roadblocked"—shown simultaneously on all networks, PBS, and interested cable stations so that people watching prime-time entertainment would be sure to see the candidates. The coalition hoped this format would promote a nightly dialogue on the issues, with candidates making news with their replies to each other's previous segments. The only requirement would be that the candidates look straight into the camera and talk. There would be no manipulation of images or unseen narrators—just candidates making their case directly to the biggest potential audience every night.

Most of the networks did eventually grant the candidates some free time in 1996, but the approach was a scattershot one. The segments varied from one to two and a half minutes, and each network chose a different time to broadcast them. A survey done by the Annenberg School of Communication immediately after the election found that only 22 percent of registered voters even knew that the free-time effort existed. Virtually everyone involved was disappointed with the results. The results from the 2000 election were similarly disheartening, as once again the networks adopted different approaches and the audiences tended to be relatively small.

Many observers believe that the experience of recent presidential elections has demonstrated the necessity of adopting a common format and time for all networks; some even advocate using the government's regulatory powers to force the networks to adopt this approach. Others point to the poor ratings of the televised debates as an example of the ineffectiveness of roadblocking political dialogue when the public just isn't very interested. You be the policymaker. Is this an experiment that the government should mandate in future presidential elections?

Politicians these days take almost every opportunity they can get to reach large audiences—even late-night comedy shows. Surveys have repeatedly shown that many young people say they learn about political affairs from these shows.

minutes per night to the exceedingly close 2000 presidential election campaign; just half the 24.6 minutes they devoted to the 1992 campaign.[34] Indeed, in the presidential election of 2000, voters had to bypass the network television newscasts and watch the TV talk shows to hear candidates deliver their messages. George Bush was on-screen for a total of 13 minutes during his appearance on *Late Night with David Letterman* on October 19, which exceeded his entire speaking time on all three network news shows during that month. Similarly, Al Gore received more speaking time on his September 14 *Letterman* appearance than he did during the entire month of September on the network evening newscasts.[35]

During the Cold War, presidents could routinely obtain coverage for their speeches on the three major networks anytime they requested it. Now, with the networks able to shunt the coverage to CNN and other cable news outlets, it is easy for them to say "no" to even the president. In May 2000, for example, Clinton was rebuffed when he asked for time on ABC, NBC, and CBS to address U.S.–China relations. "Are you crazy? It's sweeps month!" was one of the responses.[36]

Until September 11, the Bush White House was finding it harder to get media attention than any administration in a long time. A study of the first 60 days of coverage of the presidencies of Bill Clinton and George W. Bush on ABC, NBC, CBS, and PBS and on the section fronts and opinion pages of the *Washington Post*, the *New York Times*, and *Newsweek* found that there were 41 percent fewer stories on Bush than on Clinton. *Newsweek* stories on the president had decreased by 59 percent over the eight years, while network coverage was down 43 percent, and the *Post* and the *Times* had fallen off by 38 percent.[37] Although the prominence of the president increased after the September 11 terrorist attacks, there is no reason to think the trend toward less coverage of the White House has been permanently reversed.

Media Bias

Bias in the News

Many people believe that the news is biased in favor of one point of view. In recent years, Republicans have often charged that the press was against them. The charge that the media have a liberal bias has become a familiar one in American politics, and there is some limited evidence to support it. A lengthy study by the *Los Angeles Times* in the mid-1980s found that reporters were twice as likely to call themselves liberal than the general public.[38] A 2002 survey of 1,149 journalists found that 37 percent identified themselves as Democrats, compared to just 19 percent who said they were Republicans.[39]

To conclude that the news contains little explicit partisan bias is not to argue that it does not distort reality in its coverage. Former CBS News reporter Bernard Goldberg spoke for the view of many observers when he wrote in his recent best-selling book *Bias* that "real media bias comes not so much from what party they attack. Liberal bias is the result of how they see the world."[40] Goldberg argues on social issues like feminism, gay rights, and welfare that the nightly news clearly leans to the left, shaped by the cosmopolitan big-city environment in which network reporters live. He asks a telling question when he writes, "Do we really think that if the media elites worked out of Nebraska instead of New York; and if they were overwhelmingly social conservatives instead of liberals . . . do we really think that would make no difference?"[41]

Ideally, the news should mirror reality; in practice there are far too many possible stories for this to be the case. Journalists must choose which stories to cover and to what degree. The overriding bias is toward stories that will draw the largest audience. As Bernard Goldberg writes, "In the United States of Entertainment there is no greater sin than to bore the audience. A TV reporter could get it wrong from time to time. He could be snippy and snooty. But he could not be boring."[42] Surveys show that people are most fascinated by stories with conflict, violence, disaster, or scandal, as can be seen in Table 7.2. Good news is unexciting; bad news has the drama that brings in big audiences.

talking head
A shot of a person's face talking directly to the camera. Because this is visually unappealing, the major commercial networks rarely show a politician talking one-on-one for very long.

Television is particularly biased toward stories that generate good pictures. Seeing a **talking head** (a shot of a person's face talking directly to the camera) is boring; viewers will switch channels in search of more interesting visual stimulation. For example, during an unusually contentious and lengthy interview of George Bush by Dan Rather concerning the Iran-Contra scandal, CBS's ratings actually went down as people tired of watching two talking heads argue for an extended period of time.[43] A shot of ambassadors squaring off in a fistfight at the United Nations, on the other hand, will increase the ratings. Such a scene was shown three times in one day on CBS. Not once, though, was the cause of the fight discussed.[44] Network practices like these have led observers such as Lance Bennett to write that "the public is exposed to a world driven into chaos by seemingly arbitrary and mysterious forces."[45]

Are the Media Biased?

The News and Public Opinion

How does the threatening, hostile, and corrupt world often depicted by the news media shape what people believe about the American political system? For many years, students of the subject tended to doubt that the media had more than a

Table 7.2 Stories Citizens Have Tuned In and Stories They Have Tuned Out

Since 1986, the monthly survey of the Pew Research Center for the People and the Press has asked Americans how closely they have followed major news stories. As one would expect, stories involving disaster or human drama have drawn more attention than complicated issues of public policy. A representative selection of their findings is presented here. The percentage in each case is the proportion who reported following the story "very closely."

Story	Percentage
The explosion of the space shuttle *Challenger* in 1986	80%
Terrorist attacks on the World Trade Center and Pentagon	74%
Impacts of hurricanes Katrina and Rita	73%
Los Angeles riots	70%
Rescue of baby Jessica McClure from a well	69%
School shootings at Columbine High School in Colorado	68%
Iraq's invasion of Kuwait in 1990	66%
Hurricane Andrew	66%
Sniper shootings near Washington D.C.	65%
Start of hostilities against Iraq in 2003	57%
Supreme Court decision on flag burning	51%
Opening of the Berlin Wall	50%
Arrest of O. J. Simpson	48%
Nuclear accident at Chernobyl	46%
Capture of Saddam Hussein	44%
Controversy over whether Elian Gonzalez should have to return to Cuba	39%
2000 presidential election outcome	38%
Impeachment trial of President Clinton in the Senate	31%
Confirmation of John Roberts as Chief Justice	28%
Prescription drug benefit added to the Medicare program	25%
2004 Republican National Convention	22%
Release of President Bush's education plan in 2002	21%
Congressional debate about NAFTA	21%
Jack Abramoff's admission that he bribed members of Congress	18%
Passage of the Communications Deregulation Bill	12%
2003 Supreme Court decision upholding campaign finance reform	8%

Source: Pew Research Center for the People and the Press.

marginal effect on public opinion. The "minimal effects hypothesis" stemmed from the fact that early scholars were looking for direct impacts—for example, whether the media affected how people voted.[46] When the focus turned to how the media affect what Americans think about, more positive results were uncovered. In a series of controlled laboratory experiments, Shanto Iyengar and Donald Kinder subtly manipulated the stories participants saw on TV news.[47] They found that they could significantly affect the importance people attached to a given problem by splicing a few stories about it into the news over the course of a week. Iyengar and Kinder do not maintain that the networks can make something out of nothing or conceal problems that actually exist. But they do conclude that "what television news does, instead, is alter the priorities Americans attach to a circumscribed set of problems, all of which are plausible contenders for public concern."[48] Subsequent research by

Use of the Media by the American Public

Why It Matters

Media as a Business

In his classic book *Understanding Media*, Marshall McLuhan coined the famous phrase, "The medium is the message." By this, McLuhan meant that the way we communicate information can be more influential than the information itself. In the United States, news is a commodity controlled by the media, not a public service. Therefore, the news media have far more incentive to make their reports interesting than informative about policy issues. The public would probably be exposed to more policy information were it not for this incentive system.

policy agenda
The issues that attract the serious attention of public officials and other people actively involved in politics at the time.

policy entrepreneurs
People who invest their political "capital" in an issue. According to John Kingdon, a policy entrepreneur "could be in or out of government, in elected or appointed positions, in interest groups or research organizations."

Miller and Krosnick has revealed that agenda-setting effects are particularly strong among politically knowledgeable citizens who trust the media. Thus, rather than the media manipulating the public, they argue that agenda setting reflects a deliberate and thoughtful process on the part of sophisticated citizens who rely on what they consider to be a credible institutional source of information.[49]

This effect has far-reaching consequences. By increasing public attention to specific problems, the media influence the criteria by which the public evaluates political leaders. When unemployment goes up but inflation goes down, does public support for the president increase or decrease? The answer could depend in large part on which story the media emphasized. The fact that the media emphasized the country's slow economic growth in 1992 rather than the good news of low inflation and interest rates was clearly helpful to Bill Clinton's first campaign for the presidency. Similarly, the emphasis on candidate character in 2000 as opposed to the excellent economic performance under the Clinton–Gore administration clearly helped the candidacy of George W. Bush.

Much remains unknown about the effects of the media and the news on American political behavior. Enough is known, however, to conclude that media is a key political institution. The media control much of the technology that in turn controls much of what Americans believe about politics and government. For this reason, it is important to look at the American policy agenda and the media's role in shaping it.

The Media's Agenda-Setting Function

Someone who asks you "What's your agenda?" wants to know something about your priorities. As discussed in Chapter 1, governments also have agendas. John Kingdon defines **policy agenda** as "the list of subjects or problems to which government officials, and people outside of government closely associated with those officials, are paying some serious attention at any given time."[50] Interest groups, political parties, individual politicians, public relations firms, bureaucratic agencies—and, of course, the president and Congress—are all pushing for their priorities to take precedence over others. Health care, education, unemployment, and welfare reform—these and scores of other issues compete for attention from the government.

Political activists depend heavily on the media to get their ideas placed high on the governmental agenda. Political activists are often called **policy entrepreneurs**—people who invest their political "capital" in an issue (as an economic entrepreneur invests capital in an idea for making money). Kingdon says that policy entrepreneurs can "be in or out of government, in elected or appointed positions, in interest groups or research organizations."[51] Policy entrepreneurs' arsenal of weapons includes press releases, press conferences, and letter writing; convincing reporters and columnists to tell their side; trading on personal contacts; and, in cases of desperation, resorting to staging dramatic events.

The media are not always monopolized by political elites; the poor and downtrodden have access to them too. Civil rights groups in the 1960s relied heavily on the media to tell their stories of unjust treatment. Many believe that the introduction

The Internet site youtube.com has had an immediate impact on politics. Enabling Internet users to share videos and access them widely, youtube has enabled otherwise obscure home videos to get national attention. Even when speaking to small groups, politicians have to be extra careful about what they say, as anyone with a video camera can potentially post their unscripted comments on youtube.

of television helped to accelerate the movement by showing Americans—in the North and South alike—just what the situation was.[52] Protest groups have learned that if they can stage an interesting event that attracts the media's attention, at least their point of view will be heard. Radical activist Saul Alinsky once dramatized the plight of one neighborhood by having its residents collect rats and dump them on the mayor's front lawn. The story was one that local reporters could hardly resist. In 2002, graduate students at the University of California, Irvine, camped out in tents in the campus park to protest the lack of investment in on-campus housing. The prime organizer, a teaching assistant for Introduction to American Government, issued press releases and made calls to news directors urging them to come down and take a look. Soon after several stations put the sorry scene on TV, the university administration gave in to the graduate students' demands.

Conveying a long-term, positive image via the media is more important than a few dramatic events. Policy entrepreneurs—individuals or groups, in or out of government—depend on goodwill and good images. Sometimes it helps to hire a public relations firm that specializes in getting a specific message across. Groups, individuals, and even countries have hired public relations firms to improve their image and their ability to peddle their issue positions.[53]

Understanding the Mass Media

The media act as key linkage institutions between the people and the policymakers and have a profound impact on the political policy agenda. Bernard Cohen goes so far as to say, "No major act of the American Congress, no foreign adventure, no act of diplomacy, no great social reform can succeed unless the press prepares the public mind."[54] If Cohen is right, then the growth of government in America would have been impossible without the need for it being established through the media.

The Media and the Scope of Government

The media's watchdog function helps to restrict politicians. Many observers say the press is biased against whoever holds office at the moment and that reporters want to expose officeholders. They argue that reporters hold disparaging views of most public officials and believe that they are self-serving, hypocritical, lacking in integrity, and preoccupied with reelection. It is not surprising that journalists see a need to debunk public officials and their policy proposals.

The Role of the Press

As every new proposal is met with much skepticism, regular constraints are placed on the scope of what government can do. The watchdog orientation of the press can be characterized as neither liberal nor conservative but reformist. Reporters often see their job as crusading against foul play and unfairness in government and society. This focus on injustice in society inevitably encourages enlarging the scope of government. Once the media identify a problem in society—such as poverty, inadequate medical care for the elderly, or poor education for certain children—reporters usually begin to ask what the government is doing about it. Could it be acting more effectively to solve the problem? What do people in the White House and Congress (as well as state and local government) have to say about it? In this way, the media portray government as responsible for handling almost every major problem. Although skeptical of what politicians say and do, the media report on America's social problems in a manner that often also encourages government to take on more and more tasks.

Individualism and the Media

More than any other development in the past century, the rise of television broadcasting has reinforced and furthered individualism in the American political process. Candidates are now much more capable of running for office on their own by appealing to people directly through television. Individual voters can see the candidates "up close and personal" for themselves, and they have much less need for political parties or social groups to help them make their decisions.

Television finds it easier to focus on individuals than on groups. As a result, parties have declined, and candidate personality is more important than ever. Congress is difficult to cover on television because there are 535 members, but there is only one president. Doris Graber's recent study of nightly news broadcasts found that

When someone becomes an instant political celebrity it takes a police escort to get them through the hordes of cameras and reporters. Here, Monica Lewinsky leaves a federal courthouse amidst much commotion after providing evidence for the special prosecutor's investigation into charges of wrongdoing by President Clinton.

60 percent of the coverage devoted to the three branches of government was devoted to the president as compared to 31 percent for the Congress. The Supreme Court, which does not allow TV cameras to cover its proceedings and whose members rarely give interviews, is almost invisible on TV newscasts, receiving only a mere 9 percent of the coverage.[55]

Democracy and the Media

As Ronald Berkman and Laura Kitch remark, "Information is the fuel of democracy."[56] Widespread access to information could be the greatest boon to democracy since the secret ballot, yet most observers think it has fallen far short of this potential. Noting the vast increase in information available through the news media, Berkman and Kitch state, "If the sheer quantity of news produced greater competency in the citizenry, then we would have a society of political masters. Yet, just the opposite is happening."[57] The rise of the "information society" has not brought about the rise of the "informed society." For one thing, complex policy issues are not well covered in the media. The media do a far more thorough job of covering the "horse race" aspects of politics than they do of covering substantive issues.

Whenever the media are criticized for being superficial, their defense is to say that this is what people want. Network executives remark that if people suddenly started to watch in-depth shows such as PBS's *NewsHour*, then they would gladly imitate them. If the American people wanted serious coverage of the issues, networks would be happy to give it to them. Network executives claim they are in business to make a profit and that to do so, they must appeal to the maximum number of people. As Matthew Kerbel observes, "The people who bring you the evening news would like it to be informative *and* entertaining, but when these two values collide, the shared orientations of the television news world push the product inexorably toward the latter."[58] It is not their fault if the resulting news coverage is superficial, network executives argue; blame capitalism or the people—most of whom like news to be more entertaining than educational. Therefore, if people are not better informed in the high-tech age, it is largely because they do not care to hear about complicated political issues. In this sense, one can say that the people really do rule through the media.

Summary

Plenty of evidence points to the power of the media in American politics. The media are ubiquitous. There is evidence that the news and its presentation are important—perhaps the most important—shapers of public opinion on political issues. The media are important ingredients in shaping the policy agenda, and political entrepreneurs carefully use the media for this purpose.

The broadcast media have gradually replaced the print media as the principal source of news. Recently, the development of cable TV channels and Web sites has led to narrowcasting—appealing to specific segments of the mass public rather than to the entire population. The media define "news" largely as people and events that are out of the ordinary. Because of economic pressures, the media are biased in favor of stories with high drama that will attract people's interest instead of extended analyses of complex issues. With the media's superficial treatment of important policy issues, it should be no surprise that the incredible amount of information available to Americans today has not visibly increased their political awareness or participation.

Internet Resources

www.people-press.org
The Pew Center for the People and the Press regularly surveys people regarding their attitudes toward the media's coverage of politics and measures which news events people follow most closely.

www.appcpenn.org
The Annenberg Public Policy Center conducts studies that analyze the content of TV coverage of politics, which they post at this site.

www.usnpl.com
Listings for newspapers all over the country, including Web links where available.

www.cmpa.com
The Center for Media and Public Affairs posts its studies of the content of media coverage of politics at this site.

www.ammi.org/livingroomcandidate/
A great collection of classic political commercials from 1952 through 2000.

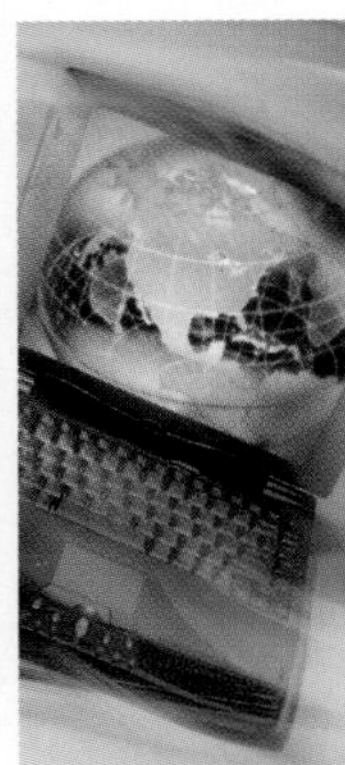

Get Connected

Campaign Advertising

Today's political campaigns rely heavily on campaign advertising to reach voters. Television stations also appear to rely on political campaigns to produce revenue for the station. The Alliance for Better Campaigns found that local television stations increased the prices of candidate ads in the two months before the 2002 elections. How much did candidates in your state spend on political advertising?

Search the Web

Go to the "In Your State" page at the Alliance for Better Campaigns' Web site, at *http://freeairtime.org/docs/index.php?DocID=21*. Look at how much the TV stations you watch earned from political advertising. Compare that amount with the amounts in neighboring states.

Questions to Ask

- How much money did your local television stations earn from campaign advertising?
- How does this compare to the amount of money stations in neighboring states earned? What might explain the differences you find?
- The Alliance for Better Campaigns advocates providing free airtime for candidates. You can read about this proposal on the organization's Web page. Does it sound like a good idea to provide free airtime to candidates?

Why It Matters

In order for voters to make informed decisions in a world with increasingly complicated issues, more detailed information is necessary. Often sound bites don't provide enough information or the right kind of information. The costs of television advertising sometimes cause candidates to end their campaigns, and some candidates can't afford to advertise on television. If television is the primary way that most voters gets political information, it is possible that some candidates' messages may not be heard.

Get Involved

Do you agree or disagree with the Alliance for Better Campaigns' goals? Send them an e-mail to let them know. The Alliance lists its state partner organizations on its Web page. Contact these state organizations to find out what they are doing in your state.

For more exercises, go to www.longmanamericangovernment.com.

For Further Reading

Baum, Matthew A. *Soft News Goes to War: Public Opinion and American Foreign Policy in the New Media Age*. Princeton, NJ: Princeton University Press, 2003. A pathbreaking examination of how people learn about major foreign policy events from entertainment news shows like *Oprah* and *Dateline*.

Bimber, Bruce, and Richard Davis. *Campaigning Online: Internet in U.S. Elections*. New York: Oxford University Press, 2003. An examination of what candidates present on their Web sites and how voters make use of this information.

Brader, Ted. *Campaigning for Hearts and Minds: How Emotional Appeals in Political Ads Work*. Chicago: University of Chicago Press, 2005. Using controlled experiments, the author shows how voters react to candidate ads that rely on enthusiasm versus fear.

Downie, Leonard Jr., and Robert G. Kaiser. *The News About the News: American Journalism in Peril*. New York: Alfred A. Knopf, 2002. A good look at how the changing economics of the news profession is altering media values and practices.

Epstein, Edward J. *News from Nowhere: Television and the News*. New York: Random House, 1973. A classic analysis of how financial considerations shape what is presented on TV news broadcasts.

Farnsworth, Stephen J., and S. Robert Lichter. *The Nightly News Nightmare*. Lanham, MD: Rowman & Littlefield, 2003. A highly critical look at how the news media cover presidential elections.

Goldberg, Bernard. *Bias: A CBS Insider Exposes How the Media Distort the News*. Washington, DC: Regnery, 2002. A best-selling account of the network news that argues there is a liberal bias on many issues, especially social policies.

Graber, Doris A. *Mass Media and American Politics*. 7th ed. Washington, DC: Congressional Quarterly Press, 2006. The standard textbook on the subject.

Hamilton, James T. *All the News That's Fit to Sell*. Princeton, NJ: Princeton University Press, 2004. An examination of how marketing considerations shape what does and does not make the news.

Iyengar, Shanto, and Donald R. Kinder. *News That Matters*. Chicago: University of Chicago Press, 1987. Two political psychologists show how the media can affect the public agenda.

Kalb, Marvin. *One Scandalous Story: Clinton, Lewinsky, and Thirteen Days That Tarnished American Journalism*. New York: Free Press, 2001. An indictment of how journalistic standards have been compromised in recent years, as illustrated by the media's coverage of the Lewinsky scandal.

Kingdon, John W. *Agendas, Alternatives, and Public Policy*. 2nd ed. New York: HarperCollins, 1995. The best overall study of the formation of policy agendas.

Mindich, David T. Z. *Tuned Out: Why Americans Under 40 Don't Follow the News*. New York: Oxford University Press, 2005. An interesting examination of why today's young people are not following political news nearly as closely as older people.

Patterson, Thomas E. *Out of Order*. New York: Knopf, 1993. A highly critical and well-documented examination of how the media covers election campaigns.

West, Darrell M. *Air Wars: Television Advertising in Election Campaigns, 1952–2004*. Washington, DC: Congressional Quarterly Press, 2005. An analysis of how TV campaign ads have evolved over the past four decades and what impact they have had on elections.

Political Parties

POLITICS IN ACTION: HOW POLITICAL PARTIES CAN MAKE ELECTIONS USER FRIENDLY FOR VOTERS In the 2006 midterm elections the Democrats won control of the House of Representatives after being in the minority for the previous 12 years. They did so largely on the basis of public discontent with the Iraq War. By voting for the opposition party voters were able to send a message of dissatisfaction even without knowing how the Democrats might approach the war differently.

The story of the 2006 midterms contrasts greatly from that of 1994, when the Republicans took control of the House of Representatives after 40 years of Democratic control. That year, 367 House Republican candidates stood on the steps of the U.S. Capitol in late September of 1994 to sign a document they titled "Contract with America." This document outlined reforms the Republicans promised to pass on the first day of the new Congress as well as 10 bills they agreed would be brought to the floor for a vote within the first 100 days of the new Republican-controlled House of Representatives. The contract was the brainchild of Newt Gingrich and Richard Armey, both of whom were college professors before they were elected to Congress. Gingrich and Armey thought the Republicans needed a stronger message in 1994 than simply saying they opposed President Clinton's policies. The contract was an attempt to offer voters a positive program for reshaping American public policy and reforming how Congress works. Without actually knowing much about the individual candidates themselves, voters would know what to expect of the signers of the contract and would be able to hold them accountable for these promises in the future. In this sense, the contract endeavored to make politics user friendly for the voters.

America's Founding Fathers were more concerned with their fear that political parties could be forums for corruption and national divisiveness than they were with the role that parties could play in making politics user friendly for ordinary voters. Thomas Jefferson spoke for many when he said, "If I could not go to heaven but with a party, I would not go there at all." In his farewell address, George Washington also warned of the dangers of parties.

Today, most observers would agree that political parties have contributed greatly to American democracy. In one of the most frequently—and rightly—quoted observations about American politics, E. E. Schattschneider said that "political parties created democracy . . . and democracy is unthinkable save in terms of the parties."[1] Political scientists and politicians alike believe that a strong party system is desirable and bemoan the weakening of American political parties in recent decades.

The strength of the parties has an impact not only on how we are governed but also on what government does. The major historical developments in the expansion or contraction of the scope of government have generally been accomplished through the implementation of one party's platform. Currently, the Democrats and Republicans differ greatly on the issue of the scope of government. Which party controls the presidency and whether the same party also controls the Congress makes a big difference.

The Meaning of Party

Almost all definitions of political parties have one thing in common: Parties try to win elections. This is their core function and the key to their definition. By contrast, interest groups do not nominate candidates for office, though they may try to influence elections. For example, no one has ever been elected to Congress as the nominee of the National Rifle Association, though many nominees have received the NRA's endorsement. Thus Anthony Downs defined a **political party** as a "team of men [and women] seeking to control the governing apparatus by gaining office in a duly constituted election."[2]

political party
According to Anthony Downs, a "team of men [and women] seeking to control the governing apparatus by gaining office in a duly constituted election."

The word *team* is the slippery part of this definition. Party teams may not be so well disciplined and single-minded as teams fielded by top football coaches. Party teams often run every which way and are difficult to lead. Party leaders often disagree about policy, and between elections the party organizations seem to all but disappear. So who are the members of these teams? A widely adopted way of thinking about parties in political science is as "three-headed political giants." The three heads are (1) the party in the electorate, (2) the party as an organization, and (3) the party in government.[3]

The *party in the electorate* is by far the largest component of an American political party. Unlike many European political parties, American parties do not require dues or membership cards to distinguish members from nonmembers. Americans may register as Democrats, Republicans, Libertarians, or whatever, but registration is not legally binding and is easily changed. To be a member of a party, you need only claim to be a member. If you call yourself a Democrat, you are one—even if you never talk to a party official, never work in a campaign, and often vote for Republicans.

The *party as an organization* has a national office, a full-time staff, rules and bylaws, and budgets. In addition to a national office, each party maintains state and local headquarters. The party organization includes precinct leaders, county chairpersons, state chairpersons, state delegates to the national committee, and officials in the party's Washington office. These are the people who keep the party running between elections and make its rules. From the party's national chairperson to its local precinct captain, the party organization pursues electoral victory.

The *party in government* consists of elected officials who call themselves members of the party. Although presidents, members of Congress, governors, and lesser officeholders may share a common party label, they do not always agree on policy. Presidents and governors may have to wheedle and cajole their own party members into voting for their policies. In the United States, it is not uncommon to put personal principle—or ambition—above loyalty to the party's leaders. These leaders are the main spokespersons for the party, however. Their words and actions personify the party to millions of Americans. If the party is to translate its promises into policy, the job must be done by the party in government.

One's party affiliation is an important part of one's political identity. Although clubs of college Republicans and college Democrats are common on campuses around the country, roughly half of college-age Americans do not have a party affiliation, preferring to call themselves Independents.

Political parties are everywhere in American politics—present in the electorate's mind, as an organization, and in government offices—and one of their major tasks is to link the people of the United States to their government and its policies.

Tasks of the Parties

The road from public opinion to public policy is long and winding. All 300 million Americans cannot raise their voices to the government and indicate their policy preferences in unison. In a large democracy, **linkage institutions** translate inputs from the public into outputs from the policymakers. Linkage institutions sift through all the issues, identify the most pressing concerns, and put these onto the governmental agenda. In other words, linkage institutions help ensure that public preferences are heard loud and clear. In the United States, there are four main linkage institutions: parties, elections, interest groups, and the media.

linkage institutions
The channels through which people's concerns become political issues on the government's policy agenda. In the United States, linkage institutions include elections, political parties, interest groups, and the media.

Kay Lawson writes that "parties are seen, both by the members and by others, as agencies for forging links between citizens and policymakers."[4] Here is a checklist of the tasks that parties perform—or should perform—if they are to serve as effective linkage institutions:

Parties Pick Candidates. Almost no one above the local level (and often not even there) gets elected to a public office without winning a party's endorsement.[5] A party's endorsement is called a *nomination*.

Parties Run Campaigns. Through their national, state, and local organizations, parties coordinate political campaigns. However, television has made it easier for candidates to campaign on their own, without the help of the party organization. For example, Ross Perot received 18.9 percent of the presidential vote in 1992 and 8.5 percent in 1996 with hardly any organizational support at all.

Why It Matters

Political Parties
Parties perform many important tasks in American politics. Among the most important are: generating symbols of identification and loyalty, mobilizing majorities in the electorate and in government, recruiting political leaders, implementing policies, and fostering stability in government. Hence, it has often been argued that the party system has to work well for the government to work well.

Parties Give Cues to Voters. Just knowing whether a candidate is a Democrat or a Republican provides crucial information to many voters. Voters can reasonably assume that if a candidate is a Republican, chances are good he or she favors conservative principles and supports President George W. Bush's policies. On the other side of the coin, it can be reasonably assumed that any Democrat opposes many of President Bush's controversial stands. A voter therefore need not do extensive research on the individual candidates but rather can rely on the informational shortcut provided by their party affiliations.

Parties Articulate Policies. Within the electorate and within the government, each political party advocates specific policy alternatives. For example, the Democratic Party has clearly supported abortion rights, and the Republican Party has repeatedly called for restrictions on abortion.

Parties Coordinate Policymaking. In America's fragmented government, parties are essential for coordination among the branches of government. Virtually all major public officials are also members of a party. When they need support to get something done, the first place they look is to their fellow partisans.

The importance of these tasks makes it easy to see why most political scientists accept Schattschneider's famous assertion that modern democracy is unthinkable without competition between political parties.

Parties, Voters, and Policy: The Downs Model

rational-choice theory
A popular theory in political science to explain the actions of voters as well as politicians. It assumes that individuals act in their own best interest, carefully weighing the costs and benefits of possible alternatives.

The parties compete, at least in theory, as in a marketplace. A party is in the market for voters; its products are its candidates and policies. Anthony Downs has provided a working model of the relationship among citizens, parties, and policy, employing a rational-choice perspective.[6] **Rational-choice theory** "seeks to explain political processes and outcomes as consequences of purposive behavior. Political actors are assumed to have goals and to pursue those goals sensibly and efficiently."[7] Downs argues that (1) voters want to maximize the chance that policies they favor will be adopted by government and that (2) parties want to win office. Thus, in order to win office, the wise party selects policies that are widely favored. Parties and candidates may do all sorts of things to win—kiss babies, call opponents ugly names, even lie and cheat—but in a democracy they will use primarily their accomplishments and policy positions to attract votes. If Party A figures out what the voters want more accurately than does Party B, then Party A should be more successful.

Deciding on a Political Party

The long history of the American party system has shown that successful parties rarely stray far from the midpoint of public opinion. In the American electorate, a few voters are extremely liberal and a few extremely conservative, but the majority are in the middle. If Downs is right, then centrist parties will win, and extremist parties will be condemned to footnotes in the history books. We frequently hear criticism that there is not much difference between the Democrats and the Republicans. Given the nature of the American political market, however, these two parties have little choice. We would not expect two competing department stores to locate at opposite ends of town when most people live on Main Street.

Downs also notes, though, that from a rational-choice perspective, one should expect the parties to differentiate themselves at least somewhat. Just as Chrysler tries to offer something different from and better than General Motors in order to build buyer loyalty, so Democrats and Republicans have to forge different identities to build voter loyalty. Two-thirds of the population currently believes that important differences do exist between the parties. When asked what those differences are, respondents most frequently comment that the Republicans favor lower taxes and less domestic spending, whereas Democrats favor more government programs to help middle-class and less advantaged Americans.

The Party in the Electorate

In most European nations, being a party member means formally joining a political party. You get a membership card to carry around, you pay dues, and you vote to pick your local party leaders. In America, being a party member takes far less work. There is no formal "membership" in the parties at all. If you believe you are a Democrat or a Republican, then you are a Democrat or a Republican. Thus, the party in the electorate consists largely of symbolic images and ideas. For most people the party is a psychological label. Most voters have a **party image** of each party; that is, they know (or think they know) what the Republicans and Democrats stand for. Liberal or conservative, pro-business or pro-labor, pro-choice or pro-life—these are some of the elements of each party's images.

party image
The voter's perception of what the Republicans or Democrats stand for, such as conservatism or liberalism.

Party images help shape people's **party identification,** the self-proclaimed preference for one party or the other. Because many people routinely vote for the party they identify with (all else being equal), even a shift of a few percentage points in the distribution of party identification is important. Since 1952, the National Election Study surveys have asked a sample of citizens, "Generally speaking, do you usually think of yourself as a Republican, a Democrat, or an Independent?" Repeatedly asking this question permits political scientists to trace party identification over time (see Table 8.1). During the last five presidential elections (1988–2004), two clear patterns have been evident. First, unlike earlier periods when Democrats greatly outnumbered Republicans, in recent elections the Democratic Party's edge in terms of identifiers in the electorate has been quite modest. In 1964 there were more than twice as many Democrats as Republicans, whereas by 2004 Republicans trailed Democrats by a mere 3 percentage points. Second, in most recent elections the most frequent response to the party identification question has been the Independent option. In 2004, 39 percent of the population called themselves Independents. As you can see in "Young People and Politics: The Parties Face an Independent Youth," survey data demonstrate that the younger one is, the more likely he or she is to be a political independent.

party identification
A citizen's self-proclaimed preference for one party or the other.

Difference Between Democrats and Republicans

People who call themselves Independents are the most likely voters to engage in the practice of **ticket splitting**—voting with one party for one office and the other

ticket splitting
Voting with one party for one office and with another party for other offices. It has become the norm in American voting behavior.

Table 8.1 Party Identification in the United States, 1952–2004[a]

YEAR	DEMOCRATS	INDEPENDENTS	REPUBLICANS
1952	48.6	23.3	28.1
1956	45.3	24.4	30.3
1960	46.4	23.4	30.2
1964	52.2	23.0	24.8
1968	46.0	29.5	24.5
1972	41.0	35.2	23.8
1976	40.2	36.8	23.0
1980	41.7	35.3	23.0
1984	37.7	34.8	27.6
1988	35.7	36.3	28.0
1992	35.8	38.7	25.5
1996	39.3	32.9	27.8
2000	34.8	41.0	24.2
2004	32.1	38.9	29.0

[a] In percentage of people; the small percentage who identify with a minor party or who cannot answer the question are excluded.
Source: Authors' analysis of 1952–2004 American National Election Study data.

YOUNG PEOPLE AND POLITICS

The Parties Face an Independent Youth

Younger people have always had a tendency to be more independent of the major political parties than older people. But this has rarely been so evident in survey data as it is now. As you can see from the 2002 survey data displayed here, 55 percent of people between the ages of 18 and 24 said they were political independents. In contrast, only about half as many people over 65 called themselves independents. As one looks down the age-groups in the table, it is clear that what varies by age is not the ratio of Democrats to Republicans but rather the likelihood of someone being an independent. Data over time indicate that as people get older, they become more likely to identify with one of the major parties. But whether this will be true for the current generation of youth remains to be seen.

Questions for Discussion

- Do you think that as the current generation of young people ages they will become more likely to identify with the major political parties?
- Because younger people are so likely to be independent, does this mean many young voters are particularly open to persuasion during campaigns? If so, why don't the Democrats and Republicans pay special attention to trying to get them on their side?
- In some states, such as New York and Florida, only voters who are registered with a party can participate in that party's primary. Given that younger people are less likely to identify with a party, does this mean their influence in primary elections is diminished in such states?

	DEMOCRAT	INDEPENDENT	REPUBLICAN
18–24	25	55	19
25–34	33	42	24
35–44	32	39	29
45–54	32	38	30
55–64	33	33	35
65+	41	28	31

Source: Authors' analysis of the 2002 General Social Survey.

party for another office. For example, the 2004 National Exit Poll found that 25 percent of Independents who voted for Bush did not support a Republican for the House of Representatives, compared to just 7 percent among Republican identifiers who voted for Bush. The result of many voters being open to splitting their tickets is that even when one party has a big edge in a state, the other party always has a decent shot at winning at least some important offices. In other words, regardless of media labels of red and blue states, the practice of ticket splitting means that no state is ever completely safe for a given party. Thus, California, Hawaii, and Vermont lean heavily toward the Democrats, but as of 2007 all the governors of these states were Republicans. On the other side of the coin, Democrats were serving as governors in heavily Republican states like Kansas, Virginia, and Oklahoma.

The Party Organizations: From the Grass Roots to Washington

An organizational chart is usually shaped like a pyramid, with those who give orders at the top and those who carry them out at the bottom. In drawing an organizational chart of an American political party, you could put the national committee and national convention of the party at the apex of the pyramid, the state party organizations in the middle, and the thousands of local party organizations at the bottom. Such a chart, however, would provide a misleading depiction of an American political party. The president of General Motors is at the top of GM on paper as well as in fact. By contrast, the chairperson of the Democratic or Republican national committee is on top on paper but not in fact.

As organizations, American political parties are decentralized and fragmented. One can imagine a system in which the national office of a party resolves conflicts among its state and local branches, states the party's position on the issues, and then passes orders down through the hierarchy. One can even imagine a system in which the party leaders have the power to enforce their decisions by offering greater influence and resources to officeholders who follow the party line and by punishing those who do not. Many European parties work just that way, but in America the formal party organizations have little such power. Candidates in the United States can get elected on their own. They do not need the help of the party most of the time, and hence the party organization is relegated to a comparatively limited role.

The major parties have different demographic bases of support. Of all social groups, African Americans tend to be the most solidly aligned with one party. Ever since the Civil Rights Act of 1964, they have voted overwhelmingly for Democratic candidates. In 2004, African American voters cast 88 percent of their votes for John Kerry.

Local Parties

The urban political party was once the main political party organization in America. From the late nineteenth century through the New Deal of the 1930s, scores of cities were dominated by **party machines**. A machine is a kind of party organization, very different from the typical fragmented and disorganized political party in America today. It can be defined as a party organization that depends on rewarding its members in some material fashion.

party machines
A type of political party organization that relies heavily on material inducements, such as patronage, to win votes and to govern.

Patronage is one of the key inducements used by party machines. A patronage job is one that is awarded for political reasons rather than for merit or competence alone. At one time, urban machines in Albany, Chicago, Philadelphia, Kansas City, and elsewhere depended heavily on ethnic group support. Some of the most fabled machine leaders were Irish politicians, including New York's George Washington Plunkett, Boston's James Michael Curley, and Chicago's Richard J. Daley. Daley's

patronage
One of the key inducements used by party machines. A patronage job, promotion, or contract is one that is given for political reasons rather than for merit or competence alone.

Chicago machine was the last survivor, steamrolling its opposition amid charges of racism and corruption. Even today there are remnants of the Chicago machine, particularly in White and ethnic neighborhoods. The survival of machine politics in Chicago can be traced to its ability to limit the scope of reform legislation. A large proportion of city jobs were classified as "temporary" even though they had been held by the same person for decades, and these positions were exempted from the merit system of hiring. At its height, the Daley machine in Chicago dispensed 40,000 patronage jobs, the recipients of which were expected to deliver at least 10 votes each on Election Day and to kick back 5 percent of their salary in the form of a donation to the local Democratic Party.[8]

Urban party organizations are also no longer very active as a rule. Progressive reforms that placed jobs under the merit system rather than at the machine's discretion weakened the machines' power. Regulations concerning fair bidding on government contracts also took away much of their ability to reward the party faithful. As ethnic integration occurred in big cities, the group loyalties that the machines often relied on no longer seemed very relevant to many people.

Mayor Richard J. Daley ruled the city of Chicago from 1955 until his death in 1976. His Cook County Democratic Party organization was highly organized at the precinct level. Members of the organization kept people in their neighborhoods happy by providing for their local needs, such as street maintenance, new stoplights, no-parking zones, and so on, and the people reciprocated on Election Day by supporting the organization's candidates.

Partly filling in the void created by the decline of the inner-city machines has been a revitalization of party organization at the county level—particularly in affluent suburbs. These county organizations distribute yard signs and campaign literature, get out the vote on Election Day, and help state and local candidates any way they can. Traditionally, local organizations relied on personal knowledge of individuals in the neighborhood who could be persuaded to support the party. Today, these organizations have access to computerized lists with all sorts of details about registered voters that they use to try to tailor their appeals to each individual. (See "Issues of the Times: Should the Political Parties Be Compiling Data About You?" printed in the Appendix of this book.)

The 50 State Party Systems

American national parties are a loose aggregation of state parties, which are themselves a fluid association of individuals, groups, and local organizations. There are 50 state party systems, and no two are exactly alike. In a few states, the parties are well organized, have sizable staffs, and spend a lot of money. Pennsylvania is one such state. In other states, however, parties are weak. California, says Kay Lawson, "has political parties so weak as to be almost nonexistent; it is the birthplace of campaigning by 'hired guns'; and it has been run by special interests for so long that Californians have forgotten what is special about that."[9]

The states are allowed wide discretion in the regulation of party activities, and how they choose to organize elections influences the strength of the parties profoundly. Some states give parties greater power than others to limit who can participate in their nomination

HOW YOU CAN MAKE A DIFFERENCE

Political Parties

Political parties offer many opportunities for you to engage in direct political action and actively participate in the political process. Though media coverage of party affairs typically focuses on both national leaders and organizations, most party activity takes place at the grassroots and state level. At the most basic level, party representatives help mobilize voters, distribute information and literature, man phone-banks, and work the polls. Party involvement gives you the chance to help noticeably sway the actions of voters and government.

Making a Difference

In preparation for its 2005 gubernatorial election, New Jersey played host to the "Be Powerful, Be Heard—Vote New Jersey Hip Hop Summit II." The summit was sponsored by hip-hop mogul Russell Simmons, who is also the Chairman of the Hip-Hop Summit Action Network (HSAN). The organization specifically targets high school and college students. The summit, with appearances by hip-hop artists like Reverend Run and Doug E. Fresh, was broadcast in schools across the state. The success of these summits is demonstrable. Following the 2004 summit, there was a 15% increase in the number of New Jersey–based young people who voted. These events encourage students to take an active role in their political futures.

What can you do:

- Become a precinct chair for your political party. As precinct chair, you direct and supervise precinct conventions—meetings of all party members in a precinct, where party policy is shaped.
- Donate time by working at a party headquarters. You could be asked to man phone-banks, to scour voter rolls for potential voters, or to put up party signs and placards.
- Organize a get-out-the-vote drive in your district. Walk through neighborhoods to inform independent and non-committed voters about the issues and the candidates.

contests. In **closed primaries** only people who have registered in advance with the party can vote in its primary, thus encouraging greater party loyalty. In contrast, **open primaries** allow voters to decide on Election Day whether they want to participate in the Democratic or Republican contests. And most antiparty of all are **blanket primaries,** which present voters with a list of candidates from all the parties and allow them to pick some Democrats and some Republicans if they like. In the case of *Democratic Party et al. v. Jones*, however, the Supreme Court ruled that for a blanket primary to be constitutional it must be officially nonpartisan, as otherwise it adulterates their candidate selection process "by opening it up to persons wholly unaffiliated with the party."

When it comes to the general election, some states promote voting according to party by listing the candidates of each party down a single column, whereas others place the names in random order. About a third of the states currently have a provision on their ballots that enables a voter to cast a vote for all of one party's candidates with a single act. This option clearly encourages straight-ticket voting and makes the support of the party organization more important to candidates in these states.

In terms of headquarters and budgets, state parties are much better organized and funded than they were several decades ago. Nevertheless, as John Bibby points

closed primaries
Elections to select party nominees in which only people who have registered in advance with the party can vote for that party's candidates, thus encouraging greater party loyalty.

open primaries
Elections to select party nominees in which voters can decide on Election Day whether they want to participate in the Democratic or Republican contests.

blanket primaries
Elections to select party nominees in which voters are presented with a list of candidates from all the parties. Voters can then select some Democrats and some Republicans if they like.

out, they mostly serve to supplement the candidates' own personal campaign organizations; thus, state party organizations rarely manage campaigns. The job of the state party, writes Bibby, is merely "to provide technical services" within the context of a candidate-centered campaign.[10]

The National Party Organizations

national convention

The meeting of party delegates every four years to choose a presidential ticket and write the party's platform.

national committee

One of the institutions that keeps the party operating between conventions. The national committee is composed of representatives from the states and territories.

national chairperson

The national chairperson is responsible for the day-to-day activities of the party and is usually handpicked by the presidential nominee.

The supreme power within each of the parties is its **national convention**. The convention meets every four years, and its main task is to write the party's platform and then nominate its candidates for president and vice president. (Chapter 9 will discuss conventions in detail.) Keeping the party operating between conventions is the job of the **national committee**, composed of representatives from the states and territories. Typically, each state has a national committeeman and a national committeewoman as delegates to the party's national committee. The Democratic committee also includes assorted governors, members of Congress, and other party officials.

Day-to-day activities of the national party are the responsibility of the party's **national chairperson**. The national party chairperson hires the staff, raises the money, pays the bills, and attends to the daily duties of the party. When asked what their biggest organizational challenge was at a 1998 joint appearance, the chairs of the Democratic and Republican parties both promptly responded "money."[11]

The chairperson of the party that controls the White House is normally selected by the president himself (subject to routine ratification by the national committee). In the early 1970s, two of the people who served for a while as chair of the Republican Party at the request of President Nixon were Bob Dole and George Bush, both of whom used this position as a means of political advancement. These days the party chairs are typically career staffers who have worked their way up through a series of behind-the-scenes jobs to the role of a visible spokesperson for the party. A recent exception to this general pattern is former presidential candidate Howard Dean, who sought after and won the job of chair of the Democratic Party after the 2004 election.

The Party in Government: Promises and Policy

Which party controls each of America's many elected offices matters because both parties and the elected officials who represent them usually try to turn campaign promises into action. As a result, the party that has control over the most government offices will have the most influence in determining who gets what, where, when, and how.

coalition

A group of individuals with a common interest on which every political party depends.

Voters are attracted to a party in government by its performance and policies. What a party has done in office—and what it promises to do—greatly influences who will join its **coalition**—a set of individuals and groups supporting it. Sometimes voters suspect that political promises are made to be broken. To be sure, there are notable instances in which politicians have turned—sometimes

180 degrees—from their policy promises. Lyndon Johnson repeatedly promised in the 1964 presidential campaign that he would not "send American boys to do an Asian boy's job" and involve the United States in the Vietnam War, but he did. In the 1980 campaign, Ronald Reagan asserted that he would balance the budget by 1984, yet his administration quickly ran up the largest deficit in American history. Throughout the 1988 campaign George Bush proclaimed, "Read my lips—no new taxes," but he reluctantly changed course two years later when pressured on the issue by the Democratic majority in Congress. Bill Clinton promised a tax cut for the middle class during the 1992 campaign, but after he was elected, he backed off, saying that first the deficit would have to be substantially reduced.

It is all too easy to forget how often parties and presidents do exactly what they say they will do. For every broken promise, many more are kept. Ronald Reagan promised to step up defense spending and cut back on social welfare expenditures, and his administration quickly delivered on these pledges. Bill Clinton promised to support bills providing for family leave, easing voting registration procedures, and tightening gun control that had been vetoed by his predecessor. He lobbied hard to get these measures through Congress again and proudly signed them into law once they arrived on his desk. George W. Bush promised a major tax cut for every taxpayer in America, and he delivered just that in 2001. In sum, the impression that politicians and parties never produce policy out of promises is largely erroneous.

In fact, the parties have done a fairly good job over the years of translating their platform promises into public policy. Gerald Pomper has shown that party platforms are excellent predictors of a party's actual policy performance in office. He tabulated

State Control and National Platforms

specific pledges in the major parties' platforms over a number of years, tabulating 3,194 specific policy pronouncements. Pomper then looked to see whether the party that won the presidency actually fulfilled its promises. Nearly three-fourths of all promises resulted in policy actions. Others were tried but floundered for one reason or another. Only 10 percent were ignored altogether.[12]

If parties generally do what they say they will, then the party platforms adopted at the national conventions represent blueprints, however vague, for action. Consider what the two major parties promised the voters in 2004 (see Table 8.2). There is little doubt that the choice between Democratic and Republican policies in 2004 was a clear one on many important issues facing the country.

Table 8.2 Party Platforms, 2004

Although few people actually read party platforms, they are one of the best written sources for what the parties believe in. A brief summary of some of the contrasting positions in the Democratic and Republican platforms of 2004 illustrates major differences in beliefs between the two parties.

REPUBLICANS	DEMOCRATS
The War in Iraq	
The best intelligence available at the time indicated that Saddam Hussein was a threat. While the stockpiles of weapons of mass destruction we expected to find in Iraq have not yet materialized, we have confirmed that Saddam Hussein had the capability to reconstitute his weapons programs and the desire to do so. . . . President Bush had a choice to make: Trust a madman or defend America. He chose defending America.	People of good will disagree about whether America should have gone to war in Iraq, but this much is clear: This administration badly exaggerated its case, particularly with respect to weapons of mass destruction and the connection between Saddam's government and Al Qaeda. This administration did not build a true international coalition. Ignoring the advice of military leaders, this administration did not send sufficient forces into Iraq to accomplish the mission.
Fighting Terrorism	
President Bush recognized that to overcome the dangers of our time, America would have to take a new approach in the world. That approach is marked by a determination to challenge new threats, not ignore them, or simply wait for future tragedy—and by a commitment to building a hopeful future in hopeless places, instead of allowing troubled regions to remain in despair and explode in violence.	The Bush doctrine of unilateral preemption has driven away our allies and cost us the support of other nations. With John Kerry as commander in chief, we will never wait for a green light from abroad when our safety is at stake, but we must enlist those whose support we need for ultimate victory.
Abortion	
We say the unborn child has a fundamental individual right to life that cannot be infringed.	We stand profoundly for a woman's right to choose, consistent with *Roe v. Wade*, and regardless of ability to pay.
Gay Marriage	
We strongly support President Bush's call for a constitutional Amendment that fully protects marriage, and we believe that neither federal nor state judges nor bureaucrats should force states to recognize other living arrangements as equivalent to marriage.	In our country, marriage has been defined at the state level for 200 years, and we believe it should continue to be defined there. We repudiate President Bush's divisive effort to politicize our Constitution by pursuing a federal marriage amendment.

Table 8.2 (Continued)

REPUBLICANS	DEMOCRATS
Health Care We must attack the root causes of high health care costs by: aiding small businesses in offering health care to their employees; empowering the self-employed through access to affordable coverage; putting patients and doctors in charge of medical decisions; and reducing junk lawsuits and limiting punitive damage awards that raise the cost of health care.	We believe that health care is a right and not a privilege. We will offer individuals and businesses tax credits to make quality, reliable health coverage more affordable. We will provide tax credits to Americans who are approaching retirement age and those who are between jobs so they can afford quality, reliable coverage. We will expand coverage for low income adults through existing federal-state health care programs.
Taxes We believe that good government is based on a system of limited taxes and spending. . . . Our party endorses the president's proposals to make tax relief permanent, so that families and businesses can plan for the future with confidence.	We must restore values to our tax code. We want a tax code that rewards work and creates wealth for more people, not a tax code that hoards wealth for those who already have it. We should set taxes for families making more than $200,000 a year at the same level as in the late 1990s.
Education The president and Republicans in Congress recognize that states and local communities are most directly responsible for the quality of education in their schools. That is why the No Child Left Behind Act stipulates that the states, not the federal government, develop an accountability plan that will work best for them.	Under Kerry and Edwards, we will offer high quality early learning opportunities, smaller classes, more after school activities, and more individualized attention for our students. . . . The federal government will meet its financial obligations for elementary and secondary education and for special education.

Source: Excerpts from party platforms as posted on the Web sites of each organization.

Party Eras in American History

While studying political parties, remember: America is a two-party system and always has been. Of course, there are many minor parties around—Libertarians, Socialists, Reforms, Greens—but they rarely have a chance of winning a major office. In contrast, most democratic nations have more than two parties represented in their national legislature. Throughout American history, one party has been the dominant majority party for long periods of time. A majority of voters identify with the party in power; thus, this party tends to win a majority of the elections. Political scientists call these periods **party eras**. The majority party does not, of course, win every election; sometimes it suffers from intraparty squabbles and loses power. Sometimes it nominates a weak candidate, and the opposition cashes in on the majority party's misfortune.

party eras
Historical periods in which a majority of voters cling to the party in power, which tends to win a majority of the elections.

critical election
An electoral "earthquake" whereby new issues emerge, new coalitions replace old ones, and the majority party is often displaced by the minority party. Critical election periods are sometimes marked by a national crisis and may require more than one election to bring about a new **party era**.

Punctuating each party era is a **critical election**.[13] A critical election is an electoral earthquake: Fissures appear in each party's coalition, which begins to fracture; new issues appear, dividing the electorate. Each party forms a new coalition—one that endures for years. A critical election period may require more than one election before change is apparent, but in the end, the party system will be transformed.

party realignment
The displacement of the majority party by the minority party, usually during a **critical election** period.

This process is called **party realignment**—a rare event in American political life that is akin to a political revolution. Realignments are typically associated with a major crisis or trauma in the nation's history. One of the major realignments, when the Republican Party emerged, was connected to the Civil War. Another was linked to the Great Depression of the 1930s, when the majority Republicans were displaced by the Democrats. The following sections look more closely at the various party eras in American history.

1796–1824: The First Party System

In the *Federalist Papers*, James Madison warned strongly against the dangers of "factions," or parties. But Alexander Hamilton, one of the coauthors of the *Federalist Papers*, did as much as anyone to inaugurate our party system.[14] To garner congressional support for his pet policies, particularly a national bank, he needed votes. From this politicking and coalition building came the rudiments of the Federalist Party, America's first political party. The Federalists were also America's shortest-lived major party. After Federalist candidate John Adams was defeated in his reelection bid in 1800, the party quickly faded. The Federalists were poorly organized, and by 1820 they no longer bothered to offer up a candidate for president. In this early period of American history, most party leaders did not regard themselves as professional politicians. Those who lost often withdrew completely from the political arena.

The party that crushed the Federalists was led by Virginians Jefferson, Madison, and Monroe, each of whom was elected president for two terms in succession. They were known as the Democratic-Republicans, or sometimes as the Jeffersonians. The Democratic-Republican Party derived its coalition from agrarian interests rather than from the growing number of capitalists who supported the Federalists. This made the party particularly popular in the largely rural South. As the Federalists disappeared, however, the old Jeffersonian coalition was torn apart by factionalism as it tried to be all things to all people.

Aaron Burr dealt a near-death blow to the Federalist Party when he killed its leader, Alexander Hamilton, in this 1804 duel. Burr, then vice president, challenged Hamilton to the duel after the former treasury secretary publicly called him a traitor.

1828–1856: Jackson and the Democrats versus the Whigs

More than anyone else, General Andrew Jackson founded the modern American political party. In the election of 1828, he forged a new coalition that included Westerners as well as Southerners, new immigrants as well as settled Americans. Like most successful politicians of his day, Jackson was initially a Democratic-Republican, but soon after his ascension to the presidency his party became known as simply the Democratic Party, which continues to this day. The "Democratic" label was particularly appropriate for Jackson's supporters because their cause was to broaden political opportunity by eliminating many vestiges of elitism and by mobilizing the masses.

Whereas Jackson was the charismatic leader, the Democrats' behind-the-scenes architect was Martin Van Buren, who succeeded Jackson as president. Van Buren's one term in office was relatively undistinguished, but his view of party competition left a lasting mark. A realist, Van Buren argued that a party could not aspire to pleasing all the people all the time. He argued that a governing party needed a loyal opposition to represent parts of society that it could not. This opposition was provided by the Whigs. The Whig Party included such notable statesmen as Henry Clay and Daniel Webster, but it was able to win the presidency only when it nominated aging but popular military heroes such as William Henry Harrison (1840) and Zachary Taylor (1848). The Whigs had two distinct wings—Northern industrialists and Southern planters—who were brought together more by the Democratic policies they opposed than by the issues on which they agreed.

1860–1928: The Two Republican Eras

In the 1850s, the issue of slavery dominated American politics and split both the Whigs and the Democrats. Slavery, said Senator Charles Sumner, an ardent abolitionist, "is the only subject within the field of national politics which excites any real interest."[15] Congress battled over the extension of slavery to the new states and territories. In *Dred Scott v. Sandford*, the Supreme Court of 1857 held that slaves could not be citizens and that former slaves could not be protected by the Constitution. This decision further sharpened the divisions in public opinion, making civil war increasingly likely.

In the late 1850s the Republicans rose as the antislavery party. Folding in the remnants of several minor parties, in 1860 the Republicans forged a coalition strong enough to elect Abraham Lincoln president and to ignite the Civil War. The "War Between the States" was one of those political earthquakes that realigned the parties. After the war, the Republican Party thrived for more than 60 years. The Democrats controlled the South, though, and the Republican label remained a dirty word in the old Confederacy.

A second Republican era was initiated with the watershed election of 1896, perhaps the most bitter battle in American electoral history. The Democrats nominated William Jennings Bryan, populist proponent of "free silver" (linking money with silver, which was more plentiful than gold, and thus devaluing money to help debtors). The Republican Party made clear its positions in favor of the gold standard, industrialization, the banks, high tariffs, and the industrial working classes, as well as its positions against the "radical" Western farmers and "silverites." "Bryan and his program were greeted by the country's conservatives with something akin to terror."[16]The *New York Tribune* howled that Bryan's Democrats were "in league with the Devil." On the other side, novelist Frank Baum lampooned the Republicans in his classic novel *The Wizard of Oz*. Dorothy follows the yellow brick road (symbolizing the gold standard) to the Emerald City (representing Washington) only to find that the Wizard (whose figure resembles McKinley) is powerless. But by clicking on her *silver* slippers (the color was changed to ruby for technicolor effect in the movie), she finds that she can return home.

Franklin Roosevelt reshaped the Democratic Party, bringing together a diverse array of groups that had long been marginalized in American political life. Many of the key features of the Democratic Party today, such as support from labor unions, can be traced to the FDR era.

Political scientists call the 1896 election a realigning one because it shifted the party coalitions and entrenched the Republicans for another generation. For the next three decades the Republicans continued as the nation's majority party, until the stock market crashed in 1929. The ensuing Great Depression brought about another fissure in the crust of the American party system.

1932–1964: The New Deal Coalition

President Herbert Hoover's handling of the Depression turned out to be disastrous for the Republicans. He solemnly pronounced that economic depression could not be cured by legislative action. Americans, however, obviously disagreed, and voted for Franklin D. Roosevelt, who promised the country a *New Deal*. In his first 100 days as president, Roosevelt prodded Congress into passing scores of anti-Depression measures. Party realignment began in earnest after the Roosevelt administration got the country moving again. First-time voters flocked to the polls, pumping new blood into the Democratic ranks and providing much of the margin for Roosevelt's four presidential victories. Immigrant groups in Boston and other cities had been initially attracted to the Democrats by the 1928 campaign of Al Smith, the first Catholic to be nominated by a major party for the presidency.[17] Roosevelt reinforced the partisanship of these groups, and the Democrats forged the **New Deal coalition**.

New Deal coalition

A **coalition** forged by the Democrats, who dominated American politics from the 1930s to the 1960s. Its basic elements were the urban working class, ethnic groups, Catholics and Jews, the poor, Southerners, African Americans, and intellectuals.

The basic elements of the New Deal coalition were the following:

- *Urban dwellers*. Big cities such as Chicago and Philadelphia were staunchly Republican before the New Deal realignment; afterward, they were Democratic bastions.
- *Labor unions*. FDR became the first president to support unions enthusiastically, and they returned the favor.
- *Catholics and Jews*. During and after the Roosevelt period, Catholics and Jews were strongly Democratic.
- *The poor*. Although the poor had low turnout rates, their votes went overwhelmingly to the party of Roosevelt and his successors.
- *Southerners*. Ever since the pre–Civil War days, White Southerners had been Democratic loyalists. This alignment continued unabated during the New Deal.
- *African Americans*. The Republicans freed the slaves, but under FDR the Democrats attracted the majority of African Americans.

As you can see in Figure 8.1, many of the same groups that supported FDR's New Deal continue to shape the party coalitions today.

The New Deal coalition made the Democratic Party the clear majority party for decades. Harry S Truman, who succeeded Roosevelt in 1945, promised a Fair Deal. World War II hero and Republican Dwight D. Eisenhower broke the Democrats'

Figure 8.1 Party Coalitions Today

The two parties continue to draw support from very different social groups, many of which have existed since the New Deal era. This figure shows the percentage identifying as Democrats and Republicans for various groups in 2004.

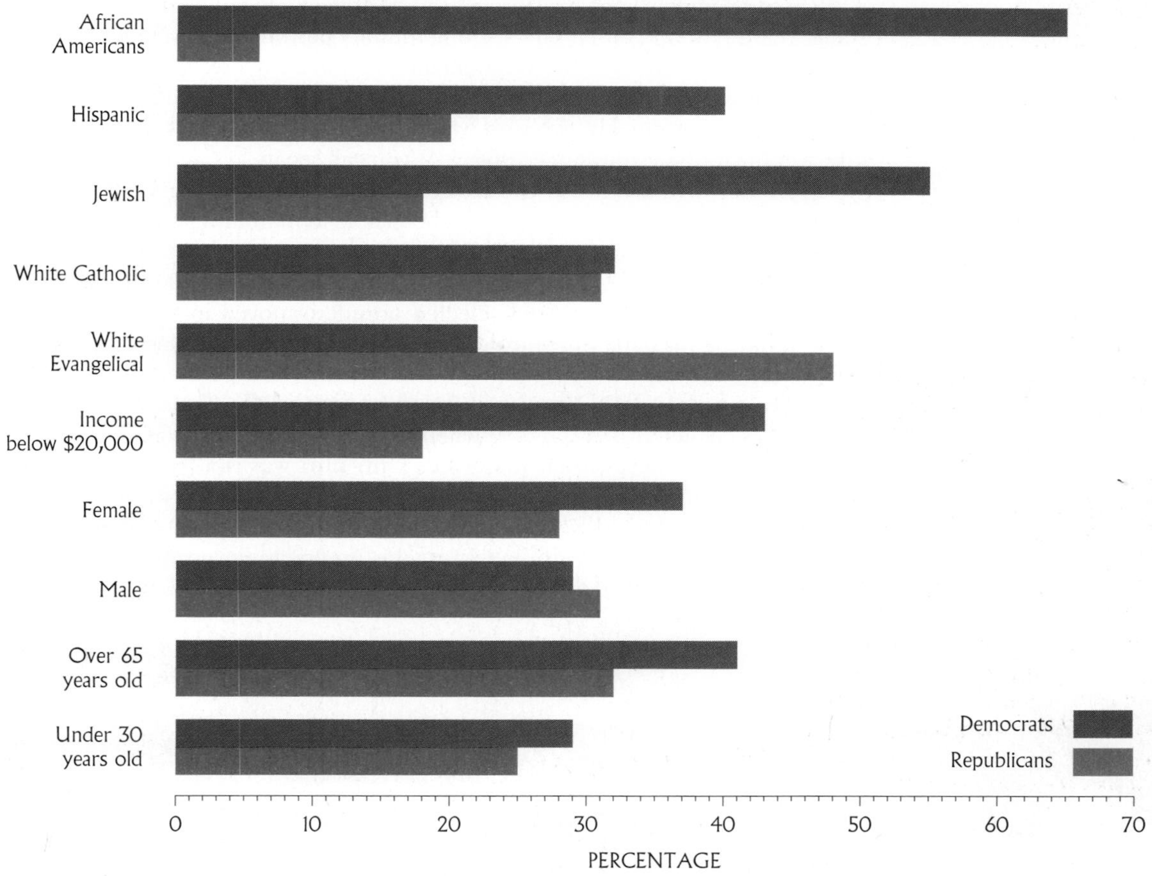

Source: Pew Research Center, *http://people-press.org/commentary/display.php3?AnalysisID=95.*

grip on power by being elected president twice during the 1950s, but the Democrats regained the presidency in 1960 with the election of John F. Kennedy. His New Frontier was in the New Deal tradition, with platforms and policies designed to help labor, the working classes, and minorities. Lyndon B. Johnson, picked as Kennedy's vice president because he could help win Southern votes, became president on Kennedy's assassination and was overwhelmingly elected to a term of his own in 1964. Johnson's Great Society programs included a major expansion of government programs to help the poor, the homeless, and minorities. His War on Poverty was reminiscent of Roosevelt's activism in dealing with the Depression. Johnson's Vietnam War policies, however, tore the Democratic Party apart in 1968, leaving the door to the presidency wide open for Republican candidate Richard M. Nixon.

Poverty and Political Parties

1968–Present: Southern Realignment and the Era of Divided Party Government

When Richard Nixon was first elected to the presidency in 1968, he formulated what became widely known as his "Southern strategy." Emphasizing his support for states' rights, law and order, and a strong military posture, Nixon hoped to win over Southern conservatives to the Republican Party, thereby breaking the Democratic Party's long dominance in the former confederacy. Party realignment in the South did not happen as quickly as Nixon would have liked, but it has taken place gradually over the four decades since 1968.[18] As you can see in "A Generation of Change: Realignment in the South," the fact that the South is now a GOP stronghold accounts for why the Republicans have been able to maintain partisan majorities in Congress in recent years.

Another noteworthy aspect of Nixon's 1968 election was that for the first time in the twentieth century, a newly elected president moved into the White House without having his party in control of both houses of Congress. Prior to 1968, most newly elected presidents had swept a wave of their fellow partisans into office with them. For example, the Democrats gained 62 seats in the House when Woodrow Wilson was elected in 1912 and 97 when FDR was elected in 1932. Nixon's inability to bring in congressional majorities with him was not to be an exception, however, but rather the beginning of a new pattern—repeated in the presidential elections won by Ronald Reagan and George Bush. For a time, it seemed that the normal state of affairs in Washington was for American government to be divided with a Republican president and a Democratic Congress.

A GENERATION OF CHANGE

Realignment in the South

One of the most significant political changes over the past generation has been the transition from Democratic to Republican majority control in the U.S. Congress. Partisan realignment in the South has been the major driving force in giving the Republicans the advantage in congressional elections today, as you can see in the table presented below. In 1987, none of the Southern delegations to the House of Representatives had a Republican majority, and the GOP controlled only 6 of the region's 22 Senate seats. A generation later, the Republicans have the edge in seven Southern state delegations to the House and have nearly tripled their number of Southern Senate seats.

The crucial role of Southerners in the Republican caucus in the Senate and the House of Representatives has been reflected in the makeup of the GOP congressional leadership in recent years. Trent Lott of Mississippi and Bill Frist of Tennessee have served as the Republicans' Majority Leader in the Senate. Georgia's Newt Gingrich served as Speaker of the House for three terms, and Texans Richard Armey and Tom DeLay have recently held the position of Republican House Majority Leader.

House of Representatives		Senate	
1987	2007	1987	2007
77D, 39R	53D, 78R	16D, 6R	5D, 17R

Bill Clinton's election in 1992 briefly restored united party government until the Republicans won both houses of Congress in the 1994 elections. After the 1994 elections, Republican leaders were optimistic that they were at last on the verge of a new Republican era in which they would control both the presidency and Congress simultaneously. On the other side, Democratic leaders were hopeful that voters would not like the actions of the new Republican Congress and would restore unified Democratic control of the government. In the end, the ambitions of both sides were frustrated as voters opted to continue divided party government in 1996. The election of George W. Bush in 2000 led to a very brief period of united Republican control of the White House and Congress. But four months after Bush took the inaugural oath, Senator James Jeffords of Vermont defected from the GOP, there by giving the Democrats the majority in the upper chamber. In 2002, the GOP regained control of the Senate, and in 2004 unified Republican control of the Congress and the presidency was ratified. But voters opted for divided government once again in 2006 by giving the Democrats majorities in both congressional chambers.

Why It Matters

Divided Party Government
When one party controls the White House and the other party controls one or both houses of Congress, divided party government exists. Given that one party can check the other's agenda, it is virtually impossible for a party to say what it is going to do and then actually put these policies into effect. This situation is bad if you want clear lines of accountability on policy, but it is good if you prefer that the two parties be forced to work out compromises.

With only about 60 percent of the electorate currently identifying with the Democrats or Republicans, it may well be difficult for either one to gain a strong enough foothold to maintain simultaneous control of both sides of Pennsylvania Avenue for very long—even with the GOP's dominance in the South. All told, both houses of Congress and the presidency have been simultaneously controlled by the same party for just 10.3 of the 40 years from 1969 to 2008.[19] The discrepancy between the patterns of presidential and congressional voting during this era of divided party government is unprecedented in American history.

Divided party government is frequently seen not only at the federal level but at the state level as well. As Morris Fiorina shows, the percentage of states that have unified party control of the governorship and the state legislature has declined substantially over the past half century.[20] Whereas 85 percent of state governments had one party controlling both houses of the legislature and the governorship in 1946, by 2007 this was the case in only 50 percent of the states. Divided government, once an occasional oddity in state capitols, is now commonplace.

The recent pattern of divided government has caused many political scientists to believe that the party system has dealigned rather than realigned. Whereas realignment involves people changing from one party to another, **party dealignment** means that people are gradually moving away from both parties. When your car is realigned, it is adjusted in one direction or another to improve its steering. Imagine if your mechanic were to remove the steering mechanism instead of adjusting it—your car would be useless and ineffective. This is what many scholars fear has been happening to the parties.

party dealignment
The gradual disengagement of people and politicians from the parties, as seen in part by shrinking **party identification**.

Third Parties: Their Impact on American Politics

The story of American party struggle is primarily the story of two major parties, but **third parties** are a regular feature of American politics and occasionally attract the public's attention. Third parties come in three basic varieties. First are parties that promote certain causes—either a controversial single issue (prohibition of alcoholic

third parties
Electoral contenders other than the two major parties. American third parties are not unusual, but they rarely win elections.

beverages, for example) or an extreme ideological position such as socialism or libertarianism. Second are splinter parties, which are offshoots of a major party. Teddy Roosevelt's Progressives in 1912, Strom Thurmond's States' Righters in 1948, and George Wallace's American Independents in 1968 all claimed they did not get a fair hearing from Republicans or Democrats and thus formed their own new parties. Finally, some third parties are merely an extension of a popular individual with presidential aspirations. Both John Anderson in 1980 and Ross Perot in 1992 and 1996 offered voters who were dissatisfied with the Democratic and Republican nominees another option.

Third Parties in American History

Although third-party candidates almost never win office in the United States, scholars believe they are often quite important.[21] They have brought new groups into the electorate and have served as "safety valves" for popular discontent. The Free Soilers of the 1850s were the first true antislavery party; the Progressives and the Populists put many social reforms on the political agenda. George Wallace told his supporters in 1968 they had the chance to "send a message" to Washington—a message of support for tougher law and order measures, which is still being felt to this day. Ross Perot used his saturation of the TV airwaves in 1992 to ensure that the issue of the federal deficit was not ignored in the campaign. In 1998, a former professional wrestler stunned the political world when he won the governorship of Minnesota as a third-party candidate. And in 2000 Green Party candidate Ralph Nader forced more attention on environmental issues and ultimately cost Gore the presidency by drawing away a small percentage of liberal votes.

Despite the regular appearance of third parties, the two-party system is firmly entrenched in American politics. Would it make a difference if America had a multiparty system, as so many European countries have? The answer is clearly yes. The

Ralph Nader challenged the two-party system in 2000 by running for president on the Green Party ticket. Exit polls show his voters preferred Gore over Bush by a margin of 5 to 2. With the margin being as close as it was in 2000, it seems readily apparent that Nader's presence in the race influenced the outcome. In 2004, Nader's Independent candidacy garnered only 0.3 percent of the vote.

most obvious consequence of two-party governance is the moderation of political conflict. If America had many parties, each would have to make a special appeal in order to stand out from the crowd. It is not hard to imagine what a multiparty system might look like in the United States. Quite possibly, African American groups would form their own party, pressing vigorously for more civil rights legislation. Environmentalists could constitute another party, vowing to clean up the rivers, oppose nuclear power, and save the wilderness. America could have religious parties, union-based parties, farmers' parties, and all sorts of others. As in some European countries, there could be half a dozen or more parties represented in Congress (see "In Focus: Multiparty Systems in Other Countries").

Third Parties

IN FOCUS

Multiparty Systems in Other Countries

One of the major reasons why the United States has only two parties represented in government is structural. America has a winner-take-all system, in which whoever gets the most votes wins the election. There are no prizes awarded for second or third place. Suppose there are three parties; one receives 45 percent of the vote, another 40 percent, and the third 15 percent. Although it got less than a majority, the party that finished first is declared the winner. The others are out in the cold. In this way, the American system discourages small parties. Unless a party wins, there is no reward for the votes it gets. Thus, it makes more sense for a small party to form an alliance with one of the major parties than to struggle on its own with little hope. In the example used here, the second- and third-place parties might merge (if they can reach an agreement on policy) to challenge the governing party in the next election.

In a system that employs proportional representation, however, such a merger would not be necessary. Under this system, which is used in most European countries, legislative seats are allocated according to each party's percentage of the nationwide vote. If a party wins 15 percent of the vote, then it receives 15 percent of the seats. Even a small party can use its voice in Parliament to be a thorn in the side of the government, standing up strongly for its principles. Such has often been the role of the Greens in Germany, who are ardent environmentalists. In 1998, they entered the government for the first time when they formed a coalition government along with Germany's Social Democratic Party. Together the coalition controlled over half the seats in the German Parliament for three years. Coalition governments are common in Europe. Italy has regularly been ruled by a coalition since the end of World War II, for example.

Even with proportional representation, not every party gets represented in the legislature. To be awarded seats, a party must always achieve a certain percentage of votes, which varies from country to country. Israel has one of the lowest thresholds at 1.5 percent. This explains why there are always so many parties represented in the Israeli Knesset. The founders of Israel's system wanted to make sure that all points of view were represented, but sometimes this has turned into a nightmare, with small extremist parties holding the balance of power.

Parties have to develop their own unique identities to appeal to voters in a multiparty system. This requires strong stands on the issues, but after the election, compromises must be made to form a coalition government. If an agreement cannot be reached on the major issues, the coalition is in trouble. Sometimes a new coalition can be formed; other times the result is the calling of a new election. In either case, it is clear that proportional representation systems are more fluid than the two-party system in the United States.

The American two-party system contributes to political ambiguity. Why should parties risk taking a strong stand on a controversial policy if doing so will only antagonize many voters? The two-party system thus throttles extreme or unconventional views.

Understanding Political Parties

Comparing Political Parties

Political parties are considered essential elements of democratic government. Indeed, one of the first steps taken toward democracy in Eastern Europe was the formation of competing political parties to contest elections. After years of one-party totalitarian rule, Eastern Europeans were ecstatic to be able to adopt a multiparty system like those that had proved successful in the West. In contrast, the founding of the world's first party system in the United States was seen as a risky adventure in the then uncharted waters of democracy. Wary of having parties at all, the Founders designed a system that has greatly restrained their political role to this day. Whether American parties should continue to be so loosely organized is at the heart of today's debate about their role in American democracy.

Democracy and Responsible Party Government

Ideally, in a democracy candidates should say what they mean to do if elected and, once they are elected, should be able to do what they promised. Critics of the American party system lament that this is all too often not the case and have called for a "more responsible two-party system."[22] Advocates of the **responsible party model** believe the parties should meet the following conditions:

responsible party model
A view favored by some political scientists about how parties should work. According to the model, parties should offer clear choices to the voters, who can then use those choices as cues to their own preferences of candidates. Once in office, parties would carry out their campaign promises.

1. Parties must present distinct, comprehensive programs for governing the nation.
2. Each party's candidates must be committed to its program and have the internal cohesion and discipline to carry out its program.
3. The majority party must implement its programs, and the minority party must state what it would do if it were in power.
4. The majority party must accept responsibility for the performance of the government.

A two-party system operating under these conditions would make it easier to convert party promises into governmental policy. A party's officeholders would have firm control of the government, so they would be collectively rather than individually responsible for their actions. Voters would therefore know whom to blame for what the government does and does not accomplish.

As this chapter has shown, American political parties fall far short of these conditions. They are too decentralized to take a single national position and then enforce it. Most candidates are self-selected, gaining their nomination by their own efforts rather than the party's. Virtually anyone can vote in party primaries; thus, parties do not have control over those who run under their labels.

In America's loosely organized party system, there simply is no mechanism for a party to discipline officeholders and thereby ensure cohesion in policymaking. As David Mayhew writes, "Unlike most politicians elsewhere, American ones at both legislative and executive levels have managed to navigate the last two centuries of history without becoming minions of party leaders."[23] American officeholders try to go along with their parties' platform whenever they can. But when the party line conflicts with their own personal opinion and/or the clear desires of their constituents, then they feel perfectly comfortable in voting against their party's leaders. As you can see in Table 8.3, even on the key issues that the House of Representatives voted on in 2004, there were numerous disagreements among members of the same party.

You Are Redrawing the Districts in Your State

Not everyone thinks that America's decentralized parties are a problem, however. Critics of the responsible party model argue that the complexity and diversity of American society are too great to be captured by such a simple model of party politics. Local differences need an outlet for expression, they say. One cannot expect Texas Democrats always to want to vote in line with New York Democrats. In the view of those opposed to the responsible party model, America's decentralized

Table 8.3 Partisan Divisions on Key House Roll Call Votes in 2004

At the end of every year, *Congressional Quarterly* selects a series of key votes for both the House and Senate on major issues of the year. These votes are chosen based on the extent to which they represent (1) a matter of major controversy, (2) a subject of presidential or political power, and (3) an issue of potentially great national impact. In the following table, you can see how Republicans and Democrats voted on the 10 key roll call votes that *Congressional Quarterly* selected for the House of Representatives in 2004.

There are a number of interesting patterns to note in these roll-call votes. First, contrary to any notions that the majority party always wins, an examination of these 10 votes finds that on half of them the minority Democrats actually contributed more votes to the winning side. In particular, measures extending unemployment benefits and providing identification cards to Mexican citizens working in the United States were passed over the objections of most Republicans. Second, only 4 of the 10 votes fit the very loose American criteria for a party-line vote: a vote in which over 50 percent of the majority party votes differently than over 50 percent of the minority party. In most European democracies a party-line vote is defined as being a vote where every member of the majority coalition votes one way and every member of the opposition votes the other way. None of the key votes in the House in 2004 met this criteria.

Key Vote	Republicans		Democrats	
	YES	NO	YES	NO
Extension of unemployment benefits	*39*	*179*	*187*	*0*
Resolution praising the Iraq War	222	2	105	90
Transportation spending	*162*	*59*	*194*	*6*
Limiting discretionary federal spending	*146*	*72*	*0*	*195*
Limits on federal search powers	18	206	192	4
Identification cards for Mexican workers	*49*	*161*	*172*	*16*
Extending tax cuts	213	0	125	65
Gay marriage prohibition	191	27	36	158
Corporate tax overhaul	207	16	73	124
Intelligence gathering overhaul	*152*	*67*	*183*	*8*

Note: Votes in italics are ones where the Democrats contributed more votes to the winning side than Republicans.
Source: "2004 Key Votes: A Mix of Hits and Misses for the Republican Leadership," *Congressional Quarterly Weekly Report*, December 11, 2004.

parties are appropriate for the type of limited government the Founders sought to create and most Americans wish to maintain.[24]

The Founding Fathers were very concerned that political parties would trample on the rights of individuals. They wanted to preserve individual freedom of action by various elected officials. With America's weak party system, this has certainly been the case. Individual members of Congress and other elected officials have great freedom to act as they see fit rather than toeing the party line.

American Political Parties and the Scope of Government

The lack of disciplined and cohesive European-style parties in America goes a long way to explain why the scope of governmental activity in the United States is not as broad as it is in other established democracies. The absence of a national health care system in America provides a perfect example. In Britain, the Labour Party had long proposed such a system, and after it won the 1945 election, all its members of Parliament voted to enact national health care into law. On the other side of the Atlantic, President Truman also proposed a national health care bill in the first presidential election after World War II. But even though he won the election and had majorities of his own party in both houses of Congress, his proposal never got very far. The weak party structure in the United States allowed many congressional Democrats to oppose Truman's health care proposal. More than four decades later, President Clinton again proposed a system of universal health care and had a Democratic-controlled Congress to work with. His experience in 1994 was much the same as Truman's. The Clinton health care bill never even came up for a vote in Congress because of the president's inability to get enough members of his own party to go along with him. Substantially increasing the scope of government in America is not something that can be accomplished through the disciplined actions of one party's members, as is the case in other democracies.

On the other hand, because it is rarely the case that one single party can ever be said to have firm control over American government, the hard choices necessary to cut back on existing government spending are rarely addressed. A disciplined and cohesive governing party might have the power to say no to various demands on the government. In contrast, America's loose party structure makes it possible for individual politicians to focus their efforts on getting more from the government for their own constituents.

Is the Party Over?

The key problem for American political parties is that they are no longer the main source of political information, attention, and affection. The party of today has rivals that appeal to voters and politicians alike, the biggest of which is the media. With the advent of television, voters no longer need the party to find out what the candidates are like and what they stand for. The interest group is another party rival. As Chapter 10 will discuss, the power of interest groups has grown enormously in

Political parties have changed greatly from the days in which they offered live political drama for the media to cover. Today, political conventions are carefully orchestrated to present the best possible image of the party ticket on television.

recent years. Interest groups, not the parties, pioneered much of the technology of modern politics, including mass mailings and sophisticated fund-raising.

The parties have clearly been having a tough time lately, but there are indications that they are beginning to adapt to the high-tech age. Although the old city machines are largely extinct, state and national party organizations have become more visible and active than ever. Two out of every five Americans call themselves Independents, but the majority still identify with a party, and this percentage seems to have stabilized.

For a time, some political scientists were concerned that parties were on the verge of disappearing from the political scene. A more realistic view is that parties will continue to play an important but significantly diminished role in American politics. Leon Epstein sees the situation as one in which the parties have become "frayed." He concludes that the parties will "survive and even moderately prosper in a society evidently unreceptive to strong parties and yet unready, and probably unable, to abandon parties altogether."[25]

Declining Political Parties

Summary

Even though political parties are one of Americans' least beloved institutions, political scientists see them as a key linkage between policymakers and the people. Parties are pervasive in politics; for each party there is a *party in the electorate*, a *party organization*, and a *party in government*. Political parties affect policy through their platforms. Despite much cynicism about party platforms, they are taken seriously when their candidates are elected.

America has a two-party system. This fact is of fundamental importance in understanding American politics. The ups and downs of the two parties constitute party competition. In the past, one party or the other has dominated the government for long periods of time. These periods were punctuated by critical elections in which party coalitions underwent realignment. Since 1968, the South has realigned from a solidly Democratic region into an area of strength for the Republicans. Overall, however, American government has experienced a unique period of party dealignment, with the result that partisan control of the presidency and Congress has frequently been divided.

Even when partisan control is united, the decentralized nature of American politics makes it difficult for them to carry out ambitious plans for major changes, such as Bill Clinton's health care reform plan or George W. Bush's plan to revamp Social Security. Some political observers would have them be far more centralized and cohesive, following the responsible party model. The loose structure of American parties allows politicians to avoid collective responsibility but also promotes individualism that many Americans value.

Internet Resources

www.rnc.org
The official site of the Republican National Committee.

www.democrats.org
The Democratic Party online.

www.lp.org
Although Libertarians rarely get more than a few percent of the vote, they are consistently getting many of their candidates on the ballot for many offices. You can learn more about their beliefs at this official site.

www.reformparty.org
The official Web site for the party founded by Ross Perot, which nominated Pat Buchanan for president in 2000.

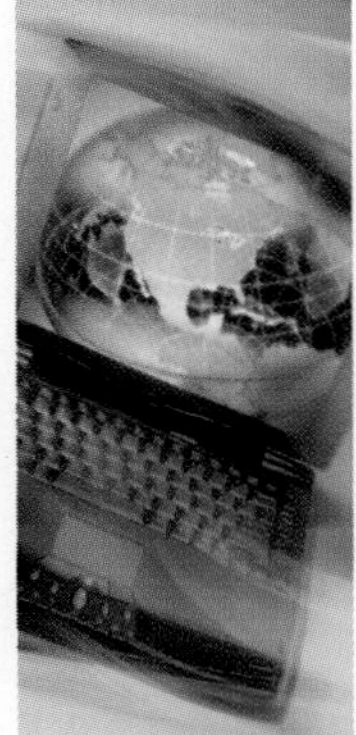

Get Connected

Third Parties

Most people have heard of the Democratic and Republican parties, but many people would be surprised to learn that there are many other parties besides these two major parties. The text notes that these other parties, called "minor parties" or "third parties," come in three basic varieties: those that promote certain causes, those that are offshoots of the major parties, and those organized around popular individuals. What do these third parties stand for? Should you identify with one of the third parties?

Search the Web

Go to the Party Matchmaking Service, *www.3pc.net/matchmaker/*, and take the quiz. Think about the questions carefully and try to answer honestly.

Questions to Ask

- According to the quiz, with which party do you have the highest compatibility? Do you already identify with this party?
- Were you surprised by the results? Why?
- Has this party ever run any candidates for office in your area of the country? If so, did the candidates win?

Why It Matters

Despite the fact that their candidates are rarely elected, third parties exist because of the diversity of ideas in America, and they play an important role in our system of government. Third parties propose policies that are often adopted by the two major parties and sometimes are enacted into law. Third parties also allow voters a "protest" vote when they don't like the Democratic or Republican candidate. In some parts of the country, third-party candidates are the only opponents faced by Democratic or Republican candidates.

Get Involved

You can find the contact information and Web page addresses of political parties at the Politics1.com Web site *www.politics1.com/parties.htm*. Research the party with which you are most compatible according to the quiz results. Are you interested in associating with this party? If so, find out how you can become an active member.

For more exercises, go to www.longmanamericangovernment.com.

For Further Reading

Black, Earl, and Merle Black. *The Rise of Southern Republicanism*. Cambridge, MA: Harvard University Press, 2002. An excellent examination of the transformation of party politics in the South.

Burden, Barry C., and David C. Kimball. *Why Americans Split Their Tickets: Campaigns, Competition and Divided Government*. Ann Arbor: University of Michigan Press, 2002. A good analysis of who splits their ticket and under what conditions they are most likely to do so.

Downs, Anthony. *An Economic Theory of Democracy*. New York: Harper & Row, 1957. An extremely influential theoretical work that applies rational-choice theory to party politics.

Green, John C., and Daniel M. Shea. *The State of the Parties*. 4th ed. Lanham, MD: Rowman & Littlefield, 2003. A diverse set of articles on numerous aspects of party politics, with an emphasis on how well the party system is working.

Hershey, Marjorie Randon. *Party Politics in America*. 12th ed. New York: Longman, 2007. The standard textbook on political parties.

Maisel, L. Sandy, ed. *The Parties Respond: Changes in the American Parties and Campaigns*. 4th ed. Boulder, CO: Westview, 2002. A good collection of readings on how parties have adapted to changes in the political system.

Mayhew, David R. *Electoral Realignments: A Critique of an American Genre*. New Haven, CT: Yale University Press, 2002. A critical look at the historical evidence concerning realignment theory.

Rosenstone, Steven, Roy Behr, and Edward Lazarus. *Third Parties in America*. 2nd ed. Princeton, NJ: Princeton University Press, 1996. An analytical study of why third parties appear when they do, and what effect they have.

Sundquist, James L. *Dynamics of the Party System*. Rev. ed. Washington, DC: Brookings Institution, 1983. One of the best books ever written on the major realignments in American history.

Wattenberg, Martin P. *The Decline of American Political Parties, 1952–1996*. Cambridge, MA: Harvard University Press, 1998. An account of the decline of parties in the electorate.

Chapter Outline

Campaigns and Voting Behavior

POLITICS IN ACTION: HOW RUNNING FOR OFFICE CAN BE MORE DEMANDING THAN GOVERNING Campaigning for any major office has become a massive undertaking in today's political world. Consider George W. Bush's grueling schedule for March 28–29, 2000, a relatively low-key period of the presidential campaign:

- The governor begins his day with an early morning flight from his home in Austin, Texas, to Dulles Airport in northern Virginia.
- On landing in Virginia, Bush goes to a reception to raise money for his campaign. After lunch, he goes to the headquarters of Sallie Mae, a corporation that helps students finance educational expenses, to give a speech about his views on government and higher education.

- Governor Bush then boards his campaign plane again for a flight to Newark, New Jersey, where he participates in another fund-raiser and gives his standard campaign speech at dinner. After dinner, he goes to Manville, New Jersey, to address the Somerset County Republican Party convention. Finally, after 15 hours of traveling and campaigning, his day ends when he checks in at the Newark Hilton at 9:30 P.M.
- The next morning, Bush goes to the North Star Academy Charter school in Newark to give another speech on education. He then rides in a limousine to New York City to give a lunch speech on foreign affairs.
- After this quick stop in New York, Bush flies to Baltimore, Maryland, to meet with the local press, attend a youth rally, and deliver his standard campaign speech yet again at a dinner event. Finally, Bush takes his fourth flight in two days—this time to Eau Claire, Wisconsin, where he arrives after 14 hours on the go.

It is often said that the presidency is the most difficult job in the world, but getting elected to the position may well be tougher. It is arguable that the long campaign for the presidency puts candidates under more continuous stress than they could ever face in the White House.

The current American style of long and arduous campaigns has evolved from the belief of reformers that the cure for the problems of democracy is more democracy. Whether this approach is helpful or harmful to democracy is a question that arouses much debate with respect to American political campaigns. Some scholars believe it is important that presidential candidates go through a long and difficult trial by fire. Others, however, worry that the system makes it difficult for politicians with other responsibilities—such as incumbent governors and senior senators—to take a run at the White House. This chapter will give you a better understanding of the pros and cons of having a nomination and campaign process that is so open and democratic.

The consequences for the scope of government are also debatable. Anthony King argues that American politicians do too little governing because they are always "running scared" in today's perpetual campaign.[1] From King's perspective, the campaign process does not allow politicians the luxury of trying out solutions to policy problems that might be immediately unpopular but would work well in the long run. The scope of government thus stays pretty much as is, given that politicians are usually too concerned with the next election to risk fundamental change. Of course, many analysts argue that officeholders' constant worry about public opinion is good for democracy and that changes in the scope of government shouldn't be undertaken without extensive public consultation.

As you read this chapter, consider whether today's nomination and campaign process provides *too much* opportunity for interaction between the public and candidates for office. Also, consider whether the entire process takes too much time and costs too much money—two very important topics of debate in American politics today.

With about half a million elected officials in this country, there is always someone somewhere running for office. One of these campaigns is for the world's most powerful office—the presidency of the United States. This chapter will focus mainly on this election campaign, although we will explore some other campaigns as well. Chapter 11 will specifically discuss the congressional election process.

There are really two types of campaigns in American politics: campaigns for party nominations and campaigns between the two nominees. These are called nomination campaigns and election campaigns. The prize for the first is garnering a party's nod as its candidate; the prize for the second is winning an office.

The Nomination Game

nomination
The official endorsement of a candidate for office by a **political party**. Generally, success in the nomination game requires momentum, money, and media attention.

campaign strategy
The master game plan candidates lay out to guide their electoral campaign.

A **nomination** is a party's official endorsement of a candidate for office. Anyone can play the nomination game, but few have any serious chance of victory. Generally, success in the nomination game requires money, media attention, and momentum. **Campaign strategy** is the way in which candidates attempt to manipulate each of these elements to achieve the nomination.

Believe it or not, not every politician wants to run for president. One reason is that campaigns have become more physically and emotionally taxing than ever. As former Speaker of the House Thomas Foley said, "I know of any number of people who I think would make good presidents, even great presidents, who are deterred from running by the torture candidates are obliged to put themselves through."[2] Running for president is an around-the-clock endurance test for over a year: sleep deprivation and strange hotel beds, countless plane rides, junk food eaten on the run, a lack of regular exercise and copious amounts of stress. As 1984 Democratic nominee Walter Mondale once said, "For four years, that's all I did. I mean, all I did. That's all you think about. That's all you talk about. . . . That's your leisure. That's your luxury. . . . I told someone, 'The question is not whether I can get elected. The question is whether I can be elected and not be nuts when I get there.'"[3]

In most advanced industrialized countries, campaigns last no more than two months according to either custom and/or law. In contrast, American campaigns seem endless; a presidential candidacy needs to be either announced or an open secret for at least a year before the election. Whoever is elected president in November of 2008 will probably have declared their candidacy by the winter of 2007.

The road to the convention is long and full of stumbling blocks. From the convention, held in the summer of election years, only one candidate emerges as each party's standard bearer.

Competing for Delegates

national party convention
The supreme power within each of the parties. The convention meets every four years to nominate the party's presidential and vice-presidential candidates and to write the party's platform.

In some ways, the nomination game is tougher than the general election game; it whittles a large number of players down to two. The goal of the nomination game is to win the majority of delegates' support at the **national party convention**, which functions to formally select presidential and vice presidential candidates and to write the party platform.

There are 50 different roads to the national convention, one through each state. From February through June of the election year, the individual state parties busily choose their delegates to the national convention via either caucuses or primaries. Candidates try to ensure that delegates committed to them are chosen to attend the convention.

The Caucus Road. Before primaries existed, all state parties selected their delegates to the national convention in a meeting of state party leaders called a **caucus**. Sometimes one or two party "bosses" ran the caucus show—often the governor of the state or the mayor of its largest city. Such state party leaders could control who went to the convention and how the state's delegates voted once they got there. They were the kingmakers of presidential politics who met in smoke-filled rooms at the convention to cut deals and form coalitions.

caucus
A meeting of all state party leaders for selecting delegates to the **national party convention**. Caucuses are usually organized as a pyramid.

Today's caucuses are different from those of the past. In the dozen states that still have them, caucuses are now open to all voters who are registered with the party. Caucuses are usually organized like a pyramid. Small, neighborhood, precinct-level caucuses are held initially—often meeting in a church, an American Legion hall, or even someone's home. At this level, delegates are chosen, on the basis of their preference for a certain candidate, to attend county caucuses and then congressional district caucuses where delegates are again chosen to go to a higher level—a state convention. At the state convention, which usually occurs months after the precinct caucuses, delegates are finally chosen to go to the national convention.

Since 1972, the state of Iowa has held the nation's first caucuses. Because the Iowa caucuses are the first test of the candidates' vote-getting ability, they usually become a full-blown media extravaganza.[4] Well-known candidates like Richard Gephardt in 2004 and John Glenn in 1984 have seen their campaigns virtually fall apart as a result of poor showings in Iowa. Most important, candidates who were not thought to be contenders have received tremendous boosts from unexpected strong showings in Iowa. An obscure former Georgia governor named Jimmy Carter took his first big presidential step by winning there in 1976. George Bush also made his first big step into the national scene with an upset victory over Ronald Reagan in Iowa in 1980. In 2004, John Kerry's surprise victory in Iowa gave a campaign that had been on the ropes newfound life. Because of the impact that Iowa's first-in-the-nation caucus can have, candidates spend more time during the nomination season there than they do in the big states like California, Texas, and Florida. Howard Dean and John Edwards went to the trouble of visiting each one of Iowa's 99 counties in their efforts to win Iowa in 2004.

The Primary Road. Today, most of the delegates to the Democratic and Republican national conventions are selected in **presidential primaries**, in which voters in a state go to the polls and vote for a candidate or delegates pledged to that candidate. As recently as the 1960s, primaries played a rather small role in the process; today, with the majority of delegates chosen in primaries, they have become essential to winning a party's presidential nomination.

presidential primaries
Elections in which voters in a state vote for a candidate (or delegates pledged to him or her). Most delegates to the **national party conventions** are chosen this way.

The increase in the number of presidential primaries occurred after the Democratic Party's disastrous 1968 national convention, which led many to rethink the delegate selection procedures then in place. As the war in Southeast Asia raged, another war of sorts took place in the streets of Chicago during the Democratic convention. Demonstrators against the war battled Mayor Richard Daley's Chicago police in what an official report later called a "police riot." Beaten up in the streets and defeated in the convention hall, the antiwar faction won one concession from the party regulars: a special committee to review the party's structure and delegate

Televised debates have become a regular part of presidential primaries. Here, candidates for the 2004 Democratic nomination are shown participating in a TV forum.

selection procedures, which they felt had discriminated against them. Minorities, women, youth, and other groups that had been poorly represented in the party leadership also demanded a more open process of convention delegate selection. The result was a committee of inquiry, which was chaired first by Senator George McGovern and later by Representative Donald Fraser, who took over when McGovern left the committee to run for president.

McGovern-Fraser Commission

A commission formed at the 1968 Democratic convention in response to demands for reform by minority groups and others who sought better representation.

The **McGovern-Fraser Commission** had a mandate to try to make Democratic Party conventions more representative. As a result of their decisions, no longer could party leaders handpick the convention delegates virtually in secret. All delegate selection procedures were required to be open, so that party leaders had no more clout than college students or anyone else who wanted to participate. One of the unforeseen results of these new rules was that many states decided that the easiest way to comply was simply to hold primary elections to select convention delegates.[5] Because state laws instituting primaries typically apply to both parties' selection of delegates, the Republican Party's nomination process was similarly transformed.

Few developments have changed American politics as much as the proliferation of presidential primaries. Presidential election watcher Theodore White calls the primaries the "classic example of the triumph of goodwill over common sense." Says White,

> *Delegates, who were supposed to be free to vote by their own common sense and conscience, have become for the most part anonymous faces, collected as background for the television cameras, sacks of potatoes packaged in primaries, divorced from party roots, and from the officials who rule states and nation.*[6]

Whereas once many of the delegates were experienced politicians who knew the candidates, today they are typically people who have worked on a candidate's

Riots at the 1968 Democratic national convention led to the creation of the McGovern-Fraser Commission, which established open procedures and affirmative action guidelines for delegate selection. These reforms have made party conventions more representative than they once were.

campaign and who owe their position as a delegate strictly to that candidate's ability to pull in primary votes.

The Democratic Party became so concerned about the lack of a role for party leaders at their conventions that starting in 1984 they automatically set aside about 15 percent of their delegate slots for public officeholders and party officials. These politicians who are awarded convention seats on the basis of their position are known as **superdelegates**. The addition of these delegates to the Democratic national convention was designed to restore an element of "peer review" to the process, ensuring participation of the people most familiar with the candidates. However, to date the primaries have proved to be far more crucial than the superdelegates.

superdelegates
National party leaders who automatically get a delegate slot at the Democratic **national party convention**.

The primary season begins during the winter in New Hampshire. Like the Iowa caucuses, the importance of New Hampshire is not the number of delegates or how representative the state is, but rather that it is traditionally the first primary.[7] At this early stage, the campaign is not for delegates, but for images—candidates want the rest of the country to see them as front-runners. The frenzy of political activity in this small state is given lavish attention in the national press. During the week of the primary, half the portable satellite dishes in the country can be found in Manchester, New Hampshire, and the networks move their anchors and top reporters to the scene to broadcast the nightly news. In recent years, over a fifth of TV coverage of the nomination races has been devoted to the New Hampshire primary.[8]

At one time, it was considered advantageous for a state to choose its delegates late in the primary season so that it could play a decisive role. However, in recent years states that have held late primaries, such as Pennsylvania and New Jersey, have found their primary results irrelevant given that one candidate had already secured the nomination by the time their primaries were held. With so much attention

frontloading
The recent tendency of states to hold primaries early in the calendar in order to capitalize on media attention.

Why It Matters

Early Delegate Contests
In baseball, no one would declare a team out of the pennant race after it lost the first two games of the season. But in the race for the presidential nomination, the results of the Iowa caucus and the New Hampshire primary frequently end the campaigns of many candidates after only a handful of national delegates have been selected. These contests are important not because of the number of delegates that are chosen but rather because they are the first indicators of public support. If a candidate does not do well in these first two contests, money and media attention dry up quickly.

being paid to the early contests, more states have moved their primaries earlier in the calendar to capitalize on the media attention. This **frontloading** of the process resulted in 71 percent of pledged Democratic delegates being chosen within six weeks of the New Hampshire primary in 2004. For 2008, at least one big state—California—has decided to move its primary back to the end of the calendar. You can learn more about this decision in "Issues of the Times: Will the Presidential Candidates Pay Any Attention to California in 2008?" printed in the *Times Reader* at the back of this book.

Week after week, the primaries serve as elimination contests, as the media continually monitor the number of delegates won. The politicians, the press, and the public all love a winner. Candidates who fail to score early wins get labeled as losers and typically drop out of the race. Usually they have little choice since losing quickly inhibits a candidate's ability to raise the money necessary to win in other states. As one veteran fundraiser put it, "People don't lose campaigns. They run out of money and can't get their planes in the air. That's the reality."[9]

In the 1980 delegate chase, a commonly used football term became established in the language of American politics. After George Bush scored a surprise victory over Ronald Reagan in Iowa, he proudly claimed to possess "the big mo"—momentum. Actually, Bush had only a little "mo" and quickly fell victim to a decisive Reagan victory in New Hampshire. But the term neatly describes what candidates for the nomination are after. Primaries and caucuses are more than an endurance contest, though they are certainly that; they are also proving grounds. Week after week, the challenge is to do better than expected. Learning from his father's experience, George W. Bush jokingly told the reporters on his campaign plane, "Please stow your expectations securely in your overhead bins, as they may shift during the trip and can fall and hurt someone—especially me."[10]

To get "mo" going, candidates have to beat people they were not expected to beat, collect margins above predictions, and—above all else—never lose to people they were expected to trounce. Momentum is good to have, but it is no guarantee of victory because candidates with a strong base sometimes bounce back. Political scientist Larry Bartels found that "substantive political appeal may overwhelm the impact of momentum."[11] Indeed, after being soundly trounced by John McCain in New Hampshire in 2000, George W. Bush quickly bounced back to win the big states necessary to get the Republican nomination.

Evaluating the Primary and Caucus System. The primaries and the caucuses are here to stay. However, many political scientists are not particularly happy with the system. Criticisms of the marathon campaign are numerous; here are a few of the most important:

American Electoral Rules: How Do They Influence Campaigns?

- *Disproportionate attention goes to the early caucuses and primaries.* Take a look at Figure 9.1, which shows how critics think America's media-dominated campaigns are distorted by early primaries and caucuses. Neither New Hampshire nor Iowa is particularly representative of the national electorate. Both are rural, both have only small minority populations, and neither is at the center of the political mainstream. Whereas Iowa is more liberal than the nation as a whole, New Hampshire is the reverse. Although Iowa and New Hampshire are not

Figure 9.1 The Inflated Importance of Iowa and New Hampshire

In 2004, the Wisconsin Advertising Project found that 48 percent of the money spent by candidates for the Democratic nomination on TV ads were run in either Iowa or New Hampshire, even though these two small states selected only about 2 percent of the convention delegates. The incredible degree to which the candidates and the media focus on these two small states has become a regular feature of the presidential nominating process. Here you can see a map of the 50 states drawn to scale in terms of the media attention their primaries and caucuses received in 1996; note how blown out of proportion Iowa and New Hampshire are on the map.

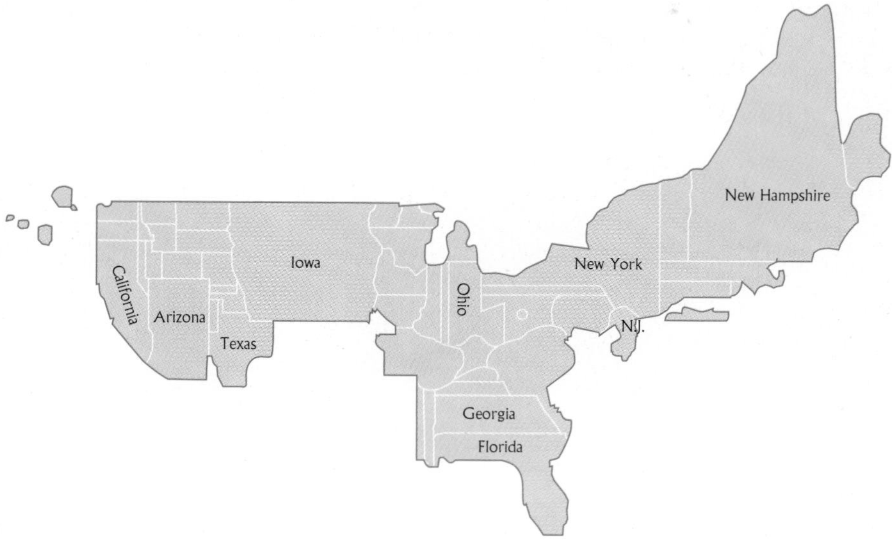

Source: Center for Media and Public Affairs, as reported in Harold W. Stanley and Richard G. Niemi, *Vital Statistics on American Politics,* 6th ed. Washington, DC: Congressional Quarterly Press, 1998, 172–74.

always "make or break" contests, they play a key—and a disproportionate—role in building momentum, money, and media attention.

- *Prominent politicians find it difficult to take time out from their duties to run.* Running for the presidency has become a full-time job. It is hard to balance the demands of serving in high public office with running a presidential campaign. Of the six Democratic candidates for the presidency in 2004 who were serving in Congress, the average voting participation rate in 2003 was a mere 52 percent—far below the average congressional attendance rate of about 90 percent.[12]
- *Money plays too big a role in the caucuses and primaries.* Momentum means money—getting more of it than your opponents do. Many people think that money plays too large a role in American presidential elections.
- *Participation in primaries and caucuses is low and unrepresentative.* Although about 50 percent of the population votes in the November presidential election, only about 20 percent casts ballots in presidential primaries. Participation in caucus states is much lower because a person must usually devote several hours to attending a caucus. Except for Iowa, where media attention usually boosts the turnout to about 20 percent, only about 5 percent of eligible voters typically show up for caucuses. Moreover, voters in primaries and caucuses are

For a number of months, Howard Dean's formidable fund-raising and high poll standing made him the front-runner in the race for the 2004 Democratic presidential nomination. But when he repeatedly screamed during a concession speech after the first delegate contest in Iowa, his reputation took a drastic hit from which his campaign never recovered.

hardly representative of voters at large; they tend to be older and more affluent than the typical citizen.

- *The system gives too much power to the media.* Critics contend that the media have replaced the party bosses as the new kingmakers. The press decides who has momentum at any given moment, and readily labels candidates as winners or losers.

Is this the best way to pick a president? Critics think not and have come up with a number of reform proposals (see "You Are the Policymaker: National and Regional Presidential Primary Proposals"). For the foreseeable future, however, states will continue to select delegates in primaries and caucuses to attend the national conventions, where the nominees are formally chosen.

national primary
A proposal by critics of the **caucuses** and **presidential primaries** systems would replace these electoral methods with a nationwide **primary** held early in the election year.

regional primaries
A proposal by critics of the **caucuses** and **presidential primaries** to replace these electoral methods with a series of primaries held in each geographic region.

The Convention Send-Off

Party conventions provided great drama in American politics for more than a century. Great speeches were given, dark-horse candidates suddenly appeared, and ballot after ballot was held as candidates jockeyed to win the nomination. Today, the drama has largely been drained from the conventions, as the winner is a foregone conclusion. No longer can a powerful governor shift a whole block of votes at the last minute. Delegates selected in primaries and open caucuses have known preferences. The last time there was any doubt as to who would win at the convention was in 1976, when Ford barely edged out Reagan for the Republican nomination. The parties have also learned that it is not in their best interest to provide high drama. The raucous conventions held by the Republicans in 1964 and

YOU ARE THE POLICYMAKER

National and Regional Presidential Primary Proposals

The idea of holding a **national primary** to select party nominees has been discussed virtually ever since state primaries were introduced. In 1913, President Woodrow Wilson proposed it in his first message to Congress. Since then, over 250 proposals for a national presidential primary have been introduced in Congress. These proposals do not lack public support; opinion polls have consistently shown that a substantial majority of Democrats, Republicans, and Independents alike favor such reform.

According to its proponents, a national primary would bring directness and simplicity to the process for the voters as well as the candidates. The length of the campaign would be shortened, and no longer would votes in one state have more political impact than votes in another. The concentration of media coverage on this one event, say its advocates, would increase not only political interest in the nomination decision but also public understanding of the issues involved.

A national primary would not be so simple, respond the critics. Because Americans would not want a candidate nominated with 25 percent of the vote from among a field of six candidates, in most primaries a runoff election between the top two finishers in each party would have to be held. So much for making the campaign simpler, national primary critics note. Each voter would have to vote three times for president—twice in the primaries and once in November.

Another common criticism of a national primary is that only well-established politicians would have a shot at breaking through in such a system. Big money and big attention from the national media would become more crucial than ever. Obscure candidates, such as Jimmy Carter in 1976, would never have a chance. Do Americans, however, really want politicians without an established reputation to become president?

Perhaps more feasible than a national primary is holding a series of **regional primaries** in which, say, states in the Eastern time zone would vote one week, those in the Central time zone the next, and so on. This would impose a more rational structure and cut down on candidate travel. A regional primary system would also put an end to the jockeying between states for an advantageous position in the primary season. In the fall of 2005, a bipartisan commission on electoral reform led by former President Jimmy Carter and former Secretary of State James Baker endorsed a plan to establish regional primaries (see *www.american.edu/ia/cfer/*).

The major problem with the regional primary proposal, however, is the advantage gained by whichever region goes first. For example, if the Western states were the first to vote, any candidate from California would have a clear edge in building momentum. Although most of the proposed plans call for the order of the regions to be determined by lottery, this would not erase the fact that regional advantages would surely be created from year to year.

Put yourself in the role of policymaker. Do the advantages of the national primary or of the regional primary proposal outweigh the disadvantages? Would either represent an improvement over the current system? Keep in mind that there are almost always unintended consequences associated with reforms.

the Democrats in 1968 and 1972 captured the public's attention, but they also exposed such divisiveness that the parties were unable to unite for the fall campaign.

Without such drama, the networks have scaled back their coverage substantially and the Nielsen ratings have fallen to new lows.[13] In 2000, ABC chose to air preseason *Monday Night Football* games on two nights when they would normally have devoted at least some time to the conventions. Even with the condensed TV coverage, the Nielsen ratings have fallen to abysmal levels.[14] About 20 million people watched John Kerry's speech to the 2004 Democratic convention, which was covered by all the major broadcast networks as well as the cable news channels. By contrast, about 31 million people tuned in to see Fantasia win the 2004 finale of *American Idol*, which was only broadcast on one network.

One can hardly blame people for tuning out the conventions when little news is made at them. Today's conventions are carefully scripted to present the party in its best light. Delegates are no longer there to argue for their causes, but rather to merely support their candidate. The parties carefully orchestrate a massive send-off for the presidential and vice-presidential candidates. The party's leaders are there in force, as are many of its most important followers—people whose input will be key during the campaign. Although conventions are no longer very interesting, they are a significant rallying point for the parties.

The conventions are also important in developing the party's policy positions and in promoting political representation. In the past, conventions were essentially an assembly of state- and local-party leaders, gathered together to bargain over the selection of the party's ticket. Almost all delegates were White, male, and over 40 years old. Lately, party reformers, especially among the Democrats, have worked hard to make the conventions far more demographically representative.

The Campaign Game

Once nominated, candidates concentrate on campaigning for the general election. These days, the word *campaign* is part of American political vocabulary, but it was not always so. The term was originally a military one: Generals mounted campaigns, using their scarce resources to achieve strategic objectives. Political campaigns are like that, too—resources are scarce, expenditures in the presidential race are limited by federal law, and both have to be timed and targeted. A candidate's time and energy are also finite. Choices must be made concerning where to go and how long to spend at each stop.

Campaigns involve more than organization and leadership. Artistry also enters the picture, for campaigns deal in images. The campaign is the canvas on which political strategists try to paint portraits of leadership, competence, caring, and other images Americans value in presidents. To project the right image to the voters, three ingredients are needed: a campaign organization, money, and media attention.

Organizing the Campaign

You Are a Professional Campaign Manager

In every campaign, there is too much to do and too little time to do it. Every candidate must prepare for nightly banquets and endless handshaking. More important, to effectively organize their campaigns candidates must do the following:

- *Get a campaign manager.* Some candidates try to run their own campaign, but they usually end up regretting it. A professional campaign manager can keep the candidate from getting bogged down in organizational details. This person also bears the day-to-day responsibility for keeping the campaign square on its message and setting its tone.

HOW YOU CAN MAKE A DIFFERENCE

Political Campaigns

Working for political campaigns is a great way to help influence government and policy, while learning, networking, and making friends at the same time. Campaign operations are of such a nature that they will accommodate and work around your employment, school, and family schedules. After all, most national campaigns need as many "boots on the ground" as possible in order to be competitive in the electoral process. A winning campaign will place candidates in office that can dramatically alter the substance and tenor of American politics. Thus, campaign workers are an integral part of instituting and shaping political change.

Making a Difference

In 2006, Virginia Senator George Allen had to apologize for what his opponent's campaign deemed demeaning and insensitive comments made by the senator about a 20-year-old campaign volunteer of Indian descent. S. R. Sidarth—a volunteer for Democrat James Webb—was following and videotaping Allen on the campaign trail (a common task for campaign volunteers). Allen referred to Sidarth as "macaca" and told him, "Welcome to America. Welcome to the real world of Virginia." After Sidarth posted footage of the incident on the Internet, an outcry went up over the Senator's comments. The incident also provoked debate over the proper treatment of volunteers working for opposition campaigns.

What you can do:

- Contact your local political party headquarters and request information on all the campaigns and candidates. This same information can be obtained by contacting your state's Secretary of State (in most states this office is charged with overseeing the state's election process and mechanism).
- Go door-to-door discussing a candidate's views.
- Work campaign booths at state fairs and other public events. You may even get the chance to give a stump speech on behalf of your candidate.
- Work at campaign headquarters where you can man phone-banks, send out mailers, act as a "gofer," or work as an aide directly for the candidate.

- *Get a fund-raiser.* Money, as this chapter will soon discuss in detail, is an important key to election victory.
- *Get a campaign counsel.* With all the current federal regulation of campaign financing, legal assistance is essential to ensure compliance with the laws.
- *Hire media and campaign consultants.* Candidates have more important things to do with their time than plan ad campaigns, contract for buttons and bumper stickers, and buy TV time and newspaper space. Professionals can get them the most exposure for their money.
- *Assemble a campaign staff.* It is desirable to hire as many professionals as the campaign budget allows, but it is also important to get a volunteer coordinator to ensure that envelopes are licked, doorbells rung, and other small but vital tasks addressed. Many campaign volunteers are typically young people, who are the most likely to have the energy for this sort of work. However, in recent years high school seniors have expressed less and less interest in participating in campaigns (see Young People and Politics: "Declining Interest in Working in Campaigns").
- *Plan the logistics.* A modern presidential campaign involves jetting around the country at an incredible pace. Good advance people handle the complicated

You Are a Presidential Campaign Consultant

YOUNG PEOPLE AND POLITICS

Declining Interest in Working in Campaigns

Walk into any campaign headquarters and chances are good that you'll find a lot of young people working away. Many of our nation's leaders got their political start working in a campaign when they were young. If you want to get involved in politics as a possible career, this is where you begin. The work is often tedious, the hours are long, and the financial rewards are usually minimal. Hence, full-time campaign work is not really suitable for either someone with an active career or a retired person. Campaign jobs have been and likely will continue to be filled primarily by young people.

Nevertheless, as you can see in the figure below, there has been a decline in interest in working on campaigns among high school seniors over the past quarter century. Whereas between 15 and 20 percent of those interviewed in the late 1970s and early 1980s said they planned to work on a campaign or had already done so, in recent years only about 10 percent have expressed an interest in campaign work.

Questions for Discussion

- At the same time that young people have been expressing less interest in working on political campaigns, they have been volunteering for community organizations at record rates. Might the decline in interest in campaigns simply be because today's young people are focusing on non-political forms of community action?
- Do you think that one reason that young people may not be very interested in working in campaigns may be that the issues discussed in recent campaigns aren't of much interest to young people? If so, what sort of issues might stimulate more young people to sign up for campaign work?
- If more young people were to volunteer for work in campaigns, what difference might it make? Do you think the tenor of recent campaigns would have been changed if more young people had been involved?

PLAN TO WORK ON A CAMPAIGN OR HAVE DONE SO

Year	Percent
2004	9.6
2003	10.2
2002	11.3
2001	9.9
2000	11.1
1999	9.4
1998	10.2
1997	12.3
1996	12.1
1995	11.0
1994	11.7
1993	13.7
1992	10.7
1991	10.5
1990	10.7
1989	13.2
1988	13.4
1987	14.5
1986	13.9
1985	15.7
1984	15.0
1983	15.7
1982	14.7
1981	17.4
1980	15.8
1979	17.2
1978	18.6
1977	20.3
1976	17.8

Source: Authors' analysis of Monitoring the Future national surveys of high school seniors.

details of candidate scheduling and see that events are well publicized and well attended.

- *Get a research staff and policy advisers.* Candidates have little time to master the complex issues reporters will ask about. Policy advisers—often distinguished academics—feed them information they need to keep up with events.
- *Hire a pollster.* Dozens of professional polling firms conduct opinion research to tell candidates how they are viewed by the voters and what is on the voters' minds.
- *Get a good press secretary.* Candidates running for major office are dogged by reporters every step of the way. The reporters need news, and a good press secretary can help them make their deadlines with stories that the campaign would like to see reported.
- *Establish a Web site.* A Web site is a relatively inexpensive way of getting a candidate's message out.

Most of these tasks cost money. Campaigns are not cheap, and the role of money in campaigns is a controversial one.

Money and Campaigning

There is no doubt that campaigns are expensive and, in America's high-tech political arena, growing more so. As the old saying goes, "Money is the mother's milk of politics." Candidates need money to build a campaign organization and to get their message out. Many people and groups who want certain things from the government are all too willing to give it; thus there is the common perception that money buys votes and influence. The following sections examine the role of money in campaigns.

The Maze of Campaign Finance Reforms

As the costs of campaigning skyrocketed with the growth of television, and as the Watergate scandal exposed large, illegal campaign contributions, momentum developed for campaign finance reform in the early 1970s. Several public interest lobbies (see Chapter 10), notably Common Cause and the National Committee for an Effective Congress, led the drive. In 1974, Congress passed the **Federal Election Campaign Act**. It had two main goals: to tighten reporting requirements for contributions and to limit overall expenditures. The 1974 act and its subsequent amendments did the following:

- *Created the* ***Federal Election Commission.*** A bipartisan body, the six-member Federal Election Commission (FEC) administers the campaign finance laws and enforces compliance with their requirements.
- *Created the* ***Presidential Election Campaign Fund.*** The FEC is in charge of doling out money from this fund to qualified presidential candidates. Money for this fund is raised via a $3 voluntary check-off box on income tax returns, which currently only about 11 percent of taxpayers do.
- *Provided partial public financing for presidential primaries.* Presidential candidates who raise $5,000 on their own in at least 20 states can get individual

Federal Election Campaign Act
A law passed in 1974 for reforming campaign finances. The act created the **Federal Election Commission**, provided public financing for presidential primaries and general elections, limited presidential campaign spending, required disclosure, and attempted to limit contributions.

Federal Election Commission
A six-member bipartisan agency created by the **Federal Election Campaign Act of 1974**. The Federal Election Commission administers and enforces campaign finance laws.

Presidential Election Campaign Fund
Funded by the $3 check-off on IRS tax forms, this fund provides a source of money for matching funds in the primaries and complete financing of Democratic and Republican presidential nominees in the general election.

matching funds
Contributions of up to $250 from individuals are matched for qualified presidential candidates in the primaries.

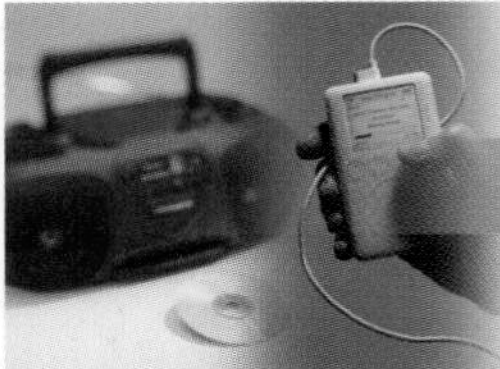

Public Campaign Financing

contributions of up to $250 matched by the federal treasury. Money received at this stage of the campaign is commonly known as **matching funds**. If presidential candidates accept federal support, they agree to limit their campaign expenditures to an amount prescribed by federal law. As you can see in "A Generation of Change: The Incredible Increase in Fundraising for Presidential Nomination Campaigns," in 2004 both Bush and Kerry declined to take matching funds so that they could raise record amounts.

- *Provided full public financing for major party candidates in the general election.* For the general election, each major party nominee gets a fixed amount of money to cover their campaign expenses. For 2004 this amounted to

A GENERATION OF CHANGE

The Incredible Increase in Fundraising for Presidential Nomination Campaigns

A generation ago, fund-raising for presidential nomination campaigns was rather limited compared to the vast sums of money that are raised by the parties' presidential nominees today. As you can see in the data displayed here, the 1988 nomination campaigns of George Bush and Michael Dukakis cost a total of $60.3 million. About 29 percent of this amount came from federal matching funds, which were designed to supplement small contributions from individuals. Acceptance of these matching funds requires candidates to limit the total amount they raise. In 1988, both Bush and Dukakis ended up spending close to the legal limit of $32 million for that year. By 2004, the cap on nomination expenditures had risen to about $52 million as the result of inflation over the years. For both the Bush and Kerry campaigns this seemed too constraining in light of what they thought they could raise on their own without matching funds. Just the donations each received from people who gave the maximum legal contribution of $2,000 enabled them to raise more than they would have been limited to had they accepted matching funds, as 61,714 people gave $2,000 to the Bush campaign and 35,891 people gave $2,000 to the Kerry campaign. All told, the two campaigns raised a stunning $500 million just to fund their activities up to their respective party conventions. Even taking inflation into account, this is about five times what the party nominees raised a generation ago.

	1988, GEORGE BUSH	1988, MICHAEL DUKAKIS	2004, GEORGE W. BUSH	2004, JOHN KERRY
Contributions from individuals	$22.6	$19.6	$271.8	$225.2
Contributions from PACs	$0.7	—	$2.9	$0.1
Federal matching funds	$8.4	$9.0	—	—
Total	$31.7 million	$28.6 million	$274.7 million	$225.3 million

Source: Federal Election Commission.

$75 million. Unlike in the primaries, the FEC pays all the costs of general election campaigns, thereby making the offer too good for anyone to turn down. Thus, although George W. Bush and John Kerry each decided not to accept federal support in the campaign for their party's nomination, they followed the practice of all previous major party nominees in taking federal money for the fall campaign.

- *Required full disclosure.* Regardless of whether they accept any federal funding, all candidates for federal office must file periodic reports with the FEC, listing who contributed and how the money was spent. In the spirit of immediate disclosure, some 2004 presidential candidates regularly posted updated campaign contribution information on their Web sites.
- *Limited contributions.* Scandalized to find out that some wealthy individuals had contributed $1 million to the 1972 Nixon campaign, Congress limited individual contributions to presidential and congressional candidates to $1,000. The McCain-Feingold Act increased this limit to $2,000 as of 2004 and provided for it to be indexed to rise along with inflation in the future.

Although the 1974 campaign reforms were generally welcomed by both parties, the constitutionality of the Federal Election Campaign Act was challenged in the 1976 case of *Buckley v. Valeo.* In this case the Supreme Court struck down the portion of the act that had limited the amount individuals could contribute to their own campaigns as a violation of free speech. This aspect of the Court ruling made it possible for Ross Perot to spend over $60 million of his own fortune on his independent presidential candidacy in 1992, and for John Kerry to loan his campaign over $7 million for the 2004 Democratic nomination contest.

Campaign Finance Reform

Another loophole was opened in 1979 with an amendment to the original act that made it easier for political parties to raise money for voter registration drives, to distribute campaign material at the grassroots level, and for generic party advertising. Money raised for such purposes is known as **soft money** and is not subject to any contribution limits. In 2000, an unprecedented amount of money flowed into the coffers of the national parties through this loophole. Nearly half a billion dollars was raised by the two parties in 2000 via soft money contributions, with many of the contributions coming in increments of hundreds of thousands of dollars. AT&T alone gave over $3 million in soft money, as did the American Federation of State, County, and Municipal Employees.

soft money
Political contributions earmarked for party-building expenses at the grass-roots level or for generic party advertising. For a time, such contributions were unlimited, until they were banned by the McCain-Feingold Act.

Senators John McCain (R-Ariz.) and Russell Feingold (D-Wis.) crusaded for years to remove the taint of large soft money campaign contributions from the political system. Their efforts finally came to fruition in 2002 when their bill was passed by the Congress and signed into law by President George W. Bush. The McCain-Feingold Act (1) banned soft money contributions, (2) increased the amount that individuals could give to candidates from $1,000 to $2,000 and indexed the latter amount to rise in the future along with inflation, and (3) barred groups from running "issue ads" within 60 days of a general election if they refer to a federal candidate and are not funded through a PAC (that is, with funds regulated by the campaign finance system). These provisions were challenged in the Courts, and in the 2003 case of *McConnell v. Federal Election Commission* the Supreme Court ruled in favor of the new law by a 5-to-4 margin.

3·22·02 THE PHILADELPHIA INQUIRER. UNIVERSAL PRESS SYNDICATE.

No sooner had the soft money loophole been closed than another loophole for big contributors opened up. Some scholars call this the "hydraulic theory of money and politics," noting that money, like water, inevitably finds its way around any obstacle. Wealthy individuals on both sides of the political spectrum found that they could make unlimited contributions to what is known as **527 groups**, which are named after the section of the federal tax code that governs these political groups. In a controversial ruling, the FEC in 2004 declined to subject 527 groups to contribution restrictions as long as their political messages did not make explicit endorsements of candidates by using phrases like "Vote for" and "Vote against." The result was that many people who had in the past given big soft money contributions to the parties decided instead to give big donations to a 527 group, such as the anti-Kerry group Swift Boat Veterans for Truth or the anti-Bush group MoveOn.org. Fifty-two individuals gave over $1 million each to a 527 group, and another 213 individuals gave over $100,000. All told, 527 groups spent about $424 million on political messages in 2004.[15]

527 Groups
Independent groups that seek to influence the political process but are not subject to contribution restrictions because they do not directly seek the election of particular candidates. Their name comes from Section 527 of the federal tax code, under which they are governed.

Even with the loopholes that have developed in campaign finance law, there is little doubt that efforts to regulate campaign contributions since 1974 have made this aspect of American politics more open and honest. All contribution and expenditure records are now open for all to examine. As Frank Sorauf writes, detailed reports of American campaign contributions and expenditures have "become a wonder of the democratic political world. Nowhere else do scholars and journalists find so much information about the funding of campaigns, and the openness of Americans about the flow of money stuns many other nationals accustomed to silence and secrecy about such traditionally private matters."[16]

The Debate Over Campaign Finance Reform

The Proliferation of PACs

The campaign reforms also encouraged the spread of **Political Action Committees**, generally known as PACs. Before the 1974 reforms, corporations were technically forbidden from donating money to political campaigns, but many wrote big checks anyway. Unions could make indirect contributions, although limits were set on how they could aid candidates and political parties. The 1974 reforms created a new, more open, way for interest groups like business and labor to contribute to campaigns. Any interest group, large or small, can now get into the act by forming its own PAC to directly channel contributions of up to $5,000 per candidate. Because *Buckley v. Valeo* extended the right of free speech to PACs, they can spend unlimited amounts indirectly, that is, if such activities are not coordinated with the campaign.

political action committees
Funding vehicles created by the 1974 campaign finance reforms. A corporation, union, or some other interest group can create a political action committee (PAC) and register it with the **Federal Election Commission**, which will meticulously monitor the PAC's expenditures.

As of 2006, the FEC reported that there were 4,217 PACs. In the 2004 congressional elections, PACs contributed $288.6 million to House and Senate candidates. Many believe that this expansion has led to a system of open graft.[17] Few developments since the Watergate crisis have generated so much cynicism about government as the explosive growth of PACs over the last three decades.

A PAC is formed when a business association, or some other interest group, decides to contribute to candidates it believes will be favorable toward its goals. The group registers as a PAC with the FEC, and then puts money into the PAC coffers. The PAC can collect money from stockholders, members, and other interested parties. It then donates the money to candidates, often after careful research on their issue stands and past voting records. One very important ground rule prevails: All expenditures must be meticulously reported to the FEC. If PACs are corrupting democracy, at least they are doing so openly.

Candidates need PACs because high-tech campaigning is expensive. Tightly contested races for the House of Representatives can sometimes cost $1 million; Senate races can easily cost $1 million for television alone. PACs play a major role in paying for expensive campaigns. Thus there emerges a symbiotic relationship between the PACs and the candidates: Candidates need money, which they insist can be used without compromising their integrity; PACs want access to officeholders, which they insist can be gained without buying votes. Justin Dart of Dart Industries, a close friend of former President Reagan, remarks of his PAC that "talking to politicians is fine, but with a little money, they hear you better."[18]

There is an abundance of PACs willing to help the candidates. There are big PACs, such as the Realtors Political Action Committee and the American Medical Association Political Action Committee. There are little ones, too, representing smaller industries or business associations: EggPAC, FishPAC, FurPAC, LardPAC, and, for the beer distributors, SixPAC.[19] Table 9.1 lists the business, labor, and ideological PACs that gave the most money to congressional candidates in 2004 and shows which party each favored.

Critics of the PAC system worry that all this money leads to PAC control over what the winners do once in office. Archibald Cox and Fred Wertheimer of Common Cause write that the role of PACs in campaign finance "is robbing our nation of its democratic ideals and giving us a government of leaders beholden to the monied interests who make their election possible."[20] On some issues, it seems clear that PAC money has made a difference. The Federal Trade Commission

Why It Matters

Money and Elections
As the 2004 primaries approached, most pundits argued that any serious candidate for the presidency needed to raise $15 million by the end of 2003 in order to be classified as a serious contender. Raising money is one concrete indicator of support before the first votes are cast. In addition, money provides a campaign with the ability to hire sufficient staff and advertising time to get its message out. A campaign that is short on money can hardly get its message out.

Table 9.1 The Big-Spending Political Action Committees (PACs)

According to an analysis of Federal Election Commission data by the Center for Responsive Politics, here are the largest business, labor, and ideological/single-issue PAC contributors to congressional candidates for the 2004 election cycle and the percentage that they gave to Republicans.

	AMOUNT CONTRIBUTED	PERCENTAGE GIVEN TO REPUBLICANS
Business		
National Association of Realtors	$3,787,083	52
National Auto Dealers	2,603,300	73
National Beer Wholesalers	2,314,000	76
National Association of Home Builders	2,201,500	67
Association of Trial Lawyers	2,181,499	6
United Parcel Service	2,142,679	72
American Medical Association	2,092,425	79
American Bankers Association	1,978,013	64
SBC Communications	1,955,116	65
Wal-Mart Stores	1,677,000	78
Labor		
Laborers Union	2,684,250	14
International Brotherhood of Electrical Workers	2,369,500	4
United Auto Workers	2,075,700	1
Carpenters & Joiners Union	2,074,560	26
Service Employees International Union	1,985,000	15
Machinists/Aerospace Workers Union	1,942,250	1
Teamsters Union	1,917,413	11
American Federation of Teachers	1,717,372	3
Ideological/Single-Issue		
Human Rights Campaign	1,165,138	9
National Rifle Association	1,026,649	85
Planned Parenthood	483,614	5
Sierra Club	388,960	6
National Pro-Life Alliance	209,600	100

Source: Center for Responsive Politics.

(FTC), for example, once passed a regulation requiring that car dealers list known mechanical defects on the window sticker of used cars. The National Association of Automobile Dealers quickly became one of the largest donors to congressional incumbents, contributing just over $1 million to candidates of both parties. Soon afterward, 216 representatives cosponsored a House resolution nullifying the FTC regulation. Of these representatives, 186 had been aided by the auto dealers' PAC.[21]

It is questionable, however, whether such examples are the exception or the rule. Most PACs give money to candidates who agree with them in the first place. For instance, the antiabortion PACs do not waste their money supporting pro-choice candidates. Frank Sorauf's careful review of the subject concludes that "there simply are no data in the systematic studies that would support the popular assertions about the 'buying' of the Congress or about any other massive influence of money on the legislative process."[22]

The impact of PAC money on presidents is even more doubtful. Presidential campaigns are, of course, partly subsidized by the public and so are less dependent on PACs. Moreover, presidents have well-articulated positions on most important issues. A small contribution from any one PAC is not likely to turn a presidential candidate's head.

Money matters in campaigns and sometimes also during legislative votes. Although the influence of PACs may be exaggerated, the high cost of running for office ensures their continuing major role in the campaign process.

Does Money Buy Victory?

Money is, of course, absolutely crucial to electoral victory; important offices are rarely won these days by candidates who spend virtually nothing. One of the last of this nonspending breed was Senator William Proxmire of Wisconsin. He was succeeded by wealthy businessman Herbert Kohl, who funded his multi-million-dollar campaign entirely out of his own pocket. As Kohl said, he was so rich that no one had to worry about him being bought by special interests.

Perhaps the most basic complaint about money and politics is that there may be a direct link between dollars spent and votes received. Few have done more to dispel this charge than political scientist Gary Jacobson. His research has shown that "the more incumbents spend, the worse they do."[23] This fact is not as odd as it at first sounds. It simply means that incumbents who face a tough opponent must raise more money to meet the challenge. When a challenger is not a serious threat (as they all too often are not), incumbents can afford to campaign cheaply.

More important than having "more" money is having "enough" money. Herbert Alexander calls this "the doctrine of sufficiency." As he writes, "Enough money must be spent to get a message across to compete effectively but outspending one's opponent is not always necessary—even an incumbent with a massive ratio of higher spending."[24] One case in point is that of the late Paul Wellstone, a previously obscure political science professor who beat an incumbent senator in 1990 despite being outspent by 5 to 1.[25] In 2004, Howard Dean was crowned by the media as the early front-runner for the Democratic presidential nomination as a result of his fundraising prowess, but John Kerry proved to be a much better vote-getter.

The Media and the Campaign

Money matters, and so does media attention. Media coverage is determined by two factors: (1) how candidates use their advertising budget and (2) the "free" attention they get as news makers. The first, obviously, is relatively easy to control; the second is harder, but not impossible. Almost every logistical decision in a campaign—where to eat breakfast, whom to include on the rostrum, when to announce a major policy

You Are a Media Consultant to a Political Candidate

proposal—is calculated according to its intended media impact. About half the total budget for a presidential or senatorial campaign is used for television advertising.

No major candidate these days can do without what political scientist Dan Nimmo calls "the political persuaders."[26] A new profession of political consultants has emerged, and for the right price, they can turn a disorganized campaign into a well-run, high-tech operation. They can do it all—polling or hiring the pollster, molding a candidate's image, advising a candidate on his or her spouse's role, handling campaign logistics, managing payrolls, and so forth. Incumbents as well as challengers turn to professional consultants for such help.

All this concern with public relations worries some observers of American politics. They fear a new era of politics in which the slick slogan and the image salesperson will dominate, an era when Madison Avenue will be more influential than Main Street. Most political scientists, however, conclude that such fears are overblown. Research has shown that campaign advertising can be a source of information about issues as well as about images. Thomas Patterson and Robert McClure examined the information contained in TV advertising and found it impressive. In fact, they concluded, viewers could learn more about candidates' stands on the issues from watching their ads than from watching the nightly news. Most news coverage emphasizes where the candidates went, how big their crowds were, and other campaign details. Only rarely do the networks delve into where candidates stand on the issues. In contrast, political ads typically address issues; a study of 230,000 candidate ads that ran in 1998 found that spots that emphasized policy outnumbered those that emphasized personal image by a 6-to-1 ratio.[27] Most candidates apparently believe that their policy positions are a crucial part of their campaign, and they are willing to pay substantial sums to communicate them to voters.

Television has been the primary way that candidates for national office have gotten out their message since about 1960. Here, President George W. Bush and First Lady Laura Bush are shown being interviewed for a joint appearance on the CNN program *Larry King Live* during the 2004 campaign.

Candidates have much less control over the other aspect of the media, news coverage. News organizations seem to believe that policy issues are of less interest to voters than the campaign itself. The result is that news coverage is disproportionately devoted to campaign strategies, speculation about what will happen next, poll results, and other aspects of the campaign game.[28] Once a candidate has taken a policy position and it has been reported on, it becomes old news. The latest poll showing Smith ahead of Jones is thus more newsworthy in the eyes of the media. Republican media consultant Roger Ailes calls this his "orchestra pit" theory of American politics: "If you have two guys on stage and one guy says, 'I have a solution to the Middle East problem,' and the other guy falls in the orchestra pit, who do you think is going to be on the evening news?"[29]

Thomas Patterson tabulated the amount of media attention to the campaign itself and the amount of attention to such substantive issues, such as the economy, in the 1976 presidential race. Examining several newspapers and newsmagazines as well as television network news, he found that the media paid roughly twice as much attention to the horse race and strategy as it did to the substance of the campaign—issues, policies, past record, and endorsements.[30] Table 9.2 shows that in recent years the major TV networks have usually focused more on the horse race than policy issues. Interestingly, the 2004 election was an exception to this general rule. Even with the race between Bush and Kerry being very close, there was just as much focus on policy matters as to who was winning and losing. The media's greater focus on policies in 2004 probably reflects the fact that the issues of the year stirred great passions and an unusual degree of viewer interest. It remains to be seen whether such public interest in candidates' policy stands can be maintained in future campaigns.

Television and Presidential Campaigns

Table 9.2 Horse-Race Versus Policy Coverage on the Network News, 1988–2004

Since 1988, the Center for Media and Public Affairs has been analyzing the content of ABC, CBS, and NBC nightly news during the fall of presidential election campaigns. For every story that has been broadcast, they have examined the content to see if it focused on the horse race and/or policy issues. The results can be seen here. Keep in mind that the numbers do not add up to 100 percent because some stories focused on both aspects, and some focused on neither.

	% OF STORIES FOCUSING ON POLICY ISSUES	% OF STORIES FOCUSING ON THE HORSE RACE
2004	49	48
2000	40	71
1996	37	48
1992	32	58
1988	39	58

Source: Stephen J. Farnsworth and S. Robert Lichter, "The *Nightly News Nightmare* Revisited: Network Television's Coverage of the 2004 Presidential Election" (paper presented at the 2005 annual meeting of the American Political Science Association), 31.

The Impact of Campaigns

Almost all politicians figure that a good campaign is the key to victory. Many political scientists, however, question the importance of campaigns. Reviewing the evidence, Dan Nimmo concluded, "Political campaigns are less crucial in elections than most politicians believe."[31] For years, researchers studying campaigns have stressed that campaigns have three effects on voters: reinforcement, activation, and conversion. Campaigns can reinforce voters' preferences for candidates; they can activate voters, getting them to contribute money or ring doorbells as opposed to merely voting; and they can convert, changing voters' minds.

Five decades of research on political campaigns leads to a single message: Campaigns mostly reinforce and activate; only rarely do they convert. The evidence on the impact of campaigns points clearly to the conclusion that the best-laid plans of campaign managers change very few votes. Given the millions of dollars spent on political campaigns, it may be surprising to find that they do not have a great effect. Several factors tend to weaken campaigns' impact on voters:

selective perception
The phenomenon that people often pay the most attention to things they already agree with and interpret them according to their own predispositions.

- Most people pay relatively little attention to campaigns in the first place. People have a remarkable capacity for **selective perception**—paying most attention to things they already agree with and interpreting events according to their own predispositions.
- Factors such as party identification—though less important than they used to be—still influence voting behavior regardless of what happens in the campaign.
- Incumbents start with a substantial advantage in terms of name recognition and an established track record.

Such findings do not mean, of course, that campaigns never change voters' minds or that converting a small percentage is unimportant. In tight races, a good campaign can make the difference between winning and losing.

As the campaign nears its end, voters face two key choices: whether to vote and, if they choose to, how to vote. The following sections investigate the ways that voters make these choices.

Whether to Vote: A Citizen's First Choice

suffrage
The legal right to vote, extended to African Americans by the **Fifteenth Amendment**, to women by the **Nineteenth Amendment**, and to people over the age of 18 by the **Twenty-sixth Amendment**.

Over two centuries of American electoral history include greatly expanded **suffrage**—the right to vote. Virtually everyone over the age of 18 now has the right to vote. The two major exceptions concern noncitizens and convicted criminals. There is no federal requirement stating that voters must be citizens, and it was quite common in the nineteenth century for immigrants to vote prior to attaining citizenship. However, no state currently permits residents who are not citizens to vote. In contrast, state law varies widely when it comes to crime and voting: Virtually all states deny prisoners the right to vote, about half extend the ban to people on parole, and 10 states impose a lifetime ban on convicted felons.

Interestingly, as the right to vote has been extended, proportionately fewer of those eligible have chosen to exercise that right. In the past 110 years, the 80 percent turnout in the 1896 election was the high point of electoral participation. In 2004, only 55 percent of the adult population voted in the presidential election, and in the 2002 midterm elections only 39 percent took part.

Deciding Whether to Vote

Realistically, when more than 120 million people vote in a presidential election, as they did in 2004, the chance of one vote affecting the outcome is very, very slight. Once in a while, of course, an election is decided by a small number of votes, as was the case in Florida in 2000. It is more likely, however, that you will be struck by lightning during your lifetime than participate in an election decided by a single vote.

The 2000 Presidential Election

Not only does your vote probably not make much difference to the outcome, but voting is somewhat costly. You have to spend some of your valuable time becoming informed, making up your mind, and getting to the polls. If you carefully calculate your time and energy, you might rationally decide that the costs of voting outweigh the benefits. Indeed, the most frequent response given by nonvoters in the 2004 Census Bureau survey on turnout was that they could not take time off from work or school that day.[32] Some scholars have therefore proposed that one of the easiest ways to increase American turnout levels would be to move Election Day to Saturday or to make it a holiday.[33]

Economist Anthony Downs, in his model of democracy, tries to explain why a rational person would ever bother to vote. He argues that rational people vote if they believe that the policies of one party will bring more benefits than the policies of the other party.[34] Thus, people who see policy differences between the parties are more likely to join the ranks of voters. If you are an environmentalist and you expect the Democrats to pass more environmental legislation than the Republicans, then you have an additional incentive to go to the polls. On the other hand, if you are truly indifferent—that is, if you see no difference whatsoever between the two parties—you may rationally decide to abstain.

Another reason why many people vote is that they have a high sense of **political efficacy**—the belief that ordinary people can influence the government. Efficacy is measured by asking people to agree or disagree with statements such as "I don't think public officials care much what people like me think." Those who lack strong feelings of efficacy are being quite rational in staying home on Election Day because they don't think they can make a difference. Yet even some of these people will vote anyway, simply to support democratic government. In this case, people are impelled to vote by a sense of **civic duty**. The benefit from doing one's civic duty is the long-term contribution made toward preserving democracy.

political efficacy
The belief that one's **political participation** really matters—that one's vote can actually make a difference.

civic duty
The belief that in order to support democratic government, a citizen should always vote.

voter registration
A system adopted by the states that requires voters to register well in advance of Election Day. Although a few states permit Election Day registration for presidential elections, advance registration dampens voter turnout.

Registering to Vote

A century ago politicians used to say, "Vote early and often." Largely to prevent corruption associated with stuffing ballot boxes, states adopted **voter registration** laws around the turn of the century, which require individuals to first place their name on an electoral roll in order to be allowed to vote. Although these laws have made it more difficult to vote more than once, they have also discouraged some people from voting at all. America's unique registration system is, in part, to blame for why Americans are significantly less likely to go to the polls than citizens of other democratic nations.

Registration procedures currently differ from state to state. In sparsely populated North Dakota, there is no registration at all, and in Minnesota, Wisconsin, Wyoming, Idaho, New Hampshire, and Maine, voters can register on Election Day. Advocates of this user-friendly procedure are quick to point out that these states all ranked near the top in voter turnout in 2004. For many years, some states—particularly in the South—had burdensome registration procedures, such as requiring people to make a trip to their county courthouse during normal business hours. As a result of the 1993 **Motor Voter Act**, this is no longer the case. The Motor Voter Act made voter registration easier by requiring states to allow eligible voters to register by simply checking a box on their driver's license application or renewal form. Nevertheless, its impact on turnout has thus far been largely disappointing. Turnout for the presidential election of 2004 was roughly the same as it was in 1992, before the Motor Voter Act was passed.

Motor Voter Act

Passed in 1993, this act went into effect for the 1996 election. It requires states to permit people to register to vote at the same time they apply for a driver's license.

Who Votes?

Voting Turnout: Who Votes?

When just over half the population votes, the necessity of studying nonvoters takes on added importance. Table 9.3 displays data regarding the turnout rates of various groups in the 2004 presidential election. This information reveals numerous demographic factors that are related to turnout:

- *Education.* People with higher-than-average educational levels have a higher rate of voting than people with less education. Highly educated people are more capable of discerning the major differences between the candidates. In addition, their educational training comes in handy in clearing the bureaucratic hurdles imposed by registration requirements.
- *Age.* Older people are far more likely to vote than younger people. Younger citizens are less likely to be registered, but even just analyzing turnout patterns among registered voters yields wide differences by age. For example, Georgia's secretary of state reported that of those on the registration rolls under 25 years of age, only 22 percent voted in 2002 as compared to 68 percent among those over 65 years of age.[35]
- *Race.* African Americans and Hispanics are underrepresented among voters relative to their share of the citizenry. This finding can largely be explained by their generally low levels of education. African Americans and Hispanics with high levels of education have a higher turnout rate than Whites with comparable educational achievement.
- *Gender.* In an earlier period many women were discouraged from voting, but today women actually participate in elections at a slightly higher rate than men.

Table 9.3 Reported Turnout Rate in 2004 by Social Groups

SOCIAL GROUPS	PERCENT
18–20	41
21–24	42
25–44	52
45–64	67
65 and over	69
No high school diploma	30
High school	52
Some college	66
College	74
White	66
African American	56
Hispanic citizens	47
Asian American citizens	44
Men	56
Women	60
Married	65
Single	47
Government workers	75
Self-employed	64
Work in private industry	57
Unemployed	46

Source: Authors' analysis of 2004 U.S. Census Bureau survey.

- *Marital status.* People who are married are more likely to vote than those who are not. This pattern is true among all age categories and generally reflects the fact that married people are more tied into their community.
- *Government employment.* Having something at stake (their jobs and the future of the programs they work on) and being in a position to know more about government impels government workers to high levels of participation.

These differences in turnout rates are cumulative. Possessing several of these traits (say, being elderly, well educated, and very religious) adds significantly to one's likelihood of voting. Conversely, being young, poorly educated, and not religious is likely to add up to a very low probability of voting. If you possess many of the demographic traits of nonvoters, then the interests of people like you are probably not drawing a great deal of attention from politicians—regardless of whether you personally vote or not. Politicians listen far more carefully to groups with high turnout rates, as they know their fate may well be in their hands. Who votes does matter.

Why It Matters

Youth Turnout

Voter turnout rates in the United States have been declining for quite some time. The very low participation rate of young people has been one of the biggest reasons for this decline. Who votes matters not only because these individuals decide who wins elections but also because politicians pay attention primarily to voters. The fact that so few young people vote means that politicians are not likely to pay too much attention to their opinions or to promote policies that will particularly help them.

Young people have one of the lowest rates of election turnout. Music stars like P. Diddy have tried to change this by actively participating in events that encourage young people to vote.

Compulsory Voting

How Americans Vote: Explaining Citizens' Decisions

mandate theory of elections
The idea that the winning candidate has a mandate from the people to carry out his or her platforms and politics. Politicians like the theory better than political scientists do.

A common explanation of how Americans vote—one favored by journalists and politicians—is that people vote because they agree more with the policy views of Candidate A than with those of Candidate B. Of course, the candidates have gone to a lot of time and trouble to get those views implanted in the public mind. Because citizens vote for the candidate whose policy promises they favor, say many journalists and politicians, the election winner has a mandate from the people to carry out the promised policies. This idea is sometimes called the **mandate theory of elections**.

Politicians, of course, are attracted to the mandate theory. It lets them justify what they want to do by claiming public support for their policies. As President Clinton said during the final presidential debate in 1992, "That's why I am trying to be so specific in this campaign—to have a mandate, if elected, so the Congress will know what the American people have voted for." Immediately after declaring victory in the 2004 presidential election, President Bush forcefully asserted that he had a mandate to enact his proposed policies over the next four years. As Bush stated, "When you win there is a feeling that the people have spoken and embraced your point of view, and that's what I intend to tell the Congress."

Political scientists, however, think very little of the mandate theory of elections.[36] Whereas victorious politicians are eager to proclaim "the people have spoken," political scientists know that the people rarely vote a certain way for the same reasons. Instead, political scientists focus on three major elements of voters' decisions: (1) voters' party identification, (2) voters' evaluation of the candidates, and (3) the match between voters' policy positions and those of the candidates and parties—a factor termed "policy voting."

Party Identification

Party identifications are crucial for many voters in that they provide a regular perspective through which they can view the political world. "Presumably," say Niemi and Weisberg, "people choose to identify with a party with which they generally agree. . . . As a result they need not concern themselves with every issue that comes along, but can generally rely on their party identification to guide them."[37] Parties tend to rely on groups that lean heavily in their favor to form their basic coalition. Even before an election campaign begins, Republicans usually assume they will not receive much support from African Americans, Jews, and Hispanic Americans. Democrats have an uphill struggle attracting groups that are staunchly Republican in their leanings, such as conservative evangelical Christians or upper-income voters. As you can see in Table 9.4, there have been substantial changes in how various groups have voted for president since the days of Kennedy versus Nixon in 1960.

With the emergence of television and candidate-centered politics, the parties' hold on voters eroded substantially during the 1960s and 1970s and then stabilized at a new and lower level.[38] In the 1950s, scholars singled out party affiliation as the best single predictor of a voter's decision. For example, it was said that many Southern Democrats would vote for a yellow dog if their party nominated one. "My party—right or wrong" was the motto that typified strong party identifiers. Today, many voters agree with the statement that "I choose the best person for the office, regardless of party," as modern technology makes it possible for them to evaluate and make their own decisions about the candidates. For these voters, election choices have become largely a matter of individual choice, and they are up for grabs in each election (the so-called floating voters). Young people are particularly likely to be up for grabs and open to the possibility of voting for candidates who are neither Democrats nor Republicans.

Candidate Evaluations: How Americans See the Candidates

All candidates try to present a favorable personal image. Using laboratory experiments, political psychologists Shawn Rosenberg and Patrick McCafferty show that it is possible to manipulate a candidate's appearance in a way that affects voters' choices. Holding a candidate's policy views and party identification constant, they find that when good pictures are substituted for bad ones, a candidate's vote-getting ability is significantly increased. Although a laboratory setting may not be representative of the real world, Rosenberg and McCafferty conclude that "with appropriate pretesting and adequate control over a candidate's public appearance, a campaign consultant should be able to significantly manipulate the image projected to the voting public."[39]

To do so, a consultant would need to know what sort of candidate images voters are most attuned to. Research by Miller, Wattenberg, and Malanchuk shows that the three most important dimensions of candidate image are integrity, reliability, and competence.[40] In 2000, one of the key factors that helped George W. Bush was that he was rated fairly positively on integrity, whereas Gore scored rather poorly on

Table 9.4 Changing Patterns in Voting Behavior: 1960 and 2004 Compared

The demographic correlates of presidential voting behavior have changed in a number of important ways since 1960. When Kennedy was elected in 1960, Protestants and Catholics voted very differently, as Kennedy's Catholicism was a major issue during the campaign. Although John Kerry was the first major party nominee since Kennedy to be of the Catholic faith, Catholics were only slightly more likely to support him than Protestants. Today, the major difference along religious lines involves how often one attends religious services, with those who attend regularly being substantially more likely to support Republican presidential candidates. The least likely group to support Republicans these days is African Americans. As you can see in data here, Kerry clearly drew more support from African Americans than did Kennedy. Another advantage that Democrats now enjoy is with female voters, who preferred Kerry by 7 percent more than men. Interestingly, women were actually slightly less likely than men to have supported the handsome JFK in 1960. Finally, the rapidly expanding Hispanic population in the United States has reshaped the electoral scene with their tendency to support Democratic candidates. Hispanics numbered only about 1 percent of voters in 1960—too small to be captured accurately in any survey—but by 2004 they accounted for 8 percent of Americans who voted for president.

	KENNEDY	NIXON	KERRY	BUSH
Protestant	36	63	40	59
Catholic	83	17	47	52
Jewish	89	11	74	25
Regularly attend religious services	49	50	39	60
Often attend religious services	36	64	49	50
Seldom attend religious services	55	44	54	45
Never attend religious services	51	49	62	36
White	48	52	41	58
African American	71	29	88	11
Hispanic	NA	NA	57	40
Male	52	48	44	55
Female	47	53	51	48
18–29	53	47	54	45
30–44	51	49	46	53
45–64	50	50	47	52
65+	39	61	47	52
No high school diploma	55	45	50	49
High school diploma	52	48	47	52
Some college	33	67	46	54
College degree	38	62	49	50

Source: 1960 National Election Study and 2004 National Voter Exit Poll.

this dimension. In addition to honesty and integrity, a good candidate should also be seen as dependable and decisive—traits that Miller, Wattenberg, and Malanchuk label as "reliability." When the Bush campaign repeatedly labeled John Kerry a "flip-flopper" during the 2004 campaign, his image of reliability clearly suffered. The personal traits most often mentioned by voters, though, involve competence.

Incumbent presidents typically score much higher on competence, as they have proven experience in dealing with national and international crises. This is one of the biggest reasons why it is so difficult to defeat a sitting president who is running for a second term.

Such evaluations of candidate personality are sometimes seen as superficial and irrational judgments. Miller and his colleagues disagree with this interpretation, arguing that voters rely on their assessments of candidates' personalities to predict how they would perform in office. If a candidate is too incompetent to carry out policy promises or too dishonest for those promises to be trusted, it makes perfect sense for a voter to pay more attention to personality than policies. Interestingly, Miller and his colleagues find that college-educated voters are actually the most likely to view the candidates in terms of their personal attributes. They argue that better-educated voters are able to make important issue-oriented inferences from these attributes (for example, that a candidate who is unreliable may not be the right person to be the commander in chief of the armed forces).

Policy Voting

Policy voting occurs when people base their choices in an election on their own issue preferences. True policy voting can only take place when four conditions are met. First, voters must have a clear view of their own policy positions. Second, voters must know where the candidates stand on policy issues. Third, they must see differences between the candidates on these issues. And finally, they must actually cast a vote for the candidate whose policy positions coincide with their own.

policy voting
Electoral choices that are made on the basis of the voters' policy preferences and on the basis of where the candidates stand on policy issues.

Given these conditions, policy voting is not always easy—even for the educated voter. Abramson, Aldrich, and Rohde analyzed responses to nine questions about policy issues in the 2000 National Election Study. They found that 51 percent of the respondents met the first three informational criteria for policy voting on the average issue. About 68 percent of the time, when someone knew the candidates' stances and saw differences between them, they voted for the candidate closest to their own position.[41] Of course, we should never expect all votes to be consistent with policy views, as many people will prefer one candidate on some policies and another candidate on other policies.

One regular obstacle to policy voting is that candidates often decide that the best way to handle a controversial issue is to cloud their positions in rhetoric. For example, in 1968 both major party candidates—Nixon and Humphrey—were deliberately ambiguous about what they would do to end the Vietnam War. This made it extremely difficult for voters to cast their ballots according to how they felt about the war. The media may not be much help, either, as they typically focus more on the "horse race" aspects of the campaign than on the policy stands of the candidates, as discussed in Chapter 7. Voters thus often have to work fairly hard just to be informed enough to potentially engage in policy voting.

In today's political world, it is somewhat easier for voters to vote according to policies than it was in the 1950s or 1960s. The key difference is that candidates are now regularly forced to take clear stands to appeal to their own party's primary voters. As late as 1968, it was still possible to win a nomination by dealing with the party bosses; today's candidates must appeal first to the issue-oriented activists in the primaries. Whatever the major issues are in the next presidential election, it is quite likely that the major contenders for the Democratic and Republican nominations will be taking stands on them in order to gain the support of these activists. Thus, what has changed is not the voters but the electoral process, which now provides much more incentive for candidates to draw clear policy distinctions between one another.

George W. Bush has taken particularly strong and clear policy stances on tax cuts, the war on terror, appointing conservative judges, and many other areas. Furthermore, rather than clouding his rhetoric in ambiguity, he has taken pride in being straightforward and plainspoken. Many scholars feel that as a result he has become a particularly polarizing figure whom many voters either love or hate. There is a wealth of survey evidence to support such a conclusion.[42]

2004: The Ratification of a Polarizing Presidency

In 2004, George W. Bush became the fourth Republican president since William McKinley to win a second term. Unlike twice-elected Republicans in the interim years—Dwight Eisenhower, Richard Nixon, and Ronald Reagan—George W. Bush was the first to repeat William McKinley's feat of winning two consecutive elections while leading the Republicans to majorities in both the Senate and the House of Representatives. The completeness of the Republican victory in 2004 led many pundits to talk of George W. Bush's presidency as ushering in a new era of Republican dominance reminiscent of the McKinley era. Whether or not this proves to be the case only time will tell. But certainly the reelection of George W. Bush will go down in history books as one of the most important and hard-fought presidential elections ever.

The intensity of the battle over the presidency in 2004 was at least partially due to the controversial way Bush gained the presidency four years earlier. Election Night 2000 provided a wild night of entertainment, full of ups and downs for everyone. The networks first reported that Al Gore had won the crucial state of Florida, but within an hour they rescinded this call. Early in the morning, they at last called Florida for Bush and declared him the president-elect. But just as Gore was ready to give his concession speech, the word broke that the networks were again rescinding their call, as the margin had narrowed to less than a thousand votes.

Because Bush's lead over Gore in the initial count was less than one-tenth of 1 percent, Florida law mandated an automatic recount. Few novelists would have dared imagine the scene of a nation watching transfixed as county-by-county recount figures came in from a state where 6 million people voted. Ultimately, with the margin between Bush and Gore down to 537 votes, the election hinged on whether the undervotes (ballots that showed no vote for president) would be examined by hand. The Gore campaign pointed out that in counties that used punch-card systems (such as Palm Beach, Miami-Dade, and Broward), 1.5 percent of the ballots showed no presidential vote, whereas only 0.3 percent of the ballots in counties that used scantrons were recorded as blank. The reason offered for this difference was that some people do not punch holes all the way through the card, thereby not fully removing the indentation—the now-famous "chad." The Gore campaign was hoping to find enough chads to turn the vote count in Gore's favor. Naturally, the Bush campaign realized this and opposed any manual recount. They argued that such a review of the ballots was inherently arbitrary and subject to manipulation and differing standards.

As with any legal dispute, this one ended up in the courts, which played a pivotal role in deciding the presidential election. The Florida Supreme Court ultimately ruled in favor of Gore's request, ordering counties to apply the standard of "the clear intention of the voter" in evaluating ballots. However, the U.S. Supreme Court in *Bush v. Gore* (2000) overruled the Florida Supreme Court and held that more precise and consistent standards for evaluating ballots would have to be applied in all counties. Most important, they ruled that there was not enough time to recount all the ballots in an orderly fashion by the time the electors were to vote. Thus, the U.S. Supreme Court ultimately determined that George W. Bush would emerge the winner.

And the Winner Is . . . Close Calls in Presidential Elections

Despite winning office by the narrowest of margins, Bush governed boldly, making numerous consequential decisions that reshaped American public policy. Many of his decisions further polarized his political allies from his political opponents. On the domestic side, his tax cuts were praised by his supporters as stimulating the economy, whereas Bush opponents frequently denounced them as a boon for millionaires that turned a budget surplus into a record budget deficit. The Bush doctrine of striking potential enemies first before they could use weapons of mass destruction was praised by supporters as keeping America safe from further strikes like those that occurred on September 11. But many opponents charged this was a reckless go-it-alone foreign policy that had alienated America from its traditional allies.

Into this maelstrom stepped John F. Kerry, a Democratic senator from Massachusetts since 1984. Kerry was used to being in the thick of battle, as both a decorated Vietnam War hero and subsequently as head of the controversial Vietnam Veterans Against the War. No sooner had Kerry wrapped up the Democratic nomination for president than George W. Bush's campaign launched a set of negative TV ads against him in order to try to define him in the public mind before he could define himself. Never before had a new nominee been attacked so early or so often.

The Kerry campaign sought to portray President Bush as a reckless leader who had rushed the country into an unnecessary war in Iraq. But it faced the problem of explaining how the senator had voted to authorize the president to use force in Iraq. When asked whether he would vote the same way again now that he knew that Iraq did not possess weapons of mass destruction, Kerry seemed to undercut his criticism of the war by saying that he would indeed. And Kerry put his foot in his mouth when he said that he initially voted for a supplemental appropriation of $87 million to fund further military operations in Iraq before he voted against it on final passage. Statements like these led the Bush campaign to charge that Kerry was a "flip-flopper" who could not be trusted to lead America in a dangerous time.

According to exit polls, strong leadership in the war on terrorism ended up being one of people's major reasons for voting for Bush. Many Bush voters also said that "moral values" was the most important issue to them. Bush's strength with evangelical white Christians was clearly instrumental in his victory, with 78 percent supporting his reelection. Voters whose top concern was taxes also favored Bush, who promised to stay the course with his tax-cutting agenda. On the other hand, Kerry won votes among those who were most concerned with the war in Iraq, the economy, health care, and education.

As shown in the electoral college results displayed in Figure 9.2, there were sharp regional divisions in the vote in 2004. Bush ran strong in the South and

Figure 9.2 The Electoral College Results for 2000 and 2004

These two maps show the number of votes each state had in the electoral college in 2000 and 2004 and which states were carried by the Democrats (green) and Republicans (rose) in 2004.

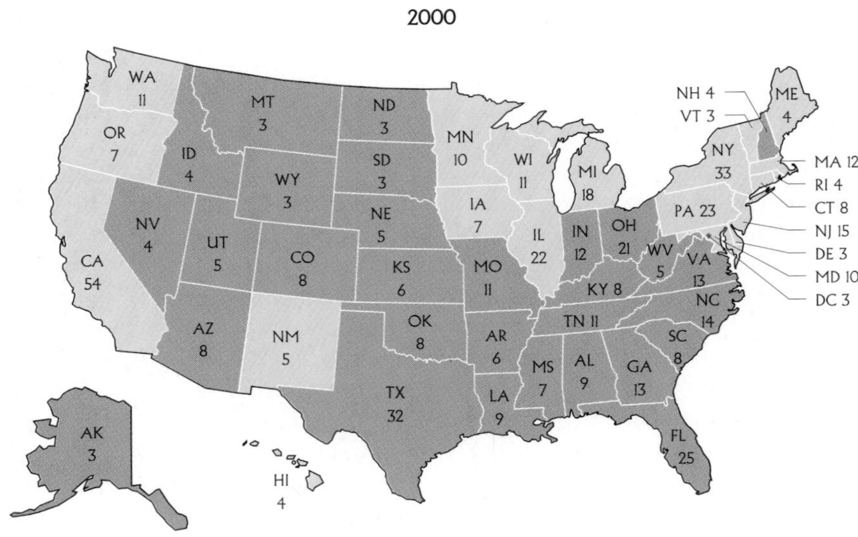

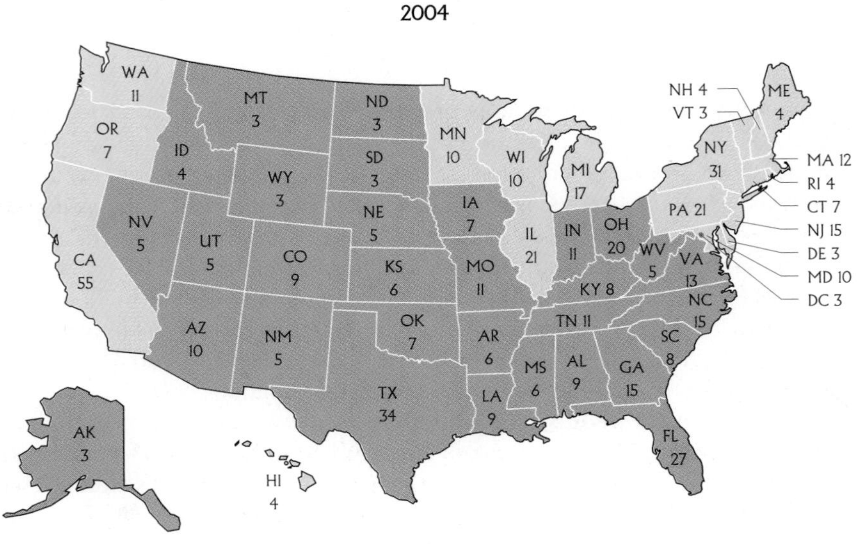

Mountain West, whereas Kerry turned in a good showing in the Northeast and the Pacific Coast states. Like the 2000 election, the electoral college winner hinged on just one big battleground state. This time it was Ohio, whose 20 electors gave Bush a victory of 286 to 252 in the electoral college, but only by a narrow margin of about 135,000 votes out of 5.5 million votes cast. Unlike in 2000, when Bush lost the popular vote to Gore by about one-half of 1 percent, this time he won the popular vote by about 3 percent (51 percent to 48 percent).

The results of the 2004 election show how important it is to understand how the electoral college works. In presidential elections, once voters make their decision it is not just a simple matter of counting the ballots to see who has won the most support nationwide. Instead, the complicated process of determining electoral college votes begins.

The Last Battle: The Electoral College

It is the **electoral college**, not the popular vote, that actually determines who becomes president of the United States. The electoral college is a unique American institution, created by the Constitution. The American Bar Association once called it "archaic, undemocratic, complex, ambiguous, indirect, and dangerous."[43] Many—but certainly not all—political scientists oppose its continued use, as do most voters.

electoral college
A unique American institution created by the Constitution, providing for the selection of the president by electors chosen by the state parties. Although the electoral college vote usually reflects a popular majority, the winner-take-all rule gives clout to big states.

Because the Founders wanted the president to be selected by the nation's elite, not directly by the people, they created the electoral college, a body of electors who are charged solely with the task of voting for the president and vice president. Fortunately, political practice since 1828 has made the vote of members of the electoral college responsive to popular majorities. Today the electors almost always vote for the candidate who won their state's popular vote. Occasionally, though, electors will exercise the right to vote their conscience, as did one West Virginia elector in 1988 who voted for Bentsen for president and Dukakis for vice president.

The Electoral College

This is how the electoral college system works today:

- Each state, according to the Constitution, has as many electoral votes as it has U.S. senators and representatives.[44] The state parties select slates of electors, positions they use as a reward for faithful service to the party.
- Aside from Maine and Nebraska, each state has a winner-take-all system.[45] Electors vote as a bloc for the winner, whether the winner got 35 percent or 95 percent of the popular vote.
- Electors meet in their states in December, following the November election, and then mail their votes to the vice president (who is also president of the Senate). The vote is counted when the new congressional session opens in January and is reported by the vice president. Thus, Dick Cheney had the duty of announcing the reelection of George W. Bush in January 2005.
- If no candidate receives an electoral college majority, then the election is thrown into the House of Representatives, which must choose from among the top three electoral vote winners. A significant aspect of the balloting in the House is that each state delegation has one vote, thus giving the one representative from

Wyoming an equal say with the 53 representatives from California. Though the Founders envisioned that the House would often have to vote to choose the president, this has not occurred since 1828.

The Electoral College

The electoral college is important to the presidential election for two reasons. First, it introduces a bias into the campaign and electoral process. Because each state gets two electors for its senators regardless of population, the less populated states are overrepresented. One of the key reasons that George W. Bush won the electoral college vote in 2000 without winning the popular vote was that he did better in the small states. Second, the winner-take-all rule means that candidates will necessarily focus on winning the states where the polls show that there appears to be a close contest. Thus, Bush and Kerry paid a great deal of attention to Florida and Ohio during the last month of the 2004 campaign but spent no time or money on states where the outcome seemed to be a foregone conclusion, such as New York and Texas.

Understanding Campaigns and Voting Behavior

Elections serve many important functions in American society. They *socialize* and *institutionalize* political activity, making it possible for most political participation to be channeled through the electoral process rather than bubbling up through demonstrations, riots, or revolutions. Because elections provide *regular access to political power*, leaders can be replaced without being overthrown. This feature gives elections *legitimacy* in the eyes of people; that is, elections are accepted as a fair and free method of selecting political leaders.

Throughout the history of American politics, election campaigns have become longer and longer as the system has become increasingly open to public participation. Reformers in both the nineteenth and twentieth centuries held that the solution to democratic problems was more democracy—or, as John Lennon sang, "Power to the people." In principle, more democracy always sounds better than less, but it is not such a simple issue in practice.

Are Nominations and Campaigns Too Democratic?

If one judges American campaigns solely by how open they are, then certainly the American system must be viewed favorably. In other countries, the process of leadership nomination occurs within a relatively small circle of party elites. Thus politicians must work their way up through an apprenticeship system. In contrast, America has an entrepreneurial system in which the people play a crucial role at every stage, from nomination to election. As a result, party outsiders can get elected in a way virtually unknown outside the United States. By appealing directly to the people, a candidate can emerge from nowhere to win the White House. For example, former one-term governor Jimmy Carter was scarcely known outside of his home state a year before his election to the presidency. After serving a number of terms as governor of Arkansas, Bill Clinton was only in a slightly better position than Carter in terms of name recognition when he announced his first campaign for the presidency in 1991. In this sense, the chance to win high office is open to almost any highly skilled politician with even a small electoral base.

There is a price to be paid for all this openness, however. The process of selecting American leaders is a long and convoluted one that has little downtime before it revs up all over again. George W. Bush had scarcely been reelected when potential candidates for 2008 started to schedule visits to Iowa and New Hampshire. Some have even called the American electoral process "the permanent campaign."[46] Many analysts wonder if people would pay more attention to politics if it did not ask so much of them. Given so much democratic opportunity, many citizens are simply overwhelmed by the process and stay on the sidelines. Similarly, the burdens of the modern campaign can discourage good candidates from throwing their hats into the ring. One of the most worrisome burdens candidates face is amassing a sufficient campaign war chest. The system may be open, but it requires a lot of fund-raising to be able to take one's case to the people.

Today's campaigns clearly promote individualism in American politics. The current system of running for office has been labeled by Wattenberg the "candidate-centered age."[47] It allows for politicians to decide on their own to run, to raise their own campaign funds, to build their own personal organizations, and to make promises about how they specifically will act in office. The American campaign game is one of individual candidates, by individual candidates, and for individual candidates.

Do Elections Affect Public Policy?

Comparing Voting and Elections

Whether elections in fact make the government pay attention to what the people think is at the center of debate concerning how well democracy works in America. In the hypothetical world of rational-choice theory and the Downs model, elections do in fact guide public policy; however, over a generation of social science research on this question has produced mixed findings. It is more accurate to describe the connection between elections and public policy as a two-way street: Elections, to some degree, affect public policy, and public policy decisions partly affect electoral outcomes. There will probably never be a definitive answer to the question of how much elections affect public policy, for it is a somewhat subjective matter. The broad contours of the answer, however, seem reasonably clear: *The greater the policy differences between the candidates, the more likely voters will be able to steer government policies by their choices.*

Of course, the candidates do not always do their best to clarify the issues. One result is that the policy stands are often shaped by what Benjamin Page once called "the art of ambiguity," in which "presidential candidates are skilled at appearing to say much while actually saying little."[48] Learning how to sidestep controversial questions and hedge answers is indeed part of becoming a professional politician, as you can observe at any presidential press conference. As long as politicians can take refuge in ambiguity (and the skimpy coverage of issues in the media does little to make them clarify their policy stands), the possibility of democratic control of policy is lessened.

When individual candidates do offer a plain choice to the voters (what 1964 Republican nominee Barry Goldwater once called "a choice, not an echo"), voters are more able to guide the government's policy direction. The voters' clear preferences for Lyndon Johnson's policies over Goldwater's in that election led to the enactment of many liberal-supported measures such as Medicare, Medicaid, federal aid to education, and the Voting Rights Act. A change of course followed in the 1980s when Ronald Reagan made clear his intention to cut the growth of domestic spending, reduce taxes, and build up American military capability. Once elected, he proceeded to do just that.

Do Campaigns Lead to Increases in the Scope of Government?

Comparing Political Campaigns

Today's long and vigorous campaigns involve much more communication between candidates and voters than America's Founders ever could have imagined. In their view, the presidency was to be an office responsible for tending to the public interest as a whole. They wished to avoid "a contest in which the candidates would have to pose as 'friends' of the people or make specific policy commitments."[49] Thus, the Founders would probably be horrified by the modern practice in which political candidates make numerous promises during nomination and election campaigns.

Because states are the key battlegrounds of presidential campaigns, candidates must tailor their appeals to the particular interests of each major state. In Iowa, for instance, promises are typically made to keep agricultural subsidies high, federal programs to help big cities are usually announced in New York, and oil industry tax breaks are promised in Texas. To secure votes from each region of the country, candidates end up supporting a variety of local interests. Promises mount as the campaign goes on, and these promises usually add up to new government programs and money. The way modern campaigns are conducted is thus one of many reasons why politicians often find it easier to expand the scope of American government than to limit it.

Elections also help to increase generalized support for government and its powers. Because voters know that the government can be replaced at the next election, they are much more likely to feel that it will be responsive to their needs. When people have the power to dole out electoral reward and punishment, they are more likely to see government as their servant instead of their master. As Benjamin Ginsberg writes, "Democratic elections help to persuade citizens that expansion of the state's powers represents an increase in the state's capacity to serve them."[50]

Therefore, rather than wishing to be protected from the state, citizens in a democracy often seek to benefit from it. It is no coincidence that "individuals who believe they can influence the government's actions are also more likely to believe, in turn, that the government should have more power."[51] Voters like to feel that they are sending a message to the government to accomplish something. It should be no surprise that as democracy has spread, government has come to do more and more, and its scope has grown.

Summary

In this age of high-tech politics, campaigns have become more media oriented and far more expensive. There are really two campaigns of importance in presidential (and other) contests: the campaign for nomination and the campaign for election.

There are two ways by which delegates are selected to the national party conventions—state caucuses and primaries. The first caucus is traditionally held in Iowa, the first primary in New Hampshire. These two small atypical American states have disproportionate power in determining who will be nominated and thus become president. This influence stems from the massive media attention devoted to these early contests and the momentum generated by winning them.

Money matters in political campaigns. As the costs of campaigning have increased, it has become more essential to raise large campaign war chests. Although federal campaign finance reform has lessened the impact of big contributors, it also allowed the proliferation of PACs. Some believe that PACs have created a system of legal graft in campaigning; others say the evidence for this view is relatively weak.

In general, politicians tend to overestimate the impact of campaigns; political scientists have found that campaigning serves primarily to reinforce citizens' views as opposed to converting them. Voters make two basic decisions at election time; the first is whether to vote. Americans' right to vote is well established, but many citizens, particularly young people, do not exercise this right today. The 2004 presidential election was another in a long string of low-turnout elections. Second, those who choose to vote must decide for whom to cast their ballots. Over a generation of research on voting behavior has helped political scientists to understand the dominant role played by three factors in voters' choices: party identification, candidate evaluations, and policy positions.

Elections are the centerpiece of democracy. Few questions are more important in understanding American government than this: Do elections matter? Under the right conditions, elections can influence public policy, and policy outcomes can influence elections. Elections also legitimize the power of the state, thereby making it easier to expand the scope of the government. For better or worse, American election campaigns are clearly the most open and democratic in the world.

Internet Resources

www.fec.gov
The Federal Election Commission's reports on campaign spending can be found at this site.

www.fundrace.org
This site allows one to look up donations from particular individuals and to map contribution patterns for particular areas.

www.umich.edu/~nes
The National Election Studies are a standard source of survey data about voting behavior. You can find information about these studies, as well as some of the results from them, at this site.

www.census.gov/population/www/socdemo/voting.html
The Census Bureau's studies of registration and turnout can be found at this address.

www.annenbergpublicpolicycenter.org/naes/
A good source of information on public views during the 2004 presidential campaign.

Get Connected

The Delegate Selection Process and Presidential Nominations

Running for president is a very demanding job. It begins years before the election. An important part of the process for each candidate involves getting delegates pledged to him or her at the national party conventions. The nomination process involves a complex procedure that is neatly outlined on a Web page called "The Green Papers."

Search the Web

Go to the Green Papers page on the nomination process for 2004, *www.thegreenpapers.com/P04/*. Find your state and examine the number of delegates selected for the Democratic and Republican national conventions in 2004. Also, look at neighboring states and then find when your state selected the delegates.

Questions to Ask

- How many delegates did your state send to the Democratic and Republican national conventions in 2004? Were they selected through a primary or a caucus or some combination of methods?
- How does your state compare with neighboring states? How about states with more or less population than yours?
- Considering your state's vote for president in 2004, will your state have more or fewer delegates to the national conventions in 2008?

Why It Matters

Presidential candidates spend much time, energy, and money trying to accumulate delegates pledged to their candidacy who will attend the national convention. The media also focus on "delegate count" as an important measure to determine which candidate is leading the presidential race. It is important for you to understand how the delegate selection process works.

Get Involved

As we get closer to the 2008 presidential election, find out how you can become a delegate from your state to your party's national convention. The political parties are particularly interested in getting younger people involved.

For more exercises, go to www.longmanamericangovernment.com.

For Further Reading

Abramson, Paul R., John H. Aldrich, and David W. Rohde. *Change and Continuity in the 2004 Elections*. Washington, DC: Congressional Quarterly Press, 2006. A good overview of voting behavior in the 2004 elections, which also focuses on recent historical trends.

Bartels, Larry M. *Presidential Primaries and the Dynamics of Public Choice*. Princeton, NJ: Princeton University Press, 1988. An excellent analysis of voters' decision-making process in the nominating season.

Bimber, Bruce, and Richard Davis. *Campaigning Online: The Internet in U.S. Elections*. New York: Oxford University Press, 2003. An interesting study of how candidates use Web sites and how voters react to them.

Campbell, Angus, et al. *The American Voter*. New York: Wiley, 1960. The classic study of the American electorate in the 1950s, which has shaped scholarly approaches to the subject ever since.

Farnsworth, Stephen J., and S. Robert Lichter, *The Nightly News Nightmare: Network Television's Coverage of U.S. Presidential Elections, 1988–2000*. Lanham, MD: Rowman & Littlefield, 2003. An interesting study of the content of TV news coverage of four recent presidential election campaigns.

King, Anthony. *Running Scared*. New York: Free Press, 1997. King argues that American politicians campaign too much and govern too little.

Malbin, Michael J., ed. *The Election After Reform: Money, Politics, and the Bipartisan Campaign Reform Act*. Lanham, MD: Rowman & Littlefield, 2006. A comprehensive set of readings that covers many aspects of how the McCain-Feingold Act worked in practice.

Martin, Fenton S., and Robert U. Goehlert. *How to Research Elections*. (Washington, DC: Congressional Quarterly, 2001. A very useful guide to many sources of information about elections.

Mayer, William G., ed. *The Making of the Presidential Candidates 2004*. Lanham, MD: Rowman & Littlefield, 2004. A good set of current readings on the presidential nomination process.

Niemi, Richard G., and Herbert F. Weisberg. *Classics in Voting Behavior*. Washington, DC: Congressional Quarterly Press, 1993. An excellent set of readings on voting that have stood the test of time.

Polsby, Nelson W., and Aaron Wildavsky. *Presidential Elections*. 11th ed. Lanham, MD: Rowman & Littlefield, 2004. The classic text on the subject.

Smith, Bradley A. *Unfree Speech: The Folly of Campaign Finance Reform*. Princeton, NJ: Princeton University Press, 2001. A provocative book that argues that most regulations concerning donations to political campaigns should be eliminated.

Sorauf, Frank J. *Inside Campaign Finance: Myths and Realities*. New Haven, CT: Yale University Press, 1992. A definitive work on the impact of money on elections, an impact that Sorauf thinks is often exaggerated.

Wattenberg, Martin P. *Where Have All the Voters Gone?* Cambridge, MA: Harvard University Press, 2002. A good review of the reasons for declining voter turnout, as well as what can be done about it.

Wolfinger, Raymond E., and Steven J. Rosenstone. *Who Votes?* New Haven, CT: Yale University Press, 1980. The classic quantitative study of who turns out and why.

CHAPTER 10

Interest Groups

Chapter Outline

POLITICS IN ACTION: HOW INTEREST GROUP LOBBYISTS WORK ON SMALL DETAILS WITH BIG PAYOFFS Just before Christmas of 2002, a very unusual quarter-page advertisement appeared in the *New York Times* and other major papers around the country. It was placed by the public interest journal titled *TomPaine.commonsense* (*www.tompaine.com*). The bold headline read, "Reward $10,000: For Information Leading to the Identification of the Eli Lilly Bandit." The story told in the advertisement was one of corporate lobbyists using their influence to get a special provision written into law at the last minute with no one watching. As a public interest journal, *TomPaine.commonsense* strives to ensure open and accountable government. They regularly seek to expose cases of corporations getting sweet deals from government policymakers. Eli Lilly & Company, a giant drug manufacturer, had gotten such a deal, and *TomPaine.commonsense* sought to at least publicize this fact, if not get to the bottom of how their lobbyists accomplished the feat.

The mystery is one worthy of Sherlock Holmes. In November 2002, Congress passed a 475-page bill creating the new Department of Homeland Security. Somehow or other, a little provision was slipped into this bill that seemingly had nothing to do with the topic of homeland security. This provision gave Eli Lilly & Company something it had badly wanted—a shield from multi-million-dollar lawsuits. Lilly was facing numerous lawsuits from parents who claim that their children's autism is linked to Thimerosal, a mercury-based preservative made by Lilly that is a common ingredient in childhood vaccines. The provision diverted those suits from state courts to a federal vaccine court, where damages are capped at $250,000. How did such a measure end up in a bill dealing with homeland security? The answer is that it was sneaked in during the conference committee negotiations, which are held behind closed doors. But who did it? That's what *TomPaine.commonsense* offered $10,000 to find out.

Strangely, in a city where knowledge is power and where people are usually eager to take credit for any political accomplishment, no one in Washington was willing to take credit for the passage of the measure helping Eli Lilly. The company's lobbyists claimed ignorance. Yes, of course they had long wanted to get something like this passed. But they claimed they had never thought of getting it into the Homeland Security Act. And Office of Management and Budget Director Mitch Daniels, a former company executive at Eli Lilly, went to considerable lengths to deny any knowledge of the matter. As of this writing, the mystery still remains, and the $10,000 reward money remains unclaimed.

The worst and oldest stereotype of a lobbyist is of someone who bribes a lawmaker to get a favorable policy decision. In contrast, whoever the Eli Lilly Bandit was, he or she used leverage with members of Congress that was probably obtained by open and legal means. The fact that Eli Lilly & Company had donated $1.6 million to the national parties and to federal candidates in the preceding two years likely had something to do with what happened. It should be noted that such donations were perfectly legal and a matter of public record.

By making the American political system so openly democratic, the means have been created for an incredible array of interests to be heard loud and clear in Washington. Some critics believe that the basic problem is that there are too many interest groups making demands on the government; others feel the real problem is that the moneyed interests get a disproportionate share of access and influence. Those who are concerned the system is too democratic often argue that the result is the frustration of any proposals for changing the existing scope of government. For those most concerned with the domination of well-off interest groups, the scope of government that results is inevitably seen as helping the rich get richer. Nevertheless, there are scholars who believe the interest group system is working pretty much as the Founders intended. James Madison argued in *Federalist Paper No. 10* that the sphere of influence must be extended in order to prevent any one group from having too much power. Whether we are far along in reaching this goal is a crucial question for you to consider when reading this chapter.

Our nation's capital has become a hub of interest group activity. On any given day, it is possible to observe pressure groups in action in many forums. In the morning, you could attend congressional hearings in which you are sure to see interest groups testifying for and against proposed legislation. At the Supreme Court, you might stop in to watch a public interest lawyer arguing for strict enforcement of environmental regulations. Take a break for lunch at a nice Washington restaurant, and you may see a lobbyist entertaining a member of Congress.

You could spend the afternoon in any department of the executive branch (such as commerce, labor, or the interior), where you might catch bureaucrats working out rules and regulations with friendly—or sometimes unfriendly—representatives of the interests they are charged with overseeing. You could stroll past the impressive headquarters of the National Rifle Association, the AFL-CIO, or the American Association of Retired Persons to get a sense of the size of some of the major lobbying organizations. To see some lobbying done on college students' behalf, you might drop by One Dupont Circle, where all the higher education groups have their offices. These groups lobby for student loans and scholarships as well as for aid to educational institutions. At dinnertime, if you are able to finagle an invitation to a Georgetown cocktail party, you may see lobbyists trying to get the ear of government officials—both elected and unelected.

All this lobbying activity poses an interesting paradox: Although turnout in elections has declined since 1960, participation in interest groups has mushroomed. As Kay Schlozman and John Tierney write, "Recent decades have witnessed an expansion of astonishing proportions in the involvement of private organizations in Washington politics."[1] This chapter will explore the factors behind the interest group explosion, how these groups enter the policymaking process and what they get out of it.

Defining Interest Groups

interest group

An organization of people with shared policy goals entering the policy process at several points to try to achieve those goals. Interest groups pursue their goals in many arenas.

The term *interest group* seems simple enough to define. Interest refers to a policy goal; a group is a combination of people. An **interest group**, therefore, is an organization of people with similar policy goals who enter the political process to try to achieve those aims. Whatever their goals—outlawing abortion or ensuring the right to one or regulating tax loopholes or creating new ones—interest groups pursue them in many arenas. Every branch of government is fair game; every level of government, local to federal, is a possible target. A policy battle lost in Congress may be turned around when it comes to bureaucratic implementation or to the judicial process.

This multiplicity of policy arenas helps distinguish interest groups from political parties. Parties fight their battles through the electoral process; they run candidates for public office. Interest groups may support candidates for office, but American interest groups do not run their own slate of candidates, as in some other countries. In other words, no serious candidate is ever listed on the ballot as a candidate of the National Rifle Association or Common Cause. It may be well known that a candidate is actively supported by a particular group, but that candidate faces the voters as a Democrat, a Republican, or a third-party candidate.

Another key difference between parties and interest groups is that interest groups are often policy specialists, whereas parties are policy generalists. Most interest groups have a handful of key policies to push: A farm group cares little about the status of urban transit; an environmental group has its hands full bringing polluters into court without worrying about the minimum wage. Unlike political parties, these groups do not face the constraints imposed by trying to appeal to everyone.

All candidates for pubic office seek to obtain the votes of various interest groups. Here, John Kerry tours a coal mine in order to learn about concerns of coal miners and to show that he cares about people like them.

Theories of Interest Group Politics

Understanding the debate over whether interest groups create problems for government in America requires an examination of three important theories, which were introduced in Chapter 1. **Pluralist theory** argues that interest group activity brings representation to all. According to pluralists, groups compete and counterbalance one another in the political marketplace. In contrast, **elite theory** argues that a few groups (primarily the wealthy) have most of the power. Finally, **hyperpluralist theory** asserts that too many groups are getting too much of what they want, resulting in government policy that is often contradictory and lacking in direction. The following sections will examine each of these three theories with respect to interest groups.

Pluralism and Group Theory

Pluralist theory rests its case on the many centers of power in the American political system. Pluralists consider the extensive organization of competing groups evidence that influence is widely dispersed among them. They believe that groups win some and lose some but that no group wins or loses all the time. Pluralist theorists offer a *group theory of politics*, which contains several essential arguments.[2]

- **Groups provide a key link between people and government.** All legitimate interests in the political system can get a hearing from government once they are organized.
- **Groups compete.** Labor, business, farmers, consumers, environmentalists, and other interests constantly make competing claims on the government.
- **No one group is likely to become too dominant.** When one group throws its weight around too much, its opponents are likely to intensify their organization and thus restore balance to the system. For every action, there is a reaction.
- **Groups usually play by the "rules of the game."** In the United States, group politics is a fair fight, with few groups lying, cheating, stealing, or engaging in violence to get their way.
- **Groups weak in one resource can use another.** Big business may have money on its side, but labor has numbers. All legitimate groups are able to affect public policy by one means or another.

Pluralists would never deny that some groups are stronger than others or that competing interests do not always get an equal hearing. Still, they can point to many

pluralist theory
A theory of government and politics emphasizing that politics is mainly a competition among groups, each one pressing for its own preferred policies.

elite theory
A theory of government and politics contending that societies are divided along class lines and that an upper-class elite will rule, regardless of the formal niceties of governmental organization.

hyperpluralist theory
A theory of government and politics contending that groups are so strong that government is weakened. Hyperpluralism is an extreme, exaggerated, or perverted form of **pluralism**.

Pluralism

cases in which a potential group organized itself and, once organized, affected policy decisions. African Americans, women, and consumers are all groups who were long ignored by government officials but who, once organized, redirected the course of public policy. In sum, pluralists argue that lobbying is open to all and is therefore not to be regarded as a problem.

Elites and the Denial of Pluralism

Whereas pluralists are impressed by the vast number of organized interests, elitists are impressed by how insignificant most of them are. Real power, elitists say, is held by relatively few people, key groups, and institutions. They maintain that the government is run by a few big interests looking out for themselves—a view that the majority of the public has usually agreed with in recent decades, as you can see in Figure 10.1.

Elitists critique pluralist theory by pointing to the concentration of power in a few hands. Where pluralists find dispersion of power, elitists find interlocking and concentrated power centers. About one-third of top institutional positions—corporate boards, foundation boards, university trusteeships, and so on—are occupied by

Figure 10.1 Perceptions of the Dominance of Big Interests

Would you say the government is pretty much run by a few big interests looking out for themselves or that it is run for the benefit of all people?

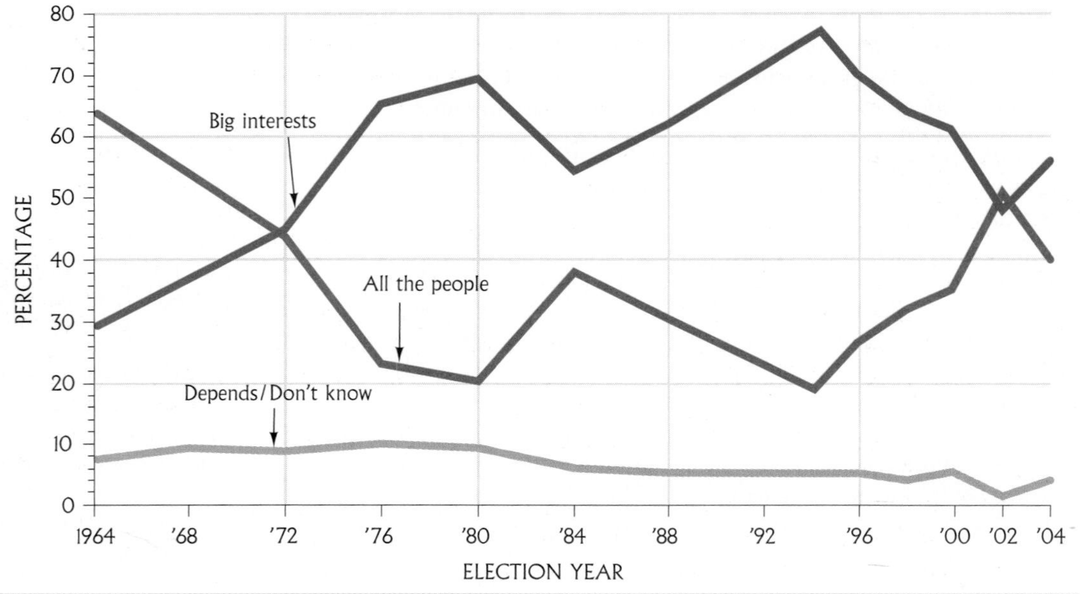

Source: Authors' analysis of 1964–2004 American National Election Study data.

people who hold more than one such position.[3] Elitists see the rise of mighty multinational corporations as further tightening the control of corporate elites. A prime example is America's giant oil companies. Robert Engler has tried to show that government has always bent over backward to maintain high profits for the oil industry.[4] When they come up against the power of these multinational corporations, consumer interests are readily pushed aside, according to elitists.

In sum, the elitist view of the interest group system makes the following assertions:

- The fact that there are numerous groups proves nothing because groups are extremely unequal in power.
- Awesome power is held by the largest corporations.
- The power of a few is fortified by an extensive system of interlocking directorates.
- Other groups may win many minor policy battles, but the corporate elites prevail when it comes to the big decisions.

Thus, even honest lobbying is a problem, say elite theorists, because it benefits a few at the expense of many.

Hyperpluralism and Interest Group Liberalism

Hyperpluralists, also critical of pluralism, argue that the pluralist system is out of control. Theodore Lowi coined the phrase *interest group liberalism* to refer to the government's excessive deference to groups. Interest group liberalism holds that virtually all pressure-group demands are legitimate and that the job of the government is to advance them all.[5]

In an effort to please and appease every interest, agencies proliferate, conflicting regulations expand, programs multiply, and, of course, the budget skyrockets. If environmentalists want clean air, government imposes clean-air rules; if businesses complain that cleaning up pollution is expensive, government gives them a tax write-off for pollution control equipment. If the direct-mail industry wants cheap rates, government gives it to them; if people complain about junk mail, the Postal Service gives them a way to take their names off mailing lists. If cancer researchers convince the government to launch an antismoking campaign, tobacco sales may drop; if they do, government will subsidize tobacco farmers to ease their loss.[6]

Interest group liberalism is promoted by the network of **subgovernments** in the American political system that exercise a great deal of control over specific policy areas. These subgovernments, which are also known as iron triangles, are composed of key interest group leaders interested in policy X, the government agency in charge of administering policy X, and the members of congressional committees and subcommittees handling policy X.

All the elements composing subgovernments have the same goal: protecting their self-interest. The network of subgovernments in the agricultural policy area of tobacco is an excellent example. Tobacco interest groups include the Tobacco Institute, the Retail Tobacco Distributors of America, and the tobacco growers. Various agencies in the Department of Agriculture administer tobacco programs,

subgovernments
A network of groups within the American political system that exercise a great deal of control over specific policy areas. Also known as iron triangles, subgovernments are composed of interest group leaders interested in a particular policy, the government agency in charge of administering that policy, and the members of congressional committees and subcommittees handling that policy.

Why It Matters

Theories of Interest Group Politics
Suppose James Madison's descendants were studying American government in order to assess how well the system he devised controls the power of special interests. They would definitely draw different conclusions depending on whether they assessed the current system using pluralist, elitist, or hyperpluralist interpretations. A pluralist interpretation could be seen as evidence that Madison's system has worked as intended. An elitist interpretation would hold that the wealthy in particular hold too much power, whereas a hyperpluralist interpretation would indicate that too many groups have too much power.

and they depend on the tobacco industry's clout in Congress to help keep their agency budgets safe from cuts. Finally, most of the members of the House Tobacco Subcommittee are from tobacco-growing regions. All these elements want to protect the interests of tobacco farmers. Similar subgovernments of group-agency-committee ties exist in scores of other policy areas.

Hyperpluralists' major criticism of the interest group system is that relations between groups and the government have become too cozy. Hard choices about national policy are rarely made. Instead of making choices between X and Y, the government pretends there is no need to choose and instead tries to favor both policies. It is a perfect script for policy gridlock. In short, the hyperpluralist position on group politics is characterized as follows:

- Groups have become too powerful in the political process as government tries to appease every conceivable interest.
- Interest group liberalism is aggravated by numerous subgovernments—comfortable relationships among a government agency, the interest group it deals with, and congressional subcommittees.
- Trying to please every group results in contradictory and confusing policy.

Ironically, the recent interest group explosion is seen by some scholars as weakening the power of subgovernments. As Morris Fiorina writes, "A world of active public interest groups, jealous business competitors, and packs of budding investigative reporters is less hospitable to subgovernment politics than a world lacking in them."[7] With so many more interest groups to satisfy and with many of them competing against one another, a cozy relationship between groups and the government is plainly more difficult to sustain.

What Makes an Interest Group Successful?

In recent years, *Fortune* magazine has issued a yearly list of the 25 most powerful interest groups in politics. Table 10.1 displays one of their lists and a quick look will probably reveal some surprises. Some of these powerful lobbying groups are relatively unknown.

Many factors affect the success of an interest group, as indicated by the diversity of groups in *Fortune*'s "Power 25." Among these factors are the size of the group, its intensity, and its financial resources. While greater intensity and more financial resources work to a group's advantage, surprisingly, smaller groups are more likely to achieve their goals than larger groups.

The Surprising Ineffectiveness of Large Groups

In one of the most often quoted statements concerning interest groups, E. E. Schattschneider wrote that "pressure politics is essentially the politics of small groups. . . . Pressure tactics are not remarkably successful in mobilizing general

Table 10.1 The Power 25

Fortune magazine has long been famous for its lists of the richest companies and individuals in the country. Lately, editors have expanded their analysis to ranking the most powerful lobbying associations. Members of Congress, prominent congressional staffers, senior White House aides, and top-ranking officers of the largest lobbying groups in Washington were asked to assess, on a scale of 0 to 100, the political clout of 87 major trade associations, labor unions, and interest groups. Here is the list of the groups that finished in the top 25 in terms of political clout in 2001.

1. National Rifle Association
2. American Association of Retired Persons
3. National Federation of Independent Business
4. American Israel Public Affairs Committee
5. Association of Trial Lawyers of America
6. AFL-CIO
7. Chamber of Commerce
8. National Beer Wholesalers Association
9. National Association of Realtors
10. National Association of Manufacturers
11. National Association of Homebuilders
12. American Medical Association
13. American Hospital Association
14. National Education Association
15. American Farm Bureau Federation
16. Motion Picture Association of America
17. National Association of Broadcasters
18. National Right to Life Committee
19. Health Insurance Association of America
20. National Restaurant Association
21. National Governors' Association
22. Recording Industry
23. American Bankers Association
24. Pharmaceutical Research and Manufacturers of America
25. International Brotherhood of Teamsters

Source: Fortune magazine.

Successful Interest Groups

interests."[8] There are perfectly good reasons why consumer groups are less effective than producer groups, patients are less effective than doctors, and energy conservationists are less effective than oil companies: Small groups have organizational advantages over large groups.

To shed light on this point, it is important to distinguish between a potential and an actual group. A **potential group** is composed of all people who might be group members because they share some common interest.[9] In contrast, an **actual group** is composed of those in the potential group who choose to join. Groups vary enormously in the degree to which they enroll their potential membership. Consumer organizations are minuscule when compared with the total number of consumers, which is almost every American. Some organizations, however, do very well in organizing virtually all their potential members. The National Beer Wholesalers Association (ranked number 8 in Table 10.1), the Tobacco Institute,

potential group
All the people who might be **interest group** members because they share some common interest. A potential group is almost always larger than an actual group.

actual group
That part of the potential group consisting of members who actually join.

and the Air Transport Association include a good portion of their potential members. Compared with consumers, these groups are tightly organized.

Economist Mancur Olson explains this phenomenon in *The Logic of Collective Action.*[10] Olson points out that all groups, unlike individuals, are in the business of providing collective goods. A **collective good** is something of value, such as clean air, that cannot be withheld from a potential group member. When the AFL-CIO wins a higher minimum wage, all low-paid workers benefit, regardless of whether they are members of the union. In other words, members of the potential group share in benefits that members of the actual group work to secure. If this is the case, an obvious and difficult problem results: Why should potential members work for something if they can get it free? Why join the group, pay dues, and work hard for a goal when a person can benefit from the group's activity without doing anything at all? A perfectly rational response is thus to sit back and let other people do the work. This is commonly known as the **free-rider problem**.

collective good

Something of value (money, a tax write-off, prestige, clean air, and so on) that cannot be withheld from a group member.

free-rider problem

The problem faced by unions and other groups when people do not join because they can benefit from the group's activities without officially joining. The bigger the group, the more serious the problem.

The bigger the group, the more serious the free-rider problem. That is the gist of **Olson's law of large groups**: "The larger the group, the further it will fall short of providing an optimal amount of a collective good."[11] Small groups thus have an organizational advantage over large ones. In a small group, members' shares of the collective good may be great enough that they will try to secure it. The old saying that "everyone can make a difference" is much more credible in the case of a relatively small group. In the largest groups, however, each member can expect to get only a tiny share of the policy gains. Weighing the costs of participation against the relatively small benefits, the temptation is always to "let somebody else do it." Therefore, as Olson argues, the larger the potential group, the less likely potential members are to contribute.

Olson's law of large groups

Advanced by Mancur Olson, a principle stating that "the larger the group, the further it will fall short of providing an optimal amount of a collective good."

This distinct advantage of small groups helps explain why consumer groups have a hard time making ends meet. Such groups claim to seek "public interest" goals, but the gains they win are usually spread thin over millions of people. In contrast, the lobbying costs and benefits for business are concentrated. Suppose, for example, that consumer advocates take the airlines to court over charges of price fixing and force the airlines to return $10 million to consumers in the form of lower prices. This $10 million settlement is spread over 300 million Americans—about 3 cents per person (actually, the benefit is a little higher if one divides only by the number of people who use airlines). The $10 million airline loss is shared by 60 carriers at over $165,000 apiece. One can quickly see which side will be better organized in such a struggle.

In sum, Olson's law of large groups explains why interest groups with relatively few members are often so effective. The power of business in the American political system is thus due to more than just money as proponents of elite theory would have us believe. Besides their financial strength, wealthy corporations also enjoy an inherent size advantage. Because there are a limited number of multinational corporations, these businesses have an easier time organizing themselves for political action than larger potential groups, such as consumers. Once well organized, large groups may be very effective, but it is much harder for them to get together in the first place.

The primary way for large potential groups to overcome Olson's law is to provide attractive benefits for only those who join the organization. **Selective benefits**

selective benefits

Goods (such as information publications, travel discounts, and group insurance rates) that a group can restrict to those who pay their annual dues.

are goods that a group can restrict to those who pay their yearly dues, such as information publications, travel discounts, and group insurance rates. The number 2 rated group in *Fortune*'s "Power 25"—the American Association of Retired Persons—has built up a membership list of 35 million senior citizens by offering a variety of selective benefits (see Figure 10.2). Similarly, Consumers Union gains most of its members not because of its efforts on behalf of product safety but by offering the selective benefit of receiving *Consumer Reports*, a monthly magazine that rates the reliability, safety, and cost effectiveness of products.

Intensity

Another way a large potential group may be mobilized is through an issue that people feel intensely about. Intensity is a psychological advantage that can be enjoyed by small and large groups alike. When a group shows that it cares deeply about an issue, politicians are more likely to listen; many votes may be won or lost on a single issue. The rise of single-issue groups (discussed in Chapter 1) has been one of the most dramatic political developments in recent years. Even college students have gotten into the act, forming groups to lobby against tuition increases in recent years, as you can read about in "Young People and Politics: The Virginia 21 Coalition."

A **single-issue group** can be defined as a group that has a narrow interest, dislikes compromise, and single-mindedly pursues its goal. Anti–Vietnam War activists may have formed the first modern single-issue group. Opponents of nuclear power plants, gun control (ranked number 1 in the "Power 25"), and abortion are some of

single-issue groups
Groups that have a narrow interest, tend to dislike compromise, and often draw membership from people new to politics. These features distinguish them from traditional **interest groups**.

Figure 10.2 The Benefits of Membership in the American Association of Retired Persons

This chart illustrates the answers given by a sample of members of the American Association of Retired Persons when they were asked why they had joined the organization.

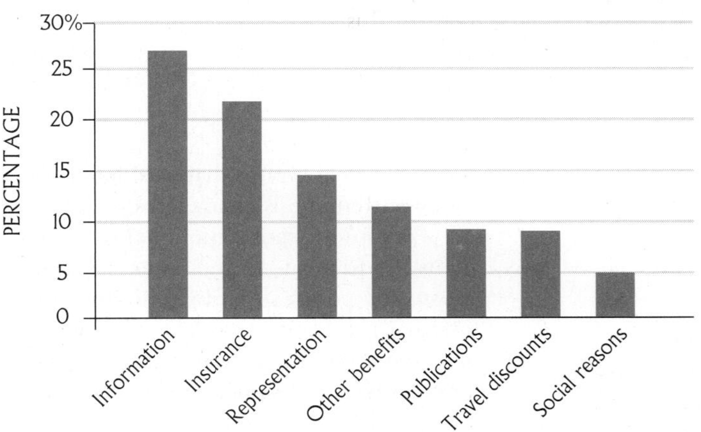

Source: American Association for Retired Persons.

YOUNG PEOPLE AND POLITICS

The Virginia 21 Coalition

As budget crunches have hit most states in recent years, many state legislatures have cut back on funding for higher education and approved sharp increases in tuition at public colleges and universities. In response, college students in some states have started to form interest groups to fight against further tuition increases. In Virginia, a group called the "21st Century Virginia Coalition," or simply "Virginia 21" for short, has recently had some success in getting the state's politicians to listen to the opinions of college students regarding funding for higher education.

Virginia 21 first entered the political scene with a campaign to garner support for a bond referendum on the 2002 Virginia ballot to provide over $900 million to state universities for capital improvements. The group raised over $17,000 to support the campaign, made roughly 20,000 telephone calls to round up votes for it, and aired a student-written and student-produced radio commercial on behalf of the referendum, which passed with overwhelming support.

One of the organization's priorities was to push for a 1 cent increase in the state's sales tax that would be dedicated to increasing funds available for education. The organization collected over 10,000 signatures for a petition titled "Fund Virginia's Future" and presented them to the state legislature. But they grabbed more attention when they dropped off over 200,000 pennies at the office of the state treasurer in support of the proposed 1 cent increase in the sales tax. The pennies weighed approximately three-quarters of a ton, and the gesture was designed to show that college students care a ton about the funding of higher education. The local media could hardly ignore such a gripping visual image.

In 2006, Virginia 21 successfully lobbied the state legislature to pass a bill designed to cut the costs of textbooks for students in Virginia colleges. The measure required public universities to come up with guidelines mandating that professors acknowledge that they are aware of the exact costs of the books they assign and to specify whether supplements sold with these books are actually required.

Virginia 21 is committed to lobbying the state legislature to substantially increase funds for higher education. It may or may not succeed in this goal, but it does seem destined to at least make sure that the views of college students are heard by policymakers. As of 2006, the Coalition had 22,000 members.

Questions for Discussion

- Would you give money and/or volunteer for a group in your state like Virginia 21? Why or why not?
- Which of the strategies of interest group lobbying discussed in this chapter do you think would be most effective for a group like Virginia 21?

Source: www.virginia21.org/.

the many such groups that exist today. All these groups deal with issues that evoke the strong emotions characteristic of single-interest groups.

Perhaps the most emotional issue of recent times has been that of abortion. As befits the intensity of the issue, activities have not been limited to conventional means of political participation. Protesting—often in the form of blocking entrances to abortion clinics—has now become a common practice for antiabortion activists. Pro-choice activists have organized as well, especially in the wake of the 1989 *Webster v. Reproductive Health Services* case, which allowed states greater freedom to restrict abortions. Both groups' positions are clear, not subject to compromise, and influence their vote. Regardless of which side candidates for political office are on, they will be taking heat on the abortion issue for years to come.

Financial Resources

One of the major indictments of the American interest group system is that it is biased toward the wealthy. When Bob Dole was the majority leader in the Senate, he once remarked that he had never been approached by a Poor People's political action committee. There is no doubt that money talks in the American political system, and those who have it get heard. All groups listed in Table 10.1 spend over a million dollars a year on lobbying and campaign contributions. A big campaign contribution may ensure a phone call, a meeting, or even a favorable vote or action on a particular policy. When Lincoln Savings and Loan Chair Charles Keating was asked whether the $1.3 million he had funneled into the campaigns of five U.S. senators had anything to do with these senators later meeting with federal regulators on his behalf, he candidly responded, "I certainly hope so."

Interest Groups and Campaign Finance

It is important to emphasize, however, that even on some of the most important issues, the big interests do not always win. An excellent example of this is the Tax Reform Act of 1986. In *Showdown at Gucci Gulch,* two reporters from the *Wall Street Journal* chronicle the improbable victory of sweeping tax reform.[12] In this case, a large group of well-organized, highly paid (and Gucci-clad) lobbyists were unable to preserve many of their most prized tax loopholes. One of the heroes of the book, former Senator Robert Packwood of Oregon, was Congress's top political action committee recipient during the tax reform struggle; he had raked in $992,000 for his reelection campaign. As chair of the Senate Finance Committee, however, Packwood ultimately turned against the hordes of lobbyists trying to get his ear on behalf of various loopholes. The only way to deal with the tax loophole problem, he concluded, was to go virtually cold turkey by eliminating all but a very few. "There is special interest after special interest that is hit in this bill," Packwood gloated, pointing out that many of them contributed to his campaign. In the end, passage of the reform bill offered "encouraging proof that moneyed interests could not always buy their way to success in Congress."[13]

How Groups Try to Shape Policy

No interest group has enough staff, money, or time to do everything possible to achieve its policy goals. Interest groups must therefore choose from a variety of tactics. The four basic strategies are lobbying, electioneering, litigation, and appealing to the public.

Lobbying

lobbying
According to Lester Milbrath, a "communication, by someone other than a citizen acting on his own behalf, directed to a governmental decision maker with the hope of influencing his decision."

The term **lobbying** comes from the place where petitioners used to collar legislators. In the early years of politics in Washington, members of Congress had no offices and typically stayed in boardinghouses or hotels while Congress was in session. A person could not call them up on the phone or make an appointment with their secretary; the only sure way of getting in touch with a member of Congress was to wait in the lobby where he was staying to catch him either coming in or going out. These people were dubbed *lobbyists* because they spent so much of their time waiting in lobbies.

Of course, merely loitering in a lobby does not make one a lobbyist; there must be a particular reason for such action. Lester Milbrath has offered a more precise definition of the practice. He writes that lobbying is a "communication, by someone other than a citizen acting on his or her own behalf, directed to a governmental decision maker with the hope of influencing his or her decision."[14] Lobbyists, in other words, are political persuaders who represent organized groups. They usually work in Washington, handling groups' legislative business. They are often former legislators themselves. Over 40 percent of members of Congress who retired between 1998 and 2004 registered as lobbyists, according to a 2005 study by Public Citizen's Congress Watch—many of them earning sums they only could have dreamed of as lawmakers.[15]

Lobbyists

There are two basic types of lobbyists. Members of the first type are regular, paid employees of a corporation, union, or association. They may hold a title such as vice president for government relations, but everyone knows that their office is in Washington for a reason, even if the company headquarters is in Houston. Members of the second type are available for hire on a temporary basis. One group may be too small to afford a full-time lobbyist; another may have a unique but temporary need for access to Congress or the executive branch. Several thousand Washingtonians are available as "lobbyists for hire."

Although lobbyists are primarily out to influence members of Congress, it is important to remember that they can be of help to them as well. Ornstein and Elder list four important ways in which lobbyists can help members of Congress.[16]

- **They are an important source of information.** Members of Congress have to concern themselves with many policy areas; lobbyists can confine themselves

Lobbyists have never been held in high esteem by the public, and they have come under especially harsh criticism in recent years. Nevertheless, lobbyists play an important role in the legislative process.

to only one area and can thus provide specialized expertise. If information is power, then lobbyists can often be potent allies.

- **They can help politicians with political strategy for getting legislation through.** Lobbyists are politically savvy people, and they can be useful consultants. When Leon Panetta served as White House chief of staff in the Clinton administration, he regularly convened a small group of Washington lobbyists to discuss how the administration should present its proposals.[17]
- **They can help formulate campaign strategy and get the group's members behind a politician's reelection campaign.** Labor union leaders, for example, often provide help in how to appeal to typical working people, and they often provide volunteers to help out in campaigns as well.
- **They are a source of ideas and innovations.** Lobbyists cannot introduce bills, but they can peddle their ideas to politicians eager to attach their name to an idea that will bring them political credit.

You Are a Lobbyist

As Richard Hall and Alan Deardorff have recently argued, lobbying can often be viewed as a form of "legislative subsidy," which they define as a "matching grant of costly policy information, political intelligence, and labor to the enterprises of strategically selected legislators."[18] They argue that the purpose of such a strategy is not to change anyone's mind but rather to help one's political allies.

Like anything else, lobbying can be done crudely or gracefully. Lobbyists can sometimes be heavy-handed. They can threaten or cajole a legislator, implying that electoral defeat is a certain result of not "going along." They can even make it clear that money flows to the reelection coffers of those who cooperate. It is often difficult to tell the difference between lobbying as a shady business and lobbying as a strictly professional representation of legitimate interests. One particular type of lobbying that has recently drawn criticism is lobbying on behalf of municipal governments, as you can read about in "Issues of the Times: Should Municipal Governments Be Hiring Lobbyists?" printed in the *Times Reader* at the back of this book.

Political scientists disagree about the effectiveness of lobbying. Much evidence suggests that lobbyists' power over policy is often exaggerated. A classic 1950s study of the influence of groups on foreign trade policy started with the hypothesis that when major business lobbies spoke, Congress listened—and acted accordingly.[19] Instead, the study found groups involved in trade policy to be ineffective, understaffed, and underfinanced. Usually the lobbyists were too disorganized to be effective. Members of Congress often had to pressure the interest groups to actively support legislation that would be in their own interest. Similarly, Milbrath concluded his own analysis of lobbying by arguing that "there is relatively little influence or power in lobbying per se."[20] Lobbyists are most effective as information sources, he claims, and are relatively ineffectual in winning over legislators.

Gun Rights and Gun Control

Plenty of other evidence, however, suggests that sometimes lobbying can persuade legislators to support a certain policy.[21] The National Rifle Association, which for years kept major gun control policies off the congressional agenda, has long been one of Washington's most effective lobbying groups.[22] In a more specific example, intensive lobbying by the nation's most wealthy senior citizens—enraged by the tax burden imposed on them by the Catastrophic Health Care Act—led Congress to repeal the act only a year after it was passed in the late 1980s.

Nailing down the specific effects of lobbying is difficult, partly because it is difficult to isolate its effects from other influences. Lobbying clearly works best on people already committed to the lobbyist's policy position. Thus, like campaigning,

For years, the National Rifle Association has successfully lobbied against gun control measures, arguing that the Second Amendment to the Constitution guarantees all citizens the right to bear arms. Charlton Heston has long been a prominent member of the group and served for a time as its president.

Gun Control

lobbying is directed toward primarily activating and reinforcing supporters. For example, antiabortion lobbyists would not think of approaching California's Barbara Boxer to attempt to convert her to their position because Boxer clearly supports the pro-choice movement. If Senator Boxer is lobbied by anyone on the abortion issue, it will be by the pro-choice faction, urging her not to compromise with the opposition.

Political Action Committees

Electioneering

Because lobbying works best with those already on the same side, getting the right people into office and keeping them there is also a key strategy of interest groups. Many groups therefore get involved in **electioneering**—aiding candidates financially and getting group members out to support them.

electioneering
Direct group involvement in the electoral process. Groups can help fund campaigns, provide testimony, and get members to work for candidates, and some form **political action committees**.

Political action committees (PACs) provide a means for groups to participate in electioneering. The number of PACs has exploded from 608 in 1974 to 4,210 in 2006, according to the Federal Election Commission. No major interest group seeking to exert influence on the electoral process these days can pass up the opportunity to funnel money honestly and openly into the campaign coffers of its supporters. For example, Major League Baseball's PAC gave $288,000 to congressional candidates and the major parties during the 2002 election cycle, mostly to members of congressional committees who were considering legislation that might impact the business of baseball. As economist Roger Noll of Stanford University remarked about the activity of baseball's PAC, "Any industry that has any kind of dependence on government is pretty much forced to do what they're doing," he said. "Unfortunately, this has become the cost of doing business."[23]

political action committees
Political funding vehicles created by the 1974 campaign finance reforms. A corporation, union, or some other interest group can create a political action committee (PAC) and register it with the Federal Election Commission, which will meticulously monitor the PAC's expenditures.

As campaign costs have risen, PACs have come along to help pay the bill. In recent years, nearly half the candidates running for reelection to the House of Representatives have received the majority of their campaign funds from PACs. Furthermore, their challengers did not enjoy this advantage. PACs gave a whopping $207 million to House incumbents during the 2003-2004 election cycle, compared to a mere $15 million to the challengers. Why does PAC money go so overwhelmingly to incumbents? The answer is that PAC contributions are basically investments for the future, and incumbents are the most likely to return the investment. When R. Kenneth Godwin and Barry J. Seldon asked a sample of PAC directors to explain why their PACs gave money to certain candidates, the top five answers were that these candidates were (1) on committees that are important to their interests, (2) very supportive of issues important to them, (3) from a district or state where they had facilities, (4) helping them with executive and regulatory agencies, and (5) in leadership positions that enabled them to influence issues that affect the PAC.[24]

Only a handful of serious congressional candidates have resisted the lure of PAC money in recent years. One candidate described his experiences trying to get on the PAC bandwagon. When Democrat Steve Sovern ran for the House from Iowa's Second District, he made the now common pilgrimage to Washington to meet with potential contributors. "I found myself in line with candidates from all over," he reported. Each PAC had eager candidates fill out a multiple-choice questionnaire on issues important to the PAC. Candidates who shared the same concerns and views and who looked like winners got the money. Sovern later reported that "the process

PACs and the Money Trails

Why It Matters

PACs

The great increase in the number of PACs over the past several decades has enabled far more groups to become involved in electioneering. If more participation is always desirable, then the increase of PACs has to be considered a positive development. But given that only groups that can successfully organize and raise substantial sums of money can take advantage of the PAC system, some obvious biases have been introduced to the electoral process because of the increased importance of PACs.

made me sick." After his defeat, he organized his own PAC called LASTPAC (for Let the American System Triumph), which urged candidates to shun PAC campaign contributions.[25] There have been serious calls to do away with PACs altogether, as discussed in "You Are the Policymaker: Should PACs Be Eliminated?"

In addition to their role in financing campaigns, interest groups also participate in elections in numerous other ways. Among these are recruiting interest groups members to run as candidates for office, issuing official group endorsements, providing volunteer labor to participate in campaign work, and sending delegates to state and national party conventions to try to influence party platforms.

Litigation

If interest groups fail in Congress or get only a vague piece of legislation, the next step is to go to court in the hope of getting specific rulings. Karen Orren has linked much of the success of environmental interest groups to their use of lawsuits. "Frustrated in Congress," she wrote, "they have made an end run to the courts, where they have skillfully exploited and magnified limited legislative gains."[26]

Environmental legislation, such as the Clean Air Act, typically includes written provisions allowing ordinary citizens to sue for enforcement. As a result, every federal agency involved in environmental regulation now has hundreds of suits pending against it at any given time. These suits may not halt environmentally troublesome practices, but the constant threat of a lawsuit increases the likelihood that businesses will consider the environmental impact of what they do.

Perhaps the most famous interest group victories in court were by civil rights groups in the 1950s. While civil rights bills remained stalled in Congress, these groups won major victories in court cases concerning school desegregation, equal housing, and labor market equality. More recently, consumer groups have used suits against businesses and federal agencies as a means of enforcing consumer regulations. As long as law schools keep producing lawyers, groups will fight for their interests in court.

One tactic that lawyers employ to make the views of interest groups heard by the judiciary is the filing of ***amicus curiae* briefs** ("friend of the court" briefs). *Amicus* briefs consist of written arguments submitted to the courts in support of one side of a case. Through these written depositions, a group states its collective position as well as how its own welfare will be affected by the outcome of the case. Numerous groups may file *amicus* briefs in highly publicized and emotionally charged cases. For example, in the case of *Regents of the University of California v. Bakke* (see Chapter 5), which challenged affirmative action programs as reverse discrimination, over 100 different groups filed *amicus* briefs. A study of participation in *amicus* briefs by Caldeira and Wright found that the Supreme Court has been accessible to a wide array of organized interests, in terms of deciding both which cases to hear and how to rule.[27]

***amicus curiae* briefs**
Legal briefs submitted by a "friend of the court" for the purpose of raising additional points of view and presenting information not contained in the briefs of the formal parties. These briefs attempt to influence a court's decision.

class action lawsuits
Lawsuits permitting a small number of people to sue on behalf of all other people similarly situated.

A more direct judicial strategy employed by interest groups is the filing of **class action lawsuits**, which enable a group of people in a similar situation to combine their common grievances into a single suit. For instance, flight attendants won a class action suit against the airline industry's regulation that all stewardesses be unmarried. As one lawyer who specializes in such cases states, "The class action is the greatest, most effective legal engine to remedy mass wrongs."[28]

YOU ARE THE POLICYMAKER

Should PACs Be Eliminated?

The effect of PAC campaign contributions on congressional votes has become a perennial issue in American politics. Critics of PACs are convinced they are distorting the democratic process and corrupting our political system in favor of those who can raise the most money. Many politicians freely admit—once they are out of office—that it is a myth to think the PACs don't want something in return. They may only want to be remembered on one or two crucial votes or with an occasional intervention with government agencies, but multiply this by the thousands of special interests that are organized today, and the worst fears of the hyperpluralists could be realized—a government that constantly yields to every special interest.

Common Cause (*www.commoncause.org*) has made it their primary mission to expose what they see as the evils of the PAC system. They argue that the influence of corporate PACs on Capitol Hill has led to "corporate welfare" and costs taxpayers billions of dollars. For example, Common Cause maintains that the timber industry prevailed against a Clinton administration proposal in 1997 to eliminate logging subsidies because of their $8 million in recent PAC contributions. Similarly, they argue that $5 million in PAC contributions from the broadcast industry led to a massive government giveaway of free digital TV licenses worth as much as $70 billion. And Common Cause and others have attributed the failure of Congress to further regulate tobacco and cigarette advertising to the more than $30 million of PAC contributions from tobacco companies over the past decade.

However, others argue that connection is not causation. They believe that most members of Congress are not affected by PAC contributions, which come largely from groups they already agree with anyway. Defenders of the PAC system also point out that the PAC system further increases participation in the political process. As opposed to individual donations, PACs—which represent groups of people—allow better representation of occupational groups. The PAC system allows people with common professional interests, such as farmers, lawyers, dentists, and college professors, to express their support of candidates jointly through political contributions.

Similarly, corporation PACs represent the interests of many stockholders and employees with common political interests. If James Madison's notion that the key to controlling the power of interest groups is to expand their sphere of participation, then PACs certainly do this according to their defenders. Beyond this, the money for today's expensive media campaigns has to come from somewhere. Those who wish to maintain the PAC system typically point to the alternative of public financing of campaigns as impractical and unpopular given the low rate of participation on the voluntary income tax check-off box.

You be the policymaker: What would you do? Would you consider eliminating PACs? Or, as a middle course, would you favor further limits on the amount of money they can donate?

Going Public

Groups are also interested in the opinions of the public. Because public opinion ultimately makes its way to policymakers, interest groups carefully cultivate their public image and use public opinion to their advantage when they can. As Ken Kollman finds, even the wealthiest and most powerful groups in America appeal to public opinion to help their cause. For example, when the government instituted a requirement for tax withholding on savings accounts, the American Bankers Association appealed to their customers to protest this to their congressional representatives. After 22 million postcards flooded into Congress, lawmakers quickly reversed the policy.[29]

Interest Groups and Representa

Paid for by the Coalition to Scare Your Pants Off

Interest groups spent over $100 million appealing to public opinion during the debate over health care in 1994. In a counter-ad produced by the Democratic National Committee, the argument was made that opponents of the Clinton health care plan were using scare tactics. You can see the tag end of the ad in this photo.

Interest groups market not only their stand on issues but also their reputations. Business interests want people to see them as "what made America great," not as wealthy Americans trying to ensure large profits. The Teamsters Union likes to be known as a united organization of hardworking men and women, not as an organization often influenced by organized crime. Farmers promote the image of a sturdy family working to put bread on the table, not the huge agribusinesses that have largely replaced family farms. In this way, many groups try to create a reservoir of goodwill with the public.

Interest groups' appeals to the public for support have a long tradition in American politics. In 1908, AT&T launched a major magazine advertising campaign to convince people of the need for a telephone monopoly. Similarly, after President Truman proposed a system of national health insurance in 1948, the American Medical Association spent millions of dollars on ads attacking "socialized medicine." In 1994, the Health Insurance Association of America ran a $15 million nationally televised ad campaign criticizing President Clinton's health care package that many analysts believe lessened public support for the reform bill. So many groups placed advertisements regarding the Clinton health care reform package and so much money was spent (over $100 million) that many observers compared this activity to a national electoral campaign.

HOW YOU CAN MAKE A DIFFERENCE

Interest Groups

For many, the best way to influence policy and make a difference in our national life is to join an interest group or help mobilize people with like-minded concerns into political lobbies. Interest group activity is an extremely effective means to bring pressure to bear on elected officials and political parties, and as a result many groups and individuals are very successful in influencing national politics. Interest groups are ideal for this, with the desire to be active, involved citizens.

Making a Difference

Take, for instance, the case of Wes Boyd and Joan Blades—two individuals whose innovative use of the Internet for political mobilization resulted in Moveon.org, a progressive political advocacy group that has in many ways altered the course of American politics. Today, Moveon boasts a membership of 3.3 million, and in 2005 raised nine million dollars for campaigns and candidates. Moveon's founders are a perfect example of how you can get involved in helping to change America's domestic and international politics and policy.

What you can do:

- Use the Internet to meet and organize others who share your social and political concerns.
- Create a political blog where you can use Internet activism to get your voice heard.
- Research the interest groups that share your views and concerns. Contact them for more information.
- Sign up for the e-mail lists and online petitions of those groups that best match your social and political outlook.

Groups often go public to make a point through carefully staged media events. Here, senior citizens rally to drive home the point that elderly people care about Medicare and expect the promise of health care to be fulfilled.

Lately, more and more organizations have undertaken expensive public relations efforts. After September 11, the media was full of ads from various groups expressing their sympathy for the victims. Some other recent examples include Phillip Morris running ads countering the arguments of anti-tobacco legislation, Microsoft condemning its prosecution by the Justice Department for alleged monopolistic practices, and Ford and Bridgestone defending themselves against charges of negligence regarding defective tires. No one knows just how effective these image-molding efforts are, but many groups seem to believe firmly that advertising pays off.

Types of Interest Groups

Whether they are lobbying, electioneering, litigating, or appealing to the public, interest groups are omnipresent in the American political system. As with other aspects of American politics and policymaking, political scientists loosely categorize interest groups into clusters. Among the most important clusters are those that deal with (1) economic issues, (2) environmental concerns, (3) equality issues, and (4) the interests of all consumers. An examination of these four distinct types of interest groups will give you a good picture of much of the American interest group system.

Economic Interests

All economic interests are ultimately concerned with wages, prices, and profits. In the American economy, government does not determine these directly. Only on rare occasions has the government imposed wage and price controls. This has usually been during wartime, although the Nixon administration briefly used wage and price controls to combat inflation. More commonly, public policy in America has economic effects through regulations, tax advantages, subsidies and contracts, and international trade policy.

Business, labor, and farmers all fret over the impact of government regulations. Even a minor change in government regulatory policy can cost industries a great deal or bring increased profits. Tax policies also affect the livelihood of individuals and firms. How the tax code is written determines whether people and producers pay a lot or a little of their incomes to the government. Because government often provides subsidies to farmers, small businesses, railroads, minority businesses, and others, every economic group wants to get its share of direct aid and government contracts. In this era of economic global interdependence, all groups worry about import quotas, tariffs (fees imposed on imports), and the soundness of the American dollar. In short, business executives, factory workers, and farmers seek to influence government because regulations, taxes, subsidies, and international economic policy all affect their economic livelihoods. The following sections discuss some of the major organized interests and their impact on economic policy.

Farm Subsidies and Domestic Policy

Labor. Labor has more affiliated members than any other interest group except the American Association for Retired Persons. About 10 million workers are members of unions belonging to the AFL-CIO—itself a union of unions. Millions of other workers belong to unions, such as the National Education Association, the Teamsters, and the Service Employees International Union, that are not affiliated with the AFL-CIO but share common interests with them.

The major aim of American union organizations, like labor unions everywhere, is to press for policies to ensure better working conditions and higher wages. Recognizing that many workers would like to enjoy union benefits without actually joining a union and paying dues, unions have fought hard to establish the **union shop**, which requires new employees to join the union representing them. In contrast, business groups have supported **right-to-work laws**, which outlaw union membership as a condition of employment. They argue that such laws deny a basic freedom—namely, the right not to belong to a group. In 1947, the biggest blow ever to the American labor movement occurred when Congress passed the Taft-Hartley Act, permitting states to adopt right-to-work laws (known as "slave labor laws" within the AFL-CIO). Most of the states that have right-to-work laws are in the South, which traditionally has had the lowest percentage of unionized workers.

union shop
A provision found in some collective bargaining agreements requiring all employees of a business to join the union within a short period, usually 30 days, and to remain members as a condition of employment.

right-to-work law
A state law forbidding requirements that workers must join a union to hold their jobs. State right-to-work laws were specifically permitted by the Taft-Hartley Act of 1947.

The American labor movement reached its peak in 1956, when 33 percent of the nonagricultural workforce belonged to a union; since then, the percentage has declined to about 13 percent. One factor behind this decline is that low wages in other countries have diminished the American job market in a number of key manufacturing areas. Steel, once made by American workers, is now made more cheaply in Korea and imported to the United States. The United Auto Workers has found its clout greatly reduced as Detroit has faced heavy competition from Japanese automakers. Some political scientists, however, believe labor's problems result from more than the decline of blue-collar industries. Paul Johnson argues that the biggest factor causing the decline in union membership is the problems unions have had in convincing today's workers they will benefit from unionization. In particular, Johnson argues that this task has become more difficult in recent years because of employers' efforts to make nonunion jobs satisfying.[30]

Business. If the elite theorists are correct, however, and there is an American power elite, it certainly must be dominated by leaders of the biggest banks, insurance companies, and multinational corporations. Elitists' views may or may not be exaggerated, but business is certainly well organized for political action. Most large firms, such as AT&T and Ford, now have offices in Washington that monitor legislative activity. Schlozman and Tierney report that 70 percent of all interest group organizations that have a Washington presence represent business.[31] Business PACs have increased more dramatically than any other category of PACs over the past several decades. Furthermore, corporate and trade PACs contributions have shifted dramatically in favor of the Republican Party and its tax-cutting and deregulatory agenda (see "A Generation of Change: How Non-Labor PACs Have Shifted to the GOP").

Different business interests compete on many specific issues, however. Both Microsoft and Google have their lobbyists on Capitol Hill pressing their competing interests. Trucking and construction companies want more highways, but railroads do not. An increase in international trade will help some businesses expand their markets, but others may be hurt by foreign competition. Business interests are generally unified when it comes to promoting greater profits but are often fragmented when policy choices have to be made.

Hundreds of trade and product associations fight regulations that would reduce their profits and seek preferential tax treatment as well as government subsidies and contracts. America's complex schedules of tariffs are monuments to the activities of the trade associations. Although they are the least visible of Washington lobbies, their successes are measured in amendments won, regulations rewritten, and exceptions made.

Environmental Interests

You Are an Environmental Activist

Among the newest political interest groups are the environmentalists. A handful, such as the Sierra Club and the Audubon Society, have been around since the nineteenth century, but many others trace their origins to the first Earth Day, April 22, 1970. On that day, ecology-minded people marched on Washington and other places to symbolize their support for environmental protection. Just two decades later, one estimate pegged the number of environmental groups at over 10,000 and their combined revenues at $2.9 billion—demonstrating "how widely and deeply green values had permeated the society."[32]

Environmental groups have promoted pollution-control policies, wilderness protection, and population control. Perhaps more significant, however, is what they

A GENERATION OF CHANGE

How Non-Labor PACs Have Shifted to the GOP

Despite the tax-cutting and deregulatory agenda advocated by Ronald Reagan and the Republican Party in the 1980s, throughout this era business and trade association PACs gave slightly more campaign contributions to Democratic than Republican candidates for the House of Representatives. The major reason for this pattern was that the Democrats had long held the majority in the House and therefore held the balance of power on the committees through which any pro-business legislation would have to pass. Many political analysts at the time argued that business groups gave money to the Republicans because they wanted to and the Democrats because they had to (in order to curry favor with the party in power).

This situation changed markedly when the Republicans became the majority party in both the House and Senate, starting in 1995. The Republican leadership in Congress started to actively encourage business interest groups and PACs to hire Republicans as part of what has become known as the "K Street Project." The idea behind this was that if the big lobbying associations on K Street in Washington, D.C., were being run by Republicans, then the contributions would naturally go the GOP's way. As you can see in the following table, this strategy has been a successful one for the Republicans over the past generation. The Republicans now receive roughly two out of every three PAC dollars that are donated to House campaigns by corporate, trade, and nonconnected PACs. Only Labor PACs have stuck with the Democrats.

	1987–1988		2003–2004	
	TOTAL CONTRIBUTIONS TO HOUSE CANDIDATES (IN MILLIONS)	% GIVEN TO REPUBLICANS	TOTAL CONTRIBUTIONS TO HOUSE CANDIDATES (IN MILLIONS)	% GIVEN TO REPUBLICANS
Corporate PACs	31.6	48	114.0	68
Trade, membership, and health PACs	28.6	42	82.7	63
Nonconnected PACs	11.3	35	51.7	65
Labor PACs	26.9	7	51.8	13
Total	102.2	34	300.2	57

Source: Federal Election Commission.

have opposed. Their hit list has included oil drilling in Alaska's Arctic National Wildlife Refuge, nuclear power plants, strip mining, and supersonic aircraft. On these and other issues, environmentalists have exerted a great deal of influence on Congress and state legislatures.

The concerns of environmentalists often come into direct conflict with energy goals. Environmentalists insist that, in the long run, energy supplies can be ensured

without harming the environment or risking radiation exposure from nuclear power plants. On the issue of nuclear power plants, their arguments have had a profound impact on public policy. No new nuclear power plants have been approved since 1977, and many that had been in the works were canceled.[33] Short-term energy needs, however, have won out over environmental concerns in many other cases. Energy producers argue that environmentalists oppose nearly every new energy project. Given that there is no sign of a major drop in energy demands, they argue that some limited risks have to be taken. What is worse, they ask: an occasional oil spill off the shore of Alaska or long lines every day at the gas pumps? Thus, despite the opposition of environmentalists, Congress subsidized the massive trans-Alaskan pipeline, which a consortium of companies use to transport oil from Alaska's North Slope. Similarly, the strip mining of coal continues despite constant objections from environmentalists. Group politics intensifies with the clash of two public interests, such as environmental protection and an ensured supply of energy.

Equality Interests

The Fourteenth Amendment guarantees equal protection under the law. American history, though, shows that this is easier said than done. Two sets of interest groups, representing minorities and women, have made equal rights their main policy goal. Chapter 5 reviewed the long history of the civil rights movement; this section is concerned with its policy goals and organizational base.

Equality at the polls, in housing, on the job, in education, and in all other facets of American life has long been the dominant goal of African American

Environmental lobbies have been successful in preventing the building of any new nuclear power plants for the last 30 years. Some of the older nuclear plants are now being destroyed, as you can see in this photo.

groups. The oldest and largest of these groups is the National Association for the Advancement of Colored People (NAACP). It argued and won the monumental *Brown v. Board of Education* case in 1954, in which the Supreme Court held that segregated schools were unconstitutional. Although the NAACP has won many victories in principle, equality in practice has been much slower in coming. Today, civil rights groups continue to push for more effective affirmative action programs to ensure that minority groups are given educational and employment opportunities. In recent years, the NAACP's main vehicle has been the Fair Share program, which negotiates agreements with national and regional businesses to increase minority hiring and the use of minority contractors.[34] As an issue, affirmative action is not as emotionally charged as was desegregation, but it too has been controversial.

When the NAACP was just beginning, suffragists were in the streets and legislative lobbies were demanding women's right to vote. The Nineteenth Amendment, ratified in 1920, guaranteed women the vote, but other guarantees of equal protection remained absent from the Constitution. More recently, women's rights groups, such as the National Organization for Women (NOW), have lobbied for an end to gender discrimination. Their primary goal has been the passage of the Equal Rights Amendment (ERA), which states that "equality of rights under the law shall not be abridged on account of sex." Although the ERA seems dead for the moment, NOW remains committed to enacting the protection that the amendment would have constitutionally guaranteed by advocating the enactment of many individual statutes. As is often the case with interest group politics, issues are rarely settled once and for all; rather, they shift to different policy arenas.

public interest lobbies
According to Jeffrey Berry, organizations that seek "a collective good, the achievement of which will not selectively and materially benefit the membership or activities of the organization."

Consumers and Public Interest Lobbies

Pluralist theory holds that for virtually every interest in society, there is an organized group. But what about the interests of all of us—the buying public? Today thousands of organized groups are championing various causes or ideas "in the public interest." These **public interest lobbies** are organizations that seek "a collective good, the

The National Organization for Women (NOW) is a relatively new interest group, founded in 1966, but has quickly become one of the best known in the country, with over a quarter of a million members. NOW can be expected to play a prominent role in issues concerning women's rights.

achievement of which will not selectively and materially benefit the membership or activists of the organization."[35] If products are made safer by the lobbying of consumer protection groups, it is not the members of such groups alone that benefit. Rather, everyone should be better off, regardless of whether or not they joined in the lobbying.

Consumer groups have won many legislative victories. In 1973, Congress responded to consumer advocacy by creating the Consumer Product Safety Commission. Congress authorized it to regulate all consumer products and even gave it the power to ban particularly dangerous ones, bearing in mind that household products are responsible for 30,000 deaths annually. Among the products the commission has investigated are children's sleepwear (some of which contained a carcinogen), hot tubs, and lawn mowers.

Consumer groups are not the only ones that claim to be public interest groups. Groups speaking for those who cannot speak for themselves seek to protect children, animals, and the mentally ill; good-government groups such as Common Cause push for openness and fairness in government; and religious groups like the Christian Coalition crusade for the protection of ethical and moral standards in American society.

Understanding Interest Groups

The problem of interest groups in America today remains much the same as James Madison defined it over 200 years ago. A free society must allow for the representation of all groups that seek to influence political decision making. Yet groups are usually more concerned with their own self-interest than with the needs of society as a whole, and for democracy to work well, it is important that they not be allowed to assume a dominant position.

Comparing Interest Groups

Interest Groups and Democracy

Madison's solution to the problems posed by interest groups was to create a wide-open system in which many groups would be able to participate. In such an extended sphere of influence, according to Madison, groups with opposing interests would counterbalance one another. Pluralist theorists believe that a rough approximation of the public interest emerges from this competition.

With the tremendous growth of interest group politics in recent years, some observers say that Madison may at last have gotten his wish. For every group with an interest, there now seems to be a competing group to watch over it—not to mention public interest lobbies to watch over them all. Robert Salisbury argues that "the growth in the number, variety, and sophistication of interest groups represented in Washington" has transformed policymaking such that it "is not dominated so often by a relatively small number of powerful interest groups as it may once have been."[36] Paradoxically, Salisbury concludes that the increase in lobbying activity has resulted in less clout overall for interest groups—and better democracy.

Elite theorists clearly disagree with this conclusion and point to the proliferation of business PACs as evidence of more interest group corruption in American politics than ever. A democratic process requires a free and open exchange of ideas in which candidates and voters should be able to hear one another out, but PACs—the source of so much money in elections—distort the process. Elite theorists particularly note that wealthier interests are greatly advantaged by the PAC system. It is true that there are over 4,000 PACs, but the relatively few big-spending ones dominate the fund-raising game. In 2004, a quarter of all PAC contributions came from just 48 PACs, each of which gave over a million dollars. In contrast, the 2,180 smallest PACs (in terms of donations made) accounted for just 10 percent of all PAC contributions.[37]

PACs can sometimes link money to politics at the highest levels. The old party machines may have bought votes in the voting booth; the new PACs are accused of buying votes in legislatures. Technology, especially television, makes American elections expensive; candidates need money to pay for high-tech campaigns, and PACs are able to supply that money. In return, they ask only to be remembered when their interests are clearly at stake.

Hyperpluralist theorists maintain that whenever a major interest group objects strongly to proposed legislation, policymakers will bend over backward to try to accommodate it. With the formation of so many groups in recent years and with so many of them having influence in Washington, hyperpluralists argue that it has been increasingly difficult to accomplish major policy change in Washington. Thus, hyperpluralist theory offers a powerful explanation for the policy gridlock often evident in American politics today.

Interest Groups and the Scope of Government

Although individualistic, Americans are also very associational. As Alexis de Tocqueville wrote in the 1830s, "Americans of all ages, all conditions, and all dispositions constantly form associations."[38] This is not at all contradictory. By joining a number of political associations, Americans are able to politicize a variety of aspects of their own individualism. The multiplicity of the American interest group structure and the openness of American politics to inputs from interest groups allow individuals many channels for political participation and thus facilitate representation of individual interests.

Although individualism is most often treated in this book as being responsible for the relatively small scope of American government, when it works its way through interest group politics, the result is just the opposite. Individual interest groups fight to sustain government programs that are important to them, thereby making it hard for politicians ever to reduce the scope of government. Both President Carter and President Reagan remarked at the end of their time in office that their attempts to cut waste in federal spending had been frustrated by interest groups. In his farewell address, Carter "suggested that the reason he had so much difficulty in dealing with Congress was the fragmentation of power and decision making that was exploited by interest groups."[39] Similarly, Reagan remarked a month before leaving office that "special interest groups, bolstered by campaign contributions, pressure lawmakers into creating and defending spending programs."[40] Above all, most special interest groups strive to maintain established programs that benefit them.

However, one can also argue that the growth in the scope of government in recent decades accounts for a good portion of the proliferation of interest groups. The more areas in which the federal government has become involved, the more interest groups have developed to attempt to influence policy. As William Lunch notes, "A great part of the increase was occasioned by the new government responsibility for civil rights, environmental protection, and greater public health and safety."[41] For example, once the government got actively involved in protecting the environment, many groups sprung up to lobby for strong standards and enforcement. Given the tremendous effects of environmental regulations on many industries, it should come as no surprise that these industries also organized to ensure that their interests were taken into account. As Salisbury writes, many groups have "come to Washington out of need and dependence rather than because they have influence."[42] He argues that interest groups spend much of their time merely monitoring policy developments in order to alert their membership and develop reactive strategies.

Summary

This chapter discusses the vast array of interest groups in American politics—all vying for policies they prefer. Pluralists see groups as the most important way people can have their policy preferences represented in government. Hyperpluralists, though, fear that too many groups are getting too much of what they want, skillfully working the many subgovernments in the American system. Elitist theorists believe that a few wealthy individuals and multinational corporations exert control over the major decisions regarding distribution of goods and services.

A number of factors influence a group's success in achieving its policy goals. Most surprising is that small groups have an organizational advantage over large groups. Large groups often fall victim to the free-rider problem, which is explained by Olson's law of large groups. Both large and small groups can benefit from the intensity of their members' beliefs. Money always helps lubricate the wheels of power, though it is hardly a surefire guarantee of success.

Interest groups use four basic strategies to maximize their effectiveness. Lobbying is one well-known group strategy. Although the evidence on its influence is mixed, it is clear that lobbyists are most effective with those legislators already sympathetic to their side. Thus, electioneering becomes critical because it helps put supportive people in office. Often today, groups operate in the judicial as well as the legislative process, using litigation in the courts when lobbying fails or is not enough. Many also find it important to project a good image, employing public relations techniques to present themselves in the most favorable light.

This chapter also examined some of the major kinds of interest groups, particularly those concerned with economic, environmental, and equality policy. Public interest lobbies claim to be different from other interest groups, representing, they say, an important aspect of the public interest. Recently there has been a rapid growth of single-interest groups, which focus narrowly on one issue and are not inclined to compromise.

The issue of controlling interest groups remains as crucial to democracy today as it was in Madison's time. Some scholars believe that the growth of interest groups has worked to divide political influence just as Madison hoped it would. Other scholars point to the PAC system as the new way in which special interests corrupt American democracy.

Internet Resources

www.aarp.org
The official site of the American Association of Retired Persons.

www.aflcio.org
The nation's largest labor association, the AFL-CIO, posts material at this site.

www.nea.org
The site of the National Education Association.

www.greenpeaceusa.org
The place to go to learn more about the activities of this environmental protection group.

www.commoncause.org
The official site of Common Cause, one of the nation's oldest and largest public affairs interest groups.

www.freespeech.org
A site for an interest group that represents young people, particularly on Social Security issues.

Get Connected

Interest Groups and PACs

Many interest groups try to influence government by getting the right people into office and helping them stay there. This process is called electioneering, aiding candidates financially and getting members of the interest group out to vote for them. In order to contribute to campaigns, interest groups create political action committees, or PACs. The costs of campaigns have risen over the past few decades, and PACs have stepped in to help with the costs. PACs typically give to incumbent candidates, especially those who serve on committees important to the group. From what interests do the U.S. senators from your state receive campaign contributions?

Search the Web

Go to the U.S. Senate Web site, *www.senate.gov*, and find the senators from your state. Also find the committees on which they serve. Develop a hypothesis about the groups that might contribute to the senators based on their committee membership. Then go to the Web site of the Center for Responsive

Politics, *www.opensecrets.org*. Look at the most recent filings for the senators. You may also want to look at the records for the senators' opponents, if they had opponents in their most recent election.

Questions to Ask

- Which interest groups contributed the most to each senator?
- Was your hypothesis supported? Did the senators receive support from groups with an interest in the senators' committees?
- Did different interest groups contribute to each of the senators? Does it appear that political party makes a difference? How about seniority or leadership position in the Senate?
- Have you heard of any of the interest groups that contributed to your senators?

Why It Matters

As the size of government has grown, so has the number of interest groups. These groups participate in politics in part by contributing money to political campaigns. Some people complain that the amount of money is hurting politics and government in the United States. You should try to learn about the interest groups that contribute to the elected public officials who represent you. It is possible that one or more of the groups advocate a position similar to your feelings on an issue.

Get Involved

Find out more about the groups that contribute to your senators by sending one or more of them an e-mail request for information. You can find a useful list of interest groups at this Web site: *www.csuchico.edu/~kcfount/*. You may want to consider joining an interest group as well.

For more exercises, go to www.longmanamericangovernment.com.

For Further Reading

Baumgartner, Frank R., and Beth L. Leech. *Basic Interests: The Importance of Groups in Politics and in Political Science.* Princeton, NJ: Princeton University Press, 1998. An excellent review and analysis of the academic literature on interest groups.

Berry, Jeffrey M. *The New Liberalism: The Rising Power of Citizen Groups.* Washington, DC: Brookings Institution, 1999. Berry argues that citizen groups have been strikingly successful in influencing the policy agenda in recent decades.

Birnbaum, Jeffrey H., and Alan S. Murray. *Showdown at Gucci Gulch: Lawmakers, Lobbyists, and the Unlikely Triumph of Tax Reform.* New York: Vintage, 1987. A fascinating account of how the 1986 tax reform bill passed over the objections of the Gucci-clad lobbyists.

Cigler, Allan J., and Burdett A. Loomis, eds. *Interest Group Politics.* 7th ed. Washington, DC: Congressional Quarterly Press, 2007. An excellent collection of original articles on the modern interest group system.

CQ Press Editors. *Public Interest Group Profiles, 2004–5.* Washington, DC: Congressional Quarterly Press, 2004. A comprehensive reference book about interest groups that provides information about internship and employment opportunities with many groups.

Dye, Thomas R. *Who's Running America?* 7th ed. Englewood Cliffs, NJ: Prentice Hall, 2002. A good summary of the elitist view of interest groups.

Herrnson, Paul S., Ronald G. Shaiko, and Clyde Wilcox, eds. *The Interest Group Connection.* 2nd ed. Washington, DC: Congressional Quarterly Press, 2005. A collection of essays on how interest groups attempt to influence elections and the three branches of government.

Kollman, Ken. *Outside Lobbying: Public Opinion and Interest Group Strategies.* Princeton, NJ: Princeton University Press, 1998. An insightful study of how many interest groups use public opinion in the lobbying process.

Lowi, Theodore J. *The End of Liberalism.* 2nd ed. New York: Norton, 1979. A critique of the role of subgovernments and the excessive deference to interest groups in the American political system.

Olson, Mancur. *The Logic of Collective Action.* Cambridge, MA: Harvard University Press, 1965. Develops an economic theory of groups, showing how the cards are stacked against larger groups.

Rozell, Mark J., Clyde Wilcox, and David Madland. *Interest Groups in American Campaigns,* 2nd ed. Washington, DC: Congressional Quarterly Press, 2006. A good review of how interest groups are playing an increasingly important role electioneering.

CHAPTER 11

Chapter Outline

Congress

POLITICS IN ACTION: LEADING IN CONGRESS As Dennis Hastert gaveled the U.S. House of Representatives into session in January 2006, he may have wondered why he wanted the job at all. Yes, he was Speaker of the House, the highest level congressional official. And, yes, he had effectively maintained a high level of unity among his Republican colleagues for most of the past seven years. Yet the previous months had been something akin to a legislative nightmare.

President George W. Bush proposed a major reform of Social Security to begin his second term, but the public rejected it and the bill never came to a vote in Congress. Lawmakers rebuffed Bush's call to make permanent his first-term tax cuts, open the Arctic to oil drilling, and liberalize immigration rules. Legislating was difficult even in the war on terrorism. Congress had balked at renewing the USA Patriot Act, forced the president to accept tighter restrictions on the treatment of detainees, and put pressure on Bush to more clearly articulate his Iraq strategy.

To make matters worse, a Texas grand jury indicted Tom DeLay, the highly effective Republican majority leader, leaving a vacuum in the leadership of the House. At nearly every crucial turn in the previous months, it was a group of Republicans who broke from the party leadership in the House and Senate and forced concessions in major legislation or stalled it altogether.

At the same time the Democrats, emboldened by their defeat of Bush's Social Security plan, were more united in their opposition to Republican policies than they had been in years. Not one Democrat in either the House or the Senate supported the budget cuts Hastert's own party demanded to pay for the recovery from Hurricane Katrina.

It is easy to sympathize with Hastert. It *is* difficult to get anything done. The movement of legislation through the congressional labyrinth is complicated. Power is fragmented within Congress, and members of Congress are often fiercely independent. Former Senate Majority Leader Howard Baker declared that moving the Senate is like "trying to push a wet noodle."

And then there is the president. Often the majority in Congress and the chief executive are of different political parties. Even if a bill passes Congress, it may be vetoed at the other end of Pennsylvania Avenue. Even when the same party controls both Congress and the presidency, disagreements within the party may hinder policymaking.

The framers of the Constitution conceived of the legislature as the center of policymaking in America. The great disputes over public policy were to be resolved there, not in the White House or the Supreme Court. Although the prominence of Congress has ebbed and flowed over the course of American history, as often as not, Congress is the true center of power in Washington.

Congress is not only our central policymaking branch but also our principal *representative* branch. As such, it lies at the heart of American democracy. How does Congress combine its roles of representing constituents *and* making effective public policy? Not very well, according to many critics. Some argue that Congress is too responsive to constituents and, especially, to organized interests and is thus unable to make difficult choices regarding public policy. Conversely, others argue that Congress is too insulated from ordinary citizens. Many critics even support efforts to force members of Congress to retire after serving just a few terms.

Other critics focus on Congress as the source of government expansion. If Congress is responsive to a multitude of interests and those interests want government policies to aid them in some way, the logical result is an increase in the size of the public sector. In addition, do the benefits of servicing constituents provide an incentive for members of Congress to tolerate—even to expand—an already big government?

Congress's tasks become more difficult each year. On any day a representative or senator can be required to make a sensible judgment about nuclear missiles, nuclear waste dumps, abortion, trade competition with China, income tax rates, the soaring costs of Social Security and Medicare, and countless other issues. President Clinton's 1993 health care reform proposal was 1,342 pages long and weighed six pounds. Just finding time to think about these issues—much less debate them—has become increasingly difficult.

Despite the many demands of the job, there is no shortage of men and women running for congressional office. The following sections will introduce you to these people.

The Representatives and Senators

Being a member of Congress is a difficult and unusual job. A person must be willing to spend considerable time, trouble, and money to obtain a crowded office on Capitol Hill. To nineteenth-century humorist Artemus Ward, such a quest was inexplicable: "It's easy to see why a man goes to the poorhouse or the penitentiary. It's because he can't help it. But why he should voluntarily go live in Washington is beyond my comprehension."

The Job

Hard work is perhaps the most prominent characteristic of a congressperson's job. Representatives and senators deeply resent common beliefs that they are overpaid, underworked, corrupt, and ineffective. Members have even commissioned their own time and motion studies of their efficiency to demonstrate that they do work hard (see Table 11.1). For example, the typical representative is a member of about six committees and subcommittees; a senator is a member of about 10. Members are often scheduled to be in two places at the same time.

There are attractions to the job, however. First and foremost is power. Members of Congress make key decisions about important matters of public policy. In addition, the salary and the perks that go with the job help make it tolerable. Members of Congress receive the following:

- A salary of $168,500 in 2007, about four times the income of the typical American family but well below that of hundreds of corporate presidents who earn several times as much
- Generous retirement benefits
- Office space in Washington and in their constituencies
- A substantial congressional staff who serve individual members, committees, and party leaders
- Handsome travel allowances to see their constituents each year, plus opportunities to travel at low fares or even free to foreign nations on congressional inquiries (what critics call "junkets")
- Franking privileges—free use of the mail system to communicate with constituents and machines that duplicate a member's signature in real ink
- Plenty of small privileges, such as free flowers from the National Botanical Gardens, research services from the Library of Congress, and access to exercise rooms and pools

Despite the salaries, perquisites, and thousands of staff members, Congress is relatively inexpensive. Per citizen, it costs Americans about the same amount to run the nation's legislature for a year as to buy a hamburger, fries, and cola at a fast-food franchise.

Table 11.1 A Day in the Life of a Member of Congress

Typical Schedule in Washington

8:00 A.M.	Budget Study Group—Chair Leon Panetta, Budget Committee
8:45 A.M.	Mainstream Forum meeting
9:15 A.M.	Meeting with Consulting Engineers Council from constituency about various issues of concern
9:45 A.M.	Meet with Soybean Association representatives regarding agriculture appropriations projects
10:15 A.M.	WCHL radio interview (by phone)
10:30 A.M.	Tape weekly radio show—budget
11:00 A.M.	Meet with former student, now an author, about intellectual property issue
1:00 P.M.	Agriculture Subcommittee Hearing—Budget Overview and General Agriculture Outlook
2:30 P.M.	Meeting with Chair Bill Ford and Southern Democrats regarding HR-5, Striker Replacement Bill, possible amendments
3:15 P.M.	Meet with Close-up students from district on steps of Capitol for photo and discussions
3:45 P.M.	Meet with professor regarding energy research programs
4:30 P.M.	Meet with constituent of Kurdish background regarding situation in Iraq
5:30–7:00 P.M.	Reception—Sponsored by National Association of Home Builders, honoring new president Mark Tipton from constituency
6:00–8:00 P.M.	Reception—Honoring retiring Representative Bill Gray
6:00–8:00 P.M.	Reception—Sponsored by Firefighters Association
6:00–8:00 P.M.	Reception—Sponsored by American Financial Services Association

Typical Schedule in Constituency

7:30 A.M.	Business group breakfast: 20 leaders of the business community
8:45 A.M.	Hoover Elementary School: sixth-grade class assembly
9:45 A.M.	National Agriculture Day: speech
10:45 A.M.	Supplemental Food Shelf: pass foodstuffs to needy families
12:00 noon	Community college: student/faculty lunch, speech and Q&A
1:00 P.M.	Sunset Terrace Elementary School: assembly fourth, fifth, and sixth grades, remarks/Q&A
	(Travel Time: 1:45 P.M.–2:45 P.M.)
2:45 P.M.	Plainview Day Care Facility: discuss changes in federal law with owner
4:00 P.M.	Town Hall meeting: American Legion
	(Travel Time: 5:00 P.M.–5:45 P.M.)
5:45 P.M.	PTA meeting: speech on education issues before Congress (also citizen involvement with national associations)
6:30 P.M.	Annual Dinner: St. John's Lutheran Church Development Activity Center
7:15 P.M.	Association for Children for Enforcement of Support meeting: discuss problems of enforcing child support payments
	(Travel Time 8:00 P.M.–8:30 P.M.)
8:30 P.M.	Students Against Drunk Driving (SADD) meeting: speech on drinking age, drunk driving, uniform federal penalties
9:30 P.M.	State university class: discuss business issues before Congress

Sources: Adapted by permission from Craig Schultz, ed., *Setting Course: A Congressional Management Guide*. Copyright © 1994 Congressional Management Foundation, Washington, D.C.; and from David E. Price, *The Congressional Experience: A View from the Hill*. Copyright © 1999 Westview Press, a division of HarperCollins Publishers. Reprinted by permission of Westview Press, a member of Perseus Books, L.L.C.

The Members

There are 535 members of Congress. An even hundred, two from each state, are members of the Senate. The other 435 are members of the House of Representatives. The Constitution specifies only that members of the House must be at least 25 years old and American citizens for seven years; senators must be at least 30 and American citizens for nine years. In addition, all members of Congress must be residents of the states from which they are elected.

Members of Congress are not typical or average Americans, however, as the figures in Table 11.2 reveal. Elite theorists are quick to point out that members come largely from occupations with high status and usually have substantial

Table 11.2 A Portrait of the 110th Congress: Some Statistics

CHARACTERISTIC	HOUSE (435 TOTAL)	SENATE (100 TOTAL)
Party		
Democrat	233	50
Republican	202	49
Independent	—	1
Gender		
Men	364	84
Women	71	16
Race		
Asian	4	2
African American	40	1
Hispanic	23	3
White and other	368	94
Religion		
Protestant	260	63
Roman Catholic	128	25
Jewish	30	13
Other and unspecified	14	1
Prior Occupation*		
Law	161	61
Business	168	27
Education	87	14
Public service/politics	172	31
Agriculture	23	6
Journalism	7	7
Real estate	36	3
Medicine	13	3
Other	61	9

*Some members specify more than one occupation.
Source: Congressional Quarterly.

incomes. Although calling the Senate a "millionaires' club" is an exaggeration, the proportion of millionaires and near millionaires is much higher in Congress than in an average crowd of 535 people. Business and law are the dominant prior occupations; other elite occupations such as academia are also well represented.

Law especially attracts persons interested in politics and provides the flexibility (and often the financial support of a law firm) to wage election campaigns. In addition, many government positions in which aspiring members of Congress can make their marks, such as district attorney, are reserved for lawyers.

Mid-Term Elections 2006

Less than 10 percent of the House are African American (compared with about 13 percent of the total population), and most (but not all) of these representatives have been elected from overwhelmingly African American constituencies. No state is predominantly African American, and there is only one African American in the Senate. There are 23 Hispanics in the House and three in the Senate. Asian and Native Americans are also underrepresented. In terms of numbers, however, women are the most underrepresented group; more than half the population is female, but only 16 senators and 71 voting representatives are female (the representative from Washington, D.C., does not vote).

How important are the personal characteristics of members of Congress? Can a group of predominantly White, upper-middle-class, middle-aged Protestant males adequately represent a much more diverse population? Would a group of more typical citizens be more effective in making major policy decisions? Because power in Congress is highly decentralized, the backgrounds of representatives and senators can be important if they influence how issues are prioritized and how officials vote on these issues. There is evidence that African American members are more active than White members in serving African American constituents,[1] and they appear to increase African American constituents' contact with and knowledge about Congress.[2] Similarly, on the average women legislators seem to be more active than men in pursuing the interests of women.[3]

Obviously, members of Congress cannot claim *descriptive* representation—that is, representing constituents by mirroring their personal, politically relevant characteristics. They may, however, engage in *substantive* representation—representing the interests of groups.[4] For example, members of Congress with a background of wealth and privilege, such as Senator Edward Kennedy, can be champions for the interests of the poor. Moreover, most members of Congress have lived in the constituencies they represent for many years and share the beliefs and attitudes of at least a large proportion of their constituents. If they do not share such perspectives, they may find it difficult to keep their seats come election time. At the same time, females and African Americans who are in Congress are achieving important positions on committees, increasing the chances of making descriptive representation effective.[5]

Congressional Elections

Congressional elections are demanding, expensive,[6] and, as you will see, generally foregone conclusions—yet the role of politician is the most universal one in Congress. Men and women may run for Congress to forge new policy initiatives, but they also enjoy politics and consider a position in Congress near the top of their

In terms of the backgrounds of members of Congress, women are the most underrepresented major demographic group. However, their numbers have been increasing. Shown here are the 14 women serving as senators in 2003–2004.

chosen profession. Even if they dislike politics, without reelection they will not be around long enough to shape policy.

Who Wins Elections?

Everyone in Congress is a politician, and politicians continually have their eyes on the next election. The players in the congressional election game are the incumbents and the challengers.

incumbents
Those already holding office. In congressional elections, incumbents usually win.

Incumbents are individuals who already hold an office. Sometime during each term, the incumbent must decide whether to run again or to retire voluntarily. Most decide to run for reelection. They enter their party's primary, almost always emerge victorious, and typically win in the November general election, too. Indeed, the most important fact about congressional elections is this: *Incumbents usually win* (see Figure 11.1). Even in a year of great political upheaval such as 1994, in which the Republicans gained eight seats in the Senate and 53 seats in the House, 92 percent of incumbent senators and 89 percent of incumbent representatives won their bids for reelection.

Not only do more than 90 percent of the incumbents seeking reelection win, but most of them win with more than 60 percent of the vote. Perhaps most astonishing is the fact that even when challengers' positions on the issues are closer to the voters' positions, incumbents still tend to win.[7]

Why Is It So Hard to Defeat an Incumbent?

The picture for the Senate is a little different. Even though senators still have a good chance of beating back a challenge, the odds of reelection are often not as handsome as for House incumbents; senators typically win by narrower margins. One reason for the greater competition in the Senate is that an entire state is almost

Figure 11.1 The Incumbency Factor in Congressional Elections

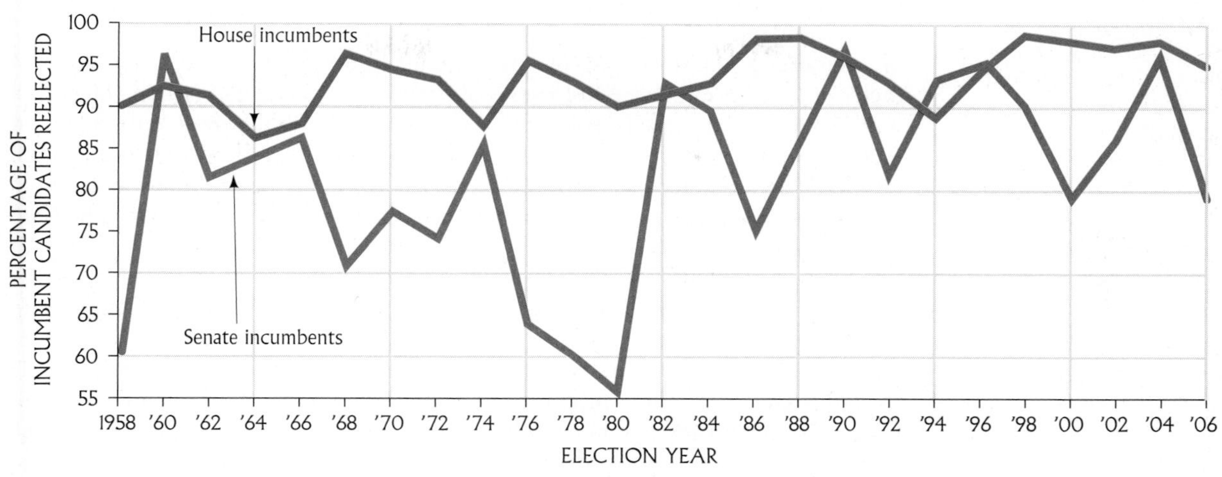

Source: Norman J. Ornstein, Thomas E. Mann, and Michael J. Malbin, *Vital Statistics on Congress, 1997–1998* (Washington, DC: Congressional Quarterly Press, 1998). Data for 1998–2006 compiled by the authors. Figures reflect incumbents running in both primary and general elections.

always more diverse than a congressional district and thus provides a larger base for opposition to an incumbent. At the same time, senators have less personal contact with their constituencies, which on average are nearly 10 times larger than those of members of the House of Representatives. Senators also receive more coverage in the media than representatives do and are more likely to be held accountable on controversial issues. Moreover, senators tend to draw more visible challengers, such as governors or members of the House, whom voters already know and who have substantial financial backing—a factor that lessens the advantages of incumbency. Many of these challengers know that the Senate is a stepping-stone to national prominence and sometimes even the presidency.

Despite their success at reelection, incumbents often feel quite vulnerable. As Thomas Mann put it, members of Congress perceive themselves as "unsafe at any margin."[8] Thus, they have been raising and spending more campaign funds, sending more mail to their constituents, visiting their states and districts more often, and staffing more local offices than ever before.[9]

The Advantages of Incumbency

There are several possible explanations for the success of incumbents. One is that voters know how their elected representatives vote on important policy issues and agree with their stands, sending them back to Washington to keep up the good work. This, however, is usually not the case. In fact, voters are rather oblivious to how their senators and representatives actually vote. One study found that only about one-fifth of Americans can make an accurate guess about how their representatives have voted on any issue in Congress.[10] As one expert put it, "Mass public knowledge of congressional candidates declines precipitously once we move beyond simple recognition, generalized feelings, and incumbent job ratings."[11]

Another possibility is that voter assessments of presidential candidates influence their voting for Congress. Most stories of presidential "coattails" (when voters support congressional candidates because of their support for the president), however, seem to be just stories.[12] Bill Clinton and George W. Bush won four presidential elections between them. Yet they received a *smaller* percentage of the vote than did almost every winning member of their party in Congress in each election. They had little in the way of coattails.

Journalists often claim that voters are motivated primarily by their pocketbooks. Yet members of Congress do not gain or lose many votes as a result of the ups and downs of the economy.[13]

What accounts for the success of congressional incumbents? Members of Congress engage in three primary activities that increase the probability of their reelection: advertising, credit claiming, and position taking.[14] In addition, the lack of strong opponents further ensures their success.

Advertising. For members of Congress, advertising means much more than placing ads in the newspapers and on television. Most congressional advertising takes place between elections in the form of contact with constituents. The goal is *visibility*.

Members of Congress work hard to get themselves known in their constituencies, and they usually succeed. Not surprisingly, members concentrate on staying visible and make frequent trips home. In a typical week, members spend at least some time in their home districts,[15] even though their districts may be hundreds of miles from Washington. Similarly, members use the franking privilege to mail newsletters to every household in their constituency.

More recently, members of Congress have employed technology to bring franking into the digital age. Congressional staffers track the interests of individual voters, file the information in a database, and then use e-mails or phone calls to engage directly with voters on issues they know they care about. Using taxpayers' money, legislators employ a new technology that allows them to call thousands of households simultaneously with a recorded message, asking people in their districts to join in on a conference call with their representative. With the push of a button, the constituent is on the line with the House member—and often 1,000 or more fellow constituents. Equally important, the lawmaker knows from the phone numbers where the respondents live and, from what they say on the call, what issues interest them. Information gathered from the events, as well as e-mails and phone calls from constituents, gets plugged into a database, giving the incumbent something a challenger could only dream of: a detailed list of the specific interests of thousands of would-be voters. E-mail then allows for personal interaction—and a free reminder of why the incumbent should be reelected.

Credit Claiming. Congresspersons also engage in credit claiming, which involves enhancing their standing with constituents through service to individuals and the district. Morris Fiorina has emphasized this close link between service and success.[16]

Members of Congress, he says, *can* go to the voters and stress their policymaking record and their stands on new policy issues on the agenda. The problem with facing the voters on one's record—past, present, and future—is that policy positions make enemies as well as friends. A member of Congress's vote for reducing government spending may win some friends, but it will make enemies of voters who happen to link that vote with service cutbacks. Besides, a congressperson can almost never show that he or she alone was responsible for a major policy. Being only one of 435 members of the House or one of 100 senators, a person can hardly promise to end inflation, cut taxes, or achieve equal rights for women single-handedly.

You Are an Informed Voter

One thing, though, always wins friends and almost never makes enemies: *servicing the constituency*. There are two ways in which members of Congress can do so: through casework and through the pork barrel. **Casework** is helping constituents as individuals—cutting through some bureaucratic red tape to give people what they think they have a right to get.

casework
Activities of members of Congress that help constituents as individuals; cutting through bureaucratic red tape to get people what they think they have a right to get.

The **pork barrel** is the mighty list of federal projects, grants, and contracts available to cities, businesses, colleges, and institutions. In the past, Congress tended to appropriate funds for grants and let institutions—such as universities—compete for funding for specific projects. In recent years, however, members of Congress have grown increasingly aggressive in "earmarking" funds that must be spent in specific districts. The Congressional Research Service reported that there were more than 15,000 such earmarks in 2005, costing about $53 billion.

pork barrel
The mighty list of federal projects, grants, and contracts available to cities, businesses, colleges, and institutions in a congressional district.

As a result of the advantages of incumbency in advertising and credit claiming, incumbents, especially in the House, are usually much better known and have a more favorable public image than do their opponents.[17] Shrewd use of the resources available to incumbents may give them an advantage, but by themselves, casework and pork barrel do not determine congressional elections.[18]

Representative Silvio Conte used a pig nose and ears to protest pork barrel spending until he wanted multi-million-dollar federal grants for his Massachusetts district. Because credit claiming is so important for reelection, members of Congress rarely pass up the opportunity to increase federal spending in their state or district.

Position Taking. Members of Congress must also engage in position taking on issues when they vote and when they respond to constituents' questions. In establishing their public images, members of Congress emphasize their personal qualities as experienced, hardworking, trustworthy representatives who have served their constituencies—an image often devoid of partisan or programmatic content. Nevertheless, all members must take policy stands, and the positions they take may affect the outcome of an election, especially if the issues are on matters salient to voters and if the candidates' stands differ from those of a majority of their constituents. This is especially true in elections for the Senate, in which issues are likely to play a greater role than in House elections.

Weak Opponents. Another advantage for incumbents is that they are likely to face weak opponents. Confronted with the advantages of incumbency, potentially effective opponents are often unlikely to risk challenging members of the House.[19] Those individuals who do run are usually not well known or well qualified and lack experience and organizational and financial backing.[20] The lack of adequate campaign funds is a special burden because challengers need money to compensate for the "free" recognition incumbents receive from their advertising and credit claiming.[21]

Campaign Spending. It costs a great deal of money to elect a Congress. The Federal Election Commission reports that in the 2003–2004 election cycle, congressional candidates spent nearly $1.2 *billion* to win the election. Challengers have to raise large sums if they hope to defeat an incumbent, and the more they spend, the more votes they receive. Money buys them name recognition and a chance to be heard. Incumbents, by contrast, already have high levels of recognition among their constituents and benefit less (but still benefit) from campaign spending; what matters most is how much their opponents spend. (In contests for open seats, the candidate who spends the most usually wins.) In the end, however, challengers are usually substantially outspent by incumbents.[22] In the House races in 2004, the typical incumbent outspent the typical challenger by a ratio of about 15 to 1. [23]

Where do campaign funds come from? And, more important, what do they buy? Although most of the money spent in congressional elections comes from individuals, about one-fourth of the funds raised by candidates for Congress comes from political action committees (PACs) (see Chapters 9 and 10). Critics of PACs offer plenty of complaints about the present system of campaign finance. Why, they ask, is money spent to pay the campaign costs of a candidate who is already heavily favored to win? Even more interesting is that PACs often make contributions *after* the election.

There is a continuous debate in America today on whether PACs "buy" votes in Congress (see "You Are the Policymaker: Should PACs Be Eliminated?" in Chapter 10). Although this question remains unresolved, everyone agrees that at the very least, PACs seek *access* to policymakers. Thus, they give most of their money to incumbents, who are likely to win anyway. When they support someone who loses, they quickly make amends and contribute to the winner. PACs want to keep the lines of communication open and create a receptive atmosphere in which to be heard. Because each PAC is limited to an expenditure of $5,000 per candidate (most give less), a single PAC can at most account for only a small percentage of a winner's total spending. If one PAC does not contribute to a candidate, there are always other PACs from which to seek funds.

Aside from the question of whether money buys influence, what does it buy the candidates who spend it? In 2000, Jon Corzine of New Jersey spent more than $60 million to win a Senate seat. However, Rick Lazio spent more than $40 million to win a Senate seat in New York—and lost. In 1994, Californian Michael Huffington spent nearly $30 million—most of it his own money—about twice the expenditures of his rival, Senator Dianne Feinstein, and still lost. In 2004, Thomas Daschle spent about $20 million in the much smaller state of South Dakota, and he lost as well. Obviously, prolific spending in a campaign is no guarantee of success.

The Role of Party Identification

At the base of every electoral coalition are the members of the candidate's party in the constituency. Most members of Congress represent constituencies in which their party is in the clear majority, and most people who identify with a party reliably vote for its candidates. Indeed, about 90 percent of voters who identify with a party vote for the House candidates of their party. State legislatures have eagerly employed advances in technology to draw the boundaries of House districts so that there is a safe majority for one party, and both demographic trends and ideological realignment in the electorate have made the constituencies of both senators and representatives less competitive.

Defeating Incumbents

In light of the advantages of incumbents, it is reasonable to ask why anyone challenges them at all. One of the main reasons is simply that challengers are often naive about their chances of winning. Because few have money for expensive polls, they rely on friends and local party leaders, who often tell them what they want to hear. Sometimes they do get some unexpected help; incumbents almost have to beat themselves, and some do.

An incumbent tarnished by scandal or corruption becomes instantly vulnerable. Clearly, voters do take out their anger at the polls. For example, representatives who bounced large numbers of checks at the House bank were much more likely to lose their seats in the 1992 elections than their more fiscally responsible colleagues.[24] In a close election, negative publicity can turn victory into defeat.[25]

Redistricting

Incumbents may also be redistricted out of their familiar turfs. After each federal census, Congress reapportions its membership. States that have gained significantly in population will be given more House seats; states that have lost substantial population will lose one or more of their seats. The state legislatures must then redraw their states' district lines; one incumbent may be moved into another's district, where the two must battle for one seat. A state party majority is more likely to move two of the opposition party's representatives into a single district than two of its own. Or an incumbent of the minority party might find his or her district split up to make it more competitive. In 2004, Republicans in Texas redrew the state's congressional boundaries for the second time since 2000, removing many Democratic constituents from the districts of Democratic representatives. In the end, the Republicans gained four seats in the state's delegation in the U.S. House of Representatives.

Finally, major political tidal waves occasionally roll across the country, leaving defeated incumbents in their wake. One such wave occurred in 1994, when the public mood turned especially sour and voters took out their frustration on Democratic incumbents, defeating 34 in the House and two in the Senate. In 2006, six senators and 23 representatives lost their seats.

Open Seats

When an incumbent is not running for reelection and the seat is open, there is greater likelihood of competition. If the party balance in a constituency is such that either party has a chance of winning, each side may offer a strong candidate—each with enough money to establish name recognition among the voters. Most of the turnover in the membership of Congress results from vacated seats.

Stability and Change

Congressional Term Limits

Because incumbents usually win reelection, there is some stability in the membership of Congress. This provides the opportunity for representatives and senators to gain some expertise in dealing with complex questions of public policy. At the same time, it also may insulate them from the winds of political change. Safe seats make it more difficult for citizens to "send a message to Washington" with their votes. Particularly in the House, it takes a large shift in votes to affect the outcomes of most elections. To increase turnover in the membership of Congress, some reformers have proposed *term limitations* for representatives and senators[26] (see "You Are the Policymaker: Should We Impose Term Limits on Members of Congress?").

How Congress Is Organized to Make Policy

Of all the senators' and representatives' roles, making policy is the toughest. Congress is a collection of generalists trying to make policy on specialized topics. Members are short on time and expertise. As amateurs in almost every subject, they are surrounded by people who know (or claim to know) more than they do—lobbyists, agency administrators, even their own staffs. Even if they had time to study all the issues thoroughly, making wise national policy would be difficult. If economists disagree about policies to fight unemployment, how are legislators to know which policies may work better than others?

When ringing bells announce a roll-call vote, representatives or senators rush into the chamber from their offices or from a hearing—often unsure of what is being voted on. Frequently, "uncertain of their position, members of Congress will seek out one or two people who serve on the committee which considered and reported the bill, in whose judgment they have confidence."[27]

The Founders gave Congress's organization just a hint of specialization when they split it into the House and the Senate. The complexity of today's issues, however, requires much more specialization. Congress tries to cope with policymaking demands through its elaborate committee system.

American Bicameralism

A **bicameral legislature** is a legislature divided into two houses. The U.S. Congress is bicameral, as is every American state legislature except Nebraska's, which has one house (unicameral). As we learned in Chapter 2, the Connecticut Compromise at the Constitutional Convention created a bicameral Congress. Each state is guaranteed two senators, and its number of representatives is determined by the population of the state (California has 53 representatives; Alaska, Delaware, Montana, North Dakota, South Dakota, Vermont, and Wyoming have just one each). By creating a

bicameral legislature
A legislature divided into two houses. The U.S. Congress and every American state legislature except Nebraska's are bicameral.

YOU ARE THE POLICYMAKER

Should We Impose Term Limits on Members of Congress?

In the late 1980s many reformers were concerned that the incumbency advantage enjoyed by legislators created, in effect, lifetime tenure, which served as a roadblock to change and encouraged ethics abuses. To increase turnover among legislators, these reformers proposed term limitations, generally restricting representatives to 6 or 12 consecutive years in office.

The movement to limit the terms of legislators spread rapidly across the country. Within a few years, 23 states enacted term limitations for members of their state legislatures. The House Republicans made terms limits for Congress part of their Contract With America in the 1994 election. Yet changing the terms of members of Congress requires changing the Constitution, which is difficult to do, and many members of Congress have fought term limitations fiercely.

Opponents of term limitations object to the loss of experienced legislators and of the American people's ability to vote for whomever they please. In addition, they add, there is plenty of new blood in the legislature: At the beginning of the 105th Congress (1997), more than half the members of the House and 40 percent of the senators had no more than four years of experience in their chambers. Moreover, recent research indicates that the movement of party fortunes in the House follows the movement of citizen preferences for public policy.*

Proponents of term limits suffered two setbacks in 1995 when Congress failed to pass a constitutional amendment on term limitations (it also failed in 1997) and when the Supreme Court, in *U.S. Term Limits, Inc. et al. v. Thornton et al.*, decided that state-imposed term limits on members of Congress were unconstitutional. In the meantime, most people seem comfortable with their own representatives and senators and appear content to reelect them again and again.

Nevertheless, many Americans support a constitutional amendment to impose term limitations on members of Congress. You be the policymaker: What would *you* do?

*Suzanna De Boef and James A. Stimson, "The Dynamic Structure of Congressional Elections," *Journal of Politics* 57 (August 1995): 630–48.

bicameral Congress, the Constitution set up yet another check and balance. No bill can be passed unless both House and Senate agree on it; each body can thus veto the policies of the other. Some of the basic differences between the two houses are shown in Table 11.3.

The House. The House is more than four times larger than the Senate and is also more institutionalized—that is, more centralized, more hierarchical, and less anarchic.[28] Party loyalty to leadership and party-line voting are more common in the House than in the Senate. Partly because there are more members, leaders in the House do more leading than do leaders in the Senate. First-term House members are more likely to be seen and not heard, and they have less power than senior representatives.[29]

Both the House and the Senate set their own agendas. Both use committees, which we will examine shortly, to winnow down the thousands of bills introduced. One institution unique to the House, however, plays a key role in agenda setting: the **House Rules Committee**. This committee reviews most bills coming from a House committee before they go to the full House. Performing a traffic cop function, the Rules Committee gives each bill a "rule," which schedules the bill on the calendar, allots time for debate, and sometimes even specifies what kind of amendments may be offered. Today, the committee usually brings legislation to the floor under rules that limit or prohibit amendments and thus the opportunities for the minority to propose changes. The Rules Committee is generally responsive to the House leadership, in part because the Speaker of the House now appoints the committee's members.

House Rules Committee
An institution unique to the House of Representatives that reviews all **bills** (except revenue, budget, and appropriations bills) coming from a House committee before they go to the full House.

The Senate. The Constitution's framers thought the Senate would protect elite interests to counteract the tendencies of the House to protect the masses. They gave the House power to initiate all revenue bills and to impeach officials; they gave the Senate

Table 11.3 House Versus Senate: Some Key Differences

CHARACTERISTIC	HOUSE OF REPRESENTATIVES	SENATE
Constitutional powers	Must initiate all revenue bills; must pass all articles of impeachment	Must give "advice and consent" to many presidential nominations; must approve treaties; tries impeached officials
Membership	435 members	100 members
Term of office	2 years	6 years
Constituencies	Smaller	Larger
Centralization of power	More centralized; stronger leadership	Less centralized; weaker leadership
Political prestige	Less prestige	More prestige
Role in policymaking	More influential on budget; more specialized	More influential on foreign affairs; less specialized
Turnover	Small	Moderate
Role of seniority	More important in determining power	Less important in determining power
Procedures	Limited debate; limits on floor amendments allowed	Unlimited debate

responsibility to ratify all treaties, to confirm important presidential nominations (including nominations to the Supreme Court), and to try impeached officials. History shows that when the same party controls each chamber, the Senate is just as liberal as—and perhaps more liberal than—the House.[30] The real differences between the bodies lie in the Senate's organization and decentralized power.

The Senate is smaller than the House and is also less disciplined and less centralized. Today's senators are more nearly equal in power than representatives are. They are also more nearly equal in power than senators have been in the past. Even incoming senators sometimes get top committee assignments; they may even become chairs of key subcommittees.

Committees and the party leadership are important in determining the Senate's legislative agenda, just as they are in the House. Party leaders do for Senate scheduling what the Rules Committee does in the House.

One activity unique to the Senate is the **filibuster**. This is a tactic by which opponents of a bill use their right to unlimited debate as a way to prevent the Senate from ever voting on a bill. Unlike their fellow legislators in the House, once senators have the floor in a debate, tradition holds that they can talk as long as they wish. Strom Thurmond of South Carolina once held forth for a full 24 hours. Working together, then, like-minded senators can practically debate forever, tying up the legislative agenda until the proponents of a bill finally give up their battle. In essence, they literally talk the bill to death.

filibuster
A strategy unique to the Senate whereby opponents of a piece of legislation try to talk it to death, based on the tradition of unlimited debate. Today, 60 members present and voting can halt a filibuster.

The power of the filibuster is not absolute, however. Sixty members present and voting can halt a filibuster by voting for *cloture* on debate, but many senators are reluctant to vote for cloture for fear of setting a precedent to be used against them when *they* want to filibuster.

At its core the filibuster raises profound questions about American democracy because it is used by a minority, sometimes a minority of one, to defeat a majority. Southern senators once used filibusters to prevent civil rights legislation.[31] More recently, the opponents of all types of legislation have used them. Indeed, during Bill Clinton's presidency, filibusters became the weapon of first resort for even the most trivial matters.

Congressional Leadership

Congressional Leadership

Leading 100 senators or 435 representatives in Congress—each jealous of his or her own power and responsible to no higher power than the constituency—is no easy task. "Few members of the House, fewer still in the Senate," Robert Peabody once wrote, "consider themselves followers."[32] Chapter 8 discussed the party in government. Much of the leadership in Congress is really party leadership. There are a few formal posts whose occupants are chosen by nonparty procedures, but those who have the real power in the congressional hierarchy are those whose party put them there.

The House. Chief among leadership positions in the House of Representatives is the **Speaker of the House**. This is the only legislative office mandated by the Constitution. In practice, the majority party selects the Speaker. Before each Congress begins, the majority party presents its candidate for Speaker, who—because this person attracts the

Speaker of the House
An office mandated by the Constitution. The Speaker is chosen in practice by the majority party, has both formal and informal powers, and is second in line to succeed to the presidency should that office become vacant.

unanimous support of the majority party—turns out to be a shoo-in. Typically, the Speaker is a senior member of the party. Nancy Pelosi of California, who has served in Congress since 1987, was elected Speaker in 2007. The Speaker is also two heartbeats away from the presidency, being second in line (after the vice president) to succeed a president who resigns, dies in office, or is convicted after impeachment.

The Power of the Speaker of the House

Years ago, the Speaker was king of the congressional mountain. Autocrats such as "Uncle Joe Cannon" and "Czar Reed" ran the House like a fiefdom. A great revolt in 1910 whittled down the Speaker's powers and gave some of them to committees, but six decades later, members of the House restored some of the Speaker's powers. Today the Speaker does the following:

- Presides over the House when it is in session
- Plays a major role in making committee assignments, which are coveted by all members to ensure their electoral advantage
- Appoints or plays a key role in appointing the party's legislative leaders and the party leadership staff
- Exercises substantial control over which bills get assigned to which committees

In addition to these formal powers, the Speaker has a great deal of informal clout inside and outside Congress. When the Speaker's party differs from the president's party, as it frequently does, the Speaker is often a national spokesperson for the party. The bank of microphones in front of the Speaker of the House is a commonplace feature of the evening news. A good Speaker also knows the members well—including their past improprieties, their ambitions, and the pressures they feel.

majority leader
The principal partisan ally of the Speaker of the House or the party's manager in the Senate. The majority leader is responsible for scheduling **bills**, influencing committee assignments, and rounding up votes in behalf of the party's legislative positions.

Leadership in the House, however, is not a one-person show. The Speaker's principal partisan ally is the **majority leader**—a job that has been the main stepping stone to the Speaker's role. The majority leader is responsible for scheduling bills in the House. More important, the majority leader is responsible for rounding up votes on behalf of the party's position on legislation. Working with the majority leader are the party's *whips*, who carry the word to party troops, counting votes before they are cast and leaning on waverers whose votes are crucial to a bill. Party whips also report the views and complaints of the party rank and file back to the leadership. The current majority leader is Steny Hoyer of Maryland.

minority leader
The principal leader of the minority party in the House of Representatives or in the Senate.

The minority party is also organized, poised to take over the Speakership and other key posts if it should win a majority in the House. The Republicans had been the minority party in the House for 40 years before 1995, although they had a president to look to for leadership for much of that period. After 12 years in the majority, they are again experiencing minority status, led by the **minority leader**, John Boehner of Ohio.

The Senate. The Constitution makes the vice president of the United States the president of the Senate; this is the vice president's only constitutionally defined job. However, even the mighty Lyndon Johnson, who had been the Senate majority leader before becoming vice president, found himself an outsider when he returned as the Senate's president. Vice presidents usually slight their senatorial chores, leaving power in the Senate to party leaders. Senators typically return the favor, ignoring vice presidents except in the rare case when their vote can break a tie.

Thus, the Senate majority leader (currently, Harry Reid of Nevada)—aided by the majority whips—is a party's workhorse, corralling votes, scheduling the

Nancy Pelosi of California was elected Speaker of the House in 2007, the first woman to serve in that post. Majority Leader Harry Reid of Nevada leads the Democrats in the Senate, which makes him the most powerful member of that body. Nevertheless, in the decentralized power structure in the upper chamber, even he must work for support and negotiate with Minority Leader Mitch McConnell of Kentucky.

floor action, and influencing committee assignments. The majority leader's counterpart in the opposition, the minority leader (currently Mitch McConnell of Kentucky), has similar responsibilities. Power is widely dispersed in the contemporary Senate; it no longer lies in the hands of a few key members of Congress who are insulated from the public. Therefore, party leaders must appeal broadly for support, often speaking to the country directly or indirectly over television.

Why It Matters

Weak Parties

Parties organize Congress, but historically they have been relatively weak. If parties are strong, they can enforce strict party loyalty and thus are better able to keep their promises to voters. At the same time, strict party loyalty makes it more difficult for members of Congress to break from the party line to represent their constituents' special needs and interests.

Congressional Leadership in Perspective. Despite their stature and power, congressional leaders cannot always move their troops. Power in both houses of Congress, but especially the Senate, is decentralized. Leaders are elected by their party members and must remain responsive to them. Except in the most egregious cases (which rarely arise), leaders cannot administer severe punishments to those who do not support the party's stand, and no one expects members to vote against their constituents' interests. Senator Robert Dole nicely summed up the leader's situation when he once dubbed himself the "Majority Pleader."

Nevertheless, party leadership, at least in the House, has been more effective in recent years. As the party contingents have become more homogeneous, there has been more policy agreement within the parties and thus more party unity in voting on the floor. Increased agreement has made it easier for the Speaker to exercise his prerogatives regarding the assignment of bills and members to committees, the rules under which the House considers legislation on the floor, and the use of an expanded whip system—all developments that have enabled the parties to advance an agenda that reflects party preferences.[33]

The Committees and Subcommittees

Will Rogers, the famous Oklahoman humorist, once remarked that "outside of traffic, there is nothing that has held this country back as much as committees." Members of the Senate and the House would apparently disagree. Most of the real

Contemporary Legislative Process

work of Congress goes on in committees, and committees dominate congressional policymaking in all its stages.

Committees regularly hold hearings to investigate problems and possible wrongdoing and to oversee the executive branch. Most of all, *they control the congressional agenda and guide legislation* from its introduction to its send-off to the president for his signature. We can group committees into four types, the first of which is by far the most important.

standing committees
Separate subject-matter committees in each house of Congress that handle **bills** in different policy areas.

joint committees
Congressional committees on a few subject-matter areas with membership drawn from both houses.

conference committees
Congressional committees formed when the Senate and the House pass a particular **bill** in different forms. Party leadership appoints members from each house to iron out the differences and bring back a single bill.

select committees
Congressional committees appointed for a specific purpose, such as the Watergate investigation.

1. **Standing committees** handle bills in different policy areas (see Table 11.4). Each house of Congress has its own standing committees; members do not belong to a committee in the other house. In the 110th Congress, the typical representative served on two committees and four subcommittees, senators averaged three committees and seven subcommittees each. Subcommittees are smaller units of a committee created out of the committee membership.
2. **Joint committees** exist in a few policy areas, such as the economy and taxation, and draw their membership from both the Senate and the House.
3. **Conference committees** are formed when the Senate and the House pass different versions of the same bill (which they typically do). Appointed by the party leadership, a conference committee consists of members of each house chosen to iron out Senate and House differences and to report back a compromise bill.
4. **Select committees** are appointed for a specific purpose. The Senate select committee that investigated Watergate is a well-known example.

Table 11.4 Standing Committees in the Senate and in the House

SENATE COMMITTEES	HOUSE COMMITTEES
Agriculture, Nutrition, and Forestry	Agriculture
Appropriations	Appropriations
Armed Services	Armed Services
Banking, Housing, and Urban Affairs	Budget
Budget	Education and the Workforce
Commerce, Science, and Transportation	Energy and Commerce
Energy and Natural Resources	Financial Services
Environment and Public Works	Government Reform
Finance	Homeland Security
Foreign Relations	House Administration
Health, Education, Labor, and Pensions	International Relations
Homeland Security and Governmental Affairs	Judiciary
Judiciary	Resources
Rules and Administration	Rules
Small Business and Entrepreneurship	Science
Veterans' Affairs	Small Business
	Standards of Official Conduct
	Transportation and Infrastructure
	Veterans' Affairs
	Ways and Means

The Committees at Work: Legislation and Oversight. With more than 11,000 bills submitted by members every two years, some winnowing is essential. Every bill goes to a committee, which has virtually the power of life and death over it. The whole House or Senate usually considers only bills that obtain a favorable committee report.

A new bill that the Speaker sends to a committee typically goes directly to a subcommittee, which can hold hearings on the bill. Sizable committee and subcommittee staffs conduct research, line up witnesses for hearings, and write and rewrite bills. Committees and their subcommittees produce reports on proposed legislation. A committee's most important output, however, is the "marked-up" (rewritten) bill itself, which it submits to the full House or Senate for debate and voting.

The work of committees does not stop when the bill leaves the committee room. Members of the committee usually serve as "floor managers" of the bill, helping party leaders hustle votes for it. They are also the "cue givers" to whom other members turn for advice. When the Senate and House pass different versions of the same bill, some committee members serve on the conference committee.

The committees and subcommittees do not leave the scene even after legislation passes. They stay busy in **legislative oversight**, the process of monitoring the bureaucracy and its administration of policy. Committees handle oversight mainly through hearings. When an agency wants a bigger budget, the relevant committee reviews its current budget. Even if no budgetary issues are involved, members of committees constantly monitor how the bureaucracy is implementing a law. Agency heads and even cabinet secretaries testify, bringing graphs, charts, and data on the progress they have made and the problems they face. Committee staffs and committee members grill agency heads about particular problems. For example, a member may ask a Small Business Administration official why constituents who are

legislative oversight
Congress's monitoring of the bureaucracy and its administration of policy, performed mainly through hearings.

Most of Congress's work takes place—and most of its members' power is wielded—in the standing committees and their numerous subcommittees. Here, a Senate committee investigates prisoner abuse in Afghanistan and Iraq.

applying for loans get the runaround. On another committee, officials charged with listing endangered species might defend the gray wolf against a member of Congress whose sheep-ranching constituents are not fond of wolves.

Oversight, one of the checks Congress can exercise on the executive branch, gives Congress the power to pressure agencies and, in extreme cases, cut their budgets in order to secure compliance with congressional wishes and even congressional whims.[34] Oversight also provides an opportunity to refine existing policies or respond to new problems.

Occasionally, congressional oversight rivets the nation's attention. In 1973 the Senate established the Select Committee on Presidential Campaign Activities to investigate the misdeeds and duplicity of the 1972 presidential campaign, otherwise known as the Watergate scandal. Following these hearings, the House Judiciary Committee conducted hearings the next year on the impeachment of President Nixon for his conduct in attempting to cover up the scandal. Shortly after the Judiciary Committee recommended three articles of impeachment, the president resigned.

Congress keeps tabs on more routine activities of the executive branch through its committee staff members. These members have specialized expertise in the fields and agencies that their committees oversee and maintain an extensive network of formal and informal contacts with the bureaucracy. By reading the voluminous reports that Congress requires of the executive and by receiving information from numerous sources—agencies, complaining citizens, members of Congress and their personal staff, state and local officials, interest groups, and professional organizations—staff members can keep track of the implementation of public policy.[35]

Why It Matters

The Committee System

The committee system in Congress is highly decentralized. As a result, it is open to the appeals of a wide range of "special" interests, especially those represented by highly paid lobbyists. If Congress were more *centralized* and only those interests cleared by the elected leadership received a hearing, special interests might be constrained. However, there is also a danger that only the interests reflecting the views of the leadership would be heard.

As the size and complexity of the national government grew in the 1960s and after numerous charges that the executive branch had become too powerful (especially in response to the widespread belief that Presidents Johnson and Nixon had abused their power), Congress responded with more oversight. The tight budgets of recent years have provided additional incentives for oversight, as members of Congress have sought to protect programs they favor from budget cuts and to get more value for the tax dollars spent on them. As the publicity value of receiving credit for controlling governmental spending has increased, so has the number of representatives and senators interested in oversight.[36]

Nevertheless, members of Congress have many competing responsibilities, and there are few political payoffs for carefully watching a government agency to see whether it is implementing policy properly. It is difficult to go to voters and say, "Vote for me. I oversaw the routine handling of road building." Because of this lack of incentives, problems may be overlooked until it is too late to do much about them. A major scandal involving the Department of Housing and Urban Development's administration of housing programs during the Reagan presidency was not uncovered until 1989, after Reagan had left office. Similarly, taxpayers could have saved well over $100 billion if Congress had insisted that the agencies regulating the savings and loan industry enforce their regulations more rigorously. More recently, there was clear evidence of fundamental problems in the operations and management of the Federal Emergency Management Agency in its response to the four hurricanes that hit Florida in 2004. Nevertheless, when hurricanes Katrina and Rita hit the next year, Congress had still not held oversight hearings.

In addition, the majority party largely determines if and when a committee will hold hearings. When the president's party has a majority in a house of Congress, that chamber is generally not aggressive in overseeing the administration because it does not wish to embarrass the president. Democrats have been critical of what they regard as timid Republican oversight of the nation's intelligence establishment and President Bush's planning and implementation of the aftermath of the war in Iraq, including the treatment of prisoners.

Getting on a Committee. One of the first worries for an incoming member of Congress (after paying off campaign debts) is getting on the right committee. Members seek committees that will help them achieve three goals: reelection, influence in Congress, and the opportunity to make policy in areas they think are important.[37]

Just after their election, new members write to the party's congressional leaders and members of their state delegation, indicating their committee preferences. Every committee includes members from both parties, but a majority of each committee's members, as well as its chair, come from the majority party in the chamber. Each party in each house has a slightly different way of picking its committee members. Party leaders almost always play a key role.

You Are a Member of Congress

Those who have supported the leadership are favored in the committee selection process, but generally the parties try to grant members' requests for committee assignments whenever possible. They want their members to please their constituents (being on the right committee should help them represent their constituency more effectively and reinforce their ability to engage in credit claiming) and to develop expertise in an area of policy. The parties also try to apportion the influence that comes with committee membership among the state delegations in order to accord representation to diverse components of the party.[38]

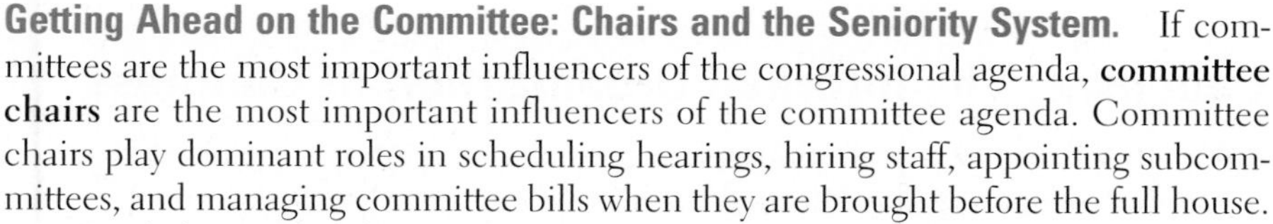

Getting Ahead on the Committee: Chairs and the Seniority System. If committees are the most important influencers of the congressional agenda, **committee chairs** are the most important influencers of the committee agenda. Committee chairs play dominant roles in scheduling hearings, hiring staff, appointing subcommittees, and managing committee bills when they are brought before the full house.

committee chairs
The most important influencers of the congressional agenda. They play dominant roles in scheduling hearings, hiring staff, appointing subcommittees, and managing committee **bills** when they are brought before the full House.

seniority system
A simple rule for picking **committee chairs**, in effect until the 1970s. The member who had served on the committee the longest and whose party controlled Congress became chair, regardless of party loyalty, mental state, or competence.

Until the 1970s, there was a simple way of picking committee chairs: the **seniority system**. If committee members had served on their committee longest and their party controlled the chamber, they got to be chairs—regardless of their party loyalty, mental state, or competence.

Woodrow Wilson, a political scientist before he became a politician, once said the government of the United States was really government by the chairs of the standing committees of Congress. The chairs were so powerful for most of the twentieth century that they could bully members or bottle up legislation at any time—and with almost certain knowledge that they would be chairs for the rest of their electoral life. Richard Fenno, a veteran congressional observer, once remarked the "performance of Congress as an institution is very largely the performance of its committees" but that the committee system is the "epitome of fragmentation and decentralization."[39] The more that power is dispersed, the more difficult it is to make coherent policy.

In the 1970s, younger members of Congress revolted. Both parties in both branches permitted members to vote on committee chairs; in 1975, the House Democrats dumped four chairs with 154 years of seniority among them. The Democrats also increased the independence of subcommittees, which limited the chairs' power and widened the distribution of authority, visibility, and resources in both chambers.[40]

Today seniority remains the *general rule* for selecting chairs, but there are plenty of exceptions. House Republicans skipped over several senior representatives when they named committee chairs in 1995 and continued to do so in subsequent Congresses. Partially in response to the problems of decentralized power in the House, the Republicans passed other prominent committee reforms when they took control in 1995. The new rules allowed committee chairs to choose the chairs of subcommittees on their committees and to hire all the committee and subcommittee staff. Some subcommittees were simply eliminated. These changes centralized more power in the committee chairs.

At the same time, the rules limited both committee and subcommittee chairs to three consecutive two-year terms as chair (Senate Republicans also adopted this rule), and committee chairs lost the power to cast proxy votes for those committee members not in attendance. The Speaker also put the committees on short leashes, giving them instructions regarding the legislation they were to report and a timetable for reporting it. In a few instances, the leadership bypassed committees by setting up separate task forces to prepare legislation.

By 1997, however, the leadership backed off. Weakened by his low ratings in the polls, Speaker Newt Gingrich gave committee chairs greater leeway to set their committee's agenda and promised to allow legislation to be first fashioned by committees. The fact remains, however, that committee chairs are not as powerful as they were before the reform era, and the party leadership in the House has much more control over legislation.

Caucuses: The Informal Organization of Congress

Although the formal organization of Congress consists of its party leadership and its committee structures, the informal organization of the House and Senate is also important. The informal networks of trust and mutual interest can spring from numerous sources. Friendship, ideology, and geography are long-standing sources of informal organization.

caucus

A group of members of Congress sharing some interest or characteristic. Most are composed of members from both parties and from both houses.

Lately, these traditional informal groupings have been dominated by a growing number of caucuses. In this context, a **caucus** is a group of members of Congress who share some interest or characteristic. There are about 300 of these caucuses, most of them containing members from both parties and some containing members from both the House and the Senate. The goal of all caucuses is to promote the interests around which they are formed. Within Congress they press for committees to hold hearings, they push particular legislation, and they pull together votes on bills they favor. They are somewhat like interest groups but with a difference: Their members are members of Congress, not petitioners to Congress on the outside looking in. Thus caucuses—interest groups within Congress—are nicely situated to pack more punch than interest groups outside Congress.[41]

The proliferation of congressional caucuses gives members of Congress an informal yet powerful means of shaping the policy agenda. Composed of legislative insiders who share similar concerns, the caucuses—such as the Black Caucus pictured here—exert a much greater influence on policymaking than most citizen-based interest groups can.

Some, such as the Black Caucus, the Congresswomen's Caucus, and the Hispanic Caucus, are based on the characteristics of their members. Others, such as the Sunbelt Caucus and the Northeast-Midwest Congressional Coalition, are based on regional groupings. Still others, such as the Republican Study Committee, are ideological groupings. And still others, such as the Steel, Travel and Tourism, Coal, and Mushroom caucuses, are based on some economic interest that is important to a set of constituencies (yes, there really is a Mushroom Caucus; it is composed of members interested in protecting the interests of mushroom growers).

This explosion of informal groups in Congress has made the representation of interests in Congress a more direct process. The caucuses proceed on the assumption that no one is a more effective lobbyist than a senator or representative. The proliferation of informal caucuses has also tended to decentralize power in Congress. In an effort to limit their importance in 1995, the new Republican majority in the House prohibited members from using appropriations for their office allowances to fund caucuses.

Congressional Staff

As we discussed earlier, members of Congress are overwhelmed with responsibilities. It is virtually impossible to master the details of the hundreds of bills on which they must make decisions each year or to prepare their own legislation. They need help to meet their obligations, so they turn to their staff.

Personal Staff. Most staff members work in the personal offices of individual members. The average representative has 17 assistants and the average senator has 40. In total, more than 11,000 individuals serve on the personal staffs of members of

Congress. (A few hundred additional staff serve the congressional leaders.) In the summer, about 4,000 interns also work in members' offices on Capitol Hill (see "Young People and Politics: Are Opportunities to Intern Biased in Favor of the Wealthy?").

Most of these staffers spend their time providing services to constituents, the casework we discussed earlier regarding congressional elections. They answer mail, communicate the member's views to voters, and help constituents solve problems. Nearly one-half of these House staffers and nearly one-third of the Senate personal staff work in members' offices in their constituencies, not in Washington. This makes it easier for people to make contact with the staff. Other personal staff help members of Congress with legislative functions, including drafting legislation, meeting with lobbyists and administrators, negotiating agreements on behalf of their bosses, writing questions to ask witnesses at committee hearings, summarizing bills, and briefing legislators. Senators, who must cover a wider range of committee assignments than members of the House, are especially dependent on staff. Indeed,

YOUNG PEOPLE AND POLITICS

Are Opportunities to Intern Biased in Favor of the Wealthy?

Many college students spend their summers working to pay for their studies during the rest of the year. Others, in contrast, serve as interns. Many of the interns have parents who support them financially during the summer. According to some experts, the focus on internships as a tool for professional success has never been greater, and about 80 percent of graduating college seniors have done a paid or unpaid internship. To some, an internship is an essential stepping-stone to career success.

Because Washington internships are in high demand, in most cases they do not pay, or they pay very little. The White House does not pay the interns who work there during the summer, in most cases the Supreme Court does not pay its undergraduate interns, and a vast majority of congressional offices do not pay the 4,000 summer interns who work on Capitol Hill, though a few, mostly on the Senate side, provide a limited stipend. To make matters worse, Washington is an expensive place to live, widening the gap between the haves and have-nots in the opportunities to gain experience as an intern. In some cases, universities or other programs provide some financial help, but most interns are left on their own.

As internships rise in importance as critical milestones along the path to success, some people question whether they are creating a class system that discriminates against students from less affluent families who must turn down unpaid internships to earn money for college expenses. To the extent that Washington internships serve as a pipeline for people to become policymakers in the nation's capital, critics fear that over time internships, like the rising costs of college tuition, will squeeze voices from the working class and even the middle class out of high-level policy debates.

Source: Jennifer Lee, "Crucial Unpaid Internships Increasingly Separate the Haves from the Have-Nots," *New York Times*, August 10, 2004.

Questions for Discussion

- Is the internship system in Washington likely to bias policymaking in the future?
- Should Congress appropriate funds so internships are more available to students from less wealthy backgrounds?

Members of Congress depend heavily on their staffs for everything from information and advice to scheduling and negotiating with other members of Congress. Here, Senator Edward Kennedy of Massachusetts confers with a staffer regarding an immigration bill.

members of both houses are now more likely to deal with each other through staff intermediaries than through personal interactions.

Committee Staff. The committees of the House and Senate employ another 2,000 or so staff members. These staff members organize hearings, research legislative options, draft committee reports on bills, write legislation, and, as we have seen, keep tabs on the activities of the executive branch. Committee staff members often possess high levels of expertise and can become very influential in policymaking. As a result, lobbyists spend a lot of time cultivating these staffers both to obtain information about likely legislative actions and to plant ideas for legislation. Sometimes, as you can see in "Issues of the Times: The Revolving Door Between Congress and Lobbying Firms," the lobbyists hire away the congressional staffers with whom they deal.

Staff Agencies. Finally, Congress has three important staff agencies that aid it in its work. The first is the *Congressional Research Service (CRS)*, administered by the Library of Congress and composed of researchers, many with advanced degrees and highly developed expertise. Each year it responds to more than 250,000 congressional requests for information and provides members with nonpartisan studies. CRS also tracks the progress of major bills, prepares summaries of bills, and makes this information available electronically.

The *Government Accountability Office* (GAO), with more than 3,200 employees, helps Congress perform its oversight functions by reviewing the activities of the executive branch to see if it is following the congressional intent of laws and by investigating the efficiency and effectiveness of policy implementation. The GAO also sets government standards for accounting, provides legal opinions, and settles claims against the government.

The *Congressional Budget Office (CBO)* (discussed in more detail in Chapter 15) focuses on analyzing the president's budget and making economic projections about the performance of the economy, the costs of proposed policies, and the economic effects of taxing and spending alternatives.

Committees, caucuses, and individual legislators follow bills from their introduction to their approval. The next sections will discuss this process, which is often termed "labyrinthine" to reflect the fact that getting a bill through Congress is very much like navigating a difficult, intricate maze.

The Congressional Process

bill

A proposed law, drafted in precise, legal language. Anyone can draft a bill, but only a member of the House of Representatives or the Senate can formally submit a bill for consideration.

Congress's agenda is, of course, a crowded one—members introduce about 11,000 bills in each Congress. A **bill** is a proposed law, drafted in precise, legal language. Anyone can draft a bill. The White House and interest groups are common sources of polished bills. However, only members of the House or the Senate can formally submit a bill for consideration. The traditional route for a bill as it works its way through the legislative labyrinth is depicted in Figure 11.2. Most bills are quietly killed off early in the process. Some are introduced mostly as a favor to a group or a constituent; others are private bills, granting citizenship to a constituent or paying a settlement to a person whose car was demolished by a postal service truck. Still other bills may alter the course of the nation.

Congress is typically a reactive and cumbersome decision-making body. Rules are piled on rules and procedures on procedures.[42] Moreover, reforms in the 1970s decentralized the internal distribution of power in Congress, making legislating more difficult. The polarized political climate of the 1980s also exacerbated the problems of legislating. Party leaders sought ways to cope with these problems, and what Barbara Sinclair has termed *unorthodox lawmaking* has become common in the congressional process, especially for the most significant legislation.[43]

In both chambers party leaders involve themselves in the legislative process on major legislation earlier and more deeply, using special procedures to aid the passage of legislation. Leaders in the House often refer bills to several committees at the same time, bringing more interests to bear on an issue but complicating the process of passing legislation. Since committee leaders cannot always negotiate compromises *among* committees, party leaders have accepted this responsibility, often negotiating compromises and making adjustments to bills after a committee or committees report legislation. On the other hand, party leaders often bypass committees altogether for high-priority legislation.

In the House, special rules from the Rules Committee have become powerful tools for controlling floor consideration of bills and sometimes for shaping the outcomes of votes. Often party leaders from each chamber negotiate among themselves instead of creating conference committees. Party leaders also use *omnibus* legislation that addresses numerous and perhaps unrelated subjects, issues, and programs to create winning coalitions, forcing members to support the entire bill to obtain the individual parts.

These new procedures are generally under the control of party leaders in the House, but in the Senate, leaders have less leverage, and *individual* senators have

Figure 11.2 How a Bill Becomes a Law

Many bills travel full circle, coming first from the White House as part of the presidential agenda, then returning to the president at the end of the process. In the interim, there are two parallel processes in the Senate and House, starting with committee action. If a committee gives a bill a favorable report, the whole chamber considers it. When the two chambers pass it in different versions, a conference committee drafts a single compromise bill.

CONGRESS

Bill introduction

HOUSE

Bill introduction
Bill is introduced by a member and assigned to a committee, which usually refers it to a subcommittee.

SENATE

Bill introduction
Bill is introduced by a member and assigned to a committee, which usually refers it to a subcommittee.

Committee action

House:

Subcommittee
Subcommittee performs studies, holds hearings, and makes revisions. If approved, the bill goes to the full committee.

Committee
Full committee may amend or rewrite the bill, before deciding whether to send it to the House floor, recommending its approval, or to kill it. If approved, the bill is reported to the full House and placed on the calendar.

Rules Committee
Rules Committee issues a rule governing debate on the House floor and sends the bill to the full House.

Senate:

Subcommittee
Subcommittee performs studies, holds hearings, and makes revisions. If approved, the bill goes to the full committee.

Committee
Full committee may amend or rewrite the bill, before deciding whether to send it to the Senate floor, recommending its approval, or to kill it. If approved, the bill is reported to the full Senate and placed on the calendar.

Leadership
Senate leaders of both parties schedule Senate debate on the bill.

Floor action

Full House
Bill is debated by full House, amendments are offered, and a vote is taken. If the bill passes in a different version from that passed in the Senate, it is sent to a conference committee.

Full Senate
Bill is debated by full Senate, amendments are offered, and a vote is taken. If the bill passes in a different version from that passed in the House, it is sent to a conference committee.

Conference action

Conference Committee
Conference committee composed of members of both House and Senate meet to iron out differences between the bills. The compromise bill is returned to both the House and Senate for a vote.

Full House
Full House votes on conference committee version. If it passes, the bill is sent to the president.

Full Senate
Full Senate votes on conference committee version. If it passes, the bill is sent to the president.

Presidential decision

President
President signs or vetoes the bill. Congress may override a veto by a two-thirds vote in both the House and Senate.

Law

retained substantial opportunities for influence (such as using the filibuster). As a result, it is often more difficult to pass legislation in the Senate.

There are, of course, countless influences on this legislative process. Presidents, parties, constituents, interest groups, the congressional and committee leadership structure—these and other influences offer members cues for their decision-making.

Presidents and Congress: Partners and Protagonists

Political scientists sometimes call the president the *chief legislator*, a phrase that might have appalled the Constitution writers, with their insistence on separation of powers. Presidents do, however, help create the congressional agenda. They are also their own best lobbyists.

Presidents have their own legislative agenda, based in part on their party's platform and their electoral coalition. Their task is to persuade Congress that their agenda should also be Congress's agenda, and they have a good chance that Congress will at least give their proposals a hearing.[44]

Presidents have many resources with which to influence Congress. (The next chapter will examine presidential leadership.) They may try to influence members directly—calling up wavering members and telling them that the country's future hinges on their votes, for example—but they do not do this often. If presidents were to pick just one key bill and spend 10 minutes on the telephone with each of the 535 members of Congress, they would spend 89 hours chatting with them. Instead, presidents wisely leave most White House lobbying to staff members and administration officials and work closely with the party's leaders in the House and Senate.

It seems a wonder that presidents, even with all their power and prestige, can push and wheedle anything through the labyrinthine congressional process. The president must win at least 10 times to hope for final passage:

1. In one House subcommittee
2. In the full House committee
3. In the House Rules Committee to move to the floor
4. On the House floor
5. In one Senate subcommittee
6. In the full Senate committee
7. On the Senate floor
8. In the House-Senate conference committee to work out the differences between the two bills
9. Back to the House floor for final passage
10. Back to the Senate floor for final passage

As one scholar put it, presidential leadership of Congress is *at the margins*.[45] In general, successful presidential leadership of Congress has not been the result of the dominant chief executive of political folklore who reshapes the contours of the political landscape to pave the way for change. Rather than creating the conditions for important shifts in public policy, the effective American leader is the less heroic *facilitator* who works at the margins of coalition building to recognize and exploit opportunities presented by a favorable configuration of political forces. Of course, presidents can exercise their veto to *stop* legislation they oppose.

Presidents are only one of many claimants for the attention of Congress, especially on domestic policy. As we will show in the next chapter, popular presidents and presidents with a large majority of their party in each house of Congress have a good chance of getting their way. Yet presidents often lose. Ronald Reagan was considered a strong chief executive, and budgeting was one of his principal tools for affecting public policy. Yet commentators typically pronounced the budgets he proposed to Congress DOA, dead on arrival. Members of Congress truly compose an independent branch.

Party, Constituency, and Ideology

Presidents come and go; the parties linger on. Presidents do not determine a congressional member's electoral fortunes; constituents do. Where presidents are less influential, on domestic policies especially, party, personal ideology, and constituency are more important.

Party Influence. On some issues, members of the parties stick together like a marching band. They are most cohesive when Congress is electing its official leaders. A vote for Speaker of the House is a straight party-line vote, with every Democrat on one side and every Republican on the other. On other issues, however, the party coalition may come unglued. In the past, votes on civil rights policies, for example, revealed deep divisions within each party.

Congressional Partisanship

Differences between the parties are sharpest on questions of social welfare and economic policy.[46] When voting on labor issues, Democrats traditionally cling together, leaning toward the side of the unions, whereas Republicans almost always vote with business. On social welfare issues—for example, the minimum wage, aid to the poor, unemployed, or uninsured, and grants for education—Democrats are more supportive of government action than are Republicans. This split between the parties should not be too surprising if you recall the party coalitions described in Chapter 8. Once in office, party members favor their electoral coalitions. Because the constituencies of House members are now more solidly Republican or Democrat, the differences between party members in the House have increased (see "A Generation of Change: Polarized Politics in Congress").

Party leaders in Congress help "whip" their members into line. Their power to do so is limited, of course. They cannot drum a recalcitrant member out of the party. Leaders have plenty of influence, however, including making committee assignments, boosting a member's pet projects, and the subtle but significant influence of providing critical information to a member.

The congressional parties can also impact who sits in Congress. The congressional campaign committees have energized both parties, helping to recruit candidates, running seminars in campaign skills, and conducting polls. They are also a source of funding, as are PACs headed by members of the party leadership.

A GENERATION OF CHANGE

Polarized Politics in Congress

In the 1970s, it was not unusual to find political analysts commenting on how Americans were growing less partisan and less ideological in their politics. Over the past quarter century, however, it is clear that the distance between the congressional parties has been growing steadily. As the parties pulled apart ideologically, they also became more homogeneous internally, as you can see in the figure in this box. In other words, Republicans in Congress became more consistently conservative, Democrats became more consistently liberal, and the distance between the center of each party increased.

By the time George W. Bush took office in 2001, the typical views of members of the parties in both chambers had moved further apart than they had been at any time since before World War I. As a result of these ideological differences between the parties in Congress, it has been more difficult to reach a compromise.

It has been especially difficult for the president, because the opposition party is generally not a fertile ground for obtaining policy support. Because of the polarized partisan divide—and thus a dwindling number of moderate-to-conservative Democrats—there have been few Democrats who were potential supporters of the Republican president in the White House.

Why did this change happen? At the core of the increased ideological distance between the parties have been increasingly divergent electoral coalitions. One important factor is that state legislatures drew the boundaries of House districts so that the partisan divisions in the constituencies of representatives became more one-sided. Most House members no longer had to worry about pleasing the center of the electorate because their own districts were either clearly conservative or liberal.

Polarization in the House and Senate, 1913–2004

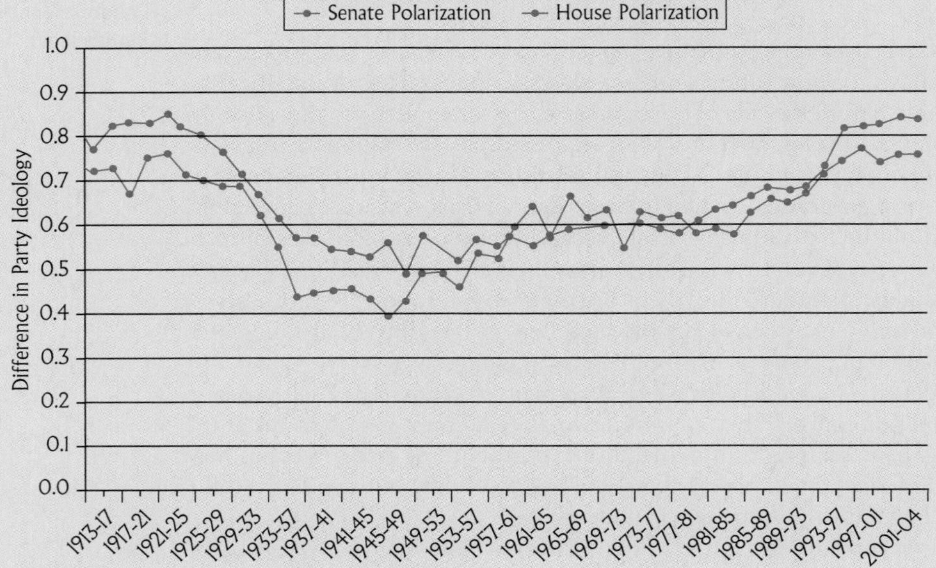

Source: Keith Poole, *http://voteview.com/Polarized_America.htm.*

In addition, liberal and conservative voters sorted themselves into the Democratic and Republican parties, respectively. There are many fewer liberal Republicans or conservative Democrats than there were a generation ago. Thus, conservatives have been more likely to support the more conservative party and liberals the more liberal party. As supporters of each party have matched their partisan and ideological views, they have made the differences between the parties more distinctive. Moreover, party loyalty among voters in congressional elections also increased, so the relationship between ideology and voting became notably stronger.

The changes in the preferences, behavior, and distribution of congressional voters gave the congressional parties more internally homogenous, divergent, and polarized electoral constituencies. These constituencies in turn elected more ideologically polarized representatives in Congress.

Source: Gary C. Jacobson, *A Divider, Not a Uniter: George W. Bush and the American Public* (New York: Longman, 2006), chapter 2.

Constituency Versus Ideology. Members of Congress are representatives; their constituents expect them to represent their interests in Washington. Sometimes this representation requires a balancing act. If some representatives favor more defense spending but suspect that their constituents do not, what are they to do? The English politician and philosopher Edmund Burke favored the concept of legislators as *trustees*, using their best judgment to make policy in the interests of the people. Others prefer the concept of representatives as *instructed delegates*, mirroring the preferences of their constituents. Actually, members of Congress are *politicos*, adopting both trustee and instructed delegate roles as they strive to be both representatives and policymakers.[47]

The best way constituents can influence congressional voting is also simple: elect a representative or senator who agrees with their views. Congressional candidates tend to take policy positions different from their opponent's. Moreover, the winners generally vote on roll calls as they said they would during their campaigns.[48] If voters use their good sense to elect candidates who share their policy positions, then constituents *can* influence congressional policy.

If voters miss their chance and elect someone out of step with their thinking, it may be difficult to influence that person's votes. It is a challenge for even well-intentioned legislators to know what people want. Some legislators pay careful attention to their mail, but the mail is a notoriously unreliable indicator of people's thinking; individuals with extreme opinions on an issue are more likely to write than those with moderate views. Some members send questionnaires to constituents, but the answers they receive are unreliable because few people respond. Some try public opinion polling, but it is expensive if professionally done and unreliable if not.

Defeating an incumbent is no easy task. Even legislators whose votes conflict with the views of their constituents tend to be reelected. Most citizens have trouble recalling the names of their congressional representatives (one study found that only 28 percent of the public could name their representatives in the House),[49] let alone keeping up with their representatives' voting records. According to one expert, "Probably less than a third of all constituents can recognize who their representatives are and what policy positions they have generally taken—and even that third tends not to evaluate incumbents on the basis of policy."[50] A National Election Study found that only 11 percent of the people even claimed to remember how their congressperson voted on a particular issue.

The Prepared Voter Kit

On some controversial issues, however, legislators ignore constituent opinion at great peril. For years, Southern members of Congress would not have dared to vote for a civil rights law. Lately, representatives and senators have been concerned about the many new single-issue groups. Such groups care little about a member's overall record; to them, a vote on one issue—gun control, abortion, gay marriage—is all that counts. Ready to pounce on one wrong vote and pour money into an opponent's campaign, these new forces in constituency politics make every legislator nervous. When issues are visible and salient to voters and easy for them to understand, their representatives are likely to be quite responsive to constituency opinion.[51]

Nevertheless, many issues are complex, obscure, and not salient to voters. On such issues legislators can safely ignore constituency opinion. On a typical issue, the prime determinant of a congressional member's vote is personal ideology. On issues where ideological divisions are sharp and constituency preferences and knowledge are likely to be weak, such as defense and foreign policy, ideology is virtually the only determinant of voting.[52] As ideological divisions weaken and constituency preferences strengthen, members are more likely to deviate from their own position and adopt those of their constituencies.[53] Thus, when they have differences of opinion with their constituencies, members of Congress consider constituency preferences but are not controlled by them.[54]

Lobbyists and Interest Groups

The nation's capital is crawling with lawyers, lobbyists, registered foreign agents, public relations consultants, and others—there are about 35,000 registered lobbyists representing 12,000 organizations—all seeking to influence Congress.[55] Several dozen groups are concerned with the single issue of protecting Alaska's environment; the bigger the issue, the more lobbyists are involved. Any group interested in influencing national policymaking—and that includes almost everyone—either hires Washington lobbyists or sends its own. Washington lobbyists can be a formidable group.

Lobbyists spend more than $2 billion on lobbying federal officials—plus millions more in campaign contributions and attempts to try to persuade members' constituents to send messages to Washington.[56] Such spending gives lobbyists a bad name, no doubt often deserved. But lobbyists have a job to do—namely, to represent the interests of their organizations. Lobbyists, some of them former members of Congress, can provide legislators with crucial policy information, political intelligence, and often with assurances of financial aid in the next campaign—making those legislators with whom they agree more effective in the legislative process.[57] They often coordinate their efforts at influencing members with party leaders who share their views. Grass-roots lobbying—such as computerized mailings to encourage citizens to pressure their representatives on an issue—is a common activity. Interest groups also distribute scorecards of how members of Congress voted on issues important to the groups, threatening members with electoral retaliation if they do not support the groups' stands.

The easiest way to frustrate lobbyists is to ignore them. Lobbyists usually make little headway with their opponents anyway: The lobbyist for General Motors arguing

Lobbyists play an important role in the legislative process, providing legislators with information and technical expertise—as well as campaign funds.

against automobile pollution controls would not have much influence with a legislator concerned about air pollution. Members of Congress can also make life uncomfortable for lobbyists. They can embarrass them, expose heavy-handed tactics, and spread the word among an organization's members that it is being poorly represented in Washington.

Congress can also regulate lobbyists. In 1995, Congress passed a law requiring anyone hired to lobby members of Congress, congressional staff members, White House officials, and federal agencies to report what issues they were seeking to influence, how much they were spending on the effort, and the identities of their clients. This law was designed to close loopholes in a 1946 law that allowed most lobbyists to avoid registering and permitted those who did to disclose only limited information about their activities. Congress also placed severe restrictions on the gifts, meals, and expense-paid travel that public officials may accept from lobbyists. In theory, these reporting requirements and restrictions not only prevent shady deals between lobbyists and members of Congress but also curb the influence of special interests. Nevertheless, slippage occurs. In 2005 and 2006, the country saw some members caught up in bribery scandals. The nation also learned of lobbyist Jack Abramoff's success in charging six Indian tribes more than $80 million for his lobbying services in less than a decade—and his extraordinary contributions to and expenditures on some representatives and senators.

There are many forces that affect senators and representatives as they decide how to vote on a bill. After his exhaustive study of influences on congressional decision making, John Kingdon concluded that none was important enough to suggest that members of Congress vote as they do because of one influence.[58] The process is as complex for individual legislators as it is for those who want to influence their votes.

Understanding Congress

Congress is a complex institution. Its members want to make sound national policy, but they also want to return to Washington after the next election. How do these sometimes conflicting desires affect American democracy and the scope of American government?

Congress and Democracy

Comparing Legislatures

In a large nation, the success of democratic government depends on the quality of representation. Americans could hardly hold a national referendum on every policy issue on the government agenda; instead, they delegate decision-making power to representatives. If Congress is a successful democratic institution, it must be a successful representative institution.

Certainly, some aspects of Congress make it very *un*representative. Its members are an American elite. Its leadership is chosen by its own members, not by any vote of the American people. Voters have little direct influence over the individuals who chair key committees or lead congressional parties. Voters in just a single constituency control the fate of committee chairs and party leaders. Voters in the other 434 House districts and the other 49 states have no real say, for example, about who chairs a committee considering new forms of energy, a committee considering defense buildups, or a committee making economic policy.

Nevertheless, the evidence in this chapter demonstrates that Congress *does* try to listen to the American people. Whom voters elect makes a difference in how congressional votes turn out; which party is in power affects policies. Linkage institutions actually link voters to policymakers. Perhaps Congress could do a better job at representation than it does, but there are many obstacles to improved representation. Legislators find it hard to know what constituents want. Groups may keep important issues off the legislative agenda. Members may spend so much time servicing their constituencies that they have little time left to represent those constituencies in the policymaking process.

Members of Congress are responsive to the people, if the people make clear what they want. For example, in response to popular demands, Congress established a program in 1988 to shield the elderly against the catastrophic costs associated with acute illness. In 1989, in response to complaints from the elderly about higher Medicare premiums, Congress abolished most of what it had created the previous year.

Representativeness Versus Effectiveness. The central legislative dilemma for Congress is combining the faithful representation of constituents with making effective public policy. Supporters see Congress as a forum in which many interests compete for a spot on the policy agenda and over the form of a particular policy—which is just as the Founders intended it to be.

Critics charge that Congress is responsive to so many interests that policy is as uncoordinated, fragmented, and decentralized as Congress itself. Interest groups grow on committees and subcommittees like barnacles on a boat. After a while, these groups develop intimacy and influence with "their" committee. Committee decisions

HOW YOU CAN MAKE A DIFFERENCE

Political Action and Congress

Because of its representative and law-making nature, Congress is often thought of as the "first branch among equals." It is the only branch of government designed to be directly accessible by the American people. American politics research shows that members of Congress are particularly concerned with constituent service and maintaining ties to voters in their districts. They understand that an angry or upset voter is more likely to work against them in an election campaign than your average satisfied voter. It follows that if you wish to help alter or change American politics and policy, accessing a member of Congress or running for Congress yourself may be excellent ways for you to have a decent impact.

Making a Difference

The Congress to Campus program sends bipartisan pairs of former members of Congress, one Democrat and one Republican, to college campuses around the country to help students understand the nobility of public service. The representatives encourage students to take an active role. They even encourage students to make their own runs for Congress. The program was founded in 1976 by the U.S. Association of Former Members of Congress to introduce students to those individuals with firsthand knowledge of representative democracy.

What you can do:

- Locate your representative's Washington and home office numbers by using the directory on Congress's own website (*http://thomas.loc.gov*). Call and set up an appointment to meet with your representative.
- Write letters or send e-mails to your representative expressing your views and concerns on the issues that matter the most to you.
- Make a run for a congressional seat yourself. Even if you lose, your run will force the representatives to address the issues that are a part of your campaign.

usually carry over to the roll-call vote. Thus, the committee system links congressional policymaking to a multiplicity of interests rather than to a majority's preferences.

In addition, some observers believe Congress is too representative—so much so that it is incapable of taking decisive action to deal with difficult problems. The agricultural committees busily tend to the interests of farmers, while committees focusing on foreign trade worry about cutting agricultural subsidies. One committee wrestles with domestic unemployment, while another makes a tax policy that encourages businesses to open new plants out of the country. One reason why government spends too much, critics say, is that Congress is protecting the interests of too many people. As long as each interest tries to preserve the status quo, Congress cannot enact bold reforms.

On the other hand, defenders of Congress point out that, because it is decentralized, there is no oligarchy in control to prevent the legislature from taking comprehensive action. In fact, Congress has enacted the huge tax cuts of 1981 and 2001, the comprehensive (and complicated) tax reform of 1986, and various bills structuring the budgetary process designed to balance the budget.[59] In recent years, Congress has also passed important trade bills, a prescription drug addition to Medicare, and a major program for elementary and secondary education.

There is no simple solution to Congress's dilemma. It tries to be both a representative and an objective policymaking institution. As long as this is true, it is unlikely that Congress will please all its critics.

Congress and the Scope of Government

If Congress is responsive to a multitude of interests and those interests desire government policies to aid them in some way, does the nature of Congress predispose it to continually increasing the scope of the public sector? Do the benefits of servicing constituents provide an incentive for members of Congress to tolerate, even to expand, an already big government? The more policies there are, the more potential ways members can help their constituencies. The more bureaucracies there are, the more red tape members can help cut. Big government helps members of Congress get reelected and even gives them good reason to support making it bigger.

Members of Congress vigorously protect the interests of their constituents. At the same time, there are many members who agree with Ronald Reagan that government is not the answer to problems but rather *is* the problem. These individuals make careers out of fighting against government programs (although these same senators and representatives typically support programs aimed at aiding *their* constituents).

Americans have contradictory preferences regarding public policy. As we have noted in previous chapters, they want to balance the budget and pay low taxes, but they also support most government programs. Congress does not impose programs on a reluctant public; instead, it responds to the public's demand for them.

Summary

According to the Constitution, members of Congress are the government's policymakers, but legislative policymaker is only one of the roles of members of Congress. They are also politicians, and politicians always keep one eye on the next election. Success in congressional elections may be determined as much by constituency service—casework and the pork barrel—as by policymaking. Senators and representatives have become so secure in their constituencies that incumbents have a big edge over challengers, making it more difficult to bring about major changes in the makeup, and thus the policies, of Congress.

The structure of Congress is so complex that it seems remarkable that legislation gets passed at all. Its bicameral division means that bills have two sets of committee hurdles to clear. Because power is often decentralized, especially in the Senate, the job of leading Congress is more difficult than ever.

Presidents try hard to influence Congress, and parties and elections can also shape legislators' choices. The impact of these factors clearly differs from one policy area to another. Party impacts are clearest on issues for which the party's coalitions are clearest, especially social welfare and economic issues. Constituencies influence policy mostly by the initial choice of a representative. Members of Congress do pay attention to voters, particularly on visible issues, but most issues do not interest voters. On these less visible issues other factors, such as lobbyists and members' individual ideologies, influence policy decisions.

Congress clearly has some undemocratic and unrepresentative features. Its members are hardly average Americans. Even so, members pay attention to popular preferences, when they can determine what they are. People inside and outside the institution, however, think Congress is ineffective. Its objective policymaking decisions and representative functions sometimes conflict, yet from time to time Congress shows that it can deal with major issues in a comprehensive fashion. Many members of Congress have incentives to increase the scope of the federal government, but the people who put those representatives in office provide these incentives.

Internet Resources

www.house.gov/
The official House Web site contains information on the organization, operations, schedule, and activities of the House and its committees. The site also contains links to the offices of members and committees and enables you to contact your representative directly.

www.senate.gov/
The official Senate Web site contains information and links similar to those for the House.

Thomas.loc.gov/
Information on the activities of Congress, the status and text of legislation, the *Congressional Record,* committee reports, and historical documents.

www.rollcall.com/
Roll Call, the online version of the Capitol Hill newspaper.

www.opensecrets.org/
Federal Election Commission data on campaign expenditures.

www.crp.org
The Center for Responsive Politics Web site with data on the role of money in politics.

www.c-span.org
Video coverage of Congress in action.

Get Connected

The Organization of Congress

Both the Senate and the House are organized into committees, where much of the real work of the Congress takes place. As the text notes, senators and representatives seek membership on committees that have something to do with their home state or district. They seek membership on the right committees because good work on the right committees will help them get reelected, make good policy, and gain influence in Congress. See whether you can pick the committees on which your local representative serves.

First, make a list of the important characteristics of your district, such as whether it is urban or rural, whether it has a lot of farming or industry, whether it has a large international airport or sits next to the ocean, or whether there is a lot of military in the district. Your list should have five or six items on it. Next, go to the House of Representatives Web site and look at the jurisdictional duties of each standing House committee. Based on your list, pick the committees on which you think your representative might serve. Once you've done that, go to your representative's Web site to see how accurate you are.

Search the Web

Go to *www.house.gov/rules/comm_jurisdiction.htm* to review the jurisdiction of the standing committees. Go to *www.house.gov/* to find your representative's Web site to check the accuracy of your picks.

Questions to Ask

- Does your representative appear to be on the kinds of committees that will allow him or her to best represent your district?
- If you could place your representative on another committee, one that might be more important to the district, which would it be? Why?
- Not all committees are focused on district-level interests. Some deal with broader issues such as foreign affairs, national defense, and tax policy. Is your representative on a committee on which he or she can influence policies critical to the nation?

Why It Matters

One job of congressional representatives is to represent the issues and concerns of their constituents. Because the committees are where most work gets done in Congress, it is important for representatives to be on a committee that will allow them to best represent their districts. Constituents also have broader interests, however, and the committees on which their representatives serve are an opportunity to influence important policies.

Get Involved

Send your representative an e-mail asking why he or she serves on certain committees. Ask why he or she serves on a committee that does not seem to fit the district and not on a committee that seems important for the district. Ask also whether your representative has any plans to change committee assignments in the future.

For more exercises, go to www.longmanamericangovernment.com.

For Further Reading

Aberbach, Joel D. *Keeping a Watchful Eye: The Politics of Congressional Oversight*. Washington, DC: Brookings Institution, 1990. A thorough study of congressional oversight of the executive branch.

Bernstein, Robert A. *Elections, Representation, and Congressional Voting Behavior*. Englewood Cliffs, NJ: Prentice Hall, 1989. Examines the issue of constituency control over members of Congress.

Binder, Sarah A. *Stalemate*. Washington, DC: Brookings Institution, 2003. Discusses the causes and consequences of legislative gridlock.

Deering, Christopher J., and Steven S. Smith. *Committees in Congress*. 3rd ed. Washington, DC: Congressional Quarterly Press, 1997. A thorough overview of the complex committee structure in the House and Senate.

Dodd, Lawrence C., and Bruce I. Oppenheimer. *Congress Reconsidered*. 8th ed. Washington, DC: Congressional Quarterly, 2005. Excellent essays covering many aspects of Congress.

Fenno, Richard F., Jr. *Home Style*. Boston: Little, Brown, 1978. How members of Congress mend fences and stay in political touch with the folks back home.

Fiorina, Morris P. *Congress: Keystone of the Washington Establishment*. 2nd ed. New Haven, CT: Yale University Press, 1989. Argues that members of Congress are self-serving in representing their constituents, ensuring their reelection while harming the national interest.

Jacobson, Gary C. *The Politics of Congressional Elections*. 6th ed. New York: Addison-Wesley Longman, 2004. An excellent review of congressional elections.

Kingdon, John W. *Congressmen's Voting Decisions*. 3rd ed. Ann Arbor: University of Michigan Press, 1989. A thorough and insightful study of congressional voting decisions.

Lee, Frances E., and Bruce I. Oppenheimer. *Sizing Up the Senate: The Unequal Consequences of Equal Representation*. Chicago: University of Chicago Press, 1999. How representation in the Senate affects how people are represented, the distribution of government benefits, and the nature of election campaigns.

Mann, Thomas E., and Norman J. Ornstein. *The Broken Branch*. New York: Oxford University Press, 2006. How Congress is failing America and how to get it back on track.

Mayhew, David R. *Congress: The Electoral Connection*. 2nd ed. New Haven, CT: Yale University Press, 2005. An analysis of Congress based on the premise that the principal motivation of congressional behavior is reelection.

Sinclair, Barbara. *Party Wars*. Norman, OK: University of Oklahoma Press, 2006. The impact of partisan polarization on congressional policy making.

Sinclair, Barbara. *Unorthodox Lawmaking*. 3rd ed. Washington, DC: Congressional Quarterly Press, 2007. Explains how Congress tries to cope with decentralization and polarization.

CHAPTER 12

The Presidency

Chapter Outline

POLITICS IN ACTION: PRESIDENTIAL POWER? As George W. Bush stood before a joint session of Congress in early 2007, he could reflect on his tenure as president. It had certainly been eventful. Elected in 2000 without even a plurality of the vote and after a protracted battle in the courts, he had to create a new administration under the difficult circumstances of a substantially shortened transition period. Once in office, he had led the successful fight on his highest priority—a major tax cut. Soon, however, his approval ratings dropped, and the Senate switched to control by the Democratic opposition.

Shortly afterward, terrorists launched a devastating attack on the United States, and the focus of his administration abruptly changed to a war on terrorism. His approval ratings rocketed to the highest on record, and his party won majorities in Congress in the midterm elections. Nevertheless, Congress was often resistant to his proposals, and members of both Congress and the press raised disturbing questions about the bureaucracy's performance regarding homeland security.

After winning reelection, he launched a campaign to reform the massive Social Security program. His efforts came to nothing. Even more frustrating were the difficulties he faced in pacifying and democratizing Iraq, and throughout his second term most Americans disapproved of his performance in office.

Powerful, strong, leader of the free world, commander in chief—these are common images of the American president. The only place in the world where television networks assign permanent camera crews is the White House. The presidency is power—at least according to popular myth. Problems are brought to their desk, they decide on the right courses of action, they issue orders, and an army of aides and bureaucrats carry out their commands.

As George W. Bush and all other presidents soon discover, nothing could be further from the truth. The main reason why presidents have trouble getting things done is that other policymakers with whom they deal have their own agendas, their own interests, and their own sources of power. Presidents operate in an environment filled with checks and balances and competing centers of power. As one presidential aide put it, "Every time you turn around people resist you."[1] Congress is beholden not to the president but to the individual constituencies of its members. Cabinet members often push their departmental interests and their constituencies (the Department of Agriculture has farmers as its constituency, for example). Rarely can presidents rely on unwavering support from their party, the public, or even their own appointees.

As the pivotal leader in American politics, the president is the subject of unending political analysis and speculation. A perennial question focuses on presidential power. World history is replete with examples of leaders who have exceeded the prescribed boundaries of their power. Can the presidency become too powerful and thus pose a threat to democracy? Or is the Madisonian system strong enough to check any such tendencies? On the other hand, is the president *strong enough* to stand up to the diverse interests in the United States? Does the president have enough power to govern on behalf of the majority?

A second fundamental question regarding democratic leaders is the nature of their relationship with the public and its consequences for public policy. The president and vice president are the only officials elected by the entire nation. In their efforts to obtain public support from the broad spectrum of interests in the public, are presidents natural advocates of an expansion of government? Do they promise more than they should in order to please the voters? As they face the frustrations of governing, do presidents seek to centralize authority in the federal government, where they have greater influence, while reducing that of the states? Does the chief executive seek more power through increasing the role of government?

Since not everyone bends easily to even the most persuasive president, the president must be a *leader*. As Richard Neustadt has argued, presidential power is the power to *persuade*.[2] To accomplish policy goals, the president must get other people—important people—to do things they otherwise would not do. To be effective, the president must have highly developed *political skills* to mobilize influence, manage conflict, negotiate, and fashion compromises. Presidential leadership has varied over the years, depending in large part on the individual who holds our nation's highest office.

The Presidents

The presidency is an institution composed of the roles presidents must play, the powers at their disposal, and the large bureaucracy at their command. It is also a highly personal office. The personality of the individual serving as president makes a difference.

Great Expectations

When a new president takes the oath of office, he faces many daunting tasks. Perhaps the most difficult is living up to the expectations of the American people. Americans expect the chief executive to ensure peace, prosperity, and security.[3] As President Carter remarked, "The President is . . . held to be responsible for the state of the economy . . . and for the inconveniences, or disappointments, or the concerns of the American people."[4] Americans want a good life, and they look to the president to provide it.

Americans are of two minds about the presidency. On the one hand, they want to believe in a powerful president, one who can do good. They look back longingly on the great presidents of the first American century—Washington, Jefferson, Lincoln—and some in the second century as well, especially Franklin D. Roosevelt.

On the other hand, Americans dislike a concentration of power. Although presidential responsibilities have increased substantially since the Great Depression and World War II, there has not been a corresponding increase in presidential authority or administrative resources to meet these new expectations. Americans are basically individualistic and skeptical of authority. According to Samuel Huntington, "The distinctive aspect of the American Creed is its antigovernment character. Opposition to power, and suspicion of government as the most dangerous embodiment of power, are the central themes of American political thought."[5] The American political culture's tenets of limited government, liberty, individualism, equality, and democracy generate a distrust of strong leadership, authority, and the public sector in general.

Presidential Power

Because Americans' expectations of the presidency are so high, who serves as president is especially important. Just who are the people who have occupied the Oval Office?

Who They Are

When Warren G. Harding, one of the least illustrious American presidents, was in office, attorney Clarence Darrow remarked, "When I was a boy, I was told that anybody could become president. Now I'm beginning to believe it." The Constitution simply states that the president must be a natural-born citizen at least 35 years old and must have resided in the United States for at least 14 years. In fact, all American presidents have been White, male, and (except for John Kennedy) Protestant. In other ways, however, the recent collection of presidents suggests considerable variety. Since World War II, the White House has been home to a Missouri haberdasher, a war hero, a Boston-Irish politician, a small-town Texas boy who grew up to

Each president has shaped the office in his own image. Lyndon Johnson's presidency was characterized by a willingness to attack a broad range of issues, from communism in Vietnam to poverty in America—and by exhaustion from grappling with so many complex problems.

become the biggest wheeler-dealer in the Senate, a California lawyer described by his enemies as "Tricky Dick" and by his friends as a misunderstood master of national leadership, a former Rose Bowl player who had spent his entire political career in the House of Representatives, a former governor who had been a Georgia peanut wholesaler, an actor who was also a former governor of California, a CIA chief and ambassador who was the son of a U.S. senator, an ambitious governor from a small state, and a former managing director of a major league baseball team who won his first election only six years before becoming president (see Table 12.1).

So far, no woman or minority group member has served as president. This situation is likely to change, however, as social prejudices diminish and as more women and minorities are elected to positions that serve as stepping-stones to the presidency.

All manner of men have occupied the Oval Office. Thomas Jefferson was a scientist and scholar who assembled dinosaur bones when presidential business was slack. Woodrow Wilson, the only political scientist ever to become president, combined a Presbyterian moral fervor and righteousness with a professor's intimidating style of leadership and speech making. His successor, Warren G. Harding, became president because Republican leaders thought he looked like one. Poker was his pastime. Out of his element in the job, Harding is almost everyone's choice as the worst American president. His speech making, said opponent William G. McAdoo, sounded "like an army of pompous phrases marching across the landscape in search of an idea." Harding's friends stole the government blind, prompting his brief assessment of the presidency: "God, what a job!"

How They Got There

No one is born to be the future president of the United States solely because of royal lineage like future kings or queens of England. Regardless of their background or character, all presidents must come to the job through one of two basic routes.

Elections: The Normal Road to the White House. Most presidents take a familiar journey to 1600 Pennsylvania Avenue: They run for president through the electoral process, which we describe in Chapter 9. The Constitution guarantees a four-year term once in office, but the **Twenty-second Amendment**, ratified in 1951, limits them to two terms.

Twenty-second Amendment

Passed in 1951, this amendment limits presidents to two terms of office.

Only 12 of the 42 presidents before George W. Bush have actually served two or more full terms in the White House: Washington, Jefferson, Madison, Monroe, Jackson, Grant, Cleveland (whose terms were not consecutive), Wilson, Franklin Roosevelt, Eisenhower, Reagan, and Clinton. A few decided against a second term ("Silent Cal" Coolidge said simply, "I do not choose to run"). Five other presidents

(Polk, Pierce, Buchanan, Hayes, and Lyndon Johnson) also threw in the towel at the end of one full term. Seven others (both the Adamses, Van Buren, Taft, Hoover, Carter, and George Bush) thought they had earned a second term, but the voters disagreed.

Succession and Impeachment. For more than 10 percent of American history, the presidency has actually been occupied by an individual who was not elected to the office. About one in five presidents got the job because they were vice president when the incumbent president either died or (in Nixon's case) resigned. In the twentieth century, almost one-third (five of 18) of those who occupied the office were "accidental presidents." The most accidental of all was Gerald Ford, who did not run for either the vice presidency or the presidency before taking office. President Nixon nominated Ford as vice president when Vice President Spiro Agnew resigned; Ford then assumed the presidency when Nixon himself resigned.

Removing a discredited president before the end of a term is not easy. The Constitution prescribes the process of **impeachment**, which is roughly the political equivalent of an indictment in criminal law. The House of Representatives may, by majority vote, impeach the president for "Treason, Bribery, or other high Crimes and Misdemeanors." Once the House votes for impeachment, the case goes to the Senate, which tries the accused president, with the chief justice of the Supreme Court presiding. By a two-thirds vote, the Senate may convict and remove the president from office.

impeachment
The political equivalent of an indictment in criminal law, prescribed by the Constitution. The House of Representatives may impeach the president by a majority vote for "Treason, Bribery, or other high Crimes and Misdemeanors."

The House has impeached only two presidents. It impeached Andrew Johnson, Lincoln's successor, in 1868 on charges stemming from his disagreement with radical Republicans. He narrowly escaped conviction. On July 31, 1974, the House Judiciary Committee voted to recommend that the full House impeach

Richard Nixon was the only American president ever to resign his office. Nixon decided to resign rather than face impeachment for his role in the Watergate scandal, a series of illegal wiretaps, break-ins, and cover-ups.

Table 12.1 Recent Presidents

PRESIDENT	TERM	PARTY	BACKGROUND	SIGNIFICANT EVENTS
Harry S Truman	1945–1953	Democrat	• U.S. senator from Missouri • Chosen as FDR's running mate in 1944 • Became president when FDR died	• Made decision to drop atomic bombs on Japan to end World War II • Presided over postwar recovery • Laid foundation for Cold War policy • Relatively unpopular during term
Dwight D. Eisenhower	1953–1961	Republican	• Commander of Allied forces in Europe in World War II • Never voted until he ran for president	• Presided over relatively Tranquil 1950s • Conservative domestic policies • Cool crisis management • Enjoyed strong public approval
John F. Kennedy	1961–1963	Democrat	• U.S. senator from Massachusetts • From very wealthy family • War hero	• Known for personal style • Presided over Cuban missile crisis • Ushered in era of liberal domestic policies • Assassinated in 1963
Lyndon B. Johnson	1963–1969	Democrat	• Senate majority leader • Chosen as Kennedy's running mate; succeeded him after the assassination	• Skilled legislative leader with a coarse public image • Launched the Great Society • Escalated the Vietnam War • Won passage of major civil rights laws • War policies proved unpopular; did not seek reelection
Richard M. Nixon	1969–1974	Republican	• U.S. senator from California • Served two terms as Eisenhower's vice president • Lost presidential election of 1960 to John F. Kennedy	• Presided over period of legislative innovation • Renewed relations with China • Ended Vietnam War • Resigned as result of Watergate scandal

Watergate

The events and scandal surrounding a break-in at the Democratic National Committee headquarters in 1972 and the subsequent cover-up of White House involvement, leading to the eventual resignation of President Nixon under the threat of **impeachment**.

Richard Nixon as a result of the **Watergate** scandal. Nixon escaped a certain vote for impeachment by resigning. In 1998, the House voted two articles of impeachment against President Clinton on party-line votes. The public clearly opposed the idea, however, and the Senate voted to acquit the president on both counts in 1999 (see "You Are the Policymaker: Should the Senate Have Convicted President Clinton?").

Constitutional amendments cover one other important problem concerning the presidential term: presidential disability and succession. Several times a president

Table 12.1 *(continued)*

PRESIDENT	TERM	PARTY	BACKGROUND	SIGNIFICANT EVENTS
Gerald R. Ford	1974–1977	Republican	• House minority leader • First person ever nominated as vice president under Twenty-fifth Amendment	• Pardoned Richard Nixon • Helped heal the nation's wounds • Lost election in 1976 to Jimmy Carter
Jimmy Carter	1977–1981	Democrat	• Governor of Georgia • Peanut farmer	• Viewed as honest but politically unskilled • Brokered peace between Egypt and Israel • Managed Iranian hostage crisis • Lost bid for reelection in 1980
Ronald W. Reagan	1981–1989	Republican	• Governor of California • Well-known actor	• Won a substantial tax cut • Led fight for a large increase in defense spending • Hurt by Iran/Contra scandal • Known as the Great Communicator
George Bush	1989–1993	Republican	• U.S. representative from Texas • Director of CIA • Ambassador to UN • Served two terms as Reagan's vice president	• Led international coalition to victory in Gulf War • Presided over end of Cold War • Popular until economy stagnated • Lost reelection bid in 1992
William J. Clinton	1993–2001	Democrat	• Governor of Arkansas • Rhodes Scholar	• Moved Democrats to center • Presided over balanced budget • Benefited from strong economy • Tenure marred by Monica Lewinsky scandal • Impeached
George W. Bush	2001–	Republican	• Governor of Texas • Son of President George Bush • Elected without plurality of the vote	• Launched war on terrorism • Won large tax cut • Established Department of Homeland Security • Began war with Iraq

has become disabled, incapable of carrying out the job for weeks or even months at a time. After Woodrow Wilson suffered a stroke, his wife, Edith Wilson, became virtual acting president. The **Twenty-fifth Amendment** (1967) clarifies some of the Constitution's vagueness about disability. The amendment permits the vice president to become acting president if the vice president and the president's cabinet determine that the president is disabled or if the president declares his own disability, and it outlines how a recuperated president can reclaim the Oval Office. Other laws specify the order of presidential succession—from the vice president, to the Speaker

YOU ARE THE POLICYMAKER

Should the Senate Have Convicted President Clinton?

Monica Lewinsky became a household name in January 1998. By the end of the year, the most intimate details of her two-year affair with President Bill Clinton were known to almost everyone in the country. The nation had to do more than live through a new soap opera of sex and politics, however. The question became whether the president should be removed from office.

In September, Independent Counsel Kenneth Starr issued a report to Congress accusing President Clinton of 11 counts of possible impeachable offenses, including perjury, obstruction of justice, witness tampering, and abuse of power. The president's detractors used the report as a basis for charging that he had broken the law, failed in his primary constitutional duty to take care that the laws be faithfully executed, betrayed the public's trust, and dishonored the nation's highest office. As a result, they argued the president should be removed from office through the process of impeachment. They also argued that other public officials would be removed from office for having an affair with a young intern. Why, they asked, should the president be held to lower standards?

The White House fought back. First, the president apologized to the nation—sort of. Then he engaged in a round of expressions of remorse before a variety of audiences. At the same time, the White House accused Starr of engaging in an intrusive investigation motivated by a political vendetta against the president. The White House argued that the president made a mistake in his private behavior, apologized for it, and should continue to do the job he was elected to do. Impeachment, the president's defenders said, was grossly disproportionate to the president's offense.

The Constitution provides only the most general guidelines as to the grounds for impeachment. Article II, Section 4, says, "The President, Vice President and all civil Officers of the United States, shall be removed from Office on Impeachment for, and Conviction of, Treason, Bribery, or other high Crimes and Misdemeanors."

Twenty-fifth Amendment
Passed in 1967, the amendment that permits the vice president to become acting president if both the vice president and the president's cabinet determine that the president is disabled. The amendment also outlines how a recuperated president can reclaim the job.

of the House, to the president pro tempore of the Senate and down through the cabinet members.

The Twenty-fifth Amendment also created a means for selecting a new vice president when the office becomes vacant (a more frequent occurrence). The president nominates a new vice president, who assumes the office when both houses of Congress approve the nomination.

Presidential Powers

Comparing Chief Executives

The contemporary presidency hardly resembles the one the Constitution framers designed in 1787. The executive office they conceived had more limited authority, fewer responsibilities, and much less organizational structure than today's presidency. The Founders feared both anarchy and monarchy. They wanted an independent executive but disagreed about both the form the office should take and the powers it should exercise. In the end, they created an executive unlike any the world had ever seen.[6]

There is agreement on at least four points regarding impeachable offenses.

1. Impeachable behavior does not have to be a crime. If the president refused to work or chose to invade a country solely to increase his public support, his actions could be grounds for impeachment, even though they would not violate the law.
2. The offense should be grave for it to be impeachable. A poker game in the White House, even though it may violate the law, would not constitute an impeachable offense.
3. A matter of policy disagreement is not grounds for impeachment. The only president who had been impeached before Clinton was Andrew Johnson, who was tried in 1868. He survived by one vote. The real issue was disagreement between the president and Congress over the policy of Reconstruction following the Civil War. Johnson's impeachment and trial are widely viewed as an abuse of impeachment power.
4. Impeachment is an inherently political process and the grounds for impeachment are ultimately whatever Congress decides they are because the Constitution assigns these calibrations to members' political judgment.

Beyond these points of agreement, we enter speculative territory. In 1974, the House Judiciary Committee passed three articles of impeachment against President Richard Nixon, but the president resigned before the House took up the charges. The three articles charged that Nixon had (1) obstructed justice, (2) abused his power, and (3) failed to comply with congressional subpoenas. The Democrats overwhelmingly supported all three articles, and the Republicans generally opposed them.

In 1998 and 1999, the tables were turned, as the Republicans supported a lower threshold for an impeachable offense, while the Democrats argued for a higher one. In December 1998, the House voted two articles of impeachment against President Clinton on nearly straight party-line votes. The articles charged him with lying to a grand jury and obstructing justice.

Most Americans felt that the president had behaved improperly, but they also felt he was doing a good job as president. Most opposed impeaching Clinton. Opinion among officeholders and journalists was more negative toward the president, however. After a Senate trial, senators voted to acquit the president. If you were a member of the Senate, would *you* have voted to convict the president?

Constitutional Powers

The Constitution says remarkably little about presidential power. The discussion of the presidency begins with these general words: "The executive power shall be vested in a president of the United States of America." It goes on to list just a few powers (see Table 12.2). The framers' invention fits nicely within the Madisonian system of shared power and checks and balances, forcing the president to persuade officials in the other branches of government.

Institutional balance was essential to the convention delegates, who had in mind the abuses of past executives (including both the king and colonial governors) combined with the excesses of state legislatures (discussed in Chapter 2). The problem was how to preserve the balance without jeopardizing the independence of the separate branches or impeding the lawful exercise of their authority. The framers resolved this problem by checking those powers they believed to be most dangerous, the ones that historically had been subject to the greatest abuse (for example, they gave Congress the power to declare war and the Senate the power to approve treaties and presidential appointments), while protecting the general spheres of authority from encroachment (the executive, for instance, was given a qualified veto). Provisions for reelection and a short term of office also encouraged presidential responsibility. For those executives who flagrantly abused their authority, impeachment was the ultimate recourse.

Table 12.2 Constitutional Powers of the President

National Security Powers
Serve as commander in chief of the armed forces
Make treaties with other nations, subject to the agreement of two-thirds of the Senate
Nominate ambassadors, with the agreement of a majority of the Senate
Receive ambassadors of other nations, thereby conferring diplomatic recognition on other governments

Legislative Powers
Present information on the state of the union to Congress
Recommend legislation to Congress
Convene both houses of Congress on extraordinary occasions
Adjourn Congress if the House and Senate cannot agree on adjournment
Veto legislation (Congress may overrule with two-thirds vote of each house)

Administrative Powers
"Take care that the laws be faithfully executed"
Nominate officials as provided for by Congress and with the agreement of a majority of the Senate
Request written opinions of administrative officials
Fill administrative vacancies during congressional recesses

Judicial Powers
Grant reprieves and pardons for federal offenses (except impeachment)
Nominate federal judges, who are confirmed by a majority of the Senate

Why It Matters

Standards of Impeachment
It is not easy to impeach a president; the threshold for an impeachable offense is a high one. This standard makes it very difficult to remove a president *between* elections. A lower threshold for impeachment would have the potential to turn the United States into a parliamentary system in which the chief executive could be changed at any time.

The Expansion of Power

Today there is more to presidential power than the Constitution alone suggests, and that power is derived from many sources. The role of the president has changed as America has increased in prominence on the world stage; technology has also reshaped the presidency. George Washington's ragtag militias were much different from the mighty nuclear arsenal that today's president commands.

Presidents themselves have taken the initiative to develop new roles for the office. In fact, many presidents have enlarged the power of the presidency by expanding the president's responsibilities and political resources. Thomas Jefferson was the first leader of a mass political party. Andrew Jackson presented himself as the direct representative of the people. Abraham Lincoln mobilized the country for war. Theodore Roosevelt mobilized the public behind his policies. He and Woodrow Wilson set precedents for presidents to serve as world leaders; Wilson and Franklin D. Roosevelt developed the role of the president as manager of the economy. The following sections explore the relationship between the president's responsibilities and resources by examining how contemporary presidents try to lead the nation.

Running the Government: The Chief Executive

Although we often refer to the president as the "chief executive," it is easy to forget that one of the president's most important roles is presiding over the administration of government. This role does not receive the same publicity as other functions do such as appealing to the public for support of policy initiatives, dealing with Congress, or negotiating with foreign powers, but it is of great importance nevertheless.

The Constitution exhorts the president to "take care that the laws be faithfully executed." In the early days of the republic, this clerical-sounding function was fairly easy. Today, the sprawling federal bureaucracy spends more than $2.5 trillion a year and numbers more than 4 million civilian and military employees. Running such a large organization would be a full-time job for even the most talented of executives, yet it is only one of the president's many jobs.

One of the resources for controlling this bureaucracy is the presidential power to appoint top-level administrators. New presidents have about 500 high-level positions available for appointment—cabinet and subcabinet jobs, agency heads, and other noncivil service posts—plus 2,500 lesser jobs. Since passage of the Budgeting and Accounting Act of 1921, presidents have had one other important executive tool: the power to recommend agency budgets to Congress.

You Are Appointing a Supreme Court Justice

The vastness of the executive branch, the complexity of public policy, and the desire to accomplish their policy goals have led presidents in recent years to pay even closer attention to appointing officials who will be responsive to the president's policies. Presidents have also taken more interest in the regulations issued by agencies. This trend toward centralizing decision making in the White House pleases those who think the bureaucracy should be more responsive to elected officials. On the other hand, it dismays those who believe that increased presidential involvement in policymaking will undermine the "neutral competence" of professional bureaucrats by encouraging them to follow the president's policy preferences rather than the intent of laws as passed by Congress.

Chapter 13 explores the president's role as chief executive further. This chapter focuses on how presidents go about organizing and using the parts of the executive branch most under their control—the vice president, the cabinet, the Executive Office of the President, and the White House staff.

The Vice President

Neither politicians nor political scientists have paid much attention to the vice presidency. Once the choice of a party's "second team" was an afterthought; now it is often an effort to placate some important symbolic constituency. Southerner Jimmy Carter selected a well-known liberal, Walter Mondale, as his running mate, and Ronald Reagan chose his chief rival, George Bush, in part to please Republican moderates.[7]

Vice presidents have rarely enjoyed the job. John Nance Garner of Texas, one of Franklin Roosevelt's vice presidents, declared that the job was "not worth a pitcher of warm spit." Once in office, vice presidents usually found that their main job is waiting. The Constitution assigns them the minor tasks of presiding over the Senate and voting in case of a tie among the senators. As George Bush put it when he was vice president, "The buck doesn't stop here." Recent presidents, though, have taken their vice presidents more seriously, involving them in policy discussions and important diplomacy.[8]

Jimmy Carter and Ronald Reagan, both Washington outsiders, chose vice presidents who had substantial Washington experience: Walter Mondale and George

Bush. To become intimates of the president, both had to be completely loyal, losing their political independence in the process. Vice President Bush, for example, was accused of knowing more about the Iran-Contra affair than he admitted, but he steadfastly refused to reveal his discussions with President Reagan on the matter.

When his turn came to choose a vice president, Bush selected Senator Dan Quayle of Indiana, considered by many a political lightweight. Albert Gore, Bill Clinton's vice president, was a Washington insider and played a prominent role in the administration. He met regularly with the president, represented him in discussions with the leaders of numerous countries, and chaired a prominent effort to "reinvent" government. George W. Bush chose Richard Cheney, who had extensive experience in high-level positions in the national government, as his vice president and assigned him a central role in his administration. Cheney has advised the president on a wide range of issues and chaired task forces dealing with major policy issues.

The Cabinet

cabinet

A group of presidential advisers not mentioned in the Constitution, although every president has had one. Today the cabinet is composed of 14 secretaries and the attorney general.

Although the Constitution does not mention the group of presidential advisers known as the **cabinet**, every president has had one. The cabinet is too large and too diverse, and its members are too concerned with representing the interests of their departments, for it to serve as a collective board of directors, however. The major decisions remain in the president's hands. Legend has it that Abraham Lincoln asked his cabinet to vote on an issue, and the result was unanimity in opposition to his view. He announced the decision as "seven nays and one aye, the ayes have it."

George Washington's cabinet was small, consisting of just three secretaries (state, treasury, and war) and the attorney general. Presidents since Washington have increased the size of the cabinet by requesting that new executive departments be established. These requests must be approved by Congress, which creates the departments. Today 14 secretaries and the attorney general head executive departments and constitute the cabinet (see Table 12.3). In addition, presidents may designate other officials (the ambassador to the United Nations is a common choice) as cabinet members.[9]

Even in making his highest level appointments, the president is subject to the constitutional system of checks and balances. President George Bush met resistance when he nominated John Tower, a former senator, to be secretary of defense. After a bitter debate (which focused on the nominee's use of alcohol and relations with women), the Senate handed the president a serious defeat by rejecting Tower. President Clinton's first nominee to serve as attorney general, Zoe Baird, withdrew from consideration after she came under fire from senators of both parties for hiring an illegal alien as her babysitter and for failing to pay Social Security taxes for her employee.

The Executive Office

Next to the White House sits an ornate building called the EEOB, or Eisenhower Executive Office Building. It houses a collection of offices and organizations loosely grouped into the Executive Office of the President.[10] Congress has created some of

Table 12.3 The Cabinet Departments

DEPARTMENT	YEAR CREATED	FUNCTION
State	1789	Makes foreign policy, including treaty negotiations
Treasury	1789	Serves as the government's banker
Defense	1947	Formed by the consolidation of the former Departments of War and the Navy
Justice	1870	Serves as the government's attorney; headed by the attorney general
Interior	1849	Manages the nation's natural resources, including wildlife and public lands
Agriculture	1862	Administers farm and food stamp programs and aids farmers
Commerce	1903	Aids businesses and conducts the U.S. census
Labor	1913	Formed through separation from the Department of Commerce; runs programs and aids labor in various ways
Health and Human Services	1953	Originally created as the Department of Health, Education, and Welfare, it lost its education function in 1979 and Social Security in 1995
Housing and Urban Development	1966	Responsible for housing and urban programs
Transportation	1966	Responsible for mass transportation and highway programs
Energy	1977	Responsible for energy policy and research, including atomic energy
Education	1979	Responsible for the federal government's education programs
Veterans Affairs	1988	Responsible for programs aiding veterans
Homeland Security	2002	Responsible for protecting against terrorism and responding to natural disasters

Members of the president's cabinet are important for both the power they exercise and the status they symbolize. President George W. Bush formed a cabinet that was representative of America's demographic diversity. Pictured here is President Bush with Attorney General Alberto Gonzales, an Hispanic, who also served as White House counsel.

Figure 12.1 Executive Office of the President

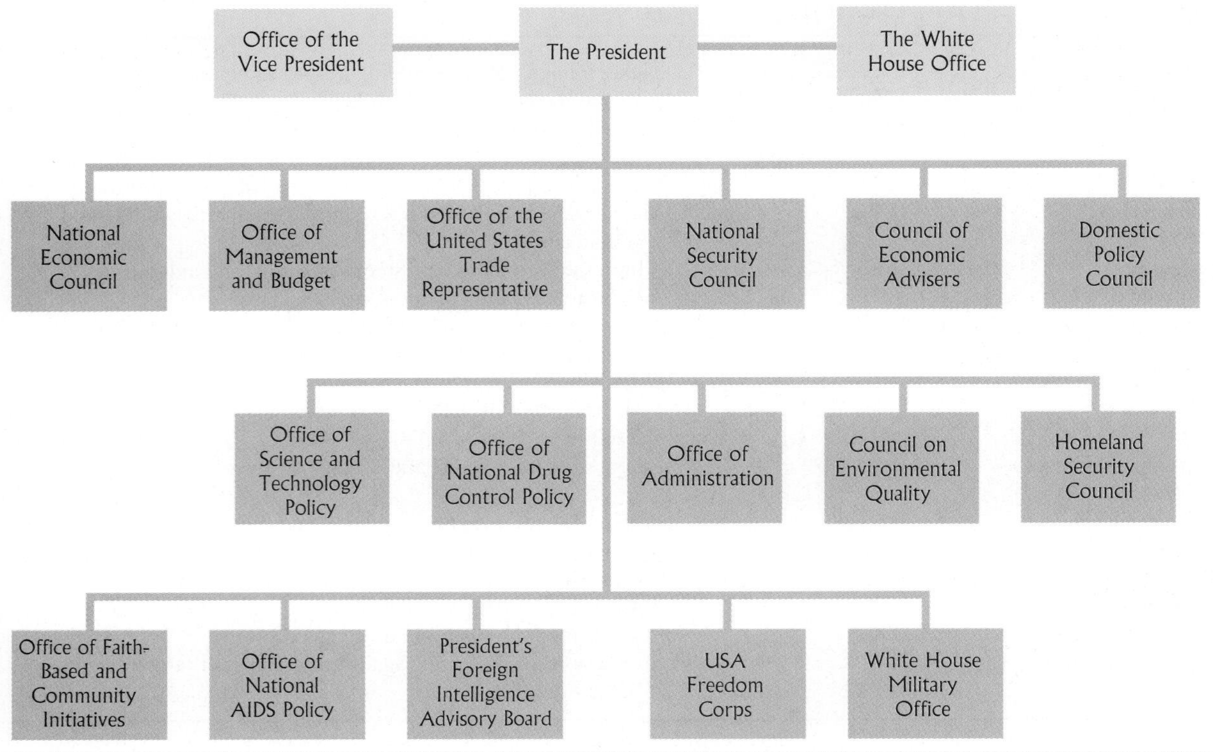

Source: White House (www.whitehouse.gov/government/); Office of the Federal Register, *The United States Government Manual, 2005/2006* (Washington, DC: U.S. Government Printing Office, 2006), 87–101; www.gpoaccess.gov/gmanual/browse-gm-05.html.

these offices by legislation, and the president has simply organized the rest. The Executive Office started small in 1939 when President Roosevelt established it, but has grown with the rest of government. Three major policymaking bodies are housed in the Executive Office—the National Security Council, the Council of Economic Advisers, and Office of Management and Budget—along with several other units that serve the president (see Figure 12.1).

National Security Council (NSC)
An office created in 1947 to coordinate the president's foreign and military policy advisers. Its formal members are the president, vice president, **secretary of state**, and **secretary of defense**, and it is managed by the president's national security assistant.

Council of Economic Advisers (CEA)
A three-member body appointed by the president to advise the president on economic policy.

- The **National Security Council (NSC)** is the committee that links the president's key foreign and military policy advisers. Its formal members include the president, vice president, and secretaries of state and defense, but its informal membership is broader. The president's special assistant for national security affairs plays a major role in the NSC and runs the council's staff. The office provides the president with information and policy recommendations, aids the president in crisis management, coordinates agency and departmental activities, and monitors the implementation of national security policy.
- The **Council of Economic Advisers (CEA)** has three members, each appointed by the president, who advise him on economic policy. They prepare

the annual *Economic Report of the President*, which includes data and analysis on the current state and future trends of the economy, and help the president make policy on inflation, unemployment, and other economic matters.

- The **Office of Management and Budget (OMB)** is composed of a handful of political appointees and more than 600 career officials, many of whom are highly skilled professionals. Its major responsibility is to prepare the president's budget (discussed in Chapter 15). President Nixon revamped the OMB in 1970 in an attempt to make it a managerial as well as a budgetary agency. Presidents also use the OMB to review legislative proposals from the cabinet and other executive agencies so that they can determine whether they want an agency to propose these initiatives to Congress. The OMB assesses the proposals' budgetary implications and advises presidents on the proposals' consistency with their overall program. The OMB also plays an important role in reviewing regulations proposed by departments and agencies.

Office of Management and Budget (OMB)
An office that grew out of the Bureau of the Budget, created in 1921, consisting of a handful of political appointees and hundreds of skilled professionals. The OMB performs both managerial and budgetary functions.

Although presidents find that the Executive Office is smaller and more manageable than the cabinet departments, it is still filled with people who often are performing jobs required by law. There is, however, one part of the presidential system that presidents can truly call their own: the White House staff.

The White House Staff

Before Franklin D. Roosevelt, the president's personal staff resources were minimal. Only one messenger and one secretary served Thomas Jefferson. One hundred years later the president's staff had grown only to 13, including clerks and secretaries. Woodrow Wilson was in the habit of typing his own letters. As recently as the 1920s, the entire budget for the White House staff was no more than $80,000 per year.

The White House staff consists of the key aides the president sees daily: the chief of staff, congressional liaison people, a press secretary, a national security assistant, and a few other administrative and political assistants. Today, there are about 600 people at work on the White House staff—many of whom the president rarely sees—who provide the chief executive with a wide variety of services ranging from making advance travel preparations to answering the avalanche of letters received each year (see Figure 12.2).

The top aides in the White House hierarchy are people who owe total loyalty to the president, and the president turns to them for advice on the most serious or mundane matters of governance. Good staff people are self-effacing, working only for the boss and shunning the limelight. Presidents rely heavily on their staffs for information, policy options, and analysis. Different presidents have different relationships with their staffs, organizing the White House to serve their own political and policy needs and decision-making styles. Most presidents end up choosing some form of *hierarchical* organization with a chief of staff at the top, whose job it is to see that everyone else is doing his or her job and that the president's time and interests are protected. A few presidents, such as John F. Kennedy, have employed a *wheel-and-spokes* system of White House management in which many aides have equal status and are balanced against one another in the process of decision

Figure 12.2 Principal Offices in the White House

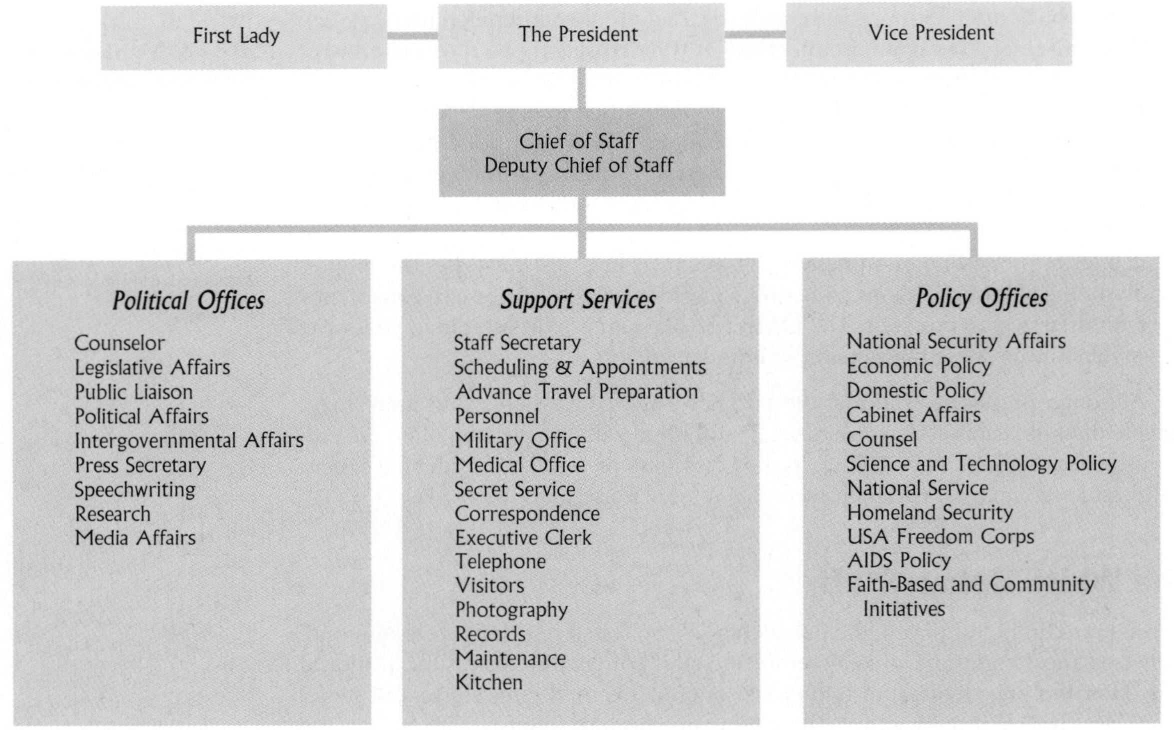

Source: Adapted from George C. Edwards III and Stephen J. Wayne, *Presidential Leadership*, 7th ed. (New York: St. Martin's Press, 2005), figure 6.2.

making.[11] Whatever the system, White House aides are central in the policymaking process—fashioning options, negotiating agreements, writing presidential statements, controlling paperwork, molding legislative details, and generally giving the president their opinions on most matters.

No presidential management styles contrasted more sharply than those of Presidents Carter and Reagan. Carter was a detail man, poring endlessly over memoranda and facts. President Reagan was the consummate delegator.

George Bush's operating style fell between the extremes of his two immediate predecessors. He consulted widely both within and outside of government, and he insisted on letting others' views reach him unfiltered by his staff. He was considerably more accessible than Reagan and devoted more energy to decision making. At the same time, he liked to delegate responsibility to his subordinates and took little initiative in domestic policy.

President Clinton, like Carter, immersed himself in the details of policy. He ran an open White House, dealing directly with a large number of aides and reading countless policy memoranda. His emphasis on deliberation and his fluid staffing system generated criticism that his White House was "indecisive" and "chaotic." George

HOW YOU CAN MAKE A DIFFERENCE

White House Internships

One of the best ways to gain experience at the highest levels of governance is to take part in the White House Internship Program. It is a highly prestigious and competitive program that allows you to actively participate in the federal government's policy decisions from inside the White House complex. While working in the Executive Office of the President, you can learn how political decisions are made and how these decisions affect the day-to-day operations of the federal government. An internship at the White House can open many doors for your future in government and politics.

Making a Difference

Three times a year, the White House selects a hundred students for its three-month internship program. For most of George W. Bush's presidency, students from Patrick Henry College received between one and five of the available spots. Located in Purcelville, Virginia, Patrick Henry boasts of a significant number of conservatives among its student population. Providing internships for these students made sense for the Bush White House. It provided a good way to reach out to their base while building a network of young political operatives.

What you can do:

- Download, fill out, and submit the White House Internship Program application from *www.whitehouse.gov/government/wh-intern.html*. In addition to this form, you will also need to submit a resumé, a personal statement, a writing sample, two letters of recommendation, and a transcript.
- Make sure that your resumé reflects your community service, academic achievements, extracurricular activities, and writing skills.
- Check to see if you have any friends or relatives with connections to the White House. Often, internships are awarded to those with "inside" connections.

W. Bush takes pride in being decisive, and he is more likely to delegate responsibility than was Clinton. Bush, however, is less likely to persist in asking probing questions. Although the Bush White House has been an orderly one, investigations into the decision making regarding the war in Iraq have found that the president's aides sometimes failed to properly vet information and follow other appropriate procedures.

Despite presidents' reliance on their staffs, it is the president who sets the tone for the White House. Although it is common to blame presidential advisers for mistakes made in the White House, it is the president's responsibility to demand that staff members analyze a full range of options and their probable consequences before they offer the president their advice. If the chief executive does not demand quality staff work, then the work is less likely to be done, and disaster or embarrassment may follow.

The First Lady

The First Lady has no official government position, yet she is often at the center of national attention. The media chronicles every word she speaks and every hairstyle she adopts. Although many people think of First Ladies as well-dressed homemakers presiding over White House dinners, there is much more to the job.

Although the First Lady has no official government position, she is often at the center of national attention. In recent years, First Ladies have taken active roles in promoting policies ranging from highway beautification and mental health to literacy and health care. Here First Lady Laura Bush reads to Washington-area students.

Abigail Adams (an early feminist) and Dolley Madison counseled and lobbied their husbands. Edith Galt Wilson was the most powerful First Lady, virtually running the government when her husband, Woodrow, suffered a paralyzing stroke in 1919. Eleanor Roosevelt wrote a nationally syndicated newspaper column and tirelessly traveled and advocated New Deal policies. She became her crippled husband's eyes and ears around the country and urged him to adopt liberal social welfare policies. Lady Bird Johnson chose to focus on one issue, beautification, and most of her successors followed this single-issue pattern. Rosalyn Carter chose mental health, Nancy Reagan selected drug abuse prevention, and Barbara Bush advocated literacy. Laura Bush, a former librarian, has also chosen to focus on increasing literacy.

In what was perhaps a natural evolution in a society where women have moved into positions formerly held only by males, Hillary Rodham Clinton attained the most responsible and visible leadership position ever held by a First Lady. She was an influential adviser to the president, playing an active role in the selection of nominees for cabinet and judicial posts, for example. Most publicly, she headed the planning for the president's massive health care reform plan in 1993 and became, along with her husband, its primary advocate.

Although many have hailed her as a model for our times, successfully combining career and family, others have criticized her as a political liability. The health plan failed to pass Congress, and many observers viewed it as a leading cause of the Democrats' crushing defeat in the 1994 congressional elections. As a result, she retreated to a more traditional role, focusing on representing the United States abroad and on advocating policies to help children and women in developing countries. In 2000, however, the voters of New York elected her to the U.S. Senate.

Presidents not only have responsibility for running the executive branch; they must also deal intensively with the legislative branch. This relationship is the topic of the following section.

Presidential Leadership of Congress: The Politics of Shared Powers

Near the top of any presidential job description would be "working with Congress." The American system of separation of powers is actually one of *shared* powers, so if presidents are to succeed in leaving their stamp on public policy, much of their time in office must be devoted to leading the legislature to support presidential initiatives.

Presidential Leadership: Which Hat Do You Wear?

Chief Legislator

Nowhere does the Constitution use the phrase *chief legislator*; it is strictly a phrase invented to emphasize the executive's importance in the legislative process. The Constitution does require that the president give a State of the Union address to Congress and instructs the president to bring other matters to Congress' attention "from time to time." In fact, as noted in Chapter 11, the president plays a major role in shaping the congressional agenda.

veto
The constitutional power of the president to send a bill back to Congress with reasons for rejecting it. A two-thirds vote in each house can override a veto.

pocket veto
A veto taking place when Congress adjourns within 10 days of having submitted a bill to the president, who simply lets it die by neither signing nor vetoing it.

The Constitution also gives the president power to **veto** congressional legislation. Once Congress passes a bill, the president may (1) sign it, making it law; (2) veto it, sending it back to Congress with the reasons for rejecting it; or (3) let it become law after ten working days by not doing anything. Congress can pass a vetoed law, however, if two-thirds of each house vote to override the president. At one point in the lawmaking process the president has the last word, however: If Congress adjourns within 10 days after submitting a bill, the president can simply let it die by neither signing nor vetoing it. This process is called a **pocket veto**. Table 12.4 shows how frequently recent presidents have used this veto.

The presidential veto is usually effective; only about 4 percent of all vetoed bills have been overridden by Congress since the nation's founding. Thus, even the threat of a presidential veto can be an effective tool for persuading Congress to give more weight to the president's views. On the other hand, the veto is a blunt instrument. Presidents must accept or reject bills in their entirety; they cannot veto only the parts they do not like (most governors have a *line-item* veto that allows them to veto particular portions of a bill). As a result, the White House often must accept provisions of a bill it opposes in order to obtain provisions that it desires. For example, in 1987, Congress passed the entire discretionary budget of the federal government in one bill (called an "omnibus" bill). President Reagan had to accept the whole package or lose appropriations for the entire government. In recent years, presidents have issued signing statements that interpret legislation and often in effect veto part of a bill (see "Issues of the Times: Are Signing Statements a Veto Power?").

Why It Matters

The President's Veto
Unlike most governors, the president does not have the power to veto parts of a bill. As a result, he cannot choose to delete what he views as wasteful items from the budget. At the same time, the lack of a line-item veto helps to maintain the delicate balance of separate institutions sharing powers.

In 1996, Congress passed a law granting the president authority to propose rescinding funds in appropriations bills and tax provisions that apply to only a few people. Opponents of the law immediately challenged it in the courts as being an unconstitutional grant of power to the president. In 1998 the Supreme Court agreed, voiding the law in *Clinton v. City of New York*.

The presidential veto is an inherently negative resource. It is most useful for preventing legislation. Much of the time, however, presidents are more interested

Table 12.4 Presidential Vetoes

PRESIDENT	REGULAR VETOES	VETOES OVERRIDDEN	PERCENTAGE OF VETOES OVERRIDDEN	POCKET VETOES	TOTAL VETOES
Eisenhower	73	2	3	108	181
Kennedy	12	0	0	9	21
Johnson	16	0	0	14	30
Nixon	26	7	27	17	43
Ford	48	12	25	18	66
Carter	13	2	15	18	31
Reagan	39	9	23	39	78
G. Bush	29	1	3	15	44
Clinton	37	2	5	1	38
G. W. Bush*	1	0	0	0	1

**Through 2006.*

in passing their own legislation. To do so, they must marshal their political resources to obtain positive support for their programs. Presidents' three most useful resources are their party leadership, public support, and their own legislative skills.

Party Leadership

No matter what other resources presidents may have at their disposal, they remain highly dependent on their party to move their legislative programs. Representatives and senators of the president's party usually form the nucleus of coalitions supporting presidential proposals and provide considerably more support than do members of the opposition party. Thus, party leadership in Congress is every president's principal task when countering the natural tendency toward conflict between the executive and legislative branches that is inherent in the government's system of checks and balances.[12]

The Bonds of Party. For most senators and representatives, being in the same political party as the president creates a psychological bond. Personal loyalties or emotional commitments to their party and their party leader, a desire to avoid embarrassing "their" administration and thus hurting their chances for reelection, and a basic distrust of the opposition party are inclinations that produce support for the White House. Members of the same party also agree on many matters of public policy, and they are often supported by similar electoral coalitions, thereby reinforcing the pull of party ties.

If presidents could rely on their party members to vote for whatever the White House sent up to Capitol Hill, presidential leadership of Congress would be rather easy. All presidents would have to do is make sure members of their party showed up to vote. If their party had the majority, presidents would always win. If their party was in the minority, presidents would only have to concentrate on converting a few members of the other party.

Slippage in Party Support. Things are not so simple, however. Despite the pull of party ties, all presidents experience at least some slippage in the support of their party in Congress. Because presidents cannot always count on their own party members for support, even on key votes, they must be active party leaders and devote their efforts to conversion as much as to mobilization of members of their party.

The primary obstacle to party unity is the lack of consensus on policies among party members, especially in the Democratic Party. Jimmy Carter, a Democrat, remarked, "I learned the hard way that there was no party loyalty or discipline when a complicated or controversial issue was at stake—none."[13]

This diversity of views often reflects the diversity of constituencies represented by party members. For many years the frequent defection of Southern Democrats from Democratic presidents (such defectors were called "boll weevils") was one of the most prominent features of American politics. When constituency opinion and the president's proposals conflict, members of Congress are more likely to vote with their constituents, whom they rely on for reelection. If the president is not popular with their constituencies, congressional party members may avoid identifying too closely with the White House.

Leading the Party. The president has some assets as party leader, including congressional party leaders, services and amenities for party members, and campaign aid. Each asset is of limited utility, however.

The president's relationship with party leaders in Congress is a delicate one. Although the leaders are predisposed to support presidential policies and typically work closely with the White House, they are free to oppose the president or lend only symbolic support; some party leaders may be ineffective themselves. Moreover,

Presidents depend heavily on their parties' leaders in Congress to pass their initiatives. They also must frequently seek support from the opposition party. Here President George W. Bush meets with Republican and Democratic leaders of the House and Senate.

party leaders, especially in the Senate, are not in strong positions to reward or discipline members of Congress on the basis of presidential support.

To create goodwill with congressional party members, the White House provides them with many amenities, ranging from photographs with the president to rides on Air Force One. Although this arrangement is to the president's advantage and may earn the benefit of the doubt on some policy initiatives, party members consider it their right to receive benefits from the White House and as a result are unlikely to be especially responsive to the president's largesse.

Just as the president can offer a carrot, so too can the president wield a stick in the form of withholding favors, although this is rarely done. Despite the resources available to the president, if party members wish to oppose the White House, the president can do little to stop them. The parties are highly decentralized, as we saw in Chapter 8. National party leaders do not control those aspects of politics that are of vital concern to members of Congress—nominations and elections. Members of Congress are largely self-recruited, gain their party's nomination by their own efforts and not the party's, and provide most of the money and organizational support needed for their elections. Presidents can do little to influence the results of these activities.

One way for the president to improve the chances of obtaining support in Congress is to increase the number of same-party members in the legislature. The phenomenon of **presidential coattails** occurs when voters cast their ballots for congressional candidates of the president's party because those candidates support the president. Most recent studies show a diminishing connection between presidential and congressional voting, however, and few races are determined by presidential coattails.[14] The change in party balance that usually emerges when the electoral dust has settled is strikingly small. In the 14 presidential elections between 1952 and 2004, the party of the winning presidential candidate gained an average of six seats (out of 435) per election in the House. In the Senate the opposition party actually gained seats in seven of the elections (1956, 1960, 1972, 1984, 1988, 1996, and 2000), and there was no change in 1976 and 1992. The net gain for the president's party in the Senate averaged less than one seat per election (see Table 12.5).

presidential coattails

The situation occurring when voters cast their ballots for congressional candidates of the president's party because they support the president. Recent studies show that few races are won this way.

What about midterm elections—those held between presidential elections? Can the president depend on increasing the number of his party members in Congress then? Actually, the picture is even bleaker than during presidential elections. As you can see in Table 12.6, the president's party typically *loses* seats in these elections. In 1986, the Republicans lost eight seats in the Senate, depriving President Reagan of a majority. In 1994, the Democrats lost eight Senate seats and 52 House seats, losing control of both houses in the process.[15] Recently, there have been exceptions. In 1998, the Democrats gained five seats in the House, and in 2002, Republicans made small gains in both houses. In 2006, however, George W. Bush's Republicans lost majorities in both houses of Congress.

To add to these party leadership burdens, the president's party often lacks a majority in one or both houses of Congress. Since 1953 there have been 30 years in which Republican presidents faced a Democratic House of Representatives and 22 years in which they encountered a Democratic Senate. President Clinton faced both a House and a Senate with Republican majorities from 1995 through 2000. George W. Bush faced a Democratic Senate from May 2001 through December 2002 and in 2007–2008.

Table 12.5 Congressional Gains or Losses for the President's Party in Presidential Election Years

Presidents cannot rely on their coattails to get their party's legislators into office to help pass White House legislative programs. The president's party typically gains few, if any, seats when the president wins an election. For instance, the Republicans lost seats in both the House and the Senate when President George W. Bush was elected in 2000.

YEAR	PRESIDENT	HOUSE	SENATE
1952	Eisenhower (R)	+22	+1
1956	Eisenhower (R)	−2	−1
1960	Kennedy (D)	−22	−2
1964	Johnson (D)	+37	+1
1968	Nixon (R)	+5	+6
1972	Nixon (R)	+12	−2
1976	Carter (D)	+1	0
1980	Reagan (R)	+34	+12
1984	Reagan (R)	+14	−2
1988	G. Bush (R)	−23	−1
1992	Clinton (D)	−10	0
1996	Clinton (D)	+9	−2
2000	G. W. Bush (R)	−2	−4
2004	G. W. Bush (R)	+3	+4
	Average	+5.6	+.7

Table 12.6 Congressional Gains or Losses for the President's Party in Midterm Election Years

For decades the president's party typically *lost* seats in midterm elections. Thus, presidents could not be certain of helping to elect members of their party once in office. The elections of 1998 and 2002 deviated from this pattern, and the president's party gained a few seats.

YEAR	PRESIDENT	HOUSE	SENATE
1954	Eisenhower (R)	−18	−1
1958	Eisenhower (R)	−47	−13
1962	Kennedy (D)	−4	+3
1966	Johnson (D)	−47	−4
1970	Nixon (R)	−12	+2
1974	Ford (R)	−47	−5
1978	Carter (D)	−15	−3
1982	Reagan (R)	−26	0
1986	Reagan (R)	−5	−8
1990	G. Bush (R)	−9	−1
1994	Clinton (D)	−52	−8
1998	Clinton (D)	+5	0
2002	G. W. Bush (R)	+6	+2
2006	G. W. Bush (R)	−30	−6
	Average	−22	−3

As a result of election returns and the lack of dependable party support, the president usually has to solicit help from the opposition party. This is often a futile endeavor, however. Nevertheless, even a few votes may be enough to give the president the required majority.

Public Support

One of the president's most important resources for leading Congress is public support. Presidents who enjoy the backing of the public have an easier time influencing Congress. Said one top aide to Ronald Reagan, "Everything here is built on the idea that the president's success depends on grassroots support."[16] Presidents with low approval ratings in the polls find it difficult to influence Congress. As one of President Carter's aides put it when the president was low in the polls, "No president whose popularity is as low as this president's has much clout on the Hill."[17] Members of Congress and others in Washington closely watch two indicators of public support for the president: approval in the polls and mandates in presidential elections.

Presidential Success in Polls and Congress

Public Approval. Members of Congress anticipate the public's reactions to their support for or opposition to presidents and their policies. They may choose to be close to or independent of the White House—depending on the president's standing with the public—to increase their chances for reelection. Representatives and senators may also use the president's standing in the polls as an indicator of presidential ability to mobilize public opinion against presidential opponents.

Public approval also makes other leadership resources more efficacious. If the president is high in the public's esteem, the president's party is more likely to be responsive, the public is more easily moved, and legislative skills become more effective. Thus public approval is the political resource that has the most potential to turn a stalemate between the president and Congress into a situation supportive of the president's legislative proposals.

Public approval operates mostly in the background and sets the limits of what Congress will do for or to the president. Widespread support gives the president leeway and weakens resistance to presidential policies. It provides a cover for members of Congress to cast votes to which their constituents might otherwise object. They can defend their votes as support for the president rather than as support for a certain policy alone.

Lack of public support strengthens the resolve of the president's opponents and narrows the range in which presidential policies receive the benefit of the doubt. In addition, low ratings in the polls may create incentives to attack the president, further eroding an already weakened position. For example, after the arms sales to Iran and the diversion of funds to the Contras made the headlines in late 1986, it became more acceptable in Congress and in the press to raise questions about Ronald Reagan's capacities as president. Disillusionment is a difficult force for the White House to combat.

The impact of public approval or disapproval on the support the president receives in Congress is important, but it occurs at the margins of the effort to build coalitions behind proposed policies. No matter how low presidential standing dips, the president still receives support from a substantial number of senators and representatives. Similarly, no matter how high approval levels climb, a significant portion of Congress will still oppose certain presidential policies. Members of Congress are unlikely to vote against the clear interests of their constituencies or the firm tenets of their ideology out of deference to a widely supported chief executive, as George W. Bush learned following the terrorist attacks of September 11, 2001. Public approval gives the president leverage, not command.[18]

In addition, presidents cannot depend on having the approval of the public, and it is not a resource over which they have much control, as we will see later. Once again, it is clear that presidents' leadership resources do not allow them to dominate Congress.

Mandates. The results of presidential elections are another indicator of public opinion regarding presidents. An electoral mandate—the perception that the voters strongly support the president's character and policies—can be a powerful symbol in American politics. It accords added legitimacy and credibility to the newly elected president's proposals. Moreover, concerns for both representation and political survival encourage members of Congress to support new presidents if they feel the people have spoken.

More important, mandates change the premises of decisions. Following Roosevelt's decisive win in the 1932 election, the essential question became *how* government should act to fight the Depression rather than *whether* it should act. Similarly, following Johnson's overwhelming win in the 1964 election, the dominant question in Congress was not whether to pass new social programs but how many social programs to pass and how much to increase spending. In 1981, the tables were turned; Ronald Reagan's victory placed a stigma on big government and exalted the unregulated marketplace and large defense efforts. Reagan had won a major victory even before the first congressional vote.

Although presidential elections can structure choices for Congress, merely winning an election does not provide presidents with a mandate. Every election produces a winner, but mandates are much less common. Even large electoral victories, such as Richard Nixon's in 1972 and Ronald Reagan's in 1984, carry no guarantee that Congress will interpret the results as mandates from the people to support the president's programs. Perceptions of a mandate are weak if the winning candidate did not stress his policy plans during the campaign or if the voters also elect majorities in Congress from the other party (of course, the winner may *claim* a mandate anyway).[19]

Legislative Skills

Presidential legislative skills come in a variety of forms, including bargaining, making personal appeals, consulting with Congress, setting priorities, exploiting "honeymoon" periods, and structuring congressional votes. Of these skills, bargaining receives perhaps the most attention from commentators on the presidency, and by examining it, one can learn much about the role that a president's legislative skills play in leading Congress.

Bargains occur in numerous forms. Reagan's budget director David Stockman recalled that "the last 10 or 20 percent of the votes needed for a majority of both houses on the 1981 tax cut had to be bought, period." The concessions for members of Congress included special breaks for oil-lease holders, real estate tax shelters, and generous loopholes that virtually eliminated the corporate income tax. "The hogs were really feeding," declared Stockman. "The greed level, the level of opportunities, just got out of control."[20]

Nevertheless, bargaining, in the form of trading support on two or more policies or providing specific benefits for representatives and senators, occurs less often and plays a less critical role in the creation of presidential coalitions in Congress than one might think. For obvious reasons, the White House does not want to encourage the type of bargaining Stockman describes, and there is a scarcity of resources with which to bargain, especially in an era where balancing the budget is a prominent goal for policymakers (discussed in Chapter 15).

Moreover, the president does not have to bargain with every member of Congress to receive support. On controversial issues where bargaining may be useful, the president usually starts with a sizable core of party supporters and may add to this group those of the opposition party who provide support on ideological or policy grounds. Others may support the president because of relevant constituency interests or strong public approval. The president needs to bargain only if this coalition does not provide a majority (or two-thirds on treaties and one-third on veto overrides).

Presidents may improve their chances of success in Congress by making certain strategic moves. It is wise, for example, for a new president to be ready to send legislation to the Hill early during the first year in office in order to exploit the "honeymoon" atmosphere that typically characterizes this period. Obviously, this is a one-shot opportunity.

An important aspect of presidential legislative strategy can be establishing priorities among legislative proposals. The goal of this effort is to set Congress' agenda. If presidents are unable to focus the attention of Congress on their priority programs, these programs may become lost in the complex and overloaded legislative process. Setting priorities is also important because presidents and their staffs can lobby effectively for only a few bills at a time. Moreover, each president's political capital is inevitably limited, and it is sensible to focus on a limited range of personally important issues; otherwise, this precious resource might be wasted.

In 1981 Ronald Reagan followed both of these strategies, moving fast and setting priorities. He had great success—obtaining passage of a large tax cut, a substantial increase in defense expenditures, and sizable decreases in the rate of spending for domestic policies. George Bush, in contrast, did not enter the White House geared for legislative action and did little to articulate his priorities. With a large budget deficit, few legislative goals, and the opposition in the majority in both the House and Senate, he did not feel it necessary or useful to focus his energies on Congress. From the outset Bush seemed destined to make his mark on foreign policy, where the president has more latitude to maneuver.

Within a month after taking office, President Clinton presented Congress with an ambitious agenda, including tax increases and both spending cuts and increases.

He proposed a major health care reform bill and the North American Free Trade Agreement later in the year. The president lacked the political capital to pass much of his agenda, however, and some of the most important proposals fell prey to Republican opposition. By failing to focus on his priorities, Clinton spent his political capital on matters of less importance. Although he engaged in an endless campaign of public appearances and congressional meetings to build support for his legislation, in the end he met with substantial disappointment. Moreover, the voters rebuffed him in the 1994 midterm elections as the Republicans captured both houses of Congress.

In his early months in office, George W. Bush followed Reagan's example of moving rapidly and focusing on his priority legislation. The White House was ready with legislation on tax cuts, education reform, and a faith-based initiative and began a process of reevaluating the nation's defense posture. Until the 9/11 attacks, the president focused on his priority proposals and met with substantial success.

The president is the nation's key agenda builder; what the administration wants strongly influences the parameters of Washington debate.[21] John Kingdon's careful study of the Washington agenda found that "no other single actor in the political system has quite the capability of the president to set agendas."[22] There are limits to what the president can do, however.

By his second year in office, Ronald Reagan's honeymoon with Congress was over, and he had lost control of the legislative agenda. Although the White House can put off dealing with many national issues at the beginning of a new president's term in order to focus on its highest priority legislation, it cannot do so indefinitely. Eventually it must make decisions about a wide range of matters. Soon the legislative

Presidents find the role of legislative leader a challenging one. Often they must compromise with opponents in Congress, as President Bill Clinton did in 1996 when he signed the welfare reform bill.

agenda is full and more policies are in the pipeline as the administration attempts to satisfy its constituents and responds to unanticipated or simply overlooked problems. Moreover, Congress is quite capable of setting its own agenda, providing competition for the president's proposals.

In general, presidential legislative skills must compete—as presidential public support does—with other, more stable factors that affect voting in Congress: party, ideology, personal views and commitments on specific policies, constituency interests, and so on. By the time a president tries to exercise influence on a vote, most members of Congress have made up their minds on the basis of these other factors.

After accounting for the status of the president's party in Congress and standing with the public, systematic studies have found that presidents known for their legislative skills (such as Lyndon Johnson) are no more successful in winning votes, even close ones, or obtaining congressional support than those considered less adept at dealing with Congress (such as Jimmy Carter).[23] The president's legislative skills are not at the core of presidential leadership of Congress. Even skilled presidents cannot reshape the contours of the political landscape and *create* opportunities for change. They can, however, recognize favorable configurations of political forces—such as existed in 1933, 1965, and 1981—and effectively exploit them to embark on major shifts in public policy.

Perhaps the most important role of presidents—and their heaviest burden—is their responsibility for national security. Dealing with Congress is only one of the many challenges presidents face in the realm of defense and foreign policy.

The President and National Security Policy

Constitutionally, the president has the leading role in American defense and foreign policy (often termed *national security policy*). Such matters, ranging from foreign trade to war and peace, occupy much of the president's time. There are several dimensions to the president's national security responsibilities, including negotiating with other nations, commanding the armed forces, waging war, managing crises, and obtaining the necessary support in Congress.

Chief Diplomat

The Constitution allocates certain powers in the realm of national security exclusively to the executive. The president alone extends diplomatic recognition to foreign governments—as Jimmy Carter did on December 14, 1978, when he announced the exchange of ambassadors with the People's Republic of China and the downgrading of the U.S. Embassy in Taiwan. The president can also terminate relations with other nations, as Carter did with Iran after Americans were taken hostage in Tehran.

The president also has the sole power to negotiate treaties with other nations, although the Constitution requires the Senate to approve them by a two-thirds vote. Sometimes presidents win and sometimes they lose when presenting a treaty to the

Senate. After extensive lobbying, Jimmy Carter persuaded the Senate to approve a treaty returning the Panama Canal to Panama (over objections such as those of one senator who declared, "We stole it fair and square"). Carter was not so lucky when he presented the SALT II treaty on arms control; it never even made it to a vote on the Senate floor. At other times senators add "reservations" to the treaties they ratify, altering the treaty in the process.[24]

In addition to treaties, presidents also negotiate *executive agreements* with the heads of foreign governments. However, executive agreements do not require Senate ratification (although they are supposed to be reported to Congress and may require implementing legislation passed by majorities of each house). Most executive agreements are routine and deal with noncontroversial subjects such as food deliveries or customs enforcement, but some, such as the Vietnam peace agreement and the SALT I agreement limiting offensive nuclear weapons, implement important and controversial policies.

Occasionally presidential diplomacy involves more than negotiating on behalf of the United States. Theodore Roosevelt won the Nobel Peace Prize for his role in settling the war between Japan and Russia. One of Jimmy Carter's greatest achievements was forging a peace treaty between Egypt and Israel. For 13 days he mediated negotiations between the leaders of both countries at his presidential retreat, Camp David.

As the leader of the Western world, the president must try to lead America's allies on matters of both economics and defense. This is not an easy task, given the natural independence of sovereign nations, the increasing economic might of other

Presidents usually conduct diplomatic relations through envoys, but occasionally they engage in personal diplomacy. Here, President Carter celebrates a peace agreement he brokered between Israeli Prime Minister Menachem Begin and Egyptian President Anwar Sadat.

countries, and the many competing influences on policymaking in other nations. As in domestic policymaking, the president must rely principally on persuasion to lead.

Commander in Chief

Because the Constitution's framers wanted civilian control of the military, they made the president the commander in chief of the armed forces. President George Washington actually led troops to crush the Whiskey Rebellion in 1794. Today, presidents do not take the task quite so literally, but their military decisions have changed the course of history. Harry Truman personally selected the target and the date for dropping atomic bombs on Japan to end World War II. Two decades later, Lyndon Johnson selected targets for bombing missions in North Vietnam. Richard Nixon made the decision to invade Cambodia in 1970. Bill Clinton joined the ranks of presidents exerting their prerogatives as commander in chief when he sent American troops to occupy Haiti, keep the peace in Bosnia, restore order in Somalia, prevent an invasion of Kuwait, and bomb Yugoslavia, Iraq, Afghanistan, and Sudan. George W. Bush ordered an attack on the Taliban government in Afghanistan—and on terrorists everywhere.

When the Constitution was written, the United States did not have—nor did anyone expect it to have—a large standing or permanent army. Today the president is commander in chief of more than 1.4 million uniformed men and women. In his farewell address, George Washington warned against permanent alliances, but today America has commitments to defend nations across the globe. Even more important, the president commands a vast nuclear arsenal. Never more than a few steps from the president is "the football," a briefcase with the codes needed to unleash nuclear war. The Constitution, of course, states that only Congress has the power to declare war, but it is unreasonable to believe that Congress can convene, debate, and vote on a declaration of war in the case of a nuclear attack. The House and Senate chambers would be gone—*literally* gone—before the conclusion of a debate.

War Powers

Perhaps no issue of executive–legislative relations generates more controversy than the continuing dispute over war powers. Although charged by the Constitution with declaring war and voting on the military budget, Congress long ago accepted that presidents make short-term military commitments of troops or naval vessels. In recent decades, however, presidents have paid even less attention to constitutional details; for example, Congress never declared war during the conflicts in either Korea or Vietnam.

War Powers Resolution
A law passed in 1973 in reaction to American fighting in Vietnam and Cambodia that requires presidents to consult with Congress whenever possible prior to using military force and to withdraw forces after 60 days unless Congress declares war or grants an extension. Presidents view the resolution as unconstitutional.

In 1973 Congress passed the **War Powers Resolution** over President Nixon's veto. As a reaction to disillusionment about American fighting in Vietnam and Cambodia, the law was intended to give Congress a greater voice in the introduction of American troops into hostilities. It required presidents to consult with Congress, whenever possible, before using military force, and it mandated the withdrawal of forces after 60 days unless Congress declared war or granted an extension.

Congress could at any time pass a concurrent resolution (which could not be vetoed) ending American participation in hostilities.

legislative veto

The ability of Congress to override a presidential decision. Although the **War Powers Resolution** asserts this authority, there is reason to believe that, if challenged, the Supreme Court would find the legislative veto in violation of the doctrine of separation of powers.

Congress cannot count the War Powers Resolution as a success, however. All presidents serving since 1973 have deemed the law an unconstitutional infringement on their powers, and there is reason to believe the Supreme Court would consider the law's use of the **legislative veto** (the ability of Congress to pass a resolution to override a presidential decision) to be a violation of the doctrine of separation of powers. Presidents have largely ignored the law and sent troops into hostilities, sometimes with heavy loss of life, without effectual consultation with Congress. The legislature has found it difficult to challenge the president, especially when American troops were endangered, and the courts have been reluctant to hear a congressional challenge on what would be construed as a political, rather than a legal, issue.[25]

Following numerous precedents, George Bush took an expansive view of his powers as commander in chief. On his own authority, he ordered the invasion of Panama in 1989 and moved half a million troops to Saudi Arabia to liberate Kuwait after its invasion by Iraq in 1990. Matters came to a head in January 1991. President Bush had given President Saddam Hussein of Iraq until January 15 to pull out of Kuwait. At that point, Bush threatened to move the Iraqis out by force. Debate raged over the president's power to act unilaterally to engage in war. A constitutional crisis was averted when Congress passed (on a divided vote) a resolution on January 12 authorizing the president to use force against Iraq.

In a sweeping assertion of presidential authority, Bill Clinton moved toward military intervention in Haiti in 1994 and essentially dared Congress to try to stop him. Congress did nothing but complain to block military action, even though a majority of members of both parties clearly opposed an invasion. In the end, the president avoided an invasion (as opposed to a more peaceful "intervention"), but Congress was unlikely to have cut off funds for such an operation had it occurred. In 1999, the president authorized the United States to take the leading role in a sustained air attack against Serbia, but Congress could not agree on a resolution supporting the use of force.

George W. Bush faced little opposition to responding to the terrorist attacks of September 11, 2001. Congress immediately passed a resolution authorizing the use of force against the perpetrators of the attacks. The next year, Congress passed a resolution authorizing the president to use force against Iraq. However, Congress was less compliant when the press revealed U.S. mistreatment of prisoners of war and the president's authorization (without a judicial warrant) of the National Security Agency to spy on persons residing within the United States.

Analysts continue to raise questions about the relevance of America's 200-year-old constitutional mechanisms for engaging in war. Some observers worry that the rapid response capabilities

The Constitution makes the president the commander in chief of the armed forces. Some presidents have involved themselves more deeply in war making than others. President George Bush made the important decisions regarding the 1991 war in the Persian Gulf but left the details to his military commanders.

afforded the president by modern technology allow him to bypass congressional opposition, thus undermining the separation of powers. Others stress the importance of the commander in chief having the flexibility to meet America's global responsibilities and combat international terrorism without the hindrance of congressional checks and balances. All agree that the change in the nature of warfare brought about by nuclear weapons inevitably delegates to the president the ultimate decision to use such weapons.

Why It Matters

War Powers
The question as to the president's war powers has never been fully resolved. Some feel we would be less likely to go to war if the president could only send troops into combat after a congressional resolution authorizing the use of force. Others see such a requirement as unduly hampering the president's ability to conduct an effective foreign policy.

Crisis Manager

The president's roles as chief diplomat and commander in chief are related to another presidential responsibility: crisis management. A **crisis** is a sudden, unpredictable, and potentially dangerous event. Most crises occur in the realm of foreign policy. They often involve hot tempers and high risks; quick judgments must be made on the basis of sketchy information. Be it American hostages held in Iran or the discovery of Soviet missiles in Cuba, a crisis challenges the president to make difficult decisions. Crises are rarely the president's doing, but handled incorrectly, they can be the president's undoing. On the other hand, handling a crisis well can remake a president's image, as George W. Bush found following the terrorist attacks of September 11, 2001.

crisis
A sudden, unpredictable, and potentially dangerous event requiring the president to play the role of crisis manager.

With modern communications, the president can instantly monitor events almost anywhere. Because situations develop more rapidly today, there is a premium on immediate action, secrecy, constant management, consistent judgment, and expert advice. Congress usually moves slowly (one might say deliberately), and it is large (making it difficult to keep secrets), decentralized (requiring continual compromising), and composed of generalists. As a result, the president—who can come to quick and consistent decisions, confine information to a small group, carefully oversee developments, and call on experts in the executive branch—has become more prominent in handling crises.

Working with Congress

With the Stroke of a Pen: The Executive Order Over Time

As America moves through its third century under the Constitution, presidents might wish the framers had been less concerned with checks and balances in the area of national security. In recent years, Congress has challenged presidents on all fronts, including intelligence operations; the treatment of prisoners of war; foreign aid; arms sales; the development, procurement, and deployment of weapons systems; the negotiation and interpretation of treaties; the selection of diplomats; and the continuation of nuclear testing.

Congress has a central constitutional role in making national security policy, although this role is often misunderstood. The allocation of responsibilities for such matters is based on the Founders' apprehensions about the concentration of power and the subsequent potential for its abuse. They divided the powers of supply and command, for example, in order to thwart adventurism in national security affairs. Congress can thus refuse to provide the necessary authorizations and appropriations for presidential actions, whereas the chief executive can refuse to act (for example, by not sending troops into battle at the behest of the legislature).

Crisis management may be the most difficult of the president's many roles. By definition, crises are sudden, unpredictable, and dangerous. Here President George W. Bush stands with firefighters and rescue workers at the World Trade Center site three days after the terrorist attacks on September 11, 2001.

Despite the constitutional role of Congress, the president is the driving force behind national security policy and provides energy and direction. Congress is well organized to deliberate openly on the discrete components of policy, but it is not well designed to take the lead on national security matters. Its role has typically been overseeing the executive rather than initiating policy. Congress frequently originates proposals for domestic policy, but it is less involved in national security policy.[26]

The president has a more prominent role in foreign affairs as the country's sole representative in dealing with other nations and as commander in chief of the armed forces (functions that effectively preclude a wide range of congressional diplomatic and military initiatives). In addition, the nature of national security issues may make the failure to integrate the elements of policy more costly than in domestic policy. Thus members of Congress typically prefer to encourage, criticize, or support the president rather than to initiate their own national security policy. If leadership occurs, it is usually centered in the White House.

Commentators on the presidency often refer to the "two presidencies"—one for domestic policy and the other for national security policy.[27] By this phrase they mean that the president has more success in leading Congress on matters of national security than on matters of domestic policy. The typical member of Congress, however, supports the president on roll-call votes about national security only slightly more than half the time. There is a significant gap between what the president requests and what members of Congress are willing to give. Certainly the legislature does not accord the president automatic support on national security policy.[28]

Nevertheless, presidents do end up obtaining much, often most, of what they request from Congress on national security issues. Some of the support they receive is the result of agreement on policy, but presidential leadership also plays an important role. That role is not one in which presidents simply bend the legislature to their will, however; rather, they lead by persuasion.

Presidents need resources to persuade others to support their policies. One important presidential asset can be the support of the American people. The following sections will take a closer look at how the White House tries to increase and use public support.

Power from the People: The Public Presidency

"Public sentiment is everything. With public sentiment nothing can fail; without it nothing can succeed." These words, spoken by Abraham Lincoln, pose what is perhaps the greatest challenge to any president—to obtain and maintain the public's support. Because presidents are rarely in a position to command others to comply with their wishes, they must rely on persuasion. Public support is perhaps the greatest source of influence a president has, for it is more difficult for other power holders in a democracy to deny the legitimate demands of a president with popular backing.

Going Public

Presidents are not passive followers of public opinion. The White House is a virtual whirlwind of public relations activity.[29] John Kennedy, the first "television president," held considerably more public appearances than did his predecessors. Kennedy's successors, with the notable exception of Richard Nixon, have been even more active in making public appearances. Indeed, they have averaged more than one appearance every weekday of the year. Bill Clinton and George W. Bush invested enormous time and energy in attempting to sell their programs to the public.

Often the White House stages the president's appearances purely to get the public's attention. When George Bush introduced his clean-air bill in 1989, he traveled to Wyoming to use the eye-catching Grand Tetons as a backdrop. He announced his support for a constitutional amendment to prohibit flag burning in front of the Iwo Jima Memorial in Arlington National Cemetery. In cases such as these, the president could have simply made an announcement, but the need for public support drives the White House to employ public relations techniques similar to those used to publicize commercial products.

George W. Bush chose to announce the end of major combat in Iraq on board the aircraft carrier the *Abraham Lincoln*. The White House's Office of Communications choreographed every aspect of the event, including positioning the aircraft carrier so the shoreline could not be seen by the camera when the president landed, arraying members of the crew in coordinated shirt colors over Bush's right shoulder, placing a banner reading "Mission Accomplished" to perfectly capture the president and the

John F. Kennedy was the first president to regularly use public appearances to seek popular backing for his policies. Despite his popularity and skills as a communicator, Kennedy was often frustrated in his attempts to win widespread support for his administration's "New Frontier" policies.

celebratory two words in a single camera shot, and timing the speech so the sun cast a golden glow on the president.

In many democracies, different people occupy the jobs of head of state and head of government. For example, the queen is head of state in England, but she holds little power in government and politics. In America, these roles are fused. As head of state, the president is America's ceremonial leader and symbol of government. Trivial but time-consuming activities—tossing out the first baseball of the season, lighting the White House Christmas tree, meeting an extraordinary Boy or Girl Scout—are part of the ceremonial function of the presidency. Meeting foreign heads of state, receiving ambassadors' credentials, and making global goodwill tours represent the international side of this role. Presidents rarely shirk these duties, even when they are not inherently important. Ceremonial activities give them an important symbolic aura and a great deal of favorable press coverage, contributing to their efforts to build public support.

Presidential Approval

Much of the energy the White House devotes to public relations is aimed at increasing the president's public approval. The White House believes that the higher the president stands in the polls, the easier it is to persuade others to support presidential initiatives. Because of the connection between public support and presidential influence, the press, members of Congress, and others in the Washington political

Figure 12.3 Average Yearly Presidential Approval

For years the Gallup Poll has asked Americans, "Do you approve or disapprove of the way [name of president] is handling his job as president?" Here you can track the percentage approving of presidential performance from Eisenhower to George W. Bush. Notice that most presidents seem to be most popular when they first enter office; later on, their popularity often erodes. Bill Clinton was an exception who enjoyed higher approval in his second term than in his first. George W. Bush had high approval following 9/11, but public support diminished steadily after that.

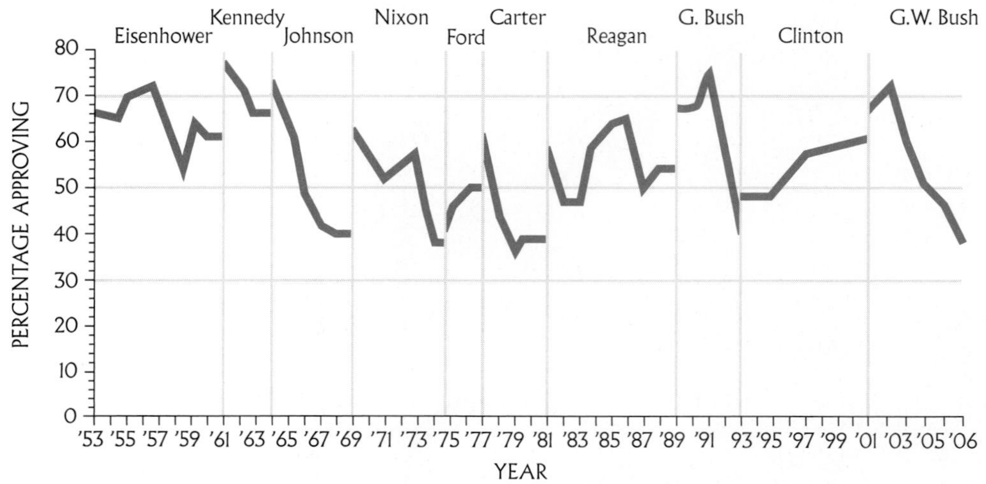

Source: George C. Edwards III, *Presidential Approval* (Baltimore: Johns Hopkins University Press, 1990); updated by the authors.

Rate the Presidents

community closely monitor the president's standing in the polls. For years, the Gallup Poll has asked Americans, "Do you approve or disapprove of the way [name of president] is handling his job as president?" You can see the results in Figure 12.3.

Presidents frequently do not have widespread public support, often failing to win even majority approval. Presidents Nixon, Ford, and Carter did not receive approval from 50 percent of the public on the average. Ronald Reagan had only a 52 percent approval level. For three years, George Bush enjoyed much higher levels of approval on the average than his predecessors did. In his fourth year, however, his ratings dropped below the 40 percent mark. President Clinton struggled to rise above the 50 percent mark in his first term, and George W. Bush was at 51 percent before the September 11, 2001, terrorist attacks. His approval skyrocketed after 9/11 but then steadily diminished and has been below 50 percent in his second term.

Presidential approval is the product of many factors.[30] At the base of presidential evaluations is the predisposition of many people to support the president. Political party identification provides the basic underpinning of approval or disapproval and mediates the impact of other factors. On average, those who identify with the president's party give approval more than 40 percentage points higher than do those who identify with the opposition party. Moreover, partisans are not inclined to approve presidents of the other party. Predispositions provide the foundations of presidential approval and furnish it with a basic stability.

Presidents also usually benefit from a "honeymoon" with the American people after taking office. Some observers believe that honeymoons are fleeting phenomena in which the public affords new occupants of the White House only a short grace period before they begin their inevitable descent in the polls. You can see in Figure 12.3 that declines do take place, but they are neither inevitable nor swift. Throughout his two terms in office, Ronald Reagan experienced considerable volatility in his relations with the public, but his record certainly does not indicate that the loss of public support is inexorable or that support cannot be revived and maintained. George Bush obtained more public support in his third year in office than in his first two years, and Bill Clinton enjoyed more approval in his second term in office than in his first.

Changes in approval levels appear to reflect the public's evaluation of how the president is handling policy areas such as the economy, war, and foreign affairs. Different policies are salient to the public at different times. For example, if international acts of terrorism on American interests are increasing, then foreign policy is likely to dominate the news and to be on the minds of Americans. If the economy turns sour, then people are going to be concerned about unemployment.

Contrary to the conventional wisdom, citizens seem to focus on the president's efforts and stands on issues rather than on personality ("popularity") or simply how presidential policies affect them (the "pocketbook"). Job-related personal characteristics of the president, such as integrity and leadership skills, also play an important role in influencing presidential approval.

Sometimes public approval of the president takes sudden jumps. One popular explanation for these surges of support is "rally events," which John Mueller defined as events that are related to international relations, directly involve the United States and particularly the president, and are specific, dramatic, and sharply focused.[31] A classic example is the 18-percentage-point rise in President George Bush's approval ratings immediately after the fighting began in the Gulf War in 1991. George W. Bush's approval shot up 39 percentage points in September 2001. Such occurrences are unusual and isolated events, however; they usually have little enduring impact on a president's public approval. President Bush, for example, dropped precipitously in the polls and lost his bid for reelection in 1992.

The criteria on which the public evaluates presidents—such as the way they are handling the economy, where they stand on complex issues, and whether they are "strong" leaders—are open to many interpretations. The modern White House makes extraordinary efforts to control the context in which the president appears in public and the way he is portrayed by the press in order to try to influence how the public views him. The fact that presidents are frequently low in the polls anyway is persuasive testimony to the limits of presidential leadership of the public. As one student of the public presidency put it, "The supply of popular support rests on opinion dynamics over which the president may exert little direct control."[32]

Policy Support

Commentators on the presidency often refer to it as a "bully pulpit," implying that presidents can persuade or even mobilize the public to support their policies if they are skilled communicators. Certainly presidents frequently do attempt to obtain public support for their policies with television or radio appearances and speeches to large groups.[33] All presidents since Truman have had media advice from experts on lighting, makeup, stage settings, camera angles, clothing, pacing of delivery, and other facets of making speeches.

Despite this aid and despite the experience that politicians have in speaking, presidential speeches designed to lead public opinion have typically been rather unimpressive. In the modern era only Franklin D. Roosevelt, John Kennedy, Ronald Reagan, and Bill Clinton could be considered especially effective speakers. The rest were not, and they appeared unimpressive under the glare of hot lights and the unflattering gaze of television cameras.

Moreover, the public is not always receptive to the president's message. Chapter 6 shows that Americans are not especially interested in politics and government; thus, it is not easy to get their attention (see "Young People and Politics: The Generation Gap in Watching the President"). Citizens also have predispositions about public policy (however ill informed) that act as screens for presidential messages. In the absence of national crises, most people are unreceptive to political appeals.[34]

The public may misperceive or ignore even the most basic facts regarding presidential policy. For example, at the end of October 1994, 59 percent of the public thought the economy was still in recession (although it was growing so fast that the Federal Reserve Board was taking strong action to cool it off), only 34 percent knew the deficit had decreased since Clinton became president (it had decreased substantially), and 65 percent thought taxes on the middle class had increased during that period (income taxes had been raised for less than 2 percent of the public).[35] Partly as a consequence of these misconceptions, Clinton was frustrated repeatedly in his efforts to obtain public support for his policy initiatives.[36]

Ronald Reagan, sometimes called the "Great Communicator," was certainly interested in policy change and went to unprecedented lengths to influence public opinion on behalf of such policies as deregulation, decreases in spending on domestic policy, and increases in the defense budget. Bill Clinton was also an extraordinarily able communicator, and he traveled widely and spoke out constantly on behalf of his policies, such as those dealing with the economy, health care reform, and free trade. Nevertheless, both presidents were typically unable to obtain the public's support for their initiatives and generally saw public opinion move against them.[37]

Mobilizing the Public

Sometimes merely changing public opinion is not sufficient, and the president wants the public to communicate its views directly to Congress. Mobilization of the public may be the ultimate weapon in the president's arsenal of resources with which to influence Congress. When the people speak, especially when they speak clearly, Congress listens.

Mobilizing the public involves overcoming formidable barriers and accepting substantial risks. It entails the double burden of obtaining both opinion support and political action from a generally inattentive and apathetic public. If the president

YOUNG PEOPLE AND POLITICS

The Generation Gap in Watching the President

If the president is to persuade the public to support him and his policies, he must have the public's attention. He has been getting less of it, however. When President Nixon went on TV to give a speech or hold a press conference in the 1970s, many viewers had little other choice but to watch him if they had their TV on at that time. Today, when regular programming is preempted on the major networks for a presidential address, most people now can turn to either the many alternatives offered via cable TV or to a videotape or DVD if they are not interested in seeing what the president has to say. As a result, presidential speeches have been viewed by a smaller percentage of the American public in recent decades. The president cannot rely on a captive audience for a speech.

A whole generation has now grown up in the narrowcasting age. The Reagan years coincided with the rise of narrowcasting. Scholars have found that people over 65 years of age were about twice as likely to view the typical Reagan speech as those under 35. In addition, older people who tuned in were also much more attentive to President Reagan. When senior citizens said they watched a speech, two out of every three said they watched the whole thing. In contrast, less than one out of every three young viewers said they watched a typical speech in its entirety. Channel surfing, as facilitated by the widespread diffusion of TV and cable remote controls during the 1980s, apparently caught on much faster with young adults—who used them to switch away from President Reagan's speeches.

The pattern of young people being less attentive to presidential messages has persisted, even for the high-profile address President Bush delivered to Congress nine days after the September 11, 2001, terrorist attacks. Older citizens were about 20 percent more likely to tune in to hear from the president than were young adults. One might expect that young people would be especially attentive to speeches regarding the onset of a war their cohorts would be asked to fight. Yet this was not the case. Young people were about 25 percent less likely to have tuned in to Bush's 2003 State of the Union speech, delivered shortly before the war with Iraq.

In sum, the audience for presidential speeches is now one that is unrepresentative of the general adult public in terms of age. When presidents address the nation in the narrowcasting age, they are actually likely to reach a much larger percentage of older than younger citizens. In some sense, then, presidents are in a less powerful position than in earlier decades. They have lost the ability to communicate directly with the American public anytime they see fit, making it more difficult to obtain the public's support.

Questions for Discussion

- Will the relative inattention to the president by today's young people persist as they age?
- Do you think presidents can govern effectively if they cannot connect to young people?

tries to mobilize the public and fails, the lack of response speaks clearly to members of Congress.

Perhaps the most notable recent example of the president's mobilization of public opinion to pressure Congress is Ronald Reagan's effort to obtain passage of his tax-cut bill in 1981. Shortly before the crucial vote in the House, the president made a televised plea for support of his tax-cut proposals and asked the people to let their representatives in Congress know how they felt. Evidently Reagan's plea worked; thousands of phone calls, letters, and telegrams poured into congressional offices. On the morning of the vote, Speaker Tip O'Neill declared, "We are experiencing a telephone blitz like this nation has never seen. It's had a devastating effect."[38] The president easily carried the day.

The Reagan administration's effort to mobilize the public on behalf of the 1981 tax cut is significant not only because of the success of presidential leadership but also because it appears to be an anomaly. In the remainder of Reagan's tenure, the president went repeatedly to the people regarding a wide range of policies, including the budget, aid to the Contras in Nicaragua, and defense expenditures. Despite high levels of approval for much of that time, Reagan was never again able to arouse many in his audience to communicate their support of his policies to Congress. Substantial tax cuts hold more appeal to the public than most other issues.

The President and the Press

Despite all their efforts to lead public opinion, presidents do not directly reach the American people on a day-to-day basis. The mass media provide people with most of what they know about chief executives and their policies. The media also interpret and analyze presidential activities, even the president's direct appeals to the public. The press is thus the principal intermediary between the president and the public, and relations with the press are an important aspect of the president's efforts to lead public opinion.

No matter who is in the White House or who reports on presidential activities, presidents and the press tend to be in conflict. George Washington complained that the "calumnies" against his administration were "outrages of common decency." Thomas Jefferson once declared that "nothing in a newspaper is to be believed." Presidents are inherently policy advocates. They want to control the amount and timing of information about their administration, whereas the press wants all the information that exists without delay. As long as their goals are different, presidents and the media are likely to be adversaries.

Because of the importance of the press to the president, the White House monitors the media closely. Some presidents have installed special televisions so they can watch the news on all the networks at once; Lyndon Johnson even had news tickers from AP, UPI, and Reuters in the Oval Office. The White House also goes to great lengths to encourage the media to project a positive image of the president's activities and policies. About one-third of the high-level White House staff members are directly involved in media relations and policy of one type or another, and most staff members are involved at some time in trying to influence the media's portrayal of the president.

The person who most often deals directly with the press is the president's *press secretary*, who serves as a conduit of information from the White House to the press. Press secretaries conduct daily press briefings, giving prepared announcements and answering questions. They and their staff also arrange private interviews with White House officials (often done on a background basis, in which the reporter may not attribute remarks to the person being interviewed), photo opportunities, and travel arrangements for reporters when the president leaves Washington.

The best-known direct interaction between the president and the press is the formal presidential press conference. Since the presidency of George Bush, however, prime-time televised press conferences have become rare events. Bill Clinton took office with an antagonistic attitude toward the national media and planned to bypass it rather than use it as part of his political strategy. After a rocky start in his press relations, the president made himself somewhat more accessible to the national press. Like Clinton, George W. Bush has relied more on travel around the country to gain television time to spread his message than on formal press conferences.

Despite their visibility, press conferences are not very useful means of eliciting information. Presidents and their staffs can anticipate most of the questions that will be asked and prepare answers to them ahead of time, reducing the spontaneity of the sessions. Moreover, the large size and public nature of press conferences reduce the candor with which the president responds to questions.

Most of the news coverage of the White House comes under the heading "body watch." In other words, reporters focus on the most visible layer of the president's personal and official activities and provide the public with step-by-step accounts. They are interested in what presidents are going to do, how their actions will affect others, how they view policies and individuals, and how they present themselves rather than in the substance of policies or the fundamental processes operating in the executive branch. Because there are daily deadlines to meet and television reporters must squeeze their stories into sound bites measured in seconds, not minutes, there is little time for reflection, analysis, or comprehensive coverage.

Bias is the most politically charged issue in relations between the president and the press. A large number of studies have concluded that the news media, including the television networks and major newspapers, are not biased *systematically* toward a particular person, party, or ideology, as measured in the amount or favorability of coverage.[39]

To conclude that the news contains little explicitly partisan or ideological bias is not to argue that the news does not distort reality in its coverage of the president. As the following excerpt from Jimmy Carter's diary regarding a visit to a U.S. Army base in Panama in 1978 illustrates, "objective" reporting can be misleading:

> *I told the Army troops that I was in the Navy for 11 years, and they booed. I told them that we depended on the Army to keep the Canal open, and they cheered. Later, the news reports said that there were boos and cheers during my speech.*[40]

We learned in Chapter 7 that the news is fundamentally superficial, oversimplified, and often overblown, all of which provides the public with a distorted view of, among other things, presidential activities, statements, policies, and options. We have also seen that the press prefers to frame the news in themes, which both simplifies complex issues and events and provides continuity of persons, institutions, and issues. Once these themes are established, the press tends to maintain them in subsequent stories. Of necessity, themes emphasize some information at the expense of other data, often determining what information is most relevant to news coverage and the context in which it is presented.

Once a stereotype of President Ford as a "bumbler" was established, every stumble was magnified as the press emphasized behavior that fit the mold. He was repeatedly forced to defend his intelligence, and many of his acts and statements were reported as efforts to "act" presidential. Once Ford was typecast, his image was repeatedly reinforced and was very difficult to overcome.[41]

News coverage of the presidency often tends to emphasize the negative (even if the negative stories are presented in a seemingly neutral manner),[42] a trend that has increased over the past 20 years.[43] In the 1980 election campaign, the press portrayed President Carter as mean and Ronald Reagan as imprecise rather than Carter as precise and Reagan as pleasant. The emphasis, in other words, was on the candidates' negative qualities. George Bush received extraordinarily negative press coverage during the 1992 election campaign, and the television networks' portrayal of the economy, for which Bush was blamed, got worse as the economy actually improved to a robust rate of growth![44]

President Clinton received mostly negative coverage during his tenure in office, with a ratio of negative to positive comments on network television of about 2 to 1.[45] When the story broke regarding his affair with Monica Lewinsky, the press engaged in a feeding frenzy, providing an extraordinary amount of information on both the affair and the president's attempts to cover it up. Little of this coverage was favorable to the president (see "A Generation of Change: Rushing to Judgment").

White House reporters are always looking to expose conflicts of interest and other shady behavior of public officials. In addition, many of their inquiries revolve around the question "Is the president up to the job?" Reporters who are confined in the White House all day may attempt to make up for their lack of investigative

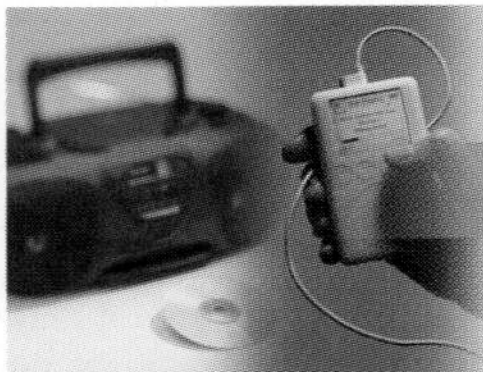

A GENERATION OF CHANGE

Rushing to Judgment

In the past, most editors were reluctant to publish analyses sharply divergent from the president's position without direct confirmation from an authoritative source who would be willing to go on the record in opposition to the White House. This approach restrained media criticism of the president. During the famous investigation of the Watergate scandal, the *Washington Post* verified all information attributed to an unnamed source with at least one other independent source. It also did not print information from other media outlets unless its reporters could independently verify that information.[46] Things have changed, however.

When the story broke about charges that President Clinton had sexual relations with a young White House intern named Monica Lewinsky, virtually all elements of the mass media went into a feeding frenzy,[47] relying as much on analysis, opinion, and speculation as on confirmed facts. Even the most prominent news outlets disseminated unsubstantiated reports of charges that those originally carrying the story had not independently verified. If one news outlet carried a charge, the rest, which did not wish to be scooped, soon picked it up. For example, the media widely reported unsubstantiated charges that members of the Secret Service had found the president and Ms. Lewinsky in a compromising position. Such reporting helped sensationalize the story, keeping it alive and undermining the president's efforts to focus the public's attention on matters of public policy.

Similarly, the press gave immediate attention to a story on the CBS television program *60 Minutes* that revealed documents regarding President George W. Bush's service in the National Guard. The documents purported to show dissatisfaction with the president's performance—or nonperformance. On closer scrutiny, however, it turned out that the documents were forgeries.

reporting with sarcastic and accusatory questioning. Moreover, the desire to keep the public interested and the need for continuous coverage may create in the press a subconscious bias against the presidency that leads to negative stories.

On the other hand, the president has certain advantages in dealing with the press. It typically portrays him with an aura of dignity and treats him with deference.[48] According to Sam Donaldson, who was generally considered an aggressive White House reporter, "For every truly tough question I've put to officials, I've asked a dozen that were about as tough as Grandma's apple dumplings."[49] Thus, when he left after serving as President Reagan's press secretary for six years, Larry Speakes told reporters they had given the Reagan administration "a fair shake."[50]

Remember that the White House can largely control the environment in which the president meets the press—even going so far as to have helicopters revved as Ronald Reagan approached them so he could not hear reporters' questions and give unrehearsed responses.

Understanding the American Presidency

Because the presidency is the single most important office in American politics, there has always been concern about whether the president is a threat to democracy. The importance of the president has raised similar concerns for the scope of government in America.

Presidential Greatness

The Presidency and Democracy

From the time the Constitution was written, there has been a fear that the presidency would degenerate into a monarchy or a dictatorship. Even America's greatest presidents have heightened these fears at times. Despite George Washington's well-deserved reputation for peacefully relinquishing power, he also had certain regal tendencies that fanned the suspicions of the Jeffersonians. Abraham Lincoln, for all his humility, exercised extraordinary powers at the outbreak of the Civil War. Since that time, political commentators have alternated between extolling and fearing a strong presidency.

Concerns over presidential power are generally closely related to policy views. Those who oppose the president's policies are the most likely to be concerned about *too much* presidential power. As you have seen, however, aside from acting outside the law and the Constitution, there is little prospect that the presidency will be a threat to democracy. The Madisonian system of checks and balances remains intact.

This system is especially evident in an era characterized by divided government—government in which the president is of one party and a majority in each house of Congress is of the other party. Some observers are concerned that there is too much checking and balancing and too little capacity to act on pressing national challenges. More potentially important legislation fails to pass under divided government than when one party controls both the presidency and Congress.[51] However, major policy change *is* possible under a divided government. One author found that major change is just as likely to occur when the parties share control as when one party holds both the presidency and a majority in each house of Congress.[52]

The Presidency and the Scope of Government

Some of the most noteworthy presidents in the twentieth century (including Theodore Roosevelt, Woodrow Wilson, and Franklin Roosevelt) have successfully advocated substantial increases in the role of the national government. Supporting an increased role for government is not inherent in the presidency, however; leadership can move in many directions.

All seven presidents since Lyndon Johnson have championed constraints on government and limits on spending, especially in domestic policy. It is often said that the American people are ideologically conservative and operationally liberal. For most of the past generation, it has been their will to choose presidents who reflected their ideology and a Congress that represented their appetite for public service. It has been the president more often than Congress who has said "no" to government growth.

Summary

Americans expect a lot from presidents—perhaps too much. The myth of the president as a powerhouse clouds Americans' image of presidential reality. Presidents mainly have the power to persuade, not to impose their will.

Presidents do not work alone. Gone are the days when the presidency meant the president plus a few aides and advisers. The cabinet, the Executive Office of the President, and the White House staff all assist today's presidents. These services come at a price, however, and presidents must organize their subordinates effectively for decision making and policy execution.

Although presidential leadership of Congress is central to all administrations, it often proves frustrating. Presidents rely on their party, the public, and their own legislative skills to persuade Congress to support their policies, but most of the time their efforts are at the margins of coalition building. Rarely are presidents in a position to create—through their own leadership—opportunities for major changes in public policy. They may, however, use their skills to exploit favorable political conditions to bring about policy change.

Some of the president's most important responsibilities fall in the area of national security. As chief diplomat and commander in chief of the armed forces, the president is the country's crisis manager. Still, disputes with Congress over war powers and presidential discretion in foreign affairs demonstrate that even in regard to national security, the president operates within the Madisonian system of checks and balances.

Because presidents are dependent on others to accomplish their goals, their greatest challenge is to obtain support. Public opinion can be an important resource for presidential persuasion, and the White House works hard to influence the public.

Public approval of presidents and their policies is often elusive, however; the public does not reliably respond to presidential leadership. The press is the principal intermediary between the president and the public, and relations with the press present yet another challenge to the White House's efforts to lead public opinion.

Internet Resources

www.whitehouse.gov/
Links to presidential speeches, documents, schedules, radio addresses, federal statistics, and White House press releases and briefings.

www.whitehouse.gov/government/eop.html
Information about the Executive Office of the President.

www.ibiblio.org/lia/president/
Links to presidents and presidential libraries.

www.ipl.org/div/potus/
Background on presidents and their administrations.

www.lib.umich.edu/govdocs/fedprs.html
Wide range of documents regarding the president's activities.

www.presidency.ucsb.edu
Presidential papers, documents, and data.

www.archives.gov/federal-register/publications/weekly-compilation.html
The *Weekly Compilation of Presidential Documents*, the official publication of presidential statements, messages, remarks, and other materials released by the White House Press Secretary.

Get Connected

Approving of the President

The White House invests a great deal of time and energy in its public relations efforts designed to increase the president's public approval. A president who is popular with the people may find it easier to enact his initiatives. Throughout a president's term in office, approval ratings rise and fall in reaction to current events in the United States and abroad as well as in response to actions taken by the president. Different polling agencies use different questions to gauge presidential approval, but most follow the pattern set by the Gallup Poll: "Do you approve of the way [name of president] is handling his job as president?"

Search the Web

Go to the Polling Report's Politics & Policy page, *www.pollingreport.com/POLPOL.htm*, and click on "White House" to access the president's job approval ratings. Compare the ratings of the president to the historical information on presidential approval ratings presented in the textbook.

Questions to Ask

- When were the president's job approval ratings the highest? The lowest? Are the ratings trending up or down for the president?
- How similar are the ratings of different polling organizations?
- What were the major reasons for changes in the president's approval?

Why It Matters

Presidents believe that public approval is the political resource that has the most potential to turn a stalemate between the president and Congress into a supportive situation for the president's legislative proposals. The White House also believes that lack of public support strengthens the resolve of the president's opponents and narrows the range in which presidential policies receive the benefit of the doubt.

Get Involved

Keep track of how presidential approval is reported in your local newspaper and on the national television networks. Also watch to see whether Congress is more responsive and press coverage is more positive when the president ranks high in the polls.

For more exercises, go to www.longmanamericangovernment.com.

For Further Reading

Burke, John P. *The Institutional Presidency*. 2nd ed. Baltimore: Johns Hopkins University Press, 2000. Examines White House organization and presidential advising.

Burke, John P., and Fred I. Greenstein. *How Presidents Test Reality*. New York: Russell Sage Foundation, 1989. Excellent work on presidential decision making.

Cooper, Phillip J. *By Order of the President*. Lawrence: University Press of Kansas, 2002. The use and abuse of executive direct action.

Edwards, George C., III. *At the Margins: Presidential Leadership of Congress*. New Haven, CT: Yale University Press, 1989. Examines the presidents' efforts to lead Congress and explains their limitations.

Edwards, George C., III. *Governing by Campaigning: The Politics of the George W. Bush Presidency*. New York: Longman, 2006. Examines the president's efforts and success in forming governing coalitions.

Edwards, George C., III. *On Deaf Ears: The Limits of the Bully Pulpit*. New Haven, CT: Yale University Press, 2003. The effect of the president's efforts to change public opinion in the White House's pursuit of popular support.

Fisher, Louis. *Constitutional Conflicts Between Congress and the President*. 4th ed. rev. Lawrence: University Press of Kansas, 1997. Presents the constitutional dimensions of the separation of powers.

Greenstein, Fred. *The Presidential Difference*. 2nd ed. New York: Free Press, 2005. Leadership styles of modern presidents.

Howell, William G. *Power Without Persuasion*. Princeton, NJ: Princeton University Press, 2003. Focuses on the use of the president's discretionary power.

Jacobs, Lawrence R., and Robert Y. Shapiro. *Politicians Don't Pander*. Chicago: University of Chicago Press, 2000. The relationship between leaders and public opinion.

Jacobson, Gary C. *A Divider, Not a Uniter: George W. Bush and the American Public*. New York: Longman, 2006. Examines the polarization of public opinion in the Bush presidency.

Neustadt, Richard E. *Presidential Power and the Modern Presidents*. New York: Free Press, 1990. The most influential book on the American presidency; argues that presidential power is the power to persuade.

Pfiffner, James P. *The Strategic Presidency*. 2nd ed. Lawrence: University Press of Kansas, 1996. Organizing the presidency.

Rudalevige, Andrew. *The New Imperial Presidency: Renewing Presidential Power After Watergate*. Ann Arbor: University of Michigan Press, 2005. The expansion of presidential power in recent decades.

The Federal Bureaucracy

Chapter Outline

POLITICS IN ACTION: REGULATING FOOD Americans do not want to worry about the safety of the food we eat. Indeed, food safety is something we take for granted. But who assures this safety? Bureaucrats. It is their job to keep our food safe from contamination. Although we rarely think about food inspections, they represent one of the most important regulatory functions of government. The fact that we rarely think about food safety is testimony to the success of bureaucrats in carrying out their tasks.[1]

Policing the food supply is not a straightforward task, however. It involves a complex web of federal agencies with overlapping jurisdictions. Twelve agencies and 35 statutes regulate food safety. Eggs in the shell fall under the purview of the Food and Drug Administration (FDA), but once cracked and processed, they come under the jurisdiction of the U.S.

Department of Agriculture (USDA). The USDA is responsible for regulating meat and poultry, while the FDA handles most other food products, including seafood and produce. Cheese pizzas are the FDA's responsibility, but if they have pepperoni on top, Agriculture inspectors step in.

Other parts of the government also play a prominent role in enforcing food safety laws. For example, the Environmental Protection Agency oversees pesticides applied to crops, the Centers for Disease Control and Prevention track food-related illnesses, and the Department of Homeland Security coordinates agencies' safety and security activities.

You Are a Federal Administrator

Is this complex system the result of bureaucratic maneuvering? No, Congress created the system layer on top of layer, with little regard to how it should work as a whole. Critics argue that the system is outdated and that it would be better to create a single food safety agency that could target inspections, streamline safety programs, and use resources more efficiently. Such proposals have generated little enthusiasm in Congress, however, where committees are sensitive about losing jurisdiction over agencies. For example, in the House, the Energy and Commerce Committee has oversight over the FDA, while the Agriculture Committee has responsibility for the USDA. Growers and manufacturers fear a single agency would impose onerous new regulations, product recalls, and fines and could be used by empire-building bureaucrats to expand their budget and regulatory authority. So little change occurs.

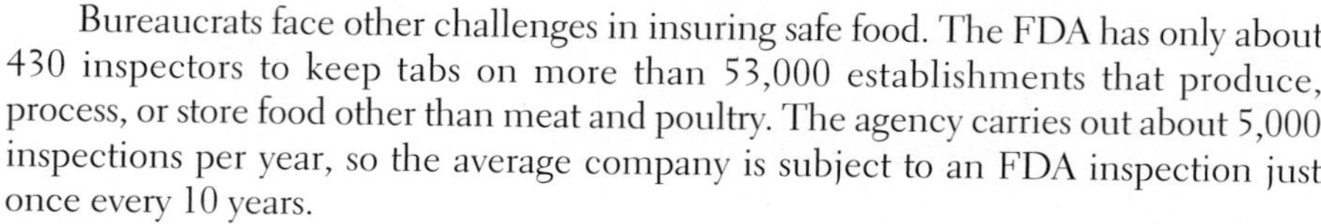
Bureaucrats face other challenges in insuring safe food. The FDA has only about 430 inspectors to keep tabs on more than 53,000 establishments that produce, process, or store food other than meat and poultry. The agency carries out about 5,000 inspections per year, so the average company is subject to an FDA inspection just once every 10 years.

Bureaucrats are central to our lives. They provide essential public services. They possess crucial information and expertise that make them partners with the president and Congress in decision making about public policy. Who knows more than bureaucrats about Social Security recipients or the military capabilities of China? Bureaucrats are also central to politics. They do much more than simply follow orders. Because of their expertise, bureaucrats inevitably have discretion in carrying out policy decisions, which is why congressional committees and interest groups take so much interest in what they do.

Bureaucratic power extends to every corner of American economic and social life, yet bureaucracies are scarcely hinted at in the Constitution. Congress creates each bureaucratic agency, sets its budget, and writes the policies it administers. Most agencies are responsible to the president, whose constitutional responsibility to "take care that the laws shall be faithfully executed" sheds only a dim light on the problems of managing so large a government. How to manage and control bureaucracies is a central problem of democratic government.

Reining in the power of bureaucracies is also a common theme in debates over the scope of government in America. Some political commentators see the bureaucracy as the prime example of a federal government growing out of control. They view the bureaucracy as acquisitive, constantly seeking to expand its size, budgets, and authority while being entwined in red tape and spewing forth senseless regulations. Others see the bureaucracy as laboring valiantly against great odds to fulfill the missions elected officials have assigned it. Where does the truth lie? The answer is less obvious than you may think. Clearly, bureaucracies require closer examination.

The German sociologist Max Weber advanced his classic conception of bureaucracy, stressing that the bureaucracy was a "rational" way for a modern society to conduct its business.[2] According to Weber, a **bureaucracy** depends on certain elements: It has a *hierarchical authority structure,* in which power flows from the top down and responsibility flows from the bottom up; it uses *task specialization* so that experts instead of amateurs perform technical jobs; and it develops extensive *rules,* which may seem extreme at times but which allow similar cases to be handled similarly instead of capriciously.

bureaucracy
According to Max Weber, a hierarchical authority structure that uses task specialization, operates on the merit principle, and behaves with impersonality. Bureaucracies govern modern states.

Bureaucracies operate on the *merit principle,* in which entrance and promotion are awarded on the basis of demonstrated abilities rather than on "who you know." Bureaucracies behave with *impersonality* so that they treat all their clients impartially. Weber's classic prototype of the bureaucratic organization depicts the bureaucracy as a well-organized machine with plenty of working but hierarchical parts.

The Bureaucrats

Bureaucrats are typically much less visible than the president or members of Congress. As a result, Americans usually know little about them. This section examines some myths about bureaucrats and explains who they are and how they got their jobs.

Some Bureaucratic Myths and Realities

Bureaucrat baiting is a popular American pastime. George Wallace, former Alabama governor and frequent presidential hopeful, warmed up his crowds with a line about "pointy-headed Washington bureaucrats who can't even park their bicycles straight." Even successful presidential candidates climbed aboard the antibureaucracy bandwagon. Jimmy Carter complained about America's "complicated and confused and overlapping and wasteful" bureaucracies, Gerald Ford complained about the "dead weight" of bureaucracies, and Ronald Reagan insisted that bureaucrats "overregulated" the American economy, causing a decline in productivity.

Any object of such unpopularity will spawn plenty of myths. The following are some of the most prevalent myths about bureaucracy:

- **Americans dislike bureaucrats.** Despite the rhetoric about bureaucracies, Americans are generally satisfied with bureaucrats and the treatment they get from them. Americans may dislike bureaucracies, but they like individual bureaucrats. Surveys have found that two-thirds or more of those who have had encounters with a bureaucrat evaluate these encounters positively. In most instances, people describe bureaucrats as helpful, efficient, fair, courteous, and working to serve their clients' interests.[3]
- **Bureaucracies are growing bigger each year.** This myth is half true and half false. The number of government employees has been expanding but not the number of *federal* employees. Almost all the growth in the number of public employees has occurred in state and local governments. The 19 million state

Bureaucrats are the scapegoats of American politics. Paperwork and red tape represent the image of bureaucracy to many Americans. Yet no society can operate without bureaucracy, and most people are satisfied with their encounters with bureaucrats.

and local public employees far outnumber the approximately 4.1 million civilian and military federal government employees (see Figure 13.1). As a percentage of America's total workforce, *federal* government employment has been shrinking, not growing; it now accounts for about 3 percent of all civilian jobs.

Of course, many state and local employees work on programs that are federally funded, and the federal government hires many private contractors to provide goods and services ranging from hot meals to weapons systems.[4] Such people provide services directly to the federal government or to citizens on its behalf. At the same time, private contractors generally lack the discretionary authority of federal employees, and high-level officials have less authority over state and local officials and private companies than they do over federal employees.

The Changing Face of the Federal Bureaucracy

- **Most federal bureaucrats work in Washington, D.C.** Only about 12 percent of federal civilian employees work in the Washington, D.C., metropolitan area. California leads the nation in federal employees, with 245,000. Texas has 166,000 and New York 133,000. About 93,000 federal civilian employees work in foreign countries and American territories.[5] You can see where federal bureaucrats work by looking in your local phone book under "U.S. Government." You will probably find listings for the local offices of the postal service, the Social Security Administration, the FBI, the Department of Agriculture's county agents, recruiters for the armed services, air traffic controllers, the Internal Revenue Service (IRS), and many others.
- **Bureaucracies are ineffective, inefficient, and always mired in red tape.** No words describing bureaucratic behavior are better known than "red tape."[6] Bureaucracy, however, is simply a way of organizing people to perform work. General Motors, a college or university, the U.S. Army, the Department of

Figure 13.1 Growth in Civilian Government Employees

The number of government employees has grown since 1965. The real growth, however, has been in the state and local sector, with its millions of teachers, police officers, and other service deliverers. Many state and local employees and programs, though, are supported by federal grants-in-aid. (Note that the figures for federal employment do not include military personnel.)

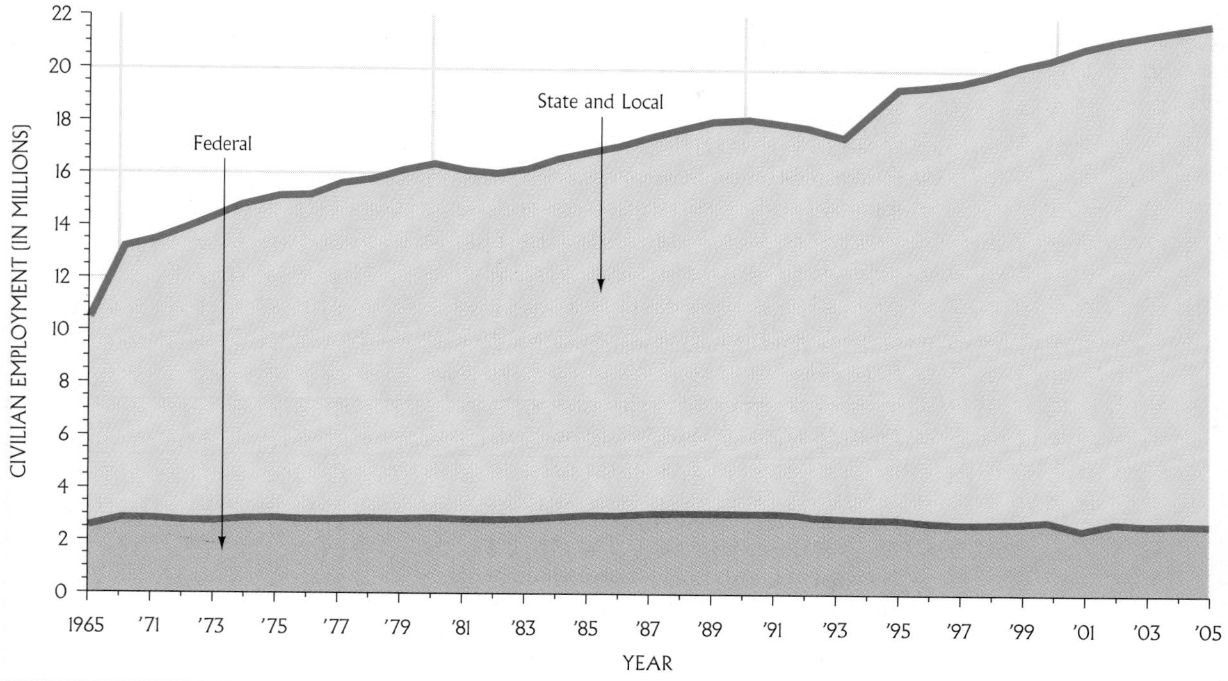

Source: Budget of the United States Government, Fiscal Year 2007: Historical Tables (Washington, DC: U.S. Government Printing Office, 2006), table 17.5.

Health and Human Services, and the Roman Catholic Church are all bureaucracies. Bureaucracies are a little like referees: When they work well, no one gives them much credit, but when they work poorly, everyone calls them unfair, incompetent, or inefficient. Bureaucracies may be inefficient at times, but no one has found a substitute for them, and no one has yet demonstrated that government bureaucracies are more or less inefficient, ineffective, or mired in red tape than private bureaucracies.[7]

Anyone who looks with disdain on American bureaucracies should contemplate life without them. Despite all the complaining about bureaucracies, the vast majority of tasks carried out by governments at all levels are noncontroversial. Bureaucrats deliver mail, test milk, issue Social Security and student loan checks, run national parks, and perform other routine governmental tasks in a perfectly acceptable manner. Most of the people who work for cities, states, and the national government are typical Americans, the type who are likely to be your neighbors.

Table 13.1 Federal Civilian Employment

EXECUTIVE DEPARTMENTS	NUMBER OF EMPLOYEES[a]
Defense (military functions)	666,700
Veterans Affairs	222,800
Homeland Security	146,600
Treasury	112,500
Justice	118,500
Agriculture	100,100
Interior	70,200
Health and Human Services	61,300
Transportation	55,400
Commerce	37,400
State	30,300
Labor	16,800
Energy	15,700
Housing and Urban Development	9,800
Education	4,300
LARGER NONCABINET AGENCIES	
U.S. Postal Service	732,348
Social Security Administration	64,000
Corps of Engineers	22,900
National Aeronautics and Space Administration	18,600
Environmental Protection Agency	17,400
Tennessee Valley Authority	12,700
General Services Administration	12,200

[a]Figures are for 2006.
Source: Budget of the United States Government, Fiscal Year 2007: Analytical Perspectives (Washington, DC: U.S. Government Printing Office, 2006), tables 24.1 and 24.3.

Most federal civilian employees work for just a few of the agencies (see Table 13.1). The Department of Defense (DOD) employs about one-fourth of federal *civilian* workers in addition to the more than 1.4 million men and women in uniform. Altogether, the DOD makes up more than half the federal bureaucracy. The Postal Service accounts for an additional 30 percent of the federal civilian employees, and the Department of Veterans Affairs, clearly related to national defense, has nearly 223,000 employees. All other functions of government, including homeland security, are handled by the remaining quarter of federal employees.

Who They Are and How They Got There

Because there are more than 2.6 million civilian bureaucrats, it is hard to imagine a statistically typical bureaucrat. Bureaucrats are male and female, all races and religions, well paid and not so well paid. Like other institutions, the federal government

Figure 13.2 Characteristics of Federal Civilian Employees[a]

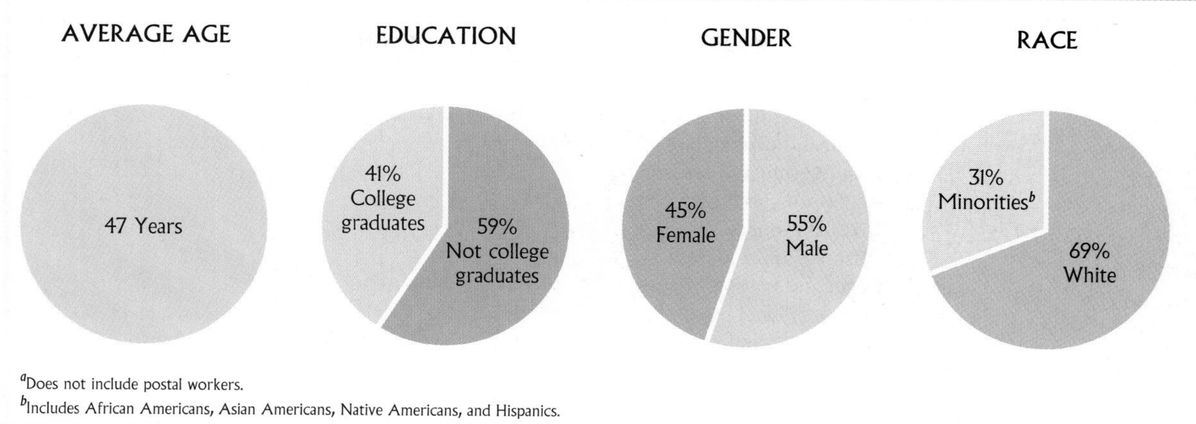

Source: Data from United States Office of Personnel Management, *The Factbook, 2005* (Washington, DC: U.S. Government Printing Office, 2006), 10–13.

has been under pressure to expand its hiring of women and minorities. Congress has ordered federal agencies to make special efforts to recruit and promote previously disadvantaged groups, but women and non-Whites still cluster at the lower ranks. As a whole, however, the permanent bureaucracy is more broadly representative of the American people than are legislators, judges, or presidential appointees in the executive branch[8] (see Figure 13.2).

Who Wants to Be a Bureaucrat?

The diversity of bureaucratic jobs mirrors the diversity of private-sector jobs, including occupations literally ranging from A to Z. Accountants, bakers, census analysts, defense procurement specialists, electricians, foreign service officers, guards in federal prisons, home economists, Indian Affairs agents, judges, kitchen workers, lawyers, missile technologists, narcotics agents, ophthalmologists, postal carriers, quarantine specialists, radiologists, stenographers, truck drivers, underwater demolition experts, virologists, wardens, X-ray technicians, youth counselors, and zoologists all work for the government (see Table 13.2).

patronage
One of the key inducements used by political machines. A patronage job, promotion, or contract is one that is given for political reasons rather than for merit or competence alone.

Civil Service: From Patronage to Protection. Until roughly 100 years ago, a person got a job with the government through the patronage system. **Patronage** is a hiring and promotion system based on political reasons rather than on merit or competence. Working in a congressional campaign, making large donations, and having the right connections helped people secure jobs with the government. Nineteenth-century presidents staffed the government with their friends and allies, following the view of Andrew Jackson that "to the victors belong the spoils." Scores of office seekers would swarm the White House after Inauguration Day. It is said that during a bout with malaria, Lincoln told an aide to "send in the office seekers" because he finally had something to give them.

The Merit System

A disappointed office seeker named Charles Guiteau helped end this "spoils system" of federal appointments in 1881. Frustrated because President James A. Garfield

Table 13.2 Full-Time Civilian White-Collar Employees of the Federal Government

SELECTED OCCUPATIONAL CATEGORIES	NUMBER OF EMPLOYEES
General administrative, clerical, and office services	363,953
Medical, hospital, dental, and public health	139,132
Engineering and architecture	123,183
Accounting and budget	115,369
Investigation	93,897
Business and Industry	87,292
Legal and kindred	86,377
Social science, psychology, and welfare	67,496
Biological sciences	58,779
Transportation	45,864
Personnel management and industrial relations	40,673
Physical sciences	33,470
Education	32,632
Supply	31,272
Information and the arts	18,197
Mathematics and statistics	13,624
Equipment, facilities, and services	12,164
Quality assurance, inspection, and grading	10,028
Library and archives	8,045
Copyright, patent, and trademark	3,864
Veterinary medical science	2,088

Source: U.S. Office of Personnel Management, *Occupations of Federal White-Collar and Blue-Collar Workers, Federal Civilian Workforce Statistics, as of September 30, 1999* (Washington, DC: U.S. Government Printing Office, 2000), table W.2.

would not give him a job, Guiteau shot and killed Garfield. The so-called Prince of Patronage himself, Vice President Chester A. Arthur, then became president. Arthur, who had been collector of the customs for New York—a patronage-rich post—surprised his critics by encouraging passage of the **Pendleton Civil Service Act** (1883), which created the federal civil service. Today, most federal agencies are covered by some sort of civil service system.

All **civil service** systems are designed to hire and promote members of the bureaucracy on the basis of merit and to create a nonpartisan government service. The **merit principle**—using entrance exams and promotion ratings to reward qualified individuals—is intended to produce an administration of people with talent and skill. Creating a nonpartisan civil service means insulating government workers from the risk of being fired when a new party comes to power. At the same time, the **Hatch Act**, originally passed in 1939 and amended most recently in 1993, prohibits civil service employees from actively participating in partisan politics while on duty. While off duty they may engage in political activities, but they cannot run for partisan elective offices or solicit contributions from the public. Employees with sensitive positions, such as those in the national security area, may not engage in political activities even while off duty.

Pendleton Civil Service Act
Passed in 1883, an Act that created a federal **civil service** so that hiring and promotion would be based on merit rather than **patronage**.

civil service
A system of hiring and promotion based on the merit principle and the desire to create a nonpartisan government service.

merit principle
The idea that hiring should be based on entrance exams and promotion ratings to produce administration by people with talent and skill.

Hatch Act
A federal law prohibiting government employees from active participation in partisan politics.

The **Office of Personnel Management** (OPM) is in charge of hiring for most federal agencies. The president appoints its director, who is confirmed by the Senate. The OPM has elaborate rules about hiring, promotion, working conditions, and firing. To get a civil service job, usually candidates must first take a test. If they pass, their names are sent to agencies when jobs requiring their particular skills become available. For each position open, the OPM will send three names to the agency. Except under unusual circumstances, the agency must hire one of these three individuals. (This process is called the "rule of three.") Each job is assigned a **GS (General Schedule) rating** ranging from GS 1 to GS 18. Salaries are keyed to rating and experience. You can see how many people are employed in each rating and their average salaries in Table 13.3.

At the very top of the civil service system are about 9,000 members of the **Senior Executive Service**, the "cream of the crop" of the federal employees. These executives earn high salaries, and the president may move them from one agency to another as leadership needs change.

Once hired, and after a probationary period, the civil service system protects civil servants—overprotects them, critics claim. Ensuring a nonpartisan civil service requires that workers have protection from dismissals that are politically motivated. Protecting all workers against political firings may also protect a few from dismissal for good cause. Firing incompetents is hard work and is unusual. According to civil service regulations, employees must exhaust their right of appeal before the government can stop their paychecks. Appeals can consume weeks, months, or even years. More than one agency has decided to tolerate incompetents, assigning them trivial or no duties, rather than invest its resources in the nearly hopeless task of discharging

Office of Personnel Management
The office in charge of hiring for most agencies of the federal government, using elaborate rules in the process.

GS (General Schedule) rating
A schedule for federal employees, ranging from GS 1 to GS 18, by which salaries can be keyed to rating and experience.

Senior Executive Service
An elite cadre of about 9,000 federal government managers, established by the Civil Service Reform Act of 1978, who are mostly career officials but include some political appointees who do not require Senate confirmation.

Table 13.3 GS Employment and Salaries

GENERAL SCHEDULE GRADE	NUMBER OF EMPLOYEES	AVERAGE SALARY
1	270	$18,081
2	955	20,963
3	8,445	23,960
4	45,327	27,315
5	100,984	31,412
6	81,255	35,666
7	130,828	39,327
8	51,413	44,771
9	123,437	47,601
10	16,975	53,493
11	180,333	57,555
12	207,566	69,655
13	174,575	83,672
14	80,205	99,285
15	41,845	119,134

Source: U.S. Office of Personnel Management, *Pay Structure of the Federal Civil Service as of March 31, 2004* (Washington, DC: U.S. Government Printing Office, 2005), table 4.

Why It Matters

The Merit System
People obtain positions in the federal bureaucracy through a merit system and are protected against losing their jobs because of their political views. If the president could appoint a substantial percentage of bureaucrats, it is likely that they would be more responsive to the president but also likely that they would be less qualified to serve the public interest than today's bureaucrats.

them. Firing incompetent female, minority, or older workers may be even more difficult than dislodging incompetent young or middle-aged White males. These groups not only have the usual civil service protections but also can resort to antidiscrimination statutes to appeal their dismissals. After a protracted battle, Congress agreed to President George W. Bush's proposal to limit job protection for employees in the Department of Homeland Security.

The Other Route to Federal Jobs: Recruiting from the Plum Book. As an incoming administration celebrates its victory and prepares to take control of the government, Congress publishes the *plum book*, which lists top federal jobs (that is, "plums") available for direct presidential appointment, often with Senate confirmation. There are about 500 of these top policymaking posts (mostly cabinet secretaries, undersecretaries, assistant secretaries, and bureau chiefs) and about 2,500 lesser positions.

All incoming presidents launch a nationwide talent search for qualified personnel. Presidents seek individuals who combine executive talent, political skills, and sympathy for policy positions similar to those of the administration. Often, the president tries to include men and women, Whites and non-Whites, people from different regions, and party members who represent different interests (although few recent presidents have appointed as high a percentage of middle-aged White males as did Ronald Reagan). Some positions, especially ambassadorships, go to large campaign contributors. A few of these appointees will be civil servants, temporarily elevated to a "political" status; most, though, will be political appointees, "in-and-outers" who stay for a while and then leave.[9]

Once in office, these administrative policymakers constitute what Hugh Heclo has called a "government of strangers." Their most important trait is their transience. The average assistant secretary or undersecretary lasts less than two years.[10] Few top officials stay long enough to know their own subordinates well, much less people in other agencies. Administrative routines, budget cycles, and legal complexities are often new to them. To these new political executives, the possibilities of power may seem endless. Nevertheless, although plum book appointees may have the outward signs of power, many of them find it challenging to exercise real control over much of what their subordinates do and have difficulty leaving their mark on policy. They soon learn that they are dependent on senior civil servants who know more, have been there longer, and will outlast them.

How Bureaucracies Are Organized

A complete organizational chart of the American federal government would be big enough to occupy a large wall. You could pore over this chart, trace the lines of responsibility and authority, and see how government is organized—at least on paper. A very simplified organizational chart of the executive branch appears in Figure 13.3. A much easier way to look at how the federal executive branch is organized is to group agencies into four basic types: cabinet departments, independent regulatory commissions, government corporations, and independent executive agencies.

Figure 13.3 Organization of the Executive Branch

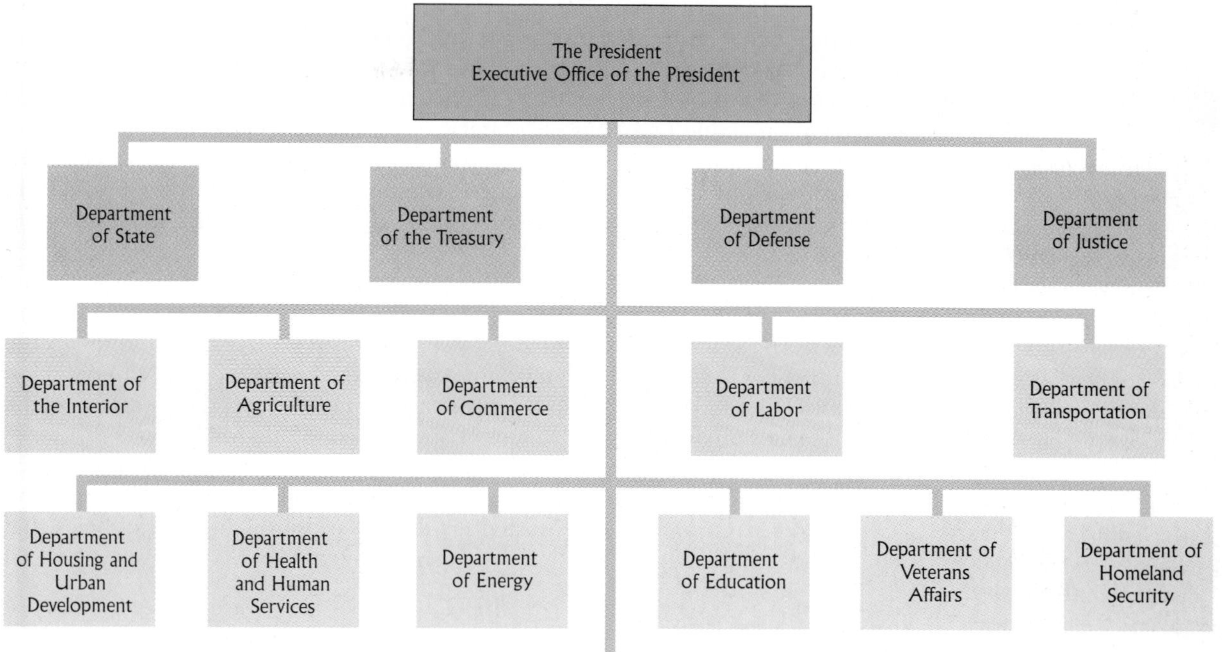

INDEPENDENT ESTABLISHMENTS AND GOVERNMENT CORPORATIONS

African Development Foundation
Broadcasting Board of Governors
Central Intelligence Agency
Commodity Futures Trading Commission
Consumer Product Safety Commission
Corporation for National and Community Service
Defense Nuclear Facilities Safety Board
Environmental Protection Agency
Equal Employment Opportunity Commission
Export-Import Bank of the United States
Farm Credit Administration
Federal Communications Commission
Federal Deposit Insurance Corporation
Federal Election Commission
Federal Housing Finance Board
Federal Labor Relations Authority
Federal Maritime Commission
Federal Mediation and Conciliation Service
Federal Mine Safety and Health Review Commission
Federal Reserve System
Federal Retirement Thrift Investment Board
Federal Trade Commission
General Services Administration
Inter-American Foundation
Merit Systems Protection Board
National Aeronautics and Space Administration
National Archives and Records Administration
National Capital Planning Commission
National Credit Union Administration
National Foundation on the Arts and Humanities
National Labor Relations Board
National Mediation Board
National Railroad Passenger Corporation (Amtrak)
National Science Foundation
National Transportation Safety Board
Nuclear Regulatory Commission
Occupational Safety and Health Review Commission
Office of the Director of National Intelligence
Office of Government Ethics
Office of Personnel Management
Office of Special Counsel
Overseas Private Investment Corporation
Peace Corps
Pension Benefit Guaranty Corporation
Postal Rate Commission
Railroad Retirement Board
Securities and Exchange Commission
Selective Service System
Small Business Administration
Social Security Administration
Tennessee Valley Authority
Trade and Development Agency
U.S. Agency for International Development
U.S. Commission on Civil Rights
U.S. International Trade Commission
U.S. Postal Service

Source: Office of the Federal Register, *United States Government Manual 2006–2007* (Washington, DC: U.S. Government Printing Office, 2006), 21.

Why It Matters

Independent Regulatory Agencies

Independent regulatory agencies, such as the Federal Reserve Board, are designed to be somewhat insulated from the influence of politics. Their independence makes them less responsive to the president and Congress than other agencies. It also provides the potential—but not the certainty—of taking a long-range view and acting in the public interest.

independent regulatory commission

A government agency responsible for some sector of the economy, making and enforcing rules to protect the public interest. It also judges disputes over these rules. Compare **government corporation** and **independent executive agency**.

The Cabinet Departments

Each of the 15 cabinet departments is headed by a secretary (except the Department of Justice, which is headed by the attorney general) chosen by the president and approved by the Senate. Undersecretaries, deputy undersecretaries, and assistant secretaries report to the secretary. Each department manages specific policy areas (see the list in Table 12.3, page 387), and each has its own budget and its own staff.

Each department has a unique mission and is organized somewhat differently. The real work of a department is done in the bureaus, which divide the work into more specialized areas (a bureau is sometimes called a *service*, *office*, *administration*, or other name).

Until the 1970s, the largest cabinet department in personnel and budget was the Department of Defense. From then until 1995, the Department of Health and Human Services (HHS) was the largest federal department in dollars spent (although the Department of Defense still had more employees). The Social Security Administration split from HHS and became an independent agency in 1995, spending one-third of the federal budget on the massive programs of Social Security and Medicare.

Sometimes status as a cabinet department can be controversial. For several years, Republicans tried to disband the Departments of Education, Energy, and Commerce, arguing that they wasted tax dollars and implemented policies that should be terminated.

The Regulatory Commissions

Each **independent regulatory commission** has responsibility for some sector of the economy, making and enforcing rules designed to protect the public interest. The independent regulatory commissions also judge disputes over these rules.[11] Some also call them the alphabet soup of American government because most such agencies are known in Washington by their initials. Some examples follow:

- *FRB (the Federal Reserve Board)*, charged with governing banks and, even more important, regulating the supply of money and thus interest rates
- *NLRB (the National Labor Relations Board)*, created to regulate labor–management relations
- *FCC (the Federal Communications Commission)*, charged with licensing radio and TV stations and regulating their programming in the public interest as well as with regulating interstate long-distance telephone rates, cable television, and the Internet
- *FTC (the Federal Trade Commission)*, responsible for regulating business practices and controlling monopolistic behavior and now involved in policing the accuracy of advertising
- *SEC (the Securities and Exchange Commission)*, created to police the stock market

Each of these independent regulatory commissions is governed by a small commission, usually with 5 to 10 members appointed by the president and confirmed by the Senate for fixed terms. The president cannot fire regulatory commission members as easily as he can cabinet officers and members of the White House staff. The

Supreme Court determined this rule after President Franklin Roosevelt fired a man named Humphrey from the FTC. Humphrey took the matter to court but died shortly afterward. The angry executors of his estate sued for back pay, and the Court held that presidents could not fire members of regulatory agencies without just cause (*Humphrey's Executor v. United States*, 1935). "Just cause" has never been defined clearly, and no member of a regulatory commission has been fired since.

Interest groups consider the rule making by independent regulatory commissions (and, of course, their membership) very important. The FCC can deny a multi-million-dollar TV station a license renewal—a power that certainly sparks the interest of the National Association of Broadcasters. The FTC regulates business practices—a power that prompts both business and consumers to pay careful attention to its activities and membership.

Interest groups are so concerned with these regulatory bodies that some critics point to the "capture" of the regulators by the regulatees.[12] It is common for members of commissions to be recruited from the ranks of the regulated. Sometimes, too, members of commissions or staffs of these agencies move on to jobs in the very industries they were regulating. Some lawyers among them use contacts and information gleaned at the agency when they represent clients before their former employers at the agency. A later section of this chapter discusses the bureaucracy's relationship with interest groups.

The Environmental Protection Agency (EPA) is an important independent executive agency, overseeing the administration of all environmental legislation. Here, EPA workers clean up hazardous waste.

The Government Corporations

The federal government also has a handful of **government corporations**. These are not exactly like private corporations in which you can buy stock and collect dividends, but they *are* like private corporations—and different from other parts of the government—in two ways. First, they provide a service that *could be* handled by the private sector. Second, they typically charge for their services, though often at rates cheaper than those the consumer would pay to a private-sector producer.

government corporation
A government organization that, like business corporations, provides a service that could be provided by the private sector and typically charges for its services. The U.S. Postal Service is an example. Compare **independent regulatory commission** and **independent executive agency**.

The granddaddy of the government corporations is the Tennessee Valley Authority (TVA). Established in 1933 as part of the New Deal, it has controlled floods, improved navigation, protected the soil against erosion, and provided inexpensive electricity to millions of Americans in Tennessee, Kentucky, Alabama, and neighboring states. Through Comsat—a modern-day government corporation that sells time-sharing on NASA satellites—you can rent time on a space satellite for radio communications. The post office, one of the original cabinet departments (first headed by Benjamin Franklin), has become the government's largest corporation: the U.S. Postal Service.

Occasionally the government has taken over a "sick industry" and turned it into a government corporation. Amtrak, the railroad passenger service, is one example. Congress grumbles about Amtrak's multi-billion-dollar subsidy (although some critics point out that billions of dollars in federal highway funds also constitute something of a subsidy for the auto industry), but members of Congress have only reluctantly agreed to let Amtrak shed its most unprofitable runs.

The Independent Executive Agencies

independent executive agency
The government not accounted for by cabinet departments, **independent regulatory commissions**, and **government corporations**. Its administrators are typically appointed by the president and serve at the president's pleasure. NASA is an example.

The **independent executive agencies** are essentially all the rest of the government—not cabinet departments, not independent regulatory commissions, and not government corporations. Their administrators typically are appointed by the president and serve at his will. The 45 to 50 of such bureaus are listed in the current issue of the *United States Government Manual.* A few of the biggest independent executive agencies (in size of budget) are the following:

- *General Services Administration* (*GSA*), the government's landlord, which handles buildings, supplies, and purchasing
- *National Science Foundation* (*NSF*), the agency supporting scientific research
- *National Aeronautics and Space Administration* (*NASA*), the agency that takes Americans to the moon and points beyond

HOW YOU CAN MAKE A DIFFERENCE

A Career in Foreign Service

In this current age of globalization, a career in foreign service can prove a rewarding and exciting experience for those Americans who wish to fulfill their civic duties. Though the word "bureaucracy" generally has a negative connotation, it is through bureaucratic organizations—like those of foreign service—that a great deal of policy is crafted and implemented. Most college graduates interested in foreign service apply to either the State Department or the Central Intelligence Agency (CIA). Both departments train their members to be "area specialists"—experts on a given region's political culture, geography, and politics. Due to its global nature, reach, and continually changing environment, the foreign service is always in need of qualified applicants from diverse backgrounds. With the chance to work on one of 250 diplomatic missions worldwide, working within a bureaucracy like the foreign service is anything but mundane!

Making a Difference

Ralph McGehee worked for the CIA from 1952 to 1977. After completing his initial training, McGehee spent fourteen years working in various field stations around the world. However, after leaving the organization, he became an outspoken critic of some of its practices. In 1983 he released *Deadly Deceit: My 25 Years in the CIA*—a book that outlines his experiences with the CIA abroad and at home. McGehee also developed CIA-BASE, a computer database of CIA figures and programs compiled from available public information. It provides a vital, easy-to-use resource for policymakers, academicians, journalists, and students.

What you can do:

- Finish college. Most foreign service organizations require that you have a college degree, though it need not be in international relations or political science.
- Download and complete an application from either the State Department (*http://careers.state.gov/general/index.html*) or the CIA (*http://www.cia.gov/employment/index.html*).
- If needed, study and prepare to take a foreign service qualifying exam. Generally, foreign service qualifying exams are required for jobs with the State Department.

Bureaucracies as Implementors

Bureaucracies are essentially *implementors* of policy. They take congressional, presidential, and sometimes even judicial pronouncements and develop procedures and rules for implementing policy goals. They also manage the routines of government, from delivering mail to collecting taxes to training troops.

What Implementation Means

Public policies are rarely self-executing. One of the few policies that administers itself is the president's decision to "recognize" a foreign government. It is entirely the chief executive's prerogative to do so, and, once it is done, diplomatic relations with the country are thereby established.

Most policies, however, are not self-executing. Congress typically announces the goals of a policy in broad terms, sets up an administrative apparatus, and leaves the bureaucracy the task of working out the details of the program. In other words, the bureaucracy is left to implement the program. **Policy implementation** is the stage of policymaking between the establishment of a policy (such as the passage of a legislative act, the issuing of an executive order, the handing down of a judicial decision, or the promulgation of a regulatory rule) and the results of the policy for individuals.[13] To paraphrase loosely a famous line about war from German General Karl von Clausewitz, "Implementation is the continuation of policymaking by other means."[14] At a minimum, implementation includes three elements:

policy implementation
The stage of policymaking between the establishment of a policy and the consequences of the policy for the people whom it affects. Implementation involves translating the goals and objectives of a policy into an operating, ongoing program.

1. Creation of a new agency or assignment of a new responsibility to an old agency
2. Translation of policy goals into operational rules and development of guidelines for the program
3. Coordination of resources and personnel to achieve the intended goals[15]

Why the Best-Laid Plans Sometimes Flunk the Implementation Test

The Scottish poet Robert Burns once wrote, "The best laid schemes o' mice and men / Gang aft a-gley [often go awry]." So, too, with the best intended public policies. Policies that people expect to work often fail. In 1996, Congress overwhelmingly passed a bill to guarantee health insurance to millions of Americans when they change or lose their jobs or lose coverage. Yet the law has been ineffective because insurance companies often charge these individuals premiums far higher than standard rates.[16] High expectations followed by dashed hopes are the frequent fate of well-intended public policies.

Program Design. Implementation can break down for several reasons. One is faulty program design. "It is impossible," said Eugene Bardach, "to implement well a policy or program that is defective in its basic theoretical conception." Consider, he suggested, the following hypothetical example:

> *If Congress were to establish an agency charged with squaring the circle with compass and straight edge—a task mathematicians have long ago shown is impossible—we could*

envision an agency coming into being, hiring a vast number of consultants, commissioning studies, reporting that progress was being made, while at the same time urging in their appropriations request for the coming year that the Congress augment the agency's budget.[17]

And the circle would remain round.[18]

Bureaucratic Reform

Lack of Clarity. Congress is fond of stating a broad policy goal in legislation and then leaving implementation up to the bureaucracies. Members of Congress can thus escape messy details and place blame for the implementation decisions elsewhere (see "Young People and Politics: Drug Offenses and Financial Aid").

Such was the case with the controversial Title IX of the Education Act of 1972,[19] which said, "No person in the United States shall, on the basis of sex, be excluded from participation in, be denied the benefits of, or be subjected to discrimination

YOUNG PEOPLE AND POLITICS

Drug Offenses and Financial Aid

In 1998, Congress wrote a provision into the law governing financial aid for college students that prohibits students who have been convicted of drug offenses from receiving grants and loans from the federal government. It does not matter whether the conviction was relatively minor or whether the conviction happened years ago—if a student has ever been convicted of a drug offense as an adult, he or she can be denied financial aid from one year to life, depending on the number of offenses and severity of conviction. Not surprisingly, the law has been a matter of contention.

The law itself might seem a bit severe, but there is more. Someone convicted of armed robbery, rape, or even murder would not be in the same predicament. Once out of prison, such a person is entitled to government grants and loans with no questions asked. But under the law, tens of thousands of would-be college students have been denied financial aid because of drug offenses, even though the crimes may have been committed long ago and the sentences already served.

Members of Congress have accused the Clinton and Bush administrations of distorting the law's intent. They argue that the Department of Education, which administers financial aid programs, should not be strict in its interpretation of the law. The department responds that Congress wrote a vague law—one that refers to "a student who has been convicted"—and that the department is faithfully implementing the letter of the law. In effect, the department is arguing that it has no discretion in the matter and cannot act on its own to make financial aid policy more just.

It might seem easy for Congress to simply change the law. No such luck. A bill to repeal the law is a long way from having enough support to come to a floor vote, much less to pass. The George W. Bush administration suggested ending the prohibition on aid for those who violated drug laws before entering college. However, it wants to continue the aid ban for those who commit such crimes while enrolled in college. Its goal, the administration said, is to discourage students from using drugs. The problem, as others see it, is that such a rule would still impose stiffer penalties for drug use than for any other crime. It would also have the effect of barring some first-time, minor offenders from getting financial aid while restoring it for more serious drug lawbreakers.

Anticipating implementation problems is difficult. Putting together coalitions within Congress is also difficult. One consequence of these difficulties is that laws are often vague—and often have unintended consequences as well.

Questions for Discussion

- How much discretion should a bureaucratic unit have to correct injustices in laws?
- Why do you think it is so difficult for Congress to anticipate problems implementing laws?

under any education program or activity receiving federal financial assistance." Because almost every college and university receives some federal financial assistance, almost all were thereby forbidden to discriminate on the basis of gender. Interest groups supporting women's athletics convinced Congress to include a provision about college athletics as well. Thus, Section 844 reads,

> *The Secretary of [Health, Education, and Welfare then, today Education] shall prepare and publish . . . proposed regulations implementing the provisions of Title IX . . . relating to prohibition of sex discrimination in Federally assisted education programs which shall include with respect to intercollegiate athletic activities reasonable provisions considering the nature of the particular sports.*

Bureaucracies are often asked to implement unclear laws. When Congress decided to prohibit gender discrimination in college athletics, for example, it left to bureaucrats the task of creating guidelines that would end discrimination while addressing the diverse needs of different sports. It took years—and several lawsuits—to establish the law's meaning.

Just what does this section mean? Proponents of women's athletics thought it meant that discrimination against women's sports was also prohibited. Some, with good reason, looked forward to seeing women's sports on an equal footing with men's. One member of the House-Senate Conference Committee proposed language specifically exempting "revenue-producing athletics" (meaning men's football and basketball) from the prohibition. The committee rejected this suggestion, but to colleges and universities with big-time athletic programs and to some alumni, the vague Section 844 called for equality in golf and swimming, not men's football and basketball programs, which could continue to have the lion's share of athletic budgets.

HEW's interpretation of the 100 or so words of Section 844 of Title IX, announced in December 1978, numbered 30 pages. The interpretation recognized that football was "unique" among college sports. If football was unique, then the interpretation implied (but did not directly say) that male-dominated football programs could continue to outspend women's athletic programs.

Supporters of equal budgets for male and female athletics were outraged. A 100-word section in a congressional statute, which prompted a 30-page interpretation by the bureaucracy, in turn prompted scores of court cases. The courts have had to rule on such matters as whether Title IX requires that exactly equivalent dollar amounts be spent on women's and men's athletics. Litigation continues to this day.

The complex case of implementing Title IX for intercollegiate athletics contains an important lesson: Policy problems that Congress cannot resolve are not likely to be easily resolved by bureaucracies.

Bureaucrats receive not only unclear orders but also contradictory ones. James Q. Wilson points out that the Immigration and Naturalization Service (INS) was supposed to keep out illegal immigrants but let in necessary agricultural workers, to carefully screen foreigners seeking to enter the country but facilitate the entry of foreign tourists, and to find and expel illegal aliens but not break up families, impose hardships, violate civil rights, or deprive employers of low-paid workers. "No organization can accomplish all of these goals well, especially when advocates of each have the power to mount newspaper and congressional investigations of the agency's 'failures.'"[20] Similarly, Congress has ordered the National Park Service to preserve the environmental quality of national parks; it has also obliged it to keep the parks accessible to tourists at the same time. The Forest Service is supposed to help timber companies exploit the lumber potential in the national forests *and* preserve the natural environment.

Lack of Resources. As noted earlier, bureaucracies are often perceived as bloated. The important issue, however, is not the size of the bureaucracy in the abstract but whether it is the appropriate size to do the job it has been assigned to do. As big as a bureaucracy may seem in the aggregate, it frequently lacks the staff—along with the necessary training, funding, supplies, and equipment—to carry out the tasks it has been assigned. Recently, for example, the news has been filled with complaints such as the following:

- U.S. troops in Iraq had insufficient numbers of body armor and armored Humvees and trucks to protect them against roadside bombs.
- The Food and Drug Administration (FDA) lacks the personnel to evaluate the safety of generic drugs that would lower the soaring cost of health care in the United States.
- Because of lack of funding, the popular Head Start program serves only about half the children who are theoretically eligible to participate.
- The Immigration and Naturalization Service (INS) lacked the personnel to track aliens who overstayed their visas or who engaged in suspicious activities such as taking flight training that did not include takeoffs and landings. The INS also lacked the resources even to identify, much less deport, more than 10 percent of the 200,000 convicted criminal aliens in the United States. It even lacked the personnel to open letters containing checks for application fees.
- In their inspections of facilities handling and storing hazardous wastes, inadequately trained inspectors for the Environmental Protection Agency (EPA) overlooked more than half the serious violations. The computer system the EPA uses to track and control water pollution is obsolete, full of faulty data, and does not take into account thousands of significant pollution sources.

Hurricane Katrina and New Orleans

- The FBI lacks computers at its headquarters that allow it to search its own databases for multiple terms such as "aviation" and "schools." It also has a serious shortage of translators for intercepted communications.
- National Guard Units have only a third of the equipment they need to respond to domestic disasters and terrorist attacks.
- The Federal Aviation Administration (FAA) lacks the proper personnel and equipment to direct the nation's air traffic safely.
- The lack of financing to maintain national parks may lead to permanent deterioration of such treasured American vacation spots as Yosemite and Yellowstone.
- The IRS lacks the appropriate computer systems to integrate the dozens of databases that contain the information necessary to collect the more than $2 trillion in taxes that finance the federal government.
- There is a shortage of epidemiologists who are trained to recognize and investigate the outbreak of infectious disease.

Agencies may also lack the *authority* necessary to meet their responsibilities. For example, many observers believe that the FDA lacks adequate powers to protect the public from dangerous drugs such as the sleeping pill Halcion and the sedative Versed. The FDA does no testing of its own and must rely entirely on the test results submitted by manufacturers. Yet it lacks the subpoena power to obtain documents when it suspects that drug companies are withholding data about adverse drug reactions or misrepresenting test results. It often lacks access to potentially damaging company documents that have been involved in private product-liability cases. Similarly, the Department of Agriculture lacks authority to close meat processing plants—even ones with serious violations of food safety standards.

Why It Matters

Bureaucratic Resources
A case can be made that some bureaucracies are too small. By substantially increasing the resources available to those who implement policies, it is possible that the quality of government services would improve.

Administrative Routine. For most bureaucrats, administration is a routine matter most of the time. They follow **standard operating procedures**, better known as SOPs, to help them make numerous everyday decisions. Standard rules save time. If a Social Security caseworker had to invent a new rule for every potential client and then have it cleared at higher levels, few clients would be served. Thus, agencies write detailed manuals to cover as many particular situations as officials can anticipate. The regulations elaborating the Internal Revenue Code compose an IRS agent's bible. Similarly, a customs agent has binders filled with rules and regulations about what can and cannot be brought into the United States duty free.

standard operating procedures
Better known as SOPs, these procedures are used by bureaucrats to bring uniformity to complex organizations. Uniformity improves fairness and makes personnel interchangeable.

SOPs also bring uniformity to complex organizations. Justice is better served when officials apply rules uniformly, as in the implementation of welfare policies that distribute benefits to the needy or in the levying of fines for underpayment of taxes. Uniformity also makes personnel interchangeable. The army, for example, can transfer soldiers to any spot in the world, and they can find out how to do their job by referring to the appropriate manual.

Routines are essential to bureaucracy. Yet they sometimes become frustrating to citizens, who term them "red tape" when they do not seem appropriate to a situation. SOPs then become obstacles to action. An October 1983 terrorist attack on their barracks outside Beirut, Lebanon, killed 241 Marines while they slept. A presidential commission appointed to examine the causes of the tragedy concluded that, among other factors contributing to the disaster, the Marines in the peacekeeping force were "not trained, organized, staffed or supported to deal effectively with the terrorist threat."[21] In other words, they had not altered their SOPs regarding security, which is basic to any military unit, to meet the unique challenges of a terrorist attack.

The FAA's protocols for hijackings assumed that the pilot of a hijacked aircraft would notify an air traffic controller that there had been a hijacking, that the FAA could identify the plane, that there would be time for the FAA and NORAD to address the issue, and that the hijacking would not be a suicide mission. As the 9/11 Commission put it, these SOPs were "unsuited in every respect" for the 9/11 terrorist hijackings.[22]

Sometimes an agency simply fails to establish routines that are necessary to complete its tasks. For example, in late 1997, the General Accounting Agency found that the FAA failed to determine whether the violations its inspectors uncovered at aircraft repair stations were ever corrected. The FAA did not keep the proper paperwork for adequate follow-up activities.

Administrators' Dispositions. Paradoxically, bureaucrats operate not only within the confines of routines but often with considerable discretion to behave independently. **Administrative discretion** is the authority of administrative actors to select among various responses to a given problem.[23] Discretion is greatest when rules do not fit a particular case, and this is often the case—even in agencies with elaborate rules and regulations.

administrative discretion
The authority of administrative actors to select among various responses to a given problem. Discretion is greatest when routines, or standard operating procedures, do not fit a case.

Although the income tax code is massive and detailed, the IRS wields vast discretion because of the complexity of the U.S. economy and the multitude of tax situations it produces. Here are a few examples:[24]

- Congress and the IRS code say that medical expenses above a certain percentage of income are deductible, but how about the expenses of a vasectomy? (The IRS said yes.)
- A girl who had been ordered to take strenuous exercise under the supervision of a doctor was enrolled by her father in $8,436 worth of ballet lessons. Was it deductible? (The IRS said no.)
- Congress and the IRS code say that business expenses are deductible, but can an airline flight attendant deduct the cost of uniforms? (The IRS said yes.)
- Are taxi expenses incurred in visiting your stockbroker a deductible expense? (The IRS said yes.)

Some administrators exercise more discretion than others. Michael Lipsky coined the phrase **street-level bureaucrats** to refer to those bureaucrats who are in constant contact with the public (often a hostile one) and have considerable discretion; they include police officers, welfare workers, and lower-court judges.[25] No amount of rules, not even the thousands of pages of IRS rules, will eliminate the need for bureaucratic discretion on some policies. The highway patrol officer who stops you can choose to issue you a warning or a ticket.

street-level bureaucrats
A phrase coined by Michael Lipsky, referring to those bureaucrats who are in constant contact with the public and have considerable **administrative discretion**.

Bureaucrats typically apply thousands of pages of rules in the performance of routine tasks, but many bureaucrats—especially street-level bureaucrats—must use administrative discretion as well. These border patrol officers, shown arresting illegal immigrants on the U.S.–Mexican border, must decide whom they will search carefully and whom they will let pass with a quick check.

Because bureaucrats will inevitably exercise discretion, it is important to understand how they use it. Ultimately, how they use discretion depends on their dispositions about the policies and rules they administer. Although bureaucrats may be indifferent to the implementation of many policies, other policies may conflict with their views or their personal or organizational interests. When people are asked to execute orders with which they do not agree, slippage is likely to occur between policy decisions and performance. A great deal of mischief may occur as well.

On one occasion, President Nixon ordered Secretary of Defense Melvin Laird to bomb a Palestine Liberation Organization hideaway, a move Laird opposed. According to the secretary, "We had bad weather for forty-eight hours. The Secretary of Defense can always find a reason not to do something."[26] The president's order was stalled for days and eventually rescinded.

Controlling the exercise of discretion is a difficult task. It is not easy to fire bureaucrats in the civil service, and removing appointed officials may be politically embarrassing to the president, especially if those officials have strong support in Congress and among interest groups. In the private sector, leaders of organizations provide incentives such as pay raises to encourage employees to perform their tasks in a certain way. In the public sector, however, special bonuses are rare, and pay raises tend to be small and across the board. Moreover, there is not necessarily room at the top for qualified bureaucrats. Unlike a typical private business, a government agency cannot expand just because it is performing a service effectively and efficiently.

In the absence of positive and negative incentives, the government relies heavily on rules to limit the discretion of implementors. As former Vice President Al Gore put it in a report issued by the National Performance Review,

> *Because we don't want politicians' families, friends, and supporters placed in "no-show" jobs, we have more than 100,000 pages of personnel rules and regulations defining in exquisite detail how to hire, promote, or fire federal employees. Because we don't want employees or private companies profiteering from federal contracts, we create procurement processes that require endless signatures and long months to buy almost anything. Because we don't want agencies using tax dollars for any unapproved purpose, we dictate precisely how much they can spend on everything from telephones to travel.*[27]

Often these rules end up creating new obstacles to effective and efficient governing, however. As U.S. forces were streaming toward the Persian Gulf in the fall of 1990 to liberate Kuwait from Iraq, the air force placed an emergency order for 6,000 Motorola commercial radio receivers. But Motorola refused to do business with the air force because of a government requirement that the company set up separate accounting and cost-control systems to fill the order. The only way the U.S. Air Force could acquire the much-needed receivers was for Japan to buy them and donate them to the United States! For an example of the impact of rules affecting implementation of policy in the war in Iraq, see "Issues of the Times: The Impact of Procurement Rules in Wartime."

Fragmentation. Sometimes responsibility for a policy is dispersed among several units within the bureaucracy. The federal government has had as many as 96 agencies involved with the issue of nuclear proliferation. Similarly, in the field of welfare, 10 different departments and agencies administer more than 100 federal human services programs. The Department of Health and Human Services has responsibility for basic welfare grants to the states to aid families, the Department of Housing and Urban Development provides housing assistance for the poor, the Department of Agriculture runs the food stamp program, and the Department of Labor administers training programs and provides assistance in obtaining employment.

The resources and authority necessary for the president to attack a problem comprehensively are often distributed among many bureaucratic units. President George W. Bush's creation of the Office of Homeland Security in 2001 dramatically illustrates the challenge of diffusion of responsibility. The president ordered the office to coordinate the implementation of a comprehensive national strategy to protect the United States from terrorist threats or attacks. This involved directing the counterterrorism efforts of 46 federal agencies, encompassing much of the federal government. Of course, each of these agencies also reported to other officials for other purposes.

One piece of the puzzle of homeland security is securing our borders. Table 13.4 lists the agencies with responsibilities for border control in 2002. As you can see, at least 33 departments and agencies had responsibility for protecting America's borders, focusing on threats ranging from illegal immigrants and chemical toxins to missiles and electronic sabotage. It is difficult to coordinate so many different agencies, especially when they lack a history of trust and cooperation. Moreover, there are often physical obstacles to cooperation, such as the largely incompatible computer systems of the INS and the Coast Guard. Once the borders have been breached and an attack has occurred, many other offices get involved in homeland security, including hundreds of state and local agencies.

Table 13.4 Departments and Agencies with Responsibility for Border Security in 2002

Department of Agriculture
- Animal and Plant Health Inspection Service

Central Intelligence Agency

Department of Commerce
- Critical Infrastructure Assurance Office
- National Oceanic and Atmospheric Administration

Department of Defense
- Defense Intelligence Agency
- Inspector General
- National Guard
- National Reconnaissance Office
- National Security Agency
- North American Aerospace Defense Command

Department of Energy
- Office of Science and Technology Policy

Environmental Protection Agency
- Office of International Activities

Department of Justice
- Bureau of Alcohol, Tobacco, and Firearms
- Drug Enforcement Administration
- Federal Bureau of Investigation
- Immigration and Naturalization Service
- Marshals Service
- Office of Special Investigations

Department of State
- Bureau of Consular Affairs
- Bureau of Intelligence and Research
- Bureau of Population, Refugees, and Migration
- Bureau for International Narcotics and Law Enforcement Agencies
- Passport Office

Postal Service

Department of Treasury
- Customs Service
- Financial Crimes Enforcement Network
- Internal Revenue Service
- Office of the Inspector General
- Secret Service

Department of Transportation
- Coast Guard
- Federal Aviation Administration
- Federal Motor Carrier Administration
- Maritime Administration

Fragmentation also allows some agencies to work at cross-purposes. For years, one agency supported tobacco farmers while another discouraged smoking. One agency encouraged the redevelopment of inner cities while another helped build highways making it easier for people to live in the suburbs. One agency helped farmers grow crops more efficiently while another paid them to produce less. As long as Congress refuses to make clear decisions about priorities, bureaucrats will implement contradictory policies.

If fragmentation is a problem, why not reorganize the government? The answer lies in hyperpluralism and the decentralization of power. Congressional committees recognize that they would lose jurisdiction over agencies if these agencies were merged with others. Interest groups (such as the nuclear power industry) do not want to give up the close relationships they have developed with "their" agencies. Agencies themselves do not want to be submerged within a broader bureaucratic unit. All these forces fight reorganization, and they usually win.[28] President Clinton's proposal to merge the Drug Enforcement Administration and the Customs Service met with immediate opposition from the agencies and their congressional allies. Pursuing the merger became too costly for the president, who had to focus on higher-priority issues.

The Department of Homeland Security

Nevertheless, under the right conditions, reorganization is possible. In 2001, congressional Democrats proposed a new Department of Homeland Security. In the summer of 2002, President George W. Bush concluded that the only way to overcome the fragmentation of agencies involved in providing homeland security was to create a new department, one that combined many of the agencies listed in Table 13.4. Congress created the new department at the end of 2002, the largest reorganization of the federal government in half a century.

Bureaucracies as Regulators

Government **regulation** is the use of governmental authority to control or change some practice in the private sector. Regulations by government pervade Americans' everyday lives and the dealings of businesses, universities, hospitals, and other institutions. Federal regulations now fill more than 200 volumes. Regulation is the most controversial role of the bureaucracies, yet Congress gives bureaucrats broad mandates to regulate activities as diverse as interest rates, the location of nuclear power plants, and food additives.

regulation
The use of governmental authority to control or change some practice in the private sector. Regulations pervade the daily lives of people and institutions.

Regulation in the Economy and in Everyday Life

The notion that the American economy is largely a "free enterprise" system, unfettered by government intervention, is about as up to date as a Model T Ford. You can begin to understand the sweeping scope of governmental regulation by examining how the automobile industry is regulated:

- The Securities and Exchange Commission regulates buying and selling stock in an automobile corporation.
- Relations between the workers and managers of the company come under the scrutiny of the National Labor Relations Board.

- The Department of Labor and the Equal Employment Opportunity Commission mandate affirmative action in hiring workers in automobile production plants because automakers are major government contractors.
- The EPA, the National Highway Traffic Safety Administration, and the Department of Transportation require pollution-control, energy-saving, and safety devices.
- Unfair advertising and deceptive consumer practices in marketing cars come under the watchful eye of the FTC.

A Full Day of Regulation. Everyday life itself is the subject of bureaucratic regulation. Almost all bureaucratic agencies—not merely the ones called independent regulatory commissions—are in the regulatory business. Consider a typical factory worker (we'll name him John Smith) who works in the city of Chicago and lives with his wife, Joan Smith, and their three young children in suburban Mount Prospect, Illinois. Federal regulations affect John's life both at work and at home. At 5:30 A.M. he is awakened by his clock radio, which is set to a country music station licensed to operate by the FCC. For breakfast he has cereal, which has passed inspection by the FDA, as has the lunch Joan packs for him. The processed meat in his sandwich is packed under the supervision of the Food Safety and Quality Service of the U.S. Department of Agriculture.

John takes the train to work and buys a quick cup of coffee before the journey. The FDA has warned that the caffeine in his coffee has caused birth defects in laboratory animals, and there is discussion in Washington about regulating it. After paying his fare (regulated by the state government), he hops aboard and shortly arrives at work, a small firm that makes refrigeration equipment for the food industry.

Most government regulation is clearly in the public interest. For example, the U.S. Department of Agriculture is charged with regulating the quality of meat products, a task it was given after novelist Upton Sinclair exposed the meat-packaging industry's unsanitary conditions at the turn of the century.

At home, Joan Smith is preparing breakfast for the children. The price of the milk she serves is affected by the dairy price supports regulated by the Agricultural Stabilization and Conservation Service. As the children play, she takes note of the toys they use, wanting to avoid any that could be dangerous. A Washington agency, the Consumer Product Safety Commission, also evaluates children's toys, regulating their manufacture and sale. The Consumer Product Safety Commission also regulates the lawn mower, the appliances, the microwave oven, and numerous other items around the Smith house.

Setting out for the grocery store and the bank, Joan encounters even more government regulations. The car has seat belts mandated by the National Highway Traffic Safety Administration, and the Department of Transportation certifies its gas mileage. The car's pollution-control devices are now in need of service because they do not meet the requirements of the EPA. The bank where Joan deposits money and writes a check is among the most heavily regulated institutions she encounters in her daily life. Her passbook savings rate is regulated by the Depository Institutions Deregulation Committee, and her account is insured by the Federal Deposit Insurance Commission.

Meanwhile, John Smith is at work assembling food-processing machinery. He and the other workers are members of the International Association of Machinists. Their negotiations with the firm are held under rules laid down by the National Labor Relations Board. Not long ago, the firm was visited by inspectors from the Occupational Safety and Health Administration (OSHA), a federal agency charged with ensuring worker safety. OSHA inspectors noted several violations and forwarded a letter recommending safety changes to the head of the firm.

Back at home, John has a beer before dinner. It was made in a brewery carefully supervised by the Bureau of Alcohol, Tobacco, and Firearms, and federal and state taxes were collected when it was sold. After dinner (almost all the food served has been transported by the regulated trucking industry), the children are sent to bed. An hour or so of television, broadcast on regulated airwaves, is followed by bedtime. A switch will turn off the electric lights, whose rates are regulated by the Illinois Commerce Commission and the Federal Energy Regulatory Commission.[29]

Regulation: How It Grew, How It Works

From the beginnings of the American republic until 1887, the federal government made almost no regulatory policies; the little regulation produced was handled by state and local authorities. Opponents disputed even the minimal regulatory powers of state and local governments. In 1877, the Supreme Court upheld the right of government to regulate the business operations of a firm. The case, *Munn v. Illinois*, involved the right of the state of Illinois to regulate the charges and services of a Chicago warehouse. During this time, farmers were seething about alleged overcharging by railroads, grain elevator companies, and other business firms. In 1887—a decade after *Munn*—Congress created the first regulatory agency, the Interstate Commerce Commission (ICC), and charged it with regulating the railroads, their prices, and their services to farmers; the ICC thus set the precedent for regulatory policymaking.

The Evolution of the Federal Bureaucracy

As regulators, bureaucratic agencies typically operate with a large grant of power from Congress, which may detail goals to be achieved but may also permit the agencies to sketch out the regulatory means. In 1935, for example, Congress created the National Labor Relations Board (NLRB) to control "unfair labor practices," but the NLRB had to play a major role in defining "fair" and "unfair." Most agencies charged with regulation must first develop a set of rules, often called *guidelines*. The appropriate agency may specify how much food coloring it will permit in a hot dog, how many contaminants it will allow an industry to dump into a stream, how much radiation from a nuclear reactor is too much, and so forth. Guidelines are developed in consultation with—and sometimes with the agreement of—the people or industries being regulated.

Next, the agency must apply and enforce its rules and guidelines, either in court or through its own administrative procedures. Sometimes it waits for complaints to come to it, as the Equal Employment Opportunity Commission does; sometimes it sends inspectors into the field, as OSHA does; and sometimes it requires application for a permit or license to demonstrate performance consistent with congressional goals and agency rules, as the FCC does. Often government agencies take violators to court, hoping to secure a judgment and fine against an offender (see "You Are the Policymaker: How Should We Regulate?"). Whatever strategy Congress permits a regulating agency to use, all regulation contains these elements: (1) *a grant of power and set of directions from Congress*, (2) *a set of rules and guidelines* by the regulatory agency itself, and (3) *some means of enforcing compliance* with congressional goals and agency regulations.

Government regulation of the American economy and society has, of course, grown in recent decades. The budgets of regulatory agencies, their level of employment, and the number of rules they issue are all increasing—and did so even during the conservative Reagan administration. As we have seen, few niches in American society are *not* affected by regulation. Not surprisingly, this situation has led to charges that government is overdoing it.

Toward Deregulation

deregulation
The lifting of restrictions on business, industry, and other professional activities for which government rules had been established and that bureaucracies had been created to administer.

Deregulation—the lifting of government restrictions on business, industry, and professional activities—is currently a fashionable term.[30] The idea behind deregulation is that the number and complexity of regulatory policies have made regulation too complicated and burdensome. To critics, the problem with regulation is that it raises prices, distorts market forces, and—worst of all—does not work. They claim that the regulatory system does the following:

- *Raises prices.* If the producer is faced with expensive regulations, the cost will inevitably be passed on to the consumer in the form of higher prices.
- *Hurts America's competitive position abroad.* Other nations may have fewer regulations on pollution, worker safety, and other business practices than the United States. Thus, American products may cost more in the international marketplace, undermining sales in other countries.

YOU ARE THE POLICYMAKER

How Should We Regulate?

Almost every regulatory policy was created to achieve some desirable social goal. When more than 6,000 people are killed annually in industrial accidents, who would disagree with the goal of a safer workplace? Who would dissent from greater highway safety when more than 40,000 die each year in automobile accidents? Who would disagree with policies to promote equality in hiring when the history of opportunities for women and minorities is one of discrimination? Who would disagree with policies to reduce industrial pollution when pollution threatens health and lives? However, there may be more than one way to achieve these—and many other—desirable social goals.

Charles L. Schultze, former chair of President Carter's Council of Economic Advisers, is—like Murray L. Weidenbaum, who held the same position under President Reagan—a critic of the current state of federal regulation. Schultze reviewed the regulatory activities of the EPA and OSHA. Neither agency's policies, he concluded, worked very well. He described the existing system as **command-and-control policy**: The government tells business how to reach certain goals, checks that these commands are followed, and punishes offenders.

Schultze advocates an **incentive system**. He argues that instead of telling construction businesses how their ladders must be constructed, measuring the ladders, and charging a small fine for violators, it would be more efficient and effective to levy a high tax on firms with excessive worker injuries. Instead of trying to develop standards for 62,000 pollution sources, as the EPA now does, it would be easier and more effective to levy a high tax on those who cause pollution. The government could even provide incentives in the form of rewards for such socially valuable behavior as developing technology to reduce pollution. Incentives, Schultze argues, use marketlike strategies to regulate industry. They are, he claims, more effective and efficient than command-and-control regulation.

Not everyone is as keen on the use of incentives as Schultze. Defenders of the command-and-control system of regulation compare the present system to preventive medicine—it is designed to minimize pollution or workplace accidents before they become too severe. Defenders of the system argue, too, that penalties for excessive pollution or excessive workplace accidents would be imposed only after substantial damage had been done. They also add that if taxes on pollution or unsafe work environments were merely externalized (that is, passed along to the consumer as higher prices), they would not be much of a deterrent. Moreover, it would take a large bureaucracy to monitor carefully the level of pollution discharged, and it would require a complex calculation to determine the level of tax necessary to encourage businesses not to pollute.

The issue of the manner of regulation is a complex one. What would *you* do?

Sources: Charles L. Schultze, *The Public Use of the Private Interest* (Washington, DC: Brookings Institution, 1977); Steven Kelman, *What Price Incentives? Economists and the Environment* (Boston: Auburn House, 1981).

- *Does not always work well.* Tales of failed regulatory policies are numerous. Regulations may be difficult or cumbersome to enforce. Critics charge that regulations sometimes do not achieve the results that Congress intended and maintain that they simply create massive regulatory bureaucracies.

President Reagan's conservative political philosophy was opposed to much government regulation, but even before the Reagan administration, sentiment favoring deregulation was building in the Washington community. Even liberals

command-and-control policy
According to Charles Schultze, the typical system of regulation whereby government tells business how to reach certain goals, checks that these commands are followed, and punishes offenders.

incentive system
According to Charles Schutze, a more effective and efficient policy than **command-and-control**; in the incentive system, market-like strategies are used to manage public policy.

sometimes joined the antiregulation chorus; for example, Senator Edward Kennedy of Massachusetts pushed for airline deregulation. The airline industry also pressed for deregulation, and in 1978 the Civil Aeronautics Board (CAB) began to deregulate airline prices and airline routes. In 1984, the CAB formally disbanded; it even brought in a military bugler to play taps at its last meeting.

Not everyone, however, believes deregulation is in the nation's best interest.[31] For example, critics point to severe environmental damage resulting from lax enforcement of environmental protection standards during the Reagan administration. Similarly, many observers attribute at least a substantial portion of the blame for the enormously expensive bailout of the savings and loan industry to deregulation in the 1980s. Many people now argue for more regulation of savings and loan institutions. Californians found that deregulation led to severe power shortages in 2001.

In addition, many regulations have proved beneficial to Americans. As a result of government regulations, we breathe cleaner air,[32] we have lower levels of lead in our blood, miners are safer at work,[33] seacoasts have been preserved,[34] and children are more likely to survive infancy.[35]

Understanding Bureaucracies

As both implementors and regulators, bureaucracies are making public policy, not just administering someone else's decisions. The fact that bureaucrats, who are not elected, compose most of the government raises fundamental issues about who controls governing and what the bureaucracy's role should be.

Bureaucracy and Democracy

Bureaucracies constitute one of America's two unelected policymaking institutions (courts are the other). In democratic theory, popular control of government depends on elections, but we could not possibly elect the more than 4 million federal civilian and military employees or even the few thousand top men and women, though they spend more than $2.5 trillion of the American gross domestic product. Furthermore, the fact that voters do not elect civil servants does not mean that bureaucracies cannot respond to and represent the public's interests. When we compare the backgrounds of bureaucrats with those of members of Congress or presidents, we find that bureaucrats are more representative than elected officials. Much depends on whether bureaucracies are effectively controlled by the policymakers citizens do elect—the president and Congress.[36]

Presidents Try to Control the Bureaucracy. Chapter 12 looked at some of the frustrations presidents endure in trying to control the government they are elected to run. Presidents try hard—not always with success—to impose their policy preferences on agencies. Following are some presidential methods of exercising control over bureaucracies:

- **Appoint the right people to head the agency.** Normally, presidents control the appointments of agency heads and subheads. Putting their people in charge is one good way for presidents to influence agency policy,[37] yet even this has its problems. President Reagan's efforts to whittle the powers of the EPA led to his appointment of controversial Anne Gorsuch to head the agency. Gorsuch had previously supported policies contrary to the goals of the EPA. When Gorsuch attempted to implement her policies, legal squabbles with Congress and political controversy ensued, ultimately leading to her resignation. To patch up the damage Gorsuch had done to his reputation, Reagan named a moderate and seasoned administrator, William Ruckelshaus, to run the agency. Ironically, Ruckelshaus demanded—and got—more freedom from the White House than Gorsuch had sought. President Clinton had no use for FBI Director Louis Freeh, who would barely talk to the president. Yet Clinton felt he could not fire him because he feared unleashing denunciations by those claiming he was purging an enemy.
- **Issue orders.** Presidents can issue **executive orders** to agencies. These orders carry the force of law and are used to implement statutes, treaties, and provisions of the Constitution.[38] Sometimes presidential aides simply pass the word that the president wants something done. These messages usually suffice, although agency heads are reluctant to run afoul of Congress or the press on the basis of a broad presidential hint. The president's rhetoric in speeches outside the bureaucracy may also influence the priorities of bureaucrats.[39]

executive orders
Regulations originating from the executive branch. Executive orders are one method presidents can use to control the bureaucracy; more often, though, presidents pass along their wishes through their aides.

- **Alter an agency's budget.** The Office of Management and Budget (OMB) is the president's own final authority on any agency's budget. The OMB's threats to cut here or add there will usually get an agency's attention. Each agency, however, has its constituents within and outside of Congress, and Congress, not the president, does the appropriating.
- **Reorganize an agency.** Although President Reagan promised, proposed, and pressured to abolish the Department of Energy and the Department of Education, he never succeeded—largely because each department was in the hands of an entrenched bureaucracy backed by elements in Congress and strong constituent groups. Reorganizing an agency is hard to do if it is a large and strong agency, and reorganizing a small and weak agency is often not worth the trouble. A massive reorganization occurred in 2002 with the creation of the Department of Homeland Security. It is not clear, however, that it has improved the implementation of policy.

Congress Tries to Control the Bureaucracy. Congress exhibits a paradoxical relationship with the bureaucracies. On the one hand (as we have seen), members of Congress may find a big bureaucracy congenial.[40] Big government provides services to constituents, who may show their appreciation at the polls. Moreover, when Congress lacks the answers to policy problems, it hopes the bureaucracies will find them. Unable itself, for example, to resolve the touchy issue of equality in intercollegiate athletics, Congress passed the ball to the Department of Health, Education, and Welfare. Unable to decide how to make workplaces safer, Congress produced

OSHA. As you saw in Chapter 11, Congress is increasingly the problem-identifying branch of government, setting the bureaucratic agenda but letting the agencies decide how to implement the goals it sets.

On the other hand, Congress has found it hard to control the government it helped create. There are several measures Congress can take to oversee the bureaucracy:

- **Influence the appointment of agency heads.** Even when the law does not require senatorial approval of a presidential appointment, members of Congress are not shy in offering their opinions about who should and should not be running the agencies. When congressional approval is required, members are doubly influential. Committee hearings on proposed appointments are almost guaranteed to produce lively debates if some members find the nominee's probable orientations objectionable.
- **Alter an agency's budget.** With the congressional power of the purse comes a mighty weapon for controlling bureaucratic behavior. At the same time, Congress knows that many agencies perform services its constituents demand. Too much budget cutting may make an agency more responsive, at the price of losing an interest group's support for a reelection campaign.
- **Hold hearings.** Committees and subcommittees can hold periodic hearings as part of their oversight responsibilities. They may parade flagrant agency abuses of congressional intent in front of the press, but the very committee that created a program usually has responsibility for oversight of it and thus has some stake in showing the agency in a favorable light. We also learned in Chapter 11 that members of Congress have other disincentives for vigorous oversight, including a desire not to embarrass the chief executive.
- **Rewrite the legislation or make it more detailed.** Every statute is filled with instructions to its administrators. To limit bureaucratic discretion and make its instructions clearer, Congress can write new or more detailed legislation. Still, even voluminous detail (as in the case of the IRS) can never eliminate discretion.

Through these and other devices, Congress tries to keep bureaucracies under its control. Never entirely successful, Congress faces a constant battle to limit and channel the vast powers it delegated to the bureaucracy in the first place.

Sometimes these efforts are detrimental to bureaucratic performance. In 2006, at least 60 House and Senate committees and subcommittees claimed jurisdiction over a portion of homeland security issues. Officials in the Department of Homeland Security have to spend a large percentage of their time testifying to these committees, and the balkanized jurisdiction has undermined the ability of Congress to perform comprehensive oversight. Moreover, different committees may send different signals to the same agency. One may press for stricter enforcement of regulations, for example, while another seeks for more exemptions.

Iron Triangles and Issue Networks. Agencies' strong ties to interest groups on the one hand and to congressional committees and subcommittees on the other further complicate efforts to control the bureaucracy. Chapter 10 illustrated that bureaucracies often enjoy cozy relationships with interest groups and with committees or subcommittees of Congress. When agencies, groups, and committees all depend on one another and are in close, frequent contact, they form what are sometimes called **iron triangles** or *subgovernments*. These triads have advantages on all sides (see Figure 13.4).

iron triangles
A mutually dependent relationship between bureaucratic agencies, interest groups, and congressional committees or subcommittees. Iron triangles dominate some areas of domestic policymaking.

There are plenty of examples of subgovernments at work. A subcommittee on aging, senior citizens' interest groups, and the Social Security Administration are likely to agree on the need for more Social Security benefits. Richard Rettig has recounted how an alliance slowly jelled around the issue of fighting cancer. It rested

Figure 13.4 Iron Triangles: One Example

Iron triangles—composed of bureaucratic agencies, interest groups, and congressional committees or subcommittees—have dominated some areas of domestic policymaking by combining internal consensus with a virtual monopoly on information in their area. The tobacco triangle is one example; there are dozens more. Iron triangles are characterized by mutual dependency in which each element provides key services, information, or policy for the others. The arrows indicate some of these mutually helpful relationships. In recent years, a number of well-established iron triangles, including the tobacco triangle, have been broken up.

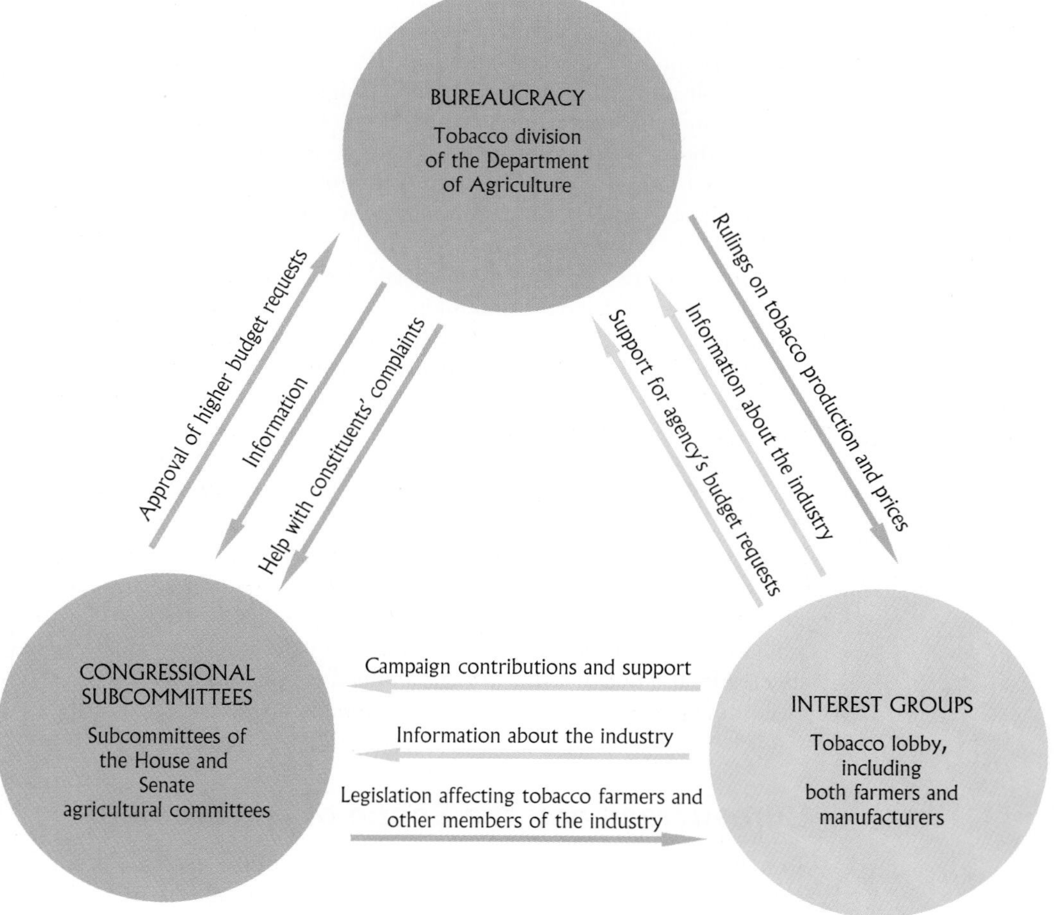

on three pillars: cancer researchers, agencies within the National Institutes of Health, and members of congressional health subcommittees.[41]

When these iron triangles shape policies for senior citizens, cancer, tobacco, or any other interest, officials make each policy independently of the others, sometimes even in contradiction to other policies. For example, for years the government supported tobacco farmers in one way or another while encouraging people not to smoke. Moreover, the iron triangles' decisions tend to bind larger institutions, such as Congress and the White House. Congress often defers to the decisions of committees and subcommittees, especially on less visible issues. The White House may be too busy wrestling with global concerns to fret over agricultural issues or cancer. Emboldened by this lack of involvement, subgovernments flourish and add a strong decentralizing and fragmenting element to the policymaking process.

The system of subgovernments is now overlaid with an amorphous system of *issue networks*. There is more widespread participation in bureaucratic policymaking, and many of the participants have technical policy expertise and are drawn to issues because of intellectual or emotional commitments rather than material interests. Those concerned with environmental protection, for example, have challenged formerly closed subgovernments on numerous fronts. This opening of the policymaking process complicates the calculations and decreases the predictability of those involved in the stable and relatively narrow relationships of subgovernments.[42]

Although subgovernments are often able to dominate policymaking for decades, they are not indestructible.[43] For example, the subgovernment pictured in Figure 13.4 long dominated smoking and tobacco policy, focusing on crop subsidies to tobacco farmers. But increasingly, these policies came under fire from health authorities, who were not involved in tobacco policymaking in earlier years. Similarly, Congress no longer considers pesticide policy, once dominated by chemical companies and agricultural interests, separately from environmental and health concerns. You can read about the evolution of another—and very powerful—iron triangle in "A Generation of Change: Nuclear Power Comes Full Circle."

You Are the President of MEDICORP

Nevertheless, there is often a cozy relationship between the components of the three sides of a subgovernment. For example, in 2003, Congress added a massive prescription drug benefit under Medicare. Representative Billy Tauzin shepherded the drug bill through the House as chair of the Energy and Commerce Committee. He then retired from Congress to head the Pharmaceutical Research and Manufacturers of America, a powerful industry lobby group, for an estimated $2 million a year. Thomas Scully, the Medicare administrator and lead negotiator for the administration, resigned his position within weeks after the passage of the bill to join a lobbying firm that represented several health care industry companies significantly affected by the new law. He also announced he would be working part time for an investment firm with interests in several more companies affected by the new law.

Bureaucracy and the Scope of Government

To many, the huge American bureaucracy is the prime example of the federal government growing out of control. As this chapter discussed earlier, some observers view the bureaucracy as acquisitive, constantly seeking to expand its size, budgets,

A GENERATION OF CHANGE

Nuclear Power Comes Full Circle

An especially vivid example of the death of an iron triangle is the case of nuclear power.* During the 1940s and 1950s, Americans were convinced that the technology that had ended World War II could also serve peaceful purposes. Nuclear scientists spoke enthusiastically about harnessing the atom to achieve all sorts of goals, eventually making electricity so inexpensive that it would be "too cheap to meter." Optimism in progress through science was the rule, and the federal government encouraged the development of nuclear power through a powerful iron triangle.

Congress established a special joint committee, the Joint Committee on Atomic Energy, and gave it complete control over questions of nuclear power. It also created a new executive agency, the Atomic Energy Commission (AEC), and together with the private companies that built the nuclear power plants and the electrical utilities that wanted to operate them, they formed a powerful subgovernment. America built more nuclear power plants than any other country in the world, and American technology was exported overseas to dozens of nations.

Nuclear power today—after the accidents at Three Mile Island and Chernobyl and the various cost overruns associated with the industry—bears almost no resemblance to that of the early 1960s when the iron triangle was at its peak. What happened? The experts lost control. When critics raised questions concerning the safety of the plants and when opponents were able to get local officials to question the policies publicly, the issue grew into a major political debate of the late 1960s, associated with the growth of environmentalism. Opposition to nuclear power destroyed two of the most powerful legs of the iron triangle. Congress disbanded the Joint Committee on Atomic Energy; a variety of congressional committees now claim some jurisdiction over nuclear power questions. Similarly, Congress replaced the AEC with two new agencies: the Nuclear Regulatory Commission and the Department of Energy.

The nuclear power industry has been devastated: No new nuclear power plants have been started in the United States since 1978, and almost all those under construction at that time have been abandoned at huge financial loss. Nuclear power provides only about 12 percent of our total energy production. In sum, the wave of environmental concern that developed in the late 1960s swept away one of the most powerful iron triangles in recent American history.

This is not the end of the story, however. The extraordinarily high price of gasoline and heating fuel in 2005 and 2006 and concerns over global warming have encouraged a reconsideration of nuclear power. The Gallup Poll has found that a majority of the public supports the use of nuclear energy to produce electricity. President George W. Bush declared on August 8, 2005, "Of all our nation's energy sources, only nuclear power plants can generate massive amounts of electricity without emitting an ounce of air pollution or greenhouse gases. And thanks to the advances in science and technology, nuclear plants are far safer than ever before. . . . We will start building nuclear power plants again by the end of this decade."

If the nuclear power industry should revive, there will be renewed calls for strict regulation—from both the bureaucracy and Congress. Whether an iron triangle reemerges from this change will depend on whether the public is attentive to the issue of nuclear power and whether it allows experts to define safety concerns as technical matters appropriate only for experts to decide.

* Frank R. Baumgartner and Bryan D. Jones, *Agendas and Instability in American Politics* (Chicago: University of Chicago Press, 1993).

and authority. Much of the political rhetoric against big government also adopts this line of argument, along with complaints about red tape, senseless regulations, and the like. It is easy to take potshots at a faceless bureaucracy that usually cannot respond.

One should keep in mind, however, that the federal bureaucracy has not grown over the past two generations, as Figure 13.1 illustrates. If one considers the fact that the population of the country has grown significantly over this period, then the federal bureaucracy has actually *shrunk* in size relative to the population it serves.

Comparing Bureaucracies

Originally, the federal bureaucracy had the modest role of promoting the economy, defending the country, managing foreign affairs, providing justice, and delivering the mail. Its role gradually expanded to include providing services to farmers, businesses, and workers. The discussion of federalism in Chapter 3 showed that as the economy and the society of the United States changed, a variety of interests placed additional demands on government. We now expect government—and the bureaucracy—to play an active role in dealing with social and economic problems. A good case can be made that the bureaucracy is actually too *small* for many of the tasks currently assigned to it—tasks ranging from the control of illicit drugs to protection of the environment.

In addition, it is important to remember that when the president and Congress have chosen to deregulate certain areas of the economy or cut taxes, the bureaucracy could not and did not prevent them from doing so. The question of what and how much the federal government should do—and thus how big the bureaucracy should be—is answered primarily at the polls and in Congress, the White House, and the courts—not by faceless bureaucrats.

Summary

Americans rarely congratulate someone for being a good bureaucrat. Unsung, taunted by cartoonists, and maligned by columnists, bureaucrats are the scapegoats of American politics. Americans may call presidents great and reelect members of Congress, but almost no one praises bureaucrats. Those who compose the bureaucracy, however, perform most of the vital services provided by the federal government.

Bureaucrats shape policy as administrators, as implementors, and as regulators. In this chapter we examined who bureaucrats are, how they got their positions, and what they do. Today, most bureaucrats working for the federal government get their jobs through the civil service system, although the president appoints a few at the very top.

In general, there are four types of bureaucracies: the cabinet departments, the independent regulatory commissions, the government corporations, and the independent executive agencies.

As policymakers, bureaucrats play two key roles. First, they are policy implementors, translating legislative policy goals into programs. Policy implementation does not always work well, and when it does not, bureaucrats usually take the blame, whether they deserve it or not. Much of administration involves a prescribed routine, but nearly all bureaucrats still have some discretion. Second, bureaucrats are regulators. Congress increasingly delegates large amounts of power to bureaucratic agencies and expects them to develop rules and regulations. Scarcely a nook or cranny of American society or the American economy escapes the long reach of bureaucratic regulation.

Although bureaucrats are not elected, bureaucracies are not necessarily undemocratic. Bureaucracies must be controlled by elected decision makers, but presidential or congressional control over bureaucracies is difficult. Bureaus have strong support from interest groups—a factor that contributes to pluralism because interest groups try to forge common links with bureaucracies and congressional committees. These subgovernments tend to decentralize policymaking, thereby contributing to fragmentation.

Although there are many critics of the increasing size of government, the federal bureaucracy has not grown over the past two generations. Instead, it has shrunk, even as the country has grown and the public has made additional demands on government.

Internet Resources

www.gpoaccess.gov/gmanual/index.html
U.S. Government Manual that provides information on the organization of the U.S. government.

www.gpoaccess.gov/fr/index.html
The *Federal Register,* which provides information on U.S. laws and regulations.

www.whitehouse.gov/government/cabinet.html
Information on federal cabinet departments.

www.whitehouse.gov/government/independent-agencies.html
Information on federal independent agencies and commissions.

www.opm.gov/feddata/
Federal employment statistics.

www.opm.gov
Office of Personnel Management Web site with information on federal jobs and personnel issues.

www.govexec.com/
The Web site for *Government Executive* magazine.

Get Connected

How Bureaucracies Are Organized

On January 24, 2003, President George W. Bush signed legislation that created a new department and the largest federal bureaucracy since 1947. The new department, called the Department of Homeland Security, was proposed first by Congress in the aftermath of the September 11, 2001, terrorist attacks. The department's mission is to better coordinate the nation's homeland defenses. Do you know how this new bureaucracy is organized? Could you contact the Department of Homeland Security if you needed to? Let us look at this department's Web page to learn more about the agency.

Search the Web

Go to *www.dhs.gov/dhspublic/faq.jsp* and review the information on that page. Then review *America at Risk: A Homeland Security Report Card* published by the Progressive Policy Institute at *www.ppionline.org/documents/HomeSecRptCrd_0703.pdf.*

Questions to Ask

- How many agencies have been combined to create the new Department of Homeland Security?
- What are some of the challenges the Progressive Policy Institute identifies for the new Department of Homeland Security?

Why It Matters

The Department of Homeland Security is the most dramatic change in the federal bureaucracy in half a century. It is likely that, as with most other agencies, citizens will come into contact with the new agency often, especially as they travel.

Get Involved

Do you have a question about the Department of Homeland Security? If so, go to *www.dhs.gov/dhspublic/contactus* and send your question. Discuss the response you get with your class. You also may follow issues related to homeland security by visiting the Web page of the U.S. House of Representatives Select Committee on Homeland Security, *http://hsc.house.gov/*.

For more exercises, go to www.longmanamericangovernment.com.

For Further Reading

Aberbach, Joel D., and Bert A. Rockman. *In the Web of Politics.* Washington, DC: Brookings Institution, 2000. Examines federal executives and the degree to which they are representative of the country and responsive to elected officials.

Arnold, Peri E. *Making the Managerial Presidency.* 2nd ed. Princeton, NJ: Princeton University Press, 1996. A careful examination of efforts to reorganize the federal bureaucracy.

Derthick, Martha, and Paul J. Quirk. *The Politics of Deregulation.* Washington, DC: Brookings Institution, 1985. Explains why advocates of deregulation prevailed over the special interests that benefited from regulation.

Edwards, George C., III. *Implementing Public Policy.* Washington, DC: Congressional Quarterly Press, 1980. A good review of the issues involved in implementation.

Goodsell, Charles T. *The Case for Bureaucracy.* 4th ed. Washington, DC: Congressional Quarterly Press, 2004. A strong case on behalf of the effectiveness of bureaucracy.

Gormley, William T., Jr. *Taming the Bureaucracy.* Princeton, NJ: Princeton University Press, 1989. Examines remedies for controlling bureaucracies.

Gormley, William T., Jr., and Steven J. Balla. *Bureaucracy and Democracy: Accountability and Performance.* Washington, DC: Congressional Quarterly Press, 2003. Discusses the accountability of unelected bureaucrats in a democracy.

Heclo, Hugh M. *Government of Strangers: Executive Politics in Washington.* Washington, DC: Brookings Institution, 1977. A study of the top executives of the federal government, who constitute (says the author) a "government of strangers."

Kerwin, Cornelius M. *Rulemaking: How Government Agencies Write Law and Make Policy.* 3rd ed. Washington, DC: Congressional Quarterly Press, 2003. Explains how agencies write regulations to implement laws.

Osborne, David, and Ted Gaebler. *Reinventing Government.* Reading, MA: Addison-Wesley, 1992. Simplistic but important view of making government more entrepreneurial and responsive to citizens.

Savas, E. S. *Privatization: The Key to Better Government.* Chatham, NJ: Chatham House, 1987. A conservative economist's argument that many public services performed by bureaucracies would be better handled by the private sector.

Wilson, James Q. *Bureaucracy.* New York: Basic Books, 1989. Presents a "bottom-up" approach to understanding how bureaucrats, managers, and executives decide what to do.

CHAPTER 14

The Federal Courts

Chapter Outline

POLITICS IN ACTION: APPEALING TO THE SUPREME COURT Say you are involved in a lawsuit regarding the application of an affirmative action policy in your college or university. A trial is held in a federal district court. After the trial, a verdict is rendered, and you lose. You are not content to accept this decision, and you appeal to the court of appeals. Once again, you lose. Now you have only two options left: accept the decision or appeal to the U.S. Supreme Court. You decide to appeal, and of the thousands of petitions for hearings presented to the Court each year, yours is one of a few dozen the Court selects.

On the day of the oral argument (there are no trials in the Supreme Court), you walk up the steep steps of the Supreme Court building, the impressive "Marble Palace" with the motto "Equal Justice Under Law" engraved over its imposing columns. The Court's surroundings and procedures suggest the nineteenth century. The justices, clothed in black robes, take their seats at the bench in front of a red velvet curtain. Behind the bench there are still spittoons, one for each justice. (Today, the spittoons are used as wastebaskets.)

Your case, like most of the cases the Court selects for oral arguments, is scheduled for about an hour. Lawyers arguing before the Court often wear formal clothing. They find a goose quill pen on their desk, purchased by the Court from a Virginia supplier. (Lawyers may take the pen with them as a memento of their day in court.) As is the norm, each side is allotted 30 minutes to present its case. The justices may—and do—interrupt the lawyers with questions. When the time is up, a discreet red light goes on at your lawyer's lectern, and he immediately stops talking.

That is the end of the hearing, but not the end of the process. You have asked the Court to overrule a policy established by your state legislature. As the Court considers doing so, it recognizes that its decision will become precedent for all such policies across the nation. Months will go by, as the justices deliberate and negotiate an opinion, before the Court announces its decision. If you win, it will take many more months for your university, aided by lower courts, to interpret the decision and implement it.

The scope of the Supreme Court's power is great, extending even to overruling the decisions of elected officials. Despite the trappings of tradition and majesty, however, the Court does not reach its decisions in a political vacuum. Instead, it works in a context of political influences and considerations, a circumstance that raises important questions about the role of the judiciary in the U.S. political system.

The federal courts pose a special challenge to American democracy. Although it is common for state judges to be elected in one fashion or another, federal judges are *appointed* to their positions—for life. The framers of the Constitution purposefully insulated federal judges from the influence of public opinion. How can we reconcile powerful courts populated by unelected judges with American democracy? Do they pose a threat to majority rule? Or do the federal courts actually function to protect the rights of minorities and thus maintain the type of open system necessary for democracy to flourish?

The power of the federal courts also raises the issue of the appropriate scope of judicial power in our society. Federal courts are frequently in the thick of policymaking on issues ranging from affirmative action and abortion to physician-assisted suicide and the financing of public schools. Numerous critics argue that judges should not be actively involved in determining public policy. Instead, the critics say, judges should focus on the settlement of routine disputes and leave the determination of policy to elected officials. On the other hand, advocates of a more aggressive role for the courts emphasize that judicial decisions have often met pressing needs—especially needs of those who are politically or economically weak—left unmet by the normal processes of policymaking. For example, we have already seen the leading role the federal courts played in ending legally supported racial segregation in the United States. To determine the appropriate role of the courts in our democracy, we must first understand the nature of our judicial system.

However impressive the Supreme Court may be, it makes only the tiniest fraction of American judicial policy. To be sure, the Court decides a handful of key issues each year. Some will shape people's lives, perhaps even decide issues of life and death. In addition to the Supreme Court, there are 12 federal courts of appeal, a Court of Appeals for the Federal Circuit, 91 federal district courts, and thousands of state and local courts. Most of America's legal business is transacted in these less august courts. This chapter focuses on federal courts and the judges who serve on them—the men and women in black robes who are important policymakers in the American political system.

The Nature of the Judicial System

The judicial system in the United States is, at least in principle, an adversarial one in which the courts provide an arena for two parties to bring their conflict before an impartial arbiter (a judge). The system is based on the theory that justice will emerge out of the struggle between two contending points of view. The task of the judge is to apply the law to the case, determining which party is legally correct. In reality, most cases never go to trial because they are settled by agreements reached out of court.

There are two basic kinds of cases: criminal law cases and civil law cases. In a *criminal law* case, the government charges an individual with violating specific laws, such as those prohibiting robbery. The offense may be harmful to an individual or to society as a whole, but in either case it warrants punishment, such as imprisonment or a fine. A *civil law* case involves a dispute between two parties (one of whom may be the government itself) and defines relationships between them. Civil law cases range from divorce proceedings to mergers of multinational companies and violations of civil rights laws. Civil law consists of both statutes (laws passed by legislatures) and common law (the accumulation of judicial decisions).

Just as it is important not to confuse criminal and civil law, it is important not to confuse state and federal courts. The vast majority of all criminal and civil cases involve state law and are tried in state courts. Criminal cases such as burglary and civil cases such as divorce normally begin and end in the state, not the federal, courts.

Participants in the Judicial System

The serenity and majesty of the U.S. Supreme Court are a far cry from the grimy urban courts where strings of defendants are bused from the local jails for their day—often only a few minutes—in court. Yet every case has certain components in common, including litigants, attorneys, and judges. Sometimes organized groups become directly involved. Judges are the policymakers of the American judicial system, and we examine them extensively in later sections of this chapter. Here we will discuss the other regular participants in the judicial process.

Litigants. Federal judges are restricted by the Constitution to deciding "cases" or "controversies"—that is, actual disputes rather than hypothetical ones. Judges do not issue advisory opinions on what they think (in the abstract) may be the meaning or constitutionality of a law. The judiciary is essentially passive, dependent on others to take the initiative.

Thus two parties must bring a case to the court before it may be heard. Every case is a dispute between a *plaintiff* and a *defendant* in which the former brings some charge against the latter. Sometimes the plaintiff is the government, which may bring a charge against an individual or a corporation. The government may charge the defendant with the brutal murder of Jones or charge the XYZ Corporation with illegal trade practices. All cases are identified with the name of the plaintiff first and the defendant second, for example, *State v. Smith* or *Anderson v. Baker*. In many (but not all) cases, a *jury*, a group of citizens (usually 12), is responsible for determining the outcome of a lawsuit.

Litigants end up in court for a variety of reasons. Some are reluctant participants—the defendant in a criminal case, for example. Others are eager for their day in court. For some, the courts can be a potent weapon in the search for a preferred policy. Not everyone can challenge a law, however. Plaintiffs must have what is called **standing to sue**; that is, they must have serious interest in a case, which is typically determined by whether they have sustained or are in immediate danger of sustaining a direct and substantial injury from another party or an action of government. Except in cases pertaining to governmental support for religion, merely being a taxpayer and being opposed to a law do not provide the standing necessary to challenge that law in court. Nevertheless, Congress and the Supreme Court have liberalized the rules for standing, making it somewhat easier for citizens to challenge governmental and corporate actions in court.

standing to sue
The requirement that plaintiffs have a serious interest in a case, which depends on whether they have sustained or are likely to sustain a direct and substantial injury from a party or an action of government.

The courts have broadened the concept of standing to sue to include **class action suits**, which permit a small number of people to sue on behalf of all other people in similar circumstances. These suits may be useful in cases as varied as civil rights, in which a few persons seek an end to discriminatory practices on behalf of all who might be discriminated against, and environmental protection, in which a few persons may sue a polluting industry on behalf of all who are affected by the air or water the industry pollutes. Following an explosion of such cases, in 1973 the Supreme Court began making it more difficult to file class action suits.

class action suits
Lawsuits permitting a small number of people to sue on behalf of all other people similarly situated.

Conflicts must not only arise from actual cases between litigants with standing in court, but they must also be **justiciable disputes**—issues that are capable of being settled by legal methods. One would not go to court to determine whether Congress should fund the Strategic Defense Initiative (SDI), because the matter could not be resolved through legal methods or knowledge.

justiciable disputes
A requirement that to be heard a case must be capable of being settled as a matter of law rather than on other grounds as is commonly the case in legislative bodies.

Groups. Because they recognize the courts' ability to shape policy, interest groups often seek out litigants whose cases seem particularly strong. Few groups have been more successful in finding good cases and good litigants than the National Association for the Advancement of Colored People (NAACP), which selected the school board of Topeka, Kansas, and a young schoolgirl named Linda Brown as the litigants in *Brown v. Board of Education* (1954). NAACP legal counsel Thurgood Marshall believed that Topeka represented a stronger case than other school districts in the United States in the effort to end the policy of "separate but equal"—meaning racially segregated—public education because the city provided segregated facilities that were otherwise genuinely equal. The courts could not resolve the case simply by insisting that expenditures for schools for White and African American children be equalized.

The American Civil Liberties Union (ACLU) is another interest group that is always seeking cases and litigants to support in its defense of civil liberties. One ACLU

Sometimes people find themselves involved in extraordinary court decisions. Linda Brown was a plaintiff in *Brown v. Board of Education,* a key civil rights case in which the Supreme Court overturned its earlier *Plessy v. Ferguson* ruling that legalized segregation.

attorney, stressing that principle took priority over a particular client, even admitted that the ACLU's clients are often "pretty scurvy little creatures. It's the principle that we're going to be able to use these people for that's important."[1] (For an example, review the case in Chapter 4 of the Nazis who tried to march in Skokie, Illinois.)

At other times groups do not directly argue the case for litigants, but support them instead with ***amicus curiae*** **("friend of the court") briefs** that attempt to influence the Court's decision, raise additional points of view, and present information not contained in the briefs of the attorneys for the official parties to the case. In controversial cases, groups may submit many such briefs to the Court: They presented 102 in the University of Michigan case on affirmative action in 2003.

amicus curiae **briefs**
Legal briefs submitted by a "friend of the court" for the purpose of raising additional points of view and presenting information not contained in the briefs of the formal parties. These briefs attempt to influence a court's decision.

Attorneys. Lawyers are indispensable actors in the judicial system. Law is one of the nation's fastest-growing professions. The United States counted about 100,000 lawyers in 1960 but has about 800,000 today. Lawyers busily translate policies into legal language and then enforce or challenge them.

Once lawyers were primarily available to the rich. Today, public interest law firms can sometimes handle legal problems of the poor and middle classes. The federally funded Legal Services Corporation employs lawyers to serve the legal needs of the poor, and state and local governments provide public defenders for poor people accused of crimes. Some employers and unions now provide legal insurance, which works like medical insurance. Members with legal needs—for a divorce, a consumer complaint, or whatever—can secure legal aid through prepaid plans. As a result, more people than ever before can take their problems to the courts. Equality of access, of course, does not mean equality of representation. The wealthy can afford high-powered attorneys who can invest many hours in their cases and arrange for testimony by expert witnesses. The poor are often served by overworked attorneys with few resources to devote to an individual case.

You Are a Young Lawyer

The audience for the judicial drama is a large and attentive one that includes interest groups, the press (a close observer of the judicial process, especially of its more sensational aspects), and the public, who often have very strong opinions about how the process works. All these participants—plaintiffs, defendants, lawyers, interest groups, and others—play a role in the judicial drama, even though many of their activities take place outside the courtroom. How these participants arrive in the courtroom and which court they go to reflect the structure of the court system.

The Structure of the Federal Judicial System

The Constitution is vague about the structure of the federal court system. Aside from specifying that there will be a Supreme Court, the Constitution left it to Congress's discretion to establish lower federal courts of general jurisdiction. In the Judiciary Act of 1789, Congress created these *constitutional courts*, and although the system has been altered over the years, America has never been without them. The current organization of the federal court system is displayed in Figure 14.1.

Congress has also established *legislative courts* for specialized purposes. These courts include the Court of Military Appeals, the Court of Claims, the Court of International Trade, and the Tax Court. Legislative courts are staffed by judges who have fixed terms of office and who lack the protections against removal or salary reductions that judges on constitutional courts enjoy. The judges apply a body of law within their area of jurisdiction but cannot exercise the power of judicial review. The following sections focus on the courts of general jurisdiction.

original jurisdiction
The jurisdiction of courts that hear a case first, usually in a trial. These are the courts that determine the facts about a case.

appellate jurisdiction
The jurisdiction of courts that hear cases brought to them on appeal from lower courts. These courts do not review the factual record, only the legal issues involved.

First, we must understand another difference among courts. Courts with **original jurisdiction** are those in which a case is heard first, usually in a trial. These are the courts that determine the facts about a case, whether it is a criminal charge or a civil suit. More than 90 percent of court cases begin and end in the court of original jurisdiction.

Lawyers can sometimes appeal an adverse decision to a higher court for another decision. Courts with **appellate jurisdiction** hear cases brought to them on

Figure 14.1 Organization of the Federal Court System

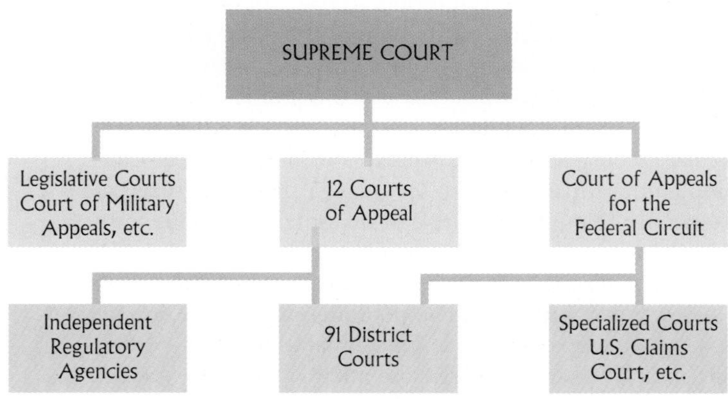

appeal from a lower court. Appellate courts do not review the factual record, only the legal issues involved. At the state level, the appellate process normally ends with the state's highest court of appeal, which is usually called the state supreme court. Appeals from a state high court can be taken only to the U.S. Supreme Court.

District Courts

The entry point for most litigation in the federal courts is one of the 91 **district courts**, at least one of which is located in each state, in addition to one in Washington, D.C., and one in Puerto Rico (there are also three somewhat different territorial courts for Guam, the Virgin Islands, and the Northern Mariana Islands). The district courts are courts of original jurisdiction; they hear no appeals. They are the only federal courts that hold trials and impanel juries. The 680 district court judges usually preside over cases alone, but certain rare cases require that three judges constitute the court. Each district court has between 2 and 28 judges, depending on the amount of judicial work within its territory.

district courts
The 91 federal courts of original jurisdiction. They are the only federal courts in which trials are held and in which juries may be impaneled.

The jurisdiction of the district courts extends to the following:

- Federal crimes
- Civil suits under federal law
- Civil suits between citizens of different states where the amount in question exceeds $75,000
- Supervision of bankruptcy proceedings
- Review of the actions of some federal administrative agencies
- Admiralty and maritime law cases
- Supervision of the naturalization of aliens

It is important to remember that about 98 percent of all the criminal cases in the United States are heard in state and local court systems, not in the federal courts. Moreover, only a small percentage of the persons convicted of federal crimes in the federal district courts actually have a trial. Most enter guilty pleas as part of a bargain to receive lighter punishment.

State and local courts handle most civil suits in the United States. Litigants settle out of court the vast majority of civil cases that commence in the federal courts. Only about 2 percent of the more than 250,000 civil cases resolved each year are decided by trials.

Diversity of citizenship cases involve civil suits between citizens of different states (such as a citizen of California suing a citizen of Texas) or suits in which one of the parties is a citizen of a foreign nation and the matter in question exceeds $75,000. Congress established this jurisdiction to protect against the possible bias of a state court in favor of a citizen from that state. In these cases, federal judges are to apply the appropriate state laws.

An elaborate supporting cast assists district judges. In addition to clerks, bailiffs, law clerks, stenographers, court reporters, and probation officers, U.S. marshals are assigned to each district to protect the judicial process and to serve the writs the judges issue. Federal magistrates, appointed to eight-year terms, issue warrants for arrest, determine whether to hold arrested persons for action by a grand jury, and set bail. They also hear motions subject to review by their district judge and, with the consent of both parties in civil cases and of defendants in petty criminal cases, preside over some trials. As the workload for district judges increases (there were more than 352,000 cases in 2003),[2] magistrates are becoming essential components of the federal judicial system.

Another important player at the district court level is the U.S. attorney. Each of the 91 regular districts has a U.S. attorney who is nominated by the president and confirmed by the Senate and who serves at the discretion of the president (U.S. attorneys do not have lifetime appointments). These attorneys and their staffs prosecute violations of federal law and represent the U.S. government in civil cases.

Most of the cases handled in the district courts are routine, and few result in policy innovations. Usually district court judges do not even publish their decisions. Although most federal litigation ends at this level, a large percentage of these cases that district court judges actually decide (as opposed to those settled out of court or by guilty pleas in criminal matters) are appealed by the losers. A distinguishing feature of the American legal system is the relative ease of appeals. U.S. law gives everyone a right to appeal to a higher court. The loser in a case only has to request an appeal to be granted one. Of course, the loser must pay a substantial legal bill to exercise this right.

Courts of Appeal

courts of appeal

Appellate courts empowered to review all final decisions of district courts, except in rare cases. In addition, they also hear appeals to orders of many federal regulatory agencies. Compare **district courts**.

Congress has empowered the U.S. **courts of appeal** to review all final decisions of district courts, except in rare instances in which the law provides for direct review by the Supreme Court (injunctive orders of special three-judge district courts and certain decisions that hold acts of Congress unconstitutional). Courts of appeal also have authority to review and enforce orders of many federal regulatory agencies, such as the Securities and Exchange Commission and the National Labor Relations Board. About 75 percent of the more than 63,000 cases filed in the courts of appeal each year come from the district courts.[3]

The United States is divided into 12 judicial circuits, including one for the District of Columbia (see Figure 14.2). Each circuit serves at least two states and has between 6 and 28 permanent circuit judgeships (179 in all), depending on the amount of judicial work in the circuit. Each court of appeal normally hears cases in panels consisting of three judges, but each may sit *en banc* (with all judges present) in particularly important cases. Decisions in either arrangement are made by majority vote of the participating judges.

There is also a special appeals court called the U.S. Court of Appeals for the Federal Circuit. Congress established this court, composed of 12 judges, in 1982 to hear appeals in specialized cases, such as those regarding patents, claims against the United States, and international trade.

The courts of appeal focus on correcting errors of procedure and law that occurred in the original proceedings of legal cases, such as when a district court judge gave improper instructions to a jury or misinterpreted the rights provided under a law. These courts are appellate courts and therefore hold no trials and hear

Figure 14.2 The Federal Judicial Circuits

Not shown are Puerto Rico (First Circuit), Virgin Islands (Third Circuit), and Guam and the Northern Mariana Islands (Ninth Circuit).

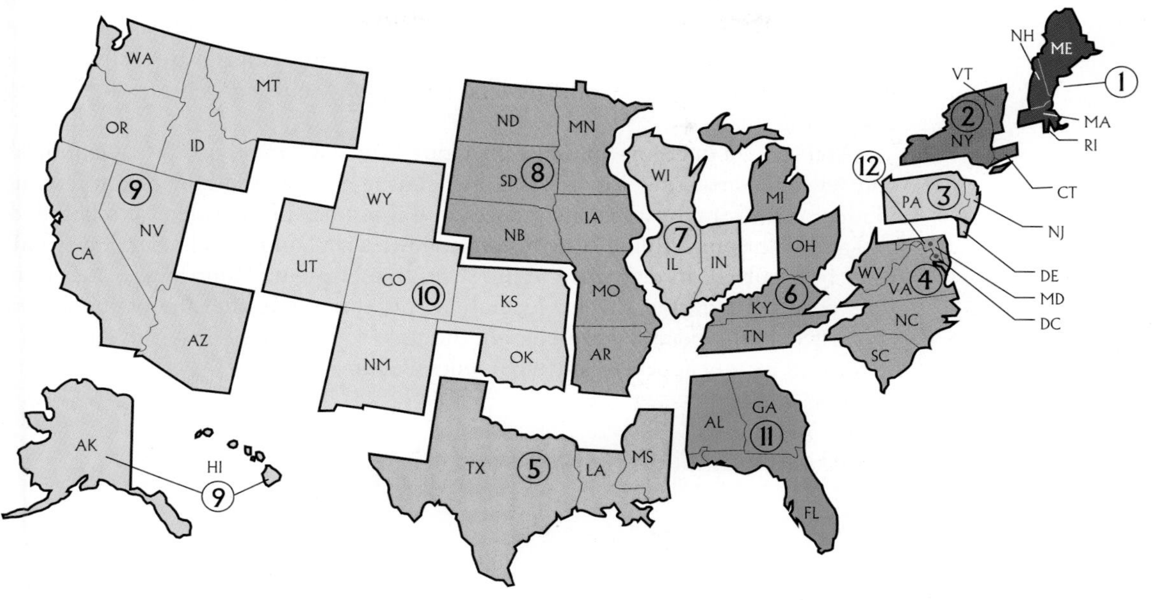

no testimony. Their decisions set precedent for all the courts and agencies within their jurisdictions.

The Supreme Court

Sitting at the pinnacle of the American judicial system is the U.S. **Supreme Court**. The Court does much more for the American political system than decide individual cases. Among its most important functions are resolving conflicts among the states and maintaining national supremacy in the law. The Supreme Court also plays an important role in ensuring uniformity in the interpretation of national laws. For example, in 1984 Congress created a federal sentencing commission to write guidelines aimed at reducing the wide disparities in punishment for similar crimes tried in federal courts. By 1989, more than 150 federal district judges had declared the law unconstitutional, and another 115 had ruled it valid. Only the Supreme Court could resolve this inconsistency in the administration of justice, which it did when it upheld the law.

Supreme Court
The pinnacle of the American judicial system. The Court ensures uniformity in interpreting national laws, resolves conflicts among states, and maintains national supremacy in law. It has both **original jurisdiction** and **appellate jurisdiction**, but unlike other federal courts, it controls its own agenda.

The Chief Justice of the Supreme Court

There are nine justices on the Supreme Court: eight associates and one chief justice (only members of the Supreme Court are called justices; all others are called judges). The Constitution does not require this number, however, and there have been as few as six justices and as many as 10. Congress altered the size of the Supreme Court many times between 1801 and 1869. In 1866, it reduced the size of the Court from 10 to seven members so that President Andrew Johnson could not nominate new justices to fill two vacancies. When Ulysses S. Grant took office, Congress increased the number of justices to nine because it was confident that he would nominate members to its liking. Since then, the number of justices has remained stable.

All nine justices sit together to hear cases and make decisions. But they must first decide which cases to hear. A familiar battle cry for losers in litigation in lower courts is, "I'll appeal this all the way to the Supreme Court!" In reality, this is unlikely to happen. Unlike other federal courts, the Supreme Court decides which cases it will hear.

You can see in Figure 14.3 that the Court does have an original jurisdiction, yet very few cases arise under it, as Table 14.1 illustrates. Almost all the business of the Court comes from the appellate process, and cases may be appealed from both federal and state courts. In the latter instance, however, a "substantial federal question" must be involved. In deference to the states, the Supreme Court hears cases from state courts only if they involve federal law, and then only after the petitioner has exhausted all the potential remedies in the state court system. Losers in a case in a state court cannot appeal to any other federal court.

Figure 14.3 The Organization and Jurisdiction of the Courts

Table 14.1 Full Opinions in the Supreme Court

TYPE OF CASE	NUMBER OF CASES
Original jurisdiction	2
Civil actions from lower federal courts	51
Federal criminal and *habeas corpus* cases	16
Civil actions from state courts	2
State criminal cases	12
Total	83

Source: "The Supreme Court, 2005 Term: The Statistics," *Harvard Law Review* 120 (November 2006): 382–84.

The Court will not try to settle matters of state law or determine guilt or innocence in state criminal proceedings. To obtain a hearing in the Supreme Court, a defendant convicted in a state court might demonstrate, for example, that the trial was not fair as required by the Bill of Rights, which was extended to cover state court proceedings by the due process clause of the Fourteenth Amendment. The majority of cases heard by the Supreme Court come from the lower federal courts.

The central participants in the judicial system are, of course, the judges. Once on the bench, they must draw on their backgrounds and beliefs to guide their decision making. Some, for example, will be more supportive of abortion or of prayer in the public schools than others. Because presidents and others involved in the appointment process know perfectly well that judges are not neutral automatons who methodically and literally interpret the law, they work diligently to place candidates on the bench who are sympathetic to presidential policies. Who are the men and women who serve as federal judges and justices, and how did they obtain their positions?

Why It Matters

Judicial Elections
The public directly elects most state and local judges. All federal judges and justices are nominated by the president and confirmed by the Senate for lifetime tenures. If we elected federal judges, their decisions on highly visible issues might be more responsive to the public—but less responsive to the Constitution.

The Politics of Judicial Selection

Appointing a federal judge or a Supreme Court justice is a president's chance to leave an enduring mark on the American legal system. Guaranteed by the Constitution the right to serve "during good behavior," federal judges and justices enjoy, for all practical purposes, lifetime positions. They may be removed only by conviction of impeachment, which has occurred a mere seven times in two centuries under the Constitution. Congress has never removed a Supreme Court justice from office, although it tried but did not convict Samuel Chase in 1805. Nor can Congress reduce the salaries of judges, a stipulation that further insulates them from political pressures.

Although the president nominates persons to fill judicial slots, the Senate must confirm each nomination by majority vote. Because the judiciary is a coequal branch, the upper house of the legislature sees no reason to be especially deferential to the executive's recommendations. Because of the Senate's role, the president's discretion is actually less important than it appears.

Popular Election of Judges

The Lower Courts

senatorial courtesy

An unwritten tradition whereby nominations for state-level federal judicial posts are not confirmed if they are opposed by a senator of the president's party from the state in which the nominee will serve. The tradition also applies to courts of appeal when there is opposition from the nominee's state senator.

The customary manner in which the Senate handles state-level federal judicial nominations is through **senatorial courtesy**. Under this unwritten tradition (which began under George Washington in 1789), the Senate does not confirm nominations for lower-court positions when they are opposed by a senator of the president's party from the state in which the nominee is to serve. In the case of judges for courts of appeal, nominees are not confirmed if opposed by a senator of the president's party from the state of the nominee's residence.

To invoke the right of senatorial courtesy, the relevant senator usually simply states a general reason for opposition. Other senators then honor their colleague's views and oppose the nomination, regardless of their personal evaluations of the candidate's merits.

Because of the strength of this informal practice, presidents usually check carefully with the relevant senator or senators ahead of time to avoid making a nomination that will fail to be confirmed. In many instances, this checking is tantamount to giving the power of nomination to these senators. Typically, when there is a vacancy for a federal district judgeship, the one or two senators of the president's party from the state where the judge will serve suggest one or more names to the attorney general and the president. If neither senator is of the president's party, then the party's state congresspersons or other state party leaders may make suggestions. Other interested senators may also try to influence a selection.[4]

Why It Matters

Senatorial Courtesy

Because of the practice of senatorial courtesy, senators actually end up nominating persons to be district court judges. If the Senate abolished this practice, it would allow the president greater freedom in making nominations and give the White House more opportunity to put its stamp on the judiciary.

Once several names have been submitted to the president, the Department of Justice and the Federal Bureau of Investigation conduct competency and background checks on these persons, and the president usually selects a nominee from those who survive the screening process. It is difficult for the president to reject the recommendation of the party's senator in favor of someone else if the person recommended clears the hurdles of professional standing and integrity. Thus, senatorial courtesy turns the Constitution on its head, and the Senate ends up making nominations, which the president then approves.

Others have input in judicial selection as well. The Department of Justice may ask sitting judges, usually federal judges, to evaluate prospective nominees. Sitting judges may also initiate recommendations to advance or retard someone's chances of being nominated. In addition, candidates for the nomination are often active on their own behalf. They have to alert the relevant parties that they desire the position and may orchestrate a campaign of support. As one appellate judge observed, "People don't just get judgeships without seeking them."[5]

The president usually has more influence in the selection of judges to the federal courts of appeal than to federal district courts. The decisions of appellate courts are generally more significant than those of lower courts, so the president naturally takes a greater interest in appointing people to these courts. At the same time, individual senators are in a weaker position to determine who the nominee will be because the jurisdiction of an appeals court encompasses several states. Although custom and pragmatic politics require that these judgeships be apportioned among the states in a circuit, the president has some discretion in doing this and therefore has a greater role in recruiting appellate judges than in recruiting district court judges. Even here, however, senators of the president's party from the state in which the candidate resides may be able to veto a nomination.

The increasing polarization of partisan politics in recent years has affected courts of appeals nominations. The time for confirmation has increased dramatically,[6] which has decreased the chances of confirmation. Senators of the opposition party have filibustered or otherwise derailed the confirmations of a number of high-profile nominations of Presidents Clinton and George W. Bush. In response, Bush appointed some judges to the courts of appeals as recess appointments. Such appointments are unusual and good only for the remainder of a congressional term. They are also likely to anger opposition senators. After the Republicans nearly voted to end the possibility of filibustering judicial nominations, 14 senators from both parties forged a deal without White House approval that allowed some—but not all—of Bush's stalled judicial nominees to receive floor votes.

The Supreme Court

The president is vitally interested in the Supreme Court because of the importance of its work and is usually intimately involved in recruiting potential justices. Nominations to the Court may be a president's most important legacy to the nation.

A president cannot have much impact on the Court unless there are vacancies to fill. Although on the average there has been an opening on the Supreme Court every two years, there is a substantial variance around this mean.[7] Franklin D. Roosevelt had to wait five years before he could nominate a justice; in the meantime, he was faced with a Court that found much of his New Deal legislation unconstitutional. More recently, Jimmy Carter was never able to nominate a justice. Between 1972 and 1984, there were only two vacancies on the Court. Nevertheless, Richard Nixon was able to nominate four justices in his first three years in office, and Ronald Reagan had the opportunity to add three new members.

Selecting Federal Judges

When the chief justice's position is vacant, the president may nominate either someone already on the Court or someone from outside to fill the position. Usually presidents choose the latter course to widen their range of options, but if they decide to elevate a sitting associate justice—as President Reagan did with William Rehnquist in 1986—the nominee must go through a new confirmation hearing by the Senate Judiciary Committee.

The president operates under fewer constraints in nominating persons to serve on the Supreme Court than in naming persons to be judges in the lower courts. Although many of the same actors are present in the case of Supreme Court nominations, their influence is typically quite different. The president usually relies on the attorney general and the Department of Justice to identify and screen candidates for the Court. Sitting justices often try to influence the nominations of their future colleagues, but presidents feel little obligation to follow their advice.

Senators also play a lesser role in the recruitment of Supreme Court justices than in the selection of lower-court judges. No senator can claim that the jurisdiction of the Court falls within the realm of his or her special expertise, interest, or sphere of influence. Presidents typically consult with senators from the state of residence of a nominee after they have decided whom to select. At this point, senators are unlikely to oppose a nomination because they like having their state receive the honor and are well aware that the president can simply select someone from another state.

Candidates for nomination usually keep a low profile. They can accomplish little through aggressive politicking, and because of the Court's standing, actively pursuing the position might offend those who play important roles in selecting nominees. The American Bar Association's Standing Committee on the federal judiciary has played a varied but typically modest role at the Supreme Court level. Presidents have not generally been willing to allow the committee to prescreen candidates before their nominations are announced. George W. Bush chose not to seek its advice at all.

Through 2006, there have been 151 nominations to the Supreme Court, and 110 persons have served on the Court. Four people were nominated and confirmed twice, eight declined appointment or died before beginning service on the Court, and 28 failed to secure Senate confirmation. Presidents have failed 20 percent of the time to appoint the nominees of their choice to the Court—a percentage much higher than for any other federal position.

Although home-state senators do not play prominent roles in the selection process for the Court, the Senate as a whole does. Through its Judiciary Committee, it may probe a nominee's judicial philosophy in great detail.

For most of the twentieth century, Supreme Court nominations were routine affairs. Only one nominee failed to win confirmation in the first two-thirds of the century. But the 1960s were tumultuous times and bred ideological conflict. Although John F. Kennedy had no trouble with his two nominations to the Court—Byron White and Arthur Goldberg—his successor, Lyndon Johnson, was not so fortunate. Johnson had to withdraw his nomination of Abe Fortas (already serving on the Court) to serve as chief justice in the face of strong opposition; therefore, the Senate never voted on Homer Thornberry, Johnson's nominee to replace Fortas as an associate justice. Richard Nixon, the next president, had two nominees rejected in a row after bruising battles in the Senate. The past generation has been even more tumultuous, punctuated by occasional periods of calm (see "A Generation of Change: Supreme Court Confirmation Politics").

In 1991, after two weeks of riveting hearings in which Clarence Thomas was charged with sexual harassment, the Senate narrowly confirmed his nomination to the Supreme Court. Historically, about one-fifth of those nominated to the Court have failed to obtain confirmation.

A GENERATION OF CHANGE

Supreme Court Confirmation Politics

Few matters are of more importance to presidents and members of Congress than the nomination of new Supreme Court justices. Over the past generation, the politics of these nominations has gone from highly contentious to relatively harmonious and, most recently, to a more mixed pattern of both consensus and conflict.

In 1987, President Reagan nominated Robert H. Bork to fill the vacancy created by the resignation of Justice Lewis Powell. Bork testified before the Senate Judiciary Committee for 23 hours. A wide range of interest groups entered the fray, mostly in opposition to the nominee, whose views they claimed were extremist. In the end, following a bitter floor debate, the Senate rejected the president's nomination by a vote of 42 to 58.

Six days after the Senate vote on Bork, the president nominated Judge Douglas H. Ginsburg to the high court. Just nine days later, however, Ginsburg withdrew his nomination after disclosures that he had used marijuana while a law professor at Harvard.

Unsuccessful Supreme Court Nominees since 1900

NOMINEE	YEAR	PRESIDENT
John J. Parker	1930	Hoover
Abe Fortas[a]	1968	Johnson
Homer Thornberry[b]	1968	Johnson
Clement F. Haynesworth Jr.	1969	Nixon
G. Harrold Carswell	1970	Nixon
Robert H. Bork	1987	Reagan
Douglas H. Ginsburg[a]	1987	Reagan
Harriet Miers[a]	2005	G. W. Bush

[a]Nomination withdrawn. Fortas was serving on the Court as an associate justice and was nominated to be chief justice.
[b]The Senate took no action on Thornberry's nomination.

In June 1991, at the end of the Supreme Court's term, Associate Justice Thurgood Marshall announced his retirement from the Court. Shortly thereafter, President Bush announced his nomination of another African American, federal appeals judge Clarence Thomas, to replace Marshall on the Court. Thomas was a conservative, so this decision was consistent with the Bush administration's emphasis on placing conservative judges on the federal bench.

The president claimed that he was not employing quotas when he chose another African American to replace the only African American ever to sit on the Supreme Court. Not everyone believed him, but liberals were placed in a dilemma. On the one hand, they favored a minority group member serving on the nation's highest court. On the other hand, Thomas was unlikely to vote the same way as Thurgood Marshall had voted. Instead, Thomas presented the prospect of strengthening the conservative trend in the Court's decisions. In the end, this ambivalence inhibited spirited opposition to Thomas, who was circumspect about his judicial philosophy in his appearances before the Senate Judiciary Committee. The committee sent his nomination to the Senate floor on a split vote.

Just as the Senate was about to vote on the nomination, however, charges of sexual harassment leveled against Thomas by University of Oklahoma law professor Anita Hill were made public. The Judicial Committee reopened hearings on the charges in response to criticism that the Senate was sexist for not seriously considering them in the first place. For several days, citizens sat transfixed before their television sets as Professor Hill calmly and graphically described her recollections of Thomas's behavior. Thomas then emphatically denied any such behavior and charged the Senate with racism for raising the issue. Ultimately, public opinion polls showed that most people believed Thomas, and he was confirmed in a 52-to-48 vote—the closest vote on a Supreme Court nomination in more than a century.

The Senate's treatment of President Clinton's two nominees harks back to the Kennedy era. Neither Ruth Bader Ginsburg nor Stephen Breyer caused much controversy. Similarly, the Senate easily confirmed George W. Bush's nomination of John Roberts as chief justice. Indeed, he was not an easy target to oppose. His pleasing and professional personal demeanor and his disciplined and skilled testimony before the Senate Judicial Committee gave potential opponents little basis for opposition.

Attention immediately turned to the president's nomination on October 2 of White House counsel Harriet Miers to replace Justice O'Connor. Bush apparently thought Miers's lack of a published record would make it easier to push her nomination through. What looked like an adroit political decision soon turned sour, however. Many of the president's most passionate supporters had hoped and expected that he would make an unambiguously conservative choice to fulfill their goal of clearly altering the Court's balance, even at the cost of a bitter confirmation battle. By instead settling on a loyalist with no experience as a judge and little substantive record on abortion, affirmative action, religion, and other socially divisive issues, the president shied away from a direct confrontation with liberals and in effect asked his base on the right to trust him on his nomination. Many conservatives were bitterly disappointed and highly critical of the president. They demanded a known conservative and a top-flight legal figure. The nomination also smacked of cronyism, with the president selecting a friend and a loyalist rather than someone of obvious merit. The comparison with Roberts only emphasized the thinness of Miers's qualifications. In short order, Miers withdrew from consideration, and the president nominated Samuel Alito.

Alito was clearly a traditional conservative and had a less impressive public presence than Roberts. Response to him followed party lines, but the nominee appeared too well qualified and unthreatening in his confirmation hearings to justify a filibuster, and without one, his confirmation was assured. The Senate confirmed Alito by a vote of 58 to 42.

It is difficult to predict the politics surrounding future nominations to the Supreme Court. One prediction seems safe, however: As long as Americans are polarized around social issues and as long as the Court makes critical decisions about these issues, the potential for conflict over the president's nominations is always present.

Nominations are most likely to run into trouble under certain conditions. Presidents whose parties are in the minority in the Senate or who make a nomination at the end of their terms face a greatly increased probability of substantial opposition.[8] Presidents whose views are more distant from the norm in the Senate or who are appointing a person who might alter the balance on the Court are also likely to face additional opposition. Equally important, opponents of a nomination usually must be able to question a nominee's competence or ethics in order to defeat a nomination. Most people do not consider opposition to a nominee's ideology a valid reason to vote against confirmation. For example, liberals disagreed strongly with the views of William Rehnquist, but he was easily confirmed as chief justice. Opponents of a nominee must usually raise questions about their legal competence and ethics in order to attract moderate senators to their side and to make ideological protests seem less partisan.

The Backgrounds of Judges and Justices

The Constitution sets no special requirements for judges or justices, but most observers conclude that the federal judiciary is composed of a distinguished group of men and women. Competence and ethical behavior are important to presidents for reasons beyond merely obtaining Senate confirmation of their judicial nominees. Skilled and honorable judges and justices reflect well on the president and are likely to do so for many years. Moreover, these individuals are more effective representatives of the president's views. Although the criteria of competence and character screen out some possible candidates, there is still a wide field from which to choose. Other characteristics then play prominent roles.

The judges serving on the federal district and circuit courts are not a representative sample of the American people. They are all lawyers (although this is not a constitutional requirement), and they are overwhelmingly White males. Jimmy Carter appointed 40 women, 37 African Americans, and 16 Hispanics to the federal bench, more than all previous presidents combined. Ronald Reagan did not continue this trend, although he was the first to appoint a woman to the Supreme Court. His administration placed a higher priority on screening candidates on the basis of ideology than on screening them in terms of ascriptive characteristics. From 1989 to 1992, George Bush continued to place conservatives on the bench, but he was much more likely to appoint women and minorities than was Reagan. Bill Clinton nominated Democrats, who are more liberal than the nominees of Reagan and Bush, and a large percentage of them were women and minorities. George W. Bush's nominees have been similar to those of his father.

Federal judges have typically held office as a judge or prosecutor, and often they have been involved in partisan politics. This involvement is generally what brings them to the attention of senators and the Department of Justice when they seek nominees for judgeships.

Like their colleagues on the lower federal courts, Supreme Court justices share characteristics that qualify them as an elite group. All have been lawyers, and all but four (Thurgood Marshall, nominated in 1967; Sandra Day O'Connor, nominated in 1981; Clarence Thomas, nominated in 1991; and Ruth Bader Ginsburg, nominated in 1993) have been White males. Most have been in their 50s and 60s when they took office, from the upper-middle or upper class, and Protestants.[9]

Most members of the federal judiciary have backgrounds atypical of most Americans. Sandra Day O'Connor, nominated in 1981, was the first woman to sit on the Supreme Court.

Race and gender have become more salient criteria in recent years. In the 1980 presidential campaign, Ronald Reagan promised to appoint a woman to the first vacancy on the Court if he were elected. In 1991, President Bush chose to replace the first African American justice, Thurgood Marshall, with another African American, Clarence Thomas. Women and minorities may serve on all federal courts more frequently in the future because of increased opportunity for legal education and decreased prejudice against their judicial activity as well as because of their increasing political clout.

Geography was once a prominent criterion for selection to the Court, but it is no longer very important. Presidents do like to spread the slots around, however, as when Richard Nixon decided he wanted to nominate a Southerner. At various times there have been what some have termed a "Jewish seat" and a "Catholic seat" on the Court, but these guidelines are not binding on the president. For example, after a half century of having a Jewish justice, the Court did not have one from 1969 to 1993.

Typically, justices have held high administrative or judicial positions before moving to the Supreme Court (see Table 14.2). Most have had some experience as a judge, often at the appellate level, and many have worked for the Department of Justice. Some have held elective office, and a few have had no government service but have been distinguished attorneys. The fact that many justices, including some of the most distinguished ones, have not had previous judicial experience may seem surprising, but the unique work of the Court renders this background much less important than it might be for other appellate courts.

Partisanship is another important influence on the selection of judges and justices. Only 13 of 110 members of the Supreme Court have been nominated by presidents of a different party. Moreover, many of the 13 exceptions were actually close to the president in ideology, as was the case in Richard Nixon's appointment of Lewis Powell. Herbert Hoover's nomination of Benjamin Cardozo seems to be one of the few cases in which partisanship was completely dominated by merit as a criterion for selection. Usually more than 90 percent of presidents' judicial nominations are of members of their own parties.

Table 14.2 Supreme Court Justices, 2007

NAME	YEAR OF BIRTH	PREVIOUS POSITION	NOMINATING PRESIDENT	YEAR OF CONFIRMATION
John G. Roberts Jr.	1955	U.S. Court of Appeals	G. W. Bush	2005
John Paul Stevens	1920	U.S. Court of Appeals	Ford	1975
Antonin Scalia	1936	U.S. Court of Appeals	Reagan	1986
Anthony M. Kennedy	1936	U.S. Court of Appeals	Reagan	1988
David H. Souter	1939	U.S. Court of Appeals	Bush	1990
Clarence Thomas	1948	U.S. Court of Appeals	Bush	1991
Ruth Bader Ginsburg	1933	U.S. Court of Appeals	Clinton	1993
Stephen G. Breyer	1938	U.S. Court of Appeals	Clinton	1994
Samuel A. Alito Jr.	1950	U.S. Court of Appeals	G. W. Bush	2006

The U.S. Supreme Court: Front row, left to right: Anthony M. Kennedy, John Paul Stevens, John G. Roberts, Antonin Scalia, and David H. Souter. Second row, left to right: Stephen G. Breyer, Clarence Thomas, Ruth Bader Ginsburg, and Samuel Alito.

The role of partisanship is really not surprising. Most of a president's acquaintances are made through the party, and there is usually a certain congruity between party and political views. Most judges and justices have at one time been active partisans—an experience that gave them visibility and helped them obtain the positions from which they moved to the courts.

Judgeships are also considered very prestigious patronage plums. Indeed, the decisions of Congress to create new judgeships—and thus new positions for party members—are closely related to whether the majority party in Congress is the same as the party of the president. Members of the majority party in the legislature want to avoid providing an opposition party president with new positions to fill with their opponents.

Ideology is as important as partisanship in the selection of judges and justices. Presidents want to appoint to the federal bench people who share their views. In effect, all presidents try to "pack" the courts. They want more than "justice"; they want policies with which they agree. Presidential aides survey candidates' decisions (if they have served on a lower court),[10] speeches, political stands, writings, and other expressions of opinion. They also glean information from people who know the candidates well. Although it is considered improper to question judicial candidates about upcoming court cases, it is appropriate to discuss broader questions of political and judicial philosophy. The Reagan administration was especially concerned about such matters and had each potential nominee fill out a lengthy questionnaire and be interviewed by a special committee in the Department of Justice. Like its predecessor, the George Bush administration was attentive to appointing conservative judges. Bill Clinton was less concerned with the ideology of his nominees, at least partly to avoid costly confirmation fights. Instead, he focused on identifying persons with strong legal credentials, especially women and minorities. George W. Bush reverted to the Reagan policy of naming clear conservatives to the federal courts.

Chief Justice John Roberts

Members of the federal bench also play the game of politics, of course, and may try to time their retirements so that a president with compatible views will choose their successor. This is one reason why justices remain on the Supreme Court for so long, even when they are clearly infirm. William Howard Taft, a rigid conservative, even feared that a successor would be named by Herbert Hoover, a more moderate conservative.[11]

Presidents are typically pleased with the performance of their nominees to the Supreme Court and through them have slowed or reversed trends in the Court's decisions. Franklin D. Roosevelt's nominees substantially liberalized the Court, whereas Richard Nixon's turned it in a conservative direction.

Nevertheless, it is not always easy to predict the policy inclinations of candidates, and presidents have been disappointed in their nominees about one-fourth of the time. President Eisenhower, for example, was displeased with the liberal decisions of both Earl Warren and William Brennan. Once, when asked whether he had made any mistakes as president, he replied, "Yes, two, and they are both sitting on the Supreme Court."[12] Richard Nixon was certainly disappointed when Warren Burger, whom he had nominated as chief justice, wrote the Court's decision calling for immediate desegregation of the nation's schools shortly after his confirmation. This turn of events did little for the president's "Southern strategy." Burger also wrote the Court's opinion in *United States v. Nixon,* which forced the president to release the Watergate tapes. Nixon's resignation soon followed.

Presidents influence policy through the values of their judicial nominees, but this impact is limited by numerous legal and "extralegal" factors beyond the chief executive's control. As Harry Truman put it, "Packing the Supreme Court can't be done . . . I've tried it and it won't work. . . . Whenever you put a man on the Supreme Court, he ceases to be your friend. I'm sure of that."[13]

There is no doubt that various women's, racial, ethnic, and religious groups desire to have their members appointed to the federal bench. At the very least, judgeships have symbolic importance for them.[14] Presidents face many of the same pressures for representativeness in selecting judges that they experience in naming their cabinet.

What is less clear is what policy differences result when presidents nominate persons with different backgrounds to the bench. The number of female and minority group judges is too few and their service too recent to serve as a sound basis for generalizations about their decisions. Many members of each party have been appointed, of course, and it appears that Republican judges in general are somewhat more conservative than Democratic judges. Former prosecutors serving on the Supreme Court have tended to be less sympathetic toward defendants' rights than other justices. It seems that background does make some difference,[15] yet for reasons that we examine in the following sections, on many issues, party affiliation and other characteristics bring no more predictability to the courts than they do to Congress.

The Courts as Policymakers

"Judicial decision making," a former Supreme Court law clerk wrote in the *Harvard Law Review*, "involves, at bottom, a choice between competing values by fallible, pragmatic, and at times nonrational men and women in a highly complex process in a very human setting."[16] This is an apt description of policymaking in the Supreme Court and in other courts, too. The next sections look at how courts make policy, paying particular attention to the role of the U.S. Supreme Court. Although it is not the only court involved in policymaking and policy interpretation, its decisions have the widest implications for policy.

Accepting Cases

Deciding what to decide about is the first step in all policymaking. Courts of original jurisdiction cannot very easily refuse to consider a case; appeals courts, including the U.S. Supreme Court, have much more control over their agendas. The approximately 8,000 cases submitted annually to the U.S. Supreme Court must be read, culled, and sifted. Figure 14.4 shows the stages of this process. At least once each week, the nine justices meet in conference, where they hammer out two important matters. First is an agenda: The justices consider the chief justice's "discuss list" and decide which cases they want to discuss. Because few of the justices can take the time to read materials on every case submitted to the Court, most rely heavily on law clerks (each justice has up to four to assist them in considering cases and writing opinions) to screen each case. If four justices agree to grant review of a case (the "rule of four"), it can be scheduled for oral argument or decided on the basis of the written record already on file with the Court.

You Are a Clerk to Supreme Court Justice Judith Gray

The most common way for the Court to put a case on its docket is by issuing to a lower federal or state court a *writ of certiorari*, a formal document that calls up a case. Until 1988, some cases—principally those in which federal laws had been found unconstitutional, in which federal courts had concluded that state laws violated the federal Constitution, or in which state laws had been upheld in state courts despite claims that they violated federal law or the Constitution—were technically supposed to be heard by the Court "on appeal." In reality, however, the Court always exercised broad discretion over hearing these and other cases.

Figure 14.4 Obtaining Space on the Supreme Court's Docket

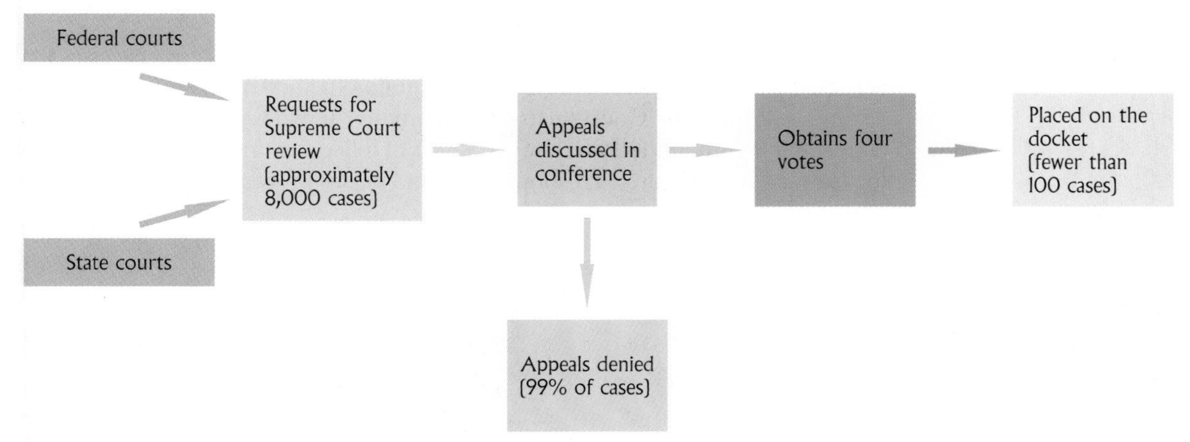

Cases that involve major issues—especially civil liberties, conflict between different lower courts on the interpretation of federal law, or disagreement between a majority of the Supreme Court and lower-court decisions—are likely to be selected by the Court.[17]

Because getting into the Supreme Court is half the battle, it is important to remember this chapter's earlier discussion of standing to sue (litigants must have serious interest in a case, having sustained or being in immediate danger of sustaining a direct and substantial injury from another party or an action of government)—a criterion the Court often uses to decide whether to hear a case. In addition, the Court has used other means to avoid deciding cases that are too politically "hot" to handle or that divide the Court too sharply,[18] as we discuss later in this chapter.

solicitor general

A presidential appointee in the Department of Justice who is in charge of the appellate court litigation of the federal government.

Another important influence on the Supreme Court is the **solicitor general**. As a presidential appointee and the third-ranking official in the Department of Justice, the solicitor general is in charge of the appellate court litigation of the federal government. The solicitor general and a staff of about two dozen experienced attorneys have four key functions: (1) to decide whether to appeal cases the government has lost in the lower courts, (2) to review and modify the briefs presented in government appeals, (3) to represent the government before the Supreme Court, and (4) to submit a brief on behalf of a litigant in a case in which the government is not directly involved.[19] Unlike attorneys for private parties, the solicitor general is careful to seek Court review only of important cases. By avoiding frivolous appeals and displaying a high degree of competence, they typically earn the confidence of the Court, which in turn grants review of a large percentage of the cases they submit.[20]

Case Overload

Ultimately, the Supreme Court decides very few cases. In recent years, the Court has made about 80 formal written decisions per year in which their opinions could serve as precedent and thus as the basis of guidance for lower courts. In a few dozen additional cases, the Court reaches a *per curiam decision*—that is, a decision without explanation. Such decisions resolve the immediate case but have no value as precedent because the Court does not offer reasoning that would guide lower courts in future decisions.[21]

Making Decisions

The second task of the justices' weekly conferences is to discuss cases actually accepted and argued before the Court. Beginning the first Monday in October and lasting until June, the Court hears oral arguments in two-week cycles: two weeks of courtroom arguments followed by two weeks of reflecting on cases and writing opinions about them. Figure 14.5 shows the stages in this process.

Figure 14.5 The Supreme Court's Decision-Making Process

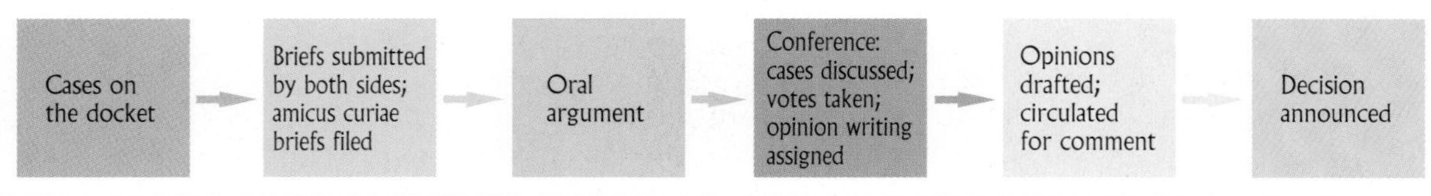

Before the justices enter the courtroom to hear the lawyers for each side present their arguments, they have received elaborately prepared written briefs from each party involved. They have also probably received several *amicus curiae* briefs from parties (often groups) who are interested in the outcome of the case but who are not formal litigants.

Amicus curiae briefs have another important role: The government, under the direction of the solicitor general, may submit them in cases in which it has an interest. For instance, a case between two parties may involve the question of the constitutionality of a federal law. The federal government naturally wants to have its voice heard on such matters, even if it is not formally a party to the case. These briefs are also a means to urge the Court to change established doctrine. For example, the Reagan administration frequently submitted *amicus curiae* briefs to the Court to try to change the law dealing with defendants' rights.

In most instances, the attorneys for each side have only a half-hour to address the Court. During this time they summarize their briefs, emphasizing their most compelling points.[22] The justices may listen attentively, interrupt with penetrating or helpful questions, request information, talk to one another, read (presumably briefs), or simply gaze at the ceiling. After 25 minutes, a white light comes on at the lectern from which the lawyer is speaking, and five minutes later a red light signals the end of that lawyer's presentation, even if he or she is in midsentence. Oral argument is over.[23]

Back in the conference room, the chief justice, who presides over the Court, raises a particular case and invites discussion, turning first to the senior associate justice. Discussion can range from perfunctory to profound and from courteous to caustic. If the votes are not clear from the individual discussions, the chief justice may ask each justice to vote. Once a tentative vote has been reached, it is necessary to write an **opinion**, a statement of the legal reasoning behind the decision.

opinion

A statement of legal reasoning behind a judicial decision. The content of an opinion may be as important as the decision itself.

Opinion writing is no mere formality. In fact, the content of an opinion may be as important as the decision itself. Broad and bold opinions have far-reaching implications for future cases; narrowly drawn opinions may have little impact beyond the case being decided. Tradition in the Supreme Court requires that the chief justice, if in the majority, write the opinion or assign it to another justice in the majority. The chief justice often writes the opinion in landmark cases, as Earl Warren did in *Brown v. Board of Education* and Warren Burger did in *United States v. Nixon*. If the chief justice is part of the minority, the senior associate justice in the majority assigns the opinion. The person assigned to write an opinion circulates drafts within the Court, justices make suggestions, and they all conduct negotiations among themselves.[24] The content of the opinion can win or lose votes. A justice must redraft an opinion that proves unacceptable to the majority of his or her colleagues on the Court.

Justices are free to write their own opinions, to join in other opinions, or to associate themselves with part of one opinion and part of another. Justices opposed to all or part of the majority's decision write *dissenting opinions*. *Concurring opinions* are those written not only to support a majority decision but also to stress a different constitutional or legal basis for the judgment. When the justices have written their opinions and taken the final vote, they announce their decision. At least six justices must participate in a case, and decisions are made by majority vote. If there is a tie (because of a vacancy on the Court or because a justice chooses not to participate), the decision of the lower court from which the case came is sustained. Five votes in agreement on the reasoning underlying an opinion are necessary for the logic to serve as precedent for judges of lower courts.

stare decisis

A Latin phrase meaning "let the decision stand." Most cases reaching appellate courts are settled on this principle.

precedent

How similar cases have been decided in the past.

The vast majority of cases that reach the courts are settled on the principle of ***stare decisis*** ("let the decision stand"), meaning that an earlier decision should hold for the case being considered. All courts rely heavily on **precedent**—the way similar cases were handled in the past—as a guide to current decisions. Lower courts, of course, are expected to follow the precedents of higher courts in their decision making. If the Supreme Court, for example, rules in favor of the right to abortion under certain conditions, it has established a precedent that lower courts are expected to follow. Lower courts have much less discretion than the Supreme Court.

The Supreme Court is in a position to overrule its own precedents, and it has done so more than 200 times.[25] One of the most famous of such instances occurred with *Brown v. Board of Education* (1954) (see Chapter 5), in which the court overruled *Plessy v. Ferguson* (1896) and found that segregation in the public schools violated the Constitution.

Judicial Review

What happens when precedents are unclear? This is especially a problem for the Supreme Court, which is more likely than other courts to handle cases at the forefront of the law. Precedent is typically less firmly established on these matters. Moreover, the justices are often asked to apply to concrete situations the vague phrases of the Constitution ("due process of law," "equal protection," "unreasonable searches and seizures") or vague statutes passed by Congress. This ambiguity provides leeway for the justices to disagree (only about one-third of the cases in which full opinions are handed down are decided unanimously) and for their values to influence their judgment.

As a result, it is often easy to identify consistent patterns in the decisions of justices. For example, if there is division on the Court (indicating that precedent is not

The content of a Supreme Court opinion may be as important as the decision itself, and justices may spend months negotiating a majority opinion. Here, William H. Rehnquist, former chief justice of the Supreme Court, prepares a written opinion.

clear) and you can identify a conservative side to the issue at hand, it is likely that Clarence Thomas will be on that side. Ruth Bader Ginsburg may very well be voting on the other side of the issue. Liberalism and conservatism have several dimensions, including freedom, equality, and economic regulation. The point is that policy preferences do matter in judicial decision making, especially in the nation's highest court[26] (see "You Are the Policymaker: The Debate over Original Intentions").

YOU ARE THE POLICYMAKER

The Debate over Original Intentions

The most contentious issue involving the courts is the role of judicial discretion. According to Christopher Wolfe, "The Constitution itself nowhere specifies a particular set of rules by which it is to be interpreted. Where does one go, then, in order to discover the proper way to interpret the Constitution?"

Some have argued for a jurisprudence of **original intent** (sometimes referred to as *strict constructionism*). This view holds that judges and justices should attempt to determine the intent of the framers of the Constitution regarding a particular matter and decide cases in line with that intent. Such a view is popular with conservatives.

Advocates of strict constructionism view it as a means of constraining the exercise of judicial discretion, which they see as the foundation of the liberal decisions, especially on matters of civil liberties, civil rights, and defendants' rights (discussed in Chapters 4 and 5).

They also see following original intent as the only basis of interpretation consistent with democracy. Judges, they argue, should not dress up constitutional interpretations with *their* views on "contemporary needs," "today's conditions," or "what is right." It is the job of legislators, not judges, to make such judgments.

Other jurists, such as former Justice William Brennan, disagree. They maintain that what appears to be deference to the intentions of the framers is simply a cover for making conservative decisions. Opponents of original intent assert that the Constitution is subject to multiple meanings by thoughtful people in different ages. Judges will differ in time and place about what they think the Constitution means. Thus, basing decisions on original intent is not likely to have much effect on judicial discretion.

In addition, Brennan and his supporters contend that the Constitution is not like a paint-by-numbers kit. Trying to reconstruct or guess the framers' intentions is very difficult. Recent key cases before the Supreme Court have concerned issues such as school busing, abortions, the Internet, and wiretapping that the framers could not have imagined; there were no public schools or buses, no contraceptives or modern abortion techniques, and certainly no computers or electronic surveillance equipment or telephones in 1787.

The Founders embraced general principles, not specific solutions, when they wrote the Constitution. They frequently lacked discrete, discoverable intent. Moreover, there is often no record of their intentions, nor is it clear whose intentions should count—those of the writers of the Constitution, those of the more than 1,600 members who attended the ratifying conventions, or those of the voters who sent them there. This problem grows more complex when you consider the amendments to the Constitution, which involve thousands of additional "framers."

Historian Jack N. Rakove points out that there is little historical evidence that the framers believed their intentions should guide later interpretations of the Constitution. In fact, there is some evidence for believing that Madison—the key delegate—left the Constitutional Convention bitterly disappointed with the results. What if Madison had one set of intentions but—like anyone working in a committee—got a different set of results?

The lines are drawn. On one side is the argument that any deviation from following the original intentions of the Constitution's framers is a deviation from principle, leaving unelected judges to impose their views on the American people. If judges do not follow original intentions, then on what do they base their decisions?

On the other side are those who believe that it is often impossible to discern the views of the framers and that there is no good reason to be constrained by the views of the eighteenth century, which reflect a more limited conception of constitutional rights. In order to cope with current needs, they argue, it is necessary to adapt the principles in the Constitution to the demands of each era.

The choice here is at the very heart of the judicial process. If you were a justice sitting on the Supreme Court and were asked to interpret the meaning of the Constitution, what would *you* do?

Sources: Christopher Wolfe, *The Rise of Modern Judicial Review* (New York: Basic Books, 1986); Raoul Berger, *Government by Judiciary: The Transformation of the Fourteenth Amendment* (Cambridge, MA: Harvard University Press, 1977); Traciel V. Reid, "A Critique of Interpretivism and Its Claimed Influence upon Judicial Decision Making," *American Politics Quarterly* 16 (July 1988): 329–56; Jack N. Rakove, ed., *Interpreting the Constitution* (Boston: Northeastern University Press, 1990); Arthur S. Miller, "In Defense of Judicial Activism," in *Supreme Court Activism and Restraint*, eds. Stephen C. Halpern and Charles M. Lamb (Lexington, MA: D.C. Heath, 1982); Stephen Breyer, *Active Liberty: Interpreting Our Democratic Constitution* (New York: Knopf, 2005); Antonin Scalia, *A Matter of Interpretation: Federal Courts and the Law* (Princeton, NJ: Princeton University Press, 1998).

original intent
A view that the Constitution should be interpreted according to the original intent of the framers. Many conservatives support this view.

The Court conveys its decisions to the press as they announce them formally in open court. Media coverage of the Court remains primitive—short and shallow. Doris Graber reports that "much reporting on the courts—even at the Supreme Court level—is imprecise and sometimes even wrong."[27] More important to the legal community, the decisions are bound weekly and made available to every law library and lawyer in the United States. There is, of course, an air of finality to the public announcement of a decision. In fact, however, even Supreme Court decisions are not self-implementing; they are actually "remands" to lower courts, instructing them to act in accordance with the Court's decisions.

Implementing Court Decisions

judicial implementation
How and whether court decisions are translated into actual policy, thereby affecting the behavior of others. The courts rely on other units of government to enforce their decisions.

Reacting bitterly to one of Chief Justice Marshall's decisions, President Andrew Jackson is said to have grumbled, "John Marshall has made his decision; now let him enforce it." Court decisions carry legal, even moral, authority, but courts must rely on other units of government to enforce their decisions. **Judicial implementation** refers to how and whether court decisions are translated into actual policy, thereby affecting the behavior of others.

You should think of any judicial decision as the end of one process—the litigation process—and the beginning of another process—the process of judicial implementation. Sometimes delay and stalling follow even decisive court decisions. There is, for example, the story of the tortured efforts of a young African American named Virgil Hawkins to get himself admitted to the University of Florida Law School. Hawkins's efforts began in 1949, when he first applied for admission, and ended unsuccessfully in 1958, after a decade of court decisions. Despite a 1956 order from the U.S. Supreme Court to admit Hawkins, continued legal skirmishing produced a 1958 decision by a U.S. district court in Florida ordering the admission of non-Whites but upholding the denial of admission to Hawkins himself. Other courts and other institutions of government can be roadblocks in the way of judicial implementation.

Charles Johnson and Bradley Canon suggest that implementation of court decisions involves several elements.[28] First, there is an *interpreting population*, heavily composed of lawyers and judges. They must correctly understand and reflect the intent of the original decision in their subsequent actions. Usually lower-court judges do follow the Supreme Court, but sometimes they circumvent higher-court decisions to satisfy their own policy interests.[29]

The Courts and School Vouchers

Second, there is an *implementing population*. Suppose the Supreme Court held (as it did) that prayers organized by school officials in the public schools are unconstitutional. The implementing population (school boards and school administrators) must then actually abandon prayers. Police departments, hospitals, corporations, government agencies—all may be part of the implementing population. With so many implementors, many of whom may disagree with a decision, there is plenty of room for "slippage" between what the Supreme Court decides and what actually occurs. Judicial decisions are more likely to be implemented smoothly if implementation is concentrated in the hands of a few highly visible officials, such as the president or state legislators.

Third, every decision involves a *consumer population*. The potential "consumers" of an abortion decision are those who want abortions (and those who oppose them); the consumers of the *Miranda* decision (see Chapter 5) are criminal defendants and their attorneys. The consumer population must be aware of its newfound rights and stand up for them.

Why It Matters

The Lack of a Judicial Bureaucracy

The federal courts lack a bureaucracy to implement their decisions. In fact, some of the Supreme Court's most controversial decisions, such as those dealing with school integration and school prayers, have been implemented only with great difficulty. If the courts had a bureaucracy to enforce their decisions, justice might be better served, but such a bureaucracy would have to be enormous to monitor, for example, every school and police station.

Congress and presidents can also help or hinder judicial implementation. The Supreme Court held in 1954 that segregated schools were "inherently unconstitutional" and the next year ordered public schools desegregated "with all deliberate speed." President Eisenhower refused to state clearly that Americans should comply with this famous decision in *Brown v. Board of Education*, which may have encouraged local school boards to resist the decision. Congress was not much help either; only a decade later, in the wake of the civil rights movement discussed in Chapter 5, did it pass legislation denying federal aid to segregated schools. Different presidents have different commitments to a particular judicial policy. In December 1984, after years of court and presidential decisions supporting busing to end racial segregation, the Reagan administration went before the Supreme Court and argued *against* school busing in a case in Norfolk, Virginia.

The fate and effect of a Supreme Court decision are complex and unpredictable. The implementation of any court decision involves many actors besides the justices, and the justices have no way of ensuring that their decisions and policies will be implemented. Courts have made major changes in public policies, however, not because their decisions are automatically implemented but because the courts both reflect and help to determine the national policy agenda.[30]

Understanding the Courts

Powerful courts are unusual; few nations have them. The power of American judges raises questions about the compatibility of unelected courts with a democracy and about the appropriate role for the judiciary in policymaking.

The Courts and Democracy

Announcing his retirement in 1981, Justice Potter Stewart made a few remarks to the handful of reporters present. Embedded in his brief statement was this observation: "It seems to me that there's nothing more antithetical to the idea of what a good judge should be than to think it has something to do with representative democracy." He meant that judges should not be subject to the whims of popular majorities. In a nation that insists so strongly that it is democratic, where do the courts fit in?

Comparing Judiciaries

In some ways, the courts are not a very democratic institution. Federal judges are not elected and are almost impossible to remove. Indeed, their social backgrounds probably make the courts the most elite-dominated policymaking institution. If democracy requires that key policymakers always be elected or be continually responsible to those who are, then the courts diverge sharply from the requirements of democratic government.

HOW YOU CAN MAKE A DIFFERENCE

The Constitution in Exile v. The Living Constitution

There are some who say the United States is in the midst of a philosophical battle—a battle regarding constitutional interpretation. There are those who believe the Constitution should be interpreted according to its original meaning, and that judges should interpret the Constitution in a manner that once again places limits on the use of federal authority. Conversely, there are others who believe the Constitution is a malleable document that should be interpreted in light of historical, social, and technological change (the "living Constitution" school). Though this debate may seem the domain of scholars and jurists, the outcome will have very real effects on the rights and freedoms you enjoy. The constitutional aspect of national politics affects everyone, including you.

Making a Difference

James Robertson is a judge for the United States District Court for the District of Columbia. He was placed on the Foreign Intelligence Surveillance Court by then Chief Justice William Rehnquist. However, on December 20, 2005, Judge Robertson resigned from his position. It was reported that Robertson's resignation was related to the Bush administration's surveillance of international communications and phone calls sent or received in the United States, without judicial warrants—a course of action in seeming violation of the spirit of the Constitution. Robertson also struck down the Bush administration's use of military tribunals as unconstitutional.

What you can do:

- Evaluate the arguments on both sides of the issue. Join and support the group that you feel is right.
- If you feel that the Constitution should limit federal power, join the Claremont Institute (http://www.claremont.org) or the Federalist Society (http://www.fed-soc.org).
- If you believe in the "living Constitution," support the American Prospect (http://prospect.org/web/index.ww) or the American Constitution Society for Law and Policy (http://www.acslaw.org).
- Contact your senator concerning judicial confirmation hearings to promote the selection of federal judges who share your views on the Constitution.

As you saw in Chapter 2, the Constitution's framers wanted it that way. Chief Justice Rehnquist, a judicial conservative, put the case as follows: "A mere change in public opinion since the adoption of the Constitution, unaccompanied by a constitutional amendment, should not change the meaning of the Constitution. A merely temporary majoritarian groundswell should not abrogate some individual liberty protected by the Constitution."[31]

The courts are not entirely independent of popular preferences, however. Turn-of-the-century Chicago humorist Finley Peter Dunne had his Irish saloonkeeper character "Mr. Dooley" quip that "th' Supreme Court follows th' iliction returns." Many years later, political scientists have found that the Court usually reflects popular majorities.[32] Even when the Court seems out of step with other policymakers, it eventually swings around to join the policy consensus,[33] as it did in the New Deal. A study of the period from 1937 to 1980 found that the Court was clearly out of line with public opinion only on the issue of prayers in public schools.[34]

Despite the fact that the Supreme Court sits in a "marble palace," it is not as insulated from the normal forms of politics as one might think. The two sides in the abortion debate flooded the Court with mail, targeted it with advertisements and protests, and bombarded it with 78 *amicus curiae* briefs in the *Webster v. Reproductive Health Services* (1989) case. Members of the Supreme Court are unlikely to cave in to interest group pressures, but they are aware of the public's concern about issues, and this awareness becomes part of their consciousness as they decide cases. Political scientists have found that the Court is more likely to hear cases for which interest groups have filed *amicus curiae* briefs.[35]

Interest groups often use the judicial system to pursue their policy goals, forcing the courts to rule on important social issues. Some Hispanic parents, for example, have successfully sued local school districts to compel them to offer bilingual education.

Courts can also promote pluralism. When groups go to court, they use litigation to achieve their policy objectives.[36] Both civil rights groups and environmentalists, for example, have blazed a path to show how interest groups can effectively use the courts to achieve their policy goals. Thurgood Marshall, the legal wizard of the NAACP's litigation strategy, not only won most of his cases but also won for himself a seat on the Supreme Court. Almost every major policy decision these days ends up in court (see "Young People and Politics: The Supreme Court Is Closer Than You Think"). Chances are good that some judge can be found who will rule in an interest group's favor. On the other hand, agencies and businesses commonly find themselves ordered by different courts to do opposite things. The habit of always turning to the courts as a last resort can add to policy delay, deadlock, and inconsistency.

What Courts Should Do: The Scope of Judicial Power

Judges and Politics

The courts "will be least in capacity to annoy or injure" the people and their liberties, wrote Alexander Hamilton in the *Federalist Papers*.[37] Throughout American history, critics of judicial power have disagreed. They see the courts as too powerful for their own—or the nation's—good. Yesterday's critics focused on John Marshall's "usurpations" of power, on the proslavery decision in *Dred Scott*, or on the efforts of the "nine old men" to kill off Franklin D. Roosevelt's New Deal legislation. Today's critics are never short of arguments to show that courts go too far in making policy.

Courts make policy on both large and small issues. In the past few decades, courts have made policies on major issues involving school busing, abortion, affirmative action, nuclear power, legislative redistricting, bilingual education, prison conditions, counting votes in the 2000 presidential election, and many other key issues.[38]

judicial restraint
A judicial philosophy in which judges play minimal policymaking roles and typically defer to the legislatures.

There are strong disagreements about the appropriateness of allowing the courts to have a policymaking role. Many scholars and judges favor a policy of **judicial restraint**, in which judges adhere closely to precedent and play minimal policymaking roles, leaving policy decisions strictly to the legislatures. These observers stress that the federal courts, composed of unelected judges, are the least democratic branch of government and question the qualifications of judges for making policy decisions and balancing interests. Advocates of judicial restraint believe that decisions such as those on abortion and prayer in public schools go well beyond the "referee" role they feel is appropriate for courts in a democracy.

judicial activism
A judicial philosophy in which judges make bold policy decisions, even charting new constitutional ground. Advocates of this approach emphasize that the courts can correct pressing needs, especially those unmet by the majoritarian political process.

On the other side are proponents of **judicial activism**, in which judges make bolder policy decisions, even charting new constitutional ground with a particular decision. Advocates of judicial activism emphasize that the courts may alleviate pressing needs—especially needs of those who are politically or economically weak—left unmet by the majoritarian political process. (For current views about

YOUNG PEOPLE AND POLITICS

The Supreme Court Is Closer Than You Think

The Supreme Court of the United States may seem remote and not especially relevant to a college student. Yet a surprising number of its most important decisions have been brought by young adults seeking protection for their civil rights and liberties. For example, we saw in Chapter 5 that in *Rostker v. Goldberg* (1981) several young men filed a suit claiming that the Military Selective Service Act's requirement that only males register for the draft was unconstitutional. Although the Court held that the requirement was constitutional, draft registration was suspended temporarily during the suit.

Students were are at the center of *Board of Regents of University of Wisconsin System v. Southworth* (2000), in which the Court upheld the University of Wisconsin's requirement of a fee to fund speakers on campus—even if the speakers advocated views that offended some students. The right of the police to search newspaper files was fought over the actions of a campus newspaper in *Zurcher v. Stanford Daily* (1978). In 1992, the Supreme Court ruled that legislatures and universities may not single out racial, religious, or sexual insults or threats for prosecution as "hate speech" or "bias crimes" (*R.A.V. v. St. Paul*). From Gregory Johnson's burning an American flag at the 1984 Republican National Convention to protest nuclear arms buildup (which the Court protected in *Texas v. Johnson* [1989]) to burning a draft card (which the Court did not protect in *United States v. O'Brien* [1968]), young people have also been pioneers in the area of symbolic speech.

Issues of religious freedom have also prominently featured college students. In *Widmar v. Vincent* (1981), the Court decided that public universities that permit student groups to use their facilities must allow student religious groups on campus to use the facilities for religious worship. In 1995, the Court held that the University of Virginia was constitutionally required to subsidize a student religious magazine on the same basis as other student publications (*Rosenberger v. University of Virginia*). However, in 2004 the Court held that the state of Washington was within its rights when it excluded students pursuing a devotional theology degree from its general scholarship program (*Locke v. Davey*).

The Supreme Court has a long history of dealing with issues of importance to young people. Often it is young adults themselves who initiate the cases—and who take them all the way to the nation's highest court.

Questions for Discussion

- Why do you think cases involving young people tend to involve civil liberties issues?
- What other issues of particular importance to young people should the Supreme Court decide?

interpreting the law, see "Issues of the Times: How Should the Courts Interpret the Law?")

It is important not to confuse judicial activism or restraint with liberalism or conservatism. In Table 14.3, you can see the varying levels of the Supreme Court's use of judicial review to void laws passed by Congress in different eras. In the early years of the New Deal, judicial activists were conservatives. During the tenure of Earl Warren as chief justice (1953–1969), activists made liberal decisions. The Courts under Chief Justices Warren Burger (1969–1986) and William

Table 14.3 Supreme Court Rulings in Which Federal Statutes Have Been Found Unconstitutional[a]

PERIOD	STATUTES VOIDED
1798–1864	2
1864–1910	33 (34)[b]
1910–1930	24
1930–1936	14
1936–1953	3
1953–1969	25
1969–1986	35
1986–present	35
Total	171

[a]In whole or in part.

[b]An 1883 decision in the *Civil Rights Cases* consolidated five different cases into one opinion declaring one act of Congress void. In 1895, *Pollock v. Farmers Loan and Trust Co.* was heard twice, with the same result both times.

Source: Henry J. Abraham, *The Judicial Process: An Introductory Analysis of the Courts of the United States, England, and France*, 7th ed. (Oxford: Oxford University Press, 1998), p. 309. Used by permission of Oxford University Press, Inc. Updated by the authors.

Rehnquist (1986–2005), conservative nominees of Republican presidents, marked the most active use of judicial review in the nation's history. In the latter period, conservative justices were the most likely to vote to void congressional legislation.[39]

The problem remains of reconciling the American democratic heritage with an active policymaking role for the judiciary. The federal courts have developed a doctrine of **political questions** as a means to avoid deciding some cases, principally those that involve conflicts between the president and Congress. The courts have shown no willingness, for example, to settle disputes regarding the War Powers Resolution (see Chapter 12).

political questions
A doctrine developed by the federal courts and used as a means to avoid deciding some cases, principally those involving conflicts between president and Congress.

Similarly, judges try to avoid deciding a case on the basis of the Constitution, preferring less contentious "technical" grounds. They also employ issues of jurisdiction, mootness (whether a case presents a real controversy in which a judicial decision can have a practical effect), standing, ripeness (whether the issues of a case are clear enough and evolved enough to serve as the basis of a decision), and other conditions to avoid adjudication of some politically charged cases. The Supreme Court refused to decide, for example, whether it was legal to carry out the war in Vietnam without an explicit declaration of war from Congress.

As you saw in the discussion of *Marbury v. Madison*, from the earliest days of the Republic, federal judges have been politically astute in their efforts to maintain the legitimacy of the judiciary and to conserve their resources. (Remember that judges are typically recruited from political backgrounds.) They have tried not to take on too many politically controversial issues at one time. They have also been much more likely to find state and local laws unconstitutional (about 1,100) than federal laws (fewer than 200, as shown in Table 14.3).[40]

Another factor that increases the acceptability of activist courts is the ability to overturn their decisions. First, the president and the Senate determine who sits on the federal bench. Second, Congress, with or without the president's urging, can begin the process of amending the Constitution to overcome a constitutional decision of the Supreme Court. Although this process does not occur rapidly, it is a safety valve. The Eleventh Amendment in 1795 reversed the decision in *Chisolm v. Georgia*, which permitted an individual to sue a state in federal court; the Fourteenth Amendment in 1868 reversed the decision in *Dred Scott v. Sandford*, which held African Americans not to be citizens of the United States; the Sixteenth Amendment in 1913 reversed the decision in *Pollock v. Farmer's Loan and Trust Co.*, which prohibited a federal income tax; and the Twenty-sixth Amendment in 1971 reversed part of *Oregon v. Mitchell*, which voided a congressional act according 18- to 20-year-olds the right to vote in state elections.

Even more drastic options are available as well. Just before leaving office in 1801, the Federalists created a tier of circuit courts and populated them with Federalist judges; the Jeffersonian Democrats took over the reins of power and promptly abolished the entire level of courts. In 1869, the Radical Republicans in Congress altered the appellate jurisdiction of the Supreme Court to prevent it from hearing a case (*Ex parte McCardle*) that concerned the Reconstruction Acts. This kind of alteration is rare, but it occurred recently. The George W. Bush administration selected the naval base at Guantánamo as the site for a detention camp for terrorism suspects in the expectation that its actions would not be subject to review by federal courts. In June 2004, however, the Supreme Court ruled that the naval base fell within the jurisdiction of U.S. law and that the habeas corpus statute that allows prisoners to challenge their detentions was applicable. In 2005, Congress stripped federal courts from hearing habeas corpus petitions from the detainees.

Finally, if the issue is one of **statutory construction**, in which a court interprets an act of Congress, then the legislature routinely passes legislation that clarifies existing laws and, in effect, overturns the courts.[41] In 1984, for example, the Supreme Court ruled in *Grove City College v. Bell* that when an institution receives federal aid, only the program or activity that actually gets the aid, not the entire institution, is covered by four federal civil rights laws. In 1988, Congress passed a law specifying that the entire institution is affected. The description of the judiciary as the "ultimate arbiter of the Constitution" is hyperbolic; all the branches of government help define and shape the Constitution.

statutory construction
The judicial interpretation of an act of Congress. In some cases where statutory construction is an issue, Congress passes new legislation to clarify existing laws.

Summary

The American judicial system is complex. Sitting at the pinnacle of the judicial system is the Supreme Court, but it is possible to exaggerate its importance. Most judicial policymaking and enforcement of laws take place in the state courts and the lower federal courts.

Throughout American political history, courts have shaped public policy with regard to the economy, liberty, equality, and, most recently, ecology. In the economic arena, until the time of Franklin D. Roosevelt, courts traditionally favored corporations, especially when government tried to regulate them. Since the New Deal, however, the courts have been more tolerant of government regulation of business, shifting much of their policymaking attention to issues of liberty and equality. From *Dred Scott* to *Plessy* to *Brown,* the Supreme Court moved from a role of reinforcing discriminatory policy toward racial minorities to a role of shaping new policies for protecting civil rights. Most recently, environmental groups have used the courts to achieve their policy goals.

A critical view of the courts claims that they are too powerful for the nation's own good and are rather ineffective policymakers besides. Throughout American history, however, judges have been important agenda setters in the political system. Many of the most important political questions make their way into the courts at one time or another. The judiciary is an alternative point of access for those seeking to obtain public policy decisions to their liking, especially those who are not in the majority.

Once in court, litigants face judges whose discretion in decision making is typically limited by precedent. Nevertheless, on questions that raise novel issues (as do many of the most important questions that reach the Supreme Court), the law is less firmly established. Here there is more leeway and judges become more purely political players, balancing different interests and linked to the rest of the political system by their own policy preferences and the politics of their selection.

The unelected and powerful federal courts raise important issues of democracy and the scope of judicial power. Yet court decisions are typically consistent with public opinion, and judges and justices have often used their power to promote democracy. Reconciling the American democratic heritage with an active policymaking role for the judiciary remains a matter of debate. The courts have been sensitive to the issue of their power and often avoid the most controversial issues, at least for a time. It has also been easier for opponents of court decisions to accept judicial power because it is possible to overturn judicial decisions.

Internet Resources

www.supremecourtus.gov/
Official site of the U.S. Supreme Court with information on its operations.

supct.law.cornell.edu/supct/
Decisions of the Supreme Court, background, schedule, and rules of the Court; also includes backgrounds of the justices serving on the Court.

www.oyez.org/oyez/frontpage
Web site that allows you to hear oral arguments before the Supreme Court. Also provides information on the Supreme Court and its docket.

www.courttv.com/trials/
Information on recent trials.

www.uscourts.gov/
Explains the organization, operation, and administration of federal courts.

www.usdoj.gov/olp/judicialnominations.htm
Information on current judicial nominations.

Get Connected

The Background of Judges and Justices

As the text notes, the Constitution sets no requirements for judges and historically judges have not represented the cultural diversity of America. For instance, federal judges have been more male and more White than the rest of the population. Advocates of race and gender equality have in recent years increased their call for greater racial and gender diversity on the federal bench. Let us look at the current list of judicial nominations and compare their background characteristics with the background characteristics detailed in Table 14.2 of the text.

Search the Web

Go to *www.usdoj.gov/olp/nominations.htm* and click on the name of the judge to view his or her biography. Do this for all the nominees.

Questions to Ask

- How does the current list of nominees compare with the characteristics outlined in Table 14.2?
- In general is President George W. Bush nominating judges who will greatly alter the general characteristics of the judiciary or not? If so, how?

Why It Matters

We want the most qualified judges to sit on the bench, and most people also want the judiciary to reflect American cultural diversity. Judges from different backgrounds, such as women and racial and ethnic minorities, may be more sensitive to the implications of issues especially relevant to their experiences.

Get Involved

Find out more about the nominees from your federal district court or federal court of appeals circuit. Contact one or both of your U.S. senators at www.senate.gov/ to tell him or her your opinions of the nominee.

For more exercises, go to www.longmanamericangovernment.com.

For Further Reading

Abraham, Henry J. *Justices, Presidents, and Senators: A History of the U.S. Supreme Court Appointments from Washington to Clinton.* Lanham, MD: Rowman & Littlefield, 1999. A readable history of the relationships between presidents and the justices they appointed.

Baum, Lawrence. *The Supreme Court.* 9th ed. Washington, DC: Congressional Quarterly Press, 2007. An excellent work on the operations and impact of the Court.

Breyer, Stephen. *Active Liberty: Interpreting Our Democratic Constitution.* New York: Knopf, 2005. Presents the "contextual" view of how justices should decide cases.

Carp, Robert A., Ronald Stidham, and Kenneth L. Manning. *Judicial Process in America.* 6th ed. Washington, DC: Congressional Quarterly Press, 2004. An overview of federal and state courts.

Ely, John Hart. *Democracy and Distrust.* Cambridge, MA: Harvard University Press, 1980. An appraisal of judicial review and an effort to create a balanced justification for the role of the courts in policymaking.

Epstein, Lee, and Jack Knight. *The Choices Justices Make.* Washington, DC: Congressional Quarterly Press, 1997. A strategic account of Supreme Court decision making.

Epstein, Lee, and Joseph F. Kobylka. *The Supreme Court and Legal Change*. Chapel Hill: University of North Carolina Press, 1992. Examines how interest groups propelled issues regarding abortion and the death penalty to the Supreme Court and how the way they framed their legal arguments affected outcomes on these issues.

Goldman, Sheldon. *Picking Federal Judges*. New Haven, CT: Yale University Press, 1997. The definitive work on backgrounds and the politics of recruiting lower-court judges.

Greenhouse, Linda. *Becoming Justice Blackmun*. New York: Times Books, 2005. Inside story of the career and daily work of a long-serving justice.

Jacob, Herbert. *Law and Politics in the United States*. 2nd ed. Boston: HarperCollins, 1995. An introduction to the American legal system with an emphasis on linkages to the political arena.

Johnson, Charles A., and Bradley C. Canon. *Judicial Policies: Implementation and Impact*. 2nd ed. Washington, DC: Congressional Quarterly Press, 1999. One of the best overviews of judicial policy implementation.

O'Brien, David M. *Storm Center*. 7th ed. New York: Norton, 2006. An overview of the Supreme Court's role in American politics.

Rowland, C. K., and Robert A. Carp. *Politics and Judgment in Federal District Courts*. Lawrence: University Press of Kansas, 1996. An important work on the operations of the federal district courts.

Scalia, Antonin. *A Matter of Interpretation: Federal Courts and the Law*. Princeton, NJ: Princeton University Press, 1998. Presents the "original intentions" view of how justices should decide cases.

Segal, Jeffrey A., and Harold J. Spaeth. *The Supreme Court and the Attitudinal Model*. Cambridge, MA: Cambridge University Press, 1993. Examines how the attitudes and values of justices affect their decisions.

CHAPTER 15

The Congress, the President, and the Budget: The Politics of Taxing and Spending

Chapter Outline

POLITICS IN ACTION: THE POLITICS OF BUDGETING In 1776, the cry of "no taxation without representation" was enough to spark a revolution. Today issues of taxes and budgetary measures continue to dominate national public policy: How much should we spend for homeland security, health care for the elderly, subsidized student loans, or cleaning up the environment? And how should we pay for these programs?

In the presidential election of 2004, George W. Bush argued that we should make temporary tax cuts permanent, while John Kerry proposed increasing taxes on the wealthiest Americans. Kerry was also more supportive of investing in new or expanded programs.

Politicians who attempt to make tough decisions about the budget risk incurring voters' wrath. In 1985, Republican senators took the lead with a reform that was designed to balance the budget. In the 1986 congressional elections, Republicans lost control of the Senate. In 1990, President George Bush bit the bullet and reversed his pledge not to raise taxes. He agreed to a budget deal with the congressional Democrats that succeeded in reducing the deficit and limiting spending. In 1992, he lost his bid for reelection.

In 1993, President Clinton followed Bush's precedent and reversed his promise to lower taxes with a program of higher taxes and spending constraints. In the 1994 elections, Republicans won majorities in both houses of Congress for the first time since 1952. They pledged to cut taxes, balance the budget, and reduce expenditures for important social welfare programs. A two-year political battle ensued between congressional Republicans and President Clinton, who vigorously opposed the scope of their proposals. In the end, little changed, and each side vowed to take its case to the American people in the 1996 elections.

The public—which typically seeks a balanced budget, little or no cut in government programs, and tax relief—split its decision. The Democrats won the presidency, but Republicans won both houses of Congress—the only time that had *ever* happened. In the 1998 elections, little changed. George W. Bush advocated a large tax cut as the centerpiece of his campaign in the 2000 presidential election and won what was perhaps the closest election in American history. Congress was also narrowly divided. It is not surprising that the battle of the budget remains at the center of American politics.

Two questions are central to public policy: *Who bears the burdens of paying for government?* and *Who receives the benefits?* Some observers are concerned that democracy poses a danger to budgeting. Do politicians seek to "buy" votes by spending public funds on things voters will like—and will remember on Election Day? Or is spending the result of demands made on government services by the many segments of American society? In addition, does the public choose to "soak the rich" with taxes that redistribute income?

Budgets are central to our theme of the scope of government. Indeed, for many programs, budgeting *is* policy. The amount of money spent on a program determines how many people are served, how well they are served, or how much of something (weapons, vaccines, and so on) the government can purchase. The bigger the budget, the bigger the government. But is the growth of the government's budget inevitable? Or are the battles over the allocation of scarce public resources actually a *constraint* on government?

The Constitution allocates various tasks to both the president and Congress, but it generally leaves to each branch the decision of whether to exercise its power to perform a certain task. There is an exception, however. Every year the president and Congress *must* appropriate funds. If they fail to do so, the government will

Because budgetary policy is so important, decision makers may be reluctant to compromise. In 1995–1996, the inability of the president and Congress to reach agreement led to the shutdown of the federal government.

come to a standstill. The army will be idled, Social Security offices will close, and food stamps will not be distributed to the poor.

Everyone has a basic understanding of budgeting. Public budgets are superficially like personal budgets. Aaron Wildavsky remarked that a budget is a document that "contains words and figures that propose expenditures for certain objects and purposes." There is more to public budgets than bookkeeping, however, because such a **budget** is a policy document allocating burdens (taxes) and benefits (expenditures). Thus "budgeting is concerned with translating financial resources into human purposes. A budget therefore may also be characterized as a series of goals with price tags attached."[1]

budget
A policy document allocating burdens (taxes) and benefits (expenditures).

Over the past 30 years, the national government has run up large annual budget deficits. A budget deficit occurs when **expenditures** exceed **revenues** in a fiscal year. In other words, the national government spends more money than it receives in taxes. As a result, the total national debt rose sharply during the 1980s, increasing from less than $1 trillion to more than $9 trillion by 2007. About 9 percent of all current budget expenditures go to paying just the *interest* on this debt.[2]

expenditures
Government spending of **revenues**. Major areas of federal spending are social services and national defense.

revenues
The financial resources of government. The individual income tax and Social Security tax are two major sources of the federal government's revenue.

The president and Congress have often been caught in a budgetary squeeze: Americans want them to balance the budget, maintain or increase the level of government spending on most policies, and keep taxes low. As a result, the president and Congress are preoccupied with budgeting, trying to cope with these contradictory demands. The distribution of the government's budget results from a very complex budgetary process. Nestled inside the tax and expenditures figures are thousands of policy choices, each prompting plenty of politics.

In this chapter you will learn how the president and Congress produce a budget, making decisions on both taxes and expenditures. In short, you will look at how government manages its money—which is, of course, really *your* money.

Why It Matters

The Progressive Income Tax
The principal source of revenue for the federal government is the income tax, which is progressive in that those with higher incomes typically pay a higher rate of taxes. What if everyone paid the same rate? Most people would probably find it unfair to pay taxes at the same rate as a millionaire. If a uniform tax rate were set at a level that everyone could afford to pay, it would have to be set very low. In this case there may not be sufficient revenues to fund critical government programs.

income tax
Shares of individual wages and corporate revenues collected by the government. The **Sixteenth Amendment** explicitly authorized Congress to levy a tax on income.

Sixteenth Amendment
The constitutional amendment adopted in 1915 that explicitly permitted Congress to levy an **income tax**.

Sources of Federal Revenue

"Taxes," said the late Supreme Court Justice Oliver Wendell Holmes Jr., "are what we pay for civilization." Despite his assertion that "I like to pay taxes," most taxpayers throughout history do not agree. The art of taxation, said Jean-Baptiste Colbert, Louis XIV's finance minister, is in "so plucking the goose as to procure the largest quantity of feathers with the least possible amount of hissing."[3] In Figure 15.1 you can see where the federal government has been getting its feathers. Only a small share comes from excise taxes (a tax levied on the manufacture, transportation, sale, or consumption of a good—for example, those on gasoline) and other sources; the three major sources of federal revenues are the personal and corporate income tax, social insurance taxes, and borrowing.

Income Tax

Millions of bleary-eyed American taxpayers struggle to the post office before midnight every April 15 to mail their income tax forms. Individuals are required to pay the government a portion of the money they earn; this portion is an **income tax**. Although the government briefly adopted an income tax during the Civil War, the first peacetime income tax was enacted in 1894. Even though the tax was only 2 percent of income earned beyond the then magnificent sum of $4,000, a lawyer opposing it called the tax the first step of a "communist march." The Supreme Court wasted little time in declaring the tax unconstitutional in *Pollock v. Farmer's Loan and Trust Co.* (1895).

In 1913, the **Sixteenth Amendment** was added to the Constitution, explicitly permitting Congress to levy an income tax. Congress was already receiving income tax revenue before the amendment was ratified, however, and the Internal Revenue Service (IRS) was established to collect it. Today the IRS receives more than 130 million individual tax returns each year. People or computers scrutinize each return. In addition, the IRS audits more than a million returns in greater detail, investigates thousands of suspected criminal violations of the tax laws, and annually prosecutes and secures the conviction of thousands of errant taxpayers or nonpayers.[4] Never a popular agency, in recent years the IRS has received substantial criticism for abusing taxpayers with its aggressive efforts to enforce the tax code. In 1998 Congress passed a law designed to rein in the IRS and make it a more consumer-oriented agency.

Corporations, like individuals, pay income taxes. Although corporate taxes once yielded more revenues than individual income taxes, this is no longer true. In 2005, corporate taxes yielded about 13 cents of every federal revenue dollar, compared with 43 cents from individual income taxes.

The income tax is generally *progressive*, meaning that those with more taxable income not only pay more taxes but also pay higher *rates* of tax on that income. As a result, the 10 percent of taxpayers with the highest incomes pay about two-thirds of all the income taxes in the country, while those in the bottom 50 percent of taxable income pay less than 4 percent of all income taxes.[5] Some people feel a progressive tax is the fairest type of taxation because those who have the most pay higher rates. Others see things differently and propose a "flat" tax, with everyone taxed at the same rate. Still others suggest that we abandon the income tax

Figure 15.1 Federal Revenues

Individual income taxes make the largest contribution to federal revenues, but more than a third comes from social insurance taxes.

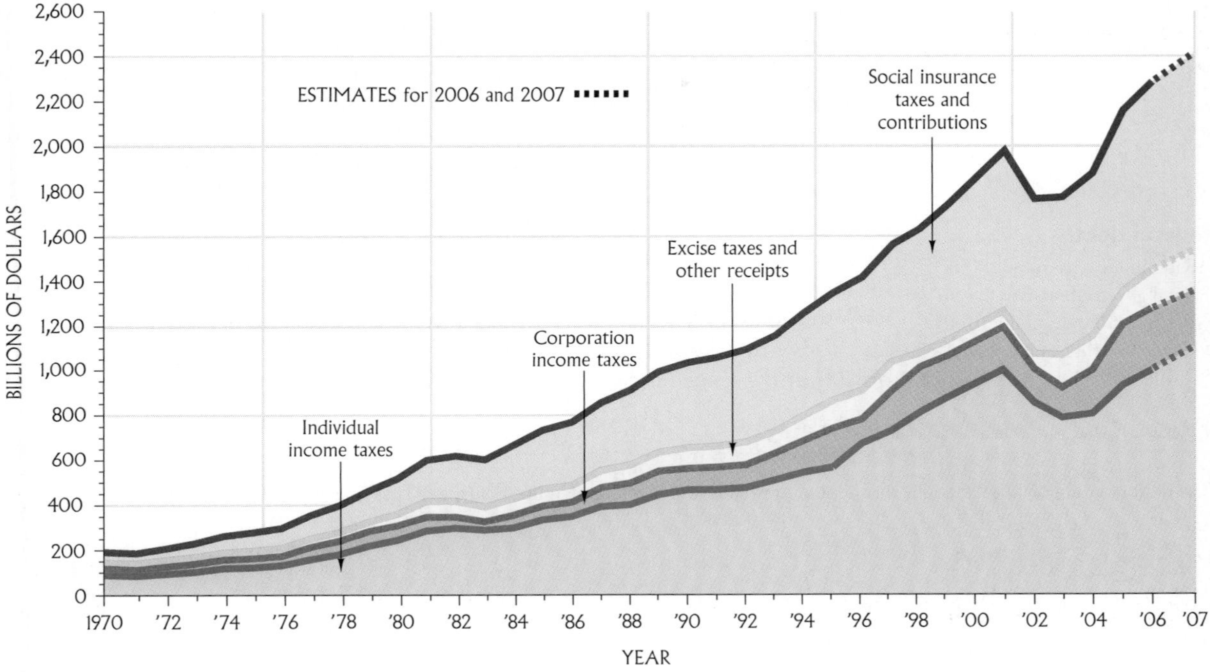

Source: Budget of the United States Government, Fiscal Year 2007: Historical Tables (Washington, DC: U.S. Government Printing Office, 2006), table 2.1.

altogether and rely on a national sales tax, much like the sales taxes in most states. As you can see, it is easy to criticize the income tax but difficult to obtain agreement on a replacement (see "Issues of the Times: Who Should Bear the Burden of Taxes?").

Social Insurance Taxes

Both employers and employees pay Social Security taxes. Money is deducted from employees' paychecks and matched by their employers. Unlike income taxes, these payments are earmarked for a specific purpose: the Social Security Trust Fund that pays benefits to the elderly, the disabled, the widowed, and the unemployed.

Social Security taxes have grown faster than any other source of federal revenue, and they will continue to grow as the population ages. In 1957, these taxes made up a mere 12 percent of federal revenues; today they account for about 37 percent. In 2007, employees and employers each paid a Social Security tax equal to 6.2 percent of the first $97,500 of earnings, and for Medicare they paid another 1.45 percent on all earnings.

Borrowing

Like families and firms, the federal government may borrow money to make ends meet. When families and firms need money, they go to their neighborhood bank, savings and loan association, or moneylender. When the federal government wants to borrow money, the Treasury Department sells bonds, guaranteeing to pay interest to the bondholder. Citizens, corporations, mutual funds, other financial institutions, and even foreign governments may purchase these bonds; there is always a lively market for government bonds. In addition, the federal government has "intragovernmental" debt on its books. This debt is what the Treasury owes various Social Security and other trust funds because the government has been using for its general purposes payroll taxes and other taxes designated to fund specific programs.

federal debt

All the money borrowed by the federal government over the years and still outstanding. Today the federal debt is more than $9 trillion.

Most government borrowing is not for its capital needs (such as a house or a factory) but for its day-to-day expenses. Most families wisely do not borrow money for their food and clothing, yet the government has largely borrowed money for its farm subsidies, its military pensions, and its aid to states and cities.

Today the **federal debt**—all the money borrowed over the years that is still outstanding—exceeds $9 *trillion* (see Figure 15.2). Nine percent of all federal

Figure 15.2 Total National Debt

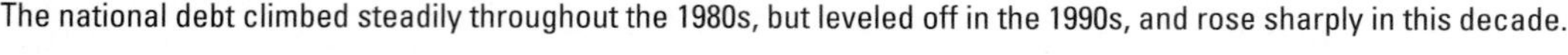

The national debt climbed steadily throughout the 1980s, but leveled off in the 1990s, and rose sharply in this decade.

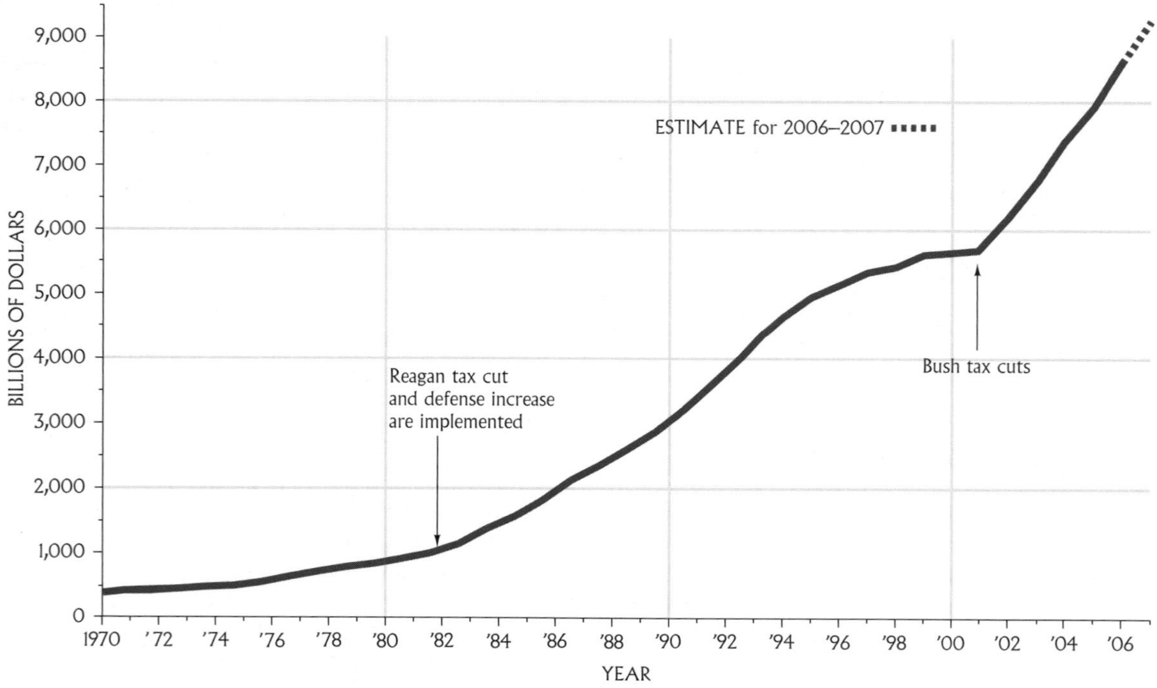

Source: Budget of the United States Government, Fiscal Year 2007: Historical Tables (Washington, DC: U.S. Government Printing Office, 2006), table 7.1.

expenditures go to paying interest on this debt rather than paying for current policies. Yesterday's consumption of public policies is at the expense of tomorrow's taxpayers because borrowing money shifts the burden of repayment to future taxpayers who will have to service the debt and pay the principal. Every dollar the government borrows today will cost taxpayers many more dollars in interest over the next 30 years. These dollars cannot be spent on health care, education, or lower taxes. Paying the interest on the debt is not optional.

Many economists and policymakers are concerned about the national debt.[6] Government borrowing may crowd out private borrowers, both individuals and businesses, from the loan marketplace. For instance, your local bank may know that you are a low-risk borrower, but it thinks the federal government is an even lower risk. Over the past 70 years a substantial percentage of all the net private savings in the country have gone to the federal government. Most economists believe that under some conditions this competition to borrow money increases interest rates and makes it more difficult for businesses to invest in capital expenditures (such as new plants and equipment) that produce economic growth. Higher interest rates also raise the costs to individuals of financing homes or purchasing with credit cards.

Deficit Spending

Large deficits also make the American government dependent on foreign investors, including other governments, to fund its debt—not a favorable position for a superpower. Foreign investors currently hold about one-fifth of the national debt.

Others say such fears are overblown and that the national debt has relatively little to do with the overall health of the U.S. economy. Our national debt, they argue, is no larger a percentage of our economy and of the total amount of money available for borrowing than in many past years. For decades a defining principle of the Republican Party was to curtail federal spending to reduce the federal deficit. In recent years, however, this philosophy has changed, and Republicans now support cutting taxes (and thus decreasing revenues), hopefully to stimulate the economy so that it produces more tax revenue in the long run. George W. Bush based his tax-cut proposals on this principle. Democrats see the issue differently, arguing that the tax cuts never replace the lost revenue and leave the country with an ever-increasing debt to service in the future.

Why It Matters

Deficit Spending

The federal government can run a deficit and borrow money to pay its current expenses. States and cities can only borrow (by issuing bonds) for long-term capital expenses such as roads and schools. If the Constitution required a balanced budget, the federal government could not borrow money to provide increased services during an economic downturn, nor could it cut taxes to stimulate the economy in such a situation.

Sometimes politicians complain that because families and businesses and even state and local governments balance their budgets, the federal government ought to be able to do the same. Such statements reflect a fundamental misunderstanding of budgeting, however. Most families do *not* balance their budgets. They use credit cards to give themselves instant loans, and they go to the bank to borrow money to purchase automobiles, boats, and, most important, homes. The mortgages on their homes are debts they owe for most of their lives.

Unlike state and local governments and private businesses, the federal government does not have a *capital budget,* a budget for expenditures on items that will serve for the long term, such as equipment, roads, and buildings. Thus, for example, when airlines purchase new airplanes or when school districts build new schools, they do not pay for them out of current income. Instead, they borrow money, often through issuing bonds. These debts do not count against the operating budget. When the federal government purchases new jets for the air force or new buildings for medical research, however, these purchases are counted as current expenditures and run up the deficit.

Despite its borrowing habits, most of the government's income still comes from taxes. Few government policies provoke more heated discussion than taxation.

Taxes and Public Policy

No government policy affects as many Americans as tax policy. In addition to raising revenues to finance its services, the government can use taxes to make citizens' incomes more nearly or less nearly equal, to encourage or discourage growth in the economy, and to promote specific interests. The following sections focus on how tax policies can promote the interests of particular groups or encourage specific activities.

Tax Loopholes. No discussion of taxes goes very far before the subject of tax loopholes comes up. Difficult to define, a *tax loophole* is presumably a tax break or tax benefit. The IRS Code, which specifies what income is subject to taxation, contains many legal exemptions, deductions, and special cases. Of course, some taxpayers benefit more from these loopholes than others. Jimmy Carter, campaigning for the presidency, called the American tax system a "national disgrace" because of its special treatment of favored taxpayers. Businesspeople, he complained, could deduct costly "three-martini lunches" as business expenses, whereas ordinary workers, carrying coffee in a Thermos and a sandwich to work, could not write off their lunch expenses.

In 1975, Texas computer magnate and 1992 and 1996 presidential candidate H. Ross Perot hired a former IRS commissioner to lobby for a change in the tax code. The proposed change would have saved Perot $15 million in taxes. The amendment passed through the House Ways and Means Committee (billionaire Perot was reported to be a generous contributor to the campaign chests of several members) but was killed on the House floor when the press reported that only Perot would benefit from the proposed provision.[7]

tax expenditures

Revenue losses that result from special exemptions, exclusions, or deductions in federal tax law.

Tax Expenditures. "Loopholes" are actually only one type of tax expenditure. The 1974 Budget Act defines **tax expenditures** as "revenue losses attributable to provisions of the federal tax laws which allow a special exemption, exclusion, or deduction." These expenditures represent the difference between what the government actually collects in taxes and what it would have collected without special exemptions. Thus tax expenditures amount to subsidies for different activities. Here are some examples:

- The government *could* send checks for billions of dollars to charities. Instead, it permits taxpayers to deduct their contributions to charities from their income. Thus, the government encourages charitable contributions.
- The government *could* give cash to families with the desire and financial means to buy a home. Instead, it permits home owners to deduct from their income the billions of dollars they collectively pay each year in mortgage interest.
- The government *could* write a check to all businesses that invest in new plants and equipment. Instead, it allows such businesses to deduct these expenses from their taxes at a more rapid rate than they deduct other expenses. In effect,

the owners of these businesses, including stockholders, get a subsidy that is unavailable to owners of other businesses.

Tax expenditures are among the most obscure aspects of a generally obscure budgetary process, partly because they receive no regular review by Congress—a great advantage for those who benefit from a tax expenditure. Few ordinary citizens seem to realize their scope; you can see the magnitude of tax expenditures in Table 15.1.

On the whole, tax expenditures benefit middle- and upper-income taxpayers and corporations. Poorer people, who tend not to own homes, can take little advantage of provisions that permit home owners to deduct mortgage interest payments. Likewise, poorer people in general can take less advantage of the exclusion of taxes on contributions to individual retirement accounts or interest on state and local bonds. Students, however, are an exception to this generalization (see "Young People and Politics: Education and the Federal Tax Code").

To some, tax expenditures such as business-related deductions, tuition tax credits, and capital gains tax rates are loopholes. To others, they are public policy choices that support a social activity worth subsidizing. Either way, they amount to the same thing: revenues that the government loses because certain items are exempted from normal taxation or are taxed at lower rates. The Office of Management and Budget

Table 15.1 Tax Expenditures: The Money Government Does Not Collect

Tax expenditures are essentially monies that government could collect but does not because they are exempted from taxation. The Office of Management and Budget estimated that the total tax expenditures in 2007 would be about $870 billion—an amount equal to more than a third of the total federal receipts. Individuals receive most of the tax expenditures, and corporations get the rest. Here are some of the largest tax expenditures and their cost to the treasury:

TAX EXPENDITURE	MAIN BENEFICIARY	COST
Exclusion of employer contributions to health care and insurance	Families	$147 billion
Deduction of mortgage interest on owner-occupied houses	Families	$80 billion
Capital gains (nonhome)	Families	$60 billion
Exclusion of individual retirement account contributions and earnings	Families	$57 billion
Exclusion of company contributions to pension funds	Families	$53 billion
Accelerated depreciation of machinery and equipment	Businesses	$52 billion
Exclusion of capital gains on home sales	Families	$49 billion
Deductions for charitable contributions	Families and businesses	$43 billion
Child credit	Families	$42 billion
Deductions for state and local taxes	Families	$40 billion
Exclusion of net imputed rental income	Businesses	$33 billion
Exclusion for interest earned on state and local government bonds	Families	$30 billion
Exclusion of Social Security benefits	Families	$28 billion
Exclusion of interest on life insurance savings	Families	$21 billion

Government could lower overall tax rates by taxing things it does not currently tax, such as Social Security benefits, pension fund contributions, charitable contributions, and the like. You can easily figure out, though, that these are not popular items to tax, and doing so would evoke strong opposition from powerful interest groups.

Source: Budget of the United States Government, Fiscal Year 2007: Analytical Perspectives (Washington, DC: U.S. Government Printing Office, 2006), tables 19.1 and 19.3.

YOUNG PEOPLE AND POLITICS

Education and the Federal Tax Code

If you think that the federal income tax is something that does not affect you much as a student, you are wrong. If you are footing the costs of higher education for yourself or your family, education tax credits can help offset these costs. On the other hand, if you think the rules for obtaining a tax credit are simple, you would also be wrong.

First, there is the Hope Credit, which applies only for the first two years of postsecondary education, such as college or vocational school. It can be worth up to $1,500 per eligible student, per year. It does not apply to graduate and professional-level programs. You are allowed 100 percent of the first $1,000 of qualified tuition and related fees paid during the tax year, plus 50 percent of the next $1,000. To receive the credit, you must be enrolled at least half time.

The Lifetime Learning Credit applies to undergraduate, graduate, and professional degree courses, including instruction to acquire or improve your job skills. If you qualify, your credit equals 20 percent of the first $10,000 of postsecondary tuition and fees you pay during the year for all eligible students, for a maximum credit of $2,000 per tax return.

The Hope Credit and the Lifetime Learning Credit are education credits you can subtract in full from your federal income tax, not just deduct from your taxable income.

Naturally, there are restrictions on claiming these credits. To qualify for either credit, you must pay postsecondary tuition and fees for yourself, your spouse, or your dependent. The credit may be claimed by the parent or the student but not by both. However, if the student was claimed as a dependent, the student cannot claim the credit. Moreover, you cannot claim both the Hope and the Lifetime Learning Credits for the same student (such as yourself) in the same year. Parents with children or attending school themselves can claim more than one Hope credit but only one Lifetime Learning Credit.

These credits are not for everyone. They are gradually reduced for those with modified adjusted gross income (MAGI) between $43,000 and $53,000 ($87,000 and $107,000 for married filing jointly) and eliminated completely for MAGI of $53,000 or more ($107,000 for married filing jointly). If a taxpayer is married, the credit may be claimed only on a joint return. In addition, the Hope Credit is not allowed for a student convicted of a felony drug offense while in school.

A taxpayer may also take a deduction for up to $4,000 of higher-education expenses, but only when opting not to use the education credits. A different deduction lets taxpayers recoup some of the cost of student loan interest. It and other deductions and credits also begin to diminish as taxpayers earn more.

Welcome to the federal tax code. As you can see, Congress has chosen to give students benefits in the tax code, but it has also been concerned that people do not abuse these benefits. Thus, even students have to face the intricacies of the federal tax code and work out the myriad tax credits and deductions that help defray the costs of a college education. In the end, however, it is worth the effort.

Questions for Discussion

- Why doesn't Congress simply appropriate money for students and send them a check instead of relying on the tax code?
- What are the obstacles to simplifying the tax code?

estimates that total tax expenditures equal more than a third of the federal government's total receipts.

Tax Reduction. The annual rite of spring—the preparation of individual tax returns—is invariably accompanied by calls for tax reform and, frequently, tax reduction. Early in his administration, President Reagan proposed a massive tax-cut bill. Standing in the way of tax cuts is never popular, and in July 1981, Congress passed Reagan's tax-cutting proposal. Over a three-year period, the federal tax bills of Americans were reduced 25 percent, corporate income taxes were also reduced, new tax incentives were provided for personal savings and corporate investment, and taxes were *indexed* to the cost of living. Indexing taxes meant that beginning in 1985, the government no longer received a larger share of income when inflation pushed incomes into higher brackets while the tax rates stayed the same. (This point is important because people with high incomes also pay a higher *percentage* of their incomes in taxes.)

Families with high incomes saved many thousands of dollars on taxes, but those at the lower end of the income ladder saw little change in their tax burden because social insurance and excise taxes (which fall disproportionately on these people) rose during the same period. Many blamed the massive deficits of the 1980s and 1990s at least partially on the 1981 tax cuts, as government continued to spend but at the same time reduced its revenues.

To deal with these deficits, in 1993 President Clinton persuaded Congress to raise the income tax rate on those in the top 2 percent of income and the top corporate income tax rate. Congress also increased a small energy tax that would be paid by all but those with low incomes.

You Are Trying to Get a Tax Cut

When budget surpluses materialized (briefly) in the late 1990s, cutting taxes was once again a popular rallying cry for some politicians, including George W. Bush. In 2001, Congress enacted a tax cut that gradually lowered tax rates over the next 10 years, and in 2003 it reduced the tax rates on capital gains and dividends. When deficits reappeared, critics charged that the president was fiscally irresponsible. The appropriate level of taxation remains one of the most vexing problems in American politics (see Figure 15.3).

Tax Reform. Gripes about taxes in America are at least as old as the Boston Tea Party. When President Reagan first revealed his massive tax simplification plan in 1985—with its proposals to eliminate many tax deductions and tax expenditures—it was met with howls of protest. The insurance industry, for example, launched a $6 million advertising campaign to save the tax deductions for fringe benefits (much of which are in the form of life and health insurance) that employers set aside for employees. A pitched battle raged between tax reformers and interest groups determined to hold on to their tax benefits.

For once, however, a tax reform plan was not derailed. Democrats were enthusiastic about tax reform. They also did not want the Republicans to get all the credit for it. In fact, the president actually had more problems obtaining the support of those in his own party and had to make an unusual trip to Capitol Hill to plead with House Republicans to support the tax bill after its initial defeat when it came to the floor.

The Senate posed an even bigger problem because the bill was loaded with special tax treatments for a wide variety of groups. While the president was on a trip abroad, the Finance Committee met behind closed doors and emerged with a bill similar in spirit to the bill supported by the president and the House. The *Tax Reform Act of 1986* was one of the most sweeping alterations in federal tax policy history. It eliminated or reduced the value of many tax deductions, removed several

Figure 15.3 How Much Is Too Much?

No one likes to pay taxes, and it is common for Americans—and citizens all over the world—to complain that taxes are too high. The figures in the accompanying graph show that the national, state, and local governments in the United States tax a smaller percentage of the resources of the country than do those in almost all other democracies with developed economies. The Scandinavian countries of Sweden and Denmark take about half the wealth of the country in taxes each year.

Comparatively, citizens in the United States have a rather light tax burden. Naturally, tax levels are related to the level of public services that governments provide. If you compare this graph with Figure 15.6, you will see that the big taxers are also the big spenders.

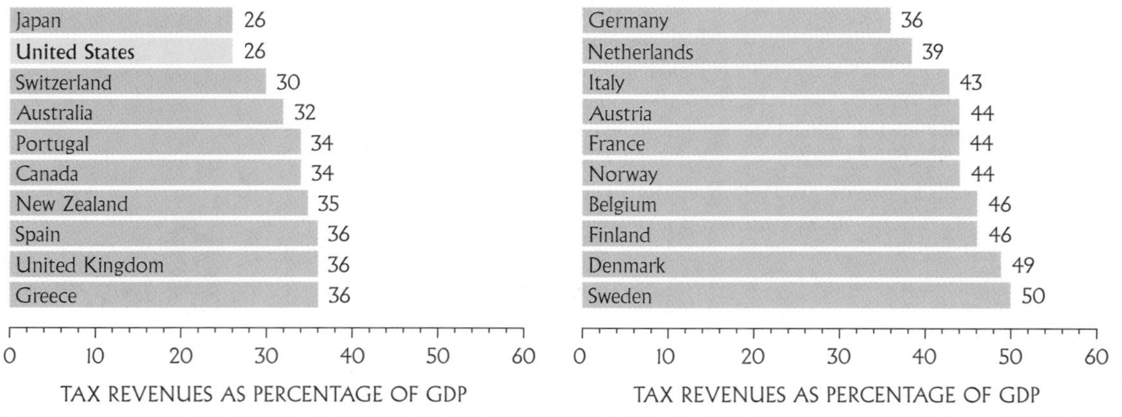

Source: Organization for Economics Cooperation and Development, 2006.

President Reagan signs the Tax Reform Act of 1986, passed with the backing of congressional leaders and administration officials. The legislation—the most wide-ranging reform of federal tax policy since the Sixteenth Amendment legalized income taxes in 1913—was implemented despite protests from numerous interest groups that did not want to lose their tax deductions.

million low-income individuals from the tax rolls, and greatly reduced the number of tax brackets (categories of income that are taxed at different rates).

Federal Expenditures

In 1932, when President Franklin D. Roosevelt took office in the midst of the Great Depression, the federal government was spending just over $3 billion a year. Today, the federal government spends that much in a single morning. Program costs once measured in the millions are now measured in billions. Comparisons over time are a little misleading, of course, because they do not account for changes in the value of the dollar. You can see in Figure 15.4 how the federal budget has grown in actual dollars.

Growth of the Budget and Federal Spending

Figure 15.4 makes two interesting points. First, the policies and programs on which the government spends money change over time. Second, expenditures keep

Figure 15.4 Federal Expenditures

The biggest category of federal expenditures is payments to individuals. National defense accounts for about one-fifth of the budget.

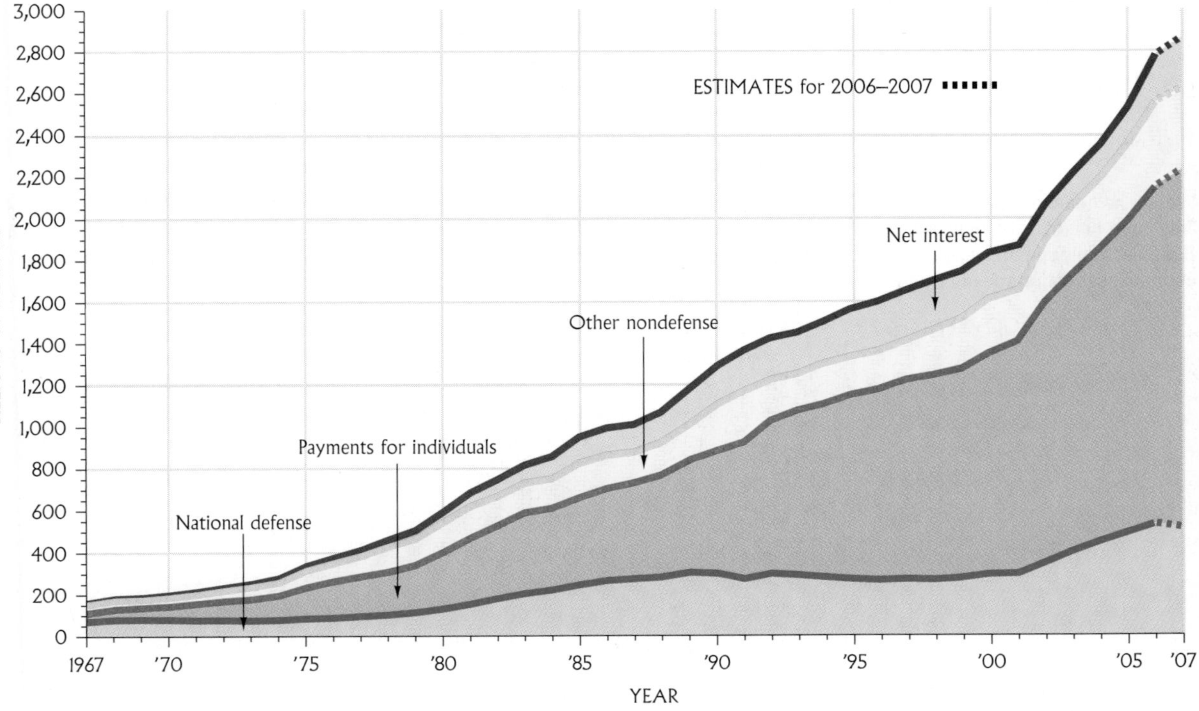

BILLIONS OF DOLLARS
3,000
2,800
2,600
2,400
2,200
2,000
1,800
1,600
1,400
1,200
1,000
800
600
400
200
0
ESTIMATES for 2006–2007
Net interest
Other nondefense
Payments for individuals
National defense
1967 '70 '75 '80 '85 '90 '95 '00 '05 '07
YEAR

Source: Budget of the United States Government, Fiscal Year 2007: Historical Tables (Washington, DC: U.S. Government Printing Office, 2006), table 6.1.

rising. The following sections explore three important questions: Why are government budgets so big? Where does the money go? and Why is it difficult to control federal expenditures?

Big Governments, Big Budgets

One answer to the question of why budgets are so large is simple: Big budgets are necessary to pay for big governments. Among the most important changes of the twentieth century is the rise of large governments.[8] Actually, as you can see in Figure 15.5, among Western nations, America has one of the *smallest* public sectors relative to the size of the economy, which is measured as the gross domestic product (GDP). Nevertheless, it is difficult to characterize the national government, with a budget of more than $2.75 trillion per year, as anything but large—some critics would say enormous.

As with other Western nations, the growth of government in the United States has been dramatic. Political scientist E. E. Schattschneider described the small beginnings of American government:

> *President Washington made his budget on a single sheet of paper. Jefferson ran his Department of Foreign Affairs with a staff of six writing clerks. . . . As late as 1822 the government spent $1,000 for the improvement of rivers and harbors and President Monroe vetoed a $9,000 appropriation for the repair of the Cumberland Road.*[9]

Figure 15.5 How Big Is Too Big?

When one hears about trillion-dollar federal budgets and budget deficits that may run $400 billion in a single year, it's easy to think of "big government." The figures in the accompanying graph, however, show that the national, state, and local governments in the United States actually spend a smaller percentage of their country's resources than those in most other democracies with developed economies. Compared with these countries, the United States has a rather modest public sector.

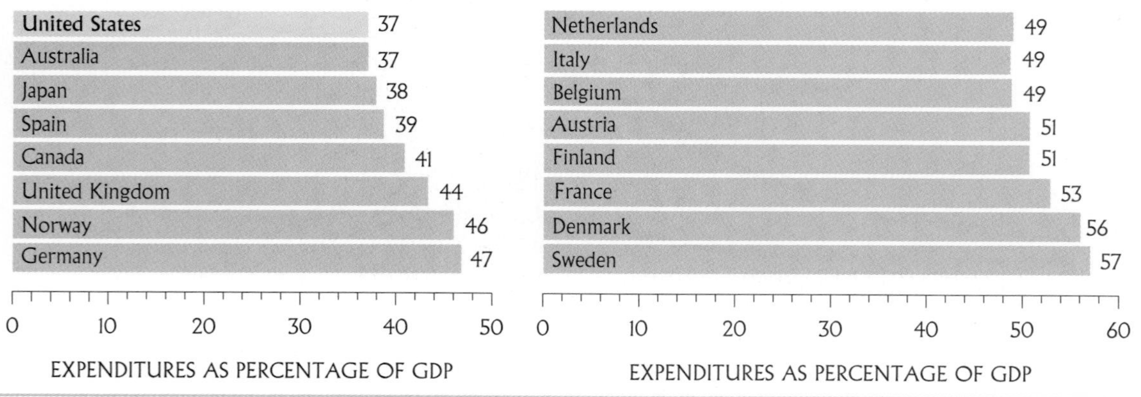

Source: Organization for Economic Cooperation and Development, 2006.

This relatively tiny government was, said Schattschneider, the "grain of mustard seed" from which today's huge government has grown. American governments—national, state, and local—spend an amount equal to one-third of the GDP. The national government's expenditures alone equal about 20 percent of the GDP.

Of course, no one knows for sure exactly why government has grown so rapidly in all the Western democracies. William Berry and David Lowery launched a major investigation into the question, but their findings were mixed. Overall, however, they found that the public sector expands principally in response to the public's preferences and changes in economic and social conditions that affect the public's level of demand for government activity.[10] This is why the rise of big government has been strongly resistant to reversal: Citizens like government services. Even Ronald Reagan, a strong leader with an antigovernment orientation, succeeded only in slowing the growth of government, not in actually trimming its size. When he left office, the federal government employed more people and spent more money than when he was inaugurated.

Two conditions associated with government growth in America are the rise of the national security state and the rise of the social service state.

The Rise and Decline of the National Security State

Forty years ago, the most expensive part of the federal budget was not its social services but its military budget. Until World War II, the United States customarily disbanded a large part of its military forces at the end of a war. After World War II, however, the Cold War with the Soviet Union resulted in a permanent military establishment and expensive military technology. Fueling the military machine greatly increased the cost of government. It was President Eisenhower—a five-star general—who coined the phrase *military industrial complex* to characterize the close relationship between the military hierarchy and the defense industry that supplies its hardware needs.

In the 1950s and early 1960s, spending for past and present wars amounted to more than half the federal budget. The Department of Defense received the majority of federal dollars. Liberals complained that government was shortchanging the poor while lining the pockets of defense contractors. Things soon changed, however. Over 15 years, from the mid-1960s to the early 1980s, defense expenditures crept downward in real dollars while social welfare expenditures more than doubled.

Although President Reagan proposed eliminating scores of domestic programs in his annual budget requests, he also urged Congress to increase the defense budget substantially. Throughout his entire second term, Congress balked, however, and in the 1990s defense expenditures decreased in response to the lessening tensions in Europe (discussed in Chapter 17). Defense expenditures increased again following the terrorist attacks on September 11, 2001, and especially with the war in Iraq. Nevertheless, the budget of the Department of Defense, once the driving force in the expansion of the federal budget, now constitutes only about one-fifth of all federal expenditures.

Payrolls and pensions for the more than 7 million persons who work for the Pentagon, serve in the reserves, or receive military retirement pay, veterans

The U.S. Air Force unveiled its new Stealth Bomber in 1989. The plane's unusual shape allows it to fly undetected by enemy radar, but such technology costs money—over $2 billion per plane. These huge expenditures contributed to substantial increases in the defense budget in the 1980s.

pensions, or disability compensation constitute a large component of the defense budget. So do the research, development, and *procurement* (purchasing) of military hardware. The costs of procurement are high, even though total military expenditures have declined as a percentage of American GDP since the end of World War II. The cost of advanced technology makes any weapon, fighter plane, or component more expensive than its predecessors. Moreover, cost overruns are common. The American fleet of Stealth Bombers cost several times the original estimate—over $2 *billion* dollars each.

Evaluating Federal Spending and Economic Policy

The Rise of the Social Service State

Social Security Act

A 1935 law passed during the Great Depression that was intended to provide a minimal level of sustenance to older Americans and thus save them from poverty.

The biggest slice of the budget pie, once reserved for defense, now belongs to *income security* expenditures, a bundle of policies extending direct and indirect aid to the elderly, the poor, and the needy. In 1935, during the Great Depression and the administration of President Franklin D. Roosevelt, Congress passed the **Social Security Act**. The act was intended to provide a minimal level of sustenance to older Americans, saving them from poverty.

In January 1940, the treasurer of the United States sent the nation's first Social Security check to Ida Fuller of Brattleboro, Vermont, in the amount of $22.54. An early entrant into the fledgling Social Security program, Fuller had contributed less than the amount of her first check to the system. By the time she died in December 1974 at the age of 100, she had collected $22,888.92 from the Social Security Administration. The typical retired worker received about $1,044 a month in 2007.

In the 1950s, disability insurance became a part of the Social Security program; thus, workers who had not retired but who were disabled could also collect benefits.

In 1965, Congress added **Medicare**, which provides both hospital and physician coverage to the elderly, to the system. Congress added an expensive prescription drug benefit to Medicare in 2003. Today, about 53 million Americans receive payments from the Social Security system each month.

Medicare
A program added to the Social Security system in 1965 that provides hospitalization insurance for the elderly and permits older Americans to purchase inexpensive coverage for doctor fees and other health expenses.

Social Security is less an insurance program than a kind of intergenerational contract. Essentially, money is taken from the working members of the population and spent on the retired members. Today, however, demographic and economic realities threaten to dilute this intergenerational relationship. In 1940, the entire Social Security system was financed with a 3 percent tax on payrolls; by 1990, the tax exceeded 15 percent. In 1945, 50 workers paid taxes to support each Social Security beneficiary. In 1990, about three workers supported each beneficiary. By the year 2025, when people born in the late 1950s will be getting their Social Security checks, only two workers will be supporting each beneficiary.

Not surprisingly, by the early 1980s the Social Security program faced a problem. As Paul Light candidly described it, "It was going broke fast."[11] And that was only the short-term problem. The aging population has added more people to the Social Security rolls annually; once there, people tend to stay on the rolls because life expectancies are increasing. Congress responded by increasing social insurance taxes so that more was coming in to the Social Security Trust Fund than was being spent. The goal was to create a surplus to help finance payments when the baby boomers retire.

In 1999, President Clinton proposed allocating much of the new budget surplus to Social Security and investing some of it in the stock market. Everyone agreed that saving Social Security was a high priority, but not everyone agreed with the president's solutions. As a result, no major changes occurred. George W. Bush faced similar resistance to his proposals for investing part of individuals' tax payments in the stock market. Nevertheless, the fiscal clock keeps ticking, and by 2018, Social Security's costs will begin to exceed its income from tax collections.

Social Security is the largest social policy of the federal government (Social Security and Medicare account for more than one-third of the federal budget).[12] However, other social service expenditures have paralleled the upward growth of income security. In health, education, job training, and many other areas, the rise of the social service state has also contributed to America's growing budget. No brief list can do justice to the range of government social programs, which provide funds for the elderly, businesses run by minority entrepreneurs, consumer education, drug rehabilitation, environmental education, food subsidies for the poor, guaranteed loans to college students, housing allowances for the poor, inspections of hospitals, and so on. Liberals often favor these programs to assist individuals and groups in society; conservatives see them as a drain on the federal treasury. In any event, they cost money—a lot of it (see Figure 15.6).

Energy Policy

The rise of the social service state and the national security state are linked with much of American governmental growth since the end of World War II. Although American social services expanded less than similar services in Western European nations, for most of the postwar period American military expenditures expanded more rapidly. Together, these factors help explain why the budget is the center of attention in American government today. Why is it so difficult to bring this increasing federal budget under control?

Figure 15.6 Trends in Social Service Spending

Social service spending has increased rapidly since the 1960s.

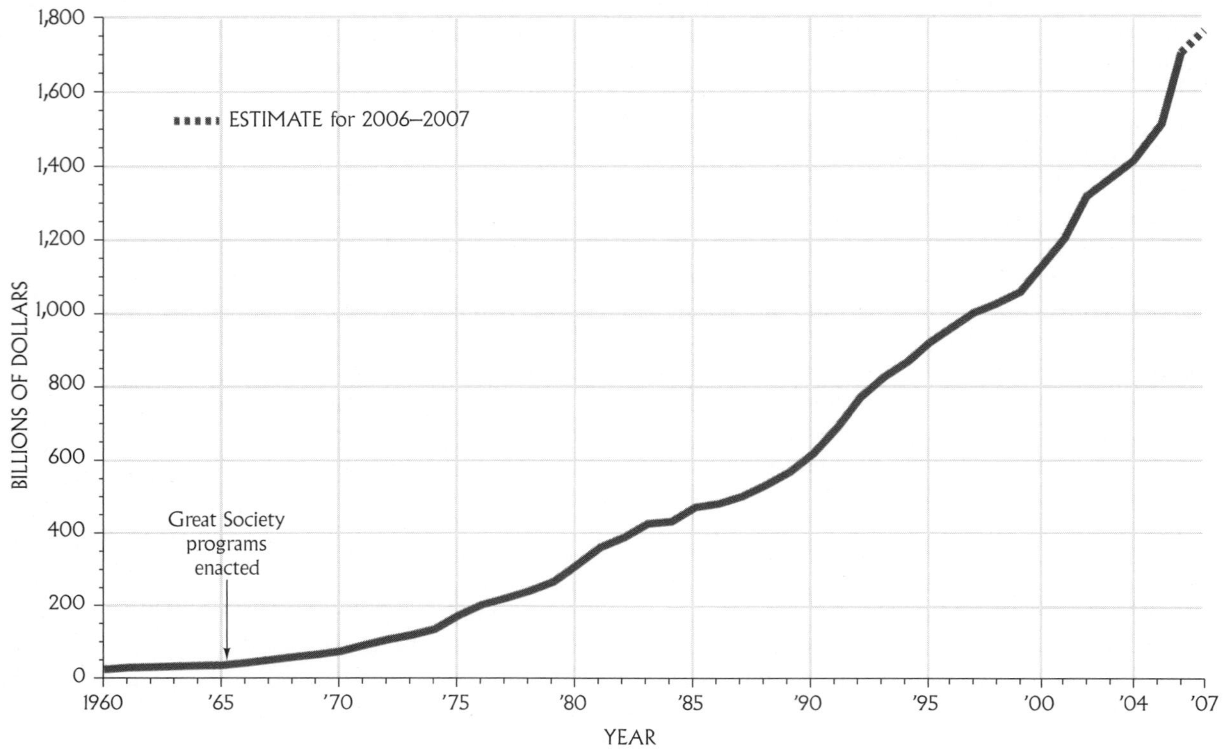

Source: Budget of the United States Government, Fiscal Year 2007: Historical Tables (Washington, DC: U.S. Government Printing Office, 2006), table 3.1.

Incrementalism

incrementalism
A description of the budgetary process where the best predictor of this year's **budget** is last year's budget plus a little bit more (an increment). According to Aaron Wildavsky, "Most of the budget is a product of previous decisions."

Sometimes political scientists use the term *incrementalism* to describe the spending and appropriations process. **Incrementalism** means simply that the best predictor of this year's budget is last year's budget plus a little bit more (an increment). According to Wildavsky and Caiden, "The largest determining factor of the size and content of this year's budget is last year's. Most of each budget is a product of previous decisions."[13] Incremental budgeting has several features:

- Very little attention is focused on the budgetary base—the amounts agencies have had over the previous years.
- Usually, agencies can safely assume they will get at least the budget they had the previous year.
- Most of the debate and most of the attention of the budgetary process are focused on the proposed increment.
- The budget for any given agency tends to grow by a little bit every year.

This picture of the federal budget is one of constant, slow growth. Expenditures mandated by an existing law or obligation (such as Social Security) are particularly likely to follow a neat pattern of increase.[14] There are exceptions, however. Paul Schulman observed that budgets for the National Aeronautics and Space Administration (NASA) were hardly incremental; they initially rose as fast as a NASA rocket but later plummeted to a fraction of their former size.[15] Incrementalism may be a general tendency of the budget, but it does not fully describe all budgetary politics. [16]

Because so much of the budgetary process looks incremental, there is a never-ending call for budgetary reform. The idea is always to make it easier to compare programs so that the "most deserving" ones can be supported and the "wasteful" ones cut. Nevertheless, the budgetary process, like all aspects of government, is affected by groups with interests in taxes and expenditures. These interests make it difficult to pare the budget. In addition, the budget is too big to review from scratch each year, even for the most systematic and conscientious members of Congress. The federal budget is a massive document, detailing annual outlays larger than the entire economies of individual countries except those of the United States, Japan, and Russia. Although efforts to check incrementalism have failed, so have attempts to reduce more rapidly rising expenses. Much of the federal budget has become "uncontrollable."

Why It Matters

"Uncontrollable" Spending

Much of the federal budget is "uncontrollable" in the sense that it does not come up for reauthorization on a regular basis. If entitlement programs were subject to annual authorizations as most other programs are, they would probably have less secure funding. We might spend less money on them and more on other services. This flexibility might please some people, especially those not receiving entitlement benefits, but those receiving Social Security and Medicare payments, for example, prefer more reliable funding.

"Uncontrollable" Expenditures

At first glance, it is hard to see how one could call the federal budget uncontrollable. After all, Congress has the constitutional authority to budget—to add or subtract money from an agency. Indeed, Presidents Reagan, Bush, and Clinton proposed and Congress adopted some proposals to cut the growth of government spending. How, then, can one speak of an uncontrollable budget?

Consider for a moment what we might call the "allowance theory" of the budget. Using this theory, a government budget works like an allowance. Mom and Dad hand Mary Jean and Tommy a monthly allowance, say $10 each, with the stern admonition, "Make that last to the end of the month because that's all we're giving you until then." In the allowance model of the budget, Congress plays this parental role; the agencies play the roles of Mary Jean and Tommy. Congress thus allocates a lump sum—say, $5.2 billion—and instructs agencies to meet their payrolls and other expenses throughout the fiscal year. When most Americans think of the government's budget, they envision the budget as a kind of allowance to the agencies.

About two-thirds of the government's budget, however, does not work this way at all. **Uncontrollable expenditures** result from policies that make some group automatically eligible for some benefit or by previous obligations of the government, such as pensions and interest on the national debt. The government does not decide each year, for example, whether it will pay the interest on the federal debt, or that it will chop the pensions earned by former military personnel in half.

uncontrollable expenditures

Expenditures that are determined not by a fixed amount of money appropriated by Congress but by how many eligible beneficiaries there are for a program or by previous obligations by the government.

Many expenditures are uncontrollable because Congress has in effect obligated itself to pay X level of benefits to Y number of recipients. Congress writes the eligibility rules; the number of people eligible and their level of guaranteed benefits

entitlements
Policies for which Congress has obligated itself to pay X level of benefits to Y number of recipients. Social Security benefits are an example.

determine how much Congress must spend. Such policies are called **entitlements**, and they range from agricultural subsidies to veterans' aid. Each year, Congress's bill is a straightforward function of the X level of benefits times the Y beneficiaries. The biggest uncontrollable expenditure of all is the Social Security system, including Medicare, which costs about a *trillion* dollars per year in 2007. The Social Security Administration does not merely provide benefits on a first-come, first-served basis until the money runs out. Instead, eligible individuals automatically receive Social Security payments. Of course, Congress can, if it desires, cut the benefits or tighten eligibility restrictions. Doing so, however, would provoke a monumental outcry from millions of elderly voters.

Balancing the Budget

In February 1998, President Clinton presented the first balanced budget in nearly 30 years. To see how this was accomplished, we must go back nearly a decade, during the tenure of George Bush. Near the end of 1990, Congress approved a major change in budgeting policy (in addition to an increase in taxes). It decided to shift its focus from controlling the size of the deficit to controlling increases in spending. Discretionary spending was divided into three categories: domestic, defense, and international. Any new spending in any of these categories had to be offset by decreases elsewhere within the category. Violations of these strictures would lead to across-the-board sequestration within the affected category. Spending for entitlement programs such as Medicare was placed on a "pay-as-you-go" basis, requiring that any expansion be paid for by a corresponding entitlement cut or revenue increase. Similarly, any tax cut was to be paid for by a compensating tax increase or entitlement cut.

President Clinton presented his first budget to Congress in 1993. After the dust cleared following a highly partisan legislative battle, the president and Congress had made a significant decrease in the deficit. There was a single cap for all discretionary spending (rather than one for each of the three components), imposing a hard freeze on appropriations, yet there was little prospect of balancing the budget in the foreseeable future.

The results of the 1994 congressional elections once again altered the budgetary game. In 1995, the new Republican majorities in each house, determined to balance the budget within seven years, argued for substantial cuts in the rate of growth of popular entitlement programs such as Medicaid and for the outright elimination of many other programs. Most Democrats strongly opposed these proposals. The president agreed with the goal of balancing the budget—but on his terms—and took his case to the voters in 1996. The outcome, as we have seen, was divided government.

In 1997, the president and Congress agreed to a budget that was to be in balance—by 2002. Each political party claimed victory, but the path to a balanced budget was eased by the booming economy, which produced more tax revenues than either side had anticipated. Indeed, the economy was so strong that the government began running surpluses. However, decreased tax revenues resulting from the economic downturn in 2000–2001 and the income tax cut of 2001 sent the budget into deficit again. Even with economic recovery, deficits persisted, partially as a

Long a goal of many elected officials, balancing the budget was aided by the booming economy that produced far more tax revenues than anticipated and the budget agreements of the 1990s that constrained spending. Here President Clinton shows how the deficit fell during his tenure.

result of decreased tax revenues and partially the result of increased spending, including spending for the war on terrorism and the occupation of Iraq. In the meantime, the budget continues as a source of conflict (see "You Are the Policymaker: Balancing the Budget").

Understanding Budgeting

Citizens and politicians alike fret about whether government is too big. In 1988, President Bush won the presidency, arguing that government had too many hands in Americans' pockets. He promised not to raise taxes to pay for more government spending. Of course, not everyone agrees that the national government is too large—even Bush backtracked on his "no new taxes" pledge by 1990 and was defeated by the more activist Bill Clinton in 1992. There is agreement on the centrality of budgeting to modern government and politics, however.

Democracy and Budgeting

Comparing Economic Policy

Almost all democracies have seen substantial growth in government in the twentieth century. One explanation for this growth is that politicians spend money to "buy" votes. They do not buy votes in the sense that a corrupt political machine pays voters to vote for its candidates; rather, policymakers spend public money on things voters will like—and will remember on Election Day. As you saw in Chapter 11, members of Congress have incentives to make government grow; they

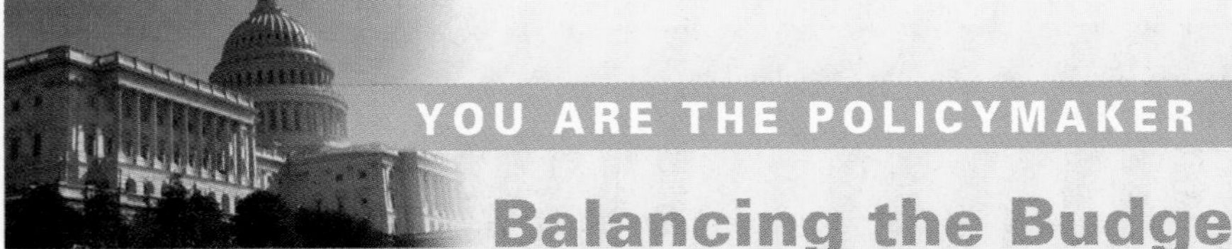

YOU ARE THE POLICYMAKER

Balancing the Budget

You have seen that the national government is running large budget deficits and that the national debt continues to grow. Here is the situation you would face as a budget decision maker: According to the OMB, in fiscal year 2007 the national government will have revenues (including Social Security taxes) of about $2,416 billion. Mandatory expenditures for domestic policy (entitlements such as Social Security and other prior obligations) total about $1,588 billion. Nondiscretionary payments on the national debt will cost another $247 billion. National defense will cost an additional $524 billion. That leaves you with just $57 billion to spend and still balance the budget. The president's proposals for discretionary domestic policy programs will take $504 billion, however. If you spend this amount, you will run a deficit of $447 billion—and you will not even have had a chance to fund any significant new programs.

What would you do? Would you drastically reduce defense expenditures? Or would you leave them alone and close down substantial portions of the rest of the government—such as programs for space and science, transportation and public works, economic subsidies and development, education and social services, health research and services, or law enforcement and other core functions of government—programs that also have broad public support? Perhaps you would show great political courage and seek a tax increase to pay for these programs.

What would *you* do?

use both constituency services and pork-barrel policies to deliver benefits to the folks back home, and government grows as a result.

Economists Allan Meltzer and Scott Richard have argued that government grows in a democracy because of the equality of suffrage. They maintain that in the private sector people's incomes are unequal, whereas in the political arena, power is much more equally distributed. Each voter has one vote. Parties must appeal to a majority of the voters. Hence, claim Meltzer and Richard, poorer voters will always use their votes to support public policies that redistribute benefits from the rich to the poor. Even if such voters cannot win in the marketplace, they can use the electoral process to their advantage.[17] Many politicians willingly cooperate with the desire of the working-class voters to expand their benefits because voters return the favor at election time. Not surprisingly, the most rapidly growing areas of expenditures are Social Security, Medicaid, Medicare, and social welfare programs, which benefit the poor more than the rich.

Many believe that elites, particularly corporate elites, oppose big government. However, Lockheed, United Air Lines, and Chrysler Corporation appealed to the government for large bailouts when times got rough. Corporations support a big government that offers them contracts, subsidies, and other benefits. A $150 billion procurement and research-and-development budget at the Department of Defense[18] benefits defense contractors, their workers, and their shareholders.

Low-income and wealthy voters alike have voted for parties and politicians who promised them benefits. When the air is foul, Americans expect government to help clean it up. When Americans get old, they expect a Social Security check. In a

HOW YOU CAN MAKE A DIFFERENCE

Federal Spending and the Pork Barrel

In 2005 Senator Ted Stevens (R, AK) earmarked $320 million in taxpayer dollars to build a bridge connecting the town of Ketchikan (population 8,900) with the Island of Gravina (population 50) so the people of Ketchikan could have easier access to Gravina's airport. Representative Allan Mollohan (D, WV) funneled $179 million in government contracts to companies that made contributions to his family-run charity. These two cases and a considerable number of others like them have prompted outrage at Congress's spending habits by Americans from all parts of the ideological spectrum.

Article I, sec. 7 of the Constitution gives the House of Representatives the sole authority to raise revenue, since the House was originally the only federal institution in which representatives were directly chosen by the people. The idea was that what representatives did with taxpayer money would be closely monitored by voters, but is this really the truth of the matter? And if not, what can you do about it?

Making a Difference

Porkbusters is one group focusing on earmarks and pork. Begun as a political weblog, Porkbusters turned into a full-fledged movement to shine a light on the federal budgetary process. The initial "blogswarm" to elected officials regarding government waste during the hurricane Katrina relief effort prompted Senator Trent Lott to exclaim "I'm getting damn tired of hearing from them . . . they have been nothing but trouble ever since Katrina."

What you can do:

- Contact your representative and senators to add your voice to the growing chorus of Americans who are beginning to demand fiscal accountability from their elected representatives (*http://www.house.gov* and *http://www.senate.gov*).
- Join one of several new watchdog movements dedicated to bringing fiscal responsibility back to the federal budgetary process, including Porkbusters (*http://www.porkbusters.org*) and Citizens Against Government Waste (*http://www.cagw.org*).
- Senator Tom Coburn (R, OK) has offered amendments to numerous spending bills to eliminate pork-laden earmarks. Look through his website to identify the earmarks that you support or reject, and contact your representatives and senators about them.
- Send an email to Senator Coburn to support or reject his call for a public database that would allow any American to easily find pork and waste in the government's budgetary process.
- Where's the pork? Visit the Citizens Against Government Waste *Congressional Pig Book* (*http://www.cagw.org*) and search for projects in your state. How did your representatives vote for these appropriations bills? Send an email to your representative expressing your support or outrage.

democracy, what people want affects what government does. Citizens are not helpless victims of big government and its big taxes; they are at least coconspirators.

Government also grows by responding to groups and their demands. The parade of political action committees is one example of groups asking government for assistance. From agricultural lobbies supporting loans to zoologists pressing for aid from the National Science Foundation, groups seek to expand their favorite part of the budget. They are aided by committees and government agencies that work to fund projects favored by supportive groups (see the discussion on iron triangles in Chapter 13).

A GENERATION OF CHANGE

Fluctuating Deficits

Annual federal deficits mushroomed during the Reagan administration (1981–1988), despite the president's oft-repeated commitment to a balanced budget. The deficit disappeared during the Clinton administration, and the nation began running a surplus in fiscal year 1998. By 2002, however, the United States was back in the red.

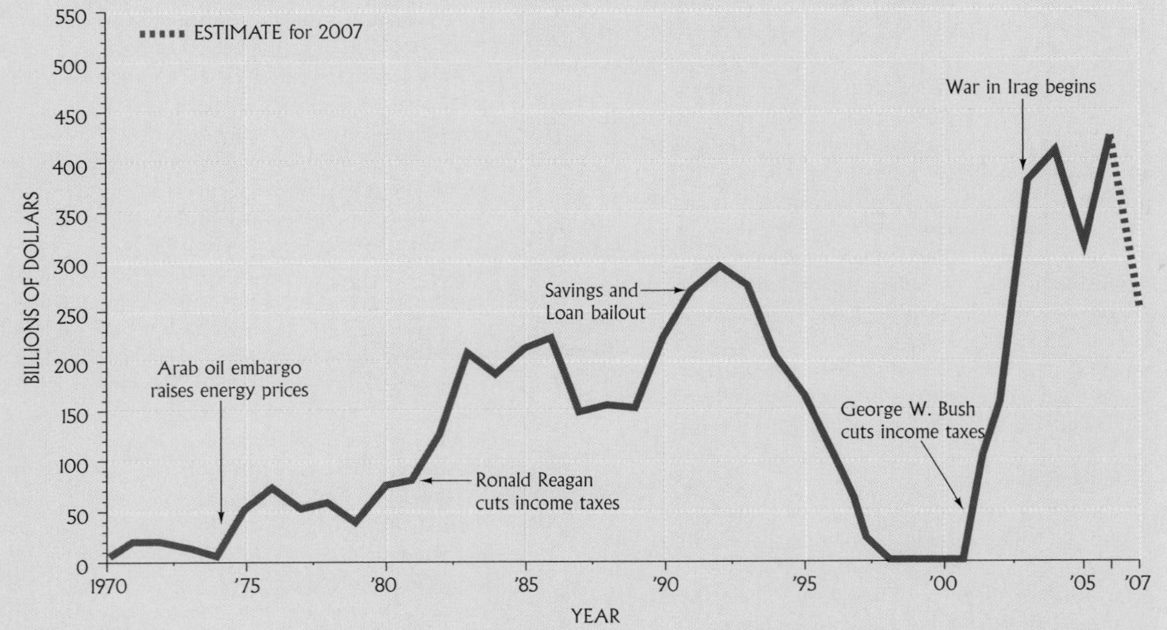

Source: Budget of the United States Government, Fiscal Year 2007: Historical Tables (Washington, DC: U.S. Government Printing Office, 2006), table 1.1. Updated by authors.

You have also seen, however, that some politicians compete for votes by promising *not* to spend money. After all, Ronald Reagan did not win election to the presidency twice by promising to raise taxes and provide more services, nor did the Republicans who took control of Congress in 1995. No country has a more open political system than the United States, but as Figures 15.3 and 15.5 demonstrate, Americans have chosen to tax less and spend less on public services than almost all other democracies with developed economies. The size of government budgets varies widely among democratic nations. Democracy may encourage government spending, but it does not compel it.

One of the most common criticisms of government is its failure to balance the budget. Public officials are often criticized for lacking the will to deal with the problem, yet it is not lack of resolve that prevents a solution to enormous budget deficits. Instead, it is a lack of consensus on policy. Americans want to spend but not pay taxes, and, being a democracy, this is exactly what the government does. The inevitable result is red ink (see "A Generation of Change: Fluctuating Deficits").

The Budget and the Scope of Government

Issues regarding the scope of government have pervaded this chapter. The reason is obvious—in many ways, the budget *is* the scope of government. The bigger the budget, the bigger the government.

The budgetary process can also limit government. One could accurately characterize policymaking in the American government since 1980 as the "politics of scarcity"—scarcity of funds, that is. Thus the budget can be a force for reining in the government as well as for expanding its role.[19] President Clinton came into office hoping to make new investments in education, worker training, and the country's physical infrastructure, such as roads and bridges. He soon found, however, that there was no money to fund new programs.

The president was reduced to speaking loudly and carrying a small budgetary stick in other policy areas as well. Because there was not enough money in the budget to pay for health care reform, he had to accept a reduced benefits package and advocate the politically difficult option of forcing employers to pay for their employees' health insurance. Welfare reform faced a similar obstacle. America's large budget deficits have been as much a constraint on government as they have been evidence of a burgeoning public sector.

Summary

When the federal government's budget consumes one-fifth of America's gross domestic product, it demands close attention. The government's biggest revenue source remains the income tax, but the Social Security tax is becoming increasingly important. Lately, much of the government's budget has been financed through borrowing. Annual deficits that sometimes exceed $400 billion have boosted the federal debt to $9 trillion in 2007.

In all Western democracies, government budgets grew during the twentieth century. In the United States, government spending also experienced significant change. Defense spending dominated the 1950s; social services spending dominated the 1990s. President Reagan, for one, wanted to reverse this trend by increasing military expenditures and cutting domestic ones. Nonetheless, much of the American budget consists of "uncontrollable" expenditures that are extremely difficult to pare. Many of these expenditures are associated with Social Security payments and with grants-in-aid.

Budget making is complex, with many actors playing many roles. The president sets the budgetary agenda, whereas Congress and its committees approve the budget itself.

Some critics believe that democracy turns politics into a bidding war for votes, increasing the size of the budget in the process. In the United States, however, many candidates campaign on *not* spending money or increasing taxes. Although larger budgets mean larger government, the budget, at least in times of substantial deficits such as those the United States experienced in the previous decade, may also serve as a constraint on further government growth.

Internet Resources

www.access.gpo.gov/eop/
The *Economic Report of the President* and the budget for the federal government.

www.irs.ustreas.gov
The Internal Revenue Service home page, containing a wealth of information about taxes.

www.whitehouse.gov/OMB/
The Office of Management and Budget home page. Clicking on the current year's budget takes you to all the current budget documents.

www.cbo.gov/
Congressional Budget Office home page, containing budgetary analyses and data.

www.taxpolicycenter.org
A joint venture of the Urban Institute and the Brookings Institution, containing many studies of budgets and taxes.

taxfoundation.org/
The Tax Foundation site with a wealth of tax information.

concordcoalition.org/
The nonpartisan Concord Coalition provides studies of budgetary issues.

Get Connected

The Budgetary Process

The process of making the federal budget is long and cumbersome. Although the Constitution gives the legislative branch the responsibility to tax and spend, the president is heavily invested in the budget process. Indeed, Congress requires the president to recommend what the federal budget should be. Its thinking was that since the executive branch was responsible for spending most of the money Congress allocated, it only made sense to ask the president to recommend a budget each year. Recommending a budget is not an easy job. Economists say that running a large deficit is bad for the economy, and so is running a large surplus. Usually, the government should spend about what it collects in taxes each year. Try putting together a budget on your own. Go to the National Budget Simulation and create a budget that reflects your values.

Search the Web

Go to the National Budget Simulation (Short Version), www.budgetsim.org/nbs/shortbudget02.html, and create your budget. Once you have made your choices, see how well you did.

Questions to Ask

- Did your budget balance, or did you have a large surplus or deficit?
- How did you make your decisions on what to change in making your budget?
- Do you think your decisions expressed conservative, liberal, or centrist values?

Why It Matters

The federal budget is more than $2.75 *trillion* (that is $2,750,000,000,000), and it is supposed to reflect the values of the nation. Because presidents recommend the annual budget to Congress, their values have a large influence on the budget.

Get Involved

How do you feel about the current federal budget? Do you think the president is recommending the right kind of budget or not? What would you change?

For more exercises, go to www.longmanamericangovernment.com.

For Further Reading

Bennett, Linda L. M., and Stephen Earl Bennett. *Living with Leviathan.* Lawrence: University Press of Kansas, 1990. Examines Americans' coming to terms with big government and their expectations of government largesse.

Berry, William D., and David Lowery. *Understanding United States Government Growth.* New York: Praeger, 1987. An empirical analysis of the causes of the growth of government in the period since World War II.

King, Ronald F. *Money, Taxes, and Politics.* New Haven, CT: Yale University Press, 1993. Explains why democratically elected officials approve tax policies that make rich people richer.

Rivlin, Alice, and Isabel Sawhill, eds. *Restoring Fiscal Sanity 2005: Meeting the Long-Run Challenge.* Washington, DC: Brookings Institution, 2005. Presents a number of reform scenarios for controlling the budget.

Rubin, Irene S. *The Politics of Public Budgeting: Getting and Spending, Borrowing and Balancing.* Washington, DC: Congressional Quarterly Press, 2006. Emphasizes how politics pervades budgetary decisions at every stage.

Schick, Allen. *The Federal Budget.* Rev. ed. Washington, DC: Brookings Institution, 2000. A useful "hands-on" view of federal budgeting.

Wildavsky, Aaron, and Naomi Caiden. *The New Politics of the Budgetary Process.* 6th ed. New York: Longman, 2007. The standard work on the budgetary process.

Chapter Outline

Social Welfare Policymaking

POLITICS IN ACTION: THE FAMILY AND SOCIAL POLICY Social policy—the topic of this chapter—is about many things. For one thing, it is about money. Our social policies represent far and away the most expensive things government funds in the United States. But social policy is also about families. Everyone knows what a family is. Or do they? What is the definition of the word "family" in America today? Is there just one definition?

Some people connect the word "family" only or mainly with marriage or with married couples with children. "Married with children" was once the norm and not just the name of a TV show. In fact, today only about 5 percent of all Americans live in the very traditional family in which dad works and mom stays home with the kids. Only 50 percent of all adults are married, and 40 percent of all mothers today have never been married. Singles will outnumber marrieds by the next census in 2010.

Yet even as the traditional family has waned, it crowds its way onto center stage of the political agenda. Politicians sometimes peddle "family values." The Republican convention that nominated President George Bush in 1988 made "family values" its theme. Later, his son President George W. Bush wanted to push marriage and spend federal funds to do so. And Americans were sharply divided about the wisdom of permitting same-sex couples to marry. People in traditional families are more likely to vote Republican; singles lean more toward Democrats.

Traditionally, families have also been among our most important economic institutions. Long before there were government programs, families had the economic responsibility for people too young or too old to work. Debates about social policy are often debates about social responsibility for dependent populations. With the rapid growth of an aged population—80- to 90-year-old Americans are the fastest-growing age-group—few families would be able to pick up financial support for their elderly relatives today. That is one reason why Social Security—a major topic of this chapter—has become the most expensive public policy in the history of the world.

Government gives lots of advantages to families—tax deductions for children, the right to share Social Security and pension benefits, and breaks on estate taxes. Even the private sector favors families. Thousands of companies, big and small, subsidize benefits for children and for spouses (to the growing annoyance of singles).

Even so, despite all the benefits that families enjoy, a lot of them still feel strapped. There were about 1.5 million individual and family bankruptcies filed in 2003. Elizabeth Warren and her daughter Amelia Warren Tyagi think they understand part of the family economic plight. Warren teaches bankruptcy courses at Harvard Law School; Tyagi is a financial consultant. In *The Two Income Trap*, they argue that more and more families these days rely on two breadwinners in large part to support schooling for their children (buying a house in the best school district even if they can barely afford it). Two incomes were once a luxury; now they have become a necessity. When a crunch comes, though, and one worker loses a job or gets ill, there is no slack in the family budget; bankruptcies are often the only alternative.[1] And these are the middle classes. David Shipler surveyed the 35 million Americans called *The Working Poor*—contrary to popular impression, most of the poor work—who are even closer to the economic margins.[2]

Social welfare policies involve the vast range of public policies that support individuals and families. The parties differ sharply on the desirable size and scope of such policies. In this chapter, we will see what the debate is about.

Americans believe strongly that people should take personal responsibility for themselves. Many are suspicious of government programs in general. Congress hammered out a major reform of public welfare in 1996 to "end welfare as we know it," in President Clinton's words. The new law was called the *Personal Responsibility and Work Opportunity Reconciliation Act* (PRWORA). While skeptical of a government "handout," Americans also believe in a "hand up." The late President Reagan, one of the most conservative of recent presidents, still favored a "safety net" of social programs, partly to signal his sympathy with poor people. President George W. Bush had a slogan about "compassionate conservatism." Even in these days of terrorism and costly wars, federal spending on social programs (about $1.6 trillion) dwarfs federal spending on the Iraq War (about $150 billion) and homeland security (about $40 billion).

Debates about social policy are debates about social responsibility. Americans believe the people are—or should be—masters of their own fate. Social policies are often called "social insurance," however, because they are intended to "insure" people against life's crises and catastrophes—serious sickness, disability, the ravages of aging, or job loss.[3] You (or you and your employer) have paid into a benefit program designed to ease the burden of aging or job loss. Social Security and unemployment compensation are social insurance programs. More than people in any other country, though, Americans believe that they are only inches away from the promise of riches. People in 44 countries were asked if they agreed that "success in life is pretty much determined by forces outside our control." Almost two-thirds of Americans—far more than in any other country—disagreed. Just after President Reagan's death, the *New York Times* looked at why Americans shared the late president's sunny optimism. Those beliefs that hard work and good luck are the most important ingredients in success help account for Americans' suspicions about social policy.[4]

What Is Social Welfare, and Why Is It So Controversial?

social welfare policies
Policies that provide benefits to individuals, either through entitlements or means testing.

Social welfare policies broadly refer to the hundreds of programs through which government provides support and assistance to specific groups of people. The Social Security check for the retired grandmother, the food stamp coupon for the poor family, the school buildings and programs, and the Medicare reimbursement for a hip replacement are but a few examples.

No public policy stimulates more argument and causes more confusion than social welfare. Here is one major confusion: Many Americans equate social welfare exclusively with government moneys given to the poor. Yet the government gives far more money to the nonpoor than to people below the poverty line. Political scientist Martin Gilens says that while "the welfare state is often associated with aid to the poor," in fact about five-sixths of all money for social programs goes to universally available benefit programs (Social Security and Medicare being the biggest examples) available to middle class and well-off Americans; only 17 percent of social spending goes to the poor. Few Americans have the slightest qualms about assisting older Americans with government programs (even though most retirees will get back in benefits many times what they put in). Handing out money to the poor may be another matter. As two political scientists put it, Americans may be humanitarians, but they are not egalitarians.[5]

entitlement programs
Government benefits that certain qualified individuals are entitled to by law, regardless of need.

Social welfare policies consist of two kinds of programs. First are the **entitlement programs** (see Chapter 14). An entitlement is any benefit provided by law and regardless of need. Entitlement programs are sometimes called "social insurance" programs because people typically pay into them and later get money back. The two biggest entitlement programs are Social Security and Medicare. You don't have to be poor to get an entitlement, nor does being rich disqualify you. Most "entitlement" programs are really social insurance—programs you (or you and your employer) contributed to in the first place. So large are federal entitlements that

HOW YOU CAN MAKE A DIFFERENCE

Faith-Based Social Welfare Policy

Since the era of the New Deal, the American polity has come to believe there is a role for the federal government in administering social welfare policy. To achieve this goal, the George W. Bush Administration introduced the controversial Faith Based and Community Initiative which will allow "faith-based community organizations" (FBCOs) to use federal funding to provide social welfare, job training, drug and alcohol rehabilitation, prisoner reentry, community outreach, etc., as an alternative to traditional social welfare and community services organizations. Proponents of the initiative believe that religiously-based social services are both more effective than traditional means and less expensive in part due to the number of volunteers who take part in service delivery. In order to ensure that these programs do not violate the principle of separation of church and state, the courts have held the programs must be narrowly tailored.

Making a Difference

Sister Ann Kendrick is the founder of the Notre Dame Mission Volunteers/Americorps program in Apopka, Florida. When Americorps announced that they were accepting faith-based groups, the Sisters of Notre Dame de Namur applied, were accepted, and started three successful programs. Today the organization boasts 20 volunteers in Apopka and 295 volunteers nationwide. They provide mentoring, tutoring, and after-school programs in poor neighborhoods. Sister Kendrick serves as the organization's co-site director. Her efforts have helped to attract a wide variety of volunteers including some who have previously benefited from the aid of the program.

What you can do:

- Contribute to organizations participating in the initiative.
- Locate FBCOs in your area by visiting the website of your state's health and human services department or agency.
- Volunteer with local church, temple, and mosque organizations. These organizations can connect you with FBCOs.

they cost $3 billion a day and leave just one-sixth of the federal budget for everything else the federal government does—fight a war in Iraq, protect the nation's borders, issue passports, aid cancer research, and so forth. While we tend to sneer at "pork-barrel" projects from members of Congress, they total by one estimate only $27.3 billion. Eliminating every one of them would save a hundredth of the federal budget dollar. The 2006 *increase* in entitlement spending is $93 billion.[6]

Means-tested programs, on the other hand, provide benefits selectively only to people with specific needs. To be eligible for means-tested programs, people have to prove that they qualify for them. Entitlement programs are rarely controversial in America. They are often overwhelmingly popular (perhaps because everyone is *entitled* to them). Means-tested programs, though, generate powerful political controversy. Much of that conflict has to do with how people see the poor and the causes of poverty. People who see the poor as mostly shiftless and irresponsible are hostile to what they see as "government handouts" to the poor. If people see poverty

means-tested programs
Government programs available only to individuals below a poverty line.

Why It Matters

Views of the Poor

Our views of the poor are likely to affect our views about the best policies for government. Americans have often distinguished between the "deserving" and the "undeserving" poor. The deserving poor are poor because of circumstances beyond their control. The undeserving poor are depicted as lazy, unwilling to work, and living off welfare benefits. These "pictures of the poor" shape our views of public policy toward the poor. Portrayals of the poor as "welfare queens" added fuel to the movement for welfare reform in 1996.

as largely beyond people's control, they are much more sympathetic to governmental assistance. Thus Americans have often distinguished between the "deserving poor" and the "undeserving poor." The deserving poor are victims of things they are not responsible for: the loss of the breadwinner, disabilities, or poor economic opportunities. The undeserving poor have presumably created their own problems and do not warrant government's help. With respect to helping the poor, "throughout the twentieth century, U.S. welfare policy was caught between two competing values: the desire to help those who could not help themselves, and the concern that charity would create dependency."[7]

Let's look, therefore, at who's rich, who's poor, who's in between—and what public policy has to do with income.

Income, Poverty, and Public Policy

Americans are a rich people. Only a handful of nations have higher per capita incomes than the United States, but most other countries have—by our standards—staggering costs of living and staggering tax rates, too. When we factor in purchasing power, only tiny Luxembourg ranks ahead of the United States. The Federal Reserve Board reported that in 2004 the median American household income was $43,200—that is, half of American households made more, and half made less than this amount. However, no industrialized country has wider extremes of income than the United States. Timothy Smeeding, the dean of American poverty researchers, says that "over the last four decades, the United States has seen large increases in income inequality. In this, it is not unique; many developed countries have experienced at least modest increases in the inequality of . . . income, but none so sustained as the United States."[8] Income is important to politics, just as it is important to people. McCarty, Poole, and Rosenthal argue that American politics is becoming more polarized and that the main "conflict is basically over income redistribution."[9] Liberals and conservatives are divided about many things, but "who gets what" is a major battleground.

Who's Getting What?

The novelist F. Scott Fitzgerald once wrote to his friend Ernest Hemingway, "The rich are different from you and me." "Yes," replied Hemingway, "they have more money." In fact, the distribution of income across segments of the American population is quite uneven. The concept of **income distribution** describes the share of national income earned by various groups in the United States. You can see in Table 16.1 how income distribution has changed in recent decades. During the 1960s and 1970s, the distribution of income was rather constant. The 1980s and 1990s, however, proved the old adage true: The rich get richer, and the poor get poorer.[10]

income distribution
The "shares" of the national income earned by various groups.

income
The amount of funds collected between any two points in time.

wealth
The value of assets owned.

Although the words *income* and *wealth* might seem similar, they are not the same thing. **Income** is the amount of money collected between any two points in time; **wealth** is the value of one's assets, including stocks, bonds, bank accounts, cars,

Table 16.1 Who Gets What? Income Shares of American Households

The following table demonstrates how much of the nation's income is received by people within each quintile (or fifth) of the population. In other words, the 3.4 percent in 2004 means that people whose income placed them in the lowest 20 percent received just 3.4 percent of the nation's income in that year, while the highest fifth got just half of the nation's income. The rich are getting richer and the poor poorer. What accounts for the growing divide between rich and poor?

INCOME QUINTILE	1960	1970	1980	1990	2004
Lowest fifth	4.9	5.5	5.1	4.6	3.4
Second fifth	11.8	12.0	11.6	10.8	8.8
Third fifth	17.6	17.4	17.5	16.6	14.8
Fourth fifth	23.6	23.5	24.3	23.8	23.0
Highest fifth	42.0	41.6	41.6	44.3	50.0

Source: U.S. Census Bureau, "Current Population Survey, 2004 and 2005 Annual Social and Economic Supplements."

houses, and so forth. Studies of wealth show even more inequality than those of income: one-third of America's wealth is held by the wealthiest 1 percent of the population, about one-third is held by the next 9 percent, and about one-third is held by the other 90 percent. For most people in the lower half of the wealth distribution, the value of their house constitutes 60 percent of their wealth.[11] *Forbes* magazine fancies itself the chronicler of the very rich and publishes an annual list of the 400 richest people in the world. In 2005, Bill Gates, Microsoft's founder, still held his edge, with a wealth of $51 billion, followed closely by Omaha investor Warren Buffett with $40 billion. Five Wal-Mart heirs, though, constituted half the top 10, with a combined wealth of $100 billion, more than Gates and Buffett put together.[12] Former British welfare mother and Harry Potter author J. K. Rowling made *Forbes*' latest list with $3 billion, making her the 128th richest person in the world.

There are a couple of hundred billionaires but a couple of million millionaires. Broker Merrill Lynch compiles an annual "World Wealth Report." It reported in 2005 that there were 8 million millionaires in the world and that their wealth had increased to a healthy $30 trillion, an 8 percent growth over the past year. These are people whose net wealth is at least $1 million, excluding real estate.[13] Americans see chief executive officers of large corporations making millions, of course, but we pay our celebrities well, too. Oprah is worth, *Forbes* says, $1.3 billion, ranking her in the top 200 richest people in the world. Even the average New York Yankee makes $4.6 million. At the other end of the income scale are the poor in America.

Who's Poor in America?

The searing images of Hurricane Katrina's victims on rooftops reminded Americans of the reality of poverty. Yet it also reinforced some stereotypes of poverty, too. TV images showed African Americans as the biggest poverty class (Whites outnumber Blacks in poverty); TV showed poverty as mostly a big-city problem (our poorest counties are in midwestern rural areas).

Few events in recent American history highlighted the gap between well-off and poor more than the 2005 Hurricane Katrina, which hit New Orleans and its suburbs. Countless pictures from New Orleans reinforced the popular image that poverty is mainly a problem for African Americans. It did, though, dramatize the realities of contemporary American poverty.

poverty line

A method used to count the number of poor people, it considers what a family must spend for an "austere" standard of living.

To count the poor, the U.S. Bureau of the Census has established the **poverty line**, which takes into account what a family must spend to maintain an "austere" standard of living. This official statistic was designed by Mollie Orshansky during the 1960s. For 2003, the Census Bureau defined a family of three as falling below the poverty level if it had an annual income below $14,824. Officially, 37 million Americans, about 12.7 percent of the population, were poor in 2003.

Estimates vary, but most experts believe that around 1 million Americans—like this man across the street from the White House—are homeless. Cuts to government programs that funded low-income housing and unemployment benefits, in addition to the deinstitutionalization of the mentally ill, forced thousands of people out into the streets during the 1980s.

The official poverty counts tend to *underestimate* the seriousness of poverty in America because it is a snapshot and not a moving picture. A count of the poor for one year can conceal millions who drop into and out of poverty. Divorce, the loss of a breadwinner, job setbacks, and the addition of a new mouth to feed can precipitate the fall below the poverty line. Rank and Hirschl looked at the overall incomes of Americans during their working lifetimes. An impressive 50.4 percent of all working Americans experienced at least a year of poverty during their lifetimes.[14]

Journalist Barbara Ehrenreich chronicled the life of millions of these "near poor" in America.[15] She took a string of low-wage jobs—working at lower-end retail stores and doing janitorial work, for example—and pieced together a meager living. Even during her short stint as a near-poor person, she was lucky: She never got sick or had to work below the minimum wage, and she had no children to feed, house, and clothe. She also had a real life to go back to. Contrary to popular impression, most of the poor work. They often have low-wage jobs, however, which still leave them poor and often without health insurance.[16]

Who's officially poor? Although the poor are a varied group, poverty is more common among some groups—African Americans, Hispanics, unmarried women, and inner-city residents—than among others. Race and ethnicity are major factors. Figure 16.1 reports the characteristics of persons in America living below the poverty line by race and ethnicity over three decades. African Americans and Hispanic Americans have a little better than a 1-in-5 chance of being in poverty. The group the Census Bureau calls "White Nonhispanic" has a less than 10 percent chance.

We began our discussion of social policy by focusing on the family. Families have a lot to do with poverty. Once poverty claimed the elderly as its main victims.

Figure 16.1 Poverty Rates by Race and Hispanic Origin: 1959–2004

Ever since the federal government started measuring the poverty rate (about 1960), poverty rates for some groups have been consistently higher than for others. African American and Hispanic groups consistently have had higher rates of poverty. In this graph, you can trace the changes in the poverty rates of groups over the past few decades.

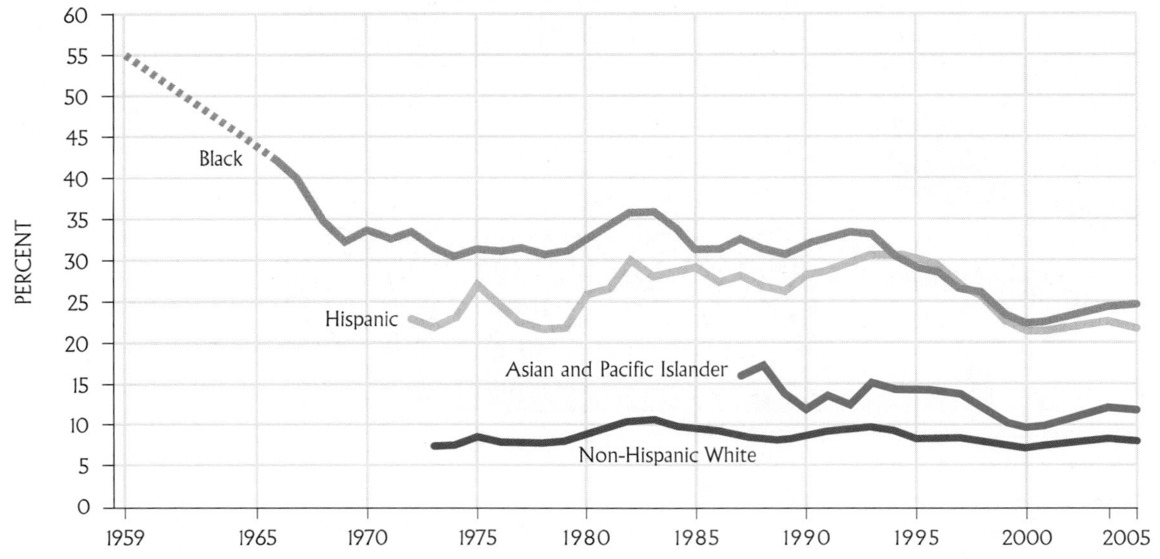

Source: U.S. Census Bureau, *Income, Poverty and Health Insurance Coverage in the United States: 2004,* August 29, 2006.

Note: The data points represent the midpoints of the respective years. Data for African Americans are not available from 1960 to 1965. Data for the other race and Hispanic origin groups are shown from the first year available. Hispanics may be of any race.

feminization of poverty
The increasing concentration of poverty among women, especially unmarried women and their children.

Now it mostly claims women and children. When Social Security was created in 1935, poverty was largely—not entirely—a problem for older Americans. For decades, the constant expansion of the Social Security system and the increase in its benefits have significantly reduced poverty among the elderly. Today, however, unmarried women and their children now greatly outnumber the elderly among the ranks of the poor. Poverty scholar Harrell Rodgers titled his study of contemporary poverty *Poor Women, Poor Children.*[17] Because of the high incidence of poverty among unmarried mothers and their children, experts on poverty often describe the problem today as the **feminization of poverty**. Female-headed families run almost a 30 percent chance of poverty, while families with two parents around have less than a 6 percent poverty rate. Having children out of wedlock, Rodgers says, is the "superhighway to poverty."[18] The unwed mother collecting welfare checks is among the most negative of all images of the poor. "Despite two decades of heated ideological controversy," Christopher Jencks says, "we don't know how much a father's absence (or a stepfather's presence) affects a child's social or emotional development. We do know, however, that not having a man in the house has serious economic consequences."[19]

Poverty cuts across all racial and ethnic groups, but is concentrated particularly among single mothers and their children.

What Part Does Government Play?

When government spends a third of our gross domestic product, it is bound to have an effect on income. Actually, politicians almost never directly debate about income distribution in America. Income distribution is hiding way off the political agenda. No party platform is likely to proclaim, "If elected, we will make the rich richer and the poor poorer." Nor will one claim, "When we are elected, we will take from the rich in order to end poverty." There are two important ways in which government does indeed affect people's incomes. One is through its taxes; the other is through its expenditures.

progressive tax
A tax by which the government takes a greater share of the **income** of the rich than of the poor—for example, when a rich family pays 50 percent of its income in taxes, and a poor family pays 5 percent.

proportional tax
A tax by which the government takes the same share of income from everyone, rich and poor alike—for example, when both a rich family and a poor family pay 20 percent.

regressive tax
A tax in which the burden falls relatively more heavily on low-income groups than on wealthy taxpayers. The opposite of a **progressive tax**, in which tax rates increase as income increases.

Taxation. "Nothing," said Benjamin Franklin, "is certain in life but death and taxes." Taxes at least became a little lower in the summer of 2001, when Congress passed President Bush's number one policy proposal, a 10-year, $1.35 trillion (that's trillion with a "t") federal income tax cut. Tax cuts are a mantra of the modern Republican Party.

There are three general types of taxes, and each can affect citizens' incomes in a different way. A **progressive tax** takes a bigger bite from the incomes of the rich than from those of the poor; an example is charging millionaires 50 percent of their income and the poor 5 percent of theirs. Second, a **proportional tax** takes the same percentage from everyone, rich and poor alike. And finally, a **regressive tax** takes a higher percentage from those at lower income levels than from the well-to-do.

A tax is rarely advocated or defended because it is regressive, but some taxes do take a bigger bite from the poor than they do the rich. Chief among these is the sales tax from which many states derive more than half their revenues. A sales tax looks proportional—6 percent of every purchase, for example, is taxed. However, since poor families spend more of their income on the necessities subject to the tax—food, clothing, and school supplies, for example—they wind up paying a higher percent of their incomes in taxes than do the rich.

In general—and even after the Bush tax cuts—federal taxes are progressive (you only have to look at the rates on your tax forms to see this). The rich send a bigger proportion of their incomes to Washington than the poor. How government helps well-off people—in contrast to poorer people—is through tax expenditures (see Chapter 14). The federal government spends about $18 billion in food stamps for the poor. By contrast, it permits individuals to deduct about $68 billion for employer-sponsored pension plans; another $67 billion is written off as interest on home mortgage interest. Few of the working poor—the folks Barbara Ehrenreich worked with, for example—can take advantage of employer pension plans or home ownership tax breaks, for example. Overall, of the $800 billion in tax breaks, people making less than $50,000 got only 15 percent of them.[20]

Earned Income Tax Credit

A "negative income tax" that provides income to very poor individuals in lieu of charging them federal income taxes.

In fact, if you are poor enough, you can get money back from the government in lieu of paying income tax. Through the **Earned Income Tax Credit** (EITC), the working poor receive a check from Washington instead of sending one. The EITC is a special tax benefit for working people who earn low incomes. In 2005, workers who were raising one child in their home and had family incomes of less than $31,030 could get an EITC of up to $2,700. The Brookings Institution estimates that the EITC puts as much as $20 billion a year into the hands of poor and near-poor families.[21]

Government Expenditures. The second way government can affect personal income is through the expenditure side of the ledger. Each year millions of government checks are mailed from federal computers to Social Security beneficiaries, retired government employees, veterans, and others. The government also provides "in-kind" benefits, something with cash value that is not cash itself, such as food stamps. About 19 million people got food stamps in 2002 (down from a high of 28.9 million in 1994). A low-interest loan for a college education is another in-kind benefit. The federal Children's Health Insurance Program—CHIP—subsidizes health care insurance for poor families with children. Together these benefits are called **transfer payments**; they transfer money from the federal treasury to individuals.

transfer payments

Benefits given by the government directly to individuals. Transfer payments may be either cash transfers, such as Social Security payments and retirement payments to former government employees, or in-kind transfers, such as food stamps and low-interest loans for college education.

Table 16.2 summarizes the major government social welfare programs that affect our incomes. Social Security and Medicare are the two major entitlement programs. They are also the most costly social welfare programs. Unemployment payments also count as entitlement programs. Companies and their employees pay into these social insurance programs to provide income in case of job loss. The other programs are means tested and are available only to the poor or the very poor.

Helping the Poor? Social Policy and Poverty

"Welfare" as We Knew It

For centuries, societies considered family welfare a private concern. Children were to be nurtured by their parents and, in turn, later nurture them in their old age. When children cast off their parents or when parents let their children go hungry,

Table 16.2 The Major Social Welfare Programs

PROGRAM	DESCRIPTION	BENEFICIARIES	FUNDING
Entitlement Programs—"Social Insurance"			
Social Security	Monthly payments	Retired or disabled people and surviving members of their families	Payroll tax on employees and employers
Medicare (Part A)	Partial payment of cost of hospital care	Retired and disabled people	Payroll taxes on employees and employers
Medicare (Part B)	Voluntary program of medical insurance (pays physicians)	Persons 65 or over and disabled Social Security beneficiaries	Beneficiaries pay premiums
Unemployment Insurance (UI)	Weekly payments; benefits vary by state	Workers who have been laid off and cannot find work	Taxes on employers; states determine benefits
The Means-Tested Programs			
Medicaid	Medical and hospital aid	The very poor	Federal grants to state health programs
Food stamps	Coupons that can be used to buy food	People whose income falls below a certain level	General federal revenues
Temporary Assistance for Needy Families (TANF)	Payment	Families with children, either one-parent families or, in some states, two-parent families where the breadwinner is unemployed	Paid partly by for states and partly by the federal government
Supplementary Security Income (SSI)	Cash payments	Elderly, blind, or disabled people whose income is below a certain amount	General federal revenues
Children's Health Insurance Program (CHIP)	Subsidies for insurance	Poor families with children	Federal and state revenues

significant social pressure was often enough to make people accept their proper family responsibilities. Governments took little responsibility for feeding and clothing the poor or anyone else. The life of the poor in America and elsewhere was grim almost beyond our imagining. In England, governments passed Poor Laws intended, historians argue, to make the life of the poor so miserable that people would do almost anything to avoid the specter, disgrace, and agony of poverty.[22] It was scarcely better in the United States.

The **Social Security Act of 1935**—the same one that created our vast entitlement program for the aged—also created a national program to assist the poor—or some of the poor. The program brought together scattered, uneven state programs

Social Security Act of 1935
Created both the Social Security Program and a national assistance program for poor children, usually called AFDC.

under a single federal umbrella. It was first called "aid to dependent children," then in 1959 "AFDC," Aid to Families with Dependent Children. The federal government established some uniform standards for the states and subsidized their efforts to help children in families with no breadwinner. However, states were free to give generous or skimpy benefits, and payments ranged widely. For the first quarter century of the program, enrollments remained small. In 1960 only 1.7 percent of all U.S. families received welfare and those typically for short periods of time. The civil rights movement of the 1960s and the succession of Lyndon Johnson to the presidency in 1963 combined to boost federal and state support for AFDC and other means-tested programs. Johnson declared a national "War on Poverty" in 1964, adding food stamps and other programs to the arsenal of poverty-fighting policies. These programs—collectively called "welfare"—came to bitterly divide Republicans from Democrats and conservatives from liberals.

The Evolution of Social Welfare Policy

If Lyndon Johnson had declared war on poverty, the late President Ronald Reagan declared war on antipoverty programs. In 1981, he persuaded Congress to cut welfare benefits, lower the number of Americans on welfare rolls, and cut benefits for many beneficiaries. Conservatives during Reagan's time—and many liberals agreed—convinced many policymakers that welfare was a failure. Conservative economist Charles Murray has offered an influential and provocative argument that the social welfare programs of the Great Society and later administrations not only failed to curb the advance of poverty but also actually made the situation worse.[23] The problem, Murray maintained, was that these public policies discouraged the poor from solving their problems. He contended that the programs made it profitable to be poor and discouraged people from pursuing means by which they could rise out of poverty. For example, Murray pointed out that poor couples could obtain more benefits if they weren't married; thus, most would not marry, a decision that leads to further disintegration of the family. Not all poverty scholars agreed. They mattered little, though, as press and politics came to shape America's condemnation of welfare. No public policy had a worse public perception than welfare. "Deadbeat dads" who ran out on their families, leaving them on welfare, and images of "welfare queens" who collected money they didn't deserve coexisted as media and popular images of a broken system.

No one could be clearer or blunter about why Americans hate welfare than political scientist Martin Gilens.[24] He found that Americans tend to see welfare recipients (wrongly) as overwhelmingly African American. Whites' welfare attitudes were strongly influenced by whether they viewed African Americans as lazy or not.[25] Negative views of African American welfare mothers were more politically potent and generated greater opposition to welfare than comparative views of White welfare mothers. The media was a major culprit here. Gilens counted magazine and newspaper stories about poor people over several decades. About a third of all welfare recipients have been African American, but the media portrayed approximately three-quarters of poor people as African American.[26] Attitudes toward welfare became "race coded." It was not a far jump to the conclusion that lots of the "undeserving poor" were on welfare. The stage for a major welfare reform was set with the 1992 presidential election. Bill Clinton, a centrist Democratic president, and the new Republican congressional majority after 1994 were gunning for the welfare system.

Ending Welfare as We Knew It: The Welfare Reforms of 1996

Bill Clinton was determined to be a "centrist" president, fearing the "tax and spend" label Republicans so eagerly applied to liberal Democrats. In the 1992 presidential election campaign, Bill Clinton promised to "end welfare as we know it" by providing two years of support—training, child care, and health care—in exchange for an agreement to return to work. The congressional Republican Party was even more enthusiastic about welfare reform than the new president. In 1995, Newt Gingrich, the new Republican Speaker of the House, launched new war-on-poverty programs. In August 1996 the president and the congressional Republicans completed a welfare reform bill that received almost unanimous backing among congressional Republicans but that was opposed by half of congressional Democrats. The law bore the lofty name of the **Personal Responsibility and Work Opportunity Reconciliation Act** (PRWORA). The major provisions of this bill were that (1) each state would receive a *fixed* amount of money to run its own welfare programs, (2) people on welfare would have to find work within two years or lose all their benefits, and (3) a lifetime maximum of five years on welfare was set.

Making a Difference: Welfare Reform

Personal Responsibility and Work Opportunity Reconciliation Act
The official name of the welfare reform law of 1996.

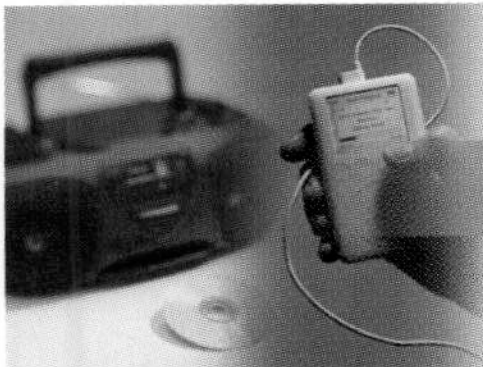

A GENERATION OF CHANGE

Declining Support for the Poor

In 2006, the United States marked the tenth anniversary of "welfare reform," the controversial law known officially as the Personal Responsibility and Work Opportunity Resolution Act of 1996. A Republican Congress, determined to reduce federal spending on the poor, sent it to a Democratic president, determined to prove that he was a "centrist" Democrat and not a "tax and spend Democrat." President Bill Clinton signed the law, fulfilling a campaign promise to "end welfare as we know it."

The name was complex and so was the law. It was intended to reduce the number of people on "welfare" and reduce government expenditures on the poor. "AFDC" was replaced by "TANF." The machinery was complex. Each state had to come up with its own plan. Many states sought or found exemptions in the PRWORA. Still, the results over a decade were breathtaking. People on welfare left the welfare rolls by the millions.

Sometimes policy change is slow or creaky. Not so "welfare reform." Here are some figures on the percent of poor Americans receiving cash assistance under AFDC or TANF when the law was passed and just a few years later:

1996	34.6%
1997	30.7%
1998	25.3%
1999	21.9%
2000	18.8%
2001	16.5%
2002	15.3%

Those figures are likely to drop even further as states purge their welfare rolls of more and more poor Americans.

The percent of Americans who are poor hasn't budged much since the PRWORA, but the percent of poor people getting federal and state financial assistance has taken a nosedive.

YOU ARE THE POLICYMAKER

Should the Government Promote Marriage?

Fifty years ago, only 4 percent of all babies were born to unmarried women; today about 33 percent are. Marriage rates are on the decline in the United States, partly because people are simply getting married later than they used to. But in the face of such changes, "family values" is a familiar refrain of politicians. The federal government even passed what is called the "Defense of Marriage Act," although it was sponsored by a twice-divorced member of Congress (it was designed to prevent gay marriages by permitting states not to recognize other states' marriages). Social scientists are nearly unanimous in showing that marriage is associated with ("associated with" is not the same thing as "caused by") substantial benefits for the partners as well as the children. Children from two-parent homes have fewer behavior problems, do better in school, and are less likely to be poor. A survey of high school seniors reports that 82 percent of girls and 73 percent of boys think it is "extremely important" to have a good marriage.

But should the government promote marriage? Oklahoma—which, despite its reputation as the "buckle of the Bible Belt," has one of the nation's highest divorce rates—uses some of its Temporary Assistance for Needy Families (TANF) funds to support workshops on marriage. A third of Oklahoma adults are divorced, compared to a fifth of all Americans. West Virginia actually gives its TANF recipients a $100 a month bonus for being married. As a part of the renewal of the welfare reform legislation in 2004, President Bush proposed spending $1.5 billion to promote marriage. Realistically, in a $2.4 trillion budget, the amount was miniscule. Still, the president argued, we should be willing to spend this for a series of demonstration projects around the country to see what worked to get and keep people married. His critics thought this was little more than a campaign initiative to please religious conservatives. Theodoro Ooms worried that "the conflict mostly isn't about research, however, but about values." She feared that it might stigmatize single parents, "many of whom do a terrific job under difficult circumstances." Unfortunately for the program, too, the Bush administration ended up paying one influential columnist, Maggie Gallagher, a $21,000 consulting fee for touting the program, a fact uncovered only much later.

One of the purposes of government is to support public goals. Liberals and conservatives alike favor government policies to reduce pollution, encourage savings, and even support home ownership. The federal government lets people deduct about $70 billion from their income tax bill for the interest on their mortgage payments. The justification: Home ownership is a valued public goal. What is so different about marriage? Couldn't government spend a bit to see if marriage can be improved? Or should government stay neutral about marriage? Or does the issue carry so much political baggage—gay marriage, for example—that marriage policy is too controversial to consider?

Sources: For information about marriage attitudes, including the survey reported here and other data, see the 2003 *State of Our Unions* report from the Rutgers University National Marriage Project, available at their Web site. See also Linda Waite and Maggie Gallagher, *The Case for Marriage: Why Married People Are Happier, Healthier and Better Off Financially* (New York: Doubleday, 2000). The Ooms quotation is from her article "Marriage Plus," *American Prospect*, April 2002. On the Oklahoma experiment, see Kim Cobb, "Oklahoma Embraces Pro-Marriage Experiment," *Houston Chronicle*, February 22, 2004, A12.

Temporary Assistance for Needy Families
Once called "Aid to Families with Dependent Children," the new name for public assistance to needy families.

Symbolically, the welfare reform policies also changed the name of "welfare as we knew it." The cash payments to poor families once called AFDC now became known as **Temporary Assistance for Needy Families** (TANF), today's name for the means-tested aid for the poorest of the poor. TANF benefits today are small and declining. The average recipient family collects about $363 monthly in TANF benefits.

In one sense, welfare reform certainly "worked." It got millions off welfare. From the act's signing in 1996 until September 2002, the number of welfare recipients declined from 12.2 million to 5 million. The welfare reform law stipulated that adults must be working in no fewer than 25 percent of the families on welfare, or else states would be subject to financial penalties at the start of 1999. Most states met this target, with the nationwide data showing that 33 percent of adults on welfare rolls were engaged in some sort of work activity by the end of 2005.[27] Even among workers, though, incomes remain pretty low. The average TANF recipient was making about $686 a month.

President George W. Bush pushed for one other welfare reform: encouraging people to marry. The welfare reform legislation permitted states to use some of their money for programs to promote marriage, and President Bush (and several states) pushed marriage as one solution to the perpetual problem of poverty. (See "You Are the Policymaker: Should the Government Promote Marriage?")

Did we win, lose, or draw what President Johnson called a "war on poverty"? For those looking for the "right" answer, the evidence is clearly mixed. Scholars disagree on how beneficial the programs were and are. One of the soundest assessments comes from economist Rebecca Blank, who warns about the fight on poverty: "Don't declare success too quickly." Very likely no one single strategy—the war on poverty, income subsidies, the EITC, welfare reform—can claim the credit for improving poverty. It is hard to beat a strong economy to help the poor.[28] The proportion of the poor has declined a little since we first started measuring poverty. But the rich get a larger share of the nation's income, and the poor a smaller one since we declared war on poverty. And the kinds of people who were poor then are still the poorest now—except for older Americans, to whom we now turn.

Why It Matters

Ending Welfare
President Clinton said that the United States should "end welfare are we know it," and that is what Congress intended with the PRWORA of 1996. In fact, the PRWORA has reduced both TANF recipients and their benefits. Welfare reform, though, took hold as the economy was moving into a recession. This made it hard for them to find jobs.

Living on Borrowed Time: Social Security

If you work, you should be regularly getting those official-looking letters about your Social Security benefits. Beginning in 1998, the federal government launched the largest mass mailing in history. The commissioner of Social Security wrote to every single American who pays Social Security taxes. The letter is titled "Your Social Security Statement." The massive computers of the Social Security Administration in Baltimore, Maryland, churned out millions of individualized letters reporting what each individual had paid year by year. The letters also reported estimated benefits. Based on what you had paid in so far, you could expect to receive—if you kept working until the retirement age—so many dollars per month.

About 75 million baby boomers will start retiring in about 2010. Chances are, they will live longer and healthier lives than any generation before—and run up even bigger costs for the Social Security system and its health care cousin, Medicare. (We discuss Medicare in the next chapter.) There are some—President George Bush is among them—who think Social Security needs some reform. It is a time bomb, most experts think, ticking away, moving inexorably toward the day when the costs will exceed the income. But what, exactly, is Social Security? Here, we examine its history—and its future.

The New Deal, the Elderly, and the Growth of Social Security

Social Security, the most expensive public policy in the United States, began modestly enough as a "pay-as-you-go" plan during Franklin Roosevelt's New Deal. Its official name is OASDI, for Old Age, Survivors and Disability Insurance. Social Security was designed in part to get older Americans out of the workforce during the Great Depression of the 1930s. At first it was "a deal that couldn't be beat."[29] The idea was that money in payroll taxes would have to come into the federal treasury before money could go out to the beneficiaries. President Roosevelt wanted a plan so fiscally solid that "no damn politician can ever scrap my social security program." Over the years, Americans have tended to believe that their Social Security payments were just getting out what was paid in. But that wasn't true even for the very first Social Security recipient, a woman named Ida May Fuller from Brattleboro, Vermont. Her total contributions were a mere $22.54, but her lifetime benefits were $22,888.92 because she lived to old age. But Ida May Fuller's deal is no longer available. Take a young woman beginning a career today at the age of 22. There will be only about two workers for every one recipient by the time she retires (in contrast to about 25 to 1 when the program began).

Where the Money Goes . . .

Social Security grew over the years, in large part because it worked. More than 90 percent of people polled, year after year, support Social Security. No one gets rich off Social Security. The mean monthly check is about $900. Still, for the cost of a tiny administrative fee to run it, Social Security got the elderly off the bottom of

No event has shaped American social welfare policy more than the Great Depression. Franklin Roosevelt's administration initiated hundreds of New Deal programs in its efforts to help citizens like these jobless men. Government spending on social welfare has continued to grow, even during the Bush administration.

the poverty ladder. In 1965, Congress tacked onto Social Security a new program, Medicare, to assist the elderly with medical costs (see Chapter 19). By the turn of the twenty-first century, Social Security and Medicare had become the most expensive public policies in the history of the world. In a decade, they will consume more than half the federal budget.

Here is how Social Security works: Government taxes workers and their employers a percent of the employee's income up to a maximum. Both employee and employer contributions are paid into the **Social Security Trust Fund**. If you work, you are contributing 6.2 percent of your wages (up to $90,000), and your employer matches it. (If you are making $90,000, you and Bill Gates are paying the same dollar amount into Social Security.) Your contributions, as well as those of more than a hundred million other workers, go into this huge government "bank account." The Trust Fund, of course, is not a literal bank account. As long as there is more money paid in than going out, the Trust Fund stays in the black. Although the sums are huge, the math is not all that complicated. Today's average Social Security payment is equal to about 36 percent of the average worker's wages. Currently, there are about 3.4 workers per recipient. Thus, the cost to each worker is about 10.5 percent of a worker's earnings (36/3.4 = 10.5). Current Social Security payroll taxes are 12.4 percent. Thus, for the moment, more money is going into the Trust Fund than is being paid out. By law, the Trust Fund can do only one thing with these moneys: invest them in U.S. treasury bonds. It cannot buy McDonald's stock or Wal-Mart stock or Joe's Hot New Internet stock. It has been earning about 6 percent a year on its investment.

Social Security Trust Fund

The "bank account" into which Social Security contributions are "deposited" and used to pay out eligible recipients.

Essential to this arithmetic is the ratio of workers to beneficiaries. The more retirees, relative to workers, the thinner the Social Security blanket stretches. If instead of 3.4 workers per beneficiary there are only 2, then the math changes. The cost to each worker rises from 10.5 percent of earnings to 18 percent of earnings (36/2 = 18)—and Social Security turns from black to red ink.[30] That will soon happen.

Thus, the Social Security program may be living on borrowed time. Americans are aging. When Social Security was first established, the life expectancy of the average American was lower than the 65 years pegged for the worker to collect benefits. Thus, the "average" American would not even live long enough to collect his or her benefits. Things changed when birthrates began to soar after World War II (the baby boomers) and better medicine kept us alive longer. Of the generation reaching age 65 in 2000, 69 percent of males lived to be 65; those who did will live another 16.2 years. Women have even longer life expectancies.

The Social Security dilemma is this: The number of Social Security contributors (the workers) is growing slowly, while the number of Social Security recipients (the retired) is growing rapidly. As the number of retirees grows and their average benefit is constantly increased to cover the cost of living (called a cost-of-living allowance), Social Security expenditures are going to increase. The more retirements and the more benefits, the higher the costs. At some point—about 2038 unless something changes—payouts will exceed income.[31] The Trust Fund's accumulated trillions will be gone. If this happens, Congress would have to use regular appropriations to pay out benefits to claimants as they retired. If taxes were not raised, a dollar that would have gone to the military or homeland security or the

Labor union members rally against the plan supported by President George W. Bush to privatize Social Security. Bush made Social Security reform a key issue of his second term.

national parks would have to be diverted to the retirees. No solution is a politically pleasant one. Cutting benefits to retirees is no more popular than raising taxes on working contributors. Hard choices lie ahead. Many young Americans suspect that Social Security is not going to be around for them anyway. (See "Young People and Politics: Social Security and UFOs.")

How George W. Bush Tried and Failed to Reform Social Security

Politicians tread gingerly on the terrain of Social Security, fearing a backlash from elderly Americans.[32] Older Americans vote far more than younger ones. About three-quarters of young people themselves agree with the statement that "voting is something older people do."[33] Elected in the squeaker of an election in 2000, the new president, George W. Bush, was nonetheless determined to behave as if he had a national mandate. Social Security reform was near the top of that mandate. George W. Bush and the Republicans proposed diverting a small portion (the suggested figure was 2 percent—that is a bit less than a third of your contribution of 6.2 percent) of Social Security contributions to private retirement funds. Each individual could, presumably, reduce his or her contribution to the Social Security system and instead put the money into a private account, a stock, a bond, or another investment. They could collect their gains—or perhaps face their losses—when they were eligible to collect Social Security. Or, perhaps, the Social Security system itself would do the investing in the stock market. Chile, Great Britain, Australia, Poland, and Brazil have done just

YOUNG PEOPLE AND POLITICS

Social Security and UFOs

The story that more young adults believe in UFOs than in the future of Social Security has been repeated so often that it has almost become an urban legend—one of those offbeat, often-told stories that just might be true. President Clinton told an audience at the University of Illinois that "there are polls that say that young people in their twenties think it's more likely that they will see UFOs than that they will ever collect Social Security." The story has been repeated by countless politicians, on ABC's *20/20*, CNN's *Capital Gang*, and elsewhere. How did such an odd "factoid" come into popular lore?

A group called Third Millennium that favors Social Security reform commissioned two surveys in 1994, one of Americans 65 and older and one of young adults. They hired pollster Frank Luntz to conduct the surveys. Luntz asked the young adults if they thought Social Security would exist by the time they retired, and only 28 percent said yes. At the very end of the questionnaire, he asked an out-of-the-blue question: "And one final question, and I ask you to take this seriously—Do you think UFOs exist?" Some 46 percent said yes. That was the basis for the claim that young people believe more in UFOs than in Social Security. (Or, in President Clinton's further embellishment, that "they will *see* UFOs.")

There was a little more to the survey than that. Interestingly, young people were more likely than seniors themselves (48 to 35 percent) to think that older people were getting "less than their fair share of government benefits." But the quirky finding about UFOs became a part of national lore. Anyone with a complaint about Social Security could trot out the isolated numbers and make something out of them.

Indeed, the "factoid" made so much news that, a few years later, the Employee Benefit Research Institute surveyed people ages 18 to 34 and asked this question: "Which do you have greater confidence in, receiving Social Security benefits after retirement or that alien life from outer space exists?" It found that 63 percent have greater confidence in getting their Social Security and 33 percent thought alien life was more likely.

Americans, even young Americans, remain pretty committed to Social Security. Fay Lomax Cook and Lawrence R. Jacobs examined public opinion about Social Security over the last two decades and found that 90 percent of the population consistently believed that we spend either "too little" or "the right amount" as a nation for Social Security. About half of all Americans were either somewhat confident or very confident about the future of Social Security, and older Americans continue to vote more heavily than younger ones.

Questions for Discussion

- In 2004, both candidates promised to protect Social Security benefits for older Americans. What could—or should—we do about younger Americans?
- How much do you plan to rely on Social Security?

Sources: The Third Millennium poll is available at their Web site, *www.third.mil.org/*. The Employee Benefit Research Institute Report is "Public Attitudes on Social Security," *EBRI News* 19 (March 1998): 1. The Lomax-Jacobs report is in the National Academy of Social Insurance, "American Attitudes Toward Social Security: Popular Claims Meet Hard Data," March 2001, 1–8.

that. Democrats feared what Franklin Roosevelt warned about, that some "damn politicians" were about to scrap the nearly sacred Social Security program.

Language matters in politics. Social Security is the most popular program in the United States. Republican intellectuals had called their program "privatization." That didn't test well. "Private accounts" and "personal accounts" were tried. "Modernization" seemed less punchy but less threatening. Business groups funded a new interest group and named it the Coalition for Protection and Modernization of America's Social Security (called "COMPASS"). It had a $20 million advertising budget.[34]

President Bush—long before the events of September 11—appointed a Commission to Strengthen Social Security. The commission was filled with advocates for the "privatization" of Social Security. The late New York Democratic Senator Daniel Patrick Moynihan, one of the few Democrats to favor privatization, and Richard Parsons, AOL-Time Warner's chief executive officer and one of the most prominent African American business leaders, cochaired the commission. Most presidential commissions release their report in the glare of television cameras, often in a showy presentation in the White House. The Moynihan–Parsons commission released its final report on December 21, 2001, while most Americans were Christmas shopping. Its warnings were dire (the warnings of almost every commission to study Social Security are dire).[35] It pushed the idea of limited privatization of Social Security. Workers could put a portion (say a third) of their contributions into the stock or bond market. The problem, the Democrats emphasized, was that permitting people to divert money from the system, even for good reason, would merely hasten its bankruptcy. The report couldn't have come at a worse time for advocates of privatization. Stocks were swooning before the commission reported and slumped further thereafter. One critic called the whole idea of privatizing Social Security the "Trillion Dollar Hustle," a plan only Wall Street could love.[36] The stock slump of the early twenty-first century eroded public and political support of the whole idea.[37] (See "Issues of the Times: Should We Privatize Social Security?")

You Are a State Legislator

Even after another close election in 2004, Bush pushed. At his first postelection news conference in 2004, President George W. Bush announced that he would make reforming Social Security his top domestic policy priority. It would be hard, he said—if it were easy, it would have been done already.

The problem with the idea was universally acknowledged. If people are putting less into the common Social Security pool, perhaps a few trillion dollars less, the Social Security System would run out of money even faster. (If you are saving $100 a month toward a new computer but start taking $10 a month out of it, your fund for the new computer is going to leak.) How to cover that gap (indeed, whether to cover the gap at all) would become the central issue of Social Security reform. If the Social Security bucket was not going to leak like a sieve, government would have to borrow trillions more to replenish it. Bush's efforts fizzled. Drained by Iraq, sidetracked by immigration politics, and weakened in the polls, Bush no longer controlled the domestic policy agenda. By 2006, Congress was wound up in a debate about immigration, leaving Social Security reform, modernization, privatization—whatever—for another president and another day.

Social Welfare Policy Elsewhere

The future of social welfare policies is just as complex (if somewhat less controversial) in other democratic countries. Most industrial nations not only provide social policy benefits but also are usually more generous with them than the U.S. government. The scope of social benefits in health, child care, parental leave, unemployment compensation, and benefits to the elderly are far greater in European nations

AMERICA IN PERSPECTIVE

Preaching Procreation and Paying for It: Family Policies in Europe and Elsewhere

Most European countries have a problem Americans would find unthinkable: shrinking populations. A country needs about 2.1 children born to each woman in order to have a stable population size. When most people were farmers, having more children was a positive benefit: More hands help with the cultivation and harvesting. In cities, more children became an economic liability. With the ready availability of birth control technologies, family size in the developed world began to shrink. In numerous European counties (heavily Catholic Spain and Italy are even extreme cases), birthrates have fallen below replacement levels. Besides, European countries are much less receptive to immigration than the United States. The American population has continued to grow, partly because of immigration but partly, too, because Americans simply have more children. European populations are withering. Having fewer children means, among other things, that fewer workers will be around to do the work and pay the taxes—including those all-important social security taxes in an aging society. Earlier in this chapter we noted that the number of workers in relation to recipients of U.S. Social Security has dropped dramatically. In Europe, the drop is even steeper.

European countries have started paying bonuses for newborns. The French government, for example, promised a "baby bonus" of nearly $900 for each newborn after January 2004; the Italians followed with an even better deal. Population in Russia is in free fall. President Putin promised Russian mothers new baby allowances. Oddly, while the Chinese government was trying to keep its families to one child per family, European governments were preaching procreation—and paying for it. Having more children became, in this sense, one's patriotic duty.

Americans might think it odd that government has any business in the bedroom. Even so, our own federal tax code is child friendly, giving tax deductions for young children that people without children cannot claim. Several liberal thinkers such as Yale law professor Bruce Ackerman have advocated that the government set up an account worth about $80,000 for each new child, financed by a small tax on the wealthy. That might even encourage more childbearing. And some religious conservatives oppose legalized contraception, fighting hard, for example, to prevent a "morning after pill" from easy access in pharmacies. Having more children means having more people to pay the taxes and get the work done.

Some of the current debate about immigration in the United States is really a debate about how many people we should have. Many European countries have already answered that question: more.

Sources: See Fred R. Harris, ed., *The Baby Bust: Who Will Do the Work? Who Will Pay the Taxes?* (Lanham, MD: Rowman & Littlefield, 2006); on baby bonuses, see Frank Ackerman and Anne Alstott, *The Stakeholder Society* (New Haven, CT: Yale University Press, 1999).

than in ours. Europeans often think of their countries as "welfare states," with all the generous benefits—and staggering taxes by U.S. standards—that this implies.[38] European old-age programs are in even bigger trouble than ours are, though, partly because their labor forces are not being replenished by immigration.[39]

Other national governments and their citizens often take quite a different approach to the problems of poverty and social welfare. Americans tend to see poverty and social welfare needs as individual rather than governmental concerns, whereas European nations tend to support greater governmental responsibility for these problems. Also, Europeans often have a more positive attitude toward government, whereas Americans are more likely to distrust government action in areas such as social welfare policy.

Comparing Social Welfare Policy

Most Americans would be amazed at the range of social benefits in the average European country. French parents, for example, are guaranteed the right to put their toddlers in *crèches* (day care centers), regardless of whether the parents are rich or poor, at work or at home. French unemployment benefits are generous by American standards (and French unemployment rates are two to three times higher than ours). In many European countries, treatments at health spas come with free or low-cost government health care policies.

Europeans pay a high price for generous benefits. Taxes in Western European nations far exceed those in the United States (see Chapter 14). There, taxes approach (or even exceed) 50 percent of income. Every problem the United States faces in funding Social Security is even bigger in Europe. In some ways, European social welfare problems are even greater because their populations are shrinking. Fewer babies mean fewer workers. Fewer workers mean fewer taxpayers. (See "America in Perspective: Preaching Procreation and Paying for It.")

As in the United States, there has been a backlash against the welfare state in Europe. Parties of the Left, advocating generous public benefits, once ruled nearly every European country. Today, conservative parties—like the Republicans in the United States—often win by bashing the welfare state.

Understanding Social Welfare Policy

Social welfare policies are going to be controversial in a capitalist, democratic political system. Very few issues divide liberals and conservatives more sharply. Americans struggle to balance individual merit and the rewards of initiative with the reality of systemic inequalities and the need to provide support to many. Citizens disagree on how much government can or should do to even out the competition and protect those who are less able or too old to compete.

Social Welfare Policy and the Scope of Government

Nothing more clearly accounts for the growth of government in America than social welfare spending. Americans tend to overestimate how much government spends on the poor. They probably underestimate how much support for the elderly costs, thinking that Social Security is merely "getting back what I paid in." Ever since the New Deal and the invention of Social Security, the growth of government has been driven by the growth of social welfare policies. Conservatives complain about the "welfare state." Even if ours is small relative to those of other nations, the American social welfare system grows generation by generation. American attitudes toward the growth of social welfare often depend on their assessment of what Schneider and Ingram call "target groups."[40] Groups viewed favorably—the elderly who have worked hard or the "deserving poor"—are one thing. The "undeserving poor" are another. Part of the debate about the scope of social welfare policies is a debate about how deserving various groups are and how big they are. We have cut back on aid to the poor, but there is no sign that the elderly will go quietly if political candidates propose cutting back on Social Security.

Democracy and Social Welfare

There is an extensive social welfare system in every major democracy. Ours, in fact, is the least extensive of all. As with other policies, competing demands have to be resolved by government decision makers, but decision makers do not act in a vacuum. They are aligned with and pay allegiance to various groups in society. These groups include members of their legislative constituencies, members of their electoral coalitions, and members of their political party. Many of these groups provide the financial assistance that the decision makers need to seek and retain political office.

In the social welfare policy arena, the competing groups are often quite unequal in terms of political resources. For example, the elderly are relatively well organized and often have the resources needed to wield significant influence in support of programs they desire. As a result, they are usually successful in protecting and expanding their programs. For the poor, however, influencing political decisions is more difficult. They vote less frequently and lack strong, focused organizations and money. In this unequal battle, cutting welfare benefits is easier than tampering with the Social Security system.

Summary

Our social welfare policies have taken two distinct paths. First are the entitlement policies, dominated by Social Security and Medicare. In the United States, we spend more money on federal entitlements than on any other single thing the government does. Rich or poor, Americans are entitled to Social Security benefits by law. The other road includes the means-tested programs, government's expenditures for poorer Americans.

You have seen in this chapter that government action and inaction can play a major role in affecting the social welfare status of many poor and elderly Americans. Entitlement programs such as Social Security and Medicare have significantly improved the lot of the elderly, but these very costly programs threaten to grow ever larger and more expensive. Programs aimed more specifically at the poor cost less (and perhaps have accomplished less), but they seem likely to remain objects of political controversy for many years to come.

As the century turned, social welfare policies were under fire more than in any period since the New Deal. A Democratic president and a Republican Congress had already reformed welfare. Social Security seemed ripe for reassessment. Like most domestic policy issues, terrorism shoved it further down the policy agenda. Neither poverty nor the Social Security crunch, though, is going away soon.

Key Terms

social welfare policies
entitlement programs
means-tested programs
income distribution
income
wealth
poverty line
feminization of poverty
progressive tax
proportional tax
regressive tax
Earned Income Tax Credit
transfer payments
Social Security Act of 1935
Personal Responsibility and Work Opportunity Reconciliation Act
Temporary Assistance for Needy Families
Social Security Trust Fund

Internet Resources

www.aecf.org
The Annie E. Casey Foundation produces a wealth of information about America's children, including its *Kid's Count* data book.

www.csss.gov
Report of the President's Commission to Strengthen Social Security.

http://marriage.rutgers.edu/publicat.htm
Rutgers University publishes an annual "State of Our Unions" report on marriages and families.

www.ssa.gov
The official site of the Social Security Administration, where you can learn about the history of the program and find out how to calculate your own benefits.

www.tanf.gov
Annual reports on the effects of the 1996 welfare reforms.

Get Connected

Insuring Children

Children tend to be the group of Americans least likely to have health insurance coverage. A provision in the Balanced Budget Act of 1997 established the State Children's Health Insurance Program (SCHIP). This program allowed each state to offer health insurance for children, up to age 19, who are not already insured. SCHIP is a state-administered program, and each state sets its own guidelines regarding eligibility and services. Let us look a little closer at the State Children's Health Insurance Program.

Search the Web

Go to the U.S. Department of Health and Human Services page on the State Children's Health Insurance Program, *www.cms.hhs.gov/home/schip.asp*. Find the link to your state's program. The department also built a Web site, "Insure Kids Now!," which provides more direct links to information about each state's insurance plan. Visit it at *www.insurekidsnow.gov/* and find the link to the Web site created by your state. Look around your state's Web site. Access some of the pages for states near your state. Also look at the page for a state that is far from your state.

Questions to Ask

- Who determines who is eligible to participate in the Children's Health Insurance Program?
- Who is eligible to participate in the program in your state? How does this compare with the eligibility in surrounding states? How about a state far away from your state?

- Can you see a relationship between who is eligible and the political culture in the states you looked at? For some help identifying the states' political cultures, you may want to consult *http://academic.regis.edu/jriley/421elazar.html/*.

Why It Matters

The State Children's Health Insurance Program was created because many families cannot afford adequate health insurance coverage. Sick children who are uninsured are often taken to hospital emergency rooms, where the care tends to be more expensive than that received from a family doctor. Usually the American taxpayer pays for the emergency room visit through the Medicaid program because the family can't afford to pay for it.

Get Involved

One of the challenges that has faced the State Children's Health Insurance Program is getting eligible children enrolled in the program. Find out if your state has experienced this problem and think about how to create an outreach plan to reach those children. You can research your state's program by searching the index of the newspaper in your state's capital or your local newspaper. The Web site *www.urban.org/urlprint.cfm?ID=7233* discusses some of the reasons why more children have not enrolled in the insurance program. Look over the items linked on *www.financeprojectinfo.org/win/HC_CHIPmisc.asp* for more information on the challenges facing the program.

For more exercises, go to www.longmanamericangovernment.com.

For Further Reading

Campbell, Andrea Louise. *How Policies Make Citizens: Senior Political Activism and the American Welfare State*. Princeton, NJ: Princeton University Press, 2003. How Social Security created a new class of political activists.

Diamond, Peter A., and Peter R. Orszag. *Saving Social Security: A Balanced Approach*. Washington, DC: Brookings Institution, 2005. Social Security needs lots of minor surgeries, not major surgery.

Ehrenreich, Barbara. *Nickel and Dimed: On (Not) Getting By in America*. New York: Owl Books, 2001. A well-educated—with a Ph.D. in biology—journalist experiences the difficulties of getting by in America while working a string of low-wage jobs.

Gilens, Martin. *Why Americans Hate Welfare: Race, Media, and the Politics of Antipoverty Policy*. Chicago: University of Chicago Press, 2000. Gilens argues that public opposition to welfare is fed by a combination of racial and media stereotyping about the true nature of America's poor.

Kotlikoff, Lawrence J., and Scott Burns. *The Coming Generational Storm*. Cambridge, MA: MIT Press, 2004. The authors argue we are rapidly shifting resources to older Americans with awful consequences.

Murray, Charles. *Losing Ground: American Social Policy, 1950–1980*. New York: Basic Books, 1984. A classic conservative argument that social policies have not worked and have actually made things worse.

Page, Benjamin I., and James R. Simmons. *What Government Can Do: Dealing with Poverty and Inequality*. Chicago: University of Chicago Press, 2000. A liberal analysis of and agenda for antipoverty policy.

Rodgers, Harrell, Jr. *American Poverty in a New Era of Reform*. 2nd ed. New York: M. E. Sharpe, 2006. Discusses what has happened to poverty since the welfare reforms.

Schieber, Sylvester J., and John B. Shoven. *The Real Deal: The History and Future of Social Security*. New Haven, CT: Yale University Press, 2000. An excellent analysis of the past, present, and future of Social Security.

Shipler, David K. *The Working Poor: Invisible in America*. New York: Knopf, 2004. How people who work still risk poverty.

National Security Policymaking

Chapter Outline

POLITICS IN ACTION: A NEW THREAT On September 11, 2001, America trembled. Terrorist attacks on the World Trade Center in New York and the Pentagon in Washington killed thousands and exposed the nation's vulnerability to unconventional attacks.

Less than 12 years after the fall of the Berlin Wall, the United States could no longer take comfort in its status as the world's only superpower. Suddenly the world seemed a more threatening place, with dangers lurking around every corner.

Communism was no longer the principal threat to the security of the United States, and our foreign policy goals suddenly changed to ending terrorism. To achieve this goal, we launched wars against Afghanistan and Iraq. The United States won the battles quite easily, but the aftermath of the wars, especially in Iraq, led to more deaths than the fighting itself and forced America to invest tens of billions of dollars in reconstruction and military occupation. Debate rages as to whether we have dealt terrorists a severe blow or whether U.S. actions have radicalized opponents and recruited new terrorists to their cause. At the same time, "rogue" states like Iran and North Korea have continued their development of nuclear weapons, threatening to make the world even less stable.

The need to answer the question of the appropriate role of the national government in national security policy is more important and perhaps more difficult than ever. America's status in the world makes leadership unavoidable. What should be the role of the world's only remaining superpower? What should we do with our huge defense establishment? Should we go it alone, or should we work closely with our allies on issues ranging from fighting terrorism and stopping nuclear proliferation to protecting the environment and encouraging trade? How should we deal with our former adversaries? Should we aid their transition to democracy?

At the same time, a number of critical areas of the world, most notably the Middle East, exhibit a frightening tendency to conflict. Should the United States get involved in trying to end conflicts resulting from ethnic, religious, and regional differences? Does the United States have a choice about involvement when the conflict could affect its ability to fight terrorism or prevent the use of nuclear weapons?

Exporting American Democracy

And just how should we decide about national security policy? Should the American people delegate discretion in this area to officials who seem more at home with complex and even exotic issues of defense and foreign policy? Or should they and their representatives fully participate in the democratic policymaking process, just as they do in domestic policy? Can the public or its representatives in Congress or in interest groups have much influence on the elites who often deal in secrecy with national security policy?

The end of the Cold War has not lessened the importance of defense and foreign policy. New and complex challenges have emerged to replace the conflict with communism. Some of these challenges, such as the fight against terrorism, are traceable to a malevolent enemy who can be contained or defeated—but many others are not.

American Foreign Policy: Instruments, Actors, and Policymakers

Foreign policy, like domestic policy, involves making choices—but the choices involved are about relations with the rest of the world. Because the president is the main force behind foreign policy, every morning the White House receives a highly confidential intelligence briefing that might cover monetary transactions in Tokyo, last night's events in some trouble spot on the globe, or Fidel Castro's health. The briefing is part of the massive informational arsenal the president uses to manage American foreign policy.

foreign policy
A policy that involves choice taking, like domestic policy, but additionally involves choices about relations with the rest of the world. The president is the chief initiator of foreign policy in the United States.

Instruments of Foreign Policy

The instruments of foreign policy are, however, different from those of domestic policy. Foreign policies depend ultimately on three types of tools: military, economic, and diplomatic.

Military. Among the oldest instruments of foreign policy are war and the threat of war. German General Karl von Clausewitz once called war a "continuation of politics by other means." The United States has been involved in only a few full-scale wars. It has often employed force to influence actions in other countries, however. Most of this influence has been close to home, in Central America and the Caribbean.

In recent years, the United States has continued to use force in limited ways around the world: to topple Saddam Hussein's regime in Iraq and the Taliban regime in Afghanistan, to oppose ethnic cleansing in the Kosovo province of Yugoslavia, to prevent the toppling of the democratic government of the Philippines, to assist a UN peacekeeping mission in Somalia, to rescue stranded foreigners and protect the U.S. embassy in Liberia, and to launch missile attacks on Baghdad in retaliation for an effort to assassinate former President Bush and for the failure to provide UN weapons inspectors access to suspected weapons sites. The United States also employed military forces to aid the democratic transfer of power in Haiti and for humanitarian relief operations in Yugoslavia, Iraq, Somalia, Bangladesh, Russia, and Bosnia.

Economic. Today, economic instruments are becoming weapons almost as potent as those of war. The control of oil can be as important as the control of guns. Trade regulations, tariff policies, and monetary policies are other economic instruments of

The United States marshaled all its instruments of foreign policy to combat terrorism following the attacks on the World Trade Center on September 11, 2001.

foreign policy. A number of studies have called attention to the importance of a country's economic vitality to its long-term national security.[1]

Diplomacy. Diplomacy is the quietest instrument of influence. It is the process by which nations carry on relationships with each other. It often evokes images of ambassadors at chic cocktail parties, but the diplomatic game is played for high stakes. Sometimes national leaders meet in summit talks. More often, less prominent negotiators work out treaties covering all kinds of national contracts, from economic relations to aid for stranded tourists.

Actors on the World Stage

If all the world's a stage, then there are more actors on it than ever before. More than 125 nations have emerged since 1945—nearly two dozen in the 1990s alone. Once foreign relations were almost exclusively transactions among nations in which leaders used military, economic, or diplomatic methods to achieve foreign policy goals. Nations remain the main actors in international politics, but today's world stage is more crowded.

International Organizations. Most of the challenges in international relations, ranging from peacekeeping and controlling weapons of mass destruction to protecting the environment and maintaining stable trade and financial networks, require the cooperation of many nations. The best-known international organization is the **United Nations** (UN). Housed in a magnificent skyscraper in New York City, the UN was created in 1945. Its members agree to renounce war and respect certain human and economic freedoms. The UN General Assembly is composed of 191 member nations. Each nation has one vote. Although not legally binding, General Assembly resolutions can achieve a measure of collective legitimization when a broad international consensus is formed on some matter concerning relations among states.

United Nations
Created in 1945, an organization whose members agree to renounce war and to respect certain human and economic freedoms. The seat of real power in the United Nations is the Security Council.

It is the *Security Council*, however, that is the seat of real power in the UN. Five of its 15 members (the United States, Great Britain, China, France, and Russia) are permanent members; the others are chosen from session to session by the General Assembly. Each permanent member has a veto over Security Council decisions, including any decisions that would commit the UN to a military peacekeeping operation. The Secretariat is the executive arm of the UN and directs the administration of UN programs. Composed of about 9,000 international civil servants, it is headed by the secretary-general. In addition to its peacekeeping function, the UN runs a number of programs focused on economic development and on health, education, and welfare.

Since 1948 there have been 60 UN peacekeeping operations, 46 of which were created by the Security Council between 1988 and 2006. In 1990, the UN Security Council backed resolutions authorizing an embargo on the shipment of goods to or from Iraq in an attempt to force its withdrawal from Kuwait. Later, it authorized the use of force to compel Iraq to withdraw. In 1992, the UN assisted famine relief in Somalia. More recently, it supported the return of the democratically elected president of Haiti and has been active in trying to end the civil war in Bosnia-Herzegovina. In 2006 there were 15 UN missions under way in Sudan, Haiti, Burundi, the Democratic Republic of the Congo, Western Sahara, India/Pakistan, Ethiopia and Eritrea, the Golan Heights, Ivory Coast, Liberia, Lebanon, Cyprus, Georgia, Kosovo, and the Middle East generally. However, the UN did not support the U.S.-led war in Iraq.

Unilateralism and Multilateralism

The United States often plays the critical role in implementing UN policies. Although President Clinton envisioned an expanded role for UN peacekeeping operations at the beginning of his term, he later concluded that the UN is often not capable of making and keeping peace, particularly when hostilities among parties still exist. He also backtracked on his willingness to place American troops under foreign commanders, always a controversial policy.

George W. Bush sought but did not receive UN sanction for the war with Iraq and has been skeptical of the organization's ability to enforce its own resolutions. Nevertheless, many countries feel that the legitimacy of the UN is crucial for their participation in peacekeeping or other operations requiring the use of force.

The UN is only one of many international organizations. For example, the International Monetary Fund helps regulate the chaotic world of international finance, the World Bank finances development projects in new nations, the World Trade Organization attempts to regulate international trade, and the Universal Postal Union helps get the mail from one country to another.

Regional Organizations. *Regional organizations* have proliferated in the post–World War II era. These are organizations of several nations bound by a treaty, often for military reasons. The **North Atlantic Treaty Organization** (NATO) was created in 1949. Its members—the United States, Canada, most Western European nations, and Turkey—agreed to combine military forces and to treat a war against one as a war against all. During the Cold War, more than a million NATO troops (including about 325,000 Americans) were spread from West Germany to Portugal as a deterrent to foreign aggression. To counter the NATO alliance, the Soviet Union and its Eastern European allies formed the Warsaw Pact. The Warsaw Pact has since been dissolved, however, and the role of NATO has changed dramatically as the Cold War has thawed. In 1999, Poland, Hungary, and the Czech Republic, former members of the Warsaw Pact, became members of NATO. In 2002, NATO invited seven additional Eastern European countries, including Slovakia, Slovenia, Bulgaria, Romania, Latvia, Estonia, and Lithuania, to join the alliance.

North Atlantic Treaty Organization
Created in 1949, an organization whose members include the United States, Canada, most Western European nations, and Turkey, all of whom agreed to combine military forces and to treat a war against one as a war against all.

Regional organizations can be economic as well as military. The **European Union** (EU) is a transnational government composed of most European nations. The EU coordinates monetary, trade, immigration, and labor policies so that its members have become one economic unit, just as the 50 United States are an economic unit. Other economic federations exist in Latin America and Africa, although none is as unified as the EU. Most EU nations have adopted a common currency, the euro.

European Union
A transnational government composed of most Western European nations that coordinates monetary, trade, immigration, and labor policies, making its members one economic unit. An example of regional organization.

Multinational Corporations. Today, a large portion of the world's industrial output comes from multinational corporations (MNCs), and they account for more than one-tenth of the global economy and one-third of world exports.[2] Sometimes more powerful (and often much wealthier) than the governments under which they operate, MNCs have voiced strong opinions about governments, taxes, and business regulations. They have even linked forces with agencies such as the Central Intelligence Agency (CIA) to overturn governments they disliked. In the 1970s, for example, several of these corporations worked with the CIA to "destabilize" the democratically elected Marxist government in Chile; Chile's military overthrew the government in 1973. Even when they are not so heavy-handed, MNCs are forces to be reckoned with in nearly all nations.

Nongovernmental Organizations. *Groups* are also actors on the global stage. Churches and labor unions have long had international interests and activities. Today, environmental and wildlife groups such as Greenpeace have also proliferated. Ecological interests are active in international as well as in national politics. Groups interested in protecting human rights, such as Amnesty International, have also grown.

You Are the Leader of Concerned Citizens for World Justice

Not all groups, however, are committed to saving whales, oceans, or even people. Some are committed to the overthrow of particular governments and operate as terrorists around the world. Airplane hijackings, assassinations, bombings, and similar terrorist attacks have made the world a more unsettled place. Conflicts within a nation or region thus spill over into world politics.

Individuals. Finally, *individuals* are international actors. Tourism sends Americans everywhere and brings to America legions of tourists from Japan, Europe, and the less developed world. Tourism creates its own costs and benefits and thus always affects the international economic system. It may enhance friendship and understanding among nations. However, more tourists traveling out of the country than arriving in the country can create problems with a country's balance of payments (discussed later in this chapter). In addition to tourists, growing numbers of students are going to and coming from other nations; they are carriers of ideas and ideologies. So are immigrants and refugees, who also place new demands on public services.

Just as there are more actors on the global stage than in the past, there are also more American decision makers involved in foreign policy problems.

The Policymakers

There are many policymakers involved with national security policy, but any discussion of foreign policymaking must begin with the president.

The President. The president, as you know from Chapter 12, is the main force behind foreign policy. As chief diplomat, the president negotiates treaties; as commander in chief of the armed forces, the president deploys American troops abroad. The president also appoints U.S. ambassadors and the heads of executive departments (with the consent of the Senate), and he has the sole power to accord official recognition to other countries and receive (or refuse to receive) their representatives.

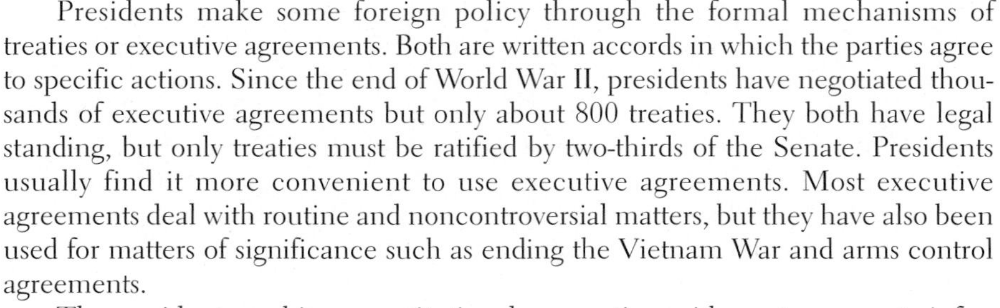

Presidents make some foreign policy through the formal mechanisms of treaties or executive agreements. Both are written accords in which the parties agree to specific actions. Since the end of World War II, presidents have negotiated thousands of executive agreements but only about 800 treaties. They both have legal standing, but only treaties must be ratified by two-thirds of the Senate. Presidents usually find it more convenient to use executive agreements. Most executive agreements deal with routine and noncontroversial matters, but they have also been used for matters of significance such as ending the Vietnam War and arms control agreements.

You Are the President

The president combines constitutional prerogatives with greater access to information than other policymakers and can act with speed and secrecy if necessary (see "Issues of the Times: Managing Crises"). The White House also has the advantages of the president's role as a leader of Congress and the public and his ability to commit the nation to a course of action. Presidents do not act alone in foreign policy, however. They are aided (and sometimes thwarted) by a huge national security bureaucracy. In addition, they must contend with the views and desires of Congress, which also wields considerable clout in the foreign policy arena—sometimes in opposition to a president.

secretary of state
The head of the Department of State and traditionally a key adviser to the president on **foreign policy**.

The Diplomats. The State Department is the foreign policy arm of the U.S. government. As the department's chief, the **secretary of state** (Thomas Jefferson was the first) has traditionally been the key adviser to the president on foreign policy matters. In over 300 overseas posts from Albania to Zimbabwe, the State Department staffs U.S. embassies and consulates, representing the interests of Americans. Once a dignified and genteel profession, diplomacy is becoming an increasingly dangerous job. The November 1979 seizure of the American embassy in Tehran and the 1998 bombing of the American embassy in Nairobi, Kenya, are extreme examples of the hostilities diplomats can face.

The more than 30,000 people working in the State Department are organized into functional areas (such as economic and business affairs and human rights and humanitarian affairs) and area specialties (a section on Middle Eastern affairs, one on European affairs, and so on), each nation being handled by a "country desk." The political appointees who occupy the top positions in the department and the highly select members of the Foreign Service who compose most of the department are heavily involved in formulating and executing American foreign policy.

Many recent presidents have found the State Department too bureaucratic and intransigent. Even its colloquial name "Foggy Bottom," taken from the part of Washington where it is located, conjures up less than an image of cooperation. Some recent presidents have bypassed institutional arrangements for foreign policy decision making and have instead established more personal systems for receiving policy advice. Presidents Nixon and Carter, for example, relied more heavily on their assistants for national security affairs (Henry Kissinger and Zbigniew Brzezinski, respectively) than on their secretaries of state. Foreign policy was thus centered in the White House and was often disconnected from what was occurring in the State Department. Critics, however, charged that this situation led to split-level government and chronic discontinuity in foreign policy.[3] President Reagan, by contrast, relied less on his assistants for national security affairs (six different men

The secretary of state is typically the president's chief foreign policy adviser, presiding over a global bureaucracy of diplomats. Here, President Bush talks with Secretary of State Condoleezza Rice.

filled the job in eight years) and more on Secretary of State George Schultz, who was a powerful player. George Bush continued this pattern, appointing his closest friend, James Baker, as secretary of state. President Clinton also relied heavily on his secretaries of state, Warren Christopher and Madeleine Albright. George W. Bush named Colin Powell, one of the most admired people in America, as secretary of state. Powell was the president's leading foreign policy adviser, but national security assistant Condoleezza Rice also played a prominent role. She replaced Powell as secretary of state in Bush's second term.

The National Security Establishment. Foreign policy and military policy are closely linked. Thus, the Department of Defense is a key foreign policy actor. Often called "the Pentagon" after the five-sided building in which it is located, Congress created the Defense Department after World War II. The new department collected the U.S. Army, Navy, and Air Force into one giant department, although they have never been thoroughly integrated and critics contend that they continue to plan and operate too independently of one another. Reforms, made law under the Goldwater-Nichols Defense Reorganization Act of 1986, have increased interservice cooperation and centralization of the military hierarchy, however. The **secretary of defense** manages a budget larger than the entire budget of most nations and is the president's main civilian adviser on national defense matters.

secretary of defense
The head of the Department of Defense and the president's key adviser on military policy; a key **foreign policy** actor.

The commanding officers of each of the services, along with a chairperson and a vice chairperson, constitute the **Joint Chiefs of Staff**. American military leaders are sometimes portrayed as aggressive hawks in policymaking, presumably eager to crush some small nation with a show of American force. Richard Betts carefully examined the Joint Chiefs' advice to the president in many crises and found them to

Joint Chiefs of Staff
The commanding officers of the armed services who advise the president on military policy.

be no more likely than civilian advisers to push an aggressive military policy.[4] On several occasions during the Reagan administration, the president's uniformed advisers cautioned against aggressive actions—including the use of military force—favored by the State Department. The military was similarly conservative regarding the use of force against Iraq in 1991[5] and intervention in the civil wars in Eastern Europe.

High-ranking officials are supposed to coordinate American foreign and military policies. Congress formed the *National Security Council (NSC)* in 1947 for this purpose. The NSC is composed of the president, the vice president, the secretary of defense, and the secretary of state. The president's assistant for national security—a position that first gained public prominence with the flamboyant, globe-trotting Henry Kissinger during President Nixon's first term—manages the NSC staff.

Despite the coordinating role assigned to the NSC, conflict within the foreign policy establishment remains common. The NSC staff has sometimes competed with rather than integrated policy advice from cabinet departments—particularly State and Defense. It has also become involved in covert operations. A scandal erupted in November 1986 when officials discovered that NSC staff were involved in a secret operation to sell battlefield missiles to Iran in return for Iranian help in gaining the release of hostages held by Iranian-backed terrorists in Lebanon. Staffers funneled some of the money from the sale secretly to anticommunist rebels (called *Contras*) fighting the Nicaraguan government, despite a congressional ban on such aid. The scandal, termed the Iran-Contra affair, resulted in the resignation of the president's assistant for national security affairs, Vice Admiral John Poindexter, and the sacking of a number of lower-level NSC officials, including Lieutenant Colonel Oliver North.

Central Intelligence Agency

An agency created after World War II to coordinate American intelligence activities abroad. It became involved in intrigue, conspiracy, and meddling as well.

All policymakers require information to make good decisions. Information on the capabilities and intentions of other nations is often difficult to obtain. As a result, governments resort to intelligence agencies to obtain and interpret such information. Congress created the **Central Intelligence Agency** (CIA) after World

The national security establishment is large, and the National Security Council is designed to integrate options and information for the president. Here, President Bush talks to national security assistant Stephen Hadley.

War II to coordinate American information- and data-gathering intelligence activities abroad and to collect, analyze, and evaluate its own intelligence. Technically, its budget and staff are secret; estimates put them at $5 billion and more than 20,000 people.

The CIA plays a vital role in providing information and analysis necessary for effective development and implementation of national security policy. Most of its activities are uncontroversial because the bulk of the material it collects and analyzes comes from readily available sources such as government reports and newspapers. However, the CIA also collects information by espionage. Most people accept the necessity of this form of information collection when it is directed against foreign adversaries. However, in the 1970s, Congress discovered that at times the agency had also engaged in wiretaps, interception of mail, and the infiltration of interest groups—in the United States. These actions violated the CIA's charter, and revelations of spying on Americans who disagreed with the foreign policy of the administration badly damaged the agency's morale and external political support.

The CIA also has a long history of involvement in other nations' internal affairs. After the end of World War II, when Eastern European nations had fallen under Moscow's shadow and Western European nations were teetering, the CIA provided aid to anticommunist parties in Italy and West Germany. It was no less busy in the developing countries where, for example, it nurtured coups in Iran in 1953 and in Guatemala in 1954. The CIA has also trained and supported armies—the most notable, of course, in Vietnam.

In the 1980s, a major controversy surrounded the CIA's activity in Central America, particularly in Nicaragua, where the Marxist government developed close ties with the Soviet Union and Cuba and embarked on a massive military buildup. Determined to undermine the regime, the Reagan administration aggressively supported armed rebels (Contras). Congressional inquiries into the Iran-Contra affair suggested that the CIA, under Director William Casey, was quietly involved in covert operations to assist the Contras.[6]

Reconciling covert activities with the principles of open democratic government remains a challenge for public officials. With the end of the Cold War, there was less pressure for covert activities and a climate more conducive to conventional intelligence gathering. Currently, Congress requires the CIA to inform relevant congressional committees promptly of current and anticipated covert operations. In the meantime, there is substantial debate on the role of the CIA in the post–Cold War era.

The failure to predict the terrorist attack on September 11, 2001, increased the intensity of this debate, with many leaders calling for an increase in covert capabilities. Perhaps more disconcerting was the CIA's conclusion that Iraq possessed weapons of mass destruction. Destroying these weapons became the principal justification for the war, and their absence was a major embarrassment for the agency and the Bush administration.

There are numerous other components of America's intelligence community. For example, the National Reconnaissance Office uses imagery satellites to monitor missile sites and other military activities around the world, and the National Security Agency (NSA) is on the cutting edge of electronic eavesdropping capabilities. In 2005, debate erupted over the NSA's monitoring of communications between the United States and overseas. Although the interception of communications focused on identifying contacts between those in the United States and terrorists abroad, there was inevitably some slippage. Critics charged the president with violating Americans' privacy and the legal mandate that the NSA obtain a warrant before listening to private messages. The White House claimed that the president possessed the power to authorize the interceptions without a warrant, that the NSA was careful to protect civil liberties, and that the program was necessary to protect Americans against terrorism.

To better coordinate the nearly 100,000 people working in 16 agencies involved in intelligence and their approximately $44 billion budget, Congress in 2004 created a director of national intelligence. The person filling this position is to be the president's chief adviser on intelligence matters. It is not easy to manage such a large number of diverse agencies, spread across numerous departments, and there are sure to be growing pains in the process.

Congress. The U.S. Congress shares with the president constitutional authority over foreign and defense policy (see Chapters 12 and 13). Congress has sole authority, for example, to declare war, raise and organize the armed forces, and appropriate funds for national security activities. The Senate determines whether treaties will be ratified and ambassadorial and cabinet nominations confirmed. The "power of the purse" (see Chapter 15) and responsibilities for oversight of the executive branch give Congress considerable clout, and each year senators and representatives carefully examine defense budget authorizations.[7]

Congress's important constitutional role in foreign and defense policy is sometimes misunderstood. It is a common mistake among some journalists, executive officials, and even members of Congress to believe that the Constitution vests foreign policy decisions solely in the president. Sometimes this erroneous view leads to perverse results, such as the Iran-Contra affair. Officials at high levels in the executive branch "sought to protect the president's 'exclusive' prerogative by lying to Congress, to allies, to the public, and to one another." Louis Fisher suggests that such actions undermined the "mutual trust and close coordination by the two branches that are essential attributes in building a foreign policy that ensures continuity and stability."[8]

American Foreign Policy: An Overview

isolationism

A **foreign policy** course followed throughout most of our nation's history whereby the United States has tried to stay out of other nations' conflicts, particularly European wars. Isolationism was reaffirmed by the Monroe Doctrine.

Throughout most of its history, the United States followed a foreign policy course called **isolationism**. This policy, articulated by George Washington in his farewell address, directed the country to stay out of other nations' conflicts, particularly European wars. The famous *Monroe Doctrine*, enunciated by President James Monroe, reaffirmed America's inattention to Europe's problems but warned European nations to stay out of Latin America. The United States—believing that its own political backyard included Central and South America—did not hesitate to send marines, gunboats, or both to intervene in South American and Caribbean affairs. When European nations were at war, however, Americans relished their distance from the conflicts. So it was until World War I (1914–1918).

In the wake of World War I, President Woodrow Wilson urged the United States to join the League of Nations, a forerunner to the UN. The U.S. Senate refused to ratify the League of Nations treaty, indicating that the country was not ready to abandon the long-standing American habit of isolationism, nor was the Senate ready to turn over its war-making authority to an international body. World War II, which forced the United States into a global conflict, dealt a deathblow to American isolationism. Most nations signed a charter for the UN at a conference in San Francisco in 1945. The United States was an original signatory and soon donated land to house the UN permanently in New York City.

The Cold War

At the end of World War II, the Allies had vanquished Germany and Japan, and much of Europe was strewn with rubble. The United States was unquestionably the dominant world power, both economically and militarily. It not only had helped to bring the war to an end but also had inaugurated a new era in warfare by dropping the first atomic bombs on Japan in August 1945. Because only the United States possessed nuclear weapons, Americans looked forward to an era of peace secured by their nuclear umbrella.

After World War II, the United States forged strong alliances with the nations of Western Europe. To help them rebuild their economies, the United States poured billions of dollars into war-ravaged European nations through a program known as the Marshall Plan—named after its architect, Secretary of State George C. Marshall. A military alliance was also forged; the creation of NATO in 1949 affirmed the mutual military interests of the United States and Western Europe, and NATO remains a cornerstone of American foreign and defense policy.

Containment Abroad and Anticommunism at Home. Although many Americans expected cooperative relations with their wartime ally, the Soviet Union, they soon abandoned those hopes. There is still much dispute about how the Cold War between the United States and the Soviet Union started.[9] Even before World War II ended, some American policymakers feared that their Soviet allies were intent on spreading communism not only to their neighbors but everywhere. All of Eastern Europe fell under Soviet domination as World War II ended. In 1946, Winston Churchill warned that the Russians had sealed off Eastern Europe with an "iron curtain."

You Are President John F. Kennedy

Communist support of a revolt in Greece in 1946 compounded fears of Soviet aggression. Writing in *Foreign Affairs* in 1947, foreign policy strategist George F. Kennan proposed a policy of "containment."[10] His **containment doctrine** called for the United States to isolate the Soviet Union—to "contain" its advances and resist its encroachments—by peaceful means if possible but with force if necessary. When economic problems forced Great Britain to decrease its support of Greece, the United States stepped in with the Truman Doctrine of helping other nations oppose communism. The Soviet Union responded with the Berlin Blockade of 1948–1949, in which it closed off land access to West Berlin (which was surrounded by communist East Germany). The United States and its allies broke the blockade by airlifting food, fuel, and other necessities to the people of the beleaguered city.

containment doctrine
A foreign policy strategy advocated by George Kennan that called for the United States to isolate the Soviet Union, "contain" its advances, and resist its encroachments by peaceful means if possible but by force if necessary.

In 1963, President John F. Kennedy looked over the Berlin Wall, which the Soviet Union had built to separate communist East Berlin from the western sectors of the city. The wall stood as the most palpable symbol of the Cold War for almost 30 years until it was torn down in 1989.

The fall of China to Mao Zedong's communist-led forces in 1949 seemed to confirm American fears that communism was a cancer spreading over the "free world." In the same year, the Soviet Union exploded its first atomic bomb. The invasion of pro-American South Korea by communist North Korea in 1950 further fueled American fears of Soviet imperialism. President Truman said bluntly, "We've got to stop the Russians now," and he sent American troops to Korea under UN auspices. The Korean War was a chance to put containment into practice. Involving China as well as North Korea, the war dragged on until July 27, 1953.

Cold War
War by other than military means usually emphasizing ideological conflict, such as that between the United States and the Soviet Union from the end of World War II until the 1990s.

The 1950s were the height of the **Cold War**. Although hostilities never quite erupted into armed battle between them, the United States and the Soviet Union were often on the brink of war. John Foster Dulles, secretary of state under Eisenhower, proclaimed a policy often referred to as "brinkmanship," in which the United States was to be prepared to use nuclear weapons in order to *deter* the Soviet Union and communist China from taking aggressive actions.

McCarthyism
The fear, prevalent in the 1950s, that international communism was conspiratorial, insidious, bent on world domination, and infiltrating American government and cultural institutions. It was named after Senator Joseph McCarthy and flourished after the Korean War.

Fear of communism affected domestic as well as foreign policy. Most Americans believed that international communism was conspiratorial, insidious, and bent on world domination and infiltrating American government and cultural institutions. Senator Joseph McCarthy exploited this atmosphere and with flimsy evidence accused scores of prominent Americans and State Department officials of being communists. **McCarthyism** flowered during the Korean War. Domestic policy in general was deeply affected by the Cold War and by anticommunist fears. A burgeoning defense budget during the Korean War and later in the 1950s was another result of the Cold War.

The Swelling of the Pentagon. The Cold War ensured that military needs and massive national security expenditures would remain fixtures in the American economy. As early as 1947, aircraft manufacturers noted that the decline of military procurement after World War II would injure the industry; to avert dislocation, they launched a campaign to sell planes to the U.S. Air Force.[11] Thus were forged some of the first links between policymakers' perceptions of the Soviet threat and corporations' awareness of potential profits from military hardware. Generals and admirals believed they needed weapons systems, and private industry was happy to supply them for a profit. Defense expenditures grew to be the largest component of the federal budget in the 1950s, consuming $13 of every $100 of the gross domestic product (GDP; the total value of all the goods and services produced annually by the United States) by 1954. Large parts of this defense budget were spent on weapons supplied by giant companies such as Westinghouse, RCA, Western Electric, and General Motors.

The interests shared by the armed services and defense contractors produced what some call a *military-industrial complex*. The phrase was coined not by a left-wing critic of the military but by President Dwight D. Eisenhower, a former five-star general. Elite theorists especially pointed to this tight alliance between business and government. Economist Seymour Melman wrote about *pentagon capitalism*, linking the military's drive to expand with the profit motives of private industry.[12] As the defense budget grew, so did the profits of aircraft producers and other defense contractors.

By the 1950s, the Soviet Union and the United States were engaged in an **arms race**. One side's weaponry goaded the other side to procure yet more weaponry, as one missile led to another. By the mid-1960s, the result of the arms race was a point of *mutual assured destruction (MAD)*, in which each side could annihilate the other, even after absorbing a surprise attack. Later sections of this chapter will examine efforts to control the arms race.

arms race
A tense relationship beginning in the 1950s between the Soviet Union and the United States whereby one side's weaponry became the other side's goad to procure more weaponry and so on.

The Vietnam War. Even though it reached its peak during the 1960s, American involvement in Vietnam began much earlier. The Korean War and the 1949 victory of communist forces in China fixed the U.S. government's attention on Asian communism. In 1950, while the Korean War raged and just after the fall of Chiang Kai-shek in China, President Truman decided to aid France's effort to retain its colonial possessions in Southeast Asia.[13]

Aided by the new communist government in China, the Vietnamese communists finally defeated the French in a battle at Dien Bien Phu in 1954. The morning after the battle, peace talks began among the participants and other major powers in Geneva, Switzerland. Although a party to the resultant agreements, the United States never accepted the Geneva agreement, which stipulated that national elections be held in Vietnam in 1956. Instead, it began supporting one noncommunist leader after another in South Vietnam, each seemingly more committed than the last to defeating communist forces in the north.

Unable to contain the forces of the communist guerillas and the North Vietnamese army with American advisers, President Johnson sent in American troops—more than 500,000 at the peak of the undeclared war. He dropped more bombs on communist North Vietnam than the United States had dropped on Germany in all of World War II. American troops and massive firepower failed to contain the North Vietnamese, however. At home, widespread protests against the war contributed to Johnson's decisions not to run for reelection in 1968 and to begin peace negotiations.

The new Nixon administration prosecuted the war vigorously, in Cambodia as well as in Vietnam, but also negotiated with the Vietnamese communists. A peace treaty was signed in 1973, but no one expected it to hold. South Vietnam's capital,

The Vietnam War Memorial is one of the most moving sights in Washington, D.C. Often called "The Wall," the memorial lists the names of more than 58,000 Americans killed during the Vietnam War.

Saigon, finally fell to the North Vietnamese army in 1975. South and North Vietnam were reunited into a single nation, and Saigon was renamed Ho Chi Minh City in honor of the late leader of communist North Vietnam.

Looking back on the Vietnam War, most Americans question its worth. It divided the nation and made citizens painfully aware of the government's ability to lie to them—and (perhaps worse) to itself. It reminded Americans that even a "great power" cannot prevail in a protracted military conflict against a determined enemy unless there is a clear objective and unless the national will is sufficiently committed to expend vast resources on the task.

The Era of Détente

Even while the United States was waging the Vietnam War, Richard Nixon—a veteran fighter of the Cold War—supported a new policy that came to be called **détente**. The term was popularized by Nixon's national security adviser and later secretary of state, Henry Kissinger.

détente

A slow transformation from conflict thinking to cooperative thinking in **foreign policy** strategy and policymaking. It sought a relaxation of tensions between the superpowers, coupled with firm guarantees of mutual security.

Détente represented a slow transformation from conflict thinking to cooperative thinking in foreign policy strategy. It sought a relaxation of tensions between the superpowers, coupled with firm guarantees of mutual security. The policy assumed that the United States and the Soviet Union had no long-range, irrevocable sources of conflict; that both had an interest in peace and world stability; and that a nuclear war was—and should be—unthinkable. Thus, foreign policy battles between the United States and the Soviet Union were to be waged with diplomatic, economic, and propaganda weapons; the threat of force was downplayed.

One major initiative emerging from détente was the *Strategic Arms Limitation Talks (SALT)*. These talks represented a mutual effort by the United States and the Soviet Union to limit the growth of their nuclear capabilities, with each power maintaining sufficient nuclear weapons to deter a surprise attack by the other. Richard Nixon signed the first SALT accord in 1972, and negotiations for a second agreement, SALT II, soon followed. After six years of laborious negotiations, President Carter finally signed the agreement and sent it to the Senate in 1979. The Soviet invasion of Afghanistan that year caused Carter to withdraw the treaty from Senate consideration, however, even though both he and Ronald Reagan insisted that they would remain committed to the agreement's limitations on nuclear weaponry.

The United States applied the philosophy of détente to the People's Republic of China as well as to the Soviet Union. After the fall of the pro-American government in 1949, the United States refused to extend diplomatic recognition to the world's most populous nation, recognizing instead the government in exile on the nearby island of Taiwan. As a senator in the early 1950s, Richard Nixon had been an implacable foe of "Red China," even suggesting that the Democratic administration had traitorously "lost" China. Nevertheless, two decades later it was this same Richard Nixon who, as president, first visited the People's Republic and sent an American mission there. President Jimmy Carter extended formal diplomatic recognition to China in January 1979. Since then, cultural and economic ties between the United States and China have increased greatly.

Not everyone favored détente, however. Even Carter called for a substantial increase in defense spending after the Soviet Union invaded Afghanistan in 1979. Few people saw more threats from the Soviet Union than did Ronald Reagan, who called it the "Evil Empire." He viewed the Soviet invasion of Afghanistan as typical Russian aggression that, if unchecked, could only grow more common. He hailed anticommunist governments everywhere and pledged to increase American defense spending.

The Reagan Rearmament

From the mid-1950s to 1981 (with the exception of the Vietnam War), the defense budget had generally been declining as a percentage of both the total federal budget and the GDP. In 1955, during the Eisenhower administration, the government was spending 61 percent of its budget for defense purposes, or about 10 percent of the GDP. By the time President Reagan took office in 1981, the government devoted less than 25 percent of the federal budget and 5.2 percent of the GDP to defense expenditures. These figures reflected a substantial cut indeed, although the decrease came about more because levels of social spending had increased than because military spending had declined. Still, Republican Richard Nixon used to boast that he was the first president in recent history who committed more of the national budget to social services than to military expenditures.

During his campaign for the presidency, Reagan argued that "we cannot negotiate arms control agreements that will slow down the Soviet military buildup as long as we let the Soviets move ahead of us in every category of armaments."

According to Reagan, America faced a "window of vulnerability" because the Soviet Union was galloping ahead of the United States in military spending.

As president, Reagan was determined to reverse the trend of diminishing defense spending and proposed the largest peacetime defense spending increase in American history: a five-year defense buildup costing $1.5 trillion. The early days of the Reagan administration were the most critical in this defense buildup. The news came down to the Pentagon rank and file quickly: President Carter's last budget had proposed a large increase in defense spending, and the Reagan administration would add $32 billion on top of that. Defense officials were ordered to find places to spend more money.[14] These heady days for the Pentagon lasted only through the first term of Reagan's presidency, however. In his second term, concern over huge budget deficits brought defense spending to a standstill. After taking inflation into account, Congress appropriated no increase in defense spending at all from 1985 to 1988.

Strategic Defense Initiative

Renamed "Star Wars" by critics, a plan for defense against the Soviet Union unveiled by President Reagan in 1983. The Strategic Defense Initiative would create a global umbrella in space, using computers to scan the skies and high-tech devices to destroy invading missiles.

In 1983, President Reagan added another element to his defense policy—a new plan for defense against missiles. He called it the **Strategic Defense Initiative** (SDI); critics quickly renamed it "Star Wars." Reagan's plans for SDI proposed creating a global umbrella in space, wherein computers would scan the skies and use various high-tech devices to destroy invading missiles. The administration proposed a research program that would have cost tens of billions of dollars over the next decade. In the face of an onslaught of criticism regarding the feasibility of SDI, its proponents reduced their expectations about the size and capabilities of any defensive shield that could be erected over the next generation. Talk of a smaller system—capable of protecting against an accidental launch of a few missiles or against a threat by some Third World country with nuclear weapons—replaced the dream of an impenetrable umbrella over the United States capable of defeating a massive Soviet nuclear strike.

The Final Thaw in the Cold War

On May 12, 1989, in a commencement address at Texas A&M University, President Bush announced a new era in American foreign policy. He termed this era one "beyond containment"; the goal of the United States would be more than containing Soviet expansion. Bush declared that it was time to seek the integration of the Soviet Union into the community of nations.

The Cold War ended as few had anticipated—spontaneously. Suddenly, the elusive objective of 40 years of post–World War II U.S. foreign policy—freedom and self-determination for Eastern Europeans and Soviet peoples and the reduction of the military threat from the East—occurred. Forces of change sparked by Soviet leader Mikhail Gorbachev led to a staggering wave of upheaval that shattered communist regimes and the postwar barriers between Eastern and Western Europe. The Berlin Wall, the most prominent symbol of oppression in Eastern Europe, came tumbling down on November 9, 1989, and East and West Germany formed a unified, democratic republic. The former Soviet Union split into 15 separate nations, and noncommunist governments formed in most of them. Poland, Czechoslovakia (splitting into the Czech Republic and Slovakia), and Hungary established democratic governments, and reformers overthrew the old-line communist leaders in Bulgaria and Romania.

Events were unfolding so fast and in so many places at once that no one was quite sure how to deal with them. President Bush declared, "Every morning I receive an intelligence briefing, and I receive the best information available to any world leader today. And yet, the morning news is often overtaken by the news that very same evening."[15]

In 1989, reform seemed on the verge of occurring in China as well as in Eastern Europe. That spring in Tiananmen Square, the central meeting place in Beijing, thousands of students held protests on behalf of democratization. Unable to tolerate challenges to their rule any longer, the aging Chinese leaders forcibly—and brutally—evacuated the square, crushing some protestors under armored tanks. It is still not clear how many students were killed and how many others arrested, but the reform movement in China received a serious setback. This suppression of efforts to develop democracy sent a chill through what had been a warming relationship between the United States and the People's Republic of China.

Reform continued elsewhere, however. On June 17, 1992, Boris Yeltsin addressed a joint session of the U.S. Congress. When the burly, silver-haired president of the new Russian republic entered the House chamber, members of Congress greeted him with chants of "Bo-ris, Bo-ris" and hailed him with numerous standing ovations.

Yeltsin proclaimed to thunderous applause,

> *The idol of communism, which spread everywhere social strife, animosity and unparalleled brutality, which instilled fear in humanity, has collapsed . . . I am here to assure you that we will not let it rise again in our land.*

The Cold War that had been waged for two generations had ended, and the West, led by the United States, had won.

The War on Terrorism

Perhaps the most troublesome issue in the national security area is the spread of terrorism—the use of violence to demoralize and frighten a country's population or government. Terrorism takes many forms, including the bombing of buildings (such as the attacks on New York and Washington on September 11, 2001; on the American embassy in Kenya in 1998; and on the World Trade Center in New York in 1993) and ships (such as the USS *Cole* in Yemen in 2000), the assassinations of political leaders (as when Iraq attempted to kill former president George Bush in 1993), and the kidnappings of diplomats and civilians (as when Iranians took Americans hostage in 1979).

It is difficult to defend against terrorism, especially in an open society. Terrorists have the advantage of stealth and surprise. Improved security measures and better intelligence gathering can help. So, perhaps, can punishing governments and organizations that engage in terrorist activities. In 1986, the United States launched an air attack on Libya in response to Libyan-supported acts of terrorism; in 1993, the United States struck at Iraq's intelligence center in response to a foiled plot to assassinate

"Surely, as the world's only superpower, we're entitled to a little mischief now and then."

former president George Bush; and in 1998, the United States launched an attack in Afghanistan on Osama bin Laden, the leader of a terrorist organization.

In his inaugural address following his reelection in 2005, the president spoke to the world, proclaiming that America would stand with those who challenge authoritarian governments and warned those governments to begin liberalizing. These exhortations appeared to represent opening another front on the war on terrorism, but the administration—including a rare press conference held by the president's father—downplayed the significance of the statements. It remains to be seen how the White House makes the inevitable trade-offs between principle and pragmatism in dealing with repressive regimes. So far, however, it appears as though the unexpected difficulties endured in Iraq since the fall of Saddam Hussein have colored the broader efforts against the "axis of evil" states of Iran and North Korea. Tehran and Pyongyang have felt freer to flout American pressure, secure in the knowledge that the U.S. military is tied down in Iraq. The White House has favored diplomacy with Tehran and Pyongyang, adopting a decidedly pragmatic turn.

Afghanistan and Iraq

9-11-2001

Following the September 11, 2001, attacks on New York and Washington, the United States declared war on terrorism. President George W. Bush made the war the highest priority of his administration, and the United States launched an attack on the Taliban regime that had been harboring terrorists in Afghanistan. The Taliban fell in short order, although many suspected terrorist members of Osama bin Laden's al-Qaeda network escaped. In the meantime, the president declared that Iran, Iraq, and North Korea formed an "axis of evil" and began laying plans to remove Iraqi President Saddam Hussein from power. In 2003, a U.S.-led coalition toppled Hussein.

Overthrowing dictators carries with it new problems, however. In the 2000 presidential campaign, George W. Bush spoke of "humility" in foreign affairs and warned against "nation building" and overextending America's military. The threat of terrorism, leading to the invasions of both Afghanistan and Iraq, caused the president to rethink these views, and the administration began talking about meeting America's "unparalleled responsibilities." One of those responsibilities has been to rebuild and democratize Iraq.

Americans in Iraq

There is broad consensus that the planning for postwar Iraq was poor. The administration presumed that Americans would be welcomed as liberators, that Iraqi oil would pay for most (if not all) of the necessary reconstruction of the country, and that the Iraqis possessed the necessary skills and infrastructure to do the job. These premises proved to be faulty, and the United States faced first chaos and then a protracted insurrection, especially in the "Sunni triangle" around Baghdad. Three years after the end of the official fighting, 130,000 American troops were still stationed in Iraq, straining our defense resources. As both U.S. expenditures on reconstruction and American casualties mounted in the period since the end of the war with Iraq, the public's support for the effort declined substantially, and the president experienced a corresponding drop in his approval ratings.

President George W. Bush has often declared that postwar Iraq is the front line in the global war on terror. The president's critics respond that the war has been a boon for extremists. Muslims consider Iraq, the seat of Islamic power for five centuries, sacred ground. The presence of foreign, non-Muslim occupiers there has become a magnet for militants hoping for an opportunity to kill Americans and other westerners. Since the war in Afghanistan, al-Qaeda has changed from an active source of planning, training, and attacks into an umbrella organization that provides an inspirational focal point for loosely affiliated terrorist groups in dozens of countries worldwide.

Some view this transformed threat as potentially more dangerous than the one posed by the original al-Qaeda. A "decapitation" strategy, focusing on the elimination of a small group of senior figures in the original al-Qaeda network, may no longer be an adequate or appropriate strategy for dealing with a threat that has, in effect, metastasized.

Formulating a new strategy to defeat al-Qaeda and its affiliates will not be easy. The use of military force alone will not neutralize this more dispersed terrorist threat. Because of the increasingly decentralized nature of the threat, the military component of the global counterterrorism campaign is more likely to resemble a war of attrition on multiple fronts than a limited number of surgical strikes against a single adversary. One consequence is that the war on terrorism is likely to persist for many years. At this point, the number of terrorist attacks worldwide is on the rise.[16] According to U.S. government figures released in April 2005, there were 651 significant international terrorist incidents in 2004, more than triple the record 175 documented in 2003. Some of the increase may be explained by improvements in data collection.

Some see the war on terrorism as responding to a tactic (terrorism) rather than to the forces that generate it. Critics also fear that the arrogation of a unilateral right to define threats and use force is squandering America's moral authority and diminishing its global credibility. They argue that the United States cannot defend itself without the help of others and thus that American national security is inextricably tied to international security.

Whichever side is right in this debate over the war on terrorism, there is no doubt that the need to fight terrorists has forced Americans to rethink some of the basic tenets of U.S. national security policy (see "A Generation of Change: Rethinking National Security Policy"). In addition, almost everyone agrees that today's complicated international environment portends an overhaul of the American national security infrastructure. Policymakers are reassessing armed

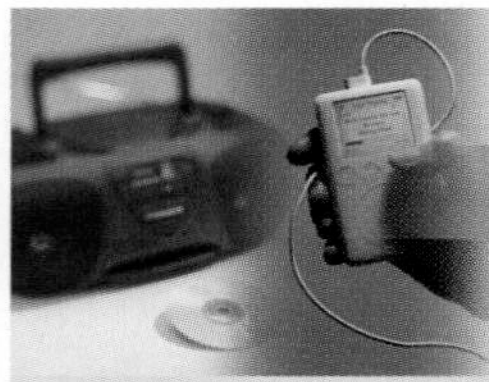

A GENERATION OF CHANGE

Rethinking National Security Policy

Despite its risks and uncertainties, the Cold War was characterized by a stable and predictable set of relations among the great powers. Now international relations have entered an era of improvisation as nations struggle to develop creative responses to changes in the global balance of power and the new challenges that have emerged.

The threat posed by terrorist groups and the hostile states supporting them has forced America to reconsider basic tenets of its national security policy. President George W. Bush believes that the strategies and institutions that kept the peace during the Cold War are not suited to a twenty-first-century campaign against terrorism. He has concluded that multilateral alliances like NATO and bilateral partnerships like that with South Korea have proven ineffective in dealing with terrorism. Thus, although the United States maintains its system of formal, structured alliances, it is also emphasizing a more fluid system of improvised alignments of nations in which the mission determines the alliance.

The national security strategy doctrine issued by the Bush administration in September 2002 was the most dramatic and far-reaching change in national security policy in a half century. The doctrine moves away from the Cold War pillars of containment and deterrence toward a policy that supports preemptive strikes against terrorists and hostile states to prevent their using chemical, biological, or nuclear weapons against the United States. When the United States found no weapons of mass destruction in Iraq, the administration expanded its formulation from precluding immediate threats to prevention of the development of threats. The strategic doctrine also explicitly advocates U.S. preeminence in military capabilities and, if necessary, unilateral action in national security policy, contrary to decades of emphasis on grounding defense policy in alliances.

The U.S. invasion of Iraq in 2003 followed directly from these premises. It was a policy designed to preempt future strikes against the United States and its allies. The absence of support from core members of NATO and the potential damage to our most enduring alliances did not deter the president. Nor did the lack of support from the United Nations, which the president feels has failed miserably—in Rwanda, in Kosovo, and most recently in its confrontation with Iraq—and needs to be made anew. Similarly, the president renounced the 1972 Anti-Ballistic Missile Treaty over the objections of Russia and China, refused to participate in the International Criminal Court, and rejected several environmental treaties.

forces and alliances, defense industries, and budgets built up since World War II in light of both the Cold War thaw and the war on terrorism.

The Politics of Defense Policy

The politics of national defense involves high stakes—the nation's security, for example. Domestic political concerns, budgetary limitations, and ideology all influence decisions on the structure of defense policy and negotiations with allies and adversaries. All public policies include budgets, people, and equipment. In the realm of national defense, these elements are especially critical because of the size of the budget and the bureaucracy as well as the destructive potential of modern weapons.

At the core of defense policy is a judgment about what the United States will defend. The central assumption of current American defense policy is that the United States requires forces and equipment sufficient to win decisively a single major conflict, defend American territory against new threats, and conduct a number of holding actions elsewhere in the world. Large military infrastructure is necessary to meet these goals.

Defense Spending

Defense spending now makes up about one-fifth of the federal budget. Although this is a much smaller percentage than in earlier years, vast sums of money and fundamental questions of public policy are still involved (see Figure 17.1). Some scholars have argued that America faces a trade-off between defense spending and social spending. A nation, they claim, must choose between guns and butter, and more guns means less butter. Evidence supporting the existence of such a trade-off is mixed, however. In general, defense and domestic policy expenditures appear to be independent of each other.[17] Ronald Reagan's efforts to increase military budgets while cutting back on domestic policy expenditures seem to have stemmed more from his own ideology than from any inevitable choice between the two.

Defense spending is a thorny political issue, entangled with ideological disputes. Conservatives advocate increases in defense spending, pointing out that many nations and terrorist organizations retain potent military capability, and insist that America maintain its readiness at a high level. They refer to the Gulf War as evidence that wars on a significant scale are still possible. In addition, they attribute the collapse of communism in Eastern and Central Europe to Western toughness and the massive increase in defense spending that occurred in the early 1980s. When the Soviet Union saw that it could not outspend the United States, they argue, it finally decided not to continue to allocate so much of its scarce resources to defense and to loosen its grip on Eastern Europe.

Liberals have supported increases in defense spending for the war on terrorism. In general, however, they are skeptical of defense spending, maintaining that the Pentagon wastes money and that the United States buys too many guns and too little butter. The most crucial aspect of national defense, they argue, is a

Why It Matters

The Defense Budget
In the twenty-first century, the United States spends about one-fifth of its national budget on defense to support a large defense establishment. This expenditure contributes to large annual budget deficits, but some argue that we should spend even more to protect the country against terrorism.

Figure 17.1 Trends in Defense Spending

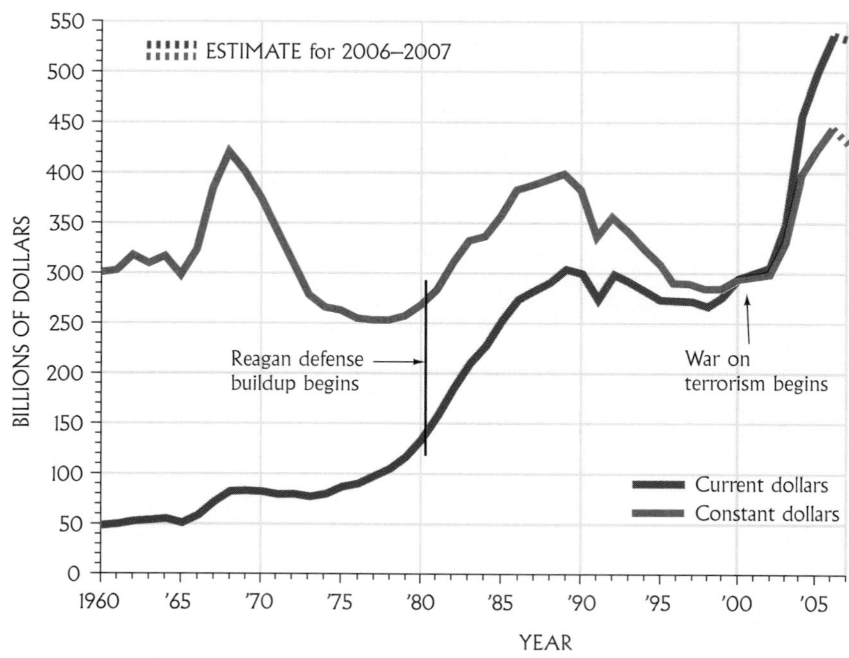

Source: Budget of the United States Government, Fiscal Year 2007: Historical Tables (Washington, DC: U.S. Government Printing Office, 2006), table 3.1.

strong economy, which is based on investments in "human capital" such as health and education. Liberals insist that the erosion of the Communist Party's authority was well under way when Gorbachev rose to power. This erosion accelerated as *glasnost* (the Russian term for the new openness of society) made the party's failures a matter of public ridicule as democratization freed new forces to challenge the existing order. They contend that Gorbachev and his reformers were responding primarily to internal, not external, pressures. Inadequacies and defects at the core of the Soviet economy—the inertia, wastefulness, and corruption inherent in the system—were the driving forces that brought change to the Soviet Union, not American defense spending.

In addition, scholars such as Paul Kennedy and David Calleo envision a new world order different from the bipolar dominance of the United States and the Soviet Union.[18] Kennedy warns of the historical dangers of "imperial overstretch," suggesting that great empires in a stage of relative economic decline compared with emerging powers accelerate their decline by clinging to vast military commitments.

Whatever its cause, the lessening of East–West tensions gave momentum to significant reductions in defense spending, what some called the *peace dividend*. Changing spending patterns is not easy, however. For example, military hardware developed during the lush years of the early 1980s has proven to be increasingly expensive to purchase and maintain. And when the assembly lines at weapons plants close down, submarine designers, welders, and others lose their jobs. These programs become political footballs as candidates compete over promises to keep weapons systems such as the *Seawolf* submarine or the Osprey helicopter in production. Ideology plays a crucial role in the basic decisions members of Congress make regarding defense spending, but once these decisions are made, liberal as well as conservative representatives and senators fight hard to help constituencies win and keep defense contracts.[19]

The trend of reductions in defense spending reversed abruptly in 2001 following the September 11 terrorist attacks. Whatever the proper level of spending, there is no question that the United States spends more on defense than the next 15 or 20 biggest spenders combined. It has overwhelming nuclear superiority, the world's dominant air force, the only truly blue-water navy (which also has impressive airpower), and a unique capability to project power around the globe. No other country in modern history has come close to this level of military predominance, and the gap between the United States and other nations is increasing with more in defense spending to support the war on terrorism. Moreover, the military advantages are even greater when one considers the quality as well as the quantity of U.S. defense capabilities. America has exploited the military applications of advanced communications and information technology and has developed the ability to coordinate and process information about the battlefield and to destroy targets from afar with extraordinary precision.

Evaluating Defense Spending

Personnel

The structure of America's defense has been based on a large standing military force and a battery of strategic nuclear weapons. The United States has more than 1.3 million men and women on active duty and about 826,000 in the national guard and reserves (see Table 17.1). There are more than 300,000 active-duty troops deployed abroad, mostly in Europe, Japan, and South Korea;[20] there were about 140,000 troops in Iraq in 2006. This is a very costly enterprise and one that frequently evokes calls to bring the troops home. Many observers believe that America's allies,

Table 17.1 Size of the Armed Forces

BRANCH	PERSONNEL[a]
Army	482,400
Navy	340,700
Air Force	334,200
Marines	175,000
Subtotal	1,332,300
Reserves	825,700
Total	2,158,000

[a]2007 estimates.

Sources: Office of Management and Budget, *Budget of the United States Government, Fiscal Year 2007: Appendix* (Washington, DC: U.S. Government Printing Office, 2006), 245–46.

especially prosperous nations such as Japan and Germany, should bear a greater share of common defense costs.

Cuts in defense spending led to reduced numbers of active-duty personnel in the armed services. As a result, the military now relies much more heavily on national guard and reserve units to maintain national security (the "Total Force" concept). The president mobilized national guard units and sent them into active duty in Bosnia, and national guard and reserve units have served in the war on terrorism, many for extended periods in Iraq.

Weapons

To deter an aggressor's attack, the United States has relied on a triad of nuclear weapons: ground-based intercontinental ballistic missiles (ICBMs), submarine-launched ballistic missiles, and strategic bombers. Both the United States and Russia have thousands of large nuclear warheads. These weapons, like troops, are costly (each Stealth bomber costs over two *billion* dollars), and they pose obvious dangers to human survival. The total cost of building nuclear weapons has been $5.5 *trillion*.[21]

The rapid drive toward democracy in Eastern Europe, combined with Moscow's economic stagnation and the Pentagon's budgetary squeeze, pushed arms reduction inexorably onto the two superpowers' discussion agenda. Substantial progress has been made to end the arms race and what was known as "the balance of terror."

During the May 1988 Moscow summit meeting, President Reagan and Mikhail Gorbachev exchanged ratified copies of a new treaty eliminating *intermediate-range nuclear forces (INF)*. Reagan, who had built his reputation on fervid anticommunism and had denounced earlier arms control efforts (such as Jimmy Carter's SALT II agreement), became the first American president to sign a treaty to reduce current levels of nuclear weapons. Under the terms of the INF treaty, more than 2,500 nuclear weapons with ranges between 300 and 3,400 miles were to be destroyed.

Superpower relations continued to improve at a dizzying pace, accelerated by the dissolution of the Soviet Union. On November 19, 1990, the leaders of 22 countries signed a treaty reducing conventional armed forces in Europe. The treaty slashed forces in Europe by 40 percent—the Soviet Union was called on to remove the most troops. A related change occurred in 1991 as the Warsaw Pact, the military alliance tying Eastern Europe to the Soviet Union, was dissolved.

On July 31, 1991, shortly before Soviet hard-liners attempted a coup to remove President Gorbachev and other reformers from power, he and President Bush signed the *Strategic Arms Reduction Treaty (START)*—after nine years of negotiations. The treaty had the distinction of being the first accord mandating the elimination of strategic nuclear weaponry. (The INF treaty banned a whole class of shorter-range nuclear arms.)

The significance of these changes was soon overshadowed by other events, however, as the democratization of Eastern Europe, the restructuring of the Soviet Union, and the deterioration of the Soviet economy substantially diminished both Russia's inclination and potential to threaten the interests of the United States and its allies. President Bush broke ground with his decision in the fall of 1991 to dismantle unilaterally some U.S. nuclear weapons, enticing President Gorbachev to follow suit shortly afterward.

In January 1993, Presidents Bush and Yeltsin signed an agreement (START II) to cut the U.S. and Russian (including those of Ukraine, Belarus, and Kazakhstan) nuclear arsenals to a total of no more than 6,500 weapons by the year 2003—less than one-third of the 20,000 long-range nuclear weapons the two possessed at the time. The agreement banned large, accurate ICBMs with multiple warheads altogether. In 2002, President George W. Bush and Russian President Vladimir Putin signed a treaty to limit strategic nuclear weapons to no more than 2,200 for each country by 2012. At the same time, President Bush stepped up efforts to build a national missile defense. To pursue this system, in December 2001 the president withdrew the United States from the Anti-Ballistic Missile Treaty that it signed with the Soviet Union in 1972.

Nuclear weapons are the most destructive in America's arsenal, but they are by no means the only weapons. Jet fighters, aircraft carriers, and even tanks are extraordinarily complex and equally costly. The perception that space-age technology helped win the Gulf War in "100 hours" and topple the Taliban regime in Afghanistan and Saddam Hussein in Iraq with few American casualties, in addition to the fact that producing expensive weapons provides jobs for American workers, means that high-tech weapons systems will continue to play an important role in America's defense posture.

Reforming Defense Policy

Directly related to rethinking national security policy is reforming the nation's military. Reevaluating weapons systems and potentially skipping a generation to produce more technologically advanced systems is part of the effort. So is changing the force structure to make the armed forces lighter, faster, and more flexible. More effectively coupling intelligence with an increasingly agile military and a greater use of Special Forces are also significant breaks from the past. New approaches to military conflict inevitably follow from such transformations.

Although progress has been made on reducing tensions between East and West, other international matters clamor for attention. Even the mightiest nation can be mired in intractable issues.

The New Global Agenda

The global agenda is changing rapidly. As military competition with communist powers has diminished, economic competition with the world has increased. The gap between domestic and foreign policy is increasingly obscure. Dealing with allies such as Japan and Germany on trade and finance is as crucial as negotiating arms reductions with Russia. Maintaining access to petroleum in the Middle East is more crucial than ever, and determining policy regarding the global environment has taken on new prominence.

Regardless of the standards one uses for measurement, the United States is the world's mightiest military power. Its very strength seems to belie an essential weakness, however. Events on the world stage often appear to counter the American script. In the long and controversial Vietnam War, 500,000 American troops were not enough. The economic vulnerability of the United States has increased. Our military might did not protect us from the deadly terrorist attacks on September 11, 2001. Oil supply lines depend on a precarious Middle Eastern peace and on the safe passage of huge tankers through a sliver of water called the Strait of Hormuz. We sometimes appear to be losing the highly publicized war on drugs to an international network of wealthy drug lords called *narco-traficantes*. Perhaps most important of all, our economy is increasingly dependent on international trade, placing us at the mercy of interest rates in Germany, restrictive markets in Japan, and currency values in China.

Why It Matters

The Only Superpower
The United States is the world's only superpower. This puts us in a strong position to defend ourselves against other nations. However, it also means that America comes under more pressure from other nations to police the world's hot spots for peacekeeping and other humanitarian purposes. Being a superpower also does not protect us against attacks by nonstate actors, such as terrorists.

There is an interesting paradox to American power: Although the United States is militarily and economically supreme, it is becoming increasingly dependent on other peoples to defeat terrorism, protect the environment, control weapons of mass destruction, regulate trade, and deal with other problems that cross national boundaries.[22] Even the effective use of U.S. military power requires military bases, ports, airfields, fuel supplies, and overflight rights that only its allies can provide.

There is much discussion in governing circles about whether America's military dominance will blind it to the need to cooperate with other nations. The George W. Bush administration has been assertive in acting unilaterally and defending U.S. interests rather than collective international interests. Many critics (including many of America's allies) complain that the United States undermines its ability to obtain the support of other countries when it fails to consult them, refuses to participate in the International Criminal Court, and rejects treaties to eliminate greenhouse gases, restrict antiballistic missile systems, prohibit land mines, and ban biological weapons testing.

The Changing Role of Military Power

From Stand-Alone to Superpower: The Evolution of Foreign Policy

Harvard political scientist Stanley Hoffman likened the plight of the United States to that of Jonathan Swift's fictional character Gulliver, the traveler seized and bound by the tiny Lilliputians.[23] For Americans, as for Gulliver, merely being big and powerful is no guarantee of dominance. Time after time and place after place, so it seems, the American Gulliver is frustrated by the Lilliputians.

One explanation for America's tribulations is that the nation's strong suit—military might—is no longer the primary instrument of foreign policy. Today military power is losing much of its utility in resolving many international issues. "Force," argue Robert Keohane and Joseph Nye, "is often not an appropriate way of achieving other goals (such as economic and ecological welfare) that are becoming more important" in world affairs.[24] Economic conflicts do not readily yield to nuclear weapons. America cannot persuade Arab nations to sell it cheap oil by bombing them, nor can it prop up the textile industry's position in world trade by resorting to military might. The United States is long on firepower at the very time when firepower is decreasing in its utility as an instrument of foreign policy.

According to Nye, it is "soft power"—the ability of a country to persuade others to do what it wants without force or coercion—that is often crucial to national security. American culture, ideals, and values have been important in helping Washington attract partners and supporters, and countries require both hard and soft power to shape long-term attitudes and preferences around the globe. Thus, security hinges as much on winning hearts and minds as it does on winning wars.[25]

Conflict among large powers, the threat of nuclear war, and the possibility of conventional war have certainly not disappeared, but grafted onto them are new issues. Former Secretary of State Henry Kissinger described the new era eloquently:

> *The traditional agenda of international affairs—the balance among major powers, the security of nations—no longer defines our perils or our possibilities. Now we are entering a new era. Old international patterns are crumbling; old slogans are uninstructive. The world has become interdependent in economics, in communications, in human aspirations.*[26]

Despite these changes, military power remains an important element in U.S. foreign policy. The end of the Cold War emboldened local dictators and reignited age-old ethnic rivalries that had been held in check by the Soviet Union. The result: The number of regional crises likely to pose a threat to peace has grown exponentially in the post–Cold War era. America's status as the only superpower has meant that Washington is the first place people look for help when trouble erupts, even in Europe's backyard, as in the case of the territory of the former Yugoslavia. One of the nation's most difficult foreign policy problems is in deciding when to send U.S. troops to police the world's hot spots.

Humanitarian Interventions. Military interventions are not always designed to increase a country's power or to defeat a threatening foe. In recent years, the United States and its allies have used military force to accomplish humanitarian ends. The most notable examples include the efforts to distribute food and then oust a ruthless and unprincipled warlord in Somalia in 1992 and 1993, restore the elected leader of Haiti in 1994, stop the ethnic warfare in Bosnia by bombing the Serbs in 1995, and protect ethnic Albanians in Kosovo by bombing Serbs in 1999.

Such interventions are often controversial because they involve violating a nation's sovereignty with the use of force. The United States is usually hesitant to intervene because such an action may cost American lives, and there may be no clear ending point for the mission. Nevertheless, there is a constant demand for U.S. intervention. The Bush administration came under intense pressure in mid-2003 to intervene to quell the violence and relieve suffering in Liberia. The crisis in Darfur in western Sudan—where, since February 2003, more than 50,000 people have been killed and over 1 million displaced—prompted new calls for international humanitarian intervention.

Economic Sanctions. An ancient tool of diplomacy, sanctions are nonmilitary penalties imposed on a foreign government in an attempt to modify its behavior. The penalties can vary broadly—a cutoff of U.S. aid, a ban on military sales, restrictions on imports, a denial of aircraft landing rights, or a total trade embargo. The implied power behind sanctions is U.S. economic muscle and access to U.S. markets.

Economic sanctions are often a first resort in times of crisis, as they are less risky than sending in troops. Sanctions are often the outgrowth of pressure from well-organized domestic political groups with ethnic, cultural, environmental, human rights, or religious grievances against a foreign regime. These groups and government officials want to curb unfair trade practices, end human rights abuses and drug trafficking, promote environmental initiatives, and stop terrorism.

There are examples of economic sanctions that accomplished the goals of their sponsors, such as the sanctions levied against South Africa in the mid-1980s that contributed to the demise of apartheid. Most experts, however, view these tools as having limited effect. The trade embargo the UN placed on Iraq after its 1990 invasion of Kuwait succeeded in isolating Iraq diplomatically and economically and prevented it from rebuilding its military to its former strength. Yet Saddam Hussein retained a firm grip on power until 2003.

Successful sanctions most often have broad international support, which is rare. Unilateral sanctions are doomed to failure. The real losers are U.S. companies that are forced to abandon lucrative markets. They are quickly replaced by their competitors around the globe. When President Carter imposed a grain embargo on the Soviet Union in 1980 in retaliation for the Soviet invasion of Afghanistan, only U.S. farmers were hurt. The Soviet Union simply bought grain elsewhere.

Economic Sanctions and Cuba

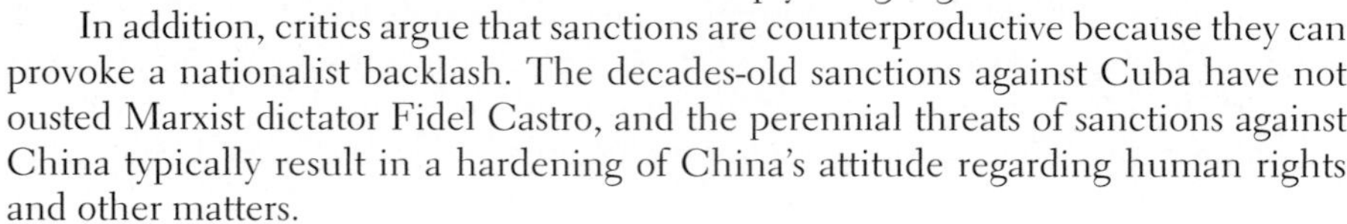
In addition, critics argue that sanctions are counterproductive because they can provoke a nationalist backlash. The decades-old sanctions against Cuba have not ousted Marxist dictator Fidel Castro, and the perennial threats of sanctions against China typically result in a hardening of China's attitude regarding human rights and other matters.

Nuclear Proliferation

The spread of technology has enabled the creation of nuclear weapons and the missiles to deliver them, encouraging U.S. officials to adopt a more assertive posture in attempting to deny these weapons of mass destruction to rogue states. American policymakers have sought to halt the spread of nuclear weapons since the signing of the Nuclear Non-Proliferation Treaty in 1968. The primary means of accomplishing this goal has been to encourage nations to agree that they would not acquire—or at least test—nuclear weapons. As you can see in Figure 17.2, only eight countries have declared that they have nuclear weapons capacities: the United States, Russia, Britain, France, China, India, North Korea, and Pakistan. Israel is widely suspected of having nuclear weapons. South Africa and three countries that used to be part of the Soviet Union—Belarus, Kazakhstan, and Ukraine—have given up nuclear weapons. Algeria, Argentina, Brazil, Libya, South Korea, Sweden, and Taiwan have ended their nuclear weapons programs. The United States actively supported the UN weapons inspections of Iraq, which faced continuous harassment and obstruction from Saddam Hussein until he was driven from power. After the United States invaded Iraq in 2003, it found that only a modest effort to develop nuclear weapons remained.

Currently, policymakers are most concerned about countries that are actively developing nuclear weapons capabilities, principally North Korea and Iran. These nations, frequently branded as "outlaw" states, pose serious threats to their neighbors

Figure 17.2 The Spread of Nuclear Weapons

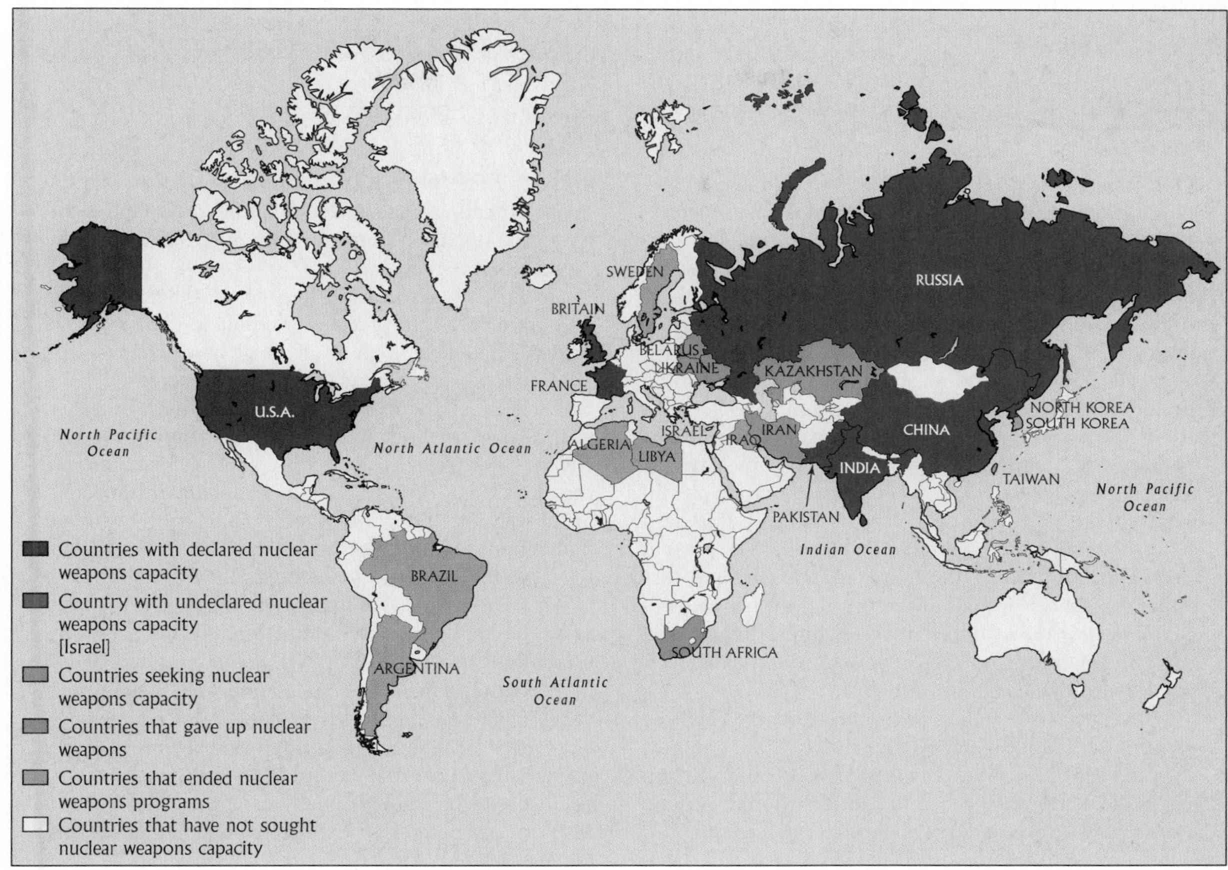

Source: Congressional Quality Weekly Report, May 28, 1998, 1,366. Updated by authors.

and perhaps to the United States as well. The United States provided aid to North Korea in return for a promise to end its nuclear weapons program, but in 2002 North Korea declared its intention to continue the program and possesses a few nuclear weapons now. It tested a nuclear weapon in 2006. Our efforts regarding Iran have been no more effective; major powers, including Russia and China, have opposed leveling sanctions against it (see "You are the Policymaker: Defanging a Nuclear Threat").

Other nations have serious security concerns when faced with hostile neighbors possessing nuclear weapons. When India resumed testing of nuclear weapons in 1998, neighboring Pakistan quickly tested its first nuclear weapons. Their possession of nuclear weapons is a matter of special concern because of their history of conflict over Kashmir. Ending the proliferation of nuclear weapons will require resolving diplomatic tensions involving undeclared and nonnuclear states. In the meantime, the United States focuses on discouraging the deployment of the nuclear weapons that have been developed.

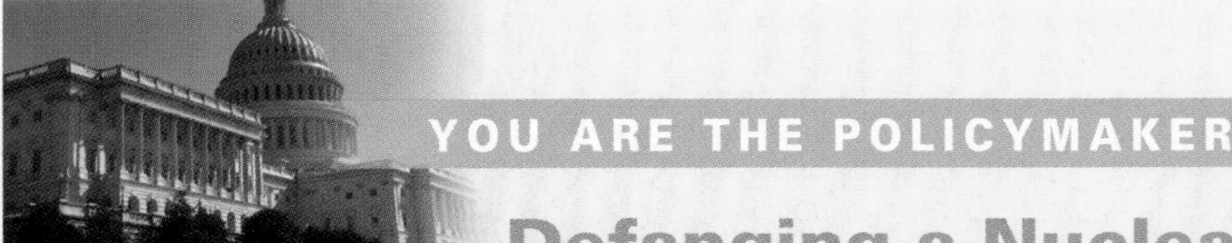

Defanging a Nuclear Threat

One of the highest priorities of U.S. foreign policy is stopping the spread of nuclear weapons, especially to countries hostile to America. Some experts estimate that Iran will need only three more years to build its first nuclear bomb. Within six to 12 months, Tehran might be able to finish the enrichment facilities that will make the Persian bomb a foregone conclusion.

Nuclear weapons in Iranian hands is not a comforting thought. The State Department has designated Iran as the world's leading sponsor of terrorism. The mullahs running the country support organizations such as Hamas, Hezbollah, and the Islamic Jihad; may be providing weapons and training to terrorists inside Iraq; and have sheltered senior members of al-Qaeda. The current president, Mahmoud Ahmadinejad, has declared that Israel should be "wiped off the map." Iran has missiles that can now reach Israel and U.S. forces in Iraq and Afghanistan and is developing missiles that can reach Western Europe and North America.

How should we deal with this threat? The first response was diplomacy. The United States and its Western European allies sought to convince Iran to stop its nuclear research, and the International Atomic Energy Agency sealed some nuclear research facilities. In 2006, however, Iran removed the seals and declared that it had every right to develop atomic energy.

We could embargo Iran's main export, oil, but that would drive up energy prices everywhere and is unlikely to receive the international support necessary for economic sanctions to succeed. Curtailing foreign travel will have little impact on a people who currently travel little outside their borders.

Another option is ordering the CIA and other agencies to encourage an overthrow of the government. The chances of succeeding in such a venture are small, however.

There are also military options. In theory, the United States could invade, but the U.S. military is overstretched with its responsibilities in Iraq. That leaves only one serious option—air strikes by Israel or the United States, possibly accompanied by commando raids. It is doubtful that bombs could eradicate Iran's nuclear program (much of which is underground), but it is possible they could set it back for years, possibly long enough for the regime to implode.

Of course, Iran is not likely to react passively to such a strike; the mullahs would almost certainly order terrorist retaliation against the United States and Israel and increase their efforts to sabotage our activities in next-door Afghanistan and Iraq. Iran could also become a rallying point for the Islamic world, which already is deeply suspicious and often disdainful of American policy. One result could be a further radicalization of millions of Muslims and an increase in the pool of potential recruits to terrorism.

As you can see, President George W. Bush faces a dilemma regarding Iran. If you were president, what would *you* do?

The International Economy

interdependency
Mutual dependency, in which the actions of nations reverberate and affect one another's economic lifelines.

Once upon a time, nations took pains to isolate themselves from the world. They erected high barriers to fend off foreign products and amassed large armies to defend their borders against intruders. Times have changed. One key word describes today's international economy: **interdependency**, a mutual reliance in which actions reverberate and affect other people's economic lifelines. The health of the American economy depends increasingly on the prosperity of its trading partners and on the smooth flow of trade and finance across borders (see "Young People and Politics: Embracing Globalization").

The *International Monetary Fund (IMF)* is a cooperative international organization of 183 countries intended to stabilize the exchange of currencies and the

YOUNG PEOPLE AND POLITICS

Embracing Globalization

The protests that regularly occur during economic summit meetings of the leaders of the world's most economically developed countries might lead you to conclude that young adults are in the forefront of opposition to globalization. Actually, the facts are quite different, according to the Pew *Global Attitudes Project* surveys.

In every country, globalization has produced some political tensions. However, strong majorities in all regions believe that increased global interconnectedness is a good thing, and globalization is more popular among the young adults of the world. Everywhere but Latin America, young people are more likely than their elders to see advantages in increased global trade and communication, and they are more likely to support "globalization."

The hesitation among some older citizens to embrace the movement toward globalization may be due in part to national pride. People in all countries and of all ages are proud of their cultures. Yet it is only in the West (North America and Western Europe) where that pride is markedly stronger among the older generations. Younger people tend to be less wedded to their cultural identities. In the United States, 68 percent of those ages 65 and older agree with the statement "our people are not perfect, but our culture is superior," while only 49 percent of those ages 18 to 29 agree. The generation gap in Western Europe is similar. The difference between generations is particularly apparent in France, where only one-fifth of those under age 30 support the notion of cultural superiority, while more than half of those ages 65 and older say French culture is superior.

Despite the general attraction of globalization, solid majorities everywhere think their way of life needs to be protected against foreign influence. In most parts of the world, that desire cuts across all age-groups. However, in the United States and Western Europe, older people are much more worried than the young about defending their country's way of life. In the United States, 71 percent of people ages 65 and older want to shield their way of life from foreign influence, while just 55 percent of those ages 18 to 29 agree. This generation gap is even greater in France, Germany, and Britain, where older people are twice as likely as young people to be worried about erosion of their way of life.

Skepticism about foreign influence is evident in widespread, intense antipathy toward immigration. Majorities in nearly every country surveyed support tougher restrictions on people entering their countries. Immigrants are particularly unpopular across Europe, especially among the older generation, where half of those surveyed *completely agree* with the need for additional immigration controls. The anti-immigrant generation gap is widest in France, where 53 percent of those ages 65 and older *completely agree* that immigration should be restricted. Only 24 percent of younger French men and women shared such strong views. Anti-immigrant sentiment also runs high in the United States, especially among older Americans. Fifty percent of those ages 65 and older strongly support new controls on entry of people into the country. Only 40 percent of young people share that intensity of sentiment.

There are many reasons why young people may be more supportive of globalization than their elders. Better educated, more widely traveled, and more accustomed to the Internet, young adults seem to be less parochial, have less fear of change, and have more appreciation for the benefits of other cultures. Partially as a result of these attitudes, we should expect the trend toward globalization to accelerate over the coming decades.

Questions for Discussion

- Do young people you know fear foreign competition?
- Do you agree that education and experience are the best explanations for the greater support of globalization among young people?

world economy. From 1997 to 1998, the decline of currencies in a number of Asian countries, including South Korea, Thailand, Indonesia, and the Philippines, threatened to force these nations to default on their debts—and throw the international economy into turmoil in the process. To stabilize these currencies, the IMF, to which the United States is by far the largest contributor, arranged for loans and credits of more than $100 billion. The IMF's intervention seems to have been successful, but the necessity of making the loans dramatically illustrates the world's economic interdependence.

International Trade. Since the end of World War II, trade among nations has grown rapidly. American exports and imports have increased 20-fold since 1970 alone (see Figure 17.3). Among the largest U.S. exporters are grain farmers, producers of computer hardware and software, aircraft manufacturers, moviemakers, heavy construction companies, and purveyors of accounting and consulting services. Foreign

Figure 17.3 Exports and Imports

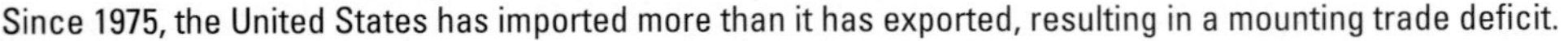

Since 1975, the United States has imported more than it has exported, resulting in a mounting trade deficit.

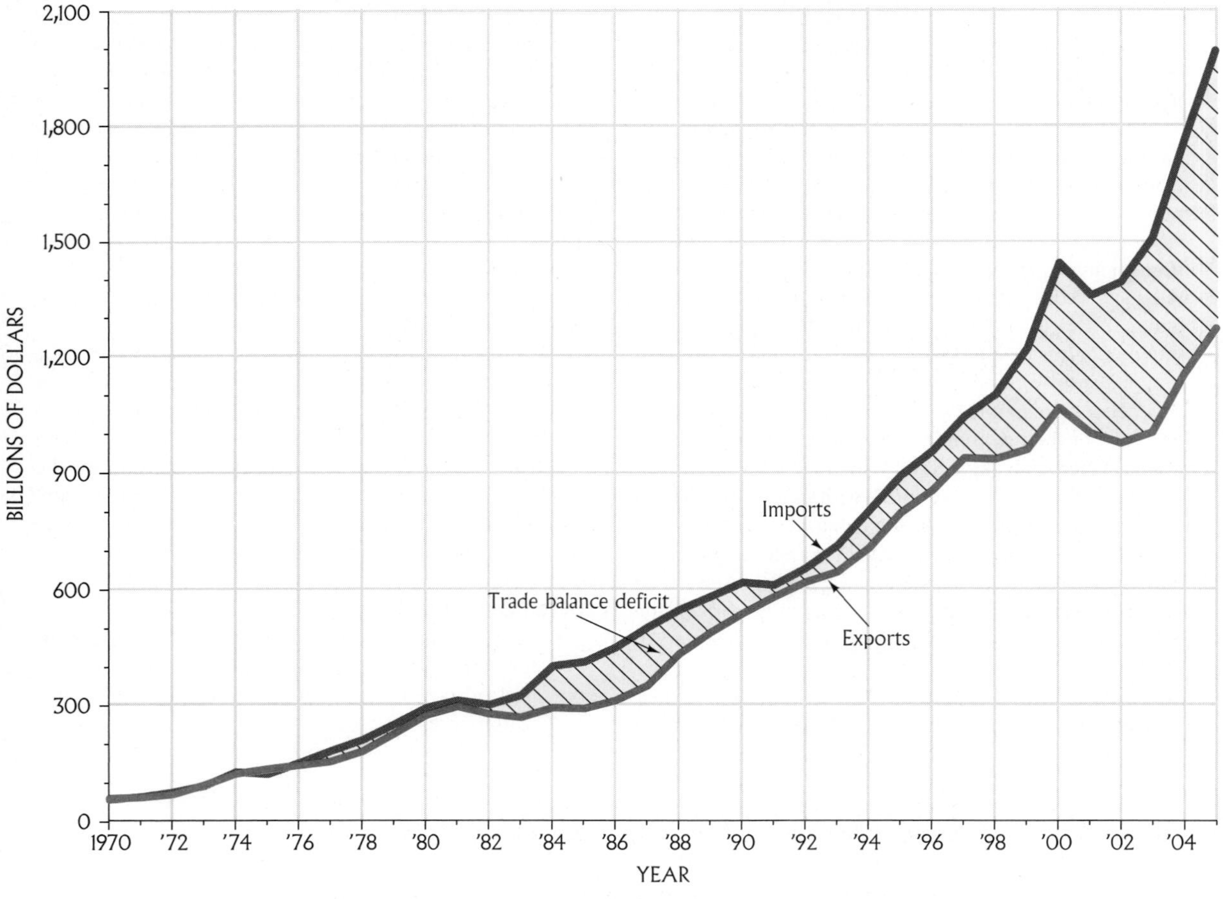

Source: U.S. Bureau of the Census, 2006.

tourist spending bolsters the U.S. travel, hotel, and recreation industries. American colleges and universities derive a significant portion of their revenue from educating foreign students. The globalization of finances has been even more dramatic than the growth of trade. Worldwide computer and communications networks link financial markets in all parts of the globe instantaneously, making it easier to move capital across national boundaries but also increasing the probability that a steep decline in the Japanese stock market will send prices plummeting on Wall Street.

Coping with foreign economic issues is becoming just as difficult—and increasingly just as important—as coping with domestic ones. In a simpler time, the main instrument of international economic policy was the **tariff**, a special tax added to the cost of imported goods. Tariffs are intended to raise the price of imported goods and thereby protect American businesses and workers from foreign competition. Tariff making, though, is a game everyone can play. High U.S. tariffs encourage other nations to respond with high tariffs on American products. The high tariffs that the government enacted early in the Great Depression (and that some say aggravated this economic crisis) were the last of their kind. Since that time, the world economy has moved from a period of high tariffs and protectionism to one of lower tariffs and freer trade.

tariff
A special tax added to imported goods to raise the price, thereby protecting American businesses and workers from foreign competition.

However, nontariff barriers such as quotas, subsidies, and quality specifications for imported products are common means of limiting imports. In recent decades, the United States has placed quotas on the amount of steel that can be imported and negotiated voluntary limits on the importation of Japanese automobiles. Such policies do save American jobs, but they also raise the price of steel and automobiles that Americans buy. American and European subsidies for agricultural products have been an obstacle to negotiating tariff reductions.

Recently, substantial progress has been made in lowering barriers to trade. In 1992, President Bush signed the *North American Free Trade Agreement (NAFTA)* with Canada and Mexico, which would eventually eliminate most tariffs among North American countries. In 1993, after a heated battle, President Clinton obtained congressional passage of the legislation implementing the agreement.

President Clinton submitted an even more important agreement to Congress in 1994. The *General Agreement on Tariffs and Trade (GATT)* is the mechanism by which most of the world's nations negotiate widespread trade agreements. In 1994, 117 nations agreed to (1) reduce tariffs 38 percent for developed countries; (2) eliminate certain nontariff barriers and subsidies; (3) broaden GATT principles to areas such as trade in services, investment, and intellectual property rights; and (4) apply more effective disciplines to agricultural trade. The GATT also included a charter to create the World Trade Organization, which would act as the arbiter of international trade disputes. In its last action, the 103rd Congress passed the legislation necessary to implement this agreement.

In 2005, Congress approved the Central American–Dominican Republic Free Trade Agreement, negotiated by the George W. Bush administration. This agreement lowered tariff barriers to American goods in a number of Central American countries and the Dominican Republic. The president also signed free trade agreements with some individual countries.

A persistent issue for the president is opening up foreign markets for U.S. goods and services. The White House is especially eager to open lucrative Japanese markets

International trade is a controversial subject. Opponents believe that it undermines U.S. laws that protect the environment and workers' rights, costs some employees their jobs, and encourages the exploitation of foreign workers. Proponents argue that everyone benefits from increased trade. Here, Seattle police face protesters during a World Trade Organization meeting in 1999.

in areas such as automobiles, auto parts, telecommunications, insurance, and medical equipment. The United States lacks the influence to *demand* that these markets be opened, however. If we refuse to trade with another nation, that nation will deny *our* exports access to its markets, and U.S. consumers will lose access to their products. In addition, millions of Americans now work in foreign-owned companies in the United States, such as Japanese automobile assembly plants. Although foreign investments and the creation of jobs are good for the United States, a by-product is that Americans have a stake in averting a trade crisis with investing nations. Those benefiting from Japanese investments, for example, may flock to Tokyo's side on some important issues.

balance of trade

The ratio of what is paid for imports to what is earned from exports. When more is imported than exported, there is a balance-of-trade deficit.

Balance of Trade. Foreign products are not free. When Americans purchase foreign products, they send dollars out of the country. When an oil tanker arrives in Houston, dollars travel to Saudi Arabia. If other nations do not buy as many American products as Americans do of theirs, then the United States is paying out more than it is taking in. If the United States puts military bases in Germany, the money that soldiers spend for a night on the town goes into German pockets. When American tourists spend their dollars abroad, they too carry American dollars away. All these instances combine to upset the **balance of trade**: the ratio of what a country pays for imports to what it earns from exports. When a country imports more than it exports, it has a balance-of-trade *deficit*. Year after year, the American balance of trade has been preceded by a minus sign, and the deficit for the balance of trade was $726 billion in 2005.[27]

The excess of imports over exports decreases the dollar's buying power against other currencies, making Americans pay more for goods that they buy from other nations. This decline in the value of the dollar, however, also makes American products cheaper abroad, thereby increasing our exports. Since the late 1980s, the

United States has experienced an export boom, reaching nearly $1.3 trillion in 2005.[28] Exports account for about 10 percent of the GDP.

A poor balance of trade also exacerbates unemployment. About 5 percent of all civilian employment in the United States is related to manufacturing exports. A substantial amount of white-collar employment—in the area of financial services, for example—is also directly tied to exports. The trade imbalance has caused not only dollars but also jobs to flow abroad. Because labor is cheaper in Mexico, Taiwan, Malaysia, and China, products made there can be priced lower than American-made products. Sometimes American firms have shut down their domestic operations and relocated in countries where labor costs are lower. The AFL-CIO claims that hundreds of thousands of American jobs have been lost to foreign competition. Under a special act guaranteeing compensation to American workers who lose their jobs to foreign competition, the Department of Labor has aided thousands of workers. The Labor Department, however, would be the first to note that short-term aid is no substitute for a long-term job.

Even so, a cheaper dollar also makes the cost of American labor more competitive. In response to this and to criticism about the balance of trade, more foreign-owned companies are building factories in the United States—just as American companies have plants around the globe. Thus, many Hondas are made in the United States, and parts for some cars manufactured by General Motors are made abroad. The web of interdependency has become so tangled that it is increasingly difficult to define "imports."

In addition, the stability of the U.S. economy and the low value of the dollar have made the United States attractive to foreign investors, who buy everything from major motion picture studios to the Rockefeller Center. Although advantages accrue to the United States when investors pour money into the country, some fear that both profits and control will move outside our borders.

Why It Matters

Economic Interdependence

The world economy is increasingly interdependent. In fact, Americans have more investments abroad than citizens of any other nation. Investments and markets in other countries provide economic opportunities for Americans, but they also make Americans more dependent on the strength of economies over which they lack control and provide increased competition for American products and American workers.

Energy. In 1973, the **Organization of Petroleum Exporting Countries** (OPEC) responded to American support of Israel in the short war against Egypt by embargoing oil shipments to the United States and Western European nations. The fuel shortages and long lines at gas stations that resulted from the 1973 oil embargo convincingly illustrated the growing interdependency of world politics.

Organization of Petroleum Exporting Countries
An economic organization consisting primarily of Arab nations that controls the price of oil and the amount of oil its members produce and sell to other nations.

More than half the world's recoverable reserves of oil lie in the Middle East; Saudi Arabia alone controls much of this resource. States such as Texas, Oklahoma, Louisiana, and Alaska produce considerable amounts of oil within the United States but not enough to meet the country's needs. America imports more than 60 percent of its annual consumption of oil from other countries, particularly from the Middle East. The United States is not as dependent on foreign sources of oil as many European countries, like France or Italy, which have virtually no oil of their own, or like Japan, which also imports all its oil. On the other hand, America's dependence on foreign oil is growing every year.

Political Corruption

America's decision to respond to Iraq's invasion of Kuwait in 1990 was based in large part by this dependence. Kuwait, although a small country, produces about 10 percent of the world's oil; its neighbor, Saudi Arabia, possesses about a quarter of the world's proven oil reserves. Following a UN embargo and ultimatum to Iraq to pull out of Kuwait, the United States and its allies poured forces into Saudi Arabia (more than a half million soldiers from the United States alone). The allied forces quickly defeated the Iraqis and liberated Kuwait.

Circumstances may again restrict the availability of oil, however, and the United States is vulnerable because of its dependence on imported oil. Yet the Middle East—and America's sources of foreign oil—remains unstable.

Foreign Aid. Presidents of each party have pressed for aid to nations in the developing world. Aside from simple humanitarian concern for those who are suffering, presidents have wanted to stabilize nations that were friendly to the United States or that possessed supplies of vital raw materials. Sometimes aid has been given in the form of grants, but often it has taken the form of credits and loan guarantees to purchase American goods, loans at favorable interest rates, and forgiveness of previous loans. At other times, the United States has awarded preferential trade agreements for the sale of foreign goods in the United States.

A substantial percentage of foreign aid is in the form of military assistance and is targeted to a few countries the United States considers to be of vital strategic significance: Israel, Egypt, Turkey, and Greece have received the bulk of such assistance in recent years. Foreign aid programs have also assisted with agricultural modernization, irrigation, and population control. Food for Peace programs have subsidized the sale of American agricultural products to poor countries (and simultaneously given an economic boost to American farmers). Peace Corps volunteers have fanned out over the globe to provide medical care and other services in less developed nations.

Nevertheless, foreign aid has never been very popular with Americans. Lacking a constituency, the president's foreign aid requests are typically cut by Congress, which currently appropriates less than 1 percent of the federal budget to economic and humanitarian foreign aid. Moreover, many people believe that the provision of economic aid to other nations serves only to further enrich the few without helping the many within a poor nation. Although the United States donates more total aid (both for economic development and military assistance) than any other country, it devotes a smaller share of its GDP to foreign economic development than any other developed nation. It is important to note, however, that the United States provides a great deal more aid through grants from private voluntary organizations, foundations, religious organizations, corporations, universities, and individuals.[29]

Understanding National Security Policymaking

National security policy is perhaps the most exotic arena of public policy, dealing with issues and nations that are often far from America's shores. Nevertheless, the themes that have guided your understanding of American politics throughout *Government in America*—democracy and the scope of government—can also shed light on the topic of international relations.

HOW YOU CAN MAKE A DIFFERENCE

Joining the Peace Corps

An institution like the Peace Corps allows young Americans to impact U.S. diplomacy while helping others at the same time. The Peace Corps helps build relationships between the United States and underdeveloped nations by providing volunteers to teach, engage in youth outreach and community development, aid in agriculture and environmental management, and assist in business development to those countries in need. A Peace Corps volunteer helps the world's disadvantaged in a very real way, and as a result the volunteer represents the American people around the globe. Foreign policy need not be conducted solely by governments, and institutions such as the Peace Corps allow interested citizens to take an active role in global politics.

Making a Difference

In 1981, Loret Miller Ruppe was appointed Director of the United States Peace Corps by President Ronald Reagan. Ruppe was the institution's longest-serving director and a champion of women in development. She is credited with revitalizing the Peace Corps during a period where there were many budget cuts in other organizations. By creating business-oriented volunteer opportunities to promote grassroots economic growth worldwide, she won the support of Republicans in Congress who generally disapproved of U.S. foreign aid programs. Also, for the first time, a large number of conservative and Republican volunteers signed up for the Peace Corps.

What you can do:

- If you are interested in joining the Peace Corps, make sure that you meet the institution's requirements. Volunteers must be 18 years of age and generally must have a four-year college degree. You must also be willing to commit to 27 months of training and service in a foreign country.
- Apply online at http://www.peacecorps.gov/index.cfm. You must provide health information, a college transcript (if applicable), and three letters of reference.

National Security Policymaking and Democracy

Comparing Foreign and Security Policies

To some commentators, democracy has little to do with America's international relations. Because domestic issues are closer to their daily lives and easier to understand, Americans are usually more interested in domestic policy than in foreign policy. This preference would seem to give public officials more discretion in making national security policy. In addition, some say, those with the discretion are elites in the State Department and unelected military officers in the Pentagon.

There is little evidence, however, that policies at odds with the wishes of the American people can be sustained; civilian control of the military is unquestionable. When the American people hold strong opinions regarding international relations—as when they first supported and later opposed the war in Vietnam—policymakers are usually responsive. Citizens in democracies do not choose to fight citizens in other democracies, and studies have found that well-established democracies rarely go to war against one another.[30]

In addition, the system of separation of powers plays a crucial role in foreign as well as domestic policy. The president takes the lead on national security matters, but you saw in Chapter 11 that Congress has a central role in matters of international relations. Whether treaties are ratified, defense budgets are appropriated, weapons systems are authorized, or foreign aid is awarded is ultimately at the discretion of the Congress—the government's most representative policymaking body. Specific issues such as the proper funding for the Strategic Defense Initiative rarely determine congressional elections, but public demands for and objections to policies are likely to be heard in Washington.

When it comes to the increasingly important arena of American international economic policy, pluralism is pervasive. Agencies and members of Congress, as well as their constituents, all pursue their own policy goals. For example, the Treasury Department and the Federal Reserve Board worry about the negative balance of trade, and the Department of Defense spends billions in other countries to maintain American troops abroad. The Departments of Agriculture and Commerce and their constituents—farmers and businesspeople—want to peddle American products abroad and generally favor freer trade. The Department of Labor and the unions worry that the nation may export not only products but also jobs to other countries where labor costs are low. Jewish citizens closely monitor U.S. policy toward Israel, whereas Greek Americans seek to limit military aid to Turkey, Greece's ancient rival. Even foreign governments hire lobbying firms and join in the political fray. As a result, a wide range of interests are represented in making foreign policy.

National Security Policymaking and the Scope of Government

America's global connections as a superpower have many implications for how active the national government is in the realm of foreign policy and national defense. The war on terrorism, treaty obligations to defend allies around the world, the nation's economic interests in an interdependent global economy, and pressing new questions on the global agenda—ranging from illicit drugs to environmental protection—demand government action.

By any standard, the scope of government in these areas is large. The national defense consumes about a fifth of the federal government's budget and requires about 2 million civilian and military employees for the Department of Defense. Even though the United States has improved relations with Eastern and Central Europe, it will remain a superpower and continue to have political, economic, and other interests to defend around the world. As long as these interests remain, the scope of American government in foreign and defense policy will be substantial.

Summary

The world—its politics and its economics—intrudes on Americans more each year. This chapter examines America's global connections and the contours of its foreign policy.

The Cold War began shortly after World War II, when the containment doctrine became the basis of American foreign policy. The Cold War led to actual wars in

Korea and Vietnam when the United States tried to contain communist advances. With containment came a massive military buildup, resulting in what some people called the *military-industrial complex*. Gradually, containment has been balanced by détente and then friendship with many of our former adversaries. This trend has accelerated with the democratization of Central and Eastern Europe and the dissolution of the Soviet Union. Nevertheless, the United States maintains an enormous defense capability, which it has put to use in the war on terrorism.

Although the United States has great military power, many of the issues facing the world today are not military issues. Nuclear proliferation and terrorism present new challenges to national security, challenges not easily met by advanced weaponry. Interconnected issues of equality, energy, and the environment have also become important. The international economic system pulls the United States deeper and deeper into the world's problems as global interdependency and its own vulnerability become more apparent.

Internet Resources

www.state.gov/
Information about the Department of State and current foreign policy issues.

www.defenselink.mil/
Information about the Department of Defense and current issues in national security policy.

www.cia.gov/cia/publications/factbook/
The CIA *World Factbook*.

www.oecd.org/home/
The Organization for Economic Cooperation and Development provides a wealth of economic information on the world's nations.

www.nato.int/
Contains background and activities of NATO.

www.un.org/
Background on the United Nations and its varied programs.

www.cfr.org
The Council on Foreign Relations is the most influential private organization in the area of foreign policy. Its Web site includes a wide range of information on foreign policy.

www.whitehouse.gov/nsc
Information about the members and functions of the National Security Council.

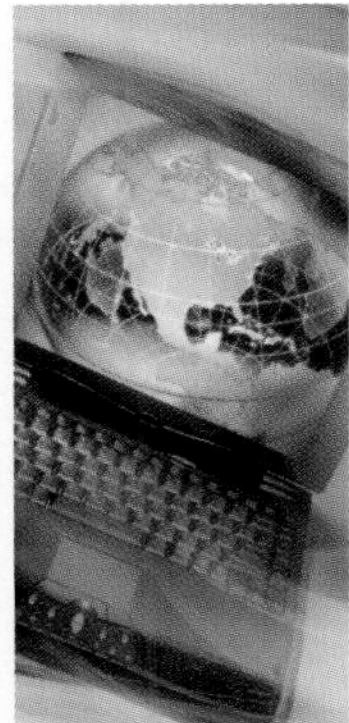

Get Connected

The Department of State

Congratulations! The president of the United States has just nominated you to be the secretary of state. You have been given advance notice that several members of the Senate Foreign Relations Committee will ask you about the "Palestinian Question" during your confirmation. Although you are aware that the relationship between Arabs and Israel has been a key element of U.S. foreign policy for decades, you want to provide the committee with some new thinking on possible answers to the Palestinian Question. One place you look for ideas is American public opinion.

Search the Web

Go to the "America's Global Role: Quick Takes" page at the Public Agenda Web site, *www.publicagenda.org/issues/angles.cfm?issue_type=americas_global_role*. There are a several graphs under the heading "Middle East" that show American public opinion about the role the United States should play in the conflict between the Palestinians and Israel. Take a look at all three graphs.

Questions to Ask

- Who do most Americans believe should take the first step in trying to end the bombings and other violence in the region?
- What should the United States do to try to help the two sides find a peaceful resolution to the decades-long conflict?
- Where should the Palestinian–Israeli conflict be on the foreign policy agenda of the United States?

Why It Matters

Israelis and Palestinians have been engaged in varying levels of conflict since Israel became an independent nation in 1948. The conflict has led to large numbers of Palestinian refugees, some of whom become terrorists. Achieving peace in the Middle East has been a foreign policy goal of the United States for decades, partly out of its long-standing support for a Jewish homeland and partly out of concern for the impact of violence in the Middle East on the supply of energy to the United States.

Get Involved

Learn a little more about the U.S. role in seeking answers to the Palestinian Question. What are the current administration's goals? How do your members of Congress feel about the potential for ending conflict between the Palestinians and the Israelis?

For more exercises, go to www.longmanamericangovernment.com.

For Further Reading

Brzezinski, Zbigniew. *The Choice: Global Domination or Global Leadership*. New York: Basic Books, 2004. An important critique of the Bush administration's national security strategy.

Daalder, Ivo H., and James M. Lindsay. *America Unbound: The Bush Revolution in Foreign Policy*. Washington, DC: Brookings Institution, 2003. A balanced analysis of the Bush administration's foreign policy.

Easterly, William. *The White Man's Burden*. New York: Penguin, 2006. Why the West's efforts to aid the rest of the world have not been more effective.

Huntington, Samuel P. *The Clash of Civilizations and the Remaking of World Order*. New York: Simon and Schuster, 1996. Argues that civilizational identities built on religious empires of the past will be the source of international turmoil in the next century.

Kagan, Donald. *On the Origins of War and the Preservation of Peace*. New York: Doubleday, 1995. Provides insights gleaned from studying the origins of great wars.

Lindsay, James M. *Congress and the Politics of U.S. Foreign Policy*. Baltimore: Johns Hopkins University Press, 1994. A useful discussion of the role of Congress in setting U.S. foreign policy.

Mandelbaum, Michael. *The Case for Goliath: How America Acts as the World's Government in the Twenty-First Century*. New York: Public Affairs, 2006. Explains the ways in which the United States provides the world critical services, ranging from physical security to commercial regulation and financial stability.

Mead, Walter Russell. *Power, Terror, Peace, and War*. New York: Alfred A. Knopf, 2004. Analyzes America's grand strategy in national security.

Nye, Joseph S., Jr. *The Paradox of American Power: Why the World's Only Superpower Can't Go It Alone*. New York: Oxford University Press, 2002. Although the United States is militarily and economically supreme, it is increasingly dependent on other nations to accomplish its goals.

Nye, Joseph S., Jr. *Soft Power: The Means to Success in World Politics*. Cambridge, MA: Harvard University Press, 2004. Argues that national security hinges as much on winning hearts and minds as it does on winning wars.

Woodward, Bob. *State of Denial*. New York: Simon and Schuster, 2006. The inside story of decision making regarding the war with Iraq and its aftermath.

Yergin, Daniel. *Shattered Peace: The Origins of the Cold War and the National Security State*. Boston: Houghton Mifflin, 1977. An excellent political history of the early years of the Cold War and containment.

Issues of the Times Reader

The New York Times nytimes.com

The Issue: How Can Young People's Interest in Politics Be Increased?

As discussed at length in Chapter 1, the problem of voter apathy—particularly among today's youth—is a matter of much concern to many close observers of American politics. For over a decade now, an organization called Rock the Vote has made appeals to young people to vote by taking advantage of celebrity endorsements, usually by rock stars, and by advertising on MTV and other media young people watch. Up until 2004, the results had been largely disappointing.

In 2004, as discussed in this article, there was much evidence that young people were more interested in the presidential campaign than they had been in quite some time. This article gives several possible explanations why.

Read All About It

Vote Drives Gain Avid Attention of Youth in '04

By Timothy Egan
September 15, 2004

PORTLAND—Four years ago, the presidential election was not even white noise to Marie Reyes. She had bigger concerns, like, um, anything except that whole Social Security lockbox thing that Al Gore and George Bush kept talking about.

"There was nothing in that election that I felt even remotely related to my life," said Ms. Reyes, who is 22.

But now, even with a full college classload, a baby and a part-time job, she spends nearly 20 hours a week in Albuquerque, her hometown, trying to get other young people to register to vote.

Ms. Reyes is part of the clipboard army scouring malls, public squares, concerts, county fairs and schools this year in search of what campaign managers consider the most malleable of electoral quarry: the young, unregistered voter.

After dismal turnout by young voters in 2000, surveys this year show that interest in the election among the young is near the highest level it has reached at any time since 18- to 20-year-olds were given the vote in 1972. And state election officials say registration of new young voters is coming in at levels they have not seen in years.

The reason for the registration jump is not just the new mood of the young but also the determined efforts of nonpartisan and partisan groups alike to add to the rolls. Here in Oregon, where the last presidential race was decided by 6,765 votes, it is elbow-to-elbow combat for potential voters.

"If I see anyone else with a clipboard, I run to get the angle," said Alden Goodman, 19, of Portland. "I've followed people onto metro trains, onto buses, and when they finally register, it's because I made it memorable."

In Wisconsin, for example, where the 2000 election was decided by 5,708 votes, more than 74,000 new voters, most of them young, have been added to the rolls by the New Voters Project, a nonpartisan group that is spending nearly $10 million to register new voters in six relatively small states where the outcome was tight in the last election. The project is financed primarily by the Pew Charitable Trusts. The clipboard legions are taking down cellphone numbers and e-mail addresses for a huge follow-through.

Of course, campaigns have tried before to lure the elusive young into active citizenship, only to be disappointed on Election Day.

But this year the tactics for getting the young to turn out have changed, while the level of political engagement is way up, reflecting new concerns of the sons and daughters of baby boomers just coming of age.

Former Gov. Howard Dean of Vermont was the first this year to tap into that group. He had his army of text-messaging and computer-blogging volunteers. Young voter participation was up sharply in the Iowa caucuses, but Dr. Dean still lost the youth vote to Mr. Kerry. As the Dean campaign flagged, the young fell away as well, and the initial enthusiasm never translated to larger youth turnout through the rest of the primary season, according to surveys of voters leaving the polls.

After failing to increase turnout with rock-star pleas and celebrity robovoice phone nags, the people involved in the major youth vote drives say they have found success with an old-fashioned strategy—ground troops—while also trying fresh pitches aimed at a "beer and babes" constituency on the Web, in bars and at convenience stores.

Rock the Vote, the big nonprofit youth registration organization that has been criticized as being ineffective despite 14 years of well-financed campaigns, is distributing a million voter registration forms, in English and Spanish, at kiosks in 5,000 convenience stores. Shoppers at 7-Eleven stores can get coupons for soft-drink discounts and voter registration forms at the same stop—"a Big Gulp and a piece of democracy to go," as Rock the Vote called it.

[W]hat has changed is not so much that the campaigns have started talking about concerns of young voters as that the issues have come around to topics that this group cares about.

The group's president, Jehmu Greene, said that more than a half-million people had downloaded registration forms from the group's site.

Another group has gone a step further. The founders of Hot or Not, a popular youth Web site at which people post photographs of themselves that are rated on a "hotness" scale, is holding a sweepstakes that will pay one registered voter $100,000 after the election; another $100,000 will go to the person who helped the winner register for the contest.

Judging by some of the marketing campaigns directed at them, young voters may seem clueless, barely tracking the major political events of a nation. But interviews and surveys showed that the problem was that the young felt disconnected from the national conversation.

"The campaigns would throw up their hands, saying, 'I don't know how to get their vote,' and so the issues agenda was always driven by the reliable interest groups," said Mr. Keeter of the Pew Center.

But what has changed is not so much that the campaigns have started talking about concerns of young voters as that the issues have come around to topics that this group cares about. Education—particularly the rising cost of college—is consistently listed at the top, followed by war and terrorism.

"I have friends and relatives fighting in Iraq, and trying to go to school," Ms. Reyes said. "These things made me think seriously about my future."

Think About It

- What, if anything, do you think particularly interested young people about the 2004 presidential race?
- Do you think the various outreach attempts discussed here really worked to get young people interested in politics? Are there other ways you can think of that might be effective in getting young people more involved in American politics in the future?

The Issue: How Is the Internet Changing Politics?

You have seen that the informal process of constitutional change is often as important as change that results from formal amendments to the Constitution. You have also seen that technology is one of the most dynamic and pervasive influences on the operation of the political system. The Internet has brought sweeping change to life for Americans—and others around the world as well. Less well understood are the changes it is bringing to politics.

Electing officials is at the heart of democracy, and *how* we elect them determines the information available to voters and who is most likely to participate in politics. The nature of political campaigns also sets a tone for our political life, influencing the winners' efforts to govern after the election as well as how candidates take their cases to the people.

Read All About It

Internet Injects Sweeping Change into U.S. Politics

By Adam Nagourney
April 2, 2006

The transformation of American politics by the Internet is accelerating with the approach of the 2006 congressional and 2008 White House elections, prompting the rewriting of rules on advertising, fund-raising, mobilizing supporters and even the spreading of negative information.

Democrats and Republicans are sharply increasing their use of e-mail, interactive Web sites, candidate and party blogs, and text-messaging to raise money, organize get-out-the-vote efforts and assemble crowds for rallies. The Internet, they said, appears to be far more efficient, and less costly, than the traditional tools of politics, notably door knocking and telephone banks.

Analysts say the campaign television advertisement, already diminishing in influence with the proliferation of cable stations, faces new challenges as campaigns experiment with technology that allows direct messaging to more specific audiences, and through unconventional means.

Those include Podcasts featuring a daily downloaded message from a candidate and so-called viral attack videos, designed to trigger peer-to-peer distribution by e-mail chains, without being associated with any candidate or campaign.

Campaigns are now studying popular Internet social networks, like Friendster and Facebook, as ways to reach groups of potential supporters with similar political views or cultural interests.

President Bush's media consultant, Mark McKinnon, said television advertising, while still critical to campaigns, had become markedly less influential in persuading voters that it was even two years ago.

"I feel like a woolly mammoth," Mr. McKinnon said.

A Pew survey released earlier this month found that 50 million Americans go to the Internet for news every day, up from 27 million people in March 2002, a reflection of the fact that the Internet is now available to 70 percent of Americans.

This means, aides said, rethinking every assumption about running a campaign: how to reach different segments of voters, how to get voters to the polls, how to raise money, and the best way to have a candidate interact with the public.

"The effect of the Internet on politics will be every bit as transformational as television was," said Ken Mehlman, the Republican national chairman. "If you want to get your message out, the old way of paying someone to make a TV ad is insufficient: You need your message out through the Internet, through e-mail, through talk radio."

On the left in particular, bloggers have emerged as something of a police force guarding against disloyalty among Democrats, as Steve Elmendorf, a Democratic consultant, learned after he told *The Washington Post* that bloggers and online donors "are not representative of the majority you need to win elections." A Daily Kos blogger wrote: "Not one dime, ladies and gentlemen, to anything connected with Steve Elmendorf. Anyone stupid enough to actually give a quote like that deserves to have every single one of his funding sources dry up."

One of the big challenges to the campaigns is not only adjusting to the changes of the past two years but also to anticipate now the kind of technological changes that might be on hand by the next presidential campaign. Among those most cited are the ability of campaigns to beam video campaign advertisements to cell phones.

If you want to get your message out, the old way of paying someone to make a TV ad is insufficient: You need your message out through the Internet, through e-mail, through talk radio.

Bloggers, for all the benefits they might bring to both parties, have proved to be a complicating political influence for Democrats. They have tugged the party consistently to the left, particularly on issues like the war, and have been openly critical of such moderate Democrats as Senator Joseph I. Lieberman of Connecticut.

Still, Democrats have been particularly enthusiastic about the potential of this technology to get the party back on track, with many Democratic leaders arguing that the Internet is today for Democrats what talk radio was for Republicans 10 years ago.

For all the attention being paid to Internet technology, there remain definite limitations to its reach. Internet use declines markedly among Americans over 65, who tend to be the nation's most reliable voters. Until recently, it tended to be more heavily used by middle- and upper-income people.

And while the Internet is efficient at reaching supporters, who tend to visit and linger at political sites, it has proved to be much less effective at swaying voters who are not interested in politics.

In this age of multitasking, voters are not as captive to a Web site as they might be to a 30-second television advertisement, or a campaign mailing. That was a critical lesson of the collapse of Mr. Dean's presidential campaign, after he initially enjoyed great Internet success in raising money and drawing crowds.

"It's very easy to look at something and just click delete," said Carl Forti, a spokesman for the National Republican Congressional Committee. "At least if they are taking out a piece of mail, you know they are taking it out and looking at it on the way to the garbage can."

Think About It

- Will Americans be less informed about candidates if there are fewer television advertisements?
- Does reliance on the Internet give active bloggers too much power to influence fund-raising and congressional votes?
- Are you concerned that reliance on the Internet will bias campaigns against older and lower income voters?
- Will the Internet make a positive contribution to civility in politics?

The Issue: Can States Compensate for Federal Inaction?

The federal system allocates responsibility for public policies in the United States. The national government manages some programs and state and local governments manage others. Usually this allocation of responsibility works reasonably well, and there is general agreement about the responsibilities of each level of government.

What happens, however, when the federal government refuses to adopt a program that people in many states desire? If the policy concerns the amount of parkland, laboratories in public schools, or the size of police forces, state and local governments may be able to act to provide the services their citizens desire—if the governments have the necessary resources.

For other policies, however, state efforts to compensate for the lack of national policy will inevitably suffer. Most people are concerned about access to health care, medical research, and environmental protection, for example. If the national government fails to provide services in these areas, it is possible for states to pass laws designed to ameliorate problems their lawmakers perceive to be pressing. Yet the federal system that decentralizes both politics and policies in the United States also creates perverse incentives that discourage states from providing the services that people desire. Thus, it is often not possible for states to compensate fully for inaction at the national level.

Read All About It

State Governments Overreach in Taking on Problems Best Solved at the National Level

By Robert H. Frank
April 13, 2006

In manufacturing, it is said, the French copy no one and no one copies the French. A parallel statement may soon apply to central elements of American public policy. In most of the world, for example, the primary responsibility for ensuring access to health care, regulating environmental quality and supporting basic scientific research is exercised by national governments. But in this country, these tasks are increasingly managed by state, and even local, governments.

Last week, for instance, Massachusetts became the first state to enact legislation trying to ensure that all its citizens have access to health care. At least 19 other states considered legislation expanding health care coverage in 2005. In January, eight states adopted new rules from the California Air Resources Board calling for a 30 percent reduction in carbon dioxide emissions from cars and light trucks by 2016, a step that Gov. George E. Pataki of New York has also pledged to take. And Maryland has just become the fifth state to authorize state spending for basic stem cell research.

In each case, there are compelling economic reasons for delegating the activities to national, rather than state or local, governments. Yet in each arena, the federal government has failed to act. It refuses to participate in international efforts to limit greenhouse gases. It makes further cuts in federal support for basic scientific research, even as the nation's share of world patents continues to decline. And about 46 million Americans currently lack any form of health insurance.

Although it is no mystery why states are beginning to take the lead in these domains, it is important to understand why the recently enacted programs are destined to fall far short f what could have been achieved at the federal level.

The explanation begins with the question of why we have multiple levels of government in the first place. Almost all of us are subject to taxation and regulation by governments at the local, state and national level. Although multi-tiered government entails substantial redundancy and inefficiency, there are good economic reasons for it.

As the economist Charles M. Tiebout explained in a seminal paper published in 1956, an important advantage of providing public services at the local level is that this enables us to better achieve our desired mix of public and private consumption.

People who like lots of parkland, well-maintained roads, large police forces and good schools can thus gather in high-tax communities that provide these amenities, while others can choose low-tax communities and spend more of their income on private consumption. Local government also minimizes the distance between citizens and the lawmakers who tax and regulate them.

But for some public services, like national defense, scale advantages rule out primary reliance on local government. Indeed, the fact that big countries can field more effective armies than small ones is the primary explanation for why large nations became the norm.

Scale advantages, however, do not explain why health care policy, environmental regulation and support for basic scientific research are best delegated to the federal government. Rather, the problem is that in each of these instances, programs at the state and local levels create perverse economic incentives.

[T]here are compelling economic reasons for delegating the activities to national, rather than state or local, governments. Yet in each arena, the federal government has failed to act.

A case in point is a proposal recently discussed in Ithaca, N.Y., where I live. Activists in this progressive upstate community (sometimes called "the People's Republic of Ithaca") called for a local income tax to finance a single-payer health care system for local residents. According to health policy experts, such a system would eliminate the substantial waste associated with attempts by insurance companies to limit authorized services and avoid covering people with chronic medical conditions.

Yet, despite this advantage, a health system operated at the local level could never work. Because people are free to move, such a plan would attract uninsured people with chronic conditions from surrounding cities, substantially raising the program's cost. In turn, the need to raise income tax rates would induce many of the community's more affluent taxpayers to flee to neighboring cities. The resulting death spiral would quickly doom the program.

Like local borders, state borders are completely permeable. So, unless a large number of other states simultaneously enact comprehensive health care legislation of their own, the new Massachusetts program will confront the same problem.

State efforts to regulate greenhouse gases and support basic scientific research are problematic for a different reason. When a pound of carbon dioxide is emitted into the atmosphere, it quickly disperses around the globe. A state that regulates greenhouse gases thus bears the entire cost of the reduction but receives only a minuscule fraction of the benefit. That fact is bound to limit political support for curbs strong enough to matter. As economists have long emphasized, effective environmental regulation requires national, or even international, collective action.

It is the same with support for basic scientific research. Residents of Maryland will bear the entire cost of any discoveries from research they finance but will reap only a small fraction of the corresponding benefits. And because of that imbalance, their incentive will be to invest too little.

My point is not that states are foolish for having extended their reach. Again, the federal government has completely dropped the ball in these domains. The recent state actions may not be the most efficient ways of dealing with our most pressing problems. But they are an unmistakable signal of voter impatience with ineffective government at the federal level.

Think About It

- Are there policies that states can adapt that do not suffer from perverse incentives?
- Why does the national government fail to act on a policy if many states wish it?
- Would it be preferable for states not to try to compensate for inaction of the national government?

The Issue: Should Universities Regulate Hate Speech?

Traditionally, we expect universities to be forums for full and candid discussion of issues. Limiting or discouraging the expression of a point of view is anathema to most university administrators, professors, and students. But what about speech that is motivated by racial, religious, or other prejudice and that includes offensive—and sometimes shocking—insults to certain categories of people? Advocates of regulating hate speech argue that hateful insults do not deserve protection because the perpetrator's intent is not to discover the truth or invite dialogue but to injure the victim. Critics of hate speech policy argue that limiting speech is too high a price to pay.

In 1992, the Supreme Court ruled in *R.A.V. v. St. Paul* that legislatures and universities may not single out racial, religious, or sexual insults or threats for prosecution as "hate speech" or "bias crimes" (although states may impose longer prison terms on people convicted of "hate crimes" without violating their rights to free speech). There are other ways to limit speech, however.

Read All About It

Hateful Name-Calling vs. Calling for Hateful Action

By Edward Rothstein
November 23, 2002

Hate speech is a confused concept. It is impossible to defend crude name-calling and insensitivity, but is it so deserving of special opprobrium? Even ordinary speech, after all, can express hatred. And even the most brutish expression of hatred can be less injurious than deceitful expressions of good will. What about this approach: if speech offends, let it be freely attacked by opposing speech. If it does more than offend but argues for hateful action—well, that is more serious.

The problem is that these priorities are often inverted. Hate speech tends to be prosecuted as a grievous violation, but arguments that can have far more hateful consequences tend to be protected as a freedom. Universities are particularly vulnerable to such contrasts, because speech grounded in argument is what a university is all about, so it is ardently defended almost regardless of content.

This leads to strange distinctions. Harvard University's English department withdrew its invitation to the poet Tom Paulin to deliver its annual Morris Gray Lecture largely because of mounting protests over what Mr. Paulin had to say about Israel. Mr. Paulin gave an interview to a Cairo-based newspaper, *Al-Ahram Weekly,* in which he said of "Brooklyn born" Jewish settlers on the West Bank: "They should be shot dead. I think they are Nazis, racists, I feel nothing but hatred for them." He also said, "I never believed that Israel had the right to exist at all." Moreover, in a poem published in *The Observer* in 2001, he referred to the Israeli army as "the Zionist SS."

But the English department was soon attacked for its awkward reversal in a new wave of protests. In a letter to *The Harvard Crimson,* Patrick Cavanagh, a Harvard psychology professor who signed a petition urging that Harvard disinvest in Israel called Harvard's president, Lawrence H. Summers, "Ayatollah Summers," accusing him of bigotry for his support of the department's retraction. (Mr. Summers has recently criticized anti-Semitism on American campuses.)

The protestors seemed to suggest that Mr. Paulin wasn't really engaged in hate speech at all. He was actually making arguments—controversial political judgments—that should be protected. The department re-reversed itself.

The confusion over hate speech was also revealed in another recent controversy. The Stanford University Law School invited the lawyer Lynne Stewart to be a Mills Public Interest Mentor in a program the school says is meant "to provide public-interest students the opportunity to meet and learn from practitioners and scholars in public service."

But Ms. Stewart, a political radical who unsuccessfully defended Sheik Omar Abdel Rahman for his responsibility in the 1993 World Trade Center bombing, was indicted last spring on charges of aiding a terrorist organization and illegally passing messages from the sheik's prison cell. In particular, in June 2000, she publicly confirmed for the sheik's fundamentalist followers in Egypt that he had called for an end to a cease-fire between those followers and the Egyptian government.

Hate speech tends to be prosecuted as a grievous violation, but arguments that can have far more hateful consequences tend to be protected as a freedom.

Ms. Stewart's assistance in that instance was not out of character. She said she believes in "violence directed at the institutions which perpetuate capitalism, racism and sexism and at the people who are the appointed guardians of those institutions." In reacting to the civilian deaths of 9/11, she said she was "pretty inured" to the idea that "in an armed struggle, people die."

When some of this became widely known, protests mounted and the dean of the law school stripped Ms. Stewart of the title Mills mentor. But her lectures and mentoring of students took place unhampered.

Yet Ms. Stewart's public service and proclamations may have caused violence (her declaration of the end of that cease-fire was indeed followed by deaths in Egypt) as well as encouraged it against American targets. Presumably, only acts of hate speech would have made her unwelcome at Stanford, but aren't her positions and actions already expressions of a virulent form of hatred?

Not all criticism of Israel is anti-Semitic, but not all criticism of Israel is not anti-Semitic. When standards of justice are applied in profoundly distorted fashion, when those distortions put the literal survival of a society at stake and when murders are taking place and explicitly encouraged, declarations are being made that may even fit university standards for "hate speech." Or perhaps the concept itself should just be retired; it leads to puritanical scrutiny in some cases and is completely ignored in others.

Think About It

- Should your university adopt a policy to limit hate speech?
- If so, how should it define hate speech?
- Is there a danger that a hate speech policy could also limit the expression of important but unpopular views?
- Is there a significant difference between hate speech and arguments advocating policies you find abhorrent?

The Issue: Affirmative Action

Nearly everyone in America supports equal opportunity for employment, promotion, or admission to universities. Few people believe any group should be at a disadvantage. However, consensus breaks down when the focus turns to equal results in obtaining these jobs or university slots. There is little support for giving some people a special advantage, even if it is to overcome past discrimination.

How do we reconcile these views with the following facts: (1) not everyone has the same chance to take advantage of a theoretical opportunity, (2) discrimination still occurs in some quarters of society, and (3) the nation is becoming more diverse and the legitimacy of institutions requires that they be broadly representative of American society?

Read All About It

What the United States Army Teaches Us About Affirmative Action

By Brent Staples
January 6, 2003, Monday

The Harvard sociologist Nathan Glazer argued fervently against affirmative action policies during the 1970's but later changed his mind. By the late 1990's, he and many other conservatives had come to see that failing to integrate the institutions that confer wealth and power would threaten the legitimacy of democracy itself.

They may have been looking at California, where the decision to outlaw the use of race in public college admissions in 1996 was initially seen as the death knell for affirmative action. But the disappearance of black and Latino faces from the state's elite public universities, and the threat of a "white out" on campuses nationwide, worried conservatives as well as liberals. Other states began to back away from proposals that would have killed off affirmative action without leaving a comparable mechanism in its place.

When race-sensitive admissions became an issue in Texas, under Gov. George W. Bush, and in Florida, under his brother Jeb, both states defused an explosive situation with plans that guaranteed admission to fixed percentages of students. As governor, George W. Bush kept diversity—and the civic peace—by guaranteeing admission to the top 10 percent of students in each high school.

The core principle behind affirmative action is that excluding black people undermines civic harmony and runs counter to American ideals. This was evident in the case of the United States Army. After years of racial strife and rigorous segregation, it transformed itself into the most fully integrated organization yet seen in this country.

The military during both World Wars consigned most black people to support jobs. The top brass commonly defended discrimination in racist terms, arguing that black men lacked the courage to fight or the intelligence to lead. These bigoted policies shadowed the military long after formal segregation was ended and nearly tore the Army apart during the 1960's and 70's. One of the pivotal figures in the transformation was Clifford Alexander, President Jimmy Carter's secretary of the Army. Early in his tenure, Mr. Alexander put a hold on a list of officers proposed for promotion to general. He was troubled, as he explained in a 1997 Op-Ed article, "because no black colonels had been promoted, even though many had achieved that rank and served with distinction."

The board that handled promotions was ordered to look at the records of eligible black colonels and to determine if they had been given lesser assignments or evaluated negatively by officers who were racially prejudiced. Once race-related blemishes were expunged, black colonels with otherwise sterling records emerged as strong candidates for promotion.

This decision was affirmative action in its purest, most elemental form. But 25 years of distortion and political warfare over this issue have made it difficult for most people to speak clearly on the subject or even to recognize affirmative action when they see it. Loaded terms such as "quotas" and "reverse discrimination" have made it all but impossible to see affirmative action as a constructive and vitally important policy for the United States.

This charged atmosphere has obscured the story of the Army's spectacular transformation. Mr. Alexander, for example, took offense when President Bill Clinton argued that Colin Powell, promoted to brigadier general during Mr. Alexander's tenure, was the product of an affirmative action program. Mr. Alexander viewed the measures he had taken as common-sense fairness but rejected the label "affirmative action." The term, he believed, implied that the black candidates for general had been less qualified than the white candidates or that they had been given some "extra" benefit. The truth, of course, is that the black officers would have been trapped in oblivion but for a strategy that allowed them to escape what were known as "nicks" on their records made by unfair superiors.

Loaded terms such as "quotas" and "reverse discrimination" have made it all but impossible to see affirmative action as a constructive and vitally important policy for the United States.

The Army also took steps to ensure that race would no longer be an obstacle to promotion. It ensured that all junior officers had a reasonable chance of getting assignments that, if performed well, made them eligible to move up. As the military historians Charles C. Moskos and John Sibley Butler wrote in "All That We Can Be: Black Leadership and Racial Integration the Army Way," the Army is "the only place in American life where whites are routinely bossed around by blacks." Twelve percent of the Army's officers are black.

The typical Army base is far more racially integrated than the average town or college campus. The rest of the country lags behind. Most black and Latino students are still confined to mediocre schools that place even excellent, hard-working students at a disadvantage in terms of standardized test scores.

Think About It

- Do you support the army's approach to affirmative action?
- Does the army's approach to promotion help get minorities into the army in the first place?
- Can the army's approach to affirmative action be used to rectify the imbalance of minorities in the nation's leading universities or in the most prestigious and lucrative positions in business?
- Do most organizations have a similar hierarchy to that in the army?

The Issue: Should Presidents Be Using Theories of Public Opinion to "Sell" Their Policies?

When George W. Bush first ran for president in 2000, he repeatedly pledged that if he were to serve as president, his administration would have no use for polls and focus groups. Implicitly criticizing the Clinton administration, he said that one couldn't govern with one's finger to the wind and be driven by the results of public opinion. Constrained by Bush's promise to govern solely by his belief in what is right, regardless of whether it is politically popular or not, his administration has sought to keep its use of public opinion data out of the limelight. Thus, when the *New York Times* revealed how public opinion data were being used to try to bolster support for the Iraq War, it became a significant news story that generated controversy.

Read All About It

Bush's Speech on Iraq War Echoes Voice of an Analyst

By Scott Shane
December 3, 2005

WASHINGTON—There could be no doubt about the theme of President Bush's Iraq war strategy speech at the Naval Academy. He used the word victory 15 times in the address; "Plan for Victory" signs crowded the podium he spoke on; and the word heavily peppered the accompanying 35-page National Security Council document titled, "Our National Strategy for Victory in Iraq."

Although White House officials said many federal departments had contributed to the document, its relentless focus on the theme of victory strongly reflected a new voice in the administration: Peter D. Feaver, a Duke University political scientist who joined the N.S.C. staff as a special adviser in June and has closely studied public opinion on the war.

Despite the president's oft-stated aversion to polls, Dr. Feaver was recruited after he and Duke colleagues presented the administration with an analysis of polls about the Iraq war in 2003 and 2004. They concluded that Americans would support a war with mounting casualties on one condition: that they believed it would ultimately succeed.

That finding, which is questioned by other political scientists, was clearly behind the victory theme in the speech and the plan, in which the word appears six times in the table of contents alone, including sections titled "Victory in Iraq is a Vital U.S. Interest" and "Our Strategy for Victory is Clear."

"This is not really a strategy document from the Pentagon about fighting the insurgency," said Christopher F. Gelpi, Dr. Feaver's colleague at Duke and co-author of the research on American tolerance for casualties. "The Pentagon doesn't need the president to give a speech and post a document on the White House Web site to know how to fight the insurgents. The document is clearly targeted at American public opinion."

Last year in an op-ed article in *The Washington Post*, noting Mr. Bush's determination to invade Iraq in 2003 in the face of doubts, Dr. Feaver wrote, "Determined commanders in chief have the mind-set and the resolve to act in spite of the political climate and military resistance."

He was recruited by the White House this year as public support for the war declined steadily in the face of mounting casualties and costs.

Based on their study of poll results from the first two years of the war, Dr. Gelpi, Dr. Feaver and Jason Reifler, then a Duke graduate student, took issue with what they described as the conventional wisdom since the Vietnam War—that Americans will support military operations only if American casualties are few.

They found that public tolerance for the human cost of combat depended on two factors: a belief that the war was a worthy cause, and even more important, a belief that the war was likely to be successful.

In their paper, "Casualty Sensitivity and the War in Iraq," which is to be published soon in the journal *International Security*, Dr. Feaver and his colleagues wrote: "Mounting casualties did not produce a reflexive collapse in public support.

Dr. Feaver was recruited after he and Duke colleagues presented the administration with an analysis of polls about the Iraq war in 2003 and 2004.

The Iraq case suggests that under the right conditions, the public will continue to support military operations even when they come with a relatively high human cost."

The role of Dr. Feaver in preparing the strategy document came to light through a quirk of technology. In a portion of the document usually hidden from public view but accessible with a few keystrokes, the plan posted on the White House Web site showed the document's originator, or "author" in the software's designation, to be "feaver-p."

Frederick Jones, an N.S.C. spokesman, said the document "reflects the broad interagency effort under way in Iraq" and "incorporates all aspects of American power," including political and economic as well as military efforts. He said major contributions to the plan came from the Departments of Defense, State, Treasury and Homeland Security, as well as the director of National Intelligence. In his news briefing on Wednesday, the White House spokesman, Scott McClellan, characterized the document as an unclassified, publicly accessible explanation of strategies that the administration has been pursuing in Iraq since 2003.

The Feaver-Gelpi hypothesis on public opinion about the war is the subject of serious debate among political scientists. John Mueller, of Ohio State University, said he did not believe that the president's speech or the victory plan—which he described as "very Feaverish, or Feaveresque"—could produce more than a fleeting improvement in public support for the war, because it was likely to erode further as casualties accumulated.

Think About It

- After this story came out, John McCain was asked on *Meet the Press* whether he was "disturbed" by the president's message being crafted by a public opinion expert. McCain responded as follows: "Well, I think you always have got to figure out how you can best put your case in a most effective fashion." Are you disturbed by the Bush administration's use of polling research in this case, or do you agree with McCain's view?
- Do you think that Dr. Feaver's research on this topic helped the Bush administration in its effort to bolster public support for the Iraq War? Why or why not?

The Issue: Can the Internet Provide the Means to Ensure Fairness in Political Reporting?

The ambitious motto of the *New York Times* is "All the news that is fit to print." In the world of the Internet, which enables journalists to post extra information beyond what can be printed in the newspaper, the question becomes how much information is enough. If some people—particularly those who were criticized in a news story—think the reporting is incomplete, they can now supplement it themselves by placing their own information and viewpoint on the Web. The result is a more free-flowing and interactive transmission of political news than ever before. But whether this is an entirely positive development is debatable, as you can see in this article.

Read All About It

Answering Back to the News Media, Using the Internet

By Katharine Q. Seelye
January 2, 2006

Never pick a fight with someone who buys ink by the barrel, or so goes the old saw. For decades, the famous and the infamous alike largely followed this advice. Even when subjects of news stories felt they had been misunderstood or badly treated, they were unlikely to take on reporters or publishers, believing that the power of the press gave the press the final word.

The Internet, and especially the amplifying power of blogs, is changing that. Unhappy subjects discovered a decade ago that they could use their Web sites to correct the record or deconstruct articles to expose what they perceived as a journalist's bias or wrongheaded narration.

But now they are going a step further. Subjects of newspaper articles and news broadcasts now fight back with the same methods reporters use to generate articles and broadcasts—taping interviews, gathering e-mail exchanges, taking notes on phone conversations—and publish them on their own Web sites. This new weapon in the media wars is shifting the center of gravity in the way that news is gathered and presented, and it carries implications for the future of journalism.

Just ask "Nightline," the ABC News program, which broadcast a segment in August about intelligent design that the Discovery Institute, a conservative clearinghouse for proponents of intelligent design, did not like very much. The next day, the institute published on its Web site the entire transcript of the nearly hourlong interview that "Nightline" had conducted a few days earlier with one of the institute's leaders, not just the brief quotes that had appeared on television.

The institute did not accuse "Nightline" of any errors. Rather, it urged readers to examine the unedited interview because, it said, the transcript would reveal "the predictable tone of some of the questions" by the staff of "Nightline."

"Here's your chance to go behind the scenes with the gatekeepers of the national media to see how they screen out viewpoints and information that don't fit their stereotypes," Rob Crowther, the institute's spokesman, wrote on the Web site.

The printing of transcripts, e-mail messages and conversations, and the ability to pull up information from search engines like Google, have empowered those whom Jay Rosen, a blogger and journalism professor at New York University, calls "the people formerly known as the audience."

All these developments have forced journalists to respond in a variety of ways, including becoming more open about their methods and techniques and perhaps more conscious of how they filter information.

"To the extent that you know there's someone monitoring every word, it probably compels you to be even more careful, which is a good thing," said Chris Bury, the "Nightline" correspondent whose interview was published by the Discovery Institute. "But readers and viewers need to realize that one interview is only one part of the story, that there are other interviews and other research and that this is just a sliver of what goes into a complete report."

Posting primary source material is becoming part of public relations strategies for interest groups, businesses and government. The Pentagon and State Department now post transcripts of interviews with top officials on their Web sites or they e-mail them to reporters, as does Vice President Dick Cheney's office.

The Pentagon and State Department now post transcripts of interviews with top officials on their Web sites or they e-mail them to reporters, as does Vice President Dick Cheney's office.

Many bloggers said reporters should publish such material as a matter of course; others questioned the need to be inundated with every scrap of unorganized, unedited information and wondered where it would stop.

Interview subjects are "annoyed that they're quoted out of context, or they did a half-hour interview and only one sentence got used. Or sometimes they're just flattered that a reporter called them," she said. "If you're one of a growing number of people with a blog, you now have a place where you can set the record straight."

Danny Schechter, executive editor of MediaChannel.org and a former producer at ABC News and CNN, said that while the active participation by so many readers was healthy for democracy and journalism, it had allowed partisanship to mask itself as media criticism and had given rise to a new level of vitriol.

"It's now O.K. to demonize the messenger," he said. "This has led to a very uncivil discourse in which it seems to be O.K. to shout down, discredit, delegitimize and denigrate the people who are reporting stories and to pick at their methodology and ascribe motives to them that are often unfair."

Reporters say that these developments are forcing them to change how they do their jobs; some are asking themselves if they can justify how they are filtering information.

While some say they are learning to accept the new interactivity, they also worry that the view of many bloggers—that reporters should post their raw material because they are filtering it through their own biases—ignores the value of traditional journalistic functions, like casting a wide net for information, coaxing it out of reluctant sources, condensing it and presenting it in an orderly way.

Think About It

- What are the possible disadvantages of making it so easy for journalists to report on every little detail and for sources to counter stories they disagree with by posting their own information? Do you think these disadvantages outweigh the advantages of greater access to information?
- Do you think editors should encourage some reporters to post more of the raw material that goes into their stories on the Web?

The Issue: Should the Political Parties Be Compiling Data About You?

Until the advent of television, the heart of political party activity revolved around an army of activists going door-to-door to try to persuade and mobilize their friends and neighbors to support the party's candidates. A good party organization would consist of activists who really knew the people they were contacting and how to best approach them. Then, television came in allowing candidates to speak directly to the people, with the result being that personal contacts were no longer necessary. Today, as this article discusses, detailed computer databases have made it possible to communicate *individualized* messages to people once again. Whether or not this is a positive development for American party politics remains to be seen.

Read All About It

The Very, Very Personal Is the Political

By Jon Gertner
February 15, 2004

Suppose, for the sake of argument, that you are called into the boss's office and asked to help sell the citizens of the United States on one of two presidential candidates in the 2004 campaign. Hard work, but what makes it especially tough is that you've been directed to try something experimental, something that's never been done before in a national election. Instead of creating a traditional political narrative for your candidate—one that highlights charisma or character, for instance, or one that hews to a message on taxes or Social Security—you've been told to focus on nothing but the people who might be persuaded to vote. . . . Think about what they like, what they do, what they consume. Think about them one by one. Name by name, address by address, phone by phone.

These are the customers you have to get to buy your Brand A over Brand B. So who are they? Where are they? Are they rich, with three kids and a jumbo mortgage? Do they own fly rods and drive minivans? Do they go to church or temple? And maybe most important, who among them has never voted, or rarely voted, or voted in ways that may deserve the special status of swing voter? To do the job right, of course, to really win this thing, you've got to find them, woo them and get them to the polls. Where to start?

These days, the first stop is a comprehensive database of U.S. voters. There are fewer than half a dozen of them. One, named Voter Vault, belongs to the Republican National Committee; another, named Datamart, belongs to the Democratic National Committee. Over the past few years, thanks to technological advances and an escalating arms race between the parties, Republicans and Democrats have gone to great lengths to make campaigning more like commercial marketing. Moreover, both parties have begun to sort through their troves of information in order to identify and then court individual voters. Variations on the new political sharpshooting have been tested successfully by the Republican and Democratic Parties in several recent statewide elections. . . .

Each party's databank has the name of every one of the 168 million or so registered voters in the country, cross-indexed with phone numbers, addresses, voting history, income range and so on—up to as many as several hundred points of data on each voter. The information has been acquired from state voter-registration rolls, census reports, consumer data-mining companies and direct marketing vendors. The parties have also amassed detailed information about the political and social beliefs that you might have shared with canvassers who have phoned or knocked on the door over the past few years. . . .

Both national committees see their detailed breakdown of the American electorate as a high-tech variation of pretelevision techniques—from the 1930's, say, or even the 1950's—when politics was driven by the one-to-one contact of a precinct worker who might know how to deliver an individualized political message simply because he knew your family, your job, your ethnicity, your values. Within the Republican Party, the 72-Hour Task Force and Voter Vault are considered proof of its return to grass-roots organizing, whereby the party will get to better understand, and keep track of, its supporters. . . .

These days, the first stop is a comprehensive database of U.S. voters.

. . . [D]ata-mining technology offers three significant advantages. First, by locating likely voters with greater accuracy, it enables campaigns to spend their dollars more wisely and efficiently. Second, it opens up innovative ways of discovering and turning out new voters. Third, it creates the option of creating a narrow or individualized message—delivered by a friend, through the mail, over the phone or on cable TV—so that parties can talk to potential supporters about exactly the things they care about most. . . .

Among privacy advocates the new databases are almost uniformly viewed as a trespass into our zone of political privacy. Oscar Gandy of the University of Pennsylvania has further noted that political targeting may effectively disenfranchise portions of the electorate that are less likely to vote, or less likely to be persuadable. Why reach out to someone a statistician or a computer program does not consider a viable target?

Meanwhile, other privacy advocates say they worry about the dangers of assembling an individualized message from voter data—a message to that 50-year-old Ford Explorer driver who likes gardening and cares about tort reform, for example. "The nightmare scenario is that the databases create puppet masters," Peter Swire, a privacy expert who worked at the Office of Management and Budget during the Clinton administration, told me. "In the nightmare, every voter will get a tailored message based on detailed information about the voter." . . . The candidate knows everything about the voter, but the media and the public know nothing about what the candidate really believes. . . .

Think About It

- After this article was printed, the *New York Times* asked online, "Should the political parties be compiling data about you?" Seventy-nine percent of those who responded clicked on "no." How would you have responded?
- What about young people? Given the information laid out in this article concerning how these computerized lists are created, do you think young people are substantially less likely to be on them? If so, might this mean that the parties will soon be concentrating even more on older people if they rely on such technology?

The Issue: Will the Presidential Candidates Pay Any Attention to California in 2008?

In 2004, states that failed to schedule their primary early in the calendar were irrelevant to the nomination process. Most of these states were stuck with dates that were traditional for them. Given the frontloading of the process, states that want to be influential have in recent decades moved their primary dates earlier and earlier. But as we look ahead to 2008, our nation's largest state—California—has surprised many observers by deciding to move its primary date three months later than it was in 2004. This represents the first time in recent history that a major state had moved its presidential primary date backward. Whether this is good or bad for California, as well as the nation as a whole, is likely to be debated for the next several years.

Read All About It

California Moves to Reschedule Its Primary from March to June

By Dean E. Murphy
August 30, 2004

SACRAMENTO—The state that helped push the presidential primary season into a fast-forward frenzy more than a decade ago is now abruptly shifting it into reverse.

A bill that would move the California presidential primary to June from March beginning in 2008 breezed through the State Legislature this week with bipartisan support.

The move would amount to unconditional surrender by the country's most delegate-rich state in the contest to influence the presidential nomination process.

"It defies logic," said Robert D. Loevy, a professor of political science at Colorado College and a scholar of presidential primaries. "You would think in a democracy with a presidency which is the top governing officer that state legislatures would be working hard to see their citizens have as much influence as possible."

California held a June primary for a half-century before the Legislature voted in 1993 to move the primary to March, largely in response to the so-called Super Tuesday primaries scheduled by Southern states in the 1980s, which were draining the California vote of its influence.

For many years, the June date made California a kingmaker in both parties, as presidential candidates methodically worked their way West in a primary system that involved far fewer contests than today. California was crucial to Barry Goldwater against Nelson Rockefeller in 1964. But the last time California played a pivotal role was in 1984, when Walter F. Mondale emerged from a tight battle with Gary Hart for the Democratic nomination.

California backers of the original June date say the three presidential elections with a March primary—in 1996, 2000 and this year—show that it failed in reviving California's fortunes. In all three of those elections, either the parties had settled on a nominee before the March primary here or candidates chose to focus their attention on other states that had also moved their primaries forward—and are much smaller and cheaper to campaign in.

Even with the move to March, California found itself behind some 20 other states in a primary sweepstakes that has states already jockeying for advantage in 2008. In New Hampshire, which has the country's first primary, state law requires that the primary be held at least one week before any other state's.

"It is a constant friction with other states where people want to keep moving their primaries to an earlier date," said Art Torres, chairman of the California Democratic Party, who supports moving the date back to June. "By the time you are done, we will have primaries at Halloween. You can never win at that level."

To make matters worse, the March elections in California have been a flop among voters: turnout this March was the lowest for any presidential primary in the state's history in percentage terms, making it difficult for candidates for offices on the same ballot to rouse interest in their races.

"People realize the March primary has been a disaster," said Susie Swatt, chief of staff for State Senator Ross Johnson, the Orange County Republican who wrote the bill.

The move would amount to unconditional surrender by the country's most delegate-rich state in the contest to influence the presidential nomination process.

In 2002, the Legislature considered another solution: separating the presidential primary from the state primary. That way the presidential vote could be held in March—or even earlier—and the primary for state and local offices could return to June. But the added cost of holding two primaries was considered too prohibitive, and the bill was vetoed by Gov. Gray Davis.

Dan Schnur, who has worked on four presidential campaigns, including that of Senator John McCain in 2000, said the March date remained a big inconvenience for local and state campaigns, particularly because it means candidates must decide whether to run much earlier. But Mr. Schnur said the biggest losers have been the voters.

"The voters' body clocks aren't ready for politics the day after the bowl games end," said Mr. Schnur, who favored the switch to March but now prefers June.

Kathy Sullivan, chairwoman of the Democratic Party in New Hampshire, said part of her longs for the old days when New Hampshire held its primary in March (when there was less snow) and California held its in June (when the vote still mattered). Ms. Sullivan said those days were probably gone forever, but she said the primary system has compensated in a way that keeps California relevant.

"People have come to recognize in this process, and I think you saw it with the Democrats in the early states this year, that we need to nominate a candidate who is going to be able to run an effective race nationwide," Ms. Sullivan said. "So people were not necessarily choosing who is best for New Hampshire or Iowa or Michigan or South Carolina."

Professor Loevy said that should not be good enough for the country's most populous state. He said California's mistake in 1993 was not moving its primary even earlier. He said a Halloween election was preferable to one in June with no meaning.

"Now they are going in exactly the wrong direction," he said.

Think About It

- After the California legislature passed this bill, the *New York Times* wrote an editorial praising California for trying to reverse the pattern of front-loading of presidential primaries. Do you agree with the position of the *New York Times* editorial board that this was a good move on California's part?
- Do you think other states will now move their primary dates back for 2008? Should they? Why or why not?

The Issue: Should Municipal Governments Be Hiring Lobbyists?

As Harold Lasswell said many years ago, "Politics is about who gets what, when, and how." Lobbyists are in business to get more of whatever there is to get from government for their clients. In recent years, the lobbying business in our nation's capital has expanded at a rapid rate, as lobbyists have found more and more clients willing to pay substantial costs to increase their chances of getting what they want from the federal government. Even relatively small municipal governments have gotten into the act, hiring lobbyists to help them get their local projects funded in Washington, as you can read about in the following article.

Read All About It

Hiring Federal Lobbyists, Towns Learn Money Talks

By Jodi Rudoren and Aron Pilhofer
July 2, 2006

TREASURE ISLAND, Fla.—Rebuffed on several requests for state and federal financing to help rebuild its crumbling bridge, this small resort town was all but resigned to raising the money by doubling the 50-cent bridge toll, increasing property taxes and issuing bonds.

But in a last-ditch gambit, city officials hired a federal lobbyist who had known the local congressman for four decades. Within weeks, the congressman, Representative C. W. Bill Young, called the mayor to say he had slipped a special $50 million appropriation, known as an earmark, into an omnibus bill.

Since that windfall three years ago, Treasure Island has continued to pay $5,000 a month to the lobbying firm, Alcalde & Fay, and has continued to reap earmarks: $500,000 to fix a sewer plant, $625,000 to repair wooden walkways over the dunes, $450,000 for pedestrian crosswalks.

"They're worth every penny they get," said Mayor Mary Maloof, who led a parade of antique cars to open the new bridge on June 10. "When we started talking about it, there were plenty of eyebrows raised that we would be doing such a thing. But it's turned out to be a valuable tool for helping us cover costs."

Cities and towns—and school districts and transit authorities and utility agencies—across the country are increasingly reaching for that same toolbox, putting lobbyists on retainer to leverage their local tax dollars into federal tax dollars.

Since 1998, the number of public entities hiring private firms to represent them in Washington has nearly doubled to 1,421 from 763, as places like Treasure Island, population 7,514, have jumped onboard with behemoths like Miami that have long had lobbyists.

Enlisted almost exclusively to land earmarks, lobbyists for local governments have boomed alongside a broader explosion in such appropriations, to 12,852 items worth $64 billion last year from 4,219 pet projects totaling $27.7 billion in 1998. The prolific earmarking does not change the overall budget's bottom line, but how the pie is cut: dollars are doled out, often in secret, at the whim of a lone legislator—often under the influence of a lobbyist—rather than through a competitive process.

Ronald D. Utt, a senior fellow at the Heritage Foundation and a frequent critic of earmarks, said he was most troubled at seeing firms solicit public clients with virtual guarantees that they could deliver "dollars for pennies" (or billions for millions).

"The mystery to me is the way they are able to promise returns," Mr. Utt said, pointing to the revolving door between Congressional appropriators' payrolls and lobby shops, as well as to lobbyists' generous campaign contributions. "It goes beyond mere influence peddling to just outright, classic third-world corruption."

Lobbyists say there is nothing improper in their political activity. In fact, they use it as a selling point. In a 2002 proposal to the City of Pembroke Pines, an Alcalde lobbyist pointed to monthly fund-raisers the firm held at its offices in Arlington, Va., and said attending events "very frequently" for Republicans and Democrats alike "does allow us to better our local government clients."

Although local officials are rarely active in the campaign-contribution race that accompanies the earmarks derby, the firm's employees have given upward of $200,000 to more than 100 politicians since 1997, nearly half in Florida and in other states where it has clusters of public clients.

Beyond any question of quid pro quo, however, some critics say the new ubiquity of private lobbyists paid with public money perverts basic democratic tenets.

Beyond any question of quid pro quo, however, some critics say the new ubiquity of private lobbyists paid with public money perverts basic democratic tenets. Of the 250 top-grossing firms in Washington, 48 have state, local and tribal governments as their leading source of revenue, far more than any other sector, according to the Center for Public Integrity, which monitors lobbying.

Tim Phillips, president of Americans for Prosperity, one of several Washington watchdog groups critical of earmarks, said it was local politicians' mandate to make their needs known—and the job of members of Congress to look out for them.

"If you're a mayor or a city councilman and you have to hire a lobbyist, what a gross admission of failure on your part," Mr. Phillips said. "I would think they have a fiduciary responsibility to not put taxpayer dollars into lobbyists when they're elected to be, really, the lobbyist for the people."

The mayors and city council members, though, point to the special appropriations as proof of their fiscal prudence.

Alcalde & Fay is one of three firms—along with Patton Boggs and the Ferguson Group—that collected $25 million from public clients in the past eight years, much more than any other lobbyists. A close look at Alcalde & Fay's 44 public clients in Florida alone shows that, since 2001, $9.8 million in lobbying fees translated into $173 million in earmarks, or a return of $18.41 on every dollar spent.

In Treasure Island, each dollar to Alcalde & Fay yielded $285.83 in federal money.

Think About It

- After this article appeared, the *New York Times* published an editorial criticizing the fact that so many municipal governments had seen fit to hire lobbyists. They wrote that this "should be an outright embarrassment to Congress," as elected lawmakers "are supposed to be best attuned to meeting the needs of their localities." Do you agree or disagree with this assessment?
- As the local politicians quoted in this article state, the price they pay to hire lobbyists to work for their municipalities is often well worth the cost. Critics would respond that this doesn't justify the procedure. What do you think?

The Issue: The Revolving Door Between Congress and Lobbying Firms

Members of Congress are extraordinarily busy and depend heavily on staff members to run their offices and committees. Whether it is helping their constituents, organizing their schedules, writing laws, or dealing with each other, representatives and senators require talented and committed staffers to do their jobs. As a result, there are thousands of congressional staffers on Capitol Hill.

What happens, however, when staffers cash in on their knowledge of the legislative process or the details of public policy and take much better paying jobs as lobbyists? For one thing, Congress loses expertise. Of equal concern is the possible conflict of interest that the revolving door between Congress and lobbying firms poses for congressional staff members. Staff members deal regularly with lobbyists on matters ranging from the details of legislation to political strategy. Does knowing that they may soon accept a lucrative position with a lobbying firm influence the advice staff members offer their congressional bosses? Finally, stories about former congressional staffers cashing in on their personal connections with members of Congress do not encourage public respect for either the legislative process or congressional ethics.

Adding to Congress's predicament is the lack of an easy solution to the revolving door.

Read All About It

Once Just an Aide, Now a King of K Street

By Anne E. Kornblut
February 5, 2006

Once, the archetype of the Capitol Hill aide was a humble policy wonk fresh from graduate school who moved to Washington to pursue a gratifying but mostly anonymous life in public service. In recent years, a more high-flying path for the Congressional aide has emerged: lobbyist-in-training.

The pay in Congressional offices still stinks. The hours are still grueling. But the job, once an end in itself, is increasingly seen as a ticket to be punched—and sometimes comes with the almost explicit promise of hitting pay dirt after a reasonably short stint. "It's the new business school," said Chris Lehane, a Democratic consultant who formed his own public relations business after serving in the Clinton White House.

Nothing has pulled the curtain back on this trend more than the story surrounding the disgraced lobbyist Jack Abramoff. With his help, several young Hill staff members jumped into the private sector after just a few years in public service, tripling their salaries overnight. In return, they used their ties to those still on the "inside" to maneuver on behalf of his business clients.

The spotlight on the case has turned attention to the widespread phenomenon of the aide-turned-lobbyist. Last week, after House Republicans elected John Boehner of Ohio as majority leader, government watchdog groups were quick to note that at least 14 former aides had turned their connections to Mr. Boehner, chairman of the Education Committee, into K Street lobbying jobs.

Democrats pounced on this figure as evidence that he was as inextricably linked to lobbyists as was his predecessor, Tom DeLay, who was forced to resign as majority leader in part because of his connections to Mr. Abramoff. (A former press secretary to Mr. DeLay, Michael Scanlon, pleaded guilty to conspiring to bribe public officials, and is cooperating in the Abramoff case after earning tens of millions of dollars through his public affairs firm.)

When did the dutiful Hill staffer become a wheeler-dealer with such amazing clout? Members of Congress have long used the revolving door to cycle out into the private sector and make big salaries. But a legislative director? Or a chief of staff?

Paradoxically, new lobbying restrictions being considered in the wake of the Abramoff scandal may only tip the scales further, making a long career on the Hill too onerous for all but the most earnest public servants.

"The first question you get whenever you move on is, 'Are you going to stay on the Hill or go off?'" said Kevin Madden, who left his job as press secretary to Representative DeLay last week and has not yet decided whether to move into the private sector or remain on Capitol Hill.

Some of the biggest names in lobbying in recent years have been former aides who emerged from Congress or the White House with extensive contacts and a deep understanding of how legislation moves.

Some aides argue that Congressional jobs will lose more luster as lobbying rules continue to tighten, shrinking the number of perks, like travel junkets, that Hill aides can take.

Ed Gillespie, the former head of the Republican National Committee who started out as a top aide to Dick Armey, the former House majority leader, is perhaps the most visible. Mr. Gillespie's firm, Quinn Gillespie & Associates, is routinely ranked in the top 10 among lobbying powerhouses; in 2004, the firm had $13.9 million in revenue, according to the magazine *Influence*, which covers the lobbying industry.

Superlobbyists might earn up to $1 million a year. Newer recruits earn at least six figures, sometimes starting as high as $200,000 a year, a great leap from the Hill, where salaries vary from office to office but where aides are lucky to break $50,000 a year. Only a small percentage of the more than 16,000 Capitol Hill staff members make more than $100,000.

"What's happened is that the disparity in salaries—between what members and staff make versus what lobbyists make downtown—it's gotten so enormous that you could be a medium-high-level Congressional staffer, and you go downtown and the first day be making more money than your boss, the senator, made," said Charlie Cook, editor of the nonpartisan *Cook Political Report*. "And I think that's sort of distorted the pecking order."

Democrats say that this disparity worsened with the so-called K Street Project, a moniker for several different Republican lobbying efforts, but generally synonymous with Mr. DeLay's insistence, after his party took control of the House in 1996, that K Street firms hire Republicans. Aides to the party's legislators had more and more access to those high-paying jobs.

Think About It

- Is Congress weakened as an institution because so many staff leave to become lobbyists?
- Should Congress substantially increase staff pay to make staff positions more attractive?
- Should Congress attempt to limit former staffers from lobbying their former bosses?

The Issue: Are Signing Statements a Veto Power?

The Constitution grants the president power to veto congressional legislation. In most instances, Congress then has the opportunity to override the president's veto. The president must veto an entire bill, however, even if he supports most of its provisions. On other occasions, Congress will not uphold a veto or the president does not wish to veto popular legislation. In any of these instances, presidents may issue a "signing statement" that reinterprets the meaning of some aspect of the legislation. In effect, such statements represent a veto of a provision because the president states that he will not implement what appears to be the intent of the law.

If the president can ignore congressional intent and if the president rather than the judiciary decides the limits of executive authority, the White House gains power. It is not surprising that some experts view signing statements as altering the constitutional balance of power between the branches.

Presidents are especially likely to employ signing statements to reject what they see as congressional attempts to limit their discretion as chief executive. George W. Bush argues that Congress has no authority to restrict his inherent power as president, so it is perfectly appropriate for him to refuse to comply with unconstitutional limitations. Of course, this view begs the question of the nature of executive power.

Read All About It

For President, Final Say on a Bill Sometimes Comes After the Signing

By Elisabeth Bumiller
January 16, 2006

Shortly after 8 p.m. on Friday, Dec. 30, the White House sent out an e-mail message with an innocuous "Statement by the President" in the subject line. As might be expected of a seemingly routine announcement released in the dead time before New Year's weekend, almost no one paid attention.

But last week, Washington opened its eyes. Mr. Bush's quiet little statement not only set off fireworks at the Supreme Court nomination hearings of Judge Samuel A. Alito Jr., but also ignited a new debate about the Bush administration's drive to expand the powers of the president.

To start at the beginning, Congress late last year passed what became known as the torture amendment, sponsored by Senator John McCain, Republican of Arizona, to ban cruel, inhumane or degrading treatment of prisoners in American custody. Mr. Bush at first opposed the amendment, but gave in when it became clear that it had overwhelming support from the two parties on Capitol Hill. The president then invited Mr. McCain, his old political nemesis, to the Oval Office to announce that he agreed with him and "to make clear to the world that this government does not torture."

But on Dec. 30, after signing the legislation into law with no ceremony at his Texas ranch, Mr. Bush issued an accompanying "signing statement"—the 8 p.m. e-mail message—that Democrats and some Republicans say asserted that he could ignore the law if he wished.

Specifically, the statement said that the administration would interpret the amendment "in a manner consistent with the constitutional authority of the president to supervise the unitary executive branch and as commander in chief and consistent with the constitutional limitations on judicial power."

Mr. McCain issued a strong statement rejecting Mr. Bush's assertion, even as the White House has repeatedly declined to say what the president meant. But Senator Edward M. Kennedy, Democrat of Massachusetts, had no doubts, and told Judge Alito at the hearings that Mr. Bush had in essence stated that "whatever the law of the land might be, whatever Congress might have written, the executive branch has the right to authorize torture without fear of judicial review."

Judge Alito, Mr. Kennedy pointed out, had in 1986, as a lawyer in the Reagan administration Justice Department, helped Edwin Meese III, then attorney general, develop a theory that signing statements could be used to advance the president's interpretation of legislation. Before then, the statements had largely been triumphal proclamations. Mr. Alito wrote at the time that the new signing statements would "increase the power of the executive to shape the law" even as they created resentment in Congress.

At his hearings, Judge Alito distanced himself from the memorandum, calling it the work of a government employee, and sidestepped questions about his current view on the statements. At this point, their legality is largely untested.

But one thing is clear: Mr. Bush has issued more than 100 of them, which scholars believe might be more than any other president. (Signing statements have been around since at least the administration of Andrew Jackson.) More significant, scholars say, Mr. Bush has greatly expanded the scope and character of the signing statement, even from the time of the Reagan administration.

Mr. Bush has greatly expanded the scope and character of the signing statement, even from the time of the Reagan administration.

"The whole history of American government is one of trying to figure out what executive power actually is, so here is the president saying, 'Well, it's my job to tell you what that power is,'" said Andrew Rudalevige, an associate professor of political science at Dickinson College in Pennsylvania and the author of *The New Imperial Presidency: Renewing Presidential Power After Watergate*.

Scholars say that many of Mr. Bush's most significant signing statements have been attached to national security and intelligence legislation and that he frequently uses them to assert that the administration regards requirements to turn over information as purely advisory.

For example, in signing the legislation that created the independent commission that investigated the Sept. 11 attacks, Mr. Bush said that while the law established "new requirements for the executive branch to disclose sensitive information," he would interpret the law "in a manner consistent with the president's constitutional authority to withhold information" for national security.

Members of the Sept. 11 commission soon learned they would have a difficult time obtaining information from the White House. "Now, we can't prove that the reason the administration held back the information was because of the signing statement, but it announced its intentions quite clearly," said Phillip J. Cooper, a professor of public administration in the Mark O. Hatfield School of Government at Portland State University in Oregon and the author of *By Order of the President: The Use and Abuse of Executive Direct Action*.

Mr. Bush also used a signing statement in November 2003 to assert that an inspector general created for oversight of the Coalition Provisional Authority, the American administration that governed Iraq, should "refrain" from audits or investigations into matters of intelligence or counterintelligence.

In December 2004, Mr. Bush used a signing statement to say that in the act that created the post of national intelligence director, he considered provisions setting forth how—and from whom—he received intelligence information to be "advisory." Or as Mr. Rudalevige put it, "The president is basically saying that those structural changes are nice, but I don't have to listen to anybody in particular."

Think About It

- Do signing statements upset the constitutional balance of power between the branches?
- Should the White House be able to reinterpret laws that affect the president's power?
- Is it possible for supporters of legislation to combat the president's interpretation of a law?

The Issue: The Impact of Procurement Rules in Wartime

Bureaucratic rules and regulations are often annoying and rarely efficient. Congress and the executive create these rules and regulations for a number of reasons, including a desire to save taxpayer money and to ensure contracts are awarded on the basis of merit rather than favoritism. As a result, the development and procurement of new items can take a considerable amount of time.

The Pentagon is by far the government's largest bureaucracy, with over 2 million civilian and uniformed personnel, and it is awash in rules and standardized procedures for doing almost everything. Regulations can be especially frustrating—and even dangerous—during war, when lives are at stake and a leisurely schedule is a luxury that the enemy does not accord our men and women in the armed forces. New conditions in war often make the need for new equipment urgent, and it is not easy to overcome regulations to acquire the equipment.

Two other related factors hinder the bureaucracy's ability to procure necessary equipment for our troops. First, Congress may not allocate the necessary funds. It generally costs more to start up a new production line than it does to buy equipment currently in production. War is expensive, and Congress may be reluctant to allocate resources to the development of new equipment. In addition, the private sector cannot start a production line without a contract promising payment. There is little potential to sell heavy-duty military equipment to the civilian sector. And if a company develops a product for the Pentagon, it is likely to be reluctant to let other companies produce it, even if it means fewer items reach the military.

Read All About It

Safer Vehicles for Soldiers: A Tale of Delays and Glitches

By Michael Moss
June 26, 2005

When Defense Secretary Donald H. Rumsfeld visited Iraq last year to tour the Abu Ghraib prison camp, military officials did not rely on a government-issued Humvee to transport him safely on the ground. Instead, they turned to Halliburton, the oil services contractor, which lent the Pentagon a rolling fortress of steel called the Rhino Runner.

State Department officials traveling in Iraq use armored vehicles that are built with V-shaped hulls to better deflect bullets and bombs. Members of Congress favor another model, called the M1117, which can endure 12-pound explosives and .50-caliber armor-piercing rounds.

Unlike the Humvee, the Pentagon's vehicle of choice for American troops, the others were designed from scratch to withstand attacks in battlefields like Iraq with no safe zones. Last fall, for instance, a Rhino traveling the treacherous airport road in Baghdad endured a bomb that left a six-foot-wide crater. The passengers walked away unscathed.

Yet more than two years into the war, efforts by United States military units to obtain large numbers of these stronger vehicles for soldiers have faltered—even as the Pentagon's program to armor Humvees continues to be plagued by delays, an examination by *The New York Times* has found.

Many of the problems stem from a 40-year-old procurement system that stymies the acquisition of new equipment quickly enough to adapt to the changing demands of a modern insurgency, interviews and records show.

Among other setbacks, the M1117 lost its Pentagon money just before the invasion, and the manufacturer is now scrambling to fill rush orders from the military. The company making one of the V-shaped vehicles, the Cougar, said it had to lay off highly skilled welders last year as it waited for the contract to be completed. Even then it was paid only enough to fill half the order.

And the Rhino could not get through the Army's testing regime because its manufacturer declined to have one of its $250,000 vehicles blown up. The company said it provided the Army with testing data that demonstrate the Rhino's viability, and is using the defense secretary's visit as a seal of approval in its contract pitches to the Defense Department.

Nearly a decade ago, the Pentagon was warned by its own experts that superior vehicles would be needed to protect American troops. The Army's vehicle-program manager urged the Pentagon in 1996 to move beyond the Humvee, interviews and Army records show, saying it was built for the cold war. Its flat-bottom-chassis design is 25 years old, never intended for combat, and the added armor at best protects only the front end from the heftier insurgent bombs, military officials concede.

But as the procurement system stumbled and the Defense Department resisted allocating money for more expensive vehicles, interviews and records show, the military ended up largely dependent on Humvees—a vast majority of which did not yet have any armor—in both combat and noncombat operations in the war.

The Pentagon has repeatedly said no vehicle leaves camp without armor. But according to military records and interviews with officials, about half of the Army's 20,000 Humvees have improvised shielding that typically leaves the underside unprotected, while only one in six Humvees used by the Marines is armored at the highest level of protection.

The Defense Department continues to rely on just one small company in Ohio to armor Humvees. And the company, O'Gara-Hess & Eisenhardt, has waged an aggressive campaign to hold onto its exclusive deal even as soaring rush orders from Iraq have been plagued by delays. The Marine Corps, for example, is still awaiting the 498 armored Humvees it sought last fall, officials told *The Times.*

In January, when military officials tried to speed production by buying the legal rights to the armor design so they could enlist other venders to help, O'Gara demurred, calling the move a threat to its "current and future competitive position," according to e-mail records obtained from the Army.

Defense Department officials defended their efforts in supplying troops with armored vehicles, saying they have managed to convert a largely unarmored fleet into one in which every vehicle in combat has some level of shielding.

The Defense Department created a task force last winter that is charged with revamping its entire fleet of light vehicles, including the Humvee.

Some say these efforts, however resolute, will suffer if the Pentagon does not also overhaul its underlying procurement system.

With insurgents using increasingly powerful bombs and bullets, American troops in Iraq have been looking beyond the Humvee. When the Marine Corps returned to Iraq last year, it settled on the Cougar as a superior vehicle to perform one of its main jobs: searching the roads for improvised explosive devices, or I.E.D.'s. The Cougar can take more than twice the explosive punch as the armored Humvee and deflect .50-caliber armor piercing bullets.

The Marines used a new ordering method called the Urgent Universal Need Statement, which allows it to skip competitive bidding, to speed the process, officials said. Even at that, the Marines Corps took two months to complete a product study, its records show. The contract took two more months to prepare. By then, one of its units in Iraq, Company E of the First Marine Division, was suffering the highest casualty rate of the war; more than half of the 21 marines killed were riding in Humvees with improvised armor or none at all.

When the Cougar order was completed in April 2004, the Marine Corps got only enough money from the Iraq war fund to buy 15 of the 27 Cougars it wanted.

Think About It

- How can the Pentagon overcome the impact of procurement rules during wartime?
- Is there any solution to the lack of funds to buy the equipment the military requests?
- Should we force private companies to share the results of product development to speed the production of essential military items?

The Issue: How Should the Courts Interpret the Law?

Judges must interpret both the Constitution and statutes. But *how* should they do so? The Constitution provides little help in answering this basic question. One source of conflict is the debate over interpreting the original intentions of the Constitution's framers. A related issue is the debate between those who favor interpreting the Constitution based on the exact text or language of the Constitution or a law and those who argue that judges should also be influenced by the purpose of a law and the effects of a decision on that purpose.

Those who support textual interpretation want clear rules of interpretation and insist that it is irresponsible to leave the law in a state of indeterminacy, changing from one year to the next. Moreover, they want to constrain the discretion of judges in interpreting the law. Those favoring an important role for context, on the other hand, argue that often there is not a clear meaning to the text of the Constitution or a statute, and ignoring the context and purpose of either leads to judicial decisions that are inconsistent with the real intent of the framers or law's drafters and do not provide for the potential of new legal understanding of laws and the Constitution.

Read All About It

Judicial Intent: The Competing Visions of the Role of the Court

By Linda Greenhouse
July 7, 2002

Labels that once comfortably described the range of views on the Supreme Court don't work so well these days. "Liberal" versus "conservative" means less than it did back when old-fashioned liberals sat on the court. And the new judicial "activism" on the right has stripped much usefulness from a handy insult once flung exclusively at liberal judges.

Yet with the court deeply divided, there remains a need to identify and analyze its current dichotomies. In fact, two justices, Antonin Scalia and Stephen G. Breyer, spent much of the term just ended engaged in a debate about how the court should approach its work. It is in terms of that debate, and in the competing visions of the judicial role emerging from it, that one of the most interesting and potentially important fault lines on the current Supreme Court can be understood.

It is a debate over text versus context. For Justice Scalia, who focuses on text, language is supreme, and the court's job is to derive and apply rules from the words chosen by the Constitution's framers or a statute's drafters. For Justice Breyer, who looks to context, language is only a starting point to an inquiry in which a law's purpose and a decision's likely consequence are the more important elements.

This debate is taking place not only in the court's opinions but, significantly, in the two justices' outside writing and speaking. Not since the Roosevelt era, when Justice Hugo L. Black (text) and Justice Felix Frankfurter (context) battled over the meaning of the Bill of Rights, has the court had two justices willing to engage each other—and the public—in a debate over basic principles.

Justice Scalia's vision is the more familiar, pungently expressed in 16 years of Supreme Court opinions and through much speaking and writing off the bench; his 1995 Tanner Lectures at Princeton became a book, "A Matter of Interpretation." He is a seeker of bright lines and boundaries, a transmitter of rules, whether derived from the framers' original understanding or from the unannotated text of federal statutes.

For Justice Scalia, constitutional principles are fixed, not evolving—"The Constitution that I interpret and apply is not living, but dead," he declared at a conference earlier this year—and Congress needs to be held to the words it wrote, not to interpretations written by committee aides or judges. "Our first responsibility is not to make sense of the law—our first responsibility is to follow the text of the law," he said from the bench. In his view, the Supreme Court's job is to give lower court judges not factors to weigh, but rules to apply.

For much of Justice Breyer's eight years on the court, his premises were not equally clear, though it was obvious that context, for him, counted far more than rules. His tone was often diffident, his doubts openly acknowledged.

It was during the past term that Justice Breyer presented an integrated theory of the role he sees for the court in society and for himself as a justice.

Not since the Roosevelt era, when Justice Hugo L. Black (text) and Justice Felix Frankfurter (context) battled over the meaning of the Bill of Rights, has the court had two justices willing to engage each other—and the public—in a debate over basic principles.

Delivering New York University Law School's James Madison Lecture last October, he said three principles should guide the court's decision-making.

First was the purpose (as opposed to text) of the constitutional provision or law under review. Second was the likely consequence of a decision, which he contrasted to "a more 'legalistic' approach that places too much weight upon language, history, tradition and precedent alone." Without mentioning Justice Scalia by name, he said the "literalist" approach leads to a result "no less subjective but which is far less transparent than a decision that directly addresses consequences in constitutional terms."

Third, Justice Breyer said, the court should bear in mind the Constitution's overall objective, that of fostering "participatory democratic self-government." The court should be wary, he said, about preempting a "national conversation" in which new legal understanding "bubbles up from below."

Justice Breyer's lecture did more than clarify his own approach. It meant that Justice Scalia was no longer the solitary voice framing the debate on the role of the court. In an influential *Harvard Law Review* article 10 years ago, Kathleen M. Sullivan described "The Justices of Rules and Standards." Justice Scalia was the quintessential and self-defined justice of rules. Justice Breyer was not on the court then, but Professor Sullivan, now dean of Stanford Law School, agreed last week that he is the quintessential justice of standards, an approach she defined as "evolutionary, pragmatic, always asking what makes sense, what would serve the purpose of the law."

Neither approach carries an ideological guarantee. Justice Black's rules (text) led him to the liberal side of the spectrum, while Justice Frankfurter's use of standards (context) had a conservative tilt. In recent cases, Justice Scalia's rules led him to write—over a dissent by Chief Justice William H. Rehnquist—that for the police to aim a thermal imaging device at a home was a search for which the framers would have required a warrant, while Justice Breyer's satisfaction that a school district's broad drug-testing policy was the product of an authentically democratic community debate led him to align with the four more conservative justices to uphold the policy.

Think About It

- How should judges interpret the Constitution and statutes?
- If judges follow the contextual approach, are they freer to make law rather than just interpret it?
- If judges follow the textual approach, will they be able to determine the intent of the Constitution's framers, who wrote the document 220 years ago?

The Issue: Who Should Bear the Burden of Taxes?

Individuals in the United States are subject to two main types of taxes: income taxes and social insurance taxes (often called "payroll"). People with higher incomes pay a higher rate of taxes on their income, and many Americans pay no income taxes at all. Americans paid payroll taxes, which support Social Security and Medicare, on the first $94,200 of income in 2006, and everyone pays the same rate (although higher income people pay a small tax for Medicare on all their income).

A perennial source of conflict in politics is the question of how high taxes should be and who should pay them. President George W. Bush made income tax reduction a priority in his first term. Republicans argued that it was quite appropriate to reduce the taxes on wealthier taxpayers because they pay most of the income taxes. Democrats responded that the president's income tax cuts increased the deficit and allocated most of the benefits to the wealthy, who ought to bear the burden of income taxation. Moreover, they say, the less well-off Americans still bear the burden of social insurance taxes. In his second term, President Bush is considering changing the basic structure of federal taxes.

Read All About It

Proposals Would Shift Burden from Wealthy to Middle Class

By Edmund L. Andrews
October 6, 2004

Almost all experts agree that the current tax code is hideously complicated and often unfair. But they also say that accomplishing any fundamental change will be hideously difficult. . .

Republican and Democratic tax experts caution that making the tax code simpler would almost certainly set off a fierce political battle over the issue of fairness, because most options under discussion would shift a substantial share of the tax burden from high-income families to middle-income earners. . . .

Supporters of a consumption tax, which can take many different forms, say it could be far simpler than today's system and would greatly increase incentives for people to save and to invest.

The options range from a flat tax on wages to some sort of national sales tax to an income tax that excludes almost all earnings from investment and business profits. Best of all, from the viewpoint of many economists, would be a pure consumption tax, which requires people to pay taxes only on the amount of money they spend each year.

To Republicans, "most of the tax reform ideas revolve around the idea of taxing consumption," said Representative Paul Ryan, Republican of Wisconsin and a staunch proponent of a major tax overhaul. "It can be a flat tax or a sales tax or anything in between, but all of those are consumption taxes."

The political obstacles, however, are enormous. An internal report by the Treasury Department in 2002, which analyzed five approaches to tax reform, concluded that either a flat income tax or a flat consumption tax would benefit higher income families at the expense of others.

"Any reform is likely to have vocal losers and largely silent winners," said the report, which was recently made public by Ron Suskind, author of a book on Paul H. O'Neill, Mr. Bush's first Treasury secretary. "In other countries, adoption of a consumption tax has led to election losses for the incumbent party.". . .

Republican tax experts acknowledge that tax reform would ignite a bitter battle over fairness.

Republican tax experts acknowledge that tax reform would ignite a bitter battle over fairness.

"Contrary to popular belief, the existing tax system is very progressive," said Kenneth Kies, a tax lobbyist and former staff director of the Joint Committee on Taxation. "The rich basically pay the income tax. It's very hard to take any of the reform options out there and do them without having a progressivity problem."

Supporters of a consumption tax or a flat income tax say such a system could still place a heavier tax burden on high-income people. A system that imposed a national sales tax or a European-style value-added tax, for example, could provide rebates to lower income people and include an extra tax for people with high incomes.

But most experts say it would be hard to design a consumption tax that did not shift some of the tax burden away from high-income taxpayers, because most taxable investment income goes to a very small slice of people at the very top of the income spectrum. Wealthy people typically spend a smaller share of their earnings than those with less income.

Leonard E. Burman, a senior analyst at the Urban Institute, estimated that half of all stock dividends in 2000 went to the top 3.8 percent of households, those with incomes higher than $200,000 a year. Wealthy people also devote a much smaller share of their incomes to consumption—about a third for families with incomes above $200,000, compared with about 93 percent for families with incomes between $20,000 and $30,000.

"You cannot do reform without spending a huge amount of money and identifying a huge number of losers," Mr. Burman said. "It's almost impossible to design a consumption tax that doesn't shift some of the tax burden from high-income tax payers.". . .

Tax reform could easily clash with Mr. Bush's call for an ownership society. Even as he called for a simpler system at the Republican convention, he proposed new tax breaks for businesses that build single-family homes and implied that he would preserve the deduction for home mortgage interest.

"You can't separate the ownership society and tax reform," said C. Eugene Steuerle, a senior fellow at the Urban Institute who coordinated the Treasury Department's last big effort at overhauling the income tax, under President Reagan in 1986. "We now have $150 billion in housing subsidies, most of that in the tax system.". . .

Think About It

- Who should bear the burden of taxes? Should the rich pay not only more taxes but also a higher rate of taxation?
- Is it appropriate for a small percentage of Americans to receive most of the benefits from a policy?
- Is it healthy for American society that a small percentage of the people pay most of the income tax?
- Should average people pay for their own Social Security and Medicare benefits, or should wealthier citizens subsidize them?

The Issues: Should We Privatize Social Security?

Social Security—the program in which workers and employees pay into an old-age pension fund—is the country's most expensive public policy. It also may be the most important policy as well because tens of millions of Americans rely heavily on it for income after they retire.

Unfortunately, the taxes paid by employees and employers do not sit in the treasury but have been spent for other purposes. In return, the Social Security system receives an IOU from the federal government. In addition, more people are retiring and living longer and there are fewer workers paying into the system for each retiree than in the past. The result is a looming budget crunch.

We could raise Social Security taxes, but this option, for obvious reasons, is not very popular. Another idea is for workers to take some of the money they now pay to Social Security and invest it in private retirement accounts. Advocates argue that this practice would allow pension funds to grow more rapidly and thus reduce the need to raise taxes. Opponents worry that private accounts are risky and could leave many elderly people without adequate income if the stock market sours.

Read All About It

AARP Opposes Bush Plan to Replace Social Security with Private Accounts

By Robert Pear
November 12, 2004

Gearing up for battle over the future of Social Security, AARP, the influential lobby for older Americans, said Thursday that it opposed President Bush's plan to divert some payroll taxes into private retirement accounts. But it supports new incentives for private accounts that supplement Social Security.

Working closely with Congress and the White House, AARP helped shape legislation adding drug benefits to Medicare last year. Social Security is an even bigger issue, politically and financially, and lawmakers said Congress was unlikely to make major changes in Social Security over the organization's objections.

Marie F. Smith, president of the organization, said, "AARP adamantly opposes replacing any part of Social Security with individual accounts." But Ms. Smith added that the group supported incentives for people to establish personal retirement accounts in addition to Social Security.

John C. Rother, the organization's policy director, said, "We favor private accounts when they are in addition to Social Security, but not as a substitute."

The fight over Social Security, pitting Mr. Bush's vision of an "ownership society" against the Democrats' determination to preserve a cornerstone of the New Deal, is reflected in a battle over the proper terminology.

The White House dislikes the word "privatization," which it sees as a misleading and imprecise way to describe Mr. Bush's ideas for Social

Security. Democrats insist that the term is accurate.

E-mail messages circulated within AARP in recent weeks indicated that the group would avoid the word whenever possible.

One message, by an editor of an AARP magazine, says, "There is a new forbidden word at AARP: Social Security privatization."

Another e-mail message, by a manager of its Web site, says, "The term 'privatization' is stricken from our vocabulary forever."

David M. Certner, the organization's director of federal affairs, said "privatization" had no fixed meaning or definition. To some people, he said, it means "getting rid of the entire program"—a goal not favored by the White House.

Martis J. Davis, a spokesman for the organization, said it was sensitive to the views of younger workers and retirees.

"Younger people think private accounts make sense," Mr. Davis said. "Polls by some organizations suggest that young people believe in flying saucers more than in Social Security. We have a problem with that. We don't want to end up being perceived as dinosaurs, and we don't want to be labeled as greedy geezers, because we are not."

In interviews this week, three Republican members of Congress—Representative E. Clay Shaw Jr. of Florida and Senators Lindsey Graham of South Carolina and John E. Sununu of New Hampshire—said Mr. Bush would make a major effort next year to overhaul Social Security.

"The election results have given new life to proposals for Social Security reform," Mr. Graham said.

Mr. Sununu said, "The president is very committed to an approach based on personal accounts."

AARP adamantly opposes replacing any part of Social Security with individual accounts.

House Democrats have begun to devise a strategy to oppose private accounts.

"Privatizing Social Security will divert trillions of dollars from the trust funds and force significant benefit cuts," said Representative Robert T. Matsui, Democrat of California.

In general, Social Security payroll taxes are credited to the Social Security trust funds, and revenues not needed to pay benefits in the current year are invested in government securities. White House officials and many Republicans in Congress say workers could get higher rates of return if some of their retirement savings were invested in private stocks and bonds rather than in government securities.

Mr. Shaw, who is chairman of the House Ways and Means subcommittee on Social Security, said private accounts were "the only way we can take care of our kids in the future, when we'll have more retirees and fewer workers."

White House officials said it was unfair to portray the president as supporting privatization.

"I do not favor 'privatization' of Social Security," Mr. Bush wrote last month in the AARP Bulletin. "Those workers who do not want a personal account would continue to receive their benefits from the federally administered Social Security system. Even those who choose a personal account would continue to draw traditional Social Security benefits."

Mr. Bush said his proposal would give workers ownership and control of their accounts, allowing them to pass wealth to their heirs. But AARP says retirees would bear a substantial investment risk and would have to accept lower guaranteed benefits under the president's plan.

The Cato Institute, a libertarian research center, established a Project on Social Security Privatization in 1995, but in 2002 it was renamed the Project on Social Security Choice.

"Republicans in Congress do not like the word 'privatization' because it does not poll well," said Michael Tanner, director of the project. "The word polls more poorly than the actual concept, in part because people do not understand what it means."

Think About It

- Do you think we should create private accounts for younger people within the Social Security system?
- If we create private accounts and the stock market crashes, what should government's response be to those who have lost a substantial portion of their life savings?
- Why do Democrats and Republicans disagree about private accounts? Do their differences reflect more basic ideologies?
- Can the United States afford to have *both* traditional Social Security benefits and private accounts?

The Issue: Managing Crises

A crisis is a sudden, unpredictable, and potentially dangerous event. Most crises focus on some aspect of national security policy. The stakes in a crisis are high, typically involving life and death. Someone must manage a crisis, and the job usually falls to the president, who can come to quick and consistent decisions, confine information to a small group, carefully oversee developments, and call on experts in the executive branch.

What makes crisis management especially difficult is that crises do not necessarily occur serially. Instead, there is often more than one crisis occurring at a time. Multiple crises raise profound questions for governing. How well can a president focus on several critical matters at the same time? What is the personal toll on a president who manages multiple crises? Equally important, what happens to domestic policy issues when crises dominate the president's time, the media and the public's attention, and perhaps the budget as well?

Read All About It

Crises, Crises Everywhere. What Is a President to Do?

By Todd S. Purdum
February 9, 2003

If, as F. Scott Fitzgerald wrote, "the test of a first-rate intelligence is the ability to hold two opposed ideas in mind at the same time and still retain the ability to function," the test of a successful presidency may be the ability to multitask in crises. In fact, it's more or less the definition of the job.

Sure, President Bush had a full week: a space disaster and a wrenching memorial service, a $2.23 trillion budget proposal to Congress, a North Korean threat of "total war," a dramatic showdown at the United Nations over Iraqi defiance of weapons inspections, a stepped-up orange-level terrorism alert based on ominous intelligence rumblings.

But the current confluence of challenging events is hardly new. Harry S. Truman faced almost nonstop crises from the moment he took office after Franklin D. Roosevelt's death in 1945. Roosevelt himself managed the Depression, then a global war, not to mention paralysis.

In 1957, Dwight D. Eisenhower was in the middle of a crisis over desegregation of Central High School in Little Rock, Ark., when the Soviet Union launched Sputnik, a silver satellite the size of a beachball, setting off a panic about preparedness in the cold war. By his own account, Richard M. Nixon managed "Six Crises" before he ever reached the White House, then created a doozy of his own in Watergate. Bill Clinton complained that it was his bad luck to be president in placid times of plenty, when greatness cannot easily emerge, then managed to become the second president in history to be impeached.

"This is what a president is—a crisis manager," said the historian Robert Dallek, who wrote a two-volume biography of Johnson and has just finished another on Kennedy. "Of course, what suffers in all of this is any domestic agenda a president has. A standard reality is that war kills reform. The Spanish-American war killed populism, World War I killed Progressivism, World War II killed the New Deal, Korea killed the Fair Deal, Vietnam the Great Society."

Mr. Bush is not the first president to govern in a 24-hour news cycle, but the endless drumbeat no doubt worsens the sense of perpetual crisis. The media, and sometimes the politicians themselves, have a tendency to inflate every event, from a school shooting to a sniper on the loose to the prospect of nuclear war, into a round-the-clock happening.

Daniel Schorr, the veteran broadcast journalist, acknowledged on NPR last week that Washington has a hard time managing multiple problems and tends to be a "one-thing-at-a-time type of town." Attention spans are short, politicians rise and fall, issues come and go.

To all appearances, Mr. Bush often seems the calmest one in the storm. For months, he has remained steadily determined to disarm Saddam Hussein, first in the face of warnings that doing so without a Middle East peace risked Arab rage, and now despite worries that North Korea is the more volatile threat.

Ronald Reagan survived an assassination attempt after just weeks in office, then went on to face recession, survive the Iran-Contra scandal and help end the cold war. Lyndon B. Johnson fared less well waging the Vietnam War while trying to build a Great Society, and was ultimately consumed by wrenching public division.

Mr. Bush is not the first president to govern in a 24-hour news cycle, but the endless drumbeat no doubt worsens the sense of perpetual crisis. The media, and sometimes the politicians themselves, have a tendency to inflate every event, from a school shooting to a sniper on the loose to the prospect of nuclear war, into a round-the-clock happening.

Harry C. McPherson Jr., who was Johnson's special counsel, said he marked the toll of White House crises in the annual albums of photographs that the Johnsons gave the senior staff at Christmas. "I got there in '65, and by '67 I looked pale and overtaxed and Johnson looked very gray."

There are costs and casualties for failing to keep up with events. The first President Bush soared to stratospheric approval ratings after the Persian Gulf War, but was seen as out of touch with a faltering economy and unemployed Americans. Jimmy Carter micromanaged the White House tennis courts but could not manage to confront a national malaise and the failure to rescue American hostages in Iran.

Sometimes the price is more personal. Everyone remembers Truman's acid letter to Paul Hume, The *Washington Post* music critic who panned the singing of his daughter, Margaret. Less well remembered is the week that led up to Truman's outburst.

On Nov. 28, 1950, Truman received word that the Chinese had plunged into the Korean War, with a quarter-million troops in a furious assault. Two days later, Truman set off a worldwide firestorm by suggesting at a news conference that the United States was prepared to use the atomic bomb in Korea. The man responsible for trying to calm that crisis was the president's press secretary, Charlie Ross, who was also his longtime friend.

On Tuesday, Dec. 5, Ross dropped dead of a heart attack, hours before Miss Truman's concert at Constitution Hall. The president kept the news from her until afterward. The next morning, when the president read Hume's assessment that Miss Truman "is flat a good deal of the time," he reached for paper and pen.

"Some day I hope to meet you," Truman wrote. "When that happens you'll need a new nose, a lot of beefsteak for black eyes, and perhaps a supporter below!"

Think About It

- How well do you think presidents have handled multiple crises?
- Are there changes the president could make in the way the White House works that would make it easier to handle crises?
- Would it be possible for the president to share the burden of managing crises?
- Is it necessary that crises abroad undermine attempts for reform at home?

Appendix

The Declaration of Independence*

In Congress, July 4, 1776

The Unanimous Declaration of the Thirteen United States of America

When in the Course of human events it becomes necessary for one people to dissolve the political bands which have connected them with another, and to assume among the powers of the earth, the separate and equal station to which the Laws of Nature and of Nature's God entitle them, a decent respect to the opinions of mankind requires that they should declare the causes which impel them to the separation.

We hold these truths to be self-evident, that all men are created equal, that they are endowed by their Creator with certain unalienable Rights, that among these are Life, Liberty and the pursuit of Happiness.—That to secure these rights, Governments are instituted among Men, deriving their just powers from the consent of the governed,—That whenever any Form of Government becomes destructive of these ends, it is the Right of the People to alter or to abolish it, and to institute new Government, laying its foundation on such principles and organizing its powers in such form, as to them shall seem most likely to effect their Safety and Happiness. Prudence, indeed, will dictate that Governments long established should not be changed for light and transient causes; and accordingly all experience hath shewn that mankind are more disposed to suffer, while evils are sufferable, than to right themselves by abolishing the forms to which they are accustomed. But when a long train of abuses and usurpations, pursuing invariably the same Object evinces a design to reduce them under absolute Despotism, it is their right, it is their duty, to throw off such Government, and to provide new Guards for their future security.—Such has been the patient sufferance of these Colonies; and such is now the necessity which constrains them to alter their former Systems of Government. The history of the present King of Great Britain is a history of repeated injuries and usurpations, all having in direct object the establishment of an absolute Tyranny over these States. To prove this, let Facts be submitted to a candid world.

He has refused his Assent to Laws, the most wholesome and necessary for the public good.

He has forbidden his Governors to pass Laws of immediate and pressing importance, unless suspended in their operation till his Assent should be obtained; and when so suspended, he has utterly neglected to attend to them.

He has refused to pass other Laws for the accommodation of large districts of people, unless those people would relinquish the right of Representation in the Legislature, a right inestimable to them and formidable to tyrants only.

He has called together legislative bodies at places unusual, uncomfortable, and distant from the depository of their Public Records, for the sole purpose of fatiguing them into compliance with his measures.

He has dissolved Representative Houses repeatedly, for opposing with manly firmness his invasions on the rights of the people.

He has refused for a long time, after such dissolutions, to cause others to be elected; whereby the Legislative Powers, incapable of Annihilation, have returned to the People at large for their exercise; the State remaining in the mean time exposed to all the dangers of invasion from without, and convulsions within.

He has endeavored to prevent the population of these States; for that purpose obstructing the Laws for Naturalization of Foreigners; refusing to pass others to encourage their migration hither, and raising the conditions of new Appropriations of Lands.

He has obstructed the Administration of Justice, by refusing his Assent to Laws for establishing Judiciary powers.

He has made Judges dependent on his Will alone, for the tenure of their offices, and the amount and payment of their salaries.

He has erected a multitude of New Offices, and sent hither swarms of Officers to harass our people, and eat out their substance.

He has kept among us, in times of peace, Standing Armies without the Consent of our legislatures.

He has affected to render the Military independent of and superior to the Civil power.

*This text retains the spelling, capitalization, and punctuation of the original.

He has combined with others to subject us to a jurisdiction foreign to our constitution, and unacknowledged by our laws; giving his Assent to their Acts of pretended Legislation:

For quartering large bodies of armed troops among us:

For protecting them, by a mock Trial, from punishment for any Murders which they should commit on the Inhabitants of these States:

For cutting off our Trade with all parts of the world:

For imposing Taxes on us without our Consent:

For depriving us in many cases, of the benefits of Trial by Jury:

For transporting us beyond Seas to be tried for pretended offences:

For abolishing the free System of English Laws in a neighboring Province, establishing therein an Arbitrary government, and enlarging its Boundaries so as to render it at once an example and fit instrument for introducing the same absolute rule into these Colonies:

For taking away our Charters, abolishing our most valuable Laws, and altering fundamentally the Forms of our Governments:

For suspending our own Legislatures, and declaring themselves invested with power to legislate for us in all cases whatsoever.

He has abdicated Government here, by declaring us out of his Protection and waging War against us.

He has plundered our seas, ravaged our Coasts, burnt our towns, and destroyed the lives of our people.

He is at this time transporting large Armies of foreign Mercenaries to compleat the works of death, desolation and tyranny, already begun with circumstances of Cruelty & perfidy scarcely paralleled in the most barbarous ages, and totally unworthy the Head of a civilized nation.

He has constrained our fellow Citizens taken Captive on the high Seas to bear Arms against their Country, to become the executioners of their friends and Brethren, or to fall themselves by their Hands.

He has excited domestic insurrections amongst us, and has endeavored to bring on the inhabitants of our frontiers, the merciless Indian Savages, whose known rule of warfare, is an undistinguished destruction of all ages, sexes and conditions.

In every stage of these Oppressions We have Petitioned for Redress in the most humble terms: Our repeated Petitions have been answered only by repeated injury. A Prince, whose character is thus marked by every act which may define a Tyrant, is unfit to be the ruler of a free people.

Nor have We been wanting in attention to our British brethren. We have warned them from time to time of attempts by their legislature to extend an unwarrantable jurisdiction over us. We have reminded them of the circumstances of our emigration and settlement here. We have appealed to their native justice and magnanimity, and we have conjured them by the ties of our common kindred to disavow these usurpations, which would inevitably interrupt our connections and correspondence. They too have been deaf to the voice of justice and consanguinity. We must, therefore, acquiesce in the necessity, which denounces our Separation, and hold them, as we hold the rest of mankind, Enemies in War, in Peace Friends.

We, therefore, the Representatives of the United States of America, in General Congress, Assembled, appealing to the Supreme Judge of the world for the rectitude of our intentions, do, in the Name, and by Authority of the good People of these Colonies, solemnly publish and declare, That these United Colonies are, and of Right ought to be Free and Independent States; that they are Absolved from all Allegiance to the British Crown, and that all political connection between them and the State of Great Britain, is and ought to be totally dissolved; and that as Free and Independent States, they have full Power to levy War, conclude Peace, contract Alliances, establish Commerce, and to do all other Acts and Things which Independent States may of right do. And for the support of this Declaration, with a firm reliance on the protection of divine Providence, we mutually pledge to each other our Lives, our Fortunes and our sacred Honor.

John Hancock

New Hampshire
Josiah Bartlett,
Wm. Whipple,
Matthew Thornton.

Massachusetts Bay
Saml. Adams,
John Adams,
Robt. Treat Paine,
Elbridge Gerry.

Rhode Island
Step. Hopkins,
William Ellery.

Connecticut
Roger Sherman,
Samuel Huntington,
Wm. Williams,
Oliver Wolcott.

New York
Wm. Floyd,
Phil. Livingston,
Frans. Lewis,
Lewis Morris.

NEW JERSEY
Richd. Stockton,
Jno. Witherspoon,
Fras. Hopkinson,
John Hart,
Abra. Clark.

PENNSYLVANIA
Robt. Morris,
Benjamin Rush,
Benjamin Franklin,
John Morton,
Geo. Clymer,
Jas. Smith,
Geo. Taylor,
James Wilson,
Geo. Ross.

DELAWARE
Caesar Rodney,
Geo. Read,
Tho. M'kean.

MARYLAND
Samuel Chase,
Wm. Paca,
Thos. Stone,
Charles Caroll of Carrollton.

VIRGINIA
George Wythe,
Richard Henry Lee,
Th. Jefferson,
Benjamin Harrison,
Thos. Nelson, jr.,
Francis Lightfoot Lee,
Carter Braxton.

NORTH CAROLINA
Wm. Hooper,
Joseph Hewes,
John Penn.

SOUTH CAROLINA
Edward Rutledge,
Thos. Heyward, Junr.,
Thomas Lynch, jnr.,
Arthur Middleton.

GEORGIA
Button Gwinnett,
Lyman Hall,
Geo. Walton.

The Federalist No. 10

James Madison

November 22, 1787

To the People of the State of New York.

Among the numerous advantages promised by a well constructed Union, none deserves to be more accurately developed than its tendency to break and control the violence of faction. The friend of popular governments, never finds himself so much alarmed for their character and fate, as when he contemplates their propensity to this dangerous vice. He will not fail therefore to set a due value on any plan which, without violating the principles to which he is attached, provides a proper cure for it. The instability, injustice and confusion introduced into the public councils, have in truth been the mortal diseases under which popular governments have every where perished; as they continue to be the favorite and fruitful topics from which the adversaries to liberty derive their most specious declamations. The valuable improvements made by the American Constitutions on the popular models, both ancient and modern, cannot certainly be too much admired; but it would be an unwarrantable partiality, to contend that they have as effectually obviated the danger on this side as was wished and expected. Complaints are every where heard from our most considerate and virtuous citizens, equally the friends of public and private faith, and of public and personal liberty; that our governments are too unstable; that the public good is disregarded in the conflicts of rival parties; and that measures are too often decided, not according to the rules of justice, and the rights of the minor party; but by the superior force of an interested and over-bearing majority. However anxiously we may wish that these complaints had no foundation, the evidence of known facts will not permit us to deny that they are in some degree true. It will be found indeed, on a candid review of our situation, that some of the distresses under which we labor, have been erroneously charged on the operation of our governments; but it will be found, at the same time, that other causes will not alone account for many of our heaviest misfortunes; and particularly, for that prevailing and increasing distrust of public engagements, and alarm for private rights, which are echoed from one end of the continent to the other. These must be chiefly, if not wholly, effects of the unsteadiness and injustice, with which a factious spirit has tainted our public administrations.

By a faction I understand a number of citizens, whether amounting to a majority or minority of the whole, who are united and actuated by some common impulse of passion, or of interest, adverse to the rights of other citizens, or to the permanent and aggregate interests of the community.

There are two methods of curing the mischiefs of faction: the one, by removing its causes; the other, by controlling its effects.

There are again two methods of removing the causes of faction: the one by destroying the liberty which is essential to its existence; the other, by giving to every citizen the same opinions, the same passions, and the same interests.

It could never be more truly said than of the first remedy, that it is worse than the disease. Liberty is to faction, what air is to fire, an aliment without which it instantly expires. But it could not be a less folly to abolish liberty, which is essential to political life, because it nourishes faction, than it would be to wish the annihilation of air, which is essential to animal life, because it imparts to fire its destructive agency.

The second expedient is as impracticable, as the first would be unwise. As long as the reason of man continues fallible, and he is at liberty to exercise it, different opinions will be formed. As long as the connection subsists between his reason and his self-love, his opinions and his passions will have a reciprocal influence on each other; and the former will be objects to which the latter will attach themselves. The diversity in the faculties of men from which the rights of property originate, is not less an insuperable obstacle to a uniformity of interests. The protection of these faculties is the first object of Government. From the protection of different and unequal faculties of acquiring property, the possession of different degrees and kinds of property immediately results: and from the influence of these on the sentiments and views of the respective proprietors, ensues a division of the society into different interests and parties.

The latent causes of faction are thus sown in the nature of man; and we see them every where brought into different degrees of activity, according to the different circumstances of civil society. A zeal for different opinions concerning religion, concerning Government and many other points, as well of speculation as of practice; an attachment to different leaders ambitiously contending for pre-eminence and power; or to persons of other descriptions whose fortunes have been interesting to the human passions, have in turn divided mankind into parties, inflamed them with mutual animosity, and rendered them much more disposed to vex and oppress each other, than to co-operate for their common good. So strong is this propensity of mankind to fall into mutual animosities, that where no substantial occasion presents itself, the most frivolous and fanciful distinctions have been sufficient to kindle their unfriendly passions, and excite their most violent conflicts. But the most common and durable source of factions, has been the various and unequal distribution of property. Those who hold, and those who are without property, have ever formed distinct interests in society. Those who are creditors, and those who are debtors, fall under a like discrimination. A landed interest, a manufacturing interest, a mercantile interest, a monied interest, with many lesser interests, grow up of necessity in civilized nations, and divide them into different classes, actuated by different sentiments and views. The regulation of these various and interfering interests forms the principal task of modern Legislation, and involves the spirit of party and faction in the necessary and ordinary operations of Government.

No man is allowed to be a judge in his own cause; because his interest would certainly bias his judgment, and, not improbably, corrupt his integrity. With equal, nay with greater reason, a body of men, are unfit to be both judges and parties, at the same time; yet, what are many of the most important acts of legislation, but so many judicial determinations, not indeed concerning the rights of single persons, but concerning the rights of large bodies of citizens, and what are the different classes of legislators, but advocates and parties to the causes which they determine? Is a law proposed concerning private debts? It is a question to which the creditors are parties on one side, and the debtors on the other. Justice ought to hold the balance between them. Yet the parties are and must be themselves the judges; and the most numerous party, or, in other words, the most powerful faction must be expected to prevail. Shall domestic manufactures be encouraged, and in what degree, by restrictions on foreign manufactures? are questions which would be differently decided by the landed and the manufacturing classes; and probably by neither, with a sole regard to justice and the public good. The apportionment of taxes on the various descriptions of property, is an act which seems to require the most exact impartiality; yet, there is perhaps no legislative act in which greater opportunity and temptation are given to a predominant party, to trample on the rules of justice. Every shilling with which they over-burden the inferior number, is a shilling saved to their own pockets.

It is in vain to say, that enlightened statesmen will be able to adjust these clashing interests, and render them all subservient to the public good. Enlightened statesmen will not always be at the helm: Nor, in many cases, can such an adjustment be made at all, without taking into view indirect and remote considerations, which will rarely prevail over the immediate interest which one party may find in disregarding the rights of another, or the good of the whole.

The inference to which we are brought, is, that the causes of faction cannot be removed; and that relief is only to be sought in the means of controlling its effects.

If a faction consists of less than a majority, relief is supplied by the republican principle, which enables the majority to defeat its sinister views by regular vote: It may clog the administration, it may convulse the society; but it will be unable to execute and mask its violence under the forms of the Constitution. When a majority is included in a faction, the form of popular government on the other hand enables it to sacrifice to its ruling passion or interest, both the public good and the rights of other citizens. To secure the public good, and private rights, against the danger of such a faction, and at the same time to preserve the spirit and the form of popular government, is then the great object to which our enquiries are directed: Let me add that it is the great desideratum, by which alone this form of government can be rescued from the opprobrium under which it has so long labored, and be recommended to the esteem and adoption of mankind.

By what means is this object attainable? Evidently by one of two only. Either the existence of the same passion or interest in a majority at the same time, must be prevented; or the majority, having such co-existent passion or interest, must be rendered, by their number and local situation, unable to concert and carry into effect schemes of oppression. If the impulse and the opportunity be suffered to coincide, we well know that neither moral nor religious motives can be relied on as an adequate control. They are not found to be such on the injustice and violence of individuals, and lose their efficacy in proportion to the number combined together; that is, in proportion as their efficacy becomes needful.

From this view of the subject, it may be concluded, that a pure Democracy, by which I mean, a Society, consisting of a small number of citizens, who assemble and administer the Government in person, can admit of no cure for the mischiefs of faction. A common passion or interest will, in almost every case, be felt by a majority of the whole; a communication and concert results from the form of Government itself; and there is nothing to check the inducements to sacrifice the weaker party, or an obnoxious individual. Hence it is, that such Democracies have ever been spectacles of turbulence and contention; have ever been found incompatible with personal security, or the rights of property; and have in general been as short in their lives, as they have been violent in their deaths. Theoretic politicians, who have patronized this species of Government, have erroneously supposed, that by reducing mankind to a perfect equality in their political rights, they would, at the same time, be perfectly equalized and assimilated in their possessions, their opinions, and their passions.

A republic, by which I mean a government in which the scheme of representation takes place, opens a different prospect, and promises the cure for which we are seeking. Let us examine the points in which it varies from pure democracy, and we shall comprehend both the nature of the cure and the efficacy which it must derive from the union.

The two great points of difference, between a democracy and a republic, are, first, the delegation of the government, in the latter, to a small number of citizens, elected by the rest; secondly, the greater number of citizens, and greater sphere of country, over which the latter may be extended.

The effect of the first difference is, on the one hand, to refine and enlarge the public views, by passing them through the medium of a chosen body of citizens, whose wisdom may best discern the true interest of their country, and whose patriotism and love of justice, will be least likely to sacrifice it to temporary or partial considerations. Under such a regulation, it may well happen, that the public voice, pronounced by the representatives of the people, will be more consonant to the public good, than if pronounced by the people themselves, convened for the purpose. On the other hand the effect may be inverted. Men of factious tempers, of local prejudices, or of sinister designs, may by intrigue, by corruption, or by other means, first obtain the suffrages, and then betray the interest of the people. The question resulting is, whether small or extensive republics are most favorable to the election of proper guardians of the public weal, and it is clearly decided in favor of the latter by two obvious considerations.

In the first place, it is to be remarked that, however small the republic may be, the representatives must be raised to a certain number, in order to guard against the cabals of a few; and that however large it may be, they must be limited to a certain number, in order to guard against the confusion of a multitude. Hence, the number of representatives in the two cases not being in proportion to that of the constituents, and being proportionally greatest in the small republic, it follows, that if the proportion of fit characters be not less in the large than in the small republic, the former will present a greater option, and consequently a greater probability of a fit choice.

In the next place, as each Representative will be chosen by a greater number of citizens in the large than in the small Republic, it will be more difficult for unworthy candidates to practise with success the vicious arts, by which elections are too often carried; and the suffrages of the people being more free, will be more likely to center on men who possess the most attractive merit, and the most diffusive and established characters.

It must be confessed, that in this, as in most other cases, there is a mean, on both sides of which inconveniences will be found to lie. By enlarging too much the number of electors, you render the representative too little acquainted with all their local circumstances and lesser interests; as by reducing it too much, you render him unduly attached to these, and too little fit to comprehend and pursue great and national objects. The Federal Constitution forms a happy combination in this respect; the great and aggregate interests being referred to the national, the local and particular, to the state legislatures.

The other point of difference is, the greater number of citizens and extent of territory which may be brought within the compass of Republican, than of Democratic Government; and it is this circumstance principally which renders factious combinations less to be dreaded in the former, than in the latter. The smaller the society, the fewer probably will be the distinct parties and interests composing it; the fewer the distinct parties and interests, the more frequently will a majority be found of the same party; and the smaller the number of individuals composing a majority, and the smaller the compass within which they are placed, the more easily will they concert and execute their plans of oppression. Extend the sphere, and you take in a greater variety of parties and interests; you make it less probable that a majority of the whole will have a common motive to invade the rights of other citizens; or if such a common motive exists, it will be more difficult for all who feel it to discover their own strength, and to act in unison with each other. Besides other impediments, it may be remarked, that where there is a consciousness of unjust or dishonorable purposes, communication is always checked by distrust, in proportion to the number whose concurrence is necessary.

Hence it clearly appears, that the same advantage, which a Republic has over a Democracy, in controlling the effects of faction, is enjoyed by a large over a small

Republic—is enjoyed by the Union over the States composing it. Does this advantage consist in the substitution of Representatives, whose enlightened views and virtuous sentiments render them superior to local prejudices, and to schemes of injustice? It will not be denied, that the Representation of the Union will be most likely to possess these requisite endowments. Does it consist in the greater security afforded by a greater variety of parties, against the event of any one party being able to outnumber and oppress the rest? In an equal degree does the increased variety of parties, comprised within the Union, increase this security? Does it, in fine, consist in the greater obstacles opposed to the concert and accomplishment of the secret wishes of an unjust and interested majority? Here, again, the extent of the Union gives it the most palpable advantage.

The influence of factious leaders may kindle a flame within their particular States, but will be unable to spread a general conflagration through the other States: a religious sect may degenerate into a political faction in a part of the Confederacy but the variety of sects dispersed over the entire face of it, must secure the national Councils against any danger from that source: a rage for paper money, for an abolition of debts, for an equal division of property, or for any other improper or wicked project, will be less apt to pervade the whole body of the Union, than a particular member of it; in the same proportion as such a malady is more likely to taint a particular county or district, than an entire State.

In the extent and proper structure of the Union, therefore, we behold a Republican remedy for the diseases most incident to Republican Government. And according to the degree of pleasure and pride, we feel in being Republicans, ought to be our zeal in cherishing the spirit, and supporting the character of Federalists.

PUBLIUS

The Federalist No. 51

James Madison

February 6, 1788

To the People of the State of New York.

To what expedient then shall we finally resort for maintaining in practice the necessary partition of power among the several departments, as laid down in the constitution? The only answer that can be given is, that as all these exterior provisions are found to be inadequate, the defect must be supplied, by so contriving the interior structure of the government, as that its several constituent parts may, by their mutual relations, be the means of keeping each other in their proper places. Without presuming to undertake a full development of this important idea, I will hazard a few general observations, which may perhaps place it in a clearer light, and enable us to form a more correct judgment of the principles and structure of the government planned by the convention.

In order to lay a due foundation for that separate and distinct exercise of the different powers of government, which to a certain extent, is admitted on all hands to be essential to the preservation of liberty, it is evident that each department should have a will of its own; and consequently should be so constituted, that the members of each should have as little agency as possible in the appointment of the members of the others. Were this principle rigorously adhered to, it would require that all the appointments for the supreme executive, legislative, and judiciary magistracies, should be drawn from the same fountain of authority, the people, through channels, having no communication whatever with one another. Perhaps such a plan of constructing the several departments would be less difficult in practice than it may in contemplation appear. Some difficulties however, and some additional expense, would attend the execution of it. Some deviations therefore from the principle must be admitted. In the constitution of the judiciary department in particular, it might be inexpedient to insist rigorously on the principle; first, because peculiar qualifications being essential in the members, the primary consideration ought to be to select that mode of choice, which best secures these qualifications; secondly, because the permanent tenure by which the appointments are held in that department, must soon destroy all sense of dependence on the authority conferring them.

It is equally evident that the members of each department should be as little dependent as possible on those of the others, for the emoluments annexed to their offices. Were the executive magistrate, or the judges, not independent of the legislature in this particular, their independence in every other would be merely nominal.

But the great security against a gradual concentration of the several powers in the same department, consists in giving to those who administer each department, the necessary constitutional means, and personal motives, to resist encroachments of the others. The provision for defense must in this, as in all other cases, be made commensurate to the danger of attack. Ambition must be made to counteract ambition. The interest of the man must be connected with the constitutional right of the place. It may be a reflection on human nature, that such devices should be necessary to control the abuses of government. But what is government itself but the greatest of all reflections on human nature? If men were angels, no government would be necessary. If angels were to govern men, neither external nor internal controls on government would be necessary. In framing a government which is to be administered by men over men, the great difficulty lies in this: You must first enable the government to control the governed; and in the next place, oblige it to control itself. A dependence on the people is no doubt the primary control on the government; but experience has taught mankind the necessity of auxiliary precautions.

This policy of supplying by opposite and rival interests, the defect of better motives, might be traced through the whole system of human affairs, private as well as public. We see it particularly displayed in all the subordinate distributions of power; where the constant aim is to divide and arrange the several offices in such a manner as that each may be a check on the other; that the private interest of every individual, may be a sentinel over the public rights. These inventions of prudence cannot be less requisite in the distribution of the supreme powers of the state.

But it is not possible to give to each department an equal power of self defense. In republican government the legislative authority, necessarily, predominates. The remedy for this inconveniency is, to divide the legislature into different branches; and to render them by different modes of election, and different principles of action, as little connected with each other, as the nature of their common functions, and their common dependence on the society, will admit. It may even be necessary to guard against dangerous encroachments by still further precautions. As the weight of the legislative authority requires that it should be thus divided, the weakness of the executive may require, on the other hand, that it should be fortified. An absolute negative, on the legislature, appears at first view to be the natural defense with which the executive magistrate should be armed. But perhaps it would be neither altogether safe, nor alone sufficient. On ordinary occasions, it might not be exerted with the requisite firmness; and on extraordinary occasions, it might be perfidiously abused. May not this defect of an absolute negative be supplied, by some qualified connection between this weaker department, and the weaker branch of the stronger department, by which the latter may be led to support the constitutional rights of the former, without being too much detached from the rights of its own department?

If the principles on which these observations are founded be just, as I persuade myself they are, and they be applied as a criterion, to the several state constitutions, and to the federal constitution, it will be found, that if the latter does not perfectly correspond with them, the former are infinitely less able to bear such a test.

There are moreover two considerations particularly applicable to the federal system of America, which place that system in a very interesting point of view.

First. In a single republic, all the power surrendered by the people, is submitted to the administration of a single government; and usurpations are guarded against by a division of the government into distinct and separate departments. In the compound republic of America, the power surrendered by the people, is first divided between two distinct governments, and then the portion allotted to each, subdivided among distinct and separate departments. Hence a double security arises to the rights of the people. The different governments will control each other; at the same time that each will be controlled by itself.

Second. It is of great importance in a republic, not only to guard the society against the oppression of its rulers; but to guard one part of the society against the injustice of the other part. Different interests necessarily exist in different classes of citizens. If a majority be united by a common interest, the rights of the minority will be insecure. There are but two methods of providing against this evil: The one by creating a will in the community independent of the majority, that is, of the society itself, the other by comprehending in the society so many separate descriptions of citizens, as will render an unjust combination of a majority of the whole, very improbable, if not impracticable. The first method prevails in all governments possessing an hereditary or self appointed authority. This at best is but a precarious security; because a power independent of the society may as well espouse the unjust views of the major, as the rightful interests, of the minor party, and may possibly be turned against both parties. The second method will be exemplified in the federal republic of the United States. While all authority in it will be derived from and dependent on the society, the society itself will be broken into so many parts, interests and classes of citizens, that the rights of individuals or of the minority, will be in little danger from interested combinations of the majority. In a free government, the security for civil rights must be the same as for religious rights. It consists in the one case in the multiplicity of interests, and in the other, in the multiplicity of sects. The degree of security in both cases will depend on the number of interests and sects; and this may be presumed to depend on the extent of country and number of people comprehended under the same government. This view of the subject must particularly recommend a proper federal system to all the sincere and considerate friends of republican government: Since it shows that in exact proportion as the territory of the union may be formed into more circumscribed confederacies or states, oppressive combinations of a majority will be facilitated, the best security under the republican form, for the rights of every class of citizens, will be diminished; and consequently, the stability and independence of some member of the government, the only other security, must be proportionally increased. Justice is the end of government. It is the end of civil society. It ever has been, and ever will be pursued, until it be obtained, or until liberty be lost in the pursuit. In a society under the forms of which the stronger faction can readily unite and oppress the weaker, anarchy may as truly be said to reign, as in a state of nature where the weaker individual is not secured against the violence of the stronger: And as in the latter state even the stronger individuals are prompted by the uncertainty of their condition, to submit to a government which may protect the weak as well as themselves: So in the former state, will the more powerful factions or parties be gradually induced by a like motive, to wish for a government which will protect all parties, the weaker as well as the more powerful. It can be little doubted, that if the state of Rhode Island was separated from the confederacy, and left to itself, the insecurity of rights under the popular form of government within such narrow limits, would be displayed by such reiterated oppressions of factious majorities, that some power altogether independent of the people would soon be called for by the voice of the very factions whose misrule had proved the necessity of it. In the extended republic of the United States, and among the great variety of interests, parties and sects which it embraces, a coalition of a majority of the whole society could seldom take place on any other principles than those of justice and the general good; and there being thus less danger to a minor from the will of the major party, there must be less pretext also, to provide for the security of the former, by introducing into the government a will not dependent on the latter; or in other words, a will independent of the society itself. It is no less certain than it is important, notwithstanding the contrary opinions which have been entertained, that the larger the society, provided it lie within a practicable sphere, the more duly capable it will be of self government. And happily for the *republican cause*, the practicable sphere may be carried to a very great extent, by a judicious modification and mixture of the *federal principle*.

PUBLIUS

The Constitution of the United States of America*

(Preamble)

We the People of the United States, in Order to form a more perfect Union, establish Justice, insure domestic Tranquility, provide for the common defence, promote the general Welfare, and secure the Blessings of Liberty to ourselves and our Posterity, do ordain and establish this Constitution for the United States of America.

Article I.

(The Legislature)

Section 1. All legislative Powers herein granted shall be vested in a Congress of the United States, which shall consist of a Senate and House of Representatives.

Section 2. The House of Representatives shall be composed of Members chosen every second Year by the People of the several States, and the Electors in each State shall have the Qualifications requisite for Electors of the most numerous Branch of the State Legislature.

No person shall be a Representative who shall not have attained to the Age of twenty five Years, and been seven Years a Citizen of the United States, and who shall not, when elected, be an Inhabitant of that State in which he shall be chosen.

Representatives and direct [Taxes][1] shall be apportioned among the several States which may be included within this Union, according to their respective Numbers [which shall be determined by adding to the whole Number of free Persons, including those bound to Service for a Term of Years, and excluding Indians not taxed, three fifths of all other Persons].[2] The actual Enumeration shall be made within three Years after the first Meeting of the Congress of the United States, and within every subsequent Term of ten Years, in such Manner as they shall by Law direct. The Number of Representatives shall not exceed one for every

[1]See Amendment XVI.
[2]See Amendment XIV.

*This text retains the spelling, capitalization, and punctuation of the original. Brackets indicate passages that have been altered by amendments.

thirty Thousand, but each State shall have at Least one Representative; and until such enumeration shall be made, the State of New Hampshire shall be entitled to chuse three, Massachusetts eight, Rhode-Island and Providence Plantations one, Connecticut five, New-York six, New Jersey four, Pennsylvania eight, Delaware one, Maryland six, Virginia ten, North Carolina five, South Carolina five, and Georgia three.

When vacancies happen in the Representation from any State, the Executive Authority thereof shall issue Writs of Election to fill such Vacancies.

The House of Representatives shall chuse their speaker and other Officers; and shall have the sole Power of Impeachment.

Section 3. The Senate of the United States shall be composed of two Senators from each State [chosen by the Legislature thereof],[3] for six Years; and each Senator shall have one Vote.

Immediately after they shall be assembled in Consequence of the first Election, they shall be divided as equally as may be into three Classes. The Seats of the Senators of the first Class shall be vacated at the Expiration of the second year, of the second Class at the Expiration of the fourth Year, and of the third Class at the Expiration of the sixth Year, so that one third may be chosen every second Year [and if Vacancies happen by Resignation, or otherwise, during the Recess of the Legislature of any State, the Executive thereof may make temporary Appointments until the next Meeting of the Legislature, which shall then fill such Vacancies].[4]

No Person shall be a Senator who shall not have attained to the Age of thirty Years, and been nine Years a Citizen of the United States, and who shall not, when elected, be an Inhabitant of that State for which he shall be chosen.

The Vice President of the United States shall be President of the Senate, but shall have no Vote, unless they be equally divided.

The Senate shall chuse their other Officers, and also a President pro tempore, in the Absence of the Vice President, or when he shall exercise the Office of President of the United States.

The Senate shall have the sole Power to try all Impeachments. When sitting for that Purpose, they shall be on Oath or Affirmation. When the President of the United States is tried, the Chief Justice shall preside: And no Person shall be convicted without the Concurrence of two thirds of the Members present.

Judgment in Cases of Impeachment shall not extend further than to removal from Office, and disqualification to hold and enjoy any Office of honor, Trust or Profit under the United States; but the Party convicted shall nevertheless be liable and subject to Indictment, Trial, Judgment and Punishment, according to Law.

Section 4. The Times, Places and Manner of holding Elections for Senators and Representatives, shall be prescribed in each State by the Legislature thereof; but the Congress may at any time by Law make or alter such Regulations, except as to the Places of chusing Senators.

[The Congress shall assemble at least once in every Year, and such Meeting shall be on the first Monday in December, unless they shall by Law appoint a different Day.][5]

Section 5. Each House shall be the Judge of the Elections, Returns and Qualifications of its own Members, and a Majority of each shall constitute a Quorum to do Business; but a smaller Number may adjourn from day to day, and may be authorized to compel the Attendance of absent Members, in such Manner, and under such Penalties as each House may provide.

Each House may determine the Rules of its Proceedings, punish its Members for disorderly Behaviour, and, with the Concurrence of two thirds, expel a Member.

Each House shall keep a Journal of its Proceedings, and from time to time publish the same, excepting such Parts as may in their judgment require Secrecy; and the Yeas and Nays of the Members of either House on any question shall, at the Desire of one fifth of those present, be entered on the Journal.

Neither House, during the Session of Congress, shall, without the Consent of the other, adjourn for more than three days, nor to any other Place than that in which the two Houses shall be sitting.

Section 6. The Senators and Representatives shall receive a Compensation for their Services, to be ascertained by Law, and paid out of the Treasury of the United States. They shall in all Cases, except Treason, Felony and Breach of the Peace, be privileged from Arrest during their Attendance at

[3]See Amendment XVII.
[4]See Amendment XVII.

[5]See Amendment XX.

the Session of their respective Houses, and in going to and returning from the same; and for any Speech or Debate in either House, they shall not be questioned in any other Place.

No Senator or Representative shall, during the Time for which he was elected, be appointed to any civil Office under the Authority of the United States, which shall have been created, or the Emoluments whereof shall have been encreased during such time; and no Person holding any Office under the United States, shall be a Member of either House during his Continuance in Office.

Section 7. All Bills for raising Revenue shall originate in the House of Representatives; but the Senate may propose or concur with Amendments as on other Bills.

Every Bill which shall have passed the House of Representatives and the Senate, shall, before it becomes a Law, be presented to the President of the United States; If he approves he shall sign it, but if not he shall return it, with his Objections to that House in which it shall have originated, who shall enter the Objections at large on their Journal, and proceed to reconsider it. If after such Reconsideration two thirds of that House shall agree to pass the Bill, it shall be sent, together with the Objections, to the other House, by which it shall likewise be reconsidered, and if approved by two thirds of that House, it shall become a Law. But in all such Cases the Votes of both Houses shall be determined by yeas and Nays, and the Names of the Persons voting for and against the Bill shall be entered on the Journal of each House respectively. If any Bill shall not be returned by the President within ten Days (Sundays excepted) after it shall have been presented to him, the Same shall be a Law, in like Manner as if he had signed it, unless the Congress by their Adjournment prevent its Return, in which Case it shall not be a Law.

Every Order, Resolution, or Vote to which the Concurrence of the Senate and House of Representatives may be necessary (except on a question of Adjournment) shall be presented to the President of the United States; and before the Same shall take Effect, shall be approved by him, or being disapproved by him, shall be repassed by two thirds of the Senate and House of Representatives, according to the Rules and Limitations prescribed in the Case of a Bill.

Section 8. The Congress shall have Power To lay and collect Taxes, Duties, Imposts and Excises, to pay the Debts and provide for the common Defence and general Welfare of the United States; but all Duties, Imposts and Excises shall be uniform throughout the United States;

To borrow Money on the credit of the United States;

To regulate Commerce with foreign Nations, and among the several States, and with the Indian Tribes;

To establish a uniform Rule of Naturalization, and uniform Laws on the subject of Bankruptcies throughout the United States;

To coin Money, regulate the Value thereof, and of foreign Coin, and fix the Standard of Weights and Measures;

To provide for the Punishment of counterfeiting the Securities and current Coin of the United States;

To establish Post Offices and post Roads;

To promote the Progress of Science and useful Arts, by securing for limited Times to Authors and Inventors the exclusive Right to their respective Writings and Discoveries;

To constitute Tribunals inferior to the supreme Court;

To define and punish Piracies and Felonies committed on the high Seas, and Offences against the Law of Nations;

To declare War, grant Letters of Marque and Reprisal, and make Rules concerning Captures on Land and Water;

To raise and support Armies, but no Appropriation of Money to that Use shall be for a longer Term than two Years;

To provide and maintain a Navy;

To make Rules for the Government and Regulation of the land and naval Forces;

To provide for calling forth the Militia to execute the Laws of the Union, suppress Insurrections and repel Invasions;

To provide for organizing, arming, and disciplining, the Militia, and for governing such Part of them as may be employed in the Service of the United States, reserving to the States respectively, the Appointment of the Officers, and the Authority of training the Militia according to the discipline prescribed by Congress;

To exercise exclusive Legislation in all Cases whatsoever, over such District (not exceeding ten Miles square) as may, by Cession of particular States, and the Acceptance of Congress, become the Seat of the Government of the United States, and to exercise like Authority over all Places purchased by the Consent of the Legislature of the State in which the Same shall be, for the Erection of Forts, Magazines, Arsenals, dock-Yards, and other needful Buildings;—And

To make all Laws which shall be necessary and proper for carrying into Execution the foregoing Powers, and all other Powers vested by this Constitution in the Government of the United States, or in any Department or Officer thereof.

Section 9. The Migration or Importation of such Persons as any of the States now existing shall think proper to admit, shall not be prohibited by the Congress prior to the Year one thousand eight hundred and eight, but a Tax or duty may be imposed on such Importation, not exceeding ten dollars for each Person.

The Privilege of the Writ of Habeas Corpus shall not be suspended, unless when in Cases of Rebellion or Invasion the public Safety may require it.

No Bill of Attainder or ex post facto Law shall be passed.

[No Capitation, or other direct, Tax shall be laid, unless in Proportion to the Census or Enumeration herein before directed to be taken.][6]

No Tax or Duty shall be laid on Articles exported from any State.

No Preference shall be given by any Regulation of Commerce or Revenue to the Ports of one State over those of another; nor shall Vessels bound to, or from, one State, be obliged to enter, clear, or pay Duties in another.

No Money shall be drawn from the Treasury, but in Consequence of Appropriations made by Law; and a regular Statement and Account of the Receipts and Expenditures of all public Money shall be published from time to time.

No Title of Nobility shall be granted by the United States: And no Person holding any Office of Profit or Trust under them, shall, without the Consent of the Congress, accept of any present, Emolument, Office, or Title, of any kind whatever, from any King, Prince, or foreign State.

Section 10. No State shall enter into any Treaty, Alliance, or Confederation; grant Letters of Marque and Reprisal; coin Money; emit Bills of Credit; make any Thing but gold and silver Coin a Tender in Payment of Debts; pass any Bill of Attainder, ex post facto Law, or Law impairing the Obligation of Contracts, or grant any Title of Nobility.

No State shall, without the Consent of the Congress, lay any Imposts or Duties on Imports or Exports, except what may be absolutely necessary for executing its inspection Laws: and the net Produce of all Duties and Imposts, laid by any State on Imports or Exports, shall be for the Use of the Treasury of the United States; and all such Laws shall be subject to the Revision and Controul of the Congress.

No State shall, without the Consent of Congress, lay any Duty of Tonnage, keep Troops, or Ships of War in time of Peace, enter into any Agreement or Compact with another State, or with a foreign Power, or engage in War, unless actually invaded, or in such imminent Danger as will not admit of delay.

[6]See Amendment XVI.

Article II.
(The Executive)

Section 1. The executive Power shall be vested in a President of the United States of America. He shall hold his Office during the Term of four Years, and, together with the Vice President, chosen for the same Term, be elected, as follows.

Each State shall appoint, in such Manner as the Legislature thereof may direct, a Number of Electors, equal to the whole Number of Senators and Representatives to which the State may be entitled in the Congress; but no Senator or Representative, or Person holding an Office of Trust or Profit under the United States, shall be appointed an Elector.

[The Electors shall meet in their respective States, and vote by Ballot for two Persons, of whom one at least shall not be an Inhabitant of the same State with themselves. And they shall make a List of all the Persons voted for, and of the Number of Votes for each; which List they shall sign and certify, and transmit sealed to the Seat of the Government of the United States, directed to the President of the Senate. The President of the Senate shall, in the Presence of the Senate and House of Representatives, open all the Certificates, and the Votes shall then be counted. The Person having the greatest Number of Votes shall be the President, if such Number be a Majority of the whole Number of Electors appointed; and if there be more than one who have such Majority, and have an equal Number of Votes, then the House of Representatives shall immediately chuse by Ballot one of them for President; and if no Person have a Majority, then from the five highest on the List the said House shall in like Manner chuse the President. But in chusing the President, the Votes shall be taken by States, the Representation from each State having one Vote; A quorum for this Purpose shall consist of a Member or Members from two thirds of the States, and a Majority of all the States shall be necessary to a Choice. In every Case, after the Choice of the President, the Person having the greatest Number of Votes of the Electors shall be the Vice President. But if there should remain two or more who have equal Votes, the Senate shall chuse from them by Ballot the Vice President.][7]

The Congress may determine the Time of chusing the Electors, and the Day on which they shall give their Votes; which Day shall be the same throughout the United States.

No Person except a natural born Citizen, or a Citizen of the United States, at the time of the Adoption of this Constitution, shall be eligible to the Office of President; neither shall any Person be eligible to that Office who shall not have attained to the Age of thirty five Years, and been fourteen Years a Resident within the United States.

[In Case of the Removal of the President from Office, or of his Death, Resignation, or Inability to discharge the Powers and Duties of the said Office, the Same shall devolve on the Vice President, and the Congress may by Law provide for the Case of Removal, Death, Resignation or Inability, both of the President and Vice President, declaring what Officer shall then act as President, and such Officer shall act accordingly, until the Disability be removed, or a President shall be elected.][8]

The President shall, at stated Times, receive for his Services, a Compensation, which shall neither be encreased nor diminished during the Period for which he shall have been elected, and he shall not receive within that Period any other Emolument from the United States, or any of them.

Before he enter on the Execution of his Office, he shall take the following Oath or Affirmation:—"I do solemnly swear (or affirm) that I will faithfully execute the Office of President of the United States, and will to the best of my Ability, preserve, protect and defend the Constitution of the United States."

Section 2. The President shall be Commander in Chief of the Army and Navy of the United States, and of the Militia of the several States, when called into the actual Service of the United States; he may require the Opinion, in writing, of the principal Officer in each of the executive Departments, upon any Subject relating to the Duties of their respective Offices, and he shall have Power to grant Reprieves and Pardons for Offences against the United States, except in Cases of Impeachment.

He shall have Power, by and with the Advice and Consent of the Senate, to make Treaties, provided two thirds of the Senators present concur; and he shall nominate, and by and with the Advice and Consent of the Senate, shall appoint Ambassadors, other public Ministers and Consuls, Judges of the supreme Court, and all other Officers of the United States, whose Appointments are not herein otherwise provided for, and which shall be established by Law: but the Congress may by Law vest the Appointment of such inferior Officers, as they think proper, in the President alone, in the Courts of Law, or in the Heads of Departments.

The President shall have Power to fill up all Vacancies that may happen during the Recess of the Senate, by granting Commissions which shall expire at the end of their next Session.

Section 3. He shall from time to time give to the Congress Information of the State of the Union, and recommend to their Consideration such Measures as he shall judge necessary and expedient; he may, on extraordinary Occasions, convene both Houses, or either of them, and in Case of Disagreement between them, with Respect to the Time of Adjournment, he may adjourn them to such Time as he shall think proper; he shall receive Ambassadors and other public Ministers; he shall take Care that the Laws be faithfully executed, and shall Commission all the Officers of the United States.

Section 4. The President, Vice President and all civil Officers of the United States, shall be removed from Office on Impeachment for, and Conviction of, Treason, Bribery, or other high Crimes and Misdemeanors.

Article III.
(The Judiciary)

Section 1. The judicial Power of the United States, shall be vested in one supreme Court, and in such inferior Courts as the Congress may from time to time ordain and establish. The Judges, both of the supreme and inferior Courts, shall hold their Offices during good Behaviour, and shall, at stated Times, receive for their Services, a Compensation, which shall not be diminished during their Continuance in Office.

Section 2. The judicial Power shall extend to all Cases, in Law and Equity, arising under this Constitution, the Laws of the United States, and Treaties made, or which shall be made, under their Authority;—to all Cases affecting Ambassadors, other public Ministers and Consuls;—to all Cases of admiralty and maritime Jurisdiction;—to Controversies to which the

[7] See Amendment XII.
[8] See Amendment XXV.

United States shall be a Party;—to Controversies between two or more States; [—between a State and Citizens of another State;—][9] between Citizens of different States,—between Citizens of the same State claiming Lands under Grants of different States, [and between a State, or the Citizens thereof, and foreign States, Citizens or Subjects.][10]

In all Cases affecting Ambassadors, other public Ministers and Consuls, and those in which a State shall be Party, the supreme Court shall have original Jurisdiction. In all the other Cases before mentioned, the supreme Court shall have appellate Jurisdiction, both as to Law and Fact, with such Exceptions, and under such Regulations as the Congress shall make.

The Trial of all Crimes, except in Cases of Impeachment, shall be by Jury; and such Trial shall be held in the State where the said Crimes shall have been committed; but when not committed within any State, the Trial shall be at such Place or Places as the Congress may by Law have directed.

Section 3. Treason against the United States, shall consist only in levying War against them, or in adhering to their Enemies, giving them Aid and Comfort. No Person shall be convicted of Treason unless on the Testimony of two Witnesses to the same overt Act, or on Confession in open Court.

The Congress shall have Power to declare the Punishment of Treason, but no Attainder of Treason shall work Corruption of Blood, or Forfeiture except during the Life of the Person attainted.

Article IV.
(Interstate Relations)

Section 1. Full Faith and Credit shall be given in each State to the public Acts, Records, and judicial Proceedings of every other State. And the Congress may by general Laws prescribe the Manner in which such Acts, Records and Proceedings shall be proved, and the Effect thereof.

Section 2. The Citizens of each State shall be entitled to all Privileges and Immunities of Citizens in the several States.

A Person charged in any State with Treason, Felony, or other Crime, who shall flee from Justice, and be found in another State, shall on Demand of the executive Authority of the State from which he fled, be delivered up, to be removed to the State having Jurisdiction of the Crime.

[No Person held to Service or Labour in one State under the Laws thereof, escaping into another, shall, in Consequence of any Law or Regulation therein, be discharged from such Service or Labour, but shall be delivered up on Claim of the Party to whom such Service or Labour may be due.][11]

Section 3. New States may be admitted by the Congress into this Union; but no new State shall be formed or erected within the Jurisdiction of any other State; nor any State be formed by the Junction of two or more States, or Parts of States, without the Consent of the Legislatures of the States concerned as well as of the Congress.

The Congress shall have Power to dispose of and make all needful Rules and Regulations respecting the Territory or other Property belonging to the United States; and nothing in this Constitution shall be so construed as to Prejudice any Claims of the United States, or of any particular State.

Section 4. The United States shall guarantee to every State in this Union a Republican Form of Government, and shall protect each of them against Invasion, and on Application of the Legislature, or of the Executive (when the Legislature cannot be convened) against domestic Violence.

Article V.
(Amending the Constitution)

The Congress, whenever two thirds of both Houses shall deem it necessary, shall propose Amendments to this Constitution, or, on the Application of the Legislatures of two thirds of the several States, shall call a Convention for proposing Amendments, which, in either Case, shall be valid to all Intents and Purposes, as Part of this Constitution, when ratified by the Legislatures of three fourths of the several States, or by Conventions in three fourths thereof, as the one or the other Mode of Ratification may be proposed by the Congress; Provided that no Amendment which may be made prior to

[9]See Amendment XI.
[10]See Amendment XI.

[11]See Amendment XIII.

the Year One thousand eight hundred and eight shall in any Manner affect the first and fourth Clauses in the Ninth Section of the first Article; and that no State, without its Consent, shall be deprived of its equal Suffrage in the Senate.

Article VI.

(Debts, Supremacy, Oaths)

All Debts contracted and Engagements entered into, before the Adoption of this Constitution, shall be as valid against the United States under this Constitution, as under the Confederation.

This Constitution, and the laws of the United States which shall be made in Pursuance thereof; and all Treaties made, or which shall be made, under the Authority of the United States, shall be the supreme Law of the Land; and the Judges in every State shall be bound thereby, any Thing in the Constitution or Laws of any State to the Contrary notwithstanding.

The Senators and Representatives before mentioned, and the Members of the several State Legislatures, and all executive and judicial Officers, both of the United States and of the several States, shall be bound by Oath or Affirmation, to support this Constitution; but no religious Test shall ever be required as a Qualification to any Office or public Trust under the United States.

Article VII.

(Ratifying the Constitution)

The Ratification of the Conventions of nine States, shall be sufficient for the Establishment of this Constitution between the States so ratifying the Same.

Done in Convention by the Unanimous Consent of the States present the Seventeenth Day of September in the Year of our Lord one thousand seven hundred and Eighty seven and of the Independence of the United States of America the Twelfth. IN WITNESS whereof we have hereunto subscribed our Names.

Go. WASHINGTON
Presid't. and deputy from Virginia

ATTEST
William Jackson
Secretary

DELAWARE
Geo. Read
Gunning Bedford jun
John Dickinson
Richard Basset
Jaco. Broom

MASSACHUSETTS
Nathaniel Gorbam
Rufus King

CONNECTICUT
Wm. Saml. Johnson
Roger Sherman

NEW YORK
Alexander Hamilton

NEW JERSEY
Wh. Livingston
David Brearley
Wm. Paterson
Jona. Dayton

PENNSYLVANIA
B. Franklin
Thomas Mifflin
Robt. Morris
Geo. Clymer
Thos. FitzSimons
Jared Ingersoll
James Wilson
Gouv. Morris

NEW HAMPSHIRE
John Langdon
Nicholas Gilman

MARYLAND
James McHenry
Dan of St. Thos. Jenifer
Danl. Carroll

VIRGINIA
John Blair
James Madison Jr.

NORTH CAROLINA
Wm. Blount
Richd. Dobbs Spaight
Hu. Williamson

SOUTH CAROLINA
J. Rutledge
Charles Cotesworth Pinckney
Charles Pinckney
Pierce Butler

GEORGIA
William Few
Abr. Baldwin

Articles in addition to, and amendment of the Constitution of the United States of America, proposed by Congress and ratified by the Legislatures of the several states, pursuant to the Fifth Article of the original Constitution.

(The first ten amendments were passed by Congress on September 25, 1789, and were ratified on December 15, 1791.)

Amendment I—Religion, Speech, Assembly, Petition

Congress shall make no law respecting an establishment of religion, or prohibiting the free exercise thereof; or abridging the freedom of speech, or of the press; or the right of the people peaceably to assemble, and to petition the Government for a redress of grievances.

Amendment II—Right to Bear Arms

A well regulated Militia, being necessary to the security of a free State, the right of the people to keep and bear Arms, shall not be infringed.

Amendment III—Quartering of Soldiers

No Soldier shall, in time of peace be quartered in any house, without the consent of the Owner, nor in time of war, but in a manner to be prescribed by law.

Amendment IV—Searches and Seizures

The right of the people to be secure in their persons, houses, papers, and effects, against unreasonable searches and seizures, shall not be violated, and no warrants shall issue, but upon probable cause, supported by Oath or affirmation, and particularly describing the place to be searched, and the persons or things to be seized.

Amendment V—Grand Juries, Double Jeopardy, Self-incrimination, Due Process, Eminent Domain

No person shall be held to answer for a capital, or otherwise infamous crime, unless on a presentment or indictment of a Grand Jury, except in cases arising in the land or naval forces, or in the Militia, when in actual service in time of War or public danger; nor shall any person be subject for the same offence to be twice put in jeopardy of life or limb; nor shall be compelled in any criminal case to be a witness against himself, nor be deprived of life, liberty, or property, without due process of law; nor shall private property be taken for public use, without just compensation.

Amendment VI—Criminal Court Procedures

In all criminal prosecutions, the accused shall enjoy the right to a speedy and public trial, by an impartial jury of the State and district wherein the crime shall have been committed, which district shall have been previously ascertained by law, and to be informed of the nature and cause of the accusation; to be confronted with the witnesses against him; to have compulsory process for obtaining witnesses in his favor, and to have the assistance of counsel for his defence.

Amendment VII—Trial by Jury in Common-law Cases

In Suits at common law, where the value in controversy shall exceed twenty dollars, the right of trial by jury shall be preserved, and no fact tried by a jury, shall be otherwise re-examined in any Court of the United States, than according to the rules of the common law.

Amendment VIII—Bails, Fines, and Punishment

Excessive bail shall not be required, nor excessive fines imposed, nor cruel and unusual punishments inflicted.

Amendment IX—Rights Retained by the People

The enumeration in the Constitution, of certain rights, shall not be construed to deny or disparage others retained by the people.

Amendment X—Rights Reserved to the States

The powers not delegated to the United States by the Constitution, nor prohibited by it to the States, are reserved to the States respectively, or to the people.

Amendment XI—Suits Against the States (Ratified February 7, 1795)

The Judicial power of the United States shall not be construed to extend to any suit in law or equity, commenced or prosecuted against one of the United States by Citizens of another State, or by Citizens or Subjects of any Foreign State.

Amendment XII—Election of the President and Vice-President (Ratified June 15, 1804)

The Electors shall meet in their respective states, and vote by ballot for President and Vice-President, one of whom, at least, shall not be an inhabitant of the same state with themselves; they shall name in their ballots the person voted for as President, and in distinct ballots the person voted for as Vice-President, and they shall make distinct lists of all persons voted for as President, and of all persons voted for as Vice-President, and of the number of votes for each, which lists they shall sign and certify, and transmit sealed to the seat of the government of the United States, directed to the President of the Senate;—The President of the Senate shall, in the presence of the Senate and House of Representatives, open all the certificates and the votes shall then be counted;—The person having the greatest number of votes for President, shall be the President, if such number be a majority of the whole number of Electors appointed; and if no person have such majority, then from the persons having the highest numbers not exceeding three on the list of those voted for as President, the House of Representatives shall choose immediately, by ballot, the President. But in choosing the President, the votes shall be taken by states, the representation from each state having one vote; a quorum for this purpose shall consist of a member or members from two-thirds of the states, and a majority of all the states shall be necessary to a Choice. [And if the House of Representatives shall not choose a President whenever the right of choice shall devolve upon them, before the fourth day of March next following, then the Vice-President shall act as President, as in the case of the death or other constitutional disability of the President.][12] —The person having the greatest number of votes as Vice-President, shall be the Vice-President, if such number be a majority of the whole number of Electors appointed, and if no person have a majority, then from the two highest numbers on the list, the Senate shall choose the Vice-President; a quorum for the purpose shall consist of two-thirds of the whole number of Senators, and a majority of the whole number shall be necessary to a choice. But no person constitutionally ineligible to the office of President shall be eligible to that of Vice-President of the United States.

[12]Amendment XX.

Amendment XIII—Slavery (Ratified on December 6, 1865)

Section 1. Neither slavery nor involuntary servitude, except as a punishment for crime whereof the party shall have been duly convicted, shall exist within the United States, or any place subject to their jurisdiction.

Section 2. Congress shall have power to enforce this article by appropriate legislation.

Amendment XIV—Citizenship, Due Process, and Equal Protection of the Laws (Ratified on July 9, 1868)

Section 1. All persons born or naturalized in the United States, and subject to the jurisdiction thereof, are citizens of the United States and of the State wherein they reside. No State shall make or enforce any law which shall abridge the privileges or immunities of citizens of the United States; nor shall any State deprive any person of life, liberty, or property, without due process of law; nor deny to any person within its jurisdiction the equal protection of the laws.

Section 2. Representatives shall be apportioned among the several States according to their respective numbers, counting the whole number of persons in each State, excluding Indians not taxed. But when the right to vote at any election for the choice of electors for President and Vice President of the United States, Representatives in Congress, the Executive and Judicial officers of a State, or the members of the Legislature thereof, is denied to any of the male inhabitants of such State, being twenty-one years of age, and citizens of the United States, or in any way abridged, except for participation in rebellion, or other crime, the basis of representation therein shall be reduced in the proportion which the number of such male citizens shall bear to the whole number of male citizens twenty-one years of age in such State.

Section 3. No person shall be a Senator or Representative in Congress, or elector of President and Vice President, or hold any office, civil or military, under the United States, or under any State, who, having previously taken an oath, as a member of Congress, or as an officer of the United States, or as a member of any State legislature, or as an executive or judicial officer of any State, to support the Constitution of the United States, shall have engaged in insurrection or rebellion against the same, or given aid or comfort to the enemies thereof. But Congress may by a vote of two-thirds of each House, remove such disability.

Section 4. The validity of the public debt of the United States, authorized by law, including debts incurred for payment of pensions and bounties for services in suppressing insurrection or rebellion, shall not be questioned. But neither the United States nor any State shall assume or pay any debt or obligation incurred in aid of insurrection or rebellion against the United States, or any claim for the loss or emancipation of any slave, but all such debts, obligations and claims shall be held illegal and void.

Section 5. The Congress shall have power to enforce, by appropriate legislation, the provisions of this article.

Amendment XV—The Right To Vote (Ratified on February 3, 1870)

Section 1. The right of citizens of the United States to vote shall not be denied or abridged by the United States or by any State on account of race, color, or previous condition of servitude.

Section 2. The Congress shall have power to enforce this article by appropriate legislation.

Amendment XVI—Income Taxes (Ratified on February 3, 1913)

The Congress shall have power to lay and collect taxes on incomes, from whatever source derived, without apportionment among the several States, and without regard to any census or enumeration.

Amendment XVII—Election of Senators (Ratified on April 8, 1913)

The Senate of the United States shall be composed of two Senators from each State, elected by the people thereof, for six years; and each Senator shall have one vote. The electors in each State shall have the qualifications requisite for electors of the most numerous branch of the State legislatures.

When vacancies happen in the representation of any State in the Senate, the executive authority of such State shall issue writs of election to fill such vacancies: *Provided*, That the legislature of any State may empower the executive thereof to make temporary appointments until the people fill the vacancies by election as the legislature may direct.

This amendment shall not be so construed as to affect the election or term of any Senator chosen before it becomes valid as part of the Constitution.

Amendment XVIII—Prohibition (Ratified on January 16, 1919)

Section 1. After one year from the ratification of this article the manufacture, sale, or transportation of intoxicating liquors within, the importation thereof into, or the exportation thereof from the United States and all territory subject to the jurisdiction thereof for beverage purposes is hereby prohibited.

Section 2. The Congress and the several States shall have concurrent power to enforce this article by appropriate legislation.

Section 3. This article shall be inoperative unless it shall have been ratified as an amendment to the Constitution by the legislatures of the several States, as provided in the Constitution, within seven years from the date of the submission hereof to the States by the Congress.[13]

Amendment XIX—Women's Right To Vote (Ratified on August 18, 1920)

The right of citizens of the United States to vote shall not be denied or abridged by the United States or by any State on account of sex.

Congress shall have power to enforce this article by appropriate legislation.

---

[13]Amendment XXI.

Amendment XX—Terms of Office, Convening of Congress, and Succession (Ratified February 6, 1933)

Section 1. The terms of the President and Vice President shall end at noon on the 20th day of January, and the terms of Senators and Representatives at noon on the 3d day of January, of the years in which such terms would have ended if this article had not been ratified; and the terms of their successors shall then begin.

Section 2. The Congress shall assemble at least once in every year, and such meeting shall begin at noon on the 3d day of January, unless they shall by law appoint a different day.

Section 3. If, at the time fixed for the beginning of the term of the President, the President elect shall have died, the Vice President elect shall become President. If a President shall not have been chosen before the time fixed for the beginning of his term, or if the President elect shall have failed to qualify, then the Vice President elect shall act as President until a President shall have qualified; and the Congress may by law provide for the case wherein neither a President elect nor a Vice President elect shall have qualified, declaring who shall then act as President, or the manner in which one who is to act shall be selected, and such person shall act accordingly until a President or Vice President shall have qualified.

Section 4. The Congress may by law provide for the case of the death of any of the persons from whom the House of Representatives may choose a President whenever the rights of choice shall have devolved upon them, and for the case of the death of any of the persons from whom the Senate may choose a Vice President whenever the right of choice shall have devolved upon them.

Section 5. Sections 1 and 2 shall take effect on the 15th day of October following the ratification of this article.

Section 6. This article shall be inoperative unless it shall have been ratified as an amendment to the Constitution by the legislatures of three-fourths of the several States within seven years from the date of its submission.

Amendment XXI—Repeal of Prohibition (Ratified on December 5, 1933)

Section 1. The eighteenth article of amendment to the Constitution of the United States is hereby repealed.

Section 2. The transportation or importation into any State, Territory, or possession of the United States for delivery or use therein of intoxicating liquors, in violation of the laws thereof, is hereby prohibited.

Section 3. This article shall be inoperative unless it shall have been ratified as an amendment to the Constitution by conventions in the several States, as provided in the Constitution, within seven years from the date of the submission hereof to the States by the Congress.

Amendment XXII—Number of Presidential Terms (Ratified on February 27, 1951)

No person shall be elected to the office of the President more than twice, and no person who has held the office of President, or acted as President, for more than two years of a term to which some other person was elected President shall be elected to the office of the President more than once. But this Article shall not apply to any person holding the office of President when this Article was proposed by the Congress, and shall not prevent any person who may be holding the office of President, or acting as President, during the term within which this Article becomes operative from holding the office of President or acting as President during the remainder of such term.

Amendment XXIII—Presidential Electors for the District of Columbia (Ratified on March 29, 1961)

Section 1. The District constituting the seat of Government of the United States shall appoint in such manner as the Congress may direct:

A number of electors of President and Vice President equal to the whole number of Senators and Representatives in

Congress to which the District would be entitled if it were a State, but in no event more than the least populous State; they shall be in addition to those appointed by the States, but they shall be considered, for the purposes of the election of President and Vice President, to be electors appointed by a State; and they shall meet in the District and perform such duties as provided by the twelfth article of amendment.

Section 2. The Congress shall have power to enforce this article by appropriate legislation.

Amendment XXIV—Poll Tax (Ratified on January 23, 1964)

Section 1. The right of citizens of the United States to vote in any primary or other election for President or Vice President, for electors for President or Vice President, or for Senator or Representative in Congress, shall not be denied or abridged by the United States or any State by reason of failure to pay any poll tax or other tax.

Section 2. The Congress shall have power to enforce this article by appropriate legislation.

Amendment XXV—Presidential Disability and Vice Presidential Vacancies (Ratified on February 10, 1967)

Section 1. In case of the removal of the President from office or of his death or resignation, the Vice President shall become President.

Section 2. Whenever there is a vacancy in the office of the Vice President, the President shall nominate a Vice President who shall take office upon confirmation by a majority vote of both Houses of Congress.

Section 3. Whenever the President transmits to the President pro tempore of the Senate and the Speaker of the House of Representatives his written declaration that he is unable to discharge the powers and duties of his office, and until he transmits to them a written declaration to the contrary, such powers and duties shall be discharged by the Vice President as Acting President.

Section 4. Whenever the Vice President and a majority of either the principal officers of the executive departments or of such other body as Congress may by law provide, transmit to the President pro tempore of the Senate and the Speaker of the House of Representatives their written declaration that the President is unable to discharge the powers and duties of his office, the Vice President shall immediately assume the powers and duties of the office as Acting President.

Thereafter, when the President transmits to the President pro tempore of the Senate and the Speaker of the House of Representatives his written declaration that no inability exists, he shall resume the powers and duties of his office unless the Vice President and a majority of either the principal officers of the executive department or of such other body as Congress may by law provide, transmit within four days to the President pro tempore of the Senate and the Speaker of the House of Representatives their written declaration that the President is unable to discharge the powers and duties of his office. Thereupon Congress shall decide the issue, assembling within forty-eight hours for that purpose if not in session. If the Congress, within twenty-one days after receipt of the latter written declaration, or, if Congress is not in session, within twenty-one days after Congress is required to assemble, determines by two-thirds vote of both Houses that the President is unable to discharge the powers and duties of his office, the Vice President shall continue to discharge the same as Acting President; otherwise, the President shall resume the powers and duties of his office.

Amendment XXVI—Eighteen-year-old Vote (Ratified on July 1, 1971)

Section 1. The right of citizens of the United States, who are eighteen years of age or older, to vote shall not be denied or abridged by the United States or by any State on account of age.

Section 2. The Congress shall have power to enforce this article by appropriate legislation.

Amendment XXVII—Congressional Salaries (Ratified on May 18, 1992)

Section 1. No law varying the compensation for the services of the Senators and Representatives, shall take effect, until an election of Representatives shall have intervened.

Presidents of the United States

YEAR	PRESIDENTIAL CANDIDATES	POLITICAL PARTY	ELECTORAL VOTE	PERCENTAGE OF POPULAR VOTE
1789	**George Washington**	—	69	—
	John Adams		34	
	Others		35	
1792	**George Washington**	—	132	—
	John Adams		77	
	Others		55	
1796	**John Adams**	Federalist	71	—
	Thomas Jefferson	Democratic-Republican	68	
	Thomas Pinckney	Federalist	59	
	Aaron Burr	Democratic-Republican	30	
	Others		48	
1800	**Thomas Jefferson**	Democratic-Republican	73	—
	Aaron Burr	Democratic-Republican	73	
	John Adams	Federalist	65	
	C. C. Pinckney	Federalist	64	
	John Jay	Federalist	1	
1804	**Thomas Jefferson**	Democratic-Republican	162	—
	C. C. Pinckney	Federalist	14	
1808	**James Madison**	Democratic-Republican	122	—
	C. C. Pinckney	Federalist	47	
	George Clinton	Independent-Republican	6	
1812	**James Madison**	Democratic-Republican	128	—
	De Witt Clinton	Federalist	89	
1816	**James Monroe**	Democratic-Republican	183	—
	Rufus King	Federalist	34	
1820	**James Monroe**	Democratic-Republican	231	—
	John Q. Adams	Independent-Republican	1	
1824	**John Q. Adams**	Democratic-Republican	84	30.5
	Andrew Jackson	Democratic-Republican	99	
	Henry Clay	Democratic-Republican	37	
	W. H. Crawford	Democratic-Republican	41	
1828	**Andrew Jackson**	Democratic	178	56.0
	John Q. Adams	National Republican	83	
1832	**Andrew Jackson**	Democratic	219	55.0
	Henry Clay	National Republican	49	
	William Wirt	Anti-Masonic	7	
	John Floyd	Independent Democrat	11	
1836	**Martin Van Buren**	Democratic	170	50.9
	William H. Harrison	Whig	73	
	Hugh L. White	Whig	26	
	Daniel Webster	Whig	14	
1840	**William H. Harrison***	Whig	234	53.0
	Martin Van Buren	Democratic	60	
	(John Tyler, 1841)			

Note: Presidents are shown in boldface.

* Died in office, succeeding vice president shown in parentheses.

YEAR	PRESIDENTIAL CANDIDATES	POLITICAL PARTY	ELECTORAL VOTE	PERCENTAGE OF POPULAR VOTE
1844	**James K. Polk**	Democratic	170	49.6
	Henry Clay	Whig	105	
1848	**Zachary Taylor***	Whig	163	47.4
	Lewis Cass	Democratic	127	
	(Millard Fillmore, 1850)			
1852	**Franklin Pierce**	Democratic	254	50.9
	Winfield Scott	Whig	42	
1856	**James Buchanan**	Democratic	174	45.4
	John C. Fremont	Republican	114	
	Millard Fillmore	American	8	
1860	**Abraham Lincoln**	Republican	180	39.8
	J. C. Breckinridge	Democratic	72	
	Stephen A. Douglas	Democratic	12	
	John Bell	Constitutional Union	39	
1864	**Abraham Lincoln***	Republican	212	55.0
	George B. McClellan	Democratic	21	
	(Andrew Johnson, 1865)			
1868	**Ulysses S. Grant**	Republican	214	52.7
	Horatio Seymour	Democratic	80	
1872	**Ulysses S. Grant**	Republican	286	55.6
	Horace Greeley**	Democratic	**	
1876	**Rutherford B. Hayes**	Republican	185	47.9
	Samuel J. Tilden	Democratic	184	
1880	**James A. Garfield***	Republican	214	48.3
	Winfield S. Hancock	Democratic	155	
	(Chester A. Arthur, 1881)			
1884	**Grover Cleveland**	Democratic	219	48.5
	James G. Blaine	Republican	182	
1888	**Benjamin Harrison**	Republican	233	47.8
	Grover Cleveland	Democratic	168	
1892	**Grover Cleveland**	Democratic	277	46.0
	Benjamin Harrison	Republican	145	
	James B. Weaver	People's	22	
1896	**William McKinley**	Republican	271	51.0
	William J. Bryan	Democratic	176	
1900	**William McKinley***	Republican	292	51.7
	William J. Bryan	Democratic	155	
	(Theodore Roosevelt, 1901)			
1904	**Theodore Roosevelt**	Republican	336	56.4
	Alton B. Parker	Democratic	140	
1908	**William H. Taft**	Republican	321	51.6
	William J. Bryan	Democratic	162	
1912	**Woodrow Wilson**	Democratic	435	41.8
	Theodore Roosevelt	Progressive	88	
	William H. Taft	Republican	8	

** Horace Greeley died between the popular vote and the meeting of the presidential electors.

(Continued)

YEAR	PRESIDENTIAL CANDIDATES	POLITICAL PARTY	ELECTORAL VOTE	PERCENTAGE OF POPULAR VOTE
1916	**Woodrow Wilson**	Democratic	277	49.2
	Charles E. Hughes	Republican	254	
1920	**Warren G. Harding***	Republican	404	60.3
	James M. Cox	Democratic	127	
	(Calvin Coolidge, 1923)			
1924	**Calvin Coolidge**	Republican	382	54.1
	John W. Davis	Democratic	136	
	Robert M. LaFollette	Progressive	13	
1928	**Herbert C. Hoover**	Republican	444	58.2
	Alfred E. Smith	Democratic	87	
1932	**Franklin D. Roosevelt**	Democratic	472	57.4
	Herbert C. Hoover	Republican	59	
1936	**Franklin D. Roosevelt**	Democratic	523	60.8
	Alfred M. Landon	Republican	8	
1940	**Franklin D. Roosevelt**	Democratic	449	54.7
	Wendell L. Willkie	Republican	82	
1944	**Franklin D. Roosevelt***	Democratic	432	53.4
	Thomas E. Dewey	Republican	99	
	(Harry S Truman, 1945)			
1948	**Harry S Truman**	Democratic	303	49.5
	Thomas E. Dewey	Republican	189	
	J. Strom Thurmond	States' Rights	39	
1952	**Dwight D. Eisenhower**	Republican	442	55.1
	Adlai E. Stevenson	Democratic	89	
1956	**Dwight D. Eisenhower**	Republican	457	57.4
	Adlai E. Stevenson	Democratic	73	
1960	**John F. Kennedy***	Democratic	303	49.7
	Richard M. Nixon	Republican	219	
	(Lyndon B. Johnson, 1963)			
1964	**Lyndon B. Johnson**	Democratic	486	61.0
	Barry M. Goldwater	Republican	52	
1968	**Richard M. Nixon**	Republican	301	43.4
	Hubert H. Humphrey	Democratic	191	
	George C. Wallace	American Independent	46	
1972	**Richard M. Nixon†**	Republican	520	60.7
	George S. McGovern	Democratic	17	
	(Gerald R. Ford, 1974)‡			
1976	**Jimmy Carter**	Democratic	297	50.1
	Gerald R. Ford	Republican	240	
1980	**Ronald Reagan**	Republican	489	50.7
	Jimmy Carter	Democratic	49	
	John B. Anderson	Independent	—	
1984	**Ronald Reagan**	Republican	525	58.8
	Walter Mondale	Democratic	13	
1988	**George Bush**	Republican	426	53.4
	Michael Dukakis	Democratic	111	

† Resigned.

‡ Appointed vice president.

YEAR	PRESIDENTIAL CANDIDATES	POLITICAL PARTY	ELECTORAL VOTE	PERCENTAGE OF POPULAR VOTE
1992	**Bill Clinton**	Democratic	370	43.0
	George Bush	Republican	168	
	H. Ross Perot	Independent	—	
1996	**Bill Clinton**	Democratic	379	49.2
	Robert Dole	Republican	159	
	H. Ross Perot	Reform	—	
2000	**George W. Bush**	Republican	271	47.8
	Al Gore	Democratic	266	
	Ralph Nader	Green		
	Patrick J. Buchanan	Reform		
2004	**George W. Bush**	Republican	286	50.7
	John Kerry	Democratic	251	
	Ralph Nader	Independent	—	

Glossary

527 groups. Independent groups that seek to influence the political process but are not subject to contribution restrictions because they do not directly seek the election of particular candidates. Their name comes from Section 527 of the federal tax code, under which they are governed. In 2004, 52 individuals gave over a million dollars to such groups, and all told spent $424 million on political messages.

A

activation. One of three key consequences of electoral campaigns for voters, in which the voter is activated to contribute money or ring doorbells instead of just voting. See also **reinforcement** and **conversion.**

actual group. That part of the potential group consisting of members who actually join. See also **interest group.**

Adarand Constructors v. Pena. A 1995 Supreme Court decision holding that federal programs that classify people by race, even for an ostensibly benign purpose such as expanding opportunities for minorities, should be presumed to be unconstitutional. Such programs must be subject to the most searching judicial inquiry and can survive only if they are "narrowly tailored" to accomplish a "compelling governmental interest."

administrative discretion. The authority of administrative actors to select among various responses to a given problem. Discretion is greatest when routines, or **standard operating procedures**, do not fit a case.

affirmative action. A policy designed to give special attention to or compensatory treatment to members of some previously disadvantaged group.

agents of socialization. Families, schools, television, peer groups, and other influences that contribute to **political socialization** by shaping formal and especially informal learning about politics.

Americans with Disabilities Act of 1990. A law passed in 1990 that requires employers and public facilities to make "reasonable accommodations" for people with disabilities and prohibits discrimination against these individuals in employment.

***amicus curiae* briefs.** Legal briefs submitted by a "friend of the court" for the purpose of raising additional points of view and presenting information not contained in the briefs of the formal parties. These briefs attempt to influence a court's decision.

Anti-Federalists. Opponents of the American Constitution at the time when the states were contemplating its adoption. They argued that the Constitution was a class-based document, that it would erode fundamental liberties, and that it would weaken the power of the states. See also **Federalists** and **U. S. Constitution**.

appellate jurisdiction. The jurisdiction of courts that hear cases brought to them on appeal from lower courts. These courts do not review the factual record, only the legal issues involved. Compare **original jurisdiction.**

arms race. A tense relationship beginning in the 1950s between the Soviet Union and the United States whereby one side's weaponry became the other side's goad to procure more weaponry, and so on.

Articles of Confederation. The first constitution of the United States, adopted by Congress in 1777 and enacted in 1781. The Articles established a national legislature, the Continental Congress, but most authority rested with the state legislatures.

B

balance of trade. The ratio of what is paid for imports to what is earned from exports. When more is imported than exported, there is a balance-of-trade deficit.

balanced budget amendment. A proposed amendment to the Constitution that would instruct Congress to hold a national convention to propose to the states a requirement that peacetime federal budgets be balanced. The amendment has been passed in varied forms by the legislatures of nearly two-thirds of the states.

Barron v. Baltimore. The 1833 Supreme Court decision holding that the **Bill of Rights** restrained only the national government, not the states and cities. Almost a century later, the Court first ruled in *Gitlow v. New York* that state governments must respect some **First Amendment rights.**

beats. Specific locations from which news frequently emanates, such as Congress or the White House. Most top reporters work a particular beat, thereby becoming specialists in what goes on at that location.

bicameral legislature. A legislature divided into two houses. The U. S. Congress and every American state legislature except Nebraska's are bicameral.

bill. A proposed law, drafted in precise, legal language. Anyone can draft a bill, but only a member of the House of Representatives or the Senate can formally submit a bill for consideration.

Bill of Rights. The first 10 amendments to the U.S. Constitution, drafted in response to some of the **Anti-Federalist** concerns. These amendments define such basic liberties as freedom of religion, speech, and press and offer protections against arbitrary searches by the police and being held prisoner without talking to a lawyer.

blanket primaries. Elections to select party nominees in which voters are presented with a list of candidates from all the parties. Voters can then select some Democrats and some Republicans if they like. See also **primaries.**

block grants. Federal grants given more or less automatically to states or communities to support broad programs in areas such as community development and social services. Compare **categorical grants.**

broadcast media. Television and radio, as compared with **print media.**

Brown v. Board of Education. The 1954 Supreme Court decision holding that school segregation in Topeka, Kansas, was inherently unconstitutional because it violated the **Fourteenth Amendment's** guarantee of **equal protection of the laws.** This case marked the end of legal segregation in the United States. See also ***Plessy v. Ferguson***.

budget. A policy document allocating burdens (taxes) and benefits (expenditures). See also **balanced budget amendment.**

bureaucracy. According to Max Weber, a hierarchical authority structure that uses task specialization, operates on the merit principle, and behaves with impersonality. Bureaucracies govern modern states.

C

cabinet. A group of presidential advisers not mentioned in the Constitution, although every president has had one. Today the cabinet is composed of 14 secretaries and the attorney general.

campaign strategy. The master game plan candidates lay out to guide their electoral campaign.

casework. Activities of members of Congress that help constituents as individuals; cutting through bureaucratic red tape to get people what they think they have a right to get. See also **pork barrel.**

categorical grants. Federal grants that can be used only for specific purposes, or "categories," of state and local spending. They come with strings attached, such as nondiscrimination provisions. Compare **block grants.**

caucus (congressional). A group of members of Congress sharing some interest or characteristic. Most are composed of members from both parties and from both houses.

caucus (state party). A meeting of all state party leaders for selecting delegates to the **national party convention.** Caucuses are usually organized as a pyramid.

census. A valuable tool for understanding demographic changes. The Constitution requires that the government conduct an "actual enumeration" of the population every ten years. See also **demography.**

Central Intelligence Agency (CIA). An agency created after World War II to coordinate American intelligence activities abroad. It became involved in intrigue, conspiracy, and meddling as well.

chains. Newspapers published by massive media conglomerates that account for almost three-quarters of the nation's daily circulation. Often these chains control **broadcast media** as well.

checks and balances. An important part of the Madisonian model designed to limit government's power by requiring that power be balanced among the different governmental institutions. These institutions continually check one another's activities. This system reflects Madison's goal of setting power against power. See also **separation of powers.**

civic duty. The belief that in order to support democratic government, a citizen should always vote.

civil disobedience. A form of **political participation** that reflects a conscious decision to break a law believed to be immoral and to suffer the consequences. See also **protest.**

civil law. The body of law involving cases without a charge of criminality. It concerns disputes between two parties and consists of both statutes and **common law.** Compare **criminal law.**

civil liberties. The legal constitutional protections against government. Although our civil liberties are formally set down in the **Bill of Rights,** the courts, police, and legislatures define their meaning.

civil rights. Policies designed to protect people against arbitrary or discriminatory treatment by government officials or individuals.

Civil Rights Act of 1964. The law that made racial discrimination against any group in hotels, motels, and restaurants illegal and forbade many forms of job discrimination. See also **civil rights movement** and **civil rights policies.**

civil rights movement. A movement that began in the 1950s and organized both African Americans and Whites to end the policies of segregation. It sought to establish equal opportunities in the political and economic sectors and to end policies that erected barriers between people because of race.

civil rights policies. Policies that extend government protection to particular disadvantaged groups. Compare **social welfare policies.**

civil service. A system of hiring and promotion based on the **merit principle** and the desire to create a nonpartisan government service. Compare **patronage.**

class action suits. Lawsuits permitting a small number of people to sue on behalf of all other similarly situated people.

closed primaries. Elections to select party nominees in which only people who have registered in advance with the party can vote for that party's candidates, thus encouraging greater party loyalty. See also **primaries.**

coalition. A group of individuals with a common interest upon which every political party depends. See also **New Deal Coalition.**

coalition government. When two or more parties join together to form a majority in a national legislature. This form of government is quite common in the multiparty systems of Europe.

cold war. War by other than military means usually emphasizing ideological conflict, such as that between the United States and the Soviet Union from the end of World War II until the 1990s.

collective good. Something of value (money, a tax write-off, prestige, clean air, and so on) that cannot be withheld from a group member.

command-and-control policy. According to Charles Schultze, the existing system of **regulation** whereby government tells business how to reach certain goals, checks that these commands are followed, and punishes offenders. Compare **incentive system.**

commercial speech. Communication in the form of advertising. It can be restricted more than many other types of speech but has been receiving increased protection from the Supreme Court.

committee chairs. The most important influencers of the congressional agenda. They play dominant roles in scheduling hearings, hiring staff, appointing subcommittees, and managing committee bills when they are brought before the full house.

common law. The accumulation of judicial decisions applied in **civil law** disputes.

comparable worth. The issue raised when women who held traditionally female jobs were paid less than men for working at jobs requiring comparable skill.

conference committees. Congressional committees formed when the Senate and the House pass a particular **bill** in different forms. Party leadership appoints members from each house to iron out the differences and bring back a single bill. See also **standing committees, joint committees,** and **select committees.**

Congressional Budget Office (CBO). A counterweight to the president's **Office of Management and Budget (OMB).** The CBO advises Congress on the likely consequences of budget decisions and forecasts revenues.

Connecticut Compromise. The compromise reached at the Constitutional Convention that established two houses of Congress: the House of Representatives, in which **representation** is based on a state's share of the U.S. population, and the Senate, in which each state has two representatives. Compare **New Jersey Plan** and **Virginia Plan.**

consent of the governed. According to John Locke, the required basis for government. **The Declaration of Independence** reflects Locke's view that governments derive their authority from the consent of the governed.

conservatism. A **political ideology** whose advocates fear the growth of government, deplore government's drag on private-sector initiatives, dislike permissiveness in society, and place a priority on military needs over social needs. Compare **liberalism.**

conservatives. Those who advocate **conservatism.** Compare **liberals.**

constitution. A nation's basic law. It creates political institutions, assigns or divides powers in government, and often provides certain guarantees to citizens. Constitutions can be either written or unwritten. See also **U. S. Constitution.**

containment doctrine. A **foreign policy** strategy advocated by George Kennan that called for the United States to isolate the Soviet Union, "contain" its advances, and resist its encroachments by peaceful means if possible, but by force if necessary.

conversion. One of three key consequences of electoral campaigns for voters, in which the voter's mind is actually changed. See also **reinforcement** and **activation.**

cooperative federalism. A system of government in which powers and policy assignments are shared between states and the national government. They may also share costs, administration, and even blame for programs that work poorly. Compare **dual federalism.**

Council of Economic Advisers (CEA). A three-member body appointed by the president to advise the president on economic policy.

courts of appeal. Appellate courts empowered to review all final decisions of district courts, except in rare cases. In addition, they also hear appeals to orders of many federal regulatory agencies. Compare **district courts.**

Craig v. Boren. In this 1976 Supreme Court decision, the Court determined that gender classification cases would have a "heightened" or "middle level" of scrutiny. In other words, the courts were to show less deference to gender classifications than to more routine classifications, but more deference than to racial classifications.

criminal law. The body of law involving a case in which an individual is charged with violating a specific law. The offense may be harmful to an individual or society and in either case warrants punishment, such as imprisonment or a fine. Compare **civil law.**

crisis. A sudden, unpredictable, and potentially dangerous event requiring the president to play the role of crisis manager.

critical election. An electoral "earthquake" whereby new issues emerge, new coalitions replace old ones, and the majority party is often displaced by the minority party. Critical election periods are sometimes marked by a national crisis and may require more than one election to bring about a new **party era.** See also **party realignment.**

cruel and unusual punishment. Court sentences prohibited by the **Eighth Amendment.** Although the Supreme Court has ruled that mandatory death sentences for certain offenses are unconstitutional, it has not held that the death penalty itself constitutes cruel and unusual punishment.

culture of poverty. Negative attitudes and values toward work, family, and success that condemn the poor to low levels of accomplishment. The view that there is a culture of poverty is most commonly held by **conservatives.**

D

Declaration of Independence. The document approved by representatives of the American colonies in 1776 that stated their grievances against the British monarch and declared their independence.

deficit. An excess of federal **expenditures** over federal **revenues.** See also **budget.**

democracy. A system of selecting policymakers and of organizing government so that policy represents and responds to the public's preferences.

demography. The science of population changes. See also **census.**

deregulation. The lifting of restrictions on business, industry, and other professional activities for which government rules had been established and that bureaucracies had been created to administer.

détente. A slow transformation from conflict thinking to cooperative thinking in **foreign policy** strategy and policymaking. It sought a relaxation of tensions between the superpowers, coupled with firm guarantees of mutual security.

district courts. The 91 federal courts of original jurisdiction. They are the only federal courts in which no trials are held and in which juries may be empaneled. Compare **courts of appeal.**

dual federalism. A system of government in which both the states and the national government remain supreme within their own spheres, each responsible for some policies. Compare **cooperative federalism.**

due process clause. Part of the **Fourteenth Amendment** guaranteeing that persons cannot be deprived of life, liberty, or property by the United States or state governments without due process of law. See also ***Gitlow v. New York.***

E

Eighth Amendment. The constitutional amendment that forbids **cruel and unusual punishment,** although it does not define this phrase. Through the **Fourteenth Amendment,** this **Bill of Rights** provision applies to the states.

elastic clause. The final paragraph of Article I, Section 8, of the Constitution, which authorizes Congress to pass all laws "necessary and proper" to carry out the enumerated powers. See also **implied powers.**

electioneering. Direct group involvement in the electoral process. Groups can help fund campaigns, provide testimony, and get members to work for candidates, and some form **political action committees (PACs).**

electoral college. A unique American institution created by the Constitution that provides for the selection of the president by electors chosen by the state parties. Although the electoral college vote usually reflects a popular majority, the winner-take-all rule gives clout to big states.

elite and class theory. A theory of government and politics contending that societies are divided along class lines and that an upper-class elite will rule, regardless of the formal niceties of governmental organization. Compare **hyperpluralism, pluralist theory,** and **traditional democratic theory.**

Engel v. Vitale. The 1962 Supreme Court decision holding that state officials violated the **First Amendment** when they wrote a prayer to be recited by New York's schoolchildren. Compare ***School District of Abington Township, Pennsylvania v. Schempp.***

entitlements. Policies for which expenditures are uncontrollable because Congress has in effect obligated itself to pay X level of benefits to Y number of recipients. Each year, Congress's bill is a straightforward function of the X level of benefits times the Y number of beneficiaries. Social Security benefits are an example.

enumerated powers. Powers of the federal government that are specifically addressed in the Constitution; for Congress, these powers are listed in Article I, Section 8, and include the power to coin money, regulate its value, and impose taxes. Compare **implied powers.**

equal protection of the laws. Part of the **Fourteenth Amendment** emphasizing that the laws must provide equivalent "protection" to all people. As one member of Congress said during debate on the amendment, it should provide "equal protection of life, liberty, and property" to all citizens.

Equal Rights Amendment. A constitutional amendment passed by Congress in 1972 and sent to the state legislatures for ratification, stating that "equality of rights under the law shall not be denied or abridged by the United States or by any state on account of sex. " Despite substantial public support and an extended deadline, the amendment failed to acquire the necessary support from three-fourths of the state legislatures.

establishment clause. Part of the **First Amendment** stating that "Congress shall make no law respecting an establishment of religion."

European Union (EU). An economic alliance of the major Western European nations, often called the Common Market. The EU coordinates monetary, trade, immigration, and labor policies.

exclusionary rule. The rule that evidence, no matter how incriminating, cannot be introduced into a trial if it was not constitutionally obtained. The rule prohibits use of evidence obtained through **unreasonable search and seizure.**

executive orders. Regulations originating from the executive branch. Executive orders are one method presidents can use to control the bureaucracy; more often, though, presidents pass along their wishes through their aides.

exit poll. Public opinion surveys used by major media pollsters to predict electoral winners with speed and precision.

expenditures. Federal spending of **revenues.** Major areas of such spending are social services and the military.

extradition. A legal process whereby an alleged criminal offender is surrendered by the officials of one state to officials of the state in which the crime is alleged to have been committed.

F

factions. Interest groups arising from the unequal distribution of property or wealth that James Madison attacked in ***Federalist Paper #10***. Today's parties or interest groups are what Madison had in mind when he warned of the instability in government caused by factions.

federal debt. All the money borrowed by the federal government over the years and still outstanding. Today the federal debt is more than $8 trillion.

Federal Election Campaign Act. A law passed in 1974 for reforming campaign finances. The act created the **Federal Election Commission (FEC),** provided public financing for presidential primaries and general elections, limited presidential campaign spending, required disclosure, and attempted to limit contributions.

Federal Election Commission (FEC). A six-member bipartisan agency created by the **Federal Election Campaign Act** of 1974. The FEC administers the campaign finance laws and enforces compliance with their requirements.

federalism. A way of organizing a nation so that two levels of government have formal authority over the same land and people. It is a system of shared power between units of government. Compare **unitary government.**

Federalist Papers. A collection of 85 articles written by Alexander Hamilton, John Jay, and James Madison under the name "Publius" to defend the Constitution in detail. Collectively, these papers are second only to the **U.S. Constitution** in characterizing the framers' intents.

Federalists. Supporters of the **U.S. Constitution** at the time the states were contemplating its adoption. See also **Anti-Federalists** and **Federalist Papers.**

Fifteenth Amendment. The constitutional amendment adopted in 1870 to extend **suffrage** to African Americans.

Fifth Amendment. The constitutional amendment designed to protect the rights of persons accused of crimes, including protection against double jeopardy, **self-incrimination,** and punishment without due process of law.

filibuster. A strategy unique to the Senate whereby opponents of a piece of legislation try to talk it to death, based on the tradition of unlimited debate. Today, 60 members present and voting can halt a filibuster.

First Amendment. The constitutional amendment that establishes the four great liberties: freedom of the press, of speech, of religion, and of assembly.

fiscal federalism. The pattern of spending, taxing, and providing grants between government units in a federal system.

foreign policy. A policy that, like domestic policy, involves choice making, but additionally involves choices about relations with the rest of the world. The president is the chief initiator of foreign policy in the United States.

formula grants. Federal **categorical grants** distributed according to a formula specified in legislation or in administrative regulations.

Fourteenth Amendment. The constitutional amendment adopted after the Civil War that states, "No State shall make or enforce any law which shall abridge the privileges or immunities of citizens of the United States; nor shall any state deprive any person of life, liberty, or property, without due process of law; nor deny to any person within its jurisdiction the **equal protection of the laws.**" See also **due process clause.**

free exercise clause. A **First Amendment** provision that prohibits government from interfering with the practice of religion.

free-rider problem. The problem faced by unions and other groups when people do not join because they can benefit from the group's activities without officially joining. The bigger the group, the more serious the free-rider problem. See also **interest group.**

frontloading. The process by which the majority of states have moved their primary dates up to the begining of the primary season over the last several elections.

full faith and credit clause. A clause in Article IV, Section 1, of the Constitution requiring each state to recognize the official documents and civil judgments rendered by the courts of other states.

G

gender gap. A term that refers to the regular pattern by which women are more likely to support Democratic candidates. Women tend to be significantly less conservative than men and are more likely to support spending on social services and to oppose the higher levels of military spending.

General Schedule rating. See **GS (General Schedule) rating.**

Gibbons v. Ogden. A landmark case decided in 1824 in which the Supreme Court interpreted very broadly the clause in Article I, Section 8, of the Constitution giving Congress the power to regulate interstate commerce, encompassing virtually every form of commercial activity. The commerce clause has been the constitutional basis for much of Congress' regulation of the economy.

Gideon v. Wainwright. The 1963 Supreme Court decision holding that anyone accused of a felony where imprisonment may be imposed, however poor he or she might be, has a right to a lawyer. See also **Sixth Amendment.**

Gitlow v. New York. The 1925 Supreme Court decision holding that freedoms of press and speech are "fundamental personal rights and liberties protected by the **due process clause** of the **Fourteenth Amendment** from impairment by the states" as well as the federal government. Compare ***Barron v. Baltimore.***

government. The institutions and processes through which **public policies** are made for a society.

government corporation. A government organization that, like business corporations, provides a service that could be provided by the private sector and typically charges for its services. The U.S. Postal Service is an example. Compare **independent regulatory agency** and **independent executive agency.**

Gregg. v. Georgia. The 1976 Supreme Court decision that upheld the constitutionality of the death penalty, stating, "It is an extreme sanction, suitable to the most extreme of crimes." The court did not, therefore, believe that the death sentence constitutes **cruel and unusual punishment.**

gross domestic product. The sum total of the value of all the goods and services produced in a nation.

GS (General Schedule) rating. A schedule for federal employees, ranging from GS 1 to GS 18, by which salaries can be keyed to rating and experience. See **civil service.**

H

Hatch Act. A federal law prohibiting government employees from active participation in partisan politics.

high-tech politics. A politics in which the behavior of citizens and policymakers and the political agenda itself are increasingly shaped by technology.

House Rules Committee. An institution unique to the House of Representatives that reviews all bills (except revenue, budget, and appropriations bills) coming from a House committee before they go to the full House.

hyperpluralism. A theory of government and politics contending that groups are so strong that government is weakened. Hyperpluralism is an extreme, exaggerated, or perverted form of pluralism. Compare **elite and class theory, pluralist theory,** and **traditional democratic theory.**

I

Impeachment. The political equivalent of an indictment in criminal law, prescribed by the Constitution. The House of Representatives may impeach the president by a majority vote for "Treason, Bribery, or other high Crimes and Misdemeanors."

implementation. The stage of policymaking between the establishment of a policy and the consequences of the policy for the people whom it affects. Implementation involves translating the goals and objectives of a policy into an operating, ongoing program. See also **judicial implementation.**

implied powers. Powers of the federal government that go beyond those enumerated in the Constitution. The Constitution states that Congress has the power to "make all laws necessary and proper for carrying into execution" the powers enumerated in Article I. Many federal policies are justified on the basis of implied powers. See also ***McCulloch v. Maryland*, elastic clause,** and **enumerated powers.**

incentive system. According to Charles Shultze, a more effective and efficient policy than **command-and-control;** in the incentive system, market-like strategies are used to manage public policy.

income. The amount of funds collected between any two points in time. Compare **wealth.**

income distribution. The "shares" of the national income earned by various groups.

income tax. Shares of individual wages and corporate revenues collected by the government. The first income tax was declared unconstitutional by the Supreme Court in 1895, but the **Sixteenth Amendment** explicitly authorized Congress to levy a tax on income. See also **Internal Revenue Service.**

incorporation doctrine. The legal concept under which the Supreme Court has nationalized the **Bill of Rights** by making most of its provisions applicable to the states through the **Fourteenth Amendment.**

incrementalism. The belief that the best predictor of this year's **budget** is last year's budget, plus a little bit more (an increment). According to Aaron Wildavsky, "Most of the budget is a product of previous decisions."

incumbents. Those already holding office. In congressional elections, incumbents usually win.

independent executive agency. The government not accounted for by **cabinet** departments, **independent regulatory agencies,** and **government corporations.** Its administrators are typically appointed by the president and serve at the president's pleasure. NASA is an example.

independent regulatory agency. A government agency responsible for some sector of the economy, making and enforcing rules supposedly to protect the public interest. It also judges disputes over these rules. Compare **government corporation** and **independent executive agency.**

interdependency. Mutual dependency, in which the actions of nations reverberate and affect one another's economic lifelines.

interest group. An organization of people with shared policy goals entering the policy process at several points to try to achieve those goals. Interest groups pursue their goals in many arenas.

intergovernmental relations. The workings of the federal system—the entire set of interactions among national, state, and local governments.

Internal Revenue Service (IRS). The office established to collect federal **income taxes,** investigate violations of the tax laws, and prosecute tax criminals.

investigative journalism. The use of in-depth reporting to unearth scandals, scams, and schemes which at times puts reporters in adversarial relationships with political leaders.

iron triangles. Entities composed of bureaucratic agencies, interest groups, and congressional committees or subcommittees, which have dominated some areas of domestic policymaking. Iron triangles are characterized by mutual dependency, in which each element provides key services, information, or policy for the others.

isolationism. A **foreign policy** course followed throughout most of our nation's history, whereby the United States has tried to stay out of other nations' conflicts, particularly European wars. Isolationism was reaffirmed by the Monroe Doctrine.

J

Joint Chiefs of Staff. The commanding officers of the armed services who advise the president on military policy.

joint committees. Congressional committees on a few subject-matter areas with membership drawn from both houses. See also **standing committees, conference committees,** and **select committees.**

judicial activism. A judicial philosophy in which judges make bold policy decisions, even charting new constitutional ground. Advocates of this approach emphasize that the courts can correct pressing needs, especially those unmet by the majoritarian political process.

judicial implementation. How and whether court decisions are translated into actual policy, affecting the behavior of others. The courts rely on other units of government to enforce their decisions.

judicial interpretation. A major informal way in which the Constitution is changed by the courts as they balance citizens' rights against those of the government. See also **judicial review.**

judicial restraint. A judicial philosophy in which judges play minimal policymaking roles, leaving that strictly to the legislatures. Compare **judicial activism.**

judicial review. The power of the courts to determine whether acts of Congress and, by implication, the executive are in accord with the **U. S. Constitution.** Judicial review was established by John Marshall and his associates in ***Marbury v. Madison***. See also **judicial interpretation.**

justiciable disputes. A constraint on the courts, requiring that a case must be capable of being settled by legal methods.

K

Korematsu v. United States. A 1944 Supreme Court decision that upheld as constitutional the internment of more than 100,000 Americans of Japanese descent in encampments during World War II.

L

leak. See **news leak.**

legislative oversight. Congress's monitoring of the bureaucracy and its administration of policy, performed mainly through hearings.

legislative veto. The ability of Congress to override a presidential decision. Although the **War Powers Resolution** asserts this authority, there is reason to believe that, if challenged, the Supreme Court would find the legislative veto in violation of the doctrine of separation of powers.

Lemon v. Kurtzman. The 1971 Supreme Court decision that established that aid to church-related schools must (1) have a secular legislative purpose, (2) have a primary effect that neither advances nor inhibits religion, and (3) not foster excessive government entanglement with religion.

libel. The publication of false or malicious statements that damage someone's reputation.

liberalism. A **political ideology** whose advocates prefer a government active in dealing with human needs, support individual rights and liberties, and give higher priority to social needs than to military needs.

liberals. Those who advocate **liberalism.** Compare **conservatives.**

limited government. The idea that certain things are out of bounds for government because of the **natural rights** of citizens. Limited government was central to John Locke's philosophy in the seventeenth century, and it contrasted sharply with the prevailing view of the divine rights of monarchs.

linkage institutions. The channels or access points through which issues and people's policy preferences get on the government's **policy agenda.** In the United States, **elections, political parties,** and **interest groups** are the three main linkage institutions.

lobbying. According to Lester Milbrath, a "communication, by someone other than a citizen acting on his own behalf, directed to a governmental decisionmaker with the hope of influencing his decision."

M

majority leader. The principal partisan ally of the Speaker of the House or the party's wheelhorse in the Senate. The majority leader is responsible for scheduling bills, influencing committee assignments, and rounding up votes in behalf of the party's legislative positions.

majority rule. A fundamental principle of **traditional democratic theory.** In a democracy, choosing among alternatives requires that the majority's desire be respected. See also **minority rights.**

mandate theory of elections. The idea that the winning candidate has a mandate from the people to carry out his or her platforms and politics. Politicians like the theory better than political scientists do.

Mapp v. Ohio. The 1961 Supreme Court decision ruling that the Fourth Amendment's protection against **unreasonable searches and seizures** must be extended to the states as well as the federal government. See also **exclusionary rule.**

Marbury v. Madison. The 1803 case in which Chief Justice John Marshall and his associates first asserted the right of the **Supreme Court** to determine the meaning of the **U.S. Constitution.** The decision established the Court's power of **judicial review** over acts of Congress, in this case the Judiciary Act of 1789.

mass media. Television, radio, newspapers, magazines, and other means of popular communication. They are a key part of **high-tech politics.** See also **broadcast media** and **print media.**

matching funds. Contributions of up to $250 for qualified presidential candidates in the primaries.

McCarthyism. The fear prevalent in the 1950s that international communism was conspiratorial, insidious, bent on world domination, and infiltrating American government and cultural institutions. It was named after Senator Joseph McCarthy and flourished after the Korean War.

McCleskey v. Kemp. The 1987 Supreme Court decision that upheld the constitutionality of the death penalty against the charges that it violated the **Fourteenth Amendment** because minority defendants were more likely to receive the death penalty than were White defendants.

McCulloch v. Maryland. An 1819 Supreme Court decision that established the supremacy of the national government over state governments. In deciding this case, Chief Justice John Marshall and his colleagues held that congress had certain **implied powers** in addition to the **enumerated powers** found in the Constitution.

McGovern-Fraser Commission. A commission formed at the 1968 Democratic convention in response to demands for reform by minority groups and others who sought better representation.

media event. Events purposely staged for the media that nonetheless look spontaneous. In keeping with politics as theater, media events can be staged by individuals, groups, and government officials, especially presidents.

Medicaid. A public assistance program designed to provide health care for poor Americans. Medicaid is funded by both the states and the national government. Compare **Medicare.**

Medicare. A program added to the Social Security system in 1965 that provides hospitalization insurance for the elderly and permits older Americans to purchase inexpensive coverage for doctor fees and other expenses. Compare **Medicaid.**

melting pot. The mixing of cultures, ideas, and peoples that has changed the American nation. The United States, with its history of immigration, has often been called a melting pot.

merit principle. The idea that hiring should be based on entrance exams and promotion ratings to produce administration by people with talent and skill. See also **civil service** and compare **patronage.**

Miami Herald Publishing Company v. Tornillo. A 1974 case in which the Supreme Court held that a state could not force a newspaper to print replies from candidates it had criticized, illustrating the limited power of government to restrict the **print media**.

Miller v. California. A 1973 Supreme Court decision that avoided defining obscenity by holding that community standards be used to determine whether material is obscene in terms of appealing to a "prurient interest."

minority leader. The principal leader of the minority party in the House of Representatives or in the Senate.

minority majority. The emergence of a non-Caucasian majority, as compared with a White, generally Anglo-Saxon majority. It is predicted that, by about 2060, Hispanic Americans, African Americans, and Asian Americans together will outnumber White Americans.

minority rights. A principle of **traditional democratic theory** that guarantees rights to those who do not belong to majorities and allows that they might join majorities through persuasion and reasoned argument. See also **majority rule.**

Miranda v. Arizona. The 1966 Supreme Court decision that sets guidelines for police questioning of accused persons to protect them against **self-incrimination** and to protect their right to counsel.

Motor Voter Act. Passed in 1993, this Act requires states to permit people to register to vote at the same time they apply for driver's licences.

N

NAACP v. Alabama. The Supreme Court protected the right to assemble peaceably in this 1958 case when it decided the NAACP did not have to reveal its membership list and thus subject its members to harassment.

narrowcasting. As opposed to the traditional "broadcasting," the appeal to a narrow, particular audience by channels such as ESPN, MTV, and C-SPAN, which focus on a narrow particular interest.

national chairperson. One of the institutions that keeps the party operating between conventions. The national chairperson is responsible for the day-to-day activities of the party and is usually hand selected by the presidential nominee. See also **national committee.**

national committee. One of the institutions that keeps the party operating between conventions. The national committee is composed of representatives from the states and territories. See also **national chairperson.**

national convention. The meeting of party delegates every four years to choose a presidential ticket and write the party's platform.

national party convention. The supreme power within each of the parties. The convention meets every four years to nominate the party's presidential and vice-presidential candidates and to write the party's platform.

national primary. A proposal by critics of the **caucuses** and **presidential primaries** systems who would replace these electoral methods with a nationwide **primary** held early in the election year.

National Security Council. An office created in 1947 to coordinate the president's foreign and military policy advisers. Its formal members are the president, vice president, **secretary of state,** and **secretary of defense,** and it is managed by the president's national security assistant.

natural rights. Rights inherent in human beings, not dependent on governments, which include life, liberty, and property. The concept of natural rights was central to English philosopher John Locke's theories about government, and was widely accepted among America's Founding Fathers. Thomas Jefferson echoed Locke's language in drafting the **Declaration of Independence.**

Near v. Minnesota. The 1931 Supreme Court decision holding that the **First Amendment** protects newspapers from **prior restraint.**

New Deal Coalition. A **coalition** forged by Franklin Roosevelt and the Democrats, who dominated American politics from the 1930s to the 1960s. Its basic elements were the urban working class, ethnic groups, Catholics and Jews, the poor, Southerners, African Americans, and Democratic intellectuals.

New Jersey Plan. The proposal at the Constitutional Convention that called for equal **representation** of each state in Congress regardless of the state's population. Compare **Virginia Plan** and **Connecticut Compromise.**

New York Times v. Sullivan. Decided in 1964, this case established the guidelines for determining whether public officials and public figures could win damage suits for libel. To do so, said the Court, such individuals must prove that the defamatory statements made about them were made with "actual malice" and reckless disregard for the truth.

news leak. A carefully placed bit of inside information given to a friendly reporter. Leaks can benefit both the leaker and the leakee.

Nineteenth Amendment. The constitutional amendment adopted in 1920 that guarantees women the right to vote. See also **suffrage.**

nomination. The official endorsement of a candidate for office by a **political party.** Generally, success in the nomination game requires momentum, money, and media attention.

North Atlantic Treaty Organization (NATO). Created in 1949, an organization whose members include the United States, Canada, most Western European nations, and Turkey, all of whom agreed to combine military forces and to treat a war against one as a war against all. Compare **Warsaw Pact.**

O

Office of Management and Budget (OMB). An office that grew out of the Bureau of the Budget, created in 1921, consisting of a handful of political appointees and hundreds of skilled professionals. The OMB performs both managerial and budgetary functions, and although the president is its boss, the director and staff have considerable independence in the budgetary process. See also **Congressional Budget Office.**

Office of Personnel Management (OPM). The office in charge of hiring for most agencies of the federal government, which uses elaborate rules in the process.

Olson's law of large groups. Advanced by Mancur Olson, a principle stating that "the larger the group, the further it will fall short of providing an optimal amount of a collective good." See also **interest group.**

open primaries. Elections to select party nominees in which voters can decide on Election Day whether they want to participate in the Democratic or Republican contests. See also **primaries.**

opinion. A statement of legal reasoning behind a judicial decision. The content of an opinion may be as important as the decision itself.

Organization of Petroleum Exporting Countries (OPEC). An economic organization, consisting primarily of Arab nations, that controls the price of oil and the amount of oil its members produce and sell to other nations. The Arab members of OPEC caused the oil boycott in the winter of 1973–1974.

original intent. A view that the Constitution should be interpreted according to the original intent of the framers. Many conservatives support this view.

original jurisdiction. The jurisdiction of courts that hear a case first, usually in a trial. These are the courts that determine the facts about a case. Compare **appellate jurisdiction.**

oversight. The process of monitoring the bureaucracy and its administration of policy, mainly through congressional hearings.

P

PACs. See **political action committees (PACs).**

party competition. The battle of the parties for control of public offices. Ups and downs of the two major parties are one of the most important elements in American politics.

party dealignment. The gradual disengagement of people and politicians from the parties, as seen in part by shrinking **party identification.**

party eras. Historical periods in which a majority of voters cling to the party in power, which tends to win a majority of the elections. See also **critical election** and **party realignment.**

party identification. A citizen's self-proclaimed preference for one party or the other.

party image. The voter's perception of what the Republicans or Democrats stand for, such as **conservatism** or **liberalism.**

party machines. A type of political party organization that relies heavily on material inducements, such as patronage, to win votes and to govern.

party neutrality. A term used to describe the fact that many Americans are indifferent toward the two major political parties. See also **party dealignment.**

party realignment. The displacement of the majority party by the minority party, usually during a **critical election period.** See also **party era.**

patronage. One of the key inducements used by **party machines.** A patronage job, promotion, or contract is one that is given for political reasons rather than for merit or competence alone. Compare **civil service** and the **merit principle.**

Pendleton Civil Service Act. Passed in 1883, an Act that created a federal **civil service** so that hiring and promotion would be based on merit rather than **patronage.**

Planned Parenthood v. Casey. A 1992 case in which the Supreme Court loosened its standard for evaluating restrictions on abortion from one of "struct scrutiny" of any restraints on a "fundamental right" to one of "undue burden" that permits considerably more regulation.

plea bargaining. A bargain struck between the defendant's lawyer and the prosecutor to the effect that the defendant will plead guilty to a lesser crime in exchange for the state's promise not to prosecute the defendant for the more serious one.

Plessy v. Ferguson. An 1896 Supreme Court decision that provided a constitutional justification for segregation by ruling that a Louisiana law requiring "equal but separate accommodations for the white and colored races" was not unconstitutional.

pluralist theory. A theory of government and politics emphasizing that politics is mainly a competition among groups, each one pressing for its own preferred policies. Compare **elite and class theory, hyperpluralism,** and **traditional democratic theory.**

pocket veto. A veto taking place when Congress adjourns within 10 days of having submitted a **bill** to the president, who simply lets it die by neither signing nor vetoing it. See also **veto.**

policy agenda. According to John Kingdon, "the list of subjects or problems to which government officials, and people outside of government closely associated with those officials, are paying some serious attention at any given time."

policy differences. The perception of a clear choice between the parties. Those who see such choices are more likely to vote.

policy entrepreneurs. People who invest their political "capital" in an issue. According to John Kingdon, a policy entrepreneur "could be in or out of government, in elected or appointed positions, in interest groups or research organizations."

policy gridlock. A condition that occurs when no coalition is strong enough to form a majority and establish policy. The result is that nothing may get done.

policy impacts. The effects a policy has on people and problems. Impacts are analyzed to see how well a policy has met its goal and at what cost.

policy implementation. See **implementation.**

policy voting. Voting that occurs when electoral choices are made on the basis of the voters' policy preferences and on the basis of where the candidates stand on policy issues.

policymaking institutions. The branches of government charged with taking action on political issues. The U.S. Constitution established three policymaking institutions—the Congress, the presidency, and the courts. Today, the power of the bureaucracy is so great that most political scientists consider it a fourth policymaking institution.

policymaking system. The process by which political problems are communicated by the voters and acted upon by government policymakers. The policymaking system begins with people's needs and expectations for governmental action. When people confront government officials with problems that they want solved, they are trying to influence the government's policy agenda.

political action committees (PACs). Funding vehicles created by the 1974 campaign finance reforms. A corporation, union, or some other interest group can create a PAC and register it with the **Federal Election Commission (FEC),** which will meticulously monitor the PAC's expenditures.

political efficacy. The belief that one's **political participation** really matters—that one's vote can actually make a difference.

political ideology. A coherent set of beliefs about politics, public policy, and public purpose. It helps give meaning to political events, personalities, and policies. See also **liberalism** and **conservatism**.

political issue. An issue that arises when people disagree about a problem and a public policy choice.

political participation. All the activities used by citizens to influence the selection of political leaders or the policies they pursue. The most common, but not the only, means of political participation in a **democracy** is voting. Other means include **protest** and **civil disobedience.**

political party. According to Anthony Downs, a "team of men [and women] seeking to control the governing apparatus by gaining office in a duly constituted election."

political questions. A doctrine developed by the federal courts and used as a means to avoid deciding some cases, principally those involving conflicts between the president and Congress.

political socialization. According to Richard Dawson, "the process through which an individual acquires his [or her] particular political orientations—his [or her] knowledge, feelings, and evaluations regarding his [or her] political world. " See also **agents of socialization.**

political system. A set of institutions and activities that link together people, politics, and policy.

politics. The process by which we select our governmental leaders and what policies these leaders pursue. Politics produces authoritative decisions about public issues.

poll taxes. Small taxes levied on the right to vote that often fell due at a time of the year when poor African American sharecroppers had the least cash on hand. This method was used by most Southern states to exclude African Americans from voting. Poll taxes were declared void by the **Twenty-fourth Amendment** in 1964.

pork barrel. The mighty list of federal projects, grants, and contracts available to cities, businesses, colleges, and institutions in the district of a member of Congress.

potential group. All the people who might be **interest group** members because they share some common interest. A potential group is almost always larger than an actual group.

poverty line. A method used to count the number of poor people; it considers what a family would need to spend for an "austere" standard of living.

precedent. How a similar court case has been decided in the past.

presidential coattails. The situation occurring when voters cast their ballots for congressional candidates of the president's party because they support the president. Recent studies show that few races are won this way.

presidential debate. A debate between presidential candidates. The first televised debate was between Richard Nixon and John Kennedy during the 1960 campaign.

Presidential Election Campaign Fund. Funded by the $3 check-off on IRS tax forms, this fund provides a source of money for **matching funds** in the primaries and complete financing of Democratic and Republican presidential nominees in the general election.

presidential primaries. Elections in which voters in a state vote for a candidate (or delegates pledged to him or her). Most delegates to the **national party conventions** are chosen this way.

press conferences. Meetings of public officials with reporters.

print media. Newspapers and magazines, as compared with **broadcast media.**

prior restraint. A government's preventing material from being published. This is a common method of limiting the press in some nations, but it is unconstitutional in the United States, according to the **First Amendment** and as confirmed in the 1931 Supreme Court case of ***Near v. Minnesota***.

Privacy Act. A law passed in 1974 stipulating that information collected by one agency of the government cannot be used by another. For example, a driving record cannot be used to deny Social Security benefits.

privileges and immunities. A clause in Article IV, Section 2, of the Constitution according citizens of each state most of the privileges of citizens of other states.

probable cause. The situation occurring when the police have reason to believe that a person should be arrested. In making the arrest, the police are allowed legally to search for and seize incriminating evidence. Compare **unreasonable searches and seizures.**

progressive tax. A tax by which the government takes a greater share of the **income** of the rich than of the poor—for example, when a rich family pays 50 percent of its income in taxes and a poor family pays 5 percent. Compare **regressive tax** and **proportional tax.**

project grants. Federal grants given for specific purposes and awarded on the basis of the merits of applications. A type of the **categorical grants** available to states and localities.

proportional representation. An electoral system used throughout most of Europe that awards legislative seats to political parties in proportion to the number of votes won in an election. Compare with **winner-take-all system.**

proportional tax. A tax by which the government takes the same share of income from everyone, rich and poor alike—for example, when a rich family pays 20 percent and a poor family pays 20 percent. Compare **progressive tax** and **regressive tax.**

protest. A form of **political participation** designed to achieve policy change through dramatic and unconventional tactics. See also **civil disobedience.**

public goods. Goods, such as clean air and clean water, that everyone must share.

public interest. The idea that there are some interests superior to the private interest of groups and individuals, interests we all have in common. See also **public interest lobbies.**

public interest lobbies. According to Jeffrey Berry, organizations that seek "a collective good, the achievement of which will not selectively and materially benefit the membership or activities of the organization." See also **lobbying** and **public interest.**

public opinion. The distribution of the population's beliefs about politics and policy issues.

public policy. A choice that **government** makes in response to a political issue. A policy is a course of action taken with regard to some problem.

R

random-digit dialing. A technique used by pollsters to place telephone calls randomly to both listed and unlisted numbers when conducting a survey. See also **random sampling.**

random sampling. The key technique employed by sophisticated survey researchers, which operates on the principle that everyone should have an equal probability of being selected for the sample. See also **sample.**

rational-choice theory. A popular theory in political science to explain the actions of voters as well as politicians. It assumes that individuals act in their own best interest, carefully weighing the costs and benefits of possible alternatives.

reapportionment. The process of reallocating seats in the House of Representatives every 10 years on the basis of the results of the census.

Red Lion Broadcasting Company v. Federal Communications Commission. A 1969 case in which the Supreme Court upheld restrictions on radio and television broadcasting. These restrictions on the **broadcast media** are much tighter than those on the **print media** because there are only a limited number of broadcast frequencies available.

Reed v. Reed. The landmark case in 1971 in which the Supreme Court upheld a claim of gender discrimination for the first time.

Regents of the University of California v. Bakke. A 1978 Supreme Court decision holding that a state university could not admit less qualified individuals solely because of their race. The Court did not, however, rule that such **affirmative action** policies and the use of race as a criterion for admission were unconstitutional, only that they had to be formulated differently.

regional primaries. A proposal by critics of the **caucuses** and **presidential primaries** to replace these electoral methods with regional primaries held early in the election year.

regressive tax. A tax in which the burden falls relatively more heavily on low-income groups than upon wealthy taxpayers. The opposite of a **progressive tax,** in which tax rates increase as income increases.

regulation. The use of governmental authority to control or change some practice in the private sector. Regulations pervade the daily lives of people and institutions.

reinforcement. One of three key consequences of electoral campaigns for voters, in which the voter's candidate preference is reinforced. See also **activation** and **conversion.**

relative deprivation. A perception by a group that it is doing less well than is appropriate in relation to a reference group. The desire of a group to correct what it views as the unfair distribution of resources, such as income or government benefits, is a frequent motivator for political activism.

representation. A basic principle of **traditional democratic theory** that describes the relationship between the few leaders and the many followers.

republic. A form of government that derives its power, directly or indirectly, from the people. Those chosen to govern are accountable to those whom they govern. In contrast to a direct democracy, in which people themselves make laws, in a republic the people select representatives who make the laws.

responsible party model. A view favored by some political scientists about how parties should work. According to the model, parties should offer clear choices to the voters, who can then use those choices as cues to their own preferences of candidates. Once in office, parties would carry out their campaign promises.

revenues. The financial resources of the federal government. The individual income tax and Social Security tax are two major sources of revenue. Compare **expenditures.**

right to privacy. The right to a private personal life free from the intrusions of government. The right to privacy is implicitly protected by the **Bill of Rights.**

right-to-work law. A state law forbidding requirements that workers must join a union to hold their jobs. State right-to-work laws were specifically permitted by the Taft-Hartley Act of 1947.

Roe v. Wade. The 1973 Supreme Court decision holding that a state ban on all abortions was unconstitutional. The decision forbade state control over abortions during the first trimester of pregnancy, permitted states to limit abortions to protect the mother's health in the second trimester, and permitted states to protect the fetus during the third trimester.

Roth v. United States. A 1957 Supreme Court decision ruling that "obscenity is not within the area of constitutionally protected speech or press."

S

sample. A relatively small proportion of people who are chosen as participants in a survey intended to be representative of the whole.

sampling error. The level of confidence in the findings of a public opinion poll. The more people interviewed, the more confident one can be of the results.

School District of Abington Township, Pennsylvania v. Schempp. A 1963 Supreme Court decision holding that a Pennsylvania law requiring Bible reading in schools violated the **establishment clause** of the **First Amendment.** Compare ***Engel v. Vitale***.

Scott v. Sandford. The 1857 Supreme Court decision ruling that a slave who had escaped to a free state enjoyed no rights as a citizen and that Congress had no authority to ban slavery in the territories.

search warrant. A written authorization from a court specifying the area to be searched and what the police are searching for.

secretary of defense. The head of the Department of Defense and the president's key adviser on military policy; a key **foreign policy** actor.

secretary of state. The head of the Department of State and traditionally a key adviser to the president on **foreign policy.**

select committees. Congressional committees appointed for a specific purpose, such as the Watergate investigation. See also **joint committees, standing committees,** and **conference committees.**

selective benefits. Goods (such as information publications, travel discounts, and group insurance rates) that a group can restrict to those who pay their yearly dues.

selective perception. The phenomenon that people often pay the most attention to things they already agree with and interpret them according to their own predispositions.

self-incrimination. The situation occurring when an individual accused of a crime is compelled to be a witness against himself or herself in court. **The Fifth Amendment** forbids self-incrimination. See also ***Miranda v. Arizona***.

senatorial courtesy. An unwritten tradition whereby nominations for state-level federal judicial posts are not confirmed if they are opposed by the senator from the state in which the nominee will serve. The tradition also applies to courts of appeal when there is opposition from the nominee's state senator, if the senator belongs to the president's party.

Senior Executive Service (SES). An elite cadre of about 11,000 federal government managers, established by the Civil Service Reform Act of 1978, who are mostly career officials but include some political appointees who do not require Senate confirmation.

seniority system. A simple rule for picking **committee chairs,** in effect until the 1970s. The member who had served on the committee the longest and whose party controlled Congress became chair, regardless of party loyalty, mental state, or competence.

separation of powers. An important part of the **Madisonian model** that requires each of the three branches of government—executive, legislative, and judicial—to be relatively independent of the others so that one cannot control the others. Power is shared among these three institutions. See also **checks and balances.**

Shays' Rebellion. A series of attacks on courthouses by a small band of farmers led by revolutionary war Captain Daniel Shays to block foreclosure proceedings.

Simpson-Mazzolli Act. An immigration law, named after its legislative sponsors, that as of June 1, 1987, requires employees to document the citizenship of their employees. Civil and criminal penalties can be assessed against employers who knowingly employ illegal immigrants.

single-issue groups. Groups that have a narrow interest, tend to dislike compromise, and often draw membership from people new to politics. These features distinguish them from traditional **interest groups.**

Sixteenth Amendment. The constitutional amendment adopted in 1913 that explicitly permitted Congress to levy an **income tax.**

Sixth Amendment. The constitutional amendment designed to protect individuals accused of crimes. It includes the right to counsel, the right to confront witnesses, and the right to a speedy and public trial.

Social Security Act. A 1935 law passed during the Great Depression that was intended to provide a minimal level of sustenance to older Americans and thus save them from poverty.

social welfare policies. Policies that provide benefits to individuals, particularly to those in need. Compare **civil rights policies.**

soft money. Political contributions earmarked for party-building expenses at the grass-roots level (buttons, pamphlets, yard signs, etc.). Unlike money that goes to the campaign of a particular candidate, such party donations are not subject to contribution limits.

solicitor general. A presidential appointee and the third-ranking office in the Department of Justice. The solicitor general is in charge of the appellate court litigation of the federal government.

sound bites. Short video clips of approximately 15 seconds, which are typically all that is shown from a politician's speech or activities on the nightly television news.

Speaker of the House. An office mandated by the Constitution. The Speaker is chosen in practice by the majority party, has both formal and informal powers, and is second in line to succeed to the presidency should that office become vacant.

standard operating procedures. Better known as SOPs, these procedures are used by bureaucrats to bring uniformity to complex organizations. Uniformity improves fairness and makes personnel interchangeable. See also **administrative discretion.**

standing committees. Separate subject-matter committees in each house of Congress that handle **bills** in different policy areas. See also **joint committees, conference committees,** and **select committees.**

standing to sue. The requirement that **plaintiffs** have a serious interest in a **case,** which depends on whether they have sustained or are likely to sustain a direct and substantial injury from a party or an action of government.

stare decisis. A Latin phrase meaning "let the decision stand." Most cases reaching appellate courts are settled on this principle.

statutory construction. The judicial interpretation of an act of Congress. In some cases where statutory construction is an issue, Congress passes new legislation to clarify existing laws.

Strategic Defense Initiative (SDI). Renamed "Star Wars" by critics; a plan for defense against the Soviet Union unveiled by President Reagan in 1983. SDI would create a global umbrella in space, using computers to scan the skies and high-tech devices to destroy invading missiles.

street-level bureaucrats. A phrase coined by Michael Lipsky, referring to those bureaucrats who are in constant contact with the public and have considerable **administrative discretion.**

subgovernments. A network of groups within the American political system which exercise a great deal of control over specific policy areas. Also know as iron triangles, subgovernments are composed of interest group leaders interested in a particular policy, the government agency in charge of administrating the policy, and the members of congressional committees and subcommittees handling that policy.

suffrage. The legal right to vote, extended to African Americans by the **Fifteenth Amendment,** to women by the **Nineteenth Amendment,** and to people over the age of 18 by the **Twenty-sixth Amendment.**

Super Tuesday. Created by a dozen or so Southern states when they held their **presidential primaries** in early March 1988. These states hoped to promote a regional advantage as well as a more conservative candidate.

superdelegates. National party leaders who automatically get a delegate slot at the Democratic **national party convention.**

supremacy clause. Article VI of the Constitution, which makes the Constitution, national laws, and treaties supreme over state laws when the national government is acting within its constitutional limits.

Supreme Court. The pinnacle of the American judicial system. The Court ensures uniformity in interpreting national laws, resolves conflicts among states, and maintains national supremacy in law. It has both **original jurisdiction** and **appellate jurisdiction,** but unlike other federal courts, it controls its own agenda.

symbolic speech. Nonverbal communication, such as burning a flag or wearing an armband. The Supreme Court has accorded some symbolic speech protection under the **First Amendment.** See ***Texas v. Johnson***.

T

talking head. A shot of a person's face talking directly to the camera. Because this is visually unappealing, the major commercial networks rarely show a politician talking one-on-one for very long. See also **sound bites.**

tariff. A special tax added to imported goods to raise the price, thereby protecting American businesses and workers from foreign competition.

tax expenditures. Defined by the 1974 Budget Act as "revenue losses attributable to provisions of the federal tax laws which allow a special exemption, exclusion, or deduction." Tax expenditures represent the difference between what the government actually collects in taxes and what it would have collected without special exemptions.

Tenth Amendment. The constitutional amendment stating that "The powers not delegated to the United States by the Constitution, nor prohibited by it to the states, are reserved to the states respectively, or to the people."

Texas v. Johnson. A 1989 case in which the Supreme Court struck down a law banning the burning of the American flag on the grounds that such action was **symbolic speech** protected by the **First Amendment.**

third parties. Electoral contenders other than the two major parties. American third parties are not unusual, but they rarely win elections.

Thirteenth Amendment. The constitutional amendment ratified after the Civil War that forbade slavery and involuntary servitude.

ticket-splitting. Voting with one party for one office and with another party for other offices. It has become the norm in American voting behavior.

traditional democratic theory. A theory about how a democratic government makes its decisions. According to Robert Dahl, its cornerstones are equality in voting, effective participation, enlightened understanding, final control over the agenda, and inclusion.

transfer payments. Benefits given by the government directly to individuals. Transfer payments may be either cash transfers, such as Social Security payments and retirement payments to former government employees, or in-kind transfers, such as food stamps and low-interest loans for college education.

trial balloons. An intentional **news leak** for the purpose of assessing the political reaction.

Twenty-fifth Amendment. Passed in 1967, the amendment that permits the vice president to become acting president if both the vice president and the president's cabinet determine that the president is disabled. The amendment also outlines how a recuperated president can reclaim the job.

Twenty-fourth Amendment. The constitutional amendment passed in 1964 that declared the poll tax void in federal elections.

Twenty-second Amendment. Passed in 1951, the amendment that limits presidents to two terms of office.

U

uncontrollable expenditures. Expenditures that are determined not by a fixed amount of money appropriated by Congress but by how many eligible beneficiaries there are for some particular program or by previous obligations of the government. Three-fourths of the federal **budget** is uncontrollable. Congress can change uncontrollable expenditures only by changing a law or existing benefit levels.

union shop. A provision found in some collective bargaining agreements requiring all employees of a business to join the union within a short period, usually 30 days, and to remain members as a condition of employment.

unitary government. A way of organizing a nation so that all power resides in the central government. Most national governments today, including those of Great Britain and Japan, are unitary governments. Compare **federalism.**

United Nations (UN). Created in 1945, an organization whose members agree to renounce war and to respect certain human and economic freedoms. The seat of real power in the UN is the Security Council.

unreasonable searches and seizures. Obtaining evidence in a haphazard or random manner, a practice prohibited by the Fourth Amendment. Both **probable cause** and a **search warrant** are required for a legal and proper search for and seizure of incriminating evidence.

unwritten constitution. The body of tradition, practice, and procedure that is as important as the written **constitution.** Changes in the unwritten constitution can change the spirit of the Constitution. **Political parties** and **national party** conventions are a part of the unwritten constitution in the United States.

urban underclass. The poorest of the poor in America. These are the Americans whose economic opportunities are severely limited in almost every way. They constitute a large percentage of the Americans afflicted by homelessness, crime, drugs, alcoholism, unwanted pregnancies, and other endemic social problems.

U.S. Constitution. The document written in 1787 and ratified in 1788 that sets forth the institutional structure of U.S. government and the tasks these institutions perform. It replaced the Articles of Confederation. See also **constitution** and **unwritten constitution.**

V

veto. The constitutional power of the president to send a bill back to Congress with reasons for rejecting it. A two-thirds vote in each house can override a veto. See also **legislative veto** and **pocket veto.**

Virginia Plan. The proposal at the Constitutional Convention that called for *representation* of each state in Congress in proportion to that state's share of the U. S. population. Compare **Connecticut Compromise** and **New Jersey Plan.**

voter registration. A system adopted by the states that requires voters to register well in advance of Election Day. Although a few states permit Election Day registration for presidential elections, advance registration dampens voter turnout.

Voting Rights Act of 1965. A law designed to help end formal and informal barriers to African American **suffrage.** Under the law, federal registrars were sent to Southern states and counties that had long histories of discrimination; as a result, hundreds of thousands of African Americans were registered and the number of African American elected officials increased dramatically.

W

War Powers Resolution. A law, passed in 1973 in reaction to American fighting in Vietnam and Cambodia, requiring presidents to consult with Congress whenever possible prior to using military force and to withdraw forces after 60 days unless Congress declares war or grants an extension. Presidents view the resolution as unconstitutional. See also **legislative veto.**

Watergate. The events and scandal surrounding a break-in at the Democratic National Committee headquarters in 1972 and the subsequent cover-up of White House involvement, leading to the eventual resignation of President Nixon under the threat of **impeachment.**

wealth. The amount of funds already owned. Wealth includes stocks, bonds, bank deposits, cars, houses, and so forth. Throughout most of the last generation, wealth has been much less evenly divided than **income.**

whips. Party leaders who work with the **majority leader** or **minority leader** to count votes beforehand and lean on waverers whose votes are crucial to a **bill** favored by the party.

White primary. One of the means used to discourage African-American voting that permitted political parties in the heavily Democratic South to exclude African Americans from primary elections, thus depriving them of a voice in the real contests. The Supreme Court declared White primaries unconstitutional in 1944.

winner-take-all system. An electoral system in which legislative seats are awarded only to the candidates who come in first in their constituencies. In American presidential elections, the system in which the winner of the popular vote in a state receives all the electoral votes of that state. Compare with **proportional representation.**

writ of habeas corpus. A court order requiring jailers to explain to a judge why they are holding a prisoner in custody.

Notes

Chapter 1

1. "The Soul of a Senator," *Time*, August 10, 1998.
2. Ganesh Sitaraman and Previn Warren, *Invisible Citizens: Youth Politics After September 11* (New York: iUniverse, Inc., 2003), ix.
3. Because the level of difficulty of the questions differed somewhat, one should only examine the differences within a year and not necessarily infer that political knowledge as a whole has decreased.
4. Stephan Earl Bennett and Eric W. Rademacher, "The Age of Indifference Revisited: Patterns of Political Interest, Media Exposure, and Knowledge among Generation X," in Stephan C. Craig and Stephan Earl Bennett, eds., *After the Boom: The Politics of Generation X* (Lanham, Md. Rowman & Littlefield, 1997), 39.
5. Michael X. Delli Carpini and Scott Keeter, *What Americans Know About Politics and Why It Matters* (New Haven, Conn.: Yale University Press, 1996), chap. 6.
6. Samuel Kernell, *Going Public: New Strategies of Presidential Leadership*, 3rd ed. (Washington, D.C.: Congressional Quarterly Press, 1997), 132.
7. Anthony Corrado, "Elections in Cyberspace: Prospects and Problems," in Anthony Corrado and Charles M. Firestone, eds., *Elections in Cyberspace: Toward a New Era in American Politics* (Washington D.C.: Aspen Institute, 1996), 29.
8. Harold D. Lasswell, *Politics: Who Gets What, When, and How* (New York: McGraw-Hill, 1938).
9. Randy Shilts, *And the Band Played On: Politics, People and the AIDS Epidemic* (New York: Penguin Books, 1987).
10. Robert A. Dahl, *Dilemmas of Pluralist Democracy* (New Haven, Conn.: Yale University Press, 1982), 6.
11. Robert A. Dahl, *A Preface to Democratic Theory* (Chicago: University of Chicago Press, 1956), 137.
12. Jacob S. Hacker and Paul Pierson, *Off Center: The Republican Revolution and the Erosion of American Democracy* (New Haven, Conn.: Yale University Press, 2005), 16.
13. American Political Science Association Task Force on Inequality and American Democracy, "American Democracy in an Age of Rising Inequality" (Washington, D.C.: American Political Science Association, 2004), 2. The entire report can be found at *www.apsanet.org/imgtest/taskforcereport.pdf*.
14. Ronald Inglehart and Christian Welzel, *Modernization, Cultural Change, and Democracy: The Human Development Sequence* (New York: Cambridge University Press, 2005), 2.
15. G. K. Chesterton, *What I Saw in America* (New York: Dodd, Mead & Co., 1922), 7.
16. Seymour Martin Lipset, *American Exceptionalism: A Double-Edged Sword* (New York: Norton, 1996), 31.
17. Ibid., 19.
18. Louis Hartz, *The Liberal Tradition in America* (New York: Harcourt, Brace, 1955).
19. Frederick Jackson Turner, *The Significance of the Frontier in American History* (New York: Readex Microprint, 1966), 221.
20. John W. Kingdon, *America the Unusual* (New York: St. Martin's/Worth, 1999), 2.
21. Seymour Martin Lipset, *The First New Nation* (New York: Norton, 1979), 68.
22. James Q. Wilson, "How Divided Are We?" *Commentary*, February 2006, 15.
23. Ibid., 21.
24. Morris P. Fiorina, *Culture War? The Myth of a Polarized America*, 2nd ed. (New York: Longman, 2006), 165.
25. Wayne Baker, *America's Crisis of Values: Reality and Perception* (Princeton, N.J.: Princeton University Press, 2005).
26. Dick Armey, *The Freedom Revolution* (Washington, D.C.: Regnery, 1995), 316.

Chapter 2

1. Gordon S. Wood, *The Radicalism of the American Revolution* (New York: Vintage, 1993), 4.
2. Clinton Rossiter, *1787: The Grand Convention* (New York: Macmillan, 1996), 60.
3. On the Lockean influence on the Declaration of Independence, see Carl L. Becker, *The Declaration of Independence: A Study in the History of Political Ideas* (New York: Random House, 1942).
4. Seymour Martin Lipset, *The First New Nation* (New York: Basic Books, 1963).
5. Gordon S. Wood, *The Creation of the American Republic, 1776–1787* (Chapel Hill: University of North Carolina Press, 1969), 3.
6. On the Articles of Confederation, see Merrill Jensen, *The Articles of Confederation* (Madison: University of Wisconsin Press, 1940).
7. Wood, *The Radicalism of the American Revolution*, 6–7.
8. "Federalist #10," in Alexander Hamilton, James Madison, and John Jay, *The Federalist Papers*, 2nd ed., ed. Roy P. Fairfield (Baltimore: Johns Hopkins University Press, 1981), 18.
9. Clavin C. Jillson and Cecil L. Eubanks, "The Political Structure of Constitution-Making: The Federal Convention of 1787," *American Journal of Political Science* 28 (August 1984): 435–58. See also Clavin C. Jillson, *Constitution Making: Conflict and Consensus in the Federal Convention of 1787* (New York: Agathon, 1988).
10. See Arthur Lovejoy, *Reflections on Human Nature* (Baltimore: Johns Hopkins University Press, 1961), 57–63.
11. "Federalist #10," *The Federalist Papers*.
12. This representation may have practical consequences. See Frances E. Lee, "Representation and Public Policy: The Consequences of Senate Appointment for the Geographic Distribution of Federal Funds," *Journal of Politics* 60 (February 1998): 34–62, and Daniel Wirls, "The Consequences of Equal Representation—The Bicameral Politics of NAFTA in the 103rd Congress," *Congress and the Presidency* 25 (autumn 1998): 129–45.
13. Cecelia M. Kenyon, ed., *The Antifederalists* (Indianapolis: Bobbs-Merrill, 1996), xxxv.
14. Rossiter, *1787*.
15. See Charles A. Beard, *An Economic Interpretation of the Constitution of the*

United States (New York: Macmillian, 1913); Robert W. Brown, *Charles Beard and the Constitution* (Princeton, NJ: Princeton University Press, 1956); Forrest B. McDonald, *We the People: The Economic Origins of the Constitution* (Chicago: University of Chicago Press, 1958); and Forrest B. McDonald, *Novus Ordo Seclorum: The Intellectual Origins of the Constitution* (Lawrence: University Press of Kansas, 1986).

16. A brilliant exposition of the Madisonian model is found in Robert A. Dahl, *A Preface to Democratic Theory* (Chicago: University of Chicago Press, 1956).
17. "Federalist #10," in Fairfield, *The Federalist Papers.*
18. "Federalist #51," in Fairfield, *The Federalist Papers.*
19. Quoted in Beard, *An Economic Interpretation of the Constitution of the United States*, 299.
20. The quote is from Amos Singletary of Massachusetts. Kenyon, *The Antifederalists*, 1.
21. Jane J. Mansbridge, *Why We Lost the ERA* (Chicago: University of Chicago Press, 1986).
22. See "Federalist #78," in Fairfield, *The Federalist Papers.*

Chapter 3

1. Thomas Anton, *Moving Money* (New York: Oxford University Press, 1982).
2. One useful introduction to federalism and intergovernmental relations is Deil S. Wright, *Understanding Intergovernmental Relations*, 4th ed. (Belmont, CA: Wadsworth, 2003). Another is David B. Walker, *The Rebirth of Federalism*, 2nd ed. (Chatham, NJ: Chatham House Press, 2000).
3. For a study of how different states enforce federal child support enforcement, see Lael R. Keiser and Joe Soss, "With Good Cause: Bureaucratic Discretion and the Politics of Child Support Enforcement," *American Journal of Political Science* 42 (October 1998): 1133–56.
4. On the states as innovators, see Jack L. Walker, "The Diffusion of Innovations in the American States," *American Political Science Review* 63 (September 1969): 880–99; Virginia Gray, "Innovation in the States: A Diffusion Study," *American Political Science Review* 67 (December 1973): 1174–85; and Richard P. Nathan and Fred C. Doolittle, *Reagan and the States* (Princeton, NJ: Princeton University Press, 1987).
5. *Alden v. Maine* (1999). See also *College Savings Bank v. Florida Prepaid Postsecondary Education Expense Board* (1999) and *Florida Prepaid Postsecondary Education Expense Board v. College Savings Bank* (1999).
6. *Federal Maritime Commission v. South Carolina Ports Authority* (2002).
7. The Fourteenth Amendment was passed *after* the Eleventh Amendment.
8. *Monroe v. Pape* (1961); *Monell v. New York City Department of Social Welfare* (1978); *Owen v. Independence* (1980); *Maine v. Thiboutot* (1980); *Oklahoma City v. Tuttle*, (1985); *Dennis v. Higgins* (1991).
9. The transformation from dual to cooperative federalism is described in Walker, *The Rebirth of Federalism*, chap. 4.
10. The classic discussion of cooperative federalism is found in Morton Grodzins, *The American System: A New View of Governments in the United States*, ed. Daniel J. Elazar (Chicago: Rand McNally, 1966).
11. See Pew Research Center poll, September 25–October 31, 1997, and Craig Volden, "Intergovernmental Political Competition in American Federalism," *American Journal of Political Science* 49 (April 2005): 327–42.
12. Office of Management and Budget, *Budget of the United States Government, Fiscal Year 2007: Analytical Perspectives* (Washington, DC: U.S. Government Printing Office, 2006), table 8.3.
13. On intergovernmental lobbying, see Donald H. Haider, *When Governments Go to Washington* (New York: Free Press, 1974), and Anne Marie Commisa, *Governments as Interest Groups: Intergovernmental Lobbying and the Federal System* (Westport, CT: Praeger, 1995).
14. U.S. House of Representatives, Committee on Ways and Means, *2004 Green Book.*
15. U.S. Department of Commerce, *Statistical Abstract of the United States, 2006* (Washington, DC: U.S. Government Printing Office, 2006), 164.
16. Michael A. Bailey, "Welfare and the Multifaceted Decision to Move," *American Political Science Review* 99 (February 2005): 125–35; Michael A. Bailey and Mark Carl Rom, "A Wider Race? Interstate Competition Across Health and Welfare Programs," *Journal of Politics* 66 (May 2004): 326–47; Paul E. Peterson and Mark Romm, "American Federalism, Welfare Policy, and Residential Choices," *American Political Science Review* 83 (September 1989): 711–28; Craig Volden, "The Politics of Competitive Federalism: A Race to the Bottom in Welfare Benefits," *American Journal of Political Science* 46 (April 2002): 352–63. But see William D. Berry, Richard C. Fording, and Russell L. Hanson, "Reassessing the 'Race to the Bottom' in State Welfare Policy" *Journal of Politics* 65 (May 2003): 327–49. Some states limit welfare payments to new residents.
17. Office of Management and Budget, *Budget of the United States Government, Fiscal Year 2007: Historical Tables* (Washington, DC: U.S. Government Printing Office, 2006), table 15.3.

Chapter 4

1. James W. Prothro and Charles M. Grigg, "Fundamental Principles of Democracy: Bases of Agreement and Disagreement," *Journal of Politics* 22 (1960): 276–94; John L. Sullivan et al., "The Sources of Political Tolerance: A Multivariate Analysis," *American Political Science Review* 75 (1981): 100–115.
2. Darren W. Davis and Brian D. Silver, "Civil Liberties vs. Security: Public Opinion in the Context of the Terrorist Attacks on America," *American Journal of Political Science* 48 (January 2004): 28–46.
3. *Widmar v. Vincent* (1981).
4. *Westside Community Schools v. Mergens* (1990).
5. *Lamb's Chapel v. Center Moriches Union Free School* (1993).
6. *Good News Club v. Milford Central School* (2001).
7. *Rosenberger v. University of Virginia* (1995).
8. *Locke v. Davey* (2004).
9. *Illinois ex rel McCollum v. Board of Education* (1948).
10. *Zorach v. Clauson* (1952).
11. *Stone v. Graham* (1980).
12. *Lee v. Weisman* (1992).
13. *Santa Fe School District v. Doe* (2000).
14. *Wallace v. Jaffree* (1985).
15. Kenneth D. Wald, *Religion and Politics in the United States*, 4th ed. (Lanham, MD: Rowman & Littlefield, 2003).

16. *Edwards v. Aguillard* (1987).
17. *Epperson v. Arkansas* (1968).
18. *McCreary County v. American Civil Liberties Union of Kentucky* (2005).
19. *Van Orden v. Perry* (2005).
20. *Lynch v. Donelly* (1984).
21. *County of Allegheny v. American Civil Liberties Union* (1989).
22. *Bob Jones University v. United States* (1983).
23. *Wisconsin v. Yoder* (1972).
24. *Boerne v. Flores* (1997).
25. *Gonzales v. O Centro Espirita Beneficente Uniao do Vegetal* (2006).
26. *R.A.V. v. St. Paul* (1992). However, states may impose longer prison terms on people convicted of "hate crimes" (crimes motivated by racial, religious, or other prejudice) without violating their rights to free speech.
27. See Fred W. Friendly, *Minnesota Rag* (New York: Random House, 1981).
28. *Hazelwood School District v. Kuhlmeier* (1988).
29. *McIntyre v. Ohio Elections Commission* (1995).
30. *Hudgens v. National Labor Relations Board* (1976).
31. *Pruneyard Shopping Center v. Robins* (1980).
32. *City of Ladue v. Gilleo* (1994).
33. *Nebraska Press Association v. Stuart* (1972).
34. *Richmond Newspapers v. Virginia* (1980).
35. Bob Woodward and Scott Armstrong, *The Brethren* (New York: Avon, 1979), 233.
36. *Jenkins v. Georgia* (1974).
37. *Osborne v. Ohio* (1990).
38. *Reno v. ACLU* (1997).
39. *Ashcroft v. Free Speech Coalition* (2002).
40. *Schad v. Mount Ephraim* (1981).
41. *Barnes v. Glen Theater, Inc.* (1991); *Erie v. Pap's A.M.* (2000).
42. Catherine MacKinnon, *Feminism Unmodified* (Cambridge, MA: Harvard University Press, 1987), 198.
43. The story of this case is told in Anthony Lewis, *Make No Law: The Sullivan Case and the First Amendment* (New York: Random House, 1991).
44. Renata Adler, *Reckless Disregard* (New York: Knopf, 1986).
45. *Tinker v. Des Moines Independent School District* (1969).
46. After Congress passed the Flag Protection Act of 1989 outlawing desecration of the American flag, the Supreme Court also found the act an impermissible infringement on free speech in *United States v. Eichman* (1990).
47. *United States v. O'Brien* (1968).
48. *Virginia v. Black* (2003).
49. *Greater New Orleans Broadcasting, Inc. v. United States* (1999).
50. *Central Hudson Gas & Electric Corporation v. Public Service Commission of N.Y.* (1980).
51. *FCC v. Pacifica Foundation* (1978).
52. *Frisby v. Schultz* (1988).
53. *Rumsfeld v. Forum for Academic and Institutional Rights, Inc.* (2006).
54. *Brigham City v. Stuart* (2006).
55. *Michigan v. Sitz* (1990).
56. *Illinois v. Caballes* (2005).
57. *Indianapolis v. Edmond* (2000).
58. *Nix v. Williams* (1984).
59. *United States v. Leon* (1984).
60. *Arizona v. Evans* (1995). See also *United States v. Payner* (1980).
61. *Hudson v. Michigan* (2006).
62. *Knowles v. Iowa* (1998).
63. *City of Indianapolis v. Edmond* (2002).
64. *Florida v. J.L.* (2002).
65. *Kyllo v. U.S.* (2001).
66. On the *Miranda* case, see Liva Baker, *Miranda: The Crime, the Law, the Politics* (New York: Atheneum, 1983).
67. *Arizona v. Fulminante* (1991).
68. The story of Gideon is eloquently told by Anthony Lewis, *Gideon's Trumpet* (New York: Random House, 1964).
69. David Brereton and Jonathan D. Casper, "Does It Pay to Plead Guilty? Differential Sentencing and the Function of the Criminal Courts," *Law and Society Review* 16 (1981–1982): 45–70.
70. *Batson v. Kentucky* (1986); *Miller-El v. Dretke* (2005).
71. *Apprendi v. New Jersey* (2000); *Blakely v. Washington* (2004); *United States v. Booker* (2005).
72. Joe Soss, Laura Langbein, and Alan R. Metelko, "Why Do White Americans Support the Death Penalty?," *Journal of Politics* 65 (May 2003): 397–421.
73. Woodward and Armstrong, *The Brethren*, 271–84.
74. *Madsen v. Women's Health Center* (1994). In 1997, the Court also upheld a 15-foot buffer zone.
75. *Hill v. Colorado* (2000).
76. *National Organization for Women v. Scheidler* (1994).
77. Although, as Chapter 16 on the judiciary will show, there is indirect accountability.

Chapter 5

1. Bland is quoted in Sidney Verba and Gary R. Orren, *Equality in America: The View from the Top* (Cambridge, MA: Harvard University Press, 1985), 25. The Adamses quotes are from Judith A. Baer, *Equality Under the Constitution: Reclaiming the Fourteenth Amendment* (Ithaca, NY: Cornell University Press, 1983), 44–47.
2. For opposing interpretations of the Fourteenth Amendment, see Baer, *Equality Under the Constitution*, and Raoul Berger, *Government by Judiciary: The Transformation of the Fourteenth Amendment* (Cambridge, MA: Harvard University Press, 1977).
3. Desmond King, *Separate but Unequal: Black Americans and the US Federal Government* (Oxford: Oxford University Press, 1995).
4. D. Garth Taylor, Paul B. Sheatsley, and Andrew M. Greeley, "Attitudes Toward Racial Integration," *Scientific American* 238 (June 1978): 42–49; Richard G. Niemi, John Mueller, and John W. Smith, *Trends in Public Opinion* (Westport, CT: Greenwood Press, 1989), 180.
5. There are a few exceptions. Religious institutions such as schools may use religious standards in employment. Gender, age, and disabilities may be considered in the few cases where such occupational qualifications are absolutely essential to the normal operations of a business or enterprise, as in the case of a men's restroom attendant.
6. On the implementation of the Voting Rights Act, see Richard Scher and James Button, "Voting Rights Act: Implementation and Impact," in *Implementation of Civil Rights Policy*, eds. Charles Bullock III and Charles Lamb (Monterey, CA: Brooks/Cole, 1984); Abigail M. Thernstrom, *Whose Votes Count?* (Cambridge, MA: Harvard University Press, 1987); and Chandler Davidson and Bernard Groffman, eds., *Quiet Revolution in the South: The Impact of the Voting Rights Act, 1965–1990* (Princeton, NJ: Princeton University Press, 1994).

7. U.S. Department of Commerce, *Statistical Abstract of the United States, 2006* (Washington, DC: U.S. Government Printing Office, 2006), 262. See David Lublin, *The Paradox of Representation: Racial Gerrymandering and Minority Interests in Congress* (Princeton, NJ: Princeton University Press, 1997), on how racial redistricting helped increase the number of minority representatives in Congress.
8. *League of United Latin American Citizens v. Perry* (2006).
9. See Dee Brown, *Bury My Heart at Wounded Knee: An Indian History of the American West* (New York: Holt, Rinehart and Winston, 1970).
10. U.S. Department of Commerce, *Statistical Abstract of the United States, 2006*, 262.
11. *White v. Register* (1973).
12. See Eleanor Flexner, *Century of Struggle* (New York: Atheneum, 1971).
13. See J. Stanley Lemons, *The Woman Citizen: Social Feminism in the 1920s* (Urbana: University of Illinois Press, 1973).
14. *Kirchberg v. Feenstra* (1981).
15. *Arizona Governing Committee for Tax Deferred Annuity and Deferred Compensation Plans v. Norris* (1983).
16. *Michael M. v. Superior Court* (1981).
17. *Kahn v. Shevin* (1974).
18. U.S. Department of Commerce, *Statistical Abstract of the United States, 2006*, 51, 387–89, 392–93.
19. *Cleveland Board of Education v. LaFleur* (1974).
20. *United Automobile Workers v. Johnson Controls* (1991).
21. *Roberts v. United States Jaycees* (1984); *Board of Directors of Rotary International v. Rotary Club of Duarte* (1987); *New York State Club Association v. New York* (1988).
22. *United States v. Virginia et al.* (1996).
23. U.S. Department of Commerce, *Statistical Abstract of the United States, 2006*, 428.
24. *Meritor Savings Bank v. Vinson* (1986).
25. *Burlington Northern & Santa Fe Railway Co. v. White* (2006).
26. *Massachusetts Board of Retirement v. Murgia* (1976).
27. *Smith v. City of Jackson* (2005).
28. *Bregdon v. Abbott* (1998).
29. *Sutton v. United Air Lines* (1999); *Albertsons v. Kirkingburg* (1999); and *Murphy v. United Parcel Service* (1999).
30. *Boy Scouts of America v. Dale* (2000).
31. Kenneth D. Wald, James W. Button, and Barbara A. Rienzo, "The Politics of Gay Rights in American Communities: Explaining Antidiscrimination Ordinances and Policies," *American Journal of Political Science* 40 (November 1996): 1152–78, examines why some communities adopt antidiscrimination ordinances and policies that include sexual orientation and others do not.
32. On the affirmative action issues raised by *Bakke* and other cases, see Allan P. Sindler, *Bakke, De Funis and Minority Admissions* (New York: Longman, 1978).
33. *Richmond v. J.A. Croson Co.* (1989).
34. *Fullilove v. Klutznick* (1980).
35. *Metro Broadcasting, Inc. v. Federal Communications Commission* (1990).
36. *Local Number 93 v. Cleveland* (1986); *United States v. Paradise* (1987).
37. *Local 28 of the Sheet Metal Workers v. EEOC* (1986).
38. *Firefighters v. Stotts* (1984).
39. *Wygant v. Jackson Board of Education* (1986).
40. Harry Holzer and David Newmark, "Assessing Affirmative Action," *Journal of Economic Literature* 38 (September 2000): 483–568.
41. See Barbara S. Gamble, "Putting Civil Rights to a Popular Vote," *American Journal of Political Science* 41 (January 1997): 245–69.

Chapter 6

1. John F. Kennedy, *A Nation of Immigrants* (New York: Harper and Row, 1964).
2. See *Statistical Abstract of the United States, 1999* (Washington, DC: U.S. Government Printing Office, 2000), 298.
3. Harold W. Stanley and Richard G. Niemi, *Vital Statistics on American Politics, 2001–2002* (Washington, DC: Congressional Quarterly Press, 2001), 61–62.
4. On the details of the 1965 Immigration Act and its unintended consequences, see Steven M. Gillon, *That's Not What We Meant to Do: Reform and Its Unintended Consequences in Twentieth-Century America* (New York: Norton, 2000), chap. 4.
5. Ronald T. Takaki, *Strangers from a Different Shore* (Boston: Little, Brown, 1989), chap. 11.
6. Judith Blake, *Family Size and Achievement* (Berkeley: University of California Press, 1989).
7. Richard Dawson et al., *Political Socialization*, 2nd ed. (Boston: Little, Brown, 1977), 33.
8. See M. Kent Jennings and Richard G. Niemi, *The Political Character of Adolescence: The Influence of Families and Schools* (Princeton, NJ: Princeton University Press), chap. 2.
9. See M. Kent Jennings and Richard G. Niemi, *Generations and Politics: A Panel Study of Young Adults and Their Parents* (Princeton, NJ: Princeton University Press, 1981).
10. "The Age of Indifference" (report of the Times Mirror Center for the People and the Press, June 28, 1990).
11. The figure on the average age of the TV news audience can be found in "A Graying, Ailing Audience," *New York Times*, February 9, 2004, C6. The figure for a typical prime-time show is cited in Robert D. Putnam, *Bowling Alone: The Collapse and Revival of American Community* (New York: Simon and Schuster, 2000), p. 221.
12. Jean M. Converse, *Survey Research in the United States: Roots and Emergence, 1890–1960* (Berkeley: University of California Press, 1987), 116. Converse's work is the definitive study on the origins of public opinion sampling.
13. Herbert Asher, *Polling and the Public: What Every Citizen Should Know* (Washington, DC: Congressional Quarterly Press, 1988), 59.
14. Quoted in Norman M. Bradburn and Seymour Sudman, *Polls and Surveys: Understanding What They Tell Us* (San Francisco: Jossey-Bass, 1988), 39–40.
15. Lawrence R. Jacobs and Robert Y. Shapiro, *Politicians Don't Pander* (Chicago: University of Chicago Press, 2000), xiii.
16. For a good summary of the evidence, see Seymour Sudman, "Do Exit Polls Influence Voting Behavior?," *Public Opinion Quarterly* 50 (fall 1986): 331–39.
17. John Mueller, "The Iraq Syndrome," *Foreign Affairs*, November/December 2005, 44–54.
18. W. Lance Bennett, *Public Opinion and American Politics* (New York: Harcourt Brace Jovanovich, 1980), 44.
19. E. D. Hirsch Jr., *Cultural Literacy* (Boston: Houghton Mifflin, 1986).

20. Michael X. Delli Carpini and Scott Keeter, *What Americans Know About Politics and Why It Matters* (New Haven, CT: Yale University Press, 1996), chap. 3.
21. W. Russell Neuman, *The Paradox of Mass Politics: Knowledge and Opinion in the American Electorate* (Cambridge, MA: Harvard University Press, 1986).
22. See Ronald Inglehart, *Modernization and Postmodernization* (Princeton, NJ: Princeton University Press, 1997), 254–55. Inglehart also shows that the decline of class voting is a general trend throughout Western democracies.
23. See Seymour Martin Lipset and Earl Raab, *Jews and the New American Political Scene* (Cambridge, MA: Harvard University Press, 1995), chap. 6.
24. Angus Campbell et al., *The American Voter* (New York: Wiley, 1960), chap. 10.
25. Norman H. Nie, Sidney Verba, and John R. Petrocik, *The Changing American Voter* (Cambridge, MA: Harvard University Press, 1976), chap. 7.
26. See, for example, John L. Sullivan, James E. Pierson, and George E. Marcus, "Ideological Constraint in the Mass Public: A Methodological Critique and Some New Findings," *American Journal of Political Science* 22 (May 1978): 233–49, and Eric R. A. N. Smith, *The Unchanging American Voter* (Berkeley: University of California Press, 1989).
27. Morris P. Fiorina, *Culture War? The Myth of a Polarized America*, 2nd ed. (New York: Longman, 2006), 127.
28. Ibid., 8.
29. This definition is a close paraphrase of that in Sidney Verba and Norman H. Nie, *Participation in America* (New York: Harper & Row, 1972), 2.
30. Tom W. Smith and Lars Jarkko, "National Pride in Cross-National Perspective," April 2001, *www.issp.org/natpride.doc*.
31. See Verba and Nie, *Participation in America*; and Sidney Verba, Kay Lehman Schlozman, and Henry E. Brady, *Voice and Equality: Civic Volunteerism in American Politics* (Cambridge, MA: Harvard University Press, 1995).
32. See Russell J. Dalton, "Citizenship Norms and Political Participation in America: The Good News Is . . . The Bad News Is Wrong" (paper prepared for the conference on Citizenship, Involvement and Democracy at the Center for Democracy and the Third Sector, Georgetown University, December 2005).
33. This letter can be found in Juan Williams, *Eyes on the Prize: America's Civil Rights Years, 1954–1965* (New York: Viking, 1987), 187–89.
34. Verba and Nie, *Participation in America*, 125.
35. Because registration procedures in Louisiana are regulated by the provisions of the Voting Rights Act, registration forms ask people to state their race and the registrars must keep track of this information. Thus, Louisiana can accurately report how many people of each race are registered and voted, which they regularly do. The 2004 data can be found at *http://sos.louisiana.gov/stats/Post_Election_Statistics/Statewide/2004_1102_sta.txt*. As these numbers take into account only registered individuals and not everyone is registered, these numbers need to be adjusted for the percentage of each race that are actually registered. The best estimates regarding this can be found at *www.census.gov/population/www/socdemo/voting/cps2004.html*.
36. See Verba and Nie, *Participation in America*, chap. 10.
37. Campbell et al., *The American Voter*, 541.
38. Morris P. Fiorina, *Retrospective Voting in America Nation Elections* (New Haven, CT: Yale University Press, 1981), 5.

Chapter 7

1. See Darrell M. West, *Air Wars: Television Advertising in Election Campaigns, 1952–1992* (Washington, DC: Congressional Quarterly Press, 1993), 48.
2. Stephen Ansolabehere and Shanto Iyengar, *Going Negative* (New York: Free Press, 1995).
3. December 1, 1969, memo from Nixon to H. R. Haldeman in Bruce Oudes, ed., *From: The President—Richard Nixon's Secret Files* (New York: Harper & Row, 1988), 76–77.
4. Mark Hertsgaard, *On Bended Knee: The Press and the Reagan Presidency* (New York: Farrar, Straus & Giroux, 1988), 34.
5. Bob Woodward, *The Agenda: Inside the Clinton White House* (New York: Simon and Schuster, 1994), 313.
6. Quoted in David Brinkley, *Washington Goes to War* (New York: Knopf, 1988), 171.
7. Theodore H. White, *The Making of the President, 1972* (New York: Atheneum, 1973), 250.
8. Sam Donaldson, *Hold On, Mr. President!* (New York: Random House, 1987), 54.
9. Marvin Kalb, *One Scandalous Story: Clinton, Lewinsky, and Thirteen Days That Tarnished American Journalism* (New York: Free Press, 2001), 6.
10. Ibid., 20.
11. Ibid., 138.
12. See the classic report by Michael J. Robinson, "Public Affairs Television and the Growth of Political Malaise: The Case of 'The Selling of the Pentagon,'" *American Political Science Review* 70 (June 1976): 409–32. See also Joseph Cappella and Kathleen Hall Jamieson, *Spiral of Cynicism: The Press and the Public Good* (New York: Oxford University Press, 1997).
13. See, for example, Michael X. Delli Carpini and Scott Keeter, *What Americans Know About Politics and Why It Matters* (New Haven, CT: Yale University Press, 1996); and Ruy A. Teixeira, *The Disappearing American Voter* (Washington, DC: Brookings Institution, 1992).
14. Leonard Downie Jr. and Robert G. Kaiser, *The News About the News: American Journalism in Peril* (New York: Knopf, 2002), 65.
15. Russell Baker, *The Good Times* (New York: William Morrow, 1989), 326.
16. See Walter Cronkite, *A Reporter's Life* (New York: Knopf, 1996), 257–58.
17. Frank Rich, "The Weight of an Anchor," *New York Times*, May 19, 2002.
18. Michael K. Bohn, *Nerve Center: Inside the White House Situation Room* (Dulles, VA: Bassey's, 2003), 59.
19. Project for Excellence in Journalism, *The State of the News Media, 2004*, *www.stateofthenewsmedia.org/index.asp* (accessed August 27, 2004).
20. Thomas Rosenstiel, "The End of Network News," *Washington Post*, September 12, 2004.
21. Doris A. Graber, *Mass Media and American Politics*, 6th ed. (Washington, DC: Congressional Quarterly Press, 2002), 44.
22. Cited in Downey and Kaiser, *The News About the News*, 239.
23. Edward J. Epstein, *News from Nowhere: Television and the News* (New York: Random House, 1973).
24. Downie and Kaiser, *The News About the News*, 137.

25. Steven Ansolabehere, Roy Behr, and Shanto Iyengar, *The Media Game: American Politics in the Television Age* (New York: Macmillan, 1993), 53.
26. For example, see Leon V. Sigal, *Reporters and Officials: The Organization and Politics of News Reporting* (Lexington, MA: D.C. Heath, 1973), 122.
27. This letter can be found in Hedrick Smith, ed., *The Media and the Gulf War: The Press and Democracy in Wartime* (Washington, DC: Seven Locks Press, 1992), 378–80. Smith's book contains an excellent set of readings on media coverage of the war.
28. Jody Powell, "White House Flackery," in *Debating American Government*, 2nd ed., ed. Peter Well (Glenview, IL: Scott, Foresman, 1988), 180.
29. Dan Rather, quoted in Hoyt Purvis, ed., *The Presidency and the Press* (Austin, TX: Lyndon B. Johnson School of Public Affairs, 1976), 56.
30. Kathleen Hall Jamieson and Joseph N. Capella, "The Role of the Press in the Health Care Reform Debate of 1993–1994," in *The Politics of News, the News of Politics*, eds. Doris Graber, Denis McQuail, and Pippa Norris (Washington, DC: Congressional Quarterly Press, 1998), 118–19.
31. This point is well argued in Kathleen Hall Jamieson, *Eloquence in an Electronic Age* (New York: Oxford University Press, 1988).
32. Quoted in Austin Ranney, *Channels of Power* (New York: Basic Books, 1983), 116.
33. Walter Cronkite, *A Reporter's Life*, 376–77.
34. "Campaign 2000 Final: How TV News Covered the General Election Campaign," *Media Monitor* 14 (November/December 2000): 3–4.
35. Ibid.
36. Michael Waldman, *POTUS Speaks: Finding the Words That Defined the Clinton Presidency* (New York: Simon and Schuster, 2000), 267.
37. Project for Excellence in Journalism, *The First 100 Days: How Bush Versus Clinton Fared in the Press* (Washington, DC: Project for Excellence in Journalism, 2001).
38. William Schneider and I. A. Lewis, "Views on the News," *Public Opinion* 8 (August/September 1985): 6–11.
39. See David Weaver et al., "The American Journalist in the 21st Century: Key Findings," *www.knightfdn.org/publications/americanjournalist/aj_keyfindings.pdf*.
40. Bernard Goldberg, *Bias: A CBS Insider Exposes How the Media Distort the News* (Washington, DC: Regnery, 2002), 5.
41. Ibid., 119.
42. Ibid., 17.
43. Michael J. Robinson and Margaret Petrella, "Who Won the George Bush–Dan Rather Debate?," *Public Opinion* 10 (March/April 1988): 43.
44. Robinson, "Public Affairs Television," 428.
45. W. Lance Bennett, *News: The Politics of Illusion*, 2nd ed. (New York: Longman, 1988), 46.
46. See Paul F. Lazarsfeld et al., *The People's Choice* (New York: Columbia University Press, 1944).
47. Shanto Iyengar and Donald R. Kinder, *News That Matters* (Chicago: University of Chicago Press, 1987).
48. Ibid., 118–119.
49. Joanne M. Miller and Jon A. Krosnick, "News Media Impact on the Ingredients of Presidential Evaluations: Politically Knowledgeable Citizens Are Guided by a Trusted Source," *American Journal of Political Science* (April 2000): 301–15.
50. John W. Kingdon, *Agendas, Alternatives, and Public Policies* (Boston: Little, Brown, 1984), 3.
51. Ibid., 3.
52. See the interview with Richard Valeriani in Juan Williams, *Eyes on the Prize* (New York: Viking, 1987), 270–71.
53. For an interesting study of how hiring a public relations firm can help a nation's TV image, see Jarol B. Manheim and Robert B. Albitton, "Changing National Images: International Public Relations and Media Agenda Setting," *American Political Science Review* 78 (September 1984): 641–57.
54. Bernard Cohen, *The Press and Foreign Policy* (Princeton, NJ: Princeton University Press, 1963), 13.
55. Doris A. Graber, *Mass Media and American Politics*, 6th ed. (Washington, DC: Congressional Quarterly Press, 2002), 275.
56. Ronald W. Berkman and Laura W. Kitch, *Politics in the Media Age* (New York: McGraw-Hill, 1986), 311.
57. Ibid., 313.
58. Matthew Robert Kerbel, *Edited for Television: CNN, ABC, and the 1992 Presidential Campaign* (Boulder, CO: Westview, 1994), 196.

Chapter 8

1. E. E. Schattschneider, *Party Government* (New York: Farrar and Rinehart, 1942), 1.
2. Anthony Downs, *An Economic Theory of* Democracy (New York: Harper & Row, 1957).
3. Marjorie Randon Hershey and Paul Allen Beck, *Party Politics in America*, 10th ed. (New York: Longman, 2003), 9.
4. Kay Lawson, ed., *Political Parties and Linkage: A Comparative Perspective* (New Haven, CT: Yale University Press, 1980), 3.
5. The major exception to this rule is nominations for the one-house state legislature in Nebraska, which is officially nonpartisan. In addition, Bernard Sanders has represented Vermont in the House as an Independent since 1990, and in 1994 Angus King was elected governor of Maine as an Independent.
6. Downs, *An Economic Theory of Democracy*.
7. Morris P. Fiorina, *Congress: Keystone of the Washington Establishment*, 2nd ed. (New Haven, CT: Yale University Press, 1989), 101.
8. See Adam Cohen and Elizabeth Taylor, *American Pharaoh* (Boston: Little, Brown, 2000), 155– 63.
9. Kay Lawson, "California: The Uncertainties of Reform," in *Party Renewal in America*, ed. Gerald Pomper (New Brunswick, NJ: Praeger, 1980), chap. 8.
10. John F. Bibby, "State Party Organizations: Coping and Adapting to Candidate-Centered Politics and Nationalization," in *The Parties Respond*, 3rd ed., ed. L. Sandy Maisel (Boulder, CO: Westview, 1998), 34.
11. Comments of Roy Romer and Jim Nicholson at the Bulen Symposium on American Politics, December 1, 1998, as noted by Martin Wattenberg.
12. Gerald M. Pomper, *Elections in America* (New York: Longman, 1980), 161. Another study of presidential promises from Kennedy through Reagan also reaches the conclusion that campaign pledges are taken seriously. See Jeff Fishel, *Presidents and Promises* (Washington, DC: Congressional Quarterly Press, 1985).
13. The term is from V. O. Key. The standard source on critical elections is Walter Dean Burnham, *Critical Elections and the Mainsprings of American Politics* (New York: Norton, 1970).

14. On the origins of the American party system, see William N. Chambers, *Political Parties in a New Nation* (New York: Oxford University Press, 1963).
15. Quoted in James L. Sundquist, *Dynamics of the Party System*, rev. ed. (Washington, DC: Brookings Institution, 1983), 88. Sundquist's book is an excellent account of realignments in American party history.
16. Ibid., 1955.
17. On Boston, see Gerald H. Gamm, *The Making of New Deal Democrats: Voting Behavior and Realignment in Boston, 1920–1940* (Chicago: University of Chicago Press, 1989).
18. See Earl Black and Merle Black, *The Rise of Southern Republicans* (Cambridge, MA: Harvard University Press, 2002).
19. For a good collection of readings on the causes and consequences of divided party government, see Gary W. Cox and Samuel Kernell, eds., *The Politics of Divided Government* (Boulder, CO: Westview, 1991).
20. See Morris P. Fiorina, *Divided Government* (New York: Macmillan, 1992).
21. Steven J. Rosenstone, Roy L. Behr, and Edward H. Lazarus, *Third Parties in America* (Princeton, NJ: Princeton University Press, 1984).
22. The classic statement on responsible parties can be found in "Toward a More Responsible Two-Party System: A Report of the Committee on Political Parties, American Political Science Association," *American Political Science Review* 44 (1950): supplement, number 3, part 2.
23. David R. Mayhew, *Divided We Govern: Party Control, Lawmaking, and Investigations, 1946–1990* (New Haven, CT: Yale University Press, 1991), 199.
24. See Evron M. Kirkpatrick, "Toward a More Responsible Party System: Political Science, Policy Science, or Pseudo-Science?," *American Political Science Review* 65 (1971): 965–90.
25. Leon Epstein, *Political Parties in the American Mold* (Madison: University of Wisconsin Press, 1986), 346.

Chapter 9

1. Anthony King, *Running Scared* (New York: Free Press, 1997).
2. R. W. Apple Jr., "Foley Assesses Presidential Elections and Tells Why He Wouldn't Run," *New York Times*, November 4, 1988, A12.
3. Paul Taylor, "Is This Any Way to Pick a President?" *Washington Post National Weekly Edition*, April 13, 1987, 6.
4. See Hugh Winebrenner, *The Iowa Precinct Caucuses: The Making of a Media Event* (Ames: Iowa State University Press, 1987).
5. See Byron Shafer, *Quiet Revolution: The Struggle for the Democratic Party and the Shaping of Post-Reform Politics* (New York: Russell Sage Foundation, 1983).
6. Theodore White, *America in Search of Itself: The Making of the President 1956–1980* (New York: Harper & Row, 1982), 285.
7. This tradition extends back to 1916. The early primary date was chosen then to coincide with the already existing town meetings. Town meetings were held in February prior to the snow melting, which in the days of unpaved roads made traveling extremely difficult in the spring. In 1916 no one could have dreamed that by holding the state's primary so early they were creating a mass media extravaganza for New Hampshire.
8. Harold W. Stanley and Richard G. Niemi, *Vital Statistics on American Politics*, 6th ed. (Washington, DC: Congressional Quarterly Press, 1998), 173. The same research also showed that New Hampshire received just 3 percent of the TV coverage during the general election—a figure far more in line with its small population size.
9. Robert Farmer, quoted in Clifford W. Brown Jr., Lynda W. Powell, and Clyde Wilcox, *Serious Money: Fundraising and Contributing in Presidential Nomination Campaigns* (New York: Cambridge University Press, 1995), 1.
10. Frank Bruni, *Ambling into History: The Unlikely Odyssey of George W. Bush* (New York: Harper Collins, 2002), 5.
11. Larry M. Bartels, *Presidential Primaries and the Dynamics of Public Choice* (Princeton, NJ: Princeton University Press, 1988), 269.
12. "Participation Vote Study: Voting on the Run," *CQ Weekly*, January 3, 2004, 22.
13. See Martin P. Wattenberg, "When You Can't Beat Them, Join Them: Shaping the Presidential Nominating Process to the Television Age," *Polity* 21 (spring 1989): 587–97.
14. Ibid.
15. Steve Weissman and Ruth Hassan, "BCRA and the 527 Groups," in *The Election After Reform: Money, Politics and the Bipartisan Campaign Reform Act*, ed. Michael J. Malbin (Lanham, MD: Rowman & Littlefield, 2006), chap. 5.
16. Frank J. Sorauf, *Inside Campaign Finance: Myths and Realities* (New Haven, CT: Yale University Press, 1992), 229.
17. See, for example, Brooks Jackson, *Honest Graft: Big Money and the American Political Process* (New York: Knopf, 1988).
18. Quoted in Jeffrey Berry, *The Interest Group Society* (Boston: Little, Brown, 1984), 162.
19. Ibid., 162–63.
20. Archibald Cox and Fred Wertheimer, "The Choice Is Clear: It's People vs. the PACs," in *Debating American Government*, 2nd ed., ed. Peter Woll (Glenview, IL: Scott, Foresman, 1988), 125.
21. This is discussed in Jeffrey M. Berry, *The Interest Group Society*, 3rd ed. (New York: Longman, 1997), 172.
22. Frank J. Sorauf, *Money in American Elections* (Glenview, IL: Scott, Foresman, 1988), 312.
23. Gary C. Jacobson, "The Effects of Campaign Spending in Congressional Elections," *American Political Science Review* 72 (June 1978): 469. For an updated analysis of this argument, see Gary C. Jacobson, "The Effects of Campaign Spending in House Elections: New Evidence for Old Arguments," *American Journal of Political Science* 34 (May 1990): 334–62.
24. Herbert E. Alexander, *Financing Politics: Money, Elections, and Political Reform*, 4th ed. (Washington, DC: Congressional Quarterly Press, 1992), 96.
25. See Dennis J. McGrath and Dane Smith, *Professor Wellstone Goes to Washington: The Inside Story of a Grassroots U.S. Senate Campaign* (Minneapolis: University of Minnesota Press, 1995).
26. Dan Nimmo, *The Political Persuaders: The Techniques of Modern Campaigning* (Englewood Cliffs, NJ: Prentice Hall, 1970).
27. Jonathan S. Krason and Daniel E. Seltz, "Buying Time: Television Advertising in the 1998 Congressional Elections," *www.brennancenter.org/programs/cmag_temp/download.html.*
28. Thomas E. Patterson, *The Mass Media Election* (New York: Praeger, 1980). See

also Thomas E. Patterson, *Out of Order* (New York: Knopf, 1993).

29. David R. Runkel, ed., *Campaign for President: The Managers Look at '88* (Dover, MA: Auburn, 1989), 136.
30. Patterson, *The Mass Media Election*, 22–25.
31. Nimmo, *The Political Persuaders*, 5.
32. A summary of these survey results can be found at *www.census.gov/population/www/socdemo/voting.html*.
33. See Martin P. Wattenberg, "Should Election Day Be a Holiday?," *Atlantic Monthly*, October 1998, 42–46.
34. Anthony Downs, *An Economic Theory of Democracy* (New York: Harper & Row, 1957), chap. 14.
35. See *www.sos.state.ga.us/elections/race_gender_age.pdf*. (accessed April 3, 2004).
36. See George C. Edwards III, *At the Margins* (New Haven, CT: Yale University Press, 1989), chap. 8.
37. Richard G. Niemi and Herbert F. Weisberg, eds., *Controversies in Voting Behavior*, 2nd ed. (Washington, DC: Congressional Quarterly Press, 1984), 164–65.
38. See Martin P. Wattenberg, *The Decline of American Political Parties, 1952–1996* (Cambridge, MA: Harvard University Press, 1998).
39. Shawn W. Rosenberg with Patrick McCafferty, "Image and Voter Preference," *Public Opinion Quarterly* 51 (spring 1987): 44.
40. Arthur H. Miller, Martin P. Wattenberg, and Oksana Malanchuk, "Schematic Assessments of Presidential Candidates," *American Political Science Review* 80 (1986): 521–540.
41. Paul R. Abramson, John H. Aldrich, and David W. Rohde, *Change and Continuity in the 2000 Elections* (Washington, DC: Congressional Quarterly Press, 2002), chap. 6.
42. See Gary C. Jacobson, "The Bush Presidency and the American Electorate," *Presidential Studies Quarterly* (2003): 701–729.
43. American Bar Association, *Electing the President* (Chicago: American Bar Association, 1967), 3.
44. The Twenty-third Amendment (1961) permits the District of Columbia to have three electors, even though it has no representatives in Congress.
45. In Maine and Nebraska, an elector is allocated for every congressional district won, and whoever wins the state as a whole wins the two electors allotted to the state for its senators.
46. Sidney Blumenthal, *The Permanent Campaign* (New York: Simon & Schuster, 1982).
47. See Martin P. Wattenberg, *The Rise of Candidate-Centered Politics: Presidential Elections of the 1980s* (Cambridge, MA: Harvard University Press, 1991).
48. Benjamin Page, *Choices and Echoes in American Presidential Elections* (Chicago: University of Chicago Press, 1978), 153.
49. James W. Caeser, *Presidential Selection: Theory and Development* (Princeton, NJ: Princeton University Press, 1979), 83.
50. Benjamin Ginsberg, *Consequences of Consent* (Reading, MA: Addison-Wesley, 1982), 194.
51. Ibid., 198.

Chapter 10

1. Kay L. Schlozman and John T. Tierney, *Organized Interests and American Democracy* (New York: Harper & Row, 1986), 1.
2. The classic work is David B. Truman, *The Governmental Process*, 2nd ed. (New York: Knopf, 1971).
3. Thomas R. Dye, *Who's Running America?*, 5th ed. (Englewood Cliffs, NJ: Prentice Hall, 1990), 170.
4. Robert Engler, *The Brotherhood of Oil* (Chicago: University of Chicago Press, 1977).
5. Theodore J. Lowi, *The End of Liberalism*, 2nd ed. (New York: Norton, 1979).
6. See Lee Fritschler, *Smoking and Politics: Policy Making and the Federal Bureaucracy* (Englewood Cliffs, NJ: Prentice Hall, 1983).
7. Morris P. Fiorina, *Congress*: Keystone of the Washington Establishment, 2nd ed. (New Haven, CT: Yale University Press, 1989), 122.
8. E. E. Schattschneider, *The Semisovereign People* (New York: Holt, Rinehart and Winston, 1960), 35.
9. Truman, *The Governmental Process*, 511.
10. Mancur Olson, *The Logic of Collective Action* (Cambridge, MA: Harvard University Press, 1965), especially 9–36.
11. Ibid., 35.
12. Jeffrey H. Birnbaum and Alan S. Murray, *Showdown at Gucci Gulch: Lawmakers, Lobbyists, and the Unlikely Triumph of Tax Reform* (New York: Vintage, 1987).
13. Ibid., 235.
14. Lester W. Milbrath, *The Washington Lobbyists* (Chicago: Rand McNally, 1963), 8.
15. See "Congressional Revolving Doors: The Journey from Congress to K Street," Public Citizen Congress Watch, July 2005. This report can be found at *www.lobbyinginfo.org/* (accessed January 4, 2006).
16. Norman Ornstein and Shirley Elder, *Interest Groups, Lobbying, and Policymaking* (Washington, DC: Congressional Quarterly Press, 1978), 59–60.
17. Peter H. Stone, "Friends, After All," *National Journal*, October 22, 1994, 2440.
18. Richard L. Hall and Alan V. Deardorff, "Lobbying as Legislative Subsidy," *American Political Science Review* 100 (February 2006): 69.
19. Raymond A. Bauer, Ithiel de Sola Pool, and Lewis A. Dexter, *American Business and Public Policy* (New York: Atherton, 1963).
20. Milbrath, *The Washington Lobbyists*, 354.
21. For a summary of recent studies on the influence of lobbying, see Frank R. Baumgartner and Beth L. Leech, *Basic Interests: The Importance of Groups in Politics and in Political Science* (Princeton, NJ: Princeton University Press, 1998), 130.
22. See Laura Langbein and Mark Lotwis, "The Political Efficacy of Lobbying and Money: Gun Control in the U.S. House, 1986," *Legislative Studies Quarterly* 15 (fall 1990): 413–40.
23. Frederic J. Frommer, "Baseball PAC Gives Thousands to Parties," Associated Press, May 13, 2003.
24. R. Kenneth Godwin and Barry J. Seldon, "What Corporations Really Want from Government: The Public Provision of Private Goods," in *Interest Group Politics*, 6th ed., eds. Allan J. Cigler and Burdett A. Loomis (Washington, DC: Congressional Quarterly Press, 2002), 219.
25. The Sovern story is told in "Taking an Ax to PACs," *Time*, August 20, 1984, 27.
26. Karen Orren, "Standing to Sue: Interest Group Conflict in Federal Courts," *American Political Science Review* 70 (September 1976): 724.
27. Gregory A. Caldeira and John R. Wright, "*Amici Curiae* Before the Supreme Court: Who Participates, When, and

How Much," *Journal of Politics* 52 (August 1990): 782–804.

28. Ronald J. Hrebenar and Ruth K. Scott, *Interest Group Politics in America*, 2nd ed. (Englewood Cliffs, NJ: Prentice Hall, 1990), 201.
29. Ken Kollman, *Outside Lobbying: Public Opinion and Interest Group Strategies* (Princeton, NJ: Princeton University Press, 1998), 33.
30. Paul Edward Johnson, "Organized Labor in an Era of Blue-Collar Decline," in *Interest Group Politics*, 3rd ed., eds. Allan J. Cigler and Burdett A. Loomis (Washington, DC: Congressional Quarterly Press, 1991), 33–62.
31. Schlozman and Tierney, *Organized Interests and American Democracy*, 68.
32. Christopher J. Bosso, "The Color of Money: Environmental Groups and the Pathologies of Fund Raising," in *Interest Group Politics*, 4th ed., eds. Allan J. Cigler and Burdett A. Loomis (Washington, DC: Congressional Quarterly Press, 1995), 102.
33. For an interesting analysis of how changes in the regulatory environment, congressional oversight, and public opinion altered the debate on nuclear power, see Frank R. Baumgartner and Bryan D. Jones, *Agendas and Instability in American Politics* (Chicago: University of Chicago Press, 1993).
34. See *www.naacp.org/departments/programs/economy/economy_index.html.*
35. Jeffrey M. Berry, *Lobbying for the People* (Princeton, NJ: Princeton University Press, 1977), 7.
36. Robert H. Salisbury, "The Paradox of Interest Groups in Washington—More Groups, Less Clout," in *The New American Political System*, 2nd ed., ed. Anthony King (Washington, DC: American Enterprise Institute, 1990), 204.
37. Mark J. Rozell, Clyde Wilcox, and David Madland, *Interest Groups in American Campaigns: The New Face of Electioneering*, 2nd ed. (Washington, DC: Congressional Quarterly Press, 2006), 87.
38. Alexis de Tocqueville, *Democracy in America*, vol. 2 (New York: Vintage, 1945), 114.
39. Hrebenar and Scott, *Interest Group Politics in America*, 234.
40. Steven V. Roberts, "Angered President Blames Others for the Huge Deficit," *New York Times*, December 14, 1988, A16.
41. William M. Lunch, *The Nationalization of American Politics* (Berkeley: University of California Press, 1987), 206.
42. Salisbury, "The Paradox of Interest Groups in Washington," 229.

Chapter 11

1. David T. Canon, *Race, Redistricting, and Representation: The Unintended Consequences of Black Majority Districts* (Chicago: University of Chicago Press, 1999).
2. Susan A. Banducci, Todd Donovan, and Jeffrey A. Karp, "Minority Representation, Empowerment, and Participation," *Journal of Politics* 66 (May 2004): 534–56.
3. There is some evidence that women state legislators in states with the highest percentage of female representatives are more likely than men to introduce and pass legislation dealing with women, children, and families. See Sue Thomas, "The Impact of Women on State Legislative Policies," *Journal of Politics* 53 (November 1991): 958–76. See also Arturo Vega and Juanita M. Firestone, "The Effects of Gender on Congressional Behavior and the Substantive Representation of Women," *Legislative Studies Quarterly* 20 (May 1995): 213–22, and Leslie A. Schwindt-Bayer and Renato Corbetta, "Gender Turnover and Roll-Call Voting in the U.S. House of Representatives," *Legislative Studies Quarterly* 29 (May 2004): 215–29.
4. On various views of representation, see Hanna Pitkin, *The Concept of Representation* (Berkeley: University of California Press, 1967).
5. Sally Friedman, "House Committee Assignments of Women and Minority Newcomers, 1965–1994," *Legislative Studies Quarterly* 21 (February 1996): 73–81; Alan Gerber, "African Americans' Congressional Careers and the Democratic House Delegation," *Journal of Politics* 58 (August 1996): 831–45.
6. An excellent review of congressional campaign costs and spending is Edie N. Goldenberg and Michael W. Traugott, *Campaigning for Congress* (Washington, DC: Congressional Quarterly Press, 1984). Another is Paul S. Herrnson, *Congressional Elections: Campaigning at Home and in Washington* (Washington, DC: Congressional Quarterly Press, 1995).
7. John L. Sullivan and Eric Uslaner, "Congressional Behavior and Electoral Marginality," *American Journal of Political Science* 22 (August 1978): 536–53.
8. Thomas Mann, *Unsafe at Any Margin* (Washington, DC: American Enterprise Institute, 1978).
9. Glenn R. Parker, *Homeward Bound* (Pittsburgh: University of Pittsburgh Press, 1986); and John R. Johannes, *To Serve the People* (Lincoln: University of Nebraska Press, 1984).
10. Patricia Hurley and Kim Q. Hill, "The Prospects for Issue Voting in Contemporary Congressional Elections," *American Politics Quarterly* 8 (October 1980): 446.
11. Mann, *Unsafe at Any Margin*, 37.
12. That presidential elections and congressional elections are not closely related is an argument made in Lyn Ragsdale, "The Fiction of Congressional Elections as Presidential Events," *American Politics Quarterly* 8 (October 1980): 375–98. For evidence that voters' views of the president affect their voting for senators, see Lonna Rae Atkeson and Randall W. Partin, "Economic and Referendum Voting: A Comparison of Gubernatorial and Senatorial Elections," *American Political Science Review* 89 (March 1995): 99–107.
13. John R. Owens and Edward C. Olson, "Economic Fluctuations and Congressional Elections," *American Journal of Political Science* 24 (August 1980): 469–93; Benjamin Radcliff, "Solving a Puzzle: Aggregate Analysis and Economic Voting Revisited," *Journal of Politics* 50 (May 1988): 440–58; Robert S. Erikson, "Economic Conditions and the Congressional Vote: A Review of the Macrolevel Evidence," *American Journal of Political Science* 34 (May 1990): 373–99; James E. Campbell, *The Presidential Pulse of Congressional Elections* (Lexington: University Press of Kentucky, 1993), 119; Gary C. Jacobson, "Does the Economy Matter in Midterm Elections?," *American Journal of Political Science* 34 (May 1990): 400–404.
14. David R. Mayhew, *Congress: The Electoral Connection* (New Haven, CT: Yale University Press, 1974).
15. Richard F. Fenno Jr., *Home Style* (Boston: Little, Brown, 1978), 32.
16. The "service spells success" argument is made in Morris P. Fiorina, *Congress: Keystone of the Washington Establishment*,

2nd ed. (New Haven, CT: Yale University Press, 1989), and, with a slightly different emphasis, in Glenn R. Parker, "The Advantages of Incumbency in Congressional Elections," *American Politics Quarterly* 8 (October 1980): 449–61.

17. Gary C. Jacobson, *The Politics of Congressional Elections*, 6th ed. (New York: Longman, 2004), 122–32; Stephen Ansolabehere, James M. Snyder Jr., and Charles Stewart III, "Old Voters, New Voters, and the Personal Vote: Using Redistricting to Measure the Incumbency Advantage," *American Journal of Political Science* 44 (January 2000): 17–34.

18. See, for example, Paul Feldman and James Jondrow, "Congressional Elections and Local Federal Spending," *American Journal of Political Science* 28 (February 1984): 147–63; Glenn R. Parker and Suzanne L. Parker, "The Correlates and Effects of Attention to District by U.S. House Members," *Legislative Studies Quarterly* 10 (May 1985): 223–42; and John C. McAdams and John R. Johannes, "Congressmen, Perquisites, and Elections," *Journal of Politics* 50 (May 1988): 412–39.

19. On strategies of challengers, see Gary C. Jacobson and Samuel Kernell, *Strategy and Choice in Congressional Elections*, 2nd ed. (New Haven, CT: Yale University Press, 1983), and Gary C. Jacobson, "Strategic Politicians and the Dynamics of U.S. House Elections, 1946–1986," *American Political Science Review* 83 (September 1989): 773–94. See also Steven D. Levitt and Catherine D. Wolfram, "Decomposing the Sources of Incumbency Advantage in the U.S. House," *Legislative Studies Quarterly* 22 (February 1997): 45–60.

20. See Gary C. Jacobson, *Money in Congressional Elections* (New Haven, CT: Yale University Press, 1980).

21. On the importance of challenger quality and financing, see Alan I. Abramowitz, Brad Alexander, and Matthew Gunning, "Incumbency, Redistricting, and the Decline of Competition in U.S. House Elections," *Journal of Politics* 68 (February 2006): 75–88; Alan I. Abramowitz, "Explaining Senate Election Outcomes," *American Political Science Review* 82 (June 1988): 385–403; and Donald Philip Green and Jonathan S. Krasno, "Salvation for the Spendthrift Incumbent," *American Journal of Political Science* 32 (November 1988): 884–907.

22. Jacobson, *The Politics of Congressional Elections*, 41–47, 132–34. See also Gary C. Jacobson, "The Effects of Campaign Spending in House Elections: New Evidence for Old Arguments," *American Journal of Political Science* 34 (May 1990): 334–62; Christopher Kenny and Michael McBurnett, "An Individual-Level Multiequation Model of Expenditure Effects in Contested House Elections," *American Political Science Review* 88 (September 1994): 699–707; Robert S. Erikson and Thomas R. Palfrey, "Campaign Spending and Incumbency: An Alternative Simultaneous Equation Approach," *Journal of Politics* 60 (May 1998): 355–73; and Alan Gerber, "Estimating the Effect of Campaign Spending on Senate Election Outcomes Using Instrumental Variables," *American Political Science Review* 92 (June 1998): 401–12.

23. Federal Election Commission.

24. Gary C. Jacobson and Michael A. Dimock, "Checking Out: The Effects of Bank Overdrafts on the 1992 House Elections," *American Journal of Political Science* 38 (August 1994): 601–24. See also Marshal A. Dimock and Gary C. Jacobson, "Checks and Choices: The House Bank Scandal's Impact on Voters in 1992," *Journal of Politics* 57 (November 1995): 1143–59, and Carl McCurley and Jeffrey J. Mondak, "Inspected by #1184063113: The Influence of Incumbents' Competence and Integrity in U.S. House Elections," *American Journal of Political Science* 39 (November 1995): 864–85.

25. John G. Peters and Susan Welch, "The Effects of Corruption on Voting Behavior in Congressional Elections," *American Political Science Review* 74 (September 1980): 697–708; Susan Welch and John R. Hibbing, "The Effects of Charges of Corruption on Voting Behavior in Congressional Elections, 1982–1990," *Journal of Politics* 59 (February 1997): 226–39.

26. On term limits, see Gerald Benjamin and Michael J. Malbin, eds., *Limiting Legislative Terms* (Washington, DC: Congressional Quarterly Press, 1992).

27. Said former House Speaker Jim Wright in *You and Your Congressman* (New York: Putnam, 1976), 190. See also Donald R. Matthews and James Stimson, *Yeas and Nays: Normal Decision-Making in the House of Representatives* (New York: Wiley, 1975), and John L. Sullivan et al., "The Dimensions of Cue-Taking in the House of Representatives: Variations by Issue Area," *Journal of Politics* 55 (November 1993): 975–97.

28. Nelson W. Polsby et al., "Institutionalization of the House of Representatives," *American Political Science Review* 62 (1968): 144–68.

29. John R. Hibbing, "Contours of the Modern Congressional Career," *American Political Science Review* 85 (June 1991): 405–28.

30. See Bernard Grofman, Robert Griffin, and Amihai Glazer, "Is the Senate More Liberal than the House? Another Look," *Legislative Studies Quarterly* 16 (May 1991): 281–96.

31. See Sarah A. Binder and Steven S. Smith, *Politics or Principle? Filibustering in the United States Senate* (Washington, DC: Brookings Institution, 1997).

32. Robert L. Peabody, *Leadership in Congress* (Boston: Little, Brown, 1976), 4.

33. On the increasing importance of party leadership in the House, see David W. Rohde, *Parties and Leaders in the Postreform House* (Chicago: University of Chicago Press, 1991); Barbara Sinclair, "The Emergence of Strong Leadership in the 1980s House of Representatives," *Journal of Politics* 54 (August 1992): 657–84; and Gary W. Cox and Matthew D. McCubbins, *Legislative Leviathan* (Berkeley: University of California Press, 1993).

34. For more on congressional oversight, see Christopher H. Foreman Jr., *Signals from the Hill* (New Haven, CT: Yale University Press, 1988), and Diana Evans, "Congressional Oversight and the Diversity of Members' Goals," *Political Science Quarterly* 109 (fall 1994): 669–87.

35. Joel D. Aberbach, *Keeping a Watchful Eye: The Politics of Congressional Oversight* (Washington, DC: Brookings Institution, 1990).

36. Aberbach, *Keeping a Watchful Eye*; Joel D. Aberbach, "What's Happened to the Watchful Eye?," *Congress and the Presidency* 29 (spring 2002): 3–23.

37. Richard F. Fenno Jr., *Congressmen in Committees* (Boston: Little, Brown, 1973), 1.

38. Useful studies of committee assignments include Kenneth Shepsle, *The Giant Jigsaw Puzzle* (Chicago: University of

Chicago Press, 1978), and Cox and McCubbins, *Legislative Leviathan*, chaps. 1, 7, and 8.

39. Richard F. Fenno Jr., "If, as Ralph Nader Says, Congress Is the 'Broken Branch,' How Come We Love Our Congressmen So Much?" in *Congress in Change*, ed. Norman Ornstein (New York: Praeger, 1975), 282.

40. For more on congressional reform, see Leroy N. Rieselbach, *Congressional Reform* (Washington, DC: Congressional Quarterly Press, 1986).

41. See Susan Webb Hammond, *Congressional Caucuses in National Policy Making* (Baltimore: Johns Hopkins University Press, 1998).

42. For a thorough discussion of rule changes and the impact of procedures, see Steven S. Smith, *Call to Order: Floor Politics in the House and Senate* (Washington, DC: Brookings Institution, 1989).

43. Barbara Sinclair, *Unorthodox Lawmaking*, 2nd ed. (Washington, DC: Congressional Quarterly Press, 2000).

44. George C. Edwards III and Andrew Barrett, "Presidential Agenda Setting in Congress," in *Polarized Politics: Congress and the President in a Partisan Era*, ed. Jon R. Bond and Richard Fleisher (Washington, DC: Congressional Quarterly Press, 2000).

45. George C. Edwards III, *At the Margins: Presidential Leadership of Congress* (New Haven, CT: Yale University Press, 1989).

46. James M. Snyder Jr. and Tim Groseclose, "Estimating Party Influence in Congressional Roll-Call Voting," *American Journal of Political Science* 44 (April 2000): 187–205; Aage Clausen, *How Congressmen Decide: A Policy Focus* (New York: St. Martin's Press, 1973).

47. See Roger H. Davidson, *The Role of the Congressman* (New York: Pegasus, 1969), and Thomas E. Cavanaugh, "Role Orientations of House Members: The Process of Representation" (paper delivered at the annual meeting of the American Political Science Association, Washington, DC, August 1979).

48. John L. Sullivan and Robert E. O'Connor, "Electoral Choice and Popular Control of Public Policy: The Case of the 1966 House Elections," *American Political Science Review* 66 (December 1972): 1256–68.

49. The *New York Times*/CBS News Poll cited in "Voters Disgusted with Politicians as Election Nears," *New York Times*, November 13, 1994, A10.

50. Robert A. Bernstein, *Elections, Representation, and Congressional Voting Behavior* (Englewood Cliffs, NJ: Prentice Hall, 1989), 99.

51. Patricia A. Hurley and Kim Quaile Hill, "Beyond the Demand-Input Model: A Theory of Representational Linkages," *Journal of Politics* 65 (May 2003): 304–26; Christopher Wlezien, "Patterns of Representation: Dynamics of Public Preferences and Policy," *Journal of Politics* 66 (February 2004): 1–24.

52. Larry M. Bartels, however, found that members of Congress were responsive to constituency opinion in supporting the Reagan defense buildup. See "Constituency Opinion and Congressional Policy Making: The Reagan Defense Buildup," *American Political Science Review* 85 (June 1991): 457–74.

53. Kim Quaile Hill and Patricia A. Hurley, "Dyadic Representation Reappraised," *American Journal of Political Science* 43 (January 1999): 109–37.

54. On the importance of ideology, see Bernstein, *Elections, Representation, and Congressional Voting Behavior.*

55. *Washington Representatives 2006* (Washington, DC: Columbia Books, 2006); *PoliticalMoneyLine*.

56. Center for Responsive Politics, 2006; *PoliticalMoneyLine*.

57. Richard L. Hall and Alan V. Deardorff, "Lobbying as Legislative Subsidy," *American Political Science Review* 100 (February 2006): 69–84.

58. John W. Kingdon, *Congressmen's Voting Decisions*, 3rd ed. (Ann Arbor: University of Michigan Press, 1989), 242.

59. See M. Darrell West, *Congress and Economic Policymaking* (Pittsburgh: University of Pittsburgh Press, 1987).

Chapter 12

1. Quoted in Thomas E. Cronin, *The State of the Presidency*, 2nd ed. (Boston: Little, Brown, 1980), 223.

2. Richard E. Neustadt, *Presidential Power and the Modern Presidents* (New York: Free Press, 1990).

3. On the public's expectations of the president, see George C. Edwards III, *The Public Presidency* (New York: St. Martin's Press, 1983), chap. 5.

4. Office of the White House Press Secretary, *Remarks of the President at a Meeting With Non-Washington Editors and Broadcasters*, September 21, 1979, 12.

5. Samuel P. Huntington, *American Politics: The Promises of Disharmony* (Cambridge, MA: Belknap, 1981), 33.

6. On the creation of the presidency, see Donald L. Robertson, *To the Best of My Ability* (New York: Norton, 1987), and Thomas E. Cronin, ed., *Inventing the American Presidency* (Lawrence: University Press of Kansas, 1989).

7. On the factors important in the presidential nominee's choice of a running mate, see Lee Sigelman and Paul J. Wahlbeck, "The 'Veepstakes': Strategic Choice in Presidential Running Mate Selection," *American Political Science Review* 91 (December 1997): 855–64.

8. See Paul C. Light, *Vice Presidential Power* (Baltimore: Johns Hopkins University Press, 1984).

9. For a study of the backgrounds of cabinet members, see Jeffrey E. Cohen, *The Politics of the U.S. Cabinet* (Pittsburgh: University of Pittsburgh Press, 1988).

10. For background on the Executive Office, see John Hart, *The Presidential Branch*, 2nd ed. (Chatham, NJ: Chatham House, 1995).

11. Two useful books on the history and functions of the White House staff are Hart, *The Presidential Branch*, and Bradley H. Patterson Jr., *The White House Staff* (Washington, DC: Brookings Institution, 2000).

12. For a discussion of presidential party leadership in Congress, see George C. Edwards III, *At the Margins: Presidential Leadership of Congress* (New Haven, CT: Yale University Press, 1989), chaps. 3–5.

13. Jimmy Carter, *Keeping Faith* (New York: Bantam, 1982), 80.

14. For a review of these studies and an analysis showing the limited impact of presidential coattails on congressional election outcomes, see Edwards, *The Public Presidency*, 83–93.

15. For evidence of the impact of the president's campaigning in midterm elections, see Jeffrey E. Cohen, Michael A. Krassa, and John A. Hamman, "The Impact of Presidential Campaigning on Midterm U.S. Senate Elections," *American Political Science Review* 85 (March 1991): 165–78. On the president's effect on congressional elections more broadly,

see James E. Campbell, *The Presidential Pulse of Congressional Elections* (Lexington: University Press of Kentucky, 1993).

16. Quoted in Sidney Blumenthal, "Marketing the President," *New York Times Magazine*, September 13, 1981, 110.
17. Quoted in "Slings and Arrows," *Newsweek*, July 31, 1978, 20.
18. Edwards, *At the Margins*, chaps. 6–7.
19. For an analysis of the factors that affect perceptions of mandates, see Edwards, *At the Margins*, chap. 8.
20. David Stockman, *The Triumph of Politics* (New York: Harper & Row, 1986), 251–65; William Greider, "The Education of David Stockman," *Atlantic*, December 1981, 51.
21. George C. Edwards III and Andrew Barrett, "Presidential Agenda Setting in Congress," in *Polarized Politics*, ed. Jon R. Bond and Richard Fleisher (Washington, DC: Congressional Quarterly Press, 2000).
22. John Kingdon, *Agendas, Alternatives, and Public Policies* (Boston: Little, Brown, 1984), 25. On presidential agenda setting, see Paul C. Light, *The President's Agenda* (Baltimore: Johns Hopkins University Press, 1991), and George C. Edwards III and B. Dan Wood, "Who Influences Whom? The President, Congress, and the Media," *American Political Science Review* 93 (June 1999): 327–34.
23. Edwards, *At the Margins*, chaps. 9–10; Jon R. Bond and Richard Fleisher, *The President in the Legislative Arena* (Chicago: University of Chicago Press, 1990), chap. 8.
24. See David Auerswald and Forrest Maltzman, "Policymaking Through Advice and Consent: Treaty Considerations by the United States Senate," *Journal of Politics* 65 (November 2003): 1097–110.
25. For an analysis of war powers and other issues related to separation of powers, see Louis Fisher, *Constitutional Conflicts Between Congress and the President*, 4th ed. rev. (Lawrence: University Press of Kansas, 1997), and Louis Fisher, *Presidential War Power* (Lawrence: University Press of Kansas, 1995).
26. See Barbara Hinckley, *Less than Meets the Eye* (Chicago: University of Chicago Press, 1994).
27. The phrase was originated by Aaron Wildavsky in "The Two Presidencies," *TransAction* 4 (December 1966): 7–14. He later determined that the two presidencies applied mostly to the 1950s. See Duane M. Oldfield and Aaron Wildavsky, "Reconsidering the Two Presidencies," in *The Two Presidencies: A Quarter Century Assessment*, ed. Steven A. Shull (Chicago: Nelson-Hall, 1991), 181–90.
28. Edwards, *At the Margins*, chap. 4.
29. See William W. Lammers, "Presidential Attention-Focusing Activities," in *The President and the Public*, ed. Doris A. Graber (Philadelphia: ISHI, 1982), 145–71, and Samuel Kernell, *Going Public*, 3rd ed. (Washington, DC: Congressional Quarterly Press, 1997), chap. 4.
30. Edwards, *The Public Presidency*, chap. 6; George C. Edwards III, *Presidential Approval* (Baltimore: Johns Hopkins University Press, 1990).
31. Mueller also included the inaugural period of a president's term as a rally event. See John E. Mueller, *War, Presidents and Public Opinion* (New York: Wiley, 1973), 208–13.
32. Kernell, *Going Public*, 169.
33. On presidents' efforts to build policy support, see Jeffrey K. Tulis, *The Rhetorical Presidency* (Princeton, NJ: Princeton University Press, 1987).
34. For a discussion of the social flow of information, see Robert Huckfeldt and John Sprague, "Networks in Context: The Social Flow of Political Information," *American Political Science Review* 81 (December 1987): 1197–216.
35. *Newsweek* poll, October 28–30, 1994, cited in "The Problem with the President," *Newsweek*, November 7, 1994, 42.
36. George C. Edwards III, "Frustration and Folly: Bill Clinton and the Public Presidency," in *The Clinton Presidency: First Appraisals*, ed. Colin Campbell and Bert A. Rockman (Chatham, NJ: Chatham House, 1995).
37. Useful comparisons over Reagan's and Clinton's tenures can be found in George C. Edwards III, *On Deaf Ears: The Limits of the Bully Pulpit* (New Haven, CT: Yale University Press, 2003), chaps. 2–3.
38. Quoted in "Tax Cut Passed by Solid Margin in House, Senate," *Congressional Quarterly Weekly Report*, August 1, 1981, 1374.
39. Two of the leading studies are found in Michael J. Robinson and Margaret A. Sheehan, *Over the Wire and on TV* (New York: Russell Sage Foundation, 1983), and Daniel C. Hallin, "The Media, the War in Vietnam, and Political Support," *Journal of Politics* 46 (February 1984): 2–24.
40. Carter, *Keeping Faith*, 179–80.
41. See Mark J. Rozell, *The Press and the Ford Presidency* (Ann Arbor: University of Michigan Press, 1992).
42. Doris A. Graber, *Mass Media and American Politics*, 5th ed. (Washington, DC: Congressional Quarterly Press, 1997), 277. On the 1992 presidential campaign, see "Clinton's the One," *Media Monitor* 6 (November 1992): 3–5.
43. Thomas E. Patterson, *Out of Order* (New York: Knopf, 1993), chap. 3.
44. Ibid., 113.
45. *Media Monitor*, May/June 1995, 2–5; Thomas E. Patterson, "Legitimate Beef: The Presidency and a Carnivorous Press," *Media Studies Journal*, spring 1994, 21–26. See also Andras Szanto, "In Our Opinion . . . : Editorial Page Views of Clinton's First Year," *Media Studies Journal*, spring 1994, 97–105; "Sex, Lies, and TV News," *Media Monitor* 12 (September/October 1998); and "TV News Coverage of the 1998 Midterm Election," *Media Monitor* 12 (November/December 1998).
46. Katherine Graham, *Personal History* (New York: Vintage, 1998).
47. See, for example, *Media Monitor*, June/July 1998.
48. Michael Baruch Grossman and Martha Joynt Kumar, *Portraying the President: The White House and the News Media* (Baltimore: Johns Hopkins University Press, 1981), chaps. 10–11.
49. Sam Donaldson, *Hold On, Mr. President* (New York: Random House, 1987), 237–38.
50. Quoted in Eleanor Randolph, "Speakes Aims Final Salvo at White House Practices," *Washington Post*, January 31, 1987, A3.
51. George C. Edwards III, Andrew Barrett, and Jeffrey S. Peake, "The Legislative Impact of Divided Government," *American Journal of Political Science* 41 (April 1997): 545–63.
52. David R. Mayhew, *Divided We Govern* (New Haven, CT: Yale University Press, 1991).

Chapter 13

1. This example is based on Allan Freedman, "Battles over Jurisdiction

Likely to Block Merger of Agencies," *Congressional Quarterly Weekly Report*, May 30, 1998, 1440.

2. H. H. Gerth and C. Wright Mills, *From Max Weber: Essays in Sociology* (New York: Oxford University Press, 1958), chap. 8.
3. See Charles T. Goodsell, *The Case for Bureaucracy*, 4th ed. (Chatham, NJ: Chatham House, 2004), chap. 2. See also Daniel Katz et al., *Bureaucratic Encounters* (Ann Arbor: Institute for Social Research, University of Michigan, 1975).
4. See Paul C. Light, *The True Size of Government* (Washington, DC: Brookings Institution, 1999), 1, 44.
5. U.S. Department of Commerce, *Statistical Abstract of the United States, 2006* (Washington, DC: U.S. Government Printing Office, 2006), 330; Office of Personnel Management, *The Factbook, 2005 Edition* (Washington, DC: U.S. Government Printing Office, 2006), 8.
6. See Herbert Kaufman, *Red Tape* (Washington, DC: Brookings Institution, 1977).
7. See Goodsell, *The Case for Bureaucracy*, 48–54.
8. Ibid., chap. 5.
9. On the transient nature of presidential appointees, see G. Calvin Mackenzie, ed., *The In-and-Outers* (Baltimore: Johns Hopkins University Press, 1987).
10. Hugh M. Heclo, *A Government of Strangers: Executive Politics in Washington* (Washington, DC: Brookings Institution, 1977).
11. On the independent regulatory agencies, see the classic work by Marver Bernstein, *Regulating Business by Independent Commission* (Princeton, NJ: Princeton University Press, 1955). See also, on regulation, James Q. Wilson, ed., *The Politics of Regulation* (New York: Basic Books, 1980), and A. Lee Fritschler and Bernard H. Ross, *Business Regulation and Government Decision-Making* (Cambridge, MA: Winthrop, 1980).
12. Bernstein, *Regulating Business by Independent Commission*, 90. For a partial test of the capture theory that finds the theory not altogether accurate, see John P. Plumlee and Kenneth J. Meier, "Capture and Rigidity in Regulatory Administration," in *The Policy Cycle*, ed. Judith May and Aaron Wildavsky (Beverly Hills, CA: Russell Sage Foundation, 1978). Another critique of the capture theory is Paul J. Quirk, *Industry Influence in Federal Regulatory Agencies* (Princeton, NJ: Princeton University Press, 1981).
13. George C. Edwards III, *Implementing Public Policy* (Washington, DC: Congressional Quarterly Press, 1980), 1.
14. Eugene Bardach, *The Implementation Game* (Cambridge, MA: MIT Press, 1977), 85; Robert L. Lineberry, *American Public Policy: What Government Does and What Difference It Makes* (New York: Harper & Row, 1977), 71. Clausewitz called war "the continuation of politics by other means."
15. Lineberry, *American Public Policy*, 70–71.
16. For another dramatic example, see Martha Derthick, *New Towns In-Town* (Washington, DC: Urban Institute Press, 1972).
17. Bardach, *The Implementation Game*, 250–51.
18. A good discussion of how policymakers ignored the administrative capacity of one important agency when assigning it new responsibilities can be found in Martha Derthick, *Agency Under Stress* (Washington, DC: Brookings Institution, 1990).
19. The implementation of the athletics policy is well documented in two articles by Cheryl M. Fields in the *Chronicle of Higher Education*, December 11 and 18, 1978, on which this account relies.
20. James Q. Wilson, *Bureaucracy* (New York: Basic Books, 1989), 158.
21. Report of the DOD Commission on Beirut International Airport Terrorist Act, October 23, 1983, December 20, 1983, 133.
22. *The 9/11 Commission Report* (New York: Norton, 2004), 17–18.
23. On administrative discretion, see Gary S. Bryner, *Bureaucratic Discretion* (New York: Pergamon Press, 1987).
24. Gerald Carson, *The Golden Egg* (Boston: Houghton Mifflin, 1977), 10. The examples given in this paragraph are from Carson.
25. Michael Lipsky, *Street-Level Bureaucracy* (New York: Russell Sage Foundation, 1980).
26. Quoted in Seymour Hersh, *The Price of Power: Kissinger in the Nixon White House* (New York: Summit, 1983), 235–36.
27. Albert Gore, *From Red Tape to Results: Creating a Government That Works Better and Costs Less* (New York: Times Books, 1993), 11.
28. For a careful analysis of efforts to reorganize the federal bureaucracy, see Peri E. Arnold, *Making the Managerial Presidency*, 2nd ed. (Princeton, NJ: Princeton University Press, 1996).
29. Based on a more elaborate account by James Worsham, "A Typical Day Is Full of Rules," *Chicago Tribune*, July 12, 1981, 1ff, with updating by the authors.
30. See Martha Derthick and Paul J. Quirk, *The Politics of Deregulation* (Washington, DC: Brookings Institution, 1985).
31. See, for example, Susan J. Tolchin and Martin J. Tolchin, *Dismantling America: The Rush to Deregulate* (New York: Oxford University Press, 1983).
32. Evan J. Ringquist, "Does Regulation Matter? Evaluating the Effects of State Air Pollution Control Programs," *Journal of Politics* 55 (November 1993): 1022–45.
33. Michael Lewis-Beck and John Alford, "Can Government Regulate Safety? The Coal Mine Example," *American Political Science Review* 74 (September 1980): 745–56.
34. Paul Sabatier and Dan Mazmanian, *Can Regulation Work? Implementation of the 1972 California Coastal Initiative* (New York: Plenum, 1983).
35. Gary Copeland and Kenneth J. Meier, "Gaining Ground: The Impact of Medicaid and WIC on Infant Mortality," *American Politics Quarterly* 15 (April 1987): 254–73.
36. See B. Dan Wood and Richard W. Waterman, *Bureaucratic Dynamics: The Role of Bureaucracy in a Democracy* (Boulder, CO: Westview, 1994).
37. A good work on this point is Richard P. Nathan, *The Administrative Presidency* (New York: Wiley, 1983).
38. See Kenneth R. Mayer, *With the Stroke of a Pen, Executive Orders and Presidential Power* (Princeton, NJ: Princeton University Press, 2001), and William G. Howell, *Power Without Persuasion* (Princeton, NJ: Princeton University Press, 2003).
39. Andrew B. Whitford and Jeff Yates, "Policy Signals and Executive Governance: Presidential Rhetoric in the War on Drugs," *Journal of Politics* 65 (November 2003): 995–1012.

40. Morris Fiorina, *Congress: Keystone of the Washington Establishment*, 2nd ed. (New Haven, CT: Yale University Press, 1989).
41. Richard A. Rettig, *Cancer Crusade* (Princeton, NJ: Princeton University Press, 1977).
42. Hugh M. Heclo, "Issue Networks and the Executive Establishment," in *The New American Political System*, ed. Anthony King (Washington, DC: American Enterprise Institute, 1978), 87–124. See also William P. Browne and Won K. Paik, "Beyond the Domain: Recasting Network Politics in the Postreform Congress," *American Journal of Political Science* 37 (November 1993): 1054–78, and John P. Heinz, Edward O. Laumann, Robert L. Nelson, and Robert L. Salisbury, *The Hollow Core: Private Interests in National Policy Making* (Cambridge, MA: Harvard University Press, 1993).
43. Frank R. Baumgartner and Bryan D. Jones, *Agendas and Instability in American Politics* (Chicago: University of Chicago Press, 1993).

Chapter 14

1. Quoted in Lawrence C. Baum, *The Supreme Court*, 4th ed. (Washington, DC: Congressional Quarterly Press, 1992), 72.
2. Administrative Office of the United States Courts.
3. Administrative Office of the United States Courts.
4. Sarah Binder and Forrest Maltzman, "The Limits of Senatorial Courtesy," *Legislative Studies Quarterly* 29 (February 2004): 5–22.
5. Quoted in J. Woodford Howard Jr., *Courts of Appeals in the Federal Judicial System: A Study of the Second, Fifth, and District of Columbia Circuits* (Princeton, NJ: Princeton University Press, 1981), 101.
6. Lauren Cohen Bell, "Senatorial Discourtesy: The Senate's Use of Delay to Shape the Federal Judiciary," *Political Research Quarterly* 55 (September 2002): 589–607.
7. See Gary King, "Presidential Appointments to the Supreme Court: Adding Systematic Explanation to Probabilistic Description," *American Politics Quarterly* 15 (July 1987): 373–86.
8. Charles R. Shipan and Megan L. Shannon, "Delaying Justice(s): A Duration Analysis of Supreme Court Confirmations," *American Journal of Political Science* 47 (October 2003): 654–68.
9. See John Schmidhauser, *Judges and Justices: The Federal Appellate Judiciary* (Boston: Little, Brown, 1978).
10. One study found, however, that judicial experience is not related to the congruence of presidential preferences and the justices' decisions on racial equality cases. See John Gates and Jeffrey Cohen, "Presidents, Supreme Court Justices, and Racial Equality Cases: 1954–1984," *Political Behavior* 10 (November 1, 1988): 22–35.
11. On the importance of ideology and partisanship considerations in judicial retirement and resignation decisions, see Deborah J. Barrow and Gary Zuk, "An Institutional Analysis of Turnover in the Lower Federal Courts, 1900–1987," *Journal of Politics* 52 (May 1990): 457–76.
12. Quoted in Henry J. Abraham, *Justices and Presidents: A Political History of Appointments to the Supreme Court*, 3rd ed. (New York: Oxford University Press, 1992), 266.
13. Ibid., 70.
14. See, for example, the important role that African-American support played in the confirmation of Clarence Thomas even though he was likely to vote against the wishes of leading civil rights organizations. L. Marvin Overby, Beth M. Henschen, Julie Walsh, and Michael H. Strauss, "Courting Constituents: An Analysis of the Senate Confirmation Vote on Justice Clarence Thomas," *American Political Science Review* 86 (December 1992): 997–1003.
15. On the impact of the background of members of the judiciary, see Robert A. Carp and C. K. Rowland, *Policymaking and Politics in the Federal District Courts* (Knoxville: University of Tennessee Press, 1983); Thomas G. Walker and Deborah J. Barrow, "The Diversification of the Federal Bench: Policy and Process Ramifications," *Journal of Politics* 47 (May 1985): 596–617; and C. Neal Tate, "Personal Attribute Models of the Voting Behavior of United States Supreme Court Justices: Liberalism in Civil Liberties and Economics Decisions, 1946–1978," *American Political Science Review* 75 (June 1981): 355–67.
16. Quoted in Nina Totenberg, "Behind the Marble, Beneath the Robes," *New York Times Magazine*, March 16, 1975, 37.
17. H. W. Perry Jr., *Deciding to Decide: Agenda Setting in the United States Supreme Court* (Cambridge, MA: Harvard University Press, 1991); Doris Marie Provine, *Case Selection in the United States Supreme Court* (Chicago: University of Chicago Press, 1980); Stuart H. Teger and Douglas Kosinski, "The Cue Theory of Supreme Court Certiorari Jurisdiction: A Reconsideration," *Journal of Politics* 42 (August 1980): 834–46.
18. Sidney Ulmer, "The Supreme Court's Certiorari Decisions: Conflict as a Predictive Variable," *American Political Science Review* (December 1984): 901–11.
19. On the solicitor general's *amicus* briefs, see Rebecca E. Deen, Joseph Ignagni, and James Meernik, "Executive Influence on the U.S. Supreme Court: Solicitor General *Amicus* Cases, 1953–1997," *American Review of Politics* 22 (spring 2001): 3–26, and Timothy R. Johnson, "The Supreme Court, the Solicitor General, and the Separation of Powers," *American Politics Research* 31 (July 2001): 426–51.
20. See Rebecca Mae Salokar, *The Solicitor General* (Philadelphia: Temple University Press, 1992).
21. Each year, data on Supreme Court decisions can be found in the November issue of the *Harvard Law Review*.
22. On the influence of oral arguments on the Supreme Court, see Timothy R. Johnson, Paul J. Wahlbeck, and James F. Spriggs II, "The Influence of Oral Arguments on the U.S. Supreme Court," *American Political Science Review* 100 (February 2006): 99–113.
23. A useful look at attorneys practicing before the Supreme Court is Kevin McGuire, *The Supreme Court Bar: Legal Elites in the Washington Community* (Charlottesville: University Press of Virginia, 1993).
24. See, for example, Forrest Maltzman and Paul J. Wahlbeck, "Strategic Policy Considerations and Voting Fluidity on the Burger Court," *American Political Science Review* 90 (September 1996): 581–92; Paul J. Wahlbeck, James F. Spriggs II, and Forrest Maltzman, "Marshalling the Court: Bargaining and Accommodation on the United States Supreme Court," *American Journal of Political Science* 42 (January 1998): 294–315; and James F. Spriggs II, Forrest Maltzman, and Paul J. Wahlbeck, "Bargaining on the U.S. Supreme Court: Justices' Responses to

Majority Opinion Drafts," *Journal of Politics* 61 (May 1999): 485–506.

25. A. P. Blaustein and A. H. Field, "Overruling Opinions in the Supreme Court," *Michigan Law Review* 57, no. 2 (1957): 151; David H. O'Brien, *Constitutional Law and Politics*, 3rd ed. (New York: Norton, 1997), 38.
26. See, for example, Jeffrey A. Segal and Harold J. Spaeth, *The Supreme Court and the Attitudinal Model* (Cambridge: Cambridge University Press, 1993); Jeffrey A. Segal and Albert O. Cover, "Ideological Values and the Votes of U.S. Supreme Court Justices," *American Political Science Review* 83 (June 1989): 557–66; Tracey E. George and Lee Epstein, "On the Nature of Supreme Court Decision Making," *American Political Science Review* 86 (June 1992): 323–37; and Jeffrey A. Segal and Harold J. Spaeth, "The Influence of Stare Decisis on the Votes of United States Supreme Court Justices," *American Journal of Political Science* 40 (November 1996): 971–1003.
27. Doris Graber, *Mass Media and American Politics*, 6th ed. (Washington, DC: Congressional Quarterly Press, 2002), 312–13.
28. Charles A. Johnson and Bradley C. Canon, *Judicial Policies: Implementation and Impact*, 2nd ed. (Washington, DC: Congressional Quarterly Press, 1999), chap. 1. See also James F. Spriggs II, "The Supreme Court and Federal Administrative Agencies: A Resource-Based Theory and Analysis of Judicial Impact," *American Journal of Political Science* 40 (November 1996): 1122–51.
29. See Richard L. Pacelle Jr. and Lawrence Baum, "Supreme Court Authority in the Judiciary," *American Politics Quarterly* 20 (April 1992): 169–91, and Donald R. Songer, Jeffrey A. Segal, and Charles M. Cameron, "The Hierarchy of Justice: Testing a Principal-Agent Model of Supreme Court–Circuit Court Interactions," *American Journal of Political Science* 38 (August 1994): 673–96.
30. However, see Gerald N. Rosenberg, *The Hollow Hope: Can Courts Bring About Social Change?* (Chicago: University of Chicago Press, 1991). Rosenberg questions whether the courts have brought about much social change.
31. William Rehnquist, "The Notion of a Living Constitution," in *Views from the Bench*, ed. Mark W. Cannon and David M. O'Brien (Chatham, NJ: Chatham House, 1985), 129. One study found, however, that judicial experience is not related to the congruence of presidential preferences and the justices' decisions on racial equality cases. See John Gates and Jeffrey Cohen, "Presidents, Supreme Court Justices, and Racial Equality Cases: 1954–1984," *Political Behavior* 10 (November 1, 1988): 22–35.
32. Richard Funston, "The Supreme Court and Critical Elections," *American Political Science Review* 69 (1975): 810; John B. Gates, *The Supreme Court and Partisan Realignment* (Boulder, CO: Westview, 1992); Thomas R. Marshall, "Public Opinion, Representation, and the Modern Supreme Court," *American Politics Quarterly* 16 (July 1988): 296–316; William Mishler and Reginald S. Sheehan, "The Supreme Court as a Countermajoritarian Institution? The Impact of Public Opinion on Supreme Court Decisions," *American Political Science Review* 87 (March 1993): 87–101; William Mishler and Reginald S. Sheehan, "Public Opinion, the Attitudinal Model, and Supreme Court Decision Making: A Micro-Analytic Perspective," *Journal of Politics* 58 (February 1996): 169–200; Roy B. Flemming and B. Dan Wood, "The Public and the Supreme Court: Individual Justice Responsiveness to American Policy Moods," *American Journal of Political Science* 41 (April 1997): 468–98; Kevin T. McGuire and James A. Stimson, "The Least Dangerous Branch: New Evidence on Supreme Court Responsiveness to Public Preferences," *Journal of Politics* 66 (November 2004): 1018–35.
33. Mario Bergara, Barak Richman, and Pablo T. Spiller, "Modeling Supreme Court Strategic Decision Making: The Congressional Constraint," *Legislative Studies Quarterly* 28 (May 2003): 247–80.
34. David G. Barnum, "The Supreme Court and Public Opinion: Judicial Decision Making in the Post–New Deal Period," *Journal of Politics* 47 (May 1985): 652–62.
35. Gregory A. Caldeira and John R. Wright, "Organized Interests and Agenda Setting in the U.S. Supreme Court," *American Political Science Review* 82 (December 1988): 1109–28.
36. On group use of the litigation process, see Karen Orren, "Standing to Sue: Interest Group Conflict in the Federal Courts," *American Political Science Review* 70 (September 1976): 723–42; Karen O'Connor and Lee Epstein, "The Rise of Conservative Interest Group Litigation," *Journal of Politics* 45 (May 1983): 479–89; and Lee Epstein and C. K. Rowland, "Debunking the Myth of Interest Group Invincibility in the Courts," *American Political Science Review* 85 (March 1991): 205–17.
37. "Federalist #78," in Hamilton, Madison, and Jay, *The Federalist Papers*.
38. Examples of judicial activism are reported in a critical assessment of judicial intervention by Donald Horowitz, *The Courts and Social Policy* (Washington, DC: Brookings Institution, 1977).
39. Paul Gerwitz and Chad Golder, "So Who Are the Activists?," *New York Times*, July 6, 2005.
40. Mario Bergara, Barak Richman, and Pablo T. Spiller, "Modeling Supreme Court Strategic Decision Making: The Congressional Constraint," *Legislative Studies Quarterly* 28 (May 2003): 247–80.
41. William N. Eskridge, "Overriding Supreme Court Statutory Interpretation Decisions," *Yale Law Journal* 101 (1991): 331–455; Joseph Ignagni and James Meernik, "Explaining Congressional Attempts to Reverse Supreme Court Decisions," *Political Research Quarterly* 10 (June 1994): 353–72. See also R. Chep Melnick, *Between the Lines: Interpreting Welfare Rights* (Washington, DC: Brookings Institution, 1994).

Chapter 15

1. Aaron Wildavsky and Naomi Caiden, *The New Politics of the Budgetary Process*, 4th ed. (New York: Longman, 2000), 2.
2. *Budget of the United States Government, Fiscal Year 2007: Historical Tables* (Washington, DC: U.S. Government Printing Office, 2007), tables 3.1 and 7.1.
3. Quoted in Gerald Carson, *The Golden Egg: The Personal Income Tax, Where It Came From, How It Grew* (Boston: Houghton Mifflin, 1977), 12.
4. Statistics on the number of returns and audits that come from the U.S. Department of Commerce, *Statistical Abstract of the United States, 2006* (Washington, DC: U.S. Government Printing Office, 2006), 324.
5. Tax Foundation, 2006.

6. An exception is Robert Eisner, who argues that if the government counted its debt as families and business firms do—that is, by balancing assets against liabilities—the government would be in pretty good shape. See *How Real Is the Federal Deficit?* (New York: Free Press, 1986).
7. Carson, *The Golden Egg*, 181–82.
8. For some perspectives on the rise of government expenditures, see David Cameron, "The Expansion of the Public Economy: A Comparative Analysis," *American Political Science Review* 72 (December 1978): 1243–61, and William D. Berry and David Lowery, *Understanding United States Government Growth* (New York: Praeger, 1987).
9. E. E. Schattschneider, *Two Hundred Million Americans in Search of a Government* (New York: Holt, Rinehart and Winston, 1969), 29–30.
10. Berry and Lowery, *Understanding United States Government Growth.*
11. Paul Light, *Artful Work: The Politics of Social Security Reform* (New York: HarperCollins, 1992), 82.
12. *Budget of the United States Government, Fiscal Year 2007: Historical Tables* (Washington, DC: U.S. Government Printing Office, 2006), tables 15.2 and 15.4.
13. Aaron Wildavsky and Naomi Caiden, *The New Politics of the Budgetary Process*, 3rd ed. (New York: Longman, 1997), 45.
14. John R. Gist, *Mandatory Expenditures and the Defense Sector* (Beverly Hills, CA: Russell Sage Foundation, 1974).
15. Paul R. Schulman, "Nonincremental Policymaking: Notes Toward an Alternative Paradigm," *American Political Science Review* 69 (December 1975): 1354–70.
16. For an extensive examination of incrementalism in federal budgeting, see Bryan D. Jones and Frank R. Baumgartner, *The Politics of Attention* (Chicago: University of Chicago Press, 2005).
17. Allen Meltzer and Scott F. Richard, "Why the Government Grows (and Grows) in a Democracy," *The Public Interest* 52 (summer 1978): 117.
18. *Budget of the United States Government, Fiscal Year 2007* (Washington, DC: U.S. Government Printing Office, 2006), Department of Defense, *www.whitehouse.gov/omb/budget/fy2007/defense.html.*
19. See James D. Savage, *Balanced Budgets and American Politics* (Ithaca, NY: Cornell University Press, 1988), for a study of the influence the principle of budget balancing has had on politics and public policy from the earliest days of U.S. history.

Chapter 16

1. Elizabeth Warren and Amelia Warrant Tyagi, *The Two Income Trap: Why Middle Class Mothers and Fathers Are Going Broke* (New York: Basic Books, 2003).
2. David K. Shipler, *The Working Poor: Invisible in America* (New York: Knopf, 2004).
3. On the decline of social insurance in the United States, see Jacob S. Hacker, "Privatizing Risk Without Privatizing the Welfare State: The Hidden Politics of Social Policy Retrenchment in the United States," *American Political Science Review* 98 (May 2004): 243–60.
4. John Leland, "Why America Sees the Silver Lining," *New York Times*, June 13, 2004.
5. Stanley Feldman and Marco R. Steenbergen, "The Humanitarian Foundation of Public Support for Social Welfare," *American Journal of Political Science* 45 (July 2001): 658–77.
6. Janie Calmes, "Budget Wish Lists Come and Go, but 'Entitlements' Outweigh All," *Wall Street Journal*, February 3, 2006, 1.
7. Alan Weil and Kenneth Finegold, "Introduction," ed. Alan Weil and Kenneth Finegold (Washington, DC: Urban Institute Press, 2002), xiii.
8. "Public Policy, Income Inequality, and Poverty: The United States in Comparative Perspective," *Social Science Quarterly* 86 (2005): 955. See also Lane Kenworthy and Jonas Pontusson, "Rising Inequality and the Politics of Redistribution in Affluent Countries," *Perspectives on Politics* 3 (September 2005): 449–72.
9. Nolan McCarty, Keith T. Poole, and Howard Rosenthal, *Income Distribution and the Realignment of American Politics* (Washington, DC: American Enterprise Institute, 1977), 1. See also their *Polarized America: The Dance of Ideology and Unequal Riches* (Cambridge, MA: MIT Press, 2006).
10. An economic analysis and explanation of the workings of the old adage can be found in Thomas Piketty and Emmanuel Saez, "Income Inequality in the United States 1913–1998," *Quarterly Journal of Economics* 113 (February 2003): 1–39.
11. Arthur Kennickell, "A Rolling Tide: Changes in the Distribution of Wealth in the United States, 1989–2001," Federal Reserve Board, May 3, 2003.
12. *Forbes*, "The 400 Richest People in America," special issue, November 2005.
13. Merrill Lynch, "The State of the World's Wealth," *World Wealth Report*, 2005.
14. Mark R. Rank and Thomas A. Hirschl, "Rags or Riches? Estimating the Probabilities of Poverty and Affluence Across the Adult American Life Span," *Social Science Quarterly* 82 (December 2001): 651–69.
15. *Nickel and Dimed: On (Not) Getting By in America* (New York: Owl Books, 2002).
16. See Shipler, *The Working Poor.*
17. Harrell Rodgers, *Poor Women, Poor Children*, 3rd ed. (New York: M. E. Sharpe, 1996).
18. Harrell Rodgers, *American Poverty in a New Era of Reform* (New York: M. E. Sharpe, 2000), 207.
19. Christopher Jencks, *Rethinking Social Policy* (New York: HarperCollins, 1992), 130.
20. "The Real State of the Budget," *Atlantic*, January/February 2003, 81.
21. Brookings Institution, *Rewarding Work*, June 2001.
22. See, for example, Francis Fox Piven and Richard Cloward, *Regulating the Poor* (New York: Pantheon, 1971). For an empirical analysis of theories of the rise of welfare that finds some support for the Piven and Cloward thesis, see Richard Fording, "The Political Response to Black Insurgency: A Critical Test of Competing Theories of the State," *American Political Science Review* 95 (March 2001): 115–30.
23. Charles Murray, *Losing Ground: American Social Policy, 1950–1980* (New York: Basic Books, 1984). Marvin Olasky, the guru of "compassionate conservatism," makes a similar argument in his *Tragedy of Human Compassion* (Chicago: Regnery, 1992). Doing good for people, especially through government, Olasky argues, is bad for them. For a contrary argument, see Benjamin Page and James R. Simmons, *What Government Can Do: Dealing with Poverty and Inequality* (Chicago: University of Chicago Press, 2000).
24. Gilens, *Why Americans Hate Welfare: Race, Media, and the Politics of Antipoverty Policy* (Chicago: University of Chicago Press, 2000).

25. Martin Gilens, "Race Coding and White Opposition to Welfare," *American Political Science Review* 90 (December 1996): 593–604.
26. Gilens, *Why Americans Hate Welfare*, chap. 5.
27. Office of Family Assistance, *TANF Fifth Annual Report*, January 20, 2006.
28. Rebecca Blank, "Fighting Poverty: Lessons from Recent U.S. History," *Journal of Economic Perspectives* 14 (spring 2000): 3–20.
29. Sylvester J. Schieber and John B. Shoven, *The Real Deal: The History and Future of Social Security* (New Haven, CT: Yale University Press, 1999), chap. 7. The Ida May Fuller story is also from Schieber and Shoven.
30. The math on Social Security is from the President's Commission to Strengthen Social Security, *Interim Report*, August 2001, 13.
31. Worse, President Bush's Commission to Strengthen Social Security argues that in about 2016, the Social Security Commission will have to begin calling in its IOUs from the federal treasury or cashing in its bonds. Social Security funds are not kept in what politicians have come to call a "lockbox." In 2016, Social Security claims would compete for regular budget dollars against national defense, homeland security, school aid, and other federal expenditures. See their *Interim Report*, August 2001.
32. Mary Louise Campbell explains how Social Security has energized one of America's most important interest groups in her *How Policies Make Citizens* (Princeton, NJ: Princeton University Press, 2002).
33. Martin Wattenberg, *Is Voting for Young People?* (New York: Pearson Longman, 2006), 4.
34. On the Republican effort to frame the debate, see Jacob S. Hacker and Paul Pierson, *Off Center* (New Haven, CT: Yale University Press), 75–79.
35. For one rare but dissenting view that argues that the Social Security "crisis" is exaggerated, partly by people who would profit from more private investment, see Dean Baker and Mark Weisbrot, *Social Security: The Phony Crisis* (Chicago: University of Chicago Press, 2000).
36. Thomas Frank, "The Trillion Dollar Hustle: Hello Wall Street, Goodbye Social Security," *Harper's*, January 2002.
37. Greg Hitt, "Social Security Plan Stalls," *Wall Street Journal*, July 23, 2002, A4.
38. Political scientist Benjamin Radcliff developed some empirical data to show that the extent of government welfare provisions is in fact positively related to people's sense of well-being from country to country. See his "Politics, Markets and Life Satisfaction: The Political Economy of Human Happiness," *American Political Science Review* 95 (December 2001): 939–52.
39. The United States, emphasizes Jacob Hacker, is not as niggardly about social benefits as liberals often think. Social spending in the United States is close to social spending levels in Europe. The major difference is that social expenditures—for health care, pensions, and other benefits—are often provided by private employers in the United States. See his *The Divided Welfare State* (New York: Cambridge University Press, 2002).
40. Anne Schneider and Helen Ingram, "The Social Construction of Target Populations," *American Political Science Review* 87 (1993): 334–47.

Chapter 17

1. See, for example, Paul Kennedy, *The Rise and Fall of the Great Powers* (New York: Random House, 1987).
2. Raymond Vernon, *In the Hurricane's Eye: The Troubled Prospects of Multinational Enterprises* (Cambridge, MA: Harvard University Press, 1998); United Nations, *World Investment Report, 2005* (New York: United Nations, 2005).
3. I. M. Destler, "National Security Management: What Presidents Have Wrought," *Political Science Quarterly* 95 (winter 1980–1981): 573–88.
4. Richard Betts, *Soldiers, Statesmen, and Cold War Crises* (Cambridge, MA: Harvard University Press, 1977), 216, table A.
5. For more on decision making regarding the Gulf War, see Bob Woodward, *The Commanders* (New York: Simon and Schuster, 1991).
6. See Bob Woodward, *Veil: The Secret Wars of the CIA, 1981–1987* (New York: Simon and Schuster, 1987).
7. A good study of the role of Congress in setting U.S. foreign policy is James M. Lindsay, *Congress and the Politics of U.S. Foreign Policy* (Baltimore: Johns Hopkins University Press, 1994). Congress's role in the defense budget process is discussed in Ralph G. Carter, "Budgeting for Defense," in *The President, Congress, and the Making of Foreign Policy*, ed. Paul E. Peterson (Norman: University of Oklahoma Press, 1994).
8. Louis Fisher, "Executive-Legislative Relations in Foreign Policy" (paper presented at the United States–Mexico Comparative Constitutional Law Conference, Mexico City, June 17, 1998), 1.
9. An excellent treatment of the origins of the Cold War is Daniel Yergin, *Shattered Peace: The Origins of the Cold War and the National Security State* (Boston: Houghton Mifflin, 1977).
10. The article was titled "Sources of Soviet Conduct" and appeared in *Foreign Affairs* (July 1947) under the pseudonym X.
11. Yergin, *Shattered Peace*, 268.
12. Seymour Melman, *Pentagon Capitalism: The Political Economy of War* (New York: McGraw-Hill, 1970).
13. Stanley Karnow, *Vietnam: A History* (New York: Penguin Books, 1983), 43. Karnow's book is one of the best of many excellent books on Vietnam. See also Frances Fitzgerald, *Fire in the Lake* (Boston: Little, Brown, 1972), and David Halberstam, *The Best and the Brightest* (New York: Random House, 1972).
14. Nicholas Lemann, "The Peacetime War," *Atlantic Monthly*, October 1984, 72.
15. Quoted in Andrew Rosenthal, "Striking a Defensive Tone, Bush Sees Virtue in Caution," *New York Times*, February 8, 1990, A10.
16. U.S. Department of State, *Country Reports on Terrorism 2004* (2005).
17. See, for example, Bruce Russett, "Defense Expenditures and National Well-Being," *American Political Science Review* 76 (December 1982): 767–77; William K. Domke, Richard C. Eichenberg, and Catherine M. Kelleher, "The Illusion of Choice: Defense and Welfare in Advanced Industrial Democracies, 1948–78," *American Political Science Review* 77 (March 1983): 19–35; and Alex Mintz, "Guns Versus Butter: A Disaggregated Analysis," *American Political Science Review* 83 (December 1989): 1285–96.
18. Kennedy, *The Rise and Fall of the Great Powers*; David Calleo, *Beyond American Hegemony: The Future of the Western Alliance* (New York: Basic Books, 1987).

For a different view, see Joseph S. Nye, *Bound to Lead* (New York: Basic Books, 1990).

19. On the importance of ideology, see studies discussed in Robert A. Bernstein, *Elections, Representation, and Congressional Voting Behavior* (Englewood Cliffs, NJ: Prentice Hall, 1989), 70–76.
20. U.S. Department of Commerce, *Statistical Abstract of the United States, 2006* (Washington, DC: U.S. Government Printing Office, 2006), 341, 343.
21. Stephen I. Schwartz, ed., *Atomic Audit: The Costs and Consequences of U.S. Nuclear Weapons Since 1940* (Washington, DC: Brookings Institution, 1998).
22. Joseph S. Nye Jr., *The Paradox of American Power: Why the World's Only Superpower Can't Go It Alone* (New York: Oxford University Press, 2002).
23. Stanley Hoffman, *Gulliver's Troubles, or the Setting of American Foreign Policy* (New York: McGraw-Hill, 1968).
24. Robert O. Keohane and Joseph S. Nye, *Power and Interdependence*, 2nd ed. (New York: HarperCollins, 1989), 27–28.
25. Joseph S. Nye Jr., *Soft Power: The Means to Success in World Politics* (Cambridge, MA: Harvard University Press, 2004).
26. Ibid., 3.
27. U.S. Department of Commerce, Bureau of the Census, 2006.
28. Ibid.
29. Carol C. Adelman, "The Privatization of Foreign Aid," *Foreign Affairs*, 82 (November/December 2003): 9–14.
30. See Bruce M. Russett, *Controlling the Sword* (Cambridge, MA: Harvard University Press, 1990), chap. 5; Thomas Hartley and Bruce M. Russett, "Public Opinion and the Common Defense: Who Governs Military Spending in the United States?," *American Political Science Review* 86 (December 1992): 905–15; Bruce M. Russett, *Grasping the Democratic Peace* (Princeton, NJ: Princeton University Press, 1993); Spencer R. Weart, *Never at War* (New Haven, CT: Yale University Press, 1998); Michael D. Ward and Kristian S. Gleditsch, "Democratizing Peace," *American Political Science Review* 92 (March 1998): 51–62; and Paul R. Hensel, Gary Goertz, and Paul F. Diehl, "The Democratic Peace and Rivalries," *Journal of Politics* 62 (November 2000): 1173–88.

Key Terms in Spanish

A

activation—acción y efecto de activar
actual group—grupo actual
administrative discretion—discreción administrativa
affirmative action—acción afirmativa
Americans with Disabilities Act of 1990—disposición legal de 1990 para ciudadanos americanos minusválidos
***amicus curiae* briefs**—instrucciones, informes, de la competencia de amigos del senado
Anti-Federalists—anti-federalistas
antitrust policy—política antimonopolio
appellate jurisdiction—jurisdicción apelatoria
appropriations bill—proyecto de ley de apropiación
arms race—carrera armamentista
Articles of Confederation—Artículos de la Confederación
authorization bill—estatuto de autorización

B

balance of trade—balance de intercambio comercial
beats—v. derrotar; recorrido de vigilancia policiaca
bicameral legislature—legislatura bi-camaral
bill—proyecto de ley; moción; cuenta
Bill of Rights—proyecto de ley de derechos
blanket primaries—cubiertas primarias
block grants—otorgamientos en conjunto
broadcast media—medios de transmisión
budget—presupuesto
budget resolution—resolución de presupuesto
bureaucracy—burocracia

C

cabinet—gabinete
campaign strategy—estrategia de campaña
capitalism—capitalismo
casework—trabajo de asistencia social
categorical grants—concesiones categorizadas
caucus—reunión del comité central o asamblea local de un partido
censorship—censura
census—censo
Central Intelligence Agency (CIA)—Agencia Central de Inteligencia
chains (newspaper chains)—cadena (cadenas periodísticas)
checks and balances—cheques y balances
city manager—aministrador de la ciudad
civic duty—deber cívico
civil disobedience—desobediencia civil
civil liberties—libertades civiles
civil rights—derechos civiles
Civil Rights Act of 1964—ley de Derechos Humanos de 1964
civil rights movement—movimiento de derechos civiles
civil service—administración pública
class action lawsuits—demanda colectiva
Clean Air Act of 1970—ley contra la contaminación del aire de 1970
closed primaries—primarias cerradas
coalition—coalición
coalition government—coalición de gobierno
cold war—guerra fría
collective bargaining—negociación colectiva
collective good—bienestar colectivo
command-and-control policy—política de ordenamiento y control
commercial speech—discurso comercial
committee chairs—presidentes de comité
comparable worth—valor comparable
conference committees—comités de conferencias
Congressional Budget and Impoundment Control Act of 1974—Ley del Presupuesto e Incautación del Congreso de 1974
Congressional Budget Office (CBO)—Oficina de Presupuesto del Congreso
Connecticut Compromise—Compromiso de Connecticut
consent of the governed—consentimiento del gobernado
conservatives—conservadores
Constitution—constitución
consumer price index (CPI)—índice de precios del consumidor
containment doctrine—doctrina o política de contención
continuing resolutions—resoluciones continuas
conversion—conversión
cooperative federalism—federalismo cooperativo
Council of Economic Advisers (CEA)—Consejo de Asesores Económicos
council of governments—consejo de gobiernos
courts of appeal—corte de apelación
crisis—crisis
critical election—elección crítica
cruel and unusual punishment—castigo cruel e inusual
culture of poverty—cultura de pobreza

D

Declaration of Independence—Declaración de Independencia
deficit—déficit
democracy—democracia
demography—demografía
deregulation—desregular, liberalizar
détente—relajación
Dillon's Rule—Regla de Dillon
direct democracy—democracia directa
direct mail—correo directo
district courts—juzgado de distrito
dual federalism—federalismo dual

E

Eighth Amendment—Octava Enmienda (constitucional)
elastic clause—cláusula flexible
electioneering—campaña electoral
electoral college—colegio electoral
elite theory—teoría de la élite
Endangered Species Act of 1973—Ley de Especies en Peligro de Extinción de 1973
entitlements—derechos
enumerated powers—poderes enumerados
environmental impact statement (EIS)—declaración de impacto sobre el ambiente
Environmental Protection Agency (EPA)—Agencia de Protección al Ambiente
equal protection of the laws—igualdad de protección de la ley
Equal Rights Amendment—enmienda de Igualdad de Derechos
establishment clause—cláusula de instauración
European Union (EU)—Unión Europea
exclusionary rule—regla de exclusión
executive orders—órdenes ejecutivas
exit poll—conteo de salida de votación
expenditures—gastos
extradition—extradición

F

factions—facciones
federal debt—deuda federal
Federal Election Campaign Act—Ley de la Campaña Federal de Elección
Federal Election Commission (FEC)—Comisión Federal Electoral
Federal Reserve System—Sistema Federal de Reserva
Federal Trade Commission (FTC)—Comisión Federal de Comercio
federalism—federalismo
Federalist Papers—Documentos Federalistas
Federalists—federalistas
Fifteenth Amendment—Quinceava Enmienda
Fifth Amendment—Enmienda Quinta
filibuster—intervención parlamentaria con objeto de impedir una votación
First Amendment—Enmienda Primera
fiscal federalism—federalismo fiscal
fiscal policy—política fiscal
Food and Drug Administration (FDA)—Departamento Administrativo de Alimentos y Estupefacientes
foreign policy—política extranjera
formula grants—fórmula de concesión
Fourteenth Amendment—Catorceava Enmienda
free exercise clause—cláusula de ejercicio libre
free-rider problem—problema de polizón
frontloading—carga frontal
full faith and credit—fe y crédito completo

G

gender gap—disparidad de género
government—gobierno
government corporations—corporaciones gubernamentales
gross domestic product—producto doméstico bruto
GS (General Schedule) rating—prorrateo programático general

H

Hatch Act—Ley Hatch
health maintenance organization (HMO)—Organización para el Manteniento de la Salud
high-tech politics—política sobre alta tecnología
home rule—regla de casa (local)
House Rules Committee—Comité de Reglas de la Cámara
House Ways and Means Committee—Comité de Formas y Medios de la Cámara
hyperpluralism—hiperpluralismo; pluralismo en exceso

I

impeachment—juicio de impugnación
implied powers—poderes implícitos
incentive system—sistema de incentivos
income—ingresos
income distribution—distribución de ingresos
income tax—impuestos sobre los ingresos
incorporation doctrine—doctrina de incorporación
incrementalism—incrementalismo
incumbents—titular en función

independent executive agencies—agencias ejecutivas independientes
independent regulatory agency—agencia regulatoria independiente
industrial policy—política industrial
inflation—inflación
initiative—iniciativa
initiative petition—iniciativa de petición
interdependency—interdependencia
interest group—grupos de interés
intergovernmental relations—relaciones intergubernamentales
investigative journalism—periodismo de investigación
iron triangles—triángulos de acero
isolationism—aislacionismo
item veto—artículo de veto

J

Joint Chiefs of Staff—Junta de Comandantes de las Fuerzas Armadas (Estado Mayor)
joint committees—comisiones
judicial activisim—activismo judicial
judicial implementation—implementación judicial
judicial restraint—restricción judicial
judicial review—revisión judicial
justiciable disputes—conflictos enjuiciables

K

Keynesian economic theory—teoría económica keynesiana

L

laissez-faire—liberalismo económico
legislative oversight—descuido legislativo
legislative veto—Veto legislativo
legitimacy—legitimidad
libel—difamación, calumnia
liberals—liberales
lieutenant governor—lugarteniente del gobernador
limited government—gobierno limitado
linkage institutions—instituciones de enlace
lobbying—cabildeo
local charter—estatutos locales; fuero local

M

majority leader—l'der de la mayoría
majority rule—gobierno de la mayoría
mandate theory of elections—mandato teórico de elecciones
mass media—medios de difusión (comunicación) masiva
McCarthyism—macartismo
McGovern-Fraser Commission—Comisión *McGovern-Fraser*
media event—evento de los medios de difusión (comunicación)
Medicaid—programa de asistencia médica estatal *Medicaid* para personas de bajos ingresos
Medicare—programa de asistencia médica estatal *Medicare* para personas mayores de 65 años
melting pot—crisol
merit plan—plan meritorio (por méritos)
merit principle—principio de mérito
minority leader—líder de la minoría parlamentaria
minority majority—majoria de la minoría
minority rights—derechos de las minorías
mixed economy—economía mixta
monetarism—monetarismo
monetary policy—política monetaria
Motor Voter Act—Ley para promoción del voto

N

narrowcasting—transmisión cerrada; monitoreo cerrado
national chairperson—director/a de comiténacional
national committee—comité nacional
national convention—convención nacional
National Environmental Policy Act (NEPA)—Ley de la Política Ambiental Nacional
national health insurance—seguro de salud nacional
National Labor Relations Act—Ley Nacional de Relaciones Laborales
national party convention—convención nacional del partido
National Security Council (NSC)—Consejo Nacional de Seguridad
national primary—primaria nacional
natural rights—derechos naturales
New Deal coalition—coalición para el Nuevo Tratado
New Jersey Plan—Plan de New Jersey
Nineteenth Amendment—Enmienda Diecinueve
nomination—nominación
North Atlantic Treaty Organization (NATO)—Tratado de las Organizaciones del Atlantico Norte

O

Office of Management and Budget (OMB)—Oficina de Gestión y Presupuesto
Office of Personnel Management (OPM)—Oficina de Gestión de Personal
Olson's law of large groups—ley de Olson de grandes grupos

open primaries—primarias abiertas
opinion—opinión
Organization of Petroleum Exporting Countries (OPEC)—Organización de Países Exportadores de Petróleo
original intent—intento original
original jurisdiction—jurisdicción original

P

party competition—competencia de partido
party dealignment—desalineamiento del partido
party eras—épocas del partido
party identification—identificación partidista
party image—imágen del partido
party machines—maquinaria partidista
party neutrality—neutralidad partidista
party platform—plataforma del partido
party realignment—realinación del partido
patronage—patrocinio
Pendleton Civil Service Act—Ley del Servicio Público de Pendleton
plea bargaining—negociación fiscal-defensa
pluralist theory—teoría pluralista
pocket veto—veto indirecto del presidente al no firmar dentro de los diez días establecidos
policy agenda—agenda política
policy entrepreneurs—política empresarial
policy gridlock—parálisis política
policy implementation—implementación política
policy voting—política de votación
policymaking institutions—instituciones de normatividad política
policymaking system—sistema de normatividad política
political action committees (PACs)—comités de acción política
political culture—cultura política
political efficacy—eficacia política
political ideology—ideología política
political issue—asunto político
political participation—participación política
political party—partido político
political questions—cuestiones políticas
political socialization—socialización política
politics—política
poll taxes—votación para impuestos
pork barrel—asignación de impuestos estatales para el beneficio de una cierta zona o grupo
potential group—grupo potencial
poverty line—límite económico mínimo para sobrevivencia
precedent—precedente
presidential coattails—acción a la sombra presidencial
presidential primaries—elecciones primarias presidenciales
press conferences—conferencias de prensa
print media—medios de comunicación impresos
prior restraint—restricción anterior
privileges and immunities—privilegiose inmunidades
probable cause—causa probable
progressive tax—impuesto progresivo
project grant—proyecto de concecsión
proportional representation—representación proporcional
proportional tax—impuesto proporcional
protest—n. protesta; v. protestar
public goods—bienes públicos
public interest lobbies—cabildeo por intereses públicos
public opinion—opinión pública
public policy—política pública

R

random-digit dialing—llamadas con números aleatorios
random sampling—muestreo aleatorio
rational-choice theory—teoría de selección racional
reapportionment—nueva distribución en la representación del congreso
recall—retirar
reconciliation—reconciliación
referendum—referendum
regional primaries—elecciones primarias regionales
regressive tax—impuesto regresivo
regulation—norma, regla
reinforcement—refuerzo
relative deprivation—privación relativa
representation—representación
republic—república
responsible party model—modelo de partido responsable
retrospective voting—votación retrospectiva
revenues—ingresos
right to privacy—derecho a la privacidad
right-to-work laws—leyes del derecho al trabajo

S

sample—muestra
sampling error—error de muestreo
search warrant—orden de cateo
secretary of defense—secretario de la defensa
secretary of state—secretario de estado
select committees—comités seleccionados
selective benefits—beneficios selectivos
selective perception—percepción selectiva
self-incrimination—auto incriminación
Senate Finance Committee—Comité Senatorial de Finanzas
senatorial courtesy—cortesía senatorial

Senior Executive Service—el de más alto rango en el servicio del ejecutivo
seniority system—sistema de antigüedad
separation of powers—separación de poderes
Shays' Rebellion—Rebelion de Shays
single-issue groups—grupos para una sola causa
Sixteenth Amendment—Enmienda Dieciséis
Sixth Amendment—Enmienda Sexta
Social Security Act—Ley de Seguridad Social
social welfare policies—políticas para el bien social
soft money—moneda débil, sin garantía
solicitor general—subsecretario de justicia
sound bites—segmentos de sonido
Speaker of the House—presidente de la cámara
standard operating procedures (SOPs)—procedimientos normales de operación
standing committees—comités permanentes
standing to sue—en posición de entablar demanda
stare decisis—variación de "decisión firme" o "decisión tomada"; la decisión se fundamenta en algo ya decidio.
statutory construction—construcción establecida por ley
Strategic Defense Initiative (SDI)—Iniciativa de Defensa Estratégica
street-level bureaucrats—burócratas de bajo nivel
subgovernments—subgobiernos
subnational government—gobierno subnacional
suffrage—sufragio
Super Tuesday—Super martes: día de votación en varios estados importantes
superdelegates—superdelegados
Superfund—superfondo; fondo de proporciones mayores
supply-side economics—economía de la oferta
supremacy clause—cláusula de supremacía
Supreme Court—Suprema Corte
symbolic speech—discurso simbólico

T

Taft-Hartley Act—Ley de Taft-Hartley
talking head—busto parlante; presentador, entrevistador
tariff—tarifa
tax expenditures—gastos de impuesto
Tenth Amendment—Enmienda Décima
term limits—periodo límite
third parties—terceras personas
Thirteenth Amendment—Enmienda Treceava
ticket-splitting—votación de candidatos de diferentes partidos para diferentes cargos
town meeting—consejo municipal de vecinos
transfer payments—transferencia de pagos
transnational corporations—corporaciones transnacionales
trial balloons—globo de prueba; proponer algo para conocer la reacción de alguien
Twenty-fifth Amendment—Enmienda veiticincoava
Twenty-fourth Amendment—Enmienda veiticuatrava
Twenty-second Amendment—Enmienda veintidoava

U

uncontrollable expenditures—gastos incontrolables
unemployment rate—nivel de desempleo; porcentage de desempleo
union shop—empresa que emplea sólo trabajadores sindicalizados
unitary governments—estados/gobiernos unitarios
United Nations (UN)—Naciones Unidas
unreasonable searches and seizures—cateos y detenciones/embargos irrazonables
urban underclass—urbanita de clase baja
U.S. Constitution—Constitución de los Estados Unidos

V

veto—veto
Virginia Plan—Plan Virginia
voter registration—registro de votantes
Voting Rights Act of 1965—Ley de Derechos del Elector de 1965

W

War Powers Resolution—Resolución de Poderes de Guerra
Water Pollution Control Act of 1972—Ley para el Control de la Contaminación de Aguas de 1972
wealth—riqueza
whips—miembro de un cuerpo legislativo encargado de hacer observar las consignas del partido
White primary—primaria blanca/sin novedad
winner-take-all system—sistema en el que el ganador toma todos los votos
writ of habeas corpus—un recurso de hábeas corpus

Acknowledgments

Text Acknowledgments

220: "Young People and Politics: How the Under-30 Crowd Learns from Different Media Sources Compared to Older Americans," from January 2004 survey. Copyright © 2004 Pew Research Center for the People and the Press. Used with permission.

243: "Party Coalitions Today," Copyright © 2004 Pew Research Center for the People and the Press. Used with permission (from *http://people-press. org/commentary/ display. php3?AnalysisID=95*).

284: "The Big-Spending PACS," © Center for Responsive Politics, *www. opensecrets. org*.

313: "The Power 25," © Fortune, Inc. 2001.

315: "The Benefits of Membership in the AARP," © American Association for Retired Persons.

339: "A Day in the Life of a Member of Congress," adapted by permission from Craig Schultz, ed., *Setting Course: A Congressional Management Guide.* Copyright © 1994 Congressional Management Foundation, Washington, D. C. and from David E. Price, *The Congressional Experience: A View from the Hill.* Copyright © 1999 Westview Press, a member of Perseus Books, L. L. C.

343: "The Incumbency Factor in Congressional Elections," from Norman J. Ornstein, et al. , *Vital Statistics on Congress, 1997–1998* (Washington, D. C. : Congressional Quarterly Press, 1998).

390: "Principal Offices in the White House," adapted from George C. Edwards III and Stephen J. Wayne, *Presidential Leadership*, 7th ed. St. Martin's Press.

488: "Supreme Court Rulings in Which Federal Statutes Have Been Found Unconstitutional," from *The Judicial Process: An Introductory Analysis of the Courts of the United States, England and France*, 7/e, by Henry J. Abraham. Copyright © 1993 by Henry J. Abraham. Used by permission of Oxford University Press, Inc.

575: "The Spread of Nuclear Weapons," from *Congressional Quarterly Weekly Report*, May 23, 1998, p. 1366. Copyright © 1998.

588: "Vote Drives Gain Avid Attention of Youth in '04" by Timothy Egan, NYT, 9/15/04. Copyright © 2004 New York Times Company, Inc. Used with permission.

590: "Internet Injects Sweeping Change into U.S. Politics," by Adam Nagourney, NYT, 4/2/06. Copyright © 2006 New York Times Company, Inc. Reprinted with permission.

592 "State Governments Overreach in Taking on Problems Best Solved at the National Level," by Robert H. Frank, NYT, 4/13/06. Copyright © 2006 New York Times Company, Inc. Reprinted with permission.

594: "Hateful Name Calling vs. Calling for Hateful Action," by Edward Rothstein, NYT, 11/23/02. Copyright © 2002 by The New York Times Co. Reprinted with permission.

596: "What the United States Army Teaches Us About Affirmative Action," by Brent Staples, NYT, 1/6/03. Copyright © 2003 New York Times Company, Inc. Used with permission.

598: "Bush's Speech on Iraq War Echoes Voice of an Analyst," by Scott Shane, NYT, 12/4/05. Copyright © 2005 New York Times Company, Inc. Used with permission.

600: "Take That, Mr. Newsman!: Answering Back to the News Media, Using the Internet," by Katharine Q. Seelye, NYT, 1/2/06. Copyright © 2006 New York Times Company, Inc. Reprinted with permission.

602: "The Very, Very Personal is the Political," Jon Gertner, *New York Times Magazine*, February 15, 2004. Copyright © 2004 Jon Gertner. Reprinted by permission.

604: "California Moves to Reschedule Its Primary from March to June," by Dean E. Murphy, NYT, 08/30/04. Copyright © 2004 New York Times Company, Inc. Used with permission.

606: "Hiring Federal Lobbyists, Towns Learn Money Talks," by Jodi Rudoren and Aron Pilhofer, NYT, 9/2/06. Copyright © 2006 New York Times Company, Inc. Reprinted with permission.

608: "Once Just an Aide, Now a King of K Street," by Anne E. Kornblut, NYT, 2/5/06. Copyright © 2006 New York Times Company, Inc. Reprinted with permission.

610: "For President, Final Say on a Bill Sometimes Comes After the Signing," by Elisabeth Bumiller, NYT, 1/16/06. Copyright © 2006 New York Times Company, Inc. Reprinted with permission.

612: "Safer Vehicles for Soldiers: A Tale of Delays and Glitches," by Michael Moss, NYT, 6/26/06. Copyright © 2006 New York Times Company, Inc. Reprinted with permission.

614: "Judicial Intent: The Competing Visions of the Role of the Court," by Linda Greenhouse, NYT, 07/07/02. Copyright © 2002 New York Times Company, Inc. Used with permission.

616: "A Clash of Goals in Bush's Efforts on the Income Tax; Proposals Would Shift Burden from Wealthy to Middle

Class," by Edmund Andrews, NYT, 10/06/04. Copyright © 2004 New York Times Company, Inc. Used with permission.

618: "AARP Opposes Bush Plan to Replace Social Security with Private Accounts," by Robert Pear, NYT, 11/12/04. Copyright © 2004 New York Times Company, Inc. Used with permission.

620: "Crises, Crises Everywhere: What is a President to Do?" by Todd S. Purdum, NYT, 02/09/03. Copyright © 2003 New York Times Company, Inc. Used with permission.

Photo Acknowledgments

Page abbreviations are as follows: (T) top, (C) center, (B) bottom, (L) left, (R) right.

2: James Leynse/Corbis; 6: AFP/Getty Images; 13: Robert Nickelsberg/Getty Images; 23: Steve Starr/Corbis; 33(L): Brown Brothers; 33(R): National Archives and Records Administration; 36: Scribner's Popular History of the U.S., 1897; 40: New York Public Library Picture Collection; 49: National Geographic Photographer George Mobley/US Capitol Historical Society; 54: Hulton Archive/Getty Images; 68: AP/Wide World Photos; 76: Stephen Frisch/Stock, Boston, LLC; 77: Steven Senne/AP/Wide World Photos; 81: Lewis Hine/Hulton|Archive Photos/Getty Images; 86: Michael Newman/PhotoEdit Inc.; 99: Christopher Lingg/The Image Works; 105: AP/Wide World Photos; 107: Dennis MacDonald/PhotoEdit; 111: Charles Ommanney/Contact Press Images; 113: Getty Images; 120: Jean-Yves Rabeuf/The Image Works; 122: Michael Newman/PhotoEdit; 134: Mobile Press Register/Corbis; 143: AP/Wide World Photos; 145: The Granger Collection, New York; 147–148: Bettmann/Corbis; 151: AP/Wide World Photos; 155: Reuters/Corbis; 157: Corbis; 160: Mark Godfrey/The Image Works; 163: Eric Risberg/AP/Wide World Photos; 164: Kim Ludbrook/EPA/Landov; 168: Steven Rubin/The Image Works; 171: Marilyn Humphries/The Image Works; 181: Allan J. Barnes; 184: AP/Wide World Photos; 188: Bob Daemmrich/Stock, Boston, LLC; 192: Jon Feingersh/Corbis; 202: Jim Cole/AP/Wide World Photos; 203: Tony Gutierrez/AP/Wide World Photos; 214: Bettmann/Corbis; 217: Reuters/Corbis; 226: AP/Wide World Photos; 227: © Tribune Media Services, Inc. All Rights Reserved. Reprinted with permission; 229: Stuart Ramso/AP/Wide World Photos; 233: Courtesy of YouTube.com; 234: Ron Sachs/CNP/Corbis; 240: Bob Daemmrich/The Image Works; 245: Rene Clement/Polaris; 246: Jean-Claude LeJeuen/Stockphoto; 249: TOLES © 2000 The Washington Post. Reprinted with permission of UNIVERSAL PRESS SYNDICATE. All rights reserved; 252: Bettmann/Corbis; 254: The Granger Collection, New York; 258: Ron Wurzer/Polaris Images; 263: Jim Ruymen/UPI/Landov; 270: Reuters/Landov; 271: AP/Wide World Photos; 272: AP/Wide World Photos; 273: AP/Wide World Photos; 274: AP/Wide World Photos; 282: AUTH © 2002 The Philadelphia Inquirer. Reprinted with permission of UNIVERSAL PRESS SYNDICATE. All rights reserved; 286: STR/AFP/Getty Images; 292: Ron Edmonds/AP/Wide World Photos; 309: AP/Wide World Photos; 317: Jim Borgman/Reprinted with special permission of King Features Syndicate; 319: Bob Daemmrich/The Image Works; 320: Phelan M. Ebenhack/AP/Wide World Photos; 324: Jeffrey Markowitz/Corbis; 325: AP/Wide World Photos; 329: Jim Borgman/Reprinted with special permission of King Features Syndicate; 330: AP/Wide World Photos; 331: Alex Wong/Getty Images; 342–353: AP/Wide World Photos; 355: Jason Reed/Reuters/Corbis; 359: AP/Wide World Photos; 361: Samantha Appleton/Aurora Photos; 369: Jack Kightlinger/AP/Wide World Photos; 369: David Schull/Bloomberg News/Landov; 379: Alex Webb/Magnum Photos, Inc.; 380: AP/Wide World Photos; 380: Eisenhower Library; 381: AP/Wide World Photos; 387: Brooks Kraft/Corbis; 392: AP/Wide World Photos; 395: Brooks Kraft/Corbis; 401: Stephen Jaffe; 403: Corbis; 405: Trippett/SIPA Press; 407: Doug Mills/AP/Wide World Photos; 409: Wayne Miller/Magnum Photos, Inc.; 433: Chuck Nacke/Woodfin Camp & Associates; 437: AP/Wide World Photos; 440: Jack Kurtz/The Image Works; 444: Jim Pickerell/Stock, Boston, LLC; 461: Carl Iwasaki/TimePix// Getty Images; 470: Reuters NewMedia Inc./Corbis; 473: Getty Images; 475: Getty Images; 480: David Hume Kennerly/ Getty Images; 485: Paul Conklin/PhotoEdit Inc.; 495: Mark Cardwell; 504: Time Life Pictures/Getty Images; 508: Philip Wallick/Corbis; 513: AFP/Getty Images; 526(T): Mario Tama/Getty Images; 526(B): Varley Charlie/Sipa Press; 527: Bettmann/Corbis; 529: Alison Wright/Corbis; 536: Bettmann/Corbis; 548: Robert Clark/Aurora Photos; 553: AFP/Getty Images; 554: Kevin Lamarque/Reuters/ Corbis; 558(L): Bettmann/Corbis; 558(R): Lionel Cironneau/AP/Wide World Photos; 560: Trippet/Sipa Press; 564: cartoonbank.com; 580: Corbis Sygma; 588: Gary I. Rothstein/Reuters/Landov; 590: Frederic Larson/ San Francisco Chronicle/Corbis; 592: Jack Kurtz/ ZUMA/Corbis; 594: James P. Blair/PhotoDisc/Getty Images; 596: Kevork Djansezian/AP/Wide World Photos; 598: Charles Dharapak/AP/Wide World Photos; 600: Ron Schwane/AP/Wide World Photos; 602: AP/Wide World Photos; 604: Barbara Davidson/Corbis; 606: Paula Illingworth/AP/Wide World Photos; 608: Gerald Herbert/ AP/Wide World Photos; 610: Paul Morse/The White House/AP/Wide World Photos; 612: Ramin Talaie/Corbis; 614: Mark Wilson/Getty Images; 616: Carah Thomas-Maskell/AP/Wide World Photos; 618: Spencer Grant/PhotoEdit Inc.; 620: Corbis Sygma.

Index